"Marco loves completeness, bo[...]
in this book and in the number[...]
or dilemma. Because of this, the[...]
well as advanced users. This is not just a book with text followed
by long listings, but rather text with screenshots and only those
parts of the code listing that are relevant."

—Bob Swart

**Dr. Bob's Review Database
of Delphi 2.X Books**

"Delphi has gained a solid reputation as a tool for developing
sophisticated Windows user interfaces and general Windows
applications. *Mastering Delphi* provides the most comprehensive
explanations of how Delphi can address these development
needs. …This is a complete … reference/tutorial for Delphi
and Windows programming."

Delphi Developer's Journal:
December 1995

"Another compendious tome to accompany Delphi, Marco
Cantù's *Mastering Delphi* isn't small and isn't lightweight.
There is something for every Delphi developer, from the
novice to the expert.

"In order to achieve this broad appeal, the author has structured the book in a way which gradually introduces those new
to Delphi to the capabilities of the language while, at the same
time, providing more experienced readers with many useful
hints, tips, and code optimizations.

"Overall, this book is to be recommended both as source of
advice and as a comprehensive tutor, with the added bonus that
the accompanying CD-ROM includes all of the sample programs
(more than 200 of them) and some more Delphi components."

*Delphi Developer's
Group Journal—UK*:
November/December 1995

"This late entry has displaced Delphi Unleashed as my favorite.
The examples are well chosen, often illustrating multiple topics,
with variations on a single program. Many include multiple
ways to treat a given task, with helpful comments on the trade-
offs. If you intend to buy just one book on Delphi, I highly
recommend this one."

*Sacra Blue The Magazine of the
Sacramento PC User's Group*:
December 1995

Mastering™ Delphi™ 3

Second Edition

Marco Cantù

SYBEX®

San Francisco • Paris • Düsseldorf • Soest

Associate Publisher: Gary Masters
Acquisitions Manager: Kristine Plachy
Acquisitions & Developmental Editor: Peter Kuhns
Editor: James A. Compton
Technical Editor: Juancarlo Añez
Graphic Illustrator: Inbar Berman
Desktop Publisher: Franz Baumhackl
Production Coordinator: Alexa Riggs
Proofreaders: Jennifer Metzger, Theresa Gonzalez, Michael Tom
Indexer: Nancy Guenther
Cover Designer: DesignSite
Cover Illustrator: Sergei Loobkoff
Cover Photograph supplied by PhotoDisc™

Screen reproductions produced with Collage Plus.

Collage Plus is a trademark of Inner Media Inc.

SYBEX is a registered trademark of SYBEX Inc.
Mastering is a trademark of SYBEX Inc.

TRADEMARKS: SYBEX has attempted throughout this book to distinguish proprietary trademarks from descriptive terms by following the capitalization style used by the manufacturer.

Netscape Communications, the Netscape Communications logo, Netscape, and Netscape Navigator are trademarks of Netscape Communications Corporation.

The author and publisher have made their best efforts to prepare this book, and the content is based upon final release software whenever possible. Portions of the manuscript may be based upon pre-release versions supplied by software manufacturer(s). The author and the publisher make no representation or warranties of any kind with regard to the completeness or accuracy of the contents herein and accept no liability of any kind including but not limited to performance, merchantability, fitness for any particular purpose, or any losses or damages of any kind caused or alleged to be caused directly or indirectly from this book.

Library of Congress Card Number: 97-65365
ISBN: 0-7821-2052-0

Manufactured in the United States of America

10 9 8 7 6

To my wife Lella, with all of my love.

ACKNOWLEDGMENTS

A lot of time has passed since I started working on the first edition of *Mastering Delphi*. Many things have happened during that period, many people got involved with my work and my life, and it is not easy to find the right words to thank all of them.

Probably the first thanks go to the Borland programmers and managers, because they've built a great product. Particular thanks go to Zack Urlocker and David Intersimone, because they have both helped me in many ways since we met many years ago, but I would also like to extend my thanks to all of Borland's Delphi team. (You can see a list of their names by opening Delphi's About box, holding down the Alt key, and typing **TEAM** or **DEVELOPERS**.) The book also owes a lot to Nan Borreson at Borland, who first suggested that I write it and has provided me with insightful information.

The next thanks are for the Sybex editors. I don't even know everyone who got involved with the book, but I want to thank them all. Special thanks go to Gary Masters, Barbara Gordon, Jim Compton, Peter Kuhns, Kristine Plachy, Franz Baumhackl, Inbar Berman, Alexa Riggs, Theresa Gonzalez, Jennifer Metzger, Michael Tom, and Molly Sharp. Other people involved with this and previous editions are John Read, Judy Jigarjian, Heather O'Connor, Thom Dyson, Jane Reh, Marilyn Smith, Dusty Bernard, Valerie Potter, Shelby Zimmerman, and Michelle Nance.

Juancarlo Añez, Tim Gooch, Alain Tadros, and Danny Thorpe reviewed the three editions of the book, suggesting improvements and new examples, revealing features I was not aware of, providing many corrections, contributing many insightful comments, and giving me advice. The book owes its quality to my technical reviewers more than to any other people, so *thank you very much indeed*.

I discussed Delphi programming with them and with many other people around the world: US, Italy, France, UK, Singapore, Holland, just to name a few countries where I've actually been. Bruce Eckel, a friend and an author of great C++ and Java books, has helped me understanding OOP languages better, and I really want to thank him for the time we've spent together.

Some magazine editors got involved with my work, including Chris Frizelle of *The Delphi Magazine*, JD Hildebrand of *Windows Tech Journal*, Bob Arnson, Kevin Weeks (who elected the first edition of the book as "the current winner of the Manhattan Phone Book Look-Alike Contest"), Jerry Coffrey of *Delphi Informant*, Giorgio Panzeri of *PcProfessionale*, and Alessandro Pedone of *Computer Programming*.

There are many others I want to thank: Norm McIntosh, who has hosted me at his house in San Francisco several times; Andrea Provaglio, an OOP expert I meet more often in the US than in Italy; Steve Tendon, who read the whole manuscript of the first edition; Bob Swart, better known as Dr. Bob; Johanna and Phil of the UK Delphi Developer's Group; Stefano Maruzzi, who taught me a lot about Windows programming, and his wife Antonella; Foo Say How, of Singapore; Giovanni Librando, who introduced me to Visual Basic (helping me to understand why Delphi is better); Glenn Field; John Howe; Mike Orriss; all the *TeamB* members of Delphi Compuserve forums; Marco Miotti, who is now in the Microsoft camp; and Ernesto Franchini, with the small team at ISS Borland. Also, a very big thank-you to all the attendees of my Delphi programming courses, seminars, and Jam Sessions.

Besides those involved with my work and the book, there are many others who helped me. First of all my wife, Lella, who never stopped supporting me in every possible way. Many of her plans, particularly for holidays and weekends, had to change because of the book. Things were really hectic at times, but she kept improving my self-confidence when things were not working out as planned and forced me to stop working from time to time.

I have to thank also many of our friends who provided opportunities for healthy breaks in the work by inviting us to their homes, to eat pizza, to see a film, or to discuss politics. The list of the friends is quite long, and includes Sandro and Monica, Stefano and Elena, Marco and Laura (and now Matteo), Chiara, Luca and Elena, Chiara and Daniele, and Laura, to name just a few. Our parents, brothers, sisters, and their families were very supportive, too. It was nice to spend some of our free time with them and our six nephews, Matteo, Andrea, Giacomo, Stefano, Andrea, and Pietro; playing with them really helped me to relax.

Finally, I would like to thank all of the people, many unknown, who enjoy life and help to build a better world. If I never stop believing in the future, it is also because of them.

CONTENTS AT A GLANCE

TABLE OF CONTENTS

5 Object Pascal as an OOP Language 185

6   Advanced Object Pascal   249

9 Creating and Handling Menus

393

11 Graphical Components   513

16   Building Database Applications 757

17   Advanced Database Access   833

Appendixes

INTRODUCTION

It all happened at once. I was a happy C++ programmer and writer when Zack Urlocker showed me a yet-to-be-released product: Delphi. The first time I saw it, I liked its fine language, its rich environment, and its ease of use. Pascal was my first serious programming language—the one I used at the university for my first projects. It took very little time to refresh my Pascal knowledge and just a little longer to grasp Object Pascal. As soon as I saw Delphi I was sure it would become a very widespread tool, and this proved to be an accurate prediction, as you probably know.

I used to write, teach, and consult about Windows programming in C and C++; now I still write, consult, and teach courses, but they mostly relate to Delphi. The previous editions of this book were a great success because Delphi itself has been so successful and was rapidly accepted by a diverse group of programmers all over the world.

From Delphi to Delphi 3

There are many programming environments you can work with, but from the very beginning, Delphi has been an outstanding choice. Some of the features that attracted me to the original version of Delphi were its form-based and object-oriented approach, its super-fast compiler, its great database support, its close integration with Windows programming, and its component technology. But the most important was the Object Pascal language, which is the foundation of all the other elements.

Delphi 2 was even better! Among its most important additions were these: the Multi-Record Object and the improved database grid; OLE Automation support and the variant data type; full Windows 95 support and integration; the long string data type; and Visual Form Inheritance.

With the release of Delphi 3, Borland has left programmers speechless. There are so many advanced new features that it is hard to choose the best ones. But I've compiled a list, in reverse order, of the ten new features I like most:

10. The Code Insight technology (Code Templates, Code Completion, Code Parameters, Tool-Tip Expression evaluation) and the enhancements in the editor

9. The DLL debugging support

8. The component templates

7. The extended common controls, including the Coolbar component

6. The new BDE Access driver, and the enhanced flexibility in the database connections

5. The inclusion of TeeChart, an improved version of QuickReport, the Decision Cube, and many other new components

4. The extended support for the Web and for distributed applications

3. The component packages technology

2. The ActiveForms

1. The interfaces and COM support

Becoming a Delphi Master (by Reading This Book)

Delphi is a great tool, but it is also a complex programming environment that involves many different elements. This book will help you master Delphi programming, including the Object Pascal language, Delphi components (both using the existing ones and developing new components), database support, and the key elements of Windows and COM programming.

You do not need an in-depth knowledge of any of these topics to read this book. Having some familiarity with Delphi will help you a lot, particularly after the introductory chapters. The book starts going in-depth in Chapter 4, so if you've never used Delphi at all, you'll have to study hard, and if you've used earlier versions of Delphi, you'll start seeing a lot of new information. In fact, you'll see new Delphi 3 features all the way from Chapter 1 through Chapter 31. There aren't just one or two final chapters or added sections at the ends of the chapters to cover new features; this book has been completely revised from the first page to the last to cover Delphi 3.

This book does require a knowledge of the basics of programming, using any language and with any operating system or environment. You should understand what variables and functions are and what the term "*loop*" means. If you've never written a program line in your life, this is not the book for you right now. First, get a solid introduction to programming, and then read this book.

The Structure of the Book

The book is divided into four parts:

- The first part, "Delphi and Object Pascal," introduces newcomers to Delphi programming and also provides many tips for more experienced users. The first three chapters focus on the Delphi development environment, and just a few examples are presented. Following chapters discuss the Object Pascal language, from a brief overview of Pascal to the advanced object-oriented features of the language. The final chapter in this part examines the key elements of Delphi's Visual Component Library (VCL).

- The second part, "Using Components," explores the use of Delphi components and forms to build Windows applications. It covers standard components, the Windows 95 controls, graphic components, menus, mouse input, graphical output, MDI (Multiple Document Interface), database programming, and many other topics. The chapters include both Delphi-specific topics and related Windows programming ideas.

- The third part, "Components and Libraries," covers Delphi component and Dynamic Link Library (DLL) development; it then looks at COM and OLE, covering Windows shell extensions, OLE Automation, ActiveX and Active-Form development, and introducing Internet programming in Delphi.

- The fourth part, "Advanced Delphi Programming," discusses some advanced Windows programming techniques, such as memory handling, using resources, printing support, file handling, Dynamic Data Exchange (DDE), and multimedia.

This book focuses on examples. After the presentation of each concept or Delphi component, you'll find an example (sometimes more than one) that shows how the feature can be used. All told, there are slightly more than 300 examples presented in the book and included on the companion CD. Most of the examples are quite simple and focus on a single feature. More complex examples are often built step-by-step, with intermediate steps including partial solutions and incremental improvements.

In this book, I've tried to skip reference material almost completely. Because Delphi provides extensive online documentation, to include lists of methods and properties of components in the book would not only be superfluous, it would also make it obsolete as soon as the software changes slightly. I suggest that you read this book with the Delphi Help files at hand, to have reference material readily available. Also, if you read it near a computer, you can test and run the programs immediately, and follow instructions as you come to them.

However, I've done my best to allow you to read the book away from a computer if you prefer (as I tend to). Screen images and the key portions of the listings should help in this direction. To see the full listings, however, you'll need to use the companion CD. When faced with a choice between displaying listings or adding new content, I chose new content. In fact, this edition has about 50 more examples than the previous edition.

Even if you tend to read books from cover to cover as I do, considering the size of this book and the various topics it covers, you might want to follow your own personal path. Use the Table of Contents and chapter introductions to find the sections best suited to your programming interests and level of experience.

The book uses just a few conventions to make it more readable. All the source code elements, such as the keywords, the names of properties, classes, and functions appear in `this font`, and listings are formatted for readability as discussed in Chapter 4. There are notes of different types, and a "New" icon added to mark specific Delphi 3 features.

The Companion CD

The companion CD holds the source code of the 300 examples discussed in the book. As I mentioned, in the text you'll mainly find small code excerpts, while on the companion CD you'll be able to see the full code. You'll also be able to run the examples immediately, since the compiled programs are already on the CD. This way, you can copy only the examples you want to modify onto your hard disk.

There are basically four ways you can browse the source code of the examples:

- You can open them in Delphi, possibly copying them first to a hard disk. In this case you'll need to remove the read-only attribute of the files on the CD before you can make any changes to them.

- You can open the CODEMD3.HTM file in the BOOKCODE directory with your favorite Web browser, and follow the links throughout the source code of the example. Every source code file, in fact, has been converted to HTML using Delphi's default syntax highlighting.

- You can open the CROSSREF.HTM file in the BOOKCODE directory with your favorite browser, to see an alphabetical list of identifiers—class, function, method, and property names, among others—from the book's examples. For each identifier, you'll find a list of links to all the source code files where it is used.

- You can use the CDVIEW application I've specifically written to browse the CD contents. This program can be used to look at the source code and run the executable files much more quickly than loading the files in Delphi (although you don't get the syntax highlighting).

The directory structure of this part of the CD is quite simple. Basically, each chapter has its own directory, with subdirectories named after each example.

NOTE In a few cases, the names of an example's project and executable files do not match the name of the directory containing them, particularly for those examples with multiple versions. In these cases, the name of the example mentioned in the text is the directory name, not the project name. Since there is a single Delphi project in each directory, it should be quite simple to find a particular example.

Besides the examples for this edition, the CD also includes all the examples from the previous editions. Since many examples are similar, you'll often find alternative coding solutions compatible with older versions of Delphi.

Third-Party Tools

On the companion CD you'll also find third-party tools, components, and documentation. Some of the tools and components are in demo or shareware versions. Of course, you'll need to register the demo and shareware components if you use them to build programs.

NOTE Many of the third-party components on the CD are Delphi 2 versions, because of the time constraints in publishing this book. You can install them in Delphi 2, and if you like them, look for an updated version on the Internet.

The CD also contains some electronic Delphi magazines, provided as Windows Help files or Acrobat files (the Acrobat reader is included, in case you don't have it).

My Own Tools

On the companion CD of this edition of *Mastering Delphi* you'll also find, for the first time, a small collection of tools I've written. They are not terribly powerful but they are certainly useful. You'll find free updates of some of these tools on my home page. The CD's Readme file provides a short overview of these tools. I've also mentioned them in the text when discussing a related topic.

The Readme Files

In addition to the main Readme file, which summarizes all the contents of the companion CD, and the Readme file in the Tools directory, most of the third-party software components provide their own Readme (or similarly named) files. These files contain important information about using the software legally and effectively, and may also direct you to online updates for the software.

How to Reach the Author

If you find any problems in the text or examples in this book, I would be happy to hear from you. You can reach me directly via electronic mail (see the address below). You can also find updates for the book and its source code on the Sybex Web site at:

`http://www.sybex.com`

and on my own Web page at:

`http://ourworld.compuserve.com/homepages/marcocantu`

My home page also hosts news and tips, the list of conferences and seminars I'll be speaking at (so we might have a chance to meet), links to other sites, and my collection of Delphi components.

I would definitely like to hear from you. Besides reporting errors and problems, please give me your unbiased opinion of the book or tell me which example you liked best and which you liked least. My e-mail address on Compuserve is `100273,2610` or `marcocantu`. From the Internet, that becomes:

`marcocantu@compuserve.com`

PART I

Delphi and Object Pascal

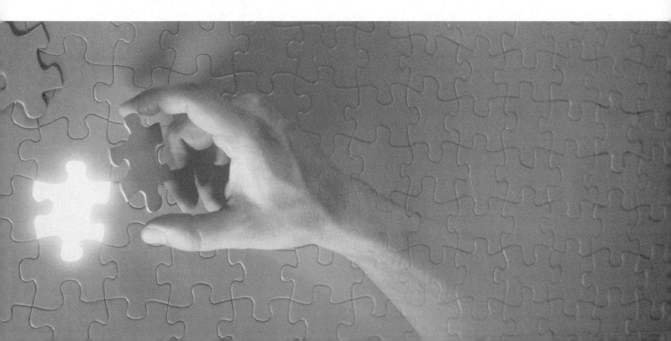

A Form Is a Window
(and an ActiveX)

- Creating a form

- Components and properties

- Program compilation

- Events and code

- Delphi as a two-way tool

- From a form to an ActiveX

In this chapter, we will build our first Windows application using Delphi. We'll also build our first ActiveForm. This chapter is a fast-paced introduction to the Delphi environment; and although it covers many basic topics, even experienced programmers may find good tips and hints (in fact, the chapter also introduces some brand-new Delphi 3 features).

Windows applications are usually based on windows. So, how are we going to create our first window? We'll do it by using a form. As the first part of the title suggests, a form really is a window in disguise. There is no real difference between the two concepts, at least from a general point of view. Later on, we'll be able to create a form of a slightly different type, called an ActiveForm. This is actually an ActiveX control based on a form, and we'll be able to use it inside a Web browser. An ActiveX control is also a window, although this special window must implement specific capabilities. Delphi 3 automatically adds these features to a specific group of forms, called ActiveForms.

> **NOTE**
>
> If you look closely, a form is always a window, but the reverse isn't always true. Some Delphi components are windows, too. A push button is a window. A list box is a window. To avoid confusion, I'll use the term *form* to indicate the main window of an application or a similar window and the term *window* in the broader sense.

Creating Your First Form

Even though you have probably already created at least some simple applications in Delphi, I'm going to show you the process again, to highlight some interesting points. Creating a form is one of the easiest operations in the system: you only need to open Delphi, and it will automatically create a new, empty form for you, as you can see in Figure 1.1. That's all there is to it.

If you already have another project open, choose File ➤ New Application to close the old project (you may be prompted to save some of the files) and open a new blank project. Believe it or not, you already have a working application. You can run it, using the Run button on the toolbar or the Run ➤ Run menu command, and it will result in a standard Windows program. Of course, this application won't be very useful, since it has a single empty window with no capabilities.

FIGURE 1.1

The empty form created when you open the Delphi environment.

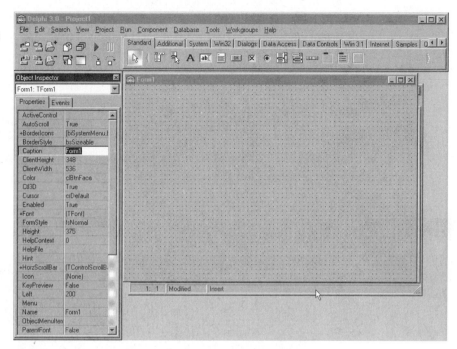

Adding a Title

Before we run the application, let's make a quick change. The title of the form is *Form1*. For a user, the title of the main window stands for the name of the application. Let's change *Form1* to something more meaningful.

When you first open Delphi, the Object Inspector window should appear on the left side of the form (see Figure 1.1 again). If it doesn't, open it by choosing View ➤ Object Inspector or pressing the F11 key. The Object Inspector shows the properties of the selected component. The window contains a tab control with two pages. The first page is labeled Properties. The other page is labeled Events and shows a list of events that can take place in the form or in the selected component.

The properties are listed in alphabetical order, so it's quite easy to find the ones you want to change. We can change the title of the form simply by changing the Caption property, which is selected by default. While you type a new caption, you can see the title of the form change. If you type *Hello*, the title of the form changes immediately, as you can see in Figure 1.2. As an alternative, you can modify the internal name of the form by changing its Name property. If you have not entered a new caption, the new value of the Name property will be used for the Caption property, too.

NOTE   Only a few of the properties of a component change while you type the new value. Most are applied when you finish the editing operation and press the Enter key (or move the input focus to a new property).

FIGURE 1.2

The Object Inspector and the form with a new title.

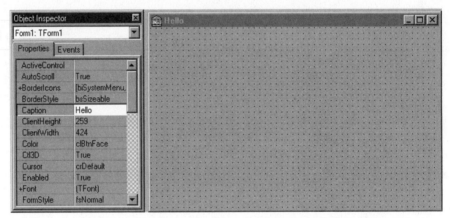

Although we haven't done much work, we have built a full-blown application, with a system menu and the default Minimize, Maximize, and Close buttons. You can resize the form by dragging its borders, move it by dragging its caption, maximize it to full-screen size, or minimize it. It works, but again, it's not very useful. If you look at the icon in the Taskbar, you'll see that something isn't right. Instead of showing the caption of the form as the icon caption, it shows the name of the project, something like *Project1*. We can fix this by giving a name to the project, which we'll do by saving it to disk with a new name.

Saving the Form

Select the Save Project or Save Project As command from the File menu, and Delphi will ask you to give a name to the source code file associated with the form, and then to name the project file. Since the name of the project should match the caption of the form (*Hello*), I've named the form source file HELLOF.PAS, which stands for *Hello Form*. I've given the project file the name HELLO.DPR.

Unfortunately, we cannot use the same name for the project and the unit that defines the form; for each application, these items must have unique names. Adding the letter *F* after the form name is a solution that was common in the 16-bit version of Delphi, because file names could not exceed 8 characters. Starting with Delphi 2, we can use long file names, so we can also name the file HELLOFORM. You could use a totally different name, or simply call it Mainform. However, with this approach you will end up with a number of forms (in different projects) that all have the same name, which can become confusing.

> **NOTE**
>
> Both files have been placed in the HELLO subdirectory of directory 01 (for Chapter 1) on the companion CD. This is the directory structure I'll use to save source files for examples throughout the book.

The name you give to the project file is used by default at run-time as the title of the application, displayed by Windows in the Taskbar while the program is running. For this reason, if the name of the project matches the caption of the main form, it will also correspond to the name on the Taskbar. You can also change the title of the application by using the Application page of the Project Options dialog box (choose Project ➤ Options), or by writing a line of code to change the Title property of the Application global object. We will discuss this global object in detail in Chapter 25.

Using Components

Now it's time to start placing something useful in our Hello form. Forms can be thought of as component containers. Each form can host a number of components or controls. You can choose a component from the Components Palette above the form, in the Delphi window. There are four simple ways to place a component on a form. If you choose the Button component from the Standard page of the Components Palette, for example, you can do any of the following:

- Click on the component, move the mouse cursor to the form, press the left mouse button to set the upper-left corner of the button, and drag the mouse to set the button's size.

- Select the component as above, and then simply click on the form to place a button of the default height and width.

- Double-click on the icon in the Components Palette, and a component of that type will be added in the center of the form.

- Shift-click on the component icon, and place several components of the same kind in the form using one of the above procedures.

Our form will have only one button, so we'll center it in the form. You can do this by hand, with a little help from Delphi. When you choose View ➤ Alignment Palette, a toolbox with alignment icons appears (see Figure 1.3).

FIGURE 1.3

The form with the centered button and the Alignment Palette toolbox.

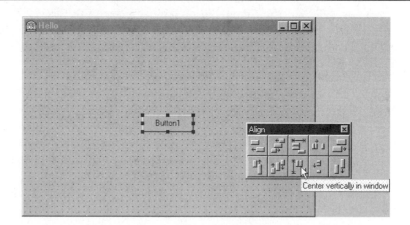

This toolbox makes a number of operations easy. It includes buttons to align controls or to center them in the form. Using the two buttons in the third column, you can place a component in the center of the form. Although we've placed the button in the center, as soon as you run the program, you can resize the form so that the button won't be in the center anymore. So the button is only in the center of the form at startup. Later on, we'll see how to make the button remain in the center after the form is resized, by adding some code. For now, our first priority is to change the button's label.

Changing Properties

Like the form, the button has a `Caption` property that we can use to change its label (the text displayed inside it). As a better alternative, we can change the name of the button. The name is a kind of internal property, used only in the code of the program. However, as I mentioned earlier, if you change the name of a button before changing its caption, the `Caption` property will have the same text as the `Name` property. Changing the `Name` property is usually a good choice, and you should generally do this early in the development cycle, before you write much code.

TIP
> It is quite common to define a naming convention for each type of component (usually the full name or a shorter version, such as "btn" for Button). If you use a different prefix for each type of component (as in "*ButtonHello*" or "*BtnHello*"), the combo box above the Object Inspector will list the components of the same kind in a group, because they are alphabetically sorted. If you instead use a suffix, naming the components "*HelloButton*" or "*HelloBtn*," components of the same kind will be in different positions on the list. In this second case, however, finding a particular component using the keyboard might be faster. In fact, when the Object Inspector is selected you can type a letter to jump to the first component whose name starts with that letter.

Besides setting a proper name for a component, you often need to change its `Caption` property. There are at least two reasons to have a caption different from the name. The first is that the name often follows a naming convention (as described in the note above) that you won't want to use in a caption. The second reason is that captions should be descriptive, and therefore they often use two or more words, as in my *Say hello* button. If you try to use this text as the `Name` property, however, Delphi will show an error message, such as the one in Figure 1.4.

The name is an internal property, and it is used as the name of a variable referring to the component. Therefore, for the `Name` property, you must follow the rules for naming an identifier in the Pascal language:

- An identifier is a sequence of letters, digits, or underscore characters of any length (although only the first 63 characters are significant).

- The first character of an identifier cannot be a number; it must be a letter or the underscore character.

- No spaces are allowed in an identifier.

- Identifiers are not case-sensitive, but usually each word in an identifier begins with a capital letter, as in *BtnHello*. But *btnhello*, *btnHello*, and *BTNHello* refer to this same identifier.

You can use the `IsValidIdent` **system function to check whether a given string is a valid identifier. The CheckId example on the companion disk calls this function while you type an identifier in its edit box, and changes the text color to indicate whether the string is valid (green) or not (red). The code of the example is quite simple, and you can look at it yourself on the disk. Try running this program to check any doubts about allowed component names.**

FIGURE 1.4

The error message shown when you try to use a space in the Name property of a component.

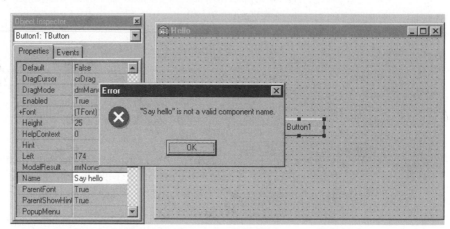

Here is a summary of the changes we have made to the properties of the button and form. At times, I'll show you the structure of the form of the examples as it appears once it has been converted in a readable format (I'll describe how to convert a form into text later in this chapter). I won't show you the entire textual description of a form (which is often quite long), but rather only its key elements. I won't include the lines describing the position of the components, their sizes, or some less important default values. Here is the code:

```
object Form1: TForm1
  Caption = 'Hello'
```

```
  OnClick = FormClick
  object BtnHello: TButton
    Caption = 'Say hello'
    OnClick = BtnHelloClick
  end
end
```

This description shows some attributes of the components and the events they respond to. We will see the code for these events in the following sections. If you run this program now, you will see that the button works properly. In fact, if you click on it, it will be pushed, and when you release the mouse button, the on-screen button will be released. The only problem is that when you press the button, you might expect something to happen; but nothing does, because we haven't assigned any action to the mouse-click yet.

Responding to Events

When you press the mouse button on a form or a component, Windows informs your application of the event by sending it a message. Delphi responds by receiving an event notification and calling the appropriate event-handler method. As a programmer, you can provide several of these methods, both for the form itself and for the components you have placed in it. Delphi defines a number of events for each kind of component. The list of events for a form is different from the list for a button, as you can easily see by clicking on these two components while the Events page is selected in the Object Inspector. Some events are common to both components.

There are several techniques you can use to define a handler for the OnClick event of the button:

- Select the button, either in the form or by using the Object Inspector's combo box (called the Object Selector), select the Events page, and double-click in the white area on the right side of the OnClick event. A new method name will appear, BtnHelloClick.

- Select the button, select the Events page, and enter the name of a new method in the white area on the right side of the OnClick event. Then press the Enter key to accept it.

- Double-click on the button, and Delphi will perform the default action for this component, which is to add a handler for the OnClick event. Other components have completely different default actions.

With any of these approaches, Delphi creates a procedure named BtnHelloClick (or the name you've provided) in the code of the form and opens the source code file in that position, as shown in Figure 1.5.

FIGURE 1.5

The Events page of the Object Inspector, and the edit window after you have created a procedure to handle the OnClick event of the HelloButton component.

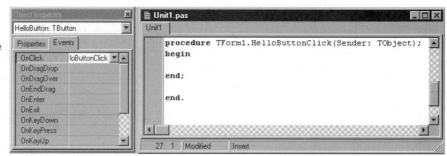

The default action for a button is to add a procedure to respond to the click event. Even if you are not sure of the effect of the default action of a component, you can still double-click on it. If you end up adding a new procedure you don't need, just leave it empty. Empty method bodies generated by Delphi will be removed as soon as you save the file. In other words, if you don't put any code in them, they simply go away.

TIP

When you want to remove an event-response method you have written from the source code of a Delphi application, you could delete all of the references to it. However, a better way is to delete all of the code from the corresponding procedure, leaving only the declaration and the begin and end keywords. The text should be the same as what Delphi automatically generated when you first decided to handle the event. When you save or compile a project, Delphi removes any empty methods from the source code and from the form description (including the reference to them in the Events page of the Object Inspector). Conversely, to keep an event-handler that is still empty, consider adding a comment to it, so that it will not be removed.

Now we can start typing some instructions between the begin and end key-words that delimit the code of the procedure. If you don't know the Object Pascal language, don't worry. We will explore its most important features in Chapters 4 and 5. Writing code is usually so simple that you don't need to be an expert in the language to start working with Delphi. For the moment, type the code below. You should type only the line in the middle, but I've included the whole source code of the procedure to let you know where you need to add the new code in the editor:

```
procedure TForm1.BtnHelloClick(Sender: TObject);
begin
  MessageDlg ('Hello, guys', mtInformation, [mbOK], 0);
end;
```

The code is very simple. There is only a call to a function, MessageDlg, to display a small message dialog box. The function has four parameters. Notice that as you type the open parenthesis, the Delphi editor will show you the list of parameters in a hint window, making it simpler to remember them.

NEW

This new feature, called *Code Parameters*, is part of the Code Insight technology introduced in Delphi 3. I'll describe it in more detail in the next chapter.

If you need more information about the parameters of this function and their meanings, you can click on its name in the edit window and press F1. This brings up the Help information. Since this is the first code we are writing, here is a summary of that description (the rest of this book, however, generally does *not* duplicate the reference information available in Delphi's Help system, concentrating instead on examples that demonstrate the features of the language and environment):

- The first parameter is the string you want to display: the message.

- The second parameter is the type of message box. You can choose mtWarning, mtError, mtInformation, or mtConfirmation. For each type of message, the corresponding caption is used and a proper icon is displayed at the side of the text.

- The third parameter is a set of values indicating the buttons you want to use. You can choose mbYes, mbNo, mbOK, mbCancel, or mbHelp. Since this is a set of values, you can have more than one of these values. Always use the proper set notation with square brackets ([and]) to denote the set, even if you have only one value, as in the line of the code above. (Chapter 4 discusses Pascal sets.)

- The fourth parameter is the help context, a number indicating which page of the Help system should be invoked if the user presses F1. Simply write 0 if the application has no help file, as in this case.

The function also has a return value, which I've just ignored, using it as if it were a procedure. In any case, it's important to know that the function returns an identifier of the button that the user clicked to close the message box. This is useful only if the message box has more than one button.

NOTE   Programmers unfamiliar with the Pascal language, particularly those who use C/C++, might be confused by the distinction between a function and a procedure. In Pascal, there are two different keywords to define procedures and functions. The only difference between the two is that functions have a return value.

After you have written this line of code, you should be able to run the program. When you click on the button, you'll see the message box shown in Figure 1.6.

FIGURE 1.6

The message box displayed when you press the "Say hello" button.

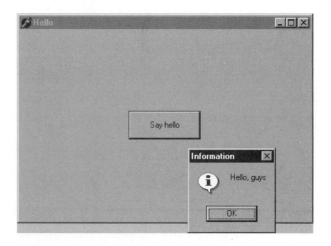

Every time the user clicks on the push button in the form, a message is displayed. What if the mouse is pressed outside that area? Nothing happens. Of course, we can add some new code to handle this event. We only need to add an OnClick event to the form itself. To do this, move to the Events page of the Object Inspector and select the form. Then double-click at the right side of the OnClick event, and you'll end up in the proper position in the edit window. Now add a new call to the MessageDlg function, as in the following code:

```
procedure TForm1.FormClick(Sender: TObject);
begin
  MessageDlg ('You have clicked outside of the button',
    mtWarning, [mbOK], 0);
end;
```

With this new version of the program, if the user clicks on the button, the hello message is displayed (Figure 1.6), but if the user misses the button, a warning message appears.

Notice that I've written the code on two lines, instead of one. The Pascal compiler completely ignores new lines, white spaces, tab spaces, and similar formatting characters. Program statements are separated by semicolons (;), not by new lines.

WARNING There is one case in which Delphi doesn't completely ignore line breaks: Strings cannot extend across multiple lines. In some cases, you can split a very long string into two different strings, written on two lines, and merge them by writing one after the other.

Compiling and Running a Program

Before we make any further changes to our Hello program, let's stop for a moment to consider what happens when you run the application. When you click on the toolbar Run button or select Run ➤ Run, Delphi does the following:

1. Compiles the Pascal source code file describing the form.

2. Compiles the project file.

3. Builds the executable (EXE) file, linking the proper libraries.

4. Runs the executable file, usually in debug mode.

The key point is that when you ask Delphi to run your application, it compiles it into an executable file. You can easily run this file from the Windows Explorer or using the Run command on the Start button.

NEW

In previous versions of Delphi, the executable file you obtained was invariably a stand-alone program. Delphi 3 still allows you to link all the required libraries into the executable file, but you can also specify the use of separate run-time packages.

Compiling this program as usual, linking all the required library code, produces an executable of about 200 Kb. For a smaller executable file, you can use the new Delphi 3 run-time packages. Simply select the Project ➤ Options menu command, move to the Packages page, and select the check box *Build with runtime packages*, as you can see in Figure 1.7. The effect of this option is to shrink the executable file to a mere 10 Kb!

FIGURE 1.7

Delphi 3 allows you to use packages to reduce the size of your executable file.

Packages are dynamic link libraries containing Delphi components (the Visual Components Library), as we'll see in more detail in Chapters 7 and 21. By using packages you can make an executable file much smaller. However, the program won't run unless the proper dynamic link libraries (such as vc130.dpl) are available on the computer where you want to run the program. The new DPL extensions stands for Delphi Package Libraries; it is the extension used by Delphi packages, which are technically DLL files. Using this extension makes it easier to recognize them (and find them on a hard disk).

If you add the size of this dynamic library to that of the small executable file, the total amount of disk space required by the program built with run-time packages is much bigger than the space required by the bigger stand-alone executable file. For this reason the use of packages is not always recommended. The great advantage of Delphi 3 over competing development tools is that you can easily choose whether to use the stand-alone executable or the small executable with run-time packages.

NOTE In both cases, Delphi executables are extremely fast to compile, and the speed of the resulting application is comparable with that of a C or C++ program. Delphi compiled code runs much faster (at least 10 times faster) than the equivalent code in interpreted or *semi-compiled* tools.

Some users cannot believe that Delphi generates real executable code, because when you run a small program, its main window appears almost immediately, as happens in some interpreted environments. To see for yourself, try this: Open the Environment Options dialog box (using Tools ➤ Options), move to the Preferences page, and turn on the Show Compile Progress option. Now select Project ➤ Build All. You'll see a dialog box with the compilation status. You'll find that this takes just a few seconds, or even less on a fast machine.

In the tradition of Borland's Turbo Pascal compilers, the Object Pascal compiler embedded in Delphi works very quickly. For a number of technical reasons, it is much faster than any C++ compiler. If you try using the new Borland C++ Builder development environment (which is very similar to Delphi) the compilation requires more time, particularly the first time you build an application. One reason for the higher speed of the Delphi compiler is that the language definition is simpler. Another is that the Pascal compilers and linkers have less work to do to include libraries or other compiled source files in a program, because of the structure of units.

Changing Properties at Run-Time

Now let's return to the Hello application, building a new version of the program, Hello2. This will allow us to see what happens when we change some properties at run-time.

> **TIP**
>
> To save the current version of the program without overwriting the previous version, you can close the project, copy all of the source files into a new subdirectory, and then delete the DSK file (if Delphi generated one). Then you can reopen the new version and modify it. If you use File ➤ Save Project As, instead, the new project will refer to (and modify) the source files of the older version. The same may happen if you forget to delete the DSK file.

In this book (as well as on the companion CD), you will find multiple versions for some complex examples that we build step-by-step. This makes it easier to understand the various steps and to test what doesn't work well in the intermediate versions. Along this line, the current example has two versions: Hello and Hello2. The different version names refer to different subdirectories where the files are stored on the companion CD.

We now want to try to change some properties at run-time. For example, we might change the text of HelloButton from *Say hello* to *Say hello again* after the first time a user clicks on it. You may also need to widen the button as the caption becomes longer. This is really simple. You only need to change the code of the HelloButtonClick procedure as follows:

```
procedure TForm1.HelloButtonClick(Sender: TObject);
begin
  MessageDlg ('Hello, guys', mtInformation, [mbOK], 0);
  HelloButton.Caption := 'Say Hello Again';
end;
```

NOTE

The Pascal language uses the := operator to express an assignment and the = operator to test for equality. At the beginning, this can be confusing for programmers coming from other languages. For example in C and C++, the assignment operator is =, and the equality test is ==. After a while, you'll get used to it. In the meantime, if you happen to use = instead of :=, you'll get an error message from the compiler.

A property such as Caption can be changed at run-time very easily, by using an assignment statement. Figure 1.8 shows the result of this operation.

FIGURE 1.8

The new caption of the button, after the change. Notice that the button is not in the center of the form, because it has been resized—a problem we will solve soon.

Most properties can be changed at run-time, and some can be changed *only* at run-time. You can easily spot this last group: They are not listed in the Object Inspector, but they appear in the Help file for the component. Some of these run-time properties are defined as read-only, which means that you can access their value but cannot change it. We'll discuss the details of property definitions in Chapter 6.

Adding Code to the Program

Our program is almost finished, but we still have a problem to solve, which will require some real coding. The button starts in the center of the form, but will not remain there when you resize the form. This problem can be solved in two radically different ways.

One solution is to change the border of the form to a thin frame, so that the form cannot be resized at run-time. Just move to the BorderStyle property of the form, and choose bsSingle instead of bsSizeable from the combo box. The other approach is to write some code to move the button to the center of the form each time the form is resized, and that's what we'll do next. Although it might seem that most of your work in programming with Delphi is just a matter of selecting options and visual elements, there comes a time when you need to write code. As you become more expert, the percentage of the time spent writing code will generally increase.

When you want to add some code to a program, the first question you need to ask yourself is Where? In an event-driven environment, the code is always executed in response to an event. When a form is resized, an event takes place: OnResize.

Select the form in the Object Inspector and double-click next to OnResize in the Events page. A new procedure is added to the source file of the form. Now you need to type some code in the editor, as follows:

```
procedure TForm1.FormResize(Sender: TObject);
begin
  BtnHello.Top := Form1.ClientHeight div 2 -
    BtnHello.Height div 2;
  BtnHello.Left := Form1.ClientWidth div 2 -
    BtnHello.Width div 2;
end;
```

To set the Top and Left properties of the button—that is, the position of its upper-left corner—the program computes the center of the frame, dividing the height and the width of the internal area or client area of the frame by 2, and then subtracts half the height or width of the button. Note also that if you use the Height and Width properties of the form, instead of the ClientWidth and ClientHeight properties, you will refer to the center of the whole window, including the caption at the top border.

This final version of the example works quite well, as you can see in Figure 1.9. This figure includes two versions of the form, with different sizes. By the way, this figure is a real snapshot of the screen. Once you have created a Windows application, you can run several copies of it at the same time by using the Explorer. By contrast, the Delphi environment can run only one copy of a program. When you run a program within Delphi, you start the integrated debugger, and it cannot debug two programs at the same time—not even two copies of the same program.

FIGURE 1.9

With the last version of the program, the Hello button always remains in the center of the form.

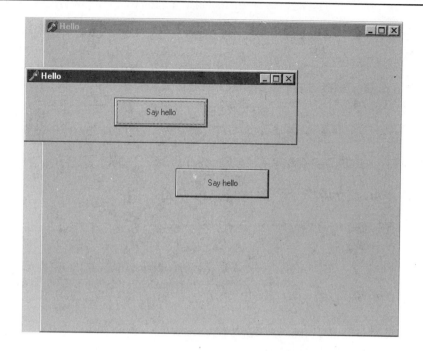

A Two-Way Tool

In the Hello example, we have written three small portions of code, to respond to three different events. Each portion of code was part of a different procedure (actually a method, as you'll learn reading Chapter 5). But where does the code we write end up? The source code of a form is written in a single Pascal language source file, the one we've named HELLOF.PAS. This file evolves and grows not only when you code the response of some events, but also as you add components to the form. The properties of these components are stored together with the properties of the form in a second file, named HELLOF.DFM.

Delphi can be defined as a two-way tool, since everything you do in the visual environment ends up in some code. Nothing is hidden away and inaccessible. You have the complete code, and although some of it might be fairly complex, you can edit everything. Of course, it is easier to use only the visual tools, at least until you are an expert Delphi programmer.

The term *two-way tool* also means that you are free to change the code that has been produced, and then go back to the visual tools. This is true as long as you follow some simple rules.

Looking at the Source Code

Let's take a look at what Delphi has generated from our operations so far. Every action has an effect—in the Pascal code, in the code of the form, or in both. When you start a new, blank project, the empty form has some code associated with it, as in the following listing.

```
unit Unit1;

interface

uses
    SysUtils, Windows, Messages, Classes, Graphics,
    Controls, Forms, Dialogs;

type
    TForm1 = class(TForm)
    private
        { Private declarations }
    public
        { Public declarations }
    end;

var
    Form1: TForm1;

implementation

{$R *.DFM}

end.
```

The file, named Unit1, uses a number of units and defines a new data type (a class) and a new variable (an object of that class). The class is named TForm1, and it is derived from TForm. The object is Form1, of the new type TForm1.

> **NOTE**
>
> *Units* are the modules into which a Pascal program is divided. When you start a new project, Delphi generates a program module and a unit that defines the main form. Each time you add a form to a Delphi program, you add a new unit. Units are then compiled separately and linked into the main program. By default, unit files have a .PAS extension and program files have a .DPR extension.

If you rename the files as suggested in the example, the code changes slightly, since the name of the unit must reflect the name of the file. If you name the file HELLOF.PAS, the code begins with

```
unit Hellof;
```

As soon as you start adding new components, the form class declaration in the source code changes. For example, when you add a button to the form, the portion of the source code defining the new data type becomes the following:

```
type
  TForm1 = class(TForm)
    Button1: TButton;
    ...
```

Now if you change the button's Name property (using the Object Inspector) to BtnHello, the code changes slightly again:

```
type
  TForm1 = class(TForm)
    BtnHello: TButton;
    ...
```

Setting properties other than the name has no effect in the source code. The properties of the form and its components are stored in a separate form description file (with a DFM extension).

Adding new event handlers has the biggest impact on the code. Each time you define a new handler for an event, a line is added to the data type definition of the form, an empty method body is added in the implementation part, and some information is stored in the form description file, too. The following listing shows the complete Pascal source code of the original Hello example:

```
unit Hellof;

interface
```

```
uses
  Windows, Messages, SysUtils, Classes, Graphics, Controls,
  Forms, Dialogs, StdCtrls;
type
  TForm1 = class(TForm)
    BtnHello: TButton;
    procedure BtnHelloClick(Sender: TObject);
    procedure FormClick(Sender: TObject);
  private
    { Private declarations }
  public
    { Public declarations }
  end;
var
  Form1: TForm1;
implementation
{$R *.DFM}
procedure TForm1.BtnHelloClick(Sender: TObject);
begin
  MessageDlg ('Hello, guys', mtInformation, [mbOK], 0);
end;
procedure TForm1.FormClick(Sender: TObject);
begin
  MessageDlg ('You have clicked outside of the button',
    mtWarning, [mbOK], 0);
end;
end.
```

It is worth noting that there is a single file for the whole code of the form, not just small fragments. Of course, the code is only a partial description of the form. The source code determines how the form and its components react to events. The form description (the DFM file) stores the values of the properties of the form and of its components. In general, source code defines the actions of the system, and form files define the initial state of the system.

The Textual Description of the Form

As I've just mentioned, along with the PAS file containing the source code, there is another file describing the form, its properties, its components, and the properties of the components. This is the DFM file, a binary file that isn't readable with an editor. However, if you load this file in the Delphi code editor, it will be converted into a textual description. This might give the false impression that the DFM file is indeed a text file. For performance reasons, Borland has decided to save the binary version, and has provided tools that allow for easy conversion to and from text. The simplest of these tools is the editor itself. In Figure 1.10, you can see the two representations of the file when loaded in two different editors.

TIP

You can open the textual description of a form simply by selecting the SpeedMenu of the form designer (that is, right-clicking on the surface of the form at design-time) and selecting the View as Text command. This closes the form, saving it if necessary, and opens the DFM file in the editor. You can later go back to the form using the View as Form command of the SpeedMenu in the editor window. The alternative is to open the DFM file directly in the Delphi editor.

To understand what is stored in the DFM file, you can look at the next listing, which shows the textual description of the form of the first version of the Hello example. This is exactly the code you'll see if you give the View as Text command in the local menu of the form:

```
object Form1: TForm1
  Left = 201
  Top = 110
  Width = 435
  Height = 300
  ActiveControl = BtnHello
  Caption = 'Hello'
  Font.Charset = ANSI_CHARSET
  Font.Color = clBlack
  Font.Height = -11
  Font.Name = 'MS Sans Serif'
  Font.Style = []
  OnClick = FormClick
  PixelsPerInch = 96
  TextHeight = 13
  object BtnHello: TButton
    Left = 161
```

```
        Top = 116
        Width = 105
        Height = 41
        Caption = 'Say hello'
        TabOrder = 0
        OnClick = BtnHelloClick
    end
end
```

FIGURE 1.10

The DFM file holds a binary description of the form, which can be converted to text using the Delphi editor.

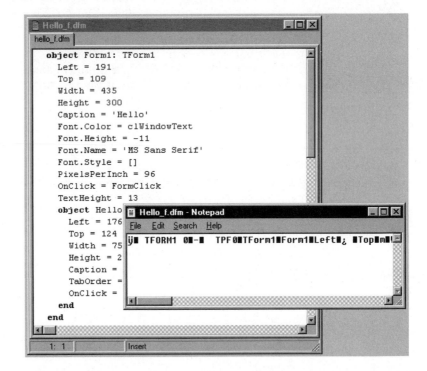

You can compare this code with what I used before to indicate the key features and properties of the form and its components. As you can see in this listing, the textual description of a form contains a number of objects (in this case, two) at different levels. The Form1 object contains the BtnHello object, as you can immediately see from the indentation of the text. Each object has a number of properties, and some methods connected to events (in this case, OnClick).

Once you've opened this file in Delphi, you can *edit* the textual description of the form, although this should be done with extreme care. As soon as you save the file, it will be turned back into a binary file. If you've made incorrect changes, this compilation will stop with an error message, and you'll need to correct the contents of your DFM file before you can reopen the form in the editor. For this reason, you shouldn't try to change the textual description of a form manually until you have a good knowledge of Delphi programming.

An expert programmer might choose to work on the text of a form for a number of reasons. For big projects, the textual description of the form is a powerful documenting tool, an important form of backup (in case someone plays with the form, you can understand what has gone wrong by comparing the two textual versions), and a good target for a version-control tool. For these reasons, Delphi also provides a DOS command-line tool, CONVERT.EXE, which can translate forms from the compiled version to the textual description and vice versa. As we will see in the next chapter, the conversion is also applied when you cut or copy components from a form to the Clipboard.

The Project File

In addition to the two files describing the form (PAS and DFM), a third file is vital for rebuilding the application. This is the Delphi project file (DPR). This file is built automatically, and you seldom need to change it, particularly for small programs. If you do need to change the behavior of a project, there are basically two ways to do so: You can use the Delphi Project Manager (see Figure 1.11) and set some project options, or you can manually edit the project file directly.

FIGURE 1.11

The Delphi Project Manager allows you to add units to a project, thus changing the contents of the project source file.

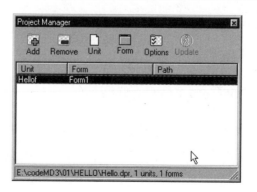

This project file is really a Pascal language source file, describing the overall structure of the program and its startup code:

```
program Hello;

uses
  Forms,
  Hellof in 'HELLOF.PAS' {Form1};

{$R *.RES}

begin
  Application.Initialize;
  Application.CreateForm(TForm1, Form1);
  Application.Run;
end.
```

You can see this file with the View ➤ Project Source menu command. As an alternative, you can click on the Select unit button of the SpeedBar or issue the equivalent menu command, View ➤ Units. When you use one of these commands, Delphi shows a dialog box with the list of the source files of the project. You can choose the project file (named Hello in the example), or any other file you are interested in seeing.

NOTE You can find more details on this code in Chapter 25, where I discuss the use of the global Application object. Some basic information about how to manage a project without editing its source file manually is provided in Chapter 2.

Building an ActiveForm

Now that we have built a simple form, we can move to a new dimension of Delphi 3 programming, building ActiveX and ActiveForm controls. I won't start discussing the technical details of OLE and ActiveX until Chapter 21, but here I want to show you how simple it is to turn our Hello form into an ActiveForm, and *activate* it into an Internet Browser.

WARNING   ActiveX and ActiveForm support is available only in the Professional and Client/Server editions of Delphi.

An ActiveX is a window control that implements several COM interfaces (as you'll learn in Part III of this book), and an ActiveForm is simply an ActiveX built using a Delphi form. ActiveX controls can be written in many languages and used by different development environments.

One of the reasons this ActiveX technology is so appealing is that once you've created a control or a form of this type, you can embed it into an HTML file, and show it inside a Web browser. If you place an ActiveX control or form on your Web page, people reaching you site will automatically download this application and run it on their computers.

In Chapter 23 we'll look in depth at this new technology, and see how to use Delphi to build ActiveX controls, while in Chapter 24 we will explore several ways you can use Delphi for Internet programming. For the moment we'll just go quickly through the steps of building your first ActiveForm.

Using Component Templates

What we have to do is create a brand new application, similar to the Hello program, with a similar button and a similar event handler. As we'll see in the next chapter, it is possible to copy a component to the Clipboard, and then paste it into another form to create a perfect clone. However, doing so you copy only the properties of the component, and not the events associated with it.

Delphi 3 allows you to copy one or more components, and install them as a new component template. This way, you also copy the code of the methods connected with the events of the component.

Simply open the Hello example, or any other one, select the component you want to move to the template (or a group of components), and then select the

Continued on next page

Using Component Templates (Continued)

Component ➤ Create Component Template menu command. This opens the Component Template Information dialog box, shown below. Here you enter the name of the template, the page of the Component Palette where it should appear, and an icon.

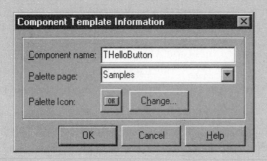

An ActiveX Library and an Active Form

We can create the ActiveForm in two steps. First we create a new project, an ActiveX Library. Simply close the current project, select the File ➤ New menu command, move to the ActiveX page, and choose ActiveX Library. Delphi will generate a new project file, which begins with the library keyword. As we'll see in Chapter 20's discussion of DLL programming, this means the compilation will generate a library instead of a program. You can now save the project to a directory of your choice (on the companion CD this is the XForm directory, and the project has the same name).

Now we can add to the library an active form. Again use the File ➤ New menu command and move to the ActiveX page (see Figure 1.12); but this time choose ActiveForm. In the resulting ActiveX Control Wizard dialog box, enter a name for the new ActiveX (I used *XForm1*), a file name (I used XFormF.Pas), and leave the check boxes as-is. Click OK, and the new form will be added to the project.

FIGURE 1.12

The ActiveX page of
the Object Repository,
activated with the File ➤
New menu command.

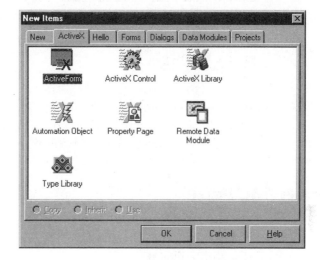

Now that we have a form, we can add a button and its code, as we've done
with the plain form earlier in this chapter. As an alternative you can *paste* into the
new form the component template we've defined (see the sidebar "Using Component Templates"): Simply move to the Samples page of the Component Palette
(or the page you've used) and select it. This copies the component into the form,
and also the code associated with its OnClick event. At this point you can try
building the program, with the Project ➤ Compile menu command. Do not try to
run it, because a library cannot be executed. Compiling this program produces a
file with the OCX extension.

Using the Project ➤ Web Deploy Options command you can provide the proper
information to generate an HTML demo file for your server. The actual HTML file
is generated by using the Project ➤ Web Deploy command. The basic information
required by the Web Deploy Options dialog box is:

- TargetDir, the directory where the OCX file (the compiler ActiveForm project) will be copied. This should be a directory managed by your Web server
  or simply another directory on your disk for local usage.

- Target URL, the URL of the OCX file. This might be simply a relative path
  from the directory of the HTML file using the ActiveForm. If the HTML and

OCX files are in the same directory, you can simply omit this or type a dot for the path (meaning the current directory).

- HTML Dir, the directory where you want Delphi to place the sample HTML page.

You can fill out other pages with the required package files, the compression and security options, and so on. The Web Deploy feature, anyway, is available only in the Client/Server Suite version of Delphi 3. If you have the Professional version you'll need to write the HTML file by hand.

The HTML Page

Once you've compiled an ActiveX control or form, you can actually test it within a Web browser. Delphi automatically generates the source code for a demo page, but I've slightly edited it:

```
<HTML>
<H2> Mastering Delphi 3 </H2>
<H1> Hello XForm </H1>
You should see your Delphi forms or controls embedded
in the form below.
<HR><center>
<OBJECT
    classid="clsid:367EDB03-8685-11D0-98D0-444553540000"
    codebase="file:XForm.ocx#version=1,0,0,0"
    width=350
    height=250
    align=center
    hspace=0
    vspace=0
>
</OBJECT>
<H2> Marco Cantù </H2>
</HTML>
```

Now you can simply place this HTML file (or the XForm.htm file from the companion CD) in the same directory as the compiled OCX file. Of course, you can move the files to different directories, and edit the HTML file with the complete

URL of the OCX file, after the command `codebase="file:..."` After this is done, you can use Microsoft's Internet Explorer (or any other ActiveX-compliant browser) to look at the result. You can see an example in Figure 1.13.

FIGURE 1.13

The ActiveForm we have built, as seen in Microsoft's Internet Explorer. I've just pressed the button.

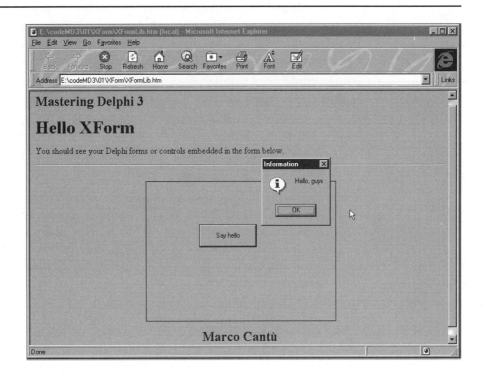

> **WARNING**
> Microsoft's Internet Explorer by default doesn't show an ActiveX unless it has the proper security signature. You can partially disable the security feature of this Internet browser (setting the Medium Safety Level in the Security options) to have it ask you if you want to show ActiveX controls or forms from uncertified sources.

What's Next

In this chapter, we created a simple program, added a button to it, and handled some basic events, such as a click with the mouse or a resize operation. Then we turned our simple form into an ActiveForm, and connected it to an HTML page. We also saw how to name files, projects, forms, and components, and how this affects the source code of the program. We looked at the source code of the simple programs we've built, although some of you might not be fluent enough in Object Pascal to understand the details.

Before we can look into more complex examples, we need to explore the Delphi development environment and study the Object Pascal language in depth. These are the topics of the other chapters of this first part of the book. The second part of the book will examine many VCL components, and in the third part we'll return to OLE, ActiveX, and Internet development.

The examples in this chapter should have shown you that Delphi is really easy to use. Now we'll start to look at the complex mechanisms behind the scenes that make this all possible. You'll see that Delphi is a very powerful tool, even though you can use it to write programs easily and quickly.

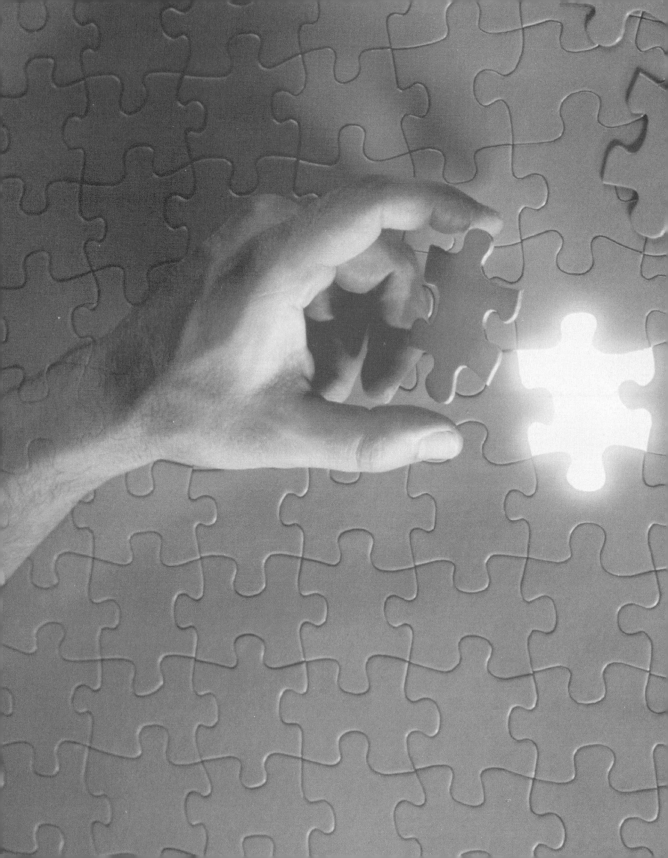

Highlights of the Delphi Environment

- Delphi menus and SpeedBars

- Form design tools

- The editor

- Code Insights

- Project management and compilation

- Tools for compiled programs

- Delphi source files

In a visual programming tool such as Delphi, the role of the environment is certainly important, at times even more important than the programming language used by its compiler or interpreter. This is a good reason to spend some time reading this chapter, or at least the sections covering new Delphi 3 features.

This chapter won't discuss all of the features of Delphi or list all of its menu commands. Instead, it will give you the overall picture and help you to explore some of the environment traits that are not obvious, while suggesting some tips that may help you. You'll find more information about specific commands and operations throughout the book.

Different Versions of Delphi

Before delving into the details of the Delphi programming environment, let's take a side step to underline two key ideas. First, there isn't a single version of Delphi; there are three of them:

- The basic version (the "Standard" edition) is aimed at Delphi newcomers and casual programmers. It has all the features required to write programs in Delphi for Windows and includes many new features not found in previous versions of Delphi. New Delphi 3 "Standard" features include new components, Code Insight, a new version of QuickReport, COM interface support, the new package architecture, component templates, DLL Debugging, and MS Access support built into the BDE.

- The second level (the "Professional" edition) is aimed at professional developers. It includes all the above features plus the TChart component, the source code of the VCL, ActiveX and ActiveForm development support, the Internet Solutions Pack, ODBC connectivity, Database Explorer, InstallShield Express, and the Open Tools API.

- The full-blown Delphi (the "Client/Server Suite" edition) is aimed at developers building client/server applications. It includes all the features of the "Professional" version plus the Decision Cube CrossTab component, extensive Web server support, SQL Links for native Client/Server BDE connection, the BDE Driver Development Kit, Open Environment's OLEnterprise and other tools for application partitioning, the SQL Monitor, the Visual Query Builder, the CASE Tool Expert, and the Data Pump Expert.

This book will cover features present in each of these versions, although the most specific target is the "Professional" version. If you own the "Standard" edition and see a description of a feature that doesn't seem to work, the problem may be a difference between the Delphi 3 versions. Of course, since the companion CD includes the executable files of all examples, you can still understand how many of these features work.

I'll cover some of the features of the Client/Server Suite, particularly in Chapter 18. However, this book does not have room to cover all of the many new features of Delphi Client/Server. Besides having different capabilities, the menu structure also has some differences between versions. For example, the Client/Server Suite includes a version control system (PVCS Version Management from Intersolv) that adds a new pull-down menu, Workgroups, to the menu bar.

Besides the different editions available, there are a number of ways to customize the Delphi environment. You can change the buttons of the SpeedBar, attach new commands to the Tools menu, hide some of the Windows or elements, and resize and move all of them. In the screen illustrations throughout the book, I'll try to use a standard user interface (as it comes out of the box); however, I have my preferences, and I generally install many add-ons, which might be reflected in some of the screen shots.

Asking for Help

Now we can really start our tour. The first element of the environment we'll explore is the Help system. Since this book teaches Delphi programming by working through a series of examples rather than listing all of the properties and methods of Delphi's components, you will want to complement the information provided here by using the reference material present in the Help files.

There are basically two ways to invoke the Help system: select the proper command in the Help pull-down menu, or choose an element of the Delphi interface or a token in the source code and press F1.

TIP
When you press F1, Delphi doesn't search for an exact match in the Help Search list. Instead, it tries to understand what you are asking. For example, if you press F1 when the text cursor is on the name of the Button1 component in the source code, the Delphi Help system automatically opens the description of the TButton class, since this is what you are probably looking for. This technique also works when you give the component a new name. Try naming the button Foo, then move the cursor to this word, press F1, and you'll still get the help for the TButton class. This means Delphi looks at the contextual meaning of the word for which you are asking help.

Note that there isn't just a single help file in Delphi. Most of the time, you'll invoke Delphi Help, but this file is complemented by an Object Pascal Help file, the Windows API Help, the Component Writer's Help, and many others (depending on your version of Delphi). These and other Help files have a common outline and a common search engine you can activate by pressing the Help Topics button while in the Help system. The Windows 95 help engine dialog box that appears allows you to browse the contents of all of the help files in the group, search for a keyword in the index, or start the Find engine. The three capabilities are available in separate pages of the Help Topics dialog box.

You can find almost everything in the Help system, but you need to know what to search for. Usually this is obvious, but at times it is not. Spending some time just playing with the Help system will probably help you understand the structure of these files and learn how to find the information you need.

The Help files provide a lot of information, both for beginner and expert programmers, and they are especially valuable as a reference tool. They list all of the methods and properties for each component, the parameters of each method or function, and similar details, which are particularly important while you are writing code. Borland also distributes reference materials in the form of Adobe Acrobat files. These are electronic versions of the printed manuals that come in the Delphi box, so you can search them for a word, and you can also print the portions you are interested in (or even the whole file if you've got some spare paper).

NOTE

The first version of Delphi included some Interactive Tutors in addition to the Help system. If you've never used Delphi (and if you have Delphi 1 installed), you might consider running these Tutors. They will guide you through Delphi's basic features and help you understand some of the terminology of the environment.

Besides the Delphi Help files, there are many sources of collections of tips and suggestions for Delphi programmers. The Delphi CD includes some FAQs (Frequently Asked Questions) and a collection of the Borland Technical Information short papers (TI). You can find updates of both at the Borland Web site (`http://www.borland.com`). Besides these official Borland documents, you'll find many more tips in Compuserve forums and Internet discussion groups. Obviously the Web is a great source of information about Delphi itself and third party products. You can find a collection of links (including my favorite Delphi Web pages) on the companion CD.

TIP

The best collection of technical information and tips on Delphi programming is *DTopics*, a big database maintained by Mike Orriss of 3K Computer Consultancy in Britain. This archive includes a specific Delphi program to browse it. You can find the latest version of both the program and the archive on many Internet sites. I couldn't include it on the companion CD because of legal copyright issues. *DTopics* is a compilation of the best messages about Delphi that have appeared in the Compuserve forums.

Delphi Menus and Commands

There are basically three ways to issue a command in the Delphi environment:

- Use the menu.

- Use the SpeedBar (or toolbar).

- Use a SpeedMenu (one of the local menus activated by pressing the right mouse button).

The Delphi menus offer many commands. I won't bore you with a detailed description of the menu structure. For this type of information, you can refer to the printed documentation or the Help file. In the following sections, I'll present some suggestions on the use of some of the menu commands. Other suggestions will follow in the rest of the chapter.

The File Menu

Our starting point is the File pull-down menu. This menu is somewhat complex, because it contains commands that operate on projects and commands that operate on source code files. Every time I open this menu, I need to think twice about what I'm doing. Some commands can be used to operate both on projects and on source code files. The commands related to projects are New, New Application, Open, Reopen, Save Project As, Save All, Close All, Add to Project, and Remove from Project. Besides these, there is also a specific Project pull-down menu. The commands related to source code files are New, New Form, New Data Module, Open, Reopen, Save, Save As, Close, and Print. Most of these commands are very intuitive, but some require a little explanation.

TIP   **Use the Reopen menu command to open projects or source code files you have worked on recently.**

The New command actually opens the New Items dialog box, also called the Object Repository. This dialog box can be used to invoke Delphi Wizards and to create items such as new applications, forms that inherit from existing forms, threads, DLLs, Delphi components, and ActiveX controls. I'll cover the Object Repository's rich set of features in the next chapter.

Another peculiar command is Print. If you are editing source code and select this command, the printer will output the text with syntax highlighting as an option. If you are working on a form and select Print from the File menu, the printer will produce the graphical representation of the form. This is certainly nice, but it can be confusing, particularly if you are working on other Delphi windows. Fortunately, two different print options dialog boxes are displayed (see Figure 2.1), so that you can check that the operation is correct.

FIGURE 2.1

The two Delphi print
options dialog boxes.

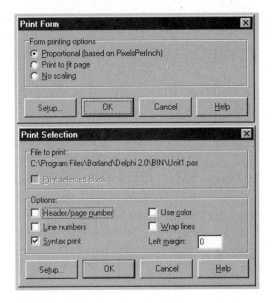

The Edit Menu

The Edit menu has some typical operations, such as Undo and Redo, and the Cut, Copy, and Paste commands, plus some specific commands for form or editor windows. There is also a new Delphi 3 command, Add to Interfaces, which relates to the development of ActiveForms. I'll cover it in Chapter 23.

The important thing to notice is that the standard features of the Edit menu (and the standard Ctrl+Z, Ctrl+X, Ctrl+C, and Ctrl+V keyboard shortcuts) work both with text and with form components. There are also some differences worth noting. For example, when you work with the editor, the first command of this pull-down menu is Undo; when you work with the form, it becomes Undelete. Unfortunately, the Form Designer has very limited Undo capabilities.

Of course, you can copy and paste some text in the editor, and you can also copy and paste components in one form, or from one form to another. You can even paste components to a different parent window of the same form, such as a panel or group box.

NEW   Besides using cut and paste commands, the Delphi 3 editor allows you to move source code by selecting and dragging words, expressions, or lines. If you drag text while pressing the Ctrl key, it will be copied instead of moved.

Copying and Pasting Components

What you might not have noticed is that you can also copy components from the form to the editor and vice versa. Delphi places components in the Clipboard along with their textual description, as you can see in Figure 2.2. You can even edit the text version of a component, copy the text to the Clipboard, and then paste it back into the form as a new component.

FIGURE 2.2

Delphi copies the textual representation of components to the Clipboard (as shown in the Clipboard Viewer), so that they are available to any text editor.

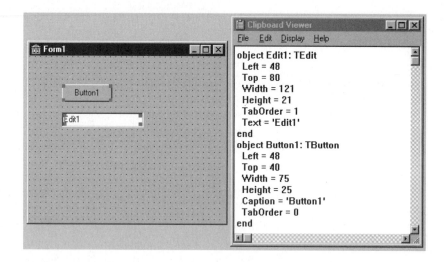

For example, if you place a button on a form, copy it, and then paste it into an editor (which can be Delphi's own source code editor or any word processor), you'll get the following description:

```
object Button1: TButton
  Left = 56
  Top = 48
  Width = 161
  Height = 57
```

```
    TabOrder = 0
    Caption = 'Button1'
  end
```

Now, if you change the name of the object, caption, or position, or add a new property, these changes can be copied and pasted back to a form. Here are some sample changes:

```
object MyButton: TButton
  Left = 200
  Top = 200
  Width = 180
  Height = 60
  TabOrder = 0
  Caption = 'My Button'
  Font.Name = 'Arial'
end
```

Copying the above description and pasting it into the form will create a button in the specified position with the caption *My Button* in an Arial font. To make use of this technique, you need to know how to edit the textual representation of a component, what properties are valid for that particular component, and how to write the values for string properties, set properties, and other special properties. When Delphi interprets the textual description of a component or form, it might also change the values of other properties related to those you've changed, and change the position of the component so that it doesn't overlap a previous copy. You can see how Delphi modifies the properties of the component by copying it back to the editor. For example, this is what you get if you paste the text above in the form, and then copy it again into the editor:

```
object MyButton: TButton
  Left = 112
  Top = 128
  Width = 180
  Height = 60
  Caption = 'My Button'
  Font.Charset = DEFAULT_CHARSET
  Font.Color = clWindowText
  Font.Height = -11
  Font.Name = 'Arial'
  Font.Style = []
  ParentFont = False
  TabOrder = 0
end
```

As you can see, some lines have been added automatically, to specify other properties of the font. Of course, if you write something completely wrong, such as this code:

```
object Button3: TButton
  Left = 100
  Eight = 60
end
```

which has a spelling error (a missing 'H'), and try to paste it into a form, Delphi will show an error indicating what has gone wrong, as you can see in Figure 2.3.

FIGURE 2.3

An error message is displayed when you try to paste a component with a property that doesn't exist or is misspelled.

You can also select several components and copy them all at once, either to another form or to a text editor. This might be useful when you need to work on a series of similar components. You can copy one to the editor, replicate it a number of times, make the proper changes, and then paste the whole group into the form again.

More Edit Commands

Along with the typical commands found on most Edit menus in Windows applications, Delphi includes a number of commands that are mostly related to forms. The specific operations for forms can also be accessed through the form Speed-Menu (the local menu you can invoke with the right mouse button) and will be covered later in the chapter.

TIP
One command not replicated in a form's local menu is Lock Controls, which is very useful for avoiding an accidental change to the position of a component in a form. For example, you might try to double-click on a component and actually end up moving it. Since there is no Undo operation on forms, protecting from similar errors by locking the controls after the form has been designed can be really useful.

The Search Menu

The Search menu has some standard commands, too, such as Search and Replace, and the new Delphi 3 Find in Files command (you can see its dialog box in Figure 2.4).

FIGURE 2.4

The new Find in Files dialog box allows you to search text in multiple files.

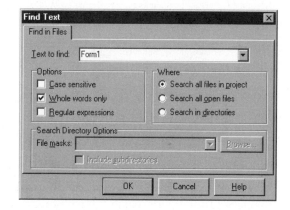

The Find in Files command allows you to search for a string in all of the source code files of a project, all the open files, or all the files in a directory (optionally including its subdirectories), depending on the radio button you check. The result of the search will be displayed in the message area at the bottom of the editor window. You can select an entry to open the corresponding file and jump to the line containing the text.

TIP

You can use the Find in Files command to search for component, class, and type definitions in the VCL source code (if your version of Delphi includes it). This is an easy way to get detailed information on a component, although using Help is generally faster and simpler.

Other commands are not so simple to understand. The Incremental Search command is one of them. When you select this command, instead of showing a dialog box where you enter the text you want to find, Delphi moves to the editor. There, you can type the text you want to search for directly in the editor message area, as you can see in Figure 2.5.

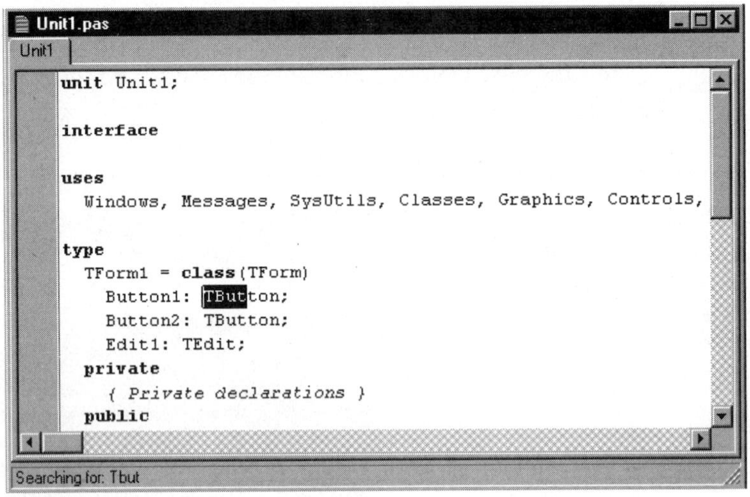

FIGURE 2.5

An example of using the
Incremental Search
command.

```
Unit1.pas                                                    _ □ ✕
Unit1
    unit Unit1;

    interface

    uses
        Windows, Messages, SysUtils, Classes, Graphics, Controls,

    type
        TForm1 = class(TForm)
            Button1: TButton;
            Button2: TButton;
            Edit1: TEdit;
        private
            { Private declarations }
        public

Searching for: Tbut
```

When you type the first letter, the editor will move to the first word starting with that letter. (But if your search text isn't found, the letters you typed won't even be displayed in the editor message area.) If that is not the word you are looking for, just keep typing; the cursor will continue to jump as you add letters. Although this command might look strange at first, it is very effective and extremely fast, particularly if you are typing and invoke it with a shortcut key (Ctrl+E if you are using the standard editor shortcuts).

The Go to Line Number command is quite intuitive. The Find Error command might seem strange at first. It is used to find a particular run-time error, not to search for a compiler error. When you are running a stand-alone program and you hit a very bad error, Delphi displays an internal address number (that is, the *logical* address of the compiled code). You can enter this value in the Find Error dialog box to have Delphi recompile the program, looking for the specific address. When it finds the address, Delphi shows the corresponding source code line. Often, however, the error is not in one of the lines of your code, but in a line of library or system code; in this (quite frequent) case the Find Error command cannot locate the offending line.

The last command on the Search menu, Browse Symbol, invokes the Object Browser, a tool you can use to explore all the symbols defined in a compiled program. To understand the output of the Object Browser, you need a good understanding of the Object Pascal language and of the Visual Component Library (VCL). We will use the Object Browser in Chapter 26.

The View Menu

The View pull-down menu combines the features you usually find in View and Window menus. There is no Window menu, because the Delphi environment is not an MDI application. Most of the View commands can be used to display one of the Windows of the Delphi environment, such as Project Manager, the Breakpoints list, or the Components command. Some of these windows are used during debugging; others when you are writing code. Most of these windows will be described later in this chapter.

NOTE It is possible to add a new item to the View menu, CPU Window, which can be used during debugging to view the Assembler code generated by the Delphi compiler, execute it step by step, and view the status of the CPU registers. You can learn more about enabling and using this window in Chapter 26.

The commands on the second part of the View menu are important, which is why they are also available on the default SpeedBar. The Toggle Form/Unit (or F12) command is used to move between the form you are working on and its source code. If you use a source code window big enough to hold a reasonable amount of text, you'll use this command often. As an alternative, you can place the two windows (the editor and the form) so that a portion of the one below is always visible. With this arrangement, you can click on it with the mouse to move it to the front.

The New Edit Window command opens a second edit window. It is the only way to view two files side by side in Delphi, since the editor uses tabs to show the multiple files you can load. Once you have duplicated the edit window, you can make each one hold a different set of files, or view two portions of the same file.

The last two commands on the View menu can be used to hide the SpeedBar or the Components palette, although this is a good way to make Delphi look silly and uncomfortable. Working on forms without the Components palette is certainly not easy. If you remove both the SpeedBar and the Components palette, the Delphi main window is reduced to a bare menu.

The Project Menu

The next pull-down menu, Project, has commands to manage a project and compile it. Add to Project and Remove from Project are used to add forms or Pascal source code files to a program and to remove them from a project.

NEW

The Client/Server version of Delphi 3 includes two more commands, Web Deploy Options and Web Deploy, which are not available in the other editions. The discussion of creating ActiveForms at the end of the last chapter gave an idea of their role.

The Compile command builds or updates the application executable file, checking which source files have changed and recompiling them when needed. With Build All, you can ask Delphi to compile every source file of the project, even if it has not been changed since the last compilation. If you just want to know whether the syntax of the code you've written is correct, but you do not want to build the program, you can use the Syntax Check command.

The next Project command, Information, displays some details about the last compilation you've made. Figure 2.6 shows the information related to the compilation of the last program presented in Chapter 1, Hello2.

FIGURE 2.6

The information about the compilation of the Hello2 example of the last chapter.

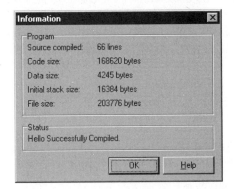

```
Information                                    [X]
┌─Program────────────────────────────────────┐
│  Source compiled:    66 lines               │
│  Code size:          168620 bytes           │
│  Data size:          4245 bytes             │
│  Initial stack size: 16384 bytes            │
│  File size:          203776 bytes           │
└─────────────────────────────────────────────┘
┌─Status─────────────────────────────────────┐
│  Hello Successfully Compiled.               │
└─────────────────────────────────────────────┘
                        [   OK   ]   [  Help  ]
```

TIP

The Compile command can be used only when you have loaded a project in the editor. If no project is active and you load a Pascal source file, you cannot compile it. However, if you load the source file *as if it were a project*, that will do the trick and you'll be able to compile the file. To do this, simply select the Open Project toolbar button and load a PAS file. Now you can check its syntax or compile it, building a DCU (Delphi Compiled Unit).

At the end of the Project menu comes the Options menu, used to set compiler and linker options, application object options, and so on. When you change the project options, you can check the Default box to indicate that the same set of options should be used for new projects. We will discuss project options again in this chapter and then throughout the book in the context of related topics.

The Run Menu

The Run menu could have been named Debug as well. Most of its commands are related to debugging, including the Run command itself. When you run a program within the Delphi environment, you execute it under the integrated debugger (unless you disable the corresponding Environment option). The Run command and the corresponding SpeedBar icon are among the most commonly used commands, since Delphi automatically recompiles a program before running it—at least if the source code has changed. Simply hit F9 as a shortcut to compile and run a program.

The next command, Parameters, can be used to specify parameters to be passed on the command line to the program you are going to run, and to provide the name of an executable file when you want to debug a DLL (DLL debugging is another new Delphi 3 feature). The remaining commands are all used during debugging, to execute the program step by step, set breakpoints, inspect the values of variables and objects, and so on. Some of these debugging commands are also available directly in the editor SpeedMenu.

NEW   Delphi 3 has a couple of new commands related to ActiveX development (and not found in the "Standard" edition). The Register ActiveX Server and Unregister ActiveX Server menu commands basically add or remove the Windows Registry information about the ActiveX control defined by the current project.

The Component Menu

The commands of the Component menu can be used to write components, add them to a package, or to install packages in Delphi. The New Component command invokes the simple Component Wizard. The three installation commands, Install Component, Import ActiveX Library, and Install Packages, can be used to add to the environment new Delphi components, packages, or ActiveX controls. Executing any of these commands adds the new components to the specified package and to the Components palette. We will discuss these menu commands in more detail in Chapters 6, 18, and 23.

Component Templates

We briefly used the Create Component Template menu item in the last chapter. When you issue this command after selecting one or more components in a form, it opens a dialog box (shown in Chapter 1) where you specify the name of the new component template, a page on the Palette, and an icon. By default, the template name is the name of the first component you've selected followed by the word *template*. The default template icon is the icon of the first component you've selected, but you can replace it with an icon file. The name you give to the component template will be used to describe it in the Components palette (when Delphi displays the fly-by hint).

All the information about component templates is stored in a single file, DELPHI32.DCT, but there is apparently no way to retrieve this information and edit a template. What you can do, however, is place the component template in a brand new form, edit it, and install it again as a component template *using the same name*. This way you can override the previous definition.

The Database Menu

The Database menu collects the Delphi database-related tools, such as the Database Form Wizard and the Database Explorer.

The Client/Server Suite edition has the SQL Explorer instead of the Database Explorer (although the menu items is invariably called Database ➤ Explore) and a menu item to start the SQL Monitor. In this edition, the Database menu is followed by the Workgroups menu. This pull-down menu can be activated in the Professional edition of Delphi by installing a Version Control System (not included in the package). Actually, if you have the Client / Server Suite edition and don't use the included VCS you should uninstall it, by removing the corresponding entry from the Windows Registry (in the Software/Borland/Delphi3.0 section). The pull-down menu takes a while to display the first time, something I find annoying.

The Tools Menu

The Tools menu simply lists a number of external programs and tools, just to make it easier to run them. You can use the Tools command to configure and add new external tools to the pull-down. As you can see in Figure 2.7, besides simply running a program, you can pass some parameters to it. Simple parameter lists can be passed directly on the command line, while complex ones can be built by clicking the Macros button in the lower part of the Tool Properties dialog box.

FIGURE 2.7

It is easy to add new applications to the Tools menu.

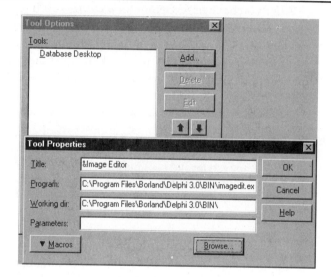

The Tools menu also includes a command to configure the Repository (discussed in the next chapter) and the Options command to configure the whole Delphi development environment. The Environment Options dialog box has many pages related to generic environment settings (the Preferences page, shown later on in Figure 2.9), packages and library settings, many editor options (in the pages Editor, Display, and Colors), a page to configure the Components Palette, one for the object Browser, and one of the new Code Insight technology. I'll discuss many of these options when covering related features.

The Help Menu

The Help menu can be used to get information about Delphi (Help ➤ Help Topics) and also to display the Delphi About box. In this window, you can hold down the

Alt key and type the letters VERSION to see the Delphi version and build number. Using other key combinations (as mentioned in the acknowledgments at the beginning of the book) you can see a list of the people involved in building Delphi. The Help menu is often populated by third-party Delphi Wizards (or Experts, as they were called in Delphi 2), although some of them add items to other Delphi pull-down menus.

The Delphi Toolbar

After you have used Delphi for a while, you'll realize that you use only a small subset of the available commands frequently. Some of these commands are probably already on the SpeedBar (Borland's name for a toolbar); some are not. If the commands you use a lot are not there, it's time to customize the SpeedBar so that it really helps you to use Delphi more efficiently.

TIP An alternative to using the SpeedBar is to use shortcut keys. Although you must remember some key combinations to use them, shortcut keys let you invoke commands very quickly, particularly when you are writing code and your fingers are already on the keyboard.

You can easily resize the SpeedBar by dragging the thick line between it and the Components Palette. But the most important operations you can do with the SpeedBar are adding, removing, or replacing the icons using the Configure command of the SpeedBar's own local menu (simply press the right mouse button over it). This operation invokes the SpeedBar Editor (shown in Figure 2.8), one of the Delphi tools with the best user interface, at least in my opinion.

To add an icon to the SpeedBar, you simply need to find it under the proper category (corresponding to a pull-down menu), and drag it to the bar. In the same way, you can drag an icon away from the SpeedBar or simply move it to another location. During these operations, you can easily leave some space between groups of icons, to make them easier to remember and select.

FIGURE 2.8

The SpeedBar Editor. Once it is open, you can drag icons from it to the SpeedBar.

The Local Menus

Although Delphi has a good number of menu items, not all of the commands are available though the pull-down menus. At times, you need to use local menus, also called SpeedMenus in Borland jargon, for specific Windows or window areas. To activate a SpeedMenu, right-click over a window, or press Alt+F10. Even if you have other alternatives, using a SpeedMenu is usually faster because you don't need to move the mouse up to the menu bar and select two levels of menus. It's also often easier, since all the SpeedMenu commands are related to the current window. Almost every window in Delphi (with the exclusion of dialog boxes) has its own SpeedMenu with related commands. I really suggest you get used to right-clicking on windows, because this is not only important in Delphi, but also has become a standard for most applications in Windows 95. Get used to it, and add SpeedMenus to the applications you build with Delphi, too.

Working with the Form Designer

Designing forms is the core of visual development in the Delphi environment. Every component you place on a form and every property you set is stored in a file describing the form (a DFM file) and has some effect on the source code associated with the form (the PAS file).

When you start a new, blank project, Delphi creates an empty form, and you can start working with it. You can also start with an existing form (using the various templates available), or add new forms to a project. A project (an application) can have any number of forms. Every time you work with a form at design-time, you are actually using Delphi's Form Designer. When you are working with a form, you can operate on its properties, on the properties of one of its components, or on those of several components at a time. To select the form or a component, you can simply click on it or use the Object Selector (the combo box in the Object Inspector), where you can always see the name and type of the selected item. You can select more than one component by Shift-clicking on the components, or by dragging a selection rectangle around the components on the form.

TIP Even when a component covers the whole surface of the form, you can still select the form with the mouse. Just press and hold Shift while you click on the selected component. This will deselect the component and select the form by default. Using the keyboard, you can press Esc to select the parent of the current component.

While you are working on a form, the SpeedMenu has a number of useful features (some of which are also available in the Edit menu). You can use the Bring to Front and Send to Back commands to change the relative position of components of the same kind (you can never bring a graphical component in front of a component based on a window, as we will see in Chapter 6). In an inherited form, you can use the command Revert to Inherited to restore the properties of the selected component to the values of the parent form.

When you have selected more than one component, you can align or size them. Most of the options in the Alignment dialog box are also available in the Alignment palette (accessible through the View ➤ Alignment Palette menu command). You can also open the Tab Order and Creation Order dialog boxes to set the tab order of the visual controls and the creation order of the nonvisual controls. You can use the Add to Repository command to add the form you are working on to a list of forms available for use in other projects. Finally, you can use the View as Text command to close the form and open its textual description in the editor. A corresponding command in the editor SpeedMenu (View as Form) will reverse the situation.

Along with specific SpeedMenu commands, you can set some form options by using the Tools ➤ Options command and choosing the Preferences page (see Figure 2.9). The options related to forms are listed under the Form Designer heading and refer to grid activation and size. The grid makes it easier to place components exactly where you want them on the form by "snapping" them to fixed positions and sizes. Without a grid, it is difficult to align two components manually (using the mouse).

FIGURE 2.9

The Preferences page of the Environment Options dialog box.

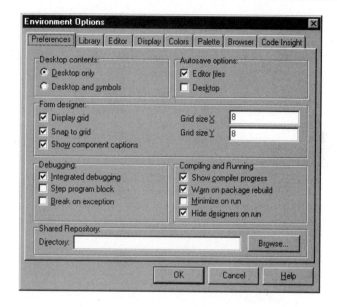

There are two alternatives to using the mouse to set the position of a component: you can either set values for the Left and Top properties, or you can use the arrow keys while holding down Ctrl. Using arrow keys is particularly useful for fine-tuning an element's position. (The Snap to Grid option works only for mouse operations.) Similarly, by pressing the arrow keys while you hold down Shift, you can fine-tune the size of a component. If you press Shift+Ctrl+an arrow key, instead, the component will be moved only at grid intervals.

Along with the commands described so far, a form's SpeedMenu offers other commands when particular components are selected. In some cases, these menu commands correspond to component properties; others contain particularly useful commands. Table 2.1 lists the commands added to the SpeedMenu of a form when some of the components are selected (the TeeChart, Quick Report and Decision Cube components add too many commands to list here). Notice that in some cases these actions are also the default action of the component, the one automatically activated when you double-click on it in the Form Designer.

TABLE 2.1   SpeedMenu Commands Added When Specific Components Are Selected

Menu Command	Components
Menu Designer	MainMenu, PopupMenu
Query Builder	Query (if the Visual Query Builder is available)
Fields Editor	Table, Query, StoredProc, ClientDataSet
Explore	Table, Query, StoredProc, Database (if the Database Explorer or SQL Explorer are available)
Define Parameters	Query, StoredProc
Database Editor	Database
Assign Local Data	ClientDataSet
UpdateSQL Editor	UpdateSQL
Execute	BatchMove
Columns Editor	DBGrid
Edit Report	Report
ImageList Editor	ImageList
New Page	Page Control
Next Page, Previous Page	Page Control, NoteBook, TabbedNotebbok
Next Frame, Previous Frame	Animate
Insert Object	OleContainer
New Button, New Separator	ToolBar
Properties, About	All the ActiveX controls
Action Editor	WebDispatcher
ResponseEditor	QueryTableProducer, DataSetTableProducer

The Component Palette

When you want to add a new component to the form you are working on, you can click on a component in one of the pages of the Component palette, and then click on the form to place the new component. On the form, you can press the left mouse button and drag the mouse to set the position and size of the component at once, or just click to let Delphi use a default size.

Each page of the palette has a number of components; each component has an icon and a name, which appears as a "fly-by" hint (just move the mouse on the icon and wait for a second). The hints show the official names of components, which I'll use in this book. They are drawn from the names of the classes defining the component, without the initial *T* (for example, if the class is TButton, the name is *Button*).

> **TIP**
>
> If you need to place a number of components of the same kind into a form, shift-click on that component in the palette. Then, every time you click on the form, Delphi adds a new component of that kind. To stop this operation, simply click on the standard selector (the arrow icon) on the left side of the Component palette.

If you are temporarily using a mouseless computer, you can add a component by using the View ➤ Components List command. Select a component in the resulting list or type its name in the edit window, and then click on the Add to Form button.

Of course, you can completely rearrange the components in the various pages of the palette, adding new elements or just moving them from page to page: select Tools ➤ Options and move to the Palette page. In this page of the dialog box, you can simply drag a component from the Components list box to the Pages list box to move that component to a different page. It's not a good idea to move components on the palette too often. If you do, you'll probably waste time trying to locate them afterwards.

> **TIP**
>
> When you have too many pages in the Component palette, you'll need to scroll them to reach a component. There is a simple trick you can use in this case: rename the pages with shorter names, so that all the pages will fit on the screen. Obvious...once you've thought about it.

The Object Inspector

When you are designing a form, you use the Object Inspector to set values of component or form properties. Its window lists the properties (or events) of the selected element and their values in two resizable columns. An Object Selector at the top of the Object Inspector indicates the current component and its data type; and you can use it to change the current selection. The Object Inspector doesn't list all of the properties of a component. It includes only the properties that can be set at design-time. As mentioned in Chapter 1, other properties are accessible only at run-time. To know about all the different properties of a component, refer to the Help files.

The right column of the Object Inspector allows only the editing appropriate for the data type of the property. Depending on the property, you will be able to insert a string or a number, choose from a list of options (indicated by an arrow), or invoke a specific editor (indicated by an ellipsis button). When a property allows only two values, such as True and False, you can toggle the value by double-clicking on it. If there are many values available, a double-click will select the next one in the list. If you double-click a number of times, all the values of the list will appear, but it is easier to select a multiple-choice value using the small combo box. For some properties, such as Color, you can enter a value, select an element from the list, or invoke a specific editor! Other properties, such as Font, can be customized either by expanding their subproperties (indicated by a plus or minus sign next to the name) or by invoking an editor. In other cases, such as with string lists, the special editors are the only way to change a property.

The subproperty mechanism is available with sets and with classes. We will see what a set is and how it works in Chapter 4, and we will discuss Object Pascal classes in Chapter 5. When you expand subproperties, each of them has its own behavior in the Object Inspector, again depending on its data type.

You will use the Object Inspector often. It should always be visible when you are editing a form, but it can also be useful to look at the names of components and properties while you are writing code. For this reason, the Object Inspector's SpeedMenu has a Stay on Top command, which keeps the Object Inspector window in front of the Form Designer and the editor.

The Alignment Palette

The last tool related to form design is the Alignment palette. You can open this palette with the View menu's Alignment Palette command. As an alternative, you can choose the components you want to align, and then issue the Align command from the SpeedMenu of the form.

The Alignment palette features a number of commands to position the various controls, center them, space them equally, and so on. To see the effect of each button, simply move the mouse over the window and look at the fly-by hints. When I'm designing complex forms, I position the Alignment palette on the far side of the screen and make sure it always stays in sight by using the Stay on Top command of its SpeedMenu.

Writing Code in the Editor

Once you have designed a form in Delphi, you usually need to write some code to respond to some of its events, as we did in Chapter 1. Every time you work on an event, Delphi opens the editor with the source file related to the form. You can easily jump back and forth between the Form Designer and the source code editor by clicking the Toggle Form Unit button on the SpeedBar, by clicking on the corresponding window, or by pressing the F12 function key.

The Delphi editor allows you to work on several source code files at once, using a "notebook with tabs" metaphor. Each page of the notebook corresponds to a different file. You can work on units related to forms, independent units of Pascal code, and project files; open the form description files in textual format; and even work on plain text files. You can jump from a page of the editor to the next by pressing the Ctrl+Tab keys (or Shift+Ctrl+Tab to move in the opposite direction).

When you work with the editor, you should probably expand its window so that you can see as many full lines of code as possible. A good approach is to size the editor so that it and the Object Inspector are the only windows that appear on the screen when you are writing code. By having the Object Inspector visible you can immediately see the names of the design-time properties of the components.

There are a number of environment options that affect the editor, mostly located in the Editor Options, Editor Display, and Editor Colors pages of the Environment Options dialog box. In the Preferences page, you can set the editor's Autosave feature. Saving the source code files each time you run the program can save the day when your program happens to crash the whole system (something not so rare as you might think). The other three pages of editor options can be used to set the default editor settings like keystroke mappings, syntax highlighting features, and font. Most of these options are fairly simple to understand.

The SpeedMenu of the edit window has some commands for debugging and others related to the editor itself, such as those to close the current page, open the file or unit under the cursor, view or hide the message pane below the window, and invoke the editor options discussed before.

Using Editor Bookmarks

The Delphi 3 editor also lets you set line bookmarks. When you are on a line of the editor, you can press Ctrl+Shift plus a number key from 0 to 9 to set a new bookmark, which then appears in the small gutter margin of the editor (see Figure 2.10). Then you can use the Ctrl key plus the number key to jump back at that line of the editor. Pressing the Ctrl+Shift+*number* toggles the status of the bookmark, so you can use this combination again to remove it.

FIGURE 2.10

The bookmarks in the gutter of the Delphi editor.

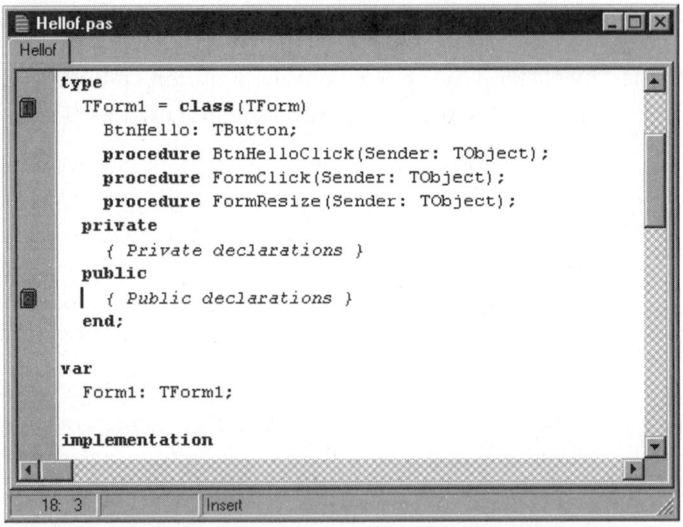

```
Hellof.pas

Hellof

type
  TForm1 = class(TForm)
    BtnHello: TButton;
    procedure BtnHelloClick(Sender: TObject);
    procedure FormClick(Sender: TObject);
    procedure FormResize(Sender: TObject);
  private
    { Private declarations }
  public
    { Public declarations }
  end;

var
  Form1: TForm1;

implementation

18: 3          Insert
```

Bookmarks are quite useful when you have a long file and you are editing multiple methods at the same time, or to jump from the class definition to the definition of a method of the class.

Borland hasn't documented bookmarks very well, probably because they have some flaws. If you set again a given bookmark, the editor moves it. This might seem reasonable, but is actually a problem: If you create a new bookmark and happen to use the number of an existing one, by error, the older bookmark will be removed. Another odd behavior is that you can add multiple bookmarks on the same line, but you'll only see the glyph of one of them. The real problem, however, is that bookmarks are not saved along with the file, nor restored when you reopen it. So they can be used only for a single editing session.

Delphi 3 Code Insight

 Delphi 3 adds to the editor several new features, collectively known as Code Insight. The basic idea of this technology is to make it easier for both newcomers and experienced programmers to write code. There are four capabilities (all new in Delphi 3) that Borland calls Code Insight:

- The Code Completion Wizard allows you to choose the property or method of an object simply by looking it up on a list, or by typing its initial letters. It also allows you to look for a proper value in an assignment statement.

- The Code Templates Wizard allows you to insert one of the predefined code templates, such as a complex statement with an inner `begin-end` block. You can also easily define new templates.

- The Code Parameter Wizard displays, in a hint or ToolTip window, the data type of a function's or method's parameters while you are typing them.

- The ToolTip Expression Evaluation is a debug-time feature. It shows you the value of the identifier, property, or expression under the mouse cursor.

I'll cover the ToolTip Expression Evaluation later in this chapter, while introducing debugging features; in the next three sections I'll give you some more details on the other three Code Insight capabilities. You can enable and disable (or configure) each of these wizards in the Code Insight page of the Environment Options dialog box.

Code Completion

There are two ways to activate this Wizard. You can simply type the name of an object, such as `Button1`, then add the dot, and wait:

```
Button1.
```

Delphi will display a list of valid properties and methods you can apply to the object, as shown in Figure 2.11. The time you have to wait before the list is displayed depends on the Code Completion Delay option, which you can configure in the Code Insight page.

FIGURE 2.11

The Code Completion
Wizard in action.

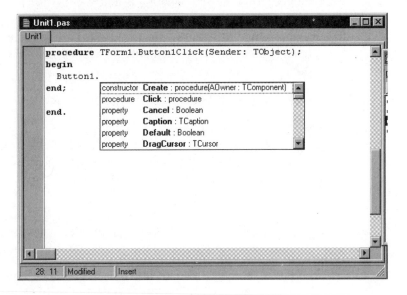

As an alternative you can type the initial portion of the property or method name, as in Button1.Ca, and then press Ctrl+SpaceBar to get the list immediately, but this time, the Wizard will try to guess which property or method you were looking for by looking at the characters you typed. You can also use this key combination in an assignment statement. If you type:

```
x :=
```

and then press Ctrl+SpaceBar, Delphi will show you a list of possible objects, variables, or constants you can use at this point in the program (that is, in the current scope).

Notice that Delphi determines the elements to show in this list dynamically, by constantly parsing the code you write in the background. So if you add a new variable to a unit, it will show up in the list.

Code Templates

Unlike the Code Completion Wizard, the Code Templates Wizard must be activated manually. You can do this by typing Ctrl+J to show a list of all of the templates.

More often, you'll first type a keyword, such as if or array, and then press Ctrl+J, to activate only the templates starting with those letters. For some keywords Borland has defined multiple templates, all starting with the keyword name (such as *ifA* and *ifB*). So if you press the keyword and then Ctrl+J, you'll get all the templates related to the keyword.

You can also use Code Templates Wizard simply to give a name to a common expression. For example, if you use the MessageDlg function often, you might want to enter a new Code Template called *mess*, type a description, and add then the following text:

```
MessageDlg ('|',
   mtInformation, [mbOK], 0);
```

Now every time you need to create a message dialog box, you simply type *mess* and then Ctrl+J, and you get the full text. The vertical line (or pipe) character indicates the position in the source code where Delphi will move the cursor after pasting the text. You should choose the position where you want to start typing to edit the code generated by the template.

As this example demonstrates, Code Templates have no direct correspondence to language keywords, but are a more general mechanism. Code Templates are saved in the DELPHI32.DCI file, so it should be possible to copy this file to make your templates available on different machines. There seems to be no easy way to merge two Code Templates files, and there are no third-party tools yet to add more templates to a machine. Those enhancements will need to wait until Borland documents the internal structure of the .DCI file.

Code Parameter

The third Code Insight technology I'll discuss here is Code Parameters, the one I was really hoping for and probably like best. Previously when I had to call an unfamiliar function I used to type the name, and then press F1 to jump to the Help system and see its parameters. Now I can simply type the function name, type the open (left) parenthesis, and the parameter names and types appear immediately on a fly-by hint window, as you can see in Figure 2.12.

Notice in this figure that the first parameter appear in boldface type. After you type the first parameter and a comma, the second parameter will be set in bold, the same with the third, and so on. This is very useful for functions with many parameters, like some functions of the Window API. Try typing *CreateWindow(* and you'll understand what I mean.

FIGURE 2.12

The new Code Parameter Wizard prompts you with the parameter types of functions and procedures while you enter them.

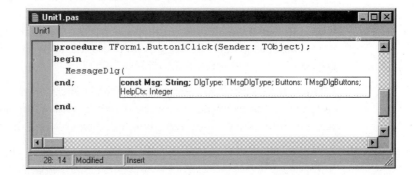

Again, the Code Parameters Wizard works by parsing your code in the background. So if you write the following procedure at the beginning of the implementation section of a unit:

```
implementation
```

```
procedure ShowInt (X: Integer);
begin
  MessageDlg (IntToStr (X),
    mtInformation, [mbOK], 0);
end;
```

you'll have full information about its parameters when you type *ShowInt(* later.

Managing Projects

In Delphi you also need to know how to manage project files. In Chapter 1, we saw that you can open a project file in the editor and edit the file. However, there are simpler ways to change some of the features of a project. For example, you can use the Project Manager window and Project Options.

The Project Manager

When a project is loaded, you can choose the View ➤ Project Manager command to open a project window. The window lists all of the forms and units that make up the current project. In Figure 2.13, you can see an example of such a window, showing a project with two different forms. The Project Manager's SpeedMenu allows you to perform a number of operations on the project, such as adding new or existing files, removing files, viewing a source code file or a form, and adding the project to the repository. Most of these commands are also available in the SpeedBar of this window.

FIGURE 2.13

The Project Manager window with its SpeedMenu.

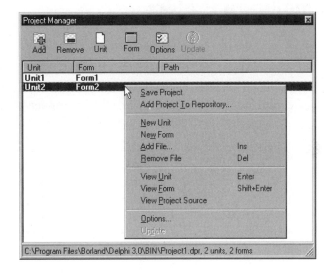

Setting Project Options

From the Project Manager (or from the Project menu), you can invoke the Project Options dialog. The first page of Project Options, named Forms, lists the forms that should be created automatically at program startup (the default behavior) and the forms that are created manually by the program. You can easily move a form from one list to the other. The next page, Application, is used to set the name of the application and the name of its Help file, and to choose its icon. Other Project Options choices relate to the Delphi compiler and linker, version information, and the use of run-time packages.

NOTE

There are two ways to set compiler options. One is to use the Compiler page of the Project Options, the other is to set or remove individual options in the source code with the {$X+} or {$X–} commands, where X is the option you want to set. This second approach is more flexible, since it allows you to change an option only for a specific source code file, or even for just a few lines of code.

All of the Project Options are saved automatically with the project, but in a separate file with a DOF extension. This is a text file you can easily edit. You should not delete this file if you have changed any of the default options.

Compiling a Project

There are several ways to compile a project. If you run it (by pressing F9 or clicking on the SpeedBar icon), Delphi will compile it first. When Delphi compiles a project, it compiles only the files that have changed. If you select Compile ➤ Build All, instead, every file is compiled, even if it has not changed. This second command is seldom used, since Delphi can usually determine which files have changed and compile them as required. The only exception is when you change some project options. In this case you have to use the Build All command to put the new options into effect.

The project lists the source code files that are part of it, and any related forms. This list is visible both in the project source and in the Project Manager, and is used to compile or rebuild a project. First, each source code file is turned into a Delphi compiled unit, a file with the same name as the Pascal source file and the DCU extension. For example, UNIT1.PAS is compiled into UNIT1.DCU.

When the source code of the project itself is compiled, the compiled units that constitute the project are merged (or linked) into the executable file, together with code from the VCL library. You can better understand the compilation steps and follow what happens during this operation if you enable the Show Compiler Progress option. You'll find this option on the Preferences page of the Environment Options dialog box, under the Compiling heading (see Figure 2.9). Although this slows down the compilation a little, the Compile window lets you see which source files are compiled each time (unless your computer is too fast; Delphi might compile several files per second on a fast PC). You can see an example of this window in Figure 2.14.

FIGURE 2.14

A compiler progress window.

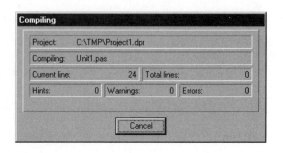

Exploring a Compiled Program

Delphi provides a number of tools you can use to explore a compiled program, including the debugger and the Browser. The following sections provide a brief introduction to these tools, which I'll cover in detail in Chapter 26.

The Integrated Debugger

Delphi has an integrated debugger with a huge number of features. However, Borland also sells a more powerful stand-alone debugger, called Turbo Debugger. For nearly all of your debugging tasks, the integrated debugger works well enough, particularly if you activate the CPU view window (see Chapter 26 for this). The stand-alone Turbo Debugger might be useful in a few special cases.

You don't need to do much to use the integrated debugger. In fact, each time you run a program from Delphi, it is executed by default in the debugger. This means that you can set a breakpoint to stop the program when it reaches a specific line of code. For example, open the Hello2 example we created in Chapter 1 and double-click on the button in the form to jump to the related code. Now set a breakpoint by clicking in the editor gutter margin, by choosing the Toggle Breakpoint command of the editor SpeedMenu, or by pressing F5.

The editor will highlight the line where you've placed the breakpoint, showing it in a different color. Now you can run the program as usual, but each time you press the button, the debugger will halt the program, showing you the corresponding line of code. You can execute this and the following lines one at a time (that is, step-by-step), look at the code of the functions called by the code, or continue running the program.

When a program is stopped, you can inspect its status in detail. Although there are many ways to inspect a value, the simplest approach is the ToolTip Expressions Evaluation introduced in Delphi 3. Simply move the mouse over the name of any variable, and you'll see its current value in a small hint window, as shown in Figure 2.15 (where you can also see a breakpoint in the editor).

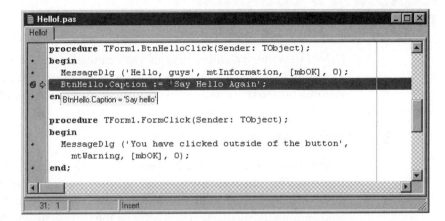

FIGURE 2.15

The ToolTip Expressions
Evaluation is the simplest
way to inspect the values
of objects and their
properties.

TIP

At times the ToolTip Expressions Evaluation seems not to work. This
may happen if the optimizing compiler has removed some sections of
generated code and placed variables in CPU registers. If you disable
the compiler optimizations, you'll get more ToolTips.

The Object Browser

Once you have compiled a program, you can run the Object Browser to explore it
(even if you are not running or debugging it). This tool allows you to see all of the
classes defined by the program (or by the units used directly and indirectly by the
program), all the global names and variables, and so on. For every class, the Object
Browser shows the list of properties, methods, and variables—both local and
inherited, private and public. The information displayed in the Object Browser may
not mean much if you're still not familiar with the Object Pascal language used by
Delphi. We'll return to the Object Browser in Chapter 26, after we've covered the
information you need to understand it properly.

Additional Delphi Tools

Delphi provides many other programming tools. For example, the Menu Designer
is a visual tool used to create the structure of a menu. There are also the various
Wizards, used to generate the structure of an application or a new form. Other tools

are stand-alone applications related to the development of a Windows application, such as the Image Editor and WinSight, a "spy" program that lets you see the Windows message flow.

There are several external database tools, such as ReportSmith, the Database Desktop, and the Database Explorer (some of which are not available in the lower-level editions of Delphi). A programmer can use other third-party tools to cover weak areas of Delphi. For example, you can use a full-blown resource editor (such as Borland's Resource Workshop), or a tool to generate Help files more easily. Here is a short list indicating where in the book I'll introduce some of the external Delphi tools:

- Several of the Wizards are covered in Chapter 3.

- The Menu Designer is described in Chapter 9.

- The Bitmap Editor is used in several chapters, starting with Chapter 11.

- Database tools are the topics of Chapters 16 and 17.

- WinSight is discussed in Chapter 26.

- Report building is described in Chapter 28.

You can also install and use many additional Delphi add-on tools from third-party vendors. You'll find demo versions of some of these tools on the companion CD, but there are many others available. Some of the add-on tools really complement Delphi nicely, and make you more productive.

The Files Produced by the System

As you have seen, Delphi produces a number of files for each project, and you should know what they are and how they are named. There are basically two elements that have an impact on how files are named: the names you give to a project and its forms, and the predefined file extensions used by Delphi for the files you write and those generated by the system. Table 2.2 lists the extensions of the files you'll find in the directory where a Delphi project resides. The table also shows when these files are created and their importance for future compilations.

TABLE 2.2   The Delphi File Extensions

Extension	File Type and Description	Creation Time	Required to Compile?
BMP ICO CUR	Bitmap file, Icon file, Cursor file: standard Windows files used to store bit-mapped images.	Development— Image Editor	When used as the value of a property, you don't need it anymore, but you'll generally keep these files anyway. Some applications load them at run-time.
DCP	Delphi Component Package: a file with symbol information for the code that was compiled into the package. It doesn't include compiled code, stored in the DCU files.	Compilation	Required when you use packages. This file is not part of a project, and is built by Delphi as a side effect of compiling a package. You'll distribute it along with DPL files.
DCU	Delphi Compiled Unit: The result of the compilation of a Pascal file.	Compilation	Only if the source code is not available. DCU files for the units you write are an intermediate step, so they make compilation faster.
DFM	Delphi Form File: A binary file with the description of the properties of a form (or a data module) and of the components it contains.	Development	Yes. As described earlier in this and the last chapter, you can convert this file into a textual format.
~DF	Backup of Delphi Form File (DFM).	Development	No. This file is produced when you save a new version of the unit related to the form (and the form file along with it).
DLL	Dynamic Link Library: another version of an executable file.	Compilation— Linking	See EXE.
DOF	Delphi Option File: A text file with the current settings for the project options. The extension was OPT in Delphi 1.	Development	Required only if special compilation options have been set.
DPK	Delphi Package: The project source code file of a package.	Development	Yes.
DPL	Delphi Package Library: a DLL including Delphi components to be used by the Delphi environment at design-time or by applications at run-time.	Compilation— Linking	See EXE. You'll distribute packages to other Delphi developers.

TABLE 2.2 The Delphi File Extensions (Continued)

Extension	File Type and Description	Creation Time	Required to Compile?
DPR	Delphi PRoject file: this file actually contains Pascal source code.	Development	Yes.
~DP	Backup of the Delphi Project file (DRP).	Development	No. This file is generated automatically when you save a new version of a project file.
DSK	Desktop file: This file contains information about the position of the Delphi windows, the files open in the editor, and other desktop settings.	Development	No. You should actually delete it if you copy the project to a new directory.
DSM	Delphi Symbol Module: Stores all the browser symbol information.	Compilation (only if option is set)	No. This file is used by the Object Browser when you have not recompiled or cannot recompile a project. Otherwise the Object Browser uses information in memory.
EXE	Executable file: The Windows application you've produced.	Compilation-Linking	No. This is the file you'll distribute. It includes all of the compiled units, the source, and forms, and can be updated by recompiling the program.
HTM	Or HTML, Hyper Text Markup Language: The file used for Internet Web pages	Web Deployment of a Delphi ActiveX	No. This is not involved in the project compilation. It can be produced again by repeating the Web Deployment process.
OCX	OLE Control eXtension: this is a special version of a DLL, containing ActiveX controls or forms.	Compilation-Linking	See EXE.
PAS	Pascal file: The source code of a Pascal unit, either a unit related to a form or a stand-alone unit.	Development	Yes.
~PA	Backup of the Pascal file (PAS).	Development	No. This file is generated automatically by Delphi when you save a new version of the source code.

TABLE 2.2   The Delphi File Extensions (Continued)

Extension	File Type and Description	Creation Time	Required to Compile?
RES	Resource file: The binary file associated with the project and usually containing its icon. You can add other files of this type to a project.	Development	Yes. The main RES file of an application can be rebuilt by Delphi according to the information in the Application page of the Project Options dialog box.
STR	String Resource file: This is a RES file including a string table generated for the resourcestring constants declared in the code (see Chapter 4).	Compilation	No, the file is built automatically by Delphi while compiling the program.
TLB	Type Library: This is a file build automatically or by the Type Library Editor for OLE server applications.	Development	This is a file OLE programs will need.

Most of these files, including the source and backup files, the project files, the options, and the desktop file, are very small. The compiled units are slightly bigger, and the executable file is often the biggest file in a project's directory, unless there are files with debugging information, such as the DSM file.

The DSM file holds Browser information to allow the use of the Object Browser, even when you have changed the source code (but always after a first successful compilation). This can be particularly useful when you accidentally introduce an error in the code, preventing the compiler from building a new version of the program. DSM files, however, can easily become quite big, so you might prevent them from being created by checking Desktop Only instead of Desktop and Symbols in the Preferences page of the Environment Options dialog box. This will also slightly reduce the compile/link time.

NEW   There are new type of files produced by Delphi 3 related to packages. As you can see in Table 2.2, DPK files are package source code files, while DPL and DCP files are the result of compiling a package. Delphi 3 can also generate OCX files, and even the HTML file required to deploy an ActiveX control or form. Other new types of files produced by the environment are the OLE type libraries (TLB) and the string resource files (STR).

The great advantage of Delphi over other visual programming environments is that most of the source code files are plain ASCII text files. We explored Pascal source code, project code, and form description files at the end of Chapter 1. Now let's take a minute to look at the structure of options and desktop files. Both types of files use a structure similar to Windows INI files, in which each section is indicated by a name enclosed in square brackets. For example, this is a fragment of the HELLO.DOF file of the Hello2 example:

```
[Compiler]
A=1
B=0
...
[Linker]
MapFile=0
MinStackSize=16384
MaxStackSize=1048576
...
[Directories]
OutputDir=
SearchPath=
```

NOTE   In Delphi 2 and Delphi 3, the option files use the DOF extension, while in Delphi 1 they used the OPT extension. These files have different contents and are not compatible between the two versions.

The initial part of this file, which I've omitted, is a long list of compiler options. The same structure is used by the desktop files, which are usually much longer. It is worth looking at what is stored in these files to understand their role. In short, a desktop file (.DSK) lists Delphi windows, indicating their position and status. For example, this is the description of the main window:

```
[MainWindow]
Create=1
Visible=1
State=0
Left=2
Top=0
Width=800
Height=97
```

These are some of the sections related to other windows:

```
[ProjectManager]
[AlignmentPalette]
[PropertyInspector]
[Modules]
[formxxx]
[EditWindowxxx]
[Viewxxx]
```

Besides environment options and window positions, the desktop file contains a number of history lists (lists of files of a certain kind), and an indication of the current breakpoints, watches, active modules, closed modules, and forms.

What's Next

This chapter presented an overview of the Delphi programming environment, including a number of tips and suggestions. Getting used to a new programming environment takes some time, particularly if it is a complex one. I could have devoted this entire book to detailing the Delphi programming environment, but I hope you'll agree that describing how to actually write programs is more useful and interesting.

A good way to learn about the Delphi environment is to use the Help system, where you can look up information about the environment elements, windows, and commands. Spend some time just browsing through the Help files. Of course, the best way to learn how the Delphi environment works is to use it to write programs. That's what Delphi is about. Now we can move on to an important feature of the Delphi environment we have only mentioned: the Object Repository and the Wizards.

CHAPTER

THREE

3

The Object Repository and the Delphi Wizards

- Delphi's Object Repository

- Reusing existing applications and forms

- The Database Form Wizard

- Other Delphi Wizards

- Configuring the Object Repository

When you start working on a new application (or simply a new form), you have two choices. You can start from scratch with a blank application or form, or you can choose a predefined model from the Object Repository. If you decide to pick an existing model from the Object Repository, you have even more alternatives. You can make a copy of an existing item (called a template in Delphi 1), you can inherit from an existing item, or you can use one of the available Wizards.

A *Wizard* is a code generator. (Borland used to call them *Experts*, but in Delphi 3 the official name has been changed to Wizards, following Microsoft tradition.) Wizards ask you a number of questions, and use your answers to create some basic code, following predefined rules. You then start working on a project or a form that already has some code and components. Usually, the code generated by these tools can be compiled immediately, and it makes up the basic structure on which you build your program or form.

The purpose of this short chapter is simply to introduce you to the Object Repository and the Delphi Wizards, and to show you how easy they are to use. We won't study the code they generate, since that will be the topic of many examples in the book. From a programming standpoint, the Wizards are really useful. The pitfall is that you might be tempted to use them without trying to understand what they do. For this reason, in some examples I'll build the code manually instead of using the corresponding Wizard.

The Object Repository

Delphi has several menu commands you can use to create a new form, a new application, a new data module, a new component, and so on. These commands are located in the File menu, and also in other pull-down menus. What happens if you simply select File ➤ New? Delphi opens the Object Repository (also called the New dialog box). The Object Repository is used to create new elements of any kind: forms, applications, data modules, libraries, thread objects, components, automation objects, and more. The Object Repository dialog box has a number of pages:

- The *New* and *ActiveX* pages allow you to create many different types of new items. At times when you create a new item, Delphi asks you the name of a new class and few other things, in a sort of *mini-Wizard*.

- The "current project" page (actually you'll see the name of the project) allows you to inherit from a form or data module included in your current project.

- The *Forms*, *Dialogs*, and *Data Modules* pages allow you to create a new element of these kinds starting from an existing one or using a Wizard.

- The *Projects* page allows you to copy the files from an existing project stored in the Repository, or use the Application Wizard.

Use the radio buttons at the bottom of the Object Repository dialog box to indicate that you want to copy an existing item, inherit from it, or use it directly without making a copy.

NOTE Chapter 5 and Appendix A introduce the concept of inheritance in object-oriented programming, and Chapter 12 discusses Delphi form inheritance in detail. In short, it is a way to add new capabilities to an existing form without making a full copy. This way, if you make a change in the original form, the inherited form will be affected, too.

When you select a Wizard instead of a template, the only available radio button is *Copy*, meaning you'll end up with a new copy, the generated code. You can tell that an item of the Object Repository corresponds to a Wizard from the light bulb glyph in its icon.

Keep in mind that I am discussing the pages of the Object Repository as they appear in Delphi Client/Server, but different editions of Delphi have fewer pages and items; and you can further customize the Repository, as we will see later on in this chapter.

TIP The Object Repository has a local menu that allows you to sort items in different ways (by name, by author, by date, or by description) and to show different views (large icons, small icons, lists, details). This last view is the only one that gives you the description, the author, and the date of the tool (as you will see in Figure 3.2, later on). This information is particularly important when looking at Wizards, projects, or forms you've added to the Repository.

The New Page

The New page of the Object Repository (shown in Figure 3.1) allows you to create several new items of the more commonly used kinds and is often an alternative to a direct menu command. Here is a list of the elements you can create from this page:

- *Application* creates a new blank project (the same as the command File ➤ New Application).

- *Component* creates a new Delphi component after you've completed the information requested by the simple Component Wizard. The same wizard can be activated with the Component ➤ New Component menu command. Chapter 18 discusses the development of new Delphi components.

- *Data Module* creates a new blank data module (the same as the command File ➤ New Data Module).

- *DLL* creates a simple DLL skeleton, as we will see in Chapter 20.

- *Form* creates a new blank form (the same as the command File ➤ New Form).

- *Package* creates a new Delphi component package. (You can also create a new package when creating a component.) Packages are covered in various chapters, but particularly in Chapter 18's discussion of component building.

- *Report* creates a new empty QuickReport form. Reports and printing are covered in Chapter 28.

- *Text* opens a new ASCII text file in the Delphi editor.

- *Thread Object* creates a new thread object after asking you to fill in the New Thread Object dialog box. Multithreading in Windows is introduced in Chapter 25.

- *Unit* creates a new blank unit, a Pascal source file not connected with a form.

- *Web Server Application* allows you to create an ISAPI/NSAPI add-in DLL, a CGI stand-alone executable, or a Win-CGI stand-alone executable. In each case Delphi creates a simple project based on a Web module (a special type of data module) instead of a form.

FIGURE 3.1

The New page of the
Object Repository.

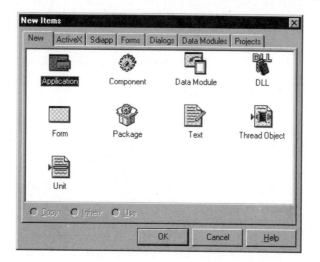

The ActiveX Page

The ActiveX page of the repository (not present in the "Standard" edition of
Delphi 3) is the starting point for creating ActiveX controls and form, and also to
manage type and control libraries. All these topics will be covered in Part III of
the book.

- *ActiveX Form* adds a new ActiveForm to the current project. An ActiveForm
  is a Delphi form you can publish as an ActiveX control, as we've seen in
  Chapter 1. This command launches the ActiveX Control Wizard.

- *ActiveX Control* opens the full-blown version of the ActiveX Control Wizard,
  which allows you to create an ActiveX control around an existing Delphi
  window-based component.

- *ActiveX Library* creates a DLL suitable for ActiveX deployment. Actually, it
  simply generates a few lines of the code of the project file.

- *Automation Object* creates a new OLE automation server object after asking
  you to fill in the simple Automation Object Wizard. This generates a few
  lines of code and opens the Type Library Editor.

- *Property Page* creates a new property page, the property editor used by
  ActiveX controls.

- *Remote Data Module* starts the development of a new data module on the server. This remote data module is accessible to client applications, which use it to access database data.

- *Type Library* open the Type Library Editor. A type library is a sort of interface that an OLE server can make available to clients to obtain fast and reliable binding of the calls to the server.

The Current Project Page

In the third page of the Object Repository, indicated by the name of the current project, you can create new forms or data modules that inherit from those of the current project. The content of this page depends exclusively on the units included in the current project. Simply create a couple of forms and then return to this page, and you'll see that its contents have already changed. Notice, however, that each time you perform an action, the Object Repository dialog box is automatically closed. So to make this test, you have to open it more than once.

The Forms Page

This page lists predefined forms. Here is a short list of the predefined forms available in Delphi (as you can see in Figure 3.2):

- *About box* is a simple About box.

- *Database form* activates the Database Form Wizard, one of the most important Delphi Wizards. This Wizard is described in detail later on in this chapter.

- *Dual list box* is a form with two different list boxes, allowing a user to select a number of elements from one list and move them to the other list by pressing a button. Along with the components, this form contains a good amount of nontrivial Pascal code.

- *Decision Cube* opens a standard form based on the new Decision Cube components. This is available only in the Client/Server Suite edition of Delphi, and is not covered in this book.

- *QuickReport Labels* creates a report form based on the QuickReport component. Again, reports are covered in Chapter 28.

- *QuickReport List* creates another form based on QuickReport, with a different layout.

- *QuickReport Master/Detail* is a third predefined report form with a more complex structure.

- *Tabbed pages* is a form based on the Windows 95 PageControl. We will discuss the use of this component in Chapter 14.

- *TeeChart Wizard* is a good starting point for the development of a form based on the TeeChart graphic component. This component is new in Delphi 3, and is discussed in Chapter 11.

FIGURE 3.2

The Forms page of the repository, showing predefined forms and Form Wizards, in the Details view.

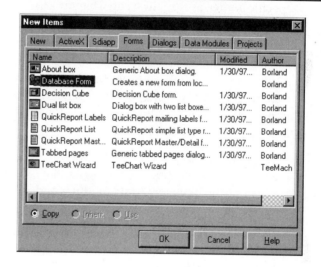

Wizards can only be executed. The other forms, by contrast, can be used in multiple ways. You can add them into a project, inherit from them (in this case the original form will be automatically added to your project), or use them directly. When you use a form or inherit from one, take care not to make any change on the original forms in the Repository.

The Dialogs Page

This page is similar to the previous one, but includes forms that are typically used as dialog boxes. Here is the list of its items:

- *Dialog with help* is available in two versions. One has the buttons on the right side of the form, and the other has them in the lower portion, as you can see from the corresponding icons.

- *Dialog Wizard* is a simple Wizard capable of generating different kinds of dialog boxes with one or more pages, as we will see later in this chapter.

- *Password dialog* is a dialog box with a simple edit box for entering a password.

- *QuickReport Wizard* creates a Print Options dialog box for a report.

- *Standard dialog* is also available in two versions, with buttons in different positions.

Dialog boxes are actually forms with a couple of special attributes, such as a specific border, as we will see in Chapter 13.

The Data Modules Page

You already know what a project and a form are, but what is a data module? It is a sort of form that never appears on screen at run-time and can be used to hold nonvisual components. It is mostly used to implement code related to database access, as we will see in Chapter 18.

This page has only a data module at start-up, *Customer Data*. If you have several forms or applications accessing the same data tables and database queries, you can easily define new data modules and add them to the repository.

The Projects Page

The last page contains project schemes you can use as the starting point for your own application. These projects often include one or more forms. Here is the list of them:

- *Application Wizard* is another simple Wizard that allows you some limited choices for the file structure and other elements of an application.

- *MDI Application* defines the main elements of a Multiple Document Interface (MDI) program. It defines a main form for the MDI frame window, with a menu, a status bar, and a toolbar. It also defines a second form that can be used at run-time to create a number of child windows. We will explore MDI applications in Chapter 15.

- *SDI Application* defines a main form with the standard attributes of a modern user interface, including a toolbar and a status bar, and also a typical About box.

- *Win95 Logo Application* defines a sample application with most of the elements required by an application to get the Windows 95 Logo. This command basically creates an SDI application with a RichEdit component in it, and adds the code needed to make the application *mail-enabled*.

When you select one of these projects, Delphi asks you to enter the name of an existing or a new directory. If you indicate a new directory, Delphi will automatically create it.

For example, we can create an SDI project based on the corresponding template. Then we can customize it, giving it a proper title, removing or adding new components, and writing some code. Some interesting components are already there, however, and there is even some ready-to-use code to make those components work properly. The menu and toolbar of the application, can be used to open some dialog boxes. File Open and File Save dialog boxes are wrapped up in components that are added to the form by the template; the About box is defined by the template as a second form.

In the simple SdiTemp example, I've decided to make just a few limited changes: I've entered a new title for the main form and some text for the labels for the About box (the property to use is `Caption` in both cases). The result is the application shown in Figure 3.3 and available on the companion CD.

FIGURE 3.3

The output of the SdiTemp example, built using the SDI project template.

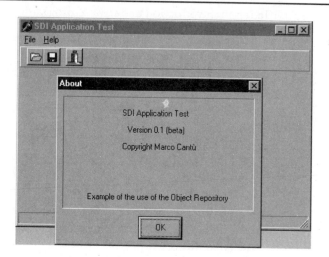

Delphi Wizards

Besides copying or using existing code, Delphi allows you to create a new form, application, or other code files, using a Wizard. Wizards (or Experts) allow you to enter a number of options and produce the code corresponding to your choices.

One of the most important predefined wizards is the Database Form Wizard, which you can activate using the Database ➤ Form Wizard menu item or the icon in the Forms page of the Object Repository. There are also some other simple Wizards in Delphi, such as the Application Wizard and the Dialog Wizard. I've listed various other Wizards in the description of the pages of the Object Repository, in the last section.

You can also buy add-on Wizards from third-party tool providers (there are some interesting ones on the companion CD) or even write your own Wizard, something I'll introduce in Chapter 19. Add-on Wizards often show up in the Help menu, but it is possible to add new menu items in other Delphi pull-down menus or install Wizards in various pages of the Object Repository.

The Database Form Wizard

In this section, I'll show you a quick example of the use of the Database Form Wizard, but I won't describe the application we build in detail. Refer to Chapter 16 for an introduction to database programming.

In this example, we'll build a database program using some of the data already available in Delphi. Note that you have to create a project first, and then start the Database Form Wizard. So you usually end up with two forms, unless you remove the original form from the project. Fortunately, one of the Wizard's options, displayed at the end, lets you select the new form generated by the Wizard as the main form.

1. As soon as you start the Database Form Wizard, you will be presented with a number of choices, which depend on the options you choose at each step. The first page, shown in Figure 3.4, lets you choose between a simple or a master detail form, and between the use of tables or queries. Leave the selections as they are by default, and move on by clicking on the Next button.

FIGURE 3.4

FIGURE 3.4

The first page of the
Database Form Wizard.

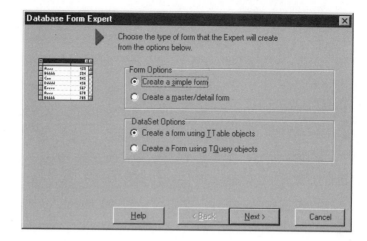

2. In the next page, shown in Figure 3.5, you can choose an existing database table to work on. In the Drive or Alias Name combo box, there should be a DBDEMOS alias. After you select this option, a number of Delphi demo database tables appear in the list. Choose the first, ANIMALS.DBF.

FIGURE 3.5

Selecting a table in the
Database Form Wizard.

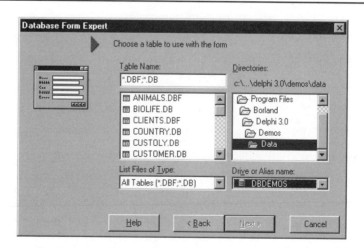

3. In the third page, you can choose the fields of the selected database table that you want to consider. To build this first example, choose all of the fields by clicking on the >> button.

4. On the next page, you can choose from various layouts. If you choose Vertical, the next page will ask you the position of the labels. The default option, Horizontal, might do.

5. The next page is the last. Leave the Generate a Main Form check box and the Form Only radio button selected, and click on the Finish button.

You can immediately compile and run the application. The result is a working database application, which allows you to navigate among many records using the buttons. This specific application (the DataExp example) even has a graphical field, displaying a bitmap with the current animal.

The output of the generated form is usually far from adequate. In this case, the image area is too small; at other times the positioning of the controls may not be satisfactory. Of course, you can easily move and resize the various components placed on the form at design-time.

To make this task easier, you can select the Table component (the one in the upper-left corner of the form) and toggle its Active property to True. Then the data of the table's first record will be displayed at design-time (as you can see in Figure 3.6). This is helpful because it allows you to see an example of the length of the field's text and the size of the image.

FIGURE 3.6

The form of the DataExp example generated by the Database Form Wizard, after some customization. Notice that I have activated the Table component, in order to see data from the database table at design-time also.

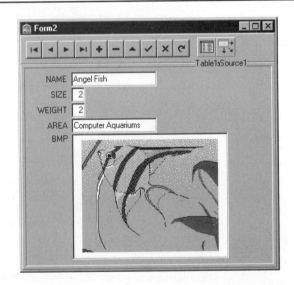

Note that the Database Form Wizard generates almost no Pascal code, besides a line used to open the table when the program starts. The capabilities of the resulting programs stem from the power of the database-related components available in Delphi, as we will see in Chapter 16.

The Application Wizard

Another interesting (although less powerful) tool is the Application Wizard. You can activate it from the Projects page of the Object Repository. The Application Wizard allows you to create the skeleton of a number of different kinds of applications, depending on the options you select.

The first page of this Wizard (see Figure 3.7) allows you to add some standard pull-down menus to the program: File, Edit, Window, and Help. If you select the File menu, the second page will ask you to enter the file extensions the program should consider. You should enter both a description of the file, such as *Text file (*.txt)*, and the extension, *txt*. (You can input several extensions, each with its own description.) These values will be used by the default File Open and File Save dialog boxes that the Application Wizard will add to the program if you select the file support option.

FIGURE 3.7

The first page of the Application Wizard.

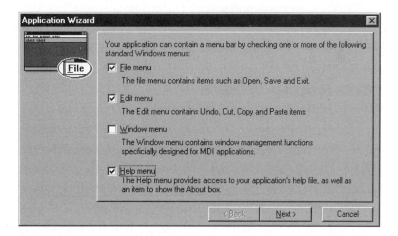

Then, if you have selected any of the pull-down menus, the Application Wizard displays a nice visual tool you can use to build a toolbar. Unfortunately, this tool is not available as a separate editor inside Delphi. You simply select one of the pull-down menus, and a number of standard buttons corresponding to the typical menu items of this pull-down menu appear (but only if the menu has been selected on the first page of the Application Wizard).

To add a new button, select one of them in the graphical list box on the right and press the Insert button. The new toolbar button will be added at the position of the small triangular cursor. You can move this cursor by clicking on one of the elements already added to the toolbar. This cursor is also used to indicate a button you want to remove from the toolbar.

When the toolbar is finished, you can move to the last page. Here you can set several other options, such as choosing MDI support, adding a status bar, and enabling hints. You can also give a name to the new application and specify a directory for the source files. The name of the application can be long, but it cannot contain white spaces (it should be a valid Pascal identifier), and the directory for the application should be an existing directory. To place the project files in a new directory, choose the Browse button, enter the new path, and the dialog box will prompt you to create the new directory.

Although it is somewhat bare and it has room for improvement, the Delphi Application Wizard is much more useful than the predefined application templates for building the first version of an application. One of its biggest advantages is that you can define your own toolbar. Another advantage is that the Application Wizard generates more code (and more comments) than the corresponding templates do. The disadvantage of this Wizard is that it generates an application with a single form. Its MDI support is limited, because no child form is defined, and the generated application has no About box.

The Dialog Wizard

Delphi's Dialog Wizard is a simple Wizard provided mostly as a demo, with its own source code. From the code of this Wizard, in theory you should be able to learn how to build other Wizards of your own. However, you can still use the Dialog Wizard as a tool to build two kinds of dialog boxes: simple dialog boxes and multiple-page dialog boxes based on the Windows 95 PageControl component (see Figure 3.8).

If you choose the simple dialog box, the Wizard will jump to the third page, where you can choose the button layout. If you choose the multiple-page dialog box, an intermediate page will appear to let you input the text of the various tabs.

This Wizard is an alternative to the corresponding form templates of the Object Repository. Its advantage is that it allows you to input the names of the PageControl tabs directly. We will explore dialog boxes in detail in Chapter 11 and the Page-Control component in Chapter 12.

FIGURE 3.8

The first page of the
Dialog Wizard.

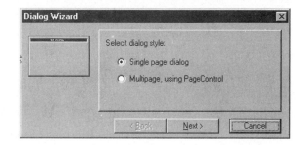

Customizing the Object Repository

Since writing a new wizard is far from simple, the typical way to customize the Object Repository is to add new projects, forms, and data modules as templates. You can also add new pages and arrange the items on some of them (not including the *New* and "current project" pages).

Adding New Application Templates

Adding a new template to Delphi's Object Repository is as simple as using an existing template to build an application. When you have a working application you want to use as a starting point for further development of two or more similar programs, you can save the current status to a template, ready to use later on.

NOTE   Although Borland now calls everything you can put in the Object Repository an *object*, from an object-oriented perspective this is far from true. For this reason I call the schemes you can save to disk for later use *templates*. Application templates, in particular, do not relate to objects or classes in any way, but are copied to the directory of your new project. *Object Repository* sounds much better than *Browse Gallery*, but besides the capability to activate form inheritance, there is not much new in this tool.

You can add a project to the Repository by using the Project ➤ Add to Repository command, or by using the corresponding item of the local menu of the Project Manager window. As a very simple example, just to demonstrate the process, the following steps describe how you can save the slightly modified version of the default SDI template (shown earlier) as a template:

1. Open the modified SdiTemp example (or any other project you are working on).

2. Select the Project ➤ Add to Repository menu command (or the Add Project to Repository command in the SpeedMenu of the Project Manager window).

3. In the Add to Repository dialog box (see Figure 3.9), enter a title, a description for the new project template, and the name of the author. You can also choose an icon to indicate the new template or accept the default image. Finally, choose the page of the Repository where you wish to add the project.

4. Click on OK, and the new template is added to the Delphi Object Repository.

FIGURE 3.9

The Add to Repository dialog box, used to define the name and descriptions of a new application template.

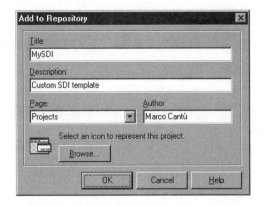

Now, each time you open the Object Repository, it will include your custom template. If you later discover that the template is not useful any more, you can remove it. You can also use a project template to make a copy of an existing project so that you can continue to work on it after saving the original version.

However, there is a simpler way to accomplish this: copy the source files to a new directory and open the new project. If you do copy the source files, do *not* copy the DSK file, which indicates the position of the Windows on the screen. The DSK file holds a list of files open in the editor, using an absolute path. This means that as soon as you open the new project and start working on it, you may well end up editing the source code files of the original project and compiling the files of the new version (the project manager stores relative paths). This will certainly surprise you when the changes you make in code or in forms seem to have no effect. Simply deleting the DSK file, or not copying it in the first place, avoids this problem.

The Empty Project Template

When you start a new project, it automatically opens a blank form, too. If you want to base a new project on one of the form objects or wizards, this is not what you want. To solve this problem, you can add an Empty Project template to the Gallery.

The steps required to accomplish this are simple:

1. Create a new project as usual.

2. Remove its only form from the project.

3. Add this project to the templates, naming it *Empty Project*.

When you select this project from the Object Repository, you gain two advantages. You have your project without a form, and you can pick a directory where the project template's files will be copied. There is also a disadvantage—you need to use the File ➤ Save Project As command to give a new name to the project, since saving the project automatically uses the default name in the template.

Adding New Form Templates to the Object Repository

Just as you can add new project templates to the Object Repository, you can also add new form templates. Simply move to the form you want to add, right-click on it, and select Add to Repository from the SpeedMenu. In the dialog box that appears (see Figure 3.10), you can choose which form of the current project should be added to the Repository, and set the title, description, author, page, and icon, as usual. Once you have set these elements and clicked on OK, the form is added to the proper page of the Object Repository.

FIGURE 3.10

FIGURE 3.10

Saving a form as a template, with the Add Form to Repository dialog box.

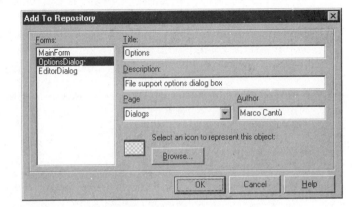

This approach is suggested if you have a complex form to make available to other applications and other programmers. They will be able to use your form as is, make a copy of it, and inherit from it. For this reason, adding forms to the Repository is far more flexible than adding projects, which can only be copied as the starting point of a new application.

The Object Repository Options

To further customize the Repository, you can use the Tools ➤ Repository command to open the Object Repository dialog box (see Figure 3.11). This dialog box is quite

FIGURE 3.11

The Object Repository Options dialog box.

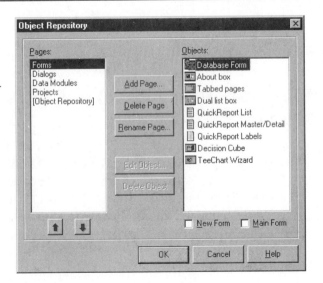

easy to use; on the left is the list of current Repository pages and on the right the list of items in each page, including both templates and Wizards. You can use this dialog to move repository items to different pages, to add new elements, or to delete existing ones.

You can use the three page-related buttons and the two buttons with arrows below the list of pages to arrange the structure of the Object Repository, adding new pages, renaming or deleting them, and changing their order. All these operations affect some of the tabs of the Object Repository itself (other tabs are fixed).

An important element of the Object Repository setup is the use of defaults:

- Use the *New Form* check box below the list of objects to designate the current form or Wizard as the default, to be used when a new form is created (File ➤ New Form). Only one object in the Object Repository can be used as a default; it is marked with a special symbol placed over its icon.

- The *Main Form* check box, instead, is used to indicate the form or Wizard used to create the main form of a new application (File ➤ New Application) when no special New Project is selected (see next bullet). The current Main form is indicated by a second special symbol.

- The New Project check box, available when you select a project object, can be used to mark the default project that Delphi uses when you issue the File ‰ New Application command. Also, the New Project is indicated by its own special symbol.

If no project is selected as New Project, Delphi creates a default project based on the form marked as Main Form. If no form is marked as the main form, Delphi creates a default project with an empty form.

When you work on the Object Repository, you work with forms and modules saved in the OBJREPOS subdirectory of the Delphi main directory. At the same time, if you directly use a form or any other object without copying it, then you end up having some files of your project in this directory. It is important to realize how the repository works, because if you want to modify a project or an object saved in the repository, the best approach is to operate on the original files, without copying data back and forth to the Repository.

Installing new DLL Wizards

Technically, new Wizards come in two different forms. Wizards may be part of components or packages, and in this case are installed the same way you install a component or a package. Other Wizards are distributed as stand-alone DLLs. In this case you should add the name of the DLL in the Windows Registry under the key:

```
Software\Borland\Delphi 3.0\Experts
```

Simply add a new string key under this, choose a name you like (it doesn't really matter) and use as text the path and filename of the Wizard DLL. You can look at the entries already present under the Experts key to see how the path should be entered.

What's Next

In this short chapter, we have seen how you can start the development of an application by using Delphi templates and Wizards. You can use one of the predefined application templates or form objects, start the Database Form Wizard, or use the other Wizards for a fast start with applications, forms, and other objects.

However, I'll rarely use these templates and Wizards in the rest of the book. With the exception of the Database Form Wizard, these tools let you build only very simple applications, which you can often put together yourself in seconds when you are an experienced Delphi programmer. For beginners, Wizards and templates provide a quick start in code development. But you are not going to *remain* a beginner, are you?

So in the remaining chapters of Part I, we need to study the Object Pascal language and explore the use of the Delphi VCL (Visual Component Library) components. After that, we'll get back to real projects, and I'll explain the code generated by the Wizards or stored in templates.

CHAPTER
FOUR

4

The Pascal Language

- Types, variables, and constants

- Delphi data types

- String handling

- Coding style

- Conditional statements and loops

- Procedures and functions

- Reference and open array parameters

- Procedural types

The Pascal language has some unique characteristics. Dr. Niklaus Wirth designed the language, naming it after the French philosopher Blaise Pascal, around 1972 as a tool for teaching the relatively new discipline of programming; but it proved to be so powerful that it came into widespread use as a language for developing practical applications.

In part, this popularity is due to the success of Borland's world-famous Turbo Pascal series of compilers, introduced in 1985. The Turbo Pascal compiler made the language particularly popular on the PC platform, thanks to its balance of simplicity and power. Now Delphi's popularity is giving new life to the Pascal language, or better, its Object Pascal successor.

When Pascal was designed, many programming languages existed, but few were in widespread use. The key idea of the new language was order, managed through a strong concept of data type, and requiring declarations and structured program controls. This book doesn't contain detailed material about Pascal, but this chapter should help you if you know basic programming concepts but are not sure how they are implemented in Pascal.

Even if you have already used the Pascal language, you should read this chapter. All of the examples are implemented using the Delphi environment, which extends the Pascal language in a number of ways. The object-oriented extensions of Object Pascal, however, are covered in the next chapter.

Types, Variables, and Constants

The original Pascal language was based on some simple notions, which have now become quite common in programming languages. The first is the notion of *data type*. The type determines the values a variable can have, and the operations that can be performed on it. The concept of type is stronger in Pascal than in C, where the arithmetic data types are almost interchangeable, and much stronger than in the original versions of BASIC, which had no similar concept.

Variables

Pascal requires all variables to be declared before they are used. Every time you declare a variable, you must specify a data type. Here are some sample variable declarations:

```
var
  Value: Integer;
  IsCorrect: Boolean;
  A, B: Char;
```

The var keyword can be used in several places in the code, such as at the beginning of the code of a function or procedure, to declare variables local to the routine, or inside a unit to declare global variables (refer to the section about scope in the next chapter for details about the scope and lifetime of variables). After the var keyword comes a list of variable names, followed by a colon and the name of the data type. You can write more than one variable name on a single line, as in the last statement above.

Once you have defined a variable of a given type, you can perform on it only the operations supported by its data type. For example, you can use the Boolean value in a test and the integer value in a numerical expression. You cannot mix Booleans and integers (as you can with the C language).

Using simple assignments, we can write the following code:

```
Value := 10;
IsCorrect := True;
```

But the next statement is not correct, because the two variables have different data types:

```
Value := IsCorrect; // error
```

If you try to compile this code, Delphi issues a compiler error with this description: *Incompatible types: 'Integer' and 'Boolean'*. Usually, errors like this are programming errors, because it does not make sense to assign a True or False value to a variable of the Integer data type. You should not blame Delphi for these errors. It only warns you that there is something wrong in the code.

Delphi error messages are now much more detailed than in the 16-bit version, and you can also enable compiler hints and warnings, which help you find errors in your programs. I strongly suggest you enable hints and warnings in the Compiler page of the Project Options dialog box.

Of course, it is often possible to convert the value of a variable from one type into a different type. In some cases, this conversion is automatic, but usually you need to call a specific system function that changes the internal representation of the data.

In Delphi you can assign an initial value to a global variable while you declare it. For example, you can write:

```
var
    Value: Integer = 10;
    Correct: Boolean = True;
```

This initialization technique works only for global variables, not for variables declared inside the scope of a procedure or method.

Constants

Pascal also allows the declaration of constants to name values that do not change during program execution. To declare a constant you don't need to specify a data type, but only assign an initial value. The compiler will look at the value and automatically use its proper data type. Here are some sample declarations:

```
const
    Thousand = 1000;
    Pi = 3.14;
    AuthorName = 'Marco Cant˘';
```

As mentioned, Delphi determines the constant's data type based on its value. In the example above, the Thousand constant is assumed to be of type SmallInt, the smallest integral type which can hold it. If you want to tell Delphi to use a specific type you can simply add the type name in the declaration:

```
const
    Thousand: Integer = 1000;
```

When you declare a constant, the compiler can choose whether to assign a memory location to the constant, and save its value there, or to duplicate the actual value each time the constant is used. This second approach makes sense particularly for simple constants.

> **WARNING**
> The 16-bit version of Delphi allows you to change the value of a typed constant at run-time, as if it was a variable. The 32-bit version still permits this behavior for backward compatibility when you enable the $J compiler directive, or use the corresponding Assignable typed constants check box of the Compiler page of the Project Options dialog box. Although this is the default, you are strongly advised *not* to use this trick as a general programming technique. Assigning a new value to a constant disables all the compiler optimizations on constants. In such a case, simply declare a variable, instead.

Resource String Constants

When you define a string constant, instead of writing:

```
const
    AuthorName = 'Marco Cantù';
```

you can write the following:

```
resourcestring
    AuthorName = 'Marco Cantù';
```

In both cases you are defining a constant; that is, a value you don't change during program execution. The difference is only in the implementation. A string constant defined with the `resourcestring` directive is stored in the resources of the program, in a string table. (Chapter 27 discusses Windows resources in detail. Generally speaking, a program that uses resources makes better use of memory and is easier to localize into different languages.)

To see this new Delphi 3 capability in action, you can look at the ResStr example later in this chapter, which has a button with the following code:

```
resourcestring
    AuthorName = 'Marco Cantù';
    BookName = 'Mastering Delphi 3';
```

```
procedure TForm1.Button1Click(Sender: TObject);
begin
  ShowMessage (BookName + #13 + AuthorName);
end;
```

The output of the two strings appears on separate lines because the strings are separated by the *newline* character (indicated by its numerical value in the #13 character type constant).

The interesting aspect of this program is that if you examine it with a resource explorer (there is one available among the examples that ship with Delphi) you'll see the new strings in the resources. You'll see how to accomplish this and learn more about resources in Chapter 27.

Delphi Data Types

In Pascal there are several predefined data types, which can be divided into three groups: *ordinal types*, *real types*, and *strings*. We'll discuss ordinal and real types in the following sections, while strings are covered later in this chapter. In this section I'll also introduce some types defined by the Delphi libraries (not predefined by the compiler), which can be considered predefined types.

Delphi also includes a *non-typed* data type, called variant. Strangely enough a variant is a type without proper type-checking. It was introduced in Delphi 2 to handle OLE automation. We'll see later in this chapter how the variant concept can be used to break Pascal's strict type-checking rules, and in Chapter 22 we'll focus on its use for OLE automation.

Ordinal Types

Ordinal types are based on the concept of order or sequence. Not only can you compare two values to see which is higher, but you can also ask for the value following or preceding a given value or compute the lowest or highest possible value.

The three most important predefined ordinal types are Integer, Boolean, and Char (character). However, there are a number of other related types that have the same meaning but a different internal representation and range of values. The following table lists the ordinal data types used for representing numbers:

Size	Signed	Unsigned
8 bits	ShortInt	Byte
16 bits	SmallInt	Word
32 bits	LongInt	
16/32 bits	Integer	Cardinal

As you can see, these types correspond to different representations of numbers, depending on the number of bits used to express the value, and the presence or absence of a sign bit. Signed values can be positive or negative, but have a smaller range of values, because one less bit is available for the value itself. You can refer to the Range example, discussed in the next section, for the actual range of values of each type.

The last group (marked as 16/32) indicates values having a different representation in the 16-bit and 32-bit versions of Delphi. Integer and Cardinal are frequently used, because they correspond to the native representation of numbers in the CPU.

Boolean values other than the Boolean type are seldom used. Some Boolean values with specific representations are required by Windows API functions. The types are ByteBool, WordBool, and LongBool.

NEW

In Delphi 3 for compatibility with Visual Basic and OLE automation, the data types ByteBool, WordBool, and LongBool represent the value True with −1, while the value False is still 0. The Boolean data type remains unchanged (True is 1, False is 0). If you've used explicit typecasts in your Delphi 2 code, porting it to Delphi 3 might result in errors.

Finally there are two different representation for characters: ANSIChar and WideChar. The first type represents 8-bit characters, corresponding to the ANSI character set traditionally used by Windows; the second represents 16-bit characters, corresponding to the new Unicode characters supported by the latest versions of Windows. Most of the time you'll simply use the Char type, which in Delphi 3 corresponds to ANSIChar. Keep in mind, anyway, that the first 256 Unicode characters correspond exactly to the ANSI characters.

The Range Example

To give you an idea of the different ranges of some of the ordinal types, I've written a simple Delphi program named Range. You can try to rebuild it or simply run it from the companion CD. Some results are shown in Figure 4.1.

The Range program is based on a simple form, which has six buttons (each named after an ordinal data type) and some labels for categories of information, as you can see in Figure 4.1. Some of the labels are used to hold static text, others to show the information about the type each time one of the buttons is pressed.

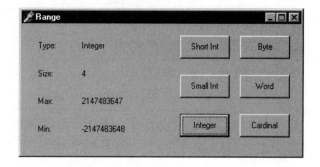

Every time you press one of the buttons on the right, the program updates the labels with the output. Different labels show the data type, number of bytes used, and the maximum and minimum values the data type can store. Each button has its own OnClick event-response method because the code used to compute the three values is slightly different from button to button. For example, here is the source code of the OnClick event for the Integer button (BtnInteger):

```
procedure TFormRange.BtnIntegerClick(Sender: TObject);
begin
  LabelType.Caption := 'Integer';
  LabelSize.Caption := IntToStr (SizeOf (Integer));
  LabelMax.Caption := IntToStr (High (Integer));
  LabelMin.Caption := IntToStr (Low (Integer));
end;
```

If you have some experience with Delphi programming, you can examine the source code of the program to understand how it works. For beginners, it's enough to note the use of three functions: SizeOf, High, and Low. The results of the last two functions are ordinals of the same kind (in this case, integers), and the result of the SizeOf function is always an integer. The return value of each of these functions is first translated into strings using the IntToStr function, then copied to the captions of the three labels.

The methods associated with the other buttons are very similar to the one above. The only real difference is in the data type passed as a parameter to the various functions. Figure 4.2 shows the result of executing this same program under Windows 95 after it has been recompiled with the 16-bit version of Delphi (the source code of this version of the Range program is available on the CD as Range16). Comparing Figure 4.1 with Figure 4.2, you can see the difference between the 16-bit and 32-bit Integer data types.

FIGURE 4.2

The output of the 16-bit version of the Range example, again showing information about integers.

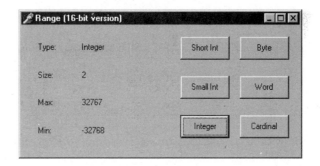

The size of the Integer type varies depending on the CPU and operating system you are using. In 16-bit Windows, an Integer variable is two bytes wide. In 32-bit Windows, an Integer is four bytes wide. For this reason, when you recompile the Range example, you get a different output.

The two different representations of the Integer type are not a problem, as long as your program doesn't make any assumptions about the size of integers. If you happen to save an Integer to a file using one version and retrieve it with another, though, you're going to have some trouble. In this situation, you should choose a platform-independent data type (such as LongInt or SmallInt). For mathematical computation or generic code, your best bet is to stick with the standard integral representation for the specific platform—that is, use the Integer type—because this is what the CPU likes best. The Integer type should be your first choice when handling integer numbers. Use a different representation only when there is a compelling reason to do so.

Ordinal Types Routines

There are some system routines (routines defined in the Pascal language and in the Delphi system unit) that work on ordinal types. They are shown in Table 4.1. C++ programmers should notice that the two versions of the Inc procedure, with one or two parameters, correspond to the ++ and += operators (the same holds for the Dec procedure).

TABLE 4.1   System Routines for Ordinal Types

Routine	Purpose
Dec	Decrements the variable passed as parameter, by one or by the value of the optional second parameter.
Inc	Increments the variable passed as parameter, by one or by the specified value.
Odd	Returns True if the argument is an odd number.
Pred	Returns the value before the argument in the order determined by the data type, the predecessor.
Succ	Returns the value after the argument, the successor.
Ord	Returns a number indicating the order of the argument within the set of values of the data type.
Low	Returns the lowest value in the range of the ordinal type passed as its parameter.
High	Returns the highest value in the range of the ordinal data type.

Notice that some of these routines, when applied to constants, are automatically evaluated by the compiler and replaced by their value. For example if you call High(X) where X is defined as an Integer, the compiler can simply replace the expression with the highest possible value of the Integer data type.

Real Types

Real types represent floating-point numbers in various formats. The smallest storage size is given by Single numbers, which are implemented with a 4-byte value. Then there are Double floating-point numbers, implemented with 8 bytes, and Extended numbers, implemented with 10 bytes. These are all floating-point data types with different precision, which correspond to the IEEE standard floating-point representations, and are directly supported by the CPU numeric coprocessor, for maximum speed.

WARNING   The Real type is available only for compatibility with older Pascal source code, but should never be used. Its 6-byte representation is not one of the IEEE standard representations for floating-point numbers.

There are also two strange data types: Comp describes very big integers using 8 bytes (which can hold numbers with 18 decimal digits); and Currency (not available in 16-bit Delphi) indicates a fixed-point decimal value with four decimal digits, and the same 64-bit representation as the Comp type. As the name implies, the Currency data type has been added to handle very precise monetary values, with four decimal places.

We cannot build a program similar to the Range example with real data types, because we cannot use the High and Low functions or the Ord function on real-type variables. Real types represent (in theory) an infinite set of numbers; ordinal types represent a fixed set of values. For this reason, it makes sense to ask for the ordinal position of the character w in the range of the Char data type, but it makes no sense at all to ask the same question about 7143.1562 in the range of a floating-point data type. Although you can indeed know whether one real number has a higher value than another, it makes no sense to ask how many real numbers exist before a given number (this is the meaning of the Ord function).

Real types have a limited role in the user interface portion of the code (the Windows side), but they are fully supported by Delphi, including the database side. The support of IEEE standard floating-point types makes the Object Pascal language completely appropriate for the wide range of programs that require numerical computations. If you are interested in this aspect, you can look at the arithmetic functions provided by Delphi in the system unit (see the Delphi Help for more details).

NOTE   Delphi also has a Math unit that defines advanced mathematical routines, covering trigonometric functions (such as the ArcCosh function), finance (such as the InterestPayment function), and statistics (such as the MeanAndStdDev procedure). There are a number of these routines, some of which sound quite strange to me, such as the MomentSkewKurtosis procedure (I'll let you find out what this is).

Date and Time

Delphi uses real types also to handle date and time information. To be more precise Delphi defines a specific TDateTime data type. This is a floating-point type, because the type must be wide enough to store years, months, days, hours, minutes, and seconds, down to millisecond resolution in a single variable. Dates are stored as the number of days since 12/30/1899 (with negative values indicating dates before 1899) in the integer part of the TDateTime value. Times are stored as fractions of a day in the decimal part of the value.

TDateTime is not a predefined type the compiler understands, but it is defined in the system unit as:

```
type
    TDateTime = type Double;
```

Using the TDateTime type is quite easy, because Delphi includes a number of functions that operate on this type. You can find a list of these functions in Table 4.2.

TABLE 4.2   System Routines for the TDateTime Type

Routine	Description
Now	Returns the current date and time into a single TDateTime value.
Date	Returns only the current date.
Time	Returns only the current time.
DateTimeToStr	Converts a date and time value into a string, using default formatting; to have more control on the conversion use the FormatDateTime function instead.
DateTimeToString	Copies the date and time values into a string buffer, with default formatting.
DateToStr	Converts the date portion of a TDateTime value into a string.
TimeToStr	Converts the time portion of a TDateTime value into a string.
FormatDateTime	Formats a date and time using the specified format; you can specify which values you want to see and which format to use, providing a complex format string.
StrToDateTime	Converts a string with date and time information to a TDateTime value, raising an exception in case of an error in the format of the string.
StrToDate	Converts a string with a date value into the TDateTime format.

TABLE 4.2   System Routines for the TDateTime Type (Continued)

Routine	Description
StrToTime	Converts a string with a time value into the TDateTime format.
DayOfWeek	Returns the number corresponding to the day of the week of the TDateTime value passed as parameter.
DecodeDate	Retrieves the year, month, and day values from a date value.
DecodeTime	Retrieves out of a time value.
EncodeDate	Turns year, month, and day values into a TDateTime value.
EncodeTime	Turns hour, minute, second, and millisecond values into a TDateTime value.

To show you how to use this data type and some of its related routines, I've built a simple example, named TimeNow. The main form of this example has a Button and a ListBox component. When the program starts it automatically computes and displays the current time and date. Every time the button is pressed, the program shows the time elapsed since the program started.

Here is the code related to the OnCreate event of the form:

```
procedure TFormTimeNow.FormCreate(Sender: TObject);
begin
  StartTime := Now;
  ListBox1.Items.Add (TimeToStr (StartTime));
  ListBox1.Items.Add (DateToStr (StartTime));
  ListBox1.Items.Add ('Press button for elapsed time');
end;
```

The first statement is a call to the Now function, which returns the current date and time. This value is stored in the StartTime variable, declared as a global variable as follows:

```
var
  FormTimeNow: TFormTimeNow;
  StartTime: TDateTime;
```

I've added only the second declaration, since the first is provided by Delphi. By default, it is the following:

```
var
  Form1: TForm1;
```

Changing the name of the form, this declaration is automatically updated. Using global variables is actually not the best approach: We'll start using a better one (using a private field of the form class) in the next chapter, when you'll learn more about classes and object-oriented programming.

The next three statements add three items to the ListBox component on the left of the form, with the result you can see in Figure 4.3. The first line contains the time portion of the TDateTime value converted into a string, the second the date portion of the same value. At the end the code adds a simple reminder.

FIGURE 4.3

The output of the TimeNow example at startup.

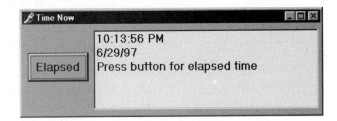

This third string is replaced by the program when the user clicks on the Elapsed button:

```
procedure TFormTimeNow.ButtonElapsedClick(Sender: TObject);
var
  StopTime: TDateTime;
begin
  StopTime := Now;
  ListBox1.Items [2] :=  FormatDateTime ('hh:nn:ss',
    StopTime - StartTime);
end;
```

This code retrieves the new time and computes the difference from the time value stored when the program started. Because we need to use a value that we computed in a different event handler, we had to store it in a global variable. We'll see in the next chapter that there are better alternatives, based on classes.

NOTE

The code that replaces the current value of the third string uses the index 2. The reason is that the items of a list box are zero-based: the first item is number 0, the second number 1, and the third number 2. More on this as we cover arrays.

Besides calling `TimeToStr` and `DateToStr` you can use the more powerful `FormatDateTime` function, as I've done in the last method above (see the Delphi Help file for details on the formatting parameters). Notice also that time and date values are transformed to strings depending on Windows international settings. Delphi reads these values from the system, and copies them to a number of global constants declared in the SysUtils unit. Some of them are:

```
DateSeparator: Char;
ShortDateFormat: string;
LongDateFormat: string;
TimeSeparator: Char;
TimeAMString: string;
TimePMString: string;
ShortTimeFormat: string;
LongTimeFormat: string;
ShortMonthNames: array[1..12] of string;
LongMonthNames: array[1..12] of string;
ShortDayNames: array[1..7] of string;
LongDayNames: array[1..7] of string;
```

More global constants relate to currency and floating-point number formatting. You can find the complete list in the Delphi Help file under the topic *Currency and date/time formatting variables*.

NEW   **Delphi 3 includes a new DateTimePicker component, described in Chapter 11.**

Specific Windows Types

The predefined data types we have seen so far are part of the Pascal language. Delphi also includes other data types defined by Windows. These data types are not an integral part of the language, but they are part of the Windows libraries. Windows types include new default types (such as `DWORD` or `UINT`), many records (or structures), several pointer types, and so on.

Among Windows data types, the most important type is represented by *handles*. The names of this data type is `THandle`, and the type is defined in the Windows unit as:

```
type
  THandle = Integer;
```

Handle data types are implemented as numbers, but they are not used as such. In Windows, a handle is a reference to an internal data structure of the system. For example, when you work with a window (or a Delphi form), the system gives you a *handle to the window*. The system informs you that the window you are working with is window number 142, for example. From that point on, your application can ask the system to operate on window number 142—moving it, resizing it, reducing it to an icon, and so on. Many Windows API functions, in fact, have a handle as the first parameter. This doesn't apply only to functions operating on windows: Other Windows API functions have as their first parameter a GDI handle, a menu handle, an instance handle, a bitmap handle, or one of the many other handle types.

In other words, a handle is an internal code you can use to refer to a specific element handled by the system, including windows, bitmaps, icons, memory blocks, cursors, fonts, menus, and so on. In Delphi, you seldom need to use handles directly, since they are hidden inside forms, bitmaps, and other Delphi objects. They become useful when you want to call a Windows API function that is not supported by Delphi.

NOTE The size of the handle data types varies in the 16-bit and 32-bit versions of Windows. The same holds true, of course, for the 16-bit and 32-bit versions of Delphi. If not used with care, this might cause compatibility problems when moving applications between the two platforms. In most cases, however, the size of handles is not an issue.

Looking at Window Handles

To complete this description, here is a simple example demonstrating Windows handles. The WHandle program has a simple form, containing just a button. In the code, I respond to the OnCreate event of the form and the OnClick event of the button, as indicated by the following textual definition of the main form:

```
object FormWHandle: TFormWHandle
  Caption = 'Window Handle'
  OnCreate = FormCreate
  object BtnCallAPI: TButton
    Caption = 'Call API'
    OnClick = BtnCallAPIClick
  end
end
```

As soon as the form is created, the program retrieves the handle of the window corresponding to the form, by accessing the Handle property of the form itself.

The numeric value of the Handle is turned into a string by calling IntToStr and added to the Caption of the form, as you can see in Figure 4.4:

```
procedure TFormWHandle.FormCreate(Sender: TObject);
begin
  Caption := Caption + ' ' + IntToStr (Handle);
end;
```

FIGURE 4.4

The WHandle example shows the handle of the form window. Every time you run this program you'll get a different value.

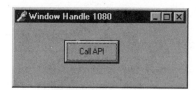

NOTE

In this procedure we can simply refer to the Caption of the form and its Handle property directly because this is actually a method of the form's class, which can access other properties and methods of the same class directly.

If you run this program several times you'll generally get different values for the handle. This value, in fact, is determined by Windows and sent back to the application. Handles are never determined by the program, and have no predefined values, but they are determined by the system, which generates new values each time you run a program.

When the user presses the button, the program simply calls a Windows API function, SetWindowText, which changes the text or caption of the window passed as the first parameter. To be more precise, the first parameter of this API function is the handle of the window we want to modify:

```
procedure TFormWHandle.BtnCallAPIClick(Sender: TObject);
begin
  SetWindowText (Handle, 'Hi');
end;
```

Notice that this code has the same effect as the previous event handler, which changed the text of the window by giving a new value to the Caption property of the form. In this case calling an API function makes no sense, because there is a simpler Delphi technique. Some API functions have no correspondence in Delphi, as we'll see in more advanced examples later in the book.

Typecasting and Type Conversions

As we have seen, you cannot assign a variable to another one of a different type. In case you need to do this, there are two choices. The first choice is *typecasting*, which uses a simple functional notation, with the name of the destination data type:

```
var
    N: Integer;
    C: Char;
    B: Boolean;
begin
    N := Integer ('X');
    C := Char (N);
    B := Boolean (0);
```

You can typecast between data types having the same size. It is usually safe to typecast between ordinal types, or between real types, but you can also typecast between pointer types (and also objects) as long as you know what you are doing.

Casting, however, is generally a dangerous programming practice, because it allows you to access a value as if it represented something else. Since the internal representations of data types generally do not match, you risk hard-to-track errors. For this reason, you should generally avoid typecasting.

The second choice is to use a type-conversion routine. The routines for the various types of conversions are summarized in Table 4.3. Some of these routines work on the data types that we'll discuss in the following sections. Notice that the table doesn't include routines for special types (such as TDateTime or variant) or routines specifically intended for formatting, like the powerful Format and FormatFloat routines.

TABLE 4.3 System Routines for Type Conversion

Routine	Description
Chr	Converts an ordinal number into an ANSI character.
Ord	Converts an ordinal-type value into the number indicating its order.
Round	Converts a real-type value into an Integer-type value, rounding its value.
Trunc	Converts a real-type value into an Integer-type value, truncating its value.

TABLE 4.3 System Routines for Type Conversion (Continued)

Routine	Description
Int	Returns the Integer part of the floating-point value argument.
IntToStr	Converts a number into a string.
IntToHex	Converts a number into a string with its hexadecimal representation.
StrToInt	Converts a string into a number, raising an exception if the string does not represent a valid integer.
StrToIntDef	Converts a string into a number, using a default value if the string is not correct.
Val	Converts a string into a number (traditional Turbo Pascal routine, available for compatibility).
Str	Converts a number into a string, using formatting parameters (traditional Turbo Pascal routine, available for compatibility).
StrPas	Converts a null-terminated string into a Pascal-style string. This conversion is automatically done for AnsiStrings in 32-bit Delphi. (See the section on strings later in this chapter.)
StrPCopy	Copies a Pascal-style string into a null-terminated string. This conversion is done with a simple PChar cast in 32-bit Delphi. (See the section on strings later in this chapter.)
StrPLCopy	Copies a portion of a Pascal-style string into a null-terminated string.
FloatToDecimal	Converts a floating-point value to record including its decimal representation (exponent, digits, sign).
FloatToStr	Converts the floating-point value to its string representation using default formatting.
FloatToStrF	Converts the floating-point value to its string representation using the specified formatting.
FloatToText	Copies the floating-point value to a string buffer, using the specified formatting.
FloatToTextFmt	As the previous routine, copies the floating-point value to a string buffer, using the specified formatting.
StrToFloat	Converts the given Pascal string to a floating-point value.
TextToFloat	Converts the given null-terminated string to a floating-point value.

The Variant Type

To provide full OLE support, the 32-bit version of Delphi includes the Variant data type. Although I'll focus on the specific use of the Variant type in the section of the book devoted to OLE programming, here I want to discuss this data type from a general perspective. The Variant type, in fact, has a pervasive effect on the whole language, and the Delphi components library also uses them in some ways not related to OLE programming.

In general, you can use variants to store any data type and perform a number of peculiar operations and type conversions. Notice that this goes against the general approach of the Pascal language and against good programming practices. A Variant is type-checked and computed at run-time. You don't have to bother with compiler type-checking, which is generally a negative thing. On the whole, you can consider the code portions using variants essentially to be interpreted code, because many operations cannot be resolved until run-time. This affects in particular the speed of the code.

Now that I've warned you against the use of the Variant type, it is time to look at what it can do. Basically, once you've declared a variant variable such as the following:

```
var
   V: Variant;
```

you can assign to it values of several different types:

```
V := 10;
V := 'Hello, World';
V := 45.55;
```

Once you have the Variant value, you can copy it to any compatible or incompatible data type. If you assign a value to an incompatible data type, Delphi performs a conversion, if it can. Otherwise it issues a runtime error. In fact, a Variant stores type information along with the data, allowing a number of runtime operations; these operations can be handy but are both slow and unsafe.

Consider the following example (VariTest on the companion CD), which is an extension of the code above. We place three edit boxes on a new form, add a couple of buttons, and then write the following code for the OnClick event of the first button:

```
procedure TForm1.Button1Click(Sender: TObject);
var
   V: Variant;
```

```
begin
  V := 10;
  Edit1.Text := V;
  V := 'Hello, World';
  Edit2.Text := V;
  V := 45.55;
  Edit3.Text := V;
end;
```

Funny, isn't it? Besides assigning a variant holding a string to the Text property of an edit component, you can assign to the Text a Variant holding an integer or a floating-point number. As you can see in Figure 4.5, everything works.

FIGURE 4.5

The output of the VariTest example after the Assign button (or Button1) has been pressed.

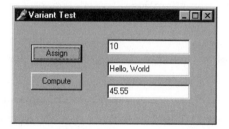

Even worse, you can use the variants to compute values, as you can see in the code related to the second button:

```
procedure TForm1.Button2Click(Sender: TObject);
var
  V: Variant;
  N: Integer;
begin
  V := Edit1.Text;
  N := Integer(V) * 2;
  V := N;
  Edit1.Text := V;
end;
```

Writing this kind of code is risky, to say the least. If the first edit box contains a number, everything works. If not, an exception is raised. Again, you can write similar code, but without a compelling reason to do so, you shouldn't use the Variant type; stick with the traditional Pascal data types and type-checking approach. For this reason, I'll rarely use the Variant type in the examples of the book.

Variants in Depth

Delphi includes a *variant record* type, TVarData, which has the same memory layout as the Variant type. You can use this to access the actual type of a variant. The TVarData structure includes the type of the Variant, indicated as VType, some reserved fields, and the actual value.

The possible types of a variant depend on the corresponding OLE type. Here is the list of the corresponding constants:

varEmpty	varNull	varSmallint	varInteger
varSingle	varDouble	varCurrency	varDate
varOleStr	varDispatch	varError	varBoolean
varVariant	varUnknown	varString	varTypeMask
varArray	varByRef		

You can find descriptions of these types in the *'Values in variants'* topic in the Delphi help system.

There are also many functions operating on variants that you can use to make specific type conversions, or ask for information about the type of a variant (see, for example, the VarType function). Most of these type conversion and assignment functions are actually called automatically when you write expressions using variants. Other *Variant support routines* (this is the name of the topic in the Help file) actually operate on variant arrays.

Variants Are Slow!

Notice also that code using the Variant type is slow, not only when you convert data types, but also when you add two Variant values holding an Integer each. They are almost as slow as the interpreted code of Visual Basic! To compare the speed of an algorithm based on variants with that of the same code based on integers, you can look at the VSpeed example on the companion CD. This program runs a loop of this kind (more on the while loop later in this chapter):

```
while n1 < 5000000 do
begin
  n2 := n2 + n1;
  Inc (n1);
end;
```

The actual loop, as you can see by looking at the source code, has some more statements to update the progress bar and let the application work properly, and is followed by the code used to time the loop. Most of those details aren't relevant at this point in the book, but since we've already discussed the TDateTime type, here is the code related to timing the loop:

```
begin
  time1 := Now;
  // loop...
  time2 := Now;
  Label1.Caption := FormatDateTime (
    'n:ss', Time2-Time1) + ' seconds';
end;
```

As you can see, I use the FormatDateTime function, and ask only for the minutes ('n') and seconds ('ss') in the format string. The speed difference is actually so great that you'll notice it even without a precise timing. Anyway, you can see the results for my own computer in Figure 4.6. The actual values depend on the computer you use to run this program, but the proportion won't change much.

FIGURE 4.6

The different speeds of the same algorithm, based on integers and variants (the actual timing varies depending on the computer), as shown by the VSpeed example.

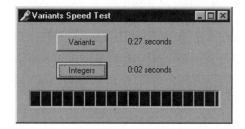

User-Defined Data Types

Along with the notion of type, one of the great ideas introduced by the Pascal language is the ability to define new data types in a program. Programmers can define their own data types by means of *type constructors*, such as subrange types, array types, record types, enumerated types, pointer types, and set types. The most important user-defined data type is the class, which is covered in the next chapter.

These types can be given a name for later use or applied to a variable directly. When you give a name to a type, you must provide a specific section in the code, such as the following:

```
type
  // subrange definition
  Uppercase = 'A'..'Z';

  // array definition
  Temperatures = array [1..24] of Integer;

  // record definition
  Date = record
    Month: Byte;
    Day: Byte;
    Year: Integer;
  end;

  // enumerated type definition
  Colors = (Red, Yellow, Green, Cyan, Blue, Violet);

  // set definition
  Letters = set of Char;
```

Similar type-definition constructs can be used directly to define a variable without an explicit type definition, as in the following code:

```
var
  DecemberTemperature: array [1..31] of Byte;
  ColorCode: array [Red..Violet] of Word;
  Palette: set of Colors;
```

WARNING In general, you should avoid using *unnamed* types as in the code above, because you cannot pass them as parameters to routines or declare other variables of the same type. The type compatibility rules of Pascal, in fact, are based on type names, not on the actual definition of the types. Two identical types are still not compatible. Get used to defining a data type each time you need a complex variable, and you won't regret the time you've spent for it.

But what do these type definitions mean? Most of you probably already know, but I'll provide some short descriptions for those who are not familiar with Pascal type constructs. I'll also try to underline the differences from the same constructs in other programming languages, so you might be interested in reading the following sections even if you are familiar with type definitions. Finally, I'll show some Delphi examples and introduce some tools that will allow you to access type information dynamically.

Subrange Types

A subrange type defines a range of values within the range of another type (hence the name *subrange*). You can define a subrange of the Integer type, from 1 to 10 or from 100 to 1000, or you can define a subrange of the Char type, as in:

```
type
  Ten = 1..10;
  OddRange = 100..1000;
  Uppercase = 'A'..'Z';
```

The last subrange above is depicted in Figure 4.7. In the definition of a subrange, you don't need to specify the name of the base type. You just need to supply two constants of that type. The original type must be an ordinal type, and the resulting type will be another ordinal type.

FIGURE 4.7

The representation of a subrange.

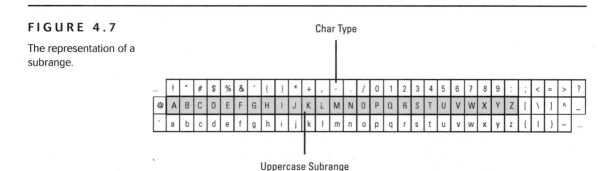

When you have defined a subrange, you can legally assign it a value within that range. This code is valid:

```
var
  UppLetter: UpperCase;
begin
  UppLetter := 'F';
```

But this one is not:

```
var
  UppLetter: UpperCase;
begin
  UppLetter := 'e'; // compile-time error
```

Writing the code above results in a compile-time error, *"Constant expression violates subrange bounds."* If you write the following code instead:

```
var
  UppLetter: Uppercase;
  Letter: Char;
begin
  Letter :='e';
  UppLetter := Letter;
```

Delphi will compile it. At run-time, if you have enabled the Range Checking compiler option (in the Compiler page of the Project Options dialog box), you'll get a *Range check error* message.

TIP

I suggest that you turn on this compiler option while you are developing a program, and then eventually disable it for the final build. This makes the program a little faster, but a little less robust. The same holds true for other run-time checking options, such as overflow and stack checking. I generally suggest leaving all these run-time checks turned on, even in a shipping program.

Enumerated Types

Enumerated types constitute another user-defined ordinal type. Instead of indicating a range of an existing type, in an enumeration you list all of the possible values for the type. In other words, an enumeration is a list of values. Here are some examples:

```
type
  Colors = (Red, Yellow, Green, Cyan, Blue, Violet);
  Suit = (Club, Diamond, Heart, Spade);
```

Each value in the list has an associated *ordinality*, starting with zero. When you apply the Ord function to a value of an enumerated type, you get this zero-based value. For example, Ord (Diamonds) returns 1.

> Enumerated types can have different internal representations. By default, Delphi uses an 8-bit representation, unless there are more than 256 different values, in which case it uses the 16-bit representation. There is also a 32-bit representation, which might be useful for compatibility with C or C++ libraries. You can actually change the default behavior, asking for a larger representation, by using the $Z compiler directive.

The Delphi VCL (Visual Component Library) uses enumerated types in many places. For example, the style of the border of a form is defined as follows:

```
type
  TFormBorderStyle = (bsNone, bsSingle, bsSizeable,
    bsDialog, bsSizeToolWin, bsToolWindow);
```

When the value of a property is an enumeration, you usually can choose from the list of values displayed in the Object Inspector:

The Delphi Help file generally lists the possible values of an enumeration. As an alternative you can use the OrdType program, in the TOOLS directory of the companion CD, to see the list of the values of each Delphi enumeration, set, subrange, and any other ordinal type. You can see an example of the output of this program in Figure 4.8.

FIGURE 4.8

Detailed information
about an enumerated
type, as displayed by the
OrdType program in the
TOOLS directory of the
companion CD.

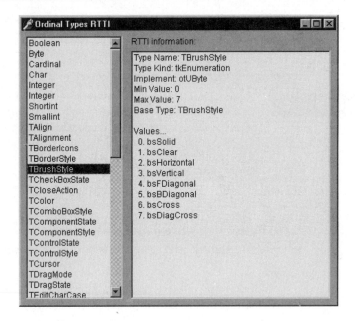

Set Types

Set types indicate the power set of an ordinal type, quite often an enumeration or
a subrange, since the base type cannot have more than 256 possible values in its
range. A variable usually holds one of the possible values of the range of a type. A
set, instead, can contain none, one, two, three, or more values of the range. It can
even include all of the values. Here is an example of a set, depicted in Figure 4.9:

```
type
    Letters = set of Uppercase;
```

Now I can define a variable of this type and assign to it some values of the original type. To indicate some values in a set, you write a comma-separated list,
enclosed within square brackets. When you have defined a variable such as

```
var
    MyLetters: Letters;
```

you can set its value with the following statements (respectively assigning several
values, a single value, and an empty value):

```
MyLetters := ['A', 'B', 'C'];
MyLetters := ['K'];
MyLetters := [];
```

FIGURE 4.9

The representation of a set.

Letters = Set of Uppercase

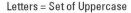

MyLetters := ['A', 'B', 'C'];

Value: 1 1 1 0 0 0 0 0 0 0 0 0 0 0 0 0 0 0 0 0 0 0 0 0 0 0 0

MyLetters := ['K'];

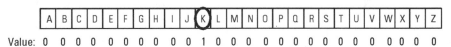

Value: 0 0 0 0 0 0 0 0 0 0 1 0 0 0 0 0 0 0 0 0 0 0 0 0 0 0

In Delphi, a `set` is generally used to indicate nonexclusive flags. For example, the following two lines of code (which are part of the Delphi library) declare an enumeration of possible icons for the border of a window and the corresponding `set` type:

```
type
    TBorderIcon = (biSystemMenu, biMinimize, biMaximize, biHelp);
    TBorderIcons = set of TBorderIcon;
```

In fact, a given window might have none of these icons, one of them, or more than one. When working with the Object Inspector, you can provide the values of a `set` by expanding the selection (double-click on the property name) and toggling on and off the presence of each value.

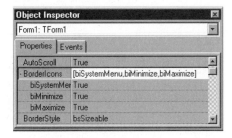

Another property based on a set type is the style of a font. Possible values indicate a bold, italic, underline, and strikethrough font. Of course the same font can be both italic and bold, have no attributes, or have them all. For this reason it is declared as a set. You can assign values to this set as follows:

```
Font.Style := []; // no style
Font.Style := [fsBold]; // bold style only
Font.Style := [fsBold, fsItalic]; // two styles
```

You can also operate on a set in many different ways, including adding two variables of the same set type (or, to be more precise, computing the union of the two set variables):

```
Font.Style := OldStyle + [fsUnderline]; // two sets
```

You'll generally use a set union to add one or more values to an existing set, as in the following code (extracted from the Choice example of Chapter 8):

```
procedure TForm1.CheckBoldClick(Sender: TObject);
begin
  if CheckBold.Checked then
    Memo1.Font.Style := Memo1.Font.Style + [fsBold]
  else
    Memo1.Font.Style := Memo1.Font.Style - [fsBold];
end;
```

Again, you can use the OrdType examples included in the TOOLS directory on the companion CD to see the list of possible values of many sets defined by the Delphi component library.

Array Types

Array types define lists of a fixed number of elements of a specific type (see Figure 4.10). For example, you can define a group of 24 integers with this code:

```
type
  DayTemperatures = array [1..24] of Integer;
```

In the array definition, you need to pass a subrange type within square brackets, or define a new specific subrange type using two constants of an ordinal type. This subrange specifies the valid indexes of the array. Since you specify both the upper and the lower index of the array, the indexes don't need to be zero-based, as is necessary in C, C++, and other programming languages.

FIGURE 4.10

The representation of an array.

DayTemperatures = Array [1..24] of Integer;

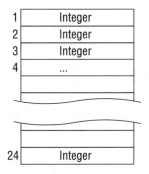

Since the `array` indexes are based on subranges, Delphi can check for their range as we've already seen. An invalid constant subrange results in a compile-time error; and an out-of-range index used at run-time results in a run-time error.

Using the array definition above, you can set the value of a `DayTemp1` variable of the `DayTemperatures` type as follows:

```
DayTemp1 [1] := 54;
DayTemp1 [2] := 52;
...
DayTemp1 [24] := 66;
DayTemp1 [25] := 67; // compile-time error
```

An array can have more than one dimension, as in the following examples:

```
type
  MonthTemps = array [1..24, 1..31] of Integer;
  YearTemps = array [1..24, 1..31, Jan..Dec] of Integer;
```

These two `array` types are built on the same core types. So you can declare them using the preceding data types, as in the following code:

```
type
  MonthTemps = array [1..31] of DayTemperatures;
  YearTemps = array [Jan..Dec] of MonthTemps;
```

This declaration inverts the order of the indexes as presented above, but it also allows assignment of whole blocks between variables. For example, the following statement copies January's temperatures to February:

```
var
  ThisYear: YearTemps;
begin
  ...
  ThisYear[Feb] := ThisYear[Jan];
```

You can also define a *zero-based* array—an array type with the lower bound set to zero. Generally, the use of more logical bounds is an advantage, since you don't need to use the index 2 to access the third item, and so on. Windows, however, uses invariably zero-based arrays (because it is based on the C language), and the Delphi component library tends to do the same.

If you need to work on an array, you can always test its bounds by using the standard Low and High functions, which return the lower and upper bounds. Using Low and High when operating on an array is highly recommended, especially in loops, since it makes the code independent of the range of the array. Later, you can change the declared range of the array indices, and the code that uses Low and High will still work. If you write a loop hard-coding the range of an array you'll have to update the code of the loop when the array size changes. Low and High make your code easier to maintain and more reliable.

TIP

Incidentally, there is no run-time overhead for using Low and High. They are resolved at compile-time into constant expressions, not actual function calls. This compile-time resolution of expressions and function calls happens also for many other simple system functions.

Delphi uses arrays mainly in the form of array properties. We have already seen an example of such a property in the TimeNow example, to access the Items property of a ListBox component. I'll show you some more examples of array properties in the upcoming section devoted to Delphi loops.

Record Types

Record types define fixed collections of items of different types. Each element, or *field*, has its own type. The definition of a record type lists all these fields, giving each a name you'll use later to access it.

Here is a small listing with the definition of a record type (see also Figure 4.11), the declaration of a variable of that type, and few statements using this variable:

```
type
  Date = record
    Year: Integer;
    Month: Byte;
    Day: Byte;
  end;
var
  BirthDay: Date;
begin
  BirthDay.Year := 1997;
  BirthDay.Month := 2;
  BirthDay.Day := 14;
```

Classes and objects can be considered an extension of the record type. Delphi libraries tend to use class types instead of record types, but there are many record types defined by the Windows API.

FIGURE 4.11

The representation of a record.

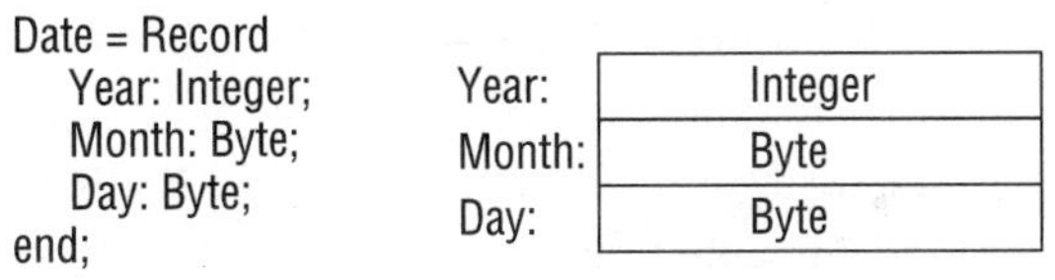

```
Date = Record
  Year: Integer;
  Month: Byte;
  Day: Byte;
end;
```

Year:	Integer
Month:	Byte
Day:	Byte

Record types can also have a variant part; that is, multiple fields can be mapped to the same memory area, even if they have a different data type. (This corresponds to a union in the C language.) Alternatively, you can use these variant fields or groups of fields to access the same memory location within a record, but considering those values from different perspectives. The main uses of this type were to store similar but different data and to obtain an effect similar to that of typecasting. The use of variant data types has been largely replaced by object-oriented and other modern techniques, although Delphi uses it in some peculiar cases.

The use of a variant record type is not type-safe and is not a recommended programming practice, particularly for beginners. Expert programmers can indeed use variant record types, and the core of the Delphi libraries makes use of them. You won't need to tackle them until you are really a Delphi expert, anyway.

Pointers

A pointer type defines a variable that holds the memory address of another variable of a given data type (or an undefined type). So a pointer variable indirectly refers to a value, as you can see in Figure 4.12. The definition of a pointer type uses a special character, the caret (^):

```
type
    PointerToInt = ^Integer;
```

FIGURE 4.12

The representation of a pointer.

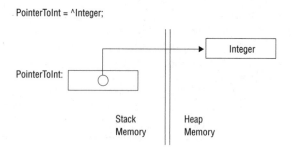

Once you have defined a pointer variable, you can assign to it the address of another variable of the same type, using the @ operator, or create a new variable on the heap with the New procedure. You'll then need to get rid of the memory you've allocated, by calling the Dispose procedure.

If a pointer has no value, you can assign the nil value to it. Then you can test whether a pointer is nil to see if it currently refers to a value. This is often used, because dereferencing an invalid pointer causes an access violation (also known as a general protection fault, or GPF). You can see an example of the effect of such an error by running the GPF example (or looking at the corresponding Figure 4.13), which executes the following code:

```
procedure TFormGPF.BtnGpfClick(Sender: TObject);
var
    P: ^Integer;
begin
    P := nil;
    ShowMessage (IntToStr (P^));
end;
```

FIGURE 4.13

The system error resulting from the access to a nil pointer, from the GPF example.

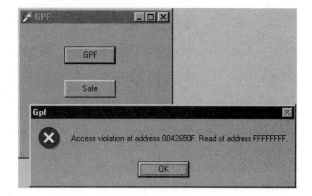

In the same program you can find an example of safe data access. In this second case the pointer is assigned to an existing local variable, and can be safely used, but I've added a safe-check anyway:

```
procedure TFormGPF.BtnSafeClick(Sender: TObject);
var
  P: ^Integer;
  X: Integer;
begin
  P := @X;
  X := 100;
  if P <> nil then
    ShowMessage (IntToStr (P^));
end;
```

As an alternative, you can dynamically allocate the memory for the pointer variable, as in the following method of the GPF example:

```
procedure TFormGPF.BtnDynamicClick(Sender: TObject);
var
  P: ^Integer;
begin
  // initialization
  New (P);
  // operations
  P^ := 20;
  ShowMessage (IntToStr (P^));
```

```
   // termination
   Dispose (P);
 end;
```

Delphi also defines a `Pointer` data type, which indicates untyped pointers (such as `void*` in the C language). If you use an untyped pointer you should use `GetMem` instead of `New`. The `GetMem` procedure is required each time the size of the memory variable is not defined.

The fact that pointers are seldom necessary in Delphi is an interesting advantage of this environment. Nonetheless, understanding pointers is important for advanced programming and for a full understanding of the Delphi object model, which uses pointers "behind the scenes."

NOTE   Although you don't use pointers often in Delphi, you do frequently use a very similar construct—namely, references. Every object instance is really an implicit pointer or reference to its actual data. However, this is completely transparent to the programmer, who uses object variables just like any other data type. We will explore the Delphi object reference model further in the next chapter.

File Types

Another Pascal-specific type constructor is the `file` type. Files are related to input/output, and they will be discussed in more detail in Chapter 29. In short, you can define a new `file` data type as follows:

```
type
  IntFile = file of Integer;
```

Then you can open a physical file associated with this structure and write integer values to it or read the current values from the file.

The use of files in Pascal is quite straightforward, but in Delphi there are also some components that are capable of storing or loading their contents to or from a file. There is some serialization support, in the form of streams, and there is also database support. I'll discuss all of these issues in future chapters.

Strings in Delphi

String handling in Delphi is quite simple, but behind the scenes the situation is quite complex. Pascal has a traditional way of handling strings, Windows has its own way, borrowed from the C language, and 32-bit versions of Delphi include support for a new long string data type, which is the default string type.

I'll start by looking at the traditional Pascal approach and then discuss Windows and Delphi approaches. Further sections will cover string conversions.

Traditional Turbo Pascal Strings

In Borland's Turbo Pascal and in 16-bit Delphi, the typical string type is a sequence of characters with a length byte at the beginning. Each string has a fixed size (which by default is the maximum, 255), although it usually holds fewer characters. Traditional Pascal strings are limited to 255 characters, and this is a real problem. Here is a 16-bit Delphi example:

```
var
  Name: string;
  Title: string [50];
```

Name is a string of 255 characters, while Title holds a maximum of 50 characters. As you can see from the use of brackets, a string type is similar to an array type. In fact, a string is almost an array of characters. This is demonstrated by the fact that you can write

```
FirstChar := Name [1];
```

to access the first character of the Name string. There are a number of functions you can use to operate on strings (refer to the Delphi Help file for a complete list). In particular, using Pascal strings, you can easily concatenate two or more strings using the plus sign:

```
FinalString := FirstString + ' ' + SecondString;
```

This expression merges the two strings, adding a blank character (a space) between them.

Delphi Long Strings

To overcome the limits of traditional Pascal strings, the 32-bit version of Delphi has introduced support for long strings. There are actually three string types:

- The ShortString type corresponds to the typical Pascal strings, as described in the section above. These strings have a limit of 255 characters and correspond to the strings in the 16-bit version of Delphi. Each element of a short string is of type ANSIChar; that is, the standard character type.

- The ANSIString type corresponds to the new variable-length, long strings. These strings are allocated dynamically and their size is almost unlimited. They are also based on the ANSIChar type.

- The WideString type is similar to the ANSIString type but is based on the WideChar type—it stores Unicode characters. This type has been introduced in Delphi 3, but is used mainly by the OLE interface units.

NOTE The VCL supports wide strings in many circumstances. However, Windows 95 has very weak support for wide strings, and some of the API functions simply don't work. On Windows NT, though, wide strings really work! To see an example of this Windows 95 problem, try the WideStr program on the CD. In this example there is a call to the SetWindowTextW API function, which is the wide string version of the SetWindowText API. This function call has absolutely no effect under Windows 95, while the same program works OK under Windows NT.

In Delphi 3 (as in Delphi 2), if you simply use the string data type, you get either short strings or ANSI strings, depending on the value of the $H compiler directive. The default is $H+, which stands for long strings (the ANSIString type), and this is what is used by the components of the Delphi library.

In theory, an ANSIString can store a maximum of two billion characters, more than some 32-bit versions of Windows actually allow for each application. As I mentioned before, these new strings are also dynamically allocated. This means that they use only as much memory as needed to hold their value. When you make a copy of the string, only the pointer is copied, making this operation extremely fast. But as soon as you change the value of one of the strings referring to the same value, the string is duplicated and only the duplicated value is affected by the change.

StrRef: An Example of Dynamic String Allocation

The StrRef example (on the companion CD) demonstrates the dynamic allocation of strings. In this example I declare two global strings:

```
var
    FormStrRef: TFormStrRef;
    Str1, Str2: string;
```

When the first of the two buttons is pressed, the program assigns a constant string to the first of the two variables, and then assign the second to the first, as you can see in the code:

```
procedure TFormStrRef.BtnAssignClick(Sender: TObject);
begin
    Str1 := 'Hello';
    Str2 := Str1;
    Label1.Caption := 'Str1: ' + Str1 +
        ' - ' + IntToStr (Integer (Str1));
    Label2.Caption := 'Str2: ' + Str2 +
        ' - ' + IntToStr (Integer (Str2));
    BtnChange.Enabled := True;
end;
```

The other statements are used to output in the Caption of two Label components the text of the two strings, along with the numerical value of the Str1 and Str2 variables. To obtain these values I've simply made a hard-coded typecast from the string type to the Integer type. Since strings are references—in practice, pointers—their value holds the actual memory location of the string.

By running this example, you should get two strings with the same content and the same memory location. Now if you change the value of one of the two strings, which one doesn't really matter, the memory location of the updated string will change. This is the effect of the *copy-on-write* technique I've just described.

Continued on next page

StrRef: An Example of Dynamic String Allocation (Continued)

We can actually produce this output by writing the following code for the OnClick event handler of the second button:

```
procedure TFormStrRef.BtnChangeClick(Sender: TObject);
begin
  Str1 [2] := 'a';
  Label1.Caption := 'Str1: ' + Str1 +
    ' - ' + IntToStr (Integer (Str1));
  Label2.Caption := 'Str2: ' + Str2 +
    ' - ' + IntToStr (Integer (Str2));
end;
```

The last two lines output the information for two strings again. As you can see, the output is actually what we were expecting.

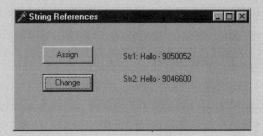

Notice that the code of the BtnChangeClick method can be executed only after the BtnAssignClick method. To enforce this, the program starts with the second button disabled (its Enabled property is set to False) at design time, and is enabled at the end of the first method.

Delphi long strings are based on a reference-counting mechanism, which keeps track of how many strings variables are referring to the same string in memory. This reference-counting is used also to free the memory when a string isn't used any more—that is, when the reference count reaches zero.

A string in memory is reallocated when you change its size, which means that a full copy of the string must be made when there is something else in the adjacent memory and the string cannot grow in the same memory location. For this reason, you can set the maximum size of the string with the SetLength procedure, effectively allocating the required amount of memory:

```
SetLength (String1, 200);
```

> **NOTE** The SetLength procedure performs a memory request, not an actual memory allocation. It reserves the required memory space for future use, without actually using the memory. This technique is based on a feature of the Windows operating systems, and is used by Delphi for all dynamic memory allocations. For example, when you request a very large array, its memory is reserved but not allocated.

Setting the length of a string is seldom necessary. The only case in which you *must* allocate memory for the long string using SetLength is when you have to pass the string as a parameter to an API function (after the proper typecast), as I'll show you shortly.

Another important point in favor of using long strings is that they are null-terminated. This means that they are fully compatible with the C language null-terminated strings used by Windows (see the next section).

All of these reasons, plus the size of the long strings, make the use of the ANSI-String type the standard in the 32-bit versions of Delphi, with the old strings available for compatibility only. Since ANSIString is the default, you can simply use the string data type in declaring strings. However, keep in mind how strings are implemented, because this has some impact on the way you write good, fast code.

C-Like Character Arrays

As an alternative to the string type, you can use a zero-based character array type to store *null-terminated* strings. A *null-terminated* string is a sequence of characters followed by a byte set to zero (or null). Character array types are typical of the C language, and they are used extensively by Windows API functions.

Since Pascal's long strings are fully compatible with C null-terminated strings, using a character array is useful mainly for compatibility with the 16-bit version of an application. You declare a character array as follows:

```
var
   Name: array [0..50] of Char;
```

and work with it as with any other array. However, there is a second way to use character array types. If the language *extended syntax* is enabled (as it is by default), a zero-based character array is compatible with PChar, a pointer to a character. You might wonder why this compatibility would be necessary. The short answer is that many Windows API functions require PChar parameters, so this compatibility rule allows you to declare character arrays, eventually fill them with values, and then pass them as parameters to these API functions.

WARNING Although many Windows functions have a PChar parameter, in most cases, declaring a PChar variable and passing it to those functions generates a very bad error. By writing such code, you end up passing an uninitialized pointer to the function, which will cause an error inside Windows code when the system tries to read or write the string. This is actually what I did on purpose to generate the "general protection fault" in the GPF example earlier in this chapter.

In general, before passing a pointer to a Windows API function, you should allocate some memory for it. In the case of PChar strings, the easiest technique is to declare an array of characters instead of a pointer, and pass that array to the function. As an alternative, you can declare the pointer and dynamically allocate memory for it (with the GetMem or NewStr functions). If you do this, remember to dispose of the memory at the end. However, it is simpler to use the new Delphi long strings, instead. Be aware that Delphi also includes a number of functions that work on null-terminated strings.

String Conversions

As already mentioned, Delphi includes many functions that operate on strings. They are listed in detail in the Help file, so I won't describe them all. Only two groups of functions are worth mentioning.

The first group includes the functions used for trimming strings, by removing white space from them. These functions were not present in the original 16-bit version of Delphi. The functions TrimLeft, TrimRight, and Trim remove leading white spaces, trailing white spaces, or white spaces at both ends of the string, respectively.

The second group consists of the conversion functions. You have already seen many functions that turn numbers into strings and vice versa, but two important cases are the StrPas function, which converts a null-terminated string into a Pascal string, and the StrPCopy function, which makes the reverse conversion. These two functions are particularly useful in the 16-bit version of Delphi.

If you need to convert a long Pascal string into a PChar, instead, a cast is enough. The reverse operation, assigning a PChar and any other character array to a string, can be done even without casting. To copy the caption of a form into a PChar string (using the API function GetWindowText) and then copy it into the Caption of the button, for example, you can write the following code:

```
procedure TForm1.Button1Click(Sender: TObject);
var
  S1: String;
begin
  SetLength (S1, 100);
  GetWindowText (Handle, PChar (S1), Length (S1));
  Button1.Caption := S1;
end;
```

You can find this code in the LongStr example on the CD. Notice that if you write this code but fail to allocate the memory for the string with SetLength, the program will probably crash.

If you are using a PChar to pass a value (and not to receive one as in the code above), the code is even simpler because there is no need to define a temporary string and initialize it. The following line of code passes the Caption property of a label as a parameter to an API function, simply by typecasting it to PChar:

```
SetWindowText (Handle, PChar (Label1.Caption));
```

NOTE
When you need to cast a WideString to a Windows-compatible type, you have to use PWideChar instead of PChar for the conversion. We'll have to use wide strings for OLE and COM programs.

String Conversion Blues

Their broad compatibility and their big size are the two key reasons to use the new strings exclusively, unless you need to maintain compatibility with the 16-bit version of Delphi. However, there are some problems that might arise when you convert a long string into a PChar.

Essentially, the underlying problem is that after this conversion, you become *responsible* for the string and its contents, and Delphi won't help you any more. Consider the following limited change to the first program code fragment above, Button1Click:

```
procedure TForm1.Button2Click(Sender: TObject);
var
  S1: String;
begin
  SetLength (S1, 100);
  GetWindowText (Handle, PChar (S1), Length (S1));
  S1 := S1 + ' is the title'; // this won't work
  Button1.Caption := S1;
end;
```

This program compiles, but when you run it, you are in for a surprise: The Caption of the button will have the original text of the window title, without the text of the constant string you have added to it. The problem is that when Windows writes to the string (within the GetWindowText API call), it doesn't set the length of the long Pascal string properly. Delphi still can use this string for output and can figure out when it ends by looking for the null terminator, but if you append further characters after the null terminator, they will be skipped altogether.

How can we fix this problem? The solution is to tell the system to convert the string returned by the GetWindowText API call back to a Pascal string. However, if you write the following code:

```
S1 := String (S1);
```

the system will ignore it, because converting a data type back into itself is a useless operation. To obtain the proper long Pascal string, you need to *recast* the string to a PChar, and let Delphi convert it back again properly to a string:

```
S1 := String (PChar (S1));
```

Actually you can skip the string conversion, because PChar-to-string conversions are automatic in Delphi. Here is the final code:

```
procedure TForm1.Button3Click(Sender: TObject);
var
  S1: String;
begin
  SetLength (S1, 100);
  GetWindowText (Handle, PChar (S1), Length (S1));
  S1 := String (PChar (S1));
  S1 := S1 + ' is the title';
  Button3.Caption := S1;
end;
```

An alternative is to reset the length of the Delphi string, using the length of the PChar string, by writing:

```
SetLength (S1, StrLen (PChar (S1)));
```

You can find three versions of this code in the LongStr example, which has three buttons to execute them. However, if you just need to access the title of a form, you can simply use the Caption property of the form object itself. There is no need to write all this confusing code, which was intended only to demonstrate the string conversion problems. There are practical cases when you need to call Windows API functions, and then you have to consider this complex situation.

Formatting Strings

Using the + operator and some of the conversion functions (such as IntToStr) you can indeed build complex strings out of existing values. However, there is a different approach to formatting numbers, currency values, and other strings into a final string. You can use the powerful Format function, or one of its companion functions.

The Format function requires as parameters a string with the basic text and some placeholders (usually marked by the % symbol) and an array of values, one of each placeholder. For example to format two numbers into a string you can write:

```
Format ('First %d, Second %d', [n1, n2]);
```

where n1 and n2 are two Integer values. The first placeholder is replaced by the first value, the second matches the second, and so on. If the output type of the placeholder (indicated by the letter after the % symbol) doesn't match the type of the corresponding parameter, a runtime error occurs. Having no compile-time type checking is actually the biggest drawback of using the Format function.

NOTE   The `Format` function uses an open-array parameter (a parameter that can have an arbitrary number of values), something I'll discuss again toward the end of this chapter. For the moment notice only the array-like syntax of the list of values passed as the second parameter.

Besides using %d, you can use one of many other placeholders defined by this function and briefly listed in Table 4.4. These placeholders provide a default output for the given data type. However you can use further *format specifiers* to alter the default output. A *width specifier*, for example, determines a fixed number of characters in the output, while a *precision specifier* indicates the number of decimal digits. For example,

```
Format ('%8d', [n1]);
```

converts the number n1 into an eight-characters string, right-aligning the text (use the – symbol to specify *left-justification*) filling it with white spaces.

TABLE 4.4   Type Specifiers for the Format Function

Type Specifier	Description
d (decimal)	The corresponding integer value is converted to a string of decimal digits.
x (hexadecimal)	The corresponding integer value is converted to a string of hexadecimal digits.
p (pointer)	The corresponding pointer value is converted to a string expressed with hexadecimal digits.
s (string)	The corresponding string, character, or PChar value is copied to the output string.
e (exponential)	The corresponding floating-point value is converted to a string based on exponential notation.
f (floating point)	The corresponding floating-point value is converted to a string based on floating-point notation.
g (general)	The corresponding floating-point value is converted to the shortest possible decimal string using either floating-point or exponential notation.
n (number)	The corresponding floating-point value is converted to a floating-point string but also uses thousands separators.
m (money)	The corresponding floating-point value is converted to a string representing a currency amount. The conversion is based on regional settings—see the Delphi Help file under *Currency and date/time formatting variables*.

The best way to see examples of these conversions is to experiment with format strings yourself. To make this easier I've written the FmtText program, which allows a user to provide formatting strings for integer and floating-point numbers.

As you can see in Figure 4.14, this program displays a form divided into two parts. The left part is for Integer numbers, the right part for floating-point numbers. Each part has a first edit box with the numeric value you want to format to a string. Below the first edit box there is a button to perform the formatting operation and show the result in a message box. Then comes another edit box, where you can type a format string. As an alternative you can simply click on one of the lines of the ListBox component, below, to select a predefined formatting string. Every time you type a new valid formatting string, it is added to the corresponding list box (note that by closing the program you lose these new items).

FIGURE 4.14

An example of the output of a floating-point value from the FmtFloat program.

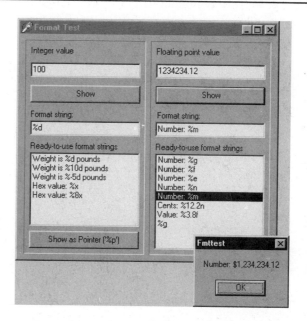

The full source code of this example is a little complex to discuss at this point of the book, but if you have already used Delphi you'll be able to understand it easily.

Coding Style

Before we move on to the subject of writing Pascal language statements, it is important to highlight a couple of elements of Pascal coding style. The question I'm addressing here is this: Besides the syntax rules, how should you write code? There isn't a single answer to this question, since personal taste can dictate different styles. However, there are some principles you need to know regarding comments, uppercase, spaces, and the so-called *pretty-printing*. In general, the goal of any coding style is clarity. The style and formatting decisions you make are a form of shorthand, indicating the purpose of a given piece of code. An essential tool for clarity is consistency—whatever style you choose, be sure to follow it throughout a project.

Comments

In Pascal, comments are enclosed in either braces or parentheses followed by a star. Delphi also accepts the C++ style comments, which can span to the end of the line:

```
{this is a comment}
(* this is another comment *)
// this is a comment up to the end of the line
```

The first form is shorter and more commonly used. The second form was often preferred in Europe because many European keyboards lack the brace symbol. The third form of comments has been borrowed from C++ and is available only in the 32-bit versions of Delphi. Comments *up to the end of the line* are very helpful for short comments and for commenting out a line of code.

> **TIP** In the listings of the book I'll try to mark comments as italic (and keywords in bold), to be consistent with the default Delphi syntax highlighting.

Having three different forms of comments can be helpful for making nested comments. If you want to comment out several lines of source code to disable them, and these lines contain some real comments, you cannot use the same comment identifier:

```
{ ... code
{comment, creating problems}
... code }
```

With a second comment identifier, you can write the following code, which is correct:

```
{  ... code
//this comment is OK
... code }
```

Note that if the open brace or parenthesis-star is followed by the dollar sign ($), it becomes a compiler directive, as in {$X+}.

> **NOTE** Actually, compiler directives are still comments. For example, {$X+ This is a comment} is legal. It's both a valid directive and a comment, although *sane* programmers will probably tend to separate directives and comments.

Use of Uppercase

The Pascal compiler (unlike those in other languages) ignores the case (capitalization) of characters. Therefore, the identifiers Myname, MyName, myname, myName, and MYNAME are all exactly equivalent. On the whole, this is definitely a positive, since in case-sensitive languages, many syntax errors are caused by incorrect capitalization.

There are a couple of subtle drawbacks, however. First, you must be aware that these identifiers really are the same, so you must avoid using them as different elements. Second, you should try to be consistent in the use of uppercase letters, to improve the readability of the code.

A consistent use of case isn't enforced by the compiler, but it is a good habit to get into. A common approach is to capitalize only the first letter of each identifier. When an identifier is made up of several consecutive words (you cannot insert a space in an identifier), every first letter of a word should be capitalized:

```
MyLongIdentifier
MyVeryLongAndAlmostStupidIdentifier
```

White Space

Other elements completely ignored by the compiler are the of spaces, new lines, and tab spaces you add to the source code. All these elements are collectively known as *white space*. White space is used only to improve code readability; it does not affect the compilation.

Unlike BASIC, Pascal allows you to write a statement on several lines of code, splitting a long instruction on two or more lines. The drawback (at least for many BASIC programmers) of allowing statements on more than one line is that you have to remember to add a semicolon to indicate the end of a statement, or more precisely, to separate a statement from the next one. Notice that the only restriction in splitting programming statements on different lines is that a string literal may not span several lines.

Again, there are no fixed rules on the use of spaces and multiple-line statements, just some rules of thumb:

- The Delphi editor has a vertical line you can place after 60 or 70 characters. If you use this line and try to avoid surpassing this limit, your source code will look better when you print it on paper. Otherwise long lines may get broken at any position, even in the middle of a word, when you print them.

- When a function or procedure has several parameters, it is common practice to place the parameters on different lines.

- You can leave a line completely white (blank) before a comment or to divide a long piece of code in smaller portions. Even this simple idea can improve the readability of the code, both on screen and when you print it.

- Use spaces to separate the parameters of a function call, and maybe even a space before the initial open parenthesis. Also keep operands of an expression separated. I know that some programmers will disagree with these ideas, but I insist: Spaces are free; you don't pay for them. (OK, I know that they use up disk space and modem connection time when you upload or download a file, but this is less and less relevant, nowadays.)

Pretty-Printing

The last suggestion on the use of white spaces relates to the typical Pascal language-formatting style, known as *pretty-printing*. This rule is simple: Each time you need to write a compound statement, indent it two spaces to the right of the rest of the current statement. A compound statement inside another compound statement is indented four spaces, and so on:

```
if ... then
  statement;

if ... then
```

```
begin
  statement1;
  statement2;
end;

if ... then
begin
  if ... then
    statement1;
  statement2;
end;
```

> **NOTE**
>
> The above formatting is based on pretty-printing, but programmers have different interpretations of this general rule. Some programmers indent the `begin` and end statements to the level of the inner code, some of them indent `begin` and end and then indent the internal code once more, other programmers put the `begin` in the line of the `if` condition. This is mostly a matter of personal taste.

A similar indented format is often used for lists of variables or data types, and to continue a statement from the previous line:

```
type
  Letters = set of Char;
var
  Name: string;
begin
  { long comment and long statement, going on in the
    following line and indented two spaces }
  MessageDlg ('This is a message',
    mtInformation, [mbOk], 0);
```

Of course, any such convention is just a suggestion to make the code more readable to other programmers, and it is completely ignored by the compiler. I've tried to use this rule consistently in all of the samples and code fragments in this book. Delphi source code, manuals, and Help examples use a similar formatting style.

Syntax Highlighting

To make it easier to read and write Pascal code, the Delphi editor has a feature called *color syntax highlighting*. Depending on the meaning in Pascal of the words you type in the editor, they are displayed using different colors. By default, keywords are in bold, strings and comments are in color (and often in italic), and so on.

Reserved words, comments, and strings are probably the three elements that benefit most from this feature. You can see at a glance a misspelled keyword, a string not properly terminated, and the length of a multiple-line comment.

You can easily customize the syntax highlight settings using the Editor Colors page of the Environment Options dialog box (see Figure 4.15). If you work by yourself, choose the colors you like. If you work closely with other programmers, you should all agree on a standard color scheme. I find that working on a computer with a different syntax coloring than the one I am used to is really difficult.

FIGURE 4.15

The dialog box used to set the color syntax highlighting.

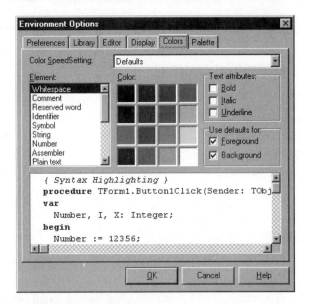

TIP   In this new edition of the book I've tried to apply a sort of syntax highlighting to the source code listings. I hope this actually makes them more readable.

Using Code Templates

Delphi 3 introduces a new feature related to source code editing. Because when writing Pascal language statement you often repeat the same sequence of keywords, Borland has provided a new feature called Code Templates, as mentioned in Chapter 2. A code template is simply a piece of code related with a shorthand. You type the shorthand, then press Ctrl+J, and the full piece of code appears.

For example, if you type **arrayd**, and then press Ctrl+J, the Delphi editor will expand your text into:

```
array[0..] of ;
```

Since the predefined code templates usually include several versions of the same construct, the shortcut generally terminates with a letter indicating which of the versions you are interested in. However, you can also type only the initial part of the shortcut. For example, if you type **ar** and then press Ctrl+J, the editor will display a local menu with a list of the available choices with a short description, as you can see in the following figure:

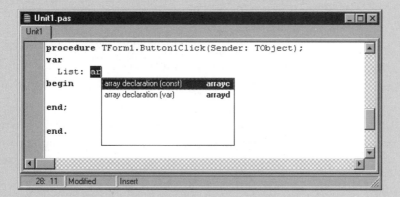

You can fully customize the code templates by modifying the existing ones or adding your own common code pieces. If you do this, keep in mind that the text of a code template generally includes the '|' character to indicate where the cursor should jump to after the operation, that is, where you start typing to complete the template with custom code.

Language Statements

Once you have defined some identifiers, you can use them in statements and in the expressions that are part of some statements. Pascal offers several statements and expressions. Let's look at expressions and operators first.

Expressions and Operators

There isn't a general rule for building expressions, since they mainly depend on the operators being used, and Pascal has a number of operators. There are logical, arithmetic, Boolean, relational, and set operators, plus some others. Expressions can be used to determine the value to assign to a variable, to compute the parameter of a function or procedure, or to test for a condition. Expressions can include function calls, too. Every time you are performing an operation on the value of an identifier, rather than using an identifier by itself, that is an expression.

Expressions are common to most programming languages. An *expression* is any valid combination of constants, variables, literal values, operators, and function results. Expressions can also be passed to value parameters of procedures and functions, but not always to reference parameters (which require a value you can assign to).

Operators and Precedence

If you have ever written a program in your life, you already know what an expression is. Here, I'll highlight specific elements of Pascal operators. You can see a list of the operators of the language, grouped by precedence, in Table 4.5.

Notice that some of the common operators have different meanings with different data types. For example, the + operator can be used to add two numbers, concatenate two strings, make the union of two sets, and even add an offset to a PChar pointer. However, you cannot add two characters, as is possible in C.

Another strange operator is div. In Pascal, you can divide any two numbers (real or integers) with the / operator, and you'll invariably get a real-number result. If you need to divide two integers and want an integer result, use the div operator instead.

TABLE 4.5 Pascal Language Operators, Grouped by Precedence

Operator	Purpose
Unary Operators (Highest Precedence)	
@	Address of the variable or function (returns a pointer)
not	Boolean or bitwise not
Multiplicative and Bitwise Operators	
*	Arithmetic multiplication or set intersection
/	Floating-point division
div	Integer division
mod	Modulus (the remainder of integer division)
as	Type-safe typecast (RTTI)
and	Boolean or bitwise and
shl	Bitwise left shift
shr	Bitwise right shift
Additive Operators	
+	Arithmetic addition, set union, string concatenation, positive value, or pointer offset addition
–	Arithmetic subtraction, set difference, negative value, or pointer offset subtraction
or	Boolean or bitwise or
xor	Boolean or bitwise exclusive or
Relational and Comparison Operators (Lowest Precedence)	
=	Test whether equal
<>	Test whether not equal
<	Test whether less than
>	Test whether greater than
<=	Test whether less than or equal to, or a subset of a set
>=	Test whether greater than or equal to, or a superset of a set
in	Test whether the item is a member of the set
is	Test whether object is type-compatible (another RTTI operator)

Set Operators

The set operators include union (+), difference (–), intersection (*),membership test (in), plus some relational operators. To add an element to a set, you can make the union of the set with another one that has only the element you need. Here's a Delphi example related to font styles:

```
Style := Style + [fsBold];
Style := Style + [fsBold, fsItalic] - [fsUnderline];
```

As an alternative, you can use the standard Include and Exclude procedures, which are much more efficient (but cannot be used with component properties of the set type, because they require an l-value parameter):

```
Include (Style, fsBold);
```

Simple and Compound Statements

A Pascal statement is *simple* when it doesn't contain any other statements. Examples of simple statements are assignment statements and procedure calls. Simple statements are separated by a semicolon:

```
X := Y + Z;   // assignment
Randomize;    // procedure call
```

As mentioned in Chapter 1, assignments in Pascal use the *colon-equal* operator, an odd notation for programmers who are used to other languages. The = operator, which is used for assignments in some other languages, is used to test for equality in Pascal.

> **NOTE** By using different symbols for an assignment and an equality test, the Pascal compiler (like the C compiler) can translate source code faster, because it doesn't need to examine the context in which the operator is used to determine its meaning. The use of different operators also makes the code easier for people to read.

Usually, statements are part of a compound statement, marked by begin and end brackets. A compound statement can appear in place of a generic Pascal statement. Here is an example:

```
begin
  A := B;
```

```
  C := A * 2;
end;
```

The semicolon after the last statement before the end isn't required, as in the following:

```
begin
  A := B;
  C := A * 2
end;
```

Both versions are correct. The first version has a useless (but harmless) semicolon. This semicolon is, in fact, a null statement; that is, a statement with no code. Notice that, at times, null statements can be used inside loops or in other particular cases.

TIP
Although these final semicolons serve no purpose, I tend to use them and suggest you do the same. Sometimes after you've written a couple of lines you might want to add one more statement. If the last semicolon is missing you should remember to add it, so it might be better to add it in the first place.

Conditional Statements

A conditional statement is used to execute either one of the statements it contains or none of them, depending on some test. There are two basic flavors of conditional statements: if statements and case statements.

If Statements

The if statement can be used to execute a statement only if a certain condition is met (if-then), or to choose between two different statements (if-then-else). The condition is described with a Boolean expression. A simple Delphi example will demonstrate how to write conditional statements. First create a new blank application, and put two check boxes and four buttons in the form. Do not change the names of buttons or check boxes, but double-click on each button to add a handler for its OnClick event. Here's a simple if statement for the first button:

```
procedure TForm1.Button1Click(Sender: TObject);
begin
  {simple if statement}
```

```
    if CheckBox1.Checked then
        ShowMessage ('CheckBox1 is checked')
end;
```

When you click on the button, if the first check box has a check mark in it, the program will show a simple message (see Figure 4.16). I've used the ShowMessage function because it is the simplest Delphi function you can use to display a short message to the user.

FIGURE 4.16

The message displayed by the IfTest example when you press the first button and the first check box is checked.

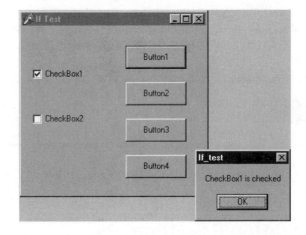

If you click the button and nothing happens, it means the check box was not checked. In general, it is better to make this more explicit, as with the code for the second button, which uses an if-then-else statement:

```
procedure TForm1.Button2Click(Sender: TObject);
begin
  {if-then-else statement}
  if CheckBox2.Checked then
    ShowMessage ('CheckBox2 is checked')
  else
    ShowMessage ('CheckBox2 is NOT checked');
end;
```

Notice that you cannot have a semicolon after the first statement and before the else keyword, or the compiler will issue a syntax error. The if-then-else statement, in fact, is a single statement, so you cannot place a semicolon in the middle of this statement.

An if statement can be quite complex. The condition can be turned into a series of conditions, or the if statement can nest a second if statement. The last two buttons of the IfTest example demonstrate these cases:

```
procedure TForm1.Button3Click(Sender: TObject);
begin
  {statement with a double condition}
  if CheckBox1.Checked and CheckBox2.Checked then
    ShowMessage ('Both check boxes are checked')
end;

procedure TForm1.Button4Click(Sender: TObject);
begin
  {compound if statement}
  if CheckBox1.Checked then
    if CheckBox2.Checked then
      ShowMessage ('CheckBox1 and 2 are checked')
    else
      ShowMessage ('Only CheckBox1 is checked')
  else
    ShowMessage (
      'Checkbox1 is not checked, who cares for Checkbox2?')
end;
```

Look at the code carefully and run the program from the CD to see if you understand everything. When you have doubts about a programming construct, writing a very simple program such as this can help you learn a lot. You can add more check boxes and increase the complexity of this small example, making any test you like.

Case Statements

If your if statements become very complex, you can replace them with case statements. A case statement consists of an expression used to select a value, a list of possible values, or a range of values. These values are constants, and they must be unique and of an ordinal type. Eventually, there can be an else statement that is executed if none of the labels correspond to the value of the selector. Here are two simple examples:

```
case Number of
  1: Text := 'One';
  2: Text := 'Two';
```

```
      3: Text := 'Three';
end;

case MyChar of
    '+' :      Text := 'Plus sign';
    '-' :      Text := 'Minus sign';
    '*', '/': Text := 'Multiplication or division';
    '0'..'9': Text := 'Number';
    'a'..'z': Text := 'Lowercase character';
    'A'..'Z': Text := 'Uppercase character';
else
    Text := 'Unknown character';
end;
```

Loops in Pascal

The Pascal language has the typical repetitive statements of most programming languages, including for, while, and repeat statements. Most of what these loops do will be familiar if you've used other languages, so I'll cover them only briefly.

The For Loop

The for loop in Pascal is strictly based on a counter, which can be either increased or decreased each time the loop is executed. Here is a simple example of a for loop used to add the first ten numbers.

```
K := 0;
for I := 1 to 10 do
  K := K + I;
```

This same for statement could have been written using a reverse counter:

```
K := 0;
for I := 10 downto 1 do
  K := K + I;
```

The for loop in Pascal is less flexible than in other languages (it is not possible to specify an increment different than one), but it is simple and easy to understand. If you want to test for a more complex condition, or to provide a customized counter, you need to use a while or repeat statement, instead of a for loop.

While and Repeat Statements

The difference between the while-do loop and the repeat-until loop is that the code of the repeat statement is always executed at least once. You can easily understand why by looking at a simple example:

```
while (I < 100) and (J < 100) do
begin
  // use I and J to compute something...
  I := I + 1;
  J := J + 1;
end;

repeat
  // use I and J to compute something...
  I := I + 1;
  J := J + 1;
until (I > 100) or (J > 100);
```

If the initial value of I or J is greater than 100, the statements inside the repeat-until loop are executed once anyway.

WARNING   The other key difference between these two loops is that the repeat-until loop has a *reversed* condition. The loop is executed until the condition is *not* met. When the condition is met, the loop terminates. This is the opposite from a while-do loop, which is executed while the condition is true. For this reason I had to reverse the condition in the code above to obtain a similar statement.

To explore the details of loops, let's look at a small Delphi example. The Loops program highlights the difference between a loop with a fixed counter and a loop with an almost random counter. Start with a new blank project, place a list box and two buttons on the main form, and give the buttons a proper name (BtnFor and BtnWhile), removing the word *Btn* from the Caption (and adding the & to activate shortcut keys). Here is a summary of the textual description of this form:

```
object Form1: TForm1
  Caption = 'Loops'
  object ListBox1: TListBox ...
  object BtnFor: TButton
    Caption = '&For'
    OnClick = BtnForClick
```

```
      end
    object BtnWhile: TButton
      Caption = '&While'
      OnClick = BtnWhileClick
    end
  end
```

Now we can add some code to the OnClick events of the two buttons. The first button has a simple for loop to display a list of numbers, as you can see in Figure 4.17. Before executing this loop, which adds a number of strings to the Items property of the list box, you need to clear the contents of the list box itself:

```
procedure TForm1.BtnForClick(Sender: TObject);
var
  I: Integer;
begin
  ListBox1.Items.Clear;
  for I := 1 to 20 do
    Listbox1.Items.Add ('String ' + IntToStr (I));
end;
```

FIGURE 4.17

Each time you press the For button of the Loops example, the list box is filled with consecutive numbers.

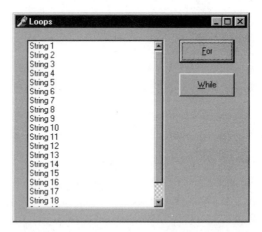

The code associated with the second button is slightly more complex. In this case, there is a while loop based on a counter, which is increased randomly. To accomplish this, I've called the Randomize procedure, which resets the random number generator, and the Random function with a range value of 100. The result of this function is a number between 0 and 99, chosen randomly. The series of random numbers control how many times the while loop is executed.

```
procedure TForm1.BtnWhileClick(Sender: TObject);
```

```
var
  I: Integer;
begin
  ListBox1.Items.Clear;
  Randomize;
  I := 0;
  while I < 1000 do
  begin
    I := I + Random (100);
    Listbox1.Items.Add ('Random Number: ' + IntToStr (I));
  end;
end;
```

Each time you click the While button, the numbers are different, because they depend on the random-number generator. Figure 4.18 shows the results from two separate button-clicks. Notice that not only are the generated numbers different each time, but so is the number of items. That is, this while loop is executed a random numbers of times. If you press the While button several times in a row, you'll see that the list box has a different number of lines.

FIGURE 4.18

The contents of the list box of the Loops example change each time you press the While button. Because the loop counter is incremented by a random value, every time you press the button the loop may execute a different number of times.

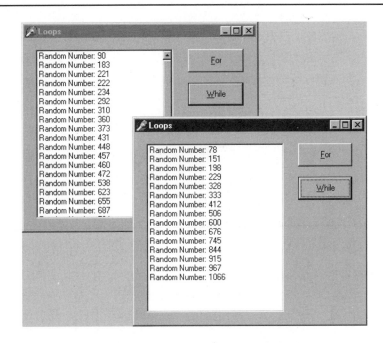

NOTE

You can alter the standard flow of a loop's execution using the `Break` and `Continue` system procedures. The first interrupts the loop; the second is used to jump directly to the loop test or counter increment, continuing with the next iteration of the loop (unless the condition is zero or the counter has reached its highest value). Two more system procedures, `Exit` and `Halt`, let you immediately return from the current function of procedure or terminate the program.

The With Statement

The last kind of Pascal statement I'll focus on is the `with` statement, which is peculiar to this programming language (and recently introduced also in BASIC) and very useful in Delphi programming.

The `with` statement is nothing but shorthand. When you need to refer to a `record` type variable (or an object), instead of repeating its name every time, you can use a `with` statement. For example, while presenting the `record` type, I wrote this code:

```
type
  Date = record
    Year: Integer;
    Month: Byte;
    Day: Byte;
  end;

var
  BirthDay: Date;

begin
  BirthDay.Year := 1997;
  BirthDay.Month := 2;
  BirthDay.Day := 14;
```

Using a `with` statement, I can improve the final part of this code, as follows:

```
begin
  with BirthDay do
  begin
    Year := 1995;
    Month := 2;
```

```
    Day := 14;
  end;
```

This approach can be used in Delphi programs to refer to components and other class types. For example, we can rewrite the final part of the last example, Loops, using a `with` statement to access the items of the list box:

```
procedure TForm1.WhileButtonClick(Sender: TObject);
var
  I: Integer;
begin
  with ListBox1.Items do
  begin
    Clear; // shortcut
    Randomize;
    I := 0;
    while I < 1000 do
    begin
      I := I + Random (100);
      // shortcut:
      Add ('Random Number: ' + IntToStr (I));
    end;
  end;
end;
```

When you work with components or classes in general, the `with` statement allows you to skip writing some code, particularly for nested fields. For example, suppose that you need to change the `Width` and the `Color` of the drawing pen for a form. You can write the following code:

```
Form1.Canvas.Pen.Width := 2;
Form1.Canvas.Pen.Color := clRed;
```

But it is certainly easier to write this code:

```
with Form1.Canvas.Pen do
begin
  Width := 2;
  Color := clRed;
end;
```

When you are writing complex code, the `with` statement can be effective and spares you the declaration of some temporary variables, but it has a drawback. It can make the code less readable, particularly when you are working with different objects that have similar or corresponding properties.

A further drawback is that using the `with` statement can allow subtle logical errors in the code that the compiler will not detect. For example:

```
with Button1 do
begin
  Width := 200;
  Caption := 'New Caption';
  Color := clRed;
end;
```

This code changes the `Caption` and the `Width` of the button, but it affects the `Color` property of the form, not that of the button! The reason is that the `TButton` components don't have the `Color` property, and since the code is executed for a form object (we are writing a method of the form) this object is accessed by default. If we had instead written:

```
Button1.Width := 200;
Button1.Caption := 'New Caption';
Button1.Color := clRed; // error!
```

the compiler would have issued an error. In general, we can say that since the `with` statement introduces new identifiers in the current scope, we might hide existing identifiers, or wrongfully access another identifier in the same scope (as in the first version of this code fragment). Even considering this kind of drawback, I suggest you get used to `with` statements, because they can be really very handy, and at times even make the code more readable. You should, however, avoid using multiple `with` statements, such as:

```
with ListBox1, Button1 do...
```

The code following this would probably be highly unreadable, because for each property defined in this block you would need to think about which component it refers to, depending on the respective properties and the order of the components in the `with` statement.

TIP   Speaking of readability, Pascal has no *endif* or *endcase* statement. If an `if` statement has a begin-end block, then the end of the block marks the end of the statement. The case statement, instead, is always terminated by an end. All these end statements, often found one after the other, can make the code difficult to follow. Only by tracing the indentations can you see which statement a particular end refers to. A common way to solve this problem and make the code more readable is to add a comment after the end statement indicating its role, as in: end; // if.

Procedures and Functions

Another important idea emphasized by Pascal is the concept of the *routine*. In Pascal, a routine can assume two forms: a procedure and a function. The only real difference between the two constructs is that a function has a return value, while a procedure doesn't.

Here are the definitions of a `procedure` and two versions of the same `function`, using a slightly different syntax:

```
procedure Hello;
begin
  ShowMessage ('Hello world!');
end;
function Double (Value: Integer) : Integer;
begin
  Double := Value * 2;
end;
// or, as an alternative
function Double2 (Value: Integer) : Integer;
begin
  Result := Value * 2;
end;
```

The use of `Result` instead of the function name to assign the return value of a function is becoming quite popular, and tends to make the code more readable, in my opinion. Once these routines have been defined, you can call them as follows:

```
Hello;
X := Double (Y);
Hello;
Z := Double2 (X);
```

Every beginning programmer knows the basics of using functions and procedures. So here I'll focus only on some slightly advanced topics.

NEW

When you call an existing Delphi function or procedure, or any VCL method, you should remember the number and type of the parameters. Delphi 3 helps you by suggesting the parameters list of a function or procedure with a fly-by hint as soon as you type its name and the open parenthesis. As introduced in Chapter 2, this new feature is called Code Parameters, and is part of the new Code Insight technology.

Reference Parameters

Pascal routines allow parameter passing by value and by reference. Passing a parameter by reference means that its value is not copied onto the stack in the formal parameter of the routine (avoiding a copy often means that the program executes faster). Instead, the program refers to the original value, also in the code of the routine. This allows the procedure or function to change the value of the parameter. Parameter passing by reference is expressed by the var keyword.

NOTE

This technique is available in most programming languages. It isn't present in C, but has been introduced in C++, where you use the & (pass by reference) symbol. In Visual Basic every parameter not specified as ByVal is passed by reference.

Here is an example:

```
procedure DoubleTheValue (var Value: Integer);
begin
  Value := Value * 2;
end;
```

In this case, the parameter is used both to pass a value to the procedure and to return a new value to the calling code. When you write:

```
var
  X: Integer;
begin
  X := 10;
  DoubleTheValue (X);
```

the value of the X variable becomes 20, because the function uses a reference to the original memory location of X, affecting its initial value.

Passing parameters by reference makes sense for predefined types, for old-fashioned strings, and for large records. Delphi objects, in fact, are *invariably* passed by reference, because they are references themselves. For this reason passing an object by reference makes little sense (apart from very special cases), because it corresponds to passing a "reference to a reference." Delphi long strings have a slightly different behavior: they behave as references, but if you change one of the string variables referring to the same string in memory, this is copied before updating it. A long string passed as a value parameter behaves as a reference only in terms of memory usage and speed of the operation. But if you modify the value of the string, the original value is not affected. On the contrary, if you pass the long string by reference, you can alter the original value.

NEW

Delphi 3 introduces a new kind of parameter, out. An out parameter has no initial value and is used only to return a value. These parameters should be used only for COM procedures and functions; in general, it is better to stick with the more efficient var parameters. Except for not having an initial value, out parameters behave like var parameters.

Constant Parameters

As an alternative to reference parameters, you can use a `const` parameter. Since you cannot assign a new value to a constant parameter inside the routine, the compiler can optimize parameter passing. The compiler can choose an approach similar to reference parameters (or a `const` reference in C++ terms), but the behavior will remain similar to value parameters, because the original value won't be affected by the routine.

In fact, if you try to compile the following (silly) code, Delphi will issue an error:

```
function DoubleTheValue (const Value: Integer): Integer;
begin
  Value := Value * 2;      // compiler error
  Result := Value;
end;
```

Open Array Parameters

Unlike C, a Pascal function or procedure always has a fixed number of parameters. However, there is a way to pass a varying number of parameters to a routine using an *open array*.

The basic definition of an open array parameter is that of a *typed open array*. This means you indicate the type of the parameter but do not know how many elements of that type the array is going to have. Here is an example of such a definition:

```pascal
function Sum (const A: array of Integer): Integer;
var
  I: Integer;
begin
  Result := 0;
  for I := Low(A) to High(A) do
    Result := Result + A[I];
end;
```

Using High(A) we can get the size of the array. Notice also the use of the return value of the function, Result, to store temporary values. You can call this function by passing to it an array of Integer expressions:

```pascal
X := Sum ([10, Y, 27*I]);
```

If you have an existing array of Integers, of any size, you can pass it directly to a routine requiring an open array parameter or, instead, you can call the Slice function to pass only a portion of the array (as indicated by its second parameter). Here is an example, where the complete array is passed as parameter:

```pascal
var
  List: array [1..10] of Integer;
  X, I: Integer;
begin
  // initialize the array
  for I := Low (List) to High (List) do
    List [I] := I * 2;
  // call
  X := Sum (List);
```

If you want to pass only a portion of the array to the Slice function, simply call it this way:

```pascal
X := Sum (Slice (List, 5));
```

You can find all the code fragments presented in this section in the OpenArr example (see Figure 4.19, below, for the form).

Type-Variant Open Array Parameters

Besides these typed open arrays, Delphi allows you to define *type-variant* or *untyped* open arrays. This special kind of array has an undefined number of values, which can be handy for passing parameter.

Technically, the construct `array of const` allows you to pass an array with an undefined number of elements of different types to a routine at once. For example, here is the definition of the Format function (we have already discussed how to use this function earlier in this chapter, without looking at its definition):

```
function Format (const Format: string;
  const Args: array of const): string;
```

The second parameter is an open array, which gets an undefined number of values. In fact, you can call this function in the following ways:

```
N := 20;
S := 'Total:';
Label1.Caption := Format ('Total: %d', [N]);
Label2.Caption := Format ('Int: %d, Float: %f', [N, 12.4]);
Label3.Caption := Format ('%s %d', [S, N * 2]);
```

Notice that you can pass a parameter as either a constant value, the value of a variable, or an expression. Declaring a function of this kind is simple, but how do you code it? How do you know the types of the parameters? The values of a type-variant open array parameter are compatible with the TVarRec type elements.

NOTE
Do not confuse the TVarRec record with the TVarData record used by the Variant type itself. These two structures have a different aim and are not compatible. Even the list of possible types is different, because TVarRec can hold Delphi data types, while TVarData can hold OLE data types.

The TVarRec record, in Delphi 3, has the following structure:

```
type
  TVarRec = record
    case Byte of
      vtInteger:      (VInteger: Integer; VType: Byte);
```

```
      vtBoolean:     (VBoolean: Boolean);
      vtChar:        (VChar: Char);
      vtExtended:    (VExtended: PExtended);
      vtString:      (VString: PShortString);
      vtPointer:     (VPointer: Pointer);
      vtPChar:       (VPChar: PChar);
      vtObject:      (VObject: TObject);
      vtClass:       (VClass: TClass);
      vtWideChar:    (VWideChar: WideChar);
      vtPWideChar:   (VPWideChar: PWideChar);
      vtAnsiString:  (VAnsiString: Pointer);
      vtCurrency:    (VCurrency: PCurrency);
      vtVariant:     (VVariant: PVariant);
      vtInterface:   (VInterface: Pointer);
  end;
```

Each possible record has the VType field, although this is not easy to see at first because it is declared only once, plus the actual Integer-size data (generally a reference or a pointer).

Using this information we can actually write a function capable of operating on different data types. In the SumAll function example, I want to be able to sum values of different types, transforming strings to integers, characters to the corresponding order value, and adding 1 for True Boolean values. The code is based on a case statement, and is quite simple, although we have to dereference pointers quite often:

```
function SumAll (const Args: array of const): Extended;
var
  I: Integer;
begin
  Result := 0;
  for I := Low(Args) to High (Args) do
    case Args [I].VType of
      vtInteger: Result :=
        Result + Args [I].VInteger;
      vtBoolean:
        if Args [I].VBoolean then
          Result := Result + 1;
      vtChar:
        Result := Result + Ord (Args [I].VChar);
      vtExtended:
        Result := Result + Args [I].VExtended^;
```

```
    vtString, vtAnsiString:
      Result := Result + StrToIntDef ((Args [I].VString^), 0);
    vtWideChar:
      Result := Result + Ord (Args [I].VWideChar);
    vtCurrency:
      Result := Result + Args [I].VCurrency^;
  end; // case
end;
```

I've added this code to the OpenArr example, which calls the SumAll function when a given button is pressed:

```
procedure TForm1.Button4Click(Sender: TObject);
var
  X: Extended;
  Y: Integer;
begin
  Y := 10;
  X := SumAll ([Y * Y, 'k', True, 10.34, '99999']);
  ShowMessage (Format (
    'SumAll ([Y*Y, ''k'', True, 10.34, ''99999'']) => %n', [X]));
end;
```

You can see the output of this call, and the form of the OpenArr example, in Figure 4.19.

FIGURE 4.19

The form of the OpenArr example, with the message box displayed when the Untyped button is pressed.

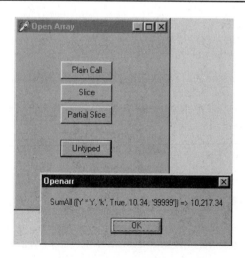

Delphi Calling Conventions

The 32-bit version of Delphi has introduced a new approach to passing parameters, known as *fastcall*: Whenever possible, up to three parameters can be passed in CPU registers, making the function call much faster. The fast calling convention (used by default in Delphi 3) is indicated by the `register` keyword.

The problem is that this is the default convention, and functions using it are not compatible with Windows: the functions of the Win32 API must be declared using the `stdcall` calling convention, a mixture of the original `pascal` calling convention of the Win16 API and the `cdecl` calling convention of the C language.

There is generally no reason not to use the new fast calling convention, unless you are making external Windows calls or defining Windows callback functions. We'll see an example using the stdcall convention before the end of this chapter. You can find a summary of Delphi calling conventions in the *Calling conventions* topic under Delphi help.

What Is a Method?

If you have already worked with Delphi or read the manuals, you have probably heard the term *method*. A method is a special kind of function or procedure that is related to a data type, a class. In Delphi, every time we handle an event, we need to define a method, generally a procedure. In general, however, the term *method* is used to indicate both functions and procedures related to a class.

We have already seen a number of methods in the examples in this and the previous chapters. Here is an empty method automatically added by Delphi to the source code of a form:

```
procedure TForm1.Button1Click(Sender: TObject);
begin
  {here goes your code}
end;
```

I will discuss methods in more detail in the next chapter when I introduce classes.

Forward Declarations

When you need to use an identifier (of any kind), the compiler must have already seen some sort of declaration to know what the identifier refers to. For this reason, you usually provide a full declaration before using any routine. However, there are cases in which this is not possible. If procedure A calls procedure B, and procedure B calls procedure A, when you start writing the code, you will need to call a routine for which the compiler still hasn't seen a declaration.

If you want to declare the existence of a procedure or function with a certain name and given parameters, without providing its actual code, you can write the procedure or function followed by the forward keyword:

```
procedure Hello; forward;
```

Later on, the code should provide a full definition of the procedure, but this can be called even before it is fully defined. Here is a silly example, just to give you the idea:

```
procedure DoubleHello; forward;

procedure Hello;
begin
  if MessageDlg ('Do you want a double message?',
      mtConfirmation, [mbYes, mbNo], 0) = mrYes then
    DoubleHello
  else
    ShowMessage ('Hello');
end;

procedure DoubleHello;
begin
  Hello;
  Hello;
end;
```

This approach allows you to write mutual recursion: DoubleHello calls Hello, but Hello might call DoubleHello, too. Of course there must be a condition to terminate the recursion, to avoid a stack overflow. You can find this code, with some slight changes, in the DoubleH example.

Although a forward procedure declaration is not very common in Delphi, there is a similar case that is much more frequent. When you declare a procedure or function in the interface portion of a unit (more on units in the next chapter), it is considered a forward declaration, even if the forward keyword is not present. Actually you cannot write the body of a routine in the interface portion of a unit. At the same time, you must provide in the same unit the actual implementation of each routine you have declared.

The same holds for the declaration of a method inside a `class` type that was automatically generated by Delphi (as you added an event to a form or its components). The event handlers declared inside a `TForm` class are `forward` declarations: the code will be provided in the `implementation` portion of the unit. Here is an excerpt of the source code of an earlier example, with the declaration of the `Button1Click` method:

```
type
  TForm1 = class(TForm)
    ListBox1: TListBox;
    Button1: TButton;
    procedure Button1Click(Sender: TObject);
  end;
```

External Declarations

Another special kind of procedure declaration is the `external` declaration. Originally used to link the Pascal code to external functions written in assembly language, the `external` directive is used in Windows programming to call a function from a DLL (a dynamic link library). In Delphi, there are a number of such declarations in the Windows unit:

```
// forward declaration
function LineTo (DC: HDC; X, Y: Integer): BOOL; stdcall;

// external declaration (instead of actual code)
function LineTo; external 'gdi32.dll' name 'LineTo';
```

This declaration means that the code of the function `LineTo` is stored in the GDI32 .DLL dynamic library (one of the most important Windows system libraries) with the same name we are using in our code. Inside an `external` declaration, in fact, we can specify that our function refers to a function of a DLL that originally had a different name.

You seldom need to write declarations like the one just illustrated, since they are already listed in the Windows unit and many other Delphi system units. The only reason you might need to write this `external` declaration code is to call functions from a custom DLL, or to call undocumented Windows functions. Chapter 20 is devoted to writing and calling DLL functions.

In the 16-bit version of Delphi, the `external` declaration used the name of the library without the extension, and was followed by the name directive (as in the code above) or by an alternative index directive, followed by the ordinal number of the function inside the DLL. The change reflects a system change in the way libraries are accessed: Although Win32 still allows access to DLL functions by number, Microsoft has stated this won't be supported in the future. Notice also that the Windows unit replaces the WinProcs and WinTypes units of the 16-bit version of Delphi.

Procedural Types

Another unique feature of Object Pascal is the presence of *procedural types*. These are really an advanced language topic, which only a few Delphi programmers will use regularly. However, since we will discuss related topics in later chapters (specifically, *method pointers*, a technique heavily used by Delphi), it's worth a quick look at them here. If you are a novice programmer, you can skip this section for now, and come back to it when you feel ready.

In Pascal, there is the concept of procedural type (which is similar to the C language concept of function pointer). The declaration of a procedural type indicates the list of parameters and eventually the return type in the case of a function. For example, you can declare the type *procedure with an integer parameter passed by reference* as:

```
type
  IntProc = procedure (var Num: Integer);
```

This procedural type is compatible with any routine having exactly the same parameters (or the same *function signature*, to use C jargon). Here is an example of a compatible routine:

```
procedure DoubleTheValue (var Value: Integer);
begin
  Value := Value * 2;
end;
```

In the 16-bit version of Delphi, routines must be declared using the `far` directive in order to be used as actual values of a procedural type.

Procedural types can be used for two different purposes: you can declare variables of a procedural type or pass a procedural type—a function pointer—as parameters to another routine. Given the preceding type and procedure declarations, you can write this code:

```
var
  IP: IntProc;
  X: Integer;
begin
  IP := DoubleTheValue;
  X := 5;
  IP (X);
end;
```

This code has the same effect as the following shorter version:

```
var
  X: Integer;
begin
  X := 5;
  DoubleTheValue (X);
end;
```

The first version is clearly more complex, so why should we use it? In some cases, being able to decide which function to call and actually calling it later on can be useful. It is possible to build a complex example showing this approach. However, I prefer to let you explore a fairly simple one, named ProcType. This example is more complex than those we have seen so far, to make the situation a little more realistic.

Simply create a blank project and place two radio buttons, a push button, and two labels in the form, as shown in Figure 4.20. This example is based on two procedures. One procedure is used to double the value of the parameter. This procedure is similar to the version I've already shown in this section. A second procedure is used to triple the value of the parameter, and therefore is named TripleTheValue:

```
procedure TripleTheValue (var Value: Integer);
begin
  Value := Value * 3;
  ShowMessage ('Value tripled: ' + IntToStr (Value));
end;
```

Both procedures display what is going on, to let us know that they have been called. This is a simple debugging feature you can use to test whether or when a certain portion of code is executed, instead of adding a breakpoint in it.

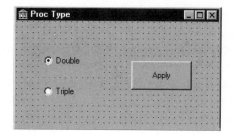

Each time a user presses the Apply button, one of the two procedures is executed, depending on the status of the radio buttons. In fact, when you have two radio buttons in a form, only one of them can be selected at a time. This code could have been implemented by testing the value of the radio buttons inside the code for the OnClick event of the Apply button. To demonstrate the use of procedural types, I've instead used a longer but interesting approach. Each time a user clicks on one of the two radio buttons, one of the procedures is stored in a variable:

```
procedure TForm1.DoubleRadioButtonClick(Sender: TObject);
begin
  IP := DoubleTheValue;
end;
```

When the user clicks on the push button, the procedure we have stored is executed:

```
procedure TForm1.ApplyButtonClick(Sender: TObject);
begin
  IP (X);
end;
```

To allow three different functions to access the IP and X variables, we need to make them visible to the whole form; they cannot be declared locally (inside one of the methods). A solution to this problem is to place these variables inside the form declaration:

```
type
  TForm1 = class(TForm)
    . . .
```

```
private
  { Private declarations }
  IP: IntProc;
  X: Integer;
end;
```

We will see exactly what this means in the next chapter, but for the moment, you need to modify the code generated by Delphi for the class type as indicated above, and add the definition of the procedural type I've shown before. To initialize these two variables with suitable values, we can handle the OnCreate event of the form (select this event in the Object Inspector after you have activated the form, or simply double-click on the form). I suggest you refer to the listing on the companion CD to study the details of the source code of this example.

A Windows Callback Function

A second and more common use of procedural types is to provide *callback* functions to a Windows API function. First of all, what is a callback function? The idea is that some API function perform a given action over a number of internal elements of the system, such as all of the windows of a certain kind. These functions, also called *enumerated* functions, require as a parameter the action to be performed on each of the elements, which is passed as a function or procedure compatible with a given procedural type. Windows uses callback functions in other circumstances, but we'll limit our study to this simple case.

Now consider the EnumWindows API function, which has the following prototype (copied from the Win32 Help file):

```
BOOL EnumWindows(
  WNDENUMPROC lpEnumFunc,  // address of callback function
  LPARAM lParam // application-defined value
  );
```

Of course this is the C language definition. We can look inside the file WINDOWS .PAS to retrieve the corresponding Pascal language definition:

```
function EnumWindows (
  lpEnumFunc: TFNWndEnumProc;
  lParam: LPARAM): BOOL; stdcall;
```

Looking in the Help file we find that the function passed as a parameter should be of the following type (again in C):

```
BOOL CALLBACK EnumWindowsProc (
  HWND   hwnd, // handle of parent window
  LPARAM lParam // application-defined value
  );
```

This corresponds to the following Delphi procedural type definition:

```
type
  EnumWindowsProc = function (Hwnd: THandle;
    Param: Pointer): Boolean; stdcall;
```

The first parameter is the handle of each main window in turn, while the second is the value we've passed when calling the EnumWindows function. Actually in Pascal the TFNWndEnumProc type is not properly defined, it is simply a pointer. This means we need to provide a function with the proper parameters, and then use it as a pointer, taking the address of the function instead of calling it. Unluckily, this also means that the compiler will provide no help in case of an error in the type of one of the parameters.

Here is the definition of a proper compatible function, which reads the title of the window into a string, then adds it to a ListBox of a given form:

```
function GetTitle (Hwnd: THandle; Param: Pointer): Boolean; stdcall;
var
  Text: string;
begin
  SetLength (Text, 100);
  GetWindowText (Hwnd, PChar (Text), 100);
  FormCallBack.ListBox1.Items.Add (
    IntToStr (Hwnd) + ': ' + Text);
  Result := True;
end;
```

The form has a ListBox covering almost its whole area, and a small panel on the top hosting a button. When the button is pressed, the EnumWindows API function is called, and the GetTitle function is passed as its parameter:

```
procedure TFormCallback.BtnTitlesClick(Sender: TObject);
var
  EWProc: EnumWindowsProc;
begin
  ListBox1.Items.Clear;
```

```
    EWProc := GetTitle;
    EnumWindows (@EWProc, 0);
  end;
```

I could have called the function without storing the value in a temporary procedural type variable first, but wanted to make clear what is going on in this example. The effect of this program is actually quite interesting, as you can see in Figure 4.21. The Callback example shows a list of all the existing main windows running in the system. Most of them are actually hidden windows you usually never see (and many have actually no caption).

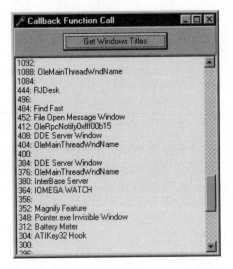

FIGURE 4.21

The output of the Callback example, listing the current main windows (visible or hidden).

What's Next

In this chapter, we have seen an overview of the basic elements of the Object Pascal language, plus an introduction to some advanced features of the language and some interesting features of the Windows systems, such as handles, API function calls, and even callback functions.

We have still not seen the object-oriented capabilities of the language Delphi is built onto, which will be detailed in the next chapter. We also have not yet considered the division of a program into units, as well as other programming techniques.

As I mentioned, this chapter was intended for people who have some programming experience, either with Pascal or another programming language. I haven't tried to explain how to use a for loop or write a conditional expression for an if statement. If these things are not clear to you, before you get started with Delphi, you should read a basic Pascal language text, or spend some time with the Delphi Help files.

This doesn't mean that you need to understand these topics perfectly. I'll show you a huge number of examples in the book, and most of them will also highlight features of the Pascal language. If you keep on reading, you will learn more about the topics we have discussed in this chapter. But the next stop is the discovery of object-oriented programming techniques, seen from the perspective of the Object Pascal language.

This actually takes three chapters: the next is devoted to the basics of object-oriented programming, Chapter 6 covers more advanced language topics related to visual programming (such as the definition of properties), and Chapter 7 provides an overview of Delphi's class library, the VCL.

Object Pascal as an OOP Language

- Object Pascal classes and objects

- Delphi's object reference model

- Information hiding and Delphi units

- The `self` keyword and class methods

- Virtual methods

- Run-Time Type Information

- Handling Exceptions

Using data types (both existing and user-defined) and writing code in small blocks (subroutines) are the essence of traditional Pascal programming. But modern versions of the Pascal language allow a completely different approach: *object-oriented programming* (OOP). OOP languages are based on three fundamental concepts: classes, inheritance, and polymorphism (or late binding). In the first part of this chapter, we'll explore how these three features are implemented in Object Pascal.

> **NOTE** For an overview of the theory behind OOP programming, refer to Appendix A. If you have no previous exposure to OOP languages, I strongly suggest you read Appendix A before delving into this chapter.

You can write Delphi applications even without knowing the details of Object Pascal. As you create a new form, add new components, and handle events, most of the related code is automatically prepared for you by Delphi. But knowing the details of the language and its implementation will help you to understand precisely what Delphi is doing and to master the language completely. From another point of view, you don't need to understand OOP, virtual methods, or polymorphism to create a complete Delphi application. However, you do need to understand these concepts to design new components.

Introducing Classes and Objects

Class and *object* are two common terms. However, since they are often misused, let's be sure that we agree on their definitions. A class is a user-defined data type, which has a state (its representation) and some operations (its behavior). A class has some internal data and some methods, in the form of procedures or functions, and usually describes the generic characteristics and behavior of a number of very similar objects. Classes are used by the programmer to arrange the source code and by the compiler to generate the application.

An object is an instance of a class or, in other words, a variable of the data type defined by the class. Objects are *actual* entities. When the program runs, objects take up some memory for their internal representation. The relationship between object and class is the same as the one between variable and type.

Unfortunately, in some languages or environments, this difference is not clear. To increase the confusion, earlier versions of the Borland Pascal compiler used the keyword object to define classes. For this reason, long-time Pascal programmers tend to use the term *object* instead of *class* to denote a type, and the term *object instance* to indicate the actual objects.

To declare a new class data type in Object Pascal, use the following syntax:

```
type
  MyNewClass = class
  end;
```

Of course, this code is not very useful, because the class does not have any data or operations. We can start adding some data as follows:

```
type
  TDate = class
    Month, Day, Year: Integer;
  end;
```

The convention in Delphi is to use the letter *T* as prefix for the name of every class you write. This is just a convention—to the compiler, *T* is just a letter like any other—but it is so common that following it will make your code easier to understand. In the book I'll try to stick with this convention. A second convention is to use a two- or three-letter code to indicate the (corporate or individual) author of a class. This convention is commonly used with components (and I'll use it that way in this book), because in Delphi you cannot install two components with the same name.

Our TDate class declaration is similar to that of a record. In fact, we can declare an object and access its three fields with a standard notation:

```
var
  ADay: TDate;
begin
  ... // object allocation is missing here
  ADay.Month := 7;
```

```
    ADay.Day := 12;
    ADay.Year := 1984;
  end;
```

Things start to get interesting when we put in some methods—functions or procedures—to add operations to the class:

```
type
  TDate = class
    Month, Day, Year: Integer;
    procedure SetValue(m, d, y: Integer);
    function LeapYear: Boolean;
  end;
```

The function and the procedure should be supplied in the code, indicating that they are part of the TDate class. To accomplish this, Object Pascal uses the dot notation again, but in a slightly different way. The syntax is ClassName.Method:

```
procedure TDate.SetValue(m, d, y: Integer);
begin
  Month := m;
  Day := d;
  Year := y;
end;

function TDate.LeapYear: Boolean;
begin
  if (Year mod 4 <> 0) then
    LeapYear := False
  else if (Year mod 100 <> 0) then
    LeapYear := True
  else if (Year mod 400 <> 0) then
    LeapYear := False
  else
    LeapYear := True;
end;
```

Once these methods have been written, we can call them as follows:

```
var
  ADay: TDate;
  Leap: Boolean;
begin
  ... // object allocation is still missing here
```

```
  ADay.SetValue (10, 10, 1997);
  Leap := ADay.LeapYear;
end;
```

The notation used is nothing strange, but it is powerful. We can write a complex function (such as LeapYear) and then access its value for every TDate object as if it were a primitive data type. Notice that ADay.LeapYear is an expression similar to ADay.Year, although its meaning is different. The first expression stands for a function call, the second stands for a direct data access. As we'll see in the next chapter, the notation used by Object Pascal to access properties is again the same.

Although the code shown here is correct, it won't work yet. Object Pascal uses an object reference model, so we need to create an instance of a TDate object first. We'll do that in the next section.

Delphi's Object Reference Model

As in most OOP languages, the class keyword is used to define a new data type, a new class. In many other languages, however, declaring a variable of a class type creates an instance of that class, an actual object. Object Pascal, instead, is based on an *object reference model*. The basic idea is that each variable of a class type, such as Day in the code fragment above, does not hold the value of the object. Rather, it contains a reference, or a pointer, to indicate the memory location where the object has been stored. You can see a scheme of the situation in Figure 5.1.

FIGURE 5.1

A graphical representation of the Object Pascal reference model.

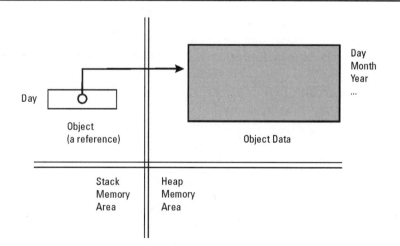

189

The reference object model is powerful, yet easier to use than other models. Other OOP languages use similar models, notably Eiffel and Java. In my opinion, adopting a reference object model was one of the best design decisions made by the Delphi development team at Borland.

The only problem with this approach is that when you declare a variable, by writing:

```
var
   ADay: TDate;
```

you don't create an object in memory, only a place to keep a reference to an object—a sort of pointer. Object instances must be created manually, at least for the objects of the classes you define. Instances of a component you place on a form are built automatically by Delphi.

To create an instance of an object, we can call its Create method, which is a constructor (a special procedure used to allocate memory for new objects and initialize them, as we'll see later on). Notice that the constructor is applied to the class, not to the object:

```
var
   ADay: TDate;
begin
   ADay := TDate.Create;
   ADay.Month := 7;
   ADay.Day := 12;
   ADay.Year := 1984;
end;
```

Where does the Create method come from? It is a constructor of the class TObject, from which all the other classes inherit (subclassing, or inheritance, will be discussed later in this chapter). In other words, writing

```
type
   TDate = class
```

is the same as writing

```
type
   TDate = class (TObject)
```

Of course, once you have created an object, you need to dispose of it. This can be accomplished by calling the Free method (yet another method of the TObject class). The following is an example of the correct code used to create, use, and dispose of an object:

```
begin
  // create
  ADay := TDate.Create;
  // use
  ADay.Month := 7;
  ADay.Day := 12;
  ADay.Year := 1999;
  if ADay.LeapYear then
    ShowMessage ('A leap year');
  // destroy
  ADay.Free;
end;
```

As long as you create objects when you need them and free them when you're finished with them, the reference object model works without a glitch. You can assign an object to another, pass an object as parameter to a function, and perform any other operation.

NEW Keeping track of object deallocation is not always simple, but Delphi 3 has some support for this when working with COM objects, as we'll see in the next chapter and in Chapter 21.

Using the TDate Class in Delphi

We've already covered a lot of ground without trying any hands-on examples, so let's go back to Delphi. The idea is to collect the TDate class code we have written so far and write a simple program using it. This way, we can make sure that it works correctly. In particular, we want to make sure that objects are initialized properly.

The LeapYear example has a simple form with two buttons, having the numbers of two years as caption. Each time one of the buttons is pressed, a TDate object is set and tested to see whether 1997 (or 1996) is a leap year. Here is the code of the OnClick event for one of the buttons:

```
procedure TForm1.Btn1997Click(Sender: TObject);
begin
  ADay.SetValue (1, 1, 1997);
```

```
    if ADay.LeapYear then
      ShowMessage ('Leap Year')
    else
      ShowMessage ('Non Leap Year');
  end;
```

The other button has similar code and produces the output in Figure 5.2.

The object ADay is a new global variable defined as:

```
var
  Form1: TForm1;
  ADay: TDate;
```

This object should be created before the button is pressed. A common approach is to use the OnCreate event of the form to create an instance of the object:

```
procedure TForm1.FormCreate(Sender: TObject);
begin
  ADay := TDate.Create;
end;
```

This method is executed before a user can press the button, and even before the form and its components are displayed on the screen. The opposite holds for the OnDestroy event, which is executed after the form is hidden from view. We can use this method to free the memory used by the object:

```
procedure TForm1.FormDestroy(Sender: TObject);
begin
  ADay.Free;
end;
```

While you are exploring the code of this example, make the following test. Comment out the code used to create an instance of the object:

```
procedure TForm1.FormCreate(Sender: TObject);
begin
  // ADay := TDate.Create;
end;
```

If you recompile the project now, you won't get a compile-time error. However, when you run the program, as soon as you press one of the buttons, the system raises an exception (indicating that you have accessed an invalid pointer), as you can see in Figure 5.3.

FIGURE 5.3

The exception error message displayed if you forget to create an instance of the object.

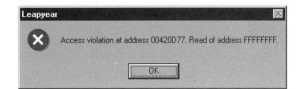

Declaring a Constructor

To allocate the memory for the object, we've called the Create method. However, before we can actually use the object, we often need to initialize it. For example, we must call the SetValue procedure of the TDate class, after we've created the object, to initialize it properly.

As an alternative we can provide a customized constructor, which creates the object and gives it an initial value. We can either provide a new version of the Create method, eventually with some parameters, or define a brand new constructor with any other name. To accomplish this you simply write a new procedure, with any name and any number of parameters, and simply use the constructor keyword instead of the procedure keyword in front of it.

A constructor is a special procedure, because when you apply it to a class Delphi automatically allocates memory for an object of that class. However, you can also apply a constructor to an object, executing the code without any memory allocation. If you do that, remember not to apply the constructor to an uninitialized variable when you want to create it. The memory allocation takes place only when the constructor is applied to a class.

The main reason to add a custom constructor to a class is to initialize its data. If you create objects without initializing them, calling methods later on may result in an odd behavior or even a run-time error. Instead of waiting for these errors to appear, you should use preventive techniques to avoid them in the first place: one such technique is the consistent use of constructors to initialize objects' data.

In the same way that a class can have a custom constructor, it can have a custom destructor, a procedure declared with the destructor keyword, which can perform some resource cleanup before an object is destroyed. Just as a constructor call allocates memory for the object, a destructor call frees the memory. Destructors are needed only for objects that acquire resources in their constructors or during their lifetime.

> **NOTE**   Instead of calling Destroy directly, a program should call Free, which calls Destroy only if the object exists—that is, if it is not nil. Keep in mind, however, that calling Free doesn't set the object to nil automatically: this is something you should do yourself!

To add a constructor to the TDate class, you can write this code:

```
type
  TDate = class
    Month, Day, Year: Integer;
    constructor Init (m, d, y: Integer);
    procedure SetValue(m, d, y: Integer);
    function LeapYear: Boolean;
  end;
```

I've chosen the name Init for the constructor, but any other name will do. You should generally use the name Create, but I wanted to stay away from it in this first example to emphasize that the name Create is no different than any other name. The important element is the presence of the constructor keyword. Then you can write the code of the constructor, as follows:

```
constructor TDate.Init (m, d, y: Integer);
begin
  Month := m;
  Day := d;
  Year := y;
end;
```

Once this is done, we can change the initialization code of the LeapYear example, to allocate memory for the ADay object and set an initial value at the same time:

```
procedure TForm1.FormCreate(Sender: TObject);
begin
  ADay := TDate.Init (1, 1, 1900);
end;
```

Looking at Objects in Memory

The approach just described is used by the Leap2 example, a new version of the LeapYear example based on a very similar form. The new example defines and uses constructors and, to demonstrate how Delphi allocates memory with constructors, also shows information about the memory location of the objects. This is not too difficult: we simply typecast the object's value—the reference—to an integer, and output the value. Here is an example of the code:

```
ShowMessage (
  'Memory location for ADay: ' +
  IntToStr (Integer (ADay)));
```

This output is performed when the object is first created (in the OnCreate event handler of the form, which means the message box will be displayed before the form), and when its value changes. In fact, when you press one of the buttons, the program calls the SetValue method, as in the LeapYear example, but when you press the other button the program simply calls the Init constructor, applying it to the object:

```
procedure TForm1.Btn1997Click(Sender: TObject);
begin
  ADay.Init (1, 1,1997);
  if ADay.LeapYear then
    ShowMessage ('Leap Year')
  else
    ShowMessage ('Non Leap Year');
  ShowMessage (
    'Memory location for ADay (after calling Init): ' +
    IntToStr (Integer (ADay)));
end;
```

As I already mentioned, applying a constructor to an object corresponds to executing its code, with no special *construction* effect. The final ShowMessage call demonstrates that the memory location of the object doesn't change.

The third button on the form, Re-Create, is instead used to create a brand new object in memory and assign it to the ADay variable:

```
procedure TForm1.BtnCreateClick(Sender: TObject);
var
  NewDay: TDate;
begin
  NewDay := TDate.Init (1, 1, 1900);
  ShowMessage (
    'Memory location for the "new" day: ' +
    IntToStr (Integer (NewDay)));
  ADay.Free;
  ADay := NewDay;
end;
```

In this case, the memory location of the object changes. If you press this button several times, you'll see that a few memory locations will be used over and over. Delphi looks for the first free memory area for the object, which can be the memory location just freed when another object was destroyed. Figure 5.4 shows the output of this program when the Re-Create button is pressed.

FIGURE 5.4

The new memory location of the TDate object, when the last button of the Leap2 example is pressed.

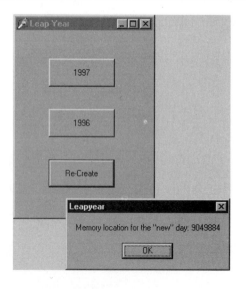

> **NOTE**
>
> When you assign an object to another object, Delphi simply copies the reference to the object in memory to the new object/reference. To copy the data of an object to the memory location of another object you should copy each field, or provide a specific method to copy the internal data. Some classes of the VCL have an `Assign` method, which does this *deep-copy*.

Classes and Information Hiding

A class can have any amount of data and any number of methods. However, for a good object-oriented approach, data should be hidden, or *encapsulated*, inside the class using it. When you access a date, for example, it makes no sense to change the value of the day by itself. In fact, changing the value of the day may result in an invalid date, such as February 30. Using methods to access the internal representation of an object limits the risk of generating erroneous situations, and allows the class writer to modify the internal representation in a future version.

The concept of encapsulation is quite simple: Just think of a class as a "black box" with a small visible portion (see Figure 5.5). The visible portion, called the *class interface*, allows other parts of a program to access and use the objects of that class. However, when you use the objects, most of their code is hidden. You seldom know which internal data the object has, and usually have no way to access it directly. Of course, you are supposed to use methods to access the data, which is shielded from unauthorized access. This is the object-oriented approach to a classical programming concept known as *information hiding*.

FIGURE 5.5

A graphical representation of the information hiding of a class.

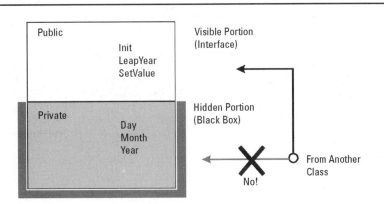

In theory, this should be nothing new for a Pascal programmer, since OOP follows the same ideas of order, type definition, and safety that are promoted by the Pascal language. In Object Pascal, there are two different constructs involved with encapsulation and protection: classes and units. Associated with classes are some special access-specifier keywords, which are discussed in the next section.

Private, Protected, and Public

Object Pascal has borrowed from C++ three access specifiers: `private`, `protected`, and `public`. A fourth one, `published`, will be discussed in the next section and detailed in the next chapter. Yet another access specifier, `automated`, is used by OLE automation, as we will see in Chapter 22.

- The `private` keyword denotes fields and methods of a class that are not accessible outside the unit (the source code file) that declares the class. This is slightly different from C++, where the `private` portion of a class cannot be accessed even by other classes defined in the same source code file.

- The `public` keyword denotes fields and methods that are freely accessible from any other portion of the code of a program, as well as in the unit in which they are defined.

- The `protected` keyword is used to indicate partially `protected` methods and fields. `Protected` elements can be accessed by the current class and all its subclasses only.

Generally, the fields of a class—that is, the data—should be `private`; the methods—the code—are usually `public`. However, this is not always the case. Methods can be `private` or `protected` if they are needed only internally to perform some partial computation. Fields can be `public` when you want an easy and direct access, and you are fairly sure that their type definition is not going to change.

> **TIP**
>
> Instead of having `public` fields, you should generally use properties, as we'll see in detail the next chapter. Properties are an extension to the encapsulation mechanism of other OOP languages, and are very important in Object Pascal.

As an example, consider this new version of the TDate class:

```
type
  TDate = class
  private
    Month, Day, Year: Integer;
  public
    procedure SetValue (m, d, y: Integer);
    function LeapYear: Boolean;
    function GetText: string;
    procedure Increase;
  protected
    function DaysInMonth: Integer;
  end;
```

In this version, the fields are now declared to be private, and there are some new methods. The first, GetText, is a function that returns a string with the date. This is the only way we have to retrieve the value of the private data (unless we use properties). You might think of adding other functions, named GetDay, GetMonth, and GetYear, which simply return the corresponding private data, but similar direct data-access functions are not always needed.

The second new method is the Increase procedure, which increases the date by one day. This is far from simple, since you need to consider the different lengths of the various months, as well as leap and non-leap years.

To simplify this (and other methods I'll add later on), I've written a function that returns the number of days in the current month, DaysInMonth. This function is not part of the public interface of this class. It doesn't make much sense to ask a specific TDate object for the number of days in its current month without knowing which month it refers to. So, I had two choices: declare the function as private or declare it as protected. I decided to use the protected keyword because I might later define a new class that would inherit from TDate and that would need to call this function.

Public and Published

Along with the public, protected, and private access directives, you can use a fourth one, called published. A published field or method is available not only at run-time, but also at design-time. In fact, every component in the Delphi Components palette has a published interface that is used by some Delphi tools, in particular the Object Inspector. This interface is accessible through some advanced techniques I'll introduce in the next chapter.

A regular use of published fields is much more important when you write a component than when you write the code of an application. Usually, the published part of a component contains no fields or methods, but has a new element of the language: properties. Properties are introduced in the next chapter.

When Delphi generates a form, it places the definitions of its components and methods in the first portion of its definition, before the public and private keywords. These fields and methods of the initial portion of the class are published. Published is the default when no special keyword is added before an element of a class.

The methods assigned to any event should be published methods, and the fields corresponding to your components in the form should be published to be automatically initialized. Only the components and methods in the initial published part of your form declaration can show up in the Object Inspector (in the list of components of the form or in the list of the available methods displayed when you select the drop-down list for an event).

You can make this experiment. Add the following declaration to the initial portion of a form (the default, published, section):

```
procedure Foo (Sender: TObject);
```

Now select the Events page in the Object Inspector, move to the OnCreate event, and click on the down arrow to select the drop-down list. The list will include the Foo method. If you cut the definition above and copy it to the public section of the form, however, the method won't show up in the Object Inspector, because Delphi doesn't generate an internal description for it. Actually, the method doesn't show up even if you add it to a new published section; the Delphi environment parses only the initial portion of the form declaration.

Classes and Units

Delphi applications, like most Pascal programs, make intensive use of *units*, or program modules. Units, in fact, were the basis of the modularity in the language before classes were introduced. But classes were built upon the concept of unit, as the visibility access rules explained in the last section clearly show.

In a Delphi application, every form generally has a corresponding unit behind it. When you add a new form to a project (with the corresponding SpeedBar button or the File ➤ New Form menu command), Delphi actually adds a new unit which defines the class for the new form.

If every form is defined in a unit, the reverse is not true. Units do not need to define forms; they can simply define and make available a collection of routines. By selecting the File ➤ New menu command, and then the Unit icon in the New page of the Object Repository, you add a new blank unit to the current project. This blank unit contains the following code, delimiting the sections a unit is divided into:

```
unit Unit1;

interface

implementation

end.
```

The concept of a unit is simple. A unit has a name (unique in each project, and corresponding to its filename), an interface section declaring what is visible to other units, and an implementation section with the real code and other hidden declarations. Finally, the unit can have an optional initialization section with some startup code, to be executed when the program using this unit is loaded into memory, and an optional finalization section, to be executed on program termination. The finalization section was added in the 32-bit version of Delphi to provide a proper cleanup of what was allocated in the initialization section of that unit.

The general structure of a unit, with all its possible sections, is the following:

```
unit unitName;

interface

// other units we need to refer to
uses
  A, B, C;

// exported type definition
type
  newType = TypeDefinition;

// exported constants
```

```pascal
const
  Zero = 0;

// global variables
var
  Total: Integer;

// list of exported functions and procedures
procedure MyProc;

implementation

uses
  D, E;

// hidden global variable
var
  PartialTotal: Integer;

// all the exported functions must be coded
procedure MyProc;
begin
  // ... code of procedure MyProc
end;

initialization
  // optional initialization part

finalization
  // optional clean-up code

end.
```

The uses clause at the beginning of the interface section indicates which other units we need to access in the interface portion of the unit. This includes the units that define the data types (classes and components) we refer to in the definition of other data types, such as the components used within a form we are defining.

The second uses clause, at the beginning of the implementation section, indicates more units we need to access only in the implementation code. When you need to refer to other units from the code of the routines and methods, you should add elements in this second uses clause instead of the first one. All the units you refer to must be present in the project directory or in a directory of the search path (you can set the search path for a project in the Directories/ Conditionals page of the project Options dialog box, as you can see in Figure 5.6).

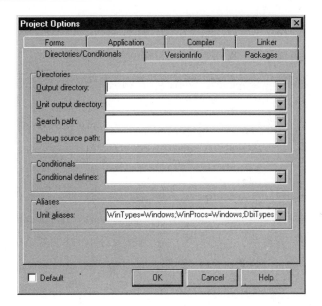

> **NOTE**
>
> C++ programmers should be aware that the uses statement doesn't correspond to an include directive. The effect of a uses statement is to import just the precompiled interface portion of the units listed. The implementation portion of the unit is considered only when that unit is compiled.

The 32-bit version of Delphi introduced a new "unit aliasing" technique. This means you can use the name of a unit in a uses statement and let the compiler actually refer to another unit. Aliases are defined in the Directories/Conditionals page of the Project Options dialog box (see again Figure 5.6).

The interface of a unit can declare a number of different elements, including procedures, functions, global variables, and data types. This last element is probably the most used in an object-oriented approach and in Delphi applications.

You can easily place a class in a unit, and this is probably the right thing to do. Delphi does this automatically each time you create a form. Do you remember the code generated for a brand-new form we looked at in Chapter 1? Here it is again:

```
unit Unit1;

interface

uses
  SysUtils, Windows, Messages, Classes,
  Graphics, Controls, Forms, Dialogs;

type
  TForm1 = class(TForm)
  private
    { Private declarations }
  public
    { Public declarations }
  end;

var
  Form1: TForm1;

implementation

{$R *.DFM}

end.
```

The only elements exported by this unit are the definition of a new data type, TForm1, and a global variable of this type, Form1. Notice the presence of the private and public keywords, and the inclusion of the form description file with the $R compiler directive.

Containing form definitions is certainly not the only use for units in Delphi. You can continue to have traditional units, with functions and procedures, and you can have units with classes that do not refer to forms or other visual elements.

To show you an example of a full-scale unit, I've further developed the TDate class. Placing this class in a unit will make it available to any application, as we will investigate soon. Before we delve into this, however, we should consider some details related to class interfaces, scope, and encapsulation in units.

The Interface of a Class

When you declare a new class type and place it in a unit, you write in the interface of the unit what is known as the *interface* of a class (that is, its declaration). The interface of a class contains the declaration of its data, its fields, and the forward declaration of its methods. The data declaration is needed to determine the size of the objects of that class, even if `private` fields won't be accessible from other units.

As a technical detail, note that it is possible to make a forward declaration of a class, without providing its implementation immediately:

```
type
  MyClass = class;
```

You cannot really start using a class without its full declaration, but you can use this new data type as a field of another class or as a parameter of a method of another class. Consider this example of two related classes:

```
type
  THusband = class;

  TWife = class
    Husband: THusband;
    ...
  end;

  THusband = class
    Wife: TWife;
    ...
  end;
```

In other OOP languages (including C++), similar code would be illegal. In Object Pascal, it is legal, thanks to object referencing. We can place a partially defined object (that is, an object of a class having only a forward reference) in another class, only because the compiler knows how much memory the object will take. In fact, every object takes up the space required for a reference or pointer. It's not surprising that in C++ you can write similar code only if you use explicit pointers.

Units and Scope

In Pascal, units are the key to encapsulation and visibility (or scope), and they are probably even more important than the `private` and `public` keywords of a class.

In fact, the effect of the `private` keyword is related to the scope of the unit containing the class.

The scope of an identifier (such as a variable, procedure, function, or a data type) is the portion of the code in which the identifier is accessible. The basic rule is that an identifier is meaningful only within its scope; that is, only within the block in which it is declared. You cannot use an identifier outside its scope. Here are some examples.

- Local variables: If you declare a variable within the block defining a routine or a method, you cannot use this variable outside that procedure. The scope of the identifier spans the whole procedure, including nested routines (unless an identifier with the same name in the nested routine hides the outer definition). The memory for this variable is allocated on the stack when the program executes the routine defining it. As soon as the routine terminates, the memory on the stack is automatically released.

- Global hidden variables: If you declare an identifier in the `implementation` portion of a unit, you cannot use it outside the unit, but you can use it in any block and procedure defined within the unit. The memory for this variable is allocated as soon as the program starts and exists until it terminates. You can use the `initialization` section of the unit to provide a specific initial value.

- Global variables: If you declare an identifier in the `interface` portion of the unit, its scope extends to any other unit that uses the one declaring it. This variable uses memory and has the same lifetime of the previous group, the only difference is in its visibility.

Any declarations in the `interface` portion of a unit are accessible from any part of the program which includes the unit in its `uses` clause. Variables of form classes are declared in the same way, so that you can refer to a form (and its public fields, methods, properties, and components) from the code of any other form. Of course, it's poor programming practice to declare everything as global. Beside an obvious memory consumption problem, using global variables makes a program less object-oriented and less easy to maintain and update. Actually, you should use the smallest possible number of global variables and objects. As you'll see in future examples, at times it is better to declare a form locally, and get rid of the corresponding global variable. The bigger a program, the more important this is.

Units and Name Clashes

The uses statement is the standard technique to access the scope of another unit. At that point you can access the definitions of the unit. But it might happen that two units you refer to declare the same identifier; that is, you might have two classes or two routines with the same name.

In this case you can simply prefix the name of the type or routine defined in the unit with the unit name. For example, you can refer to the ComputeTotal procedure defined in the given Totals unit as Totals.ComputeTotal. This is not required very often, and you are strongly advised against using the same name for two different things in a program.

However, if you look into the VCL library and the Windows files, you'll find that some Delphi functions have the same name as (and generally different parameters than) some Windows API functions available in Delphi itself. An example is the simple Beep procedure.

If you create a new Delphi program, add a button, and write the following code:

```
procedure TForm1.Button1Click(Sender: TObject);
begin
  Beep;
end;
```

As soon as you press the button you'll hear a short sound. Now, move to the uses statement of the unit, and change the code from this:

```
uses
    Windows, Messages, SysUtils, Classes, ...
```

to this very similar version (simply moving the SysUtils unit before the Windows unit):

```
uses
    SysUtils, Windows, Messages, Classes, ...
```

If you now try to recompile this code, you'll get a compiler error: *Not enough actual parameters*. The problem is that the Windows unit defines another Beep function with two parameters. Stated more generally, what happens in the definitions of the first units you include in the uses statement might be hidden by corresponding definitions of later units. The safe solution is actually quite simple:

```
procedure TForm1.Button1Click(Sender: TObject);
begin
  SysUtils.Beep;
end;
```

This code will compile regardless of the order of the units in the uses statements. There are few other name clashes in Delphi, simply because Delphi code is generally hosted by methods of classes. Having two methods with the same name in two different classes doesn't create any problem. The problems arise only with global routines.

Encapsulating Changes

One of the key ideas of encapsulation is to reduce the number of global variables used by a program. A global variable can be accessed from every portion of a program. For this reason, a change in a global variable affects the whole program. On the other hand, when you change the representation of a field of a class, you only need to change the code of some methods of that class, and nothing else. For this reason, we can say that information hiding refers to *encapsulating changes*.

Let me clarify this idea with an example. In the LeapYear example, I added a TDate object to the var declarations of the unit interface. This object can be accessed from any other portion of this unit, but also from any other unit of the application, because it has been declared in the interface portion of the unit. In our small program, this was fine. However, in a complex application, developed by several programmers, other units might use this object. In this case, changing the TDate object's name or the way it is used could ruin the whole program.

To avoid this situation, I could have declared the object of the TDate class as a field of the class describing the form:

```
type
  // new data type, a TDate
  TDate = class
  private
    Month, Day, Year: Integer;
  public
    constructor Init (m, d, y: Integer);
    function LeapYear: Boolean;
  end;

  TForm1 = class(TForm)
    Btn1997: TButton;
    Btn1996: TButton;
    procedure FormCreate(Sender: TObject);
    procedure FormDestroy(Sender: TObject);
    procedure Button1995Click(Sender: TObject);
```

```
    procedure Button1996Click(Sender: TObject);
private
  { Private declarations }
  ADay: TDate; // new private declaration!
public
  { Public declarations }
end;

var
  Form1: TForm1;
```

If I add it as a `private` field, the TDate object won't be accessible from outside the unit, unless I provide a proper method to do so. And if I write an access method, and later decide to change the meaning or the representation of the object, I can just change the code of the access method accordingly, without any effect on the rest of the program's code.

Of course, declaring the three fields of the TDate class as `private` improves the encapsulation performed by the program and makes it more object-oriented. To accomplish this, however, we also need to add some methods to the class, so that we can access these `private` fields.

NOTE   There is a second difference between adding a field to the form class and declaring a global variable in the unit. In the first case, in fact, if you create two form objects of the same class you end up with two copies of the data, while unit data is shared among all of the objects of the form class. Of course, this difference makes sense only for secondary forms of a program you might want to create in multiple copies. The main form of a program is generally unique.

A Unit for the TDate Class

Throughout this chapter, we have developed a couple of examples with simple versions of a TDate class. The final version of this class will have some more functions, and we will place it in a unit. This is the interface of the class, inside the `interface` portion of the unit:

```
unit Dates;

interface
```

```
type
  TDate = class
  private
    Month, Day, Year: Integer;
  public
    constructor Init (m, d, y: Integer);
    procedure SetValue (m, d, y: Integer);
    function LeapYear: Boolean;
    procedure Increase;
    procedure Decrease;
    procedure Add (NumberOfDays: Integer);
    procedure Subtract (NumberOfDays: Integer);
    function GetText: string;
  protected
    function DaysInMonth: Integer;
  end;
```

The aim of the new methods is quite easy to understand:

- Increase and Decrease change the value of the date to the day after or before.

- Add and Subtract change the date by adding or subtracting the number of days passed as parameter, instead of a single day. For example, if the value of the current object is 3/8/1997, adding 10 days makes it 3/18/1997.

- GetText returns a string with the formatted date, using the Format function and some format specifiers to set the number of digits and to pad the number with zeros.

The following rather long listing shows the source code of some of the member functions of this class. You can find the full code of the unit in the companion CD as part of the ViewDate example used to test this class:

```
function TDate.DaysInMonth: Integer;
begin
  case Month of
    1, 3, 5, 7, 8, 10, 12:
      DaysInMonth := 31;
    4, 6, 9, 11:
      DaysInMonth := 30;
    2:
      if (LeapYear) then
```

```
        DaysInMonth := 29
      else
        DaysInMonth := 28;
    else
      // if the month is not correct
      DaysInMonth := 0;
  end;
end;

procedure TDate.Increase;
begin
  // if this day is not the last of the month
  if (Day < DaysInMonth) then
    Inc (Day) // increase the value by 1
  else
  // if it is not in December
    if Month < 12 then
    begin
      // Day 1 of next month
      Inc (Month);
      Day := 1;
    end
    else
    begin
      // else it is next year New Year's Day
      Inc (Year);
      Month := 1;
      Day := 1;
    end;
end;

function TDate.GetText: string;
begin
  {format the text, converting the integers to
  strings with a fixed number of characters}
  GetText := Format ('%.2d.%.2d.%4d',
    [Month, Day, Year]);
end;

procedure TDate.Add (NumberOfDays: Integer);
var
  N: Integer;
```

```
begin
  // increase the day n times
  for N := 1 to NumberOfDays do
    Increase;
end;
```

To test this unit, we can create a new example. The new form will have a caption to display a date and four buttons, which can be used to modify the date. You can see the main form of the ViewDate example at run-time in Figure 5.7. Notice that to work properly, the label component has a big font, it is as wide as the form, it has the Alignment property set to taCenter, and its AutoSize property is set to False, as you can see in the textual description of the form:

FIGURE 5.7

The output of the View-Date example at startup.

```
object DateForm: TDateForm
  Caption = 'Dates'
  Font.Name = 'MS Sans Serif'
  Font.Style = []
  OnCreate = FormCreate
  OnDestroy = FormDestroy
  object LabelDate: TLabel
    Alignment = taCenter
    AutoSize = False
    Caption = 'date'
    Font.Height = -27
    Font.Name = 'Arial'
    Font.Style = [fsBold]
  end
```

```
object BtnIncrease: TButton
  Caption = '&Increase'
  OnClick = BtnIncreaseClick
end
object BtnDecrease: TButton
  Caption = '&Decrease'
  OnClick = BtnDecreaseClick
end
object BtnAdd10: TButton
  Caption = '&Add 10'
  OnClick = BtnAdd10Click
end
object BtnSubtract10: TButton
  Caption = '&Subtract 10'
  OnClick = BtnSubtract10Click
end
end
```

We can write the startup code of this program in the OnCreate event. In the corresponding method, we create an instance of the TDate class, initialize this object, and then show its textual description in the Caption of the label, as shown in Figure 5.7.

```
procedure TDateForm.FormCreate(Sender: TObject);
begin
  TheDay := TDate.Init(5, 1, 1997);
  LabelDate.Caption := TheDay.GetText;
end;
```

TheDay is now a private field of the TDateForm data type. By the way, the name for the class, TDateForm, is automatically chosen by Delphi when we change the Name property of the form to DateForm.

When one of the four buttons is pressed, you need to apply the corresponding method to the TheDay object, then display the new value of the date in the label. Here are two examples:

```
procedure TDateForm.BtnIncreaseClick(Sender: TObject);
begin
  TheDay.Increase;
  LabelDate.Caption := TheDay.GetText;
end;
```

```
procedure TDateForm.BtnAdd10Click(Sender: TObject);
begin
  TheDay.Add(10);
  LabelDate.Caption := TheDay.GetText;
end;
```

TIP
As you can see in Figure 5.7, the four buttons of the form have the first letter underlined, which means that those characters can be used as shortcut keys. To obtain this effect, just add the & character in front of the letter in the Caption of the button, as you can see in the code for the buttons shown earlier. Pressing a shortcut key is a quick way to change the date. When you hold down one of the four underlined keys, the date will change rapidly.

If it still isn't clear to you how the program works, refer to its full source code on the companion CD and try to change it. For example, you can add new buttons to increase or decrease the date by a higher number of days. Try adding a Next Year button—one that will also work with leap years.

Units and Programs

A Delphi application consists of two kinds of source code files: there are one or more units and one program file. The units can be considered secondary files, which are referred to by the main part of the application, the program. In theory, this is true. In practice, the program file is usually an automatically generated file with a limited role. It simply needs to start up the program, running the main form. As we have already seen in Chapters 1 and 2, the code of the program file, or Delphi project file (.DPR), can be edited either manually or by using the Project Manager and some of the Project Options related to the application object and the forms.

The structure of the program file is usually much simpler than the structure of the units. For example, here is the source code of the ViewDate program file:

```
program ViewDate;

uses
  Forms,
  DateF in 'DATEF.PAS' {DateForm},
  Dates in 'DATES.PAS';
```

```
begin
  Application.Initialize;
  Application.CreateForm(TDateForm, DateForm);
  Application.Run;
end.
```

As you can see, there is simply a uses section and the main code of the application, enclosed by the begin and end keywords. The program's uses statement is particularly important, because it is used to manage the compilation and linking of the application.

> **NOTE** In 32-bit versions of Delphi, the code of the project has one more line of text than it did in the 16-bit version. The new line, Application .Initialize, usually does nothing, and it is not actually necessary. The only time this is used is if the project includes a subclass of TAutoObject (which makes the application an OLE automation server)—in which case the Initialize method updates the system registry. More about this topic in Chapter 22.

Inheriting from Existing Types

It is quite common to need a slightly different version of an existing class. For example, you might need to add a new method or change an existing one slightly. You can do this easily by modifying the original code, unless you are already using the same class in another unit of your program. In that case, making changes can create problems for the other unit. You should avoid modifications that can affect other units, particularly in big applications.

A typical alternative is to make a copy of the original type definition, change its code to support the new features, and give a new name to the resulting type. This might work, but it also might create problems: in duplicating the code you duplicate also the bugs, and if you want to add a new feature, you'll need to add it two or more times, depending on the number of copies of the original code you've made. This approach results in two completely different data types, and so the compiler cannot help you take advantage of the similarities between the two types.

To solve these kinds of problems in expressing similarities between classes, Object Pascal allows you to define a new class directly from an existing one. This technique is known as *inheritance* (or *subclassing*, or *derivation*) and is one of the fundamental elements of object-oriented programming languages. To inherit from an existing class, you only need to indicate that class at the beginning of the declaration of the subclass. For example, Delphi does this automatically each time you create a new form:

```
type
    TForm1 = class(TForm)
    end;
```

This simple definition indicates that the TForm1 class inherits all the methods, fields, and other elements of the TForm class. You can apply to an object of the TForm1 type each public method of the TForm class. If you look up TForm in the Help file, you'll see that this class has a number of methods. TForm, in turn, inherits some of its methods from another class, and so on, up to the TObject class. (For an introduction to the TObject class see the next chapter.)

NOTE In 32-bit versions of Delphi, a form can be a subclass of another form you have built. This powerful technique is known as *visual form inheritance*. I'll discuss visual form inheritance in Chapter 13, after we look at programs with multiple forms.

As a simple example of inheritance, we can change the ViewDate program slightly, deriving a new class from TDate and modifying one of its functions, GetText. You can find this code in the companion disk in the DATES.PAS file of the ViewD2 example.

```
type
    TNewDate = class (TDate)
    public
        function GetText: string;
    end;
```

In this example, TNewDate is derived from TDate. It is common to say that TDate is an *ancestor* class or a *parent* class (or a *base* class, to use the C++ terminology) of

TNewDate, and that TNewDate is a *subclass*, *descendant* class, or a *child* class (or a *derived* class, to use another C++ term) of TDate.

WARNING   Different object-oriented programming languages use different terms to denote inheritance and the classes involved. Unfortunately, there isn't a common jargon for all object-oriented languages—or better, for object-oriented *programmers*.

When I first implemented the new version of the GetText function I used a constant array of month names, defined in the implementation section of the unit, to output the description of the date:

```
// definition of the month names
const
  MonthNames: array [1..12] of string =
    ('January', 'February', 'March', 'April',
    'May', 'June', 'July', 'August', 'September',
    'October', 'November', 'December');

function TNewDate.GetText: string;
begin
  GetText := Format ('%s %d, %d',
    [MonthNames[Month], Day, Year]);
end;
```

Later, I realized it was much better to use the predefined month names available in Windows, which depend on Windows regional settings. Many of these regional settings are copied by Delphi into constants defined in the library, such as LongMonth-Names, ShortMonthNames, and many others you can find under the *Currency and date/time formatting variables* topic in the Delphi Help file. Here is a better version of the GetText method:

```
function TNewDate.GetText: string;
begin
  GetText :=  Format ('%s %d, %d',
    [LongMonthNames[Month], Day, Year]);
end;
```

Using regional information, the ViewD2 program automatically adapts itself to different user settings of Windows. If you run this same program on a computer with regional settings referring to a language other than English, it will automatically show month names in that language. To test this behavior, you just need to change the regional settings; you don't need a new version of Windows.

This code works only if it is written in the same unit as the TDate class, since we access private fields of the ancestor class. If we want to place the descendant class in a new unit, we need either to declare the three fields as protected or to add three simple methods in the ancestor class to read the values of the three private fields.

Once we have defined the new class, we need to use this new data type in the code of the form of the ViewD2 example. Simply define the TheDay object of type TNewDate and call its constructor in the FormCreate method:

```
type
  TDateForm = class(TForm)
    . . .
  private
    TheDay: TNewDate; // updated declaration
  end;

procedure TDateForm.FormCreate(Sender: TObject);
begin
  TheDay := NewDate.Init (7, 4, 1997); // updated
  DateLabel.Caption := TheDay.GetText;
end;
```

Without any other changes, the new ViewD2 example will work properly. The TNewDate class has inherited methods to increase the date, add a number of days, and so on. So the older code calling these methods still works. Actually, even to call the new version of the GetText method we don't need to change the source code! The Delphi compiler will automatically bind that call to a new method. The source code of all the other event handlers remains exactly the same, although its meaning changes considerably, as the new output demonstrates (see Figure 5.8).

FIGURE 5.8

The output of the
ViewD2 program, with
the name of the month
depending on regional
settings.

Inheritance and Type Compatibility

Pascal is a strictly typed language. This means that you cannot assign an integer value to a Boolean variable, at least not without making an explicit typecast, which can result in meaningless data. The rule is that two values are compatible only if they are of the same data type, or (to be more precise) if their data type has the same name.

There is an important exception to this rule in the case of class types. If you declare a class, such as TAnimal, and derive from it a new class, say TDog, you can assign an object of type TDog to a variable of type TAnimal. That is because a dog is an animal! So, although this might surprise you, the following constructor calls are both legal:

```
var
  MyAnimal, MyAnimal2: TAnimal;
begin
  MyAnimal := TAnimal.Create;
  MyAnimal2 := TDog.Create;
  ...
```

As a general rule, you can use an object of a descendant class each time an object of an ancestor class is expected. However, the reverse is not legal; you cannot use an object of an ancestor class when an object of a descendant class is expected. In code terms:

```
MyAnimal := MyDog;  // This is OK
MyDog := MyAnimal;  // This is an error!!!
```

Before we look at the implications of this important feature of the language, let me start building an example, Animals1, that I'll extend later on. The two classes of this example are defined as follows (in the ANIM.PAS unit):

```
type
  TAnimal = class
  public
    constructor Create;
    function GetKind: string;
  private
    Kind: string;
  end;

  TDog = class (TAnimal)
  public
    constructor Create;
  end;
```

The two Create methods simply set the value of kind, which is returned by the GetKind function:

```
constructor TAnimal.Create;
begin
  Kind := 'An animal';
end;

function TAnimal.GetKind: string;
begin
  GetKind := Kind;
end;

constructor TDog.Create;
begin
  Kind := 'A dog';
end;
```

To show an example of the use of these classes, I've built a simple form with two RadioButton components, a Button component, and a Label component with centered text and a big font, as you can see in Figure 5.9 and in the following partial listing:

```
object FormAnimals: TFormAnimals
  Caption = 'Animals'
  OnCreate = FormCreate
```

```
    OnDestroy = FormDestroy
    object LabelKind: TLabel
      Alignment = taCenter
      AutoSize = False
      Caption = 'Kind'
      Font.Height = -16
      Font.Name = 'Arial'
      Font.Style = [fsBold]
    end
    object BtnKind: TButton
      Caption = '&Kind'
      OnClick = BtnKindClick
    end
    object RbtnAnimal: TRadioButton
      Caption = '&Animal'
      Checked = True
      OnClick = RbtnAnimalClick
    end
    object RbtnDog: TRadioButton
      Caption = '&Dog'
      OnClick = RbtnDogClick
    end
  end
```

FIGURE 5.9

The form of the
Animals1 example at
design time.

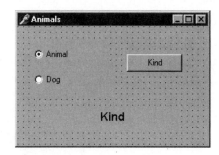

The form has some fields, which store the values of an animal, a dog, and a
generic object, MyAnimal:

```
type
  TFormAnimals = class(TForm)
    ...
  private
    MyAnimal, AnAnimal: TAnimal;
```

```
    ADog: TDog;
  end;
```

The instances of these objects are created and initialized when the form is created:

```
procedure TFormAnimals.FormCreate(Sender: TObject);
begin
  AnAnimal := TAnimal.Create;
  ADog := TDog.Create;
  MyAnimal := AnAnimal;
end;
```

The OnClick event handlers of the two radio buttons serve to change the object associated with the generic MyAnimal variable. Here is one of them:

```
procedure TFormAnimals.RbtnDogClick(Sender: TObject);
begin
  MyAnimal := ADog;
end;
```

Finally, the Kind button calls the GetKind method for the current animal and displays the result in the label:

```
procedure TFormAnimals.BtnKindClick(Sender: TObject);
begin
  KindLabel.Caption := MyAnimal.GetKind;
end;
```

The output of this method is shown in Figure 5.10. Remember to destroy the two objects (ADog and AnAnimal) in the FormDestroy method. If this type compatibility rule is clear, we can now focus on taking full advantage of it, by discussing late binding.

FIGURE 5.10

The output of the Animals1 program when the Dog radio button is selected.

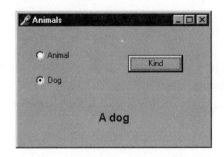

Late Binding and Polymorphism

Pascal functions and procedures are usually based on *static binding* or *early binding*. This means that a method call is resolved by the compiler or the linker, which replaces the call with a call to the specific memory location where the function or procedure resides (this is known as the address of the function).

Object-oriented programming languages, including Object Pascal, allow the use of another form of binding, known as *dynamic binding* or *late binding*. In this case, the actual address of the method to be called is determined at run-time. The advantage of this technique is known as *polymorphism*. The basic idea of polymorphism is that you write the call to a method, applying it to a variable, but which method is actually called depends on the type of the object the variable relates to. Delphi cannot determine until run-time the actual class of the object the variable refers to, simply because of the type compatibility rule discussed in the previous section.

NOTE   The term *polymorphism* is quite a mouthful. A glance at the dictionary tells us that in a general sense it refers to something having more than one shape or form. In the OOP sense, then, it refers to the fact that there may be several versions of a given method, and that a single method call can refer to each of these versions.

For example, suppose that a class and its subclass (let's say TAnimal and TDog) both define a method, and this method has late binding. Now you can apply this method to a generic variable, such as MyAnimal, which at run-time can refer either to an object of class TAnimal or to an object of class TDog. The actual method to call is determined at run-time, depending on the class of the current object.

The Animals2 example extends the Animals1 example to demonstrate this technique. In the new version of the program, the TAnimal and the TDog classes have a new method, Verse (to output and hear the sound made by the selected animal). This method is defined as virtual in the definition in the TAnimal class and is later overridden in the definition in the TDog class, by the use of the virtual and override keywords:

```
type
  TAnimal = class
  public
```

```
    constructor Create;
    function GetKind: string;
    function Verse: string; virtual;
  private
    Kind: string;
  end;

  TDog = class (TAnimal)
  public
    constructor Create;
    function Verse: string; override;
  end;
```

Of course, the two methods should be implemented. Here is a simple approach:

```
uses
  MMSystem;

function TAnimal.Verse: string;
begin
  Verse := 'Verse of the animal';
  PlaySound ('Anim.wav', snd_Async, 0);
end;

function TDog.Verse: string;
begin
  Verse := 'Arf Arf';
  PlaySound ('dog.wav', snd_Async, 0);
end;
```

NOTE This example uses a call to the PlaySound API function, defined in the MMSystem unit. The first parameter of this function is the name of the sound file you want to execute; the second and third parameters indicate the behavior of the function. We'll discuss simple multimedia applications in Chapter 31.

Now what is the effect of the call MyAnimal.Verse? It depends. If the MyAnimal variable currently refers to an object of the TAnimal class, it will call the method TAnimal.Verse (shorthand used to indicate the Verse method of the TAnimal class).

If it refers to an object of the TDog class, it will call the method TDog.Verse instead. This happens only because the function is virtual, and so it has late binding.

The call to MyAnimal.Verse will work for an object instance of any descendant of the TAnimal class, even classes that are defined after or outside the scope of this method call. The compiler doesn't need to know about all the descendants in order to make the call compatible with them; only the ancestor class is needed. In other words, this call to MyAnimal.Verse is compatible with all future TAnimal subclasses that haven't been created yet.

This is the key technical reason that leads to the assumption that object-oriented programming languages favor reusability. You can write some code that uses the classes of a hierarchy without any knowledge of the actual classes of the hierarchy itself. In other words, the hierarchy—and the program—is still extensible, even when you've written thousands of lines of code using it. Of course, there is one condition: the ancestor classes of the hierarchy need to be designed very carefully.

The Animals2 program demonstrates the use of these new classes and has a form similar to that of the previous example. The Button component this time has the Caption *'Verse'*, and a new internal Name (BtnVerse). The Name of the label becomes LabelVerse. This code is executed by clicking on the button:

```
procedure TFormAnimals.BtnVerseClick(Sender: TObject);
begin
  LabelVerse.Caption := MyAnimal.Verse;
end;
```

In Figure 5.11, you can see an example of the output of this program. By running it you'll also hear the corresponding sounds produced by the PlaySound API call.

FIGURE 5.11

The output of the Animals2 example.

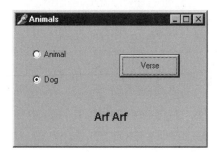

If you compare it with the previous version, you may very well say, "So what?" The output and the behavior of the two programs are similar, but something behind the scenes is quite different. In Animals1, there was a call to a function, GetKind, that simply returned the value of a field. In Animals2, there is a single call, MyAnimal.Verse, that at times refers to a method of a class and at other times refers to a method of another class. This is an interesting and powerful technique. The same compiled code calls one of two functions depending on the actual type of an object at run-time.

To appreciate this fully, consider that the two or more methods can be complex and completely different from each other. Virtual methods can also be called by other methods of the same class, and they can call other virtual or static methods.

Overriding and Redefining Methods

As we have seen before, to override a late-bound method in a descendant class, you need to use the override keyword. Notice, however, that this can take place only if the method was defined as virtual in the ancestor class. Otherwise, if it was a static method, there is no way to activate late binding, other than by changing the code of the ancestor class.

The rules are simple: A method defined as static remains static in every subclass, unless you hide it with a new virtual method having the same name. A method defined as virtual remains late-bound in every subclass. There is no way to change this, because of the way the compiler generates different code for late-bound methods.

To redefine a static method, you simply add a method to a subclass having the same parameters or different parameters than the original one, without any further specifications. To override a virtual method, you must specify the same parameters and use the override keyword:

```
type
  MyClass = class
    procedure One; virtual;
    procedure Two; {static method}
  end;

  MySubClass = class (MyClass)
    procedure One; override;
    procedure Two;
  end;
```

There are typically two different ways to override a method. One is to replace the method of the ancestor class with a new version. The other is to add some more code to the existing method. This can be accomplished by using the `inherited` keyword to call the same method of the ancestor class. For example, you can write:

```
procedure MySubClass.One;
begin
  // new code
  ...
  // call inherited procedure MyClass.One
  inherited One;
end;
```

You might wonder why you need to use the `override` keyword. In other languages, when you redefine a method in a subclass, you automatically override the original one. However, having a specific keyword allows the compiler to check the correspondence between the names of the methods of the ancestor class and the subclass (misspelling a redefined function is a common error in other OOP languages), check that the method was virtual in the ancestor class, and so on.

Furthermore, if you define a static method in any class inherited by a class of the library, even if the library is updated with a new virtual method having the same name as a method you've defined, there will be no problem. Since your method is not marked by the `override` keyword it will be considered as a separate method, and not a new version of the one added to the library (something that would probably break your code).

Virtual versus Dynamic Methods

In Delphi, there are basically two different ways to use *late binding* with a method. You can declare the method as `virtual`, as we have seen before, or declare it as `dynamic`. The syntax of these two keywords is exactly the same, and the result of their use is also the same. What is different is the internal mechanism used by the compiler to implement late binding.

`Virtual` methods are based on a virtual method table (VMT, also known as *vtable*). A virtual method table is an array of method addresses. For a call to a `virtual` method, the compiler generates code to jump to an address stored in the *nth* slot in the object's virtual method table.

Virtual method tables allow a fast execution of the method calls. Their main drawback is that they require an entry for each virtual method for each descendant class, even if the method is not overridden in the subclass. At times, this has the effect of propagating virtual method table entries throughout a class hierarchy (even for methods that aren't redefined). This might require a lot of memory just to store the same method address a number of times.

Dynamic method calls, on the other hand, are dispatched using a unique number indicating the method. The search for the corresponding function is generally slower than the simple one-step table lookup for virtual methods. The advantage is that dynamic method entries only propagate in descendants when the descendants override the method. For large or deep object hierarchies, using dynamic methods instead of virtual methods can result in significant memory savings and causes just a minimal speed penalty.

From a programmer's perspective, the difference between these two approaches lies only in a different internal representation and slightly different speed or memory usage. Beside this, virtual and dynamic methods are the same.

Here are some rules of thumb:

- If the method is going to be overridden by nearly every descendant, make it virtual.

- If the method is not going to be overridden very often, but still needs late binding for flexibility, make it dynamic, especially if there will be a lot of descendant classes.

- If the method might be called many times per second, make it virtual. Otherwise, there is no real speed difference in using dynamic.

Of course, this assumes that you have already decided the method must use late binding. Static methods are the fastest form of method dispatch, and this is the reason they are the default.

Message Handlers

A late-bound method can be used to handle a Windows message, too, although the technique is somewhat different. For this purpose Delphi provides yet another directive, message, to define message-handling methods. This method must be a procedure with a single var parameter. It is followed by the message directive plus an index, which is the number of the Windows message they refer to, or a corresponding mnemonic constant. For example:

```
type
  TForm1 = class(TForm)
    . . .
    procedure WMMinMax (var Message: TMessage);
      message WM_GETMINMAXINFO;
  end;
```

The name of the procedure and the actual type of the parameters are up to you, although there are a number of predefined record types for the various Windows messages. This technique can be extremely useful for veteran Windows programmers, who know all about Windows messages and API functions. In Chapter 10, I'll show you the example (called MinMax) from which the code fragment above was taken.

NOTE   The ability to handle Windows messages and call API functions as you do when you are programming Windows with the C language may horrify some programmers and delight others. But in Delphi, when writing Windows applications, you will seldom need to use message methods. Only when you are writing complex components in Delphi will you have to deal with low-level messages and API calls.

Abstract Methods

The abstract keyword is used to declare methods that will be defined only in subclasses of the current class. The abstract directive fully defines the method; it is not a forward declaration. If you try to provide a definition for the method, the compiler will complain:

```
type
  AbstractClass = class
    function F: Integer; virtual; abstract;
  end;
```

In Object Pascal, you can create instances of classes that have abstract methods. However, Delphi's 32-bit compiler issues a warning message when you create an instance of a class containing abstract methods.

NOTE   C++ uses a more strict approach: in this language you cannot create instances of abstract classes—classes that have pure virtual functions.

If you happen to call an abstract method, Delphi will issue a run-time error and terminate your application. Unlike most run-time errors, the run-time error 201 ("Call to abstract method") does not raise a standard exception. A call to an abstract method (a method that has no implementation) is considered a severe error, worthy of a fatal exit after the corresponding exception is raised.

You might wonder why you would want to use abstract methods. The reason lies in the use of polymorphism. If class TAnimal has the abstract method, Verse, every subclass can redefine it. The advantage is that you can now use the generic MyAnimal object to refer to each animal defined by a subclass, and invoke this method. If this method was not present in the interface of the TAnimal class, the call would not have been allowed by the compiler, which performs static type checking. In other words, using a generic MyAnimal object you can call only the method defined by its own class, TAnimal.

In other words, you cannot call methods provided by subclasses, unless the parent class has at least the declaration of this method—in the form of an abstract method. The next example, Animals3, demonstrates the use of abstract methods and some other features of polymorphism. I've written a new version of the ANIM .PAS file, declaring three classes: TAnimal, TDog, and TCat. Here are the interfaces of these classes:

```
type
  TAnimal = class
  public
    constructor Create;
    function GetKind: string;
    function Verse: string; virtual; abstract;
  private
    Kind: string;
  end;

  TDog = class (TAnimal)
  public
    constructor Create;
    function Verse: string; override;
    function Eat: string; virtual;
  end;
```

```
TCat = class (TAnimal)
public
  constructor Create;
  function Verse: string; override;
  function Eat: string; virtual;
end;
```

The most interesting portion is the definition of the class TAnimal, which includes a virtual abstract method, Verse. It is also important to notice that each derived class overrides this definition and adds a new virtual method, Eat. What are the implications of these two different approaches? To call the Verse function, we can simply write the same code as in the previous version of the program:

```
LabelVerse.Caption := MyAnimal.Verse;
```

How can we call the Eat method? We cannot apply it to an object of the TAnimal class. The statement

```
LabelVerse.Caption := MyAnimal.Eat;
```

generates the compiler error *Field identifier expected.*

To solve this problem, you can use Run-Time Type Information (RTTI) to cast the TAnimal object to a TCat or TDog object; but without the proper cast, the program will raise an exception. You will see an example of this approach in the next section. Adding the method definition to the TAnimal class is a typical solution to the problem, and the presence of the abstract keyword favors this choice.

To test our three new classes, we can modify the form of the previous version slightly, adding a new radio button for the new kind of animal. Along with adding the required code for the TCat class, I've made some other changes.

The two previous versions of the program created an object of each type at the beginning, then assigned the existing objects to the MyAnimal variable when the user selected one of the radio buttons. Now only one object exists at a time. The form has just a private field, MyAnimal, initialized in the OnCreate event handler with the statement MyAnimal := TDog.Create. Each of the OnClick event handlers of the radio buttons removes the current object and creates a new one:

```
procedure TFormAnimals.RbtnDogClick(Sender: TObject)
begin
  MyAnimal.Free;
  MyAnimal := TDog.Create;
end;
```

The code of the VerseButtonClick method remains the same, still calling MyAnimal.Verse and showing the result in the caption (besides playing the sound file). When you run this program, either the label will display the sound made by a dog or a cat (see Figure 5.12), or you'll experience a serious run-time error that will stop your application and possibly make the system unstable (if you click the Animal button, calling the abstract method of the TAnimal class).

> **NEW**
>
> Besides abstract classes (classes with abstract methods), Delphi 3 allows you to define *interfaces*—pseudo-classes with *only* abstract methods. Such a class is also called a *purely* abstract class. We'll start covering interfaces in Chapter 6, and see many more details in Chapter 21.

FIGURE 5.12

The output of the Animals3 example when the Cat radio button is selected.

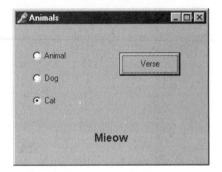

Run-Time Type Information

The Object Pascal type-compatibility rule for descendant classes allows you to use a descendant class where an ancestor class is expected. As I mentioned earlier, the reverse is not possible.

Now suppose that the TDog class has an Eat method, which is not present in the TAnimal class. If the variable MyAnimal refers to a dog, it should be possible to call the function. But if you try, and the variable is referring to another class, the result is an error. By making an explicit typecast we could cause a nasty run-time error (or worse, a subtle memory overwrite problem), since the compiler cannot determine if the type of the object is correct, and the methods we are calling actually exist.

To solve the problem, we can use techniques based on run-time type information (RTTI). Essentially, because each object "knows" its type and its parent class, we can ask for this information with the is operator or using some of the methods of the TObject class (discussed in the next chapter). The parameters of the is operator are an object and a class type, and the return value is a Boolean:

```
if MyAnimal is TDog then
  . . .
```

The is expression evaluates as True only if the MyAnimal object is currently referring to an object of class TDog, or a type descendant from TDog. This means that if you test whether a TDog object is of type TAnimal, the test will succeed. In other words, this expression evaluates as True if you can safely assign the object (MyAnimal) to a variable of the data type (TDog).

Now that you know for sure that the animal is a dog, you can make a safe type-cast (or type conversion). You can accomplish this direct cast by writing the following:

```
if MyAnimal is TDog then
begin
  MyDog := TDog (MyAnimal);
  Text := MyDog.Eat;
end;
```

This same operation can be accomplished directly by the second RTTI operator, as, which converts the object only if the requested class is compatible with the actual one. The parameters of the as operator are an object and a class type, and the result is an object converted to the new class type. We can write the following:

```
MyDog := MyAnimal as TDog;
Text := MyDog.Eat;
```

If we only want to call the Eat function, we might also use another shorter notation:

```
(MyAnimal as TDog).Eat;
```

The result of this expression is an object of the TDog class data type, so you can apply to it any method of that class. The difference between the traditional cast and the use of the as cast is that the second one raises an exception if the type of the object is not compatible with the type you are trying to cast it to. The exception raised is EInvalidCast (exceptions will be described in the next section).

To avoid this exception, use the is operator and, if it succeeds, make a plain typecast (in fact there is no reason to use is and as in sequence, doing the type check twice):

```
if MyAnimal is TDog then
  TDog(MyAnimal).Eat;
```

Both RTTI operators are very useful in Delphi because you often want to write generic code that can be used with a number of components of the same type or even of different types. When a component is passed as a parameter to an event-response method, a generic data type is used (TObject), so you often need to cast it back to the original component type:

```
procedure TForm1.Button1Click(Sender: TObject);
begin
  if Sender is TButton then
    ...
end;
```

This is a common technique in Delphi, and I'll use it in a number of examples throughout the book. Besides its use with is and as expressions, the term RTTI refers to a number of operations you can do on any class or object. I'll introduce some of these techniques in the next chapter, but the more advanced ones are beyond the scope of this book. If you are interested, they are discussed in the *Delphi Developer's Handbook*, by Marco Cantù and Tim Gooch (Sybex, 1997).

The two RTTI operators, is and as, are extremely powerful, and you might be considering using them as a standard programming construct. Although they are indeed powerful, you should probably limit their use to special cases. When you need to solve a complex problem involving several classes, try using polymorphism first. Only in special cases, where polymorphism alone cannot be applied, should you try using the RTTI operators to complement it. *Do not use RTTI instead of polymorphism.* This is both bad programming practice and results in slower programs. RTTI, in fact, has a high negative impact on performance, since it must walk the hierarchy of classes to see if the typecast is correct. As we have seen, virtual method calls require just a memory lookup, which is much faster.

Handling Exceptions

The last interesting feature of Object Pascal we will cover in this chapter is *exception handling*. The idea of exceptions is to make programs more robust by adding the capability of handling software or hardware errors. A program can survive such errors or terminate gracefully, allowing the user to save data before exiting.

There are several alternative ways to cope with errors, including extensive testing of function return codes. However, testing each time and for each function to see if something wrong has happened is boring and error-prone. Function-result error codes are problematic because each call to a routine must be checked for an error situation, and if such a situation exists, the current routine must be cleaned up and the error condition reported to the caller of the current routine. Each function in the call chain is responsible for passing the error information on to the next. If one routine in the call chain neglects to pass on the error information, your code will not be informed of errors, thus breaking down the whole process.

Exceptions solve this problem by removing the reporting mechanism from your normal code. If a particular body of code is not interested in error conditions, it doesn't need to do anything to ensure that error reporting works smoothly. Exceptions enable you to write more compact code that is less cluttered by maintenance chores unrelated to the actual programming objective. Exceptions also allow you to separate the code that discovers an error condition from the code that reports the error condition.

Exceptions are a plus also because they define a uniform and universal error-reporting mechanism, which is also used by Delphi libraries (and the environment itself). At run-time, Delphi raises exceptions when something goes wrong. If your code has been written properly, it can acknowledge the problem and try to solve it; otherwise, the exception is passed to its calling code, and so on. Eventually, if no part of your code handles the exception, Delphi handles it, by displaying a standard error message and trying to continue the program.

The whole mechanism is based on four keywords:

- `try` delimits the beginning of a protected block of code.

- `except` delimits the end of a protected block of code, and introduces the exception-handling statements, with this syntax form:

    on *exception-type* **do** *statement*

- `finally` is used to specify blocks of code that must always be executed, even when exceptions occur.

- `raise` is the statement used to generate an exception. Most exceptions you'll encounter in your Delphi programming will be generated by the system, but you can also `raise` exceptions in your own code when it discovers invalid or inconsistent data at run-time. The `raise` keyword can also be used inside a handler to *re-raise* an exception; that is, to propagate it to the next handler.

Here is an example of a simple protected block:

```
function Divide (A, B: Integer): Integer;
begin
  try
    {the following statement is protected because
    it can generate an error if B equals 0}
    Result := A div B;
  except
    on EDivByZero do
      Result := 0;
  end;
end;
```

In the exception-handling statement, we catch the `EDivByZero` exception, which is defined by Delphi. There are a number of these exceptions referring to run-time problems (such as a division by zero or a wrong dynamic cast), to Windows resource problems (such as out-of-memory errors), or to component errors (such as a wrong index). Programmers can also define their own exceptions. Simply create a new subclass of the default exception class or one of its subclasses:

```
type
  EArrayFull = class (Exception);
```

When you add a new element to an array and this is already full (probably due to an error in the logic of the program), you can raise the corresponding exception by creating an object of this class:

```
if MyArray.Full then
  raise EArrayFull.Create ('Array full');
```

This `Create` method (inherited from the `Exception` class) has a string parameter to describe the exception to the user. You don't need to worry about destroying the object you have created for the exception, since it will be deleted automatically by the exception-handler mechanism.

The at Keyword

There is another keyword involved in exception handling, but one that is used infrequently: the at keyword. It can be used in a raise statement, to indicate which machine code location should be indicated as the one causing the exception. The syntax is:

```
raise object at location
```

For example, in the SYSUTILS.PAS source code, you can see the expression:

```
raise OutOfMemory at ReturnAddr
```

The error will be reported as if it was encountered in the code calling this procedure, and not in the procedure itself; that is, in the location returned by the system ReturnAddr function. This will inform the run-time module that the exception was indeed raised by the caller function. Of course, this kind of code makes sense only in special cases related to the system.

An Example of the Use of Exceptions

The code presented in this example and the previous Divide function are part of a sample program you can experiment with to test exceptions. The program is named Except, and it displays the simple form shown in Figure 5.13. The form has four buttons, each with an intuitive name and an OnClick event handler.

FIGURE 5.13

The form of the Except example at design-time.

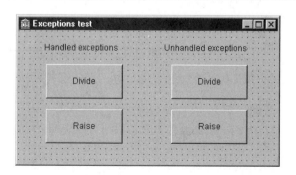

Each time a user presses one of the buttons, an exception is generated, either by making a division by zero or by an explicit raise statement. The two events of the two buttons on the left have the proper exception-handling code. But those on the right do not bother handling the exceptions. Pressing the various buttons you can see how the program behaves.

TIP   When you run a program in the debugger, the debugger will stop the program by default when an exception is encountered. This is normally what you want, of course, since you'll know where the exception took place and can see the call of the handler step by step. In the case of this test program, however, this behavior will confuse the program's execution. In fact, even if the exception is properly handled by the code, the debugger will stop the program execution. Then moving step-by-step through the code, you can see how it is handled. If you just want to let the program run when the exception is properly handled, run the program from the Windows Explorer, or temporarily disable the Break on Exception debugging feature in Delphi's Environment Options.

The first Divide button calls the Divide function, in a slightly different version than the one described earlier:

```
procedure TForm1.ButtonDivide1Click(Sender: TObject);
begin
  Divide (10, 0);
end;
```

```
{protected version of the div operator}
function Divide (A, B: Integer): Integer;
begin
  try
    {the following statement is protected because it
    can generate an error if B equals 0}
    Result := A div B;
  except
    on EDivByZero do
    begin
      Result := 0;
      MessageDlg ('Divide by zero corrected',
        mtError, [mbOK], 0);
    end;
```

```
    on E: Exception do
    begin
      Result := 0;
      MessageDlg (E.Message,
        mtError, [mbOK], 0);
    end;
  end; // end except
end;
```

This code generates an exception, which is trapped immediately. Notice that there are two different exception handlers after the same try block. You can have any number of these handlers, which are evaluated in sequence. For this reason, you need to place the broader handlers (the handlers of the ancestor exception classes) at the end.

In fact, using a hierarchy of exceptions, a handler is called also for the subclasses of the type it refers to, as any procedure will do. This is polymorphism in action again. But keep in mind that using a handler for every exception, such as the one above, is not usually a good choice. It is better to leave unknown exceptions to Delphi. The default exception handler in the VCL displays the error message of the exception class in a message box, and then resumes normal operation of the program.

Another important element is that you can use the exception object you receive in the handler. In the example above, I've written something like:

```
on E: Exception do
  MessageDlg (E.Message, mtError, [mbOK], 0);
```

The object E of class Exception receives the value of the exception object passed by the raise statement. When you work with exceptions, remember this rule: You raise an exception creating an object and handle it indicating its type. This has an important benefit, because as we have seen, when you handle a type of exception, you are really handling exceptions of the type you specify plus each descendant type.

TIP   Delphi defines a hierarchy of exceptions, and you can choose to handle each specific type of exception in a different way, or handle groups of them together. Refer to Chapter 7 for a graph of the hierarchy of Delphi exception classes.

A message box (see Figure 5.14) is displayed only because we generate it in the code, with the MessageDlg call. On the other hand, if we simply make a division by zero, Delphi will handle this exception, displaying a standard message box (see Figure 5.15). This happens when you press the second Divide button, executing the following code:

```
procedure TForm1.ButtonDivide2Click(Sender: TObject);
var
  A, B, C: Integer;
begin
  A := 10;
  B := 0;
  {generates an exception, which is not handled}
  C := A div B;
  {we have to use the result, or the optimizer will
  remove the code and the error, too}
  Caption := IntToStr (C);
end;
```

FIGURE 5.14

The first Divide button of the Except example raises an exception and handles it directly.

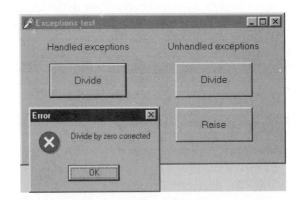

FIGURE 5.15

The second Divide button of the Except example raises an exception and leaves it to Delphi to handle.

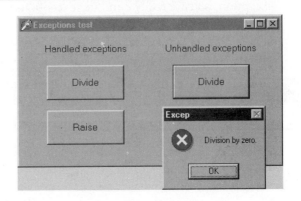

The other two buttons are even simpler. They call a function that invariably raises an exception. Again, the first button handles it, without even showing a message box to the user, and the second button doesn't seem to care. When the user presses the first Raise button, nothing seems to happen. This is exactly what is meant by handling an exception!

```
{fake procedure: the array is always full}
procedure AddToArray (N: Integer);
begin
  raise EArrayFull.Create ('Array full');
end;

procedure TForm1.ButtonRaise1Click(Sender: TObject);
begin
  try
    // this procedure raises an exception
    AddToArray (24);
  except
    // simply ignores the exception
    on EArrayFull do; // do nothing
  end;
end;

procedure TForm1.ButtonRaise2Click(Sender: TObject);
begin
  // unguarded call
  AddToArray (24);
end;
```

Exceptions and the Stack

When the program raises an exception and the current routine doesn't handle it, what happens to your function call stack? The program starts searching for a handler among the functions already on the stack. This means that the program exits from existing functions and does not execute the remaining statements. To understand how this works, you can either use the debugger or add a number of simple message boxes to the code, to be informed when a certain source code statement is executed. In the next example, Except2, I've followed this second approach.

For example, when you press the Raise2 button in the form of the Except2 example, an exception is raised and not handled, so that the final part of the code will never be executed:

```
procedure TForm1.ButtonRaise2Click(Sender: TObject);
begin
  // unguarded call
  AddToArray (24);
  ShowMessage ('Program never gets here');
end;
```

Notice that this method calls the AddToArray procedure, which raises the exception. The final code of this procedure is not executed, either:

```
procedure AddToArray (N: Integer);
begin
  raise EArrayFull.Create ('Array full');
  ShowMessage ('Program never gets here');
end;
```

If you run the Except2 program, you'll never see these messages, unless you comment out the raise statements (I suggest that you try this, so that you can see the difference between when the exception is raised and when it is not).

When the exception is handled, the flow starts again after the handler, and not after the code that raises the exception. Consider this modified method:

```
procedure TForm1.ButtonRaise1Click(Sender: TObject);
begin
  try
    // this procedure raises an exception
    AddToArray (24);
    ShowMessage ('Program never gets here');
  except
  on EArrayFull do
      ShowMessage ('Handle the exception');
  end;
  ShowMessage ('Exception has already been handled');
end;
```

The last ShowMessage call will be executed right after the second one, while the first is always ignored. I suggest that you run the program, change its code, and experiment with it to fully understand the program flow when an exception is raised. You can find its complete source code on the companion disk, as Except2.

The Finally Block

There is a fourth keyword for exception handling that I've mentioned but haven't used so far, `finally`. A `finally` block is used to perform some actions (usually cleanup operations) that should always be executed. In fact, the statements in the `finally` block are processed whether or not an exception takes place. The plain code following a `try` block, instead, is executed only if an exception was not raised, or if it was raised and handled. In other words, the code in the `finally` block is always executed after the code of the `try` block, even if an exception has been raised. Consider this function:

```
function ComputeBits (A, B: Integer): Integer;
var
  Bmp: TBitmap;
begin
  try
    Bmp := TBitmap.Create;
    // compute bits ...
    Result := A div B;
    Bmp.Free;
  except
    on EDivByZero do
    begin
      Result := 0;
      MessageDlg ('Error in ComputeBits',
        mtError, [mbOK], 0);
    end;
  end; // end except
end;
```

This code is fundamentally flawed. When B is zero and the exception is raised, the statement used to free the bitmap won't be executed at all. The program jumps from the code generating the exception to the corresponding handler, skipping statements in between.

One might think of placing the resource deallocation code at the end of the function, after the `try` block, but if an exception is raised and not handled, the `try` block won't be executed. The solution to the problem is to use the `finally` statement:

```
function ComputeBits (A, B: Integer): Integer;
var
  Bmp: TBitmap;
begin
```

```
  Bmp := TBitmap.Create;
  try
    // compute bits ...
    Result := A div B;
  finally
    Bmp.Free;
  end; // end finally
end;
```

When the program executes this function, it always calls the Free method of the TBitmap object, whether an exception occurs (of any sort) or not. The drawback to this version of the function is that it doesn't handle the exception. Strangely enough, this is not possible. A try block can be followed by either an except or a finally statement, but not both of them at the same time. The typical solution is to use two nested try blocks. Give the internal one a finally statement, and give the external one an except statement or vice versa, as the situation requires. Here is an example:

```
function ComputeBits (A, B: Integer): Integer;
var
  Bmp: TBitmap;
begin
  Bmp := TBitmap.Create;
  MessageDlg ('Bitmap created',
    mtWarning, [mbOK], 0);
  try try
    // compute bits ...
    Result := A div B;
    MessageDlg (
      'Code not reached (if the exception is raised)',
      mtWarning, [mbOK], 0);
  finally
    Bmp.Free;
    MessageDlg ('Bitmap destroyed',
      mtWarning, [mbOK], 0);
  end; // end finally
  except

    on E: EDivByZero do
      // re-raise the exception, changing its message
      raise EDivByZero.Create ('Error in ComputeBits');

  end; // end except
end;
```

WARNING In theory in the program above it should be possible to change the `Message` property of the exception object (`E.Message := 'Error in ComputeBits';`) and then re-raise the same exception object, by calling `raise`; with no further parameters. However, in 32-bit Delphi this doesn't always work, depending on the context and the version. So the "official" approach is to raise a new exception object of the same type, as in the code above. This always works, at least.

To demonstrate that this code works as I've described, I've written a program around this function. The new example is called Except3, and it has just two buttons (see the output in Figure 5.16, when a user clicks on the first button). Its code contains two versions of the do-nothing `ComputeBits` function, one similar to the last version above and the other having only the `finally` block. Since the function shows a number of message boxes, you are informed of the allocation and deallocation of the bitmap, and of the flow of execution.

FIGURE 5.16

The three message boxes displayed by the Except3 program, when the first button is pressed. Notice the order of execution.

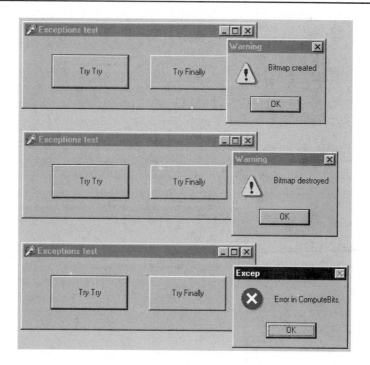

You should protect blocks with the `finally` statement, to avoid resource or memory leaks in case an exception is raised. Handling the exception is probably less important, since Delphi can survive most of them. The difference between the two versions of the `ComputeBits` function of the Except3 example is that in the first one the program customizes the error message, using the code I've just shown. To understand this program, run it, see what it does, and try to change its behavior. As an alternative, look at Figure 5.16, which shows the three messages displayed when a user presses the button labeled Try Try.

What's Next?

In this chapter, we have discussed object-oriented programming in Object Pascal. We have considered the definition of classes, the use of methods, encapsulation, inheritance, the definition of units, run-time type information, and exception handling. Certainly this is quite a lot for a single chapter, and if you have no previous exposure to OOP, the presentation here may be too concise. Again, you can refer to Appendix A for a short introduction to OOP, but I also suggest that you spend some time with a book fully devoted to this subject, one that also includes some theory. To become a fluent Delphi programmer, the ideas presented in this chapter should be enough. You may want to come back to this chapter, and the next two, after you've read Part II ("Using Components").

If you want to become an *expert* Delphi programmer, however, read the following two chapters with care. They'll introduce you to many advanced topics of the Object Pascal language, to the structure of the VCL, and to some brand-new features introduced in Delphi 3.

CHAPTER

SIX

6

Advanced Object Pascal

- The self keyword

- Class methods and data

- Method pointers

- Class references

- Defining properties and events

- Building your first Delphi component

In the last chapter we explored the basic features of Object Pascal as an object-oriented programming language. We discussed classes, inheritance, and polymorphism, the foundations of any OOP language. This chapter focuses on advanced topics of Object Pascal, and shows how the language has been extended to support component development and the COM model (the foundation of OLE). Some of the features discussed in this chapter are brand-new Delphi 3 features, not available in previous versions, but many others are little-known advanced features already available in Delphi 2.

I suggest you read this chapter through: although some of the topics might not have an immediate application for you, they will ultimately help you understand how Delphi works and how your programs interact with the system. This chapter and the next, in fact, focus on how Delphi's component library is built upon the Object Pascal language and its many extensions.

> **NOTE**
>
> If you are new to Delphi and to OOP, you may want to skip this chapter (and possibly also Chapter 7) for the moment. You can return to these two chapters before you reach the third part of the book, which focuses on component development and the OLE/COM technology.

The Self Keyword

The self keyword refers to an implicit parameter automatically passed to any method when it is called. Self can be defined as a reference to the current object (the current instance of the class) and is used by the language to refer to the fields of that specific object inside a method. In fact, when you declare several objects of the same class, each time you apply a method to one of the objects, the method will operate only on its own data and not affect the other objects.

For example, here is a method we encountered in the last chapter:

```
procedure Date.SetValue(m, d, y: Integer);
begin
  Month := m;
  Day := d;
  Year := y;
end;
```

In a method like this, Month really refers to the Month field of the current object, something you might express as:

```
Self.Month := m;
```

This is actually how the Delphi compiler translates the code, *not* how you are supposed to write it. The self keyword is a fundamental language construct used by the compiler, but at times it is used by programmers to resolve name conflicts and to make tricky code more readable. If you have ever used an object-oriented programming language, you should already have encountered the concept of self, maybe with a different name, such as the keyword this in C++.

All you really need to know about self is that it is a hidden parameter of every method in Object Pascal, and its presence is part of what distinguishes a method from a procedure or function that is not related to a class. The technical implementation of a call to a method differs from that of a call to a generic subroutine. Methods have an extra hidden parameter, self. But since all this happens behind the scenes, you do not need to know much about how self works for now.

TIP
> If you look at the definition of the TMethod data type in the VCL, you'll see that it is a record with a Code field and a Data field. The first is a pointer to the function's address in memory, the second the value of the self parameter for the method. We'll discuss method pointers shortly.

Creating Components Dynamically

In Delphi, the self keyword is often used when you need to refer to the current form explicitly in one of its methods. The typical example is the creation of a component at run-time, where you must pass the owner of the component to its Create constructor, and assign the same value to its Parent property (the difference between Owner and Parent properties is discussed in the next chapter). In both cases, you have to supply the current form as parameter or value, and the best way to do this is to use the self keyword.

To demonstrate this kind of code I've written the CreateC example (the name stands for *Create Component*). This program has a simple form with no components, and a handler for its OnMouseDown method. I've used OnMouseDown instead of OnClick because the first event handler has as parameter the position of the mouse click. I need this information to create a button component in that position. Here is the code of the method:

```
procedure TForm1.FormMouseDown(Sender: TObject; Button: TMouseButton;
  Shift: TShiftState; X, Y: Integer);
var
  Btn: TButton;
begin
  Btn := TButton.Create (self);
  Btn.Parent := self;
  Btn.Left := X;
  Btn.Top := Y;
  Btn.Width := Btn.Width + 50;
  Btn.Caption := Format ('Button in %d, %d', [X, Y]);
end;
```

The effect of this code is to create buttons at mouse-click positions, with a caption indicating the exact location, as you can see in Figure 6.1. In the code above, notice in particular the use of the self keyword, as parameter of the Create method and as value of the Parent property.

FIGURE 6.1

The output of the CreateC example, which creates Button components at run-time.

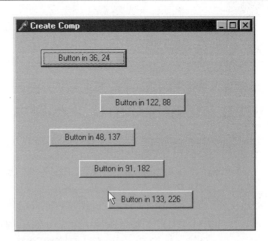

Notice also that it is very common to write code like the above method using a with statement, as in the following listing:

```
procedure TForm1.FormMouseDown(Sender: TObject; Button: TMouseButton;
  Shift: TShiftState; X, Y: Integer);
begin
  with TButton.Create (self) do
```

```
begin
  Parent := self;
  Left := X;
  Top := Y;
  Width := Width + 50;
  Caption := Format ('Button in %d, %d', [X, Y]);
end;
end;
```

Class Methods and Class Data

When you define a field in a class, you actually specify that the field should be added to each object instance of that class. Each instance has its own independent representation (referred to by the self pointer). In some cases, however, it might be useful to have a field that is shared by all the objects of a class.

Other object-oriented programming languages have formal constructs to express this, such as static in C++. In Object Pascal, this is not needed, because the encapsulation is always provided at the unit level. For this reason, if you simply add a variable in the implementation portion of a unit, it behaves as a class variable—a single memory location shared by all of the objects of a class.

If you need to access this value from outside the unit, you might use a method of the class. However, this forces you to apply this method to one of the instances of the class. An alternative solution is to declare a *class method*. A class method is a method that cannot access the data of any single object, but can be applied to a class as a whole rather than to a particular instance. A class method is a method related to the class, not to its objects or instances.

TIP

Technically, in Object Pascal, in a class method the self hidden parameter refers not to an object of the class (as in an ordinary method) but to the underlying class. This is known as a *class reference*.

Class methods are present in several object-oriented languages, and they are implemented in C++ using static member functions. To declare a class method in Object Pascal, you simply add the `class` keyword in front of the word `function` or `procedure`:

```
type
  MyClass = class
    class function ClassMeanValue: Integer;
```

The use of class methods is not very common in Object Pascal, because you can obtain the same effect by adding a procedure or function to a unit declaring a class. Object-oriented purists will definitely prefer the use of a class method over a routine unrelated to a class. And actually the VCL uses class methods quite often, although there are also many global subroutines. Class methods can also be virtual, so they can be overridden and used to obtain polymorphism.

> **NOTE**
>
> The *pure* object-oriented programming languages, such as Java or Small-Talk, do not allow for global subroutines, but force you to use class methods invariably. Although this is regarded as a good OOP approach, I find that it doesn't really make the code cleaner. On the contrary, it forces programmers to mix OOP code with non-OOP code, and even to write an otherwise useless class only to have a class method available. I think this is not a benefit, but a drawback of such languages.

A Class with an Object Counter

When class data (or unit data, to be more precise) is used to maintain general information related to the class (such as the number of objects created or a list of these objects), you can use class methods to access that data (such as to return the number of objects in the class or offer a way to navigate the list of objects). This is exactly the aim of the next simple example.

The CountObj program is an extension of the previous example, CreateC. The new form is still quite bare, but I've added some new code. In particular I've added a brand-new class, which inherits from the TButton class of the VCL and adds a new feature, namely object counting. This is the declaration of the new class:

```
type
  TCountButton = class (TButton)
    constructor Create (AOwner: TComponent); override;
    destructor Destroy; override;
    class function GetTotal: Integer;
  end;
```

> **NOTE**
>
> To be more precise this example should have overridden the `NewInstance` method, instead of overriding the `Create` constructor. In fact it is legal to call `Create` several times upon an already created object, to repeat the initialization code without creating a brand-new object. This happens by applying the constructor to an already created object (as in `MyObject1.Create`) instead of a class (as in `MyObject1 := TMyClass.Create`).

Every time an object is created, before calling the constructor of the base class, the program increments the counter. Every time an object is destroyed, the counter is decreased:

```
constructor TCountButton.Create (AOwner: TComponent);
begin
  inherited;
  Inc (TotBtns);
end;

destructor TCountButton.Destroy;
begin
  Dec (TotBtns);
  inherited Destroy;
end;
```

> **TIP**
>
> In theory when you call the inherited version of the `Create` constructor you should specify the method name and its parameters again. In practice, the shorthand code above does exactly the same! I've explicitly used the more traditional approach in the destructor, simply because it has no parameters and is simple to write anyway.

The counter itself is a variable declared in the `implementation` portion of the unit, and so is not accessible outside the unit. Only the class method allows us to read its current value:

```
implementation

var
  TotBtns: Integer = 0;
```

```
class function TCountButton.GetTotal: Integer;
begin
  Result := TotBtns;
end;
```

Notice that you can directly initialize this variable when it is defined.

Now we can create objects of this new type by changing the code of the FormMouseDown method slightly:

```
procedure TForm1.FormMouseDown(Sender: TObject; Button: TMouseButton;
  Shift: TShiftState; X, Y: Integer);
begin
  with TCountButton.Create (self) do
  begin
    Parent := self;
    Left := X;
    Top := Y;
    Width := Width + 60;
    Caption := Format ('%d Button in %d, %d',
      [GetTotal, X, Y]);
  end;
end;
```

Every time a TCountButton object is created, the current number of objects is displayed at the beginning of its caption. We can call the GetTotal class method for the newly created object (notice that we are inside a with statement), just as we call any plain method. However, we can call the same method without a valid object instance. This is what we do when the interval of a timer I've added to the form elapses:

```
procedure TForm1.Timer1Timer(Sender: TObject);
begin
  Caption := Format ('CountObj: %d custom buttons',
    [TCountButton.GetTotal]);
end;
```

The Caption property in this code refers to the caption of the form. You can see the effect of this call in Figure 6.2. The drawback of this example is that we can only create objects, and never destroy them, so we see the total number of *live* objects always increasing and never reducing its value.

FIGURE 6.2

The output the CountObj example, after a couple of TCountButton objects have been created.

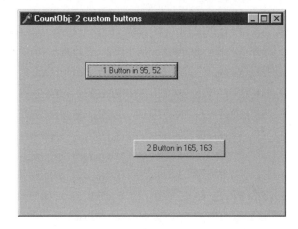

To see that the number of objects in existence goes down to zero, we can try to check the number of objects after the form has been destroyed, along with the TCountButton objects it owns. This is the code I've added at the end of the unit:

```
initialization
  MessageBox (0, PChar (Format (
    'There are %d CountButton objects',
    [TCountButton.GetTotal])),
    'Initialization', mb_OK);
finalization
  MessageBox (0, PChar (Format (
    'There are %d CountButton objects',
    [TCountButton.GetTotal])),
    'Finalization', mb_OK);
end.
```

WARNING

In the finalization code above I had to use a Windows API function (MessageBox) instead of a Delphi procedure (such as ShowMessage). The latter would make the program simply stop, and if you executed it in the debugger, it would also completely stop Windows 95 from running. Actually the finalization code of our unit is executed after some of the Delphi global objects have been destroyed, so it is better not to rely on them. I've used the same code in the initialization section, and in another method we'll soon add the form class, simply for consistency. Using ShowMessage in the initialization section works fine.

In both cases the program simply shows a Windows message box indicating the number of objects in existence, obtained by calling the GetTotal class method. If you run the program, in both cases the number in the output is zero. To test that everything actually works, I've added the same code in the handler of the OnDestroy event of the form, triggered while the form is being destroyed:

```
procedure TForm1.FormDestroy(Sender: TObject);
begin
  MessageBox (0, PChar (Format (
    'There are %d CountButton objects',
    [TCountButton.GetTotal])),
    'Destroy', mb_OK);
end;
```

If you now run the program, you'll see that when the FormDestroy method is executed all of the objects you've created still exist, but right after that, the objects are destroyed, and the count decreases to zero. We'll see a more complete example, in which we'll be able to destroy the buttons at run-time, after we discuss method pointers.

Method Pointers

Another Delphi addition to the Object Pascal language is the concept of *method pointers*. A method pointer type is like a procedural type, but one that refers to a method. Technically, a method pointer type is a procedural type that has an implicit self parameter. In other words, a method pointer stores two addresses: the address of the method code, and the address of an object instance (data). The address of the object instance will show up as self inside the method body. Again, this explains the definition of the TMethod type noted earlier, as a record with a Code field and a Data field.

The declaration of a method pointer type is similar to that of a procedural type, except that it has the keywords of object at the end of the declaration:

```
type
  IntProceduralType = procedure (Num: Integer);
  IntMethodPointerType = procedure (Num: Integer) of object;
```

When you have declared a method pointer, such as the one above, you can have a field type of this kind in an object:

```
type
  MyClass = class
    Value: Integer;
```

```
      Operation: IntMethodPointerType;
   end;
```

You can later assign this field any other type-compatible method—any other method of the same kind (procedure or function) and with parameters of the same data type. For example, you can declare another class having a method with the same integer parameter:

```
type
   AnotherClass = class
      X: Integer;
      procedure Add (N: Integer);
   end;
```

If you now declare a couple of objects of the two classes, such as

```
var
   MyObject: MyClass;
   AnotherObject: AnotherClass;
```

you can then make the assignment:

```
MyObject.Operation := AnotherObject.Add;
```

At this point, if you call the method

```
MyObject.Operation;
```

you end up calling the Add method on object AnotherObject.

At first glance, the goal of this overly complicated technique may not be clear, but this is one of the cornerstones of Delphi component technology. The secret is in the word *delegation*. If someone has built an object that has some method pointers, you are free to change the behavior of such pre-built objects simply by assigning a new method to them. Does this sound familiar? It should.

When you add an OnClick event handler for a button, Delphi does exactly this. The button has a method pointer, named OnClick, and you can directly or indirectly assign a method of the form to it. When a user clicks on the button, this method is executed, even if you have defined it inside another class (typically, in the form).

What follows is a listing that does exactly what the previous code fragments did, with names of classes, methods, and parameters slightly modified. What is important is that the new code is very similar to the code actually used by Delphi components:

```
type
   TNotifyEvent = procedure (Sender: TObject) of object;
```

```
MyButton = class
  OnClick: TNotifyEvent;
end;

TForm1 = class (TForm)
  procedure OnButton1Click (Sender: TObject);
  Button1: MyButton;
end;

var
  Form1: TForm1;
```

Now inside a procedure, you can write:

```
MyButton.OnClick := Form1.OnButton1Click;
```

The only real difference between the code fragment above and the actual code of the VCL is that OnClick is a property name, and the actual data it refers to is called FOnClick. An event that shows up in the Events page of the Object Inspector, in fact, is nothing more than a property of a method pointer type.

The Updated Counter Example

Now that we know how to use method pointers, we can update the CountObj example by using them. The name of the new example is CountOb2. What I want to do is to add a handler for the OnKeyPress event of the new objects I create dynamically. This is actually quite simple: Add the following code in the form class declaration:

```
procedure ButtonKeyPress(Sender: TObject; var Key: Char);
```

The parameters are those required for an event of this kind. If you select the OnKeyPress event for a component of a form, in fact, and press the F1 key to invoke the Help file, you'll find the following declaration:

```
TKeyPressEvent = procedure (Sender: TObject;var Key: Char) of object;
property OnKeyPress: TKeyPressEvent;
```

As you can see in this last line, the event is based on the TKeyPressEvent method pointer type listed in the line before. Therefore we need to write a method that complies with this method pointer type, like the one I've written above.

To connect this method with the OnKeyPress event of the buttons we create dynamically, we need just one line of code in the FormMouseDown method:

```
with TCountButton.Create (self) do
```

```
begin
  ...
  // set the event handler
  OnKeyPress := ButtonKeyPress;
  // grab the input focus
  SetFocus;
end;
```

The second line of code moves the input focus to the newly created button. (More on the input focus and on keyboard input in general in Chapters 8 and 10.)

Now we can write the actual code of the ButtonKeyPress method. There is no method skeleton automatically generated by Delphi, so we have to write all the code by hand, including the procedure declaration in the implementation section of the unit:

```
procedure TForm1.ButtonKeyPress(Sender: TObject; var Key: Char);
begin

end;
```

Of course we also need to *fill* this method declaration with some actual code. What I want to do in this example is to destroy the button when the user presses the Backspace key. Since keyboard input is sent to the control that has the input focus, you can simply click on a button or use the Tab key to select the button you want to destroy, and then press the Backspace key.

The first approach I tried was simply to destroy the object passed as Sender parameter, which is the object that received the event:

```
procedure TForm1.ButtonKeyPress(Sender: TObject;
  var Key: Char);
begin
  if Key = #8 then
    Sender.Free
end;
```

This code generates an exception. We simply cannot destroy an object while we are processing one of its events. What we can do is save the object we want to destroy in a private field of the form class, and later destroy it. This is the version of the code actually used in the example:

```
procedure TForm1.ButtonKeyPress(Sender: TObject;
  var Key: Char);
```

```
begin
  // if user pressed backspace
  if Key = #8 then
    // set this as the object to destroy
    ToDestroy := Sender as TButton;
end;
```

In this code ToDestroy is a private field of the form of the TButton data type:

```
private
  ToDestroy: TButton;
```

This field is automatically set to nil (no object to destroy) when the form is first created (this is the default initialization for class fields). When the user presses the Backspace key the current button object (the Sender of the ButtonKeyPress method) is stored in the ToDestroy field. Now we can add a Timer component to the form; and every time the timer interval elapses, we can test for a button to destroy, and eventually destroy it:

```
procedure TForm1.Timer1Timer(Sender: TObject);
begin
  // if there is an object to destroy
  if Assigned (ToDestroy) then
  begin
    // moves the input focus to the next control
    SelectNext (ToDestroy, True, True);
    // destroy the object
    ToDestroy.Free;
    // no more objects to destroy
    ToDestroy := nil;
  end;
  // update the form caption
  Caption := Format ('CountObj: %d custom buttons',
    [TCountButton.GetTotal]);
end;
```

To make the program behave a little better, before destroying an object I move the input focus to the next control, by calling the SelectNext method. Then I call the Free method of the object, which in turn invokes the destructor Destroy. Since the destructor is virtual, the program invokes the overridden destructor of the TButtonCount class, which decrements the object counter. For this reason I've placed the code to destroy the object before the code that updates the form caption.

Destroying Objects Once and Only Once

This example brings us to a different topic: every object you create should be destroyed, but if you try to destroy the same object twice, you get an exception. These problems had many faces, and while exploring it we'll cover the relationship between the Free method and the Destroy destructor, the use of the Assigned function to test if an object exists, and the reason for setting objects to nil. Having a clear understanding of all of these topics is fundamental for writing safe programs.

First let me recap what a destructor is. A *destructor* is a method that deallocates an object's memory. We can write some code for a destructor, generally overriding the Destroy destructor, to let the object execute some code before it is destroyed. In your code, of course, you don't have to handle memory deallocation—this is something Delphi does for you.

Destroy is simply a virtual destructor of the TObject class. Most of the classes requiring custom clean-up code when the objects are destroyed override this virtual method. The reason you should never define a new destructor is that objects are usually destroyed by calling the Free method, and this method calls the Destroy virtual destructor (including the eventually overridden version) for you.

As I've just mentioned, Free is simply a method of the TObject class, inherited by each other class. The Free method basically checks whether the current object (self) is not nil before calling the Destroy virtual destructor. Here is its pseudo-code (the actual code in the RTL source code files is written in assembler):

```
procedure TObject.Free;
begin
  if self <> nil then
    Destroy;
end;
```

Continued on next page

Destroying Objects Once and Only Once (Continued)

Next, we can turn our attention to the `Assigned` function. When we pass a pointer to this function, it simply tests whether the pointer is `nil`. So the following two statements are equivalent, at least in most cases:

```
if Assigned (ToDestroy) then ...
if ToDestroy <> nil then ...
```

Notice that these statements test only whether the pointer is not `nil`, and do not check if it is a valid pointer. If you write the following code:

```
ToDestroy.Free;
if ToDestroy <> nil then
   ToDestroy.DoSomething;
```

the test will be satisfied, and you'll get an error on the line with the call to the method of the object. It is important to realize that calling `Free` doesn't set the object to `nil`.

Automatically setting an object to `nil` is not possible: you might have several references to the same object, and Delphi doesn't track them. At the same time, inside a method (such as `Free`) we can operate on the object, but we don't know the memory address of the variable we've used to call the method. In other words, inside the `Free` method or any other method of a class, we know the memory address of the object (`self`) but we don't know the memory location of the variable referring to the object, as `ToDestroy`. Therefore, the `Free` method cannot affect the `ToDestroy` variable.

Consider this example:

```
ToDestroy.Free;
...
ToDestroy.Free;
```

Continued on next page

Destroying Objects Once and Only Once (Continued)

Of course, you are probably not going to write that, but it can result from executing the same method twice in a row. This is how we can translate it:

```
if ToDestroy <> nil then
  ToDestroy.Destroy;
...
if ToDestroy <> nil then
  ToDestroy.Destroy;
```

Since the ToDestroy variable is never set to nil, the second call to the Destroy method will be executed even when the object has already been destroyed, and an exception will be raised. To make a test, try removing the assignment to nil in the CountOb2 example, and you'll get such an error.

To sum things up, here are a couple of guidelines:

- Always call Free to destroy objects.
- Always set object references to nil after calling Free, unless the reference is going out of scope immediately afterwards.

Class References

Having looked at several topics related to methods, we can now move on to the topic of *class references*, and extend our example of dynamically creating components even further. The first point to notice is that a class reference isn't a class, it isn't an object, it isn't a reference to an object; it is a simply a reference to a class type.

A class reference type determines the type of a class reference variable. Sounds confusing? A few lines of code might make this a little clearer. Suppose you have defined a class:

```
type
  MyClass = class
    ...
  end;
```

You can now define a new class reference type, related to that class:

```
type
  MyClassRef = class of MyClass;
```

Now you can declare variables of both types:

```
var
  AClassRef: MyClassRef;
  AnObject: MyClass;
```

The first variable refers to an object, the second to a class:

```
AClassRef := MyClass;
AnObject := MyClass.Create;
```

You may wonder what class references are used for. In general, class references allow you to manipulate a class data type at run-time. You can use a class reference in any expression where the use of a data type is legal. Actually, there are not many such expressions, but the few cases are interesting. The simplest case is the creation of an object. We can rewrite the two lines above as follows:

```
AClassRef := MyClass;
AnObject := AClassRef.Create;
```

This time I've applied the Create constructor to the class reference instead of to an actual class; I've used a class reference to create an object of that class.

> **NOTE** Class references remind us of the concept of *metaclass* available in other OOP languages. In Object Pascal, however, a class reference is not a class, but only a type pointer. Therefore, the analogy with metaclasses (classes describing other classes) is a little misleading. Actually TMetaclass is also the term used in Borland C++Builder.

Class reference types wouldn't be as useful if they didn't support the same type compatibility rule that applies to class types. When you declare a class reference variable, such as MyClassRef above, you can then assign to it that specific class and also any subclass. So if MyNewClass is a subclass of my class, you can also write:

```
AClassRef := MyNewClass;
```

Delphi declares a lot of class references in the run-time library and the VCL, including the following:

```
TClass = class of TObject;
ExceptClass = class of Exception;
TComponentClass = class of TComponent;
TControlClass = class of TControl;
TFormClass = class of TForm;
```

In particular, the TClass class reference type can be used to store a reference any class you write in Delphi, because every class is ultimately derived from TObject. The TFormClass reference, instead, is used in the source code of most Delphi projects. The CreateForm method of the Application object, in fact, requires as parameter the class of the form to create:

```
Application.CreateForm(TForm1, Form1);
```

The first parameter is a class reference, the second an actual object.

Creating Components at Run-Time Using Class References

What is the *practical* use of class references in Delphi? Being able to manipulate a data type at run-time is a fundamental element of the Delphi environment itself. When you add a new component to a form by selecting it from the Components palette, you select a data type and create an object of that data type. Or, at least, this is what Delphi does for you behind the scenes.

To give you a better idea of how class references work, I've built a simple example, named ClassRef. The form of this example is quite simple. It has three radio buttons, placed inside a panel in the upper portion of the form. When you select one of these radio buttons and click on the form, you'll be able to create new components of the three types indicated by the button labels: radio buttons, push buttons, and edit boxes.

To make this program run properly, you need to change the names of the three components. The form must also have a class reference field. You should declare a new class reference type first:

```
type
  TControlClass = class of TControl;
```

Actually this is simply a redeclaration, since the same class reference type is already present in the VCL. The next step is to add two new private fields to the form:

```
private
  ClassRef: TControlClass;
  Counter: Integer;
```

The first field stores a new data type every time the user clicks on one of the three radio buttons. Here is one of the three methods:

```
procedure TForm1.RadioButtonRadioClick(Sender: TObject);
begin
  ClassRef := TRadioButton;
end;
```

The other two radio buttons have OnClick event handlers similar to this one, assigning the value TEdit or TButton to the ClassRef field. A similar assignment is also present in the handler of the OnCreate event of the form, used as an initialization method.

The interesting part of the code is executed when the user clicks on the form. Again, I've chosen the OnButtonDown event of the form to have the position of the mouse click:

```
procedure TForm1.FormMouseDown(
  Sender: TObject; Button: TMouseButton;
  Shift: TShiftState; X, Y: Integer);
var
  NewCtrl: TControl;
  MyName: String;
begin
  // create the control
  NewCtrl := ClassRef.Create (self);
  // hide it temporarily, to avoid flickering
  NewCtrl.Visible := False;
  // set parent and position
  NewCtrl.Parent := self;
  NewCtrl.Left := X;
  NewCtrl.Top := Y;
  // compute the unique name (and caption)
  Inc (Counter);
  MyName := ClassRef.ClassName + IntToStr (Counter);
  Delete (MyName, 1, 1);
  NewCtrl.Name := MyName;
```

```
  // now show it
  NewCtrl.Visible := True;
end;
```

The first line of the code for this method is the key. It creates a new object of the class data type stored in the `ClassRef` field. We accomplish this simply by applying the `Create` constructor to the class reference. Now you can set the value of the `Parent` property, set the position of the new component, give it a name (which is automatically used also as `Caption` or `Text`), and make it visible.

Notice in particular the code used to build the name; to mimic Delphi's default naming convention, I've taken the name of the class with the expression `ClassRef.ClassName`. (The meaning of this class method of the `TObject` class will be described in the next chapter.) Then I've added a number at the end of the name and removed the initial letter of the string. For the first radio button, the basic string is `TRadioButton`, plus the *1* at the end, and minus the *T* at the beginning of the class name—*RadioButton1*. Sounds familiar?

You can see two examples of the output of this program in Figure 6.3. Notice that the naming is not exactly the same as used by Delphi. Delphi uses a separate counter for each type of control; I've used a single counter for all of the components. If you place a radio button, a push button and an edit box in a form of the ClassRef example, their names will be *RadioButton1*, *Button2*, and *Edit3*.

FIGURE 6.3

Two examples of the output of the ClassRef example, in two different windows.

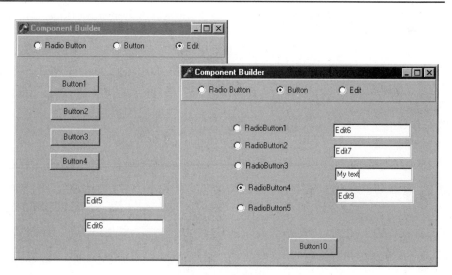

Interface and Multiple Inheritance

In the last chapter, we saw that the Delphi inheritance model doesn't support multiple inheritance: each class can have only a single base class. We also saw that in Delphi you can create an *abstract class*; that is, a class with one or more abstract methods. Now Delphi 3 adds some new features to this picture.

> **NOTE**   The techniques covered in this section are used to implement COM objects, and I'll cover them in more detail in Chapters 21 through 24. For the moment, let's consider them simply as language elements.

Declaring an Interface

Besides declaring abstract classes (classes with abstract methods), in Delphi 3 you can also write a *purely abstract declaration* of a class; that is, a sort of class declaration with only virtual abstract methods. This is accomplished using a new keyword, `interface`. For this reason we refer to these class declarations as *interfaces*, and not as classes. Technically, in fact, an interface is not a class, although it may resemble one. Here is the definition of a new interface:

```
type
  ICanFly = interface
    ['{10000000-0000-0000-0000-000000000000}']
    function TakeOff: string;
    function Fly: string;
    function Land: string;
  end;
```

> **TIP**   As class names generally start with the letter T, interface names generally start with the letter I. Of course, this is just another convention. To function properly, each interface requires a numeric identifier, like the one above. You'll learn more about these identifiers (technically indicated by the term GUID, Globally Unique Identifier) in Chapter 21. Here I've just used an almost arbitrary value.

This interface is not terribly useful until you start inheriting actual classes from it. A class inheriting from an interface must implement all of its methods, possibly declaring them as virtual:

```
type
  TAirplane = class (TInterfacedObject, ICanFly)
    function TakeOff: string; virtual;
    function Fly: string; virtual;
    function Land: string; virtual;
    destructor Destroy; override;
  end;
```

As any class inherits from the TObject class, any interface inherits from the IUnknown interface (more on this interface in Chapter 21). Since ICanFly inherits from IUnknown, the TAirplane class must implement the methods of both these interfaces. Delphi includes a special class, TInterfacedObject, which gives a default light-weight implementation to the methods of the IUnknown interface. For this reason, I've inherited the TAirplane class also from TInterfacedObject.

WARNING Actually the compiler doesn't accept a class that inherits only from an interface. To get around this you might simply inherit from the interface and the TObject class, writing: TAirplane = class (TObject, ICanFly).

Now we can implement the methods of the TAirplane class:

```
function TAirplane.TakeOff: string;
begin
  Result := 'Fasten your seat belts. '#13#10+
    ' The plane is taking off.';
end;

function TAirplane.Fly: string;
begin
  Result := 'Flying plane in the sky.';
end;

function TAirplane.Land: string;
begin
  Result := 'Flaps out. Clear for landing.';
end;
```

```
destructor TAirplane.Destroy;
begin
  MessageBox (0, 'Airplane destroyed',
    'Anim MI', mb_ok);
end;
```

I've added this destructor so we'll be able to see when an object of this class is destroyed. The Destroy method uses the MessageBox API function so that we'll see the message at the very end of program execution, as we did in the CountObj example earlier in this chapter. Once this is done, we can write an example that uses the class, just like any other class. There is really no difference:

```
procedure TForm1.ButtonAirClick(Sender: TObject);
var
  Air1: TAirplane;
begin
  Air1 := TAirplane.Create;
  Memo1.Lines.Add (Air1.TakeOff);
  Memo1.Lines.Add (Air1.Fly);
  Memo1.Lines.Add (Air1.Land);
  Memo1.Lines.Add ('');
  Air1.Free;
end;
```

You can see the result of this code in Figure 6.4, which shows the effect of pressing the first button on the left. We'll discuss the other buttons of the AnimMI example throughout this section.

FIGURE 6.4

The effect of pressing the Airplane test button of the AnimMI example.

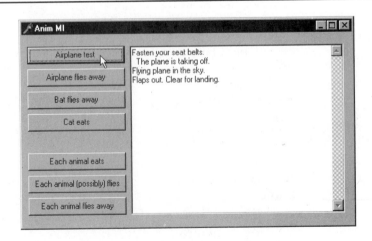

In the last code fragment I declared an object of the TAirplane class and used it as usual. However, once you've declared a new interface type you can also declare a variable of the interface type. This variable is similar to a class type variable, and you can also assign to it objects of a class that implements the interface. For example, you can write:

```
procedure TForm1.ButtonAirIntClick(Sender: TObject);
var
  Fly1: ICanFly; // interface
begin
  Fly1 := TAirplane.Create;
  Memo1.Lines.Add (Fly1.TakeOff);
  Memo1.Lines.Add (Fly1.Fly);
  Memo1.Lines.Add (Fly1.Land);
  Memo1.Lines.Add ('');
end;
```

What is important to notice in this method is that there is no code to destroy the object we create. However, if you run this code (pressing the second button of the form), it will produce the same output as the previous method, including the call to the destructor. This is proved by the fact that the corresponding message box is displayed.

As soon as you assign an object to an interface variable, Delphi automatically checks to see if the object implements that interface, and in this case calls the _AddRef method, which increases the reference count of the interface variable. At the end of the method, when the interface variable goes out of scope, Delphi calls the _Release method which decreases the reference count, checks whether the reference count is zero, and in this case destroys the object.

In other words, in Delphi 3 objects referenced by interface variables are reference-counted, and are they automatically deallocated when no interface variable refers to them any more.

WARNING This doesn't take into account that an object variable might still refer to the object: for this reason you should never mix objects and references.

Using an Interface as Parameter

What is interesting is that we can use a sort of polymorphism on interfaces. In fact, we can write a function that operates on an interface, like the following FlyAway function:

```
function FlyAway (F: ICanFly): string;
begin
    Result := F.TakeOff + #13#10 + F.Fly + #13#10 +
    F.Fly + ' ...over and over... ' + #13#10 +
    F.Land;

end;
```

In the code above, the characters #13#10 are used to add a new line in the memo component. Now we can generate the same output as the ButtonAirClick method above, by writing:

```
procedure TForm1.ButtonAirFAClick(Sender: TObject);
var
  Air1: ICanFly;
begin
  Air1 := TAirplane.Create;
  Memo1.Lines.Add (FlyAway (Air1));
  Memo1.Lines.Add ('');
end;
```

WARNING When you pass an interface as a parameter, Delphi automatically increases and then decreases its reference count. If you don't properly initialize the reference count (for example, if you declare the variable of the TAirplane type), it can be automatically destroyed as execution returns from the function call, making the object invalid in the following lines.

Writing a Second Interface

All of the code discussed above is in the AnimMI example. The name stands for *Animals Multiple Inheritance*, and although the airplane has little to do with animals, I'm going to use the ICanFly interface again, and also some other features including the FlyAway function. I decided to put all of the code of this section of the chapter in a single example, writing the classes in a separate unit from the form. The form, as you saw in Figure 6.4, has a memo component for the output and a group of buttons whose captions describe what they do.

I've basically added another interface for the animals, and then written a very simple class to define mammals:

```
type
  IMammal = interface
    ['{20000000-0000-0000-0000-000000000000}']
    function Eat: string;
  end;

  TMammal = class (TInterfacedObject, IMammal)
    function Eat: string; virtual; abstract;
    destructor Destroy; override;
  end;
```

This definition indicates that mammals can eat. (Of course, you can say the same for other kinds of animals. I could have implemented many other methods, but I preferred to keep the example as simple as possible.) Notice that the class above inherits again from TInterfacedObject. However, we also need to implement at least one interface in the TMammal class to be able to use interface-related techniques, such as interface querying. This is the destructor of the TMammal class, which will be used also for its subclasses:

```
destructor TMammal.Destroy;
var
  S: String;
begin
  S := ClassName + ' object gone';
  MessageBox (0, PChar (S), 'TMammal.Destroy', mb_OK);
end;
```

From TMammal I've inherited the TCat class, with the following code:

```
type
  TCat = class (TMammal)
    function Eat: string; override;
  end;

function TCat.Eat: string;
begin
  Result := 'The cat is eating a (Microsoft) mouse.';
end;
```

Again, I can simply use objects of this class and call their methods as usual:

```
procedure TForm1.ButtonCatClick(Sender: TObject);
var
  Cat1: IMammal;
begin
  Cat1 := TCat.Create;
  Memo1.Lines.Add (Cat1.Eat);
  Memo1.Lines.Add ('');
end;
```

Once again, using the interface type variable instead of a plain class type variable we don't need to destroy the object manually.

Implementing Both Interfaces

Now comes the interesting part. You can have a mammal that implements also the ICanFly interface, namely a bat:

```
type
  TBat = class (TMammal, ICanFly)
    function Eat: string; override;
    function TakeOff: string; virtual;
    function Fly: string; virtual;
    function Land: string; virtual;
  end;
```

Again, I've implemented the three methods of this class, and can now use them as in the ButtonCatClick method described at the end of the previous section. However, I can also write the following code, which calls the FlyAway function to operate on the ICanFly interface (you can see the effect of this code in Figure 6.5):

```
procedure TForm1.ButtonBatFAClick(Sender: TObject);
var
  FlAnim: ICanFly;
begin
  FlAnim := TBat.Create;
  Memo1.Lines.Add (FlyAway (FlAnim));
  Memo1.Lines.Add ('');
end;
```

FIGURE 6.5

The effect of calling
the FlyAway function
for a bat, in the AnimMI
example.

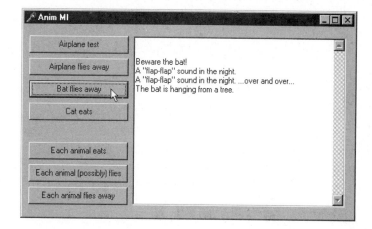

In this method I've again used a variable of an interface type. Notice, however, that I could have used both a variable of the IMammal type or one of the ICanFly type, since the TBat class implements both these interfaces. For example you can also write the above method as follows:

```
procedure TForm1.ButtonBatFAClick(Sender: TObject);
var
  FlAnim: IMammal;
begin
  FlAnim := TBat.Create;
  Memo1.Lines.Add (FlyAway (FlAnim as ICanFly));
  Memo1.Lines.Add ('');
end;
```

This code uses the as operator to ask the object for a different interface, namely ICanFly. The as operator for interfaces used here has little in common with the as RTTI operator used by objects and classes. When the second operand of the as operator is an interface, Delphi calls a special method common to all interfaces, QueryInterface, to test whether that interface is supported and *convert* the interface object to the new value. Actually this same call takes place also when you assign an object to an interface variable, as in the first line of the last method, which can also be written as:

```
FlAnim := TBat.Create as IMammal;
```

This example demonstrates that I can have a single function, FlyAway, which works on any object implementing the ICanFly interface, either bats or airplanes.

Notice that we obtain something similar to polymorphism even if TBat and TAirplane do not inherit from each other. We can say that they both implement the same interface, which is similar to (but not the same as) saying that they inherit from the same abstract base class.

Now the nice side of the example is that I can also use polymorphism on the TMammal class and its derived classes. The main form of the AnimMI example, in fact, has a field storing an array of animals:

```
private
    Animals: array [1..3] of IMammal;
```

These objects are created when the program starts, in the OnCreate event handler of the form. This method also activates the reference counting and outputs a line of text describing the operation:

```
procedure TForm1.FormCreate(Sender: TObject);
begin
  Animals[1] := TCat.Create;
  Animals[2] := TBat.Create;
  Animals[3] := TCat.Create;
end;
```

The three animals are then automatically destroyed when they go out of scope; that is, when the Form1 object is destroyed. Again, you can confirm this behavior thanks to the message box displayed by the destructor of the TMammal class. Now when one of last three buttons is pressed, the program can do some operations on each of the animals of the array. The first of these buttons, labeled *Each animal eats*, shows yet another simple example of how polymorphism works:

```
procedure TForm1.ButtonAllEatClick(Sender: TObject);
var
  I: Integer;
begin
  for I := 1 to 3 do
    Memo1.Lines.Add (Animals[I].Eat);
  Memo1.Lines.Add ('');
end;
```

If I want to call the Fly method or the FlyAway function for all the objects of the array also implementing the ICanFly interface, however, I have a small problem to solve. I cannot call Fly directly, and if I use the as conversion it might fail, raising an exception with the message *Interface not supported*.

I have to check whether the interface is supported before using as. This can be done by calling the `QueryInterface` method explicitly. This method requires as parameters the interface you want to convert to and an interface variable that will hold the resulting object. After this call we can actually use its result, instead of doing another as conversion:

```
procedure TForm1.ButtonAllFlyClick(Sender: TObject);
var
  I: Integer;
  Fly1: ICanFly;
begin
  for I := 1 to 3 do
  begin
    Animals[i].QueryInterface (ICanFly, Fly1);
    if Assigned (Fly1) then
      Memo1.Lines.Add (Fly1.Fly);
  end;
  Memo1.Lines.Add ('');
end;
```

Instead of testing the final value of the interface parameter of the `QueryInterface` method, calling `Assigned (Fly1)`, we can test the result of the method call. In fact, `QueryInterface` returns zero if the interface was found or the error code `E_NoInterface` if it was not found. Since testing for zero to see if a method succeeds seems quite odd, in the method of the last button I've checked whether the result was different than `E_NoInterface`. The `ButtonAllFAClick` method uses a slightly different approach than the previous `ButtonAllFlyClick` method:

```
procedure TForm1.ButtonAllFAClick(Sender: TObject);
var
  I: Integer;
begin
  for I := 1 to 3 do
    if Animals[i].QueryInterface (
        ICanFly, Fly1) <> E_NoInterface then
      Memo1.Lines.Add (FlyAway(Fly1));
  Memo1.Lines.Add ('');
end;
```

For the moment, consider that this is a very interesting extension of the Object Pascal language. You can find something very similar in other OOP languages, in particular Java. The Java implementation of interfaces is a little more flexible, while the Delphi implementation is strictly connected with COM objects. For this reason we'll re-start from this point of the discussion in Chapter 21.

> **NOTE**   Java and Object Pascal really have more in common than most people think. Most programmers think that Java is similar to C++, and this is true if you refer only to syntax. If you think of the object reference model, the single inheritance model, the presence of a common ancestor for all of the classes, the way exception handling works, and the concept of interfaces, you can see that Java and Object Pascal have many more ideas in common than they have with C++. Actually, both Java and Object Pascal have taken some of their features from earlier OOP languages, including the little-known Eiffel.

Defining Properties

Now that we have looked at the intricacies of interfaces, we can focus for the rest of the chapter on other extensions of the Object Pascal language specifically tailored for visual, component-based programming. This section covers properties; later on, we'll look at events and build a first simple component.

Properties are attributes that determine the status and behavior of an object. A property is basically a name that is mapped to some read and write methods or that accesses some data directly. In other words, every time you read the value of a property or change it, you might be accessing a field (even a private one) or might be calling a method. For example, here is the definition of a property for a date object:

```
property Month: Integer read FMonth write SetMonth;
```

To access the value of the Month property, this code has to read the value of the private field FMonth, while to change the value it calls the method SetMonth. Different combinations are possible (for example, we could also use a method to read the value or directly change a field in the write directive), but the use of a method to change the value of a property is very common. Here are some alternatives:

```
property Month: Integer read GetMonth write SetMonth;
```

```
property Month: Integer read FMonth write FMonth;
```

When you write code that accesses a property, it is important to realize that a method might be called, because some of these methods take some time to execute. They also can produce a number of side effects, often including a (slow) repainting of the component on the screen. Although property side effects are seldom documented, you should be aware that they exist, particularly when you are trying to optimize your code.

The `write` directive of a property can also be omitted, making it a *read-only* property. Technically you can also omit the `read` directive and define a *write-only* property, but this happens rarely. Another distinction is between *design-time* properties and *run-time only* properties. Design-time properties are declared in a `published` section of the class declaration. Anything that is declared in the `public` section is not available at design-time—it is run-time only. All the read-only properties must be defined in the `public` section (or in the `protected` or `private` sections) because published properties must be *read-write*.

To know the value of a `published` property at design-time, or to change it, you can use the Object Inspector; this is how Delphi's visual programming environment gives you access to properties. At run-time, you can access any public or published property by reading or writing its value.

Remember that the Object Inspector lists only the design-time properties of a component, omitting the run-time only properties. For a complete list of the properties of a component, refer to the Delphi Help files, not to the Object Inspector.

To summarize, along with the properties listed in the Object Inspector (design-time), there are other properties (run-time only), some of which can only be read (read-only). The description of each property in the Help file tells which kind of property it is. The Delphi Help system uses some symbols to indicate published and read-only properties, as you can see in Figure 6.6. Notice that these symbols have changed since the Delphi 2 Help file. Actually the overall structure of the Help file has changed, making it much easier to navigate through the list of properties of a component class and its base classes.

FIGURE 6.6

The different symbols
used by the new Delphi 3
Help file to mark differ-
ent kinds of properties.

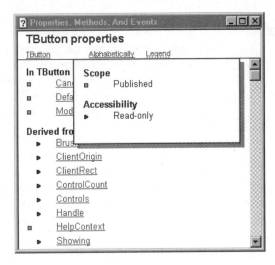

Note that you can usually assign a value to a property or read it, and even use properties in expressions, but you cannot always pass a property as a parameter to a procedure or method. This is because a property is not a memory location, so it cannot be used as a var parameter, it cannot be passed by reference.

Not all of the VCL classes have properties. Properties are present in components and in other subclasses of the TPersistent class, because properties usually can be streamed and saved to a file. A DFM file, in fact, is nothing but a collection of published properties of the components on the form. Delphi has extensive support for saving this kind of information, as you'll see in Chapter 29.

NOTE
Properties are a very sound OOP mechanism, a very well-thought-out application of the idea of encapsulation. Essentially, you have a name that hides the implementation of how to access the information of a class (either accessing the data directly or calling a method). In fact, using properties you end up with an interface that is very unlikely to change. At the same time if you only want to allow users access to some fields of your class, you can easily wrap those fields into properties instead of making them public. You have no further code to write (coding simple Get and Set methods is terribly boring), and at the same time you are still able to change the implementation of your class. Even if you replace the direct data access with access methods, you won't have to change the source code that uses these properties at all. You'll only need to recompile it. Think of this as the concept of encapsulation raised to the maximum power!

Adding Properties to the TDate Class

In the last chapter we developed a class, TDate. Now we can extend it by using properties. This new example, DateProp, is basically an extension of the ViewD2 example from Chapter 5. This is the new declaration of the class, with a couple of new methods (used to set the values of the properties) and four properties:

```
type
  TDate = class
  private
    FMonth, FDay, FYear: Integer;
  protected
    function DaysInMonth: Integer;
    procedure SetMonth (Value: Integer);
    procedure SetDay (Value: Integer);
  public
    constructor Init (m, d, y: Integer);
    procedure SetValue (m, d, y: Integer);
    function LeapYear: Boolean;
    procedure Increase;
    procedure Decrease;
    procedure Add (NumberOfDays: Integer);
    procedure Subtract (NumberOfDays: Integer);
    function GetText: string;
    // properties:
    property Day: Integer read FDay write SetDay;
    property Month: Integer read FMonth write SetMonth;
    property Year: Integer read FYear write FYear;
    property Text: string read GetText;
  end;
```

To follow the standard notation, I've changed the name of the local fields, prefixing them with the letter *F*. The Day and Month properties read their value directly and store it using two corresponding methods. I've added these methods in order to check for the range of the two values, using the following code:

```
procedure TDate.SetMonth (Value: Integer);
begin
  if (Value >= 1) and (Value <= 12) then
    FMonth := Value
  else
    raise EDateOutOfRange.Create ('Month out of range');
end;
```

```
procedure TDate.SetDay (Value: Integer);
begin
  if (Value >= 1) and (Value <= DaysInMonth) then
    FDay := Value
  else
    raise EDateOutOfRange.Create ('Day out of range');
end;
```

To write this code, I've defined a custom exception class, which is raised every time a value is out of range:

```
type
  EDateOutOfRange = class (Exception);
```

The Year property simply reads and writes the corresponding private field. Having written these methods with constraints on the values, we can update the SetValue method and the Init constructor to use them:

```
procedure TDate.SetValue (m, d, y: Integer);
begin
  FYear := y;
  // check the ranges
  SetMonth (m);
  SetDay (d);
end;
```

The fourth property, Text, maps only to a method. The information returned by reading this read-only property is not stored in the object but is computed each time, using a function that was already part of the class (actually I've used the textual description of the month, which was part of an inherited class in the ViewD2 example).

TIP

What is important to acknowledge in the definition of this property is that some properties do not map directly to data. They are simply computed. This happens not only for read-only properties, but also for read-write properties. In fact, we could extend this example by adding a SetText method to turn a string into a date, and use it to set the new value of the FMonth, FDay, and FYear fields.

Having updated the class with the new properties, we can now update the example to use properties when appropriate. For example we can use the Text property:

```
procedure TDateForm.BtnIncreaseClick(Sender: TObject);
begin
  TheDay.Increase;
  LabelDate.Caption := TheDay.Text;
end;
```

Actually, I've added to the form of the example three edit boxes, where the user can read or write the values of the three main properties (as you can see in Figure 6.7). This happens when a button is pressed:

```
procedure TDateForm.ButtonReadClick(Sender: TObject);
begin
  EditYear.Text := IntToStr (TheDay.Year);
  EditMonth.Text := IntToStr (TheDay.Month);
  EditDay.Text := IntToStr (TheDay.Day);
end;
```

FIGURE 6.7

The updated form of the DateProp example at run-time.

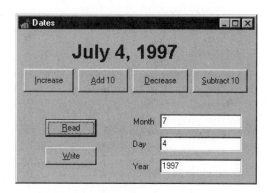

A second button does the reverse operation:

```
procedure TDateForm.ButtonWriteClick(Sender: TObject);
begin
  TheDay.Year := StrToInt (EditYear.Text);
  TheDay.Month := StrToInt (EditMonth.Text);
  TheDay.Day := StrToInt (EditDay.Text);
  // update the label
  LabelDate.Caption := TheDay.Text;
end;
```

If we try to use this example (rather than the final code provided on the companion disk), we are in for a surprise. In fact, if the current object refers to 5/1/1997 and we try to set the illegal date 6/31/1998, we end up with 6/1/1998! The reason is that we set year, month, and day in turn, and when an exception is raised we skip the wrong value, and any following ones. But we end up setting the year anyway. This might be the desired behavior, since we might indicate to the users of this class that they are supposed to check whether a date is valid before trying to use it. However, checking for a valid date requires a lot of code we have already written. So we can try improving the class.

I've updated the SetValue method to take care of the problem. Basically I store the initial values, and reassign them if an exception is raised. I actually re-raise the exception at the end to let the user see the error message:

```
procedure TDate.SetValue (m, d, y: Integer);
var
  OldY, OldM: Integer;
begin
  // store the old value
  OldY := FYear;
  OldM := FMonth;
  // passing the new value
  try
    FYear := y;
    // check the ranges
    SetMonth (m);
    SetDay (d);
  except
    on EDateOutOfRange do
    begin
      // reset the values
      FYear := OldY;
      FMonth := OldM;
      // let the error show up
      raise;
    end;
  end;
end;
```

In the form, I've used this method, instead of accessing properties directly:

```
procedure TDateForm.ButtonWriteClick(Sender: TObject);
begin
  TheDay.SetValue (StrToInt (EditMonth.Text),
    StrToInt (EditDay.Text),
```

```
    StrToInt (EditYear.Text));
  // update the label
  LabelDate.Caption := TheDay.Text;
end;
```

This leaves us with one concern. Classes and components should be easy to use without complex preconditions. However, this is not the case with the TDate class. A solution we might choose is to make the three properties read-only, so that programmers must use our correct SetValue method to change the date. This is not a bad solution, but it won't allow us to publish the properties and see them in the Object Inspector (as we'll do later on in this chapter). In the end, I decided to leave the code as it is, although it is a little risky.

NOTE The SetValue method of this class and the three properties have the same relationship as the SetBounds method of the TControl classes has with the Left, Top, Width, and Height properties. Actually in some special circumstances the same problem described above arises with these positional properties of controls.

Events in Delphi

When a user does something with a component, such as clicking on it, the component generates an event. Other events are generated by the system, as a response to a method call or a property change on that component (or even on a different one). For example, if you set the focus on a component, the component currently having the focus loses it, triggering the corresponding event.

Technically, most Delphi events are triggered when a corresponding Windows message is received, although the events do not match the messages on a one-to-one basis. Delphi events tend to be higher-level than Windows messages, as is the case of mouse dragging (there are no specific mouse dragging messages in Windows).

From a theoretical point of view, an event is the result of a message sent to a window, and this window (or the corresponding component) is allowed to respond to the message. Following this approach, to handle the click event of a button, we would need to subclass the TButton class and add the new event handler.

In practice, creating a new class is too complex to be a reasonable solution. In Delphi, the event handler of a component usually is a method of the form that holds that component, not of the component itself. In other words, the component relies on its owner, the form, to handle its events. This technique is called *delegation*, and it is a fundamental of the Delphi component-based model.

Events Are Properties

Another important concept is that events are properties. This means that to handle an event of a component, you assign a method to the corresponding event property, as we've done in the CountOb2 example earlier in this chapter. When you double-click on an event in the Object Inspector, a new method is added to the owner form, and assigned to the proper event property of the component.

This is the reason why it is possible for several events to share the same event handler, or change an event handler at run-time. To use this feature, you don't need much knowledge of the language. In fact, when you select an event in the Object Inspector, you can press the arrow button on the right of the event name to see a drop-down list of "compatible" methods—a list of methods having the same method pointer type. Using the Object Inspector, it is easy to select the same method for the same event of different components or for different, compatible events of the same component.

> **NOTE**
>
> The Object Inspector reads the list of available compatible methods from the source code of your form class definition: If you add a new published method in the initial part of the form class declaration (before the `public` keyword) with the parameters of a valid event handler, it will automatically be listed in the Object Inspector when you select an event with a compatible handler.

Adding an Event to the TDate Class

As I've added some properties to the TDate class, I can add one event. The event is going to be very simple. It will be called OnChange, and it can be used to warn the user of the component that the value of the date has changed. To define an event we simply define a property corresponding to it, and add some data to store the actual method pointer the event refers to. These are the new definitions I've added to the class:

```
type
  TDate = class
  private
    FOnChange: TNotifyEvent;
    ...
  protected
    procedure DoChange; virtual;
    ...
  public
    property OnChange: TNotifyEvent
      read FonChange write FOnChange;
    ...
  end;
```

The property definition is actually very simple. A user of this class can assign a new value to the property, and hence to the FOnChange private field. The class doesn't assign a value to this FOnChange field. It is the user of the component that does the assignment. The TDate class simply calls the method stored in the FOnChange field when the value of the date changes. Of course the call takes place only if the event property has been assigned. This is accomplished by the DoChange method:

```
procedure TDate.DoChange;
begin
  if Assigned (FOnChange) then
    FOnChange (self);
end;
```

This method in turn is called every time one of the values changes. Here is one example:

```
procedure TDate.SetMonth (Value: Integer);
begin
  if (Value >= 1) and (Value <= 12) then
  begin
    FMonth := Value;
    DoChange;
  end
  else
    raise EDateOutOfRange.Create ('Month out of range');
end;
```

I've changed each method of the class that changes the date in the same way. I've also added a write procedure for the Year property, since changing the year should trigger the event as well:

```
procedure TDate.SetYear (Value: Integer);
begin
  FYear := Value;
  DoChange;
end;
```

Now if we look at the program that uses this class, we can simplify its code considerably. First we add a new custom method to the form class:

```
type
  TDateForm = class(TForm)
    ...
    procedure DateChange(Sender: TObject);
```

The code of this method simply updates the label with the current value of the Text property of the TDate object:

```
procedure TDateForm.DateChange;
begin
  LabelDate.Caption := TheDay.Text;
end;
```

This event handler is then installed in the FormCreate method:

```
procedure TDateForm.FormCreate(Sender: TObject);
begin
  TheDay := TDate.Init (7, 4, 1997);
  LabelDate.Caption := TheDay.Text;
  // assign the event handler for future changes
  TheDay.OnChange := DateChange;
end;
```

Well, this seems a lot of work. Was I lying when I told you that the event handler would save us some coding? No. Now, after we've added some code, we can totally forget about updating the label when we change some of the data of the object. Here, as an example, is the handler of the OnClick event of one of the buttons:

```
procedure TDateForm.BtnIncreaseClick(Sender: TObject);
begin
  TheDay.Increase;
end;
```

The same simplified code is present in many other event handlers. Once we have installed the event handler, we don't have to remember to update the label continuously, which is a potential source of errors in the program. Also note that we had to write some code at the beginning because this is not a component installed in Delphi, but simply a class. With a component, you simply select the event handler in the Object Inspector and write the line of code to update the label. That's all.

How difficult is it to write a new component in Delphi? It's actually so simple, I'm going to show you how to do it in the next section.

Creating a TDate Component

The next step, actually a very simple one, is to turn our TDate class into a component. First, we have to inherit our class from the TComponent class, instead of the default TObject class. Here is the specific code:

```
type
  TDate = class (TComponent)
    ...
  public
    constructor Create (AOwner: TComponent); override;
```

As you can see, the second thing I had to do was to add a new constructor to the class, overriding the default constructor for components to provide a suitable initial value. In the code of this constructor I simply set the date to today's date:

```
constructor TDate.Create (AOwner: TComponent);
var
  Y, D, M: Word;
begin
  inherited Create (AOwner);
  // today...
```

```
    DecodeDate (Now, Y, M, D);
    FYear := Y;
    FMonth := M;
    FDay := D;
  end;
```

Having done this, we need to add to the unit that defines our class (the file DATES.PAS in the DATECOMP directory) a Register procedure. This is required in order to add the component to Delphi's Component Palette. Simply declare the procedure, which requires no parameters, in the interface portion of the unit, then write this code in the implementation section:

```
procedure Register;
begin
  RegisterComponents ('Md3', [TDate]);
end;
```

This code adds the new component to the *Md3* page of the Palette, creating the page if necessary. By the way, this is the same page I'll use for all the components built in the book.

The last step is to install the component. For this simple example we won't create a new package. Instead, we can install the component in the default *Delphi User's Components* package (a file named DCLUSR30.DPK and stored in the LIB directory of Delphi). We'll see how to build new packages in Chapter 18.

So you can select the Component ➤ Install Component menu item, choose the *Into existing package* page (this should be the default), select the DCLUSR30.DPK package file name, and enter the unit file name of the component, DATES.PAS. Now simply press the OK button and Delphi will update the package, compile it, and ask you to install it in Delphi (if you haven't already done so).

If you now move to the Components Palette, it should have a new *Md3* page with the new component. This will be shown using the default icon for Delphi components. At this point you can place the component on the form of a new application, and start manipulating its properties in the Object Inspector, as you can see in Figure 6.8. You can also handle the OnChange event in a much easier way than in the last example.

Besides trying to build your own custom example using this component (something I really suggest you do) you can now open the DateComp example, which is an updated version of the example we've built step by step in the last few sections of this chapter. This is basically a simplified version of the DateEvt example, since now the event handler is directly available in the Object Inspector.

FIGURE 6.8

The properties of our
new TDate component in
the Object Inspector.

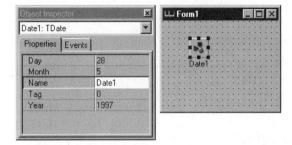

WARNING   Important: If you open the DateComp example before installing the new
component, Delphi won't recognize the component as it opens the form,
and will give you an error message. You won't be able to compile the
program or make it work until you install the new component.

What's Next

In this chapter we explored some of the more advanced topics related to the
Object Pascal language, such as method pointers, class references, properties and
events, and the new Delphi 3 interfaces.

The next step is to look into the structure of the VCL hierarchy. That will complete the foundations of Delphi programming, which we need to do before
exploring examples using the various components (something we'll start doing
in Chapter 8). In the next chapter we'll cover the structure of the VCL, and also
complete the coverage of the language with a discussion of the TObject class. Actually, this special class is part of the language and not of the VCL, but I've decided
to cover it in the next chapter anyway, along with other base classes, such as the
TComponent class we've just used.

7

The Visual Component Library

■ The TObject class

■ The VCL hierarchy of classes

■ Delphi components and objects

■ An overview of VCL properties, methods, and events

■ Types of Delphi collections

Delphi has a number of ready-to-use, standard routines, but also a larger and much more important set of classes. Some of them are component classes, showing up in the Components Palette, while others are more general-purpose classes. In this chapter, we'll focus on the structure of the Delphi class library, with an overview of some general-purpose classes. The use of the components and other classes related to Windows and database programming is the subject of Part II.

The Delphi system library is called the *Visual Component Library*, or *VCL* for short, although it includes more than components. This chapter delves into some intricacies of the VCL. If you would like to skip the VCL details for now, and continue with simpler information about the use of the Delphi components, you can go directly to the next chapter. Remember to come back to this chapter when you are ready to leverage your Delphi programming knowledge.

The TObject Class

At the heart of Delphi is a hierarchy of classes. Every class in the system is a subclass of the TObject class, so the whole hierarchy has a single root. This allows you to use the TObject data type as a replacement for the data type of any class type in the system. For example, event handlers usually have a Sender parameter of type TObject. This simply means that the Sender object can be of any class, since every class is ultimately derived from TObject. The typical drawback of such an approach is that to work on the object, you need to know its data type. In fact when you have a variable or a parameter of the TObject type you can apply to it only the methods and properties defined by TObject. If this variable or parameter happens to refer to an object of the TButton type, for example, you cannot directly access its Caption property. The typical solution to this problem is the use of the is and as RTTI operators, to check the data type and do the actual type conversion. For example, if the Sender parameter of the TObject type refers to a button you can write

```
(Sender as TButton).Caption
```

The advantage of this approach is that when the type conversion fails, Delphi raises an exception. This makes the code safe.

Since there isn't a specific Object Pascal syntax to write *generic* classes (known as *template* classes in the C++ language jargon), the TObject type and RTTI are used instead. To be honest, I don't miss C++ templates. Object Pascal's approach is much easier and equally powerful. I know that the use of *untyped* containers is often regarded as an unsafe approach because of the required type conversions, but by using RTTI and controlled casts, we can avoid any problems. We will discuss generic classes later in this chapter, when we focus on some container classes of the VCL.

Since the TObject class is the "mother of all classes," let's take a quick look at its definition in the Delphi source code. Note that I've grouped the methods in a logical way and added some comments:

```
type
  TObject = class
    // construction and destruction (commonly used)
    constructor Create;
    procedure Free;
    destructor Destroy; virtual;

    // construction and destruction (others)
    class function InitInstance(Instance: Pointer): TObject;
    class function NewInstance: TObject; virtual;
    procedure CleanupInstance;
    procedure FreeInstance; virtual;

    // type information and parent classes
    class function InstanceSize: Longint;
    function ClassType: TClass;
    class function ClassInfo: Pointer;
    class function ClassName: ShortString;
    class function ClassNameLs
    class function ClassParent: TClass;
    class function InheritsFrom(AClass: TClass): Boolean;
            (const Name: string): Boolean;

    // message handling and dispatching
    procedure Dispatch(var Message);
    procedure DefaultHandler(var Message); virtual;
```

```
      // access to published elements
      class function MethodAddress(const Name: ShortString): Pointer;
      class function MethodName(Address: Pointer): ShortString;
      function FieldAddress(const Name: ShortString): Pointer;

      // interface support
      function GetInterface(const IID: TGUID; out Obj): Boolean;
      class function GetInterfaceEntry(const IID: TGUID): PInterfaceEntry;
      class function GetInterfaceTable: PInterfaceTable;
      function SafeCallException(ExceptObject: TObject;
        ExceptAddr: Pointer): Integer; virtual;
    end;
```

The TObject class has a number of methods that you can use on any object, including those of classes that you define. Most of the methods of the TObject class are often used by the system, and they become particularly useful if you need to write a tool to extend the Delphi programming environment.

Some of the TObject methods can have a role when writing generic Windows applications. For example, the ClassName method returns a string with the name of the class. Because it is a class method, you can apply it both to an object and to a class. Suppose you have defined a TDate class and a Date1 object of that class. Then the following statements have the same effect:

```
Text := Date1.ClassName;
Text := TDate.ClassName;
```

There are occasions to use the name of a class, but it might also be useful to retrieve a class reference to the class itself or to its base class. We can do this with the ClassType and ClassParent methods. Once you have a class reference, you can use it as if it were an object; for example, to call the ClassName method.

Another method that might be useful is InstanceSize, which returns the run-time size of an object. Although you might think that you can use the SizeOf global function for this information, that function actually returns the size of an object reference—a pointer, which is invariably four bytes—instead of the size of the object itself.

Showing Class Information

To illustrate the use of some of the methods of the TObject class, I've written a small example called ObjUse. To build it yourself, place a button and a list box in the form of a new, blank application. Then add to the project the unit defining the

TDate class we wrote in Chapter 5, and add a uses statement referring to it in the code of the main form of the new project.

Then add to the form class a new method, sending to the Listbox component a description of the class of the generic object passed as parameter. Here is a possible implementation of this ShowInfo method:

```
procedure TForm1.ShowInfo (Obj: TObject);
begin
  // add class name
  ListBox1.Items.Add ('Class Name: ' + Obj.ClassName);
  // add parent class name, if any
  if Obj.ClassParent <> nil then
  begin
    ListBox1.Items.Add ('Parent Class Name: ' +
      Obj.ClassParent.ClassName);
    // add grandparent class name, if any
    if Obj.ClassParent.ClassParent <> nil then
      ListBox1.Items.Add ('Grandparent Class Name: ' +
        Obj.ClassParent.ClassParent.ClassName);
  end;
  // add the size of object and reference
  ListBox1.Items.Add ('Object Size: ' +
    IntToStr (Obj.InstanceSize));
  ListBox1.Items.Add ('Reference Size: ' +
    IntToStr (SizeOf (Obj)));
  // indicate if this is a component or not
  if Obj.InheritsFrom (TComponent) then
    ListBox1.Items.Add ('This is a component')
  else
    ListBox1.Items.Add ('This is NOT a component');
end;
```

Now, when the user clicks on the button, we can call the ShowInfo method for three different objects: a TDate object we are creating on the spot, the self object (the form), and the Sender object (the button generating the event):

```
procedure TForm1.ShowButtonClick(Sender: TObject);
var
  Day: TDate;
begin
  {create an instance and show some information}
  Day := TDate.Init (6, 1, 1995);
  ShowInfo (Day);
  ListBox1.Items.Add ('');
```

```
{show the same information about the form and the sender}
ShowInfo (self);
ListBox1.Items.Add ('');
ShowInfo (Sender);
{free memory}
Day.Free;
{disable the button, to avoid a second click}
ShowButton.Enabled := False;
end;
```

When you run this program, the list box will contain the names of the three classes followed by a description, as shown in Figure 7.1.

FIGURE 7.1

The output of the ObjUse example.

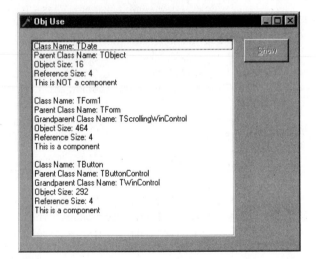

The VCL Hierarchy

The VCL defines a number of subclasses of TObject. Many of these classes are actually subclasses of other subclasses, forming a very complex hierarchy. Unless you are interested in developing new components, you'll use only the *terminal* classes of this hierarchy—the leaf nodes of the hierarchy tree—which are fully documented in the Delphi Help system. However, if you want to look at the full structure of the system, you can use the Object Browser (a tool discussed in more detail in Chapter 26), refer to the VCL-hierarchy posters that Borland and other third-party companies have distributed, or also refer to some of the figures in this chapter. To see some output from the Object Browser, you can look at Figure 7.2.

FIGURE 7.2

An example of the output of the Object-Browser, showing some classes of the VCL hierarchy.

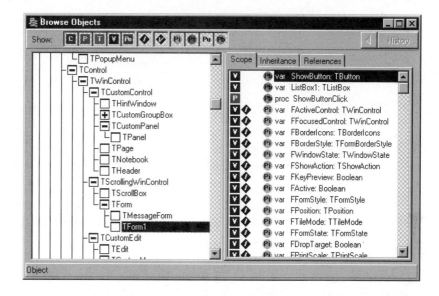

NOTE   You can see a complete tree of the VCL classes by running the VclHiera example in the Tools directory. For more information refer to the companion CD's Readme file.

We can divide the VCL hierarchy into three main areas: components, generic objects, and exceptions. We'll look into each of them in the next three sections.

Components

Components are the central elements of Delphi applications. When you write a program, you basically choose a number of components and define their interactions. That's all there is to most of Delphi programming.

There are different kinds of components in Delphi. Most components are included in the Components Palette, but some of them (including the classes TForm and TApplication) are not. Technically, components are subclasses of the TComponent class. As such, they can be streamed in a DFM file (since they inherit from the TPersistent class, which implements streaming) and they may have published properties and events you can manipulate visually. We saw a simple example of building a component at the end of the last chapter.

NOTE   We will use most of the Delphi components in the examples throughout this book. I'll try to present the components in logical groups, to cover related topics in each chapter. This grouping only partially matches the pages of the Components Palette.

In Figure 7.3 you can see a graph with the part of the VCL hierarchy related to components. This graph is not complete, because there are too many components to fit in a page, and also because my aim is just to show you the global structure of this hierarchy.

In fact, there are standard names used to indicate groups of components, as you can see in the reduced graph of Figure 7.4. These groups indicate components with a similar internal structure:

- *Controls* or *visual components* are all the classes that descend from *TControl*. Controls have a position and a size on the screen, and show up in the form at design time in the same position they'll have at run-time. Controls have two different specifications, window-based or graphical:

  - *Window-based controls* or *windowed controls* are visual components based on a system window. From a technical point of view, this means that these controls have a window handle. From a user perspective, windowed controls can receive the input focus and can contain other controls. This is the biggest group of components in the Delphi VCL.

  - *Graphical controls,* or *nonwindowed controls* are visual components that are not based on a window. Therefore, they have no handle, cannot receive the focus, and cannot contain other controls. These controls are painted by their parent form, which sends them mouse-related and other events. Examples of nonwindowed controls are the Label and the SpeedButton components. There are just a few controls in this group, but they are critical to minimizing the use of system resources, particularly for components used often and in number, such as labels or toolbar buttons.

- *Nonvisual components* are all the components that are not controls—all the classes descend from TComponent but not from TControl. At design-time, a nonvisual component appears on the form as an icon (eventually with a caption below it). At run-time, some of these components are visible at times (for example, the standard dialog boxes), and others are invisible (for example, the database table component). In other words, nonvisual components are not visible themselves at run-time, although they might manage something that is visual, such as a dialog box.

FIGURE 7.3

The first part of the VCL hierarchy: Components.

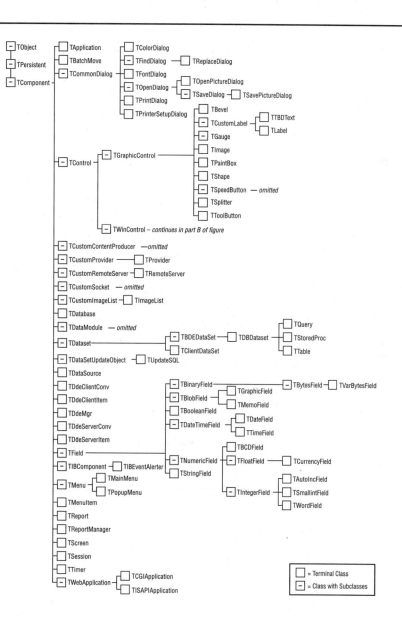

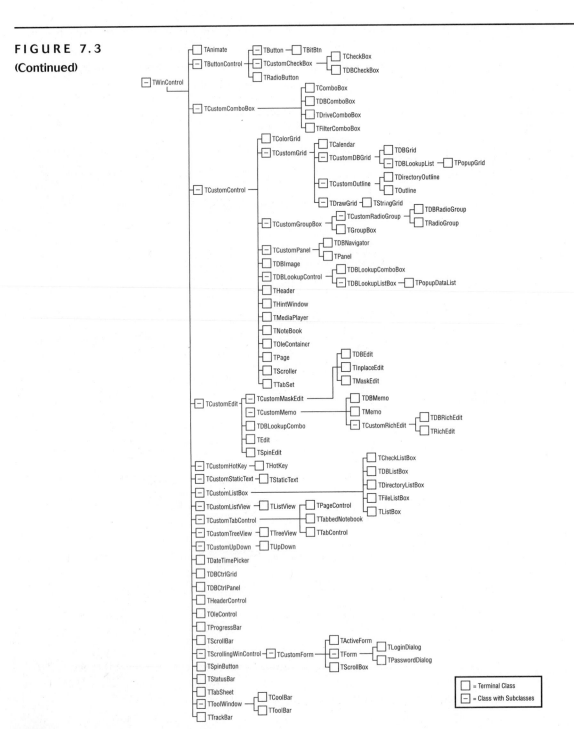

FIGURE 7.3
(Continued)

FIGURE 7.4

A graphical representation of the groups of components.

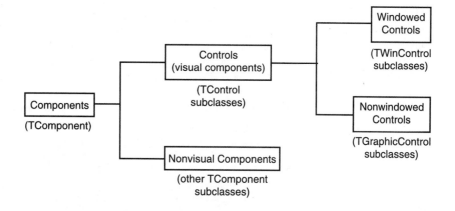

TIP

You can use an environment option, Show Component Captions, to see the name of a nonvisual component right under its icon. This helps to locate them, particularly if you have several components of the same kind on a form (all indicated by the same icon).

Objects

Although the VCL is basically a collection of components, there are other classes that do not fit in this category, because they do not descend from TComponent. You can the see most important of these classes in Figure 7.5.

All the noncomponent classes are often identified (by the Delphi help files and documentation, among others sources) as *objects*, although this is not a precise definition. There are two main uses for these classes. Generally, noncomponent classes define the data type of component properties, such as the Picture property of an image component (which is a TGraphic object) or the Items property of a list box (which is a TStrings object). These classes generally inherit from TPersistent, so they are *streamable*, and can have sub-properties and even events.

The second use of noncomponent classes is a direct use. In the Delphi code you write, you can allocate and manipulate objects of these classes. You might do this for a number of purposes, including to store a copy of the value of a property in memory and modify it without changing the original component, to store a list of values, to write complex algorithms, and so on. You'll see several examples in the book that show how to use noncomponent classes directly.

FIGURE 7.5

The second part of the VCL hierarchy: Objects. Part B shows the new COM-related classes.

```
TObject
    TAggregatedObject ── TConnectionPoints
                         TContainedObject ── TConnectionPoint
    TAutomation
    TBDECallback
    TBits
    TBookmarkList
    TChangeLink
    TComponentError ── TDefaultError
    TComponentList
    TConversion
    TCustomModule
    TDataSetDesigner
    TDBError
    TDesigner ── TFormDesigner
    TDragObject ── TDragControlObject
    TFieldDef
    TFieldDefs
    TFiler ── TReader
             TWriter
    TIndexDef
    TIndexDefs
    TIniFile
    TInterface ── interface classes omitted
    TList
    TLookupList
    TMask
    TPaintControl
    TParamList
    TParser
    TPersistent
    TPrinter
    TPropertyEditor ── property editor hierarchy omitted
    TRegistry ── TRegIniFile
    TRegistryClass
    TSessionList          TBitmapImage
    TSharedImage          TIconImage
    TStream               TMetafileImage
    TSynchroObject ── TCriticalSection
    TThread           THandleEvent ── TEvent ── TSimpleEvent
    TThreadList
```

```
    TCanvas ── TControlCanvas
              TMetafileCanvas
    TClipboard
    TCollection ── omitted
    TCollectionItem ── omitted
    TColumnTitle
    TControlScrollBar
    TDataLink ── omitted
    TDateTimeColors
    TGraphic ──────────── TBitmap
    TGraphicsObject        TIcon
    THTMLTagAttribute ── omitted    TBrush    TMetafile
    TIconOptions                    TFont     TOleGraphic
    TListItem                       TPen
    TListItems
    TOutlineNode
    TParaAttributes
    TParam
    TParams
    TPicture
    TStrings ── TStringGridStrings    TIndexFiles
               TStringList           TTabList
    TTextAttributes
    TTreeNode
    TTreeNodes
```

```
    TBlobStream
    TCustomMemoryStream ── TMemoryStream
    THandleStream ── TFileStream    TResourceStream
    TOleStream
    TStringStream
    TVirtualStream
    TWinSocketStream
```

□ = Terminal Class	
⊟ = Class with Subclasses	

(A)

(B)

```
TObject
    TComObject          TActiveXPropertyPage
                        TTypedComObject ── TAutoObject ── TActiveXControl ── TActiveFormControl
    TComClassFactory    TActiveXPropertyPageFactory
                        TTypedComObjectFactory ── TAutoObjectFactory ── TActiveXControlFactory ── TActiveFormFactory
    TComServerObject ── TComServer
    TInterfacedObject   TAdapterNotifier
                        TAutoIntfObject ── omitted
                        TCustomAdapter ── omitted
                        TOleForm
```

There are several groups of noncomponent classes in the VCL:

- *Graphic-related objects*: TBitmap, TBrush, TCanvas, TFont, TGraphic, TGraphicsObject, TIcon, TMetafile, TPen, and TPicture. Some of these classes are discussed in Chapters 10 and 11.

- *Stream/file-related objects*: TBlobStream, TFileStream, THandleStream, TIniFile, TMemoryStream, TFiler, TReader, and TWriter. Some of these classes are covered in Chapter 29.

- *Lists and collections*: TList, TStrings, TStringList, TCollection, and TCollectionItem. We will focus on collections in a later section of this chapter.

- COM-related classes (shown in part B of Figure 7.5). This is an important new area of Delphi programming. COM-related classes are covered in Chapters 21 to 24.

Exceptions

The third main part of the VCL classes consists of the exception classes. We discussed exception handling in Chapter 5, so I won't repeat the details here. You can see the hierarchy of the exception classes in Figure 7.6.

All exception classes are subclasses of the Exception class. Here is the definition of this class:

```
type
  Exception = class(TObject)
  private
    FMessage: string;
    FHelpContext: Integer;
  public
    constructor Create(const Msg: string);
    constructor CreateFmt(const Msg: string;
      const Args: array of const);
    constructor CreateRes(Ident: Integer);
    constructor CreateResFmt(Ident: Integer;
      const Args: array of const);
    constructor CreateHelp(const Msg: string;
      AHelpContext: Integer);
    constructor CreateFmtHelp(const Msg: string;
      const Args: array of const; AHelpContext: Integer);
```

```
constructor CreateResHelp(Ident: Integer;
  AHelpContext: Integer);
constructor CreateResFmtHelp(Ident: Integer;
  const Args: array of const; AHelpContext: Integer);
property HelpContext: Integer
  read FHelpContext write FHelpContext;
property Message: string
  read FMessage write FMessage;
end;
```

Two things are worth noticing in this definition. The first is the presence of many different constructors, having as parameters a `string`, the resource identifier of a string, a format string, a format string extracted from the resources, and combinations of those. The second is the `Message` property, which can be used to access the message defined in the constructor. Other constructors define the `HelpContext` property, too.

To see how these elements are used, turn back to the examples of exception handling at the end of Chapter 5. More examples of exceptions are presented in the rest of the book, whenever resource allocation is involved or there is a need for their use.

Using VCL Classes

The VCL classes are documented in the various Delphi help files. I was about to say *fully documented*, but I'm not very confident of that: past experience with Delphi 1 and 2 has demonstrated that some classes, properties, or methods are missing from the documentation or are only partially documented. In some cases this is deliberate, because Borland thinks features might change in future releases. In other cases they are simply details that were missed in the effort of documenting hundreds of classes.

For each class of the VCL, you can generally use its properties and handle its events (if it is a component or persistent object), or call its methods. Using properties and events is generally easier.

Some of the properties, events, and methods of the VCL classes are defined at the highest level of the class hierarchy, and therefore are available for any component. The next section provides an overview of these common properties and events, with a detailed description and some simple examples (see Delphi's Help system for a complete reference.) Starting in the next chapter, we'll see other specific properties that various components have, and I'll show you examples of the use of almost all of the components in the Component palette.

FIGURE 7.6

The third part of the VCL hierarchy: Exceptions.

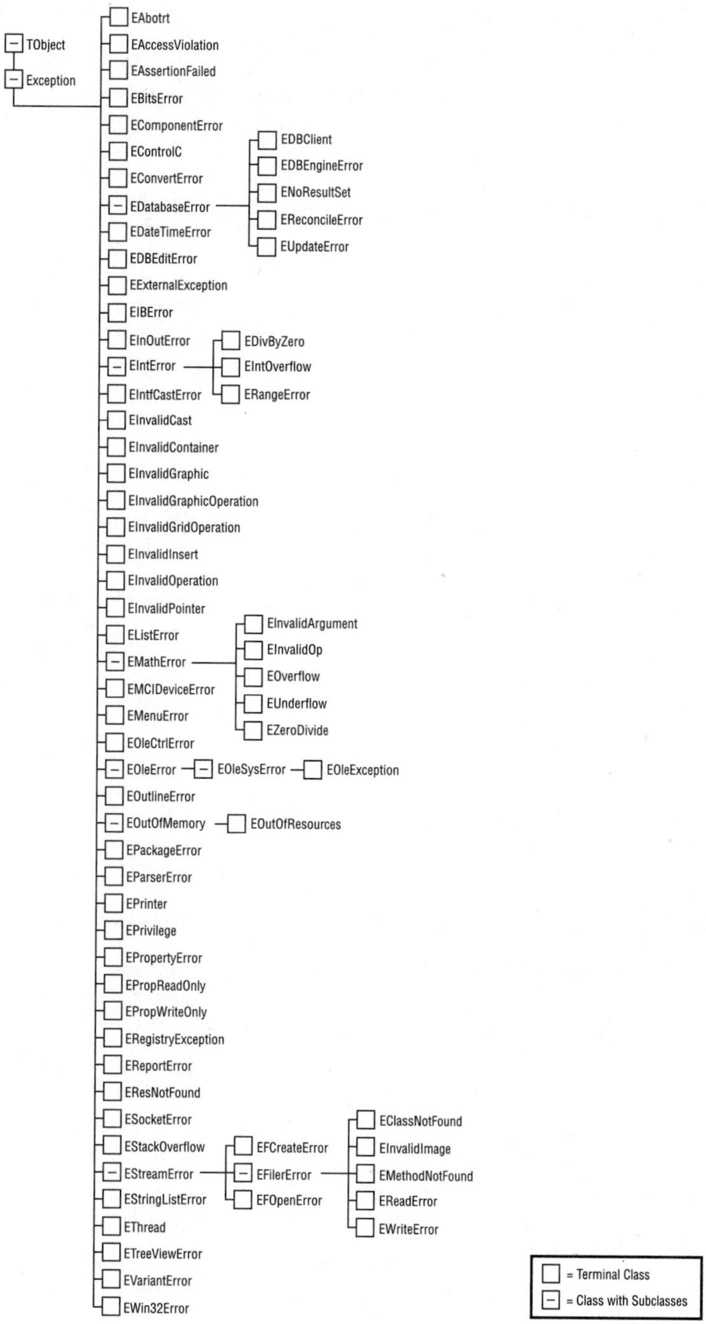

- TObject
- Exception
  - EAbotrt
  - EAccessViolation
  - EAssertionFailed
  - EBitsError
  - EComponentError
  - EControlC
  - EConvertError
  - EDatabaseError
    - EDBClient
    - EDBEngineError
    - ENoResultSet
    - EReconcileError
    - EUpdateError
  - EDateTimeError
  - EDBEditError
  - EExternalException
  - EIBError
  - EInOutError
  - EIntError
    - EDivByZero
    - EIntOverflow
    - ERangeError
  - EIntfCastError
  - EInvalidCast
  - EInvalidContainer
  - EInvalidGraphic
  - EInvalidGraphicOperation
  - EInvalidGridOperation
  - EInvalidInsert
  - EInvalidOperation
  - EInvalidPointer
  - EListError
  - EMathError
    - EInvalidArgument
    - EInvalidOp
    - EOverflow
    - EUnderflow
    - EZeroDivide
  - EMCIDeviceError
  - EMenuError
  - EOleCtrlError
  - EOleError — EOleSysError — EOleException
  - EOutlineError
  - EOutOfMemory — EOutOfResources
  - EPackageError
  - EParserError
  - EPrinter
  - EPrivilege
  - EPropertyError
  - EPropReadOnly
  - EPropWriteOnly
  - ERegistryException
  - EReportError
  - EResNotFound
  - ESocketError
  - EStackOverflow
  - EStreamError
    - EFCreateError
    - EFilerError
      - EClassNotFound
      - EInvalidImage
      - EMethodNotFound
      - EReadError
      - EWriteError
    - EFOpenError
  - EStringListError
  - EThread
  - ETreeViewError
  - EVariantError
  - EWin32Error

☐ = Terminal Class
⊟ = Class with Subclasses

Common VCL Properties

Although each component has its own set of properties, you may have already noticed that some properties are common to all of them. Table 7.1 lists some of the common properties along with very short descriptions.

TABLE 7.1   Some Properties Available in Most Components

Property	Available For	Description
Align	Some controls	Determines how the control is aligned in its parent control area.
BoundsRect	All controls	Indicates the bounding rectangle of the control (run-time only).
Caption	Most controls	The caption of the control.
ComponentCount	All components	The number of components owned by the current one (run-time only).
ComponentIndex	All components	The position of the component in the list of components of the owner (run-time only).
Components	All components	An array of the components owned by the current one (run-time only).
ControlCount	All controls	The number of child controls of the current one (run-time only).
Controls	All controls	An array of the child controls of the current one (run-time only).
Color	Most controls	Indicates the color of the surface or the background.
Ctrl3D	Most components	Determines whether the control has a three-dimensional look.
Cursor	All controls	The cursor used when the mouse pointer is over the control.
DragCursor	Most controls	The cursor used to indicate that the control accepts dragging.
DragMode	Most controls	Determines the drag-and-drop behavior of the control.
Enabled	All controls and some nonvisual components	Determines whether the control is active or is inactive (or grayed).

TABLE 7.1   Some Properties Available in Most Components (Continued)

Property	Available For	Description
Font	All controls	Determines the font of the text displayed inside the component.
Handle	All windowed controls	The handle of the system window used by the control (run-time only).
Height	All controls	The vertical size of the control.
HelpContext	All controls and the dialog components	A context number used to invoke the context-sensitive help automatically.
Hint	All controls	The string used to display fly-by hints for the control.
Left	All controls	The horizontal coordinate of the upper-left corner of the component.
Name	All components	The unique name of an instance of the component, which can generally be used in the source code.
Owner	All components	Indicates the owner component (run-time only).
Parent	All controls	Indicates the parent control (run-time only).
ParentColor	Most controls	Determines if the component uses the same Color of the parent.
ParentCtl3D	Most components	Determines whether the component uses the same Ctrl3D as the parent.
ParentFont	All controls	Determines whether the component uses the same Font as the parent.
ParentShowHint	All controls	Determines whether the component uses the same ShowHint as the parent.
PopupMenu	All controls	The pop-up menu used when the user *right-clicks* on the control.
ShowHint	All controls	Determines whether hints are enabled.
Showing	All controls	Determines whether the control is currently *showing* on the screen; that is, if it is visible the parent is visible, and its parent, and so on (run-time only).
TabOrder	All windowed controls	Determines the tab order in the parent control.

TABLE 7.1   Some Properties Available in Most Components (Continued)

Property	Available For	Description
TabStop	All windowed controls	Determines whether the user can move the control with the Tab key.
Tag	All components	A long integer available to store custom undefined data.
Top	All controls	The vertical coordinate of the upper-left corner of the component.
Visible	All controls	Determines whether the control is visible (see also the Showing property).
Width	All controls	The horizontal size of the control.

Since there is inheritance among components, it is interesting to see in which ancestor classes the most common properties are introduced. You can look at Figure 7.7 for an overview of the properties introduced by the topmost classes of the VCL hierarchy. The following sections provide basic descriptions of the most common properties.

The Name Property

Every component in Delphi should have a proper name. The name must be unique within the owner component, which is generally the form into which you place the component. This means that an application can have two different forms, each with a component with the same name, although you might want to avoid this practice to prevent confusion. It is generally better to keep component names unique throughout an application.

NOTE   Technically, it is possible to have a component without a name, but this makes sense only for components you create dynamically. Delphi uses the name of a component to associate it with the corresponding field of the form class. For this reason you should never change the name of a component at run-time.

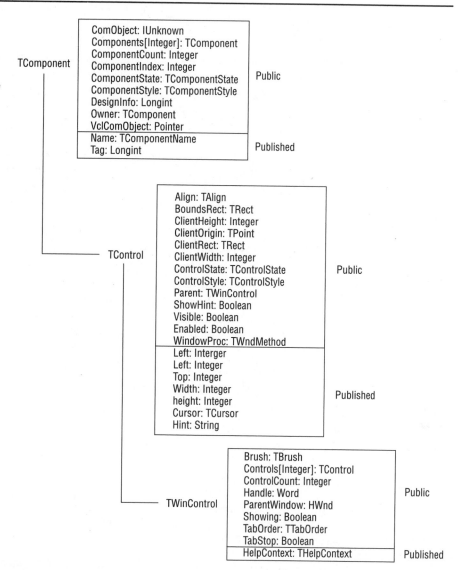

FIGURE 7.7

The properties introduced by the topmost classes of the VCL hierarchy, and available in all of the subclasses.

TComponent

ComObject: IUnknown
Components[Integer]: TComponent
ComponentCount: Integer
ComponentIndex: Integer
ComponentState: TComponentState
ComponentStyle: TComponentStyle
DesignInfo: Longint
Owner: TComponent
VclComObject: Pointer

Public

Name: TComponentName
Tag: Longint

Published

TControl

Align: TAlign
BoundsRect: TRect
ClientHeight: Integer
ClientOrigin: TPoint
ClientRect: TRect
ClientWidth: Integer
ControlState: TControlState
ControlStyle: TControlStyle
Parent: TWinControl
ShowHint: Boolean
Visible: Boolean
Enabled: Boolean
WindowProc: TWndMethod

Public

Left: Interger
Left: Integer
Top: Integer
Width: Integer
height: Integer
Cursor: TCursor
Hint: String

Published

TWinControl

Brush: TBrush
Controls[Integer]: TControl
ControlCount: Integer
Handle: Word
ParentWindow: HWnd
Showing: Boolean
TabOrder: TTabOrder
TabStop: Boolean

Public

HelpContext: THelpContext

Published

Setting a proper value for the Name property is very important: if it's too long, you'll need to type a lot of code to use the object; if it's too short, you may confuse different objects. Usually the name of a component has a prefix with the component type: this makes the code more readable and allows Delphi to group components in the combo box of the Object Inspector, where they are sorted by name. There are three important elements related to the Name property of the components:

- First, the value of the Name property is used to define the name of the object in the declaration of the form class. This is the name you're generally going to use in the code to refer to the object. For this reason, the value of the name property must be a legal Pascal identifier, as we saw in the CheckId example of Chapter 1.

- Second, as mentioned in Chapter 1, if you set the Name property of a control before changing its Caption property, the new name is copied to the caption. That is, if the name and the caption are identical, then changing the name will also change the caption.

- Third, Delphi uses the name of the component to create the default name of the methods related to its events. If you have a Button1 component, its default OnClick event handler will be called Button1Click, unless you specify a different name. If you later change the name of the component, Delphi will modify the names of the related methods accordingly. For example, if you change the name of the button to MyButton, the Button1Click method automatically becomes MyButtonClick.

Anyway, keep in mind that besides accessing a component by name, you can use the Components and Controls properties of its form. Here is an example of the code you can use to add to a list box the names of all the components of a form:

```
procedure TForm1.Button1Click(Sender: TObject);
var
  I: Integer;
begin
  ListBox1.Items.Clear;
  for I := 0 to ComponentCount - 1 do
    ListBox1.Items.Add (Components [I].Name);
end;
```

This code uses the ComponentCount property, which holds the total number of components owned by the current form, and the Components property, which is actually the list of the owned components. When you access a value from this list you get a value of the TComponent type. For this reason you can directly use only the properties common to all components, such as the Name property. To use other specific properties, you have to use the proper type-downcast (as).

NOTE In Delphi, there are some components that are also component containers: the GroupBox, the Panel, the Windows 95 Page control, the Notebook, the TabbedNotebook and, of course, the Form component. When you use these controls, you can add other components inside them. In this case, the container is the parent of the components (as indicated by the Parent property), while the form is their owner (as indicated by the Owner property). You can use the Controls property of a form or group box to navigate the child controls, and you can use the Components property of the form to navigate all the owned components, regardless of their parent.

Using the Components property we can always access each component of a form. If you need access to a specific component, however, instead of comparing each name with the name of the component you are looking for, you can let Delphi do this work, by using the FindComponent method of the form.

Properties Related to Component Size and Position

Other important properties, common to all controls, are those related to their size and position. The position of a component is determined by its Left and Top properties, and its size (available only for controls) is determined by the Height and Width properties. All components have a position because when you reopen an existing form at design-time, you want to be able to see the icons for the non-visual components exactly in the same position where you've placed them.

An important feature of the position of a component is that, like any other coordinate in Windows, it always relates to the client area of its parent component (which is the component indicated by its Parent property). For a form, the client area is the surface included within its borders (but without the borders themselves). It would have been messy to work in screen coordinates, although there are some ready-to-use methods that convert the coordinates between the form and the screen and vice versa.

Note, however, that the coordinates of a control might also be relative to a panel and another *container* component. If you place a panel in a form, and a button in a panel, the coordinates of the button relate to the panel, and not to the form containing the panel. In fact, in this case, the parent component of the button is the panel.

Activation and Visibility Properties

There are two basic properties you can use to let the user activate or hide a component. The simplest is the `Enabled` property. When a component is disabled (when `Enabled` is set to `False`), there is usually some visual hint to specify this state to the user. At design-time, the "disabled" property does not always have an effect, but at run-time, disabled components are generally grayed, as you can see in Figure 7.8. If you want to see how the disabled elements behave, you can run the program used to generate the figure. It is named Disabled and is available on the companion disk.

FIGURE 7.8

The user interface of some common controls when they are enabled (on the left) and disabled (on the right).

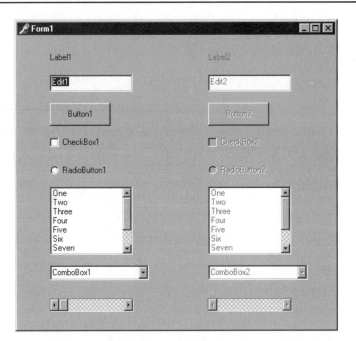

TIP

To disable all of the controls in the right column, you can simply select all of them (by Shift-clicking on them, or by dragging a rectangle around them) and toggle the `Enabled` property of all the selected components at once.

For a more radical approach, you can completely hide a component, either by using the corresponding Hide method or by setting its Visible property to False. Notice, however, that reading the status of the Visible property does not tell you if the control is actually visible. In fact, if the container of a control is hidden, even if the control is set to Visible, you cannot see it. For this reason, there is another property, Showing, which is a run-time and read-only property. You can read the value of Showing to know if the control is really visible to the user; that is, if it is visible, its parent control is visible, the parent control of the parent control is visible, and so on.

The Customizable Tag Property

The Tag property is a strange one, because it has no effect at all. It is merely an extra memory location, present in each component class, where you can store custom values. The kind of information stored and the way it is used are completely up to you.

It is often useful to have an extra memory location to attach information to a component without needing to define your component class. Technically, the Tag property stores a long integer so that, for example, you can store the entry number of an array or list that corresponds to an object. Using typecasting, you can store in the Tag property a pointer, an object, or anything else that is four bytes wide. This allows a programmer to associate virtually anything with a component using its tag.

> **NOTE**
>
> Experienced Windows programmers might find a relationship between the Tag property of Delphi components and the extra bytes attached to windows. Both elements can be used to associate some user-defined information with a predefined structure, but the similarity ends quickly. Using Delphi's Tag property is much easier than using extra bytes, and is also a lot faster than digging up the Windows extra bytes.

We'll see examples of the use of this property in several examples in future chapters, including the Numbers example in Chapter 8, the RichNot2, BitMenu, and ODMenu examples in Chapter 9, and some more examples in Chapter 25.

The User Interface: Color and Font

Two properties often used to customize the user interface of a component are Color and Font. There are several properties related to the color. The Color property itself usually refers to the background color of the component. Also, there is a Color property for fonts and many other graphic elements. Many components also have a ParentColor and a ParentFont property, indicating whether the control should use the same font and color of their parent component, usually the form. You can use these properties to change the font of each control on a form by setting only the Font property of the form itself.

When you set a font, either by entering values for the attributes of the property in the Object Inspector or by using the standard font selection dialog box, you can choose one of the fonts installed in the system. The fact that Delphi allows you to use all the fonts installed on your system has both advantages and drawbacks. The main advantage is that if you have a number of nice fonts installed, your program can use any of them. The drawback is that if you distribute your application, these fonts might not be available on your users' computers.

If your program uses a font that your user doesn't have, Windows will select some other font to use in its place. A program's carefully formatted output can be ruined by the font substitution. For this reason, you should probably rely only on Windows' standard fonts (such as MS Sans Serif, System, Arial, Times New Roman, and so on). The alternative is to ship some fonts with your application, if the font's user license allows it.

There are a number of ways to set the value of a color. The type of this property is TColor. For properties of this type, you can choose a value from a series of predefined name constants or enter a value directly. These are the possible values:

clAqua	clBlack	clBlue	clDkGray
clFuchsia	clGray	clGreen	clLime
clLtGray	clMaroon	clNavy	clOlive
clPurple	clRed	clSilver	clTeal
clWhite	clYellow		

As a better alternative, you can use one of the colors used by Windows for system elements, such as the background of a window, a highlighted menu, the active caption, and so on. You can see a list of these values, along with a short description, in Table 7.2.

TABLE 7.2   Colors Used by Windows for System Elements

Color Constant	Windows Color for...
cl3DdkShadow	The 3D dark shadow effect
cl3Dlight	The 3D light effect
clActiveBorder	The border of the active window
clActiveCaption	The title bar of the active window
clAppWorkSpace	The application work space
clBackground	The Windows background
clBtnFace	The face of the buttons
clBtnHighlight	The highlighting of a button
clBtnShadow	The shadow cast by a button
clBtnText	Text on a button
clCaptionText	The text on the title bar of the active window
clGrayText	The text that is dimmed
clHighlight	The background of the selected text
clHightlightText	The selected text
clInactiveBorder	The border of inactive windows
clInactiveCaption	The title bar of inactive windows
clInactiveCaptionText	The text on the title bar of an inactive window
clInfoBk	The background color of the hint window
clInfoText	Text of the hint window
clMenu	The background of menus
clMenuText	The text of menus items
clScrollBar	The scroll bars
clWindow	The background of a window
clWindowFrame	The frame of a window
clWindowText	The text of a window

Another option is to specify a TColor as a number (a four-byte hexadecimal value) instead of using a predefined value. If you use this approach, you should know that the low three bytes of this number represent RGB color intensities for blue, green, and red, respectively. For example, the value $00FF0000 corresponds to a pure blue color, the value $0000FF00 to green, the value $000000FF to red, the value $00000000 to black, and the value $00FFFFFF to white. Specifying intermediate values, you can obtain any of the 16 million possible colors.

Instead of using these hexadecimal values directly, I suggest that you use the RGB function, which has three parameters ranging from 0 to 255, the first for the amount of red, the second for the amount of green, and the last for the amount of blue. Using the RGB function makes programs generally more readable than using a single hexadecimal constant.

> **NOTE**
>
> RGB is *almost* a Windows API function. It is defined by the Windows-related units and not by Delphi units, but a similar function does not exist in the Windows API. In C, there is a macro that has the same name and effect, so this is a welcome addition to the Pascal interface to Windows.

The highest-order byte of the TColor type is used to indicate which palette should be searched for the closest matching color, but this is far too advanced a topic to discuss here. The same byte is also used by sophisticated imaging programs to carry transparency information for each display element on the screen. Regarding palettes and color matching, notice that Windows sometimes replaces an arbitrary color with the closest available solid color, at least in video modes that use a palette. This is always the case with fonts, lines, and so on. At other times, Windows uses a dithering technique to mimic the requested color by drawing a tight pattern of pixels with the available colors. In 16-color adapters (VGA), but also at higher resolutions, you often end up seeing confused patterns of pixels of different colors, and not the color you had in mind.

Common VCL Methods

Component methods are just like any other methods. There are procedures and functions you can call to perform the corresponding action. As mentioned earlier, you can often use methods to accomplish the same effect as reading or writing a property. Usually, the code is easier to read and to understand when you use properties. However, not all methods have corresponding properties. Most of them are procedures, which actually execute an action, instead of reading or writing a value. Again, there are some methods available in all of the components, other methods that are shared only by controls (visual components), and so on. Table 7.3 lists some common component methods. We'll see examples of using most of these methods throughout the book.

TABLE 7.3   Some Methods Available for Most VCL Components

Method	Available For	Description
BeginDrag	All controls	Starts manual dragging.
BringToFront	All controls	Puts the control in front of all others.
CanFocus	All controls	Determines whether the control can receive the focus.
ClientToScreen	All controls	Translates client coordinates into screen coordinates.
ContainsControl	All controls	Determines whether a certain control is contained by the current one.
Create	All components	Creates a new instance (constructor).
Destroy	All components	Destroys the instance (destructor). You should actually call Free.
Dragging	All controls	Indicates whether the controls are being dragged.
EndDrag	All controls	Manually terminates dragging.
FindComponent	All components	Returns the component in the Components array property having a given name (we've just used it in the NameProp example).
Focused	All windowed controls	Determines whether the control has the focus.
Free	All components	Deletes the object from memory (forms should use the Release method).
GetTextBuf	All controls	Retrieves the text (or caption) of the control.
GetTextLen	All controls	Returns the length of the text (or caption) of the control.
HandleAllocated	All controls	Returns True if a system handle has been allocated for the control.

TABLE 7.3   Some Methods Available for Most VCL Components (Continued)

Method	Available For	Description
HandleNeeded	All controls	Allocates a corresponding system handle if one doesn't already exist.
Hide	All controls	Makes the control invisible (the same as setting the Visible property to False).
InsertComponent	All components	Adds a new element to the list of owned components.
InsertControl	All controls	Adds a new element to the list of controls that are the children of the current one.
Invalidate	All controls	Forces a repaint of the control.
RemoveComponent	All components	Removes a component from the Components list.
ScaleBy	All controls	Scales the control by a given percentage.
ScreenToClient	All controls	Translates screen coordinates into client coordinates.
ScrollBy	All controls	Scrolls the contents of the control.
SendToBack	All controls	Puts the control behind all the others.
SetBounds	All controls	Changes the position and size of the control (faster than accessing the related properties one by one).
SetFocus	All controls	Gives the input focus to the control.
SetTextBuf	All controls	Sets the text (or caption) of the control.
Show	All controls	Makes the control visible (the same as setting the Visible property to True).
Update	All controls	Immediately repaints the control, if there are pending painting requests.

Common VCL Events

Just as there is a set of properties common to all components, there are some events that are available for all of them. Table 7.4 provides short descriptions of these events. Again, this table is meant only as a starting point. We'll see examples using most of these events throughout the book.

TABLE 7.4   Some Events Available for Most Components

Event	Available For	Description
OnChange	Many components	Occurs when the object or its data change.
OnClick	Most controls	Occurs when the left mouse button is clicked over the component.
OnDblClick	Many controls	Occurs when the user double-clicks with the mouse over the component.
OnDragDrop	Most controls	Occurs when a dragging operation terminates over the component; it is sent by the component that *received* the dragging operation.
OnDragOver	Most controls	Occurs when the user drags the mouse over the component.
OnEndDrag	Most controls	Occurs when the dragging terminates; it is sent by the component that *started* the dragging operation.
OnEnter	All windowed controls	Occurs when the component is activated; that is, the component receives the focus.
OnExit	All windowed controls	Occurs when the component loses the focus.
OnKeyDown	Some windowed controls	Occurs when the user presses a key on the keyboard; it is sent to the component with the input focus.
OnKeyPress	Some windowed controls	Occurs when the user presses a key; it is sent to the component with the input focus.
OnKeyUp	Some windowed controls	Occurs when the user releases a key; it is sent to the component with the input focus.
OnMouseDown	Most controls	Occurs when the user presses one of the mouse buttons; it is sent to the component under the mouse cursor.
OnMouseMove	Most controls	Occurs when the user moves the mouse over a component; it is sent to the component under the mouse cursor.
OnMouseUp	Most controls	Occurs when the user releases one of the mouse buttons; it is sent to the component under the mouse cursor.
OnStartDrag	Most controls	Occurs when the user starts dragging; it is sent to the component *originating* the dragging operation.

Using Delphi Collections

Among the various noncomponent classes, an important group is *collections*. There are basically three different collection classes in Delphi:

- TList defines a list of pointers, which can be used to store objects of any class. A TList is far more flexible than an array, because it can be dynamically expanded at run-time.

- TStrings is an abstract class to represent all forms of string lists, regardless of their storage implementations. This class defines an abstract list of strings. For this reason, TStrings objects are used only as properties of components capable of storing the strings themselves, such as a list box.

- TStringList, a subclass of TStrings, defines a list of strings with their own storage. You can use this class to define your own lists of strings in a program.

- TCollection defines a homogeneous list of objects, which are owned by the collection class. The objects in the collection must be descendants of the TCollectionItem class. If you need a collection storing specific objects, you have to create both a subclass of TCollection and a subclass of TCollectionItem.

Borland has chosen to name some of these classes *lists*, and I'll follow the same convention; but they are actually dynamic arrays, not the traditional linked lists. All these lists have a number of methods and properties. You can operate on lists using the array notation ("[" and "]"), both to read and to change elements. Other properties include the Count property, as well as typical access methods, such as Add, Insert, Delete, Remove, and search methods (for example, IndexOf).

Notice that TStringList and TStrings objects have both a list of strings and a list of objects associated with the strings. This opens up a number of different uses for these classes. For example, you can use them for dictionaries of associated objects or to store bitmaps or other elements to be used in a list box.

> **NOTE**
>
> The TListbox component actually uses a TStringList object when it needs to store strings while its window handle is invalid; it uses a TStrings object when it finally associates with a Windows list box control, which stores its own strings.

The two classes of lists of strings also have some ready-to-use methods to store or load their contents to or from a text file, `SaveToFile` and `LoadFromFile`. To iterate on a list, you can use a simple `for` loop based on its index, as if it were an array (or, as an alternative, use the `List` array property).

Using Lists of Objects and Data

We can write an example focusing on the use of the generic `TList` class. When you need a list of any kind of data, you can generally declare a `TList` object, fill it with the data, and then access the data while casting it to the proper type. The ListDemo example demonstrates just this. It also shows the pitfalls of this approach. Its form has two private variables, holding two lists:

```
private
  ListNum, ListDate: TList;
```

These list objects are created when the form itself is created:

```
procedure TForm1.FormCreate(Sender: TObject);
begin
  Randomize;
  ListNum := TList.Create;
  ListDate := TList.Create;
end;
```

Two buttons of the form add a random number and a random date to the respective lists (of course, I've included the unit containing the date class in the project):

```
procedure TForm1.ButtonAddNumClick(Sender: TObject);
begin
  ListNum.Add (Pointer (Random (10000)));
end;
```

```
procedure TForm1.ButtonAddDateClick(Sender: TObject);
begin
  ListDate.Add (TDate.Init (1 + Random (12),
    1 + Random (31), 1900 + Random (200)));
end;
```

By the way, notice that when we use the `TDate` component, the `Init` call above might raise an exception when the values correspond to an invalid date. When you extract the items from the list, you have to cast them back to the proper type, as in the following two methods, connected with the two List buttons (you can see the effect of the second one in Figure 7.9):

```
procedure TForm1.ButtonListNumClick(Sender: TObject);
var
  I: Integer;
begin
  ListBox1.Clear;
  for I := 0 to ListNum.Count - 1 do
    Listbox1.Items.Add (IntToStr (Integer (ListNum [I])));
end;

procedure TForm1.ButtonListDateClick(Sender: TObject);
var
  I: Integer;
begin
  ListBox1.Clear;
  for I := 0 to ListDate.Count - 1 do
    Listbox1.Items.Add ((
      TObject(ListDate [I]) as TDate).GetText);
end;
```

FIGURE 7.9

The list of dates shown by the ListDemo example

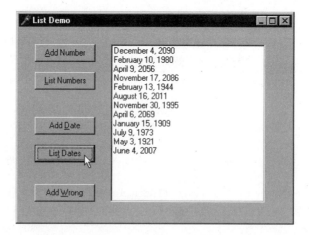

At the end of the code above, to be able to do an as downcast, I first need to hard-cast the pointer returned by the TList into a TObject reference. This kind of expression can result in an invalid typecast exception, or generate a memory error when the pointer is not a reference to an object.

To demonstrate that things can indeed go wrong, I've added one more button, which adds a TButton object to both lists, actually it adds the button you've just pressed:

```
procedure TForm1.ButtonWrongClick(Sender: TObject);
begin
  // add a button to both lists
  ListNum.Add (Sender);
  ListDate.Add (Sender);
end;
```

If you press this button and then update one of the lists, you'll get an error. The list of dates raises an exception, while the list of numbers considers the object address as if it were a number, with the result you can see in Figure 7.10.

> **WARNING**
>
> When you destroy a list of objects, you should remember to destroy all of the objects of the list first. I've accomplished this in the FormDestroy method of the form. List objects are not automatically maintained and destroyed by Delphi.

FIGURE 7.10

If you add an object to the list of numbers of the ListDemo example, you actually get its address.

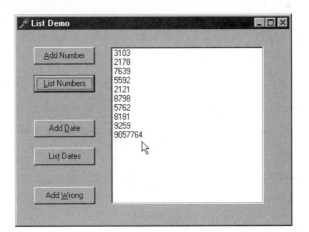

Studying the VCL
Source Code

In this chapter, we have barely scratched the surface of the VCL. To learn more about the library classes—the components—just go on reading the book. If you really want to delve into the details and study the implementation of the components, there is another path to explore: the VCL source code, included in the Professional and Client/Server Suite versions of Delphi.

These versions of Delphi come with the source code of the run-time library (RTL) and the VCL library. You can study the VCL source code if you want a detailed understanding of what a component does. However, do not take this approach in learning how to *use* components. Looking at the source code is useful for learning how to write new components and how to extend existing ones. Before you attempt this, you should be fluent in Delphi and Windows programming.

If you want to spend some time browsing through Delphi source code, consider using the Object Browser or the integrated debugger, instead of loading the files in an editor. To let these tools see the VCL source code, you need to add its path (usually C:\Program Files\Borland\Delphi 3.0\Source\VCL) to the Search Path option in the Directories page of the Project Options dialog box. When you rebuild a project after setting this option, the VCL source code will be compiled, and full information about it will be available in the Object Browser. To make this work you also need to have debug information turned on and good amount of RAM on the computer.

The main advantage of compiling the VCL along with a project is that you can use the integrated debugger to trace the execution both through your code and the VCL source code. Using the Object Browser, you can see where in the source code each class is defined and referenced, and open the editor on the proper file (and the right line) with a mouse-click. I will discuss these tools in more detail in Chapter 26.

What's Next

As we have seen in this chapter, Delphi includes a full-scale class library that is just as complete as Microsoft's MFC C++ class library. Delphi's VCL, of course, is much more component-oriented, and its classes offer a higher-level abstraction over the Windows API than the C++ libraries usually do.

To use components you only need a clear understanding of the terminal nodes of the VCL hierarchy; that is, the components that show up in the Components Palette plus a few others. You really don't need a deeper knowledge of the VCL internals to use components; this knowledge is only necessary to write new components or modify existing ones.

This chapter ends Part I of the book, which covered the foundations of Delphi programming. Part II is fully devoted to examples of the use of the various components. We'll start in Chapter 8 with traditional Windows controls, then look at menus in Chapter 9, the TForm class and graphical output in Chapter 10, and then graphical components, toolbars, status bars, dialog boxes, MDI applications, and finally database-related components in later chapters.

PART II

Using Components

CHAPTER
EIGHT

8

A Tour of the Basic Components

- Clicking a button or another component

- Adding colored text to a form

- Dragging from one component to another

- Accepting input from the user

- Creating a simple editor

- Making a choice with radio buttons and list boxes

- Allowing multiple selections

- Choosing a value in a range

Now that you've been introduced to the Delphi environment and have seen an overview of the Object Pascal language and the Visual Component Library, we are ready to delve into the central part of the book: the use of components. This is really what Delphi is about. Visual programming using components is the key feature of this development environment.

The system comes with a number of ready-to-use components. I will not describe every component in detail, examining each of its properties and methods. If you need this information, you can find it easily in the Help system. The aim of Part II of this book is to show you how to use some of the features offered by the Delphi predefined components to build applications. In fact, this chapter and those following will be based heavily on sample programs. These examples tend to be quite simple—although I've tried to make them meaningful—in order to focus on only a couple of features at a time.

I'll start by focusing on a number of basic components, such as buttons, labels, list boxes, edit fields, and other related controls. Some of the components discussed in this chapter are present in the Standard page of the Delphi Components palette; others are in different pages. I'm not going to describe all the components of the Standard page, either. My approach will be to discuss, in each chapter, logically related components, ignoring the order suggested by the pages of the Components palette.

Windows' Own Components

You might have asked yourself where the idea of using components for Windows programming came from. The answer is simple: Windows itself has some components, usually called controls. A *control* is technically a predefined window with a specific behavior, some properties, and some methods (although traditional C language code used to access the predefined components in Windows by sending and receiving messages). These controls were the first step in the direction of component development. The second step was probably Visual Basic controls, and the third step is Delphi components.

NOTE

Actually Microsoft's third step is its ActiveX controls (an extension of the older OCX technology), the natural successor of VBX controls. In Delphi you can use both ActiveX and native components, but if you look at the technology, Delphi components are really ahead of the ActiveX controls. It is enough to say that Delphi components use OOP to its full extent, while ActiveX controls do not fully implement the concept of inheritance. We have already seen a couple of simple examples, but I'll focus on the details of using and writing ActiveX controls in Chapter 23.

Windows 3.1 has six kinds of predefined controls, generally used inside dialog boxes. They are buttons (push buttons, check boxes, and radio buttons), static labels, edit fields, list boxes, combo boxes, and scroll bars. Windows 95 adds a number of new predefined components, such as the list view, the status bar, the spin button, the progress bar, the tab control, and many others. These controls were already used by programmers, who had to re-implement them each time. Windows 95 developers can use the standard common controls provided by the system, and Delphi 3 developers have the advantage of having corresponding easy-to-use components.

NEW

Delphi 3 includes several more common controls than Delphi 2 did. As we'll see later on, there is now an Animate component and a Toolbar component. There are also new components for common controls Microsoft has added to Windows after the release of Windows 95, like the CoolBar and the DateTimePicker components.

The standard system controls are the basic components of each Windows application, regardless of the programming language used to write it, and are very well known by every Windows user. Delphi literally wraps these Windows predefined controls in some of its basic components—including those discussed in this chapter.

Clicking a Button

In the first chapter of this book, we built small applications based on a button. Clicking on that button caused a "*Hello*" message to appear on the screen. The only other operation that program performed was moving the button so that it always appeared in the middle of the form. Since then we've seen other examples that used buttons as a way to perform a given action (using their OnClick event).

Now we are going to build another form with several buttons and change some of their properties at run-time; in this example, clicking a button will usually change a property of another button. To build the Buttons program, I suggest you follow the instructions closely at first and then make any changes you want. Of course, you can read the description in the book and then work on the source files on the companion CD, if you prefer.

The Buttons Example

First, open a new project and give it a name by saving it to disk. I've given the name BUTTONF.PAS to the unit describing the form and the name BUTTONS.DPR to the project. Now you can create a number of buttons, let's say six.

> **TIP**
>
> Instead of selecting the component, dragging it to the form, and then selecting it again to repeat the operation, you can take a shortcut. Simply select the component by clicking on the Components palette while holding down Shift. The component will remain selected, as indicated by a little border around it. Now you can create a number of instances of that component.

Even if you use the grid behind the form, you might need to use the Edit ➤ Align command to arrange the buttons properly. Remember that to select all six buttons at a time, you can either drag a rectangle around them or select them in turn, holding down the Shift key. In this case, it's probably better to select a column of three buttons at a time and arrange them as shown in Figure 8.1.

Now that we have a form with six buttons, we can start to set their properties. First of all, we can give the form a name (ButtonsForm) and a caption (*Buttons*). The next step is to set the text, or Caption property, of each button. Usually, a button's Caption describes the action performed when a user clicks on it. We want to follow this rule, adding the number of the button at the beginning of each caption. So if

FIGURE 8.1

The six aligned buttons
used to build the example.

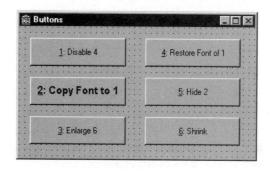

the first button disables button number four (which is the one on the same row), we can name it *1: Disable 4*. Following the same rule, we can create captions for the other buttons.

For a summary of the properties of the components of this form, you can refer to its textual description:

```
object ButtonsForm: TButtonsForm
  Caption = 'Buttons'
  object Button1: TButton
    Caption = '&1: Disable 4'
    OnClick = Button1Click
  end
  object Button2: TButton
    Caption = '&2: Copy Font to 1'
    Font.Color = clBlack
    Font.Height = -15
    Font.Name = 'Arial'
    Font.Style = [fsBold]
    ParentFont = False
    OnClick = Button2Click
  end
  object Button3: TButton
    Caption = '&3: Enlarge 6'
    OnClick = Button3Click
  end
  object Button4: TButton
    Caption = '&4: Restore Font of 1'
    OnClick = Button4Click
  end
  object Button5: TButton
    Caption = '&5: Hide 2'
```

```
      OnClick = Button5Click
    end
    object Button6: TButton
      Caption = '&6: Shrink'
      OnClick = Button6Click
    end
  end
```

Notice that every button has an underlined shortcut key, in this case the number of the button. Simply by placing an ampersand (&) character in front of each caption, as in '*&1: Disable 4*', we can create buttons that can be used with the keyboard. Just press a number below 7, and one of the buttons will be selected, although you won't see it pressed and released.

The final step, of course, is to write the code to provide the desired behavior. We want to handle the OnClick event of each button. The easiest code is that of Button2 and Button4. When you press Button2, the program copies the font of this button (which is different from the standard font of the other buttons) to Button1, and then disables itself:

```
procedure TButtonsForm.Button2Click(Sender: TObject);
begin
  Button1.Font := Button2.Font;
  Button2.Enabled := False;
end;
```

Pressing Button4 restores the original font of the button. Instead of copying the font directly, we can restore the font of the form, using the ParentFont property of the button. The event also enables Button2, so that it can be used again to change the font of Button1:

```
procedure TButtonsForm.Button4Click(Sender: TObject);
begin
  Button1.ParentFont := True;
  Button2.Enabled := True;
end;
```

To implement the Disable and Hide operations of Button1 and Button5, we might use a Boolean variable to store the current status. As an alternative, we can decide which operation to perform while checking the current status of the button—the status of the Enabled property. The two methods use two different approaches, as you can see in the following code:

```
procedure TButtonsForm.Button1Click(Sender: TObject);
begin
  if not Button4.Enabled then
  begin
    Button4.Enabled := True;
    Button1.Caption := '&1: Disable 4';
  end
  else
  begin
    Button4.Enabled := False;
    Button1.Caption := '&1: Enable 4';
  end;
end;

procedure TButtonsForm.Button5Click(Sender: TObject);
begin
  Button2.Visible := not Button2.Visible;
  if Button2.Visible then
    Button5.Caption := '&5: Hide 2'
  else
    Button5.Caption := '&5: Show 2';
end;
```

You can see the results of this code in Figure 8.2. The last two buttons have *unconstrained* code. This means that you can shrink Button6 so much that it will eventually disappear completely:

```
procedure TButtonsForm.Button3Click(Sender: TObject);
begin
  Button6.Height := Button6.Height + 3;
  Button6.Width := Button6.Width + 3;
end;

procedure TButtonsForm.Button6Click(Sender: TObject);
begin
  Button6.Height := Button6.Height - 3;
  Button6.Width := Button6.Width - 3;
end;
```

It would have been quite easy, in any case, to check the current size of the button and prevent its reduction or enlargement by more than a certain value.

FIGURE 8.2

In the form of the Buttons example, you can hide or disable some buttons, or reduce the size of one of them.

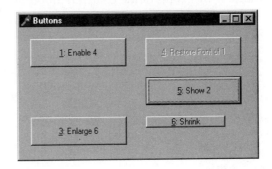

Clicking the Mouse Button

Up to now we have based the examples on the OnClick event of buttons. Almost every component has a similar click event. But what exactly is a click? And how is it related to other events, such as OnMouseDown and OnMouseUp?

First, consider the click. At first sight you might think that to generate a click, a user has to press and release the left mouse button on the control. This is certainly true, but the situation is more complex. When the user clicks the left mouse button on a button component, the component is graphically pressed, too. However, if the user moves the cursor (holding down the left mouse button) outside the button surface, this button will be released. If the user now releases the left mouse button outside the button area, no effect—no click—takes place. On the other hand, if the user places the cursor back on the button, it will be *pressed* again, and when the mouse button is released, the click will occur. If this is not clear, experiment with a button; any button in any Windows application will do.

Now to the second question. In Windows, the behavior just described is typical of buttons, although Delphi has extended it to most components, as well as to forms. In any case, the system generates more basic events—one each time a mouse button is pressed, and another each time a button is released. In Delphi, these events are called OnMouseDown and OnMouseUp. Since the mouse has more than one button, these same events are generated when the user presses any mouse button.

You might want different actions to occur, depending on the mouse button. For this reason, these event handlers include a parameter indicating which button was pressed. These methods also include another parameter, indicating whether some special key (such as Shift or Ctrl) has been pressed and, finally, two more values indicating the x and y positions where the action took place. This is the method corresponding to this event for a form:

```
procedure TForm1.FormMouseDown(
    Sender: TObject; Button: TMouseButton;
    Shift: TShiftState; X, Y: Integer);
```

Most of the time, we do not need such a detailed view, and handling the mouse-click event is probably more appropriate. In Chapter 10, I'll show you a more detailed example of mouse input.

Adding Colored Text to a Form

Now that you have played with buttons for a while, it's time to move to a new component, labels. Labels are just text, or comments, written in a form. Usually, the user doesn't interact with a label at all—or at least not directly. It doesn't make much sense to click on a label (although in Delphi this is technically possible). Keep in mind, however, that not all of the text you see in a form corresponds to a label. A form (and any other component) can simply output text on its surface, for example using the TextOut method.

We use labels to provide descriptions of other components, particularly edit fields and list or combo boxes, because they have no title. If you open a dialog box in any Windows application, you'll probably see some text. These are *static controls* (in Windows terms) or *labels* (in Delphi terms).

NEW

Windows implements labels as windows of the static class. Delphi, instead, implements labels as non-windowed, graphical components. This is very important since it allows you to speed up form creation and save some Windows resources. However, Delphi 3 also includes a new component that corresponds to the Windows label, the StaticText component. This component has similar properties and the same events, and Borland seems to have added it mainly for ActiveX support. We will use this component in the next example.

Besides using labels for descriptions, we can use instances of this component to improve and add some color to the user interface of our application. This is what we are going to do in the next example, LabelCo. The basic idea of this application is to test a couple of properties of the label component at run-time. Specifically, we want to alter the background color of the label, the color of its font, and the alignment of the text.

The LabelCo Example

The first thing to do is to place a big label in the form and enter some text. Write something long. I suggest you set the WordWrap property to True, to have several lines of text, and the AutoSize property to False, to allow the label to be resized freely. It might also be a good idea to select a large font, to choose a color for the font, and to select a color for the label itself.

To change the font color, background color, and alignment properties of the label at run-time, we can use buttons. Instead of placing these buttons directly on the form, we can place a Panel component in the form, and then place the five buttons over (or actually inside) the panel. We need two to change the colors and three more to select the alignment—left, center, or right. Placing the buttons inside the panel, this last control will become the Parent component of the buttons: the coordinates of the buttons will be relative to the panel, so that moving the panel will move the buttons, hiding the Panel will hide the buttons, and so on.

NOTE　We discussed the difference between the Parent and the Owner properties of a component in the last chapter, and you can refer to that discussion if this difference is not yet clear to you.

Making the label and the panel child components of the form allows us to align them (something you cannot do with buttons). Simply set the Align property of the Panel to alTop, and the Align property of the Label to alClient, and the two components will take up the full client area of the form. What's interesting is that when we resize the form, the two components will adjust their size and position correspondingly. Notice, by the way, that the StaticText component has no Align property.

The last component we have to place on the form is a ColorDialog component (you can find it in the Dialogs page of the Components palette). This component invokes the standard Windows Color dialog box. The resulting form is shown in Figure 8.3, and in the following listing:

```
object ColorTextForm: TColorTextForm
  Caption = 'Change Color and Alignment'
  object Label1: TLabel
    Align = alClient
    Alignment = taCenter
    Caption = 'Push the buttons...' // omitted
    Color = clYellow
    Font.Color = clNavy
    Font.Height = -40
    Font.Name = 'Arial'
    WordWrap = True
  end
  object Panel1: TPanel
    Align = alTop
    object BtnFontColor: TButton...
    object BtnBackColor: TButton...
    object BtnLeft: TButton...
    object BtnCenter: TButton...
    object BtnRight: TButton...
  end
  object ColorDialog1: TColorDialog...
end
```

FIGURE 8.3

The form of the colored label example at run-time.

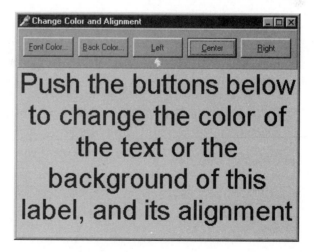

343

NOTE   The two buttons used to change the color will display a dialog box, instead of performing an action directly. For this reason at the end of their Caption there is an ellipsis (...), which is the standard Windows convention for button and menu items to indicate the presence of a dialog box.

Now it's time to write some code. The click methods for the three alignment buttons are very simple. The program has to change the alignment of the label, as in:

```
procedure TColorTextForm.BtnLeftClick(Sender: TObject);
begin
  Label1.Alignment := taLeftJustify;
end;
```

The other two methods should use the values taCenter and taRightJustify instead of taLeftJustify. You can find the names of these three choices in the Alignment property of the label, in the Object Inspector.

Writing code to change the color is a little more complex. In fact, we can provide a new value for the color, maybe choosing it from a list with a series of possible values. We might solve this problem, for example, by declaring an array of colors, entering a number of values, and then selecting a different element of the array each time. However, a more professional solution needs even less code: using the Windows standard dialog box to select a color.

The Standard Color Dialog Box

To use the standard Color dialog box, move to the Dialogs page of the Delphi Components palette, select the ColorDialog component, and place it anywhere on the form. The position has no effect, since at run-time this component is not visible inside the form. (There is a more detailed presentation of these standard dialog boxes in Chapter 13, although I'll use them often before.) Now we can use the component, writing the following code:

```
procedure TColorTextForm.BtnFontColorClick(Sender: TObject);
begin
  ColorDialog1.Color := Label1.Font.Color;
```

```
if ColorDialog1.Execute then
    Label1.Font.Color := ColorDialog1.Color;
end;
```

The three lines in the body of the procedure have the following meanings: with the first, we select the background color of the label as the initial color displayed by the dialog box; with the second, we run the dialog box; with the third, the color selected by the user in the dialog box is copied back to the label. We do this last operation only if the user closes the dialog box by pressing the OK button (in which case the Execute method returns True). If the user presses the Cancel button (and Execute returns False), we skip this last statement. To change the color of the label's text, we write similar code, referring this time to the Label1.Font .Color property. (The complete source code for the form LabelCo example is on the CD in the file LABELF.PAS.)

You can see the Color dialog box in action in Figure 8.4. This dialog box can also be expanded by clicking on the Define Custom Colors button.

FIGURE 8.4

The dialog box used to select the color of the label and its text (in this case, the user is changing the color of the text).

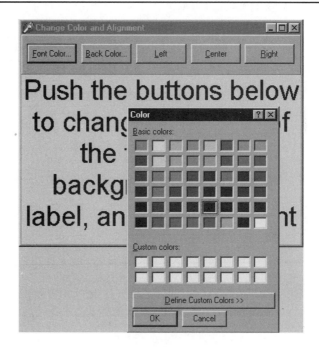

345

Dragging from One Component to Another

Before we try out other Delphi components, it's helpful to examine a particular technique: *dragging*. The dragging operation is quite simple and is increasingly common in Windows. In Windows 95 you can drag files and programs from a folder to another, drop them on the desktop, or perform similar dragging operations on files and folders with the Windows Explorer. You usually perform this operation by pressing the mouse button on one component (or window) and releasing it on another component (or window). When this operation occurs, you can provide some code, usually for copying a property, a value, or something else to the destination component.

As an example, consider the form in Figure 8.5. There are four color labels, with the name of each color as text, and a destination label, with some descriptive text. Actually the destination label is implemented with a StaticText component. This component has a special value for the Border property, sbsSunken, with a *lowered* effect. A similar capability is not available for plain labels. The aim of this example, named Dragging, is to be able to drag the color from one of the labels on the left to the static text, changing its color accordingly. The components have very simple properties, as the following textual description of the form summarizes:

```
object DraggingForm: TDraggingForm
  Caption = 'Dragging'
  Font.Color = clBlack
  Font.Height = -16
  Font.Name = 'Arial'
  Font.Style = [fsBold]
  object LabelRed: TLabel
    Alignment = taCenter
    AutoSize = False
    Caption = 'Red'
    Color = clRed
    DragMode = dmAutomatic
  end
  object LabelAqua: TLabel...
  object LabelGreen: TLabel...
  object LabelYellow: TLabel...
  object StaticTarget: TStaticText
    Alignment = taCenter
```

```
        AutoSize = False
        BorderStyle = sbsSunken
        Caption = 'Drag colors here to change the color'
        Font.Height = -32
        OnDragDrop = StaticTargetDragDrop
        OnDragOver = StaticTargetDragOver
    end
end
```

FIGURE 8.5

The form of the Dragging example.

After preparing the labels by supplying the proper values for the names and caption, as well as a corresponding color, you have to enable dragging. You can do this by selecting the value dmAutomatic for the DragMode property of the four labels on the left and responding to a couple of events in the destination label.

NOTE

As an alternative to the automatic dragging mode, you might choose the manual dragging mode. This is based on the use of the BeginDrag and EndDrag methods. This technique will be shown in the Nodes example in Chapter 11. Other examples in the book will show how to handle dragging manually, simply by providing a handler for events related to moving the mouse and pressing and releasing mouse buttons.

The Code for the Dragging Example

The first event I want to consider is OnDragOver, which is called each time you are dragging and move the cursor over a component. This event indicates that the component accepts dragging. Usually, the event takes place after a determination of whether the Source component (the one that originated the dragging operation) is of a specific type:

```
procedure TDraggingForm.StaticTargetDragOver(
  Sender, Source: TObject; X, Y: Integer;
  State: TDragState; var Accept: Boolean);
begin
  Accept := Source is TLabel;
end;
```

This code accepts the dragging operation, activating the corresponding cursor, only if the Source object is really a Label component. Notice the use of the is dynamic type checking operator.

The second method we have to write corresponds to the OnDragDrop event:

```
procedure TDraggingForm.StaticTargetDragDrop(
  Sender, Source: TObject;  X, Y: Integer);
begin
  StaticTarget.Color := (Source as TLabel).Color;
end;
```

To read the value of the Color property from the Source object, we need to cast this object to the proper data type, in this case TLabel. We have to perform a type conversion—technically speaking, a type downcast (a typecast from a base class to a derived class, down through the hierarchy). As discussed in Chapter 5, a type downcast is not always safe. In fact, the idea behind this cast is that we receive the parameter Source of type TObject, which is really a label, and want to use it as a TLabel object, where TLabel is a class derived fromTObject. However, in general, we face the risk of down-casting to TLabel an object that wasn't originally a label but, say, a button. When we start using the button as a label, we might have run-time errors.

In any case, when we use the as typecast, a type check is performed. Had the type of the Source object not been TLabel, an exception would have been raised. In this particular case, however, we haven't much to worry about. In fact, the OnDragDrop event is received only when the Accept parameter of the OnDragOver method is set to True, and we make this only if the Source object really is a TLabel.

Accepting Input from the User

We have seen a number of ways a user can interact with the application we write using a mouse: mouse clicks, mouse dragging, and so on. What about the keyboard? We know that the user can use the keyboard instead of the mouse to select a button by pressing the key corresponding to the underlined letter of the caption (if any).

Aside from some particular cases, Windows can handle keyboard input directly. Defining handlers for keyboard-related events isn't a common operation, anyway. In fact, the system provides ready-to-use controls to build edit fields and a simple text editor. Delphi has several slightly different components in this area: Edit, Mask-Edit, Memo, RichText, and the related data-aware controls. The two basic components are Edit and Memo.

An Edit component allows a single line of text and has some specific properties, such as one that allows only a limited number of characters or one that shows a special password character instead of the actual text. A Memo component, as we will see in a while, can host several lines of text.

Our first example of the Edit component, named Focus, will demonstrate a feature common to many controls, the *input focus*. In Windows, it's fairly simple to determine which is the active main window: it is in front of the other windows, and the title bar is a different color. It is not as easy to determine which window (or component) has the input focus. If the user presses a key, which component is going to receive the corresponding keyboard input message? It can be the active window, but it can also be one of its controls. Consider a form with several edit fields. Only one has the input focus at a given time. A user can move the input focus by using Tab or by clicking with the mouse on another component.

Handling the Input Focus

What's important for our example is that each time a component receives or loses the input focus, it receives a corresponding event indicating that the user either has reached (OnEnter) or has left (OnExit) the component. So we can add some methods to the form to take control over the input focus and display this information in a label or a status bar.

Besides three edit boxes, the form has also some labels indicating the meaning of the three edit fields (*First name*, *Last name*, and *Password*). You can see the form used for this example in Figure 8.6. For the output of the status information I've used a specific Windows 95 component, the StatusBar, but using a label or a panel would have had a similar effect. In fact, you can use the StatusBar component as a single-line output tool, by setting its SimplePanel property to True. Here is a summary of the properties for this example:

```
object FocusForm: TFocusForm
  Caption = 'Focus'
  object Label1: TLabel
    Caption = '&First name:'
    FocusControl = EditFirstName
  end
  object Label2: TLabel
    Caption = '&Last name:'
    FocusControl = EditLastName
  end
  object Label3: TLabel
    Caption = '&Password:'
    FocusControl = EditPassword
  end
  object EditFirstName: TEdit
    TabOrder = 0
    OnEnter = EditFirstNameEnter
  end
  object EditLastName: TEdit
    TabOrder = 1
    OnEnter = EditLastNameEnter
  end
  object EditPassword: TEdit
    PasswordChar = '*'
    TabOrder = 2
    OnEnter = EditPasswordEnter
  end
  object ButtonCopy: TButton
    Caption = '&Copy Last Name to Title'
    TabOrder = 3
    OnClick = ButtonCopyClick
    OnEnter = ButtonCopyEnter
  end
  object StatusBar1: TStatusBar
    SimplePanel = True
  end
end
```

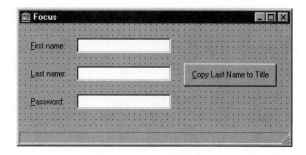

As you can see, the form also contains a button we can use to copy the text of the `LastNameEdit` to the form's caption. This is just an example of how to work with text entered in an edit box. As you can see in the following code, before using the `Text` property of an edit box, it's a good idea to test whether the user has actually typed something or if the edit field is still empty:

```
procedure TFocusForm.ButtonCopyClick(Sender: TObject);
begin
  if EditLastName.Text <> '' then
    FocusForm.Caption := EditLastName.Text;
end;
```

Now we can move to the most interesting part of the program. We can write a comment in the status bar each time the focus is moved to a different control, as in Figure 8.7.

> **TIP**
>
> Displaying text in the status bar as the focus moves from control to control is a good way to guide the user through the steps of an application.

To accomplish this, we need four methods, one for each of the Edit components and one for the button, referring to the `OnEnter` event. Here is the code of one of the methods (the other three event handlers are very similar):

```
procedure TFocusForm.EditFirstNameEnter(Sender: TObject);
begin
  StatusBar1.SimpleText := 'Entering the first name...';
end;
```

FIGURE 8.7

One of the messages
shown in the status bar
when the Focus program
is running. Notice the
form's new caption.

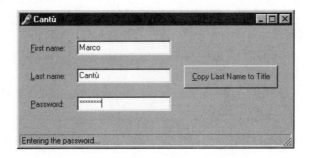

You can test this program with the mouse or use the keyboard. If you press the
Tab key, the input focus cycles among the Edit components and the button, without
involving the labels. To have a proper sequence, you can change the TabOrder
property of the windowed component. You can change this order either by entering
a proper value for this property in the Object Inspector or (much better and easier)
by using the Edit Tab Order dialog box, which can be called using the Tab Order
command on the form's SpeedMenu. If you open this dialog box for the Focus
example, you can see the output shown in Figure 8.8. Notice that the status bar is
listed but you cannot actually move onto it using the Tab key.

FIGURE 8.8

The Edit Tab Order dialog
box for the main form of
the Focus example.

A second way to select a component is to use a shortcut key. It is easy to place a
shortcut key on the button, but how can you jump directly to an edit box? It isn't
possible directly (the Text of the edit box changes as a user types), but there is an
indirect way. You can add the shortcut key—the ampersand (&)—to a label, then
set the FocusControl property of the label to the corresponding Edit component.

TIP In Windows 95, the edit controls automatically have a local menu displayed when the user presses the right mouse button over them. Although you can easily customize such a menu in Delphi (as we will see in the next chapter), it is important to realize that this is standard behavior in Windows 95.

A Generic OnEnter Event Handler

The problem with this code is that we have to write four different OnEnter event handlers, copying four strings to the text of the StatusBar component. To add more edit boxes to the example, you would need to add more event handlers, copying the code over and over. And if you wanted to provide a slightly different output (for example, by changing the output of the StatusBar allowing for multiple panels), you would need to change the code many times.

The alternative solution is to write a single event handler for the OnEnter event of each edit box (and the button, too). We simply need to store the message for the status bar in a property, then refer to this property for the Sender object. A good technique is to use the Hint property, which is actually designed for providing descriptions to the user. (We will discuss the Hint property in depth in Chapter 12.)

Simply store the proper messages in the Hint property of the edit boxes and of the button, then remove the current OnEnter event handler, and install this method for each of them:

```
procedure TFocusForm.GlobalEnter(Sender: TObject);
begin
  StatusBar1.SimpleText := (Sender as TControl).Hint;
end;
```

Notice you cannot write Sender as TEdit because the control might be a button as well. The solution is to typecast to a common ancestor class of TButton and TEdit, which defines the Hint property, as you can see in the code above.

Entering Numbers

We saw in the previous example that it is very easy to use an Edit component to ask the user to input some text, although it must be limited to a single line. In general, it's quite common to ask users for numeric input, too. To accomplish this, you can use the MaskEdit component (in the Additional page of the Components palette) or simply use an Edit component and then convert the input string into an integer, using the standard Pascal Val procedure or the Delphi IntToStr function.

This sounds good, but what if the user types a letter when a number is expected? Of course, these conversion functions return an error code, so we can use it to test whether the user has really entered a number. The second question is, when can we perform this test? Maybe when the value of the edit box changes, when the component loses focus, or when the user clicks on a particular button, such as the OK button in a dialog box. As you'll see, not all of these techniques work well.

There is another, radically different, solution to the problem of allowing only numerical input in an edit box. You can look at the input stream to the edit box and stop any non-numerical input. This technique is not foolproof (a user can always paste some text into an edit box), but it works quite well and is easy to implement. Of course, you can improve it by combining it with one of the other techniques.

The next example, Numbers, shows some of the techniques you can use to handle numerical input with an Edit component, so you can compare them easily. This example is meant as an exercise to discuss keyboard input and the input focus. To handle numerical input in an application you'll generally use specific components, as the SpinEdit or the UpDown controls available in Delphi. We will see an example of the use of another even more sophisticated control for keyboard input, the MaskEdit component.

In this example we're going to compare the effect of testing the input at different stages. First of all, build a form with five edit fields and five corresponding labels, describing in which occasion the corresponding Edit component checks the input, as shown in Figure 8.9. The form also has a button to check the contents of the first edit field. The contents of the first edit box are checked when the Check button is pressed. In the handler of the OnClick event of this button, the text is first converted into a number, using the Val procedure, which eventually returns an error code. Depending on the value of the code, a message is shown to the user:

```
procedure TNumbersForm.CheckButtonClick(Sender: TObject);
var
  Number, Code: Integer;
begin
  if Edit1.Text <> '' then
  begin
    Val (Edit1.Text, Number, Code);
    if Code <> 0 then
    begin
```

```
      Edit1.SetFocus;
      MessageDlg ('Not a number in the first edit',
         mtError, [mbOK], 0);
    end
    else
      MessageDlg ('OK, the number in the first edit box is' +
         IntToStr (Number), mtInformation, [mbOK], 0);
  end;
end;
```

If an error occurs, the application moves the focus back to the edit field before showing the error message to the user, thus inviting the user to correct the value. Of course, in this sample application a user can ignore this suggestion and move to another edit field.

FIGURE 8.9

The error displayed when the second edit box loses the focus and the user has entered letters.

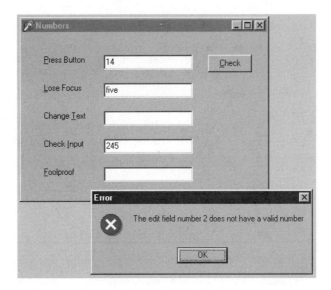

The same kind of check is made on the second edit field when it loses the focus. In this case, the message is displayed automatically, but only if an error occurs (see Figure 8.9). Why bother the user if everything is fine? The code here differs from that of the first edit field; it makes no reference to the Edit2 component but always refers to the generic Sender control, making a safe typecast. To indicate the number of each button, I've used the Tag property, entering the number of the edit control.

TIP

As you can see in the following listing, instead of casting the Sender parameter to the TEdit class several times in the same method, it is better to do this operation once, saving the value in a local variable of the TEdit type. The type checking involved with these casts, in fact, is quite slow.

This method is a little more complex to write, but we will be able to use it again for a different component. Here is its code:

```
procedure TNumbersForm.Edit2Exit(Sender: TObject);
var
  Number, Code: Integer;
  CurrEdit: TEdit;
begin
  CurrEdit := Sender as TEdit;
  if CurrEdit.Text <> '' then
  begin
    Val (CurrEdit.Text, Number, Code);
    if Code <> 0 then
    begin
      CurrEdit.SetFocus;
      MessageDlg ('The edit field number ' +
        IntToStr (CurrEdit.Tag) + ' does not have a valid number',
        mtError, [mbOK], 0);
    end;
  end;
end;
```

TIP

In the 32-bit versions of Delphi, this code produces a warning message (a hint) when compiled, because the Number variable is not used after a value has been assigned to it. To avoid these hints, you can ask the compiler to disable its generation inside a specific method using the $HINTS compiler directive. Simply write {$HINTS OFF} before the method and {$HINTS ON} after it, as I've done in the source code of this example.

The third Edit component makes a similar test each time its content changes (using the OnChange event). Although we have checked the input on different occasions—using different events—the three functions are very similar to each other. The idea is to check the string once the user has entered it.

For the fourth Edit component, I want to show you a completely different technique. We are going to make a check *before* the Edit even knows that a key has been pressed. The Edit component has an event, OnKeyPress, that corresponds to the action of the user. We can provide a method for this event and test whether the character is a number or the Backspace key (which has a numerical value of 8, so we can refer to it as the character #8). If not, we change the value of the key to the null character (#0), so that it won't be processed by the edit control, and produce a little warning sound:

```
procedure TNumbersForm.Edit4KeyPress(
  Sender: TObject; var Key: Char);
begin
  {check if the key is a number or backspace}
  if not (Key in ['0'..'9', #8]) then
  begin
    Key := #0;
    Beep;
  end;
end;
```

The fourth Edit component accepts only numbers for input, but it is not foolproof. A user can copy some text to the Clipboard and paste it into this Edit control with the Shift+Ins key combination (but not using Ctrl+V), avoiding any check. To solve this problem, we might think of adding a check for a change to the contents, as in the third edit field, or a check on the contents when the user leaves the edit field, as in the second component. This is the reason for the fifth, Foolproof edit field: it uses the OnKeyPress event of the fourth edit field, the OnChange method of the third, and the OnExit event of the second, thus requiring no new code.

To reuse an existing method for a new event, just select the Events page of the Object Inspector, move to the component, and instead of double-clicking to the left of the event name, select the button in the combo box at the right. A list of names of old methods compatible with the current event—having the same number of parameters—will be displayed, as you can see in Figure 8.10.

FIGURE 8.10

The Edit5 component uses methods already written for other components. All compatible methods are displayed when you select the small combo box button of the Object Inspector.

If you select the proper methods, the fifth component will combine the features of the third and the fourth. This is possible because in writing these methods, I took care to avoid any reference to the control to which they were related.

The technique I used was to refer to the generic Sender parameter and cast it to the proper data type, which in this case was TEdit. As long as you connect a method of this kind to a component of the same kind, no problem should arise. Otherwise, you should make a number of type checks (using the is operator), which will probably make the code more complex to read. My suggestion is to share code only between controls of the same kind.

Notice also that to tell the user which edit box has incorrect text, I've added to each Edit component a value for the Tag property, as I mentioned before. Every edit box has a tag with its number, from 1 to 5.

Sophisticated Input Schemes

In the last example, we saw how an Edit component can be customized for special input purposes. The components could really accept only numbers, but handling complex input schemes with a similar approach is not straightforward. For this reason, Borland has supplied a ready-to-use *masked edit component*, an edit component with an input mask stored in a string.

For example, to handle numbers of no more than five digits, we can set the EditMask property to 99999. (The character 9 stands for *non-compulsory digit*; refer to the Delphi documentation for the meaning of the various characters and symbols in the edit mask.) I suggest that you don't enter a string directly in this property, but instead always open the associated editor by clicking on the small ellipses button. The Input Mask editor has a test window and includes sample masks for commonly used input values (see Figure 8.11).

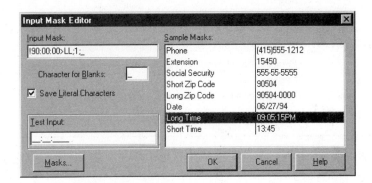

Notice that the Input Mask editor allows you to enter a mask, but it also asks you to indicate a character to be used as a placeholder for the input and to decide whether to save the *literals* present in the mask, together with the final string. For example, you can choose to have the parentheses around the area code of a phone number only as an input hint or to save them with the string holding the resulting number. These two entries in the Input Mask editor correspond to the last two fields of the mask (separated, by default, with semicolons).

To see more default input masks, you can press the Masks button, which allows you to open a mask file. The predefined files hold standard codes grouped by country. For example, if you open the Italian group, you can find the taxpayer number (or *fiscal code*, which is used like social security numbers in the U.S.). This code is a complex mix of letters and numbers (including the consonants representing name, birth date, area code, and more), as its mask demonstrates:

```
LLLLLL00L00L000L
```

In this kind of code, L stands for a letter and 0 for a number. While you can look these up in the Help file, there is a summary of these codes in the following Mask1 example (in Figure 8.12).

The form of this example includes a MaskEdit and an Edit component. The Edit is used to change the EditMask property of the first one at run-time. To accomplish this, I've just written a couple of lines of code to copy the text of the property into the edit box at the beginning (the OnCreate event) and reverse the action each time the plain edit box changes (Edit1Change):

```
procedure TForm1.FormCreate(Sender: TObject);
begin
  Edit1.Text := MaskEdit1.EditMask;
end;

procedure TForm1.Edit1Change(Sender: TObject);
begin
  MaskEdit1.EditMask := Edit1.Text;
end;
```

FIGURE 8.12

An example of the output of the Mask1 program.

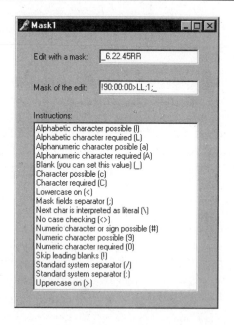

As you can see in Figure 8.12, the form also has a list box with the description of the most important codes used to build the mask.

Creating a Simple Editor

Edit components can handle a limited amount of text, and only on a single line. If you need to accept longer text input, you should use the Memo component. A Memo component is like an Edit component, but it can span several lines, contain scroll bars to move through the text, and contain more text.

The easiest way to use a Memo is as a text editor, as you'll see in the next example, Notes. The idea is to implement an editor covering all of the window (or form) which contains it, to resemble Windows' own Notepad. The only other feature we will implement is to give the user the option of choosing the font for the editor.

Both parts are very easy to implement. Create a new project and place a Memo component on the form. Delete its text, remove the border, and set the `Alignment` property to `alClient`, so that it will always cover the whole client area—the internal surface—of the form. Also add both scroll bars, horizontal and vertical, selecting the value `ssBoth` for the memo's `ScrollBars` property. Here is the summary:

```
object NotesForm: TNotesForm
  Caption = 'Notes'
  object Memo1: TMemo
    Align = alClient
    BorderStyle = bsNone
    Font.Height = -19
    Font.Name = 'Times New Roman'
    ScrollBars = ssBoth
    OnDblClick = Memo1DblClick
  end
  object FontDialog1: TFontDialog...
end
```

The Font Dialog Box

The second portion of the program involves the font. In the same way we used the standard Color dialog box in a previous example, we can use the standard Font selection dialog box provided by Windows. Just move to the Dialogs page of the Components palette and select the FontDialog component. Place it anywhere on the form, and add the following code when the user double-clicks inside the Memo:

```
procedure TNotesForm.Memo1DblClick(Sender: TObject);
begin
  FontDialog1.Font := Memo1.Font;
```

```
if FontDialog1.Execute then
   Memo1.Font := FontDialog1.Font;
end;
```

This code copies the current font to the corresponding property of the dialog component so it will be selected by default. Then it executes the dialog box (see Figure 8.13). At the end, the Font property will contain the font the user selected. If the user presses the OK button, the third line of the above code copies the font back to the Memo.

FIGURE 8.13

The Font dialog box for the Notes program.

This program is more powerful than it appears at first glance. For example, it allows copy and paste operations using the keyboard—this means you can copy text from your favorite word processor—and can handle the color of the font. Why not use it to place a big and colorful message on your screen?

Creating a Rich Editor

Although you can choose a font in the Notes program, all of the text you have written will have the same font. Windows 95 has a new control that can handle the Rich Text Format (RTF). A new Delphi component, RichEdit, encapsulates the behavior of this standard control.

You can find an example of a complete editor based on the RichEdit component among the examples that ship with Delphi. (The example is named RichEdit, too). Here, we'll only change the previous program slightly by replacing the Memo component with a RichEdit, and allow a user to change the font of the selected portion of the text, not the whole text.

The RichNote example has a RichEdit component filling its client area. However, the component has no double-click event, so I added a button to select the font and placed it in a panel aligned to the top of the form, making a very simple toolbar. Here is the textual description of some of the properties of the three components:

```
object RichEdit1: TRichEdit
  Align = alClient
  HideScrollBars = False
  ScrollBars = ssBoth
end
object Panel1: TPanel
  Align = alTop
  object Button1: TButton
    Caption = '&Font...'
  end
end
```

Notice the caption of the button, which has an ampersand for the shortcut key, and an ellipsis at the end to indicate that pressing it will open a dialog box. When the user clicks on the button, if some text is selected, the program shows the standard Font dialog box using the default font of the RichEdit component as the initial value. At the end, the selected font is copied to the attributes of the current selection. The DefAttributes and SelAttributes properties of the RichEdit component are not of the TFont type, but they are compatible, so we can use the Assign method to copy the value:

```
procedure TForm1.Button1Click(Sender: TObject);
begin
  if RichEdit1.SelLength > 0 then
  begin
    FontDialog1.Font.Assign(RichEdit1.DefAttributes);
```

```
        if FontDialog1.Execute then
          RichEdit1.SelAttributes.Assign(FontDialog1.Font);
    end
    else
      ShowMessage ('No text selected');
  end;
```

The RichEdit component has other attributes related to fonts and paragraph formatting. We will use this component in further examples of the book; however, the simple code above is enough to let users produce much more complex output than the Memo component allows. You can see a funny example in Figure 8.14.

Making Choices

There are two standard Windows controls that allow the user to choose different options. The first is the *check box*, which corresponds to an option that can be selected freely (unless it has been disabled). The second control is the *radio button*, which corresponds to an exclusive selection. For example, if you see two radio buttons with the labels *A* and *B*, you can select *A* or select *B*, but not both of them at the same time. The other characteristic of a multiple choice is that you *must* check one of the radio buttons.

If the difference between check boxes and radio buttons is still not clear, an example might help you. In Figure 8.15, you see the output of the Choice example. There are three check boxes to select the style *Bold*, *Italic*, or *Underlined*, and three radio buttons to choose a font (*Times New Roman*, *Arial*, or *Courier*). There is also a memo field with some text to show the effect of the user selections immediately.

FIGURE 8.15

The output of the Choice example.

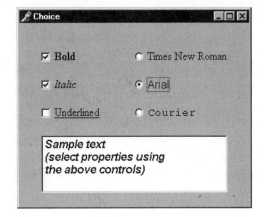

The difference between the use of the check boxes and the radio buttons should be obvious. The text might be bold and italic at the same time, but it cannot be Arial and Courier at once. A user must choose only one font (and cannot choose none) but can select each of the styles independently from the other two (including no style at all).

This program requires some simple code. Each time the user clicks on a check box or radio button, we have to create a corresponding action. For the text styles, we have to look at the Check property of the control and add or remove the corresponding element from the memo's Font property Style set:

```
procedure TForm1.CheckBoldClick(Sender: TObject);
begin
  if CheckBold.Checked then
    Memo1.Font.Style := Memo1.Font.Style + [fsBold]
  else
    Memo1.Font.Style := Memo1.Font.Style - [fsBold];
end;
```

The other two check boxes have similar code for their `OnClick` events. The basic code for the radio buttons is even simpler since you cannot deselect a radio button by clicking on it:

```
procedure TForm1.RadioTimesClick(Sender: TObject);
begin
  Memo1.Font.Name := 'Times New Roman';
end;
```

Grouping Radio Buttons

Radio buttons represent exclusive choices. However, a form might contain several groups of radio buttons. Windows cannot determine by itself how the various radio buttons relate to each other. The solution, both in Windows and in Delphi, is to place the related radio buttons inside a container component. The standard Windows user interface uses a group box control to hold the radio buttons together, both functionally and visually. In Delphi, this control is implemented in the GroupBox component. However, Delphi has a second, similar component that can be used specifically for radio buttons: the RadioGroup component. A RadioGroup is a group box with some radio button *clones* painted inside it. The term *clone* in this context refers to the fact that the RadioGroup component is a single control, a single window, which paints elements similar to radio button on its own surface. It is not a control with other controls inside it.

Using the radio group is probably easier than using the group box, but I'll use the more traditional approach to show you the code you can write to work with controls that have been placed inside another control. The fact that you have some controls inside another control is also a good reason *not* to follow this approach in real programs, because you end up with more windows on the screen, wasting system resources, and resulting in slightly slower code. Also, the RadioGroup component can automatically align its radio buttons, and you can easily add new choices at run-time. You can see the differences between the two approaches in the next example.

The rules for building a group box with radio buttons are very simple. Place the GroupBox component in the form, then place the radio buttons in the group box. The GroupBox component contains other controls and is one of the container components used most often, together with the Panel component. If you disable or hide the group box, all the controls inside it will be disabled or hidden.

You can continue handling the individual radio buttons, but you might as well navigate through the array of controls owned by the group box. As discussed in the last chapter, the name of this property referring to this array of controls is `Controls`. Another property, `ControlCount`, holds the number of elements. These two properties can be accessed only at run-time.

The Phrases1 Example

If you've ever tried to learn a foreign language, you probably spent some time repeating the same silly and useless phrases over and over. Probably the most typical, when you learn English, is the infamous *"The book is on the table."* To demonstrate radio buttons, the Phrases1 example creates a tool to build such phrases by choosing among different available options. The form is shown in Figure 8.16.

FIGURE 8.16

The form of the Phrases1 example.

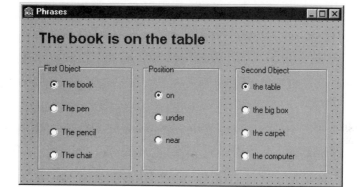

This form is quite complex. If you rebuild it, remember that you must place the GroupBox components first and the radio buttons later. After doing this, you have to enter a proper caption for each element, as you can see in Figure 8.16. The last selection is based on a radio group component, instead of a group box holding some radio buttons (as you can see in the textual description of the form below). In this case you create the options by entering a list of values in the Items property.

Remember that you also need to add a label, select a large font for it, and enter text corresponding to the radio buttons that are checked at design-time. This is an important point: When you place some radio buttons in a form or in a group box, remember to check one of the elements at design-time. One radio button in each group should always be checked, and the ItemIndex property of the radio group, indicating the current selection, should have a proper value.

Here is the textual description of the form with a summary of this information:

```
object Form1: TForm1
  Caption = 'Phrases'
  object Label1: TLabel
    Width = 243
    Caption = 'The book is on the table'
    Font.Height = -21
    Font.Name = 'Arial'
    Font.Style = [fsBold]
  end
  object GroupBox1: TGroupBox
    Caption = 'First Object'
    object RadioBook: TRadioButton
      Caption = 'The book'
      Checked = True
      OnClick = ChangeText
    end
    object RadioPen: TRadioButton
      Caption = 'The pen'
      OnClick = ChangeText
    end
    object RadioPencil: TRadioButton...
    object RadioChair: TRadioButton...
  end
  object GroupBox2: TGroupBox
    Caption = 'Position'
    object RadioOn: TRadioButton
      Caption = 'on'
      Checked = True
      OnClick = ChangeText
    end
    object RadioUnder: TRadioButton...
    object RadioNear: TRadioButton...
  end
```

```
object RadioGroup1: TRadioGroup
  Caption = 'Second Object'
  Items.Strings = (
    'the table'
    'the big box'
    'the carpet'
    'the computer')
  OnClick = ChangeText
end
end
```

Now we have to write some code so that when the user clicks on the radio buttons, the phrase changes accordingly. There are different ways to do this. One is to follow the same approach as in the last example, providing a method for each button's OnClick event. Then we need to store the various portions of the phrase in some of the form's variables, change the portion corresponding to that button, and rebuild the whole phrase.

An alternative solution is to write a single method that looks at which buttons are currently checked and builds the corresponding phrase. This single method must be connected to the OnClick event of every radio button and of the Radio-Group component, a task we can easily accomplish. Select each of the radio buttons on the form (clicking on each one while you hold down the Shift key) and enter the name of the method in the Object Inspector. Since the method used to compute the new phrase doesn't refer to a specific control, you might name it yourself, simply entering a name in the second column of the Object Inspector next to the OnClick event. Here is the code of this single complex method:

```
procedure TForm1.ChangeText(Sender: TObject);
var
  Phrase: string;
  I: integer;
begin
  {look at which radio button is selected
  and add its text to the phrase}
  for I := 0 to GroupBox1.ControlCount - 1 do
    if (GroupBox1.Controls[I] as TRadioButton).Checked then
      Phrase := (GroupBox1.Controls[I] as TRadioButton).Caption;

  {add the verb and blank spaces}
  Phrase := Phrase + ' is ';
```

```
{repeat the operation on the second group box}
for I := 0 to GroupBox2.ControlCount - 1 do
  with GroupBox2.Controls[I] as TRadioButton do
    if Checked then
       Phrase := Phrase + Caption;

{retrieve the radio group selection, and display
the result in the label}
Label1.Caption := Phrase + ' ' +
   RadioGroup1.Items [RadioGroup1.ItemIndex];
end;
```

The ChangeText method starts looking at which of the first group of radio buttons is selected, then moves on to adding a verb and the proper spaces between words. To determine which control in a group box is checked, the procedure scans these controls in a for loop. The for loop ranges from 0 to the number of controls minus 1, because the Controls array is zero-based, and tests whether the Checked property of the radio button is True. A cast is required to perform this operation—we cannot use the Checked property on a generic control. When the checked radio button has been found, the program simply copies its caption to the string. At this point, the for loop might terminate, but since only one radio button is checked at a time, it is safe to let it reach its natural end—testing all the elements. The same operation is repeated two times, but you can see that the second time a with statement is used to make the code shorter and more readable.

As you can see from the final portion of the method above, if you are using the RadioGroup component, the code is much simpler. This control, in fact, has an ItemIndex property indicating which radio button is selected and an Items property with a list of the text of the fake radio buttons. Overall, using a radio group is very similar to using a list box (as we will see in the next example), aside from the obvious difference in the user interface of the two components.

A List with Many Choices

If you want to add many selections, radio buttons are not appropriate, unless you create a really big form. The usual number of radio buttons is no more than 5 or 6. Another problem is that although you can disable a radio button, the elements of a group are usually fixed. Only when using a radio group can you have some flexibility. For both of these problems, the solution is to use a list box. A list box can host a large number of choices in a small space, because it can contain a scroll bar to show on screen only a limited portion of the whole list. Another advantage of a list box is that you can easily add new items to it or remove some of the current items. List boxes are extremely flexible and powerful.

TIP Another important feature is that by using the ListBox component, you can choose between allowing only a single selection, a behavior similar to a group of radio buttons, and allowing multiple selections, which is similar to a group of check boxes. The next version of this example will have a multiple-selection list box.

For the moment, let's focus on a single-selection list box. We might use a couple of these components to change the Phrases1 example slightly. Instead of having a number of radio buttons to select the first and second objects of the phrase, we can use two list boxes. Besides allowing us to have a larger number of items, the advantage is that we can allow the user to insert new objects in the list and prevent selection of the same object twice, to avoid a phrase such as "The book is on the book." As you might imagine, this example is really much more complicated than the previous one and will require some fairly complex code.

The Form of the Phrases2 Example

As usual, the first step is to build a form (see Figure 8.17). You can start with the form from the last example and remove the two group boxes on the sides and replace them with two list boxes. The radio buttons inside the group boxes will be deleted automatically. I've also replaced the central group box with a radio group. Actually, there's not much left from the previous example!

Now, add some strings to the Items property of both list boxes. For the example to work properly, the two list boxes should have the same strings; you can copy and paste them from the editor of the Items property of one list box to the editor of the same property of the other component. To improve the usability of the program, you might sort the strings in the list boxes, setting their Sorted property to

True. Remember also to add a couple of labels above the list boxes, to describe their contents.

FIGURE 8.17

The form of the second version of the Phrases example.

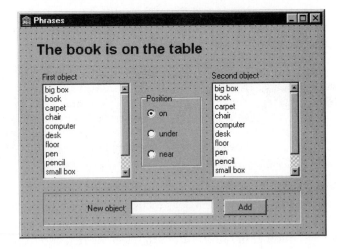

In the lower part of the form (see Figure 8.17 again), I've also added an edit field, with its label, and a button, and a bevel around them to group them visually (the bevel is just a graphical component, not a container). As we will see later, when a user presses the button, the text in the Edit control is added to both list boxes. This operation will take place only if the text of the edit box is not empty and the string is not already present in the list boxes.

Here is the textual description of the components of this updated form (which is really very different from the previous version):

```
object Form1: TForm1
  Caption = 'Phrases'
  OnCreate = FormCreate
  object Label1: TLabel... // as in Phrases1
  object Label2: TLabel
    Caption = 'First object'
  end
  object Label3: TLabel
    Caption = 'Second object'
  end
  object ListBox1: TListBox
    Items.Strings = (
```

```
        'big box'
        'book'
        'carpet'
        'chair'
        'computer'...)
      Sorted = True
      OnClick = ChangeText
    end
    object RadioGroup1: TRadioGroup
      Caption = 'Position'
      Items.Strings = (
        'on'
        'under'
        'near')
    end
    object ListBox2: TListBox... // identical to ListBox1
    object Bevel1: TBevel...
    object Label4: TLabel
      Caption = 'New object'
    end
    object EditNew: TEdit...
    object ButtonAdd: TButton
      Caption = 'Add'
      OnClick = ButtonAddClick
    end
  end
end
```

Working with the List Boxes

Once you have built this or a similar form, you can start writing some code. The first thing to do is to provide a new ChangeText procedure, connected with the OnClick event of the radio group and of the two list boxes. This procedure is simpler than in the previous example. In fact, to retrieve the selected text from the list box, you only need to get the number of the item selected (stored in the run-time property ItemIndex) and then retrieve the string at the corresponding position of the Item array, as the Phrases1 program did.

Here is what the code for the procedure looks like initially (this is just a temporary version, different from the one on the companion CD):

```
procedure TForm1.ChangeText(Sender: TObject);
var
  Phrase: String;
```

```
begin
  Phrase := 'The ';
  Phrase := Phrase + ListBox1.Items [ListBox1.ItemIndex];
  Phrase := Phrase + ' is ';
  Phrase := Phrase + RadioGroup1.Items [RadioGroup1.ItemIndex];
  Phrase := Phrase + ' the ';
  Phrase := Phrase + ListBox2.Items [ListBox2.ItemIndex];
  Label1.Caption := Phrase;
end;
```

This program, however, won't work properly because, at the beginning, no item is selected in either list box. To solve this problem, we can add some code to the form's OnCreate event. In this code, we can look for the two default strings, book and table, and select them. You should do this operation in two steps. First, you need to look for the string's index in the array of strings, with the IndexOf method. Then you can use that value as the index of the currently selected item:

```
procedure TForm1.FormCreate(Sender: TObject);
var
  N : Integer;
begin
  N := ListBox1.Items.IndexOf ('book');
  ListBox1.ItemIndex := N;
  N := ListBox2.Items.IndexOf ('table');
  ListBox2.ItemIndex := N;
end;
```

Removing a Selected String from the Other List Box

Once this part of the program works, we have two more problems to solve: We must remove the selected string from the other list box (to avoid using the same term twice in a phrase), and we must write the code for the click event on the button.

The first problem is more complex, but I'll address it immediately since the solution of the second problem will be based partially on the code we write for the first one. Our aim is to delete from a list box the item currently selected in the other list box. This is easy to code. The problem is that once the selection changes, we have to restore the previous items, or our list boxes will rapidly become empty.

A good solution is to store the two currently selected strings for the two list boxes in two private fields of the form, String1 and String2:

```
type
  TForm1 = class(TForm)
  ...
  private
    String1, String2: String;
  end;
```

Now we have to change the code executed at startup and the code executed each time a new selection is made. In the FormCreate method, we need to store the initial value of the two strings and remove them from the other list box; the first string should be removed from the second list box, and vice versa. Since the Delete method of the TStrings class requires the index, we have to use the IndexOf function again to determine it:

```
procedure TForm1.FormCreate(Sender: TObject);
var
  N : Integer;
begin
  String1 := 'book';
  String2 := 'table';

  {delete the selected string from the other list box
  to avoid a double selection}
  ListBox2.Items.Delete (ListBox2.Items.IndexOf (String1));
  ListBox1.Items.Delete (ListBox1.Items.IndexOf (String2));

  {select the two strings in their respective list boxes}
  N := ListBox1.Items.IndexOf (String1);
  ListBox1.ItemIndex := N;
  N := ListBox2.Items.IndexOf (String2);
  ListBox2.ItemIndex := N;
end;
```

WARNING The code to select the string should be executed after calling Delete, because removing an element before the one currently selected will alter the selection. The fact is that the selection is just a number referring to a string, not the reverse, as it should probably be. By the way, this doesn't depend on Delphi implementation but on the behavior of list boxes in Windows.

Things get complicated when a new item is selected in one of the list boxes. The ChangeText procedure has some new code at the beginning, executed only if the click took place on one of the list boxes (remember that the code is also associated with the group box). For each string, we have to check whether the selected item has changed and, in this case, add the previously selected string to the other list box and delete the new string. Here is the new version of the ChangeText method:

```
procedure TForm1.ChangeText(Sender: TObject);
var
  TmpStr: String;
begin
  // if a list box has changed
  if Sender is TListBox then
  begin
    // get the text of the first string
    TmpStr := ListBox1.Items [ListBox1.ItemIndex];
    // if the first one has changed
    if TmpStr <> String1 then
    begin
      // update the strings in ListBox2
      {1.} ListBox2.Items.Add (String1);
      {2.} ListBox2.Items.Delete (
             ListBox2.Items.IndexOf (TmpStr));
      {3.} ListBox2.ItemIndex :=
             ListBox2.Items.IndexOf (String2);
      {4.} String1 := TmpStr;
    end;
    // get the text of the second string
    TmpStr := ListBox2.Items [ListBox2.ItemIndex];
    // if the second one has changed
    if TmpStr <> String2 then
    begin
      // update the strings in ListBox1
      ListBox1.Items.Add (String2);
      ListBox1.Items.Delete (ListBox1.Items.IndexOf (TmpStr));
      ListBox1.ItemIndex := ListBox1.Items.IndexOf (String1);
      String2 := TmpStr;
    end;
  end;
  // build the phrase with the current strings
  Label1.Caption := 'The ' + String1 + ' is ' +
```

```
        RadioGroup1.Items [RadioGroup1.ItemIndex] +
        ' the ' + String2;
    end;
```

What is the effect of the first part of this code? Here is a detailed description of the operations, referring to a new selection in the first list box. The procedure stores the selected element of the first list box in the temporary string TmpStr. If this is different from the older selection, String1, four operations take place (refer to the numbers in the listing above):

1. The previously selected string, String1, is added to the other list box, ListBox2.

2. The new selection, TmpStr, is removed from the other list box.

3. The selected string of the other list box, String2, is reselected in case its position has been changed by the two preceding operations.

4. Once the two lists contain the correct elements, we can store the new value in String1 and use it later on to build the phrase.

We perform the same steps for the other list box a few lines later. Notice that we don't need to access the list boxes again to build the phrase at the end of the OnChange method, since String1 and String2 already contain the values we need. You can see the resulting output in Figure 8.18.

FIGURE 8.18

The Phrases2 example. Notice that the string selected in one list box is not present in the other one.

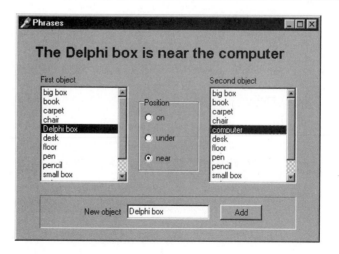

377

Implementing the OnClick event for the Add button is quite simple. The only precautions we have to take are to test whether there is actually some text in the edit box or if it is empty and to check whether the string is already present in one of the two list boxes. Checking only one of the list boxes will miss a correspondence between the text of the edit box and the item currently selected in the other list box.

To make this check, we can ask both ListBox components for the index of the new string; if it is not present in the list—if there is no match—the value –1 will be returned. Otherwise, the IndexOf function returns the correct index, starting with 0 for the first element. In technical terms, we can say that the function returns the zero-based index of the element, or the error code –1 if it is not found. Here is the code:

```
procedure TForm1.ButtonAddClick(Sender: TObject);
begin
  {if there is a string in the edit control and
  the string is not already present in one of the lists}
  if (EditNew.Text <> '') and
    (ListBox1.Items.IndexOf(EditNew.Text) < 0) and
    (ListBox2.Items.IndexOf(EditNew.Text) < 0) then
  begin
    {add the string to both list boxes}
    ListBox1.Items.Add (EditNew.Text);
    ListBox2.Items.Add (EditNew.Text);
    {reselects the current items properly}
    ListBox1.ItemIndex := ListBox1.Items.IndexOf (String1);
    ListBox2.ItemIndex := ListBox2.Items.IndexOf (String2);
  end
  else
    MessageDlg ('The edit control is empty or contains'
      + ' a string which is already present',
      mtError, [mbOK], 0);
end;
```

In the final part of this method's code, we need to reselect the current item of each list box since the position of the selected item might change. This happens if the new item is inserted before the one that is currently selected—that is, if it has a lower sort order.

Allowing Multiple Selections

A list box can allow the selection of either a single element or a number of elements. We make this choice in setting up a list box by specifying the value of its Multiple property. As the name implies, setting Multiple to True allows multiple selections. There are really two different kinds of multiple selections in Windows and in Delphi list boxes: *multiple selection* and *extended selection*. In the first case a user selects multiple items simply by clicking on them, while in the second case the user can use the Shift and Ctrl keys to select multiple consecutive or nonconsecutive items. This second choice is determined by the Extended-Select property.

While setting up a multiple-selection list box is very simple, the problems start to appear when you have to write the code. Accessing the selected item of a single-selection list box is simple. The ItemIndex property holds the index of the selected item, and the selected string can be retrieved with a simple expression:

```
ListBox2.Items[ListBox2.ItemIndex];
```

In a multiple-selection list box, on the other hand, we do not know how many items are selected, or even whether there is any item selected. In fact, a user can click on an item to select it, drag the cursor to select a number of consecutive items in the list, or click the mouse button on an item while holding down Ctrl key to toggle the selection of a single item without affecting the others. Using this last option, a user can even deselect all the items in a list box.

A program can retrieve information on the currently selected items by examining the Selected array. This array of Boolean values has the same number of entries as the list box. Each entry indicates whether the corresponding item is selected, as shown in the schema of Figure 8.19.

For example, to know how many items are selected in a list box, we need to scan the Selected array, usually with a for loop ranging from 0 to the number of items in the list minus one:

```
SelectCount := 0;
for ListItem := 0 to ListBox1.Items.Count - 1 do
  if ListBox1.Selected[ListItem] then
    Inc (SelectCount);
```

FIGURE 8.19

A schema of the relationship between the Selected and Items properties in a multiple-selection list box.

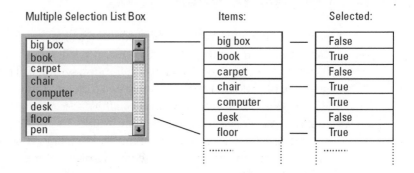

Actually, the ListBox component has an undocumented SelCount property, you can use to obtain exactly the information computed in the code above. We won't use this code in the next example, anyway, but a more complex version.

The Third Version of the Phrases Example

With this information, we can build a new version of the Phrases example, allowing a user to select several items in the first list box. The only real difference between the form of this new version and that of the last one is the value of the MultiSelect property in the first list box is not set to True.

In addition, the label at the top of the form has been enlarged, enabling the WordWrap property and disabling the AutoSize property, to accommodate longer phrases. Since the example's code is complex enough, I've removed the portion used to delete from a list box the item selected in the other list box. In the case of multiple selections, this would have been really complicated.

The main problem we face is building the different phrases correctly. The basic idea is to scan the Selected array each time and add each of the selected objects to the phrase. However, we need to place an *"and"* before the name of the last object, omitting the comma if there are only two. Moreover, we need to decide between singular and plural (*is* or *are*) and provide some default text if no element is selected. As you can see from Table 8.1 (and in Figure 8.20), building these phrases is not simple. In fact, if we store the phrase *"The book and the computer,"* when we need to add a third item, we must go back and change it.

TABLE 8.1   Possible Strings Built by the Phrases3 Example

Items Selected	SelectCount	Phrase
(none)	0	Nothing is
book	1	The book is
book, computer	2	The book and the computer are
book, computer, pen	3	The book, the computer, and the pen are
book, computer, pen, small box	4	The book, the computer, the pen, and the small box are

FIGURE 8.20

An example of the output of the Phrases3 program.

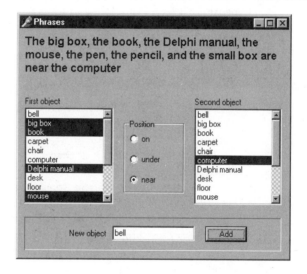

An alternative idea is to create two different phrases, one valid if no other elements will be added, the other prepared to host future objects (without the *and*). In the code, the TmpStr1 string is the tentative final statement, while TmpStr2 is the temporary string used to add a further element. At the end of the loop, TmpStr1 holds the correct value. As you can see in the code below, in case only two items are selected we have to build the phrase in a slightly different way, removing the comma before the *and* conjunction.

Notice when scanning a sorted list box that the objects are always added to the resulting string in alphabetical order, not in the order in which they were selected. You can study how this idea has been implemented by looking at the new version of the ChangeText method, in the following code (and by studying Table 8.2, which describes step-by-step how the strings are built):

```
procedure TForm1.ChangeText(Sender: TObject);
var
  Phrase, TmpStr1, TmpStr2: String;
  SelectCount, ListItem: Integer;
begin
  SelectCount := 0;
  {look at each item of the multiple selection list box}
  for ListItem := 0 to ListBox1.Items.Count - 1 do
    if ListBox1.Selected [ListItem] then
    begin
      {if the item is selected increase the count}
      Inc (SelectCount);
      if SelectCount = 1 then
      begin
        {store the string of the first selection}
        TmpStr1 := ListBox1.Items.Strings [ListItem];
        TmpStr2 := TmpStr1;
      end
      else if SelectCount = 2 then
      begin
        {add the string of the second selection}
        TmpStr1 := TmpStr1 + ' and the ' +
          ListBox1.Items.Strings [ListItem];
        TmpStr2 := TmpStr2 + ', the ' +
          ListBox1.Items.Strings [ListItem];
      end
      else // SelectCount > 2
      begin
        {add the string of the further selection}
        TmpStr1 := TmpStr2 + ', and the ' +
          ListBox1.Items.Strings [ListItem];
        TmpStr2 := TmpStr2 + ', the ' +
          ListBox1.Items.Strings [ListItem];
      end;
    end;
  {build the first part of the phrase}
```

```
if SelectCount > 0 then
  Phrase := 'The ' + TmpStr1
else
  Phrase := 'Nothing';
if SelectCount <= 1 then
  Phrase := Phrase + ' is '
else
  Phrase := Phrase + ' are ';
{add the text of the radio button}
Phrase := Phrase +
  RadioGroup1.Items [RadioGroup1.ItemIndex];
{add the text of the second list box}
Phrase := Phrase + ' the ' +
  ListBox2.Items [ListBox2.ItemIndex];

Label1.Caption := Phrase;
end;
```

TABLE 8.2 The Process of Building the Strings Step-by-Step

Items Selected	Steps	TmpStr1 (Tentative Final Statement)	TmpStr2 (Temporary Statement)
book	1	book	book
+ computer	2	book and the computer	book, the computer
+ pen	3	book, the computer, and the pen	book, the computer, the pen
+ small box	4	book, the computer, the pen, and the small box	book, the computer, the pen, the small box

The other procedures of the program change only slightly. The FormCreate method is simplified because we do not need to delete the selected item from the other list box. The Add method is simplified because both list boxes always have the same items and because the multiple-selection list box creates no problems with the selection if you add a new element.

An alternative solution to handle the status of multiple-selection list boxes is to look at the value of the ItemIndex property, which holds the number of the item of the list having the focus. If a user clicks on several items while holding down Ctrl, each time a click event takes place, you know which of the items have been selected or deselected—you can easily determine which of the two operations took place by looking at the value of the Selected array for that index. The problem is that if the user selects a number of elements by dragging the mouse, this method won't work. You need to intercept the dragging events, and this is considerably more complex than the technique described earlier.

Using a CheckListBox Component

 A further extension to the Phrases example is the use of the CheckListBox component, a new component introduced by Borland in Delphi 3. This is basically a list box with a custom output (or an *owner-draw* list box, to use the proper technical term). Each item of the list is preceded by a check box. A user can select a single item of the list, but can also click on the check boxes to toggle their status.

If the component has the AllowGrayed property set to True, then each check box can be non-selected, grayed, or selected. Clicking on the check box alternates these three possible conditions. To check the current status of each item you can use the Checked and the State property. Both are array properties. The first, Checked, is a Boolean property you should use when AllowGrayed is set to False. The second, State, is a property of the TCheckBoxState data type:

```
type
  TCheckBoxState = (cbUnchecked, cbChecked, cbGrayed)
```

This property should be used when AllowGrayed is set to True, to distinguish among the three different states of each item. Apart from these properties, the specific user interface, and the new OnClickCheck event, this component behaves as a ListBox.

As I mentioned at the beginning of this section, to show you an example of the use of this component I've further updated the Phrases3 example, building the Phrases4 version. I've basically replaced the first multiple selection list box with the new CheckListBox component, set its Sorted property to True, and copied the Items. Then I've updated the code, replacing the ListBox1 object with the CheckListBox1 object, and replacing the Selected property of the first with the Checked property of the second in the ChangeText method. Here is an excerpt of the new version of this method:

```
for ListItem := 0 to CheckListBox1.Items.Count - 1 do
  if CheckListBox1.Checked [ListItem] then
  begin
    {if the item is selected increase the count}
    Inc (SelectCount);
```

```
if SelectCount = 1 then
begin
  {store the string of the first selection}
  TmpStr1 := CheckListBox1.Items.Strings [ListItem];
  TmpStr2 := TmpStr1;
end
else if SelectCount = 2 then ...
```

You can see the output of the program with the new component in Figure 8.21. The important point is that this component makes it more obvious to the user that the list box allows multiple selections. The plain list box, in fact, gives no clue of this fact.

FIGURE 8.21

The output of the Phrases4 example, with the new CheckListBox component.

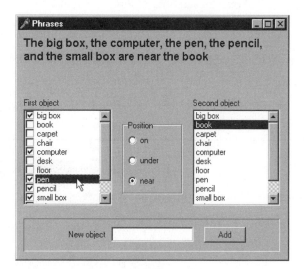

Many Lists, Little Space

List boxes take up a lot of screen space, and they offer a fixed selection. That is, a user can choose only among the items in the list box and cannot make any choice that the programmer did not specifically foresee.

You can solve both problems by using a ComboBox control. A combo box is similar to an edit box, and you can often enter some text in it. It is also similar to a list box, with a drop-down arrow that displays a list box. Even the name of the control suggests that it is a combination of two other controls, an Edit and a ListBox.

However, the behavior of a ComboBox component might change a lot, depending on the value of its Style property. Here is a short description of the various styles:

- The csDropDown style defines a typical combo box, which allows direct editing and displays a list box on request.

- The csDropDownList style defines a combo box that does not allow editing. By pressing a key, the user selects the first word starting with that letter in the list.

- The csSimple style defines a combo box that always displays the list box below it. This version of the control allows direct editing.

- The csOwnerDrawFixed and csOwnerDrawVariable styles define combo boxes based on an owner-draw list—that is, a list containing graphics determined by the program rather than simple strings.

To see the difference between the first three types, you can run the Combos example, which I'll describe in a moment. As you can see in Figure 8.22 and better appreciate by testing the program, Combos displays three combo boxes having three different styles: drop-down, drop-down list, and simple.

FIGURE 8.22

The output of the Combos example, with the three basic types of combo boxes.

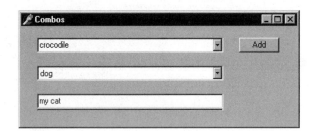

This program is very simple. Each combo box has the same basic strings—the names of more than 20 different animals. The first combo box contains an *Add* button. If the user presses the button, any text entered in the combo box is added to its list, provided it is not already present. This is the code associated with the OnClick event of the button:

```
procedure TForm1.ButtonAddClick(Sender: TObject);
begin
with ComboBox1 do
  if (Text <> '') and (Items.IndexOf (Text) < 0) then
```

```
      Items.Add (Text);
  end;
```

You can use the second combo box to experiment with the automatic lookup technique. If you press a key, the first of the names in the list starting with that letter will be selected. By pressing ↑ and ↓, you can further navigate in the list without opening it. This navigation technique of using initial letters and arrows can be used with each of the combo boxes.

The third combo box is a variation of the first. Instead of adding the new element when the Add button is pressed, that action is performed when the user presses ↵. To test for this event, we can write a method for the combo box's OnKeyPress event and check whether the key is ↵, which has the numeric code 13. The remaining statements are similar to those of the button's OnClick event:

```
procedure TForm1.ComboBox3KeyPress(
  Sender: TObject; var Key: Char);
begin
  {if the user presses the Enter key}
  if Key = Chr (13) then
    with ComboBox3 do
      if (Text <> '') and (Items.IndexOf (Text) < 0) then
        Items.Add (Text);
end;
```

NEW

There is a new Delphi 3 component with a user interface similar to that of a ComboBox. It is the new DateTimePicker component, which I'll cover in Chapter 11.

Choosing a Value in a Range

The last basic component I want to explore in this chapter is the scroll bar. Scroll bars are usually associated with other components, such as list boxes and memo fields, or are associated directly with forms. Notice, however, that when a scroll bar is associated with another component, it is really a portion of that component—one of its properties—and there is little relationship to the ScrollBar component itself. Forms having a scroll bar have no ScrollBar component. A portion of their border is used to display that graphical element. Forms with scroll bars will be discussed in Chapter 14.

Direct usage of the ScrollBar component is quite rare, especially with the new TrackBar component of Windows 95. However, there are cases in which it can play a role. The typical example is to allow a user to choose a numerical value in a large range (since a TrackBar is generally used for smaller ranges).

Most Windows programming books describe scroll bars using the example of selecting a color, and this book is no exception. But if you've seen a typical Windows example, you'll notice something very interesting: using Delphi, you can build this example in about one-fourth the time and writing a minimal amount of code.

The Scroll Color Example

The ScrollC example—the name stands for scroll color—has a simple form with three scroll bars and three corresponding labels, a track bar with its own label, and some shape components to show the current color. Each scroll bar refers to one of the three fundamental colors, which in Windows are red, green, and blue (RGB). Each label displays the name of the corresponding color and the current value.

Scroll bars have a number of peculiar properties. You can use Min and Max to determine the range of possible values; Position holds the current position; and the LargeChange and SmallChange properties indicate the increment caused by clicking on the bar or on the arrow at the end of the bar, respectively. You can see a graphical description of these properties, with the values used in the example, in Figure 8.23.

FIGURE 8.23

A graphical description of some properties of a scroll bar (the values are borrowed from the ScrollC example).

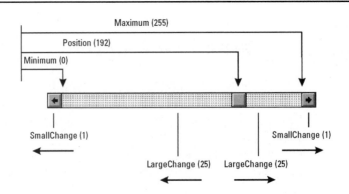

In the ScrollC example, the value of each bar ranges from 0 to 255. The range is determined by the fact that each color is a DWORD with the lower three bytes representing the Red, Green, and Blue values (as discussed in Chapter 7). The initial value of 192 has been chosen for the position because with settings of 192 for red, 192 for green, and 192 for blue, you get the typical light gray, which is the default value for the color of the form and of the shapes. Here is the textual description of one of these three ScrollBar components:

```
object ScrollBarRed: TScrollBar
  LargeChange = 25
  Max = 255
  Position = 192
  OnScroll = ScrollBarRedScroll
end
```

The TrackBar components has similar properties (Min, Max, Position):

```
object TrackBar1: TTrackBar
  Max = 30
  Min = 1
  Orientation = trHorizontal
  Frequency = 1
  Position = 25
  TickMarks = tmBottomRight
  TickStyle = tsAuto
  OnChange = TrackBar1Change
end
```

This control is used, in this example, to set the LargeChange property of the three scrollbars, with the following code:

```
procedure TFormScroll.TrackBar1Change(Sender: TObject);
begin
  LabelScroll.Caption := 'Scroll by ' +
    IntToStr(TrackBar1.Position);
  ScrollBarGreen.LargeChange := TrackBar1.Position;
  ScrollBarRed.LargeChange := TrackBar1.Position;
  ScrollBarBlue.LargeChange := TrackBar1.Position;
end;
```

When one of the scroll bars changes (the OnScroll event), the program has to update the corresponding label and the color of the shapes. The first of these shapes is used to show the color as it is determined by the three RGB values of the scroll bars. Assigning the color to the Color property of the brush used to fill the surface of the shape, we obtain a dithered color, an approximation of the real tint made with the colors available on the video adapter. The same color is assigned to the Color property of the pen of the second shape, resulting in the closest approximation of the requested color. Pens, in fact, do not use dithering, but rather the closest *pure* color. You can see the difference in Figure 8.24, and by running this example, although the effect might change depending on your video adapter.

FIGURE 8.24

The output of the ScrollC example.

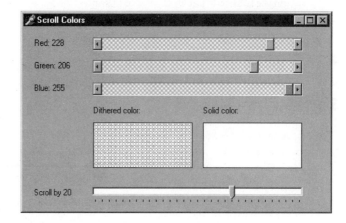

If you browse through the code of the program, notice also that there is a third shape component used to mimic the border of the second shape. The real border of this shape, in fact, is enlarged to fill its whole surface, using a very wide pen. This way we use the color of the pen—the wide border—to actually fill the shape. Here is the code corresponding to one of the scroll bars:

```
procedure TFormScroll.ScrollBarRedScroll(Sender: TObject;
  ScrollCode: TScrollCode; var ScrollPos: Integer);
begin
  LabelRed.Caption := 'Red: ' + IntToStr(ScrollPos);
  Shape1.Brush.Color := RGB (ScrollBarRed.Position,
    ScrollBarGreen.Position, ScrollBarBlue.Position);
  Shape2.Pen.Color := RGB (ScrollBarRed.Position,
    ScrollBarGreen.Position, ScrollBarBlue.Position);
end;
```

You need to copy this code once for each scroll bar and correct the name of the label and its output text. The second and third statements always remain the same.

They are based on a Windows function, RGB, which takes three values in the range 0–255 and creates a 32-bit value with the code of the corresponding color.

It is interesting to note that the OnScroll event has three parameters: the sender, the kind of event (ScrollCode), and the final position of the thumb (ScrollPos). This type of event can be used for very precise control of the user's actions. The ScrollCode parameter indicates if the user is dragging the thumb (scTrack, scPosition, or scEndScroll), has clicked on one of the two final arrows (scLineUp or scLineDown), has clicked on the bar in one of the two directions (scPageUp or scPageDown), or is trying to scroll out of the range (scTop or scBottom).

What's Next

In this chapter, we have started to explore some of the basic components available in Delphi. These components correspond to the standard Windows controls and some of the new Windows 95 common controls, and are extremely common in applications (with the exception of the stand-alone scroll bars). Of course, when you start adding more advanced Delphi components to an application, you can easily build more complex and colorful user interfaces and more powerful programs.

We will explore some of the advanced components in future chapters (particularly Chapters 11 and 12), but the next two chapters are devoted to two specific and important topics: the use of menus and a detailed description of forms. After these two in-depth discussions, which will also include information about the mouse input and the direct output on a canvas, we will move back to the use of other components, including the graphical versions of list boxes, outlines, grids, and more.

CHAPTER
NINE

9

Creating and Handling Menus

- The structure of a menu

- Using menu templates

- Checking, disabling, and modifying menus at run-time

- Creating menu items at run-time

- A custom menu check mark

- Bitmap menu items and owner-draw menu items

- The system menu

- Pop-up menus

The sample programs we have built so far have lacked one of the most important user-interface elements of any Windows application: the menu bar. Although our forms have each had a system menu, its use has been very limited. In practical applications, however, the menu bar is a central element in the development of a program. While the user can click and sometimes drag the mouse to select options, most complex tasks usually involve menu commands. Consider the applications you use and the number of menu commands you issue in those programs (including those invoked by a shortcut key, such as Ctrl+C, which is equivalent to the Edit ➤ Copy command in most applications).

Menus are so important that almost any real Windows application has at least one. In fact, an application can also have several menus that change at run-time (more on this later), various local menus (usually activated with a right mouse click), and even a customized system menu.

The Borland programmers who created Delphi considered menus so important that they have placed the corresponding components in the Standard page of the Components palette.

The Structure of the Main Menu

Before looking at the use of menus in Delphi, let me recap some general information about menus and their structure. Usually, a menu has two levels. A menu bar, appearing below the title of the window, contains the names of the pull-down menus, each of which in turn contains a number of items. However, the menu structure is very flexible. It is possible to place a menu item directly in the menu bar and to place a *second level* pull-down menu inside another pull-down menu.

You should avoid placing commands directly on the menu bar, because users tend to select the elements of the menu bar to explore the structure of the menu. They do not expect to issue a command this way. If, for some reason, you really need to place a command in the menu bar, at least place the standard exclamation mark after it (as you can see in Figure 9.1). Using an exclamation mark is a standard hint, but most users have never seen this "convention," so it's best to avoid the whole situation altogether and simply have a pull-down menu with a single menu item. A typical example is a Help menu with a single About menu item.

FIGURE 9.1

Besides the typical two-level menu structure, a pull-down menu can be placed inside another pull-down (above) and a menu item in the menu bar (below).

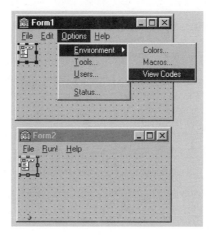

Putting a pull-down menu inside another pull-down menu—a second-level pull-down—is far more common, and Windows in this case provides a default visual clue, a small triangular glyph at the right of the menu (see Figure 9.1 again). Many applications use this technique, particularly in Windows 95, because the system makes heavy use of multilevel menus (consider the Start button's Programs menu). However, keep in mind that selecting a menu item in a second-level pull-down takes more time and can become tedious.

Many times, instead of having a second-level pull-down, you can simply group a number of options in the original pull-down and place two separator bars, one before and one after the group. You can see an exaggerated multilevel menu in Figure 9.2, or you can test it directly by running the Levels example on the companion disk. Since this is a demonstration of what you should try to *avoid*, I won't list the structure of the menu here. (For an example of related menu options grouped by separators, glance ahead to Figure 9.3.)

FIGURE 9.2

The multilevel menu of the Levels example.

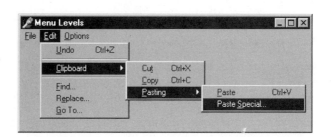

Different Roles of Menu Items

Now let's turn our attention to menu items, regardless of their position in the menu structure. There are three fundamental kinds of menu items:

- *Commands* are menu items used to execute an action. They have no special visual clue.

- *State-setters* are menu items used to toggle an option on and off, to change the state of a particular element. These commands usually have a check mark on the left to indicate they are active. In this case, selecting the command produces the opposite action.

- *Dialog menu items* are menu items that cause a dialog box to appear. The real difference between these and the other menu items is that a user should be able to explore the possible effects of the corresponding dialog box and eventually abort it by choosing the Cancel button. These commands should have a visual clue, consisting of an ellipsis (three dots) after the text.

TIP

In Windows 95, besides the traditional state-setters with a check mark, you can also have radio menu items with a bullet check mark. These menu items represent alternative selections, just as RadioButton components do, and simply checking one of them disables the other elements of the group. We'll explore radio menu items in an example later on.

Building a Menu with the Menu Designer

Delphi includes a special editor for menus, the Menu Designer. To invoke this tool, place a MainMenu component on a form and double-click on it. Don't worry too much about the position of the menu component on the form, since it doesn't affect the result; the menu is always placed properly, below the form's caption.

NOTE

To be more precise, the form displays, below its caption, the menu indicated in its Menu property, which is set by default as soon as you create the first main menu component of the form. If the form has more than one main menu component, this property should be set manually and can be changed both at design-time and at run-time.

The Menu Designer is really powerful: It allows you to create a menu simply by writing the text of the commands, to move the items or pull-down menus by dragging them around, and to set the properties of the items easily. It is also very flexible, allowing you to place a command directly in the menu bar (this happens each time you do not write any element in the corresponding pull-down menu) or to create second-level pull-down menus. To accomplish this, select the Create Submenu command on the Menu Designer's SpeedMenu (the local menu invoked with the right mouse button).

Another very important feature available through the Menu Designer is the ability to create a menu from a template. You can easily define new templates of your own. Simply create a menu, and use the Save As Template command on the SpeedMenu to add it to the list. This makes sense particularly if you need to have a similar menu in two applications or in two different forms of the same application.

The Standard Structure of a Menu

If you've used Windows applications for some time, you have certainly noticed that the structure of an application's menu is not an invention of its programmers. There are a number of standard Windows guidelines describing how to arrange the commands in a menu. You can infer most of these rules by looking at the menus of some of the best-selling applications.

An application's menu bar should start with a File pull-down, followed by Edit, View, and then some commands specific to the application. The final part of the sequence includes Options, Tools, and Window (in MDI, or Multiple Document Interface, applications) and always terminates with Help. Each of these pull-down menus has a standard layout, although the actual items depend on the application. The File menu, for example, usually has commands such as New, Open, Save, Save As, Print, Print Setup, and Exit.

Shortcut Keys and Hotkeys

A common feature of menu items is that they contain an underlined letter, generally called a *hotkey*. This letter, which is often the first letter of the text, can be used to select the menu using the keyboard. Pressing Alt plus the underlined key selects the corresponding pull-down menu. By pressing another underlined key on that menu, you issue a command.

Of course, each element of the menu bar must have a different underlined character. The same is true for the menu items on a specific pull-down menu. (Obviously, menu items on different pull-down menus can have the same underlined letter.) To indicate the underlined key, you simply place an ampersand (&) before it, as in Save &As... or &File. In these examples, the underlined keys would be A for Save As and F for File.

Menu items have another standard feature: shortcut keys. When you see the shorthand description of a key, or key combination, beside a menu item, it means you can press those keys to give that command. Although giving menu commands with the mouse is easier, it tends to be somewhat slow, particularly for keyboard-intensive applications, since you have to move one of your hands from the keyboard to the mouse. Pressing Alt and the underlined letter might be faster, but it still requires two operations. Using a shortcut key usually involves pressing a special key and another key at the same time (such as Ctrl+C). Windows doesn't even display the corresponding pull-down menu, so this results in a faster internal operation, too.

In Delphi, associating a shortcut key with a menu item (pull-down menus cannot have a shortcut key) is very easy. You simply select a value for the ShortCut property, choosing one of the standard combinations: Ctrl or Shift plus almost any key.

You might even add shortcut keys to a program without adding a real menu. For example, you can create a pop-up menu, connect it to a form (by setting the PopupMenu property of the form), set the Visible property of all of its items to False, and add the proper shortcut keys; a user will never see the menu, but the shortcuts (documented in your Help system, of course) will work. If this is not clear, you can look at the HShort example (the name stands for "Hidden Shortcut") on the companion CD.

Using the Predefined Menu Templates

To let you start developing an application's menu following the standard guidelines, Delphi contains some predefined menu templates. The templates include two different File pull-down menus, an Edit menu (including OLE commands), a Window menu, and two Help menus. There is also a complete MDI menu bar template, which has the same four menu categories.

Using these standard templates brings you some advantages. First of all, it is faster to reuse an existing menu than to build one from scratch. Second, the menu template follows the standard Windows guidelines for naming menu commands, for using the proper shortcuts, and so on. Of course, using these menus makes sense in a file-based application. But if the program you are writing doesn't handle files, has no editing capabilities, and is not MDI, you'll end up using only the template Help pull-down menu.

Responding to Menu Commands

To build the MenuOne example, the first example with a menu, we will extend the LabelCo example of the last chapter (its original form was shown in Figure 8.3). The new version of the form has been extended with a MainMenu component. This menu bar has four pull-down menus: the File pull-down with only the Exit option, the View pull-down with only the Toolbar menu item, the Options menu with various options, and the Help menu with the About menu item. You can see the menu bar in the Menu Designer in Figure 9.3.

FIGURE 9.3

The menu bar of the MenuOne application.

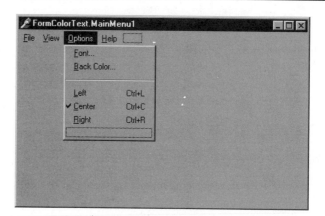

To add the separator in the Options pull-down menu, simply insert a hyphen as the text of the command. Do not change the Break property. (Except for rare situations, the Break property will make a mess of your menu. You are better off forgetting that this property even exists.)

TIP
Of course, the Break property has its uses, or it would not have been added to the component. You can better understand it if I use different names for its possible values, NewLine or NewColumn. If an item on the menu bar has the mbMenuBarBreak (or NewLine) value, this item will be displayed in a second or subsequent line. If a menu item has the mbMenuBreak (or NewColumn) value, this item will be added to a second or subsequent column of the pull-down. Neither of these features are used very often.

The Code Generated by the Menu Designer

Once you have built this menu, take a look at the list of components displayed by the Object Inspector, or open the DFM file with the textual description of the form, which will also contain a textual description of the menu structure. Here is the portion of the textual description of the form related to the menu and its items:

```
object MainMenu1: TMainMenu
  object File1: TMenuItem
    Caption = '&File'
    object Exit1: TMenuItem
      Caption = 'E&xit'
      OnClick = Exit1Click
    end
  end
  object View1: TMenuItem
    Caption = '&View'
    object Toolbar1: TMenuItem
      Caption = '&Toolbar'
      Checked = True
      OnClick = Toolbar1Click
    end
  end
  object Options1: TMenuItem
    Caption = '&Options'
    object Font1: TMenuItem
      Caption = '&Font...'
      OnClick = Font1Click
    end
```

```
    object BackColor1: TMenuItem
      Caption = '&Back Color...'
      OnClick = BackColor1Click
    end
    object N1: TMenuItem
      Caption = '-'
    end
    object Left1: TMenuItem
      Caption = '&Left'
      ShortCut = 16460 // stands for Ctrl+L
      OnClick = Left1Click
    end
    object Center1: TMenuItem
      Caption = '&Center'
      Checked = True
      ShortCut = 16451 // stands for Ctrl+C
      OnClick = Center1Click
    end
    object Right1: TMenuItem
      Caption = '&Right'
      ShortCut = 16466 // stands for Ctrl+R
      OnClick = Right1Click
    end
  end
  object Help1: TMenuItem
    Caption = '&Help'
    object About1: TMenuItem
      Caption = '&About Menu One...'
      OnClick = About1Click
    end
  end
end
```

As you can see in the listing above, there is a specific component for each menu item, one for each pull-down menu, and, surprisingly, even one for each separator. Delphi builds the names of these components automatically when you insert the menu item's label. The rules are simple:

- Any blank or special character (including ampersands and hyphens) is removed.

- If there are no characters left, the letter N is added.

- A number is always added at the end of the name (1 if this is the first menu item with this name, a higher number if not).

All of these new components are listed in the Object Inspector, and you can select them directly or navigate among them by opening the Menu Designer and selecting menu items visually. Actually each of these items is also listed as a component in the class definition of the form:

```
type
  TFormColorText = class(TForm)
    MainMenu1: TMainMenu;
    Options1: TMenuItem;
    Font1: TMenuItem;
    BackColor1: TMenuItem;
    N1: TMenuItem;
    Left1: TMenuItem;
    Center1: TMenuItem;
    Right1: TMenuItem;
    Help1: TMenuItem;
    About1: TMenuItem;
    File1: TMenuItem;
    Exit1: TMenuItem;
    View1: TMenuItem;
    Toolbar1: TMenuItem;
    ...
```

TIP

If there are menu items your code will not refer to (such as the separators), you can actually delete the fields declaring these objects (as N1 above). They will be created anyway, since they are listed in the form definition file, but you won't be able to access them easily from within the source code of the form. Since the objects are created anyway, you won't save much memory, though (only the space for the reference inside the form class), but removing useless statements may improve code readability.

To respond to menu commands, you should define a method for the OnClick event of each menu item. The OnClick event of the pull-down menus is used only in special cases—for example, to check whether the menu items below should be disabled. The OnClick event of the separators is totally useless, because it will never be activated.

> **TIP**
>
> Once you have defined the main menu of a form and it is displayed below the caption, you can add a new method for the OnClick event of a menu command simply by selecting it in the menu bar. If a handler is already present, Delphi will show you the corresponding portion of the source code; otherwise, a new method will be added to the form.

The Code of the MenuOne Example

The code of the MenuOne example is very simple, and is similar to that of the LabelCo example it extends. The OnClick event of the menu command for the background color and of the corresponding toolbar button are connected to the same method:

```
object BtnBackColor: TButton
  Caption = '&Back Color...'
  OnClick = BackColor1Click
end
```

This method has the same code as the earlier version.

The menu command and button related to the font are both connected to the Font1Click method, which this time displays the font selection dialog box, not the color selection dialog box. Notice that the code is quite compact, because it uses a with statement:

```
procedure TFormColorText.Font1Click(Sender: TObject);
begin
  with FontDialog1 do
  begin
    Font := Label1.Font;
    if Execute then
      Label1.Font := Font;
  end;
end;
```

The other three menu items of the Options pull-down menu (and the last three buttons of the toolbar) have basically the same code as the LabelCo example: the code of their OnClick event handlers simply set the Alignment property of the label. This works fine, but the resulting application doesn't follow the standard user-interface guidelines. Each time you have a series of choices in a menu, the selected choice should have a check mark beside it.

To accomplish this, you need to create two different operations. First, you have to place a check mark near the default choice, Center, changing the value of the menu item's Check property in the Object Inspector. Second, you should correct the code so that each time the selection changes, the check mark is properly set (as shown in Figure 9.4):

```
procedure TFormColorText.Left1Click(Sender: TObject);
begin
  Label1.Alignment := taLeftJustify;
  Left1.Checked := True;
  Center1.Checked := False;
  Right1.Checked := False;
end;
```

The other two methods are similar. You can simply copy the source code of the last three statements, paste this text twice into the other two methods, and correct the values of the three Checked properties so that each time one of them is set to True. Removing the check marks from the other items of the group can be handled in more efficient ways, but the real solution is to use radio menu items, instead of check marks. We'll look at this technique later on.

The View ➤ Toolbar menu item is a typical item with a check mark, set when the toolbar is visible. Here is its code:

```
procedure TFormColorText.Toolbar1Click(Sender: TObject);
begin
  Panel1.Visible := not Panel1.Visible;
  Toolbar1.Checked := Panel1.Visible;
end;
```

The program toggles the status of the Visible property of the panel, then sets the check mark—the Checked property—of the menu item accordingly. You should only remember to set the initial value of this property, to match the initial status of the panel. The Help ➤ About and File ➤ Exit commands simply show a message box or call the Close method of the form, respectively. They are so simple I won't show their source code here. (You can find it in the MenuOneF.PAS file on the CD.)

FIGURE 9.4

The check mark in the
pull-down menu of the
MenuOne example indi-
cates the current
selection.

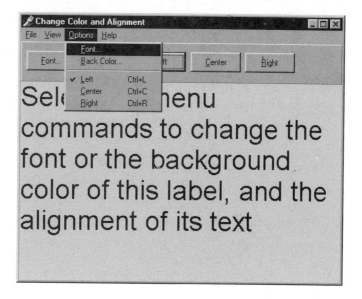

Modifying the Menu
at Run-Time

You can perform a number of operations in Windows to change the structure of a
menu at run-time. We'll start by examining in detail the operations you can do on
a single menu item, then move to pull-down menus, build a flexible main menu,
and change the default bitmap for the check mark.

Changing Menu Items at Run-Time

It is important to note that menu items can change at run-time. For example,
when a menu command cannot or should not be selected, it is usually grayed. In
this case, the user has no way to issue that command. You shouldn't generally
hide a menu item when it is not available, but simply disable it. This standard
technique lets users know that the command is currently not available.
Otherwise, they might think the menu command was somewhere else in the
menu structure, and keep looking for it.

Another visual change is the use of the check mark, which applications can toggle on and off easily, as we've seen in the last example. At times, to implement a state-setter menu item, you can change the text of the menu item altogether, which might result in an easier interface. For example, suppose an application has a Show Toolbar command. If you select it, a toolbar will appear and a check mark will be added to the item. This means that if you again select the Show Toolbar command, the toolbar will disappear: The command you issue has the opposite effect as its name. To avoid this problem, you might use two different captions for the two states of the menu item, such as *Show Toolbar* and *Hide Toolbar*.

When the user can select more than two choices, it is better to use multiple menu items with a check mark, or even better the new radio menu item user interface, which is becoming the standard approach.

Three properties are commonly used to modify a menu item:

- We used the Checked property in the example above to add or remove a check mark beside the menu item.

- The Enabled property can be used to gray a menu item so that it cannot be selected by a user (but it remains visible).

- The last property of this group is the Caption, the text of the menu item, which can be modified to reflect the actual effect of a command, as discussed above.

I'll demonstrate the use of these properties by extending the MenuOne example (the name of the new project is MenuOne2) with new menu items. I've added two new menu items to the View pull-down menu (Hide Label and Fixed Font) and two new menu items in the Options pull-down menu (Fixed View and Disable Help), plus a couple of new separators.

The Hide Label menu item demonstrates the use of different captions for an item depending on the status of the program. Here is its OnClick event handler:

```
procedure TFormColorText.HideLabel1Click(Sender: TObject);
begin
  Label1.Visible := not Label1.Visible;
  if Label1.Visible then
    HideLabel1.Caption := 'Hide &Label'
  else
    HideLabel1.Caption := 'Show &Label'
end;
```

Disabling Menu Items and Hiding Pull-Down Menus

The other three new menu items of the MenuOne2 example are used to disable or hide other menu items or pull-down menus. The View ➤ Fixed Font command is used to disable the Options ➤ Font menu item (as you can see in Figure 9.5):

```
procedure TFormColorText.FixedFont1Click(Sender: TObject);
begin
  ToggleCheck (FixedFont1);
  Font1.Enabled := not Font1.Enabled;
end;
```

FIGURE 9.5

A disabled menu item is still there, but cannot be selected. This screen-shot is taken from the MenuOne2 example.

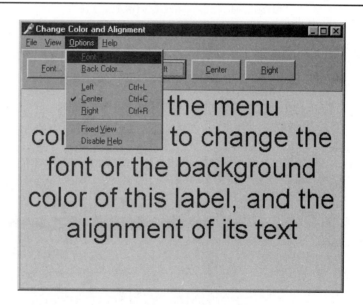

This method calls the custom `ToggleCheck` procedure I've written as a shortcut to the code for toggling the check mark (something all these three final menu commands do). Here is its simple code:

```
procedure ToggleCheck (Item: TMenuItem);
begin
  Item.Checked := not Item.Checked;
end;
```

I've already advised you against hiding menu items (by turning off their Visible property), because users will probably try to find them in a different pull-down menu. Menu items should generally be disabled when you want to prevent users from calling them. Hiding entire pull-down menus, however, is a common practice. In many applications the pull-down menus you see reflect the window you are working on. Technically, it is possible to disable a pull-down menu as well, but this is not very common. The last two menu items I've added to the program do these two operations, as you can see in their corresponding OnClick event handlers:

```
procedure TFormColorText.FixedView1Click(Sender: TObject);
begin
  ToggleCheck (FixedView1);
  View1.Visible := not View1.Visible;
end;

procedure TFormColorText.DisableHelp1Click(Sender: TObject);
begin
  ToggleCheck (DisableHelp1);
  Help1.Enabled := not Help1.Enabled;
end;
```

In Figure 9.6 you can see the effect of these two operations. The View pull-down menu has been removed, and the Help pull-down menu is grayed.

FIGURE 9.6

The form of the MenuOne2 example at run-time, with one pull-down menu disabled and one hidden.

Using Radio Menu Items

In addition to using check marks, in Windows 95 and in Windows NT 4.0, you can use radio menu items. These provide not only a different user interface, but also different behavior (basically simpler code, since the system does some of the work for us). A notable example of this new user-interface feature is the View menu of the Windows Explorer.

In Delphi, simply set the RadioItem property of a MenuItem component to True and you get the new check mark for the item. If you set this property for several consecutive menu items and set their GroupIndex property to the same value, they'll use the new mark and behave as radio buttons, as you can see in Figure 9.7. This means that only one of the menu items in the group will be selected at a time. Instead of having to deselect all other items manually, as you did in the first version of the MenuOne example, now you can simply select the proper menu item, and the rest is automatic.

FIGURE 9.7

The glyph of the new radio menu items, from the MenuOne3 example.

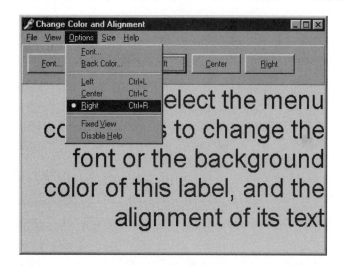

Here is how you can implement this feature, in the third version of the MenuOne example (which also has another feature I'll discuss in the next section). The following listing shows the updated textual description of this group of menu items:

```
object Options1: TMenuItem
  Caption = '&Options'
  ...
```

```
object Left1: TMenuItem
  Caption = '&Left'
  GroupIndex = 1
  RadioItem = True
  OnClick = Left1Click
end
object Center1: TMenuItem
  Caption = '&Center'
  Checked = True
  GroupIndex = 1
  RadioItem = True
  OnClick = Center1Click
end
object Right1: TMenuItem
  Caption = '&Right'
  GroupIndex = 1
  RadioItem = True
  OnClick = Right1Click
end
```

This code will work as is, but we can actually simplify it. Here is the new version of the Right1Click method:

```
procedure TFormColorText.Right1Click(Sender: TObject);
begin
  Label1.Alignment := taRightJustify;
  // Left1.Checked := False; // now useless
  // Center1.Checked := False; // now useless
  Right1.Checked := True;
end;
```

I've simply commented out the two useless statements, instead of deleting them, to let you see the differences from the older version.

Creating Menu Items Dynamically

The run-time changes on menu items and pull-down menus we've seen so far were all based on the direct manipulation of some properties. These components, however, also have some interesting methods, such as Insert and Remove, that you can use to make further changes.

The basic idea is that each object of the TMenuItem class—which Delphi uses for both menu items and pull-down menus—contains a list of menu items. Each of these items has the same structure, in a kind of recursive way. A pull-down menu has a list of submenus, and each submenu has a list of submenus, each with its own list of submenus, and so on.

The properties you can use to explore the structure of an existing menu are Items, which contains the actual list of menu items, and Count, which contains the number of subitems. Adding new menu items (or entire pull-down menus) to a menu is fairly easy. Slightly more complex is the handling of the commands related to the new menu items. Basically, you need to write a specific message-response method in your code (without any help from the Delphi environment), and then assign it to the new menu item by setting its OnClick property. As an alternative, you can have a single method used for several OnClick events and use its Sender parameter to determine which menu command the user issued.

All these features are demonstrated by the MenuOne3 example. As soon as you start this program, it creates a new pull-down with menu items used to change the size of the font of the big label hosted by the form. Instead of creating a bunch of menu items with captions indicating sizes ranging from 8 to 48, you can let the program do this repetitive work for you. I could have created the pull-down at design-time, and then added the menu items dynamically, but I prefer showing you the complete code, so that you can apply it to other cases.

To create a new menu item (or pull-down) you simply call the Create constructor of the TMenuItem class:

```
var
  PullDown: TMenuItem;
begin
  PullDown := TMenuItem.Create (self);
```

Then you can simply set its Caption and other properties, and finally insert it in the proper parent menu. The new pull-down should be inserted in Items of the MainMenu1 component. You can calculate the position, knowing the index is zero-based, or you can ask the main menu component for the previous pull-down menu:

```
Position := MainMenu1.Items.IndexOf (Options1);
MainMenu1.Items.Insert (Position + 1, PullDown);
```

The menu items of this pull-down are created in a while loop (I don't use a for loop because I want to provide only one menu item for every four possible sizes: 8, 12, 16, and so on). The code to create each item is slightly more complex simply because I want to turn them into radio items, but the basic structure of the code is very simple:

```
var
  Item: TMenuItem;
  I: Integer;
begin
  ...
  I := 8;
  while I <= 48 do
  begin
    Item := TMenuItem.Create (self);
    Item.Caption := IntToStr (I);
    PullDown.Insert (PullDown.Count, Item);
    I := I + 4;
  end;
```

To insert an item at the end I call the `Insert` method passing the number of items (`PullDown.Count`) as a parameter. You can see the final structure of the pull-down menu in Figure 9.8.

FIGURE 9.8

The Size pull-down menu of the MenuOne3 example is created at run-time, along with all of its menu items.

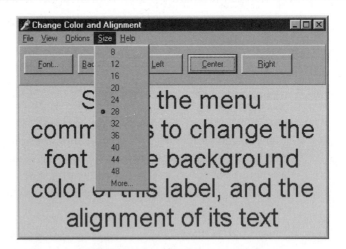

As you can see, the program adds one extra item at the end of the menu, used to set a different size than those listed. The `OnClick` event of this last menu item is handled by the `Font1Click` method, which shows the font selection dialog box:

```
Item := TMenuItem.Create (self);
Item.Caption := 'More...';
```

```
Item.OnClick := Font1Click;
PullDown.Insert (PullDown.Count, Item);
```

Also the `OnClick` events of the other menu items are connected with a method, but this time it is a method you have to define manually, by adding its declaration to the form class:

```
type
  TFormColorText = class(TForm)
    ...
  public
    procedure SizeItemClick(Sender: TObject);
end;
```

The method should have the proper signature (or parameters list). Here is the code of the method, which is based on the `Sender` parameter:

```
procedure TFormColorText.SizeItemClick(Sender: TObject);
begin
  with Sender as TMenuItem do
    Label1.Font.Size := StrToInt (Caption);
end;
```

As you can see, this code doesn't set the proper check mark (or radio item mark) next to the selected item. The reason is that the user can select a new size by changing the font. For this reason, we can use a different approach, and handle the `OnClick` event of the pull-down menu. This event is activated just before showing the pull-down menu, so we can use it to set the proper check mark at that time:

```
procedure TFormColorText.SizeClick (Sender: TObject);
var
  I: Integer;
  Found: Boolean;
begin
  Found := False;
  with Sender as TMenuItem do
  begin
    // look for a match, skipping the last item
    for I := 0 to Count - 2 do
      if StrToInt (Items [I].Caption) =
        Label1.Font.Size then
      begin
        Items [I].Checked := True;
        Found := True;
        System.Break; // skip the rest of the loop
```

```
      end;
    if not Found then
      Items [Count - 1].Checked := True;
  end;
end;
```

This code scans the items of the pull-down menu we have activated (the Sender), skipping only the final one, and checks whether the caption matches the current Size of the font of the label. If no match is found, the program checks the last menu item, to indicate that a different size is active.

Of course we have to set this SizeClick event handler at run-time, when the pull-down menu is created. So we can finally look at the complete source code of the FormCreate method, which sums up all the features I have discussed in this section:

```
procedure TFormColorText.FormCreate(Sender: TObject);
var
  PullDown, Item: TMenuItem;
  Position, I: Integer;
begin
  // create the new pulldown menu
  PullDown := TMenuItem.Create (self);
  PullDown.Caption := '&Size';
  PullDown.OnClick := SizeClick;
  // compute the position and add it
  Position := MainMenu1.Items.IndexOf (Options1);
  MainMenu1.Items.Insert (Position + 1, PullDown);
  // create menu items for various sizes
  I := 8;
  while I <= 48 do
  begin
    // create the new item
    Item := TMenuItem.Create (self);
    Item.Caption := IntToStr (I);
    // make it a radio item
    Item.GroupIndex := 1;
    Item.RadioItem := True;
    // handle click and insert
    Item.OnClick := SizeItemClick;
    PullDown.Insert (PullDown.Count, Item);
    I := I + 4;
  end;
  // add extra item at the end
```

```
    Item := TMenuItem.Create (self);
    Item.Caption := 'More...';
    // make it a radio item
    Item.GroupIndex := 1;
    Item.RadioItem := True;
    // handle click by showing the font dialog box
    Item.OnClick := Font1Click;
    PullDown.Insert (PullDown.Count, Item);
  end;
```

Creating Menus and Menu Items Dynamically

When you want to create a menu or a menu item dynamically, you can use the corresponding components, as I've done in the MenuOne3 example. As an alternative, you can also use some global functions available in the Menus unit:

```
function NewMenu(Owner: TComponent; const AName: string;
  Items: array of TMenuItem): TMainMenu;
function NewPopupMenu(Owner: TComponent;
  const AName: string; Alignment: TPopupAlignment;
  AutoPopup: Boolean; Items: array of TMenuitem):
  TPopupMenu;
function NewSubMenu(const ACaption: string;
  hCtx: Word; const AName: string;
  Items: array of TMenuItem): TMenuItem;
function NewItem(const ACaption: string;
  AShortCut: TShortCut; AChecked, AEnabled: Boolean;
  AOnClick: TNotifyEvent; hCtx: Word;
  const AName: string): TMenuItem;
function NewLine: TMenuItem;
```

The NewMenu and NewPopupMenu functions, in particular, should be used to create brand-new menus. Calling the constructors of the corresponding classes, in fact, doesn't always work properly.

Short and Long Menus

If you don't like creating menu items dynamically, but still need to have a very flexible menu, there are a couple of good alternatives. You can create a large menu with all the items you need, then hide all the items and pull-down menus you do not want at the beginning. To add a new command you need only show it. This solution is a follow-up to what we have done up to now.

You can also create several menus, possibly with common elements, and exchange them as required. This approach is demonstrated in this section. A typical example of a form having two menus is one that uses two different sets of menus (long and short) for two different kinds of users (expert and inexperienced). This technique was common in major Windows applications for some years but has since been replaced by other approaches, such as letting each user redefine the whole structure of the menu.

The idea is simple and its implementation straightforward:

1. Prepare the full menu of the application, adding a menu item with the Caption *'Short'*.

2. Add this menu to the Delphi menu template.

3. Place a second MainMenu component on the form, and copy its structure from the template.

4. In the second menu, remove the items corresponding to advanced features and change the Caption of the special item from *'Short'* to *'Long'*.

5. In the Menu property of the form, set the MainMenu component you want to use when the application starts, choosing one of the two available. Note that this operation has an effect on the form at design-time, too.

6. Write the code for the Short and Long commands so that when they are selected, the menu changes.

If you follow these steps, you'll end up with an application similar to TwoMenus (see Figure 9.9), which can change its menu at run-time. The example has two different MainMenu components, with useless "dummy" menu items, plus the Short and Long commands.

FIGURE 9.9

The long and short
menus of the TwoMenus
example.

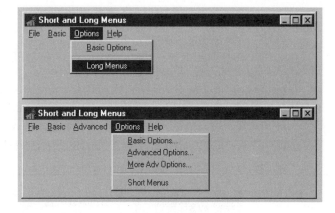

The application does nothing apart from changing the main menu when the
Short Menu or Long Menu items are selected. Here is the code for the Short Menu
item:

```
procedure TForm1.ShortMenus1Click(Sender: TObject);
begin
  {activate short menu}
  Form1.Menu := MainMenu2;
end;
```

Graphical Menu Items

Besides the run-time changes on a menu's structure I've listed so far, which are all
directly available in Delphi, there are a number of operations you can perform on
menus using the Windows API. In fact, there are several API functions referring
to menus.

In particular, using Windows API functions for menus lets us add some graphics
to them. We can customize the check mark, replace the strings with bitmaps, and
even paint in the menu items.

Customizing the Menu Check Mark

As I've just mentioned, there are a number of ways to customize a menu in Windows. In this section, I'm going to show you how you can customize the check

mark used by a menu item, using two bitmaps of your own. This example, New-Check, involves using bitmaps and calling a Windows API function.

First I should explain why we need two bitmaps, not just one. If you look at a menu item, it can have either a check mark or nothing. In general, however, Windows uses two different bitmaps for the checked and unchecked menu item. I've prepared two bitmaps, of 16 x 14 pixels, using the Delphi Image Editor (see Figure 9.10). You can easily run this program from the Tools menu, but you can prepare the bitmaps with any editor, including Windows Paintbrush. The bitmaps should be stored in two BMP files in the same directory as the project.

FIGURE 9.10

One of the two new check marks in the Delphi Image Editor.

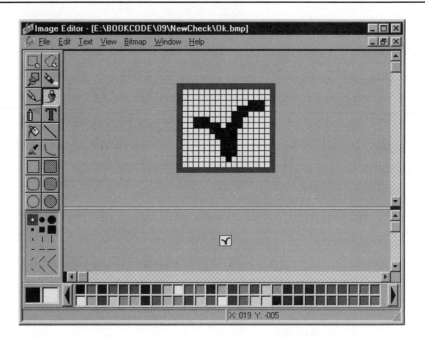

The NewCheck example has a very simple form, with just two components, a MainMenu and a label:

```
object Form1: TForm1
  Caption = 'New Check'
  Menu = MainMenu1
  OnCreate = FormCreate
  OnDestroy = FormDestroy
  object Label1: TLabel
```

```
      Alignment = taCenter
      AutoSize = False
      Caption = 'OFF'
      Font.Height = -96
      Font.Name = 'Arial'
      Font.Style = [fsBold]
    end
    object MainMenu1: TMainMenu
      object Command1: TMenuItem
        Caption = '&Command'
        OnClick = Command1Click
        object Toggle1: TMenuItem
          Caption = '&Toggle'
          OnClick = Toggle1Click
        end
      end
    end
  end
```

As you can see in the listing above, the menu item has a single command (Toggle), which will be used to change the text of the label from 'ON' to 'OFF' and change the check mark, too:

```
procedure TForm1.Toggle1Click(Sender: TObject);
begin
  Toggle1.Checked := not Toggle1.Checked;
  if Toggle1.Checked then
    Label1.Caption := 'ON'
  else
    Label1.Caption := 'OFF';
end;
```

The most important portion of the code of this example is the call to the SetMenuItemBitmaps Windows API function:

```
function SetMenuItemBitmaps (Menu: HMenu;
  Position, Flags: Word;
  BitmapUnchecked, BitmapChecked: HBitmap): Bool;
```

This function has a number of parameters:

- The first parameter is the pull-down menu we refer to.

- The second parameter is the position of the menu item in that pull-down menu.

- The third parameter is a flag that determines how to interpret the previous parameter (Position).

- The last two parameters indicate the bitmaps that should be used.

Notice that this function changes the check mark bitmaps only for a specific menu item. Here is the code you can use in Delphi to call the function (see Figure 9.11 for an example of the output):

```
procedure TForm1.Command1Click(Sender: TObject);
begin
  SetMenuItemBitmaps (Command1.Handle,
    Toggle1.Command, MF_BYCOMMAND,
    Bmp2.Handle, Bmp1.Handle);
end;
```

FIGURE 9.11

The NewCheck example at run-time. Notice the new check mark.

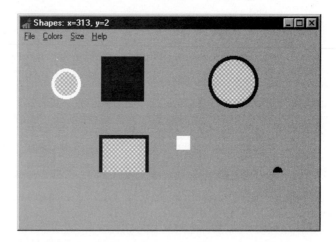

This call uses two bitmap variables that are defined in the code and the names of some components (Command1 is the name of the pull-down, and Toggle1 is the name of the menu item). The code above shows that it is usually very easy to pass the handle of an element to a Windows function—just use its Handle property.

At first I thought this function could be called when the form was created, after the two bitmaps had been loaded from the file, but it cannot. Delphi changes the default Windows behavior somewhat, forcing the application to reassociate the bitmap with the menu items each time they are displayed. The solution I've found is to execute this call each time the pull-down menu is selected—that is, on the OnClick event of the pull-down.

The only thing left is to load the bitmaps. You need to add two fields of the TBitmap type to the form class, create an instance of the two objects, and then load the bitmaps from the two BMP files. This is done only once, when the form is created:

```
procedure TForm1.FormCreate(Sender: TObject);
begin
  Bmp1 := TBitmap.Create;
  Bmp2 := TBitmap.Create;
  Bmp1.LoadFromFile ('ok.bmp');
  Bmp2.LoadFromFile ('no.bmp');
end;
```

The two bitmaps should also be destroyed when the program terminates (in the handler of the OnDestroy event of the form):

```
procedure TForm1.FormDestroy(Sender: TObject);
begin
  Bmp1.Free;
  Bmp2.Free;
end;
```

Notice that to run this program, you need to have the two BMP files in the same directory as the executable file. The bitmaps, in fact, are loaded at run-time and are not embedded by Delphi in the EXE file. As an alternative I could have used two nonvisible Image components to hold the images.

> **NOTE**
> You can indeed include a bitmap in the resources of an application and in its executable file in order to be able to ship the application in a single file. This process, however, is slightly more complex, so I've decided not to use it for the moment. Later chapters (starting with Chapter 11) include examples of the use of resources to store a bitmap. Chapter 27 is devoted entirely to Windows resources.

Bitmap Menu Items

Instead of placing a bitmap close to a menu item to indicate the status of its Checked property, as we've done in the previous section, you can actually replace the text of a menu item with a bitmap. In specific cases this can make an application easier to use. Figure 9.12 shows a bitmap menu from the BitMenu example I'll build in this section.

FIGURE 9.12

The Shape pull-down menu of the BitMenu example is based on bitmaps instead of strings.

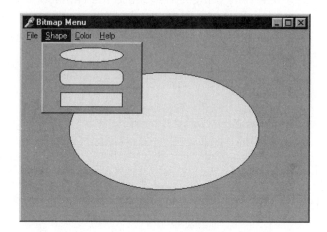

BitMenu is a very simple program. I've put a shape in the middle of a form and added a menu to set the kind of shape (rectangle, rounded rectangle, or ellipse), and its color. Here is the textual description of the form and its menu:

```
object Form1: TForm1
  Caption = ' Bitmap Menu'
  Menu = MainMenu1
  OnCreate = FormCreate
  OnDestroy = FormDestroy
  OnResize = FormResize
  object ShapeDemo: TShape...   // default properties
  object MainMenu1: TMainMenu
    object File1: TMenuItem...
      object Exit1: TMenuItem...
            end
    object Shape1: TMenuItem
      Caption = '&Shape'
      object Ellipse1: TMenuItem
        Caption = 'Ellipse'
        OnClick = Ellipse1Click
      end
      object RoundRec1: TMenuItem
        Caption = 'RoundRec'
        OnClick = RoundRec1Click
      end
      object Rectang1: TMenuItem
        Caption = 'Rectang'
```

```
          OnClick = Rectang1Click
        end
      end
    object Color1: TMenuItem
      Caption = '&Color'
      object Red1: TMenuItem
        Caption = 'Red'
        OnClick = Red1Click
      end
      object Green1: TMenuItem
        Caption = 'Green'
        OnClick = Green1Click
      end
      object Blue1: TMenuItem
        Caption = 'Blue'
        OnClick = Blue1Click
      end
    end
    object Help1: TMenuItem...
      object About1: TMenuItem...
  end
end
```

I've listed the complete description of the menu items because their captions will play an important role in the code, as you'll see shortly. As a second step I've made the program work, by handling the various menu commands. Here are two examples from the two main pull-down menus:

```
procedure TForm1.Red1Click(Sender: TObject);
begin
  ShapeDemo.Brush.Color := clRed;
end;


procedure TForm1.Ellipse1Click(Sender: TObject);
begin
  ShapeDemo.Shape := stEllipse;
end;
```

I've also written a handler for the OnResize event of the form, to resize the shape depending on the actual size of the form. Instead of setting its four positional properties (Left, Top, Width, and Height) I've called the SetBounds method. This approach leads to faster code.

Now that we've written the code of the program, it is time to turn the menu items into bitmaps. To accomplish this I've prepared a bitmap file for each of the three shapes and one for each of the three base colors. Technically these bitmaps can have any size, but to make them look nice they should generally be wide and low (the typical size of a menu item).

Having prepared the six bitmap files, each named with the caption of its menu items (plus the .BMP extension), I've written a handler for the OnCreate event of the form, and replaced the text of the items of the fake standard menu with bitmaps. This can be accomplished by calling the ModifyMenu API function:

```
function ModifyMenu (hMnu: HMENU;
    uPosition, uFlags, uIDNewItem: UINT;
    lpNewItem: PChar): BOOL; stdcall;
```

The first parameter is the handle of the menu we are working on (typically a pull-down menu), the second is the position of the item we want to modify, the third is some menu flags indicating the effect of other parameters, the fourth is the identifier of the menu item (stored by Delphi in the Command property), and the last is the new string for the menu item. How can we use this to set a bitmap, instead? We simply pass the handle of a bitmap in the last parameter (instead of the string), and use the mf_Bitmap menu flag among the values of the uFlags parameter.

Now you are ready to look at the source code, which is based on two for loops. I wanted to make the code as generic as possible, so that adding a new kind of shape or color will be pretty straightforward:

```
procedure TForm1.FormCreate(Sender: TObject);
var
    I: Integer;
    Bmp: TBitmap;
begin
    // load the bitmaps for the shapes
    for I := 0 to Shape1.Count - 1 do
    begin
        Bmp := TBitmap.Create;
        Bmp.LoadFromFile (Shape1.Items [I].Caption + '.bmp');
        ModifyMenu (Shape1.Handle,Shape1.Items [I].MenuIndex,
            mf_ByPosition or mf_Bitmap,
            Shape1.Items [I].Command, Pointer (Bmp.Handle));
        Shape1.Items [I].Tag := Integer (Bmp);
    end;
```

```
// load the bitmaps for the colors
for I := 0 to Color1.Count - 1 do
begin
  Bmp := TBitmap.Create;
  Bmp.LoadFromFile (Color1.Items [I].Caption + '.bmp');
  ModifyMenu (Color1.Handle, Color1.Items [I].MenuIndex,
    mf_ByPosition or mf_Bitmap, Color1.Items [I].Command,
    Pointer (Bmp.Handle));
  Color1.Items [I].Tag := Integer (Bmp);
end;
end;
```

TIP

In the two calls to the ModifyMenu **API function in the code above, we've used the** mf_ByPosition **flag in the third parameter, and passed the position of the item in the second parameter. However, we still need to pass the menu command as the fourth parameter, because this will be the command of the new menu item. If we don't, we'll lose the connection between the menu item and its Delphi event handler.**

As you can see I save the reference to each bitmap object I create in the Tag property of the corresponding menu item. The only reason I have to save the bitmap objects is to be able to destroy them when the application terminates:

```
procedure TForm1.FormDestroy(Sender: TObject);
var
  I: Integer;
begin
  for I := 0 to Shape1.Count - 1 do
    TBitmap (Shape1.Items [I].Tag).Free;
  for I := 0 to Color1.Count - 1 do
    TBitmap (Color1.Items [I].Tag).Free;
end;
```

As an alternative I could have saved the bitmap objects in an array (declared as a field of the form), and then destroyed each of the objects of the array at the end.

When you run this program, the Shape pull-down menu looks nice. The Color pull-down menu, however, is not working properly. As soon as you select it, in fact, the colors are displayed properly. But when you move over a menu item (as you can see by running the program) its colors are reversed by the menu item selection. Reversing the color you are asking for results in a very odd user interface: to select the color blue you have to click on an item that has temporarily turned to yellow!

Basically, you can use only black-and-white or gray-scaled bitmaps in a menu item. Color bitmaps create a lot of problems. If you want to obtain this effect, you should use an owner-draw menu item, as described in the next section.

Owner-Draw Menu Items

In Windows, the system is usually responsible for painting buttons, list boxes, edit boxes, menu items, and similar elements. Basically these controls know how to paint themselves. As an alternative, however, the system allows the owner of these controls, generally a form, to paint them. This technique, available for buttons, list boxes, combo boxes, and menu items, is called *owner-draw*.

Actually in Delphi the situation is slightly more complex. The components can take care of painting themselves also in this case (as is the case for the TBitBtn class for bitmap buttons), and eventually activate corresponding events. If you don't think about the internal details, owner-draw techniques for list boxes and combo boxes require you simply to write the handler for a couple of events.

Delphi provides no support for owner-draw menu items, though. So in this case we have to use the standard Windows approach, and handle a couple of system messages in our form (this technique was introduced in Chapter 5). Here is the definition of these methods in the source code of the ODMenu example, an extension of the BitMenu example discussed in the last section:

```
type
  TForm1 = class(TForm)
    ...
  public
    procedure WmMeasureItem (var Msg: TWmMeasureItem);
      message wm_MeasureItem;
    procedure WmDrawItem (var Msg: TWmDrawItem);
      message wm_DrawItem;
  end;
```

The wm_MeasureItem message is sent by Windows once for each menu item when the pull-down menu is displayed to determine the size of each item. The wm_DrawItem message is sent when an item has to be repainted. This happens when Windows first displays the items, and each time the status changes; for example, when the mouse moves over an item, it should become highlighted. In fact, to paint the menu items, we have to consider all the possibilities, including drawing the highlighted items with specific colors, drawing the check mark if required, and so on.

In the ODMenu example I'll handle the highlighted color, but skip other advanced aspects (such as the check marks). I've modified the CreateForm method to call the ModifyMenu API function passing the mfOwnerDraw menu flag. I also pass a code as the last parameter, to distinguish the various items. The other parameters are the same as in the previous version of the example:

```
procedure TForm1.FormCreate(Sender: TObject);
var
  I: Integer;
begin
  ...
  // turn the menu items into owner-draw items
  for I := 0 to Color1.Count - 1 do
  begin
    ModifyMenu (Color1.Handle,Color1.Items [I].MenuIndex,
      mf_ByPosition or mf_OwnerDraw,Color1.Items [I].Command,Pointer
(I));
  end;
end;
```

Now we have to write the code of the two owner-draw message handlers. The WmMeasureItem method receives as a parameter (in the corresponding TWmMeasureItem structure) a pointer to the Windows MeasureItemStruct structure (you can see the details of this structure in the Windows API help file). From this last structure we use the CtlType field, which stores the type of element we are measuring, to check whether this operation pertains to a menu. If it does, we use the ItemWidth and ItemHeight fields to set the width and height of the item. Since all items have the same size, the code is quite simple. The last thing we have to do is to provide a return value for the message, indicating we have handled it, in the Result field of the message structure. Here is the complete code:

```
procedure TForm1.WmMeasureItem (var Msg: TWmMeasureItem);
begin
  inherited;
  with Msg.MeasureItemStruct^ do
    if CtlType = odt_Menu then
    begin
      ItemWidth := 80;
```

```
        ItemHeight := 30;
        Msg.Result := 1; // we've handled it
    end;
  end;
```

Drawing a menu item is slightly more complex, since to write Delphi code we have to create a TCanvas object, which encapsulates a Windows *device context* handle. Since we have to free this object to avoid memory leaks, I've used a try-finally statement to destroy it even if an error occurs:

```
Canvas1 := TCanvas.Create;
Canvas1.Handle := hDC;
try
  ...
finally
  Canvas1.Free;
end;
```

The code assigns to the Handle property of this TCanvas object the hDC field passed by the message in the DrawItemStruct structure (there is, again, a pointer to this structure passed in one of the fields of the TWmDrawItem parameter of the message-handler method). This hDC field passes to our code the handle to the device context (the painting area, the Canvas) of the pull-down menu we are going to paint.

Once we have set up the drawing mechanism, we can start with the actual code. First we have to check the state of the menu item, stored in the ItemState field. If this includes the ods_Selected flag (a condition we can test by checking the result of a bitwise and expression); then we have to paint the background of the menu item using the Windows system color for the highlighted items, clHighlight. Otherwise, we use the standard color for menus, clMenu.

NOTE   As discussed in Chapter 7, some of the Delphi constants for colors correspond to the Windows system color. These colors are not fixed, but reflect the current color setting made by the user.

Once we've assigned to the Brush of the canvas the background color, we can easily paint it by calling the FillRect method. This method has one single parameter, corresponding to the rectangle we have to erase. This information is available in the rcItem field of the DrawItemStruct structure. Notice, by the way, that if you don't limit your drawing area to this rectangle, you can paint over other menu items as well!

The second step is drawing the actual colored areas, which don't depend on the status of the menu item, since we want each color to show up properly even if the item is selected. By looking to the ItemData field, the code retrieves the code passed as the last parameter of the ModifyMenu function call, used to make the menu item owner-draw. Depending on the value of this field, the program sets a proper value for the Color of the Brush using a simple case statement. At this point we only have to paint the area, by calling the Rectangle function and passing, in the four parameters, a smaller area than the full surface of the menu item. In fact we need to reserve a border with the background color. In the example the border is 5 pixels wide.

Here, finally, is the complete source code of the WmDrawItem method:

```
procedure TForm1.WmDrawItem (var Msg: TWmDrawItem);
var
  Canvas1: TCanvas;
begin
  inherited;
  with Msg.DrawItemStruct^ do
    if CtlType = odt_Menu then
    begin
      // create a canvas for painting
      Canvas1 := TCanvas.Create;
      Canvas1.Handle := hDC;
      try
        // set the background color and draw it
        if (ods_Selected and ItemState <> 0) then
          Canvas1.Brush.Color := clHighlight
        else
          Canvas1.Brush.Color := clMenu;
        Canvas1.FillRect (rcItem);
        case ItemData of
          0: Canvas1.Brush.Color := clRed;
          1: Canvas1.Brush.Color := clLime;
          2: Canvas1.Brush.Color := clBlue;
        end;
        Canvas1.Rectangle (rcItem.Left + 5, rcItem.Top + 5,
          rcItem.Right - 10, rcItem.Bottom - 10);
```

```
        finally
          Canvas1.Free;
        end;
      end;
  end;
```

You can see the effect of this code in Figure 9.13. I suggest you run this program along with the BitMenu program, to see the differences in the way the colored menu items are painted. Actually, looking at these two examples one might think of using the owner-draw technique also for menu items with black-and-white bitmaps.

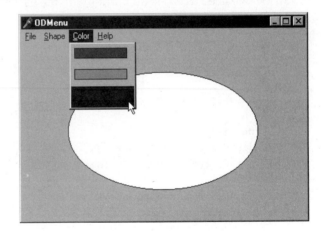

Customizing the System Menu

In some circumstances, it is interesting to add menu commands to the system menu itself, instead of (or besides) having a menu bar. This might be useful for secondary windows, toolboxes, windows requiring a large area on the screen, and for "quick-and-dirty" applications. Adding a single menu item to the system menu is straightforward:

```
AppendMenu (GetSystemMenu (Handle, FALSE),
  MF_SEPARATOR, 0, '');
AppendMenu (GetSystemMenu (Handle, FALSE),
  MF_STRING, idSysAbout, '&About...');
```

The code fragment above (extracted from the SysMenu example) adds a separator and a new item to the system menu item. The GetSystemMenu API function, which requires as a parameter the handle of the form, returns a handle to the system menu. The AppendMenu API function is a general-purpose function you can use to add menu items or complete pull-down menus to any menu (the menu bar, the system menu, or an existing pull-down menu). When adding a menu item, you have to specify its text and a numeric identifier. In the example I've defined this identifier as:

```
const
    idSysAbout = 100;
```

In the SysMenu example, this code is executed in the OnCreate event handler, and it produces the system menu you can see in Figure 9.14.

FIGURE 9.14

The new item of the Sysmenu example's system menu, added in the form's OnCreate event handler.

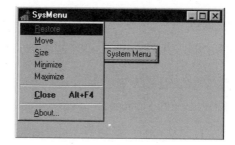

Adding a menu item to the system menu is easy, but how can we handle its selection? Selecting a normal menu generates the wm_Command Windows message. This is handled internally by Delphi, which activates the OnClick event of the corresponding menu item component. The selection of system menu commands, instead, generates a wm_SysCommand message, which is passed by Delphi to the default handler. Windows usually needs to do something in response to a system menu command.

We can intercept this command and check to see whether the command identifier (passed in the CmdType field of the TWmSysCommand parameter) of the menu item is our idSysAbout. Since there isn't a corresponding event in Delphi, we have to define a new message response method to the form class:

```
public
    procedure WMSysCommand (var Msg: TMessage);
        message wm_SysCommand;
```

The code of this procedure is not very complex. We just need to check whether the command is our own and call the default handler:

```
procedure TForm1.WMSysCommand (var Msg: TWMSysCommand);
begin
  if Msg.CmdType = idSysAbout then
    ShowMessage ('Mastering Delphi: SysMenu example');
  inherited;
end;
```

To build a more complex system menu, instead of adding and handling each menu item as we have just done, we can follow a different approach. Just add a MainMenu component to the form, create its structure (any structure will do), and write the proper event handlers. Then reset the value of the Menu property of the form, removing the menu bar. This way we have a MainMenu component but nothing on the screen.

Now we can add some code to the SysMenu example to add each of the items from the hidden menu to the system menu. This operation takes place when the button of the form is pressed. The corresponding handler uses generic code that doesn't depend on the structure of the menu we are appending to the system menu:

```
procedure TForm1.Button1Click(Sender: TObject);
var
  I: Integer;
begin
  // add a separator
  AppendMenu (GetSystemMenu (Handle, FALSE), MF_SEPARATOR, 0, '');
  // add the main menu to the system menu
  with MainMenu1 do
    for I := 0 to Items.Count - 1 do
      AppendMenu (GetSystemMenu (self.Handle, FALSE),
        mf_Popup, Items[I].Handle, PChar (Items[I].Caption));
  // disable the button
  Button1.Enabled := False;
end;
```

This code uses the expression self.Handle to access the handle of the form. This is required because we are currently working on the MainMenu1 component, as specified by the with statement.

The menu flag used in this case, mf_Popup, indicates that we are adding a pull-down menu. In this function call the fourth parameter is interpreted as the handle of the pull-down menu we are adding (in the previous example we passed the identifier of the menu, instead). Since we are adding to the system menu items with sub-menus, the final structure of the system menu will have two levels, as you can see in Figure 9.15.

FIGURE 9.15

The second-level system menu items of the Sys-Menu example are the result of copying a complete main menu to the system menu.

> **WARNING**
>
> The Windows API uses the terms *pop-up menu* and *pull-down menu* interchangeably. This is really odd, because most of us use the terms for two different things, the local menus and the secondary menus of the menu bar. Apparently, they've done this because these two elements are implemented with the same kind of internal windows; and the fact that they are two distinct user-interface elements is probably something that was later conceptually built over a single basic internal structure.

Once you have added the menu items to the system menu, you need to handle them. Of course you can check for each menu item in the WMSysCommand method, or you can try building a smarter approach. Since in Delphi it is easier to write a handler for the OnClick event of each item, as usual, we can look for the item corresponding to the given identifier in the menu structure. Delphi helps us by providing a FindItem method.

When we have found the menu item (and if we have found something), we can call its Click method (which invokes the OnClick handler). Here is the code I've added to the WMSysCommand method:

```
var
  Item: TMenuItem;
begin
  ...
```

```
Item := MainMenu1.FindItem (Msg.CmdType, fkCommand);
if Item <> nil then
  Item.Click;
```

In this code, The CmdType field of the message structure that is passed to the WMSysCommand procedure holds the command of the menu item being called.

You can also use a simple if or case statement to handle one of the system menu's predefined menu items that have special codes for this identifier, such as sc_Close, sc_Minimize, sc_Maximize, and so on. For more information, you can see the description of the wm_SysCommand message in the Windows API Help file, available in Delphi.

> **NOTE**
>
> This application works but has one glitch. If you click the right mouse button over the TaskBar icon representing the application, you get a plain system menu (actually even different than the default one). The reason is that this system menu belongs to a different window, the window of the Application global object. I'll discuss the Application object, and update this example to make it work with the TaskBar icon, in Chapter 25.

Building a Complete Menu

Now that we know how to write a menu, disable and check menu items, and so on, we are ready to build the menu for a full-fledged application. Do you remember the RichNote example of the last chapter? It was a simple editor based on a RichEdit component. You could use it to write and change the font of the selected text, but that was all. Now we want to add a menu and implement a number of features, including a complete scheme for opening and saving the text files. In fact, we want to be able to ask the user to save any modified file before opening a new one, to avoid losing any changes. Sounds like a professional application, doesn't it?

First of all, we need to build the menu, following the standard. The main menu starts with two standard pull-down menus, File and Edit, with the typical menu items. Then there are two specific pull-down menus, Font and Paragraph, with menu items to set the text font and alignment. The last two pull-down menus,

Options and Help, are *almost* standard: Their names are standard, but their menu items are not. The Options menu has commands to change the background color and to count the characters, and the Help menu has only the About menu item.

In this example, we want to implement most but not all of the commands of the menu. You'll see examples using all the Clipboard commands (the items of the Edit pull-down menu) will be implemented in Chapter 30. The following table shows the complete structure of the menu:

&File	&Edit	F&ont	&Paragraph	&Options	&Help
&New	Cu&t	&Times New Roman	&Left Aligned	&Background Color	&About RichNote...
&Open...	&Copy	&Courier New	&Right Aligned	&Read Only	
&Save	&Paste	&Arial	&Centered	&Count chars...	
Save&As...		&Bold			
&Print...		&Italic			
E&xit		&Small			
		&Medium			
		&Large			
		More &Fonts...			

Having added a complete menu, we can now get rid of the simple panel and the font button of the RichNote example. The only visual component left in the form of the RichNot2 version will be the RichEdit component, which is aligned with the client area. Then there is the MainMenu component, and four components for standard dialog boxes (OpenDialog, SaveDialog, FontDialog, and ColorDialog).

The File Menu

As I mentioned when we began working through the RichNot2 example, the most complex part of this program is implementing the commands of the File pull-down menu—New, Open, Save, and Save As. In each case, we need to track whether the current file has changed, saving the file only if it has. We should prompt the user to save the file each time the program creates a new file, loads an existing one, or terminates.

To accomplish this, I've added two fields and three methods to the class describing the form of the application:

```
private
  FileName: string;
  Modified: Boolean;
public
  function SaveChanges: Boolean;
  function Save: Boolean;
  function SaveAs: Boolean;
```

The FileName string and the Modified flag are set when the form is created and changed when a new file is loaded or the user renames a file with the Save As command. These two flags are initialized when the form is first created:

```
procedure TFormRichNote.FormCreate(Sender: TObject);
begin
  FileName := '';
  Modified := False;
end;
```

The value of the flag changes as soon as you type new characters in the RichEdit control (in its OnChange event handler):

```
procedure TFormRichNote.RichEdit1Change(Sender: TObject);
begin
  Modified := True;
end;
```

When a new file is created, the program checks whether the text has been modified. If so, it calls the SaveChanges function, which asks the user whether to save the changes, discard them, or skip the current operation:

```
procedure TFormRichNote.New1Click(Sender: TObject);
begin
  if not Modified or SaveChanges then
  begin
    RichEdit1.Text := '';
    Modified := False;
    FileName := '';
    Caption := 'RichNote - [Untitled]';
  end;
end;
```

If the creation of a new file is confirmed, some simple operations take place, including using 'Untitled' instead of the file name in the form's caption.

Short-Circuit Evaluation

The expression `if not Modified or SaveChanges then` requires some explanation. By default, Pascal performs what is called "short-circuit evaluation" of complex conditional expressions. The idea is simple: if the expression `not Modified` is true, we are sure that the whole expression is going to be true, and we don't need to evaluate the second expression. In this particular case, the second expression is a function call, and the function is called only if `Modified` is True. This behavior of `or` and `and` expressions can be changed by setting a Delphi compiler option called Complete Boolean Eval. You can find it on the Compiler page of the Project Options dialog box.

The message box displayed by the `SaveChanges` function has three options (see Figure 9.16). If the user selects the Cancel button, the function returns `False`. If the user selects No, nothing happens (the file is not saved) and the function returns `True`, to indicate that although we haven't actually saved the file, the requested operation (such as creating a new file) can be accomplished. If the user selects Yes, the file is saved and the function returns `True`.

FIGURE 9.16

The message box displayed by the RichNot2 example when the text of the RichEdit control has been changed and has not been saved.

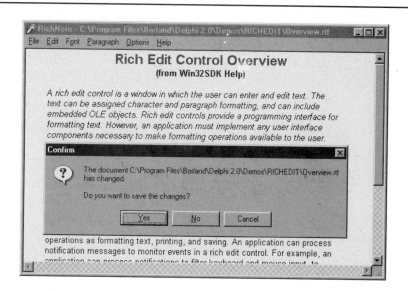

In the code of this function, notice in particular the call to the `MessageDlg` function used as the value of a `case` statement:

```
function TFormRichNote.SaveChanges: Boolean;
begin
  case MessageDlg (
    'The document ' + filename + ' has changed.' +
    #13#13 + 'Do you want to save the changes?',
    mtConfirmation, mbYesNoCancel, 0) of
  idYes:
    // call Save and return its result
    Result := Save;
  idNo:
    // don't save and continue
    Result := True;
  else // idCancel:
    // don't save and abort operation
    Result := False;
  end;
end;
```

TIP In the MessageDlg call above, I've added explicit newline characters (#13) to improve the readability of the output. As an alternative to using a numeric character constant, you can call Chr(13).

To actually save the file, another function is invoked: Save. This method saves the file if it already has a proper file name or asks the user to enter a name, calling the SaveAs functions. These are two more internal functions, not directly connected with menu items:

```
function TFormRichNote.Save: Boolean;
begin
  if Filename = '' then
    Result := SaveAs // ask for a file name
  else
  begin
    RichEdit1.Lines.SaveToFile (FileName);
    Modified := False;
    Result := True;
  end;
end;
```

```
function TFormRichNote.SaveAs: Boolean;
begin
  SaveDialog1.FileName := Filename;
  if SaveDialog1.Execute then
  begin
    Filename := SaveDialog1.FileName;
    Save;
    Caption := 'RichNote - ' + Filename;
    Result := True;
  end
  else
    Result := False;
end;
```

I use two functions to perform the Save and SaveAs operations (and do not call the corresponding menu handler directly) because I need a way to report a request to cancel the operation from the user. To avoid code duplication, the handlers of the Save and SaveAs menu items call the two functions too, although they ignore the return value:

```
procedure TFormRichNote.Save1Click(Sender: TObject);
begin
  if Modified then
    Save;
end;

procedure TFormRichNote.Saveas1Click(Sender: TObject);
begin
  SaveAs;
end;
```

Opening a file is much simpler. Before loading a new file, the program checks whether the current file has changed, asking the user to save it with the SaveChanges function, as before. The Open1Click method is based on the OpenDialog component, another default dialog box provided by Windows and supported by Delphi:

```
procedure TFormRichNote.Open1Click(Sender: TObject);
begin
  if not Modified or SaveChanges then
    if OpenDialog1.Execute then
    begin
      Filename := OpenDialog1.FileName;
      RichEdit1.Lines.LoadFromFile (FileName);
```

```
        Modified := False;
        Caption := 'RichNote - ' + FileName;
      end;
  end;
```

The only other detail related to file operations is that both the OpenDialog and SaveDialog components of the NotesForm have a particular value for their `Filter` and `DefaultExt` properties, as you can see in the following fragment from the textual description of the form:

```
object OpenDialog1: TOpenDialog
  DefaultExt = 'rtf'
  FileEditStyle = fsEdit
  Filter = 'Rich Text File (*.rtf)|*.rtf|Any file (*.*)|*.*'
  Options = [ofHideReadOnly, ofPathMustExist,ofFileMustExist]
end
```

The string used for the `Filter` property (which should be written on a single line) contains four pairs of substrings, separated by the | symbol. Each pair has a description of the type of file that will appear in the File Open or File Save dialog box, and the filter to be applied to the files in the directory, such as `*.RTF`. To set the filters in Delphi, you can simply invoke the editor of this property, which displays a list with two columns (see Figure 9.17).

FIGURE 9.17

The standard Open File dialog box in the RichNot2 program. On the left you can see the value of the Filter property in the Object Inspector and the Filter Editors.

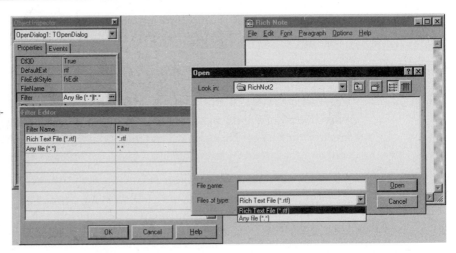

The file-related methods above are also called from the `FormCloseQuery` method (the handler of the `OnCloseQuery` event), which is called each time the user tries to close the form, terminating the program. We can make this happen in various ways—by double-clicking on the system menu icon, selecting the system menu's Close command, pressing the Alt+F4 keys, or calling the `Close` method in the code, as in the File ➤ Exit menu command.

In `FormCloseQuery`, you can decide whether or not to actually close the application by setting the `CanClose` parameter, which is passed by reference. Again, if the current file has been modified, we call the `SaveChanges` function and use its return value. Again we can use the short-circuit evaluation technique:

```
procedure TFormRichNote.FormCloseQuery(Sender: TObject;
  var CanClose: Boolean);
begin
  CanClose := not Modified or SaveChanges;
end;
```

The last menu item of the File menu is the Print command. I'll discuss printing in detail in Chapter 28, but since the RichEdit component includes print capabilities and they are very simple to use, I've decided to implement it anyway. Here is the code, which actually produces a very nice printout:

```
procedure TFormRichNote.Print1Click(Sender: TObject);
begin
  RichEdit1.Print (FileName);
end;
```

The Paragraph Menu

Compared to the File menu, the other pull-down menus of this example are simpler. The code of the Paragraph menu is based on some properties of its items. Here is their textual description (extracted from the DFM file):

```
object Paragraph1: TMenuItem
  Caption = '&Paragraph'
  object LeftAligned1: TMenuItem
    Caption = '&Left Aligned'
    Checked = True
    GroupIndex = 1
    RadioItem = True
```

```
      OnClick = RightAligned1Click
    end
  object RightAligned1: TMenuItem
    Caption = '&Right Aligned'
    GroupIndex = 1
    RadioItem = True
    OnClick = RightAligned1Click
  end
  object Centered1: TMenuItem
    Caption = '&Centered'
    GroupIndex = 1
    RadioItem = True
    OnClick = RightAligned1Click
  end
end
```

As you can see, the program uses radio menu items, by giving to the three items the same value for the GroupIndex property and setting the RadioItem property to True. The menu items also share the same RightAligned1Click method for their OnClick event. Here is the code of the method, which is based on the correspondence between the position of the menu items in the pull-down (indicated by their MenuIndex property) and the order of the values of the TAlignment enumeration. It is a trick, but it works. Here is the code:

```
procedure TFormRichNote.RightAligned1Click(Sender: TObject);
begin
  RichEdit1.Paragraph.Alignment :=
    TAlignment ((Sender as TMenuItem).MenuIndex);
  (Sender as TMenuItem).Checked := True;
end;
```

First, this procedure sets the alignment of the current paragraph (the paragraph including the selected text or the editor cursor), then it checks the current menu item—the menu item that has activated the method (the Sender object). As you can see, this code relies on some controlled typecasts, based on the as keyword: this is what you have to do any time you want to write generic code (that is, to attach the same methods to events of different components).

Notice that setting the check mark for the current menu item is correct only until you change the selection or the current line in the text. For this reason, we can handle the OnSelectionChange event of the RichEdit component, and update the check mark of the Paragraph menu each time:

```
procedure TFormRichNote.RichEdit1SelectionChange(Sender: TObject);
begin
  Paragraph1.Items [Integer (RichEdit1.Paragraph.Alignment)].
    Checked := True;
end;
```

The Font Menu

The Font pull-down menu is built on the same concept, but it has two groups of radio items, plus items with a standard check mark. Each group, then, uses a different approach to handle the menu item selection with a single event response method. You can see the details of the properties of the menu items directly in the RichForm .DFM source code file on the CD (this listing was too long to reproduce here).

The code of the first group of menu items (used to select the font) is based on a simple trick: the name of the font to select corresponds to the Caption of the menu item, without the initial & character:

```
procedure TFormRichNote.TimesRoman1Click(Sender: TObject);
var
  FontName: string;
begin
  // get the font name and remove the &
  FontName := (Sender as TMenuItem).Caption;
  Delete (FontName, 1, 1);
  // change selected text font
  if RichEdit1.SelLength > 0 then
    RichEdit1.SelAttributes.Name := FontName;
  (Sender as TMenuItem).Checked := True;
end;
```

This code acts on the current selection (using the SelAttributes property of the RichEdit1 component), as the RichNote example in Chapter 8 did. Notice that you can easily extend this code by adding new menu items consisting of the name of the font preceded by the & character. Then you'll necessarily have to set the same value for the GroupIndex property of the previous items (in this case 1). So if you simply set the RadioItem property to True and connect the OnClick event to the Times-Roman1Click method, they'll behave just like the existing font selection menu items.

The second group of items controls the selection of the bold and italic styles. This is accomplished by two similar but separate methods. Here is one of them:

```
procedure TFormRichNote.Bold1Click(Sender: TObject);
begin
  Bold1.Checked := not Bold1.Checked;
  if RichEdit1.SelLength > 0 then
    with RichEdit1.SelAttributes do
      if Bold1.Checked then
        Style := Style + [fsBold]
      else
        Style := Style - [fsBold];
end;
```

The last part of the menu has another group of radio menu items, used to set the size of the font. These menu items refer to a font size in the caption and have the same value stored in their Tag property. This makes the code very easy to write. Again, there is a single method for the three menu items, but you can add new items to this group with very little effort:

```
procedure TFormRichNote.Large1Click(Sender: TObject);
begin
  if RichEdit1.SelLength > 0 then
    RichEdit1.SelAttributes.Size :=(Sender as TMenuItem).Tag;
  (Sender as TMenuItem).Checked := True;
end;
```

The last item of this menu simply activates the Font dialog box. Notice that the font returned by this dialog box cannot be assigned directly to the SelAttributes property; we need to call the Assign method, instead:

```
procedure TFormRichNote.More1Click(Sender: TObject);
begin
  FontDialog1.Font := RichEdit1.Font;
  if FontDialog1.Execute then
    RichEdit1.SelAttributes.Assign (FontDialog1.Font);
  // update the check marks
  RichEdit1SelectionChange (self);
end;
```

All the commands of this menu affect the status of the current selection, setting the check boxes and radio items properly, as you can see in Figure 9.18. The method above, instead, calls the RichEdit1SelectionChange method. This is the handler of the OnSelectionChange event of the RichEdit component.

FIGURE 9.18

The check marks and radio items of the Font menu of the RichNot2 example indicate the status of the current selection.

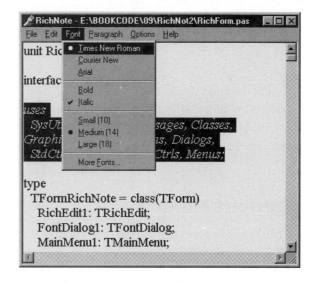

This method scans some of the groups to determine which element has to be checked. As in other examples before, this code has been written so that you can easily extend it for new menu items (the listing also includes the code used to reset the paragraph alignment, discussed earlier):

```
procedure TFormRichNote.RichEdit1SelectionChange(Sender: TObject);
var
  FontName: string;
  I: Integer;
begin
  // check the font name radio menu item
  FontName := '&' + RichEdit1.SelAttributes.Name;
  for I := 0 to 2 do
    with Font1.Items [I] do
      if FontName = Caption then
        Checked := True;
  // check the bold and italic items
  Italic1.Checked :=
    fsItalic in RichEdit1.SelAttributes.Style;
  Bold1.Checked :=
    fsBold in RichEdit1.SelAttributes.Style;
  // check the font size
  for I := Small1.MenuIndex to Large1.MenuIndex do
    with Font1.Items [I] do
      if Tag = RichEdit1.SelAttributes.Size then
```

```
        Checked := True;
    // check the paragraph style
    Paragraph1.Items [Integer (RichEdit1.Paragraph.Alignment)].
        Checked := True;
    end;
```

This method doesn't work perfectly. When you set a custom font, the selection doesn't change properly (because the current item remains selected). To fix it, we should remove any radio check mark when the value is not one of the possible selections, or add new menu items for this special case. The example is complex enough, so I think we can live with this minor inconvenience.

The Options Menu

The last pull-down menu of the RichNot2 example is the Options menu. This menu has three unrelated commands used to customize the user interface, and to determine and display the length of the text. The first command displays a color selection dialog box, used to change the color of the background of the RichEdit component:

```
procedure TFormRichNote.BackColor1Click(Sender: TObject);
begin
  ColorDialog1.Color := RichEdit1.Color;
  if ColorDialog1.Execute then
    RichEdit1.Color := ColorDialog1.Color;
end;
```

The second command can be used to mark the text as read-only. In theory this property should be set depending on the status of the file on the disk. In the example, instead, the user can toggle the read-only attribute manually:

```
procedure TFormRichNote.ReadOnly1Click(Sender: TObject);
begin
  RichEdit1.ReadOnly := not RichEdit1.ReadOnly;
  ReadOnly1.Checked := not ReadOnly1.Checked;
end;
```

The last menu item activates a method to count the number of characters in the text and display the total in a message box. The core of the method is the call to the GetTextLen function of the RichEdit control. The number is extracted and formatted into an output string:

```
procedure TFormRichNote.Countchars1Click(Sender: TObject);
begin
  MessageDlg (Format (
```

```
     'The text has %d characters', [RichEdit1.GetTextLen]),
     mtInformation, [mbOK], 0);
  end;
```

The handler of the OnClick event of this last item of the Options menu terminates the example. As mentioned at the beginning, this was a rather long and complex example, but its purpose was to show you the implementation of the menu commands of a real-world application. In particular, I explained in detail the File pull-down menu because this is something you'll probably need to handle in any file-related application.

Now we are ready to delve into another topic involving menus, the use of local menus activated by the right mouse button click.

Pop-Up Menus

In Windows 95, it is common to see applications that have special local menus you activate by clicking the right mouse button. The menu that is displayed—a pop-up menu, in common Windows terminology—usually depends on the position of the mouse click. These menus tend to be easy to use since they group only the few commands related to the element that is currently selected. They are also usually faster to use than full-blown menus because you don't need to move the mouse up to the menu bar and then down again to go on working.

In Delphi, there are basically two ways to display pop-up menus, using the corresponding component. You can let Delphi handle them automatically or you can choose a manual technique. I'll explore both approaches, starting with the first, which is the simplest one.

To add a pop-up menu to a form, you need to perform a few simple operations. Create a PopupMenu component, add some menu items to it, and select the component as the value of the form's PopupMenu property. That's all. Of course, you should also add some handlers for the OnClick events of the local menu's various menu items, as you do with an ordinary menu.

An Automatic Local Menu

To show you how to create a local menu, I've built an example that is an extension of the Dragging example of Chapter 8. The new example is named Local1. I've added a first PopupMenu component to the form and connected it using the

PopupMenu property of the form itself. Once this is done, running the program and clicking the right mouse button on the form displays the local menu.

Then, I've added a second pop-up menu component, with two levels, to the form, and I've attached it to the StaticText component on the right, LabelTarget. To connect a local menu to a specific component, you simply need to set its PopupMenu property. You can see the result in Figure 9.19. The four methods related to the first group of commands of the Colors pull-down menu just select a color:

```
procedure TDraggingForm.Aqua1Click(Sender: TObject);
begin
  LabelTarget.Color := clAqua;
end;
```

The Transparent command selects the color of the parent form as the current color, setting the value of the ParentColor property to True.

FIGURE 9.19

The checked Alignment pull-down menu of the second pop-up in the Local1 example.

The last command of the pull-down menu, User Defined, presents the standard Color Selection dialog box to the user. The three commands of the pop-up menu's second pull-down change the alignment of the text of the big label and add a check mark near the current selection, deselecting the other two menu items. Here is one of the three methods:

```
procedure TDraggingForm.Center1Click(Sender: TObject);
begin
  LabelTarget.Alignment := taCenter;
  Left1.Checked := False;
  Center1.Checked := True;
  Right1.Checked := False;
end;
```

A pop-up menu, in fact, can use all the features of a main menu and can have checked, disabled, or hidden items, and more. I could have also used radio menu items for this pop-up menu, but this doesn't seem to be a very common approach.

Modifying a Pop-Up Menu When It Is Activated

Why not use the same technique to display a check mark near the selected color? It is possible, but it's not a very good solution. In fact, there are six menu items to consider, and the color can also change when a user drags it from one of the labels on the left of the form. For this reason, and to show you another technique, I've followed a different approach.

Each time a pop-up menu is displayed, the OnPopup event is sent to your application. In the code of the corresponding method, you can place the check mark on the current selection of the color, independently from the action used to set it:

```
procedure TDraggingForm.PopupMenu2Popup(Sender: TObject);
var
  I: Integer;
begin
  {unchecks all menu items
    (not required for radio menu items)}
  with Colors1 do
    for I := 0 to Count - 1 do
      Items[I].Checked := False;
```

```
{checks the proper item}
case LabelTarget.Color of
  clRed: Red1.Checked := True;
  clAqua: Aqua1.Checked := True;
  clGreen: Green1.Checked := True;
  clYellow: Yellow1.Checked := True;
else
  if LabelTarget.ParentColor then
    Transparent1.Checked := True
  else
    UserDefined1.Checked := True;
  end;
end;
```

This method's code requires some explanation. At the beginning, the menu items are all unchecked by using a for loop on the Items array of the Colors1 menu. The advantage of this loop is that it operates on all the menu items, regardless of their number. Then the program uses a case statement to check the proper item.

Handling Pop-Up Menus Manually

In the Local1 example, we saw how to use automatic pop-up menus. As an alternative, you can set the AutoPopup property to False or not connect the pop-up menu to any component, and use the pop-up menu's Popup method to display it on the screen. This procedure requires two parameters: the x and y values of the position where the menu is going to be displayed. The problem is that you need to supply the *screen* coordinates of the point, not the client coordinates, which are the usual coordinates relative to the form's client area.

As an example, I've taken an existing application with a menu—the third version of the MenuOne example, described in this chapter—and added a peculiar pop-up menu. The idea is that there are two different pop-up menus, one to change the colors and the other to change the alignment of the text. Each time the user right-clicks on the caption, one of the two pop-up menus is displayed. In real applications, you'll probably have to decide which menu to display depending on the status of some variable. Here, I've followed a simple (and arbitrary) rule: Each time the right mouse button is clicked, the pop-up menu changes. My aim is to show you how to do this in the simplest possible way.

The two pop-up menus are very simple, and correspond to actions already available in the main menu (and connected with the same event handlers). Actually, I've built these pop-up menus by copying the main menu to a menu template and then pasting from it. The only change I've made is to remove the shortcut keys.

When the user clicks the right mouse button over the label, which takes up the whole surface of the form, a method displays one of the two menus. Instead of using the OnClick event, I've trapped the OnMouseDown event of the label. This second event passes as parameters the coordinates of the mouse click.

These coordinates are relative to the label, so you have to convert them to screen coordinates by calling the ClientToScreen method of the label:

```
procedure TFormColorText.Label1MouseDown(Sender: TObject;
  Button: TMouseButton; Shift: TShiftState; X, Y: Integer);
var
  ClientPoint, ScreenPoint: TPoint;
begin
  if Button = mbRight then
  begin
    ClientPoint.X := X;
    ClientPoint.Y := Y;
    ScreenPoint := Label1.ClientToScreen (ClientPoint);
    Inc (ClickCount);
    if Odd (ClickCount) then
      PopupMenu1.Popup (ScreenPoint.X, ScreenPoint.Y)
    else
      PopupMenu2.Popup (ScreenPoint.X, ScreenPoint.Y);
  end;
end;
```

In this procedure, you first have to check whether the right mouse button was clicked. The second step is to translate the coordinate of the position of the mouse click from client coordinates to screen coordinates. Screen coordinates are required by the PopupMenu component's Popup method.

The last thing we have to do is provide the proper check marks for the menu items of the second pop-up menu. A solution is to copy the current check marks of the main menu to the pop-up before displaying it:

```
if Odd (ClickCount) then
  PopupMenu1.Popup (ScreenPoint.X, ScreenPoint.Y)
else
begin
  {set the check marks as in the main menu}
  Left2.Checked := Left1.Checked;
```

```
  Center2.Checked := Center1.Checked;
  Right2.Checked := Right1.Checked;
  PopupMenu2.Popup (ScreenPoint.X, ScreenPoint.Y);
end;
```

An alternative solution—the one I've actually implemented in the Local2 example—is to set this check mark every time you set the check marks of the main menu, as in the following code:

```
procedure TFormColorText.Left1Click(Sender: TObject);
begin
  Label1.Alignment := taLeftJustify;
  Left1.Checked := True;
  Left2.Checked := True;
end;
```

In a more general application you might want to write a generic routine to apply the check marks more consistently, but in this example one of these two simple techniques will do.

What's Next

In this chapter, we have seen how to create main menus and pop-up menus in Delphi. We've discussed the standard guidelines for the names of the pull-down menus and of the menu items, shortcut keys, check marks, graphical menus, local menus, and many other topics. You can explore in other directions, as well. For example, you can create a menu dynamically (at run-time) or copy portions of a menu to another menu, as in the SysMenu example. We will see further examples of the use of menus, particularly in Chapters 13 and 15, when we will explore menu-merging techniques. I'll update the SysMenu example in Chapter 25, and use menus quite often in each of the following chapters.

The next step, however, is to explore in depth one of the most common elements of Delphi programming, forms. We've already used forms many times, but there are still many new features to discuss, and quite important ones. Then we'll move on to graphical components, toolbars, status bars, dialog boxes, and so on.

CHAPTER

TEN

10

Back to the Form

- The hidden application window

- Form styles and topmost forms

- Border styles and border icons

- Positioning and scaling forms

- Creating forms

- Closing forms

- Mouse and keyboard input

- Drawing and painting

If you've read all the chapters up to this point, you should now be able to use Delphi's basic components and to create and use menus. So let's turn our attention to the central element of development in Delphi: the form. We have used forms since the first chapter, but I've never described in detail what you can do with a form, which properties you can use, or which methods of the TForm class are particularly interesting.

In this chapter, we'll look at some of the properties and styles of forms and at their size and position. We'll also devote some time to input and output on a form, including an in-depth discussion of painting and drawing techniques. Let me start this chapter with a general, theoretical discussion of forms and windows.

Forms versus Windows

Do you remember the title of the first chapter of this book? It was "A Form Is a Window and..." and at the beginning of the text I explained that there is a sort of correspondence between the forms we create in Delphi and the windows in Windows. Now it's time to look into the details of this correspondence.

In Windows, most elements of the user interface are windows. For this reason, in Delphi most components are also based on windows—most of them, but not all. Of course, this is not what a user perceives. The distinction is not obvious, so you should study the following definitions carefully. Then we can make some further observations.

- From a user standpoint, a window is a portion of the screen surrounded by a border, having a caption and usually a system menu, that can be moved on the screen, closed, and at times also minimized and maximized. Windows move on the screen or inside other windows, as in MDI applications. These user windows can be divided into two general categories: main windows and dialog boxes.

- Technically speaking, a window is an entry in an internal memory area of the Windows system, often corresponding to an element visible on the screen, that has some associated code. One of the Windows system libraries contains a list of all the windows that have been built by every application and assigns to each of them a unique number (usually known as a *handle*). Some of these windows are perceived as such by users (see the first definition above), others have the role of controls or visual components, others are temporarily created by the system (for example, to show a pull-down menu), and still others are created by the application but remain hidden from the user.

The common denominator of all windows is that they are known by the Windows system and refer to a function for their behavior; each time something happens in the system, a notification message is sent to the proper window, which responds by executing some code. Each window of the system, in fact, has an associated function (generally called its *window procedure*), which handles the various messages the window is interested in.

In a Delphi application, these lower-level messages are turned into events by the system. But at times, as we have already seen in some examples, we handle low-level messages directly in a form. Delphi allows us to work at a higher level than the system, making application development much easier.

NOTE   The memory area of the Windows system allocated to listing all the windows that have been built is limited. Building too many windows reduces the so-called *system resources*. Windows 3.1 had a severe limit to the number of windows available in the system. In Windows 95, this limit has been greatly enlarged, and in Windows NT it doesn't even exist. Once there are too many windows in the system (counting all the controls and hidden windows, as well), you cannot create even one more window, something that will block most applications. This is why, in Delphi, there are a number of non-windowed components, including labels. This approach lets you save a lot of this system memory without having to worry about or even know about it.

With these general definitions in mind, we can now move back to Delphi and try to understand the role of forms. Forms represent windows from a user standpoint and can be used to build main windows, MDI windows, and dialog boxes. Their behavior depends mostly on their code, but also on a couple of very important properties I'll discuss in a moment. Many other components are based on windows, but only forms define windows from a user's point of view. The other windowed components, or controls, can be defined as windows only according to the second, technical definition.

Take as an example the first application in Chapter 1, Hello. Using the WinSight tool that comes with Delphi, you can see the list of the windows of the system; notice in particular the windows created by the application, as shown in Figure 10.1 (for more details on WinSight and the information it can deliver, see Chapter 26). These include the following windows:

- A main window, the form, with the title *Hello*. It is an overlapped window of class TForm1.

- A child window, the button inside the form, with the title *Say Hello*. This is a child window of class TButton.

- A hidden main window, the application window, entitled *Hello*. This is a pop-up window of class TApplication.

Notice that the names in brackets in WinSight, which are internal names of the system, correspond to the names of the classes of the Delphi components.

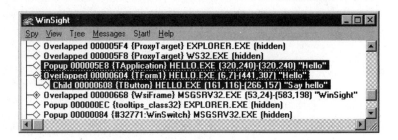

FIGURE 10.1

The windows of the Hello application as they appear in WinSight.

Overlapped, Pop-Up, and Child Windows

To understand the role of the various windows of this program, we need to look at some technical elements related to the Windows environment. These are not simple concepts, but I think they are worth knowing about.

Each window you create has one of three general styles that determine its behavior. These styles are overlapped, pop-up, and child:

- *Overlapped* windows are main windows of the application, which behave as you would probably expect.

- *Pop-up* windows are often used for dialog boxes and message boxes and can be considered a holdover from older versions of the system. In fact, in Windows 1.0, the windows were not overlapped but tiled, and only the pop-up windows could cover other windows. Pop-up windows are generally very similar to overlapped windows.

- The third group, *child* windows, was originally used for controls inside a dialog box. You can use this style for any window that cannot move outside the client area of the parent window. The obvious extension is to use child windows to build MDI applications, but, as we will see in Chapter 15, Microsoft added a fix-up technique to allow this behavior, which is not automatic.

It is important to note that, technically speaking, only child windows can have a parent. Any other window, however, can have an owner. An *owner* is a window that has a continuous message exchange with the windows it owns—for example, when the window is reduced to an icon, when it is activated, and so on. Usually a parent is also the owner, but it forces its child to live inside its client area. The child windows don't use screen coordinates; instead, they use the client area coordinates of their parent window—they borrow pixels not from the screen to display themselves but from their parent window.

WARNING The Windows API uses the same term (*Parent*) to indicate both the parent and the owner. Even the `GetParent` API function can return both items. Within the system, however, the two handles (that of the parent window and that of the owner window) are stored separately. This is indeed very odd, and causes a lot of confusion.

In Delphi, forms are all overlapped windows, even the dialog boxes, and the windowed components (the controls) you place inside a form are all owned by the form. However, their parent can be either the form or one of the special *container* components, such as the GroupBox or the Panel. When you place a radio button inside a group box, the group box is its parent, but the form is its owner. What about pop-up windows? In Delphi, they are used only for the hidden application window. In the system they are used for message boxes and pop-up or pull-down menus, just to mention two examples.

The Application Is a Window

From the analysis of the WinSight information, you might have noticed something very strange: The application is a window! The main form of a program works so well it appears to be the main window of the application. Instead, forms are connected to an owner, the application window. This window is hidden from sight unless you minimize the form, which makes the application window appear on the Taskbar (or as an icon in older versions of Windows).

> **NOTE** We noticed in previous chapters that the system menu of the Taskbar icon is different from the system menu of the form, and that the title of the Taskbar icon doesn't always match the caption of the main form.

What are the role and effect of this hidden main window? The role of the application object is to provide some startup code before you create any form, or even before you decide which form to create, as you can see with the View ➤ Project Source command after you've created or loaded a project.

The window related to the Application object—the application window—serves to keep together all the windows of an application. The fact that all the top-level forms of a program have this hidden owner window, for example, is fundamental when the application is activated. In fact, when the windows of your program are behind other windows, clicking on one window in your application will bring all of your application's windows to the front. In other words, the hidden application window is used to connect the different forms of the application.

The Application object, which is one of the few components not present in the Components Palette, has some properties, including the name of the executable file and the title of the application. The Title is usually the name of the executable file without the extension. You can see the application's Title in the Windows Taskbar. The same name appears when you scan the running applications with the Alt+Tab keys. To avoid a discrepancy between the two titles, you can change the application's title at design-time, in the Application page of the Project Options dialog box. At run-time, you can copy the form's caption to the title of the application with this code:

```
Application.Title := Form1.Caption;
```

In most applications, you simply don't care about the application window, apart from setting its Title and icon, and handling some of its events. However, there are some interesting uses of this global object and its window, as we'll see in Chapter 25.

WARNING   The presence of the hidden application window causes some other strange behavior in Windows. For example, Delphi applications do not tile or cascade properly. This is a less important issue in 32-bit versions of Windows.

Setting Form Styles

Among the properties of a form, two of them determine the fundamental rules of its behavior: `FormStyle` and `BorderStyle`. The first of these two special properties allows you to choose between a normal SDI form—*SDI* stands for *Single Document Interface*—and one of the windows that make up an MDI application—*MDI* stands for *Multiple Document Interface*.

These are the possible values of the `FormStyle` property:

- `fsNormal`: The form is a normal SDI window or a dialog box.

- `fsMDIChild`: The form is an MDI child window.

- `fsMDIForm`: The form is an MDI parent window—that is, the frame window of the MDI application.

- `fsStayOnTop`: The form is an SDI window, but it always remains on top of all other windows except for any that also happen to be *stay-on-top* windows.

Since an application following the Multiple Document Interface standard needs Windows of two different kinds (frame and child), two values of the `FormStyle` property are involved. To build an MDI application, you can use the standard application template or look at Chapter 15, which focuses on the MDI in detail. For now, though, it might be interesting to explore the use of the `fsStayOnTop` style.

Creating Topmost Forms

To create a topmost form (a form whose window is always on top), you need only set the FormStyle property, as indicated above. This property has two different effects, depending on the kind of form you apply it to:

- The main form of an application will remain in front of every other application (unless other applications have the same topmost style, too).

- A secondary form will remain in front of any other form of the application it belongs to. The windows of other applications are not affected, though.

Before we look at an example, consider that topmost windows can be useful, but they can also be very disappointing. When a topmost window is maximized, activating another application (for example, by pressing Alt+Tab) has almost no effect. My advice is to use topmost windows sparingly, and mostly for secondary windows, such as a toolbox. You can actually test this effect by setting the topmost attribute of many windows of the Delphi environment, using the window's local menu.

TIP

It is important to keep in mind that since the Delphi development environment is built in Delphi, its windows follow the same approach as the windows of the applications you build with it.

Building a topmost window is very easy. The Top example allows a user to toggle the topmost attribute on and off. The form of the example has only a menu component with a closing command, a menu item used to toggle the topmost style (initially set), and a multiple Help ➤ About menu command. This is used to test the behavior of message boxes when you have a topmost form.

When the user selects Style ➤ Stay on Top, the topmost style is toggled, together with the check mark (which is initially set):

```
procedure TForm1.StayOnTop1Click(Sender: TObject);
begin
  if FormStyle = fsStayOnTop then
    FormStyle := fsNormal
  else
    FormStyle := fsStayOnTop;
```

```
    StayOnTop1.Checked := not StayOnTop1.Checked;
  end;
```

When you execute this method, you can see some flickering on the screen when the topmost style is set or removed. This occurs because Delphi has to destroy and re-create the same window each time you toggle the value of the Topmost property.

The two menu items of the Help pull-down invoke a message box, using two different techniques. The first calls the MessageDlg VCL function, while the second calls the MessageBox API function. Strangely enough, the second works but the call to MessageDlg doesn't. According to the VCL documentation, to show a modal dialog from a topmost window you should first *normalize* it. This is the code that is supposed to work:

```
procedure TForm1.AboutMessageDlg1Click(Sender: TObject);
begin
  Application.NormalizeTopMosts;
  MessageDlg ('This is a MessageDlg',
    mtInformation, [mbOK], 0);
  Application.RestoreTopMosts;
end;
```

It doesn't seem to work in the current Delphi "build," although Borland may have fixed the problem by the time you read this.

WARNING When a topmost form displays a modal message box, that box may show up behind the form. However, since the message box is modal you cannot interact with the form, you can't even move it! So you are stuck. The only solution at this point is to use the Spacebar key or the Esc key or Alt+F4 to close the message box blindly.

Avoiding Topmost Flickering

To avoid the negative effect of topmost flickering, we can forget for a second what we know about Delphi and this form property and ask ourselves how we could have toggled the topmost attribute using the Windows API. There are a number of possible techniques. The topmost attribute is technically an extended Windows style (ws_ex_Topmost). For a style, we can use the SetWindowLong API function, which allows a programmer to change a number of window attributes at run-time.

A second approach is to use the SetWindowPos API function, which has seven parameters but in our case is easy to use. In fact, there are some flags we can use to toggle the topmost attribute, and we can ignore most of the parameters. To make a window a topmost window, we can write

```
SetWindowPos (Handle, hwnd_TopMost, 0, 0, 0, 0,
  swp_NoMove or swp_NoSize);
```

NOTE   SetWindowPos is a strange function. It requires the handle of the window you want to operate on, the handle of a second window or a special flag (to set the *z-order* of a window, a term indicating the relative position of windows along a *z*-axis coming out of the screen), two position-related parameters (x and y), two size parameters (cx and cy, the width and the height), and some flags. The strange thing is that you can use the flags to indicate which of the parameters make sense and should be used. For example, if you write swp_NoMove, the third and fourth parameters will be ignored (for this reason, I've just written some zeros in my code).

To get the opposite effect, removing the topmost style, simply replace hwnd_TopMost with hwnd_NoTopMost in the function call. The new version of the example is named Top2. Its form is the same as the previous one, aside from the fact that the topmost property is not enabled at first, and the corresponding menu check mark is off. Here is the code for the new version of the StayOnTop1Click method:

```
procedure TForm1.StayOnTop1Click(Sender: TObject);
begin
  if StayOnTop1.Checked then
    SetWindowPos (Handle, hwnd_NoTopMost,
      0, 0, 0, 0, swp_NoMove or swp_NoSize)
  else
    SetWindowPos (Handle, hwnd_TopMost,
      0, 0, 0, 0, swp_NoMove or swp_NoSize);
  StayOnTop1.Checked := not StayOnTop1.Checked;
end;
```

Notice that this time I've decided to test the status of the menu item's check mark to determine the current status of the form. In fact, the value of the FormStyle property always remains fsNormal, even when the topmost style of the form has been set. Remember that some properties of Delphi components duplicate information available in Windows and do not retrieve it every time you access it. This is always true for properties not having a direct correspondence in the system, such as a form's style.

If you experiment with Top and Top2, you'll notice that the second version has no flickering at all. Although Delphi is a great environment, at times, if you know what you are doing, you can bypass undesired behavior by using a direct call to the Windows API. With this said, you might wonder why Borland hasn't followed this approach. Well, there are a number of very good reasons. The technique based on the SetWindowPos API shown above works only in some circumstances, and doesn't work properly with secondary forms. However it seems that for my main topmost form the MessageBox and MessageDlg calls behave in the same odd way as the last example.

To sum up, if you have just a single window, you can use the approach shown above; otherwise, I suggest you stay with the Delphi solution. Better yet, consider avoiding the topmost flag for a main form whenever possible.

The Border Style

The second property of a form I want to focus on is BorderStyle. This property refers to a visual element of the form, but it has a much more profound influence on the behavior of the window. The BorderStyle property of a form has six possible values, as you can see in Figure 10.2:

- bsSizeable: The form has a standard thick border that a user can drag to resize it. This is the default style.

- bsDialog: The form has a standard dialog box border, which is thick but not resizable. A form with this style behaves like a dialog box—it really *is* a dialog box.

- bsSingle: The form has a thin border and cannot be resized; it is also known as a *fixed* border. Unlike Windows 3.1, Windows 95 displays no clear visible difference between a thin and a thick border.

- bsToolWindow: The form has a thin caption (with a smaller font), and only a miniature Close button. This is a special style for non-resizable toolboxes.

- bsSizeToolWin: The form has a thin caption, as with the style above, but is also resizable.

- bsNone: The form has no border or any of the traditional elements (caption, Minimize and Maximize buttons, system menu).

FIGURE 10.2

Sample forms with the
different border styles,
created by the Borders
example.

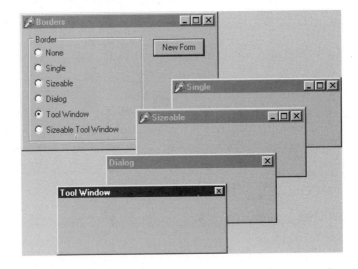

Setting the BorderStyle property at design-time produces no visible effect.
There are good reasons for this. How could you resize the form with the mouse if
it were turned into a dialog box? When you run the application, though, the form
will have the border you requested.

> **NOTE**
>
> Several component properties do not take effect at design-time,
> because they would prevent you from working on the component while
> developing the program. For example, if setting the Visible property of
> a component to False at design-time actually hid the component, it
> would not have been possible for you to operate on it. For the same
> reasons, at design-time a form is always resizable, whichever is the
> value for the BorderStyle property.

The Effect of the Border Style Property

At design-time, the form is always shown with the default value of the BorderStyle
property, bsSizeable. This corresponds to a Windows style known as *thick frame*.
When a main window has a thick frame around it, a user can resize it by dragging
its border. This is made clear by the special *resize* cursors (with the shape of a
double-pointer arrow) displayed when the user moves the mouse onto this thick
window border.

A second important choice for this property is bsDialog. If you select it, the form uses as its border the typical dialog-box frame—a thick frame that doesn't allow resizing. In addition to this graphical element, note that if you select the bsDialog value, the form becomes a dialog box. This involves a number of changes. For example, the items on its system menu are different, and the form will ignore some of the elements of the BorderIcons set property.

When are you supposed to use this kind of frame? There are two possibilities: when you are actually building a dialog box (see Chapter 13) or when you want to use a dialog box as the application's main window.

We can give four more values to the BorderStyle property. The style bsSingle can be used to create a main non-resizable window. Many applications based on windows with controls (such as data-entry forms) and many games use this value, simply because resizing these forms makes no sense. Enlarging a form to see an empty area or reducing its size to make some components less visible often doesn't help a program's user (although Delphi's automatic scroll bars partially solve the last problem). The value fsNone is used only in very special situations and inside other forms. You'll never see an application with a main window that has no border or caption (except as an example to show you that this makes no sense).

The last two values, bsToolWindow and bsSizeToolWin are related to the specific Win32 extended style Ws_ex_ToolWindow. This new style (not available in 16-bit Windows) turns the window into a floating toolbox, with a small title font and close button. This style should not be used for the main window of an application.

The Borders Example

To test the effect and behavior of the different values of the BorderStyle property, I've written a simple program called Borders. You've already seen its output, in Figure 10.2. However, I suggest you run this example and experiment with it for a while to understand all the differences in the forms.

The main form of this program is simple containing only a radio group and a button. There is also a secondary form, with no components and the Position property set to poDefaultPosOnly. This affects the initial position of the secondary form we'll create by pressing the button (I'll discuss the Position property later in this chapter). Here are the properties of this form's components:

```
object Form1: TForm1

  Caption = 'Borders'
  object BtnNewForm: TButton
```

```
      Caption = 'New Form'
      OnClick = BtnNewFormClick
    end
    object BorderRadioGroup: TRadioGroup
      Caption = ' Border '
      ItemIndex = 2
      Items.Strings = (
        'None'
        'Single'
        'Sizeable'
        'Dialog'
        'Tool Window'
        'Sizeable Tool Window')
    end
  end
```

The code of the program is very simple: when you press the button, a new form is created, depending on the selected item of the radio group:

```
procedure TForm1.BtnNewFormClick(Sender: TObject);
var
  NewForm: TForm2;
begin
  NewForm := TForm2.Create (Application);
  NewForm.BorderStyle := TFormBorderStyle (
    BorderRadioGroup.ItemIndex);
  NewForm.Caption := BorderRadioGroup.Items[
    BorderRadioGroup.ItemIndex];
  NewForm.Show;
end;
```

This code actually uses a trick: It casts the number of the selected item into the TFormBorderStyle enumeration. Everything works simply because I've given the radio buttons the same order as the values of this enumeration:

```
type
  TFormBorderStyle = (bsNone, bsSingle, bsSizeable,
    bsDialog, bsToolWindow, bsSizeToolWin);
```

The BtnNewFormClick method then copies the text of the radio button to the caption of the secondary form. This program refers to TForm2, the secondary form defined in a secondary unit of the program, saved as SECOND.PAS. For this reason, to compile the example you must add the following lines to the implementation section of the unit of the main form:

```
uses
  Second;
```

As mentioned in Chapter 5, whenever you need to refer to another unit of a program, place the corresponding uses statement in the implementation portion instead of the interface portion if possible. This speeds up the compilation process, results in cleaner code (because the units you include are separate from those included by Delphi), and never generates circular references between different units. To accomplish this, you can also use the File ➤ Use Unit menu command.

The Border Icons

Another important element of a form is the presence of icons on its border. By default, a form in Windows 3.1 had in its caption a system menu, a Minimize box, and a Maximize box. In Windows 95 a window has a small icon replacing the system menu and a Close button on the far right, near the Minimize and Maximize buttons.

You can set different options using the BorderIcons property, a set with four possible values: biSystemMenu, biMinimize, biMaximize, and biHelp.

NOTE

The new biHelp border icon enables the "What's this?" help. When this style is included and the biMinimize and biMaximize styles are excluded, a question mark appears in the form's title bar. If you click on this question mark and then click on a form or component, Delphi activates the help about that object inside a pop-up window. (Writing a help system and associating it with a Delphi application are topics not covered in this book.)

Again, I've written a simple program, named BIcons, to demonstrate the behavior of a form with different border icons and to show how to change this property at run-time. The form of this example is very simple: it has only a menu, with a pull-down containing four menu items, one for each of the possible elements of the set of border icons.

Each time you select one of the menu commands, its check mark and the corresponding border icon are toggled. This could be accomplished by writing four methods, one for each menu command, but instead I've written a single method, connected with the three commands, that reads the check marks on the menu items to determine the value of the BorderIcons property. This code is therefore also a good exercise in working with sets:

```
procedure TForm1.SetIcons(Sender: TObject);
var
  BorIco: TBorderIcons;
begin
  (Sender as TMenuItem).Checked :=
    not (Sender as TMenuItem).Checked;
  if SystemMenu1.Checked then
    BorIco := [biSystemMenu]
  else
    BorIco := [];
  if MaximizeBox1.Checked then
    Include (BorIco, biMaximize);
  if MinimizeBox1.Checked then
    Include (BorIco, biMinimize);
  if Help1.Checked then
    Include (BorIco, biHelp);
  BorderIcons := BorIco;
end;
```

By running the BIcons example, you can easily set and remove the various visual elements of the form's border. You'll immediately see that some of these elements are closely related: if you remove the system menu, all of the borders icons will disappear; if you remove either the Minimize or the Maximize button, it will be grayed; if you remove both these buttons, they will disappear. Notice also that in these last two cases, the corresponding items of the system menu are automatically disabled. This is the standard behavior for any Windows application. When the Maximize and Minimize buttons have been disabled, you can activate the Help button, as you can see in Figure 10.3.

FIGURE 10.3

The Help button displayed by the BIcons example. Notice that the system menu reflects the presence or absence of the form's minimize or maximize buttons.

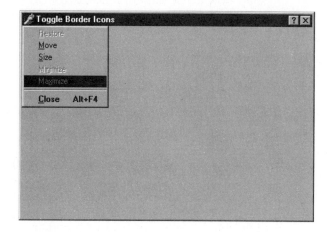

Setting More Windows Styles

The border style and border icons are indicated by two different properties in Delphi, and they can be used to set the initial value of the corresponding user interface elements. Besides changing the user interface, we have seen that these properties affect the behavior of a window. It is important to know that these border-related properties and the FormStyle property mainly correspond to different settings in the *style* and *extended style* of a window. These two terms reflect two parameters of the CreateWindowEx API function Delphi uses to create forms.

It is important to acknowledge this, because Delphi allows you to modify these two parameters freely, by overriding the CreateParams virtual method:

```
public
  procedure CreateParams (
    var Params: TCreateParams); override;
```

This is the only way to use some of the peculiar window styles that are not directly available through form properties. For a list of window styles and extended styles see the API Help under the topics *CreateWindow* and *CreateWindowEx*. You'll notice that the Win32 API has a number of new styles for these functions, including those related to tool windows.

To show how to use this approach, I've written a simple example, called Transpar, that lets you create a useless and very awkward transparent window:

```
procedure TForm1.CreateParams (var Params: TCreateParams);
begin
  inherited CreateParams (Params);
  Params.ExStyle := Params.ExStyle or ws_EX_Transparent;
end;
```

If you run this program, you will wonder why you would ever need a window that cannot even paint its border properly. Well, I'm puzzled too, although I guess this can be used to place a large invisible window in front of all others, intercepting all the mouse messages. I know of some particular uses for this style when it is used for controls.

Setting window styles can be used for other reasons in Delphi. For example, you can remove the caption of a window, leaving its border. An example of a window without a caption is a splash screen (we will build one in Chapter 13), although special window styles are more common in the definition of a new component than in a main window.

When you create a form with a number of components, it is common to make the form non-resizable to avoid having some of the components fall outside the visible portions of the form. This is not a big problem, because Delphi automatically adds scroll bars to the form so you can reach every control easily (form scrolling is one of the subjects of Chapter 14).

Be aware of this problem when you create a big form: If you build a form on a high-resolution screen, it might be bigger than the available screen size. This is a pity, and it is more common that you might expect. If you can, never build a form larger than 640 × 480 pixels.

If you have to build a bigger form and using scroll bars is not a solution, Delphi has some nice scaling features. There are two basic techniques:

- The form's ScaleBy method allows you to scale the form and each of its components. You can use this method at startup after you've determined the screen resolution, or it can be used in response to a specific request by the user, by means of a command you can add to the form's menu.

- The PixelsPerInch and Scaled properties allow Delphi to resize an application automatically when the application is run with a different screen resolution. Of course, you can change the values of these properties manually, as described in the next section, and let the system scale the form only when you want.

In both cases, to make the form scale its window, be sure to also set the Auto-Scroll property to False. Otherwise, the contents of the form will be scaled, but the form border itself will not.

Manual Form Scaling

Each time you want to scale a form, including its components, you can use the ScaleBy method, which has two integer parameters, a multiplier and a divisor—a fraction. You can apply the same method to a single component. For example, with the statement:

```
ScaleBy (3, 4);
```

the size of the current form is divided by 4 and multiplied by 3; that is, the form is reduced to three-quarters of its original size. Generally, it is easier to use percentage values. The same statement can be written as:

```
ScaleBy (75, 100);
```

When you scale a form, all the proportions are maintained, but if you go below or above certain limits, the text strings can alter their proportions slightly. Notice that if you reduce the size of a form too much, most of the components will become unusable or even disappear completely. The problem is that in Windows, components can be placed and sized only in whole pixels, while scaling almost always involves multiplying by fractional numbers. So any fractional portion of a component's origin or size will be truncated.

To avoid similar problems, you should let a user perform only a limited number of scaling operations, or re-create the form from scratch before each new scaling so that round-off errors do not accumulate.

WARNING   If you apply the ScaleBy method to a form, the form won't actually be scaled. Only the components inside the form will change their size. As I mentioned before, to overcome this problem, you should disable the form's AutoScroll property. What is the relationship between scaling and scrolling? My guess is that if scrolling is enabled, the component can be moved outside the form's visible area without many problems; otherwise, the form is resized, too.

I've built a simple example, Scale, to show how you can scale a form manually, responding to a request by the user. The form of this application (see Figure 10.4) has two buttons, a label, an edit box, and a component we have not yet used: the Windows 95 UpDown control.

FIGURE 10.4

The form of the Scale
example after a scaling
with 50 and 200.

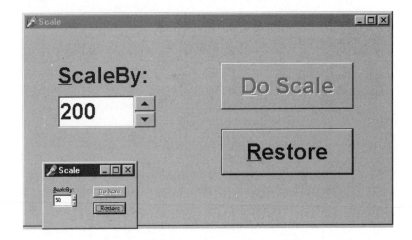

The UpDown component connects to the edit box (using its Associate property): now a user can type only numbers in the box, click on the two small arrows to increase or decrease the number in the edit box by a fixed amount (indicated by the Increment property of the UpDown component), and extract the text of the edit box (Edit1.Text) or the value of the number (UpDown1.Position). You can also set a range for the possible values, as you can see in the textual description of the form components:

```
object Form1: TForm1
  AutoScroll = False
  Caption = 'Scale'
  Font.Height = -16
  Font.Name = 'Arial'
  Font.Style = [fsBold]
  object Label1: TLabel
    Caption = '&ScaleBy:'
  end
  object ScaleButton: TButton...
  object RestoreButton: TButton...
```

```
object UpDown1: TUpDown
  Associate = Edit1
  Min = 30
  Max = 300
  Increment = 10
  Position = 100
  Wrap = False
end
end
```

When you press the ScaleButton button, the current input value is used to determine the scaling percentage of the form:

```
procedure TForm1.ScaleButtonClick(Sender: TObject);
begin
  AmountScaled := UpDown1.Position;
  ScaleBy (AmountScaled, 100);
  UpDown1.Height := Edit1.Height;
  ScaleButton.Enabled := False;
  RestoreButton.Enabled := True;
end;
```

This method stores the current input value in the form's `AmountScaled` private field and enables the Restore button, disabling the one that was pressed. Later, when the user presses the Restore button, the opposite scaling takes place, by calling `ScaleBy (100, AmountScaled)`. In both cases, I've added a line of code to set the `Height` of the UpDown component to the same `Height` as the edit box it is attached to. This prevents small differences between the two.

TIP

If you want to scale the text of the form properly, including the captions of components, the items in list boxes, and so on, you should use True-Type fonts exclusively. The system font and other bitmapped fonts do not scale well. The font issue is important because the size of many components depends on that of their captions, and if the caption does not scale well, the component might not work properly. For this reason, in the Scale example I've used an Arial font.

Automatic Form Scaling

Instead of playing with the ScaleBy method, you can ask Delphi to do the work for you. When Delphi starts, it asks the system for the screen resolution and stores the value in the PixelsPerInch property of the Screen object, a special global object of the VCL, available in any application. At design-time, the PixelsPerInch value of the screen, which is a read-only property, is copied to any form of the application. Delphi then uses the value of PixelsPerInch, if the Scaled property is set to True, to resize the form when the application starts.

Therefore, the same application running at a different screen resolution automatically scales itself, without any specific code. Although automatic scaling has problems in some special cases, if you comply with the following rules you should get good results:

- Set the Scaled property of forms to True.
- Use only TrueType fonts.
- Use Windows small fonts on the computer you use to develop the forms.
- Set the AutoScroll property to False, if you want to scale the form, and not just the controls inside it.

Scaling and Fonts

Both automatic scaling and that performed by the ScaleBy method operate on components by changing the size of the font. The size of each control, in fact, depends on the font it uses.

With automatic scaling, the value of the form's PixelsPerInch property (the design-time value) is compared to the current system value (indicated by the corresponding property of the Screen object), and the result is used to change the font of the components on the form. Actually, to improve the accuracy of this code, the final height of the text is compared to the design-time height of the text, and its size is eventually adjusted if they do not match.

Continued on next page

Scaling and Fonts (Continued)

It is important to keep in mind that scaling depends more on font size than on screen resolution. Even at the same screen resolution, two different computers can be set up with system fonts of different sizes (such as the standard small fonts and large fonts). For example, at the 800 x 600 screen resolution, using small fonts the PixelPerInch ratio is 96, using large fonts it is 120. This means that a Delphi program will try to adapt to the new resolution.

Setting the Form's Position and Size

If you don't set specific values for the PixelsPerInch property, you might expect your form to appear on the screen as you designed it. This is the default behavior, but you can modify it by setting some more properties.

One of them is the Position property, which indicates the initial position of the form on the screen when it is first created (and has no meaning when the form is active). Some of its choices depend on a feature of the Windows environment: using a specific flag, Windows can position new windows using a standard arrangement, which follows the cascade layout. Here are the possible values of the property:

- poDesigned: The form appears in the same position and at the same size you designed it. The properties that determine this attribute are Left, Top, Height, and Width, although you usually set them by dragging the caption or the form's borders.

- poDefault: Windows determines the form's position and size by using a cascade layout, ignoring the design-time attributes completely. If you run the application a number of times in a row, each time its form moves down and to the right of the screen, and if it is resizable, it is reduced each time. After a number of windows have been created, the original position is used again. Notice that this option works only for a main window (bsSizeable or bsFixed), not for a dialog box.

- poDefaultPosOnly: The form uses the size you determined at design-time, but Windows chooses its position on the screen, again using the same algorithm. I've used this approach in the Borders example, to create several secondary forms in different positions.

- poDefaultSizeOnly: The form is displayed in the design position, but Windows determines its size. The right border of the form is always near the right side of the screen, and the bottom border of the form is always near the bottom of the screen, regardless of the form's position. This value is seldom used.

- poScreenCenter: The form is always displayed in the center of the screen, with the size you set at design-time.

WARNING
If you do develop a Delphi application using a high-resolution video mode, be careful not to leave the Position property of your forms set to poDefault. Otherwise, if you design a form in the lower-right portion of the screen, a user running your application at a lower-resolution video mode might not be able to see the form (it might show up completely off-screen).

The second parameter that affects the initial size and position of a window is its *state*. You can use the WindowState property at design-time to display a maximized or minimized window at startup. This property, in fact, can have only three values: wsNormal, wsMinimized, and wsMaximized. The meaning of this property is intuitive. If you set a minimized window state, it will be displayed as a minimized window (separate from the entry in the Windows 95 Taskbar); if you set a maximized window state, it will be displayed full-screen.

WARNING
Notice that if you change the default values of the border icons or set a fixed-size border for the form, it is always displayed as required by the WindowState property. In other words, if you set this property to wsMaximized, it will be displayed full-screen even if it has a dialog border, and a dialog box usually cannot be maximized.

Minimizing and Maximizing a Form

Of course, you can maximize or minimize a window at run-time, too. Simply change the value of the WindowState property. This is exactly what happens in the example I've written, which demonstrates both the default position of a form, as determined by the system, and the use of the WindowState property at run-time. The Position example has a simple form with four buttons, used to minimize, maximize, and restore the form, as you can see in Figure 10.5.

When the user presses the Maximize button, a simple statement is executed:

```
procedure TForm1.BtnMaximizeClick(Sender: TObject);
begin
  WindowState := wsMaximized;
end;
```

FIGURE 10.5

The form of the Position example. Notice the status of the buttons.

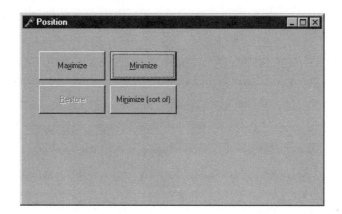

The Restore button sets the property to wsNormal. Since the two buttons are exclusive, you have to disable the one that is not available. For example, if a window is maximized, pressing the Maximize button again has no effect, so we can disable it. Simple? Not at all. If you disable the Maximize button when it is pressed and enable it again when the Restore button is pressed, using the Maximize button of the form's border will mess things up. We need a different approach.

Since we are in an event-based system, we should look for an event. In our example, we can use the OnResize event, which is called each time the form is resized, and this happens when we maximize, minimize, or restore it. Here is the code I've written for this event:

```
procedure TForm1.FormResize(Sender: TObject);
begin
  if WindowState = wsMaximized then
  begin
    BtnMaximize.Enabled := False;
    BtnRestore.Enabled := True;
  end
  else
  begin
    BtnMaximize.Enabled := True;
    BtnRestore.Enabled := False;
  end;
end;
```

Notice that this code is executed also when the application starts, and for this reason the buttons are all enabled at design-time, and the program will disable the Restore button as soon as it starts. What about the Minimize button? Since in a minimized form the buttons are not visible at all, changing their state would be useless. So we have no problem with the button states.

We have a different problem, instead. Setting the WindowState property to wsMinimized creates a minimized window that is not placed in the Taskbar. This is not what we are supposed to do with the main form of a program. You can test this behavior by pressing the button with the caption *Minimize (sort of)*. If you press the Minimize button on the caption, instead, you'll notice a different behavior: the minimized form will move to the Taskbar.

The solution to this problem is to call a method of the Application global object to minimize the form:

```
procedure TForm1.BtnMinimizeClick(Sender: TObject);
begin
  Application.Minimize;
end;
```

There is also a Restore method in the TApplication class that you can use when you need to restore a form, although most often the user will do this with a standard Windows operation (using the Restore system menu command, clicking on the icon in the Taskbar, and so on).

The minimize and maximize operations are associated by default with some system sounds and a visual effect. In a Delphi application most of these sounds are not played, and the visual effect is missing. You can easily solve the first problem by calling the PlaySound API function, passing as a parameter the name of a system sound (as shown in Chapter 31). The visual effect is more difficult to obtain, and I won't discuss it in the book.

The Size of a Form and Its Client Area

At design-time, there are two ways to set the size of a form: setting the value of the Width and Height properties, or dragging its borders. At run-time, if the form has a resizable border, the user can resize it, and in any case, the program can resize it by changing the value of the two-dimensional properties.

However, if you look at a form's properties, you can see that there are two properties referring to its width and two referring to its height:

- Height is the height of the form, including the borders.
- Width is the width of the form, including the borders.
- ClientHeight is the height of the internal area of the form, excluding the borders, the caption, and the menu bar.
- ClientWidth is the width of the internal area of the form, excluding its borders.

Two of these properties refer to the client area of the form, which is its internal portion, within (and excluding) its borders and the eventual menu. This is the area you can use to place components on the form, to create output, and to receive user input.

In Windows, it is also possible to create output and receive input from the non-client area of the form—that is, its border. Painting on the border and getting input when you click on it is really a complex issue. If you are interested in this topic, look in the Help file at the description of such Windows messages as wm_NCPaint, wm_NCCalcSize, and wm_NCHitTest and the series of non-client messages related to the mouse input, such as wm_NCLButtonDown. The difficulty of this approach is in combining your code with the default Windows behavior. However, Delphi lets you process these low-level Windows messages without any problem, something that most visual programming environments do not allow at all.

Since you might be interested in having a certain available area, at times it makes sense to set the *client* size of a form instead of its global size. This is straightforward, since as you set one of the two client properties, the corresponding form property changes accordingly. When you modify the value of ClientHeight, the value of Height immediately changes.

The Maximum and Minimum Size of a Form

When you choose a resizable border for a form, users can generally resize the form as they like and also maximize it to full-screen. Windows informs you that the form's size has changed with the wm_Size message, which generates the OnResize event. OnResize takes place after the size of the form has already been changed. Modifying the size again in this event (if the user has reduced or enlarged the form too much) is silly. A preventive approach is better suited to this problem.

Before we look at how to set the possible maximum and minimum sizes of a window, let me recap a couple of ideas. First of all, if you want a window of a fixed size, you should avoid a resizable border and choose instead the fixed border or the dialog border. Second, if some of the controls go out of the border and the AutoScroll property is set to True, Delphi automatically adds the scroll bars to the form so you can reach them anyway.

Nonetheless, it is often useful to set a limit on the form size, particularly the minimum size. Delphi does not include a property to set this value, but you can easily handle the proper Windows message in the form to obtain this effect.

The message we must use is wm_GetMinMaxInfo. The parameter of the corresponding method should be of the type TWMGetMinMaxInfo (the types of the message's parameters are defined in the Messages unit). This structure contains a field that is a pointer to the MinMaxInfo structure, defined in the Windows unit as

```
type
  PMinMaxInfo = ^TMinMaxInfo;
  TMinMaxInfo = record
    ptReserved: TPoint;
    ptMaxSize: TPoint;
    ptMaxPosition: TPoint;
    ptMinTrackSize: TPoint;
    ptMaxTrackSize: TPoint;
  end;
```

The fields of this structure are complex, but only because it is a very powerful tool:

- `ptReserved` is an undocumented field, reserved for Windows' internal use.
- `ptMaxSize` is a point holding, in the x field, the maximized width of the window, and in the y field, its maximized height.
- `ptMaxPosition` is a point indicating the position of the window (that is, its upper-left corner) when it is maximized.
- `ptMinTrackSize` indicates the minimum width and height of the window when a user resizes it.
- `ptMaxTrackSize` specifies the maximum width and height of the window.

When you receive this message, the structure has some default values, so you need to change only the fields you are interested in. In the MinMax example, I've decided to fix both the minimum and the maximum *tracking* size of the window and disable its Maximize button. In fact, letting the user maximize the window without making it full-screen (see Figure 10.6) makes sense only in a few cases— for example, in the Delphi main window.

FIGURE 10.6

The window of the Min-Max example is quite small but has the typical restore button of maximized windows.

The form of the MinMax example is very simple, having no components at all. The only change you have to make from the default is to disable the `biMaximize` border icon. To handle window-size tracking you have to add a message response procedure and write some code. In the type definition of the TForm1 class, you have to define the new procedure as

```
public
  procedure GetMinMax (var MinMaxMessage: TWMGetMinMaxInfo);
    message wm_GetMinMaxInfo;
```

Notice the message directive, which connects the procedure directly with the Windows message. The second step is to write the code of this procedure, setting the proper values in the structure pointed to by the MinMaxInfo field of the MinMax-Message parameter. To make it easy to access a number of fields of this structure, we can use a with statement, which uses the structure pointed to by the MinMaxInfo pointer. Inside this with statement you can easily access the various fields:

```
procedure TForm1.GetMinMax (
  var MinMaxMessage: TWMGetMinMaxInfo);
begin
  with MinMaxMessage.MinMaxInfo^ do
  begin
    ptMinTrackSize.x := 150;
    ptMinTrackSize.y := 150;
    ptMaxTrackSize.x := 300;
    ptMaxTrackSize.y := 300;
  end;
end;
```

The effect of this code is simple. A user cannot reduce the window below a certain limit or enlarge it too much, as you can see by running this program.

Automatic Form Creation

Up to now we have ignored the issue of form creation. We know that when the form is created, we receive the OnCreate event and can change or test some of the initial form's properties or fields. But the form is invariably created. The statement responsible for this is in this project's source file (or .DPR file, available through the View ▶ Project menu command):

```
begin
  Application.Initialize;
  Application.CreateForm(TForm1, Form1);
  Application.Run;
end.
```

To skip the automatic form creation, you can either modify this code or, better, use the Forms page of the Project Options dialog box (see Figure 10.7). In this dialog box, you can decide whether the form should be automatically created. If you disable the automatic creation, the project's initialization code becomes the following:

```
begin
  Applications.Initialize;
  Application.Run;
end.
```

FIGURE 10.7

The Forms page of the Delphi Project Options dialog box.

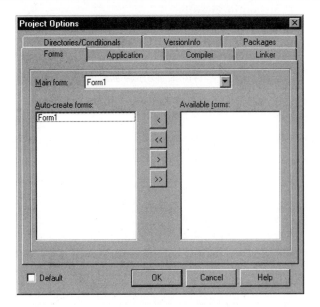

If you now run this program, nothing happens, and it terminates immediately because no main window is created. So, what is the effect of the call to the application's CreateForm method? It creates a new instance of the class passed as the first parameter and assigns it to the variable passed as the second parameter.

Something else happens behind the scenes. When CreateForm is called, if there is currently no main form, the current form is assigned to the application's MainForm property. For this reason, the form indicated as *Main form* in the dialog box shown in Figure 10.7 (above) corresponds to the first call to the application's CreateForm method (that is, when several forms are created at startup).

The same holds for closing the application. Closing the main form terminates the application, regardless of the other forms. If you want to perform this operation from the program's code, simply call the Close method of the main form, as we've done several times in past examples.

Closing a Form

When you close the form using the method just described or by the usual means (Alt+F4, the system menu, or the Close button), the OnCloseQuery event is called. In this event, you can ask the user to confirm the action, particularly if there is unsaved data in the form. I used this approach in the RichNot2 example in the preceding chapter.

Just as a reminder, I've written another small example, Close, which includes the following code:

```
procedure TForm1.FormCloseQuery(Sender: TObject;
  var CanClose: Boolean);
begin
  if MessageDlg ('Are you sure you want to exit?',
      mtConfirmation, [mbYes, mbNo], 0) = idNo then
    CanClose := False;
end;
```

The Close example has a form with a button to close it (you can see the result of the call of the previous method in Figure 10.8). If OnCloseQuery indicates that the form should still be closed, the OnClose event is called. The third step is to call the OnDestroy event, which is the opposite of the OnCreate event, and is generally used to deallocate objects related to the form and free the corresponding memory.

FIGURE 10.8

The first close-confirmation dialog box of the Close example.

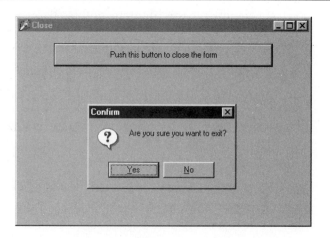

So what is the use of the intermediate OnClose event? In this method you have another chance to avoid closing the application, or you can specify alternative "close actions." The method, in fact, has an Action parameter passed by reference. You can assign the following values to this parameter:

- caNone: The form is not allowed to close. This corresponds to setting the CanClose parameter of the OnCloseQuery method to False.

- caHide: The form is not closed, just hidden. This makes sense if there are other forms in the application; otherwise, the program terminates. This is the default for secondary forms.

- caFree: The form is closed, freeing its memory, and the application eventually terminates if this was the main form. This is the default action for the main form.

- caMinimize: The form is not closed, but only minimized. This is the default action for MDI child forms.

In the Close example, I've written a method for the OnClose event, too. This procedure asks users once again if they really want to exit:

```
procedure TForm1.FormClose(Sender: TObject;
  var Action: TCloseAction);
begin
  if MessageDlg ('Are you REALLY SURE you want to exit?' +
      Chr(13) + '(This is your last chance to remain with us!)',
      mtConfirmation, [mbYes, mbNo], 0) = idNo then
    Action := caNone
  else
    Action := caFree;
end;
```

I've written this second request just to demonstrate that there are two possible solutions to the "stop closing" problem. I don't advise ever writing something similar, since your application's users will get really angry. What might happen is that in the OnClose event you might request other forms of your program if they are ready to close, calling their own OnCloseQuery event handlers manually. In general, however, it is preferable to handle all the requests for closing in the OnCloseQuery, and use OnClose only to specify eventual close actions.

TIP

When you shut down Windows, the `OnCloseQuery` event is activated, and you can use it to stop the shut-down process. In this case, the `OnClose` event is not called even if `OnCloseQuery` sets the `CanClose` parameter to `True`.

When you build applications with a single main form, handling the `OnClose` event is not a particular problem. As you add other forms to a program, they are often created at startup by the project code and destroyed only when the program terminates. In this case, the default close action, which corresponds to hiding the form, makes sense. However, when you create forms dynamically, perhaps because you need several forms of the same kind in a single program, you should also take care of deleting a form when it is closed, eventually using the `caFree` value as the closing action (more on this topic in the chapters dealing with multiple forms, particularly Chapters 13 and 15).

Having discussed some special capabilities of forms, I'll now move to a very important topic: input and output within a form. If you decide to make limited use of components, you might write complex programs as well, receiving input from the mouse and the keyboard, and drawing directly on the surface of the form.

Supervising Keyboard Input

Generally, forms don't handle keyboard input directly. If a user has to type something, your form should include an edit component or one of the other input components. If you want to handle keyboard shortcuts, you can use those connected with menus, as I demonstrated with the HShort example in the last chapter (which used a hidden popup menu to activate some shortcut keys).

At other times, however, you might want to handle the keyboard in particular ways for a specific purpose. What you can do in these cases is turn on the `Key-Preview` property of the form. Then, even if you have some input controls, the form's `OnkeyPress` event will always be activated for any keyboard input operation. The keyboard input will then reach the destination component, unless you stop it in the form by setting the character value to zero (not the character *0*, but the value 0 of the character set, indicated as #0).

The example I've built to demonstrate this, KPreview, has a form with no special properties (not even `KeyPreview`), a radio group with four options, and some edit boxes (see Figure 10.9):

```
object Form1: TForm1
  Caption = 'Key Preview'
  OnKeyPress = FormKeyPress
  object RadioPreview: TRadioGroup
    Caption = 'Preview Options'
    ItemIndex = 0
    Items.Strings = (
      'None'
      'Enter = Tab'
      'Type in Caption'
      'Skip vowels')
    OnClick = RadioPreviewClick
  end
  object Edit1: TEdit...
  object Edit2: TEdit...
  object Edit3: TEdit...
end
```

By default the program does nothing special, except when the different radio buttons are used to enable the key preview:

```
procedure TForm1.RadioPreviewClick(Sender: TObject);
begin
  KeyPreview := RadioPreview.ItemIndex <> 0;
end;
```

FIGURE 10.9

The KPreview program allows you to type into the caption of the form (among other things).

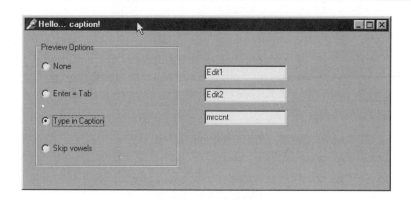

Now we'll start receiving the OnKeyPress events, and we can do one of the three actions requested by the three special buttons of the radio group. The action depends on the value of the ItemIndex property of the radio group component. This is the reason the event handler is based on a case statement:

```
procedure TForm1.FormKeyPress(Sender: TObject; var Key: Char);
begin
  case RadioPreview.ItemIndex of
    ...
```

In the first case if the value of the Key parameter is #13, which corresponds to the Enter key, we disable the operation (setting Key to zero) and then mimic the activation of the Tab key. There are many ways to accomplish this, but the one I've chosen is quite particular. I send the CM_DialogKey message to the form, passing the code for the Tab key (VK_TAB):

```
1: //  Enter = Tab
  if Key = #13 then
  begin
    Key := #0;
    Perform (CM_DialogKey, VK_TAB, 0);
  end;
```

NOTE The CM_DialogKey message is an internal undocumented Delphi message, something which is really beyond the scope of this book, but is discussed in other texts, including the *Delphi Developer's Handbook*, which I've co-written with Tim Gooch (Sybex, 1997).

To type in the caption of the form, the program simply adds the character to the current Caption, as you can see in Figure 10.9. There are two special cases: when the Backspace key is pressed, the last character of the string is removed (by copying to the Caption all the characters of the current Caption but the last one); and when the Enter key is pressed, the program stops the operation, by resetting the ItemIndex property of the radio group control:

```
2: //  Type in Caption
begin
  if Key = #8 then // backspace: remove last char
    Caption := Copy (Caption, 1,
      Length (Caption) - 1)
```

```
    else if Key = #13 then // enter: stop operation
      RadioPreview.ItemIndex := 0
    else // anything else: add character
      Caption := Caption + Key;
    Key := #0;
  end;
```

Finally, if the last radio item is selected, the code checks whether the character is a vowel (by testing for its inclusion in a constant *vowel set*). In this case the character is skipped altogether:

```
3: // Skip vowels
   if Key in ['a', 'e', 'i', 'o', 'u',
       'A', 'E', 'I', 'O', 'U'] then
     Key := #0;
```

Getting Mouse Input

When a user presses one of the mouse buttons over a form (or over a component, by the way), Windows sends the application some messages. Delphi defines some events to write code in response to these messages. The two basic events are as follows:

- OnMouseDown is received when one of the mouse buttons is pressed;

- OnMouseUp is received when one of the buttons is released.

Another fundamental system message is related to mouse movement. The event is OnMouseMove. Although it should be easy to understand the meaning of the three messages—down, up, and move—the question that might arise is, how do they relate to the OnClick event we have often used up to now?

We have often used the OnClick event for components, but it is also available for the form. Its general meaning is that the left mouse button has been pressed and released on the same window or component. However, between these two actions, the cursor might have been moved outside the area of the window or component, while the left mouse button was held down. If you press the mouse button at a certain position and then move it away and release it, no click is involved. In this case, the window receives *only* a down message, some move messages, and an up message. Another difference is that the click event relates only to the left mouse button.

The Mouse Buttons

Most of the mouse types connected to a Windows PC have two mouse buttons, and at times even three. Usually we refer to these buttons as the left mouse button, which is the most used; the right mouse button; and the middle mouse button:

- The left mouse button is *the* mouse button. It is used to select elements on screen, to give menu commands, to click buttons, to select and move elements (*dragging*), to select and activate (usually with a double-click), and so on.

- The right mouse button is used for local pop-up menus. Many applications used this approach in the past, but Windows 95 has made local menus the standard effect of right-clicking.

- The middle button is seldom used because most users either don't even have it or don't have a proper software driver. Some CAD programs use the middle button. If you want to support this button, it should be optional, or else you should be ready to provide your customers with a free three-button mouse and the corresponding driver.

Keep in mind that users can customize their mouse buttons, switching the left and right buttons, and turning a single click on the middle button into a double-click of the left button. When you refer to events related to a mouse button in your code what matters is not the physical button, but rather its meaning.

Using Windows without a Mouse

While I am on this topic, consider the following statement: a user should always be able to use any Windows application without the mouse. This is not an option; it is a Windows programming rule. Of course, it might be easier to use an application with a mouse, but it should never be mandatory. In fact, there are users who for several reasons might not have a mouse connected to their system, such as travelers with a small laptop and no space, workers in industrial environments, and bank clerks with a number of other peripherals around.

There is another reason, already mentioned in this chapter in respect to the menu, to support the keyboard: using the mouse is nice, but it tends to be slower. If you are a skilled touch typist, you won't use the mouse to drag a word of text; you'll use shortcut keys to copy and paste it, without moving your hands from the keyboard.

For all these reasons, you should always set up a proper tab order for a form's components, remember to add keys for buttons and menu items for keyboard selection, use shortcut keys on menu commands, and so on. An exception to this rule might be a graphics program. However, be aware that you can use even a program such as Paintbrush without the mouse—although I don't recommend it.

The Parameters of the Mouse Events

Since I'm going to build a graphics program, too, I will focus only on the use of the mouse. The first event we need to consider for the first minimal version of the Shapes program is OnMouseDown. The related method has a number of parameters, as shown in the following declaration:

```
procedure TShapesForm.FormMouseDown (
   Sender: TObject; Button: TMouseButton;
   Shift: TShiftState; X, Y: Integer);
```

In addition to the usual Sender parameter, there are four more parameters:

- Button indicates which of the three mouse buttons has been pressed. Possible values are mbRight, mbLeft, and mbCenter. These are exclusive values because the purpose of this parameter is to determine which button generated the message.

- Shift indicates which *mouse-related keys* were pressed when the event occurred. These mouse-related keys are Alt, Ctrl, and Shift, plus the mouse buttons themselves. This parameter is of a set type since several keys (and mouse buttons) might be pressed at the same time. This means you should test for a condition using the in expression, not for equality.

- X and Y indicate the coordinates of the position of the mouse, in *client area* coordinates of the current window (a form or a control). The origin of the *x* and *y*-axes of these coordinates is the upper-left corner of the client area of the window receiving the event (again, a form or a control).

Click and Draw: The Shapes1 Example

We can start writing our example, Shapes1, with a simple OnMouseDown event handler. As you can see from the class name, the form of this example, which has no components, has been renamed ShapesForm:

```
procedure TShapesForm.FormMouseDown(
   Sender: TObject; Button: TMouseButton;
   Shift: TShiftState; X, Y: Integer);
```

```
begin
  if Button = mbLeft then
    Canvas.Ellipse (X-10, Y-10, X+10, Y+10);
end;
```

If the user presses the left mouse button, the program draws a circle on the surface of the form, using as its center the position of the mouse. To draw the circle,
we have to use the Ellipse procedure since neither Windows nor Delphi has a
function to draw a circle. The Ellipse method requires four parameters representing the opposite sides of the bounding rectangle, as shown in Figure 10.10.

FIGURE 10.10

The bounding rectangle
of an ellipse.

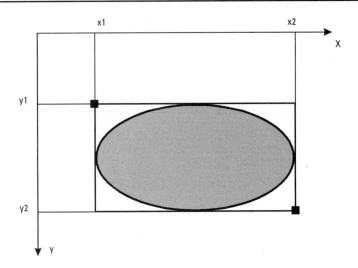

To draw on the form, we use a very special property: Canvas. A TCanvas object
has two distinctive features: it holds a collection of drawing tools (such as a pen,
a brush, and a font) and it has a number of drawing methods, which use the current tools. More on the canvas in the next section.

Before we look into the problems of painting, let me add a couple of new
features to the bare program. First of all, I want to allow the user to draw shapes
of different forms depending on the keys pressed with the left mouse button. You
can accomplish this by checking the value of the procedure's third parameter, corresponding to the OnMouseDown event:

```
procedure TShapesForm.FormMouseDown(
  Sender: TObject; Button: TMouseButton;
  Shift: TShiftState; X, Y: Integer);
```

```
begin
  if Button = mbLeft then
    if ssShift in Shift then
      Canvas.Rectangle (X-10, Y-10, X+10, Y+10)
    else
      Canvas.Ellipse (X-10, Y-10, X+10, Y+10);
end;
```

Now, if the user presses the Shift key and the left mouse button, the program draws a small square instead of a small circle (see Figure 10.11). You might further customize this example by drawing lines or rectangles with rounded corners. See the description of the TCanvas class in the Delphi Help file for a list of the available drawing methods.

> **NOTE** Experienced Windows programmers should note that a Delphi canvas technically represents a Windows device context. The methods of the TCanvas class are similar to the GDI functions of the Windows API.

FIGURE 10.11

The output of the Shapes1 example.

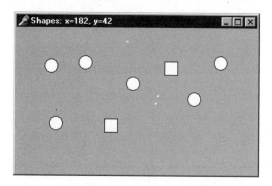

To end the first version of the Shapes program, we can add a new feature. I want to show the position of the mouse in client-area coordinates to allow more precise drawing. As soon as the mouse moves over the form, the OnMouseMove event is sent to our program. By providing a method for this event, we can transform the x and y values we receive as parameters into a string and display it. Since our application has no status bar nor any other control, we can use the form's caption for the output (see the title of the window in Figure 10.11):

```
procedure TShapesForm.FormMouseMove(Sender: TObject;
  Shift: TShiftState; X, Y: Integer);
```

```
begin
  Caption := Format ('Shapes: x=%d, y=%d', [X, Y]);
end;
```

Now our drawing program is slightly more interesting. But the real advantage is that you can use this example to understand how the mouse works. Make this test: Run the program and resize the Windows on the desktop so that the form of the Shapes program is behind another window and inactive, but with the title visible. Now move the mouse over the form, and you'll see that the coordinates change. This means that the OnMouseMove event is sent to the application even if its window is not active, and it proves what I have already mentioned: mouse messages are always directed to the window under the mouse, with only a few exceptions.

Drawing on the Form

Using Shapes1, you can draw a number of circles and squares on the surface of the form, as shown earlier in Figure 10.11. This looks like it works fairly well, but it doesn't. There are several related problems. If you cover your form with another window, the shapes will disappear. If you reduce the size of the form, the shapes outside the new smaller surface will disappear, too; and if you enlarge the form again, they won't reappear. Try playing with this program to see what I mean.

Why does this happen? It depends on Windows' default behavior. As you draw on a window, Windows does *not* store the resulting image. When the window is covered, its contents are usually lost.

NOTE   Why doesn't Windows store the contents of each window in a bitmap? The answer is simple: to spare memory. A color bitmap for a 300 x 400 image at 256 colors requires about 120 KB. By increasing the color count or the number of pixels, you can easily have full-screen bitmaps of about 1 MB and reach 4 MB of memory for a 1280 x 1024 resolution at 16 million colors. If storing the bitmap was the default choice, running half a dozen simple applications will require at least 8 MB of memory, if not 16 MB.

There are some techniques in both Windows and Delphi to save the contents of a form in a bitmap. In Windows, these techniques require some coding; in Delphi, they require the use of the proper components. In this chapter, focusing on forms and on direct output, I'll follow the usual Windows drawing technique, based on painting, which is the focus of the next section. In the next chapter I'll show you how to use the Image component to store the current output of a form in a bitmap.

The Drawing Tools

For the moment, let me improve the application by playing with the drawing tools available in a Canvas. Here is a list of these drawing tools (or *GDI objects,* from the Graphics Device Interface, one of the Windows system libraries) of a canvas:

- The Brush property determines the color of the enclosed surfaces. The brush is used to fill closed shapes, such as circles or rectangles. The properties of a brush are its Color, its Style, and eventually its Bitmap.

- The Pen property determines the color and size of the lines and of the borders of the shapes. The properties of a pen are its Color, its Width, and its Style, which includes several dotted and dashed lines (available only if the Width is 1 pixel).

- The Font property determines the font used to write text in the form, using the TextOut method of the canvas. A font has a Name, a Size, a Style, a Color, and so on.

Brushes, pens, and fonts (but also forms and most other components) have a Color property. However to change the color of an element properly using non-standard colors (such as the color constants in Delphi), you should know how Windows treats the color. In theory, Windows uses 24-bit RGB colors. This means you can use 256 different values for each of the three basic colors (red, green, and blue), obtaining an impressive number of different shades.

However, you or your users might have a video adapter that cannot display such a variety of colors, although this is increasingly less frequent. In this case, Windows uses either a technique called *dithering,* which basically consists of using a number of pixels of the available colors to simulate the requested one; or it approximates the color, using the nearest available one. For the color of a brush (and the background color of a form, which is actually based on a brush) Windows uses the dithering technique; for the color of a pen or font, it uses the nearest solid color.

In terms of pens, you can read (but not change) the current pen position with the PenPos property of the canvas. The pen position determines the starting point of the next line the program will draw, using the LineTo method. To change it, you can use the canvas's MoveTo method. Other properties of the canvas affect lines and colors, too. Interesting examples are CopyMode and ScaleMode. Another property you can manipulate directly to change the output is the array of pixels, which you can use to access (read) or change (write) the color of any individual point on the surface of the form.

Drawing Shapes

Now we want to improve the Shapes application. We need to add a menu to choose the color of the shapes and of their borders—that is, the color of the brush and the pen, respectively—and the size of the shape and of its border. The code needed to implement these commands is quite simple, although somewhat longer than usual. Here is the structure of the menu, extracted from the textual description of the form:

```
object MainMenu1: TMainMenu
  object File1: TMenuItem
    object New1: TMenuItem
    object N1: TMenuItem
    object Exit1: TMenuItem
  object Colors1: TMenuItem
    object PenColor1: TMenuItem
    object BrushColor1: TMenuItem
  object Size1: TMenuItem
    object IncreasePenSize1: TMenuItem
    object DecreasePenSize1: TMenuItem
    object N2: TMenuItem
    object IncreaseShapeSize1: TMenuItem
    object DecreaseShapeSize1: TMenuItem
  object Help1: TMenuItem
    object AboutShapes1: TMenuItem
```

The form initializes and stores only the current radius of the circle (used also as the value of half of the side of the square—that is, the *radius* of the square):

```
private
  Radius: Integer;
```

All the other values set by the menu commands are directly saved in properties of the Canvas property of the form. Increasing or decreasing the Radius (which is set to 5 in the FormCreate method) is quite simple. The only special feature is to disable the Decrease menu item to avoid having a negative size:

```
procedure TShapesForm.IncreaseShapeSize1Click(Sender: TObject);
begin
  Radius := Radius + 5;
  DecreaseShapeSize1.Enabled := True;
end;

procedure TShapesForm.DecreaseShapeSize1Click(Sender: TObject);
begin
  Radius := Radius - 5;
  if Radius < 10 then
    DecreaseShapeSize1.Enabled := False;
end;
```

If you want, you can add similar checks to avoid values that are too large. The code used to change the pen size is similar, but is based on the Width property of the Pen of the Canvas:

```
procedure TShapesForm.IncreasePenSize1Click(Sender: TObject);
begin
  Canvas.Pen.Width := Canvas.Pen.Width + 2;
  DecreasePenSize1.Enabled := True;
end;

procedure TShapesForm.DecreasePenSize1Click(Sender: TObject);
begin
  Canvas.Pen.Width := Canvas.Pen.Width - 2;
  if Canvas.Pen.Width < 3 then
    DecreasePenSize1.Enabled := False;
end;
```

To change the colors of the border (the pen) or the surface (the brush) of the shape, I've used the standard Color dialog box. Here is one of the two methods:

```
procedure TShapesForm.PenColor1Click(Sender: TObject);
begin
  ColorDialog1.Color := Canvas.Pen.Color;
  if ColorDialog1.Execute then
    Canvas.Pen.Color := ColorDialog1.Color;
end;
```

All this information is then used directly or indirectly whenever the program draws a new shape:

```
procedure TShapesForm.FormMouseDown(Sender: TObject;
  Button: TMouseButton;
  Shift: TShiftState; X, Y: Integer);
begin
  if Button = mbLeft then
    if ssShift in Shift then
      Canvas.Rectangle (X - Radius, Y - Radius,
        X + Radius, Y + Radius)
    else
      Canvas.Ellipse (X - Radius, Y - Radius,
        X + Radius, Y + Radius);
end;
```

The only really strange portion of the code is the method the program uses to clear the surface of the form when the File ➤ New command is called:

```
procedure TShapesForm.New1Click(Sender: TObject);
begin
  Repaint;
end;
```

This code simply calls the Repaint method of the form. This method repaints the whole surface of the window, erasing its contents. The effect, of course, is that you lose any previous output since it was not stored. This program, in fact, has the same big problem as the previous version (as you can see in Figure 10.12). If you move another window over this form or reduce its size, you lose its contents. We need a way to store the contents and repaint the window on request.

> **NOTE**   Curiously enough, the contents of the form are also erased if you open the Color dialog box to its maximum extent (by pressing the Define Custom Colors button) or you move this dialog box, but it remains on screen if you open only the basic version of the dialog box and don't move it. In fact, when small areas are covered (by menus, message boxes, or small dialog boxes), Windows actually saves the bitmap of the corresponding area of the form being covered. When these elements become too big, however, Windows doesn't save the surface and later asks the program to redraw the area. Windows experts will recognize this as the effect of the cs_SaveBits class style.

FIGURE 10.12

The output of the Shapes2 program is improved over the last version, but it is still flawed, as you can see in the right portion of the window.

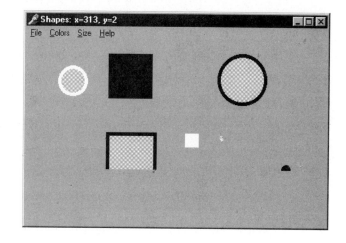

Drawing and Painting in Windows

It's time to face the problems related to *drawing* and *painting* in Windows. What do I (and other authors) mean by these two terms?

- *Drawing* is what we have done up to now in the Shape application. You access the form's canvas and call some of its methods. Since the image is not saved, the form can lose part or all of its contents, as shown earlier in Figure 10.12. The output might change because the image is not saved and the application doesn't know how to redraw it.

- *Painting* is what we will do to let the application repaint its whole surface under any of the possible conditions. If we provide a method to redraw the contents of the form and this method is automatically called when a portion of the form has been hidden and needs repainting, we will be able to re-create the output properly.

Painting is the common approach to handling output in Windows, aside from particular graphics-oriented programs that store the form's whole image in a bitmap (as I'll describe in the next chapter). The approach used to implement painting has a very descriptive name: *store and paint*. In fact, when the user presses a mouse button or performs any other operation, we need to store the position and other elements; then, in the painting method, we use this information to actually paint the corresponding image.

Since this approach takes two steps, we must be able to execute these two operations in a row, asking the system to repaint the window—without waiting for a portion of the window to become invalid because some other window has been placed above it. You can use several methods (which can be applied to both forms and controls) to invoke repainting; the first two correspond to the Windows API functions, while the latter two have been introduced by Delphi:

- The Invalidate method informs Windows that the entire surface of the form should be repainted. The most important thing is that Invalidate does *not* enforce a painting operation immediately. Windows simply stores the request and will respond to it only after the current procedure has been completely executed and as soon as there are no other events pending in the system. Windows deliberately delays the painting operation since it is one of the most time-consuming operations. At times, with this delay, it is possible to paint the form only after a number of changes have taken place, avoiding a number of consecutive calls to the (slow) paint method.

- The Update method asks Windows to update the contents of the form, repainting it immediately. However, remember that this operation will take place only if there is an *invalid area*. This happens if the Invalidate method has just been called or as the result of an operation by the user. If there is no invalid area, a call to Update has no effect at all. For this reason, it is common to see a call to Update just after a call to Invalidate. This is exactly what is done by the two new Delphi methods, Repaint and Refresh.

- The Repaint method calls Invalidate and Update in sequence. As a result, it activates the OnPaint event immediately. There is a slightly different version of this method called Refresh. For a form the effect is the same; for components it might be slightly different.

> **TIP**
>
> The Repaint and Refresh methods are totally interchangeable. Borland pretended there was a difference in the Delphi 1 help file, but there is not. Contrary to what the documentation used to say, to avoid erasing the form's background, you need to set the csOpaque flag in the undocumented ControlStyle property of the form (or of the component you want to use).

When you need to ask the form for a repaint operation, you should generally call Invalidate, following the standard Windows approach. This is particularly important when you need to request this operation frequently, because if Windows takes too much time to update the screen, the requests for repainting can be accumulated into a simple repaint action. The wm_Paint message in Windows is a sort of low-priority message. To be more precise, if a request for repainting is pending but other messages are waiting, the other messages are handled before the system actually performs the paint action.

On the other hand, if you call Repaint several times, the screen must be repainted each time before Windows can process other messages, and since paint operations are slow, this can actually make your application less responsive. There are times, however, when you want the application to repaint a surface as quickly as possible. In these less-frequent cases, calling Repaint is the way to go.

Painting a Single Shape

The first version of the Shapes example was capable of drawing only simple circles and squares, with no support for color or other frills. I've implemented it again using the *store and draw* technique in order to demonstrate this approach with a simple program rather than a complex one.

When the user presses the left mouse button, we need to store three values: the two coordinates of the center of the shape and a Boolean indicating whether the shape is a circle or a square. For this reason I've added two local fields to the form of the Shapes3 example:

```
type
  TShapesForm = class(TForm)
    ..
  private
    Center: TPoint;
    Circle: Boolean;
  end;
```

These values are set by the FormMouseDown method, which then calls the Invalidate method:

```
procedure TShapesForm.FormMouseDown(
  Sender: TObject; Button: TMouseButton;
  Shift: TShiftState; X, Y: Integer);
begin
  if Button = mbLeft then
```

```
begin
  // store the center and the kind of shape
  Center.X := X;
  Center.Y := Y;
  Circle := not (ssShift in Shift);
  // ask to repaint the form
  Invalidate;
  end;
end;
```

The call to the Invalidate method indirectly activates FormPaint, the method associated with the OnPaint event of the form. This procedure draws a shape, using the current values:

```
procedure TShapesForm.FormPaint(Sender: TObject);
begin
  if Circle then
    Canvas.Ellipse (Center.X - 10, Center.Y - 10,
      Center.X + 10, Center.Y + 10)
  else
    Canvas.Rectangle (Center.X - 10, Center.Y - 10,
      Center.X + 10, Center.Y + 10);
end;
```

The initial values of the private fields are set at the beginning, in the FormCreate method. The coordinates of the center are set at a negative offset, so that at the beginning, the shape is not visible. In fact, the OnPaint method is executed also at startup. As you can see by running the program, Shapes3 allows you to draw only one shape at a time. This last version of the Shapes program we have built is probably the most robust, but it is not by any means the best. However, you might merge its code with that of the Shape2 example to allow a user to choose the color and size of the current shape.

We can further improve this program (or the modified version I've just suggested) by storing not only the last shape, but a number of them, and not only the position and type, but also the color, the size, and all the other attributes we need to repaint them properly when required by the system.

Painting a List of Shapes

There is a simple solution in Delphi to the problem of storing a number of elements: Use a TList object, which can store a list of objects of any other kind.

This is what I've done in the Shapes4 example, which is a mix of the second and third versions of the program, with the support for a number of shapes. In particular, the new version uses the same form and the same menu structure as the Shapes2 example.

The program defines a custom TShapeData data type to store the attributes of each shape:

```
type
  TShapeData = class
    Circle: Boolean;
    X, Y, Size, PenSize: Integer;
    PenColor, BrushColor: TColor;
  end;
```

The form has a TList object data member, named ShapesList, which is initialized in the OnCreate event handler:

```
procedure TShapesForm.FormCreate(Sender: TObject);
begin
  Radius := 5;
  ShapesList := TList.Create;
end;
```

The program adds a new object to the list each time the user creates a new shape by pressing the left mouse button:

```
procedure TShapesForm.FormMouseDown(
  Sender: TObject; Button: TMouseButton;
  Shift: TShiftState; X, Y: Integer);
var
  Shape: TShapeData;
  InvRect: TRect;
begin
  if Button = mbLeft then
  begin
    Shape := TShapeData.Create;
    if ssShift in Shift then
      Shape.Circle := False
    else
      Shape.Circle := True;
    Shape.X := X;
    Shape.Y := Y;
    Shape.Size := Radius;
```

```
      Shape.PenSize := Canvas.Pen.Width;
      Shape.PenColor := Canvas.Pen.Color;
      Shape.BrushColor := Canvas.Brush.Color;
      ShapesList.Add (Shape);
      Invalidate;
    end;
  end;
```

In the method corresponding to the OnPaint event, all the shapes currently stored in the list are painted. Since the painting code affects the properties of the Canvas, we need to store the current values and reset them at the end. Why? A user might have changed the current color from that of the last shape, and if we fail to save and restore the current color, at the end of the loop the Canvas will have the attributes of the last shape:

```
procedure TShapesForm.FormPaint(Sender: TObject);
var
  I, OldPenW: Integer;
  CurShape: TShapeData;
  OldPenCol, OldBrushCol: TColor;
begin
  // store the current Canvas attributes
  OldPenCol := Canvas.Pen.Color;
  OldPenW := Canvas.Pen.Width;
  OldBrushCol := Canvas.Brush.Color;

  // repaint each shape in the list
  for I := 0 to ShapesList.Count - 1 do
  begin
    CurShape := ShapesList.Items [I];
    with CurShape do
    begin
      Canvas.Pen.Color := PenColor;
      Canvas.Pen.Width := PenSize;
      Canvas.Brush.Color := BrushColor;
      if Circle then
        Canvas.Ellipse (X-Size, Y-Size, X+Size, Y+Size)
      else
        Canvas.Rectangle (X-Size, Y-Size, X+Size, Y+Size);
    end;
  end;
```

```
// reset the current Canvas attributes
Canvas.Pen.Color := OldPenCol;
Canvas.Pen.Width := OldPenW;
Canvas.Brush.Color := OldBrushCol;
end;
```

The other methods of the TShapeForm class are simple. The program asks the user to confirm some operations, such as exiting from the program or removing all the shapes from the list (with the File ➤ New command):

```
procedure TShapesForm.New1Click(Sender: TObject);
begin
  if (ShapesList.Count > 0) and (MessageDlg (
    'Are you sure you want to delete all the shapes?',
    mtConfirmation, [mbYes, mbNo], 0) = idYes) then
  begin
    ShapesList.Clear;
    Refresh;
  end;
end;
```

This time, the output looks great (see Figure 10.13), and whatever happens to the window, the shapes are always repainted in the proper position.

FIGURE 10.13

The output of the Shapes4 example.

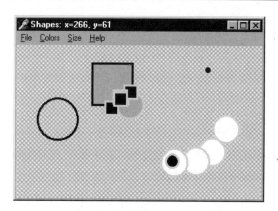

The only drawback is that when you have a number of shapes on the form, if you add a new shape, the program takes some time to redisplay them all, and the drawing tends to flicker. Instead of invalidating, erasing, and repainting the whole surface of the form, you might consider doing the same operation for only a smaller portion of it. To accomplish this, Delphi offers no specific support, but you can call the InvalidateRect function of the Windows API:

```
procedure InvalidateRect(Wnd: HWnd;
  Rect: PRect; Erase: Bool);
```

The three parameters indicate the handle of the window (that is, the Handle property of the form), the rectangle you want to repaint, and a flag indicating whether or not you want to erase the area before repainting it. In the Shapes4 program's FormMouseDown procedure, we can replace the call to Invalidate with the following code:

```
var
  InvRect: TRect;
begin
  ...
  {standard code:}
  // Invalidate;

  {optimized code:}
  InvRect := Rect (X - Radius - Shape.PenSize,
  Y - Radius - Shape.PenSize, X + Radius + Shape.PenSize,
  Y + Radius + Shape.PenSize);
  InvalidateRect (Handle, @InvRect, False);
end;
```

This code is already present in the Shapes4 example on the companion disk. You can comment it and uncomment the previous call to see the difference. I suggest you experiment with the two versions of the example to get an idea of why calling InvalidateRect is really a great benefit to a slow graphical program. The key idea is that if Repaint or Invalidate is called, the surface of the form is erased, and then each shape is repainted.

Invalidating only a small portion of the window, instead, makes any flicker less noticeable, because it involves only a smaller area and because Windows can redraw it more quickly. In fact—and this is an important thing to acknowledge—*paint operations are limited by a clipping rectangle*, which usually has the size of the form, but in this case is limited to the invalidated area. *Windows automatically skips every output operation outside the clipping rectangle*, avoiding any time-consuming video driver access.

To be more precise, I should have used the term *clipping region* instead of *clipping rectangle,* because this area can have any complex form. If you want more details, you can see the description of the InvalidateRegion and CreateRegion API functions in the Windows Help file.

> **TIP**
>
> The area you invalidate with the InvalidateRect call should be big enough for the last shape, including its eventual thick border (unless the pen style is psInsideFrame). For this reason, I've added the size of the pen (as you can see in the code fragment above), although half the size of the pen would have probably been enough.

Delphi Output Components

We have made four versions of the Shapes example, using almost no components, aside from a standard color-selection dialog box. As an alternative, we could have used two Delphi components: PaintBox and Shape. What are these two components for?

- You use the PaintBox component when you need to paint on a certain area of a form and that area might move on the form. For example, PaintBox is useful for painting on a dialog box without the risk of mixing the area for the output with the area for the controls. The PaintBox might fit within other controls of a form, such as a toolbar or a status bar, and avoid any confusion or overlapping of the output. In the Shapes example, using this component made no sense, because we always worked on the whole surface of the form.

- You use the Shape component to paint shapes on the screen, exactly as we have done up to now. We could indeed use the Shape component instead of our manual output, but I really wanted to show you how to accomplish some direct output operations. Our approach was not much more complex than the one Delphi suggests. Using the Shape component would have been useful to extend the example, allowing a user to drag shapes on the screen, remove them, and work on them in a number of other ways. You can see an example of the use of the Shape component in the MdiDemo4 example in Chapter 15.

What's Next

Since Chapter 1 we have seen that a form is a window, but until this chapter we had not explored any of a form's properties. Now we know how to handle the size and position of a form, how to resize it, how to get mouse input, and how to paint on the surface of the form. I've also mentioned the existence of two global objects, Application and Screen, which will be further explored in Chapter 25.

Other chapters in the book will describe topics related to forms. In particular, Chapters 12 through 15 cover the use of toolbars and status bars, building a dialog box and an application with multiple forms, scrolling forms, building forms with multiple pages, splitting forms, and building MDI applications. As you can see from this list, forms play a central role in Delphi programming, and we still have to explore a number of topics related to them.

Before we go on to these topics, however, in the next chapter you'll see how to use a number of other components, including the graphical components mentioned in the last section of this chapter, and many other graphical components, such as buttons, list boxes, and grids. (I never said you could learn Delphi programming in two days. But if you take the time—and read the rest of this book—you can achieve a true mastery of this complex subject.)

CHAPTER
ELEVEN

11

Graphical Components

- Bitmap buttons
- Animated buttons
- An image viewer
- The Animate control
- Drawing over a bitmap
- Graphical list boxes
- The TreeView and ListView controls
- The Mines game
- Building a font grid
- The color selection grid
- Using TeeChart
- The DateTimePicker common control

In addition to the basic controls borrowed from Windows, Delphi offers a number of more powerful components that have a modern user interface. Some of these controls are the graphical versions of traditional components (such as buttons or list boxes), others are brand-new elements. Some of them are new Windows 95 common controls, others are defined by Delphi and are also available in the 16-bit version of the Borland development environment. We will start exploring some of these advanced controls in this chapter, and we will continue to look at them for several more chapters.

We saw in the last chapter that it is easy to draw on the surface of a form. The same operation is possible for other components, too. However, we have also seen that the Windows painting model is far from simple. For this reason, having ready-to-use graphical controls is a big advantage over the traditional approach. You can improve your application's user interface with very little effort by using graphical buttons, grids, and outlines and, at the same time, adding powerful capabilities to the application in almost no time.

Improving the User Interface with Graphics

The user interface of early Windows applications was very different from what we see today. With Windows 3.1, a number of techniques to improve the user interface became common, including toolbars, graphical buttons, graphical list boxes, and so on. The 16-bit Windows API did not directly support these elements, and they required a lot of coding. Now things have changed. Windows 95 includes a number of improved graphical controls, ready for applications to use. Delphi has still other graphical and complex components, including grids.

I'll briefly describe some of these components and show their use in simple examples, as usual. Before we start looking at the code, however, consider that while some graphics can improve a program and make it seem more professional, too many colors and too many graphics can be counterproductive. The user interface of Windows and those of applications running in this environment follow specific rules, defined by Microsoft and known as *Windows Style Guides*. Without referring to this document, you can easily understand what these rules dictate by looking at the mainstream Windows applications.

Slight differences from the rules can improve a program, but diverging too much from the standard might backfire. If one application behaves differently from the others, a user might conclude that it isn't working properly. Of course, you can write a manual to explain the details of your choices, but how many users will read your manual before they start using the program? An important point, however, is that the *standard* for a user interface is a moving target. Each time someone (read *Microsoft*) writes down the details, a new application with a new feature comes out, thus changing the standard.

Consider this example: A couple of years ago, there were no toolbars. Then some toolbars with big buttons containing text and graphics were introduced. The next standard was to have smaller buttons, and maybe several lines of them. A couple of months later, every application allowed users to change the buttons on the toolbar. More time passed, and an application without *tool tips* (the yellow hint messages that appear when the cursor pauses over a button) was considered old. Then came dockable toolbars (that is, toolbars you can drag to different positions on the screen), an increased use of color (originally forbidden), and the new *Internet Explorer*-like toolbar buttons, now available also in Delphi 3.

A Bitmap in a Button

One of the simplest and most common ways you can improve an application's user interface is to make the buttons more colorful and, at the same time, more intuitive. Several years ago, Borland started to place bitmaps in buttons to highlight their meanings. For example, OK buttons have a green check mark on them, and Cancel buttons have a red cross. Delphi offers two kinds of graphical buttons:

- The BitBtn (bitmap button) component usually has some graphics and some text, as did the old Borland buttons. The behavior of BitBtn buttons is similar to the Button components—that is, they implement push buttons. You can choose one of the typical Borland buttons with a corresponding return value for these buttons in a modal form or dialog box.

- The SpeedButton component allows both graphics and text, but you'll often use it with only a glyph. As the name implies, speed buttons are mainly used in toolbars (or SpeedBars, to use the Borland term). Their behavior can mimic push buttons, check boxes with off and on states, and even radio buttons. They also allow you to use different glyphs for the various states.

The key technical difference between the BitBtn component and the SpeedButton component is that the first is based on a Windows button, using the owner-drawn technique (internally) to paint on its surface, and the second is a graphical component, not based on a window (it has no window handle). For this reason, speed buttons make a more limited use of system resources, which is particularly important when you need many buttons. Note also that speed buttons cannot receive the input focus (you cannot select them with the Tab key), and for this reason you should generally avoid using them in generic forms or dialog boxes. In this section, I'll focus on bitmap buttons, leaving the speed buttons for the next chapter, which is entirely devoted to SpeedBars (or toolbars) and status bars.

Once you have created an object with the BitBtn component, you can simply use the Kind property to select a default text, glyph, and return value. The available choices are the values of the TBitBtnKind enumeration:

```
type
  TBitBtnKind = (bkCustom, bkOK, bkCancel,
    bkHelp, bkYes, bkNo, bkClose, bkAbort,
    bkRetry, bkIgnore, bkAll);
```

If you select a custom button, you have to supply the button's Caption and Glyph properties; otherwise, a default glyph and caption are shown. Other properties let you arrange the position of text and graphics (Layout) and set the space between them (Spacing).

Another important concept is the idea of *transparent color*. When you prepare a bitmap for a button or other graphical component, the color found in the lower-left corner pixel of the bitmap is considered the transparent color. For this reason, many applications and Delphi itself use bitmaps with a dark yellow background (the clOlive color), a color seldom used in the bitmap itself. This value determines which color of the glyph should be considered transparent and replaced by the button's background color. If you use this approach, the system will be able to use the default colors (light gray, dark gray, and so on) for the various states of the button, always integrating your bitmap seamlessly.

A Car in a Button

To experiment with graphical buttons, we'll build a simple and almost useless example, Cars, having a number of bitmap buttons with different behaviors. The program will have a *two-state* button that changes its text and its image each time it is pressed. It will also have a group of three buttons, only one of which is active at a time. The last two buttons are simpler. One of them, however, has its text and its caption reversed, for symmetry, as you can see in Figure 11.1.

FIGURE 11.1

The output of the Cars example. The image of the car can be moved outside of the bevel.

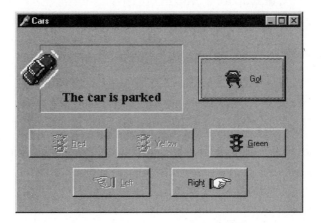

Besides the bitmap buttons, the form contains a label, an Image component, and a Bevel component. We have never used these two components, so I'll describe them briefly (and then move back to the example):

- You can use the Image component to display images on the background of the form, possibly behind other components. To load the bitmap for an image from a file or to store it in a new file, you simply call the LoadFromFile and SaveToFile methods of the component's Picture property. You can choose to show the image in its original size or stretch it to the size of the component. Since Image components support only click events, they can be considered static elements. Later in this chapter, we'll use this component again to build an image viewer.

- The Bevel component defines a 3D effect you can use to make some of the form's controls stand out or to group them. It defines *beveled* boxes, frames or lines (see its Shape property) that can be either lowered or raised, as described by the Style property. Bevels have no events at all, so their only use is to improve the user interface. As we will see in detail in the next chapter, there is another component, Panel, that is similar to a bevel but with much more functionality. Along with TPanel's extra capabilities comes additional resource overhead, so do not use a panel when a bevel is enough.

The form of the Cars example has a number of bitmap buttons, plus a bevel in the upper-left portion, with an image and a label inside. Note that once you select a bitmap for a property of a component, this bitmap is copied into the textual description as a stream of hexadecimal numbers. Here is an example:

```
object CarImage: TImage
  Picture.Data = {
    07544269746D617076020000424D760200000000000076
    0000020000000010004000000000000200000000000000
```

And so on for about 20 lines. This means you do not need the bitmap to compile or to run the application: Everything is included in the DFM file. However, in the following and in later textual descriptions of forms including bitmaps I'll refer to the file, so you can rebuild the example (in case you really don't you like typing hexadecimal numbers!). By the way, the bitmaps are all included on the companion CD, each in its own directory. Here, then, is the textual description of the form of the Cars example:

```
object CarsForm: TCarsForm
  ActiveControl = CarButton
  Caption = 'Cars'
  OnCreate = FormCreate
  OnDestroy = FormDestroy
  object CarLabel: TLabel
    Alignment = taCenter
    AutoSize = False
    Caption = 'The car is parked'
    Font.Height = -19
    Font.Name = 'Times New Roman'
    Font.Style = [fsBold]
  end
  object Bevel1: TBevel...
  object CarImage: TImage
    Picture.Data = {Cars.bmp}
    Stretch = True
  end
  object CarButton: TBitBtn
    Caption = 'G&o!'
    OnClick = CarButtonClick
    Glyph.Data = {Cars2.bmp}
    Spacing = 12
  end
  object GreenButton: TBitBtn
    Caption = '&Green'
    Enabled = False
```

```
    OnClick = GreenButtonClick
    Glyph.Data = {LightG.bmp}
  end
  object RedButton: TBitBtn
    Caption = '&Red'
    TabOrder = 3
    OnClick = RedButtonClick
    Glyph.Data = { LightR.bmp}
  end
  object YellowButton: TBitBtn
    Caption = '&Yellow'
    Enabled = False
    OnClick = YellowButtonClick
    Glyph.Data = {LightY.bmp}
  end
  object LeftButton: TBitBtn
    Caption = '&Left'
    TabOrder = 4
    OnClick = LeftButtonClick
    Glyph.Data = {Left.bmp}
  end
  object RightButton: TBitBtn
    Caption = 'Righ&t'
    OnClick = RightButtonClick
    Glyph.Data = {Right.bmp}
    Layout = blGlyphRight
  end
end
```

When the Left or Right button is pressed, the image is moved to the left or right until it bounces against the form's border (or almost the border, since some pixels are left):

```
procedure TCarsForm.LeftButtonClick(Sender: TObject);
begin
  {move the car, but not outside the area of the form}
  RightButton.Enabled := True;
  CarImage.Left := CarImage.Left - 10;
  {when the left border of the image is less than ten
  pixels from the left border of the form, which is at 0}
  if CarImage.Left < 10 then
```

```
begin
  RightButton.SetFocus;
  LeftButton.Enabled := False;
end;
end;
```

As you can see in Figure 11.1, this approach is far from good; the limit should be set on the border of the bevel. This simple change is left to you as an exercise.

When any of the three buttons with a traffic-light bitmap is pressed, the code simply disables the button and enables another one, following a round-robin approach: the green button follows the red button, the yellow button follows the green button, and the red button follows the yellow button. Here is one of the three methods:

```
procedure TCarsForm.RedButtonClick(Sender: TObject);
begin
  {after the red, green}
  GreenButton.Enabled := True;
  GreenButton.SetFocus;
  RedButton.Enabled := False;
end;
```

Notice that there is a call to the SetFocus method of the GreenButton object before the RedButton is disabled. When disabled, the button loses the focus anyway, but it will move almost randomly to other buttons. If you then call SetFocus it will move again with a distracting flash effect. If the SetFocus method is instead called before the button is disabled, we can decide which button is going to receive the focus and move it there immediately. The advantage of moving the focus to the next related button is that if you click on the button by pressing the spacebar, you can tap the spacebar a number of times and see the focus move from button to button, in a particular order.

The same happens with the Left and Right buttons. If you press the spacebar repeatedly, the image will bounce against the border and then move back since the focus is set on the button corresponding to the opposite direction. Notice that you can also use shortcut keys (defined using the & in the button captions) to give a command. Even when you change button captions at run-time (see also the code below) remember to set the & properly, to keep shortcuts consistent.

The example's most complex piece of code is that of the button with the car picture. The effect of clicking this button is to change the Glyph and the Caption of the button itself, the Picture of the Image component, and the Caption of the label below it. The code also sets the value of a private Boolean field of the form, CarStopped, to keep track of the current status.

To avoid loading a bitmap for the image and one for the button each time, with a statement such as

```
CarButton.Glyph.LoadFromFile ('cars2.bmp');
```

I've added to the form two bitmap objects, storing the two graphical images. The form has three fields:

```
private
  CarStopped: Boolean;
  Car1Bmp, Car2Bmp: TBitmap;
```

These private fields are initialized when the form is created:

```
procedure TCarsForm.FormCreate(Sender: TObject);
begin
  {set the flag and load the two bitmaps of the car}
  CarStopped := True;
  Car1Bmp := TBitmap.Create;
  Car2Bmp := TBitmap.Create;
  Car1Bmp.LoadFromFile ('cars.bmp');
  Car2Bmp.LoadFromFile ('cars2.bmp')
end;
```

After this initialization, we can use the two bitmap objects to set a value for the image and the graphical button. Of course, there are two alternative versions, which depend on the value of the CarStopped flag. There is also a special case. If the car is not moving and the red light is on—that is, the RedButton is enabled—you cannot go. A warning message is displayed, and nothing happens. Here is the first part of the source code of the CarButton click method:

```
procedure TCarsForm.CarButtonClick(Sender: TObject);
begin
  {a car should not start if the light is red}
  if CarStopped then
    if RedButton.Enabled then
      MessageDlg ('No turn on red, please!',
        mtWarning, [mbOK], 0)
    else {if was stopped and it is not red}
    begin
      {change the bitmaps and captions}
```

```
        CarButton.Glyph := Car1Bmp;
        CarButton.Caption := 'St&op';
        CarImage.Picture.Graphic := Car2Bmp;
        CarLabel.Caption := 'The car is on the road';
        CarStopped := False;
    end
else {if the car was moving, regardless of the lights}
    ...
```

The second part of the code does the same, using the other bitmap and different text. Notice that for this code to work you really need to keep the two car bitmaps in the directory of the executable file, since they are loaded at run-time. Also keep in mind that you have to free the two TBitmap objects in the OnDestroy event handler of the form.

An Animated Bitmap in a Button

As you saw in the previous example, bitmap buttons are easy to use and can produce better-looking applications than the standard push buttons (the Button component). To further improve the visual effect of a button, we can also think of *animating* the button. There are basically two kinds of animated buttons—buttons that change their glyph slightly when they are pressed and buttons having a moving image, regardless of the current operation. I'll show you a simple example of each kind, Fire and World. Each of these examples will have a couple of slightly different versions.

A Two-State Button

The first example, Fire, has a very simple form, containing only a bitmap button. This button has the Caption "Fire" and is connected to a Glyph representing a cannon. Imagine such a button as part of a game program. As the button is pressed, the glyph changes to show a firing cannon, as you can see in Figure 11.2. As soon as the button is released, the default glyph is loaded again. In between, the program displays a message if the user has actually clicked the button. (A user might press the button and then move the mouse away and release it. In this case, the OnClick event doesn't take place, but the bitmap is temporarily changed anyway.)

FIGURE 11.2

The image displayed
by the Fire example when
the button is pressed,
and the "Boom" message.

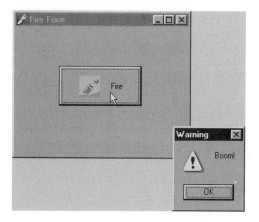

To write this program, we need to handle three of the button's events:
OnMouseDown, OnMouseUp, and OnClick. The code of the three methods is
extremely simple:

```
procedure TForm1.BitBtnFireMouseDown(Sender: TObject;
  Button: TMouseButton; Shift: TShiftState; X, Y: Integer);
begin
  {load firing cannon bitmap}
  if Button = mbLeft then
    BitBtnFire.Glyph.LoadFromFile ('fire2.bmp');
end;

procedure TForm1.BitBtnFireMouseUp(Sender: TObject;
  Button: TMouseButton; Shift: TShiftState; X, Y: Integer);
begin
  {load default cannon bitmap}
  if Button = mbLeft then
    BitBtnFire.Glyph.LoadFromFile ('fire.bmp');
end;

procedure TForm1.BitBtnFireClick(Sender: TObject);
begin
  MessageDlg ('Boom!', mtWarning, [mbOK], 0);
end;
```

When you hold down the left mouse button over the bitmap button, the bitmap
button is pressed. If you then move the mouse cursor away from the button while

holding down the mouse button, the bitmap button is released, but it doesn't get an OnMouseUp event, so the firing cannon remains there. If you later release the left mouse button outside the surface of the bitmap button, it receives the OnMouseUp event anyway.

Windows follows this rule: all mouse events are sent to the window or component behind the cursor. So how can we send a mouse event to the button if we release it outside its surface? This behavior depends on the *mouse capture*. A window can decide to capture all of the following input of the mouse, independently of the current window below the cursor. This is the default behavior of all the buttons in Windows, when they are pressed. So we can state the rule above more correctly: all mouse events are sent to the window or component behind the cursor or to the window, if any, that has captured the mouse input.

TIP You can capture the mouse using the Windows API SetCapture function and later stop this operation with ReleaseCapture. Capturing the mouse can be very interesting in some applications and is the basis for every dragging operation, as we will see in later chapters (Chapter 14 in particular).

Many Images in a Bitmap

The Fire example used a manual approach. I loaded two bitmaps and changed the value of the Glyph property when I wanted to change the image. The BitBtn component, however, can also handle a number of bitmaps automatically. You can prepare a single bitmap that contains a number of images (or glyphs) and set this number as the value of the NumGlyphs property. All such "sub-bitmaps" must have the same size since the overall bitmap is divided into equal parts.

If you provide more than one glyph in the bitmap, they are used according to the following rules:

- The first bitmap is used for the released button, the default position.

- The second bitmap is used for the disabled button.

- The third bitmap is used when the button is clicked.

- The fourth bitmap is used when the button remains down, as in buttons behaving as check boxes.

Usually you provide a single glyph and the others are automatically computed from it, with simple graphical changes. However, it is easy to provide a second, a third, and a fourth customized picture. If you do not provide all four bitmaps, the missing ones will be computed automatically from the first one. However, only the last or the last two bitmaps can be missing. You can't specify a normal and a pressed image without including the disabled bitmap between them.

In our example, the new version of Fire (named Fire2), we only need the first and third glyphs of the bitmap but are obliged to add the second bitmap, too. To see how this glyph (the second of the bitmap) can be used, I've added a check box to disable the bitmap button. To build the new version of the program, I've prepared a bitmap of 32 x 96 pixels (see Figure 11.3) and used it for the Glyph property of the bitmap. To my surprise, the NumGlyphs property was *automatically* set to 3 since the bitmap is three times wider than it is high.

FIGURE 11.3

The bitmap with three images of the Fire2 example, as seen in the Delphi Image Editor.

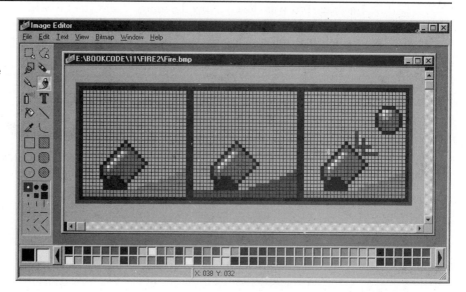

Then I removed the BitBtnFireMouseDown and BitBtnFireMouseUp methods, which are now useless. The next step was to add a check box, used to enable and disable the button (so we can see the glyph corresponding to the disabled status) and to write a line of code for its OnClick event:

```
procedure TForm1.CheckBox1Click(Sender: TObject);
begin
  BitBtnFire.Enabled := CheckBox1.Checked;
end;
```

I've also added some sound capabilities, playing a .WAV file when the button is pressed (with a call to the PlaySound function of the MMSystem unit). The code is very simple, so I'll skip any details about sound and multimedia and refer you to Chapter 31:

```
procedure TForm1.BitBtnFireClick(Sender: TObject);
begin
  PlaySound ('Boom.wav', 0, snd_Async);
  MessageDlg ('Boom!', mtWarning, [mbOK], 0);
end;
```

When you run the program, there are two ways to change the bitmap in the button. You can disable the bitmap button by using the check box (see Figure 11.4), or you can press the button to see the cannon fire. If you compare the output of this program with Figure 11.2, showing Fire, you will notice a remarkable difference. In the first version, the image with the firing cannon remained on the button until the message box was closed. Now the image is shown only while the button is pressed. As soon as you move outside the surface of the button, or release the button after having pressed it (activating the message box), the first glyph is displayed.

FIGURE 11.4

The enabled and disabled bitmap buttons of the Fire2 example, in two different copies of the application.

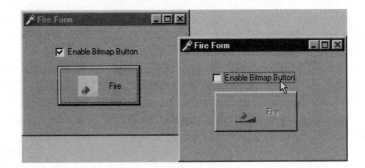

The Rotating World

The second example of animation, World, has a button featuring the earth, which slowly rotates, showing the various continents. You can see some samples in Figure 11.5, but, of course, you should run the program to see its output. In the previous example, the image changed when the button was pressed. Now the image changes by itself, automatically. This occurs thanks to the presence of a Timer component, which receives a message at fixed time intervals. For a detailed discussion of timers and related topics, see Chapter 25.

FIGURE 11.5

Some examples of the running World program.

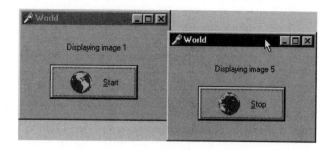

Here is a summary of the properties of the components of this example:

```
object WorldForm: TWorldForm
  Caption = 'World'
  OnCreate = FormCreate
  object Label1: TLabel
    Caption = 'Displaying image 1'
  end
  object WorldButton: TBitBtn
    Caption = '&Start'
    OnClick = WorldButtonClick
    Glyph.Data = {W1.bmp}
    Spacing = 15
  end
  object Timer1: TTimer
    Enabled = False
    Interval = 500
    OnTimer = Timer1Timer
  end
end
```

The timer component is started and stopped (enabled and disabled) when the user presses the bitmap button with the world image. The button has a *'Start'* Caption, which changes to *'Stop'* when the timer is active. So by pressing the button, you start or stop the animation:

```
procedure TWorldForm.WorldButtonClick(Sender: TObject);
begin
  if Timer1.Enabled then
  begin
    Timer1.Enabled := False;
    WorldButton.Caption := '&Start';
```

```
    end
    else
    begin
      Timer1.Enabled := True;
      WorldButton.Caption := '&Stop';
    end;
  end;
```

As you can see in Figure 11.5, a label above the button indicates which of the images is being displayed. I added the label as a debugging tool when I started writing this program, but then I decided to leave it there. You might replace it with information on time zones or something else. Each time the timer message is received, the image and label change:

```
procedure TWorldForm.Timer1Timer(Sender: TObject);
begin
  Count := (Count mod 16) + 1;
  Label1.Caption := 'Displaying image ' +
    IntToStr (Count);
  WorldButton.Glyph.LoadFromFile (
    'w' + IntToStr (Count) + '.bmp');
end;
```

In this code, Count is a field of the form that is initialized to 1 in the FormCreate method. At each timer interval, Count is increased modulus 16 and then converted into a string (preceded by the letter *w*).

NOTE   The modulus operation returns the remainder of the division between integers. This means that Count mod 16 invariably returns a value in the range 0–15. Adding one to this return value, we obtain the number of the bitmap, which is in the range 1–16.

The reason for this limit is simple: I had 16 bitmaps of the earth to display. Naming the bitmap files W1.BMP, W2.BMP, and so on, makes it easy for the program to access them, building the strings with the name at run-time.

A List of Bitmaps, the Use of Resources, and a PaintBox

The World program works, but it is very slow, for a couple of reasons. First of all, at each timer interval, it needs to read a file from the disk, and although a disk cache can make this faster, it is certainly not the most efficient solution. Besides reading the file from disk, the program has to create and destroy Windows bitmap objects, and this takes some time, too. The second problem depends on how the image is updated: When you change the button's bitmap, the component is completely erased and repainted. This causes some flickering, as you can see by running the program.

To solve the first problem (and to show you a different approach to handling bitmaps), I've added a TList object, storing a list of bitmaps, to the form of the second version of the example, World2:

```
type
  TWorldForm = class(TForm)
    ...
  private
    Count: Integer;
    BitmapsList: TList;
  end;
```

All the bitmaps are loaded when the program starts and destroyed when it terminates. At each timer interval, the program shows one of the list's bitmaps in the bitmap button. By using a list, we avoid loading a file each time we need to display a bitmap, but we still need to have all the files with the images in the directory with the executable file. A solution to this problem is to move the bitmaps from independent files to the application's resource file. This is easier to do than to explain.

Resources are graphical or textual data connected to a Windows program. The most important resources in Delphi include bitmaps, icons, fonts, string tables, and the images of the forms. (Note that an application's resources have nothing to do with free system resources—the two uses of the term are completely unrelated!) We will discuss resources in detail in Chapter 27, but we'll use them often in graphical examples before then (and we'll use them often again in this chapter).

TIP

There are basically three reasons to use resources in Windows applications. The first is that some of them refer to graphical elements and require proper editors; the second and more important reason is that resources are handled in memory in a special way (see Chapter 26 for more information on memory in Windows); the third is that to localize a Windows application, you usually translate the text of the resources into a different language, without changing the source code.

To use the resources instead of the bitmap files, we need first of all to copy the bitmap to the resource file. If you want to do a tedious operation, you can use the Delphi Image Editor to create a brand new resource file, open each of the bitmap files, and copy-and-paste the bitmap into the resource file.

WARNING

Do not add the new bitmaps to the WORLD.RES file of the program. This file is automatically updated by Delphi in some circumstances, deleting the current contents!

As a better alternative, you can write a resource script (an .RC file) listing the names of the bitmap files and of the corresponding resources. Just select the File ➤ New command to open the Object Repository, then click on the Text icon in the New page. In the blank text field Delphi generates, write the following code:

```
W1  BITMAP  "W1.BMP"
W2  BITMAP  "W2.BMP"
W3  BITMAP  "W3.BMP"
// ... and so on
```

Once you have prepared the RC file (I've named it WORLDBMP.RC), you can compile it into a .RES file using the resource compiler included in Delphi (the BRCC32 command-line application you can find in the BIN directory of Delphi):

```
BRCC32 WORLDBMP.RC
```

Then add a compiler directive to the source code of the program to include the new resource file. We can place it in the unit describing the form, just after the directive to include the form resource (the DFM file):

```
{$R *.DFM}
{$R WORLDBMP.RES}
```

Once you have properly defined the resources of the application, you need to load the bitmaps from the resources. Delphi components do not support this operation directly, but you can easily accomplish it using the Windows API Load-Bitmap function. This function requires two parameters: a handle to the application, known as HInstance, which is available in Delphi as a global variable; and a string with the name of the resource.

NEW

Delphi 3 defines a new global variable, MainInstance, which refers to the HInstance of the main executable file. In most cases you can use one or the other interchangeably.

Of course, you need to pass to the LoadBitmap API function a PChar string, not a Pascal string, so a conversion might be required. This is the code of the FormCreate method:

```
procedure TWorldForm.FormCreate(Sender: TObject);
var
  I: Integer;
  Bmp: TBitmap;
  BmpName: string;
begin
  Count := 1;

  {load the bitmaps from the resources of the
  application to the list of TBitmap objects}
  BitmapsList := TList.Create;
  for I := 1 to 16 do
  begin
    Bmp := TBitmap.Create;
    BmpName := 'W' + IntToStr (I);
    {load the bitmap from the resources:
    LoadBitmap is a Windows API function}
    Bmp.Handle := LoadBitmap (HInstance, PChar (BmpName));
    BitmapsList.Add (Bmp);
  end;
end;
```

One problem remains to be solved. How can we obtain a smooth transition from
one image of the world to the following one? I tried to work it out using the TBitBtn
class, but there were many obstacles. After a while, I figured out a completely different solution. Why not paint the bitmaps in a canvas using the Draw method?
Unfortunately, the bitmap button's canvas is not directly available, so I added a
new component, PaintBox, to the form. Again, things weren't working. You cannot
place the PaintBox component inside a button; only inside a form. Even if you place
it over the button, Delphi will connect the PaintBox component to the form, thus
hiding it behind the button. The PaintBox component, in fact, is not based on a window. It uses its parent control—in this case, the form. The solution? Very easy, once
you think about it—change the Parent of the PaintBox component at run-time, by
writing this code (in the FormCreate method), and place it in the proper position:

```
PaintBox1.Parent := WorldButton;
PaintBox1.SetBounds (
  WorldButton.Margin,
  (WorldButton.Height - Bmp.Height) div 2,
  Bmp.Width + 2,
  Bmp.Height + 2);
```

The horizontal position of the PaintBox depends on the Margin of the icon of
the bitmap button. The PaintBox has the size of a bitmap and is vertically
centered in the button. Once the PaintBox component is properly set, you can
simply paint over it in the Timer1Timer method:

```
procedure TWorldForm.Timer1Timer(Sender: TObject);
begin
  Count := (Count mod 16) + 1;
  Label1.Caption := Format ('Displaying image %d', [Count]);

  {draw the current bitmap in the canvas placed
  over the bitmap button}
  PaintBox1.Canvas.Draw (1, 1,
    BitmapsList.Items[Count-1]);
end;
```

This code copies the bitmap to the surface of the PaintBox component—that is, the surface of its parent component, the bitmap button. Another thing to do is to define a proper FormDestroy method to deallocate each of the bitmaps:

```
procedure TWorldForm.FormDestroy(Sender: TObject);
begin
  {free each element and the list itself}
  BitmapsList.Clear;
  BitmapsList.Free;
end;
```

The last problem is to move the position of the PaintBox when the left mouse button is pressed or released over it (that is, in the OnMouseDown and OnMouseUp events of the button). Besides moving the PaintBox, we should update the glyph of the bitmap, because Delphi will automatically display it while redrawing the button. It you fail to do so, you'll see the initial image until the timer interval doesn't elapse (something that might take a while if you've stopped it!). Here is the code of the two methods:

```
procedure TWorldForm.WorldButtonMouseDown(Sender: TObject;
  Button: TMouseButton; Shift: TShiftState; X, Y: Integer);
begin
  if Button = mbLeft then
  begin
    {paint the current image over the button}
    PaintBox1.Left := PaintBox1.Left + 2;
    PaintBox1.Top := PaintBox1.Top + 2;
    WorldButton.Glyph.Assign (
      BitmapsList.Items[Count-1]);
  end;
end;

procedure TWorldForm.WorldButtonMouseUp(Sender: TObject;
  Button: TMouseButton; Shift: TShiftState; X, Y: Integer);
begin
  if Button = mbLeft then
  begin
    PaintBox1.Left := PaintBox1.Left - 2;
    PaintBox1.Top := PaintBox1.Top - 2;
    WorldButton.Glyph.Assign (
      BitmapsList.Items[Count-1]);
  end;
end;
```

WARNING

Placing a PaintBox component in front of a button creates a problem: when you click on its surface, the button is not pressed. To improve the program, I've connected the `OnClick` event of the `PaintBox1` component to the method used to handle the `OnClick` event of the button. This works, but if you click on that area, you won't see the button being pressed. To make the button behave better, we should probably dispatch any mouse operation on the PaintBox component (including `OnMouseDown`, `OnMouseMove`, and `OnMouseUp`) to it, but this might well generate further problems.

The Animate Control

There is a better way to obtain animation than displaying a series of bitmaps in sequence. Use the Windows 95 Animate common control. Borland has added a Delphi component encapsulating it in Delphi 3. The Animate control is based on the use of AVI (Audio Video Interleaved) files, a series of bitmaps similar to a movie.

NOTE

Actually, the Animate control can display only those AVI files that have a single video stream, are uncompressed or compressed with RLE8 compression, and have no palette changes; and if they have sound, it is ignored. In practice, the files corresponding to this requirement are those made of a series of computer bitmaps, not those based on an actual film.

The Animate control can have two different sources for its animation:

- It can be based on a AVI file with the requirements indicated in the note above: this is obtained by setting a proper value for the `FileName` property.

- It can use a special internal Windows 95 animation, part of the common controls library: this is obtained by choosing one of the possible values of the `CommonAVI` property (which is based on an enumeration).

If you simply place an Animate control on a form, choose an animation using one of the methods just described, and finally set its `Active` property to `True`, you'll start seeing the animation performed even at design time. By default, the animation runs continuously, restarting it as soon as it is done. However, you can regulate this effect by using the Repetitions property. Setting it to -1 causes the infinite repetition.

You can also specify the initial and final frame of the sequence, with the StartFrame and StopFrame properties. These three properties (initial position, final position, and number of repetitions) correspond to the three parameters of a method you'll often use with a Animate control, the Play method. As an alternative, you can set the properties and then call the Start method. At run-time you can also access the total number of frames using the FrameCount property: you can use this to execute the animation from the beginning to the end. Finally, for finer control, you can use the Seek method, which displays a specific frame.

I've used all of these methods in a simple demo program, which can use both files or the Windows 95 standard animations. The program allows you to choose a file or one of the animations by using a ListBox. I've added an item to this ListBox for each element of the TCommonAVI enumeration, and used the same order:

```
object ListBox1: TListBox
  Items.Strings = (
    '[Use an AVI file]'
    'Find Folder'
    'Find File'
    'Find Computer'
    'Copy Files'
    'Copy File'
    'Recycle File'
    'Empty Recycle'
    'Delete File')
  OnClick = ListBox1Click
end
```

Thanks to this structure, when the user clicks on the ListBox, I can simply cast the number of the selected items to the enumerated data type to get the proper value for the CommonAVI property:

```
procedure TForm1.ListBox1Click(Sender: TObject);
begin
  Animate1.CommonAVI := TCommonAVI (ListBox1.ItemIndex);
  if (ListBox1.ItemIndex = 0) and
      OpenDialog1.Execute then
    Animate1.FileName := OpenDialog1.FileName
end;
```

As you can see, when the first item is selected (the value is caNone) the program automatically loads an AVI file, using an OpenDialog component. The most important component of the form is the Animate control. Here is its textual description:

```
object Animate1: TAnimate
  AutoSize = False
  Align = alClient
  CommonAVI = caFindFolder
  OnOpen = Animate1Open
end
```

I've aligned it to the client area, so that a user can easily resize it depending on the actual size of the frames of the animation. As you can see I've also defined a handler for an event of this component, OnOpen:

```
procedure TForm1.Animate1Open(Sender: TObject);
begin
  LblFrames.Caption := 'Frames ' +
    IntToStr (Animate1.FrameCount);
end;
```

When a new file (or common animation) is opened, the program simply outputs the number of its frames in a label. This label is hosted together with several buttons and a few SpinEdit controls into a big panel, acting as a toolbar. You can see them in the design-time form of Figure 11.6.

FIGURE 11.6

The form of the AnimCtrl example at design-time. The Animate control is actually showing an animation, even before running the program.

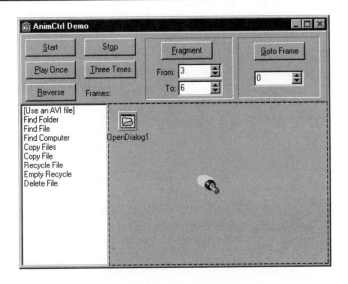

The Start, Stop, and Play Once buttons have the simplest code:

```
procedure TForm1.BtnStartClick(Sender: TObject);
begin
  Animate1.Active := True;
end;

procedure TForm1.BtnStopClick(Sender: TObject);
begin
  Animate1.Stop;
end;

procedure TForm1.BtnOnceClick(Sender: TObject);
begin
  Animate1.Play (0, Animate1.FrameCount, 1);
end;
```

Things start getting more interesting with the code used to play the animation three times, or place only a fragment of it. Both of these methods are based on the Play method:

```
procedure TForm1.BtnTriceClick(Sender: TObject);
begin
  Animate1.Play (0, Animate1.FrameCount, 3);
end;

procedure TForm1.BtnFragmentClick(Sender: TObject);
begin
  Animate1.Play (SpinEdit1.Value, SpinEdit2.Value, -1);
end;
```

The last two button event handlers are based on the Seek method, instead. The Goto button simply moves to the frame indicated by the corresponding SpinEdit component, while the Reverse buttons move to each frame in turn starting with the last one, pausing between each of them:

```
procedure TForm1.BtnGotoClick(Sender: TObject);
begin
  Animate1.Seek (SpinEdit3.Value);
end;
```

```
procedure TForm1.BtnReverseClick(Sender: TObject);
var
  Init: TDateTime;
  I: Integer;
begin
  for I := Animate1.FrameCount downto 0 do
  begin
    Animate1.Seek (I);
    // wait 30 milliseconds
    Init := Now;
    while Now < Init + EncodeTime (0, 0, 0, 30) do
      Application.ProcessMessages;
  end;
end;
```

You can extend this last method to control the speed of the animation, just choosing a different *waiting* time. However, the whole idea of the AVI file generally implies that the animation should proceed at its own pace.

An Image Viewer

The Image component introduced earlier in this chapter is usually considered to be an image viewer. You can easily load into it a bitmap file (BMP), an icon (ICO), or a Windows metafile (WMF). Bitmap and icon files are well-known formats. Windows metafiles, however, are not so common. They are a collection of graphical commands, similar to a list of GDI function calls that need to be executed to rebuild an image. Metafiles are usually referred to as *vector graphics* and are similar to the graphics file formats used for clip-art libraries.

> **NOTE**
>
> To produce a Windows metafile, a program should call GDI functions, redirecting their output to the file. Later on, this metafile can be *played* or executed to call the corresponding functions, thus producing a graph. The advantage of metafiles is the limited amount of storage required compared to other graphical formats, and the device-independence of their output.

To build a full-blown image viewer program, ImageV, around the Image component we need only a form with an image filling the whole client area, a simple menu, and an OpenDialog component:

```
object ViewerForm: TViewerForm
  Caption = 'Image Viewer'
  Menu = MainMenu1
  object Image1: TImage
    Align = alClient
  end
  object MainMenu1: TMainMenu
    object File1: TMenuItem...
      object Open1: TMenuItem...
      object N1: TMenuItem...
      object Exit1: TMenuItem...
    object Options1: TMenuItem
      object Stretch1: TMenuItem
      object Center1: TMenuItem
    object Help1: TMenuItem
      object AboutImageViewer1: TMenuItem
  end
  object OpenDialog1: TOpenDialog
    FileEditStyle = fsEdit
    Filter = 'Bitmap (*.bmp)|*.bmp|
      Icon (*.ico)|*.ico|Metafile (*.wmf)|*.wmf'
    Options = [ofHideReadOnly, ofPathMustExist,
      ofFileMustExist]
  end
end
```

Surprisingly, this application requires very little coding, at least for a first basic version. The File ➤ Exit and Help ➤ About commands are trivial, and the File ➤ Open command has the following code:

```
procedure TViewerForm.Open1Click(Sender: TObject);
begin
  if OpenDialog1.Execute then
  begin
    Image1.Picture.LoadFromFile (OpenDialog1.FileName);
    Caption := 'Image Viewer - ' + OpenDialog1.FileName;
  end;
end;
```

The fourth and fifth menu commands, Options ➤ Stretch and Options ➤ Center, simply toggle the component's Stretch property (see Figure 11.7 for the result) or Center property and add a check mark to themselves. Here is the OnClick event handler of the Stretch1 menu item:

```
procedure TViewerForm.Stretch1Click(Sender: TObject);
begin
  Image1.Stretch := not Image1.Stretch;
  Stretch1.Checked := Image1.Stretch;
end;
```

Keep in mind that when stretching an image you can change its width-to-height ratio, altering the shapes, and that not all images can be properly stretched. Stretching black-and-white or 256-color bitmaps doesn't always work correctly.

FIGURE 11.7

The ImageV program displaying the regular and stretched versions of the bitmap used in the Fire2 example.

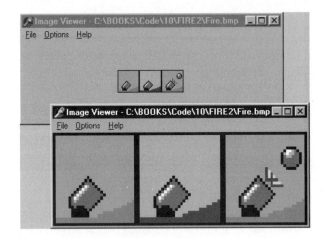

Besides this problem, the application has some other drawbacks. If you select a file without the proper extension, the Image component will raise an exception. The behavior of the exception handler provided by the system is good enough: the wrong image file is not loaded and the program can safely continue. Another problem is that if you load a large image, the viewer has no scroll bars. You can maximize the viewer window, but this might not be enough. The Image components do not handle them automatically, but the form can do it. I'll further extend this example to include scroll bars in Chapter 14.

Drawing in a Bitmap

In the last chapter, I mentioned that by using an Image component, you can draw images directly in a bitmap. Instead of drawing on the surface of a window, you draw in a bitmap in memory; then the bitmap is copied to the surface of the window. The advantage is that instead of having to repaint the image each time an OnPaint event occurs, the component copies the bitmap back to video.

Technically, a TBitmap object has its own canvas. By drawing on this canvas, you can change the contents of the bitmap. As an alternative, you can work on the canvas of an Image component connected to the bitmap you want to change. You might think of choosing this approach instead of the typical painting approach if any of the following conditions are true:

- The program has to support freehand drawing or very complex graphics (such as fractal images).

- The program should be very fast in drawing a number of images.

- You and your users have a lot of RAM or are going to use only a few applications.

- You are a lazy programmer.

The last point is interesting because painting generally requires more code than drawing, although it allows more flexibility. In a graphics program, for example, if you use painting, you have to store the location and colors of each shape. On the other hand, you can easily change the color of an existing shape or move it. These operations are very difficult with the painting approach and may cause the area behind an image to be lost. If you are working on a complex graphical application, you should probably choose a mix of the two approaches. For casual graphics programmers, the choice between the two approaches involves a typical speed-versus-memory decision: painting requires less memory; storing the bitmap is faster.

Drawing Shapes

Now that you've been introduced to the use of the Image component to paint on a bitmap in Delphi, let's look at an example. What better than a new version of the Shapes series of examples from the last chapter? The idea is simple. I've taken version 2 of the Shapes example, the one having colored shapes but still no support to save them—that is, with drawing but without painting. Then I placed an Image component on its form, covering the whole client area, and I redirected all the output operations to the canvas of this Image component.

In this example, Shapes5, I've also added some new menu items to save the image to a file and to load an existing bitmap. To accomplish this, I've added to the form a couple of default dialog components, OpenDialog and SaveDialog. One of the properties I had to change was the background color of the form. In fact, when you perform the first graphical operation on the image, it creates a bitmap, which has a white background by default. If the form has a gray background, each time the window is repainted, some flickering occurs. For this reason, I've chosen a white background for the form, too.

The code of this example is still quite simple, considering the number of operations and menu commands. The drawing portion is linear and very close to Shapes2, except that the mouse events now relate to the image instead of to the form, and that the canvas of the image is used:

```
procedure TShapesForm.Image1MouseDown(Sender: TObject;
  Button: TMouseButton; Shift: TShiftState; X, Y: Integer);
begin
  {draw a form in x:y, using the current radius}
  if Button = mbLeft then
    if ssShift in Shift then
      Image1.Canvas.Rectangle (
        X - Radius, Y - Radius,
        X + Radius, Y + Radius)
  ...
```

To avoid overly complex file support, I decided to implement the File ➤ Load and File ➤ Save As commands, and not handle the Save command, which is generally more complex. I've only added a Changed field to the form to know if an image has changed, and checked this value a number of times (before asking the user to confirm). To add full-blown file saving support, you should incorporate the relevant code from the RichNot2 example of Chapter 9.

The handler of the OnClick event of the File ➤ New menu item calls the FillArea method to paint a big white rectangle over the whole bitmap. In this code you can also see how the Changed field is used:

```
procedure TShapesForm.New1Click(Sender: TObject);
var
  Area: TRect;
  OldColor: TColor;
```

```
begin
  if not Changed or (MessageDlg (
    'Are you sure you want to delete the current image?',
    mtConfirmation, [mbYes, mbNo], 0) = idYes) then
  begin
    {repaint the surface, covering the whole area,
    and resetting the old brush}
    Area := Rect (0, 0, Image1.Picture.Width,
      Image1.Picture.Height);
    OldColor := Image1.Canvas.Brush.Color;
    Image1.Canvas.Brush.Color := clWhite;
    Image1.Canvas.FillRect (Area);
    Image1.Canvas.Brush.Color := OldColor;
    Changed := False;
  end;
end;
```

Of course, the code has to save the original color and restore it later on. A realignment of the colors is required also by the File ➤ Load command response method. When you load a new bitmap, in fact, the Image component creates a new canvas, with the default attributes. For this reason, the program saves the pen's colors and size and copies them later to the new canvas:

```
procedure TShapesForm.Load1Click(Sender: TObject);
var
  PenCol, BrushCol: TColor;
  PenSize: Integer;
begin
  if not Changed or (MessageDlg (
      'Are you sure you want to delete the current image?',
      mtConfirmation, [mbYes, mbNo], 0) = idYes) then
    if OpenDialog1.Execute then
    begin
      PenCol := Image1.Canvas.Pen.Color;
      BrushCol := Image1.Canvas.Brush.Color;
      PenSize := Image1.Canvas.Pen.Width;
      Image1.Picture.LoadFromFile (OpenDialog1.Filename);
      Image1.Canvas.Pen.Color := PenCol;
      Image1.Canvas.Brush.Color := BrushCol;
      Image1.Canvas.Pen.Width := PenSize;
      Changed := False;
    end;
end;
```

Saving the current image is much simpler, instead:

```
procedure TShapesForm.Saveas1Click(Sender: TObject);
begin
  if SaveDialog1.Execute then
  begin
    Image1.Picture.SaveToFile (
      SaveDialog1.Filename);
    Changed := False;
  end;
end;
```

Finally here is the code of the OnCloseQuery event of the form, which uses the Changed field:

```
procedure TShapesForm.FormCloseQuery(Sender: TObject;
  var CanClose: Boolean);
begin
  if not Changed or (MessageDlg (
      'Are you sure you want to delete the current image?',
      mtConfirmation, [mbYes, mbNo], 0) = idYes) then
    CanClose := True
  else
    CanClose := False;
end;
```

Shapes5 is an interesting program (see Figure 11.8), with bare but working file support. The real problem is that the Image component creates a bitmap of its own size. When you increase the size of the window, the Image component is resized, but not the bitmap in memory. Therefore, you cannot draw on the right and bottom areas of the window. There are a number of possible solutions: Use the Windows wm_GetMinMaxInfo message to set the maximum size of the form (as shown in Chapter 10), use a fixed border, visually mark the *drawing area* on the screen, and so on. However, I've decided to leave the program as-is since it does its job of demonstrating how to draw in a bitmap well enough.

FIGURE 11.8

The Shapes5 example has limited but working file support: you can load an existing bitmap, draw shapes over it, and save it to disk.

Graphical Lists

It has become common to see Windows applications with graphical list boxes, particularly lists of files. To draw in a standard list box in Windows 3.1, you had to declare it as owner-drawn and provide some painting code. Windows 95 introduces some new common controls, such as ListView and TreeView, which can display graphical lists and hierarchical information. In Delphi, you can still have an owner-drawn list box, but you'll generally use the Windows 95 common controls. As an alternative there are also some native Delphi components, such as the Outline, the FileListBox, and the DirectoryListBox components.

If you use the common controls in your application, users will already know how to interact with them, and they will regard the user interface of your program as a very modern one. TreeView and ListView are the two key components of Windows 95 Explorer, and you can assume that many users will be familiar with them. The drawback of the common controls is that you won't be able to recompile your application with the 16-bit version of Delphi and run it on 16-bit versions of Windows. Using a component such as Outline, instead, your application will be portable between the various versions of Delphi and between 16-bit and 32-bit versions of Windows.

Having said this, I'll show you a simple owner-draw list box, a comparative example of the use of a TreeView and an Outline, and one focusing on the ListView component. The examples presented here tend to be quite simple: I'll use these components to build more complex examples in later chapters.

Drawing a List of Colors

As we have already seen for menus, list boxes have an owner-draw capability, which means a program can paint the items of a list box. While Delphi provides limited support for owner-draw menus, obliging us to do Windows API calls and handle Windows messages directly, the TListbox class (like the TCombobox class) provides explicit support, making the code much simpler.

To create an owner-draw list box, we first need to set its Style property to the lbOwnerDrawFixed or lbOwnerDrawVariable. The first value indicates that we are going to set the height of the items of the list box by specifying the ItemHeight property, and that this will be the height of each and every item. The second owner-draw style indicates a list box with items of different heights. In this case the component will trigger the OnMeasureItem event for each item, to ask the program their heights.

In the ODList example, I'll stick with the first, simpler, approach. The aim of this example is to store color information along with the items of the list box, then draw the items in colors (instead of using a single color for the whole list). Here are the properties of the components of the main form of this example:

```
object ODListForm: TODListForm
  Caption = 'Owner-draw Listbox'
  Font.Color = clBlack
  Font.Height = -32
  Font.Name = 'Arial'
  Font.Style = [fsBold]
  Position = poDefault
  OnCreate = FormCreate
  TextHeight = 37
  object ListBox1: TListBox
    Align = alClient
    Style = lbOwnerDrawFixed
    OnDblClick = ListBox1DblClick
    OnDrawItem = ListBox1DrawItem
  end
  object ColorDialog1: TColorDialog...
end
```

As you can see, I've set a big font for the form, and the lbOwnerDrawFixed value for the Style of the list box. Notice the value of the TextHeight attribute of the form, which corresponds to the pixels required to display the text. This is the value we should use for the ItemHeight property of the list box. A better solution is to compute this value at·run-time, so that if we later change the font at design-time we don't have to remember to set the height of the items accordingly.

> **NOTE**   I've just described TextHeight as an *attribute* of the form, not a property. And in fact it isn't a property, but a local value of the form. If this is not a property, you might ask, how does Delphi saves it in the DFM file? Well, the answer is that Delphi's streaming mechanism is based on properties plus special *property-clones* created by the DefineProperties method. This is really an advanced topic, not covered in this book. You can refer to the Delphi Help file for some information, or to advanced Delphi books (including the *Delphi Developer's Handbook*) for the details.

Since `TextHeight` is *not* a property, although it is listed in the form description, we cannot access it directly. Studying the VCL source code, I found that this value is computed by calling a private method of the form, `GetTextHeight`. Since it is private, we cannot call this function. What we can do is to duplicate its code (which is actually quite simple) in the `FormCreate` method of the form:

```
ListBox1.ItemHeight := Canvas.TextHeight('0');
```

The next thing we have to do is add some items to the list box. Since this is a list box of colors, we want to add color names to the `Items` of the list box and the corresponding color values to the `Objects` data storage related to each item of the list. Instead of adding the two values separately, I've written a procedure to add new items to the list:

```
procedure TODListForm.AddColors (Colors: array of TColor);
var
  I: Integer;
begin
  for I := Low (Colors) to High (Colors) do
    ListBox1.Items.AddObject (
      ColorToString (Colors[I]),
      TObject(Colors[I]));
end;
```

This method uses an open-array parameter, a technique described in Chapter 4. For each item passed as a parameter we add the name of the color to the list, and its value to the related data, by calling the `AddObject` method. The string corresponding to the color is obtained by calling Delphi `ColorToString` function, which returns a string with the corresponding color constant, if any, or a string with the hexadecimal value of the color. The color data is added to the list box after casting its value to the `TObject` data type (a 4-byte reference), as required by the `AddObject` method.

TIP Besides `ColorToString`, which converts a color value into the corresponding string with the identifier or the hexadecimal value, there is also a Delphi function to convert a properly formatted string into a color, `StringToColor`.

In the ODList example this method is called in the OnCreate event handler of the form (after setting the height of the items):

```
procedure TODListForm.FormCreate(Sender: TObject);
begin
  ListBox1.ItemHeight := Canvas.TextHeight('0');
  AddColors ([clRed, clBlue, clYellow, clGreen, clFuchsia, clLime,
    clGray, RGB (213, 23, 123), RGB (0, 0, 0)]);
end;
```

The code used to draw the items is not particularly complex: We simply have to retrieve the color associated with the item, set it as the color of the font, and then draw the text:

```
procedure TODListForm.ListBox1DrawItem(
  Control: TWinControl; Index: Integer;
  Rect: TRect; State: TOwnerDrawState);
begin
  with Control as TListbox do
  begin
    // erase
    Canvas.FillRect(Rect);
    // draw item
    Canvas.Font.Color := TColor (Items.Objects [Index]);
    Canvas.TextOut(Rect.Left, Rect.Top, Listbox1.Items[Index]);
  end;
end;
```

You can see an example of the output of this program at startup in Figure 11.9. The example actually allows you also to add new items, by double-clicking on the list box:

```
procedure TODListForm.ListBox1DblClick(Sender: TObject);
begin
  if ColorDialog1.Execute then
    AddColors ([ColorDialog1.Color]);
end;
```

If you try using this capability you'll notice that some colors you add are turned into color names (one of the Delphi color constants), while others are converted into hexadecimal numbers. The same is true for the last two items added by the FormCreate method. As you can see in Figure 11.9, one of them results in a number, and one in the name of a constant.

Although using an owner-draw list box is quite simple, Delphi provides components that implement this capability, and other advanced ones. In particular, the Outline and TreeView components use graphics to build multilevel lists of values.

FIGURE 11.9

The output of the ODList example, with a colored owner-draw list box.

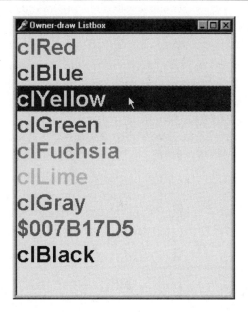

The Outline of the Book

First, I'll use the Outline component, demonstrating some its features. The Outline component allows you to add a bitmap before the text of the list items and to build a graphical hierarchy of items. To create a simple list of elements, you only need to add them to the Lines property and provide a specific bitmap in the PictureLeaf property.

The use of the outline makes particular sense when you have hierarchical information to display. I've taken as an example the table of contents of the previous edition of this book, and I've built the BookOut example with it. (Because of publishing time constraints, the example cannot be built around this edition of the book.)

WARNING

When I started writing the example, my intention was to call it Outline. However, after trying to do so, I realized the Pascal compiler was not able to refer properly to the Outline unit of the system because it was hidden by the name of the program file. The moral of this story is that you should avoid duplicate identifiers in general, but especially unit and module names (including those of the VCL).

Before we look at the example, let me describe some of the properties and styles of the Outline component. The Lines property has the textual version of the contents of the control, and you can access it at design-time. The Items property has the same information, but in a hierarchical structure, and is accessible only at run-time.

When you enter the text of an outline or read it from a text file, you can leave either a space or a tab in front of an item's text to indicate its level of indentation. To work on this list of strings at design-time you can open the String Editor connected to the property and eventually load a text file from it.

TIP

When you are using the Delphi String List Editor, by pressing Tab you move the focus to one of the buttons below instead of entering a tab in the text. To enter a tab in front of an item, use Ctrl+Tab.

Once you have defined the outline's text, you can set its style. The OutlineStyle property has six possible values:

- osPictureText defines an outline with the open-folder picture for the expanded nodes, the closed-folder picture for the collapsed nodes, or the leaf picture for the items without further sub-items.

- osTreePictureText defines an outline with open and closed pictures, also having some lines to highlight the tree of items and the different indentation levels.

- osPlusMinusText defines an outline having only the plus and minus pictures.

- `osPlusMinusPictureText` defines an outline with both open and closed pictures, and plus and minus pictures.

- `osText` defines an outline having only text, with no glyphs.

- `osTreeText` defines an outline having only the graphical tree and the text, with no bitmaps.

You can see the effect of these properties by running the BookOut example. Each version of the outline shows the text with the proper indentation. A second relevant property is `Options`, which you can use to define the presence of a tree root (`ooDrawTreeRoot`), choose the activation of a focus rectangle (`ooDrawFocusRect`), or stretch the standard bitmaps (`ooStretchBitmap`) to fit in the size of the item, which depends on the height of the component's font. If you don't set the `ooStretchBitmap` option, the bitmaps are displayed as they are, possibly cutting out a portion or leaving a large white border around them. When you select a big font or big bitmaps, this option can come in handy. These properties can be changed at run-time using the BookOut example, as you can see in the output of Figure 11.10.

FIGURE 11.10

The BookOut program allows you to configure many properties of an outline, as you can see by comparing the two examples here.

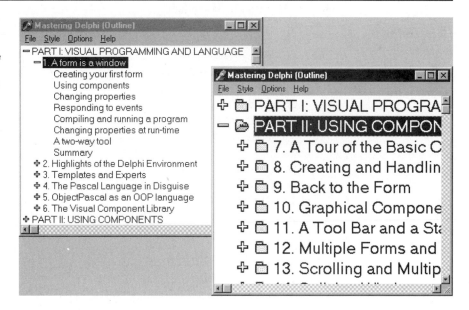

Having seen the main elements of an Outline component, we can now move to the example I've built to show how it can be used. Again, the BookOut example will allow you to test the different styles of the outline, which can be activated by means of the application's menu. The simple form of the BookOut example contains an outline that fills the form's whole client area, and a menu:

```
object Form1: TForm1
  Caption = 'Mastering Delphi (Outline)'
  Menu = MainMenu1
  object Outline1: TOutline
    Lines.Nodes = (
      'PART I: VISUAL PROGRAMMING AND LANGUAGE'
      #9'1. A form is a window '
      #9#9'Creating your first form'
      #9#9'Using components'
      // and so on... )
    Options = []
    Align = alClient
    BorderStyle = bsNone
    ItemSeparator = '\'
  end
  object MainMenu1: TMainMenu
    object File1: TMenuItem...
      object Exit1: TMenuItem...
    object Style1: TMenuItem...
      object PictureText1: TMenuItem
        Caption = '&Picture Text'
        GroupIndex = 1
        RadioItem = True
        OnClick = PictureText1Click
      end
      object PlusMinusPictureText1: TMenuItem...
      object PlusMinusText1: TMenuItem...
      object Text1: TMenuItem...
      object TreePictureText1: TMenuItem
        Caption = 'T&ree Picture Text'
        Checked = True
        GroupIndex = 1
        RadioItem = True
        OnClick = TreePictureText1Click
      end
      object TreeText1: TMenuItem...
    object Options1: TMenuItem...
      object DrawTreeRoot1: TMenuItem...
```

```
        object DrawFocusRect1: TMenuItem...
        object StretchBitmaps1: TMenuItem...
        object N1: TMenuItem...
        object Font1: TMenuItem
      object Help1: TMenuItem...
        object About1: TMenuItem...
    end
    object FontDialog1: TFontDialog...
  end
```

The code of the application is simple, too. It contains only commands to toggle on and off some styles of the outline, with the proper check marks or radio items beside the selected menu items. The menu items of the Style menu are mutually exclusive and use a radio menu item. The code of their OnClick event handlers is very simple, as you can see in the following method:

```
procedure TForm1.PictureText1Click(Sender: TObject);
begin
  Outline1.OutlineStyle := osPictureText;
  PictureText1.Checked := True;
end;
```

The menu items of the Options pull-down, instead, work independently of each other. They do not correspond to alternative values, but to items of a set. For this reason checking if they are active and activating or removing them requires several operations:

```
procedure TForm1.DrawTreeRoot1Click(Sender: TObject);
begin
  if ooDrawTreeRoot in Outline1.Options then
    Outline1.Options := Outline1.Options - [ooDrawTreeRoot]
  else
    Outline1.Options := Outline1.Options + [ooDrawTreeRoot];

  DrawTreeRoot1.Checked := not DrawTreeRoot1.Checked;
end;
```

To set a new font with the last menu item of this pull-down, the program activates a FontDialog component, as usual.

NOTE   Stretching the outline bitmaps while using a bit form seems to produce an odd output in this version of Delphi.

A Tree of Chapters

Now we can try to build a similar example, using the TreeView component instead of the Outline component. There isn't a direct way to load the text into this component, so we'll have to write this code by ourselves. The TreeView has a flexible user interface (with support for editing and dragging elements), but also a more standard one, because it is the user interface of the Windows Explorer. There are a number of properties and various ways to customize the bitmap of each line, or of each kind of line. The TreeView, in fact, is connected with a TImageList component. This allows a programmer to associate a number of bitmaps with the TreeView, and to set an index for each node or item.

In this first example using a TreeView, I'll just build a program very similar to the last one. This new example, called ChapTree, is based on a form with a TreeView component aligned to the whole client area, and a menu with some commands corresponding to properties you can toggle on and off. There is also a command to change the font:

```
object Form1: TForm1
  Caption = 'Chapters Tree'
  Menu = MainMenu1
  OnCreate = FormCreate
  object TreeView1: TTreeView
    Align = alClient
  end
  object MainMenu1: TMainMenu
    object File1: TMenuItem...
      object Exit1: TMenuItem...
    object Options1: TMenuItem...
      object Root1: TMenuItem...
      object Buttons1: TMenuItem...
      object Lines1: TMenuItem...
      object N1: TMenuItem...
      object Font1: TMenuItem...
    object Help1: TMenuItem...
      object About1: TMenuItem...
  end
  object FontDialog1: TFontDialog...
end
```

In this example, I could load the structure of the nodes of the TreeView at design time, as I've done in the previous example, thanks to a welcome Delphi 3 addition in the property editor of the TreeView `Items` property (see Figure 11.11), which you can use to build the structure of the data. In this case, however, I've decided to load it in the TreeView data at startup.

FIGURE 11.11

The TreeView Items property editor.

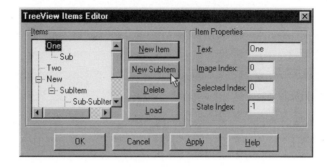

The `Items` property of this new component has many member functions you can use to alter the hierarchy of strings. For example, we can build a two-level tree with the following lines:

```
var
  Node: TTreeNode;
begin
  Node := TreeView1.Items.Add (nil, 'First level');
  TreeView1.Items.AddChild (Node, 'Second level');
```

Using these two methods (`Add` and `AddChild`) we can build a complex structure at run-time. But how do we load the information? Instead of accessing a file directly (which isn't that difficult in itself, by the way) I decided to create a memo component at run-time, load a text file with the saved form of the outline from the previous example, and parse it. Basically, the program counts the number of tabulators (character #9), and adds a new item to the tree at the proper level. If there are no tabulators, the new item is connected to the root; otherwise, it is connected with the last item of the previous level. Sounds complex? The code actually isn't too convoluted:

```
procedure TForm1.FormCreate(Sender: TObject);
var
  Node, Node1, Node2: TTreeNode;
  Memo: TMemo;
  I: Integer;
```

```
begin
  // initialize node variables (just in case)
  Node := nil;
  Node1 := nil;
  Node2 := nil;
  // create a temporary memo control
  Memo := TMemo.Create (self);
  try // finally: memo should be destroyed
    Memo.Parent := self;
    Memo.Width := 1000;
    try // except file not found
      Memo.Lines.LoadFromFile ('toc.txt');
    except
      on E: EFOpenError do
      begin
        MessageDlg ('File "TOC.TXT" not found'#13 +
          'The ChaptTree will be terminated',
          mtError, [mbOK], 0);
        // terminate the program
        Halt;
      end; // on E: EFOpenError do
    end; // except

    for I := 0 to Memo.Lines.Count - 1 do
      if Memo.Lines[I][1] <> #9 then
        Node := TreeView1.Items.Add (nil, Trim(Memo.Lines[I]))
      else if Memo.Lines[I][2] <> #9 then
        Node1 := TreeView1.Items.AddChild (Node, Trim (Memo.Lines[I]))
      else if Memo.Lines[I][3] <> #9 then
        Node2 := TreeView1.Items.AddChild (Node1, Trim (Memo.Lines[I]))
      else if Memo.Lines[I][4] <> #9 then
        TreeView1.Items.AddChild (Node2, Trim (Memo.Lines[I]));
  finally
    Memo.Free;
  end;
end;
```

As you can see, I've used both a try-except block to handle the *file-not-found* situation and a try-finally block to ensure the destruction of the temporary memo component. Assigning the nodes to nil was done mainly to get rid of compiler warnings, but is also a sort of safety net in case the code is wrong. The other notable instruction is the use of the Trim function to remove white spaces and tabulators from the strings. You can see the result of running this code in Figure 11.12. Notice that this component allows direct editing of the text of each node or leaf of the tree.

TIP In case of an error that prevents the program from initializing properly (for example, if the file TOC.TXT is not found), you should stop the program immediately, to avoid showing the user an empty and useless form. To terminate the program I've called the Halt global procedure.

FIGURE 11.12

The output of the Chap-Tree example.

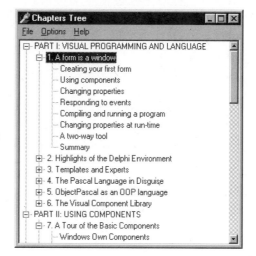

The Nodes of the Outline

As we have seen for the TreeView, there is also a list of objects (of type TOutlineNode) at the core of the Outline component. Each of these objects has some text, possibly some data, and a bunch of other properties. For example, Level indicates the level of indentation of an item, and FullPath indicates the name, including all the parent items. If you plan advanced use of the Outline component, study the node classes in detail. Instead of boring you with a list of all the operations you can do on an outline, I will show you a slightly more advanced example of the use of this component.

The example, named Nodes, is a kind of geography game. The main form of the program (see Figure 11.13) has two graphical list boxes. The list on the left contains a number of countries, states, and country organizations (such as the "European Community" or "NAFTA"). Of course, this is not a full list: if you live in a state or country that is not present, please add it to the list. The list on the right contains the seven continents. The aim of the game is to drag items from the left outline to the proper position in the hierarchy on the right. To accomplish this, you need to select an element in the left outline and drag it over the parent node in the right outline. For example, you can select "Brazil" and drag it over "South America."

FIGURE 11.13

The Nodes program is an advanced example of the use of the Outline component.

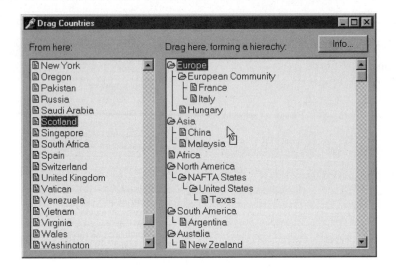

Other elements should be dragged to a lower level. For example, "England" should be placed under "United Kingdom," which should go under "European Community," which should be under "Europe." When you have done this, you can get information on an item by pressing the Info button. This information includes the full path of the item, as you can see in Figure 11.14.

FIGURE 11.14

The information about the "United Kingdom" item, including its full path, as displayed by the Nodes example.

Building the example's form is quite simple: just two Outline components, two labels, and a button. The two outlines have no special attributes. I've only removed the root node and added the text of the items. Notice that automatic dragging has not been enabled—I decided to use manual dragging instead.

TIP
If you select automatic dragging for a list box or similar component, your code should handle the selection of elements. To allow a user to both select items and drag them, you have to use manual dragging, calling the BeginDrag method and passing to it the False parameter. In this case, dragging is not started immediately, and a click properly selects a new item.

Handling the dragging manually is easy. When the user presses the left mouse button over the first outline component (if it is not empty), the program calls the BeginDrag method:

```
procedure TForm1.Outline1MouseDown(
  Sender: TObject; Button: TMouseButton;
  Shift: TShiftState; X, Y: Integer);
begin
  if (Outline1.ItemCount > 0) and (Button = mbLeft) then
    OutLine1.BeginDrag (False);
end;
```

As soon as the button is released, the program automatically calls the EndDrag method of the first outline. The second outline component defines a simple handler for the OnDragOver event, and performs the real work in the OnDragDrop event:

```
procedure TForm1.Outline2DragDrop(
  Sender, Source: TObject; X, Y: Integer);
var
  Current: Integer;
begin
  Current := Outline2.GetItem (X, Y);
  if Current > 0 then
  begin
    Outline2.AddChild (Current, Outline1.
      Lines[Outline1.SelectedItem - 1]);
    Outline2.Items [Current].Expanded := True;
```

```
    Outline1.Delete (Outline1.SelectedItem);
  end
  else
    MessageDlg ('You''ve not dragged over an item',
      mtError, [mbOk], 0);
end;
```

This last method, the heart of the program, is quite complex. When the user drags a new element, the program first determines the item of the destination outline on which the element was dropped, using the GetItem function and the coordinates passed by the event. Then the program selects this item as the outline's current item—that is, the item that will be affected by the following call to the AddChild method. The -1 is needed because the Lines array is zero-based, while the items are numbered starting from 1. It is possible to extract the text of the item directly from the Lines array only because the items of the source list have no indentation. The Lines value for an indented item, in fact, might have a tab character at the beginning. Windows displays this as a vertical line (in this case calling the Trim function can do the trick). After the element is copied to the destination outline, it should be deleted from the source outline, and its new parent node should be expanded to show the new element.

The only other complex method is the one that computes the string to display as information about the item (see again Figure 11.13). This string includes the item's full path, its level, and whether it is an intermediate node:

```
procedure TForm1.ButtonInfoClick(Sender: TObject);
var
  Node: TOutlineNode;
  Text: string;
begin
  Node := Outline2.Items [Outline2.SelectedItem];
  Text := Format ('Item: %s'#13'Level: %d',
    [Node.FullPath, Node.Level]);
  if Node.HasItems then
  begin
    Text := Text + #13'* Has sub-items';
    if Node.Expanded then
      Text := Text + ' and is expanded';
  end;
  MessageDlg (Text, mtInformation, [mbOk], 0);
end;
```

A Graphical List

When you use a TreeView component, besides creating a structure, you can also provide bitmaps for each node and leaf of the structure. Actually, you can provide bitmaps both indicating the status of the element (for example, the selected item) and describing the contents of the item in a graphical way. Consider again the Windows Explorer application: the tree of directories in the left pane has glyphs to indicate open or closed folders (the status of the item), but it also has special bitmaps for the recycle bin, the system itself, the network, and so on.

Instead of showing you an example of a graphical TreeView, I'll use another component: the ListView, another powerful Windows 95 common control. What the two components have in common is the way they connect bitmaps to the items, although the ListView component is more complex because it connects both a small and a large bitmap to each item of the list.

How do we connect the images to a list or tree? We need to use a specific component, TImageList. An image list is a sort of interface to a bitmap having various sub-images, each corresponding to an item in the image list. If you have a number of bitmaps ready, you can place an ImageList component in a form and activate the Image List Editor using the local menu of the component. As you can see in Figure 11.15, this special editor allows you to add many bitmaps to the ImageList, defining some of their properties.

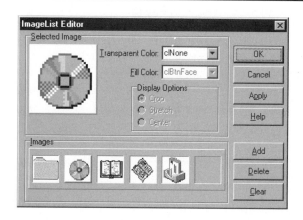

FIGURE 11.15

The ImageList Editor allows you to create a list, adding bitmaps of the same size to it.

Before you use the Image List Editor, however, you should set the Height and Width of the bitmaps in the list, using the two properties with those names in the ImageList (this is a non visual component, so it doesn't use size-related properties itself). It is important to do this operation up front, because if you do it later you'll lose the contents of the image list, without even a warning. Once you have set a size, in fact, all the images of the list will be of that size. I've used this approach to build the `ImageList1` component for the RefList example, after setting the width and height to 32. This image list, in fact, is used for the `LargeImages` property of a list view component.

To define the `SmallImages` property, I've used an alternative approach: I've created a single big bitmap (16 × 80 pixels) with all the images inside. Then I've added the bitmap to a resource file, and I've written some code to load it all at once (not one image at a time). I've actually created this second ImageList component at run-time (assigning it as owner the form—see the parameter of the Create constructor—so that I don't have to manually destroy it at the end). Here is the code of the handler for the `OnCreate` event of the form:

```
procedure TForm1.FormCreate(Sender: TObject);
var
  ImageList2: TImageList;
begin
  ImageList2 := TImageList.Create (self);
  ImageList2.ResourceLoad(rtBitmap,
    'SmallImages', clOlive);
  ListView1.SmallImages := ImageList2;
  ListView1.Arrange (arDefault);
end;
```

After the definition of the two image lists, I've added some items to the list using the complex editor of the `Items` property. You can define items and so-called sub-items, which are displayed only in the detailed view (when you set the `vsReport` value of the `ViewStyle` property). For each item, you can indicate the index of a sub-image in the image list; this image (in the small or large version) will be used in conjunction with the list item. In Figure 11.16 you can see an example of the use of the Items property editor, with the values I've provided for my RefList example, a list of references to books, magazines, CD-ROMs, and similar resources.

Since I've added some sub-items to the list, I also need to edit their captions and the size of the columns used to display them. The `Columns` property of the ListView has a specific editor for this. When the definition of the properties of the ListView component is completed, you can write code to toggle between different views and to perform other standard operations on the component. You can refer to the RefList example on the CD for the details, but setting the `Items` and `Columns` properties at design-time and assigning the proper image lists at run-time is all we need to do to have a working list view. You can see some examples of its output in Figure 11.17.

FIGURE 11.16

The Items property editor of the ListView component.

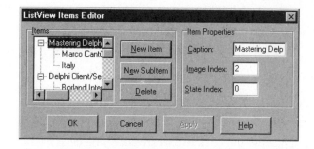

FIGURE 11.17

Different examples of the output of a ListView component, obtained by changing the ViewStyle property.

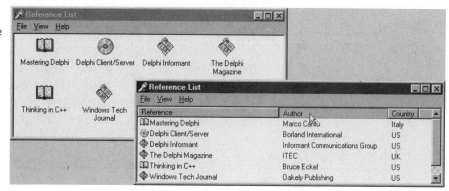

In the RefList example, you can easily change the style of the list view component using the View menu. This menu has four radio menu items, each setting one of the four possible values of the ViewStyle property of the component. Here is one of the four OnClick event handlers (the other three are very similar):

```
procedure TForm1.LargeIcons1Click(Sender: TObject);
begin
ListView1.ViewStyle := vsIcon;
LargeIcons1.Checked := True;
end;
```

Graphical Grids

Another interesting group of Delphi graphical components is represented by grids. The system contains different grid components: a grid of strings, one of images, database-related grids, and a grid of colors. The first two kinds of grids are particularly useful since they allow you to represent a lot of information and let the user navigate it. Of course, grids are extremely important in database programming, as we will see in Chapters 16 and 17, which are devoted to databases and client-server programming, respectively.

The DrawGrid and StringGrid components are closely related. In fact, the TStringGrid class is a subclass of TDrawGrid. What is the use of these grids? Basically, you can store some values, either in the strings related to the StringGrid or in other data structures, and then display selected values, using specific criteria. While grids of strings can almost be used as they are (since they already provide editing capabilities), the grids of generic objects usually require more coding.

Grids, in fact, define display organization, not storage. The only grid that stores the data it displays is the StringGrid. All other grids are just viewers, not containers. The basic structure of a grid includes a fixed number of columns and rows, which indicate the non-scrollable region of the grid (as you can see in Figure 11.18). Grids are among the most complex components available in Delphi, as indicated by the high number of properties and methods they have. There is a plethora of options and properties for grids, controlling both their appearance and their behavior.

FIGURE 11.18

When you place a new grid component on a form, it contains one fixed row and one fixed column by default.

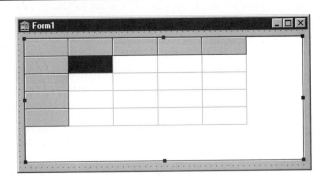

Regarding the user interface, the grid can have lines of different sizes, or it can even have no lines. You can set the size of each column or row independently of the others because the RowSize, ColWidth, and RowHeight properties are arrays. Regarding user actions, you can let the user resize the columns and the rows (goColSizing and goRowSizing), drag entire columns and rows to a new position (goRowMoving and goColumnMoving), select automatic editing, and allow range selections. Since various options allow users to perform a number of operations on grids, there are also a number of events related to grids, such as OnColumnMoved, OnDrawCell, or OnSetEditText.

The most important event is probably OnDrawCell. In response to this event, a program has to paint a certain cell of the grid. Only string grids can automatically display their contents. The DrawGrid, in fact, doesn't have support for storing data. It is simply a tool for arranging a portion of the screen to display information in a regular format. It is a simple tool but, at the same time, a powerful one. Methods like CellRect, which returns the rectangle corresponding to the area of a cell, or MouseToCell, which returns the cell in a specific location, are a joy to use, considering that they handle resizable rows and columns and scrollable grids.

What can you use a grid for? Building a spreadsheet is probably the first idea that comes to mind, but Delphi already includes an OCX component with spreadsheet capabilities. I've decided to use the two grids to build two examples, presented in the next two sections. The StringGrid is used in a program that shows the fonts installed in the system, and the DrawGrid in a program that emulates the MineSweeper game.

> **NOTE**
>
> Delphi is good for games, too. The fact that you can build Windows games in Delphi should not be underestimated, even if your business is completely different. Games and other entertainment programs, in fact, demand more in terms of system and development tools than any other category of software, databases included. So being good for games means that Delphi is a very good development environment.

After the MineSweeper clone comes a simple example of the use of another, completely different grid, the ColorGrid.

A Grid of Fonts

If you place a StringGrid component on a form and set its options properly, you have a full working editor of strings arranged in a grid, with no programming at all. To make the example more interesting, I've decided to draw each cell of the grid with a different font, varying both its size and its type. You can see the result of this program, FontGrid, in Figure 11.19.

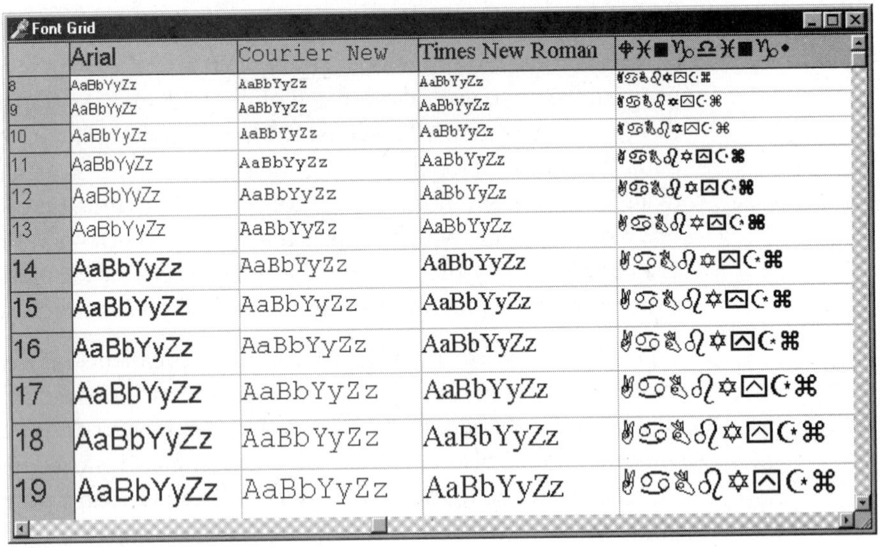

FIGURE 11.19

An example of the output of the FontGrid application.

The form of this program is very simple. You need only place a grid component on a form, align it with the client area, set a few properties and options, and let the program do the rest. The number of columns and rows and their size, in fact, are computed at run-time. The important properties you need to set are Default-Drawing, which should be False to let us paint the grid as we like, and Options:

```
object Form1: TForm1
  Caption = 'Font Grid'
  OnCreate = FormCreate
  object StringGrid1: TStringGrid
    Align = alClient
    ColCount = 20
    DefaultColWidth = 200
    DefaultDrawing = False
    RowCount = 20
    Options = [goFixedVertLine, goFixedHorzLine,
      goVertLine, goHorzLine, goDrawFocusSelected,
      goColSizing, goColMoving, goEditing]
    OnDrawCell = StringGrid1DrawCell
  end
end
```

As usually happens in Delphi, the simpler the form is, the more complex the code. This example follows that rule, although it has only two methods, one to initialize the grid at startup and the other to draw the items. The editing, in fact, has not been customized and takes place using the system font. The first of the two methods is `FormCreate`. At the beginning, this method uses the global `Screen` object to access the fonts installed in the system.

NOTE
The `Screen` global variable holds an object of type `TScreen`, which in turn holds a number of pieces of information about the attributes of the screen, the fonts installed in the system, and the forms of the current application. Chapter 25 contains a specific section about the `Screen` object.

The grid has a column for each font, plus a fixed column with numbers representing font sizes. The name of each column is copied from the `Screen` object to the first row of each column (which has a zero index):

```
procedure TForm1.FormCreate(Sender: TObject);
var
  I, J: Integer;
begin
  StringGrid1.ColCount := Screen.Fonts.Count + 1;
  StringGrid1.ColWidths [0] := 50;

  for I := 1 to Screen.Fonts.Count do
  begin
    {write the name of the font in the first row}
    StringGrid1.Cells [I, 0] :=
      Screen.Fonts.Strings [I-1];

    {compute maximum required size of column,
    getting the width of the text with the
    biggest size of the font in that column}
    StringGrid1.Canvas.Font.Name :=
      StringGrid1.Cells [I, 0];
    StringGrid1.Canvas.Font.Size := 32;
    StringGrid1.ColWidths [I] :=
      StringGrid1.Canvas.TextWidth ('AaBbYyZz');
  end;
  ...
```

In the last part of the code above, the program computes the width of each column by evaluating the space occupied by the custom string of text "AaBbYyZz," using the font in the column (written in the first row, Cells [I, 0]) and the biggest size used by the program (32). To compute the space required by the text, you can apply the TextWidth and TextHeight methods to a canvas with the proper font selected.

The rows, instead, are always 26 and have an increasing height, computed with the approximate formula: 15 + I x 2. In fact, computing the highest text means checking the height of the text in each column, certainly too complex an operation for this example. The approximate formula works well enough, as you can see in Figure 11.19, and by running the program. In the first cell of each row, the program writes the size of the font, which corresponds to the number of the line plus seven.

The last operation is to store the string "AaBbYyZz" in each non-fixed cell of the grid. To accomplish this, the program uses a nested for loop. Expect to use nested for loops often when working with grids. Here is the second part of the FormCreate method:

```
{defines the number of columns}
StringGrid1.RowCount := 26;
for I := 1 to 25 do
begin
  {write the number in the first column}
  StringGrid1.Cells [0, I] := IntToStr (I+7);
  {set an increasing height for the rows}
  StringGrid1.RowHeights [I] := 15 + I*2;
  {insert default text in each column}
  for J := 1 to StringGrid1.ColCount do
    StringGrid1.Cells [J, I] := 'AaBbYyZz'
end;
StringGrid1.RowHeights [0] := 25;
end;
```

Now we can study the second method, StringGrid1DrawCell, which corresponds to the grid's OnDrawCell event:

```
procedure TForm1.StringGrid1DrawCell(Sender: TObject;
  Col, Row: Longint; Rect: TRect; State: TGridDrawState);
```

This method has a number of parameters:

- Col and Row refer to the cell we are currently painting;

- Rect is the area of the cell we are going to paint;

- State is the state of the cell, a set of three flags, which can be active at the same time: gdSelected (the cell is selected), gdFocused (the cell has the input focus), and gdFixed (the cell is in the fixed area, which usually has a different background color). Knowing the state of the cell is important because this usually affects its output.

The DrawCell method paints the text of the corresponding element of the grid, with the font used by the column and the size used for the row. Here is the listing of this method:

```
procedure TForm1.StringGrid1DrawCell(
  Sender: TObject; Col, Row: Integer;
  Rect: TRect; State: TGridDrawState);
begin
  {select a font, depending on the column}
  if Col = 0 then
    StringGrid1.Canvas.Font.Name := 'Arial'
  else
    StringGrid1.Canvas.Font.Name :=
      StringGrid1.Cells [Col, 0];

  {select the size of the font, depending on the row}
  if Row = 0 then
    StringGrid1.Canvas.Font.Size := 14
  else
    StringGrid1.Canvas.Font.Size := Row + 7;

  {select the background color}
  if gdSelected in State then
    StringGrid1.Canvas.Brush.Color := clHighlight
  else if gdFixed in State then
    StringGrid1.Canvas.Brush.Color := clBtnFace
  else
    StringGrid1.Canvas.Brush.Color := clWindow;

  {output the text}
  StringGrid1.Canvas.TextRect (
    Rect, Rect.Left, Rect.Top,
    StringGrid1.Cells [Col, Row]);

  {draw the focus}
  if gdFocused in State then
    StringGrid1.Canvas.DrawFocusRect (Rect);
end;
```

The font's name is retrieved by the first row (row 0) of the same column. The font's size is computed by adding 7 to the number of the row. The fixed columns use some default values, instead. Having set the font and its size, the program selects a color for the background of the cell, depending on its possible states: selected, fixed, or normal (that is, no special style).

The value of the style's gdFocused flag is used a few lines later to draw the typical focus rectangle—a rectangle with a thin dotted line. When everything is set up, the program can perform some real output, drawing the text and eventually drawing the focus rectangle, with the last two statements of the StringGrid1DrawCell method above.

> **TIP**
>
> To draw the text in the grid's cell, I've used the TextRect method of the canvas instead of the more common TextOut method. The reason is that TextRect clips the output to the given rectangle, preventing drawing outside this area. This is particularly important in the case of grids because the output of a cell should not cross its borders. Since we are painting on the canvas of the whole grid, when we are drawing a cell, we can end up corrupting the contents of neighboring cells, too.

As a final observation, remember that when you decide to draw the contents of a grid's cell, you should not only draw the default image, you should also provide a different output for the selected item, properly draw the focus, and so on. In the ODList example, showing an owner-draw list, we could skip this code because Delphi handles these special cases for us.

Mines in a Grid

The StringGrid component uses the Cells array to store the values of the elements and also has an Objects property to store custom data for each cell. The DrawGrid component, instead, doesn't have a predefined storage. For this reason, in the next example, I'm going to define a two-dimensional array to store the value of the grid's cells—that is, of the playing field.

The Mines example is a clone of the MineSweeper games included with Windows. If you have never played this game, I suggest you try it and read its rules in the Help file since I'll give only a basic description. When the program starts, it displays an empty field (a grid) in which there are some hidden mines. By clicking the left mouse button on a cell, you test whether or not there is a mine in that position. If you find a mine, it explodes, and the game is over. You have lost.

If there is no mine, the program indicates in the cell the number of mines in the eight other cells surrounding it. Knowing the number of mines near the cell, you have a good hint for the following turn. To help you further on, when a cell has zero mines in the surrounding area, the number of mines for these cells is automatically displayed, and if one of them has zero surrounding mines, the process is repeated. So if you are lucky, with a single click you might uncover a good number of mines (see Figure 11.20).

FIGURE 11.20

The Mines program after a single lucky click. A group of cells with no mines is displayed at once.

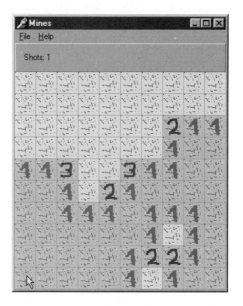

When you think you have found a mine, simply click on the cell with the right mouse button, positioning a flag. The program does not say whether your inference is correct; the flag is only a hint for your future attempts. If you later change your mind, you can again right-click on the cell to remove the flag. When you have placed a flag on each of the mines, you have won, and the game terminates.

Those are the rules of the game. Now we have to implement them, using a DrawGrid as starting point. In this example, the grid is fixed and cannot be resized or modified in any way at run-time. In fact, it has square cells of 30 × 30 pixels, which will be used to display bitmaps of the same size.

The code of this program is complex, and it is not easy to find a starting point to describe it. For this reason, I've added more comments than usual to the source code on the companion CD so you can browse through it to understand what it does. Nonetheless, I'll describe its most important elements, highlighting the key methods and algorithms used and trying to follow its logical flow. If you can, I suggest you follow this description after you've printed the listing of the example, or with its source code on a monitor nearby.

First of all, the program's data is stored in two arrays (declared as `private` fields of the form):

```
Display: array [0 .. NItems - 1, 0 .. NItems -1] of Boolean;
Map: array [0 .. NItems - 1, 0 .. NItems -1] of Char;
```

The first is an array of `Boolean` values that indicate whether an item should be displayed or remain hidden. Notice that the number of rows and columns of this array is `NItems`. You can freely change this constant, but you should resize the grid accordingly. The second array, `Map`, holds the positions of the mines and flags and the numbers of the surrounding mines. It uses character codes instead of a proper enumeration data type, for the advantage of using the digits 0–8 to indicate the number of mines around the cell. Here is a list of the codes:

- *M: Mine* indicates the position of a mine that the user still has not found.

- *K: Known mine* indicates the position of a mine already found by the user and having a flag.

- *W: Wrong mine* indicates a position where the user has set a flag but where there is no mine.

- *0 to 8: Number of mines* indicates the number of mines in the surrounding cells.

The first method I'll explore is `FormCreate`, executed at startup. This method initializes a number of fields of the form class, fills the two arrays with default values (using two nested `for` loops), and then sets the mines in the grid. For the number of times defined in a constant (that is, the number of mines), the program adds a new mine in a random position. However, if there was already a mine, the loop should be executed once more since the final number of mines in the `Map` array should equal the requested one. If not, the program will never terminate, since it tests when the number of mines found equals the number of mines added to the grid. The following is the code of the loop, which can be executed more than NMines times, thanks to the use of the MinesToPlace integer variable, which is increased when we try to place a mine over an existing one:

```
Randomize;
{place 'NMines' non-overlapping mines}
MinesToPlace := NMines;
while MinesToPlace < 0 do
begin
  X := Random (NItems);
  Y := Random (NItems);
  {if there isn't a mine}
  if Map [X, Y] <> 'M' then
  begin
    {add a mine}
    Map [X, Y] := 'M';
    Dec (MinesToPlace)
  end;
end;
```

The last portion of the initialization code computes the number of surrounding mines for each cell that doesn't have a mine. This is accomplished by calling the ComputeMines procedure for each cell. The code of this function is fairly complex since it has to consider the special cases of the mines near a border of the grid. The effect of this call is to store in the Map array the character representing the number of mines surrounding each cell.

The next logical procedure is DrawGrid1MouseUp, called when the mouse button is released over a cell (there were some problems with the focus using the mouse-down event, so I decided on the mouse-up event). This method first computes the cell on which the mouse has been clicked, with a call to the grid's MouseToCell method. Then there are three alternative portions of code: a small one when the game has ended, and the other two for the two mouse buttons.

When the left mouse button is pressed, the program checks whether there is a mine (hidden or not), and if there is, it displays a message and terminates the program with an explosion (see Figure 11.21).

If there is no mine, the program sets the Display value for the cell to True, and if there is a 0, it starts the FloodZeros procedure. This method displays the eight items near a visible cell having a value of 0, repeating the operation over and over if one of the surrounding cells also has a value of 0. This recursive call is complex because you have to provide a way to terminate it. If there are two cells near each other, both having a value of 0, each one is in the surrounding area of the other, so they might continue forever to ask the other cell to display itself and its surrounding cells. Again, the code is complex; and the best way to study it may be to step through it in the debugger.

FIGURE 11.21

Ouch! You have stepped on a mine.

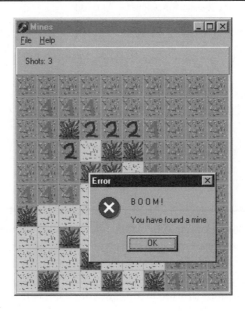

If the right mouse button was pressed, the program changes the status of a cell from M (Hidden mine) to K (Known mine) and vice versa (in case in that location there is actually a mine), or from a number to W (Wrong mine) and vice versa (in case there isn't a mine there). The right mouse button action is to toggle the flag on the screen, so a user can always remove an existing flag, if he thinks his earlier decision was wrong. When all the mines have been found, the program terminates with a congratulations message.

A very important piece of code is at the end of the OnMouseUp event response method. Each time the user clicks on a cell and its contents change, that cell should be repainted. If you ask to repaint the whole grid, the program will be slower. For this reason, I've used the Windows API function InvalidateRect, introduced in Chapter 10's Shapes4 example:

```
MyRect := DrawGrid1.CellRect (Col, Row);
InvalidateRect (DrawGrid1.Handle, @MyRect, False);
```

The last important method is DrawGrid1DrawCell. We already used this painting procedure in the last example, so you should remember that it is called for each cell that needs repainting. Fundamentally, this method extracts the code corresponding to the cell, which shows a corresponding bitmap, loaded from a file. Once again, I've prepared a bitmap for each of the images in a new resource file, included in the form's code with this directive:

```
{$R BITMAPS.RES}
```

Recall that when using resources, the code tends to be faster than when using separate files, and again, we end up with a single executable file to distribute. The bitmaps have names corresponding to the code in the grid, with a character ('M') in front since the name '0' would have been invalid. The bitmaps can be loaded and drawn in the cell with this code:

```
StrPCopy (Name, 'M' + Code);
Bmp.Handle := LoadBitmap (HInstance, Name);
DrawGrid1.Canvas.Draw (Rect.Left, Rect.Top, Bmp);
```

Of course, this takes place only if the cell is visible, if Display is True. Otherwise, a default undefined bitmap is displayed (the bitmap name is 'UNDEF'). Loading the bitmaps from the resources each time seems slow, so the program could have stored all the bitmaps in a list in memory, as I did in the World2 example earlier in this chapter. However, this time, I've decided to use a different, although slightly less efficient, approach: a cache. This makes sense because we already use resources instead of files to speed up things.

The bitmap cache of Mines is small since it has just one element, but its presence speeds up the program considerably. The program stores the last bitmap it has used and its code; then, each time it has to draw a new item, if the code is the same, it uses the cached bitmap. Here is the new version of the code above:

```
if not (Code = LastBmp) then
begin
  StrPCopy (Name, 'M' + Code);
  Bmp.Handle := LoadBitmap (HInstance, Name);
  LastBmp := Code;
end;
DrawGrid1.Canvas.Draw (Rect.Left, Rect.Top, Bmp);
```

Increasing the size of this cache will certainly improve its speed. You can consider a list of bitmaps as a big cache, but this is probably useless since some bitmaps (those with high numbers) are seldom used. As you can see, some improvements can be made to speed up the program, and much can also be done to improve its user interface. If you have understood this version of the program, I think you'll be able to improve it considerably.

Choosing Colors

The last example using grids is much simpler than the previous ones. It uses ColorGrid, a component of the Samples page of the Component Palette. This component doesn't have much in common with the other grids, and its use is straightforward. It can be used every time you want to let a user choose one or two colors (foreground and background, by default) without using the standard Color dialog box. The ColorGrid is particularly handy when you want to let a user choose a color and show an immediate preview of the result. Delphi itself uses this control in the Colors page of the Environment Options dialog box, the page used to customize syntax highlighting.

A ColorGrid has a number of cells, each with a color, and uses the left and right mouse clicks to select two colors, namely a foreground color with the left mouse button and a background color with the right mouse button. Two properties, ForegroundIndex and BackgroundIndex, hold the values of the current colors, which the user automatically changes by clicking, but only if they are active.

The only other peculiar property is GridOrdering, which indicates the structure of the grid—the number of lines and rows. Since the color grid always has 16 colors, you can choose a vertical or horizontal line, two lines of 8 colors, or a 4×4 square grid. I've built a simple example, ColGrid, which has a grid and a text label, using the colors indicated in the grid (see Figure 11.22). Its source code is just two lines. Each time a user clicks on the grid, the two colors are copied to the label:

```
procedure TForm1.ColorGrid1Change(Sender: TObject);
begin
  Label1.Color := ColorGrid1.BackgroundColor;
  Label1.Font.Color := ColorGrid1.ForegroundColor;
end;
```

FIGURE 11.22

The ColGrid example,
based on a ColorGrid
component.

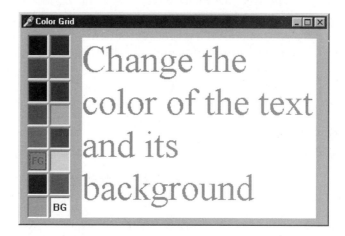

Using TeeChart

 A final component we examine in this chapter is the TeeChart component, a VCL based charting component build by David Berneda and licensed to Borland for inclusion in the Developer and Client/Server versions of Delphi 3. Previous versions of Delphi included business graphic controls, but they were OCX controls, not Delphi native ones. Moreover, TeeChart is a really powerful charting component, well worth its inclusion in the package.

The TeeChart component is very complex: Delphi includes a Help file and other reference material for this component, so I won't spend time listing all of its features. I'll just build a couple of examples here, and use the component again in a database example in Chapter 16. TeeChart, in fact, comes in three versions: the stand-alone component (in the Additional page of the Component Palette), the data-aware version (in the Data Controls page), and the Report version (in the QuickReport page).

> **NOTE** Of course, it would be simpler to build an example using the TeeChart Wizard, but seeing all the steps will give you a better understanding of this component's structure.

The TeeChart component provides the basic structure for charting, and support the framework and the visual container for charts. The actual charts, however, are objects of class `TChartSeries`, or derived classes. Once you've places the TeeChart component on a form, you should create one or more series. To accomplish this you can open the Chart Component Editor: select the component, right-click to show the local menu of the form designer, and choose the Edit Chart command. Now press the Add button, and choose the graph (or series) you want to add among the many available (as you can see in Figure 11.23).

FIGURE 11.23

The TeeChart Gallery allows you to choose the type of graph, or series.

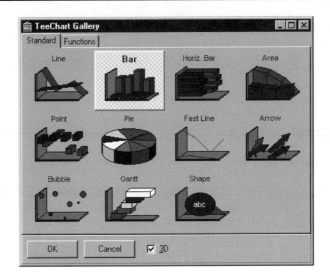

As soon as you create a new series, a new object of a `TChartSeries` subclass is added to your form. This is the same behavior as the MainMenu component, which adds objects of the `TMenuItem` class to the form (or of the Table component, which adds objects of the `TField` subclasses, as we'll see in Chapter 16). You can then edit the properties of the `TSeries` object in the Chart Component Editor, or select the `TChartSeries` object in the Object Inspector (with the Object Selector combo box) and edit its many properties.

The different `TChartSeries` subclasses—that is, the different kinds of graph— have different properties and methods (although some of them are common). Keep in mind that a graph can have multiple series: if they are all of the same type they will probably integrate better, as in the case of multiple bars. Anyway, you can also have a complex layout with graph of different types visible at the same time. At times, this is an extremely powerful option.

Building a First Example

To build my example I've placed a TeeChart component in a form, and then simply added four 3D Bar series; that is, four objects of the TBarSeries class. Then I've set up some global properties, such as the title of the chart and so on. Here is a summary of this information, taken from the textual description of the form:

```
object Chart1: TChart
  AnimatedZoom = True
  Title.Text.Strings = (
    'Simple TeeChart Demo for Mastering Delphi')
  BevelOuter = bvLowered
  object Series1: TBarSeries
    SeriesColor = clRed
    Marks.Visible = False
  end
  object Series2: TBarSeries
    SeriesColor = clGreen
    Marks.Visible = False
  end
  object Series3: TBarSeries
    SeriesColor = clYellow
    Marks.Visible = False
  end
  object Series4: TBarSeries
    SeriesColor = clBlue
    Marks.Visible = False
  end
end
```

Next I've added to the form a string grid and a push button labeled *Update*. This button is used to copy the numeric values of the string grid to the chart. The grid is based on a 5×4 matrix, plus a line and a column for the titles. Here is its textual description:

```
object StringGrid1: TStringGrid
  ColCount = 6
  DefaultColWidth = 50
  Options = [goFixedVertLine, goFixedHorzLine,
    goVertLine, goHorzLine, goEditing]
  ScrollBars = ssNone
  OnGetEditMask = StringGrid1GetEditMask
end
```

The value 5 for the RowCount property is a default, and doesn't show up in the textual description. (The same holds for the value of 1 for the FixedCols and FixedRows properties.) An important element of this string grid is the edit mask used by all of its cells. This is set using the OnGetEditMask event:

```
procedure TForm1.StringGrid1GetEditMask(Sender: TObject;
  ACol, ARow: Longint; var Value: string);
begin
  // edit mask for the grid cells
  Value := '09;0';
end;
```

There is actually one more component, a check box used to toggle the visibility of the marks of the series (the *marks* are small yellow tags describing each value). You can see the form at design time in Figure 11.24. In this case the series are populated with random values, a nice feature of the component which allows you to preview the output without having to enter any actual data.

FIGURE 11.24

The Graph1 example, based on the TeeChart component, at design-time.

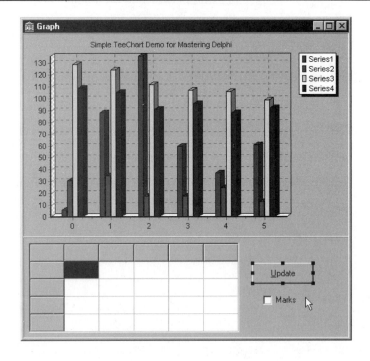

Adding Data to the Chart

Now we simply have to initialize the data of the string grid, and copy it to the series of the chart. This takes place in the handler of the OnCreate event of the form. This method fills the fixed items of the grid and the series names, then actually fills the data portion of the string grid, and finally calls the handler of the OnClick event of the *Update* button, to update the chart:

```
procedure TForm1.FormCreate(Sender: TObject);
var
  I, J: Integer;
begin
  with StringGrid1 do
  begin
    {fills the fixed column and row,
    and the chart series names}
    for I := 1 to 5 do
      Cells [I, 0] := Format ('Group%d', [I]);
    for J := 1 to 4 do
    begin
      Cells [0, J] := Format ('Series%d', [J]);
      Chart1.Series [J-1].Title := Format ('Series%d', [J]);
    end;

    {fills the grid with random values}
    Randomize;
    for I := 1 to 5 do
      for J := 1 to 4 do
        Cells [I, J] := IntToStr (Random (100));
  end; // with

  // update the chart
  UpdateButtonClick (self);
end;
```

We can access the series using the component name (as Series1) or using the Series array property of the chart, as in Chart1.Series[J-1]. In this expression notice that the actual data in the string grid starts at row and column one—the first line and column, indicated by the zero index, are used for the fixed elements—while the chart Series array is zero-based.

Another example of the update of each series is present in the handler of the OnClick event of the check box, which toggles the visibility of the marks:

```
procedure TForm1.ChBoxMarksClick(Sender: TObject);
var
  I: Integer;
begin
  for I := 1 to 4 do
    Chart1.Series [I-1].Marks.Visible :=
      ChBoxMarks.Checked;
end;
```

But the really interesting code is in the UpdateButtonClick method, which updates the chart. To accomplish this, the program first removes the existing data of each chart, then it adds new data (or *data points*, to use a jargon term):

```
procedure TForm1.UpdateButtonClick(Sender: TObject);
var
  I, J: Integer;
begin
  for I := 1 to 4 do
  begin
    Chart1.Series [I-1].Clear;
    for J := 1 to 5 do
      Chart1.Series [I-1].Add (
        StrToInt (StringGrid1.Cells [J, I]),
        '', Chart1.Series [I-1].SeriesColor);
  end;
end;
```

The parameters of the Add method (used when you don't want to specify an X value, but only an Y value) are the actual value, the label, and the color. In this example the label is not used, so I've simply omitted it. As color I could have use the default value, clTeeColor, to get the proper color of the series. You might use specific colors to indicate different ranges of data.

Once you've build the graph, TeeChart allows you a lot of viewing options. You can easily zoom into the view (simply indicate the area with the left mouse button), zoom out (using the mouse in the opposite way, dragging towards the top left corner), and use the right mouse button to pan the view. You can see an example of zooming in Figure 11.25.

FIGURE 11.25

The form of the Graph1 example at run-time. Notice that I've zoomed into the graph.

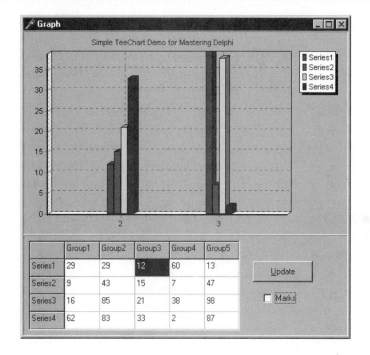

Creating Series Dynamically

The Graph1 example shows some of the capabilities of the TeeChart component, but it is based on a single, fixed type of graph. I could have improved it by allowing some customization of the shape of the vertical bars; instead I decided to go for a more general approach, allowing user to choose different kind of series, different kinds of graphs.

The TeeChart component initially has the same attributes as the previous example. The form, instead, now has four combo boxes, one for each row of the string grid. Each combo box has four values (Line, Bar, Area, and Point) corresponding to the four types of series I want to handle. Actually to handle these combo boxes in a more flexible way in the code, I've added an array of these controls to the private fields of the form:

```
private
  Combos: array [0..3] of TComboBox;
```

This array is filled with the actual component in the `FormCreate` method, which also selects the initial item of each of them. Here is the new code of `FormCreate`:

```
// fill the Combos array
Combos [0] := ComboBox1;
Combos [1] := ComboBox2;
Combos [2] := ComboBox3;
Combos [3] := ComboBox4;

// show the initial chart type
for I := 0 to 3 do
  Combos [I].ItemIndex := 1;
```

TIP

This example demonstrates a common way to create an array of controls in Delphi, something Visual Basic programmers often long for. Actually Delphi is so flexible that array of controls are not built-in: you can create them as you like. This approach relies on the fact that you can generally associate the same event handler to different events, something that VB doesn't allow you to do.

All these combo boxes share the same `OnClick` event handler, which destroys each of the current series of the chart, creates the new ones as requested, then updates their properties and data:

```
procedure TForm1.ComboChange(Sender: TObject);
var
  I: Integer;
  SeriesClass: TChartSeriesClass;
  NewSeries: TChartSeries;
begin
  // destroy the existing series (in reverse order)
  for I := 3 downto 0 do
    Chart1.Series [I].Free;
  // create the new series
  for I := 0 to 3 do
  begin
    case Combos [I].ItemIndex of
      0: SeriesClass := TLineSeries;
      1: SeriesClass := TBarSeries;
      2: SeriesClass := TAreaSeries;
    else // 3: and default
      SeriesClass := TPointSeries;
    end;
```

```
    NewSeries := SeriesClass.Create (self);
    NewSeries.ParentChart := Chart1;
    NewSeries.Title :=
      Format ('Series %d', [I + 1]);
  end;
  // update the marks and update the data
  ChBoxMarksClick (self);
  UpdateButtonClick (self);
end;
```

The central part of this code is the `case` statement, which stores a new class in the `SeriesClass` class reference variable, used to create the new series objects, and set their `ParentChart` and `Title`. I could have also used a call to the `AddSeries` method of the chart in each case branch, and then set the `Title` with another `for` loop. In fact a call such as:

```
Chart1.AddSeries (TBarSeries.Create (self));
```

creates the series objects and sets its parent chart at the same time.

Notice that this new version of the program allows you to change the type of graph for each series independently. You can see an example of the resulting effect in Figure 11.26.

FIGURE 11.26

Various kinds of graphs, or chart series, displayed by the Graph2 example.

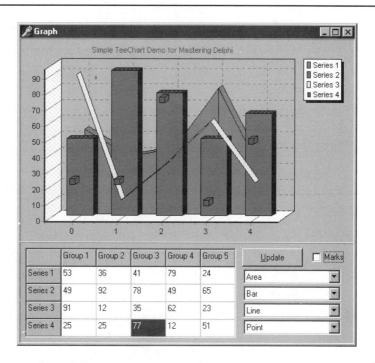

The DateTimePicker New Common Control

There is one more graphical component I want to cover briefly in this chapter, the DateTimePicker control. This is a new control added recently by Microsoft to the Windows 95 common controls library (and distributed with Microsoft Internet Explorer). Keep in mind that users must have the updated version of this library to be able to use this control.

The DateTimePicker is a simple input tool for date and time values. It allows you to edit the time (the default value is the current time) by incrementing one of its portions (hour, minute, second) either by using the arrow keys or by using a small up-down button. To select a date you have one more choice: use the combo box style and show a pull-down calendar, like the one you can see in Figure 11.27.

FIGURE 11.27

The output of the simple PickDate example, with the drop-down calendar. You can use it to enter a new date.

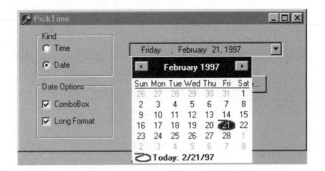

This figure is the output of a very simple example, named PickDate, I've built around the component to let you test its key features. Two radio buttons and two check boxes lets you toggle the value of the Kind property (which can be dtkTime or dtkDate), of the DateFormat property (either dfLong or dfShort) and of the DateMode property (which can be dmComboBox or dmUpDown). These last two properties actually make sense only if the control is showing a date. When it is showing a time they are ignored.

You can look at the source code of the example on the companion CD. As you'll see, it also includes two buttons, which simply display in a dialog box the date or the time you have picked. This is accomplished by reading the value of the Date and Time properties of the DateTimePicker control (a TDate and a TTime value, respectively), and converting them to a string using the DateToStr and

TimeToStr Delphi function. We have already used some of these functions with the TDateTime data type in Chapter 4. Here is the simple code of the OnClick event handler of one of the two buttons:

```
procedure TForm1.Button1Click(Sender: TObject);
begin
  MessageDlg ('The time is ' +
    TimeToStr (DateTimePicker1.Time),
    mtInformation, [mbOK], 0);
end;
```

What's Next

In this chapter, we have explored a number of different Delphi components, including outlines, grids, bitmap buttons, and some Windows 95 common controls, such as the TreeView and the ListView. Of course, there are other components of this kind, including those of the Sample pages of the Component Palette.

You can also create or buy new components and add them to Delphi. We will explore this topic briefly at the end of the book. What is important is that when components are well documented, using them is usually fairly simple. There is nothing to understand, aside from the meanings of the properties and methods. What is required of a great Delphi programmer is a good knowledge of the basics and some imagination in mixing different components on a form to build an application.

With a little imagination, Delphi programmers can easily build complex toolbars and status bars out of the existing components, as we will do in the next chapter, although Delphi 3 also includes specific components. The standard graphical components provide basic capabilities, but it is quite simple to extend both their user interface and their behavior. We'll use again some of the graphical components described in this chapter, building more complex programs with them.

A Toolbar, a CoolBar, and a Status Bar

One of the distinctive features of many Windows applications is the presence of a toolbar at the top of the window and a status bar at its bottom. The toolbar might have a variety of names, such as SpeedBar or control bar, depending on the application's producer. (Some of these names are trademarks.) Whatever name you give it, a toolbar usually contains a number of small buttons you can click on to give commands or to toggle options on and off. At times, a toolbar can also contain a combo box, an edit box, or some other control. The toolbars of the latest generation of big applications usually can be moved to the left or right of the window, or even taken away and used as a *toolbox*, a small floating window with an array of buttons.

Recently Microsoft Internet Explorer has introduced a new kind of toolbar, with transparent and flat buttons, and a specific behavior. They are called CoolBars, and Delphi 3 includes a specific Windows 95 component for using them. But this is just one of the many new features of Delphi in this area.

A status bar, by contrast, usually has one or more areas with a textual description of the current status of the program. You might have an area to display mouse coordinates; to show the selected font; or to display hints, error messages, and so on. What should go in a status bar really depends on the application.

Grouping Controls with Panels

To create a simple toolbar or status bar in Delphi, you can use the Panel component, adding a number of buttons or other panels inside it, or you can use the specific components. I'll start by using a panel and then explore the specific approaches.

A panel can be considered a tool for dividing the client area of a frame into different portions and for grouping other components. Although a panel can have its own text, it rarely does. Instead, panels can make good use of their three-dimensional aspect to improve the look of the application. In this respect, a panel is similar to a bevel, although this last component has a less important role and much less functionality (a bevel is a graphical component, and cannot be a parent for other controls).

From a graphical point of view, a panel can be described as a *double-bevel* since it has two elements of this kind you can play with (see the properties BevelInner and `BevelOuter`). Combined with the different values for the `BevelWidth`, this allows for a variety of effects, as you can see by playing with these properties or running the PanBord example you can find on the companion CD. Usually, when you create a panel, you place it in a particular area of the form, changing the value of the `Align` property. For a typical toolbar, use the value `alTop`; to mimic a status bar, use the value `alBottom`. You might also choose vertical panels.

Besides other common properties, the Panel component can handle hints; `Hint` and `ShowHints` are the two most relevant properties. The terms *hints* usually refers to short messages displayed near the cursor when the user moves the mouse over a toolbar button (these are also called *fly-by hints*); but the same term is used for descriptions displayed in the status bar.

> **WARNING** Using the same term for two slightly different things generates some confusion, but Delphi uses the same internal mechanism for both kinds of hints, so we have to stick with this naming. More about this later on.

Hints are not available only in panels. Every form can have hints for some or all of the components it contains. We will see an example of a plain form with hints later in this chapter.

Building a Toolbar with a Panel

To build a simple toolbar, you just need to place a panel at the top of a form's client area and place a number of SpeedButton components inside it. A *speed button* is similar to a bitmap button, a component described in the last chapter. Like bitmap buttons, speed buttons can have a `Caption` and a `Glyph`, although often they have only the graphical element.

The main difference is in the behavior. Bitmap buttons are like push buttons (that is, the Button component) and are mainly used inside dialog boxes. Speed buttons can behave like push buttons, check boxes, or radio buttons, and they can have different bitmaps depending on their status. There are also important technical differences between a SpeedButton and bitmap button. The first is a graphical component, has no window handle (thus consuming no Windows resources), cannot receive the input focus, has no tab order, and is faster to create and paint.

If you simply select the SpeedButton component and place an instance in the panel—the toolbar—you end up with a graphical push button. Toolbar buttons tend to be quite small, around 20 × 20 pixels. You cannot write much text in such a limited space. A glyph, on the other hand, can be meaningful even if it is small. Consider, in any case, that 20 × 20-pixel glyphs on a small screen can be quite small as well.

A First Toolbar

Once you have added a speed button, you might simply write some code for its OnClick event. This is the default operation you obtain by double-clicking on it in the form at design-time. In the Toolbar example, I've prepared a musical note glyph and added the following code to the button:

```
procedure TToolbarForm.SpeedButtonNoteClick(Sender: TObject);
begin
  Beep;
end;
```

Now we can add a group of speed buttons that will work like radio buttons. Just place some more speed buttons on the panel, select all of them, and give their GroupIndex properties the same value. All the buttons having the same Group-Index become mutually exclusive selections, similar to radio buttons. One of these buttons should always be selected, so remember to set the Down property to True for one of them at design-time or as soon as the program starts.

As an alternative, you can have a group of mutually exclusive buttons that can all be *up*—that is, a group from which the user can select one option or leave them all unselected. With this approach the user will need to click on the selected button to deselect it, rather than simply click another button. You can choose this behavior by setting the AllowAllUp property for all the buttons of the group to True (the default is False). In this case, of course, at startup the buttons can all be in the up position.

As an example of the two approaches, you can add two different groups of speed buttons to the panel (or toolbar). In the Toolbar example (see the form in Figure 12.1), I've added three exclusive buttons to determine the alignment of a label's text and three more buttons to determine its style. One of the alignment buttons should always be selected, since the text must always have an alignment. The methods corresponding to the three OnClick events of these buttons have the following structure:

```
procedure TToolbarForm.SpeedButtonLeftClick(Sender: TObject);
begin
  Label1.Alignment := taLeftJustify;
end;
```

FIGURE 12.1

The form of the Toolbar example.

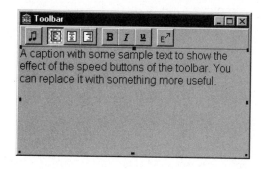

On the other hand, the three speed buttons for style (those of the second group) can all be off since the text style can be "normal." This use of the styles is far from perfect since they are not usually considered exclusive selections—you can have "bold italic" text—but I've decided to depart from the common behavior for this simple example. The problem in this portion of the code is that you cannot simply select the style when the button is pressed. You also have to deselect it, resetting the normal style, when the button is released. In the methods responding to the click events of these speed buttons, we have to write something like this:

```
procedure TToolbarForm.SpeedButtonBoldClick(Sender: TObject);
begin
  if SpeedButtonBold.Down then
    Label1.Font.Style := [fsBold]
  else
    Label1.Font.Style := [];
end;
```

I could have used three independent speed buttons behaving like check boxes, or *toggle buttons*, instead of this second group of buttons. In fact the three attributes are not really exclusive. But how do you add to the toolbar a speed button that works as a check box? Is there a special property? If you look at the properties of the SpeedButton component, you'll find nothing. In fact, the solution is already at hand: to create a toggle button we define a group that has only one button and that allows all its buttons (that is, all one of them) to be deselected.

In practice, you accomplish this by adding a new speed button, giving it a specific value for the GroupIndex property (different from the indexes of the other groups), and choosing True for the AllowAllUp property. That's all you need to have a fully working check box. The code corresponding to this last speed button is simple:

```
procedure TToolbarForm.SpeedButtonBigClick(Sender: TObject);
begin
  if SpeedButtonBig.Down then
    Label1.Font.Size := 24
  else
    Label1.Font.Size := 12;
end;
```

As you press this button, it remains down (see Figure 12.2); when you press it again, it is released. Test the example to see the behavior of the various buttons and groups of buttons. As a summary of this example, here is the textual description of the form:

```
object ToolbarForm: TToolbarForm
  Caption = 'Toolbar'
  object Label1: TLabel
    Align = alClient
    AutoSize = False
    Caption = 'A caption ...'
    WordWrap = True
  end
  object Panel1: TPanel
    Align = alTop
    object SpeedButtonNote: TSpeedButton
      Glyph.Data = {note.bmp}
      OnClick = SpeedButtonNoteClick
    end
    object SpeedButtonLeft: TSpeedButton
      GroupIndex = 1
      Down = True
```

```
      OnClick = SpeedButtonLeftClick
    end
    object SpeedButtonCenter: TSpeedButton...
    object SpeedButtonRight: TSpeedButton...
    object SpeedButtonBold: TSpeedButton
      AllowAllUp = True
      GroupIndex = 2
      OnClick = SpeedButtonBoldClick
    end
    object SpeedButtonItalic: TSpeedButton...
    object SpeedButtonUnderline: TSpeedButton...
    object SpeedButtonBig: TSpeedButton
      AllowAllUp = True
      GroupIndex = 3
      OnClick = SpeedButtonBigClick
    end
  end
end
```

FIGURE 12.2

The last speed button of
the Toolbar example
behaves like a check box.

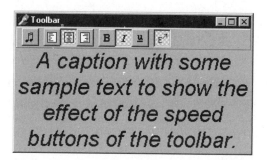

Enabling and Disabling Toolbar Buttons

This simple example has more or less standard behavior. Every button has its own glyph, which is used both for selected and deselected check boxes or radio buttons. However, you can also give each speed button a number of different glyphs (that is, different bitmaps), reflecting the button's status, without having to change the bitmap manually. We saw the differences between these two approaches in the two versions of the Fire example in the last chapter.

To test this feature, I've prepared a second version of the toolbar example, Toolbar2. In this version, I've added a menu with some items that can be used to disable some of the speed buttons or even hide the whole toolbar. The Toolbar pull-down menu contains a command to hide the whole toolbar. It calls the following method:

```
procedure TToolbarForm.Visible1Click(Sender: TObject);
begin
  {hide or display the toolbar, setting the menu item check mark}
  Panel1.Visible := not Panel1.Visible;
  Visible1.Checked := not Visible1.Checked;
end;
```

This code toggles the value of two Boolean properties, one to accomplish the required action and the second to add or remove the check mark beside the menu item. Two similar statements are also present in the commands used to disable or enable specific speed buttons:

```
procedure TToolbarForm.DisableSound1Click(Sender: TObject);
begin
  {disable or enable button and set menu check mark}
  SpeedButtonNote.Enabled := not SpeedButtonNote.Enabled;
  DisableSound1.Checked := not DisableSound1.Checked;
end;
```

When you disable one of these speed buttons, Delphi automatically paints a *grayed* version of the bitmap you have supplied (actually, the color of a grayed item depends on the system colors), as you can see by comparing Figure 12.3 with Figure 12.2.

In this example, Delphi generates three versions of the bitmaps: normal, pressed, and disabled. However, I've decided to supply a custom version of the glyphs of the last button, preparing the bitmap shown in Figure 12.4, with four different portions. For this button, I just needed two glyphs, one for the normal button and one for the pressed button, but I had to provide two more glyphs for the other states because the *Stay Down* glyph is the fourth. By preparing more glyphs, I was able to animate the button. If you run the program and press the button, the bitmap will change immediately and will later change again, after the click event (see Figure 12.3 again).

FIGURE 12.3

FIGURE 12.3

The output of the Toolbar2 example, with some disabled toolbar buttons, and a different bitmap for the last button.

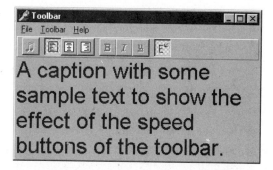

FIGURE 12.4

The bitmap used for the last speed button of the toolbar in the Toolbar2 example.

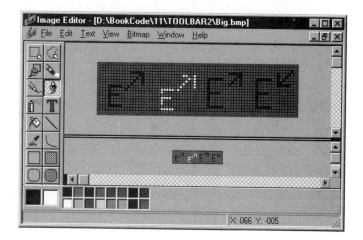

NOTE

In the Toolbar example, I've used gray-scale bitmaps, but you can make intensive use of color in speed buttons. This is becoming more common in major applications.

Adding Hints to the Toolbar

Another element becoming quite common in toolbars is the *fly-by hint*, also called *balloon help*—some text that briefly describes the speed button that is currently under the cursor. This text is usually displayed in a yellow box after the mouse cursor has remained steady over a button for a set amount of time. To add hints to an application's toolbar, simply set the ShowHints property of the Panel component used as the toolbar to True.

You can also change the default value of the HintColor, StraightHintPause, HintHidePause, and HintShortPause properties of the Application global object. The Toolbar3 example actually allows a user to customize the hint background color by selecting a specific menu item (Toolbar ➤ Hint Color), with the following event handler:

```
procedure TToolbarForm.HintColor1Click(Sender: TObject);
begin
  ColorDialog1.Color := Application.HintColor;
  if ColorDialog1.Execute then
    Application.HintColor := ColorDialog1.Color;
end;
```

In this example, I've added a proper value for the Hint property of the various speed buttons of the previous version. In the same Toolbar3 example I've made another change: I've set the Flat property of all the SpeedButton components to True, obtaining a new user interface effect.

NEW The Flat property has been added to Delphi 3 to mimic the new look and feel of Microsoft applications. Delphi 3 also includes some specific toolbar components I'll discuss later in this chapter.

Even if we don't write any new Pascal code, the updated version of the program works very well and makes the example look quite professional and modern (see Figure 12.5). However, we can still do something to improve the program: make a context-sensitive hint and allow users to toggle the new Flat style on and off.

Context-sensitive hints, in this example, make sense for the last button. The Hint of this button, in fact, is "*Expand*," which is appropriate only when the button is not pressed. When it is down, the Hint should become "*Shrink*" or something similar. We can accomplish this by adding two lines of code to the SpeedButtonBigClick method, to change the Hint each time the status of the button changes:

```
procedure TToolbarForm.SpeedButtonBigClick(Sender: TObject);
begin
```

FIGURE 12.5

The output of the
Toolbar3 example, with
the fly-by hints and the
new *flat* style.

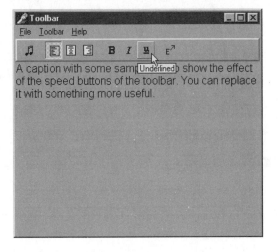

```
    if SpeedButtonBig.Down then
    begin
      Label1.Font.Size := 24;
      SpeedButtonBig.Hint := 'Shrink';
    end
    else
    begin
      Label1.Font.Size := 12;
      SpeedButtonBig.Hint := 'Expand';
    end;
  end;
```

The other change is to add a menu command to toggle the flat style of the buttons. (We'll do this just to accommodate those users who don't like the new style.) To toggle the new style you have to change it for each of the speed buttons. To do this we can use the `Controls` property of the `Panel1` component (the toolbar) which lists the controls having the panel as parent; that is, the speed buttons. Here is the code:

```
procedure TToolbarForm.FlatStyle1Click(Sender: TObject);
var
  I: Integer;
begin
  FlatStyle1.Checked := not FlatStyle1.Checked;
  for I := 0 to Panel1.ControlCount - 1 do
```

```
      (Panel1.Controls [I] as TSpeedButton).Flat :=
         FlatStyle1.Checked;
  end;
```

We'll look at further extensions of the Toolbar example in a while, but let's move sideways to discuss forms and hints first.

Adding Customized Hints to a Form

Just as we have added hints to an application's toolbar, we can add hints to forms, or to the components of a form, without the need to add a panel. I'll show you a simple example of adding fly-by hints to an existing program, Phrases3. The new version, Phrases4, shows hints when you move over the components contained by the form, as you can see in Figure 12.6.

As you can see in the figure and by running the program, the hints are usually displayed below the component, which works well for the buttons of a toolbar but is not always the best solution for the components of a form. If you add a hint to the form itself, it will be displayed below the window. If you add it to the label at the top, it will be shown far away from its text because the surface of the label, at least at the beginning, has enough space to show three lines. The only way to display hints near the mouse position, and not below the current component, is to customize hints, as we'll do in the next section.

Customizing Hints

We have seen that it is easy to add hint support to a toolbar or a form. It is also easy to customize the way hints are displayed. The simplest thing you can do is change the value of the HintColor property of the Application object (as I've done in the Toolbar3 example) and the three properties related to the hint pause, HintPause, HintHidePause, and HintShortPause. The first defines the amount of time the cursor should remain on a component before hints are displayed, the second how long the hint will be displayed, and the third how long the system should wait to display a hint if another hint has just been displayed.

FIGURE 12.6

The output of the
Phrases4 example,
with the hint displayed
when the mouse is over
the first list box.

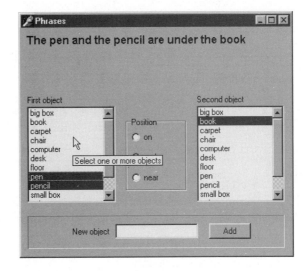

To obtain more control over their display, you can customize hints even further by assigning a method to the application's OnShowHint event. You cannot do this with the Object Inspector, because the Application object doesn't show up in the list. Instead, you need to add a new method to the form manually and then assign it to the OnShowHint property of the Application object at startup (for example, when the form is created).

The method you have to define has some interesting parameters, such as a string with the text of the hint, a Boolean flag for its activation, and a structure with further information:

```
TShowHintEvent = procedure (
  var HintStr: string;
  var CanShow: Boolean;
  var HintInfo: THintInfo) of object;
```

Each of the parameters is passed by reference, so you have a chance to change it. The last parameter is a structure, with the indication of the control, the position of the hint, its color, and other information:

```
THintInfo = record
  HintControl: TControl;
  HintPos: TPoint;
  HintMaxWidth: Integer;
```

```
    HintColor: TColor;
    CursorRect: TRect;
    CursorPos: TPoint;
  end;
```

You can modify the values of this structure, for example, to change the position of the hint window before it is displayed. This is what I've done in the Phrases4 example. If you look again at Figure 12.6 you can see that the position of the hint is not the usual position below the control, but is close to the center of its client area. To accomplish this you have to add a new method to the form, with the parameters indicated above for the type TShowHintEvent:

```
public
  procedure ShowHint (var HintStr: string;
    var CanShow: Boolean; var HintInfo: THintInfo);
```

This method should be connected to the OnShowHint event of the Application when the form is created:

```
procedure TForm1.FormCreate(Sender: TObject);
begin
  ...
  Application.OnShowHint := ShowHint;
end;
```

Next we have to write the code of the new method. Here is what you can write to show the hints of the big label on the top and the two list boxes in the center of their surface:

```
procedure TForm1.ShowHint (var HintStr: string;
  var CanShow: Boolean; var HintInfo: THintInfo);
begin
  with HintInfo do
    if (HintControl = Label1) or
       (HintControl = ListBox1) or
       (HintControl = ListBox2) then
      HintPos := HintControl.ClientToScreen (Point (
        HintControl.Width div 2, HintControl.Height div 2));
end;
```

The code is a little convoluted because it has to retrieve the center of the generic control (the HintInfo.HintControl), and then convert its coordinates to screen coordinates, applying the ClientToScreen method to the control itself. As I've mentioned, this code produces the effect shown in Figure 12.6.

Multiple Hints for a Control

We can further update the Phrases4 example in a different way. The RadioGroup control in the middle of the form has three radio buttons. However, these are not stand-alone components, but simply radio button clones painted on the surface of the radio group. What if we want to add a hint for each of them?

The CursorRect field of the THintInfo record can be used for this purpose. It indicates the area of the component the cursor can move over without disabling the hint. When the cursor moves outside this area, Delphi hides the hint window. If we specify a different text for the hint and a different area for each of the radio buttons, we can in practice provide three different hints. Since computing the actual position of each radio button isn't easy, I've simply divided the surface of the radio group into three equal parts, one for each radio button. The text of the radio button (not the selected item, but the item under the cursor) is then added to the text of the hint:

```
procedure TForm1.ShowHint (var HintStr: string;
  var CanShow: Boolean; var HintInfo: THintInfo);
var
  RadioItem, RadioHeight: Integer;
  RadioRect: TRect;
begin
  with HintInfo do
    if (HintControl = Label1) ... // as before
    else
    if HintControl = RadioGroup1 then
    begin
      RadioHeight := RadioGroup1.Height div 3;
      RadioItem := CursorPos.Y div RadioHeight;
      HintStr := 'Choose the ' +
        RadioGroup1.Items [RadioItem] + ' button';
      RadioRect := RadioGroup1.ClientRect;
      RadioRect.Top := RadioRect.Top +
        RadioHeight * RadioItem;
      RadioRect.Bottom := RadioRect.Top + RadioHeight;
      // assign the hints rect and pos
      CursorRect := RadioRect;
      HintPos := RadioGroup1.ClientToScreen (
        RadioRect.BottomRight);
    end;
end;
```

The final part of the code builds the rectangle for the hint, starting with the rectangle corresponding to the client area of the component, and moving its Top and Bottom values to the proper section of the RadioGroup1 component. The bottom-right corner of this rectangle is then used to determine the position of the hint, as you can see in Figure 12.7.

FIGURE 12.7

The Radio Group of the Phrases4 example shows a different hint depending on the radio button the mouse is over.

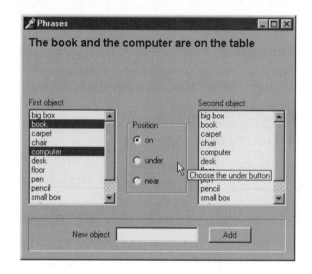

Adding Features to a Toolbar

The Toolbar example we built in three steps contained a standard toolbar, although it had buttons with different behaviors, changing bitmaps, and hints. We can extend this example in two directions. The first is to add some new features to the toolbar panel, such as a combo box, a pop-up menu, and so on. The second is to implement a *dockable* or *draggable* toolbar—a toolbar you can position on any side of the form at run-time.

A Combo Box in a Toolbar

The first extension is the ComboBar example, which has a combo box in its toolbar. A number of common applications use combo boxes in toolbars to show lists of styles, fonts, font sizes, and so on. Our program is along the same lines, but it follows a slightly different approach: it uses a combo box to let the user choose a font and an edit box connected with an UpDown component for setting the font size. You can see an example of this program's form at run-time in Figure 12.8.

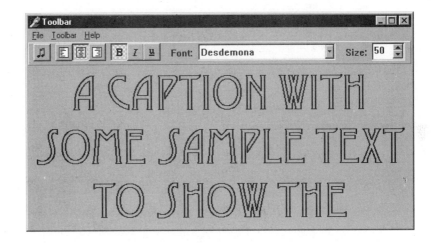

The form of this example is similar to that of the previous version, ToolBar3, although it lacks some of the advanced features. I've removed the Size speed button and added a combo box and an edit box with its UpDown component, each with its own label. The three new components and their labels have a proper message in the Hint property. The form has another component, a pop-up menu, connected with the panel and having almost the same menu commands as the menu bar's Toolbar pull-down. To make this new pop-up menu work without much effort, I simply connected the OnClick events of its items with the methods of the corresponding items of the main menu, using the Object Inspector.

The original methods associated with these commands add and remove the check marks only from the items of the Toolbar pull-down, not from the items of the pop-up menu. I could have changed these methods to operate also on the items of the pop-up menu, but I decided to follow a different approach. When the pop-up menu is going to be displayed, I copy to its items the current check marks of the corresponding items of the main menu:

```
procedure TToolbarForm.PopupMenu1Popup(Sender: TObject);
begin
  DisableSound2.Checked := DisableSound1.Checked;
```

```
    DisableStyles2.Checked := DisableStyles1.Checked;
  end;
```

The rest of the new code refers to the new components placed on the toolbar. The combo box is filled when the application starts, copying the names of the currently available fonts from the Screen object (as we did in the FontGrid example in Chapter 11):

```
procedure TToolbarForm.FormCreate(Sender: TObject);
begin
  ComboBox1.Items := Screen.Fonts;
  {select the current font}
  ComboBox1.ItemIndex :=
    ComboBox1.Items.IndexOf (Label1.Font.Name);
end;
```

Notice the last statement of the method, used to select the current font of the label into the combo box. When a new element of the combo box is selected, the reverse action takes place: The text of the current item of the combo box is copied to the name of the label's font:

```
procedure TToolbarForm.ComboBox1Change(Sender: TObject);
begin
  Label1.Font.Name :=
    ComboBox1.Items [ComboBox1.ItemIndex];
end;
```

Something similar takes place for the UpDown control. You can access the current value of the UpDown and the edit box by using the Position property of the UpDown control and copying it to the Size field of the label's Font property. This operation can take place when the edit box changes:

```
procedure TToolbarForm.Edit1Change(Sender: TObject);
begin
  Label1.Font.Size := UpDown1.Position;
end;
```

A Toolbar You Can Drag

Another improvement to the Toolbar example is to allow the user to drag the toolbar to a different area of the screen. Some Windows applications have toolbars that can be placed only below the menu or at the bottom of the window, others allow vertical bars, and some even have the choice of turning the toolbar into a toolbox—

that is, a small floating window. In the following example, DragTool, I'm going to explore all of these choices.

To accomplish this, the panel used as the toolbar should support automatic dragging, and the label should accept dragging. So first of all, set the DragMode property of Panel1 to dmAutomatic, and then add an OnDragOver event method to the label covering the form, setting the Accept reference parameter to True. To indicate the possible positions of the toolbar, I used the TAlign data type defined by the VCL as follows:

```
type
  TAlign = (alNone, alTop, alBottom,
    alLeft, alRight, alClient);
```

The value alNone will be used to indicate the toolbox (no toolbar). This data type is the return value of a GetBarPos function, which returns the different code depending on the value of the X and Y parameters, which represent form coordinates:

```
function TToolbarForm.GetBarPos (X, Y: Integer): TAlign;
begin
  if X < DragSize then
    GetBarPos := alLeft
  else if Y < DragSize then
    GetBarPos := alTop
  else if X > ClientWidth - DragSize then
    GetBarPos := alRight
  else if Y > ClientHeight - DragSize then
    GetBarPos := alBottom
  else
    GetBarPos := alNone;
end;
```

In this code, DragSize is a constant, defined by the program, that should be less than the height (or width) of the toolbar. Once the dragging ends, we have to move the toolbar to the new position. This is the interesting part of the program, but it is probably easier than you might imagine.

Let me start with a simple case. What is the code you have to write to move the toolbar from the top to the bottom of the form? You should change only the value of the Align property of the panel:

```
Panel1.Align := alBottom;
```

Notice that we can simply ignore the form's other components only because there is a label aligned with the client area; that is, it covers the whole area of the form, excluding the rectangle taken up by the toolbar. To restore Panel1 to the top, the reverse action is required. When you move the toolbar to another location (see Figure 12.9), a similar action should be performed, using the return value of the GetBarPos function directly:

```
ReqPos := GetBarPos (X + Label1.Left, Y + Label1.Top);
Panel1.Align := ReqPos;
```

FIGURE 12.9

In the DragTool example, a user can drag the toolbar to a side of the form.

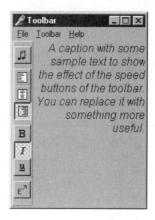

In turning the panel into a vertical one, the problem is not in the panel itself but in the speed buttons it hosts. We need to move each of the buttons to a new location; otherwise, only the first will be visible. Again, this seems more complex than it is. To move a button from the horizontal bar to the vertical bar, you can simply exchange its Top coordinate with its Left coordinate. If you think about it a bit, you should understand why. Luckily, to move the buttons back to a horizontal bar, we only have to perform exactly the same operation again. Here is the code of the RotateSpeedbar procedure:

```
procedure TToolbarForm.RotateSpeedbar;
var
  I, X, Y: Integer;
begin
  for I := 0 to Panel1.ControlCount - 1 do
  begin
    {reverse X and Y}
```

```
    X := Panel1.Controls.Top;
    Y := Panel1.Controls.Left;
    Panel1.Controls.Top := Y;
    Panel1.Controls.Left := X;
  end;
end;
```

The method inverts the X and Y values for each of the controls of the bar, scanning the `Controls` array `ControlCount` times. Of course, this code works well only for *square* controls. If you have a combo box on the toolbar, it will fail. When should you call this method? Only when the old and the new toolbar are one vertical and the other horizontal, or vice versa:

```
if (ReqPos in [alTop, alBottom]) <>
   (BarPos in [alTop, alBottom]) then
   RotateSpeedBar;
```

In this `if` test, `BarPos` is the current position of the toolbar. With this code, we can now move the SpeedBar to each of the four sides of the form. The last thing we have to do is let the user turn the toolbar into a toolbox, as shown in Figure 12.10. To accomplish this, I've added a second form to the project, named it ToolBox, and set its `BorderStyle` property to `bsToolWindow` and its `FormStyle` property to `fsStayOnTop`.

FIGURE 12.10

The toolbar of the Drag-Tool example.

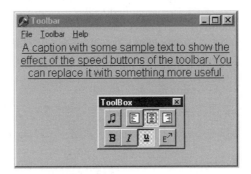

At first I thought I could have copied the speed buttons from the panel to the other window, but then I realized that keeping their attributes in sync would have been a nightmare. So I decided to leave the toolbox form empty and copy the speed buttons into it when they are needed. If the dragging operation terminates in the central portion of the form, I show the toolbox, hide the toolbar, rotate the speed buttons if they are vertical, and then call the MoveButtons method.

The code also sets a private Boolean field of the form, BoxOn, to True, to indicate that the toolbox is visible:

```
if ReqPos = alNone then
begin
  Panel1.Visible := False;
  BoxOn := True;
  if BarPos in [alLeft, alRight] then
    RotateSpeedbar;
  {move buttons to the toolbox}
  MoveButtons (ToolBox);
  ToolBox.Show;
end
```

The MoveButtons procedure has two different actions: First it moves the button to the TWinControl passed as a parameter, then it places the speed buttons on two lines, or moves them back to one line (I'll also use the same method to restore the position of the speed buttons):

```
procedure TToolbarForm.MoveButtons (Win: TWinControl);
var
  I, J: Integer;
begin
  {move the speed buttons to a new parent component}
  for I := 0 to ComponentCount - 1 do
    if Components is TSpeedButton then
      TSpeedButton (Components).Parent := Win;
    if Win = ToolBox then
    begin
      {place the buttons on two lines}
      for J := 0 to Win.ControlCount - 1 do
        if Win.Controls [J].Left > 110 then
        begin
          Win.Controls [J].Left :=
            Win.Controls [J].Left - 112;
          Win.Controls [J].Top := 30;
        end;
    end
    else
    begin
```

```
{place back the buttons on one line}
for J := 0 to Win.ControlCount - 1 do
  if Win.Controls [J].Top = 30 then
  begin
    Win.Controls [J].Left :=
      Win.Controls [J].Left + 112;
    Win.Controls [J].Top := 2;
  end;
  end;
end;
```

Once the toolbox is visible, you cannot drag it into a side of the form to turn it into a toolbar. If you don't want the toolbox anymore just close it, and the toolbar will be displayed again in its former position. The code to accomplish this is in the OnClose event of the toolbox:

```
procedure TToolBox.FormClose(Sender: TObject;
  var Action: TCloseAction);
begin
  ToolbarForm.Panel1.Visible := True;
  ToolbarForm.BoxOn := False;
  ToolbarForm.MoveButtons (ToolbarForm.Panel1);
  if ToolbarForm.BarPos in [alLeft, alRight] then
    ToolbarForm.RotateSpeedbar;
end;
```

The Toolbar Windows 95 Control

 Delphi 3 introduces a specific Toolbar component, which encapsulates the corresponding Windows 95 common control. This component provides a toolbar, with its own buttons, and has some extended capabilities compared to a home-made toolbar. A good example of the use of this component is Microsoft's latest version of the Internet Explorer, which actually has a Toolbar inside a Coolbar, another new component I'll cover in a while.

We can start exploring this component by rebuilding the familiar Toolbar example using the new specific component instead of a panel. This is quite easy. Start with a brand-new form and place on it a Toolbar component from the Windows 95 page of the Component Palette. What you have is a plain toolbar. To add buttons into it, select the local menu of the component, and choose one of the two custom menu items, New Button or New Separator. You can see an example of a Toolbar under construction in Figure 12.11.

FIGURE 12.11

To create a toolbar you can place the corresponding component on a form and then use the two special commands of its local menu.

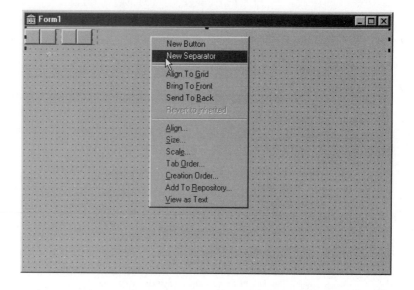

The Toolbar is populated with objects of the TToolButton class. These are *internal* objects, just as a TMenuItem is an internal object of a MainMenu component. These objects have a fundamental property, Style, which determines their behavior:

- The tbsButton style indicates a standard push button.

- The tbsCheck style indicates a button with the behavior of a check box, or that of a radio button if the button is Grouped with the others in its block (determined by the presence of separators).

- The tbsDropDown style indicates a drop-down button, a sort of check box. The drop-down portion, however, is not directly supported but must be prepared separately using another component.

- The tbsSeparator style indicates a separator.

The next step is to provide bitmaps for the buttons. You accomplish this by adding one or more ImageList components to the form, loading the bitmaps in the ImageList, and then connecting the ImageList with the Images property of the toolbar. By default the images will be assigned to the buttons in the order they appear, but you can change this quite easily, by setting the ImageIndex property of each toolbar button. You can prepare further ImageLists for special conditions of the buttons, and assign them to the DisabledImages and HotImages properties of the toolbar. The first group is used for the disabled buttons, the second for the button currently under the mouse. This last group of images is usually more colorful, as you can see by running the CoolBar example discussed in the next section.

In the RealBar example, however, I've created a toolbar with just the standard image list. This example is a new version of the example we've already seen, this time based on a *real* toolbar—a TToolbar component. You can see the form of this example at design-time in Figure 12.12, and see some excerpts of its textual description in the following listing:

```
object ToolBar1: TToolBar
  AllowAllUp = False
  AutoSize = True
  Flat = True
  Images = ImageList1
  ShowCaptions = True
  ShowHint = True
  object TbNote: TToolButton
    Hint = 'Play Note'
    Caption = 'Note'
    ImageIndex = 0
    OnClick = TbNoteClick
  end
  object TbSeparator1: TToolButton
    Style = tbsSeparator
  end
  object TbLeft: TToolButton
    Hint = 'Align Left'
    Caption = 'Left'
    Down = True
    Grouped = True
    ImageIndex = 1
    Style = tbsCheck
```

```
      OnClick = TbLeftClick
  end
  object TbCenter: TToolButton...
  object TbRight: TToolButton...
  object TbSeparator2: TToolButton...
  object TbBold: TToolButton...
  object TbItalic: TToolButton...
  object TbUnderlined: TToolButton...
  object TbSeparator3: TToolButton...
  object TbSize: TToolButton...
    Hint = 'Resize Text'
    Caption = 'Size'
    ImageIndex = 7
    Wrap = True
    Style = tbsCheck
    OnClick = TbSizeClick
  end
end
```

FIGURE 12.12

The Toolbar component of the RealBar example at design-time.

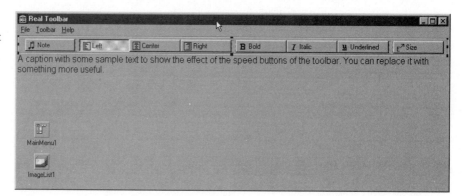

The Toolbar component is quite flexible. You can put captions on the buttons or not, show them on the left of the image or below it, and choose between the traditional buttons and the new flat style. The Toolbar pull-down menu of the RealBar example allows a user to change these features at run-time, as you can see in Figure 12.13.

FIGURE 12.13

The Toolbar of the Real-Bar example can be customized in a number of ways, making it quite different from the original design-time version (shown in Figure 12.12).

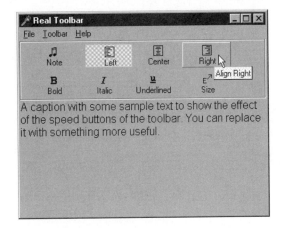

The code of these three buttons simply toggles some of the properties of the toolbar component, and then places check marks on the corresponding menu items. The first command also disables the second one, since it makes no sense to move the caption when it is not visible:

```
procedure TRealBarForm.Captions1Click(Sender: TObject);
begin
  Toolbar1.ShowCaptions := not Toolbar1.ShowCaptions;
  Captions1.Checked := Toolbar1.ShowCaptions;
  CaptionBelow1.Enabled := Toolbar1.ShowCaptions;
end;
```

The other two menu commands have very simple handlers, and you can look up their code on the companion disk.

A Really Cool Toolbar

In addition to the Toolbar component, Delphi 3 features the CoolBar component, which encapsulates a brand-new Windows common control, introduced by Microsoft with Internet Explorer 3.0 and part of the updated COMCTRLS.DLL library.

The CoolBar component is a basically collection of TCoolBand objects. Unlike the toolbar buttons, these objects do not appear as stand-alone objects in the form, but are simply a collection of sub-items. They appear in the Object Inspector only when you select the editor of the Bands property of the CoolBar, as you can see in Figure 12.14. You simply create one or more bands, then set their attributes.

FIGURE 12.14

The property editor of the Bands property of the CoolBar component works in conjunction with the Object Inspector.

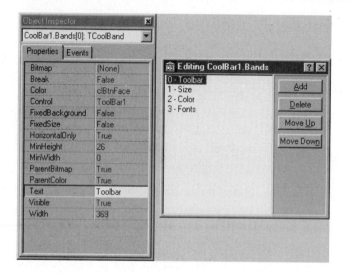

Using the CoolBar component is really simple: You can set a bitmap for its background, add some bands using the editor for the Bands property, and then assign to each band an existing component or component container. You can use any window-based control (not graphic controls), but only some of them will show up properly. If you want to have a bitmap on the background of the Cool-Bar, for example, you need to use partially transparent controls.

The typical component used in a CoolBar is the Toolbar (which can be made completely transparent) but combo boxes, edit boxes, and animation controls are also quite common. This is often inspired by the user interface of the Internet Explorer, the first Microsoft application featuring the CoolBar component.

You can place one band on each line or all on the same line, each one using a part of the available surface, and automatically enlarged by clicking on its title. It is easier to use this new component than to explain it. Try it yourself, or follow the description below, in which we build a new version of our Toolbar example based on a CoolBar control. You can see the form of this example at run-time in Figure 12.15.

FIGURE 12.15

The form of the CoolBar example at run-time.

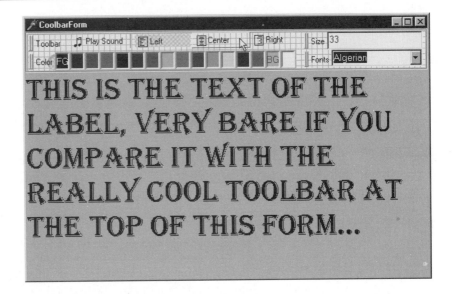

The CoolBar example has a TCoolBar component with four bands, two for each of the two lines. The first band includes a subset of the toolbar of the previous example, this time adding an ImageList for the highlighted images; the second has an edit box used to set the font of the text; the third has a ColorGrid component, used to choose the font color and that of the background; and the last band has a ComboBox control with the available fonts. Here is the textual description of the CoolBar component of the example:

```
object CoolBar1: TCoolBar
  AutoSize = True
  BandBorderStyle = bsNone
  Bands = <
    item
      Control = ToolBar1
      HorizontalOnly = True
      Text = 'Toolbar'
    end
    item
      Control = Edit1
      Text = 'Size'
```

```
        end
        item
          Control = ColorGrid1
          HorizontalOnly = True
          Text = 'Color'
        end
        item
          Control = ComboBox1
          Text = 'Fonts'
        end>
      BorderWidth = 1
      Bitmap.Data = {...}
      ShowHint = True
    end
```

The code of the program is quite simple, so I won't discuss it. The new CoolBar component is really thrilling, and Microsoft is increasingly using it in its applications, so having it easily available in Delphi is a real plus. By the way, Delphi 3 includes an example (named CoolStuf) of the use of the CoolBar component in building an Internet Browser, a real clone of the user interface of the Microsoft Internet Explorer.

Creating a Status Bar

Building a status bar is even simpler than building a toolbar. Delphi includes a specific StatusBar component, based on the corresponding Windows 95 common control. Although you can use a bottom-aligned Panel component for the same purpose, I suggest you rely on the StatusBar component. This component can be used almost as a panel when its SimplePanel property is set to True. In this case you can use the SimpleText property to output some text. The real advantage of this component, however, is that it allows you to define a number of sub-panels by simply activating the editor of its Panels property, as you can see in Figure 12.16. Each sub-panel has its own graphical attributes, customizable using the editor. Another feature of the status bar component is the "size grip" area added to the lower-right corner of the bar, which is useful to resize the form itself. This is a typical element of the Windows 95 user interface.

FIGURE 12.16

The StatusBar Panels
editor.

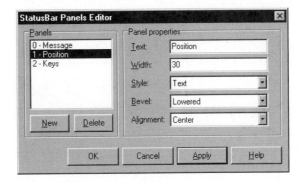

There are a number of uses for a status bar. The most common is to display
information about the menu item currently selected by the user. Besides this, a
status bar often displays information about the status of a program (hence the
name). For example, you might display the position of the cursor in a graphical
application, the current line of text in a word processor, the status of the lock
keys, the time and date, or other information.

Menu Hints in the Status Bar

The first example, Status1, has a status bar capable of displaying the description
of the current menu item and the status of the Caps Lock key. These are the properties of the StatusBar component:

```
object StatusBar1: TStatusBar
  Panels = <
    item
      Width = 300
    end
    item
      Width = 36
    end
    item
      Width = 100
    end>
  SimplePanel = False
end
```

The form has a main menu, of course, and when the user moves to the menu to select an element, the program displays a description of the current command in the status bar, as you can see in Figure 12.17.

FIGURE 12.17

The simple status bar of the Status1 example displays a description of the current menu item.

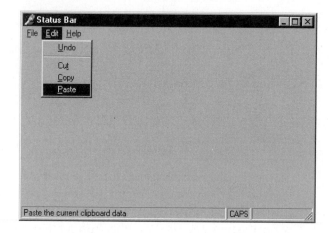

To obtain this effect, you need to take two steps. First, input a string as a Hint property of each item or pull-down of the main menu. Second, write some code to handle the application's OnHint event. You need to add a new method to the form manually and then assign it to the OnHint event of the Application object at startup (for example, when the form is created):

```
procedure TForm1.FormCreate(Sender: TObject);
begin
  Application.OnHint := ShowHint;
end;
```

In the form's interface, you can add the following definition:

```
procedure ShowHint(Sender: TObject);
```

This procedure copies the current value of the application's Hint property, which temporarily contains a copy of the selected item's hint, to the status bar:

```
procedure TForm1.ShowHint(Sender: TObject);
begin
  StatusBar1.Panels[0].Text := Application.Hint;
end;
```

This is all you need to do to display a hint indicating the effect of a menu in the status bar. To display the status of the Caps Lock key, or of any other key, you have to call the GetKeyState API function, which returns a state number. If the low-order bit of this number is set (that is, if the number is odd), then the key is pressed. When do we check this state? We can do it every time the user presses a key on the form, or we can add a timer and make the check every second. This second approach has an advantage, because the user might press the Caps Lock key while working with a different application and this should be indicated on the status bar of our program, too. However, using a timer makes the response to pressing the key quite slow. So I've decided to write a simple procedure CheckCapslock and then call it in both event handlers:

```
procedure TForm1.CheckCapslock;
begin
  if Odd (GetKeyState (VK_CAPITAL)) then
    StatusBar1.Panels[1].Text := 'CAPS'
  else
    StatusBar1.Panels[1].Text := '';
end;

procedure TForm1.FormKeyDown(Sender: TObject;
  var Key: Word; Shift: TShiftState);
begin
  CheckCapslock;
end;

procedure TForm1.Timer1Timer(Sender: TObject);
begin
  CheckCapslock;
end;
```

Speed Button Hints in the Status Bar

We can easily extend this application by adding a toolbar to it and providing a way to display a description of the speed buttons when the mouse moves over them. Recall that the Hint property of the speed buttons is already used to display the yellow fly-by hints near the buttons. How can we use the same property for two different strings? Strangely enough, this problem has a direct solution: write a simple string divided into two portions by a separator, the | character. For example, you might enter the following as the value of the Hint property:

```
'Help|Activate the help of the application'
```

The first portion of the string, *Help*, is used by fly-by hints, the second portion by the status bar. This takes place automatically when you have written the code described in the first version of the status bar.

> **TIP**
>
> When the hint for a control is made up of two strings, you can use the GetShortHint and GetLongHint methods to extract the first (short) and second (long) substrings from the string you pass as a parameter, which is usually the value of the Hint property.

For example, in Status2, I copied the form of Status1 and its code; then I pasted the toolbar of an older application. I've also removed the sub-panels of the status bar, and set its SimplePanel property to True. Then I changed the code of the ShowHint method as follows:

```
procedure TForm1.ShowHint(Sender: TObject);
begin
  StatusBar1.SimpleText := Application.Hint;
end;
```

Finally, I set the value of the Hint property of the graphical buttons, and without changing the code I've been able to show both hints at once, as you can see in Figure 12.18.

FIGURE 12.18

The output of Status2, with speed buttons having both a fly-by hint and a status bar description.

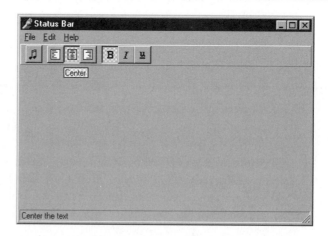

TIP

To build the example above, I copied a group of components from one application to another. This is quite simple, as mentioned in Chapter 2. Open the source application, select a number of components (in this case, the panel and some of the speed buttons it contains), copy them to the Clipboard, and then move to the destination form and paste them in. As an alternative, you can use a component template.

What's Next?

In this chapter, we have examined a specific topic: the definition of a toolbar and a status bar for simple SDI applications. We have seen that we can use specific Windows 95 controls (encapsulated by the ToolBar, CoolBar, and StatusBar Delphi components) or simply a Panel component with SpeedButtons.

Actually, there is a different approach for building a toolbar or a status bar in Delphi, using the Application Expert or one of the Application templates. When these projects are generated, the application's main form has both a working toolbar and a working status bar.

You can consider this chapter the first step toward building professional applications. We will take other steps in the following chapters; but you already know enough to make your programs similar to some best-selling Windows applications, which may be very important for your clients. Now that the elements of the main form of our programs are properly set up, we can consider adding secondary forms and dialog boxes. This is the topic of the next chapter, although we already saw how simple it is to add a second form to a program to build a toolbox. In the next chapter we'll also explore visual form inheritance, a very powerful Delphi technique.

Multiple Forms and Dialog Boxes

■ Modal and modeless forms

■ How to merge form menus

■ Modal and modeless dialog boxes

■ Predefined dialog boxes

■ Extensible dialog boxes

■ Building a splash screen

■ Visual Form Inheritance

Up to this point, the programs in this book have each consisted of a single form. Although it is possible to build fully functional applications with one form and a number of components, it is far more common to have more than one form. Usually, applications have a main window, some floating toolboxes or palettes, and a number of dialog boxes that can be invoked through menu commands or command buttons. More complex applications might have an MDI structure—a frame window with a number of child windows inside its client area. The development of MDI applications will be discussed in Chapter 15. This chapter focuses on applications having more than one form or having dialog boxes.

Dialog boxes are not a new subject. We have already used a number of default dialog boxes to select colors, fonts, and files, and we've used some message boxes, by calling the `MessageDlg` function. In this chapter, you will see how you can define your own dialog boxes.

Dialog Boxes versus Forms

Before presenting examples of applications with multiple forms and applications with user-defined dialog boxes, let me begin with a general description of these two alternatives and their differences.

We have already seen a correspondence between forms in Delphi and Windows as perceived by the user (see the definitions in the section "Forms versus Windows" in Chapter 10). Since dialog boxes are a particular kind of window, you expect dialog boxes in Delphi to be based on forms, too. This is indeed the case. Once we have added a second form to a program, we can display it as a form or as a dialog box. Something slightly different might take place behind the scenes in Delphi and in Windows, but it won't matter to us.

When you write a program, there is really no big difference between a dialog box and a second form, aside from the border and other user-interface elements you can customize.

What users associate with a dialog box is the concept of a *modal window*—a window that takes the focus and must be closed before the user can move back to the main window. This is true for message boxes and usually for dialog boxes, as well. However, you can also have nonmodal—or *modeless*—dialog boxes. So if you think that dialog boxes are just modal forms, you are on the right track, but your description is not precise. In Delphi (as in Windows), you can have modeless dialog boxes and modal forms. We have to consider two different elements:

- The form's border and its user interface determine whether it looks like a dialog box.

- The use of two different functions (Show or ShowModal) to display the second form determines its behavior (modeless or modal).

By combining these two elements, we can build any kind of secondary form. This is what we will do in this chapter, before looking at other related topics.

Adding a Second Form to a Program

Now we are ready to dive into an example. To experiment with modeless forms, we will add a second form to an application. (You'll see how to create a modal form when we move on to dialog boxes.) The example, Phones, is simple: The main form (Form1) has a list of phone numbers; the secondary form (Form2) has a list of e-mail addresses. (Of course, to build this program, I've just invented a list of fictitious names, phone numbers, and e-mail addresses. Any resemblance to existing people or references is unintentional.)

TIP
To add a second form to an application, you simply click on the New Form button on the Delphi toolbar or use the File ➤ New Form menu command. As an alternative you can select File ➤ New, move to the Forms or Dialogs page, and choose one of the available form templates or form Wizards. In most of the examples in this chapter, we will start with a blank main form and one or more blank secondary forms.

You can see the two forms in Figure 13.1. If you have two forms in a project, you can use the Select Form or the Select Unit button of the toolbar to navigate through them at design-time. You can also choose which form is the main one and which forms should be automatically created at startup using the Forms page of the Project Options dialog box (see Figure 13.2).

Once you have prepared the two forms, you need to add some code to the program to make them work properly. In both forms, I've added a button. In the first form, the button is used to show the second window, and in the second form, it is used to close the form. In fact, you can close the second form and continue with the first one. The opposite is not possible: as soon as you close the main form of a Delphi application, the program terminates.

The two forms of the Phones example at run-time.

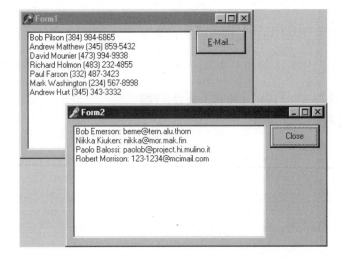

FIGURE 13.2

The Forms options of the Phones project.

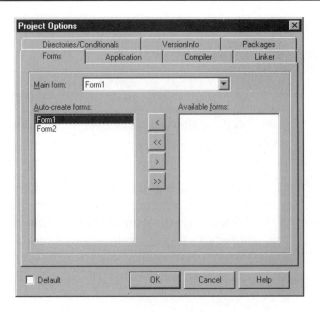

To run the second form when the user presses `Button1`, you should write this simple code:

```
procedure TForm1.Button1Click(Sender: TObject);
begin
  Form2.Show;
end;
```

If you use the Show function, the second form will be displayed as modeless, so you can move back to the first one while the second is still visible. Notice that the code simply displays the form; it doesn't create it. In fact, the form is created by the project file, as indicated in the Forms page of the Project Options dialog box. If you look at the project file's code, you can see that both forms are included (*used*) and that both are created, using the application's `CreateForm` method. The first form created becomes the application's main form:

```
program Phones;

uses
  Forms,
  Unit1 in 'UNIT1.PAS' {Form1},
  Unit2 in 'UNIT2.PAS' {Form2};

begin
  Application.Initialize;
  Application.CreateForm(TForm1, Form1);
  Application.CreateForm(TForm2, Form2);
  Application.Run;
end.
```

If you now compile this application, Delphi will issue an error message, but it will also offer to fix the problem, as you can see in Figure 13.3. To compile the code of the first form, in fact, you need to include the unit containing the second form (in this case, Unit2) with a `uses` statement, possibly in the implementation portion. As an alternative, you can select the first form and issue the File ➤ Use Unit menu command.

FIGURE 13.3

The request from the compiler to add the proper *uses* statement to the code of the main form.

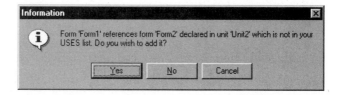

To close the second form, you might use its system menu or click on the Close button, calling the following method:

```
procedure TForm2.CloseButtonClick(Sender: TObject);
begin
  Close;
end;
```

When you run this code, Delphi does not close the secondary form, but instead simply hides it. This is what we need, since we want to be able to display the secondary form again without having to re-create it. In other cases, you need to override the OnClose event and actually destroy the form, to avoid having too many forms in memory at the same time.

Modal and Modeless Forms

As you saw in the previous section, adding a second form to a program (and a third, and so on) is really simple, so let's try something more complex. Let's expand this example into a generic one, allowing a user to open a number of modal or modeless forms. The main form of the Modes program has two buttons, used to create modal and modeless forms. Once you have added two new forms to the project—I've named them ModalForm and ModelessForm—you can write the following methods, corresponding to the two OnClick events of the two buttons, which create a new form on the fly:

```
procedure TMainAppForm.ModalButtonClick(Sender: TObject);
var
  Modal: TModalForm;
begin
  Modal := TModalForm.Create (Application);
  try
    Modal.ShowModal;
  finally
    Modal.Free;
  end;
end;
```

```
procedure TMainAppForm.ModelessButtonClick(Sender: TObject);
var
  NonModal: TModelessForm;
begin
  NonModal := TModelessForm.Create (Application);
  NonModal.Show;
end;
```

When the modal form is created and executed by means of ShowModal, it remains active until you close it. This means that the call to the ShowModal function does not return until the form is closed. During this time, the application's main form remains *disabled*. You cannot click the two buttons or interact with the form in any way. Once the modal form has been closed, the ShowModal function terminates and the code deletes the object from memory. (Since the ShowModal call can raise an exception, to be sure of the object deallocation, you should write it in a finally block.)

The behavior of the modeless form is different. The Show procedure—notice that this is a procedure, while ShowModal is a function—returns immediately. Of course, we cannot delete the object from memory since the corresponding window is currently on the screen (for this reason, the form will free itself when it is closed). We can, instead, press the Modeless button again to create a second modeless form, then a third form, a fourth, and so on. There is practically no limit, apart from the Windows resource limits (which are very high in 32-bit versions of Windows).

The main form can display secondary forms. What can you do with these forms? They both have a Close button, as you can see in Figure 13.4. The two Close buttons are connected with a simple method that calls the Close procedure. The modal form has also a second button, to create another *nested* modal form. The OnClick method for this button has the same code as the main form's ModalButtonClick method.

An important element of this program is that each time you create an object of a form class in your code, you should disable the automatic form creation, using the Forms page of the Project Options dialog box (already shown in Figure 13.2). You can also remove the declaration of a global variable for the form that Delphi automatically adds in the interface section of the unit describing the form.

FIGURE 13.4

The modal and modeless forms of the Modes program at run-time.

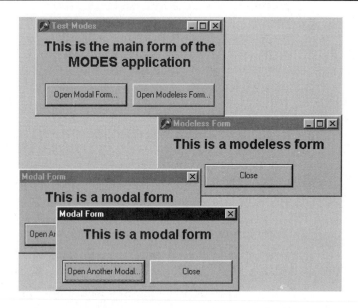

Two Forms, Two Menus

Now we can go back to our Phones example and try to add a menu to the forms, building the Phones2 program. The easiest thing to do is to add a menu to each of the forms. To show that this approach works with both a modal and a modeless form, I've added to the older version of the program the code to create the second form as either modal or modeless, using the two menu items of the EMail Form pull-down menu.

To show the secondary form, you need only apply either the ShowModal or the Show method to it. In fact, the forms of this program are both created by the project's code at startup. When the program shows the second form as modal, the main form is automatically disabled, together with its menu. When the form is displayed as modeless, you should disable its menu manually. Since there is only one form, trying to show it twice won't be a good choice.

```
procedure TForm1.ShowModeless1Click(Sender: TObject);
begin
  ShowModal1.Enabled := False;
  ShowModeless1.Enabled := False;
  Form1.CloseModeless1.Enabled := True;
  Form2.Show;
end;
```

When the form is displayed, the first two items of the EMail Form pull-down menu are disabled and the third is enabled (it was disabled at design-time), as shown in Figure 13.5.

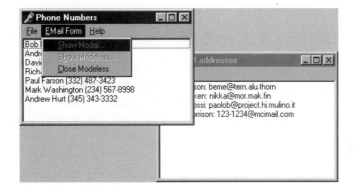

Notice that in the figure, the menu items have different colors because the first is currently selected (although it is grayed). When you select this last menu item, the modeless form is closed, calling its Close method. So what happens to the menu items? Shouldn't we re-enable them when the Close Modeless menu item is called? We might do so, but the program won't work properly. In fact, there are a number of ways to close the second modeless form, including the Close command of its own menu. Instead of repeating the code to enable the menu items in a number of places, you can write it in the second form's OnClose event:

```
procedure TForm2.FormClose(Sender: TObject;
  var Action: TCloseAction);
begin
  Form1.ShowModal1.Enabled := True;
  Form1.ShowModeless1.Enabled := True;
  Form1.CloseModeless1.Enabled := False;
end;
```

Notice that this method of the second form refers to the first one; that is, it needs access to some properties of the TForm1 class. For this reason, the second form should use the first one. In this case, the uses statements *must* be in the implementation section of the unit. Otherwise the program would cause a circular reference between the two units, with each unit referring to the other one in its interface portion. If the two units refer to each other, but the uses statements are in the implementation portion, there is no problem, because the other unit will be considered only when the first one is compiled.

This example demonstrates that on the whole, handling modal forms is usually easier than handling modeless forms, since you do not need to change the behavior of the main window. In fact, the user cannot interact with the main form when the modal form is open, and you don't need to keep track of the open or closed forms, as you do with modeless forms.

Merging Form Menus

In the preceding version of the Phones program, each of the two forms had its own menu bar. Delphi, however, provides a way to merge the menu bars of two or more forms automatically. In this technique, the application's main window has a menu bar, as usual. The other forms have a menu bar with the `AutoMerge` property enabled, so their menu bar won't be displayed in the form but will instead be merged with the one from the main window.

These are the rules for menu merging: Each pull-down menu has a `GroupIndex` property. When menu bars are merged, the pull-down menus are arranged as follows:

- If two elements of the different menu bars have the same `GroupIndex`, those of the original menu are removed.

- Elements are ordered by ascending `GroupIndex` values.

For example, in Figure 13.6, you can see how the menus of the two forms of the Phones3 example are merged. The pull-down menus of the main form have

FIGURE 13.6

The two menu bars of the Phones3 example and how they are merged.

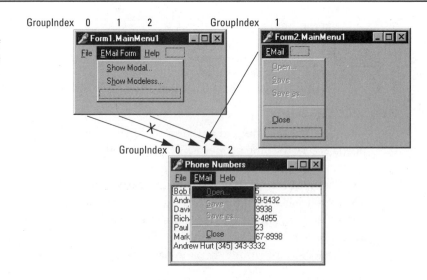

indexes 0, 1, and 2. The only pull-down of the second form has an index 1, so it replaces the pull-down with the corresponding index of the main form's menu. Consider, however, that menu merging makes sense only for modeless forms. If you display the second form as modal, you cannot access the main window's menu bar, so Delphi doesn't perform any merging.

Using menu merging is extremely simple, at least at first glance. If you open Phones2 again, set the AutoMerge property of the second form's main menu to True, and set proper values for the GroupIndex properties, as indicated in the following list, the program will almost work:

Form	Pull-Down Menu	GroupIndex
Form1	File	0
	EMail Form	1
	Help	2
Form2	EMail	1

In fact there is still a problem: when the form is displayed as modal, its menu is not accessible. We can solve the first problem easily by adding a statement to set the value of the AutoMerge property of the second form's menu dynamically.

However, instead of simply setting this property, I want to use a more radical and dynamic approach, to show you one more example of dynamic form creation. We will create and destroy the secondary form each time it should be shown or hidden. This requires a number of simple changes in the source code. First of all, you need to disable automatic form creation using the Forms page of the Project Options dialog box. To show the form as modal, we have to create it, set its properties, and later destroy it:

```
procedure TForm1.ShowModal1Click(Sender: TObject);
begin
  Form2 := TForm2.Create (Self);
  Form2.MainMenu1.AutoMerge := False;
  Form2.ShowModal;
  Form2.Free;
end;
```

The approach used for the modeless activation is slightly different. The form is created but not destroyed:

```
procedure TForm1.ShowModeless1Click(Sender: TObject);
begin
  Form2 := TForm2.Create (Self);
```

```
    Form2.MainMenu1.AutoMerge := True;
    Form2.Show;
  end;
```

Notice that from the previous version, I've removed the code used to disable some menu items, since the whole pull-down menu is completely hidden. For this reason, I've also removed the last item, Close. The modeless form is destroyed when it is closed if you set the `Action` parameter of the `OnClose` event to `caFree`:

```
procedure TForm2.FormClose(Sender: TObject;
  var Action: TCloseAction);
begin
  Action := caFree;
end;
```

The rest of the code of this Phones3 example is the same as in Phones2, although there isn't much left after the last changes I've made.

Creating a Dialog Box

I stated earlier in this chapter that a dialog box is not very different from other forms. There is a very simple trick to build a dialog box instead of a form. Just select the `bsDialog` value for the form's `BorderStyle` property. With this simple change, the interface of the form becomes like that of a dialog box, with no system icon, no Minimize or Maximize boxes, and the proper system menu you can activate by right-clicking over the caption. Of course, such a form has the typical dialog box thick border, which is non-resizable. (See the Borders example in Chapter 10 for a comparison of the border styles.)

Once you have built a dialog box form, you can display it as a modal or modeless window using the two usual show methods (the `Show` procedure and the function `ShowModal`). Modal dialog boxes, however, are more common than modeless ones. This is exactly the reverse of forms: modal forms should generally be avoided since a user won't expect them. The following table lists the complete schema of the various combinations of styles:

Window Type	Modal	Modeless
Form	Never	Usual, in SDI applications
Dialog box	Most common kind of secondary form	Used, but not very common

Sometimes, an alternative to the use of too many secondary forms is to build multipage forms, a new kind of user interface that is spreading rapidly among Windows applications. You can do this easily using Delphi's Notebook and Page-Control components, as we'll see in Chapter 14.

Modal Dialog Boxes

Since modal dialog boxes are more common than modeless ones, I'll concentrate on them first. As an example, we'll build a typical Options dialog box. The main form of this example, named Dialog1, has two labels, and you can use the dialog box to hide or show them. You can see the main form and the dialog box at run-time in Figure 13.7.

The dialog box also has two standard bitmap buttons, with the default glyphs for OK and Cancel. Using these default buttons is usually a good idea because you can set a single property (Kind) instead of a number of them, including the Caption, the Glyph, the return value (ModalResult), and others. As a consequence—and an important one—you get a standard user interface. Here is a summary of the properties of the dialog box form and its components:

```
object ConfigureDialog: TConfigureDialog
  BorderStyle = bsDialog
  Caption = 'Choose configuration'
  object BitBtn1: TBitBtn
    Kind = bkOK
  end
  object BitBtn2: TBitBtn
    Kind = bkCancel
  end
  object CheckBox1: TCheckBox
    Caption = 'Show &first label'
    State = cbChecked
  end
  object CheckBox2: TCheckBox
    Caption = 'Show &second label'
    State = cbChecked
  end
end
```

The code of this application is quite simple. After you have included the unit describing the dialog box form in the code of the main form, you can simply call ShowModal to display the dialog box. This is not very useful by itself. In fact, we do not respond to any actions the user might have taken in the dialog box.

FIGURE 13.7

The main form and the
dialog box of the Dialog1
example.

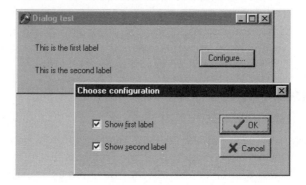

Each time the dialog box is executed, the status of the two check boxes should be used to determine which of the labels should be visible. However, if the user terminates the dialog box by pressing the Cancel button, the values should not be considered. So we need to make the assignments only if the return value of the ShowModal function (that is, the modal result) is mrOk:

```
procedure TForm1.ConfigureButtonClick(Sender: TObject);
begin
  if ConfigureDialog.ShowModal = mrOk then
  begin
    Label1.Visible := ConfigureDialog.CheckBox1.Checked;
    Label2.Visible := ConfigureDialog.CheckBox2.Checked;
  end;
end;
```

If you open the dialog box, set some options, and press the Cancel button, the new values are not considered; but the next time you open the dialog box, you'll see the options you set before pressing the Cancel button, not the currently active options. For this reason, we need to set up the dialog box properly each time it is executed. Here is the final code of the Dialog1 example:

```
procedure TForm1.ConfigureButtonClick(Sender: TObject);
begin
  {copy current values to the dialog box}
  ConfigureDialog.CheckBox1.Checked := Label1.Visible;
  ConfigureDialog.CheckBox2.Checked := Label2.Visible;
  if ConfigureDialog.ShowModal = mrOk then
  begin
    {copy new dialog box values in the main form}
    Label1.Visible := ConfigureDialog.CheckBox1.Checked;
```

```
      Label2.Visible := ConfigureDialog.CheckBox2.Checked;
    end;
  end;
```

This is one of the approaches you can follow when you run a modal dialog box. These are the steps:

1. Set the initial values each time you run the dialog box.

2. Show the dialog box.

3. If the OK button was pressed, copy the new values back to the form.

Of course, this is not the only possible technique. As an alternative, you can set up the values of the dialog box only the first time, store the current values each time you run it, and reset the values to the current ones when the user quits the dialog box with the Cancel button. In our example, we could have written

```
procedure TForm1.ConfigureButtonClick(Sender: TObject);
var
  old1, old2: Boolean;
begin
  {store the old values of the dialog box}
  old1 := ConfigureDialog.CheckBox1.Checked;
  old2 := ConfigureDialog.CheckBox2.Checked;
  if (ConfigureDialog.ShowModal = mrOk) then
  begin
    {set the new values in the form}
    Label1.Visible := ConfigureDialog.CheckBox1.Checked;
    Label2.Visible := ConfigureDialog.CheckBox2.Checked;
  end
  else
  begin
    {restore the old values of the dialog box}
    ConfigureDialog.CheckBox1.Checked := old1;
    ConfigureDialog.CheckBox2.Checked := old2;
  end;
end;
```

The advantage here is that the code that saves and restores the old values can be moved into the code of the dialog box. This is useful if there are several places in the code where you can show the same dialog box. In this case, the code to set up and even show the dialog box can be written in a custom method of the dialog box form, and the OnClick method of the dialog box's OK button should copy the proper final values to some fields or properties of the main form. This is a change of perspective: instead of having a main form accessing values and properties of the dialog box, we can have a dialog box getting values from the main form and setting them into it directly.

Closing a Dialog Box

What happens when the user clicks on OK or Cancel? The code should close the dialog box, returning the proper value to the application. You can indicate the return value by setting the ModalResult property of the button the user clicks to terminate the dialog box. As a side effect, when you assign a value to this property of the form, the modal dialog box is automatically closed.

Notice that the ModalResult value becomes exactly the return value of the ShowModal method that was used to show the modal dialog box. So that we don't need to code this by hand, each button component, including bitmap buttons, has a ModalResult property. If you do not handle a button's OnClick event, it automatically uses its ModalResult value to set the corresponding property of its parent form.

A Modeless Dialog Box

The second example of dialog boxes shows a more complex modal dialog box that uses the standard approach, as well as a modeless dialog box. The main form of the Dialog2 example has five labels with names (see Figure 13.8):

```
object Form1: TForm1
  ActiveControl = StyleButton
  Caption = 'Modal & modeless dialogs'
  object Bevel1: TBevel...
  object Label1: TLabel
    Caption = 'Name'
    OnClick = LabelClick
    OnDblClick = LabelDoubleClick
  end
  object Label2: TLabel
    Caption = 'Name'
    OnClick = LabelClick
    OnDblClick = LabelDoubleClick
  end
```

```
object Label3: TLabel... // the same
object Label4: TLabel... // the same
object Label5: TLabel... // the same
object Label6: TLabel
  Alignment = taCenter
  AutoSize = False
  Caption = 'Double-click on a name to change it
    or click on the button below to modify text style'
  WordWrap = True
end
object StyleButton: TButton
  Caption = '&Style...'
  OnClick = StyleButtonClick
end
end
```

FIGURE 13.8

The three forms (a main
form and two dialog
boxes) of the Dialog2
example at run-time.

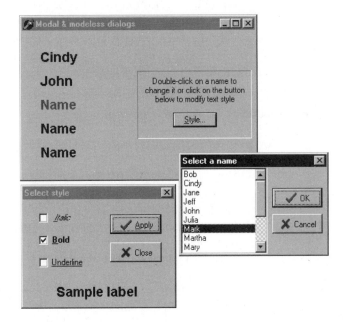

If the user clicks on a name, its color turns to red; if the user double-clicks on
it, the program displays a modal dialog box with a list of names to choose from. If
the user clicks on the Style button, a modeless dialog box appears, allowing the
user to change the font style of the main form's labels. The five labels of the main

form are connected to two methods, one for the OnClick event and the second for the OnDoubleClick event. The first method turns the last label a user has clicked on to red, resetting all the others to black. Notice that the same method is associated with all of the labels:

```
procedure TForm1.LabelClick(Sender: TObject);
begin
  {set the color of all the labels to black}
  Label1.Font.Color := clBlack;
  Label2.Font.Color := clBlack;
  Label3.Font.Color := clBlack;
  Label4.Font.Color := clBlack;
  Label5.Font.Color := clBlack;
  {set the color of the clicked label to red}
  (Sender as TLabel).Font.Color := clRed;
end;
```

The second method common to all of the labels is the handler of the OnDoubleClick event. The LabelDoubleClick method selects the Caption of the current label (indicated by the Sender parameter) in the list box of the dialog, and then shows the modal dialog box. If the user closes the dialog box by clicking on OK and an item of the list is selected, the selection is copied back to the label's caption:

```
procedure TForm1.LabelDoubleClick(Sender: TObject);
begin
  with ListDial.Listbox1 do
  begin
    {select the current name in the list box}
    ItemIndex := Items.IndexOf (Sender as TLabel).Caption);
    {show the modal dialog box, checking the return value}
    if (ListDial.ShowModal = mrOk) and (ItemIndex >= 0) then
      {copy the selected item to the label}
      (Sender as TLabel).Caption := Items [ItemIndex];
  end;
```

Notice that all the code used to customize the modal dialog box is in the LabelDoubleClick method of the main form. The form of this dialog box has no added code. Here is its textual form description:

```
object ListDial: TListDial
  BorderStyle = bsDialog
  Caption = 'Select a name'
```

```
object ListBox1: TListBox
  Align = alLeft
  Items.Strings = (
    'Bob'
    'Cindy'
    ...)
  Sorted = True
end
object BitBtn1: TBitBtn
  Kind = bkOK
end
object BitBtn2: TBitBtn
  Kind = bkCancel
end
end
```

TIP

When you write generic code in a method connected to components of the same kind, there is no need to test that the Sender is a component of that kind, with a statement like if Sender is TLabel. In fact, Sender is always a label. And if by any chance it is not, you'll get a run-time error when the as statement is executed. This means that our assumption (that the method is connected to components of the same kind) is wrong, and we'll be grateful to see the error, and correct the program.

The modeless dialog box, instead, has a lot of coding behind it. The main form simply runs it when the Style button is clicked (notice that the button caption ends with three dots to indicate that when it is pressed, the program will open a dialog box), by callings its Show method. You can see the dialog box running in Figure 13.8 above, and its textual form description below:

```
object StyleDial: TStyleDial
  BorderStyle = bsDialog
  Caption = 'Select style'
  object LabelSample: TLabel
    Alignment = taCenter
    Caption = 'Sample label'
  end
  object ApplyBitBtn: TBitBtn
    Caption = '&Apply'
    ModalResult = 1 // mrOK
    OnClick = ApplyBitBtnClick
  end
```

```
    object CloseBitBtn: TBitBtn
      Caption = 'Close'
      ModalResult = 2 // mrCancel
      OnClick = CloseBitBtnClick
    end
    object ItalicCheckBox: TCheckBox
      Caption = '&Italic'
      Font.Style = [fsItalic]
      OnClick = ItalicCheckBoxClick
    end
    object BoldCheckBox: TCheckBox
      Caption = '&Bold'
      Font.Style = [fsBold]
      OnClick = BoldCheckBoxClick
    end
    object UnderlineCheckBox: TCheckBox
      Caption = '&Underline'
      Font.Style = [fsUnderline]
      OnClick = UnderlineCheckBoxClick
    end
  end
```

Notice the names of the two buttons, Apply and Close, which usually replace the OK and Cancel buttons in a modeless dialog box. (The fastest way to obtain these buttons is to select the bkOK or bkCancel value for the Kind property, and then edit the Caption.) At times, you may see a Cancel button that works as a Close button, but the OK button in a modeless dialog box usually has no meaning at all. Instead, there might be one or more buttons that perform specific actions on the main window, such as Apply, Change Style, Replace, Delete, and so on.

If the user clicks on one of the check boxes of this modeless dialog box, the style of the sample label's text at the bottom changes accordingly. You accomplish this by adding or removing the specific flag to or from the set indicating the style, as in the following OnClick event handler:

```
procedure TStyleDial.ItalicCheckBoxClick(Sender: TObject);
begin
  if ItalicCheckBox.Checked then
    LabelSample.Font.Style :=
      LabelSample.Font.Style + [fsItalic]
  else
    LabelSample.Font.Style :=
      LabelSample.Font.Style - [fsItalic];
end;
```

When the user selects the Apply button, the program copies the style of the sample label to each of the form's labels, rather than considering the values of the check boxes:

```
procedure TStyleDial.ApplyBitBtnClick(Sender: TObject);
begin
  Form1.Label1.Font.Style := LabelSample.Font.Style;
  Form1.Label2.Font.Style := LabelSample.Font.Style;
  ...
```

As an alternative, instead of referring to each label directly you can look for it by calling the FindComponent method of the form, pass the label name as a parameter, and then cast the result to the TLabel type. The advantage of this approach is that we can create the names of the various labels with a for loop:

```
procedure TStyleDial.ApplyBitBtnClick(Sender: TObject);
var
  I: Integer;
begin
  for I := 1 to 5 do
    (Form1.FindComponent ('Label' + IntToStr (I)) as TLabel).
      Font.Style := LabelSample.Font.Style;
end;
```

TIP

The ApplyBitBtnClick method could also be written by scanning the Controls array in a loop, as I've already done in other examples. I decided to use the FindControl method, instead, to show you a new technique.

This second version of the code is certainly slower, because it has more operations to do, but you won't notice the difference, because it is very fast anyway. Of course, this second approach is also more flexible: In case you add a new label you only need to fix the higher limit of the for loop, provided all the labels have consecutive numbers. Notice that when the user clicks on the Apply button, the dialog box does not close. Only the Close button has this effect. Consider also that this dialog box needs no initialization code because the form is not destroyed, and its components maintain their status each time the dialog box is displayed.

Using Predefined Dialog Boxes

Besides building your own dialog boxes, Delphi allows you to use some default dialog boxes of different kinds. Some are predefined by Windows, others are simple dialog boxes (such as message boxes) displayed by a Delphi routine. Delphi also includes template forms and form Wizards you can use to create dialog boxes, as discussed in Chapter 3.

Windows Common Dialogs

The Delphi Components palette contains a page of dialog box components. Each of these dialog boxes—known as *Windows common dialogs*—is defined in the library COMMDLG.DLL, which first appeared in Windows 3.1. I have already used some of these dialog boxes in several examples in the previous chapters, so you are probably already familiar with them. Basically, you need to put the corresponding component on a form, set some of its properties, run the dialog box (with the Execute method), and retrieve the properties that have been set while running it.

The Open Dialog Component   In this section we will build a kind of test program, CommDlg, to highlight some of the features of the common dialog boxes. In fact, by setting some of the properties and options, you can obtain very different versions of the same dialog box, altering its behavior and its user interface more than you might expect. For example, the OpenDialog component can be customized by setting different filters, by checking whether the extension of the selected file matches the default extension (using the ofExtensionDifferent flag of the Options property), and by allowing multiple selections.

Here is the code of the two methods used to create a version of the dialog that checks for a specific extension and a version for selecting multiple files (shown in Figure 13.9):

```
procedure TCommDlgForm.TextFiles1Click(Sender: TObject);
begin
  with OpenDialog1 do
  begin
    Filter := 'Text File (*.txt)|*.txt';
    DefaultExt := 'txt';
    Filename := '';
    Options := [ofHideReadOnly, ofFileMustExist,
```

FIGURE 13.9

The *ofAllowMultiSelect* option of the OpenDialog component allows a user to select multiple files, as shown by the CommDlg example.

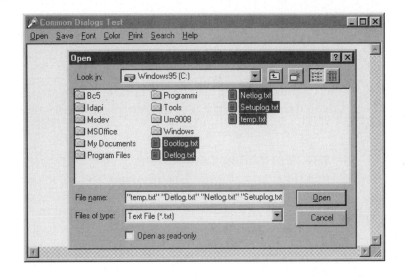

```
      ofPathMustExist];
  if Execute then
    if ofExtensionDifferent in Options then
      MessageDlg (
        'Not a file with the .TXT extension',
        mtError, [mbOK], 0)
    else
      Memo1.Lines.LoadFromFile (FileName);
  end;
end;

procedure TCommDlgForm.MultipleSelection1Click(Sender: TObject);
var
  I: Integer;
begin
  with OpenDialog1 do
  begin
    Filter :=
      'Text File (*.txt)|*.txt|Any File (*.*)|*.*';
    Filename := '';
    Options := [ofAllowMultiSelect,
      ofPathMustExist, ofCreatePrompt];
    if Execute then
      for I := 0 to Files.Count - 1 do
        if MessageDlg (
```

```
            'Open file ' + Files.Strings [I] + '?',
            mtConfirmation, [mbYes, mbNo], 0) = idYes then
        Memo1.Lines.LoadFromFile (Files.Strings [I]);
    end;
  end;
```

Of course, having a single memo as a viewer, at the end of the last operation you'll see only the last file you've opened. The SaveDialog component is used in similar ways.

The Font Dialog Component   The FontDialog component can be shown in four different variations. The first menu item of the Font pull-down activates only TrueType fonts and shows the portion of the dialog related to the special effects. The second menu item allows any font and disables the effects (see Figure 13.10). A third version disables the initial setting of the styles and the size selections.

What changes in the code used to show these three different versions is the value given to the Options property before executing the dialog box. Here are the three assignments:

```
Options := [fdEffects, fdTrueTypeOnly, fdForceFontExist];
Options := [fdForceFontExist];
Options := [fdEffects, fdNoOEMFonts, fdNoStyleSel,
  fdNoSizeSel, fdForceFontExist];
```

The last version of the Font selection common dialog box is more interesting. In this version I activate the Apply button of the dialog box, simply by providing an event handler for its OnApply event and using the fdApplyButton option. At the end of the method we have to remove this event handler (by setting it to nil) to let the program use the same dialog component again without this effect. A Font dialog box with an Apply button (see Figure 13.11) behaves almost like a modeless dialog box (but isn't one):

```
procedure TCommDlgForm.Apply1Click(Sender: TObject);
begin
  with FontDialog1 do
  begin
    OnApply := FontDialogApply;
    Options := [fdEffects, fdForceFontExist, fdApplyButton];
    Execute;
    OnApply := nil;
  end;
end;
```

FIGURE 13.10

A partially disabled Font common dialog (without the effects portion), one of the versions of this dialog box shown by the CommDlg example.

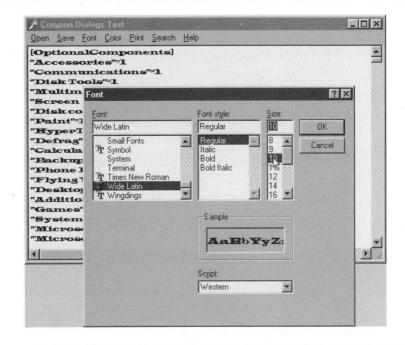

FIGURE 13.11

The Font selection dialog box with an Apply button.

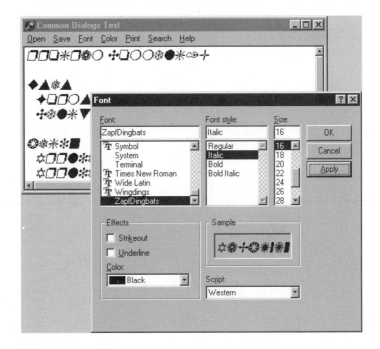

When the user presses the Apply button, the associated event handler is executed. This simply copies the current Font of the dialog box to the same property of the Memo1 component. Keep in mind that the button is part of the dialog box, but its event handler is written in the program's main form. This is really useful, as it lets us change the behavior of the dialog box without having to customize the component.

The Color Dialog Component   The ColorDialog component is used with different options, to show the dialog fully open at first or to prevent it from opening fully. These settings are the cdFullOpen or cdPreventFullOpen values of the Options property.

The Find Dialog and Replace Dialog Components   The Find and Replace dialog boxes are truly modeless dialogs. I've implemented only a limited version of the Find and Replace methods. These methods are connected to the buttons of the two dialog boxes, as in the case of the Apply button in the Font dialog box (see Figure 13.12). The FindDialog1Find method looks for a match (using the Pos system function) in the text of the memo. To be more precise, it searches the text of the memo that follows the current selection:

```
procedure TCommDlgForm.FindDialog1Find(Sender: TObject);
var
  FoundPos, InitPos: Integer;
begin
  {search in the text after the current selection}
  InitPos := Memo1.SelStart + Memo1.SelLength;
  FoundPos := Pos (FindDialog1.FindText,
    Copy (Memo1.Text, InitPos + 1,
      Length (Memo1.Text) - InitPos));
  if FoundPos > 0 then
  begin
    {activate the component, and select the text}
    Memo1.SetFocus;
    Memo1.SelStart := InitPos + FoundPos - 1;
    Memo1.SelLength := Length (FindDialog1.FindText);
  end
  else
  begin
    MessageDlg ('Text not found',
      mtInformation, [mbOK], 0);
  end;
end;
```

TIP

The code above adds or subtracts 1 from position values, because the Pos function considers 1 as the first character of the string, while the SelStart property is a zero-based position. By the way, to write similar code with 16-bit Delphi, you had to scan each line of the memo, because the Pos function worked only on Pascal strings of up to 255 characters. In 32-bit Delphi, we can simply treat the full text of the memo as a single long Pascal string.

FIGURE 13.12

The standard Find dialog box, partially implemented in the CommDlg example.

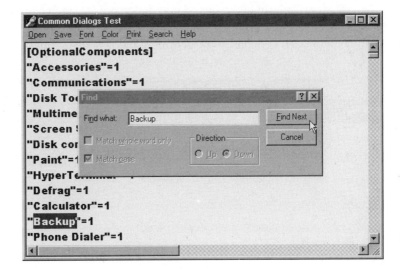

The Find operation for the Replace dialog box is so similar that I can simply call the previous method after an assignment:

```
procedure TCommDlgForm.ReplaceDialog1Find(Sender: TObject);
begin
  FindDialog1.FindText := ReplaceDialog1.FindText;
  FindDialog1Find (ReplaceDialog1);
end;
```

The best solution would probably have been to write a single Find method to be called to implement the code of the Replace routine, as well. Instead I've written a separate method for the Replace button, with just one new line (as indicated in the code fragment below:

```
if FoundPos > 0 then
begin
  ...
  Memo1.SelText := ReplaceDialog1.ReplaceText;
end
```

The other dialog boxes are simply executed, after setting a few options (if any). You can further customize the dialog boxes, and eventually extend this example, by choosing between a normal and 3D effect, asking users to confirm their choices (particularly in the file-related dialog boxes), and so on. I suggest you explore this subject, first by studying the details of the example and then by adding further customized versions of the common dialog boxes.

NEW

There are two more components on the Dialogs page of the Component Palette of Delphi 3, the OpenPictureDialog and the SavePictureDialog components. These components are variations of the OpenDialog and SaveDialog components, specifically aimed at opening and saving graphical files. The new dialog boxes, in fact, show a preview of the graphical files while you select them.

A Parade of Message Boxes

The Delphi message boxes and input boxes are another set of predefined dialog boxes. There are basically six Delphi procedures and functions you can use to display simple dialog boxes:

- The MessageDlg function shows a customizable message box, with one or more buttons and usually a bitmap. We have used this function quite often in previous examples.

- The MessageDlgPos function is similar to the MessageDlg function. The difference is that the message box is displayed in a given position, not in the center of the screen.

- The ShowMessage procedure displays a simpler message box, with the application name as the caption, and just an OK button. The ShowMessageFmt procedure is a variation of ShowMessage, which has the same parameters of the Format function. It corresponds to calling Format inside a call to ShowMessage.

- The ShowMessagePos procedure does the same, but you also indicate the position of the message box.

- The InputBox function asks the user to input a string. You provide the caption, the query, and a default string.

- The InputQuery function asks the user to input a string, too. The only difference between this and the InputBox function is in the syntax. The InputQuery function has a Boolean return value that indicates whether the user has clicked on OK or Cancel.

The first two message boxes are more complex and have a higher number of parameters, including a set of buttons, the type of message box, a help context code (useful if there is a Help button), and eventually the position. The MessageDlg and MessageDlgPos functions can display different types of message boxes, depending on the value of the second parameter, of type TMsgDlgType:

```
type
  TMsgDlgType = (mtWarning, mtError, mtInformation,
    mtConfirmation, mtCustom);
```

Each type of message box has its own glyph (a yellow exclamation point, a red stop sign, a blue 'i', a green question mark, or no bitmap, respectively). These message boxes can also have one or more buttons, as indicated by the following set type:

```
type
  TMsgDlgBtn = (mbYes, mbNo, mbOK, mbCancel,
    mbAbort, mbRetry, mbIgnore, mbAll, mbHelp);
  TMsgDlgButtons = set of TMsgDlgBtn;
```

To demonstrate the various message box options available in Delphi, I've written another sample program, with a similar approach to the preceding CommDlg example. In this example, MBParade, you have a high number of choices (radio buttons, check boxes, edit boxes, and spin edit controls) to set before you press one of the buttons that displays a message box. You can get a better idea of the program by looking at its form in Figure 13.13.

FIGURE 13.13

The main form of the
MBParade example, with
a sample message box.

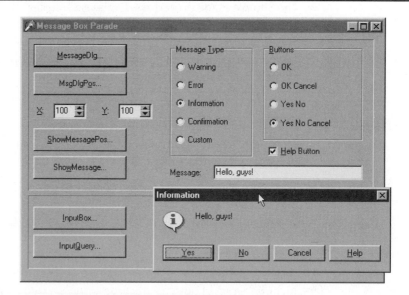

For a `MessageDlg` box, you can choose the style of the message box, its buttons
(including the Help button), and the message. The two positional functions use
the values of the two spin edit controls. What's interesting is that if you choose a
custom type and include only the OK button, the `MessageDlg` box degrades to a
`ShowMessage` box.

The basic structure of the program is the following. The form has two fields
storing the current value of some of the available options:

```
private
  MsgDlgType: TMsgDlgType;
  MsgButtons: TMsgDlgButtons;
```

Whenever the user selects one of the radio buttons, the corresponding flag is set, as
in the two following methods associated with the radio buttons of the two groups:

```
procedure TForm1.RadioWarningClick(Sender: TObject);
begin
  MsgDlgType := mtWarning;
end;


procedure TForm1.RadioOKCancelClick(Sender: TObject);
begin
```

```
    MsgButtons := mbOkCancel;
  end;
```

These fields are used when you press one of the buttons to show the message boxes. Here is the method that calls the `MessageDlgPos` function:

```
procedure TForm1.ButtonMsgDlgPosClick(Sender: TObject);
begin
  if CheckHelp.Checked then
    Include (MsgButtons, mbHelp);
  MessageDlgPos (Edit1.Text, MsgDlgType, MsgButtons,
    0, SpinX.Value, SpinY.Value);
end;
```

The input boxes use only the values in the three edit boxes in the second half of the form. Aside from the fact that the code used to execute them is different, their output is exactly the same (see Figure 13.14). Here are the two calls:

```
procedure TForm1.ButtonInputBoxClick(Sender: TObject);
begin
  EditValue.Text := InputBox (EditCaption.Text,
    EditPrompt.Text, EditValue.Text);
end;
```

```
procedure TForm1.ButtonInputQueryClick(Sender: TObject);
var
  Text: String;
begin
  Text := EditValue.Text;
  if InputQuery (EditCaption.Text,
      EditPrompt.Text, Text) then
    EditValue.Text := Text;
end;
```

Having said this, I think you can easily understand the rest of the source code just by reviewing it. What's more important, however, is to run it, so that you can see a quick overview of the effect of the parameters of the various functions.

TIP   Although Delphi message boxes are graphically superior to the default Windows message boxes, you can always choose between the two. To display a message box, you can use the Windows API `MessageBox` function, which has parameters similar to the Delphi `MessageDlg` function.

FIGURE 13.14

The main form of the
MBParade example, with
an InputQuery message
box open.

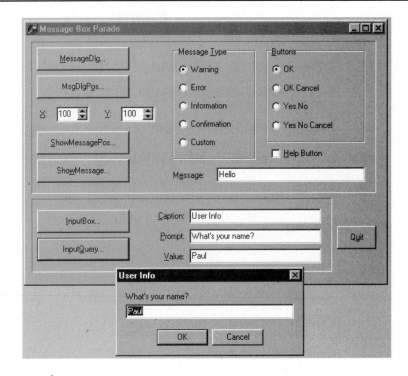

Extensible Dialog Boxes

Some dialog boxes display a number of components to the user. At times, you can divide them into logical pages, which Delphi supports through the TabControl and Notebook components (discussed in Chapter 14). At other times, some of the dialog box controls can be temporarily hidden to help first-time users of an application. There are basically two approaches for displaying advanced information only when the user asks for it: build a secondary dialog box, displayed when the user presses a button with an Advanced label on it, or increase the size of the dialog box to host new controls when the user presses a More button.

The second approach is certainly more interesting but requires a little more care. I'll use it to extend the first example on dialog boxes (Dialog1) and build the

More example. First of all, we need to extend the dialog box with new controls: a More button (see Figure 13.15) and a whole new portion of the form with two new check boxes labeled *italic* and *bold* and used to change the font style of the main form's text. Once you have added the new controls, you need to resize the dialog box so that the new elements are outside its visible surface:

```
object ConfigureDialog: TConfigureDialog
  BorderStyle = bsDialog
  Caption = 'Choose configuration'
  ClientHeight = 106 // notice this value !!!
  OnActivate = FormActivate
  OnCreate = FormCreate
  object Label1: TLabel
    Top = 112 // out of range !!!
    AutoSize = False
    Caption = 'Here comes the rest of the dialog
      box, with some new controls...'
  end
  object BitBtn1: TBitBtn
    Kind = bkOK
  end
  object BitBtn2: TBitBtn
    Kind = bkCancel
  end
  object CheckBox1: TCheckBox...
  object CheckBox2: TCheckBox...
  object BitBtn3: TBitBtn
    Caption = '&More >>'
    OnClick = BitBtn3Click
  end
  object ItalicCheckBox: TCheckBox
    Top = 152 // out of range !!!
    Caption = '&Italic'
    Enabled = False
  end
  object BoldCheckBox: TCheckBox
    Top = 152  // out of range !!!
    Caption = '&Bold'
    Enabled = False
  end
end
```

FIGURE 13.15

The dialog box of the
More example at design-
time. Some of the com-
ponents are invisible
because they are
beyond the border.

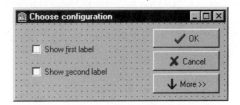

The components outside the visible area (marked above with comments) should
be disabled, otherwise the user might press the Tab key and move onto them
even if they are not visible. As an alternative you might disable their TabStop
property. These properties (Enabled or TabStop) are then set to True when the
form is enlarged.

Now we need to add some code to the application to handle the two new check
boxes and to resize the form when a user clicks on the More button. To prepare
the resize effect, we need a couple of fields in the form (named OldHeight and
NewHeight) to store the two different heights of the client area of the form. We can
set up their values when the form is first created:

```
procedure TConfigureDialog.FormCreate(Sender: TObject);
begin
  OldHeight := ClientHeight;
  NewHeight := ItalicCheckBox.Top +
    ItalicCheckBox.Height + BitBtn1.Top;
end;
```

I determined the new height by adding to the bottom of the check box (its Top
plus its Height property) the margin above the topmost bitmap button. The real
dialog box resizing takes place when the More button is pressed. Here is a first
version:

```
procedure TConfigureDialog.BitBtn3Click(Sender: TObject);
begin
  BitBtn3.Enabled := False;
  BoldCheckBox.Enabled := True;
  ItalicCheckBox.Enabled := True;
  ClientHeight := NewHeight;
end;
```

The result it produces is shown in Figure 13.16. If you want a more spectacular effect, you might increase the height a pixel at a time instead of setting the final value at once. If you write a `for` loop increasing the client height and repainting the form each time, the new controls will appear with a nice effect, only a little slower. The last line of the `BitBtn3Click` method above becomes

```
for I := ClientHeight to NewHeight do
begin
  ClientHeight := I;
  Update;
end;
```

FIGURE 13.16

The dialog box of the More example, once it has been resized.

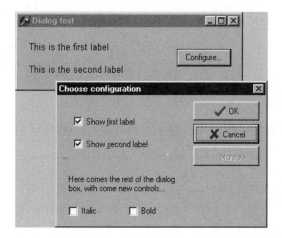

Each time the dialog box is activated (`OnFormActivate` event), we reset its height, disable the hidden components (to avoid letting the user Tab to them), and enable the More button:

```
procedure TConfigureDialog.FormActivate(Sender: TObject);
begin
  ClientHeight := OldHeight;
  BitBtn3.Enabled := True;
  BoldCheckBox.Enabled := False;
  ItalicCheckBox.Enabled := False;
end;
```

This code is required so that each time the dialog box is displayed it starts in the default *small* configuration.

Including About Boxes

Windows applications usually have an About box, where you can display information such as the version of the product, a copyright notice, and so on. The simplest way to build an About box is to use the `MessageDlg` function. With this method you can show only a limited amount of text and no special graphics.

Therefore, the usual method for creating an About box is to use a simple dialog box, such as the one generated with one of the Delphi default templates. I say *simple* because when you have designed the form with a logo and so on, you seldom need much code. At most, some code might be required to display system information, such as the version of Windows or the amount of free memory, or some user information, such as the registered user name.

Using the System About Box

A strange alternative is to use the standard dialog box of many Windows applications. If you select the About box of the Explorer or any application that comes with Windows, you can see that they all use the same dialog box. This is a system dialog box that was already present in Windows 3.1, although it was not documented. In the Win32 API and in 32-bit Delphi the use of this dialog box is partially documented: you can use the `ShellAbout` function of the Shell-Api unit to display the system dialog box and customize it a little bit. This function is called in the ShAbout example when the user presses the only button of the main form:

```
procedure TForm1.Button1Click(Sender: TObject);
begin
  ShellAbout (Handle,
    'About ShellAbout Test#makes funny programs like',
    'Portions Copyright 1996 Marco Cantù',
    Application.Icon.Handle);
end;
```

What is not documented in the Windows API help file is that the first string parameter requires two parts separated by the # character, as you can see in the code above. The first part of this parameter is used as the title of the system About box, while the second part is displayed between standard (and fixed) lines of text. The effect is quite funny, as you can see in Figure 13.17. I do not think this is really useful, because the text of the dialog box will be plagued by the presence of the Microsoft name, something you won't like to have in your own applications.

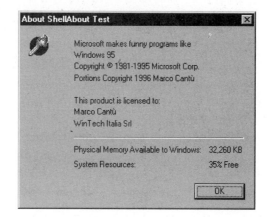

Building a Custom Hidden Screen

It looks like we'll just have to build our own About box. While we do that, we can add a hidden credit screen, such as Delphi and many other applications have. You might want to add a hidden credit screen for a number of reasons. If you work in a big company, this might be your way to prove that you worked on that project, which might help you in finding a new job (if the project was successful). At times, a hidden About box can be fun to see, and they sometimes also provide a good occasion for making jokes about your competitors. A more serious reason is that a hidden credit screen can be used to demonstrate who wrote the program, as a sort of legal copyright.

I've written a simple example, showing how you might implement a hidden screen. As you can see in Figure 13.18, the dialog box has a Panel component containing two Label components. The panel might contain any number of components to display graphics and text. Some of the strings might even be computed at run-time. The only added feature required to show the hidden credits is a PaintBox component covering part of the form.

FIGURE 13.18

The About box of the
Credits example at
design-time.

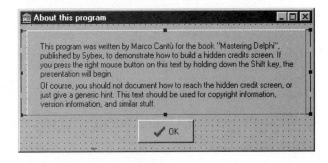

When the user makes a specific complex action (in this case, right-clicking on
the upper label while holding down the Shift key), the panel is hidden and something appears on the screen. A simple solution is to have some text painted on the
surface of the form—that is, on its canvas:

```
procedure TAboutBox.Label1MouseDown(Sender: TObject;
  Button: TMouseButton;
  Shift: TShiftState; X, Y: Integer);
begin
  if (Button = mbRight) and (ssShift in Shift) then
  begin
    Panel1.Visible := False;
    PaintBox1.Canvas.Font.Name := 'Arial';
    PaintBox1.Canvas.Font.Size := 20;
    PaintBox1.Canvas.TextOut (40, 50, 'Author: Marco Cantù');
    PaintBox1.Canvas.TextOut (40, 100, 'Version 1.0');
  end;
end;
```

To build a more spectacular hidden screen, we might scroll some text in a for loop,
as I've done in the final version of the Credits example. Notice that the position of
the lines depend on the height of the text, retrieved by calling the TextHeight
method of the Canvas of the PaintBox component:

```
Panel1.Visible := False;
LineH := PaintBox1.Canvas.TextHeight ('0');
    for I := 0 to 100 + LineH * 10 do
      with PaintBox1.Canvas do
      begin
        // empty lines are used to delete descendants
        TextOut (40, 100 - I, 'CREDITS example from:');
```

```
TextOut (40, 100 + LineH - I, '"Mastering Delphi"');
TextOut (40, 100 + LineH * 2 - I, '                          ');
...
// wait 5 milliseconds
Delay (0, 5);
  end;
Panel1.Visible := True;
```

You can see the effect of this code in Figure 13.19. To avoid a scrolling rate that's too fast, particularly on faster computers, inside the for loop I've added a call to a Delay procedure, which requires as parameters the seconds and milliseconds you want to wait for. This Delay procedure simply checks the current time, then waits in a while loop until the required seconds and milliseconds have elapsed:

```
procedure Delay (Seconds, MilliSec: Word);
var
  TimeOut: TDateTime;
begin
  TimeOut := Now + EncodeTime (0,
    Seconds div 60, Seconds mod 60, MilliSec);
  // wait until he TimeOut time
  while Now < TimeOut do
    Application.ProcessMessages;
end;
```

Inside the loop I call the ProcessMessages method of the Application global object to let Windows generate and dispatch the needed paint messages. This Delay procedure is a fairly generic one, so you can use it in other examples quite easily.

FIGURE 13.19

The hidden credits screen of the About box of the Credits example.

> **TIP**
>
> Consider another aspect of the preceding example. We have written some code to draw on the surface of a dialog box. Although it is not very common, dialog boxes can have graphical output and respond to mouse input just like any other form. In fact, a dialog box *is a form.*

Now that I've suggested this idea, don't spend so much time preparing astounding hidden credit screens that you neglect writing the rest of the code for your applications. Although you can save some time by programming with Delphi, you can probably think of better ways to use that time!

Building a Splash Screen

Another typical technique used in applications is to have an initial screen, displayed before the main form is shown. This makes the application seem more responsive, because you show something to the user while the program is loading, but it also makes a nice visual effect. Sometimes, this same window is displayed as the application's About box.

For an example in which a splash screen is particularly useful, I've built a program displaying a list box filled with prime numbers. The prime numbers are computed on program startup, so that they are displayed as soon as the form becomes visible:

```
procedure TForm1.FormCreate(Sender: TObject);
var
  I: Integer;
begin
  for I := 1 to 10000 do
    if IsPrime (I) then
      ListBox1.Items.Add (IntToStr (I));
end;
```

This method calls an `IsPrime` function I've added to the program. This is not a very efficient function, but I actually need it to be slow to show my point:

```
function IsPrime (N: Integer): Boolean;
var
  Test: Integer;
begin
  IsPrime := True;
  for Test := 2 to N - 1 do
    if (N mod Test) = 0 then
```

```
  begin
    IsPrime := False;
    break; {jump out of the for loop}
  end;
end;
```

The numbers are added to a list box that covers the full client area of the form and allows multiple columns to be displayed, as you can see in Figure 13.20. This is the summary of the form's textual description:

```
object Form1: TForm1
  Caption = 'Prime Numbers'
  Menu = MainMenu1
  OnCreate = FormCreate
  object ListBox1: TListBox
    Align = alClient
    Columns = 5
  end
  object MainMenu1: TMainMenu
    object File1: TMenuItem...
      object Exit1: TMenuItem...
    object Help1: TMenuItem...
      object About1: TMenuItem...
  end
end
```

FIGURE 13.20

The main form of the Splash example, with the About box activated from the menu.

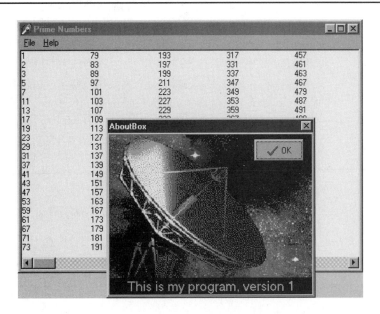

As you can see by running the Splash0 example, the problem with this program is that the initial operation, which takes place in the FormCreate method, takes a lot of time. When you start the program it takes several seconds (on a standard Pentium machine) to display the main form. If your computer is very fast or very slow you can change the higher limit of the for loop of the FormCreate method, to make the program faster or slower.

This program has a simple dialog box with an image component, a simple caption, and a bitmap button, all placed inside a panel taking up the whole surface of the About box. This form is displayed when you select the Help ➤ About menu item.

Actually, the code of the OnClick event handler for this About box is quite interesting. The dialog box is not created at startup (I've disabled it in the Forms page of the Project Options dialog box), but only the first time it is requested. After it has been displayed, however, the code doesn't destroy it, since it might be needed later on. How do I determine whether the form has to be created? Simply by calling the Assigned method, which tests whether the object is nil:

```
procedure TForm1.About1Click(Sender: TObject);
begin
  if not Assigned (AboutBox) then
    AboutBox := TAboutBox.Create (Application);
  AboutBox.ShowModal;
end;
```

This is a general technique for delaying the creation of a form until it is required, without destroying it each time it is used. But what we really want is to display this About box while the program starts. You can see this effect by running the Splash1 or the Splash2 examples, which show a splash screen using two different techniques.

First of all I've added a method to the TAboutBox class. This method, called MakeSplash, changes some properties of the form to make it suitable for a splash form. Basically it removes the border and caption, hides the OK button, makes the border of the panel thick (to replace the border of the form), and then shows the form, repainting it immediately (see Figure 13.21 for the effect):

```
procedure TAboutBox.MakeSplash;
begin
  BorderStyle := bsNone;
  BitBtn1.Visible := False;
  Panel1.BorderWidth := 3;
  Show;
  Update;
end;
```

FIGURE 13.21

The form of the splash screen of the Splash1 example is slightly different than the original About box (shown in Figure 13.20).

This is my program, version 1

This method is called after creating the form in the project file of the Splash1 example. This code is executed before creating the other forms (in this case only the main form), and the splash screen is then removed before running the application. These operations take place within a `try-finally` block. Here is the complete source code of the project file for the Splash2 example:

```
program Splash;

uses
  Forms,
  MainSpF in 'MainSpF.pas' {Form1},
  AboutF in 'AboutF.pas' {AboutBox};

{$R *.RES}

var
  SplashAbout: TAboutBox;

begin
  Application.Initialize;
  // create and show the splash form
  SplashAbout := TAboutBox.Create (Application);
  try
    SplashAbout.MakeSplash;
    // standard code...
    Application.CreateForm(TForm1, Form1);
    // get rid of the splash form
    SplashAbout.Close;
```

```
    finally
      SplashAbout.Free;
    end;
    Application.Run;
  end.
```

This approach makes sense only if the startup code is slow, and your application's main form takes a while to create, to execute its startup code (as in this case), or to open database tables.

An alternative approach is to keep the splash form on the screen a little longer, and use a timer to get rid of it after a while. I've implemented this second technique in the Splash2 example. This example also uses a different approach for creating the splash form: Instead of creating it in the project source code, it is created at the very beginning of the FormCreate method of the main form:

```
procedure TForm1.FormCreate(Sender: TObject);
var
  I: Integer;
  SplashAbout: TAboutBox;
begin
  // create and show the splash form
  SplashAbout := TAboutBox.Create (Application);
  SplashAbout.MakeSplash;
  // standard code...
  for I := 1 to 10000 do
    if IsPrime (I) then
      ListBox1.Items.Add (IntToStr (I));
  // get rid of the splash form, after a while
  SplashAbout.Timer1.Enabled := True;
end;
```

The timer is enabled just before terminating the method. After its interval has elapsed (in the example, 3 seconds) the OnTimer event is activated, and the splash form handles it by closing and destroying itself:

```
procedure TAboutBox.Timer1Timer(Sender: TObject);
begin
  Close;
  Free;
end;
```

There is one more thing to fix. The Main form will be displayed later and in front of the splash form, unless you make this a topmost form. For this reason I've added one line to the MakeSplash method of the about box of the Splash2 example:

```
FormStyle := fsStayOnTop;
```

Visual Form Inheritance

One of the most important innovations introduced by Delphi 2 was visual form inheritance. In short, you can simply inherit a form from an existing one, adding new components or altering the properties of the existing ones. But what is the real advantage of visual form inheritance?

Well, this mostly depends on the kind of application you are building. If it has a number of forms, some of which are very similar to each other or simply include common elements, then you can place the common components and the common event handlers in the base form and add the specific behavior and components to the subclasses. For example, you can prepare a standard parent form with a toolbar, a logo, default sizing and closing code, and the handlers of some Windows messages, and use it as the parent class for each of the forms of an application.

You can also use visual form inheritance to customize an application for different clients, without duplicating any source code or form definition code: just inherit the specific versions for a client from the standard forms. The same approach can be used to localize an application in a different language: simply inherit the local version of each form, translating the captions of the components. You can also try placing some data access components in a base form, but it is often better to *use* a secondary form, or a Data Module, with the database components, than to inherit from it.

Remember that the main advantage of visual inheritance is that you can later change the original form and automatically update all the derived forms. This is a well-known advantage of inheritance in object-oriented programming languages. But there is a side effect: polymorphism. You can add a virtual method in a base form and override it in a subclassed form. Then you can refer to both forms and call this method for each of them.

WARNING Although Visual Form Inheritance is a very powerful technique, it has some pitfalls. A couple of suggestions might help you alleviate the problems: first, never change the name of a component , either in the base or the derived form; second, always open the parent form of the form you're visually editing. The problems mainly relate to desynchronization between components of a base and a derived form.

Inheriting from a Base Form

The rules governing visual form inheritance are quite simple, once you have a clear idea of what inheritance is. Basically, a subclass form has the same components as the parent form, plus some new components, and you can change the properties of the inherited components. If you change a property of a component in the inherited form, any modification in the parent form will have no effect. However, you can re-synchronize the two values by using the Revert to Inherited local menu command of the Object Inspector. The same thing is accomplished by setting the two properties to the same value and recompiling the code. An alternative technique is to open the textual description of the inherited form and remove the line that changes the value of the property (we will look at the structure of this file in a second). Besides inheriting components, the new form inherits all the methods of the base form, including the event handlers. You can add new handlers in the inherited form, and also override existing handlers.

To describe how visual form inheritance works, I've built a very simple example, called VFI. I'll describe step-by-step how to build it. First, start a new project, and add four buttons to its main form. Then select File ➤ New and choose the page with the name of the project in the New Items dialog box (see Figure 13.22). Here you can choose the form from which you want to inherit. The new form has the same four buttons. Here is the initial textual description of the new form:

```
inherited Form2: TForm2
  Caption = 'Form2'
end
```

And here is its initial class declaration, where you can see that the base class is not the usual TForm, but the actual base class form:

```
type
  TForm2 = class(TForm1)
  private
    { Private declarations }
  public
    { Public declarations }
  end;
```

FIGURE 13.22

The New Items dialog box allows you to create an inherited form.

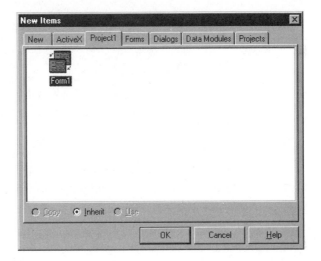

Notice the presence of the inherited keyword, and the fact that the form indeed has some components, although they are defined in the base class form. If you move the form and add the caption of one of the buttons, the textual description will change accordingly:

```
inherited Form2: TForm2
  Left = 313
  Top = 202
  Caption = 'Form2'
  inherited Button2: TButton
    Caption = 'Beep...'
  end
end
```

Only the properties with a different value are listed (and by removing these properties from the textual description of the inherited form, you can reset them to the value of the base form, as I mentioned before). I've actually changed the captions of most buttons, as you can see in Figure 13.23.

FIGURE 13.23

The two forms of the VFI example at run-time.

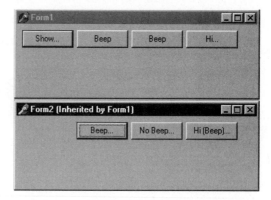

Each of the buttons of the first form has an OnClick handler, with simple code. The first button shows the inherited form, calling its Show method; the second and the third buttons call the Beep procedure; and the last button displays a simple message calling ShowMessage ('Hi').

What happens in the inherited form? The first thing I'd like to do is to remove the first button, since the secondary form is already visible. However, you cannot delete a component from an inherited form. An alternative solution is to leave the component there, but set its Visible property to False. The button will still be there, but not visible (as you can guess from Figure 13.23). The other three buttons will be visible, but with different handlers. This is simple to accomplish. If you select the OnClick event of a button in the inherited form (by double-clicking on it), you'll get an empty method slightly different from the default one:

```
procedure TForm2.Button2Click(Sender: TObject);
begin
  inherited;
end;
```

The inherited keyword stands for a call to the corresponding event handler of the base form. Notice that this keyword is always added by Delphi, even if the handler is not defined in the parent class (and this is reasonable, because it might be defined later) or if the component is not present in the parent class (which doesn't seem like a great idea to me).

It is very simple to execute the code of the base form, and perform some other operations:

```
procedure TForm2.Button2Click(Sender: TObject);
begin
  inherited;
  ShowMessage ('Hi');
end;
```

This is not the only choice. An alternative approach is to write a brand-new event handler and not execute the code of the base class, as I've done for the third button of the VFI example:

```
procedure TForm2.Button3Click(Sender: TObject);
begin
  ShowMessage ('Hi');
end;
```

Still another choice includes calling a base class method after some custom code has been executed, calling it when a condition is met, or calling the handler of a different event of the base class, as I've done for the fourth button:

```
procedure TForm2.Button4Click(Sender: TObject);
begin
  inherited Button3Click (Sender);
  inherited;
end;
```

Probably, this won't be very common, but you must be aware that you can do it. Of course, you can consider each method of the base form as a method of your form, and call it freely. This example allows you to explore some features of visual form inheritance, but to see its true power you'll need to look at a complex real-world example, something I'm not going to show you. There is something else I want to show you here: *visual form polymorphism*.

Polymorphic Forms

The problem is simple. If you add an event handler to a form, and then change it in an inherited form, there is no way to refer to the two methods using a common variable of the base class, because the event handlers use static binding by default.

Confusing? Here is an example. Suppose you want to build a bitmap viewer form and a text viewer form in the same program. The two forms have similar elements, a similar toolbar, a similar menu, an OpenDialog component, and different components for viewing the actual data. So you can decide to build a base class form containing the common elements and inherit the two forms from it. You can see the three forms at design-time in Figure 13.24.

FIGURE 13.24

The base form and the two inherited forms of the PoliForm example at design-time.

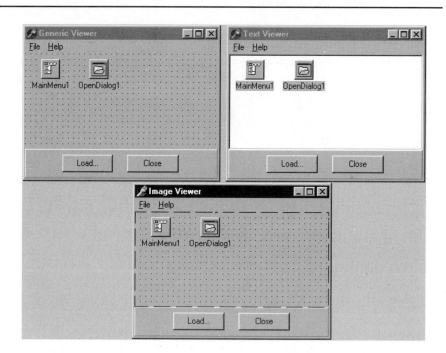

Here is the textual description of the main form:

```
object ViewerForm: TViewerForm
  Caption = 'Generic Viewer'
  Menu = MainMenu1
  object Panel1: TPanel
    Align = alBottom
    object ButtonLoad: TButton...
    object CloseButton: TButton...
  end
  object MainMenu1: TMainMenu
```

```
    object File1: TMenuItem...
      object Load1: TMenuItem...
      object N1: TMenuItem...
      object Close1: TMenuItem...
    object Help1: TMenuItem...
      object AboutPoliform1: TMenuItem...
    end
  object OpenDialog1: TOpenDialog...
end
```

The two inherited forms have only minor differences, but they feature a new component, either an image viewer (TImage) or a text viewer (TMemo):

```
inherited ImageViewerForm: TImageViewerForm
  Caption = 'Image Viewer'
  object Image1: TImage [0]
    Align = alClient
  end
  inherited OpenDialog1: TOpenDialog
    Filter = 'Bitmap file|*.bmp|Any file|*.*'
  end
end

inherited TextViewerForm: TTextViewerForm
  Caption = 'Text Viewer'
  object Memo1: TMemo [1]
    Align = alClient
  end
  inherited OpenDialog1: TOpenDialog
    Filter = 'Text files|*.txt|Any file|*.*'
  end
end
```

The main form includes some common code. The Close button and the File ➤ Close command call the Close method of the form. The Help ➤ About command shows a simple message box. The Load button of the base form has the following code:

```
procedure TViewerForm.ButtonLoadClick(Sender: TObject);
begin
  ShowMessage ('Error: File loading code missing');
end;
```

675

The File ➤ Load command, instead, calls another method:

```
procedure TViewerForm.Load1Click(Sender: TObject);
begin
  LoadFile;
end;
```

This method is defined in the TViewerForm class as:

```
public
  procedure LoadFile; virtual; abstract;
```

Because this is an abstract method, we will need to redefine it (and override it) in the inherited forms:

```
type
  TImageViewerForm = class(TViewerForm)
    Image1: TImage;
    procedure ButtonLoadClick(Sender: TObject);
  public
    procedure LoadFile; override;
  end;
```

The code of this LoadFile method simply uses the OpenDialog1 component to ask the user to select an input file, and loads it into the image component:

```
procedure TImageViewerForm.LoadFile;
begin
  if OpenDialog1.Execute then
    Image1.Picture.LoadFromFile (
      OpenDialog1.Filename);
end;
```

The other inherited class has similar code, loading the text into the memo component. The project has one more form, a main form with two buttons, used to reload the files in each of the viewer forms. The main form is the only form created by the project when it starts. The generic viewer form is never created: it is only a generic base class, containing common code and components of the two subclasses. The forms of the two subclasses are created in the OnCreate event handler of the main form:

```
procedure TMainForm.FormCreate(Sender: TObject);
var
  I: Integer;
```

```
begin
  FormList [1] := TTextViewerForm.Create (Application);
  FormList [2] := TImageViewerForm.Create (Application);
  for I := 1 to 2 do
    FormList[I].Show;
end;
```

See Figure 13.25 for the resulting forms (with text and image already loaded in the viewers). FormList is a polymorphic array of forms, declared in the TMainForm class as

```
private
  FormList: array [1..2] of TViewerForm;
```

FIGURE 13.25

The PoliForm example at run-time.

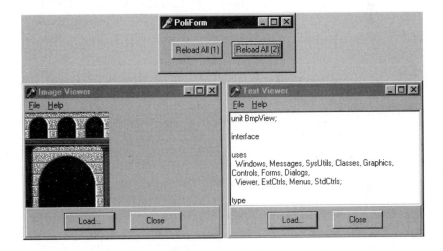

Note that to make this declaration in the class, you need to add the Viewer unit (but not the specific forms) in the uses clause of the interface portion of the main form. The array of forms is used to load a new file in each viewer form when one of the two buttons is pressed. The two handlers of the two buttons' OnClick events use different approaches:

```
procedure TMainForm.ReloadButton1Click(Sender: TObject);
var
  I: Integer;
begin
```

```
    for I := 1 to 2 do
        FormList.ButtonLoadClick (self);
end;

procedure TMainForm.ReloadButton2Click(Sender: TObject);
var
  I: Integer;
begin
  for I := 1 to 2 do
    FormList.LoadFile;
end;
```

The second button simply calls a virtual method, and it will work without any problem. The first button calls an event handler and will always reach the generic TFormView class (displaying the error message of its ButtonLoadClick method). This happens because the method is static, not virtual.

Is there a way to make this approach work? Sure: Declare the ButtonLoadClick method of the TFormView class as virtual, and declare it as overridden in each of the inherited form classes, as we do for any other virtual method:

```
type
  TViewerForm = class(TForm)
    // components and plain methods...
    procedure ButtonLoadClick(Sender: TObject); virtual;
  public
    procedure LoadFile; virtual; abstract;
  end;
...
type
  TImageViewerForm = class(TViewerForm)
    Image1: TImage;
    procedure ButtonLoadClick(Sender: TObject); override;
  public
    procedure LoadFile; override;
  end;
```

Simple, isn't it? This trick really works, although it is never mentioned in Borland documentation. This ability to use virtual event handlers is what I actually mean by visual form polymorphism.

What's Next

In this chapter, we have explored many ways to build applications that have more than one form. We have seen how you can create a secondary modal or modeless form, or a modal dialog box. The most important point to remember is that in Delphi, dialog boxes are just plain forms with a special border and a couple of other attributes—nothing more.

Besides the basic examples, we have delved into some advanced topics, such as dynamically building a number of forms, creating extensible dialog boxes, and visual form inheritance. We've explored the common dialogs and the Delphi message boxes, and built special About boxes, with hidden credits or used as a splash screen.

Another enhancement, the use of the increasingly widespread notebook metaphor, will be one of the topics of the next chapter. The Options dialog boxes of most modern Windows applications follow the notebook style. Another occasion for discussing programs with multiple windows will be Chapter 15, devoted to MDI applications. In the database chapters, we'll also discuss applications with multiple synchronized views of the same table.

Scrolling, Multipage Forms, and Splitting

- Scroll bar handling

- Scrolling and form coordinates

- The Windows 95 PageControl and TabControl components

- Borland-style notebooks with tabs

- Tabs without a notebook

- A notebook without tabs

- Different approaches to splitting forms

- The Splitter component

In the beginning, the user interface of Windows applications was very simple. Over the years, the most widespread applications and the system itself introduced new features and elements to improve it. For example, to improve ease of use, toolbars and status bars were added. Another leading idea has been to mimic common metaphors, based on tools we use every day; one such metaphor is a notebook with tabs to move among various pages or areas. Delphi has a number of these elements. Tabs are used in Options dialog boxes, in the editor, in the Object Inspector, and in the Component Palette.

Many applications have similar approaches in their dialog boxes. Some applications, including leading spreadsheets, even use the notebook metaphor for their main windows. The use of notebooks and tabs has become so important that Microsoft has added direct system support for them in Windows 95.

But before delving into notebooks and multipage forms, we will discuss a simpler but effective technique to use when you need to cram several components into a form: scrolling.

When Forms Are Too Big

When you build a simple application, a single form might hold all of the components you need. As the application grows, you may need to squeeze in the components, increase the size of the form, or add new forms. If you reduce the space occupied by the components, you might add some capability to resize them at runtime, eventually splitting the form into different areas. If you choose to increase the size of the form, you might use scroll bars to let the user move around in a form that is bigger than the screen.

Finally, if you choose to add a new form, there are basically three approaches:

- Create secondary forms and dialog boxes, as described in Chapter 13.

- Use Windows 95 PageControls or Delphi's Notebook component to create forms with multiple pages, as described in this chapter.

- Follow the typical Windows MDI approach, which will be the focus of Chapter 15.

Multipage forms have been used in dialog boxes in Windows applications at least since Microsoft WinWord 2.0 and Quattro Pro for Windows. The latest generation of Microsoft applications has introduced a new kind of notebook approach for dialog boxes, with tabs above the pages. This has become a standard in Windows 95, although the user interface of the Windows 95 TabControl is slightly different than its past incarnations.

Delphi 2 has both a TabControl and a PageControl component, based on Windows 95 common controls, and a custom Notebook component, which can be combined with a custom Tab component to build a notebook with tabs. The Notebook component, however, can also be used in conjunction with other elements, as we will see later in this chapter.

Scrolling a Form

Adding a scroll bar to a form is simple. In fact, you don't need to do anything. If you place a number of components in a big form and then reduce its size, a scroll bar will be added to the form automatically, as long as you haven't changed the value of the `AutoScroll` property, which by default is set to `True`.

Along with `AutoScroll`, forms have two properties, `HorzScrollBar` and `VertScrollBar`, which can be used to set several properties of the two `TFormScrollBar` objects associated with the form. The `Visible` property indicates whether the scroll bar is present, the `Position` property determines the initial status of the scroll thumb, and the `Increment` property determines the effect of clicking one of the arrows at the ends of the scroll bar. The most important property, however, is `Range`.

The `Range` property of a scroll bar determines the virtual size of the form in one direction, not the actual range of values of the scroll bar. At first, this might be somewhat confusing. Here is an example to clarify how the `Range` property works. Suppose that you need a form with a number of components, and so the form needs to be 1000 pixels wide. We can use this value to set the "virtual range" of the form, changing the range of the horizontal scroll bar. See Figure 14.1 for an illustration of the virtual size of a form implied by the range of a scroll bar. If the width of the client area of the form is smaller than 1000 pixels, a scroll bar will appear. Now you can start using it at design-time to add new components in the "hidden" portion of the form.

FIGURE 14.1

A representation of the
virtual size of a form
implied by the range of a
scroll bar.

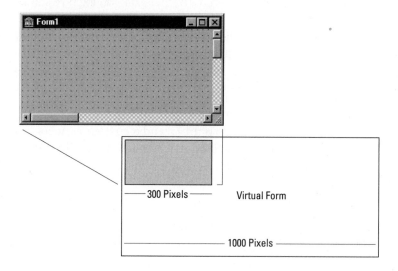

300 Pixels   Virtual Form

1000 Pixels

The Position property of the scroll bar ranges from 0 to 1000 minus the current
size of the client area. In fact, if the client area of the form is 300 pixels wide, you can
scroll 700 pixels to see the far end of the form (the thousandth pixel).

The Scroll Testing Example

I've built an example, Scroll1, which has a virtual form of 1000 pixels. To accomplish this, I simply set the range of the horizontal scroll bar to 1000:

```
object Form1: TForm1
  Width = 458
  Height = 368
  HorzScrollBar.Range = 1000
  VertScrollBar.Range = 305
  AutoScroll = False
  Caption = 'Scrolling Form'
  OnResize = FormResize
  ...
```

The form of this example has been filled with a number of meaningless list boxes,
and I could have obtained the same scroll bar range by placing the rightmost list
box so that its position (Left) plus its size (Width) would equal 1000.

The interesting part of the example is the presence of a toolbox window
displaying the status of the form and of its horizontal scroll bar. This second form

has four labels, two with fixed text and two with the actual output. Besides this, the secondary form (called Status) has a bsToolWindow border style and is a topmost window. You should also set its Visible property to True, to have its window automatically displayed at startup:

```
object Status: TStatus
  BorderIcons = [biSystemMenu]
  BorderStyle = bsToolWindow
  Caption = 'Status'
  FormStyle = fsStayOnTop
  Visible = True
  object Label1: TLabel...
    ...
```

There isn't much code in this program. Its aim is to update the values in the toolbox each time the form is resized or scrolled (as you can see in Figure 14.2). The first part is extremely simple. You can handle the OnResize event of the form, and simply copy a couple of values to the two labels. Notice that the labels are part of another form, so you need to prefix them with the name of the form instance, Status:

```
procedure TForm1.FormResize(Sender: TObject);
begin
  Status.Label3.Caption := IntToStr(ClientWidth);
  Status.Label4.Caption := IntToStr(HorzScrollBar.Position);
end;
```

FIGURE 14.2

The output of the Scroll1 example.

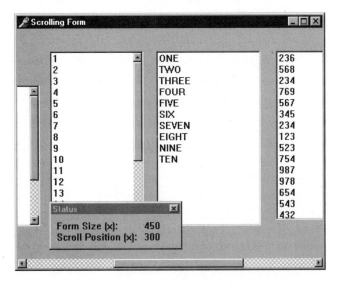

If we wanted to change the output each time the user scrolls the contents of the form, we could not use a Delphi event-handler, because there isn't an OnScroll event for forms (although there is one for stand-alone ScrollBar components). Omitting this event makes sense, because Delphi forms handle scroll bars automatically in a powerful way. In comparison, in Windows, scroll bars are extremely low-level elements, requiring a lot of coding. Handling the scroll event makes sense only in special cases, such as when you want to keep track precisely of the scrolling operations made by a user.

> **NOTE** Once again, what I really like in Delphi is that handling a Windows message that is not supported by the environment requires only one more line of code. I've never seen something so nice in any other visual environment.

Here is the code we need to write. First, add a method declaration to the class, and associate it with the Windows horizontal scroll message (wm_HScroll):

```
public
  procedure FormScroll (var ScrollData: TWMScroll);
    message wm_HScroll;
```

Then write the code of this procedure, which is almost the same as the code of the FormResize method we've seen before:

```
procedure TForm1.FormScroll (var ScrollData: TWMScroll);
begin
  inherited;
  Status.Label3.Caption := IntToStr(ClientWidth);
  Status.Label4.Caption := IntToStr(HorzScrollBar.Position);
end;
```

It's important to add the call to inherited, which activates the method related to the same message in the base class form. Notice that the inherited keyword in Windows message handlers calls the method of the base class we are overriding, which is the one associated with the corresponding Windows message (even if the procedure name is different). Without this call, the form won't have its default scrolling behavior; that is, it won't scroll at all.

Automatic Scrolling

The scroll bar's Range property can seem strange until you start to use it consistently. When you think about it a little, you'll start to understand the advantages of this approach. First of all, the scroll bar is automatically removed from the form when the client area of the form is big enough to accommodate the virtual size; and when you reduce the size of the form, the scroll bar is added again.

This feature becomes particularly interesting when the AutoScroll property of the form is set to True. In this case, the extreme positions of the rightmost and lower controls are automatically copied into the Range properties of the form's two scroll bars. Automatic scrolling works well in Delphi. In the last example, the virtual size of the form would be set to the right border of the last list box. This was defined with the following attributes:

```
object ListBox6: TListBox
  Left = 832
  Width = 145
end
```

Therefore, the horizontal virtual size of the form would be 977 (which is the sum of the two above values). This number is automatically copied into the Range field of the HScrollBar property of the form, unless you change it manually to have a bigger form (as I've done for the Scroll1 example, setting it to 1000 to leave some space between the last list box and the border of the form). You can see this value in the Object Inspector, or make the following test: Run the program, size the form as you like, and move the scroll thumb to the rightmost position. When you add the size of the form and the position of the thumb, you'll always get 1000, the virtual coordinate of the rightmost pixel of the form, whatever the size.

Scrolling an Image

An advantage of the way automatic scrolling works in Delphi is that if the size of a single big component contained in a form changes, scroll bars are added or removed automatically. A good example is the use of the Image component. If the AutoSize property of this component is set to True and you load a new picture into it, the component automatically sizes itself, and the form eventually adds or removes the scroll bars.

An example will probably help clarify how image scrolling works. Do you remember the image viewer we built in Chapter 11? Its form showed a bitmap loaded from a file, either stretching it to fit the size of the form or leaving it in its original size. The problem is that when the original size is too big to fit in the form, part of the bitmap remains hidden. The solution to this problem is simple. We can set the AutoSize property of the Image component to True and disable its alignment with the client area. You should also set a small initial size for the image. You don't need to make any adjustments when you load a new bitmap, because the size of the Image component is automatically set for you by the system. Simply write the following code:

```
procedure TViewerForm.Open1Click(Sender: TObject);
begin
  if OpenDialog1.Execute then
    Image1.Picture.LoadFromFile (OpenDialog1.FileName);
end;
```

You can see in Figure 14.3 that scroll bars are actually added to the form. The figure shows two different copies of the program. The difference between the copy of the program on the left and the one on the right is that the first has an image smaller than its client area, so no scroll bars were added. When you load a larger image in the program, two scroll bars will automatically appear, as in the example on the right.

FIGURE 14.3

In the ImageV2 example, the scroll bars are added automatically to the form when the whole bitmap cannot fit into the client area of the form displayed.

Some more coding is required to disable the scroll bars and change the alignment of the image when the Stretch menu command is selected, and to restore them when this feature is disabled. Again, we do not act directly on the scroll bars themselves, but simply change the alignment of the panel, using its Stretch property, and manually calculate the new size using the size of the picture currently loaded (this code mimics the effect of the AutoSize property, which works only when a new file is loaded):

```
procedure TViewerForm.Stretch1Click(Sender: TObject);
begin
  Image1.Stretch := not Image1.Stretch;
  Stretch1.Checked := Image1.Stretch;
  if Image1.Stretch then
    Image1.Align := alClient
  else
  begin
   Image1.Align := alNone;
   Image1.Height := Image1.Picture.Height;
   Image1.Width := Image1.Picture.Width;
  end;
end;
```

Scrolling and Form Coordinates

As we have seen in the examples in the two previous sections, forms can automatically scroll their components. But what happens if you paint directly on the surface of the form? Some problems arise, but their solution is at hand. Suppose that we want to draw some lines on the virtual surface of a form, as shown in Figure 14.4.

FIGURE 14.4

The lines to draw on the virtual surface of the form.

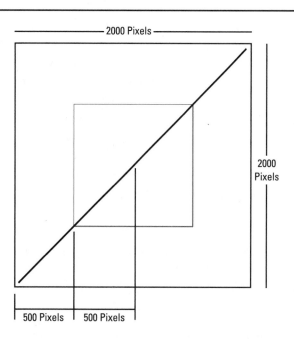

Since you probably do not own a monitor capable of displaying 2000 pixels on each axis, you can create a smaller form, add two scroll bars, and set their Range property, as I've done in the Scroll2 example. Here is the textual description of the form:

```
object Form1: TForm1
  HorzScrollBar.Range = 2000
  VertScrollBar.Range = 2000
  ClientHeight = 336
  ClientWidth = 472
  OnPaint = FormPaint
end
```

If we simply draw the lines using the virtual coordinates of the form, the image won't display properly. In fact, in the OnPaint response method, we need to compute the virtual coordinates ourselves. Fortunately, this is easy, since we know that the virtual X1 and Y1 coordinates of the upper-left corner of the client area correspond to the current positions of the two scroll bars:

```
procedure TForm1.FormPaint(Sender: TObject);
var
  X1, Y1: Integer;
begin
  X1 := HorzScrollBar.Position;
  Y1 := VertScrollBar.Position;
  {draw a yellow line}
  Canvas.Pen.Width := 30;
  Canvas.Pen.Color := clYellow;
  Canvas.MoveTo (30-X1, 30-Y1);
  Canvas.LineTo (1970-X1, 1970-Y1);
  {draw a blue line}
  Canvas.Pen.Color := clNavy;
  Canvas.MoveTo (30-X1, 1970-Y1);
  Canvas.LineTo (1970-X1, 30-Y1);
  {draw a fuchsia square}
  Canvas.Pen.Color := clFuchsia;
  Canvas.Brush.Style := bsClear;
  Canvas.Rectangle (500-X1, 500-Y1, 1500-X1, 1500-Y1);
end;
```

You can see an example of the output of the program in Figure 14.5. Try using the program and changing the drawing functions, but remember to use coordinates relative to the virtual origin of the form by subtracting the virtual coordinates X1 and Y1 (which refer to the scroll bar position). You might also try to use plain coordinates to see what happens. You'll find that the output of the program is not correct—it won't scroll, and the same image will always remain in the same position, regardless of scrolling operations.

FIGURE 14.5

An example of the output of the Scroll2 example.

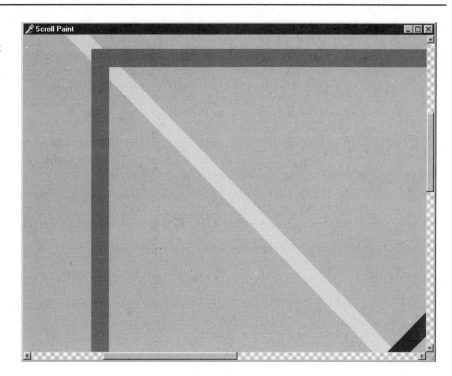

Building Notebooks with Delphi

There are three ways to build a notebook with tabs to change the current page:

- Use the Windows 95 PageControl component.

- Use a Notebook component together with a TabSet component.

- Use the TabbedNotebook component, which is still available in 32-bit versions of Delphi for compatibility purposes only.

The main difference between the three approaches is in the user interface of these components, as you can see in the figures in the following sections. In general, since the PageControl and TabControl components are based on a Windows common control, you should probably use them unless you have compatibility problems or some other special reason not to do so. Technically speaking, the TTabControl class is built around the Windows 95 tab control, providing little else than the capability to show its own tabs. The TPageControl class is based on a tab control plus some panels (tab sheets), and provides more capabilities.

If you only need a tab, without the notebook or pages, you can use the TabControl or TabSet component. If you need the pages without the tabs, you can use the PageControl (hiding the tabs) or use the Notebook component by itself.

PageControls and TabSheets

There are three components used to handle pages and tabs in Windows 95, which are represented in Delphi by the TabControl and PageControl components, and by the TabSheet component used inside a PageControl. The TabControl is used to build stand-alone tabs (not connected with pages; I'll use it later in a specific example). The PageControl component is used to build an application or a dialog box using the common multipage or notebook metaphor.

As usual, instead of duplicating the Help system's list of properties and methods of the PageControl component, I've built an example that stretches its capabilities and allows you to change its behavior at run-time. The example, called Pages, has a PageControl with three pages. To build it yourself, you can simply place the control on a new form, then select it and use the local menu to add new pages or tab sheets. Then add components and set their properties as indicated by the following textual description of the form:

```
object Form1: TForm1
  Caption = 'Pages Test'
  OnCreate = FormCreate
  object PageControl1: TPageControl
    ActivePage = TabSheet1
    Align = alClient
    object TabSheet1: TTabSheet
      Caption = 'Pages'
      object Label3: TLabel...
      object ListBox1: TListBox...
    end
```

```
object TabSheet2: TTabSheet
  Caption = 'Tabs Size'
  object Label1: TLabel...
  object EditWidth: TEdit...
  object UpDown1: TUpDown
    Associate = EditWidth
    Min = 0
    Max = 2000
    Position = 0
  end
  object Label2: TLabel...
  object EditHeight: TEdit
    Text = '0'
  end
  object UpDown2: TUpDown
    Associate = EditHeight
    Min = 0
    Max = 2000
    Position = 0
  end
  object CheckBoxMultiLine: TCheckBox...
  object CheckBoxVisible: TCheckBox...
    Caption = '&Last Tabs &Visible'
    State = cbChecked
  object BitBtnApply: TBitBtn...
end
object TabSheet3: TTabSheet
  Caption = 'Tabs Text'
  object Memo1: TMemo...
  object BitBtnChange: TBitBtn
    Caption = '&Change'
    Enabled = False
    OnClick = BitBtnChangeClick
  end
end
end
object BitBtnPrevious: TBitBtn...
object BitBtnNext: TBitBtn...
end
```

Each TabSheet object has its own Caption, which is displayed as the sheet's tab. You can use the same local menu to change pages. You can also do this by clicking on the tab directly and then clicking back on the surface of the form to select the TabSheet. You can see the local menu of the PageControl component in Figure 14.6, together with the first page. This page holds a list box and a small caption, and shares two buttons with the other pages.

FIGURE 14.6

The first sheet of the PageControl of the Pages example, with its local menu.

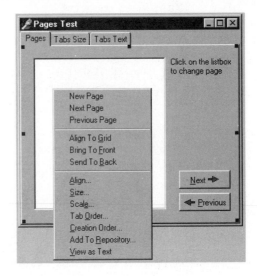

If you place a component on a page, it is available only in that page. How can you have the same component (in this case, two bitmap buttons) in each of the pages, without duplicating it? Simply place the component on the form, outside of the PageControl (or before aligning it to the client area) and then move it in front of the pages, calling the Bring to Front command of the form's local menu. The two buttons I've placed in each page can be used to move back and forth between the pages and are an alternative to using the tabs. Here is the code associated with one of them:

```
procedure TForm1.BitBtnNextClick(Sender: TObject);
begin
  PageControl1.SelectNextPage (True);
end;
```

The other button calls the same procedure, passing False as its parameter to select the previous page. Notice that there is no need to check whether we are in the first or last page, because the SelectNextPage method considers the last page to be the one before the first, and will move you directly between those two pages.

Now that we have defined the use of the common component, we can focus on the first page again. It has a list box, which at run-time will hold the name of the tabs. If a user clicks on an item of this list box, the current page changes. This is the third method available to change pages (after tabs and buttons). The list box is filled in the FormCreate method, associated with the OnCreate event of the form, copying the caption of each page (the Page property stores a list of TabSheet objects):

```
for I := 0 to PageControl1.PageCount - 1 do
  ListBox1.Items.Add (PageControl1.Pages.Caption);
```

When you click on a list item, you can select the corresponding page:

```
procedure TForm1.ListBox1Click(Sender: TObject);
begin
  PageControl1.ActivePage :=
    PageControl1.Pages [ListBox1.ItemIndex];
end;
```

The second page hosts two edit boxes (connected with two UpDown components), and two check boxes, as you can see in Figure 14.7. The user can input a number (or choose it by clicking on the up and down buttons with the mouse or pressing ↑ or ↓ while the corresponding edit box has the focus) and check the boxes, then press the Apply button to make the changes:

```
procedure TForm1.BitBtnApplyClick(Sender: TObject);
begin
  {set tabs width, height, and lines}
  PageControl1.TabWidth := StrToInt (EditWidth.Text);
  PageControl1.TabHeight := StrToInt (EditHeight.Text);
  PageControl1.MultiLine := CheckBoxMultiLine.Checked;
  {show or hide the last tab}
  TabSheet3.TabVisible := CheckBoxVisible.Checked;
end;
```

With this code we can change the width and height of each tab (remember that 0 means the size is computed automatically from the space taken by each string), and choose to have either multiple lines of tabs or two small arrows to scroll the tab area. You can also hide the last tab on the PageControl, which corresponds to the TabSheet3 component.

FIGURE 14.7

The second page of the example can be used to size and position the tabs: Here you can see large tabs on multiple lines.

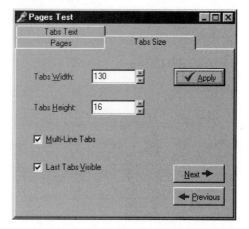

If you hide one of the tabs by setting its TabVisible property to False, you cannot reach that tab by clicking on the Next and Previous buttons, which are based on the SelectNextPage method. Instead, you should use the FindNextPage function, as shown below in this new version of the OnClick event handler of the NextButton component:

```
procedure TForm1.BitBtnNextClick(Sender: TObject);
begin
  PageControl1.ActivePage :=
    PageControl1.FindNextPage (
      PageControl1.ActivePage, True, False);
end;
```

> **WARNING** When you change the height of the tabs of a PageControl or set multiple lines at run-time, every component in the page is moved downwards, and might even slip out of the visible area. At the same time, if you have components that are not children of the PageControl but are placed in front of it (as with the two bitmap button in the Pages example), they will not move and might hide other components of a specific page.

The last page has a memo component, again with the names of the pages (added in the FormCreate method). You can edit the names of the pages and press the Change button to change the text of the tabs, but only if the number of strings matches the number of tabs:

```
procedure TForm1.BitBtnChangeClick(Sender: TObject);
var
  I: Integer;
begin
  if Memo1.Lines.Count <> PageControl1.PageCount then
    MessageDlg ('One line per tab, please', mtError, [mbOK], 0)
  else
    for I := 0 to PageControl1.PageCount -1 do
      PageControl1.Pages [I].Caption := Memo1.Lines [I];
  BitBtnChange.Enabled := False;
end;
```

Another feature we might add to the example is a way to add new pages at run-time and to place some components inside them. We might also add a pull-down menu listing the pages, to offer a fourth technique to change pages.

TIP

Whenever you write a form based on a PageControl or notebook, remember that the first page displayed at run-time is the page you were in before the code was compiled. This means that if you are working on the third page, and then compile and run the program, it will start with that page. A common way to solve this problem is to add a line of code in the FormCreate method to set the PageControl or notebook to the first page. This way, the current page at design-time doesn't determine the initial page at run-time.

A Notebook with a Tab Set

The standard approach to building a notebook with tabs in 16-bit Delphi was to use the two separate components, the Notebook and the TabSet. This might still be a useful approach, because it is very flexible and because it is highly compatible between the 16-bit and the 32-bit versions of Delphi. A program using the PageControl, in fact, cannot be recompiled in 16-bit Delphi. To describe the Notebook and TabSet components in detail, I've written an example similar to the previous one and named it Tab1.

To create this form, you can place a Notebook component on the form, then place a TabSet component on the form, align the TabSet to the bottom of the form (alBottom), and align the Notebook with the client area (alClient). Now you can name the pages of the notebook by selecting the Pages property and entering some values in the corresponding editor. The next step is to prepare the tabs by entering some strings for the Tabs property. It is a good idea to use the same names for the pages of the notebook and for the tabs of the TabSet component. However, the names you use for the TabSet component are not particularly important, since they are not visible. The important thing is that the tabs themselves must have meaningful names, because they are visible to the user.

To connect the notebook to the tab set, you need to write at least one line of code in response to the OnChange event of the TabSet component:

```
procedure TForm1.TabSet1Change(Sender: TObject;
  NewTab: Integer; var AllowChange: Boolean);
begin
  Notebook1.PageIndex := NewTab;
end;
```

TIP

In the OnChange response method, you should use the NewTab parameter and not the current index of the tab, because this field contains the older value, the one before the click took place. In fact, the OnChange method can even be used to prohibit the page change by setting the AllowChange parameter, which is passed by reference, to False.

As an alternative, you can activate the pages by using their names (the ActivePage property of the notebook) instead of their index (the PageIndex property). This works only if the names of the pages match those of the tabs:

```
procedure TForm1.TabSet1Change(Sender: TObject;
  NewTab: Integer; var AllowChange: Boolean);
begin
  Notebook1.ActivePage := TabSet1.Tabs [NewTab];
end;
```

To make this program interesting, we need to add some components to the various pages. At design-time, to work on the various pages of the notebook you must change the value of its PageIndex property; you can't just click on the tabs as with the PageControl component. As soon as you enter a new value for the PageIndex or the ActivePage property in the Object Inspector, the visible page of the notebook changes accordingly. A better alternative is to select the notebook in the Form Designer, and activate the SpeedMenu, which has commands to move to the next or previous page.

Now that we know how to change the active page at design-time, what's in the pages of this example? Again, I decided to fill the pages with some controls we can use to change the properties of these two components. You can see a summary of these components in the following textual description of the form of the Tab1 example:

```
object Form1: TForm1
  Caption = 'Tab Test App'
  OnCreate = FormCreate
  object Notebook1: TNotebook
    Align = alClient
    object TPage
      Caption = 'One'
      object Label1: TLabel...
      object ListBox1: TListBox...
    end
    object TPage
      Caption = 'Two'
      object Label2: TLabel...
      object GroupBox1: TGroupBox
        Caption = 'Dithering'
        object RadioButton1: TRadioButton
          Caption = 'On'
          OnClick = RadioButton1Click
        end
        object RadioButton2: TRadioButton
          Caption = 'Off'
          Checked = True
          OnClick = RadioButton2Click
        end
      end
    end
    object TPage
      Caption = 'Three'
      object Label3: TLabel...
      object ColorGrid1: TColorGrid...
```

```
      end
      object TPage
        Caption = 'Four'
        object Label4: TLabel...
        object Memo1: TMemo...
        object ChangeButton: TButton...
      end
      object TPage
        Caption = 'Five'
        object Label5: TLabel...
        object Label6: TLabel
          Caption = 'Hello !'
          Font.Color = clRed
          Font.Height = -96
        end
      end
    end
    object TabSet1: TTabSet
      Align = alBottom
      DitherBackground = False
      Tabs.Strings = (
        'Pages'
        'Dithering'
        'Colors'
        'Tabs'
        'Hello')
      OnChange = TabSet1Change
    end
  end
```

The first page—would you guess it?—holds a list box with the names of the pages, filled when the form is created with the names of the pages of the notebook. This time the code is simpler, because both components are based on a TStringList object:

```
procedure TForm1.FormCreate(Sender: TObject);
begin
  ListBox1.Items := Notebook1.Pages;
  Memo1.Lines := TabSet1.Tabs;
  {reset the page}
  Notebook1.PageIndex := 0;
end;
```

We can also simplify the code to change between pages when the user clicks on an item in the list box. As we change the active page of the notebook, we must only remember to select the proper tab as well, since the page and tab index synchronization is not automatic:

```
procedure TForm1.ListBox1Click(Sender: TObject);
begin
  Notebook1.PageIndex := Listbox1.ItemIndex;
  TabSet1.TabIndex := Listbox1.ItemIndex;
end;
```

The second page has two radio buttons to activate or disable the dithering effect of the background of the TabSet control. The third page contains a ColorGrid component you can use to select the background color of the form, used also for the notebook. Therefore, it might be a good idea to use it for the background of the tab set and for the active tab, too. The important idea is that to provide the proper three-dimensional effect, the color of the active tab should always match the color of the notebook, so that it seems like an extension of its surface (see Figure 14.8). The second color, the foreground color, is used for the inactive tabs:

```
procedure TForm1.ColorGrid1Change(Sender: TObject);
begin
  Form1.Color := ColorGrid1.BackgroundColor;
  TabSet1.BackGroundColor := ColorGrid1.BackgroundColor;
  TabSet1.SelectedColor := ColorGrid1.BackgroundColor;
  TabSet1.UnselectedColor := ColorGrid1.ForegroundColor;
end;
```

FIGURE 14.8

An example of the new colors and the dithering effect you can set for the notebook and the tab of the Tab1 example.

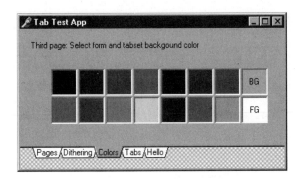

The fourth page allows a user to change the text of the tabs (but not of the memo pages). It contains a memo field, which is initialized as usual in the Form-Create method (see the code above). Here is the code of the Change button:

```
procedure TForm1.ChangeButtonClick(Sender: TObject);
begin
  if Memo1.Lines.Count <> TabSet1.Tabs.Count then
    MessageDlg (
      Format('Not %d lines!', [TabSet1.Tabs.Count])',
      mtError, [mbOk], 0)
  else
    TabSet1.Tabs := Memo1.Lines;
end;
```

If you write longer and more descriptive names for the pages, the TabSet component can add two "mini" scroll buttons to move among the tabs when they do not fit into the width of the Tab control, working similarly to the PageControl tabs. This example and the Pages example we've discussed before highlight two interesting points:

- You are not limited to the use of tabs to change the page of a PageControl or notebook. The list box on the first page that we have used for this purpose could be placed on one side and used as a page selector, as we will do in the next section.

- It is quite simple to edit the text of the tabs. This technique might be used to allow a user to configure the application.

Changing the Page of a Notebook

The example we have just finished can be further extended in a number of directions, particularly in providing alternative ways to change the page of the notebook. The same could be said for the Pages example. However, when you use the standard Windows 95 component, it is not as important to examine many other techniques to change the page as it is when you are using a less-standard user interface. If you are building a completely custom user interface, a notebook can easily be used without tabs.

The technique we'll try first is to add a list box similar to the one on the first page of the notebook, and to make it always visible in the window. Then all you need to do is click on this list box to change to another page. The second addition will be a menu to select the page.

To build the Tab2 example, we can add a new list box on the left or right side of the form. To accomplish this, we need to resize the various components, disable their top alignment, and choose a fixed border for the frame so that it cannot be resized. You can see an example of the final form in Figure 14.9. At program startup, we can initialize the new list box with the same text as the labels of the TabSet component.

FIGURE 14.9

The Tab2 program shows the selected page both in the tab, in the list box on the left, and with a radio check mark in the Page pull-down menu.

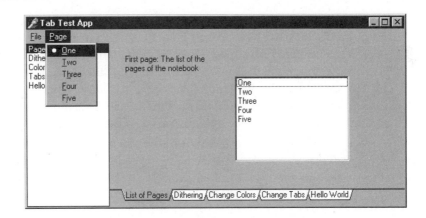

We can handle the click on an element of the new list box (ListBox2) by writing a code fragment similar to the one used for the first list box. (If you simply copy and paste this code, remember to change the list box numbers.) Even better, we can write a single version of the code to act with both list boxes, and connect it with the click event of both of them:

```
procedure TForm1.ListBox1Click(Sender: TObject);
begin
  {works with both list boxes}
  Notebook1.PageIndex := (Sender as TListBox).ItemIndex;
  TabSet1.TabIndex := (Sender as TListBox).ItemIndex;
end;
```

With this code, when the list box selection changes, we select a new page and activate the proper tab. The second technique introduced in Tab2 is to add a pull-down menu to select the various pages. The OnClick event for each menu item is associated with a single method, MenuPage, which is based on a simple trick: The name of each menu item corresponds to the name of a page of the notebook. This simplifies the code quite a bit:

```
procedure TForm1.MenuPage(Sender: TObject);
begin
  Notebook1.ActivePage := (Sender as TMenuItem).Name;
  TabSet1.TabIndex := Notebook1.PageIndex;
  ListBox2.ItemIndex := Notebook1.PageIndex;
  CheckCurrentPage;
end;
```

This approach also makes the program easily extensible, because you don't need to write new code or change it when new pages and the corresponding menu items are added. Only the first statement above contains the action related to the menu item selection. The other two statements are needed to update the list box and tab selections. The last statement invokes a procedure I've defined, named CheckCurrentPage. This method places a check mark on the menu item corresponding to the currently selected page, as already shown in Figure 14.9. This method should remove the check mark from every menu item (setting the Checked property of each of them to False), and then enables the one corresponding to the current page, maybe using a case statement based on Notebook1.PageIndex. This is actually how I originally wrote this example.

To write a better CheckCurrentPages procedure and to improve the user interface, you can use radio menu items for the Pages pull-down menu and remove the five lines above used to deselect each possible item. In fact, you can also remove the case statement, because the number of the active page corresponds to the number of the menu item you have to select. Here is the final version of this method:

```
procedure TForm1.CheckCurrentPage;
begin
  Page1.Items [NoteBook1.PageIndex].Checked := True;
end;
```

Of course, you will seldom need three different ways to select the page of a notebook, as I've included in the Tab2 example, but a couple of choices might be useful to satisfy the tastes of different users. The aim of this example was to show you some alternatives you can apply also to the PageControl component (in particular the selection of pages using a pull-down menu).

Tabbed Notebooks

A third alternative to the use of the PageControl and the TabSet and Notebook components is the use of the TabbedNotebook component. This component has a user interface quite similar to the Windows 95 PageControl, but it was also available in the 16-bit version of Delphi, so it can be used for Windows 3.1 applications, too.

The example I've built to show the use of the TabbedNotebook, named SimTab, is similar to—although somewhat simpler than—the Pages and Tab1 examples shown earlier. As you can see in Figure 14.10, the first page of this multipage form has a list box with the names of the pages. There is also a Close button, which should be present on every page of the notebook. Again, I placed the button on the form, not on the notebook, and then moved it over the notebook.

FIGURE 14.10

The first page of the SimTab example.

I placed the button in the bottom-center of the form, and I've selected a non-resizable dialog border for the form. The other pages of the notebook in the SimTab example allow you to change the font of the tab captions and the number of tabs per row. The last two pages are almost empty.

The code of this example is fairly simple. In fact, the TabbedNotebook component handles page changing automatically, like the PageControl. This means that we don't need to change the active page each time the user clicks on a tab, as is the case in the Tab1 and Tab2 examples. Again, however, we can implement more than one technique to change the page. As a recurring example, we can fill the list box of the first page with the names of the pages, and then move to another page when the user clicks on the corresponding element in the list box.

To change the page in the tabbed notebook, we can set the name of the page or its index, as with the other multipage components. Since the list box has a zero-based ItemIndex property, indicating the selected item, we can simply write the following code:

```
TabbedNotebook1.PageIndex := ListBoxPages.ItemIndex;
```

The other two pages of the notebook can be used to change the font and arrangement of the tabs. To change the font when the user clicks on the corresponding button, you can simply use a FontDialog component, and use the selected value to change the font of the tabs:

```
if FontDialog1.Execute then
    TabbedNotebook1.TabFont := FontDialog1.Font;
```

The program also changes the Caption of a test label to show the name of the current font, and an example of how the font will look. For the last operation—changing the number of tabs per row—I've simply added a SpinEdit component and a button. The code is simple. When the user clicks the button, the value of the SpinEdit component is used as the new number of tabs per row:

```
TabbedNotebook1.TabsPerRow := SpinEdit1.Value;
```

WARNING Unfortunately, this code does not work as documented—changing the TabsPerRow property has no effect on the tabs! I've decided to leave the wrong code in the example anyway, hoping Borland will fix this, even if it is an old property retained only for backward-compatibility with Delphi 1.

Notebooks without Tabs and Tabs without Notebooks

The interface of the PageControl is getting quite common, and the Notebook and TabSet components naturally fit with each other. However, using the two components together is not the only choice. As the title of this section suggests, you can write applications with tabs but without a multipage component, or with notebooks but without any sort of tabs or list to select the page from. Here are some examples, some of which will be fully implemented in the following sections.

The TabControl (or TabSet) alone can be used in various ways: in a multipage editor (such as the editor in Delphi), in a multipage bitmap viewer, to select a disk drive in a file viewer, in a three-dimensional spreadsheet, or to select a form in a multiple-form program. Delphi uses tabs to select pages in the Component palette, too.

A notebook can be used without tabs if you instead use a list box or a menu (as shown in the Tab2 example). As an alternative, you can use a TreeView component instead of a list, obtaining an effect similar to a multipage explorer. Another alternative to the use of a tab is to add buttons to navigate through the notebook, as partially demonstrated by the Pages example. There are basically two ways to use buttons for navigation:

- Add a row of buttons with commands such as First, Next, Previous, and Last, similar to database navigation commands. A special case of this is the development of Experts or Wizards. In these applications the form is based on a notebook and usually has a button to move to the next page, and one to go back to the previous page. Typically it is possible to move to the following page only after you have selected some options. The order of the pages (and even their presence) might depend on your past selections.

- Add specific buttons in the various pages of the notebook to move to other relevant pages. This solution is similar to the use of hyperlinks, and you can use specific portions of the text or of an image instead of push buttons to launch the move.

A Presentation in a Notebook

Our first example is a notebook without a tab, called NoteOnly. It has both a row of buttons at the bottom and some buttons in the pages to give specific navigation commands. The four buttons in the row at the bottom of the form are placed on a panel, so that the notebook can take up the rest of the client area of the form. Probably the best way to understand this example is to run it. It is a presentation about traveling in Italy.

Each page usually has a button to move to the next step, as you can see in Figure 14.11, but at times you have two or more choices. There is nothing else besides buttons, and their code is quite simple. Usually, when you select a button, a new page of the notebook is chosen. Some more coding is required to disable the buttons that are currently meaningless. For example, after a user clicks on the First button, you should disable the first two buttons (since the user is already at the first page and there are no previous pages) and enable the other two buttons in case they had been disabled.

FIGURE 14.11

A couple of pages of the NoteOnly example, featuring a simple presentation about Italy.

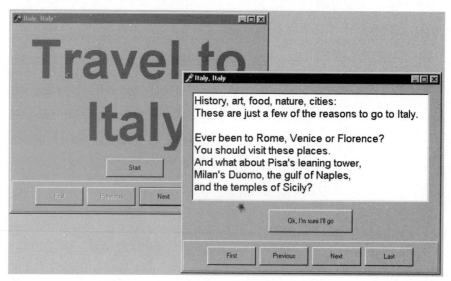

Slightly more complex is the case of the Next and the Previous buttons. You should check whether the notebook has reached the first or the last page, and disable or enable the various buttons accordingly. The real problem here is that we also need to enable and disable some of the buttons on the button row when the navigational buttons of the various pages of the notebook are clicked, to avoid inconsistent behavior.

An Image Viewer with Tabs

Now that we've gone through an example of a notebook without tabs, we are ready to explore the opposite situation: a tab that is not attached to a notebook. Often, you'll find another component connected to a tab. For example, you might attach a tab set to a panel, an image, one of the various kinds of grids, or other types of components. In our next example, TabOnly, we want to display a bitmap in an Image component. The image that appears depends on the selection in the tab above it (as you can see in Figure 14.12). This is a simple example. The form has a TabControl component aligned to the whole client area, and an Image component inside the TabControl and covering its client area. The other two components are a main menu and a File Open dialog box that allows multiple selections:

```
object Form1: TForm1
  Caption = 'Bitmap Viewer'
  object TabControl1: TTabControl
    Align = alClient
    Tabs.Strings = ('None')
    OnChange = TabControl1Change
    object Image1: TImage
      Align = alClient
    end
  end
  object OpenDialog1: TOpenDialog
    Options = [ofAllowMultiSelect, ofPathMustExist,
      ofFileMustExist, ofShareAware]
    Title = 'Select one or more images'
  end
  object MainMenu1: TMainMenu
    object File1: TMenuItem...
      object Open1: TMenuItem...
      object N1: TMenuItem...
      object Exit1: TMenuItem...
    object Help1: TMenuItem...
      object AboutImageViewer1: TMenuItem...
  end
end
```

At the beginning, the TabControl has only a fake tab, describing the situation (*No file selected*). When the user selects File ➤ Open, the dialog box is displayed. The user can select a number of files, and the array of strings with the names of the files (the Files property of the OpenDialog1 component) is used as the text for the tabs (the Tabs property of TabControl1):

```
procedure TForm1.Open1Click(Sender: TObject);
begin
  if OpenDialog1.Execute then
  begin
    TabControl1.Tabs := OpenDialog1.Files;
    TabControl1.TabIndex := 0;
    TabControl1Change (TabControl1);
  end;
end;
```

FIGURE 14.12

The interface of the bitmap viewer in the TabOnly example.

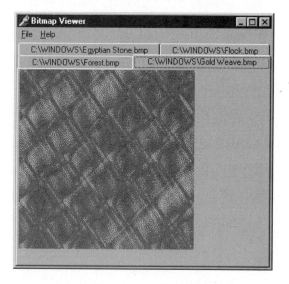

After we display the new tabs, we have to update the image so that it matches the first tab. To accomplish this the program calls the method connected with the OnChange event of the TabControl, which loads the file corresponding to the current tab in the image component:

```
procedure TForm1.TabControl1Change(Sender: TObject);
begin
  Image1.Picture.LoadFromFile (
    TabControl1.Tabs [TabControl1.TabIndex]);
end;
```

This example works, but not very well. One of the problems is that displaying the whole path makes the tabs very big, so that they will take up a lot of screen space (because I've set the Multiline property of the TabControl to True). To correct this problem, the program defines a set of hidden temporary strings, so that the path name can be removed from the tabs. Another problem is that if you select a file that doesn't contain a bitmap, an error will occur. However, the program will warn the user with a standard exception, ignore the file, and continue its execution.

The last problem involves usability. This program is not very suitable for browsing the hard disk looking for a bitmap, because you need to execute the OpenDialog over and over again. A better idea is to have a list of directories directly on the form and allow the user to browse through it. This is easy to do in Delphi, since there is a DirectoryListBox component readily available. By using some advanced system components and only a few lines of code, we can build a full-fledged image browser.

An Image Browser with Tabs

To build our new TabOnly2 example—the image browser—place in a new form a DriveComboBox with a DirectoryListBox below it, as shown in Figure 14.13. On the right of the form, place a TabControl with an Image component inside it. I've also added a Bevel component behind them, to improve the user interface.

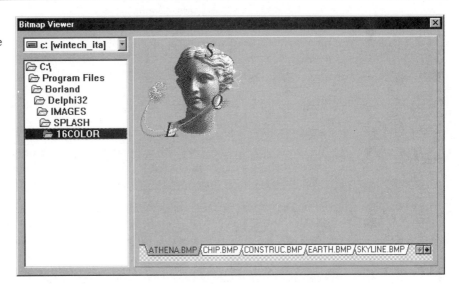

The idea behind this program is that as the user selects a new directory, the tabs should immediately display the names of bitmap files in that directory. First, we need to connect the combo box with the names of the drives and with the directory list box, so that each change in the combo box is reflected in the other component. This can be easily done by setting the DirList property of the DriveComboBox component. The second step is to load the names of the bitmap files in the tabs each time the selection in the directory list box changes. We might do this manually, by accessing DOS functions, or we can use another component to solve the problem. The latter solution is more Delphi-oriented, and also much easier, so I've chosen to follow it.

Just place a FileListBox component on the form, and reduce its size so that it will be invisible, place it behind another component, or simply set its Visible property to False. Then change the value of the Mask property of the file list box to *.*bmp*. Now add a method for the OnChange event of the directory list box, and write the following code:

```
procedure TForm1.DirectoryListBox1Change(Sender: TObject);
begin
  with FileListBox1 do
    if Items.Count = 0 then
    begin
      TabControl1.Tabs.Clear;
      Image1.Visible := False;
      TabControl1.Tabs.Add ('None');
    end
    else
    begin
      Image1.Visible := True;
      TabControl1.Tabs := FileListBox1.Items;
    end;
end;
```

Using this method, each time the user selects a new directory (or a new disk), the directory shown in the file list box changes. Then, if there are some items in this directory, the array of strings is copied to the tab set. As an alternative, the *None* string is added to an empty tab set, and the image with the old bitmap is temporarily hidden. When the tabs display the names of the files, we can use a statement very similar to that of the TabOnly example to load the corresponding bitmap in the picture of the Image component:

```
procedure TForm1.TabControl1Change(Sender: TObject);
begin
  with TabControl1 do
    if Tabs [TabIndex] <> 'None' then
      Image1.Picture.LoadFromFile (Tabs [TabIndex]);
end;
```

A Multipage Toolbar

Our last example before we move on to form-splitting defines a notebook with tabs used to build a multipage toolbar. Building a multipage toolbar, in general, is easy. You only need to place a number of speed buttons in the pages of a PageControl or a notebook. You can see an example of such a toolbar in Figure 14.14 or experiment with it running the MultiBar example, which is based on a Notebook and a TabSet component. I decided not to enter the text for the tabs of the TabSet component, but to simply copy the names of the pages into the tabs of the notebook at run-time:

```
procedure TForm1.FormCreate(Sender: TObject);
begin
  TabSet1.Tabs := Notebook1.Pages;
end;
```

Of course, to make the tabs work properly, you should also connect them to the notebook as usual:

```
procedure TForm1.TabSet1Change(Sender: TObject;
  NewTab: Integer; var AllowChange: Boolean);
begin
  Notebook1.PageIndex := NewTab;
end;
```

FIGURE 14.14

The output of the Multi-Bar example at run-time.

Notice that the tabs of this example mimic the names of possible pull-down menus. A better solution might be to provide two or three toolbars corresponding to different environment situations (file editing, folder handling, other tools, and so on). The program might automatically change the toolbar page when the context changes, but the user is still free to select a different page of the toolbar. Having a multipage toolbar, such as the Delphi Component Palette, might be a better alternative than having many toolbars using up all of the screen real estate, as many applications do.

> **TIP**
>
> I've borrowed all of the bitmaps for the examples in this chapter from the Delphi Image Library, a collection of graphic files usually available in the `Delphi 3.0/Images` directory and its subdirectories.

A problem in building a similar example is that you need to select the bitmap for each button manually, which can be extremely boring. A solution is to give names to the buttons, so that they can later load a bitmap having the same name at run-time. If you follow this approach, another improvement might come from storing the bitmaps as resources inside the executable file, instead of as external BMP files. Another problem with this example is that it uses a huge amount of Windows memory. An alternative solution might be to load the bitmaps dynamically one page at a time, destroying the buttons as soon as the page is hidden.

Form Splitting Techniques

There are several ways to implement form splitting techniques in Delphi, and in Delphi 3 there is even direct support for this with a specific component, Splitter, found in the Additional page of the Component Palette. Nonetheless, I'd like to cover some additional approaches you can use, including direct mouse message handling.

> **TIP**
>
> The new TCoolBar component (covered in Chapter 11) can also function as a splitter, although this is not its primary role.

I'll build essentially the same example several times, starting with the official approach, then discussing the use of the HeaderControl component, and finally focusing on low-level mouse-dragging operations. The example used each time is based on a form with three list boxes containing names of animals. These list boxes support font changing with a mouse double-click.

Splitting with a Splitter

Of course, we start with the most natural approach, the use of a Splitter component. To build the Split1 example, simply place in a form a Listbox component, then a Splitter component, a second Listbox, another Splitter, and a final Listbox component. The form has also a simple toolbar with two SpeedButton components and two combinations of label, edit box, and UpDown control. The form includes also a FontDialog and a ColorDialog component, as you can see in the textual description:

```
object Form1: TForm1
  Caption = 'Split (with the Splitter component)'
  object ListBox1: TListBox
    Align = alLeft
```

```
    Font.Height = -64
    Items.Strings = (
      'Whale'
      'Elephant'
      ...)
    OnDblClick = OnListClick
  end
  object Splitter1: TSplitter
    // Align = alLeft {default, not listed}
    Cursor = crHSplit
    Beveled = False
  end
  object ListBox2: TListBox
    Align = alLeft
    Font.Height = -32
    Items.Strings = (
      'Dog'
      'Cat'
      ...)
    OnDblClick = OnListClick
  end
  object Splitter2: TSplitter...// similar to Splitter1
  object ListBox3: TListBox
    Align = alClient
    Font.Height = -12
    Items.Strings = (
      'Lizard'
      'Ant'
      ...)
    OnDblClick = OnListClick
  end
  object Panel1: TPanel
    Align = alTop
    object SpeedBeveled: TSpeedButton...
    object SpeedColor: TSpeedButton...
    object LabelMin: TLabel...
    object EditMin: TEdit...
    object UpDownMin: TUpDown
      Associate = EditMin
      Min = 10
      Max = 200
      Increment = 10
      Position = 30
```

```
      OnClick = UpDownMinClick
    end
    object LabelWidth: TLabel...
    object EditWidth: TEdit...
    object UpDownWidth: TUpDown...// similar to UpDownMin
  end
  object ColorDialog1: TColorDialog...
  object FontDialog1: TFontDialog...
end
```

By simply placing these two splitter components, you give your form the complete functionality of moving and sizing the controls it hosts at run-time. The Width, Beveled, and Color properties of the splitter components determine their appearance, and in the Split1 example you can use the toolbar to change them. Another relevant property is MinSize, which determines the minimum size of the various components of the form. During the splitting operation (see Figure 14.15) a line marks the final position of the splitter, but you cannot drag this line over a certain limit.

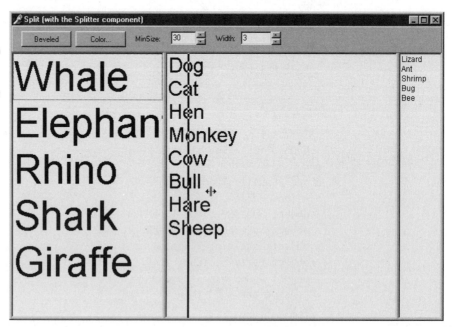

I suggest you try using the example, so that you'll fully understand how the splitter affects its adjacent controls and the other controls of the form. The code of the example is so simple I won't even list it in the text. You can refer to the companion disk for the details.

Horizontal Splitting

The Splitter component can also be used for horizontal splitting, instead of the default vertical splitting. However, this approach is a little more complicated. Basically you can place a component on a form, align it to the top, and then place the splitter on the form. By default, it will be left-aligned. Choose the alTop value for the Align property, then resize the component manually, changing the Height property in the Object Inspector (or by resizing the component).

You can see a form with a horizontal splitter in the SplitH example. This program has two memo components you can open a file into, and a splitter dividing them. It also features a status bar, which keeps track of the current height of the two memo components. Here is the textual description:

```
object Form1: TForm1
  Caption = 'Horizontal Splitter'
  OnResize = Splitter1Moved
  object MemoUp: TMemo
    Align = alTop
    ScrollBars = ssVertical
    OnDblClick = MemoDblClick
  end
  object Splitter1: TSplitter
    Cursor = crVSplit
    Align = alTop
    OnMoved = Splitter1Moved
  end
  object MemoDown: TMemo
    Align = alClient
    ScrollBars = ssVertical
    OnDblClick = MemoDblClick
  end
  object StatusBar1: TStatusBar...
  object OpenDialog1: TOpenDialog
end
```

When you double-click on a memo the program loads a text file into it (notice the structure of the with statement):

```
procedure TForm1.MemoDblClick(Sender: TObject);
begin
  with Sender as TMemo, OpenDialog1 do
    if Execute then
      Lines.LoadFromFile (FileName);
end;
```

The program also handles the OnMoved event of the splitter (it is the only event of this component) to update the text of the status bar. The same code is executed whenever the form is resized:

```
procedure TForm1.Splitter1Moved(Sender: TObject);
begin
  StatusBar1.Panels[0].Text := Format (
    'Upper Memo: %d - Lower Memo: %d',
    [MemoUp.Height, MemoDown.Height]);
end;
```

You can see the effect of this code by looking at Figure 14.16, or by running the SplitH example.

FIGURE 14.16

The status bar of the SplitH example indicates the position of the horizontal splitter component.

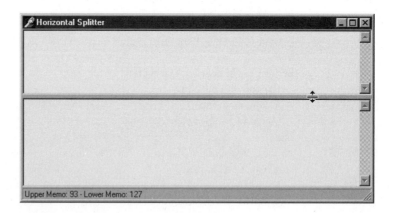

Alternative Splitting Components

After these two examples of the official Delphi 3 approach to splitting, I'll show you some alternative solutions. Although these techniques made more sense before the Splitter component was introduced, they provide an opportunity to discuss some new components you can use for splitting: the Header Control and the Panels, with the use of some dragging techniques. Later on I'll show a further solution that's based on Windows mouse messages rather than on Delphi components.

Splitting with a Header

Using the HeaderControl is another common technique to implement a vertical splitter. As an alternative (for compatibility with Windows 3.1), you can use Delphi's own Header component.

If you place a HeaderControl component on a form, it will be automatically aligned with the top of the form. Then you can add the three list boxes to the rest of the client area of the form. The first list box can be aligned on the left, but this time you cannot align the second and third list box as well. The problem is that the sections of the header can be dragged outside of the visible surface of the form. If the list boxes use an automatic alignment, they cannot move outside the visible surface of the form, as the program requires.

Now we can define the sections of the header, using the specific editor of the Sections property. As you can see in Figure 14.17, this property editor allows you to change various settings besides the names of the sections. You can set the alignment of the text; the current, minimum, and maximum size of the header; and so on. Setting the limit values is really a powerful tool, which allows us to avoid handling this issue at run-time within our code.

FIGURE 14.17

The editor of the Sections property of the Header-Control component.

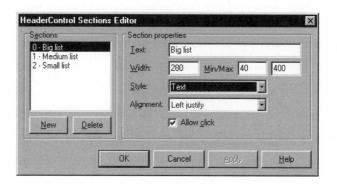

The only problem is with the last section of the header. We want the third list box to fill up the client area, if possible, but the header usually has some empty space after the last section. For this reason, in the Split2 example I've made the last section of the header very big (see Figure 14.18). Here are the values of the properties of the HeaderControl, taken from the textual description of the form:

```
object HeaderControl1: THeaderControl
  Sections = <
  item
    MaxWidth = 400
    MinWidth = 40
    Text = 'Big list'
    Width = 280
  end
  item
    MaxWidth = 400
    MinWidth = 40
    Text = 'Medium list'
    Width = 180
  end
  item
    MaxWidth = 1000
    MinWidth = 40
    Text = 'Small list'
    Width = 1000
  end>
  OnSectionClick = HeaderControl1SectionClick
  OnSectionResize = HeaderControl1SectionResize
end
```

As you can see in the listing above, I've decided to handle two events: OnSectionResize and OnSectionClick. In the first handler, I simply resize the three list boxes according to the width of the three sections:

```
procedure TForm1.HeaderControl1SectionResize(
  HeaderControl: THeaderControl; Section: THeaderSection);
begin
  ListBox1.Width := HeaderControl1.Sections[0].Width;
  ListBox2.Left := ListBox1.Width;
  ListBox2.Width := HeaderControl1.Sections[1].Width;
  ListBox3.Left := ListBox2.Width + ListBox2.Left;
  ListBox3.Width := Form1.Width -
    HeaderControl1.Sections[0].Width -
    HeaderControl1.Sections[1].Width;
end;
```

FIGURE 14.18

The output of the Split2
example.

WARNING I've written `Form1.Width` instead of accessing the property directly, because the handler of the `OnSectionTrack` event of the `THeaderControl` component (called while the user is dragging the separators) has `Width` as one of its parameters. This parameter hides the corresponding property of the form.

Along with this event, we need to handle the resizing of the form, using the following code (remember that the first list box is automatically aligned):

```
procedure TForm1.FormResize(Sender: TObject);
begin
  ListBox2.Height := ListBox1.Height;
  ListBox3.Height := ListBox1.Height;
  HeaderControl1SectionResize(HeaderControl1,
    HeaderControl1.Sections [0]);
end;
```

After setting the height of the list boxes, this method simply calls the previous one, passing parameters that we won't use in this example. The second method of the HeaderControl, the click on the sections, is used to sort the contents of the corresponding list box. The problem is, how do you know which section was clicked? The best way I've figured out (there may be a better one) is to compare the section object passed as a parameter with the section objects of the Sections list property of the HeaderControl:

```
procedure TForm1.HeaderControl1SectionClick(
  HeaderControl: THeaderControl; Section: THeaderSection);
begin
  if Section = HeaderControl1.Sections[0] then
    ListBox1.Sorted := True;
  if Section = HeaderControl1.Sections[1] then
    ListBox2.Sorted := True;
  if Section = HeaderControl1.Sections[2] then
    ListBox3.Sorted := True;
end;
```

Of course this code doesn't provide the default Windows behavior of sorting the elements when you click on the header, and then sorting them in the reverse order if you click again. To implement this you should write your own sorting algorithm.

NOTE   As an alternative to the header control, and for compatibility with the 16-bit version of Delphi, you can use the Header component. You can see an example of the use of this component (very similar to the example we've just described) in the OldHead directory. The Sections property of the header this time is a plain StringList, but now we should handle the OnSizing event to limit the movement at a certain boundary.

Splitting with Panels

In our next example, Split3, the splitter is based on a Panel component instead of on the Splitter component. I've included this example to show you how Delphi handles advanced dragging operations.

To build this third version, place the three list boxes on the form, and then add two thin vertical panels in between (see Figure 14.19). Now align every component, except the third list box, to the left. The third list box, as you can probably guess, is aligned with the client area. Note that you should set the alignment of the components in the proper order, starting from the first list box, moving on to the first panel, then the second list box, the second panel, and finally the third list box.

FIGURE 14.19

The form of the Split3 example at design-time. Notice the panels between the list boxes.

This time, we need to solve the problem by using the automatic dragging features of any Delphi component. The two panels of this example support automatic dragging—their DragMode property is set to dmAutomatic—and they have the special *horizontal-splitting* cursor (crHSplit) for both the standard and the custom cursor. The three list boxes use the same cursor for dragging, too.

Each panel accepts the dragging of the panel or panels near its borders, and immediately provides the proper resizing of the list boxes. As a further enhancement, no list box can be made less than 40 pixels wide. For example, only the first panel can be dragged over the first list box (Source = Panel1), and the cursor horizontal coordinate (X) cannot be less than 40 pixels:

```
procedure TForm1.ListBox1DragOver(
  Sender, Source: TObject; X, Y: Integer;
  State: TDragState; var Accept: Boolean);
begin
  if (Source = Panel1) and (X > 40) then
  begin
    Accept := True;
    ListBox1.Width := X;
```

```
      end
    else
      Accept := False;
  end;
```

Accept should be set to True again also when a panel is dragged over itself—that is, when the user presses the left mouse button over the panel but doesn't move it away from it. This is required to display the drag cursor instead of the no-drag cursor:

```
procedure TForm1.PanelDragOver(
  Sender, Source: TObject; X, Y: Integer;
  State: TDragState; var Accept: Boolean);
begin
  if Source = Sender then
    Accept := True
  else
    Accept := False;
end;
```

This time, the program tests whether the component that originated dragging (Source) is the same one that is receiving the drag event (Sender). If this is the case, we are dragging a panel onto itself, and not over another panel. Because we have written the method with this generic code (without references to specific panels), we can use it for both panels.

The first panel can also be dragged onto the second list box. In this case, we should still resize the first list box, enlarging it, but we need to check that the third one doesn't shrink below a certain limit:

```
procedure TForm1.ListBox2DragOver(
  Sender, Source: TObject; X, Y: Integer;
  State: TDragState; var Accept: Boolean);
begin
  if (Source = Panel1) and (ListBox3.Width > 40) then
  begin
    Accept := True;
    ListBox1.Width := ListBox1.Width + X;
  end
  ...
```

Now X is relative to the second list box, so we can use it as an increment for the size of the first one. The maximum-width test performed by this code is far from perfect, since it checks to see if the third list box was big enough, not if it still will be more than 40 pixels after the current mouse-move message. The code could test whether the future size of the third list box will be big enough, but in this example, that is probably not necessary. If we end up with a list box that is 30 pixels wide, it isn't a big problem. We could easily fix this by increasing the value we test for (such as using 45 instead of 40, considering an average of 5 pixels for each mouse move message).

NOTE   Actually, no one can say what the movement of the mouse is between two consecutive mouse-move messages. The system cannot send a message for each movement of a single pixel, unless you move the mouse really slowly. The move messages are discrete, not continuous. Their generation depends on system timers and similar hardware-related parameters, but they are added to a message queue. For this reason, an application receives mouse-move messages at a rate that depends on the total workload of the system. The idea of an average of 5 pixels per movement is almost a random guess.

The same ListBox2DragOver method should also test to see if the second panel is being dragged over the second list box, checking that the list box is not reduced too much. Also, the third list box has an OnDragOver event handler, related to the second panel, as you can see in the final code (on the companion disk).

Drawing a Split Line

In the preceding example, I moved or resized the list boxes during the dragging operation, and not at the end. The advantage of this approach is that the user always has a clear picture of what is going on. The disadvantage is that the contents of the list boxes must be repainted several times, often with a nasty flickering, and if you resize the list boxes quite fast, the program will delay the window update, showing you large gray areas.

In the Split1 example, based on a *real* splitter component, we dragged a big vertical line, indicating the possible final position of the splitter, without actually moving the components until the end of the dragging operation. This is the approach I've cloned in the next version of our example, Split4.

To add a splitter line, we could draw a thick gray line on the list box in the current horizontal position. The problem is that we will need to delete that gray splitter line as soon as the splitter is moved. To accomplish this, the program needs to remember where the line was and be able to restore the previous contents of the list box (its text). A solution is to draw a line using the pmNot pen mode, which reverses the current output. This is useful because, by reversing the output twice, we can easily restore the original drawing. To obtain this effect, for each list box, write the following initialization code:

```
ListBox1.Canvas.Pen.Width := 5;
ListBox1.Canvas.Pen.Mode := pmNot;
```

The form of Split4, shown in Figure 14.20, has the same components as the previous version, but a more complex source code.

FIGURE 14.20

The line splitter of the Split4 example.

First, notice that I've written two custom methods. The DrawDragLine method is used to draw the new line and eventually delete the old one. The other method, DeleteDragLine, is used to delete the current line when dragging ends. To draw or delete a line, these functions use the MoveTo and LineTo methods of the canvas of the current list box (passed as a parameter) or of the old list box. Here is the code of the two methods:

```
procedure TForm1.DrawDragLine (
  List: TListBox; X: Integer; State: TDragState);
begin
  {if there is currently a line...}
  if OldList <> nil then
  begin
    {delete the previous line, redrawing onto it}
    OldList.Canvas.MoveTo (OldX, 0);
    OldList.Canvas.LineTo (OldX, ClientHeight);
  end;

  if not (State = dsDragLeave) then
  begin
    {if the user is not leaving the list box,
    draw the new line and store the older values}
    List.Canvas.MoveTo (X, 0);
    List.Canvas.LineTo (X, ClientHeight);
    OldX := X;
    OldList := List;
  end
  else
  begin
    {if the user is leaving the list box, then do
    *not* draw and set old values to nil/invalid}
    OldX := -10;
    OldList := nil;
  end;
end;

procedure TForm1.DeleteDragLine (List: TListBox);
begin
  {delete the old line and reset the invalid position}
  if OldList <> nil then
  begin
    OldList.Canvas.MoveTo (OldX, 0);
    OldList.Canvas.LineTo (OldX, ClientHeight);
    OldX := -10;
    OldList := nil;
  end;
end;
```

Notice that the line-drawing procedure tests the value of the State parameter passed by the dragging event, checked for with dsDragLeave. If the mouse cursor is leaving the list box, then the line is not drawn. Instead, the OldList and OldX private fields of the form are set to nil and a random negative value, respectively. Another important part of the Split4 example is the test to see whether the OldList object is currently storing a list box or is nil. This test is done before any call to a method of the object. If you don't do this, you risk accessing an undefined object, which will raise an exception.

In the code of the three OnDragOver events, you can see something similar to the code in the Split3 example. We check to see if the list box should accept dragging from the current panel (except for ListBox2, which can accept input from both), and then we also test whether the current position is within the permitted range. When the splitter is within the range, the program calls the line drawing (or even better, *moving*) method. When the splitter goes out of the proper area, the program removes the last line, calling DeleteDragLine.

As usual, to test whether the position is valid, we check whether X is less than 40; if not, the last list box has enough space. To make this last check, however, we need to compute the size of the third list box, since it doesn't change continuously during the dragging operation as in the other examples. The simplest way to compute whether the third list box is large enough is to test whether the increase in width (X) will leave it at more than 40 pixels, as you can see in the full listing on the companion disk. Here is a simpler case:

```
procedure TForm1.ListBox1DragOver(
  Sender, Source: TObject; X, Y: Integer;
  State: TDragState; var Accept: Boolean);
begin
  Accept := False;
  if Source = Panel1 then
    if X > 40 then
    begin
      Accept := True;
      DrawDragLine (ListBox1, X, State);
    end
    else
      DeleteDragLine (ListBox1);
end;
```

The new width of the list box being dragged is set only when the dragging operation ends, as in the following code:

```
procedure TForm1.ListBox1DragDrop(
  Sender, Source: TObject; X, Y: Integer);
begin
  DeleteDragLine (ListBox1);
  ListBox1.Width := X;
end;
```

As you can see, there is no test of any sort, since dropping can take place only if dragging is allowed. However, in the OnDragDrop method of the second list box, we need to consider which panel originated the dragging:

```
procedure TForm1.ListBox2DragDrop(
  Sender, Source: TObject; X, Y: Integer);
begin
  DeleteDragLine (ListBox2);
  if Source = Panel1 then
    ListBox1.Width := ListBox1.Width + X
  else
    ListBox2.Width := X;
end;
```

Although the code of this example is more complex, and it took some time to devise the whole schema, the effect is worth the effort. A particular challenge was handling the case of two consecutive dragging operations on two different list boxes (which takes place only after a fast mouse movement). To handle this situation, I introduced the idea of the OldList object.

Direct Mouse Handling in a Form

The fifth and final version of this same splitting example is less Delphi-oriented and more Windows-oriented. It uses no components other than the list boxes. Without splitters, panels, or headers, and without the mouse-dragging support offered by Delphi for components (forms cannot originate dragging operations in the VCL), the form must receive and handle Windows mouse messages directly. The other disadvantage of this approach is that we need to leave some space between the list boxes, to allow the user to operate on the form, and so we lose the automatic alignment features. On the other hand, we have very precise control; although to keep this example simple I haven't taken advantage of that to implement a splitter line, as in Split4.

NOTE Again, the purpose of this example is not to show an odd way to implement a splitter, but to demonstrate how to handle mouse dragging operations with the bare Windows API.

So here we are with three list boxes and a form. You don't see much of the form, just two small vertical areas between the list boxes we will use as a splitter. The form uses the crHSplit cursor as standard cursor. When the user presses the left mouse button on the form (that is, on one of the two thin vertical areas), the program starts some dragging code, which continues until the user releases the mouse button. During this time, any mouse movement has the effect of moving the list boxes, simulating a corresponding movement in the splitter area. Before we discuss the code of this example, however, let's take a moment for an overview of how Delphi implements dragging and capturing the mouse input.

Dragging and Clipping the Mouse

As we discussed in Chapter 10, Windows has three basic groups of mouse messages: those related to pressing a button, those related to releasing the button, and those related to moving the mouse. Delphi components also add the concept of the left-button click. But there is no concept of dragging. So how can you implement it, and how has Borland implemented it in Delphi? The idea behind dragging is quite simple. The program receives a sequence of button-down, mouse-move, and button-up messages. When the button is pressed, dragging begins, although the real actions take place only when the user moves the mouse (without releasing the mouse button) and when dragging terminates (when the button-up message arrives).

The problem with this basic approach is that it is not reliable. A window usually receives mouse events only when the mouse is over its client area; so if the user presses the mouse button, moves the mouse onto another window, and then releases the button, the second window will receive the button-up message.

There are two solutions to this problem. One (seldom used) is mouse clipping. Using a Windows API function (namely `ClipCursor`), you can force the mouse not to leave a certain area of the screen. When you move it outside the specified area, it stumbles against an invisible barrier. The second (more common) solution is to capture the mouse. When a window captures the mouse, all the subsequent mouse input is sent to that window, as we saw in Chapter 11's Fire example. This is the approach we will use for the Split5 example.

The Dragging Code

The code of Split5 is built around three methods: `FormMouseDown`, `FormMouse-Move`, and `FormMouseUp`. Pressing the left mouse button over the form (that is, over a one of the thin vertical areas used for splitting) starts the process, setting a couple of `Boolean` fields of the form, named `Dragging` and `FirstSplit`. The first variable is used to indicate that dragging is in action, and this variable will be used by the other two methods. The second variable indicates which of the two splitters the user is currently dragging (`True` indicates the first one; `False` the second). Here is the code:

```
procedure TForm1.FormMouseDown(
  Sender: TObject; Button: TMouseButton;
  Shift: TShiftState; X, Y: Integer);
begin
  if Button = mbLeft then
  begin
    Dragging := True;
    SetCapture (Handle);
    if X <= ListBox2.Left then
      FirstSplit := True
    else
      FirstSplit := False;
  end;
end;
```

An important action of this method is the call to the `SetCapture` API function. When dragging is active, as indicated by the corresponding variable (`Dragging`), and the user moves the mouse, the program performs a number of actions, but the idea is simple—resize the list boxes, unless we are out of range:

```
procedure TForm1.FormMouseMove(Sender: TObject;
  Shift: TShiftState; X, Y: Integer);
begin
```

```
if Dragging then
  if FirstSplit then
  begin
    if (X > 40) and
      (X < ClientWidth - ListBox3.Width - 40) then
    begin
      ListBox1.Width := X - 2;
      ListBox2.Left := X + 2;
      ListBox2.Width := ListBox3.Left -
        ListBox2.Left - 4;
    end;
  end
  else
    {similar code for the second split}
    ...
```

Notice that this time X is expressed in form coordinates, not the coordinate of the list box over which we are dragging the splitter. If we are within the range, the list boxes are moved and arranged properly. In this example, when the first splitter is dragged, the first list box is enlarged and the second is reduced by a corresponding amount. The third list box is not involved. This behavior is different from the previous example, which emulated the Header component. Remember also that some space (4 pixels) should be left free between the list boxes to implement the splitter.

If we move out of the range, the dragging operation terminates, calling the ReleaseCapture API function, and setting the value of the Dragging field to False. The same thing happens when the mouse button is released:

```
procedure TForm1.FormMouseUp(
  Sender: TObject; Button: TMouseButton;
  Shift: TShiftState; X, Y: Integer);
begin
  if Dragging then
  begin
    ReleaseCapture;
    Dragging := False;
  end;
end;
```

What's Next

In the first part of this chapter, we saw how Delphi handles form scrolling, and how you can work with it. We have seen how to paint on a scrolling surface and how to track scrolling operations by the user. In the second part, we focused on other techniques you can use to increase the number of components you can display on a form, using various forms of multiple-page components. We saw how to use the new Windows 95 PageControl and TabControl components, and how you can connect a Tab-Set to a Notebook component. In the third part we discussed splitting techniques, based on the new Splitter component, on the use of the Header Control, and on panels. We also discussed direct handling of mouse-related Windows messages. Delphi components are very flexible. Rather than sticking with a fixed design, you can choose from the many options available.

The notebook metaphor allows us to build complex applications, with many forms (or pages) and a simple user interface, generally better then using several windows moving on the screen, and possibly hidden from view. Another approach to building complex applications with several forms is the MDI technique. This will be the topic of the next chapter, Chapter 15.

C H A P T E R

F I F T E E N

Creating MDI Applications

■ Frame and child windows

■ The Window menu

■ MDI applications with multiple child windows

■ MDI applications with different child windows

■ Implementing a bouncing square

So far, we've covered how to handle simple Delphi applications that have a single main form, as well as more complex applications that have a number of different forms and dialog boxes. We have also seen that scrolling, splitting, and layering (that is, using notebooks) are techniques you can use to display a lot of information and components in a single form.

Besides using dialog boxes, or secondary forms, and squeezing components into a form, there is a third approach that is common in Windows applications: MDI (*Multiple Document Interface*). MDI applications are made up of a number of forms that appear inside a single main form. In this chapter, we'll start with some general and technical information about MDI development in Windows. Then we'll build an MDI program in Delphi step by step.

MDI in Windows: A Technical Overview

In the early days of Windows, each application was made up of a number of different windows floating around the screen. This was with the second version of the environment, since the first version of the Microsoft operating system could only *tile* its windows, not overlap them. A few years later, Microsoft introduced a technique to have a full-blown window (we might call it a *form*) living inside another window, usually called the *frame*. This model is known as Multiple Document Interface (or MDI) because an application generally uses a *child window* for each document. If you use Windows Notepad, you can open only one text document, because Notepad isn't an MDI application. But with your favorite word processor, you can probably open a number of different documents, each in its own child window, because it is an MDI application. All these windows referring to the documents are usually held by a *frame*, or *application*, window. Although it is quite common to think of MDI as a technique for allowing users to work on a number of documents or files at the same time, this is not always the case. In Windows 3.1, the Program Manager and File Manager, for example, used MDI to display system information, not documents. Other applications use MDI to display various views of the same data in different windows.

NOTE When Windows 3.0 was released, Microsoft really stressed the use of MDI. By the time Windows 3.1 came out, Microsoft had started to acknowledge that many users were not comfortable with this interface. With the advent of different approaches to the user interface, and particularly with the release of Windows 95, MDI is becoming less common. For example, the Windows 95 Explorer is an SDI (*Single Document Interface*) application. However, MDI won't disappear quickly, simply because there are too many applications following this approach (including most office suites), and many users have become familiar with this interface.

This section provides a short overview of MDI, in technical Windows terms. Just forget Delphi for a moment, and I'll try to give you an idea of what MDI really is (not what an MDI application looks like). If you've never built an MDI application and you want a quick start, you might consider skipping this section for now.

You know that the idea behind MDI is to have a child window similar to a main window, but placed inside another window. What you might not know is that to make this work, Windows requires a complex structure. If you simply place a window inside another one as a child window, a lot of strange things happen. If you don't believe me, try running the Child example. Figure 15.1 shows the output of this application. When you run this program, you'll find that things are funny when you try to work with the windows. Notice that the active child window does not have an active title bar. Clicking inside the client area of the child window doesn't activate it. Maximizing a child window has a weird effect.

FIGURE 15.1

The output of the Child application. It looks almost like an MDI application, but doesn't actually work like one.

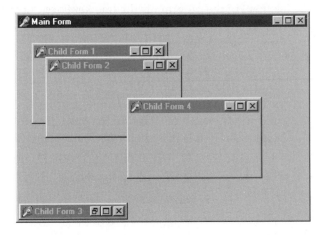

This example defines two forms: a main form and a child form. When the user clicks in the main form, a new child form is created, with the following code:

```
procedure TMainForm.FormClick(Sender: TObject);
var
  NewForm: TChildForm;
begin
  {increase the child window counter}
  Inc (Counter);

  {create a new form and define it
  as child of the current form}
  NewForm:= TChildForm.Create (self);
  NewForm.Parent := self;

  {add the number to the caption, and move it slightly}
  NewForm.Caption := NewForm.Caption + ' ' +
    IntToStr (Counter);
  NewForm.Left := (Counter * 20) mod 500;
  NewForm.Top := (Counter * 20) mod 450;

  {show the form}
  NewForm.Show;
end;
```

In this procedure, Counter is an integer, a private field of the form, and TChildForm is the data type of the form defined in a second unit, CHILDF.PAS. This second form is a plain default form, without any special properties, as is the main form. The Counter value is used to give a different name to each form, and to make sure that they won't all be placed in the same position. But the key element of the program is the line NewForm.Parent := self, which assigns to the Parent property of the new form the main form, self. This makes the new form a child of the main window.

As you can see, this program appears to be an MDI application, but it is not. Some of its problems are that the active child doesn't have an active title bar, the child windows are moved to the front only if you select their borders, and the child windows are not maximized properly. Note that this strange behavior is not Delphi's fault. It is the default Windows behavior. This misbehaving application can be corrected by handling a number of Windows messages to make it have the desired behavior, but there is an easier solution: use the MDI approach. MDI was introduced to fix just these kinds of problems.

Although the MDI structure is not simple, it gives programmers a number of benefits automatically. For example, Windows handles a list of the child Windows in one of the pull-down menus of the application, and there are specific Delphi methods that activate the corresponding MDI functionality, to tile or cascade the child windows. The following is the technical structure of an MDI application in Windows:

- The main window of the application acts as a frame, or a container. This window requires a proper menu structure and some specific coding (at least when programming with the API).

- A special window, known as the *MDI client*, covers the whole client area of the frame window, providing some special capabilities. For example, the MDI client handles the list of child windows. Although this might seem strange at first, the MDI client is one of the Windows predefined controls, just like an edit box or a list box. The MDI client window does not have the typical elements of the interface of a window, such as a caption or border, but it is visible. In fact, you can change the standard system color of the MDI work area (called the "Application Background") in the Appearance page of the Display Properties dialog box of Windows 95.

- There are a number of child windows, of the same kind or of different kinds. These child windows are not placed in the frame window directly, but each is defined as a child of the MDI client window, which in turn is a child of the frame window. (We might say that the child windows are the "grand-children" of the frame.)

When you program using the Windows API, some work is usually required to build and maintain this structure, and other coding is needed to handle the menu properly. As you'll see in this chapter, these tasks become much easier with Delphi.

Frame and Child Windows in Delphi

Delphi makes the development of MDI applications easy, even without considering the MDI application template. You only need to build at least two forms, one with the FormStyle property set to fsMDIForm, and the other with the same property set to fsMDIChild. That's all, almost.

A First Delphi MDI Demo

Once the two forms have these two values for the `FormStyle` property, you need to provide a way to create one or more child windows. This can be done by adding a menu with a New menu item and writing the following code:

```
procedure TMainForm.New1Click(Sender: TObject);
var
  ChildForm: TChildForm;
begin
  ChildForm := TChildForm.Create (Application);
  ChildForm.Show;
end;
```

> **NOTE**
> When you create a new form you can pass either `Application` or the parent form (`self`) as the parameter of the `Create` constructor. Most of the time, a program will work fine in both cases, but there are some differences. The parameter you pass indicates the owner of the form, the one that will destroy the form when it is closed. In some cases this relationship also affects the behavior of the windows (for example, when you minimize one), particularly in an application with many forms.

In the above code, I've named the two forms `MainForm` and `ChildForm`. Since you refer to the `TChildForm` class, the unit defining it should be included in this source code. In the MdiDemo1 example, this second file is simply `CHILD.PAS`.

To create an even better program, you can name the pull-down menu containing this item Window, and use it as value of the `WindowMenu` property of the form. Of course, you can choose any other name for the menu item, but "Window" is standard. With these simple operations, which might require less than a minute, I have built the first MDI demo program. To make this program work properly, we need to take a few more steps. First, notice that only the first form (the main form) should be created automatically at startup. You can set this in the Forms page of the Project Options dialog box. Then, we can add a number to the title of any child window when it is created:

```
procedure TMainForm.New1Click(Sender: TObject);
var
  ChildForm: TChildForm;
begin
  WindowMenu := Window1;
  Inc (Counter);
```

```
ChildForm := TChildForm.Create (self);
ChildForm.Caption := ChildForm.Caption + ' ' +
  IntToStr (Counter);
ChildForm.Show;
end;
```

This first version of the MdiDemo application performs some of the common tasks of MDI applications. Figure 15.2 shows an example of this program's output. You can open a number of child windows, minimize or maximize each of them, close them, and use the Window pull-down menu to navigate among them.

FIGURE 15.2

An example of the output of the MdiDemo1 program.

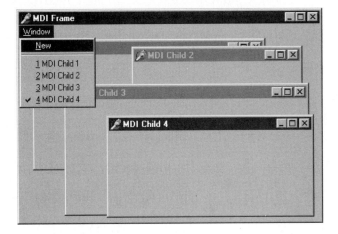

As you can see in Figure 15.2, Delphi has already added the list of child windows, using their names, in the Window menu. If you create more than nine child windows, a More Windows menu item is added to the pull-down menu; when you select this menu item, you'll see a dialog box (provided by Windows, not part of your program) with a complete list of the child windows.

Now suppose that we want to close some of these child windows, to unclutter the client area of our program. Click on the Close box of some of the child windows and they are minimized! What is happening here? Remember that when you close a window, you generally hide it from view. The closed forms in Delphi still exist, although they are not visible. In the case of child windows, simply hiding them won't work, because the MDI Window menu and the list of windows will still list existing child windows, even if they are hidden. For this reason, Delphi simply minimizes the MDI child windows when you try to close them. To solve this problem, we need to delete the child windows when they are closed, as we will do in the next version of this example.

MdiDemo1 has another problem: its Window pull-down menu is somewhat bare. We should add some commands to tile or cascade the child windows, and to arrange their icons. This is standard in any Windows MDI application, and it is simple to implement in Delphi.

Building a Complete Window Menu

Our first task is to define a better menu structure for the example. Typically the Window pull-down menu has at least three items, titled *Cascade*, *Tile*, and *Arrange Icons*.To handle the menu commands, we can use some of the predefined methods that are available in forms that have the fsMDIForm value for the Form-Style property:

- The Cascade method cascades the open MDI child windows. The child forms are arranged starting from the upper-left corner of the client area of the frame windows, and moving toward the lower-left corner. The windows overlap each other. Iconized child windows are also arranged (see Arrange-Icons below).

- The Tile method tiles the open MDI child windows. The child forms are arranged so that they do not overlap. The client area of the frame windows is divided into equal portions for the different windows, so that they can all be shown on the screen, no matter how many windows there are. Figure 15.3 shows an example of five child windows tiled on the screen. The Tile method will also arrange iconized child windows.The default behavior is horizontal tiling, although if you have several child windows, they will be arranged in several columns. This default can be changed by using the TileMode property.

- The TileMode property determines how the Tile procedure should work. The only two choices are tbHorizontal, for horizontal tiling, and tbVertical, for vertical tiling. Some applications use two different menu commands for the two tiling modes; other applications offer only one Tile menu command but check whether the Shift key is pressed when the user selects it. This actually confuses most users, so you'll probably want to keep your application simple, with one tiling option.

- The `ArrangeIcons` procedure arranges all the iconized child windows, starting from the lower-left corner of the client area of the frame window, and moving to the upper-right corner. Open forms are not moved.

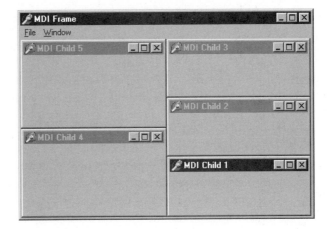

These procedures and properties are useful for handling the Window menu of an MDI application. For example you can write the following code:

```
procedure TMainForm.Cascade1Click(Sender: TObject);
begin
  Cascade;
end;
```

The other menu command handlers of the program are simple, too. There are also some other interesting methods and properties related strictly to MDI in Delphi:

- `ActiveMDIChild` is a run-time and read-only property of the MDI frame form, and holds the active child window. The user can change this value by selecting a new child window, or by the program can change it using the `Next` and `Previous` procedures.

- The `Next` procedure activates the child window following the active one in the internal order.

- The `Previous` procedure activates the child window preceding the active one in the internal order.

- The ClientHandle property holds the Windows handle of the MDI client window, which covers the client area of the main form.

- The MDIChildCount property stores the current number of child windows.

- The MDIChildren property is an array of child windows. You can use this and the MDIChildCount property to cycle among all of the child windows, for example using a for loop. This can be useful for finding a particular child window, or to operate on each of them.

Note that the internal order of the child windows is the reverse order of activation. This means that the last child window selected is the active window (the first in the internal list), the second-to-last child window selected is the second, and the first child window selected is the last. This order determines how the windows are arranged on the screen. The first window in the list is the one above all others, while the last window is below all others, and probably hidden away. You can imagine an axis (the z-axis) coming out of the screen towards you. The active window has a higher value for the z-coordinate, and thus covers other windows. For this reason, the Windows ordering schema is known as the *z-order*.

To make the list of child windows work properly, we need to add a few lines of code to the OnClose event of the child window, as mentioned earlier:

```
procedure TChildForm.FormClose(Sender: TObject;
  var Action: TCloseAction);
begin
  Action := caFree;
end;
```

Up to now, we have focused on the frame window, but the form used for the child windows has no components and very little code. The frame window usually doesn't change much in the different MDI examples (besides having a toolbar, a status bar, and similar enhancements). Usually, most of the code goes in the child forms. Now it's time to look at a real example of using child windows.

Building a Child Window

In the last two examples, we have seen how to build the structure of an MDI application in Delphi, focusing on the frame window. Thus, we've obtained a program with the typical MDI behavior, but no real functionality. What can we do with the child form? The answer is anything we can do with a form. We can add a number of components, build editors, add graphics programs, and so on. Any of the programs we have built up to now could be turned into an MDI application (although this wouldn't make much sense for some of them).

Our first example is an MDI version of a simple graphical program (similar to the second version of the Shape program we built in Chapter 10), named MdiDemo3. This program can display a circle in the position where the user clicked one of t he mouse buttons. Figure 15.4 shows an example of the output of the MdiDemo3 example. The program includes a Circle menu, which allows the user to change the color of the surface of the circle, as well as the color and size of its border. What is interesting here is that to program the child form, we do not need to consider the existence of other forms or of the frame window. We simply write the code of the form, and that's all. The only special care required is for the menus of the two forms.

FIGURE 15.4

The output of the MdiDemo3 example, with a child window that displays circles and a flexible menu bar. Notice the different menu bars at startup and when a child window has been created.

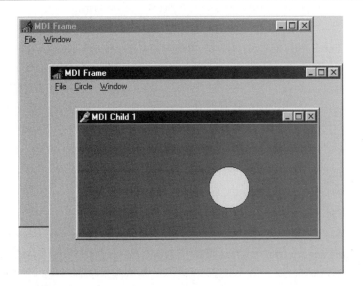

If we prepare a main menu for the child form, once this is displayed on the screen, it replaces the main menu of the frame window. An MDI child window, in fact, cannot have a menu of its own. But the fact that a child window can't have any menus should not bother you, because this is the standard behavior of MDI applications. You can use the menu bar of the frame window to display the menus of the child window. Even better, you can merge the menu bar of the frame window and that of the child form. For example, in this program, the menu of the child form can be placed between the frame window's File and Window pull-down menus. You can accomplish this using the following GroupIndex values:

- File pull-down menu, main form: 1
- Window pull-down menu, main form: 3
- Circle pull-down menu, child form: 2

Using these settings for the menu group indexes, the menu bar of the frame window will have either two or three pull-down menus. At startup, the menu bar has two menus. As soon as you create a child window, there are three menus, and when the last child window is closed (destroyed), the Circle pull-down menu disappears. You can see this in Figure 15.4, but you should also spend some time testing this behavior by running the program.

The source code of the main form is the same as for the previous version of the program. The code of the child window has been only slightly changed from Chapter 9. If you look at the source code (on the companion disk), it is interesting to notice how the menu commands of the running program pertain to the two forms, and that in the source code, each form handles its own commands, regardless of the existence of other elements.

The data of the child form, particularly the coordinates of the center of the circle, must be declared using some fields of the form, and not other variables declared inside the unit. In fact, we need a specific memory location to store the center of the circle for each child window.

NOTE
Storing the child form's data is simple to implement in Delphi, but not in Windows programming using the API. Traditional Windows code requires complex schemes to store the data of the child Windows of an MDI application. I'll spare you the details, but I thought you should be aware of this great advantage of object-oriented programming in an operating system and a user interface that are not truly object-oriented.

MDI Applications with Different Child Windows

A common approach in complex MDI applications is to include child Windows of different kinds (that is, based on different child forms). We can extend the previous example to highlight some problems you may encounter with this approach. For this example, we need to build a new child form. Any form would do, but I wanted to use this example to show you something new: limited multitasking. To do that, I decided to use a form that contains a bouncing square.

Adding a Bouncing Shape

The square, a Shape component, moves around the client area of the form at fixed time intervals, using a Timer component, and bounces on the edges of the form, changing its direction. This turning process is determined by a fairly complex (compared with most of the examples in this book) algorithm. The idea is that the square has its own position and is associated with a Dir (direction) value—another member of the form class—which can assume one of the following values:

```
type
  Directions = (up_right, down_right,
    down_left, up_left);
```

When the period elapses, the square is moved in the corresponding direction:

```
procedure TBounceChildForm.Timer1Timer(Sender: TObject);
begin
  case Dir of
    up_right: begin
      Shape1.Left := Shape1.Left + 3;
      Shape1.Top := Shape1.Top - 3;
    end;
    ...
```

This accounts for the movement. The real problem is to make the square bounce on the edges of the form. In short, each time the square reaches an edge, we must change its direction. To determine when the shape has reached an edge, you can check its top and right values against zero and the bottom and right values against the size of the client area. The bottom and right values are not directly available, but you can compute them by adding the height of the shape to its top value (or the width to the left value):

```
if Shape1.Top <= 0 then ...
if Shape1.Top + Shape1.Height >= ClientHeight then ...
if Shape1.Left <= 0 then ...
if Shape1.Left + Shape1.Width >= ClientWidth then ...
```

You might try making these checks at the end of the code in order to increase the current values, but that would not work. In fact, to make the square move gracefully, you should choose a good (and more complex) pattern. For example, suppose that we want each turn to be at 90 degrees, so that the square doesn't bounce back in the same direction as its approach, as illustrated in Figure 15.5.

FIGURE 15.5

The proper path of the Shape object, which should turn 90 degrees each time it bounces against a border.

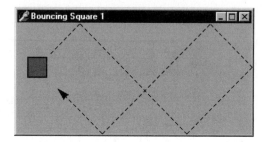

The idea is that if the form is itself a square, the shape should always move clockwise, or always counterclockwise, depending on the initial direction. If the form is a rectangle, the two kinds of turns alternate, as you can see in Figure 15.5. (Of course, you can see this behavior in action by running the MdiDemo4 program.) To obtain this behavior, we need to write some code to change the current direction in each of the different branches of the case statement mentioned before. In fact, the next direction of the square when it has reached a border of the form depends on the current direction. Here is only the first part of the rather long Timer1Timer method, the key method of this form:

```
procedure TBounceChildForm.Timer1Timer(Sender: TObject);
begin
  case Dir of
    up_right:
    begin
```

```
    Shape1.Left := Shape1.Left + 3;
    Shape1.Top := Shape1.Top - 3;
    if Shape1.Top <= 0 then
      Dir := down_right;
    if Shape1.Left + Shape1.Width >= ClientWidth then
      Dir := up_left;
  end;
  ...
```

The Menu of the New Child Form

Like any child form, the one in our example will have its own menu bar, which is merged with the menu bar of the frame window. The menu structure is quite simple, although it has two different pull-down menus. The first pull-down menu, Square, has two commands to change the color of the square or to retrieve its position. The code of the first method should be obvious, so here is the second:

```
procedure TBounceChildForm.GetPosition1Click(
  Sender: TObject);
begin
  MessageDlg (
    'The top-left corner of the square was in the position ('
    + IntToStr (Shape1.Left) + ', ' + IntToStr (Shape1.Top)
    + ').', mtInformation, [mbOk], 0);
end;
```

Since we use the color selection dialog box for only one color (the color used to fill the square), we don't need to store it in a separate variable. Of course, we need to initialize this value, along with the starting direction, in the FormCreate method.

The second pull-down menu, Movements, has two commands to start or stop the movement of the shape. This can be accomplished easily by enabling or disabling the timer. Besides this, each of the two methods disables the corresponding command, and enables the opposite one (it makes no sense to start a moving shape, or stop one that has already been stopped). Here is the first:

```
procedure TBounceChildForm.Start1Click(Sender: TObject);
begin
  Timer1.Enabled := True;
  Start1.Enabled := False;
  Stop1.Enabled := True;
end;
```

Changing the Main Form

Now that the bouncing square form is complete, we need to integrate it into the MDI application. The main form must provide a menu command to create a child form of this new kind and to check the group indexes of the pull-down menus. I've slightly changed the structure of the menu of this form. The File pull-down menu here has a second New menu item, which is used to create a child window of the new kind. The code uses the same child window counter as the other form. As an alternative, you could use two different counters for the two kinds of child windows.

As soon as a form of this kind is displayed on the screen, its menu bar is automatically merged with the main menu bar. When you select a child form of one of the two kinds, the menu bar changes accordingly. Once all the child windows are closed, the original menu bar of the main form is reset. By using the proper menu group indexes, we let Delphi accomplish everything automatically, as you can see in the two windows shown in Figure 15.6.

FIGURE 15.6

The menu bar of the MdiDemo4 application changes automatically to reflect the currently selected child window.

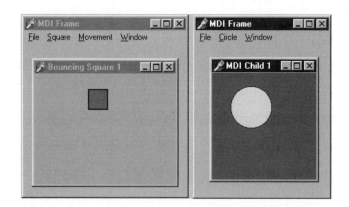

I've added a few other menu items in the main form. One menu choice is used to close every child window, a second tiles the child windows horizontally instead of vertically, and another shows some statistics about them. The methods connected to these menu items use some specific MDI properties of the form, such as the TileMode property, the MDIChildCount property, and the MDIChildren array. Two of these methods are quite interesting, because they show how to take an action on each of the child windows. For example, the CloseAllClick procedure has the following code:

```
procedure TMainForm.CloseAllClick(Sender: TObject);
```

```
var
  I: Integer;
begin
  for I := 0 to MDIChildCount - 1 do
    MDIChildren [I].Close;
end;
```

Another example is in the method related to the Count command. In this procedure, the array is scanned to count the number of child Windows of each kind. This is accomplished using the RTTI operator is:

```
procedure TMainForm.Count1Click(Sender: TObject);
var
  NBounce, NCircle, I: Integer;
begin
  NBounce := 0;
  NCircle := 0;
  for I := 0 to MDIChildCount - 1 do
    if MDIChildren is TBounceChildForm then
      Inc (NBounce)
    else
      Inc (NCircle);
  MessageDlg (
    Format ('There are %d child forms.'#13 +
      '%d are Circle child windows and ' +
      '%d are Bouncing child windows',
      [MDIChildCount, NCircle, NBounce]),
    mtINformation, [mbOk], 0);
end;
```

Once these values are computed, they are shown on the screen with the MessageDlg function, as you can see in the code above and in the corresponding Figure 15.7.

FIGURE 15.7

The output of the Count menu command of the MdiDemo4 example, indicating the number of child Windows of each kind.

A Fast Start with MDI

In this chapter, we have built some MDI applications in Delphi from scratch. Taking this approach allowed us to learn the details of MDI in Windows and of Delphi's support for this approach. However, the "from-scratch" approach is not the best way to go when you need to build a real MDI application. Delphi provides an MDI Application template, and you can also use one of the Wizards to build the initial code of an MDI application quickly. We'll look at the framework each of these tools produces, and then see how to build an application starting with the code generated by Delphi.

To use the MDI Application template, just issue the File ➤ New command in the Delphi environment, choose the Projects page, and then MDI Application. Select a directory for the project, and Delphi will copy the files you need for a simple MDI application, with a toolbar, a status bar, and a menu, into that directory. (I've included the generated files in the MdiTemp directory of the current chapter, together with the generated executable file, for your convenience.)

The form generated by the template contains standard elements: a main menu, a Panel component used as a toolbar, a StatusBar component, and some system dialog boxes. The source code of the form has some interesting elements. I suggest you generate the code and study it with some care. First, notice the code of the FormCreate method:

```
procedure TMainForm.FormCreate(Sender: TObject);
begin
  Application.OnHint := ShowHint;
  Screen.OnActiveFormChange := UpdateMenuItems;
end;
```

The first statement activates the hints at the application level, as we have seen in Chapter 11. It works together with the ShowHint procedure, which displays the hints in the StatusBar component. The second statement of the FormCreate method is something new. What is the Screen object? What is this OnActiveFormChange event? You might remember that I've used the Screen global object in a couple of programs in earlier chapters. This object provides access to the list of fonts installed in the system. The Screen object handles a lot of information related to the output of the application, including the available fonts and a list of the forms in the application. We will see some more details about the TScreen class in Chapter 25. For the moment, it is enough to know that the OnActiveFormChange event takes place each time the active form of the application changes.

The OnActiveFormChange event refers to the active form or window of the application, not the active application. In other words, this event is not activated when the user changes the active window among all of the Windows applications that are running; the event is activated when the user changes the active form within the current application. It is an application-wide event, not a system-wide one. To execute some code when the active Windows application changes, you can use the OnActivate event of the Application object. Do not confuse this with the OnActivate event of a form, which takes place when the form itself becomes active. You can use the OnActiveFormChange event of the Screen object instead of the OnActivate event of each of the different forms, obtaining a similar effect.

As with events of the Application object, events of the Screen object must be set in the code. Notice that this operation is canceled, setting the event to nil, inside the FormDestroy method. By the way, the effect of the UpdateMenuItems procedure is to enable or disable some of the menu items when there are no more child windows:

```
procedure TMainForm.UpdateMenuItems(Sender: TObject);
begin
  FileCloseItem.Enabled := MDIChildCount > 0;
  FileSaveItem.Enabled := MDIChildCount > 0;
  CutItem.Enabled := MDIChildCount > 0;
  CopyItem.Enabled := MDIChildCount > 0;
  ...
```

Another interesting part of the source code generated by Delphi is the way file opening is handled. There is a CreateMDIChild method, responsible for creating a new child form and giving it a title, using the value of its parameter:

```
procedure TMainForm.CreateMDIChild(const Name: string);
var
  Child: TMDIChild;
begin
  { create a new MDI child window }
  Child := TMDIChild.Create(Application);
  Child.Caption := Name;
end;
```

This method is called by the procedure related to both the New and Open commands on the File menu:

```
procedure TMainForm.FileOpenItemClick(Sender: TObject);
begin
  if OpenDialog.Execute then
    CreateMDIChild(OpenDialog.FileName);
end;
```

The files are not automatically opened: only the file name is used! You might extend this by merging into this program the code of the Notes example, the RichNote example, or that of the image viewer example.

What's Next

There are many things we could do to further explore MDI support in Windows, but I think that this chapter is enough for an overview. In particular, I've decided not to show you more MDI examples, because this kind of model is being de-emphasized in Windows 95. With this chapter, we have concluded the specific study of multiple-form applications, which we started in Chapter 13 when we explored secondary forms (modal and modeless) and dialog boxes. We have also seen some examples of notebook-based applications, the use of form-splitting techniques, and in this chapter, MDI. In some cases, each of these techniques are valid solutions, so you will need to decide which approach to use. I've given equal coverage to each of these techniques, although I have my preferences: few secondary forms, more dialog boxes, MDI if it is needed, and notebooks whenever possible.

Now we can move forward to a very hot Delphi programming topic: building database applications. This will take the next two chapters, which will try to cover most of the fundamental topics of Delphi database programming. It is possible to write a specific book about this, so the description won't be exhaustive, but you should be able to get a comprehensive overview of this key element of Delphi development.

After these two database chapters we'll be able to start looking into Delphi behind the scenes, and focus on topics such as the construction of Delphi components and ActiveX controls.

CHAPTER
SIXTEEN

16

Building Database Applications

- Delphi's database components

- Constructing database applications manually

- The DBGrid and multi-record objects

- The use of the Database Form Wizard

- Query and table field manipulation

- Forms with more than one database table

Database support is one of the key features of the Delphi programming environment. Many programmers spend most of their time writing data-access code, and this needs to be the most robust portion of a database application. This chapter provides an overview of Delphi's extensive support for database programming. You can create very complex database applications, starting from a blank form or one generated by Delphi's Database Form Wizard.

What you won't find here is a discussion of the theory of database design. I'm assuming that you already know the fundamentals of database design and have already designed the structure of a database. I won't delve into database-specific problems; my goal is to help you understand how Delphi supports this kind of programming.

We'll begin with an explanation of how data access works in Delphi, and then review the database components that are available in Delphi. Then we'll move on to some basic examples to see how the components work. After that, we'll delve into some more advanced features, such as getting information about the tables at run-time, creating new tables with Delphi code, using graphics fields, and building forms with more than one table.

> **NOTE** Besides accessing data in local databases, the Delphi Client/Server Suite edition can be used to connect to SQL databases on server computers. This topic will be introduced in the next chapter, together with other advanced topics related to Delphi database architecture, such as data modules.

Data, Files, Databases, and Tables

On a computer, permanent data—including database data—is always stored in files. There are several techniques you can use to accomplish this storage. The two most common approaches are to store a whole database in what appears to the file system as a single file, or to store each table, index, and any other elements of the database in a separate file, usually on the same directory.

Delphi can use both approaches; or more precisely, it uses a custom approach that works well with both underlying structures. You always refer to a database with its name or an *alias*, which is a sort of a nickname of a database, but this reference can be to a database file or to a directory containing files with tables. It just depends on the data format you are using. But Delphi is not tied to a specific data format. It can use dBASE or Paradox tables, and access SQL (Structured Query Language) server databases or databases in other formats via the Microsoft ODBC (Open Database Connectivity) standard.

TIP You can define new aliases for databases by using the Database Explorer or the Database Engine Configuration utility. It is also possible to define them by writing code in Delphi that calls the `DbiAddAlias` function of the BDE.

Delphi database applications do not have direct access to the data sources they reference. Delphi interfaces with the Borland Database Engine (BDE), which does have direct access to a number of data sources, including dBASE, Paradox, ASCII, FoxPro, and Access tables (using the appropriate drivers).

NEW Support for Microsoft Visual FoxPro and Microsoft Access tables is brand new in Delphi 3. It was not available in previous versions of Delphi.

The BDE can also interface with Borland's SQL Links, a tool that allows access to a number of local and remote SQL servers. Delphi ships with the Local InterBase for Windows, from Borland. Remote servers include Oracle, Sybase, Informix, InterBase, and DB2. If you need access to a different database or data format, the BDE can interface with ODBC drivers. Although ODBC can provide access to data sources, this is usually the least efficient method. Use ODBC only as a last choice. See Figure 16.1 for an illustration of how database access works in Delphi.

The fact that generally Delphi applications don't access to data directly but use the BDE basically means that you will need to install the BDE along with your applications on your clients' computers. This is not difficult, since Delphi includes the "lite" version of an installation program (InstallShield) that can be used to prepare installation disks for the BDE, along with your own application. The BDE files are required—your Delphi database applications won't work without them—but you can distribute them freely.

NEW

Delphi 3 has increased support for the development of database applications that don't access the BDE. Delphi 3 includes a ClientDataSet component you can use to access data from an OLE server, running on a different computer. Besides this, third-party developers are likely to release new lightweight database engines that will replace the BDE and generally work with a specific database format only. There were already similar tools for earlier versions of Delphi, but they were far less integrated into the VCL.

FIGURE 16.1

The overall picture of data access in Delphi.

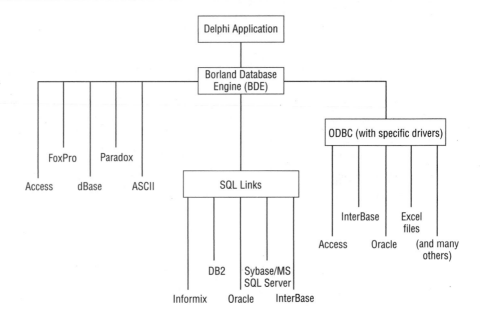

What Is a Table?

In general, we can use the term *database* to refer to a collection of tables. But what exactly is a table? Although most of you probably know the answer, I'll recap the basic information for the database newcomers.

A table in a database can be compared to a file of records in Pascal. A table has many records, or *rows*, and many columns, one for each field of the record. You can see the structure of a table, with its key elements labeled, in Figure 16.2.

Notice that in a table there are the concepts of *current record* (the record a user is operating in) and *current field* (the active field of the current record).

FIGURE 16.2

The schema of a database table. The table has been loaded in the Database Explorer.

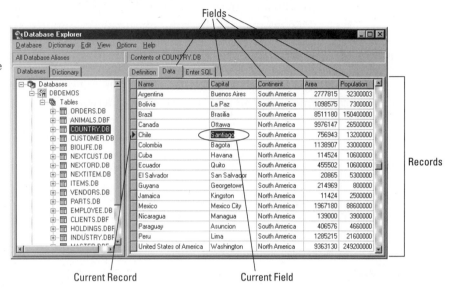

The structure of a table can be clearly seen when you load it in a table viewer program, such as the Database Desktop or the Database Explorer included in Delphi. This last is the tool I used to create the image in Figure 16.2.

NOTE

The sample table shown in Figure 16.2, COUNTRY.DB, is part of the Delphi examples (in the directory DEMOS\DATA, also indicated by the DBDEMOS alias, set up by Delphi during the installation). Many of my examples will use this Delphi database. This way, instead of needing to build new ones, you already have these files available. In some examples, however, I'll show you how to build tables from scratch.

The first row of the table shows the names of the various fields, such as Name, Capital, Continent, and so on. Below them are the actual values of these fields in the various rows of the table. You can also see that there are visual hints indicating the current record and the current field.

Operations on Database Data

Once you have a database table, you can perform a number of actions, such as edit values, insert new records, and delete existing records. You can also perform operations on a window that contains a copy of some of the database data, and then later copy that data back into the database. You'll see these two steps in the code of many of the database application examples.

The problem of synchronizing the values seen by the user with the real data is complicated by the fact that several users might be accessing a database at the same time from different computers on a network. To avoid conflicts, databases have some form of locking to prevent two users from changing the same database data at the same time. However, you seldom need to deal with this issue directly. The BDE and the databases you connect to shield you from most of the details of database handling and data processing.

Delphi offers a uniform view of database access, but you must be aware that not all databases support the same features.

> **NOTE**　In the 32-bit versions of the BDE, databases have the concept of a *transaction* (a sequence of database operations treated as a single indivisible one) and of *transaction rollback* (the process of ignoring a transaction and returning to the preceding situation). This is a feature of SQL server databases that is now also available for local tables.

Delphi Database Components

Delphi includes a number of components related to databases. The Data Access page of the Components palette contains components used to interact with databases. Most of them are nonvisual components, since they encapsulate database connections, tables, queries, and similar elements. Fortunately, Delphi also provides a number of predefined components you can use to view and edit database data. In the Data Controls page, there are visual components used to view and edit the data in a form. These controls are called *data-aware* controls.

To access a database in Delphi, you generally need a data source, described by the DataSource component. The DataSource component, however, does not indicate the data directly; it refers either to a table, to the result of a query, or to a stored procedure. Therefore, you also need a Table, Query, or StoredProc component in the form, as you can see in the scheme shown in Figure 16.3. What this figure does not show is that the DataSource component can be connected to either a table or a query, but not to both at the same time. Instead, multiple data-aware controls are usually connected to a single data source.

FIGURE 16.3

The role of the DataSource component is to connect multiple data-aware controls with one data set.

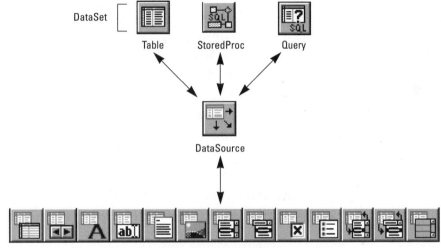

As soon as you have placed a Table or Query component on the form, you can use the DataSet property of the DataSource component to refer to it. For this property, the Object Inspector lists the available data sets of the current form, or of other forms connected with the current one (using the File ➤ Uses Form command). In other words, a database application must provide a DataSource component and one of the data set components, in one of its forms.

> **NOTE**
>
> By "data set component," I mean either a TTable, a TQuery, or a TStored-Proc object, which are all subclasses of the TBDEDataSet class, which is a subclass of the TDatSet class. In Delphi 3 there is a fourth inherited class, TClientDataSet. The new version of Delphi has also a more complex class hierarchy for data sets. Again, these intermediate classes can be useful for companies implementing new forms of data access in Delphi.

Tables and Queries

The simplest way to specify data access in Delphi is to use the Table component. A Table object simply refers to a database table. When you use a Table component, you need to indicate the name of the database you want to use in its `DatabaseName` property. You can enter the name itself, an alias, or the path of the directory with the table files. The Object Inspector lists the available names, which depend on the aliases installed in the BDE.

You also need to indicate a proper value in the `TableName` property. Again this can be an internal name or the name of the file holding the table. The Object Inspector lists the available tables of the current database (or directory), so you should generally select the `DatabaseName` property first, and the `TableName` property soon afterwards.

Two other relevant properties of the Table component are `ReadOnly`, used to prevent any changes in the data, and `Exclusive`, used to forbid concurrent access to a networked table from several applications at the same time. There are also properties related to indexes and master tables. We will focus on these last properties again at the end of this chapter, in the MastDet example.

A second data set available in Delphi is the Query component. A query is usually more complex than a table, because it requires a SQL language command. However, you can customize a query using SQL more easily than you can customize a table (as long as you know at least the basic elements of SQL, of course).

> **NOTE**
>
> SQL is a standard language for writing database queries and generally interacting with a database. If you are not fluent in SQL, you can refer to Appendix B for a description of its basic commands. If you remember at least the key elements, however, you can probably read the simple SQL examples in this book without worrying too much about the details. The Client/Server Suite of Delphi includes a specific tool to create SQL queries, called the Visual Query Builder, which is discussed in Chapter 17.

The Query component has a `DatabaseName` property like the Table component, but it does not have a `TableName` property. The table is indicated inside the SQL statement, stored in the SQL property. As we will see in an example later in this chapter, this SQL statement can also include parameters, specified with the Parameters property. You can set the SQL statement both at design-time, by opening the

SQL string editor, or at run-time. For example, you can write a simple SQL statement like this:

```
select * from Country
```

where Country is the name of a table, and the star symbol (*) indicates that you want to use all of the fields in the table. If you are fluent in SQL, you might use the Query component more often, but the efficiency of a table or a query varies depending on the database you are using. The Table component tends to be faster on local tables, while the Query component tends to be faster on SQL servers, although this is not always the case.

In a simple example, you can use either a Table or Query component to achieve the same effects. In general, tables tend to be used to browse through most of the fields of a table. Queries are generally used when you have particularly complex restrictive clauses, and when you want the database server (and not the client, the Delphi application) to browse through the data.

Queries are also often used to join two or more tables and see the result as if it were a single table stored in the database. While a Table component refers to a current table of the database, a SQL statement (and therefore a Query component) produces a table as its result. This allows you to browse through a table that is not in the database, but is the result of a join, a selection, or other computations. Of course, these computations take time. Complex operations, such as table joins, might really take quite a while.

The third data set component is StoredProc, which refers to local procedures of a SQL server database. You can run these procedures and get the results in the form of a database table. Stored procedures can only be used with SQL servers, and won't be covered in the book.

The Status of a Data Set

When you operate on a data set in Delphi (such as a table or a query), you can work in different states, indicated by a specific State property, which can assume several different values:

- dsBrowse indicates that the data set is in normal browse mode, used to look at the data and scan the records.

- dsEdit indicates that the data set is in edit mode. A data set enters this state when the program calls the Edit method or the DataSource has the AutoEdit property set to `True`, and the user starts editing a data-aware control, such as a DBGrid or DBEdit. When the changed record is posted, the data set exits the `dsEdit` state.

- `dsInsert` indicates that a new record is being added to the data set. Again, this might happen when calling the Insert method, moving to the last line of a DBGrid, or using the corresponding command of the DBNavigator component.

- `dsInactive` is the state of a closed data set.

- `dsSetKey` indicates that we are preparing a search on the data set. This is the state between a call to the `SetKey` method and a call to the `GotoKey` or `GotoNearest` methods (see the Search example later in this chapter).

- `dsCalcFields` is the state of a data set while a field calculation is taking place, that is, during a call to an `OnCalcFields` event handler. Again, I'll show this in an example.

- `dsNewValue`, `dsOldValue`, and `dsCurValue` are the states of a data set when an update of the cache is in progress.

- `dsFilter` is the state of a data set while setting a filter, that is during a call of an `OnFilterRecord` event handler.

In simple examples, the transitions between these states are handled automatically, but it is important to understand them because there are many events referring to the state transitions. You can refer to some examples later in this chapter (such as HandGri2 and Navig1) to see some of this state information. Other examples will explore DataSet events in detail.

Other Data-Access Components

Along with the Table, Query, StoredProc, and DataSource, there are some other components in the Data Access page of the Components palette:

- The Database component is used for transaction control, security, and connection control. It is generally used only to connect to remote databases in client/server applications, or to avoid the overhead of connecting to the same database in several forms.

- The Session component provides global control over database connections for an application, including a list of existing databases and aliases and an event to customize database log-in.

- The BatchMove component is used to perform batch operations, such as copying, appending, updating, or deleting values, on one or more databases.

- The UpdateSQL component allows you to write SQL statements to perform various update operations on the data set, when using a read-only query (that is when working with a complex query). This component is used as the value of the UpdateObject property of tables or queries.

- The Report component is an interface to Borland's ReportSmith application included in some versions of Delphi.

- The ClientDataSet is a new Delphi 3 component used on the client side of applications which use distributed database access.

- Provider and RemoteServer are two new Delphi 3 components used on the server side of applications based on distributed database access. This is a fairly advanced topic not covered in this book.

These can be considered advanced database components, and some of them are of little use in a local environment. We will use some of these components in this chapter and the next one, but we won't focus on them in great detail.

Delphi Data-Aware Controls

We have seen how it is possible to connect a data source to a database, using either a table or query, but we still do not know how to view the data. For this purpose, Delphi provides many components that resemble the usual Windows controls, but are data-aware. For example, the DBEdit component is similar to the Edit component, and the DBCheckBox component corresponds to the Check-Box component. You can find all of these components in the Data Controls page of the Delphi Components palette:

- DBGrid is a grid capable of displaying a whole table at once. It allows scrolling and navigation, and you can edit the grid's contents. It is an extension of the other Delphi grid controls.

- DBNavigator is a collection of buttons used to navigate and perform actions on the database. The buttons perform basic actions, so you can easily replace them with your own toolbar.

- DBLabel displays the contents of a field that cannot be modified. It is a data-aware Label graphical control.

- DBEdit lets the user edit a field (change the current value), using an Edit control.

- DBMemo lets the user see and modify a large text field, eventually stored in a memo or BLOB (which stands for Binary Large OBject) field. It resembles the Memo component.

- DBRichEdit is a new Delphi 3 component that lets the user edit a formatted text file, and is based on a Windows 95 RichEdit control.

- DBImage shows a picture stored in a BLOB field, and is a extension of an Image component.

- DBListBox and DBComboBox let the user select a single value from a specified set. If this set is extracted from another database table or is the result of another query, you should use the DBLookupListBox or DbLookupComboBox components instead. These last two components replace the DBLookupList and DBLookupCombo controls of Delphi 1, still available in the Win 3.1 page of the Components Palette.

- DBCheckBox can be used to show and toggle an option, corresponding to a Boolean table field, and extends the CheckBox component.

- DBRadioGroup provides a series of choices, with a number of exclusive selection radio buttons, as the RadioGroup control.

- DBChart is an extension of the Chart component, added to Delphi 3.

- DBCtrlGrid is a multi-record grid, which can host a number of other data-aware controls. These controls are duplicated for each record of the data set.

All of these components are connected to a data source using the corresponding property, DataSource. Many of them refer to a specific field of the data source, as indicated by the DataField property. Once you select the DataSource property, the DataField property will have a list of values available in the drop-down combo box of the Object Inspector. Except for these and a few other specific properties, the properties of the Data Controls page components are similar to those of the corresponding standard controls.

Now let's turn to the job of building database applications. First we'll see how to create such an application by hand, and then later we'll try using the Database Form Wizard.

Building Database Applications by Hand

Now that we know the role of Delphi's various database components, we are ready to start building an application, or actually, a series of simple examples. We will use both tables and queries, and we'll also use a number of data-aware controls. The first example shows the simplest approach, with the use of a DBGrid component.

A Database Grid

Our first database example, called HandGrid, uses the table shown earlier in Figure 16.2, which lists American countries with their capitals and population. To make things simple, we can use a grid to display all of the data in the table. To begin, open a new form and place on it a Table, a DataSource, and a DBGrid component. This last component can be aligned with the whole client area. To connect the three elements to each other and to the proper database table, use DataSource1 as the value of the DataSource property for the DBGrid component, use Table1 as the value of the DataSet property for the DataSource component, and use DBDEMOS as the value of the DatabaseName property and COUNTRY.DB as the value of the Table-Name property for the Table component.

If you set the Active property of the table to True, the data will appear in the form at design-time (this technique is usually called *live-data* design). When a grid displays live data, you can even use its scroll bars to navigate through the records and view the other fields also at design-time, as you can see in Figure 16.4.

FIGURE 16.4

The form of the HandGrid example with live data at design-time.

In Figure 16.4 you can also see the captions of the Table1 and DataSource1 components. Captions are very useful when you have several similar components, as often happens in database applications. To enable the captions, use the *Show component captions* check box in the Preferences page of the Environment Options.

You can see a summary of the components of this form and their properties in the following textual description of its form:

```
object Form1: TForm1
  ActiveControl = DBGrid1
  Caption = 'Hand Grid'
  object DBGrid1: TDBGrid
    Align = alClient
    DataSource = DataSource1
  end
  object Table1: TTable
    Active = True
    DatabaseName = 'DBDEMOS'
    TableName = 'COUNTRY.DB'
  end
  object DataSource1: TDataSource
    DataSet = Table1
  end
end
```

Now we can run the program, and it will show the same data we could already see at design-time. The difference now is that we can also edit the values, writing new text in each of the cells. This is possible because the DBGrid component's Options property includes the flag dgEditing and the ReadOnly property is set to False. You are working directly on the database data, so if you make a change, it will become permanent.

Besides changing the current values of a record, this program also allows you to insert or append new records. To insert a new row in a given position, press the Insert key with the cursor positioned there. To append a new record at the end, just move the cursor below the last element of the grid (go to the last record and press ↓). You can also press Ctrl+Del to delete the current record, after you confirm the action. Try using this program for a while (maybe after making a backup copy of the original database), and test how it works when you toggle the various flags of the Options property of the grid on and off.

What about the code of the program? Up to this point, there is none. The Pascal file contains only the usual declarations of the objects used by the form, automatically added by Delphi. So without writing any code at all, we have created an application that can be used to perform a relevant number of operations on a table. This is really a nice side of Delphi database programming.

Customizing the DBGrid

In the first version of Delphi, there was no simple way to customize the output of the DBGrid. In 32-bit versions of Delphi, there is an easy-to-use yet very powerful property: Columns. This property has a custom editor with a number of capabilities (see Figure 16.5).

FIGURE 16.5

The DBGrid Columns Editor.

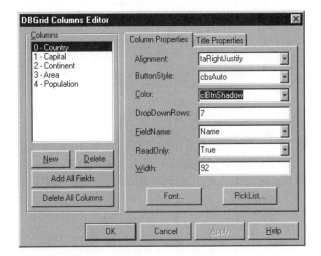

You can easily choose the fields of the table you want to see in the grid as columns, then set a number of column properties (color, font, width, alignment, and so on) for each field and title properties such as the caption, font, and colors. This allows you to customize a grid easily, in a number of ways. Some of the more advanced properties, such as ButtonStyle and DropDownRows, can be used to provide custom editors for the cells of a grid or a drop-down list (we will see how at the end of this chapter).

In the HandGri2 example, I've taken the grid from the HandGrid example and changed the caption of the first column and the font of the first and third. I've also chosen a dark gray background and a white font color for the first column. You can see the result in Figure 16.6.

FIGURE 16.6

The output of the Hand-
Gri2 example.

> **NOTE**
>
> Notice that once you have defined the Columns property of the DBGrid,
> you can size the columns at design-time simply by dragging the lines sep-
> arating them. The same capability is optionally available at run-time, and
> can be set along with many others using the Options property of the grid.

The Table State

There are many more things you can do to customize grids, and we'll explore
some of them in the rest of this chapter. For the moment I want to add a really
interesting feature (and some code) to the example. If you look at the caption
of the form in Figure 16.6 you'll notice something new: the title of the form indicates the status of the Table component. How do we get this information? Simply
by handling the OnStateChange event of the DataSource component, and not an
event of the Table itself. In this event handler, the HandGri2 example merely outputs the current status, determined using a simple case statement:

```
procedure TForm1.DataSource1StateChange(Sender: TObject);
var
  Title: string;
begin
  case Table1.State of
    dsBrowse: Title := 'Browse';
    dsEdit: Title := 'Edit';
    dsInsert: Title := 'Insert';
  else
    Title := 'Other state';
```

```
  end;
  Caption := 'Hand Grid - ' + Title;
end;
```

The code consider only the three states the Table component of this program can have as the user interacts with the corresponding DBGrid.

Using DBEdit Controls

The HandGri2 example works well, but we want to try using other controls, such as edit boxes, and we want to see specific information rather than all the data in our database. The next example, called Navig1, is similar to the previous one, but it uses some DBEdit components and some labels, along with the table and the data source. We also need to add a brand new component, the DBNavigator. Figure 16.7 shows the form of the Navig1 example at design-time (with live data).

FIGURE 16.7

The three DBEdit and the DBNavigator components of the Navig1 example, with live data.

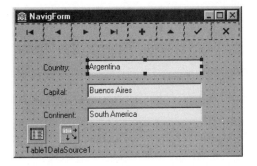

TIP

You can use the standard Windows Copy and Paste commands to copy components such as the Table and some data-aware controls, with all their properties, from one form to another or from one example to another. In this case, the trick is really helpful, because you can copy the two components along with their database connections and all their other properties you've set.

Again, we need to connect the three data-aware controls to the data source by setting their `DataSource` property, and also indicate a specific field for each of the three edit boxes in their `DataField` property (Name, Capital, and Continent are the fields for this example). If you have already connected the data source to the table and the edit boxes to the data source, you can simply select a field in the list displayed by the Object Inspector for the DataField property. When this connection is made, if the Active property of the Table is set to True the values of the first record's fields appear automatically in the edit boxes (see Figure 16.7).

Another step we can take is to disable some of the buttons of the DBNavigator control, by removing some of the elements of the VisibleButtons set. The meanings of the buttons are shown in Table 16.1.

TABLE 16.1   The Meanings of the Buttons of the DBNavigator Control

Button	Meaning
nbFirst	Go to the first record.
nbPrior	Go to the previous record.
nbNext	Go to the next record.
nbLast	Go to the last record.
nbInsert	Insert a new blank record in the current position.
nbDelete	Delete the current record.
nbEdit	Allow the editing of the current record.
nbPost	Post (store) the changes that occurred in the current edit action.
nbCancel	Cancel the changes in the current edit action.

You can see the graphical representation of the various buttons of the navigator, along with the descriptions of their actions, in Figure 16.8. The symbols of some of these buttons are not very intuitive, but they feature automatic fly-over hints, so that a user can see the function of a button just by moving the mouse over it.

FIGURE 16.8

The buttons of the DBNavigator component.

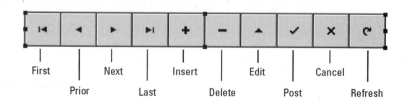

774

TIP Of course, you can turn off the ShowHint property to disable the fly-over hints of the navigator. As a better alternative, you can provide a customized description for their text, using the Hints string list. This can be useful when you need to translate an application into another language (or to write it directly in another language, as I often do). The strings you insert are used for the buttons in order: the first string is used for the first button, the second for the second, and so on. If some buttons are not visible, you can provide empty strings (just a blank space), as place-holders.

In the Navig1 program, I've used only some of the buttons, disabling the delete and refresh operations. I've also aligned the navigator to the top of the form, and set its Flat property to True to activate the new flat button style (as discussed in Chapter 12). You can run it and test whether it works properly, and look at the caption again: I've copied to this example the OnStateChange event handler of the HandGri2 example's DataSource component.

Notice that when the program is running at the beginning or when you jump to the first or to the last record of the table, two of the navigator's buttons will be disabled automatically. However, if you move step-by-step to the first or last record, the buttons are disabled only when you try to move beyond those records. The navigator only realizes at this point that there are no more records in that direction. The same happens when you use the DBGrid's vertical scroll bar. Other buttons are automatically enabled and disabled when you enter the edit state, or exit from it.

Using a Query

In the first two examples, we have used a Table component, and we have browsed through all of the records in the table. For our next example, called Navig2, we'll remove the Table component and add a Query component instead. We can connect the query to the usual DBDEMO database alias and enter the text of a simple SQL statement. As we have already seen, we can select all of the fields of all of the records in the table by writing the following code:

```
select * from Country
```

When this query has been entered, you can activate the Query component, setting the Active property to True, and the values of the fields of the first record should appear again in the edit boxes. Of course, this happens only if the SQL statement you have inserted is correct. Otherwise, Delphi will issue an error message, and the query won't be activated.

NOTE If you want to change the current SQL statement of a query at design-time or at run-time, you need to set the Active property of the component to False first, then change the value, and then set it to True again, reactivating the connection between the data-aware controls and the data. As an alternative you can call the Close and Open methods, which have exactly the same effect.

Of course, this example won't be particularly interesting. Why use the Query component instead of the Table component if all we want is to select an entire table? We can take advantage of the new component by adding some radio buttons to select different queries at run-time. I decided to add four radio buttons—that is, four different options.

The first button is used to select the default SQL statement, and it is checked at startup. The second and third buttons can be used to choose only the records that have a specific value, either North America or South America, for their Continent field. To accomplish this, we need to add a where clause to the SQL statement, as we will see shortly. The last radio button allows a user to enter the text of the where statement, writing a custom condition in the edit box next to the radio button (for a description of the where clause in SQL you can refer to Appendix B).

Letting a user type in a statement is slightly dangerous, since entering the wrong text can cause an error. But Delphi is robust enough to withstand this risk, thanks to its exception handling. For the first time in this chapter, we need to write some code. The code is necessary to change the value of the SQL property of the Query component when a new radio button is checked. Each time we do this operation, we must remember to call the Close and Open methods of the Query component, or to set the value of the Active property to False and True. Here is the code associated with the first radio button:

```
procedure TNavigForm.RadioButton1Click(Sender: TObject);
begin
  Query1.Close;
  Query1.Sql.Clear;
  Query1.Sql.Add('select * from Country');
  Query1.Open;
end;
```

Notice that the SQL property is not a string, but has a TStrings type. This can be used to build very long queries (the text limit for an array of strings is high) and to define different portions of the query in different places of the code and merge them. I've chosen to follow a more traditional approach, with a query made of a single line of text. The second and third radio buttons share the same code, which uses their Caption property to build the text of the SQL statement:

```
procedure TNavigForm.RadioButton2Click(Sender: TObject);
begin
  Query1.Close;
  Query1.Sql.Clear;
  Query1.Sql.Add ('select * from Country');
  Query1.Sql.Add ('where Continent = "' +
    (Sender as TRadioButton).Caption + '"');
  Query1.Open;
end;
```

This code defines a SQL statement by adding two strings. SQL code can be formatted freely, as Pascal source code, so I could have used one or three strings, as well.

> **TIP**
> In the SQL statements above I've used a double quotation mark for strings. It is also possible to use single quotation marks. However, to have a single quotation mark inside a Pascal string, you have to use two consecutive single quotation marks. For this reason, in the code above, we would have had triple and even quadruple quotation marks.

For the last radio button, the code is simpler, since we only need to merge the default statement with the text of the edit box:

```
procedure TNavigForm.RadioButton4Click(Sender: TObject);
begin
  Query1.Close;
  if (Edit1.Text <> '') then
  begin
    Query1.Sql.Clear;
    Query1.Sql.Add ('select * from Country');
    Query1.Sql.Add ('where ' + Edit1.Text);
  end;
  Query1.Open;
end;
```

This code is executed any time the edit box is not empty, based on the assumption that the text is a correct SQL statement (the program doesn't check this assumption at all). To improve the program slightly, the last radio button is automatically disabled each time the edit box has no text. This check takes place in the OnChange event of the Edit component :

```
procedure TNavigForm.Edit1Change(Sender: TObject);
begin
  RadioButton4.Enabled := Edit1.Text <> '';
end;
```

When you run this program, you can choose any of the four buttons and see immediately the effect on the current record. Notice that the navigator works on the resulting table of the query, so that it correctly considers Canada to be the first North American country in alphabetic order. The Custom edit box can be used in a number of different ways. Figure 16.9 shows two different examples of its use. One example shows a single country of the database selected, and the other shows the result of selecting a population range. If you write something meaningless, or just make a small syntax error, the program will stop with an error message.

One last thing to notice in this example is that by default, you cannot edit the result data of a query. To make this possible you have to set the RequestLive property of the Query to True. This makes the data fully editable only when some given conditions are met. Simple queries referring to a single database table can generally be "live," while complex queries joining several tables generally cannot.

FIGURE 16.9

Two copies of the Navig2 example with a custom SQL where clause. In the form on the left, a single country is selected. In the window on the right the program select all the countries with a large population.

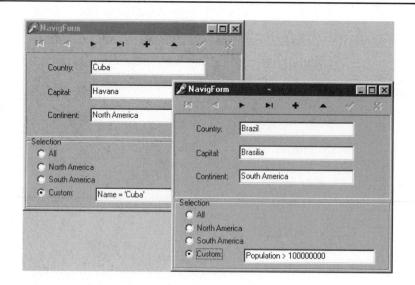

> **NOTE**
> As an alternative to the use of where SQL statements, you can use a table and set a range of records you want to consider. The range should be based on an indexed field, and of course is not terribly flexible. Another powerful alternative is to filter a data set. Simply set the Filtered property of a Table or Query to True, and provide a proper condition in the Filter property. As an alternative, the program will call the OnFilterRecord event of the data set component to determine which records to show.

A Query with Parameters

The last version of our navigator example demonstrates the use of query parameters. All of the queries in the previous version were very similar. Instead of building a new query each time, we can write a query with a parameter, and simply change the value of the parameter.

If we decide to choose North American or South American countries, for example, we can write the following statement:

```
select * from Country where Continent = :Continent
```

In this SQL clause, :Continent is a parameter. We can set its data type and startup value, using the special editor of the Params property of the Query component. You can access this editor from the Object Inspector or through the Define Parameters command on the form's SpeedMenu when the Query component is selected in the form. When the Parameters editor is open, as shown in Figure 16.10, you see a list of the parameters defined in the SQL statement of the Query component. For each of these parameters, you can set a data type and provide an initial value.

FIGURE 16.10

The Parameters editor of a Query component.

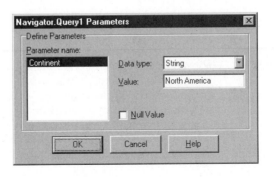

Using this approach makes the new version of this example extremely simple. Its form is a reduced version of the previous example's form, with only two radio buttons. Its most significant code is the response method for the OnClick event of both radio buttons. Here is its code:

```
procedure TNavigForm.RadioButton2Click(Sender: TObject);
begin
  Query1.Close;
  Query1.Params[0].AsString :=
    (Sender as TRadioButton).Caption;
  Query1.Open;
end;
```

This method copies the caption of the radio button to the first parameter of the query. The first parameter is number 0, since the Params array is zero-based, and you should access its value as a string. This AsString property is common to parameter and field arrays of the database components. As we will see in more detail later in the chapter, these are arrays of elements that can have different data types, so one of the *As* conversion properties is always required.

We can add a second method to this program to take advantage of a specific feature of parameterized queries. To react faster to a change in the parameters, these queries can be optimized, or *prepared*. Simply call the Prepare method before the program first opens the query. In our example, Navig3, we have to set the Active property of the Query to False at design-time, and then write the following OnCreate handler for the form:

```
procedure TNavigator.FormCreate(Sender: TObject);
begin
  Query1.Prepare;
  Query1.Open;
end;
```

NOTE   Prepared parameterized queries are very important when you work on big tables and a complex query. In fact, to optimize such a query, many databases create temporary indexes. Instead of creating an index each time you open it, a prepared query can set up this optimization only once at the beginning, saving a lot of time when a parameter changes. The only drawback is that some SQL servers can optimize the queries themselves, so that your suggestions (the call to Prepare) won't be terribly useful, and won't really speed up the code at all, simply because it is already as fast as it can be.

Using the Database Form Wizard

We have been able to build some simple examples by placing database components on the main form of the application and then connecting them. Often, this operation requires some time. For this reason, Delphi has a Database Form Wizard tool (called Database Form Expert in previous versions of Delphi), which provides a fast start in the development of a database application. You had a brief introduction to this tool in Chapter 3, which provided an overview of Delphi's Object Repository. Now we are ready to use it and understand the code it generates.

Just to gain some confidence in using this tool, we can try to rebuild the first example in this chapter, HandGrid, using the Wizard. The new example is named ExpGrid. Create a new, blank project, and start the Database Form Wizard. In the Wizard, select a simple form based on a table, choose the COUNTRY.DB table in the DBDEMOS database, select all the fields, and choose a grid. One of these steps is shown in Figure 16.11. Now you can generate the code, remove the older blank form from the project (probably Form1), compile the program, give proper names to the files, and run it. This program is similar to the one we built before, but this time the process was much simpler and faster.

FIGURE 16.11

The second step of building the new version of the grid of countries using the Database Form Wizard.

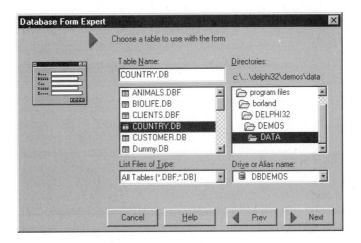

The Wizard is even faster when your form is based on labels and edit fields, instead of on a single grid. In this case, placing all of the components on the form, aligning them, and so on requires more time. But when you use the Database Form Wizard, you can simply choose a vertical or a horizontal layout. If you use a vertical layout, you can decide whether to place the label above or to the left of the corresponding edit field. We will use this approach in an example later in this chapter.

Before we use the Wizard to build new examples, let's take a moment to study the code that it has generated for us. The form of the ExpGrid program has six components, as you can see by opening the project on the companion CD or generating a new one on the fly.

There is a table, connected with the data, a data source associated with the table, a navigator (hosted by two nested panels), and a grid aligned to the remaining area. The two panels are used to place the navigator near the right border of the form, but not too close to the border (not aligned to the right). The code generated for this example is simple. The only predefined method corresponds to the OnCreate event of the form; it is used to activate the table, and simply calls Table1.Open.

Although the Database Form Wizard doesn't generate much code, using its various options we can obtain complex forms, including master detail forms based on tables or SQL queries. Unfortunately, it is not possible to customize the Database Form Wizard, mainly because the source code of this add-on tool is not included.

Accessing the Data Fields

Before we try to build more attractive and complex examples, there are few more technical elements we should explore. Up to now, we have included all of the fields in the source database tables. You probably noticed that the Database Form Wizard lets you choose the fields you want to use. Suppose that we have already built an example. How could we remove a field? How can we add new fields, such as calculated fields? In trying to solve these problems, we face a more general question: How do we access the values—the fields—of the current record from a program? How can we change them without direct editing by the user?

The answer to all of these questions lies in the concept of *field*. Field components (instances of class TField or of one of its subclasses) are nonvisual components that are fundamental for each Delphi database application. Data-aware controls are directly connected to these Field objects, which correspond to database fields.

In the examples we have built up to now, the TField components were automatically created by Delphi at run-time. This happens each time a data set component is open. These fields are stored in the Fields array property of tables and queries, which is an array of fields. We can access these values in our program by number (accessing the array directly) or by name (using the FieldByName method):

```
Table1.Fields[0].AsString
Table1.FieldByName('Name').AsString
```

As an alternative, the field components can be created at design-time, using the Fields Editor. In this case, you can also set a number of properties for these fields at design-time. These properties affect the behavior of the data-aware controls using them, both for visualization and for editing. When you define new fields at design-time, they are listed in the Object Inspector, just like any other component.

To try this, we can access the Fields Editor of the table we generated in the last example. To open the Fields Editor for a table, select the Table object on the form, activate its local menu with a right mouse button click, and choose the Fields Editor command. An empty Fields Editor appears. Now you have to activate the local menu of this editor, to access its capabilities. The simplest operation you can do is to select the Add command, which allows you to add any other fields in the database table to the list of fields. Figure 16.12 shows the Add Fields dialog box, which lists all the fields that are still available. These are the database table fields that are not already present in the list of fields in the editor.

FIGURE 16.12

The Fields editor with the
Add Fields dialog box.

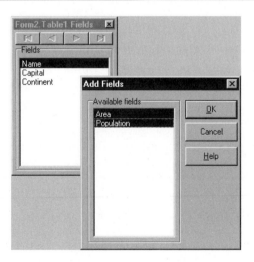

The Define command of the Fields Editor, instead, lets you define a new calculated field, a lookup field, or a field with a modified type. In this dialog box, you can enter a descriptive field name, which might include blank spaces. Delphi generates an internal name—the name of the field component—that you can further customize. Next, select a data type for the field. If this is a calculated field or a lookup field, and not just a copy of a field redefined to use a new data type, simply check the proper radio button. We'll see how to define a calculated field in the next section, and a lookup field at the end of this chapter.

> **NOTE**
> A TField component has both a Name property and a FieldName property. The Name property is the usual component name. The FieldName property is the name of the column in the database table, or the name you define for the calculated field. It can be more descriptive, and it allows blank spaces. The FieldName property of the TField component is copied to the DisplayLabel property by default, but it can be changed to any suitable text. The field name is used, among other things, to search a field in the FieldByName method of the TDataSet class.

All of the fields that you add or define are included in the Fields Editor, and can be used by data-aware controls, or displayed in a database grid. If a field of the original database table is not in this list, it won't be accessible. When you use the Fields Editor, Delphi adds the declaration of the available fields to the class of the form, as new components (much as the Menu Designer adds TMenuItem components to the form). The component of the TField class, or better of its subclasses, are not visible on the form, but can be selected in the Object Inspector. Of course, you can also refer to these components in the code of your program, to change their properties at run-time or get or set their value.

In the Fields Editor you can also drag the fields to a different position to change their order. Proper field ordering is particularly important when you define a grid, which arranges its columns using this order.

> **TIP**
> An even better feature of the Fields Editor is that you can drag fields from this editor to the surface of a form and have Delphi automatically create a data-aware control (such as a DBEdit, a DBMemo, or a DBImage). This is a very fast way to generate custom forms, and I suggest you try it out if you've never used it before. This is my preferred way to build database-related forms.

The Hierarchy of Field Classes

Before we look at an example, let's go over the use of the TField class. The importance of this component should not be underestimated. Although it is often used behind the scenes, its role in database applications is fundamental. As I already mentioned, even if you do not define specific objects of this kind, you can always access the fields of a table or a query using their Fields array property or their FieldByName method. Both the Fields property and the FieldByName function return you an object of type TField, so you sometimes have to use the as operator to downcast their result to its actual type (like TFloatField, or TDateField) before accessing specific properties of these subclasses.

The FieldAcc example is an extension of the ExpGrid example, with three speed buttons in the toolbar panel, accessing various Field properties at run-time. The first button changes the formatting of the population column of the grid. To do this we have to access the DisplayFormat property, a specific property of the TFloatField class. For this reason we have to write:

```
procedure TForm2.SpeedButton1Click(Sender: TObject);
begin
  (Table1.FieldByName ('Population') as
    TFloatField).DisplayFormat := '###,###,###';
end;
```

When you set field properties related to data input or output, the change applies to every record in the table. When you set properties related to the value of the field, instead, you always refer to the current record only. For example, we can output the population of the current country in a message box by writing:

```
procedure TForm2.SpeedButton2Click(Sender: TObject);
begin
  ShowMessage (Table1.FieldByName('Name').AsString +
    ': ' + Table1.FieldByName('Population').AsString);
end;
```

When you access the value of a field, you can use a series of *As* properties to handle the current field value using a specific data type (if this is available, otherwise an exception is raised):

```
AsBoolean: Boolean;
AsDateTime: TDateTime;
AsFloat: Double;
AsInteger: LongInt;
AsString: string;
```

These properties can be used to read or change the value of the field. Changing the value of a field is possible only if the DataSet is in edit mode. As an alternative to the *As* properties indicated above, you can access the value of a filed by using its Value property, which is defined as a variant. Although at times this can be handy, using variants can slow down a program considerably, as detailed in Chapter 4.

Most of the other properties of the TField component, such as Alignment, DisplayLabel, DisplayWidth, and Visible, reflect elements of the field's user interface and are used by the various data-aware controls, particularly DBGrid. In the FieldAcc example, clicking on the third speed button changes the Alignment of every field:

```
procedure TForm2.SpeedButton3Click(Sender: TObject);
var
  I: Integer;
begin
  for I := 0 to Table1.FieldCount - 1 do
    Table1.Fields[I].Alignment := taCenter;
end;
```

This affects the output of the DBGrid, and of the DEdit control I've added to the toolbar, which shows the name of the country. You can see this effect, along with the new display format, in Figure 16.13.

There are several field class types in the VCL. Delphi automatically uses one of them depending on the data definition in the database, when you open a table at run-time or when you use the Fields Editor at design-time. Table 16.2 shows the complete list of subclasses of the TField class.

FIGURE 16.13

The output of the Field-Acc example after the Center and Format buttons have been pressed.

Name	Capital	Continent	Area	Population
Argentina	Buenos Aires	South America	2777815	32,300,003
Bolivia	La Paz	South America	1098575	7,300,000
Brazil	Brasilia	South America	85111968	150,400,000
Canada	Ottawa	North America	9976147	26,500,000
Chile	Santiago	South America	756943	13,200,000
Colombia	Bagota	South America	1138907	33,000,000
Cuba	Havana	North America	114524	10,600,000
Ecuador	Quito	South America	455502	10,600,000
El Salvador	San Salvador	North America	20865	5,300,000
Guyana	Georgetown	South America	214969	800,000

TABLE 16.2   The Subclasses of TField

Subclass	Base Class	Definition
TStringField	TField	Text data of a fixed length (it may be up to 255 characters, depending on the database type).
TNumericField	TField	Generally not used directly. This is the base class of all the numeric field classes.
TIntegerField	TNumericField	Whole numbers in the range of long integers (32 bits).
TSmallIntField	TIntegerField	Whole numbers in the range of integers (16 bits).
TWordField	TIntegerField	Whole positive numbers in the range of words or unsigned integers (16 bits).
TAutoIncField	TIntegerField	Whole positive number connected with an auto-increment field of a table, a special field automatically assigned a different value for each record.
TFloatField	TNumericField	Floating-point numbers (8 byte).
TCurrencyField	TFloatField	Currency values, with the same range as real numbers.
TBCDField	TNumericField	Real numbers, with a fixed number of digits after the decimal point.
TBooleanField	TField	Boolean value.
TDateTimeField	TField	Date and time value.
TDateField	TDateTimeField	Date value.
TTimeField	TDateTimeField	Time value.
TBinaryField	TField	Generally not used directly. This is the base class of the next two classes.
TBytesField	TBinaryField	Arbitrary data and no size limit.
TVarBytesField	TBytesField	Arbitrary data, up to 64K characters.
TBlobField	TField	Binary data and no size limit (BLOB stands for Binary Large OBject).
TMemoField	TBlobField	Text of arbitrary length.
TGraphicField	TBlobField	Graphic of arbitrary length.

NOTE   The availability of any particular field type, and the correspondence with the data definition, depend on the database in use. For example, InterBase doesn't support BCD, so you'll never get a BCDField for a table on the InterBase server. The range and precision of floating-point fields and the size of decimal fields also vary among different SQL servers, creating problems for building portable applications.

Adding a Calculated Field

Now that you've been introduced to the use of TField objects and seen an example of their run-time use, it is time to build a simple example based on the declaration of field objects at design-time using the Fields Editor. We can start again from the last example we built, ExpGrid, and add a calculated field. The COUNTRY.DB database table we are accessing has both the population and the area of each country, so we can use this data to compute the population density.

To build the new example, named Calc, select the Table component in the form and open the Fields editor (using the form's SpeedMenu). In this editor, choose the Add command and select some of the fields (I've decided to include them all). Now select the Define command and enter a proper name and data type (TFloatField) for the new calculated field, as you can see in Figure 16.14.

Of course, we also need to provide a way to calculate the new field. This is accomplished in the OnCalcFields event of the Table component, which has the following code (at least in a first version):

```
procedure TForm2.Table1CalcFields(DataSet: TDataSet);
begin
  Table1PopulationDensity.Value :=
    Table1Population.Value / Table1Area.Value;
end;
```

FIGURE 16.14

The definition of a calculated field in the Calc example.

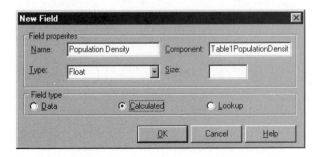

Everything fine? Not at all! If you enter a new record and do not set the value of the population and area, or if you accidentally set the area to zero, the division will raise an exception, making it quite problematic to continue using the program. As an alternative we could have handled every exception of the division expression, and simply set the resulting value to zero:

```
try
    Table1PopulationDensity.Value :=
        Table1Population.Value / Table1Area.Value;
except
  on Exception do
      Table1PopulationDensity.Value := 0;
end;
```

However, we can do even better. We can check if the value of the area is defined—if it is not null—and if it is not zero. It is better to avoid using exceptions when you can anticipate the possible error conditions:

```
if not Table1Area.IsNull and
    (Table1Area.Value <> 0) then
    Table1PopulationDensity.Value :=
        Table1Population.Value / Table1Area.Value
else
    Table1PopulationDensity.Value := 0;
```

The code of the `Table1CalcFields` method above (in each of the three versions) accesses some fields directly. This is possible because I used the Fields Editor, and it automatically created the corresponding field declarations, as you can see in this excerpt of the interface declaration of the form:

```
type
    TCalcForm = class(TForm)
        Table1: TTable;
        Table1PopulationDensity: TFloatField;
        Table1Area: TFloatField;
        Table1Population: TFloatField;
        Table1Name: TStringField;
        Table1Capital: TStringField;
        Table1Continent: TStringField;
        procedure Table1CalcFields(DataSet: TDataset);
        ...
```

Each time you add or remove fields in the Fields Editor, you can see the effect of your action immediately in the grid present in the form. Of course, you won't see the values of a calculated field at design-time; they are available only at runtime, since they result from the execution of compiled Pascal code.

Since we have defined some components for the fields, we can use them to customize some of the visual elements of the grid. For example, to set a display format that adds a comma to separate thousands, we can use the Object Inspector to change the DisplayFormat property of some field components the to "###,###,###". This change has an immediate effect on the grid at design-time.

NOTE The display format I've just mentioned (and used also in the previous example) uses the Windows International Settings to format the output. When Delphi translates the numeric value of this field to text, the comma in the format string is replaced by the proper ThousandSeparator character. For this reason, the output of the program will automatically adapt itself to different International Settings. On computers that have the Italian configuration, for example, the comma is replaced by a period.

After working on the table components and the fields, I've customized the DBGrid using its Columns property editor. I've set the Population Density column to read-only and set its ButtonStyle property to cbsEllipsis, to provide a custom editor. When you set this value, a small button with an ellipsis is displayed when the user tries to edit the grid cell. Pressing the button invokes the OnEditButtonClick event of the DBGrid:

```
procedure TCalcForm.DBGrid1EditButtonClick(
  Sender: TObject);
begin
  MessageDlg ('To change the population density,'#13 +
    'edit the Population or the Area',
    mtInformation, [mbOK], 0);
end;
```

Actually, I haven't provided a real editor, but rather a simple message describing the situation, as you can see in Figure 16.15, where you can note the values of the calculated fields. To create an editor, you might build a secondary form to handle special data entries.

FIGURE 16.15

The output of the Calc example. Notice the Population Density calculated column, the ellipsis button, and the message displayed when you select it.

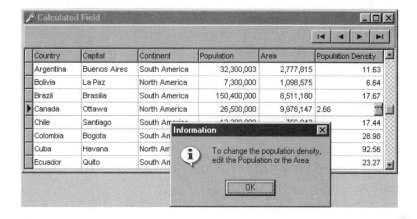

A second column I've customized is Continent. For this field, I want to offer a closed selection, with just two alternatives. To accomplish this, simply click on the PickList button and enter the names of the continents you want to support; then set the number of values (there are just a few) in the DropDownRows property. Without any further change, a drop-down list is displayed when you try to edit the values in this column, as you can see in Figure 16.16.

FIGURE 16.16

The drop-down list defined by setting the PickList of a DBGrid's column.

Country	Capital	Continent	Population	Area	Population Density
Argentina	Buenos Aires	South America	32,300,003	2,777,815	11.63
Bolivia	La Paz	North America ▼	7,300,000	1,098,575	6.64
Brazil	Brasilia	North America	150,400,000	8,511,180	17.67
Canada	Ottawa	South America	26,500,000	9,976,147	2.66
Chile	Santiago	South America	13,200,000	756,943	17.44
Colombia	Bogota	South America	33,000,000	1,138,907	28.98
Cuba	Havana	North America	10,600,000	114,524	92.56
Ecuador	Quito	South America	10,600,000	455,502	23.27

You can see the final values of the items of the Columns property in the corresponding editor or in the textual description of the form (where this TCollection object is marked by angle brackets). The Columns property of the DBGrid and the properties of the field objects determine the appearance of the grid. These properties are among the key elements of the DFM file of the form of example, partially listed below. Notice also the two nested panels generated by the Form Wizard to show the Navigator component in the top-right corner of the form:

```
object CalcForm: TCalcForm
  Caption = 'Calculated Field'
  OnCreate = FormCreate
  object Panel1: TPanel
    Align = alTop
    object Panel2: TPanel
      Align = alRight
      BevelOuter = bvNone
      object DBNavigator: TDBNavigator
        DataSource = DataSource1
        VisibleButtons = [nbFirst, nbPrior, nbNext, nbLast]
      end
    end
  end
  object DBGrid1: TDBGrid
    Align = alClient
    Columns = <
      item
        FieldName = 'Name'
      end
      item
        DropDownRows = 3
        FieldName = 'Continent'
        PickList.Strings = (
          'North America'
          'South America')
      end
      ...
      item
        ButtonStyle = cbsEllipsis
        FieldName = 'Population Density'
        ReadOnly = True
      end>
    DataSource = DataSource1
    OnEditButtonClick = DBGrid1EditButtonClick
  end
  object DataSource1: TDataSource
    DataSet = Table1
  end
  object Table1: TTable
```

```
Active = True
OnCalcFields = Table1CalcFields
DatabaseName = 'DBDEMOS'
TableName = 'country.db'
object Table1Name: TStringField
  DisplayLabel = 'Country'
  FieldName = 'Name'
end
...
object Table1Area: TFloatField
  FieldName = 'Area'
  DisplayFormat = '###,###,###'
end
object Table1PopulationDensity: TFloatField
  Calculated = True
  FieldName = 'Population Density'
  DisplayFormat = '###.##'
end
end
end
```

Using Fields to Manipulate a Table

TField components can be used to access data and manipulate a table at run-time. We have seen only a limited example of direct data access; in the previous example, we used the value of two fields to calculate a third one. Now we will build some simple examples that will allow us to use the fields to search elements in a table, operate on the values, and access information about the tables of a database. There are many more possible uses of field components, but this should give you an idea of what can be done.

Looking for Records in a Table

For this example and the following ones, we need a new form, this time connected to EMPLOYEE.DB, another of the sample Delphi tables. To prepare the form, which has a number of edit fields, you can use the Database Form Wizard or drag the fields from the Fields Editor and add the corresponding labels.

If you generate the form with the Database Wizard, first get rid of the DBNavi-gator in the toolbar, so you can experiment with some manual table navigation. Instead of the default Delphi component, we can add a group of six navigational SpeedButtons. The two buttons on the side (marked << and >>) are used to move to the first or last record in the table, and the two in the middle (marked < and >) move to the next or previous record. The other two buttons, indicated by a –5 and a +5 caption, are used to move five records backward or forward. (I chose this number arbitrarily.)

Since there are several SpeedButtons, and we'll add more, I've given each of them a meaningful name, such as `SpeedButtonFirst` or `SpeedButtonNext`. Each button has some code associated with its `OnClick` event. Basically, these six meth-ods call some navigational procedures of the Table component. Here are the six calls, extracted from the source code of the example, and in the same order as the buttons:

```
Table1.First;
Table1.MoveBy (-5);
Table1.Prior;
Table1.Next;
Table1.MoveBy (5);
Table1.Last;
```

Moving around in a table is simple. What makes the code complex is handling the `Enabled` property of the toolbar buttons. Each button used to move toward the end of the table (the last three buttons) should be disabled when we reach the end. The opposite should happen for the three buttons used to move toward the beginning.

We can test whether we have reached either extreme of the table by using the `BOF` (Beginning Of File) and `EOF` (End Of File) properties of the table. The problem is that there are a number of ways to reach the end of the table and to leave it. For this reason, I've written some procedures to enable and disable the two groups of buttons. Here is one of them:

```
procedure TSearchForm.DisableNextButtons;
begin
  SpeedButtonLast.Enabled := False;
  SpeedButtonNext.Enabled := False;
  SpeedButtonMoveOn.Enabled := False;
end;
```

This procedure is called when the end of file is reached. Here is a procedure that can take place when we click on the Next button:

```
procedure TSearchForm.SpeedButtonNextClick(Sender: TObject);
begin
  Table1.Next;
  EnablePriorButtons;
  if Table1.EOF then
    DisableNextButtons;
end;
```

With this code, we always enable the first three buttons (there isn't much time penalty if they were already enabled) and disable the last three if the EOF property is True. You can see the rest of the code used to enable and disable the buttons in the complete source code of the example on the companion CD.

Once the navigation SpeedButtons are set, we can improve this example by adding search capabilities. We want to be able to enter a name in an edit box and jump to the corresponding record.

Before continuing with the discussion of the example, take a look at its final form in Figure 16.17. Notice in particular the structure of the scroll box inside the panel, which contains the data-aware edit boxes. These controls were created by the Database Form Wizard, and they work very well, since you can freely resize the form without any problems. When the form becomes too small, scroll bars will appear automatically in the area holding the edit boxes.

FIGURE 16.17

An example of a best-match search using the Search application.

The searching capabilities are activated by the two new SpeedButtons and their associated edit controls. The first button is used for an exact match, and the second for a nearest search. In both cases, we want to compare the text in the edit box with the Last Name fields of the Employee table. The Table component has methods to accomplish this, such as GotoKey, FindKey, GotoNearest, and Find-Nearest.

For non-indexed fields, or as a general technique, you can use the Locate method. The Locate method uses the optimal access: if an index is available it uses the index for a faster search, otherwise it does a plain sequential search.

To use the first group of search methods, you need to set the IndexFieldNames property of the Table component to the proper value (in this case you can directly select the string *LastName;FirstName* in the drop-down list). Were the index not defined, you would have had to add a secondary index using the Database Desktop or the Database Explorer. You can use this last tool to see the indexes currently available for a table.

The Find Methods

When the index is properly set, we can make the actual search. The simplest approach is to use the FindNearest method for the approximate search and the FindKey method to look for an exact match:

```
procedure TSearchForm.SpeedButtonGoNearClick(Sender: TObject);
begin
  Table1.FindNearest ([EditName.Text]);
  EnableAllButtons;
end;

procedure TSearchForm.SpeedButtonGotoClick(Sender: TObject);
begin
  if not Table1.FindKey ([EditName.Text]) then
    MessageDlg ('Name not found', mtError, [mbOk], 0)
  else
    EnableAllButtons;
end;
```

Both find methods use as parameters an array of constants. Each array element corresponds to an indexed field. In our case, we pass only the value for the first field of the index, so the other fields will not be considered.

The Goto Methods

The FindNearest and FindKey methods are easy to use. To better understand how they work, though, we can look at the usage of the GotoNearest and GotKey methods. These last two methods, in fact, map very closely to the actual low-level BDE calls. The simplest of the two is the best-guess search of the GotoNearest speed button:

```
procedure TSearchForm.SpeedButtonGoNearClick(Sender: TObject);
begin
  Table1.SetKey;
  Table1.FieldByName('LastName').AsString := EditName.Text;
  Table1.GotoNearest;
  EnableAllButtons;
end;
```

As you can see in this code, each search on a table is done in three steps:

1. Start up the search state of the table.

2. Set a target value for each lookup field. In this example, I've set the value of the LastName field. I've used the FieldByName method instead of a direct access (Table.Fields[1]), because the code is more readable this way.

3. Start the lookup process, moving the current record to the requested position.

You can see an example of the effect of this search in Figure 16.17 above. In the code there is also one statement to enable all of the navigational buttons of the toolbar.

The code used to call the other search method, using an exact-match algorithm, is similar. The differences are in these two statements:

```
procedure TSearchForm.SpeedButtonGotoClick(Sender: TObject);
begin
  Table1.SetKey;
  Table1.FieldByName('LastName').AsString := EditName.Text;
  Table1.KeyFieldCount := 1;
  if not Table1.GotoKey then
    MessageDlg ('Name not found', mtError, [mbOK], 0)
  else
    EnableAllButtons;
end;
```

As I've mentioned before, this code requires a proper index for the table. Notice the value set for the KeyFieldCount property, which indicates that I want to use just the first of the two fields that contribute to the index. The second difference is that the GotoNearest procedure always succeeds, moving the cursor to the closest match (a closest match always exist, even if it is not very close). On the other hand, the GotoKey method fails if no exact match is available, and you can check the return value of this function, and eventually warn the user of the error.

FindKey performs exactly the same steps as the GotoKey version of the above code. FindKey and GotoKey provide equivalent functionality, except that the former is easier to use and the latter provides for better error handling.

The Locate Method

If the table doesn't have an index on the field you are searching for (at least for local tables), you cannot use the two techniques above. A third, more general, technique is to use the Locate method. This approach (first introduced in Delphi 2) is very handy in any case, because if there is an index on the field you are searching, Locate automatically uses it; otherwise it does a plain (and slower) search.

Using Locate is quite simple: Just provide a first string with the fields you want to search, and a second string with the values you are searching for. Here is an example of its use, extracted again from the Search program:

```
if not Table1.Locate ('LastName', EditName.Text, []) then
  MessageDlg ('Name not found', mtError, [mbOk], 0)
else
  EnableAllButtons;
```

In the Search example, on the companion CD, you'll find the three versions of the code.

The Total of a Table Column

So far in our examples, the user can view the current contents of a database table and manually edit the data or insert new records. Now we will see how we can change some data in the table through the program code. The idea behind this example is quite simple. The Employee table we have been using has a Salary field. A manager of the company could indeed browse through the table and change the salary of a single employee. But which will be the total expense for salaries for the company? And what if the manager wants to give a 10 percent salary increase (or decrease) to everyone?

These are the two aims of the Total example, which is an extension of the previous program. The toolbar of this new example has two more buttons and a SpinEdit component. There are few other minor changes from the previous example.

I opened the Fields Editor of the table and removed the Table1Salary field, which was defined as a TFloatField. Then I selected the New Field command and added the same field, with the same name, but using the TCurrencyField data type. This is not a calculated field; it's simply a field converted into a new (but equivalent) data type. Using this new field type the program will default to a new output format, suitable for currency values.

Now we can turn our attention to the code of this new program. First, let's look at the code of the total button, which is the one with the dollar signs (*$$*) in Figure 16.18. This button lets you calculate the sum of the salaries of all the employees, then edit some of the values and compute a new total. Basically, we need to scan the table, reading the value of the Table1Salary field for each record:

```
procedure TSearchForm.SpeedButtonTotalClick(
  Sender: TObject);
var
  Total: Real;
begin
  Total := 0;
  Table1.First;
  while not Table1.EOF do
  begin
    Total := Total + Table1Salary.Value;
    Table1.Next;
  end;
  MessageDlg ('Sum of new salaries is ' +
    Format ('%m', [Total]), mtInformation, [mbOK], 0);
end;
```

This code works, as you can see from the output in Figure 16.18, but it has a number of problems. One problem is that the record pointer is moved to the last record, so the previous position in the table is lost. To avoid this problem, we need to store the current position of the record pointer in the table, and restore it at the end. This can be accomplished using a *table bookmark*, a special variable storing the position of a record in a database table. We need to declare a variable of the TBookmark data type, and initialize it while getting the current position from the table:

```
var
  Bookmark: TBookmark;
begin
  Bookmark := Table1.GetBookmark;
```

FIGURE 16.18

The output of the Total program, showing the total salaries of the employees.

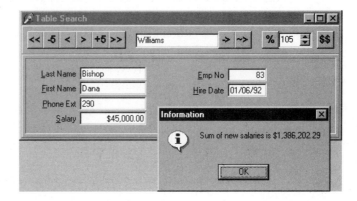

At the end of the `SpeedButtonTotalClick` method, we can restore the position and delete the bookmark with the following two statements:

```
Table1.GotoBookmark (Bookmark);
Table1.FreeBookmark (Bookmark);
```

Another side effect of the program is that, although we will restore the record pointer to the initial position, we might see the records scrolling while the routine browses through the data. This can be avoided by disabling the controls connected with the table during browsing. The table has a `DisableControls` method we can call before the `while` loop starts and an `EnableControls` method we can call at the end, after the record pointer is restored.

TIP

Disabling the data-aware controls connected with a table during long operations not only improves the user interface (since the output is not changing constantly), it also speeds up the program considerably. In fact, the time spent to update the user interface is much greater than the time spent performing the calculations. To test this, try commenting out the `DisableControls` and `EnableControls` methods of the Total example, and see the speed difference.

Finally, we face some dangers from errors in reading the table data, particularly if the program were reading the data from a server using a network. If any problem occurs while retrieving the data, an exception takes place, the controls remain disabled, and the program cannot resume its normal behavior. So we should use a `try-finally` block. Actually, if you want to make the program 100 percent error-proof you should use two nested `try-finally` blocks. Including this change and the two discussed above, here is the resulting code:

```
procedure TSearchForm.SpeedButtonTotalClick(
  Sender: TObject);
var
  Bookmark: TBookmark;
  Total: Real;
begin
  Bookmark := Table1.GetBookmark;
  try
    Table1.DisableControls;
    Total := 0;
    try
      Table1.First;
      while not Table1.EOF do
      begin
        Total := Total + Table1Salary.Value;
        Table1.Next;
      end;
    finally
        Table1.EnableControls;
  end
  finally
    Table1.GotoBookmark (Bookmark);
    Table1.FreeBookmark (Bookmark);
  end;
  MessageDlg ('Sum of new salaries is ' +
    Format ('%m', [Total]), mtInformation, [mbOK], 0);
end;
```

I've written this code to show you an example of a loop to browse the contents of a table, but it would be faster to use a SQL query to sum (or batch-modify) the data (see Appendix B for an example). SQL statements can be used to query and update local tables, which is usually faster than bringing the data all the way back into the application. When you use a SQL server, the advantage of a SQL call to compute the total is even greater.

Editing a Table Column

The code of the method connected to the OnClick event of the % SpeedButton is similar to the one we have just seen. This method also scans the table, computing the total of the salaries, as the previous method did. Although it has just two more statements, there is a key difference. When you increase the salary, you actually change the data in the table. The two key statements are within the while loop:

```
while not Table1.EOF do
begin
  Table1.Edit;
  Table1Salary.Value := Round (Table1Salary.Value *
    SpinEdit1.Value) / 100;
  Total := Total + Table1Salary.Value;
  Table1.Next;
end;
```

The first statement brings the table into edit mode, so that changes to the fields will have an immediate effect. The second statement computes the new salary by multiplying the old one by the value of the SpinEdit component (by default, 105), and dividing it by 100. That's a five percent increase, although the values are rounded to the nearest dollar. With this program, you can change salaries by any amount—even double the salary of each employee—with the click of a button. Note that when you do this, you permanently alter the contents of the table. There is no way to restore it at the end, other than trying to make the reverse operation, which is not always easy, because of the rounding of the values and the approximation of floating-point computations.

If this table is stored on a database that supports transactions, however, you might start a transaction before the update loop, run through all the updates, and then either commit or cancel the transaction. That would guarantee that either all the salaries get updated or none do. Of course, after the changes are committed, you can't undo them.

Exploring the Tables of a Database

In our examples so far, we have always accessed a database table by setting its name at design-time. But what if you do not know which table your program will be connected to? At first, you might think that if you do not know the details of the database at design-time, you won't be able to create forms and operate on the table. This is not true. Setting everything at design-time is certainly easier. Changing almost anything at run-time requires you to write some more code. This is what I've done in the next example, called Tables, which demonstrates how to access the list of databases available to the BDE, how to access the list of the tables for each database, and how to select which fields to view from a specific table.

Choosing a Database and a Table at Run-Time

The first part of the program for this example is quite simple. I've prepared a form with two list boxes. Each list box, and a corresponding label, is placed inside a panel. Each label is aligned to the top of the panel, and each list box to the client area. The first panel, then, is aligned to the left, and the second panel is aligned to the client area. In between there is a Splitter component. All of these components make it easy for users to resize the form in many ways. I suggest you use this approach regularly for the forms of your programs.

When the program starts, it copies the names of the databases in the first list box, using the following code:

```
procedure TMainForm.FormCreate(Sender: TObject);
var
  DBNames: TStringList;
begin
  DBNames := TStringList.Create;
  Session.GetDatabaseNames (DBNames);
  ListBox1.Items := DBNames;
  DBNames.Free;
end;
```

As an alternative, you can directly assign the value to the items of the list box:

```
procedure TMainForm.FormCreate(Sender: TObject);
begin
  Session.GetDatabaseNames (ListBox1.Items);
end;
```

The key element is the call to the GetDatabaseNames procedure of the Session global object. An object of class TSession is automatically defined and initialized by each Delphi database application (even if you don't define one), and to access its methods you only need to refer to the DBTables unit in the uses statement. The first version of this procedure fills the string list object you pass to it as a parameter, so you need to create that object first. After the call, you can copy all of the strings to a list box at once. The alternative, as you saw above, is to pass the value of the list box Item property as parameters to the GetDatabaseNames function.

When you click on one of the database names in the first list box, the second one is filled with the names of the available tables. This time, the code is based on another method of the TSession class, GetTableNames. This method has five parameters: the name of a database, a filter string, two Boolean values indicating whether to include the table file extensions (for local tables only) and whether to include system tables in the list (for SQL databases only), and a list of strings that will be filled with the names of the tables. Here is the code the program executes when the user double-clicks on an item in the first list box:

```
procedure TMainForm.ListBox1DblClick(Sender: TObject);
var
  CurrentDB: string;
begin
  CurrentDB := ListBox1.Items [ListBox1.ItemIndex];
  Session.GetTableNames (CurrentDB, '',
    True, False, ListBox2.Items);
end;
```

You can see the effect of this code in Figure 16.19. As you have seen, the key for this kind of operation is the global Session object, which holds information about the current database activity.

FIGURE 16.19

When you double-click on a database name in the Tables example, the second list box shows the available tables.

A Table Viewer

The next step in the program is to view the contents of one of the tables the program has listed. To accomplish this, we need to define a second form, based on a DBGrid component. Using a grid, we can easily view all of the fields in a database without needing to create a number of controls at run-time. To avoid cluttering the main form, and to build a more flexible program, I've placed the DBGrid component in a second form. The basic idea is that each time the user double-clicks on one of the table names in the second list box of the main form, a new secondary form is created, showing the data in the table. A new form is created each time the user views a table's data, so we need to disable the automatic definition of a form at program startup. Although this creation is controlled by some of the code of the project files, you can change it through the Project Options dialog box. Select the Forms page, and remove the GridForm from the Auto Create forms list.

The advantage of not having a single global object for the second form is that we can create a number of them at run-time. These forms are modeless, which means that we can return to the main form and open another table view without closing the first one.

When the user double-clicks on the second list box in the main form, the code creates a TGridForm object, connects the Table1 component of this form to the proper database and table, and shows the form:

```
procedure TMainForm.ListBox2DblClick(Sender: TObject);
var
  CurrentDB, CurrentTable: string;
  GridForm: TGridForm;
begin
  CurrentDB := ListBox1.Items [ListBox1.ItemIndex];
  CurrentTable := ListBox2.Items [ListBox2.ItemIndex];
  GridForm := TGridForm.Create (self);

  {connect the table component to the selected
  table and activate it}
  GridForm.Table1.DatabaseName := CurrentDB;
  GridForm.Table1.TableName := CurrentTable;
  GridForm.Table1.Open;
  try
    {set the title and call a custom
    initialization method, then show the form}
    GridForm.Caption := Format ('Table: %s - %s',
```

```
    [CurrentDB, CurrentTable]);
  GridForm.FillFieldsCombo;
  GridForm.Show;
except on Exception do
  GridForm.Close;
end;
end;
```

This code displays a new form showing the table data, as you can see in Figure 16.20, where two forms of this kind are visible at the same time. Notice that the code above simply creates the form and never destroys it. It is the responsibility of a form to delete itself, in its OnClose event handler, setting the Action reference parameter to caFree.

FIGURE 16.20

The Tables program can be used to open two or more grid-based table viewers.

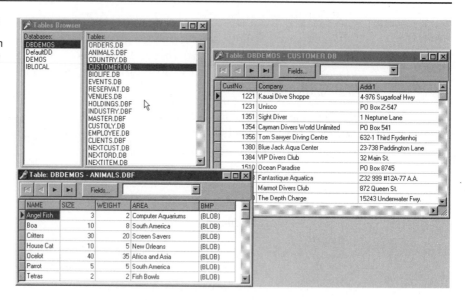

The program sets the caption of the form using the name of the table and database, and it also calls a custom method of the form, FillFieldsCombo. As we will see in a while, this method simply fills a combo box with the names of the fields of the table (hence the name). Basically, this is an initialization method of the form to be called after it is created.

However, this code can't go in the OnCreate event of the form, because the form is created before its Table1 component is properly set up. Instead of trying to find the best event to use (OnShow and OnActivate were two good choices), I've just written a custom method called from the main form. The fact that Windows is event-driven should not compel you to write event-response methods only. At times, good old-fashioned methods—not connected to any event or Windows messages, but directly called from another portion of the code—work better and are easier to understand (and debug). This moves our attention to the code of the DBGrid form. Here is the code of the custom `FillFieldsCombo` method:

```
procedure TGridForm.FillFieldsCombo;
var
  I: Integer;
begin
  for I := 0 to Table1.FieldCount - 1 do
    ComboBox1.Items.Add (Table1.Fields.FieldName);
end;
```

In this procedure, we see how it is possible to access the third element of a database program. After a list of databases and a list of tables within a database, this code lists the fields of a table, storing them in the combo box I've placed in the toolbar of this form. A possible extension to this program would be to generate a form based on data-aware controls, chosen depending on the type of field.

NOTE   Besides accessing the field definition using the `Fields` array of a data set, you can use the `FieldDefs` array, which contains only the field definition, not the data. `FieldDefs` allows you to access the field definition even if the table is still closed (although you should call the `Update` method of the `FieldDefs` to read in the data). This property also allows you to define the structure of a table, as we will see in the following `CreateG` example.

What is the purpose of this combo box? Each time a user selects an element, the corresponding field is either shown or hidden, depending on its current state:

```
procedure TGridForm.ComboBox1Change(Sender: TObject);
begin
  {toggle the visibility of the field}
  Table1.FieldByName (ComboBox1.Text).Visible :=
    not Table1.FieldByName (ComboBox1.Text).Visible;
end;
```

Notice the use of the `FieldByName` method to retrieve the field using the current selection of the combo box, and the use of the Visible property. Once a field becomes invisible, it is immediately removed from the grid associated with the table. Therefore, by simply setting this property, we change the grid automatically. You might also consider allowing the user to customize the grid further, by giving access to some values of the Columns property at run-time.

A Field Editor

The combo box we have placed in the toolbar of the GridForm works, but if you need to select several fields in a big table, it is slow and error-prone. As an alternative, I've created a small field-editor form. This is the third form of the Tables example, named FieldsForm. This form is displayed as a modal form, so we can use a single global object every time. The new form has no code of its own. When the Fields button of the grid form's toolbar is clicked, the multiple selection list box of the FieldsForm (which is the only relevant component) is filled with the names of the fields of the Table1 component. At the same time, the code selects the list box items corresponding to visible fields, as you can see in Figure 16.21.

FIGURE 16.21

The list box can be used to select the table fields to show in the grid.

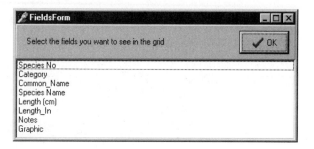

The user can toggle the selection of each item in this list box while the modal form is active. When it is closed, the other form retrieves the values of the selected items, and sets the Visible property of the fields accordingly. Here is the complete code of this method:

```
procedure TGridForm.SpeedButton1Click(Sender: TObject);
var
  I: Integer;
begin
  for I := 0 to Table1.FieldCount - 1 do
  begin
    FieldsForm.FieldsList.Items.Add (
      Table1.Fields [I].FieldName);
    if Table1.Fields [I].Visible then
      FieldsForm.FieldsList.Selected [I]  := True;
```

```
  end;
FieldsForm.ShowModal;
for I := 0 to Table1.FieldCount - 1 do
  Table1.Fields.Visible [I] :=
      FieldsForm.FieldsList.Selected [I] ;
FieldsForm.FieldsList.Clear;
end;
```

This code ends the description of this complex example. We have seen that you can write database applications that do most of the work at run-time, although this approach is slightly more complex. There are many other things we could have done. I've just chosen basic features to avoid making the program too complex.

A Better User Interface for the Table Browser

After writing this program, I came up with an alternative user interface. The new program, Tables2, has almost the same code and capabilities as the previous version, but the database list box is replaced by a database combo box, and the DBGrid is added directly to the main form, instead of to a separate form. Also, this time I've added a Splitter component between the label and the DBGrid. You can see the output of this program in Figure 16.22.

FIGURE 16.22

The output of the Tables2 program, which integrates the DBGrid in the main form.

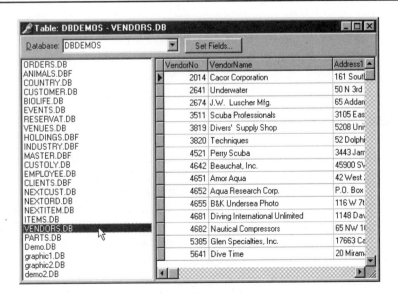

When the program starts, it fills the combo box, then fills the list box (forcing the selection of the first item of the combo box), and then shows a table in the DBGrid (simulating the selection of the first item of the list box):

```
procedure TMainForm.FormCreate(Sender: TObject);
begin
  Session.GetDatabaseNames (ComboBox1.Items);
  // force an initial list in the listbox
  ComboBox1.ItemIndex := 0;
  ComboBox1Change (self);
  // force an initial selection in the DBGrid
  ListBox1.ItemIndex := 0;
  ListBox1Click (self);
end;
```

When this initialization code is executed, or when a user selects a new table, the grid contents are updated. This is the code of the OnClick event of the list box:

```
procedure TMainForm.ListBox1Click(Sender: TObject);
begin
  Table1.Close;
  Table1.DatabaseName := ComboBox1.Text;
  Table1.Tablename := Listbox1.Items [Listbox1.ItemIndex];
  Table1.Open;
  Caption := Format ('Table: %s - %s',
    [Table1.DatabaseName, Table1.Tablename]);
end;
```

The toolbar panel of this main form hosts also the Fields button. If you press this button the program shows the Fields form, as in the Tables example.

Creating a Table

When you start a new project, you should sit down first and design the structure of the database tables used by your application. This is not an easy task. Also, in even moderately complex programs, a flaw in the database design can lead to incredible problems. If your previous database programming experience is limited, you should consider reading one of the many books on this topic before you start writing a complex database application with Delphi.

Once you have developed your database, you need to create the tables. There are basically two choices. The simplest method is to use the stand-alone Database Desktop applications. The other approach is to write some code in Delphi to create the tables. With the Database Desktop tool you can define a new table with the following steps:

1. Choose the File ➤ New ➤ Table menu command.

2. In the resulting dialog box, select the table type (such as Paradox 7 or dBASE for Windows).

3. The Create Table dialog box displayed at this point will depend on the table type you've selected. Besides indicating the names and types of the fields, you'll be able to add primary and secondary indexes, referential constraints, validity checks, and other features. In Figure 16.23, you can see the Create Table dialog box for a Paradox 7 table.

4. At the end, save the new table in a specific directory, or even better choose one of the already defined BDE aliases.

5. You can now open the table and input test values for it, or simply leave it empty.

FIGURE 16.23

The Paradox 7 version of the Create Table dialog box of the Database Desktop application.

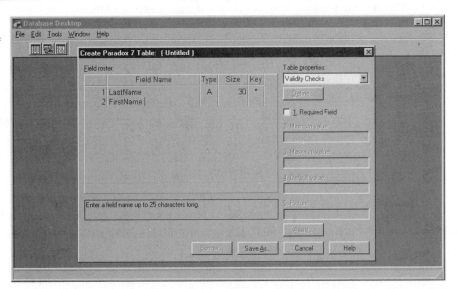

Creating Tables Dynamically

Now suppose that the structure of our table is simple, and that we want to allow the user to create a number of tables of the same kind (or of a similar type). We can use a Delphi application and create tables in its code. This is the aim of the next example, which also uses a graphic field for the first time in this book. (Incidentally, this is also the first example that uses the Clipboard, a topic discussed in detail in Chapter 30.)

> **NOTE** Graphic, memo, and BLOB fields in Delphi are handled exactly like other fields. Just connect the proper editor or viewer, and most of the work is done behind the scenes by the system. I assume that you have already seen the Delphi graphical example, which shows fish. If not, try running the DEMOS\DB\FISHFACT example that ships with Delphi and see how it works.

The name of this example is CreateG, where *G* stands for graphics. Its goal is to allow a user to capture images on the screen and store them in database tables. Note that these tables will probably become quite big after a while, so if you have limited disk space, beware of using this program.

Each time you run CreateG, it asks you if you want to create a new table or use an existing one. If you want to create a new table, you should provide a table name that doesn't exist so that you won't override existing, valuable data. If you load an existing table, you must use a table with the proper fields: a description of the image, the date and time it was saved, and the image itself.

When a suitable table has been created or selected, the program displays its main form, as shown in Figure 16.24. You can now capture an image on the screen, copying it to the Clipboard. This step is not performed by the program. You can just press the PrintScreen key to capture a bitmap of the whole screen or the Alt+PrintScreen combination for a bitmap of the current active window. Or you can use any program or technique to create a bitmap, and then copy it to the Clipboard.

After the image has been copied to the Clipboard, click on the Add button or select the Record ➤ Add menu command, and the program will ask you for a description of the image, read the system time, copy the bitmap from the Clipboard, and insert the new record in the table. If something went wrong, you can use the Delete button, or the Record ➤ Delete menu command, to remove the current record. Of course, you can always browse through the records of the table (which are sorted by description). Finally, you can use the check box to stretch the image or view it (or a portion of it) in the default scale.

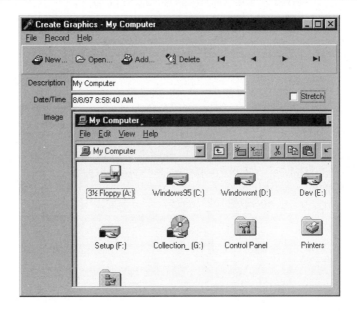

FIGURE 16.24

The main form of the CreateG example at run-time. Notice that image stretching is disabled.

After you're done with the table, you can create a new one by clicking on the New button or selecting the File ➤ New menu command, or reopen an existing table by clicking on the Open button or using the File ➤ Open menu command. Of course, there are many ways to improve this program, such as making the screen capture automatic or checking the contents of the Clipboard. However, the features it does have demonstrate the concepts, and the example is already complex enough.

The Form and Its Startup Code

Let's begin by taking a look at the main form of this program, which has two Table components. We are going to use the second table, which is not connected to a DataSource component, inside a search algorithm. The form has some data-aware controls, and a toolbar with four speed buttons plus a Navigator control, all having the Flat property set to True. The components have no special properties, so I'll omit the textual description of the form.

When the program starts, it displays a simple message dialog box, as shown in Figure 16.25. This lets the user choose between creating a new table or using an existing one. The message dialog box, displayed in the FormCreate method before the main form becomes visible, has three choices:

```
procedure TGraphForm.FormCreate(Sender: TObject);
var
  Code: Word;
begin
  Code := MessageDlg (
    'Do you want to create a new table?' +
    #13'(choose No to load an existing table,' +
    #13'Cancel to quit)',
    mtConfirmation, mbYesNoCancel, 0);
  if Code = idYes then
    New1Click (self)
  else if Code = idNo then
    Open1Click (self)
  else
    Application.Terminate;
end;
```

FIGURE 16.25

The message dialog box shown at program startup.

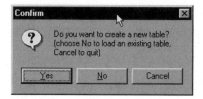

If the user selects the Yes button, the program creates a new table, calling the handler of the corresponding menu item. If the user selects No, the program loads an existing table, again by activating the code of a menu selection. If the user selects Cancel, the application terminates. The central pieces of code of this program are in the two methods New1Click and Open1Click.

Creating a New Table

To create a new table in Delphi, you can call the CreateTable method of a Table component. However, before you do this, you need to set some properties of this component. You must specify a database name, a table name, the names and types of the fields, and the name of an index.

The database name is set to the alias DBDEMOS at design-time. You can change it, but if you do, you need to replace this string with the new one in several places in the source code. We request the table name from the user, with the InputQuery function. When the user has entered a name, we need to verify whether a table with the same name already exists. In fact, the CreateTable method of the TTable class eventually overrides a table that has the same name as the new one. How do we check if the name is already in use? We can call a method of the Session global object, as we did in the last example. Here is the first part of the code of this method:

```
procedure TGraphForm.New1Click(Sender: TObject);
var
  TableName: string;
  TbNames: TStringList;
begin
  {request the name of the new table from the user,
  raising an exception if Cancel is pressed}
  TableName := '';
  if InputQuery ('New Table',
    'Enter a new table name:', TableName) then
  begin
    if TableName = '' then
      raise EMyDatabaseError.Create (
        'Invalid table name');

    {if the table already exists in the DBDEMOS
    database, do not overwrite it}
    TbNames := TStringList.Create;
    Session.GetTableNames ('DBDEMOS', '',
      False, False, TbNames);
    if TbNames.IndexOf (TableName) >= 0 then
      raise EMyDatabaseError.Create (
        'Table already exists');
```

The IndexOf method of the string list returns the index of the string, or –1 if the string does not exist. If the string exists, the program raises an exception to stop further execution of this method. EMyDatabaseError is a new exception class I've defined in the code of this program as follows:

```
type
  EMyDatabaseError = class (EDatabaseError)
  end;
```

The same exception is raised in the New1Click method if the user has clicked the Cancel button of the InputQuery dialog box. As you can see in the following code, however, this exception is raised only if the method was activated by the OnCreate event handler. The program can determine this by looking at the value of the Sender parameter:

```
if InputQuery... then
  ...
else
  // if OnCreate called this method
  if Sender = self then
    raise EMyDatabaseError.Create (
    'Table creation aborted by the user');
```

All these exceptions are checked in the FormCreate method. If an error occurs in one of the two possible procedures, New1Click or Open1Click, the program shows an error message and restarts the custom initialization code, asking again for the user to choose between a new or an existing table. Here is the final complete code of the FormCreate method:

```
procedure TGraphForm.FormCreate(Sender: TObject);
var
  Code: Word;
  Done: Boolean;
begin
  Done := False;
  while not Done do
  try
    Code := MessageDlg (
      'Do you want to create a new table?' +
      #13'(choose No to load an existing table,' +
      #13'Cancel to quit)',
      mtConfirmation, mbYesNoCancel, 0);
    if Code = idYes then
      New1Click (self)
    else if Code = idNo then
      Open1Click (self)
    else
      Application.Terminate;
    Done := True
  except
    on E: EMyDatabaseError do
```

```
      ShowMessage (E.Message);
  end; // end of try-except and while blocks
end;
```

Now we can move back to the second part of the New1Click method. If the table does not already exist, the program can create it. First it has to store the name of the table in the Table1 component, and also set the TableType property with the value ttParadox (or any other table type). The next step, which is the most complex one, is to define the three fields of the table. We need to use the FieldDefs property (the list of field definitions) of the Table component, and call the Add method three times. The Add method adds a new field to the structure of the table. The Add method of the IndexDefs property is used to define a primary index. Here is the second part of the New1Click method:

```
{close the current table}
Table1.Close;

{set the name and type of the new table}
Table1.TableName := TableName;
Table1.TableType := ttParadox;

{define the three fields and the index}
with Table1.FieldDefs do
begin
  Clear;
  Add ('Description', ftString, 50, True);
  Add ('Time', ftDateTime, 0, False);
  Add ('Graphics', ftGraphic, 0, False);
end;
Table1.IndexDefs.Clear;
Table1.IndexDefs.Add('DescrIndex', 'Description',
  [ixPrimary, ixUnique]);

{create the table using the above definitions}
Table1.CreateTable;
Table1.Open;
Caption := 'Create Graphics - ' + TableName;
```

As you can see in the last three lines above, after the program has set up the attributes of the table, it can create it, calling the CreateTable method, and then it can open the table. Since the data source and the other data-aware controls are already connected, once the table is open, we can start working with it.

Choosing an Existing Table with the Proper Fields

The second time you run the program, you can choose an existing table instead of creating a new one. The loading code is handled by the Open1Click method. This code starts by filling the list box of a dialog box with the names of the available tables.

I initially thought that simply accessing the dialog box components as usual was enough, but when I tried, I invariably got an error. What's wrong? The problem is that the code we are writing can be called from the initialization code, part of the OnCreate method of the main form. If you remember, the code of the typical project file of a Delphi program calls the CreateForm procedure a number of times (once for each form created at startup). One of the effects of calling this method is that the OnCreate method is executed.

For this reason, during the OnCreate event of the main form, the dialog box form has still not been created. Accessing one of its components results in a run-time error. The compiler knows nothing about the order of execution of the events and of the initialization code. To solve the problem, simply disable the automatic creation of TablesForm in the Project Options dialog box (in the Forms page), and then manually create the form before accessing any components in it.

Now we can move to the core of this procedure. The code retrieves the list of database tables with a call to the GetTableNames method of the Session global object (as we've already done in the past), but instead of copying the whole string list to the list box, it performs a test on each item. Basically the program assigns the name of each table to the Table2 component, and then checks its FieldDefs property (after updating it). Here is the first part of the procedure:

```
procedure TGraphForm.Open1Click(Sender: TObject);
var
  TbNames: TStringList;
  I: Integer;
  TableFound: Boolean;
begin
  {create the form of the dialog box,
  before filling its list box with the table names}
  TablesForm := TTablesForm.Create (Application);

  {retrieve the list of tables from the database}
  TableFound := False;
  TbNames := TStringList.Create;
```

```
Session.GetTableNames ('DBDEMOS', '',
  True, False, TbNames);

{check if the table has the proper fields,
that is, if it was created by this program.
The code uses a secondary table object}
for I := 0 to TbNames.Count - 1 do
begin
  Table2.TableName := TbNames [I];
  Table2.FieldDefs.Update;
  if (Table2.FieldDefs.Count = 3) and
    (Table2.FieldDefs[0].DataType = ftString) and
    (Table2.FieldDefs[1].DataType = ftDateTime) and
    (Table2.FieldDefs[2].DataType = ftGraphic) then
  begin
    {table fields match: add the table to the list}
    TablesForm.Listbox1.Items.Add (Table2.TableName);
    TableFound := True;
  end;
end;
```

When a table passes the test, it is added to the list box of the dialog box, and a proper flag (TableFound) is set. If any table is found, the dialog box is displayed on the screen, as shown in Figure 16.26. When the dialog box is closed (by clicking on OK), the selected list box item is copied to the TableName property of the of Table1 component, which in turn is connected to the data-aware controls of the main form. If no table passes the test, an exception is raised. Here is the second part of the Open1Click method:

```
{if no table was found, raise an exception}
if not TableFound then
  raise EMyDatabaseError.Create (
    'No table with the proper structure');

{otherwise, show the dialog box}
TablesForm.ListBox1.ItemIndex := 0;
if TablesForm.ShowModal = idOK then
begin
  {if OK was pressed, open the table}
  Table1.Close;
  Table1.TableName := TablesForm.ListBox1.Items [
    TablesForm.ListBox1.ItemIndex];
  Table1.Open;
```

```
          Caption := 'Crete Graphics - ' +
            Table1.TableName;
      end
      else
        // if OnCreate called this method
        if Sender = self then
          raise EMyDatabaseError.Create (
            'Table selection aborted by the user');
    end;
```

FIGURE 16.26

The TablesForm dialog box allows a user to choose only from the tables that have the proper fields.

Adding or Removing Records

Once a table is open, we can simply insert new records. This happens when the user clicks on the Add button in the main form of the program or selects the corresponding menu item. The code of this button's OnClick method is quite simple. The procedure asks the user to enter a description (which must be unique), and then creates a new record at the end of the table:

```
procedure TGraphForm.Add1Click(Sender: TObject);
var
  Descr: string;
begin
  if InputQuery ('New record',
    'Enter the description:', Descr) then
  begin
    Table1.Insert;
    EditDescription.Text := Descr;
    EditDate.Text := DateTimeToStr (Now);
    DBIMage.PasteFromClipboard;
```

```
      Table1.Post;
    end;
  end;
```

Notice that the values are copied to the data-aware controls, and not directly to the fields. In this case, we can use the PasteFromClipboard method to fill the DBImage component with the bitmap currently in the Clipboard. The other two methods of the main form, one to delete the current record and the other to stretch the image, are very simple:

```
procedure TGraphForm.Delete1Click(Sender: TObject);
begin
  if MessageDlg (
    'Are you sure you want to delete the current record?',
     mtConfirmation, [mbYes, mbNo], 0) = idYes then
    Table1.Delete;
end;

procedure TGraphForm.CheckBox1Click(Sender: TObject);
begin
  DBImage.Stretch := CheckBox1.Checked;
end;
```

That is all. What we have built is a program based on the file metaphor, with File ➤ New and File ➤ Open menu commands. Although it uses this metaphor, it is actually based on database tables, which can indeed be files (as in the case of a Paradox database) but can also be implemented as portions of a single big file, as in the case of Microsoft Access or InterBase databases.

A Multi-Record Grid

So far we have seen that you can either use a grid to display a number of records of a database table or build a form with specific data-aware controls for the various fields, accessing the records one by one. There is a third alternative: Use a multi-record object (a DBCtrlGrid), which allows you to place many data-aware controls in a small area of a form and automatically duplicate these controls for a number of records.

Here is what we can do to build the Multi1 example. Create a new blank form, place a Table component and a DataSource component in it, and connect them to the COUNTRY.DB table. Now place a DBCtrlGrid on the form, set its size and the number of rows and columns, and place two edit components connected with the Name and Capital fields of the table. To place these DBEdit components, you can also open the Fields Editor and drag the two fields to the control grid. At design-time you simply work on the active portion of the grid (see Figure 16.27, on the right), and at run-time you can see these controls replicated a number of times (see Figure 16.27, on the left).

FIGURE 16.27

The DBCtrlGrid of the Multi1 example at design-time (on the right) and at run-time (on the left).

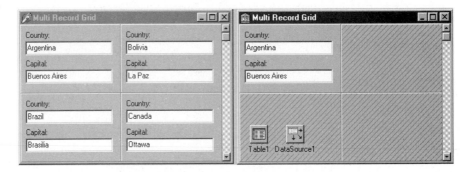

Here are the most important properties of the DBCtrlGrid object and the other components of this example:

```
object Form1: TForm1
  Caption = 'Multi Record Grid'
  object DBCtrlGrid1: TDBCtrlGrid
    ColCount = 2
    DataSource = DataSource1
    RowCount = 2
    object DBEdit1: TDBEdit
      DataField = 'Name'
      DataSource = DataSource1
    end
    object DBEdit2: TDBEdit...
  end
  object Table1: TTable
    Active = True
    DatabaseName = 'DBDEMOS'
    TableName = 'COUNTRY.DB'
  end
  object DataSource1: TDataSource
```

```
      DataSet = Table1
  end
end
```

Actually, you can simply set the number of columns and rows. Then each time you resize the control, the width and height of each panel are set accordingly. What is not available is a way to align the grid automatically to the client area of the form.

Moving Control Grid Panels

To improve the last example, we might resize the grid using the FormResize method. We could simply write the following code (in the Multi2 example):

```
procedure TForm1.FormResize(Sender: TObject);
begin
  DBCtrlGrid1.Height := ClientHeight - Panel1.Height;
  DBCtrlGrid1.Width := ClientWidth;
end;
```

This works, but it is not what I want. I'd like to increase the number of panels, not enlarge them. To accomplish this we can define a minimum height for the panels and compute how many panels can fit in the available area each time the form is resized. For example, in Multi2, I've added one more statement to the FormResize method above, which now becomes:

```
procedure TForm1.FormResize(Sender: TObject);
begin
  DBCtrlGrid1.RowCount :=
    (ClientHeight - Panel1.Height) div 100;
  DBCtrlGrid1.Height := ClientHeight - Panel1.Height;
  DBCtrlGrid1.Width := ClientWidth;
end;
```

Instead of doing the same for the columns of the control grid component, I've added a TrackBar component to a panel. When the position of the trackbar changes (the range is from 2 to 10), the program sets the number of columns of the control grid and resizes it. In fact, if you simply set the number of columns, they'll have the same width as before. Here is the code of the trackbar's OnChange event handler:

```
procedure TForm1.TrackBar1Change(Sender: TObject);
begin
```

```
LabelCols.Caption := Format (
  '%d Columns', [TrackBar1.Position]);
DBCtrlGrid1.ColCount := TrackBar1.Position;
DBCtrlGrid1.Width := ClientWidth;
end;
```

This code and the `FormResize` method above allow you to change the configuration of the control grid at run-time in a number of ways. You can see an example of a crammed version of the form in Figure 16.28.

FIGURE 16.28

The output of the Multi2 example, with an excessive number of columns.

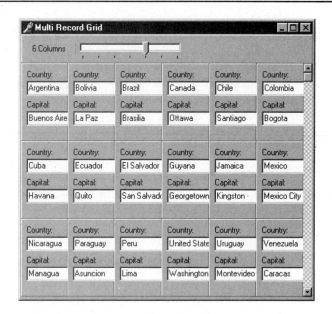

Building a Master Detail Form with the Wizard

When you run the Database Form Wizard, it asks whether you want to create a form based on a single table or a master detail form. A master detail form involves two tables, with a one-to-many relationship. You can define this behavior by using a proper SQL statement, or with some properties of the Table component. Either way, you can let the Wizard generate the code for you. This is exactly what you'll see in the next example.

Since we're using the sample tables available in Delphi, there are not many choices for building a master detail form. Our example will use the Customer and Order tables, which are also used by some Delphi sample programs.

Here are the steps to build the MastDet example:

1. Start a new project and run the Database Form Wizard.

2. In the first page of the Wizard, choose a master detail form and Table objects.

3. Choose CUSTOMER.DB from DBDEMOS as the master table. Choose some of the fields, and select the horizontal or vertical layout.

4. As the detail table, select ORDERS.DB. Choose some of the fields from this table, and select the default grid layout.

5. You are now on a crucial page of the Database Form Wizard, shown in Figure 16.29. Select the CustNo index, then select the same field in the two lists of fields.

6. Click on the Add button to define a join.

7. Generate the form (as the main form), without selecting the Form and Data-Module radio button, and the program is finished. You can run it immediately to see its effect.

FIGURE 16.29

This page of the Database Form Wizard lets you specify master-detail relationships between two tables.

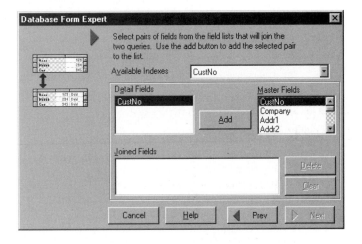

In Figure 16.30 you can see an example of the output of this program (MastDet) at run-time. In the figure, I've increased the size of the form and moved some of the components, but the form's behavior is exactly the same as the one generated by the Wizard. Each time you select a new customer, the grid below displays only the orders pertaining to that customer.

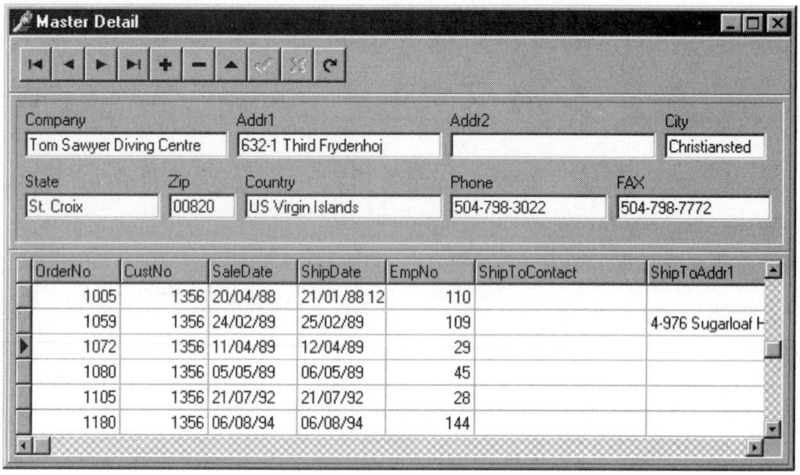

FIGURE 16.30

The MastDet example, a program fully generated by the Delphi Database Form Wizard.

How does this program work? The answer is very simple. If you look at the properties of the two Table components in the Object Inspector, you can see the following values:

```
object Table1: TTable
  DatabaseName = 'DBDEMOS'
  TableName = 'customer.db'
end
object Table2: TTable
  DatabaseName = 'DBDEMOS'
  TableName = 'orders.db'
  IndexFieldNames = 'CustNo'
  MasterFields = 'CustNo'
  MasterSource = DataSource1
end
```

The second table has a master source (the data source connected with the first table), and relates to a specific field, which provides the cross-reference.

A Master Detail Structure with Queries

The previous example used two tables to build a master detail form, because this is exactly what we asked for. As an alternative, you can define this type of join using a SQL statement. This is easy, since once again, the Database Form Wizard can generate the code for us. Simply run the Wizard once more, this time selecting a TQuery instead of a TForm.

For this example, I've joined the ORDERS.DB table with ITEMS.DB table, which describes each item in each order. The two tables can be joined using the OrderNo field. When you generate the code, the program, named Orders, behaves exactly like the previous one. This time, however the trick is in the SQL statements of the second query object:

```
select
  items."OrderNo",
  items."ItemNo",
  items."PartNo",
  items."Qty"
from
  items
where
  "items"."OrderNo" =: "OrderNo"
```

As you can see, this SQL statement uses a parameter, OrderNo. This parameter is connected directly to the first query, because the DataSource property of Query2 is set to DataSource1, which is connected to Query1. In other words, the second query is considered to be a data control connected to the first data source. Each time the current record in the first data source changes, the Query2 component is updated, just like any other component connected to DataSource1. The field used for the connection, in this case, is the field having the same name as the query parameter.

Providing a Closed Selection in a Combo Box

The form of the Orders example generated with the Database Form Wizard can be improved (you won't find the original version on the companion CD, only the customized one). In the customized version, I've moved some of the editor boxes and labels to place them in two columns, and moved some other elements, but in particular, I've solved a problem that this form had.

In the original version, when you view the records or enter new data, you need to work with the customer number, which is not the most natural way—most users will prefer to work with customer names. However, in the database, the names of the customers are stored in a different table, to avoid duplicating the customer data for each order of the same customer. To get around working with customer numbers, I placed a new component in the form, a DBLookupComboBox control. This component can be connected to two data sources at the same time, one with the actual data and a second with the display data. Basically, we want to connect it with the CustNo value of `DataSource1`, the master query, but let it show the information extracted from another table, `CUSTOMER.DB`.

To accomplish this, I removed the DBEdit component connected to the customer number and replaced it with a DBLookupComboBox component and a DBText component. DBText is a sort of label, or text that can't be edited. Then I added a new data source (`DataSource3`) connected to a table (`Table1`), which relates to the `CUSTOMER.DB` file. For the program to work, you need to set several properties of the DBLookupComboBox1 component. Here is a list of the relevant values:

```
object DBLookupComboBox1: TDBLookupComboBox
  DataField = 'CustNo'
  DataSource = DataSource1
  KeyField = 'CustNo'
  ListField = 'Company'
  ListSource = DataSource3
end
```

The first two properties determine the main connection, as usual. The other three properties determine the secondary source (`ListSource`), the field used for the join (`KeyField`), and the information to display (`ListField`). Besides entering the name of a single field, you can provide multiple fields: Only the first field is displayed as combo box text, but if you set a large value for the `DropDownWidth` property, the pull-down list of the combo box will include multiple columns of data. You can see this output of the form in Figure 16.31.

TIP
If you set the index of the table connected with the DBLookupComboBox to the Company field, the drop-down list will show the companies in alphabetical order, and not following the customer number order. This is what I've done in the example.

FIGURE 16.31

The output of the Orders example, with the BDLookupComboBox showing multiple fields in its drop-down list.

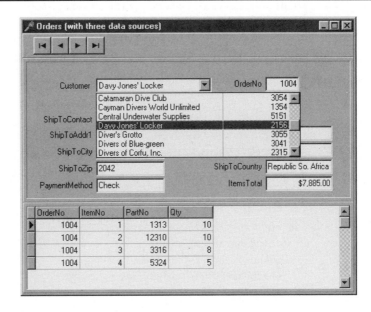

What about the code of this program? Well, there is none. Everything works just by setting the correct properties. The three joined data sources do not need custom code.

A Lookup in a Grid

Because I've placed a lookup field in a form (using the DBLookupComboBox component), I can add a drop-down lookup list in a DBGrid component. We saw in the Calc example how to provide a drop-down list in a field of the DBGrid, by customizing the `Columns` property to provide a closed selection. (To do this we press the PickList button in the Columns editor). However, to customize the grid by adding a lookup list, which refers to a secondary data source, we need to follow a completely different approach. In fact, we have to define a lookup field using the Fields Editor.

As an example, I've taken the MastDet form just described and turned it into the MastDet2 form. In the original version of this form, the grid displayed the code number of the employee who took the order. Why not show the employee name, instead, and let the user choose it from a drop-down list of employees?

To accomplish this, I added a Table and DataSource component, referring to the EMPLOYEE.DB database table. Then I've opened the Fields Editor for the second table, the one with the orders, and I've added all the fields. I've selected the EmpNo field, and set its Visible property to False, to remove it from the grid (we cannot remove it altogether because it is used to build the cross-reference with the corresponding field of the Employee table).

Now it is time to define the lookup field. If you've followed the preceding steps, you can issue the New Fields command in the local menu of the Fields Editor, and define the new field in the resulting dialog box, as you can see in Figure 16.32. Simply enter a name (such as Employee) and check the Lookup radio button. Once this is done, select the field in the Object Inspector and set its lookup properties as follows:

```
object Table2Employee: TStringField
  FieldName = 'Employee'
  Lookup = True
  LookupDataSet = Table3
  KeyFields = 'EmpNo'
  LookupKeyFields = 'EmpNo'
  LookupResultField = 'LastName'
end
```

FIGURE 16.32

The dialog box used to define a new look-up field.

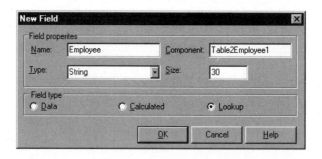

This is all that is needed to make the drop-down list work (see Figure 16.33) and to view the value of the cross-references field at design-time, too. Notice that there is no need to customize the Columns property of the grid, because the drop-down button and the value of seven rows are taken by default. This doesn't mean you cannot use this property to further customize these and other visual elements of the grid.

FIGURE 16.33

The output of the Mast-Det2 example, with the drop-down list inside the grid displaying values taken from another database table.

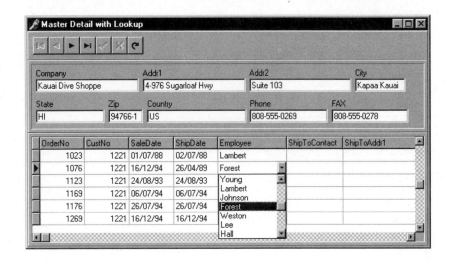

What's Next?

In this chapter, we have seen a number of examples of database access from Delphi programs. We have reviewed the basics of navigating in a table, entering new values, finding values, and using the grid and navigator components. In the last part of the chapter, we explored some more advanced features, such as building tables and creating table viewers at run-time to let the user select the fields he or she wants to see. We have seen an example of the use of a graphics field, and some examples of joins.

Is this all there is to say about Delphi database programming? Not at all. Delphi database support is very extensive and complete. The purpose of this chapter was to give you an idea of what you can do. What you don't find in this chapter is a discussion of database design principles, and I deliberately didn't attempt to design a full-scale database. Database design is the subject of many whole books by itself. What I'll focus on in the next chapter (still devoted to databases) is a more general picture, with some elements of client/server programming, the Visual Query Builder, data modules, the Data Dictionary and more.

CHAPTER SEVENTEEN

Advanced Database Access

- The local InterBase server

- The Visual Query Builder

- Table joins with the Visual Query Builder

- Data modules

- Table ranges and filters

- Using the Data Dictionary

- Database transactions

- Handling database errors

In Chapter 16, we went through a number of examples of developing database applications. All of those applications accessed data stored in dBASE or Paradox tables; that is, in the usual files. This is certainly good enough for a simple program, but if you need your application to be robust and safe, you might think of moving your data to a SQL server. (See Appendix B for a short overview of the SQL language.) The SQL server can reside on a server computer connected to a network, or it can be on the same local machine you are using to develop your programs. Delphi includes the local Windows version of Borland's SQL server, InterBase.

In this chapter, we will explore some of the details of using a SQL server. If you do not own the Client/Server Suite edition of Delphi, you might be tempted to skip this chapter. However, some of the tools described here (such as the local InterBase server) are available in every Delphi box. The second part of the chapter covers other advanced database features, such as the data modules and the data dictionary. These features do not strictly relate to client/server development, although they provide interesting benefits in that area.

Accessing a SQL Server

The local SQL server can be used both as a target platform and as a development platform. When you use it as a target platform, you end up installing a copy of the InterBase server (provided you have a license for it), along with your program and the BDE libraries your program needs.

> **NOTE**　Realize that the local InterBase server is a single-user implementation, not a full-scale multiuser SQL server. Local InterBase is useful for deploying applications that need to run on stand-alone machines (not networked), without giving up the advantages of SQL queries or writing a separate version of the application to use local tables. Borland also sells full-scale versions of InterBase, which can run on Windows NT or UNIX machines.

Often, you'll use the local InterBase only as a development platform. Instead of developing the application right on a network, you can build it on a local machine, and then simply change the destination database at the end. This might also be the intermediate step between a local version using files (a prototype of your program) and a fully developed client/server version (your final application).

Developing a Delphi application that accesses a remote server is really not very different from developing a Delphi application that accesses local tables. Once the server database has been set up, and you have defined the proper tables, you use the remote server almost seamlessly from within the development environment. There are, however, some differences. For example, the user must generally log in to access the database. Another key element of SQL servers is the presence of a more powerful transaction control (since the 32-bit version of the Borland Database Engine includes only a simple transaction control for Paradox and dBASE tables). Other features include the execution of stored procedures and increased efficiency in using queries rather than tables. Indexing and optimization techniques might even depend on the specific SQL server.

Some of the issues related to these differences can be handled using Delphi's database components. For example, the Database and Session components allow you to customize the database log-in procedure and to determine how a transaction should interact with another simultaneous transaction accessing the same tables (the *transaction-isolation level*). Although you are not required to have these two components in your Delphi applications, using them might increase the control you have over the server environment.

Another specific SQL server component is the StoredProc component. This allows a program to execute a procedure present on the server database, eventually passing some parameters and retrieving a return value. A third useful component for database manipulation is BatchMove, which allows a program to copy, append, or delete groups of records or an entire table from two different databases. The interesting element is that one of these databases can be a local table and the other a SQL server.

A First InterBase Application

Now let's get to work and build a simple Delphi application using the local InterBase engine. We'll create this program using the Database Form Expert, to demonstrate that you can use this approach in developing a client/server application. (Everything we have seen in the previous chapter really works as I've described for SQL servers.)

To build this program, create a new Delphi project, then choose Database ➤ Form Expert. Select a simple form based on a query. Move to the next page and choose the IBLOCAL alias (which should point to the `Mastsql.gdb` InterBase file in the `Delphi 3\Demos\Data` subdirectory. At this point, the InterBase local server will prompt you with a log-in dialog box. If you have not worked with the local InterBase server before, the default log-in name you should type will be *'SYSDBA'*. Enter the default password, *'masterkey'*, and you are ready to go on using the Database Form Expert as usual. For example, to rebuild the IbEmp example, you should choose the Employee table as the one to access.

Notice, in this case, that tables are not files. The pseudo List Files of Type combo box just lets you choose between User Tables or All Tables, including system tables. Continue with the Expert, selecting the only two fields in this table and a layout (I chose vertical, with labels on top). Then generate the form.

Customize the form as you like. I activated table editing (by setting the `RequestLive` property of the Query component to `True`), moved some of the components around on the screen, resized the form, and set the `Flat` property of the Navigator component to `True`. I also gave the form a new name and caption. An example of the output of the program, named IbEmp and included on the companion CD, is shown in Figure 17.1.

FIGURE 17.1

The IbEmp program at run-time. Notice the log-on dialog box, requiring a user to type in the proper password, before the main form of the program is displayed.

Each time you run this program, it requests your user name and password (see Figure 17.1 again). To skip this, you can add a database component to the form and set the corresponding properties. As an alternative, you might handle the `OnLogin` event of this component and enter some values in the `LoginParams` property. Either way allows you to bypass the log-in prompt, but is that what you really want to do?

Keep in mind that having a log-in prompt is one of the key features of database security. You might consider skipping it while you're developing your program, but you'll usually want to require the end users to log in before using the application. In this example, I used a local SQL database, installed on the same computer I used to develop the Delphi application. This is not the only choice. I could have developed a real client/server application, following the same steps but using a remote server connected to my computer via a network.

Accessing a Remote SQL Server

The only real difference between using a local database and accessing a SQL server is that you need the Client/Server Suite version of Delphi, with its SQL Links. Actually, you can access most SQL servers through ODBC, but this is far from the best choice if efficiency is an issue. SQL Links is basically an extension of the Borland Database Engine. As explained in Chapter 16 (and illustrated in Figure 16.1), the BDE can directly access some data sources, such as Paradox and dBASE tables, or it can interface with ODBC (Open Database Connectivity) drivers or SQL Links.

Since there are a number of layers involved in connecting Delphi to a SQL server with either the BDE or ODBC, you need to take several steps to install and configure everything. You can install the BDE along with Delphi or separately, and it can be configured using the BDE Configuration utility. With the Configuration utility, you can define aliases, install new ODBC drivers, and set parameters used to connect to the various databases.

The second layer is SQL Links, which you can also configure with the BDE Configuration utility. After this layer there is the network, which requires the installation of a proper network protocol. The last step is to configure the SQL server.

InterBase Server Tools

Delphi includes applications that can be used to set up, configure, and maintain both the local InterBase engine and remote servers. Here, I'll briefly describe these tools. For a full description of their capabilities, refer to the Borland documentation, which is quite extensive in this area.

Server Manager   The Server Manager can be used for administering InterBase local or remote databases and servers. With Server Manager, you can manage database security (authorize new users, change user passwords, and remove user authorizations), back up a database, perform maintenance tasks, and execute other related operations. Figure 17.2 shows an example of using the Server Manager to add a user.

FIGURE 17.2

The InterBase Server Manager tool, while adding a new user (me).

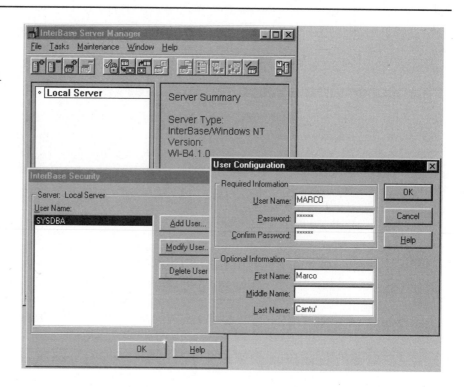

Windows ISQL   The Windows InterBase ISQL (Interactive SQL) application can be used to execute a SQL statement on a local or remote InterBase server. You can start ISQL, connect to an existing local or remote database, and enter a SQL statement. For example, you could connect to the IBLOCAL alias, and enter this statement:

```
select First_Name, Last_Name
from employee
where Job_Code = "Eng"
```

This SQL command outputs the first and last name of every employee in the Engineering (*Eng*) department, as you can see in Figure 17.3.

Windows ISQL can be used to view the contents of a database, but its real role is in database setup and maintenance. You can define new tables, add indexes, write procedures (the stored procedures), and so on. This is all done using Inter-Base SQL, so it is probably not for the casual user.

FIGURE 17.3

The result of executing a SQL statement in the Windows ISQL application.

NOTE

Note that the SQL language recognized by InterBase is much wider than the language features I discuss in Appendix B and the standard SQL you can use with the BDE. Any SQL server usually implements some specific advanced capabilities not included in the ANSI SQL standard.

Database Explorer and Database Desktop Another tool you can use with local and remote InterBase servers is the Database Explorer application. It offers the easiest way to navigate through existing tables or databases, as well as to insert and delete records and modify existing values. Along with the Database Explorer there is the Database Desktop. Both can be considered table viewers and configuration tools, while the Server Manager and Windows ISQL can be considered database configuration and definition tools. These tools overlap: you can run a SQL query over an InterBase database using Windows ISQL, the Database Explorer, and the Database Desktop (not to mention the Visual Query Builder). For instance, with the Database Explorer you can execute a SQL statement similar to the one I used in the previous Windows ISQL example (Figure 17.3). This example of the use of the Database Explorer is shown in Figure 17.4.

FIGURE 17.4

The result of a SQL query on employees using the Database Explorer.

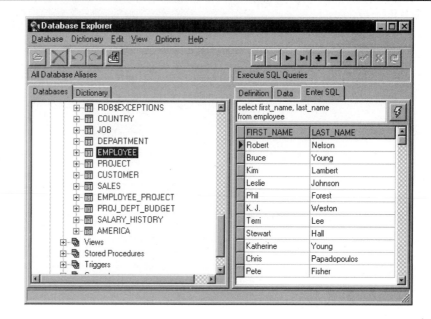

By simply selecting the Data and SQL tabs, you can see all of the data or select just some fields or records. For more information about the Database Explorer and the InterBase server tools, refer to the Borland online documentation and manuals. Now we will continue with some examples using Delphi—and some code.

Moving an Existing Program to the SQL Server

We've seen that developing a new Delphi database application using a server is similar to developing an application based on local files. What is involved in expanding or upgrading an application based on local files to one that works with a SQL server? It takes very little to make it work. To take advantage of all the SQL server's features, including transaction processing, it takes just a little more work. In this section, we'll see what is involved in moving an existing Delphi database application based on a local table to the local InterBase server. This is usually a first step in its move to a remote SQL server. The second step is much simpler.

As an example, let's go through the steps for upgrading the Calc example presented in Chapter 16. The new version will include a viewer of the COUNTRY.DB table with a calculated field, and it will be connected to the local InterBase server. To upsize the program, proceed in two steps:

1. Copy the tables manually or write a program to copy the table from a Paradox file to an InterBase database.

2. Update the program to have it use the new table.

Copying a Table

There are basically two ways to copy a Paradox table to a SQL server. One is to use one of the interactive tools, such as the Database Explorer. The other method is to write a program in Delphi, based on the BatchMove component. I've chosen the second approach, because this will let you follow the examples and run them without having to do other operations. You'll generally follow the same approach with your users. To build the MoveCoun example (the name is short for Move Country), place two Table components, a BatchMove component, and a Button control in a form.

The first table should be connected with the original Paradox table (COUNTRY.DB), and we can immediately open it (set its Active property to True). The second table should relate to the target database, indicating the name of the new table. I could not choose *Country* as the target name, because there is already a table with this name in the IBLOCAL database. I decided to use *Americas*, because there are only American countries in that table. Once each table is properly set up, use them for the Source and Destination properties of the BatchMove component.

The last step is to choose a proper value for the Move property of the BatchMove component. The default is batAppend, which appends records to an existing destination table. But you can set any of the following values:

- batUpdate, which updates only matching records.

- batAppendUpdate, which both appends and updates.

- batCopy, which creates the destination table, copying the source table "as is."

- batDelete, which deletes matching records.

The batCopy parameter is what we are looking for. Set it, select the BatchMove component, activate the form's SpeedMenu, and choose the Execute command. Delphi will create the new table (after asking for login information, since the destination table relates to an InterBase database). We have made the copy of the table without even compiling the program! As an alternative, we can write one line of code for the OnClick event of the button:

```
procedure TForm1.ButtonMoveClick(Sender: TObject);
begin
  BatchMove1.Execute;
end;
```

The real code, as I mentioned, is in the properties of the form, here listed as usual in textual format. Notice that we have two DataSet components and no DataSource component:

```
object Form1: TForm1
  Caption = 'Move Countries'
  object ButtonMove: TButton
    Caption = 'Move'
    OnClick = ButtonMoveClick
  end
  object BatchMove1: TBatchMove
    Destination = Table2
    Source = Table1
  end
  object Table1: TTable
    Active = True
    DatabaseName = 'DBDEMOS'
    TableName = 'COUNTRY.DB'
  end
  object Table2: TTable
    DatabaseName = 'IBLOCAL'
    TableName = 'AMERICAS'
  end
end
```

This is certainly nice, but I would like to show you some more details. For this reason, I used the default batAppend mode in the program and created the table in the code. This approach is only slightly more complex. Before you call the CreateTable method of the Table2 component, you need to copy the structure of the first table to Table2. Here is the complete code:

```
procedure TForm1.ButtonMoveClick(Sender: TObject);
begin
  // update the UI
  ButtonMove.Enabled := False;

  // copy the data
  Table2.FieldDefs := Table1.FieldDefs;
  Table2.IndexDefs.Assign (Table1.IndexDefs);
  Table2.CreateTable;
  Table2.Open;
  BatchMove1.Execute;
end;
```

At the beginning of this method, the button is disabled, so that the user can make only one copy each time the program is executed. Run the program, click on the button, and fill in the login dialog box. Now you are ready for the second step of the upsizing process.

Porting the Application

Now that the table has been moved to the InterBase local server, we can turn our attention to improving the Calc application. I've named the new version Calc2. Open the old application (or a copy), select the Table component, set its Active property to False, and then choose the IBLOCAL database and the Americas table (which should appear in the list of available tables in the Object Inspector). Activate the table again, and the live data is back, as you can see in Figure 17.5. But now we are accessing a SQL server. When you run the program, the new calculated field will appear, exactly as it did in the previous version. The example works, and it is so simple that performance is not a concern.

The next version of the example, Calc3, uses a Query instead of a Table component. Simply remove the table and add a query. Connect the data source with the query and write the proper SQL statement. Since we are exploring the development of client/server applications, we will try using another tool included in Delphi: the Visual Query Builder. (As an alternative to this tool, you can enter the resulting SQL statement in the corresponding property of the Query component.)

FIGURE 17.5

The form of the Calc2 example at design time. This program accesses an InterBase table.

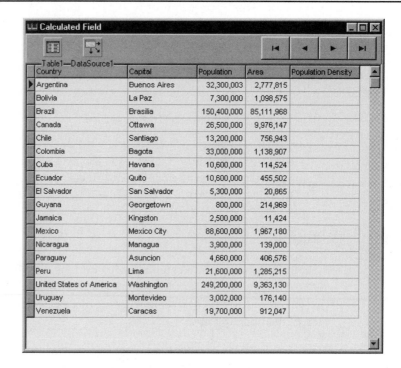

Using the Visual Query Builder

Running the Visual Query Builder is simple: just select the Query component and activate the local SpeedMenu of the Form Designer by pressing the right mouse button (on the form). Select the Query Builder menu item and fill in the login fields, choosing a database and entering a password. In the dialog box that follows, choose only the Americas table. Then close the dialog box. Now we are ready to work.

As you can see in Figure 17.6, the Visual Query Builder has a lower area where you build the query and an upper area for the tables you are using. The buttons on the toolbar of the Visual Query Builder are used to create a new query, open an existing one or save it, set some options, select more tables, add calculated columns, show the text or the result of the query, and accept or cancel it.

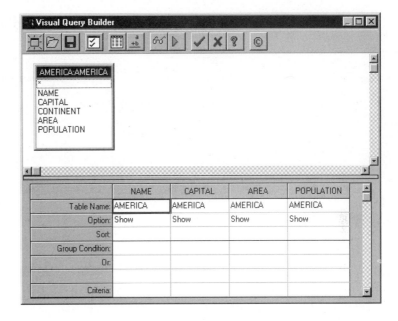

FIGURE 17.6

The main screen of the Visual Query Builder, with one table and some of its fields selected.

To define a query, for example, you can drag some fields from one of the tables in the upper portion to the bottom part, adding them to the result. In the lower part of the window you can set the sort order of the table resulting from the query, filter the records, and set a number of other advanced features. As we will see in an example later in this chapter, when you have more than one table loaded in the Visual Query Builder, you can also join them graphically.

Another thing you can do is define calculated fields directly in the query, and we'll use this feature in building our Calc3 example. Click on the Expression button in the toolbar. In the Expression dialog box, give the expression a name (I chose Density), double-click on the Population field, and then on the division sign (/), and finally on the Area field.

The expression appears in the Expression box at the bottom of the dialog box, as shown in Figure 17.7. If it's correct, you can eventually save the text of the query to a file, and then save the query itself into the SQL property of the table simply by clicking on the Close button. A new field will be added to the resulting table of the query. Now you can click on the Execute button to see the result, and the calculated field will be there as if it were an original field of the table.

FIGURE 17.7

The Expression dialog box of the Visual Query Builder can be used to define calculated fields.

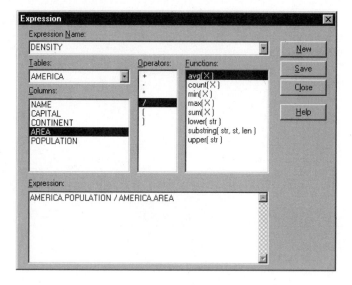

You can also look at the code of the SQL query, pressing the button with the glasses icon, which is now the following:

```
select
    Americas.Name,
    Americas.Capital,
    Americas.Area,
    Americas.Population ,
    ( Americas.Population / Americas.Area ) as Density
from
    Americas Americas
order by
    Americas.Name
```

Click on the SpeedButton with the check mark, and the text of the query will be copied back to the Query component in the form. Now activate it, and you'll see the fields of the form in the grid, including the calculated field, at design-time.

There is still a minor problem, however. The division calculation we have written in the SQL query expression results in a floating-point number with several decimal places. In the expression used to calculate the field in the earlier versions, we called the Round function, which is not available in SQL.

The problem is that the default grid is not wide enough to accommodate the most significant digits, and the values displayed on the screen seem to be wrong. To solve the problem, we simply need to define the fields for the query and set the proper format string for the `DisplayFormat` property. Indicate the thousands separators for the area and the population (with the value ###,###,###) and then set the number of decimal digits for the population density (with the value ###.# ##). Then you can size the grid columns properly, as you can see in Figure 17.8.

NAME	CAPITAL	AREA	POPULATION	DENSITY
Argentina	Buenos Aires	2,777,815	32,300,003	11.628
Bolivia	La Paz	1,098,575	7,300,000	6.645
Brazil	Brasilia	8,511,180	150,400,000	17.671
Canada	Ottawa	9,976,147	26,500,000	2.656
Chile	Santiago	756,943	13,200,000	17.439
Colombia	Bogota	1,138,907	33,000,000	28.975
Cuba	Havana	114,524	10,600,000	92.557
Ecuador	Quito	455,502	10,600,000	23.271
El Salvador	San Salvador	20,865	5,300,000	254.014
Guyana	Georgetown	214,969	800,000	3.721
Jamaica	Kingston	11,424	2,500,000	218.838
Mexico	Mexico City	1,967,180	88,600,000	45.039
Nicaragua	Managua	139,000	3,900,000	28.058
Paraguay	Asuncion	406,576	4,660,000	11.462

From Porting to Upsizing

In the Calc3 example, we have obtained two interesting advantages. The first and most evident advantage is that now we can display a calculated field at run-time. This is possible because we do not need compiled Pascal code to make this computation; the server does it, while processing a SQL statement.

This is a key point. We have actually moved some computation from the client application to the server. This means that you can move computations from the client computer to the server computer, which can usually handle the huge amount of data involved in big queries more quickly and efficiently. Although we are currently running both the client and the server code on the same computer, this doesn't modify the general perspective. This is what real client/server programming means: distributing the workload of an application between a client computer and a server computer. The client should be primarily involved in the user interface, and the server in data processing.

As a consequence of this approach, the Calc3 application should run slightly faster than the previous version, although in such a simple case, the difference isn't noticeable. This is one of the points that marks the difference between simply changing an application so that it can connect to a remote database, and upgrading an application to take advantage of a client/server platform. There are other elements in the picture as well. The SQL server can be used to improve robustness and data consistency and to speed up the access from multiple users at the same time, just to mention a few ideas. On the whole, moving your data and making the application work with the remote server is just the first step of the process, although a very important one.

Joining Tables with the Visual Query Builder

In the last section, we saw that owners of the Delphi Client/Server Suite can take advantage of a special tool, the Visual Query Builder. We used it to create a SQL query with a calculated field. Now we will explore another feature of this tool: its ability to define table joins graphically.

A Join with Three Tables

The form of the project, named SqlJoin, includes only three items: a Query component, a data source, and a grid aligned to the client area. Basically, we want to display some information about the employees involved in each project, using the data stored in the IBLOCAL database.

The database contains an Order table, which is related to several other tables, including the table of the employees (to indicate who took the order) and the table of the customers. (We used a similar table at the end of the last chapter, although we were working with local tables at that time.)

To have some readable information, we need to join this table with the Customer table, which contains the name and address of each customer, and the Employee table, which stores information about each employee. Using the Visual

Query Builder, we can express these two joins simply by selecting the three tables and dragging a field onto the corresponding field of the other table. Next, choose some fields for the output. You can see the query I've built with this tool in Figure 17.9.

FIGURE 17.9

The query of the SqlJoin example in the Visual Query Builder.

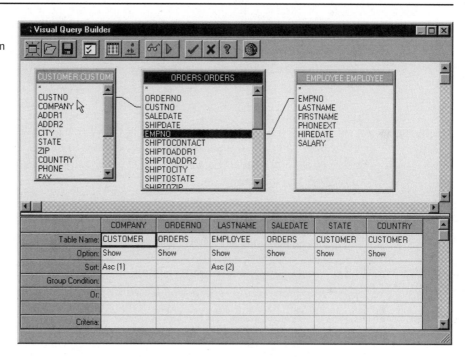

Here are the SQL statements corresponding to this graphical query:

```
select
    Customer.Company, Orders.Orderno, Employee.Lastname,
    Orders.Saledate, Customer.State, Customer.Country
from
    Employee Employee, Customer Customer, Orders Orders
where
    (Customer.Custno = Orders.Custno) and
    (Employee.Empno = Orders.Empno)
order by
    Customer.Company, Employee.Lastname
```

In the output, we use fields from only two tables. The third table is just used to perform two joins with corresponding codes in the other tables.

> **WARNING**
>
> When you have built a query with the Visual Query Builder, you can indeed see its text in the SQL property of the corresponding Query object. However, if you make any change there, you cannot access the query structure in the Query Builder any more. To avoid this risk, I suggest that you always save the query to a file before you exit from the Visual Query Builder, so that you can restore the structure later.

In the output of this program, but also in the table at design-time (see Figure 17.10), you can see why the database has been structured to divide the project information between several tables. You can see that there are employees working on several projects at the same time.

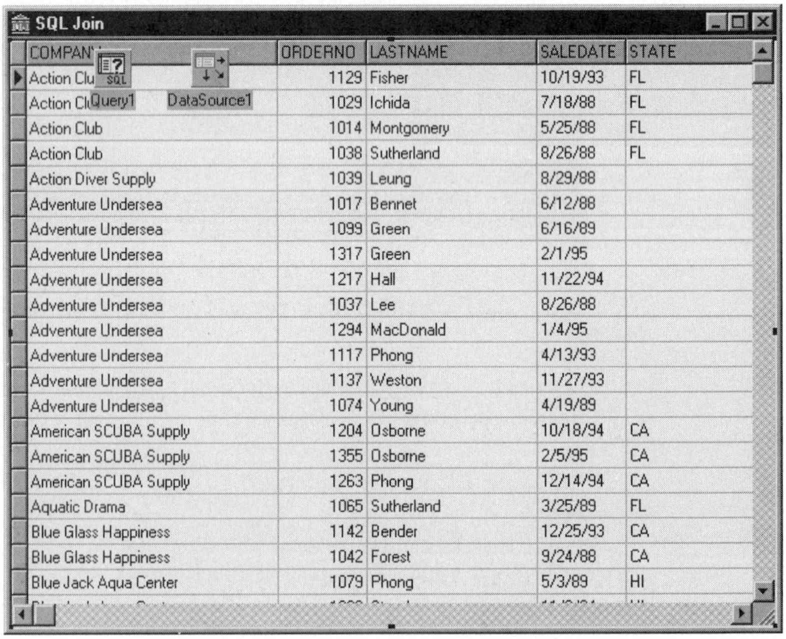

FIGURE 17.10

The form of the SqlJoin example at design time, with the data retrieved from three different tables.

COMPANY	ORDERNO	LASTNAME	SALEDATE	STATE
Action Clu	1129	Fisher	10/19/93	FL
Action Clu	1029	Ichida	7/18/88	FL
Action Club	1014	Montgomery	5/25/88	FL
Action Club	1038	Sutherland	8/26/88	FL
Action Diver Supply	1039	Leung	8/29/88	
Adventure Undersea	1017	Bennet	6/12/88	
Adventure Undersea	1099	Green	6/16/89	
Adventure Undersea	1317	Green	2/1/95	
Adventure Undersea	1217	Hall	11/22/94	
Adventure Undersea	1037	Lee	8/26/88	
Adventure Undersea	1294	MacDonald	1/4/95	
Adventure Undersea	1117	Phong	4/13/93	
Adventure Undersea	1137	Weston	11/27/93	
Adventure Undersea	1074	Young	4/19/89	
American SCUBA Supply	1204	Osborne	10/18/94	CA
American SCUBA Supply	1355	Osborne	2/5/95	CA
American SCUBA Supply	1263	Phong	12/14/94	CA
Aquatic Drama	1065	Sutherland	3/25/89	FL
Blue Glass Happiness	1142	Bender	12/25/93	CA
Blue Glass Happiness	1042	Forest	9/24/88	CA
Blue Jack Aqua Center	1079	Phong	5/3/89	HI

According to the standard database design rules (also called *normalization* rules), no information should be duplicated. For this reason, we cannot store employee data in the Orders tables. Nor can we store customer information in the Orders table, since the same customer does many orders. The only theoretically sound approach is to divide the data into three tables, as is done in this database.

> **NOTE** If you do not know what I mean by *database normalization rules*, you should study some database design before delving into the development of complex database applications—with Delphi or any other tool. There are many books devoted to this topic, including some on database theory for university courses.

A Join with More Tables

This program is already an interesting example of joining three tables, but there is still some information that is not set properly. For example, we might want to retrieve sales information about the products. Since each order may include more than one item, we can add the Items table to our join to see which products were ordered by which customer. The Items table, however, has only the code of the product associated with each order. We should refer to the Parts table for the product names. So we end up with five intertwined tables, as you can see in Figure 17.11. This is the corresponding SQL statement:

```
select
    Parts.Description, Items.Qty, Customer.Company,
    Orders.Saledate, Employee.Lastname
from
    Orders Orders, Customer Customer, Parts Parts,
    Items Items, Employee Employee
where
    (Customer.Custno = Orders.Custno) and
    (Employee.Empno = Orders.Empno) and
    (Items.Partno = Parts.Partno) and
    (Items.Orderno = Orders.Orderno)
order by
    Parts.Description, Customer.Company
```

FIGURE 17.11

The query of the SqlJoin2 example in the Visual Query Builder.

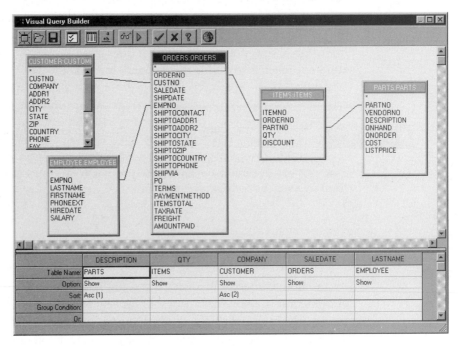

Data Modules

Client/server programming is a very interesting form of application partitioning, where you split the code and workload between two different logical levels, and generally, also, between two different computers. On one side, you have the database data, and on the other side you have the Delphi program accessing it. In the last few years, another approach has been developed to partition applications better, the *three-tier* approach. On one side you have the data, on another side you have the user interface, and on a third side you have some rules and criteria governing how data is accessed and modified by a program.

> **NOTE**
>
> The three-tier approach is a comprehensive technique for client/server development, and I won't discuss its details and advantages here; I'll merely outline its key points. Again, a full discussion of database development in general is beyond the scope of this book.

We can consider the data access components (Table, Query, Data Access, and so on) as part of this third, intermediate level. These nonvisual components do not pertain to the user interface, but can be used to set field properties, add calculated fields, check new data being posted to the tables, and so on. Using these components, we can implement some of the rules of our data access, although other rules are imposed by the database itself. In the Delphi programs we have built so far, these visual components were intertwined with the data-access components, following the typical two-tier approach. All the data-related components were on a single form, and all their code was in the methods of the corresponding form class. To implement the three-tier approach, we can place the data-access components on a separate form from the data controls, and then refer from one form to the other (using File ➤ Use Unit). This way we can connect the data-aware controls to the proper tables or queries at design-time.

The problem with this approach is that we need to create the forms containing the data-access components and never show them. The Delphi alternative to this hidden form is to use the data modules (which can be described as a sort of *hidden form*, containing nonvisual components). The data modules can hold both the data-access components and the methods related to their events, thus separating the database access from the user interface portion of the program.

In Delphi 3, data modules can constitute a building block for three-tier applications. In fact they can be executed locally (as we'll see in the following examples) but also encapsulated in objects to be executed on a server computer. In order to have the client run the user interface forms, a departmental server the data module, and a bigger server the database, you have to build a *physical three-tier* application, something that Delphi 3 allows you to do but is beyond the scope of this book.

Creating a Data Module

To create a new data module, simply create a new default application, and then add a data module to it by selecting File ➤ New Data Module (if you use the Database Form Expert, you can use the corresponding options of the last page to create both a form and a data module for its data access components). The data module will appear on the screen as an empty white window, where you can add components as usual. There are two key differences: First, you cannot add a control to a data module; second, the data module window is only a design-time representation of a container for the module's components, as you can see in Figure 17.12.

The TDataModule class derives directly from TComponent, so it is completely unrelated to the Windows concept of a window. The limited similarity between a form and a data module is obvious if you note that the last class has just a few properties and events. For this reason, it's useful to think of data modules as *components and method containers in memory*.

What do data modules and forms have in common? What makes them look so similar to a Delphi developer? Like forms, data modules relate to specific Object Pascal units for their definition and to form definition (DFM) files that list the components included in the module and their properties:

```
object DataModule2: TDataModule2
  Height = 159
  Width = 196
  object Table1: TTable...
  object DataSource1: TDataSource...
end
```

The structure of the Delphi unit for a data module is very similar to that of a form. The key difference is in the parent class:

```
type
  TDataModule2 = class(TDataModule)
```

Another thing forms and data modules have in common is that they can both be created either when the application starts or later. In fact, they are even listed in the Forms page of the Project Options.

> You might think that data modules relate only to the development of database applications. This is certainly the most common case, but you can take advantage of separate code modules for other purposes, too. An example is handling system components, such as DDE components. Each time you have some nonvisual components that do not strictly relate to a form or that can be used in multiple forms, you can use secondary data modules. At times this alternative is preferable to visual form inheritance, in particular when you want to mimic multiple inheritance (that is, to add different capabilities implemented in various modules to a form).

A Data Module for Multiple Views

A typical example of the use of a data module is to provide different views of the same data and to keep the views in sync. This is what I've done in the TwoViews example. Later on, I'll extend this example by adding data rules and filtering capabilities to the program. In the TwoViews example, I've created two forms and a data module. Then I placed a table related to the CUSTOMER.DB file of the DBDEMOS database and the data source. The data module of this application is very simple; here is its textual definition:

```
object DataModule2: TDataModule2
  object Table1: TTable
    Active = True
    DatabaseName = 'DBDEMOS'
    TableName = 'CUSTOMER.DB'
  end
  object DataSource1: TDataSource
    DataSet = Table1
  end
end
```

Then I built a toolbar for the main form of the program, using a panel aligned to the top, a speed button, and a DBNavigator. The speed button has a proper glyph and is used to show the secondary form. The rest of the form is filled with a DBGrid. After using the data module from the form, you can set the DataSource property of both the DBNavigator and the DBGrid to DataModule2.DataSource1.

> **TIP**
>
> Before you use another unit in a form, you should properly name the unit to which you want to refer. In fact, if you use a unit (for example, Unit2), and then rename it when you first save the file, the connection will be lost, and you'll need to manually replace all the references to the renamed unit, even if Delphi built those uses statements automatically or with the File ➤ Use Unit command.

The second view is based on a form with many DBEdit components, one for each field of the database table except the last. Instead of placing a number of DBEdit components and connecting each of them, you can select the table component in the data module, open the fields editor, add all the fields, select all of them except the last, and then drag the selected fields to the secondary form. With this simple operation, Delphi will arrange all the proper DBEdit and Label components on the form at once. I've actually set the Visible property of the secondary form to True, so that it becomes immediately visible when the program starts, as you can see in Figure 17.13.

FIGURE 17.13

The TwoViews program at run-time, with the two synchronized forms referring to the same record.

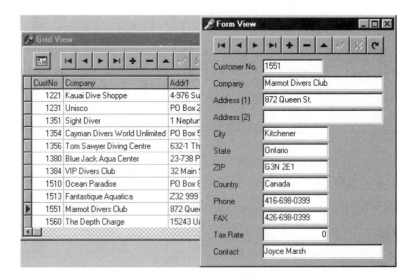

If you display both forms, they are kept in synch. Using one of the two navigators affects both forms. In fact the navigator is connected to neither of them: it relates to the data source in the data module, and the visual components of both forms are affected by any change in the common data access components. Edit one form, and the other will be updated as soon as you accept the changes. Add a new record, and the action will take place on both forms.

Notice that you can also navigate through the records at design-time. While you scroll the grid, the data in the secondary form will change, allowing you, for example, to size the DBEdit components if any field of the current record is too long to fit in the available space.

Setting Field Properties and Initial Values

Using a data module to keep two forms in synch can be handy and is quite simple. We want to add to the program some more capabilities related to the data itself, not the specific viewer. For example, in the data module we can edit the properties of the fields, using a special value for the EditMask properties of the Table1Phone and Table1FAX field components. This customization will affect the output and the editing of these fields in both forms at the same time.

To accomplish something a little more complex, we can introduce a rule in the table, or at least a suggestion to the users. We want to automatically provide a new unique value for the customer number and make it the current highest value plus one for this field. I've accomplished this by adding some code to the data module in a second version of the program, TwoView2.

Basically, I want to set the proper value of the Table1CustNo field each time the user inserts or appends a new record to the table. To accomplish this you can handle the OnNewRecord event of the table as follows:

```
procedure TDataModule2.Table1NewRecord(DataSet: TDataSet);
begin
  Table1CustNo.Value := Max + 1;
end;
```

The question is, how do I compute the Max value? I can simply browse the table, as we did in the last chapter, and check for the highest value of the CustNo field. However, I cannot do this in the event handler above, because this will put the table back in tsBrowse mode from the tsInsert mode. An alternative is to compute the highest value again each time the user inserts a new record, using the OnBeforeInsert event:

```
procedure TDataModule2.Table1BeforeInsert(DataSet: TDataSet);
begin
  ComputeMax;
end;
```

This ComputeMax procedure simply scans the table looking for the maximum value. Here is the code of this method, which also handles exceptions with a try-finally block, uses a bookmark, and disables/enables controls:

```
procedure TDataModule2.ComputeMax;
var
  Bookmark: TBookmark;
begin
  Bookmark := Table1.GetBookmark;
  try
    Table1.DisableControls;
    Max := 0;
    try
      Table1.First;
      while not Table1.EOF do
      begin
        if Table1CustNo.AsInteger > Max then
          Max := Table1CustNo.AsInteger;
        Table1.Next;
      end;
    finally
      Table1.EnableControls;
    end;
  finally
    Table1.GotoBookmark (Bookmark);
    Table1.FreeBookmark (Bookmark);
  end;
end;
```

By adding some methods to the data module, we move toward the structure of a three-tier application. This code, in fact, is completely independent from the user interface (the two views). The code of this example is very simple, but it is meant to highlight this important idea.

Standard Table Filtering

Now I want to add to the application the capability of filtering the records in both views (again using the data module). The simplest filtering capability in Delphi tables is to set a range of values for an indexed field. For example, I've ordered the table of the TwoView2 example using the *ByCompany* secondary index (just select this value for the IndexName property). Then I've chosen all records between two values supplied by the user, by writing the following:

```
Table1.SetRange (['Abacus'], ['Custom']);
```

As an alternative you can set key values as in the GotoKey method, calling the SetRangeStart, SetRangeEnd, and ApplyRange methods in sequence. Usually it is much simpler to call SetRange and pass it two arrays of values, with the same number of items (and the same order) as the fields in the current index. When you want to stop applying the range, simply call the CancelRange method.

Actually, in the TwoView2 program I haven't indicated a fixed range of values, as suggested above, but added a new dialog box to ask the user for the initial and final value of the range. I could have used the toolbar of the main form, instead of a dialog box, but I wanted again to relate the code used to set the range to the data module itself, not to a specific form used to view the data. To do that, I've prepared a form with a check box and two edit controls, and added a new custom method to the data modules, with the following code:

```
procedure TDataModule2.ChooseRange;
begin
  with FormRange do
    if ShowModal = mrOK then
      if CheckBoxRange.Checked then
        Table1.SetRange ([Edit1.Text], [Edit2.Text])
      else
        Table1.CancelRange;
end;
```

This means a data module has no visual components, but can rely on specific forms or dialog boxes to provide some direct input/output capabilities. Each form can now call this method as it happens with a click on the new Range button of the toolbar of the main form:

```
procedure TForm1.RangeSpeedButtonClick(Sender: TObject);
begin
  DataModule2.ChooseRange;
end;
```

You can see the effect of setting a custom filter, along with the new dialog box, in Figure 17.14. Adding this dialog box is another way to customize the interaction between data and forms, working on the data access layer in between. Although I've added some user interface capabilities to the data module, notice that this dialog box doesn't show any database data, but only some visualization options. For this reason we can reasonably say it belongs to the data module, the third tier.

FIGURE 17.14

The dialog box used to set a range on the table, and the result of this operation on the grid.

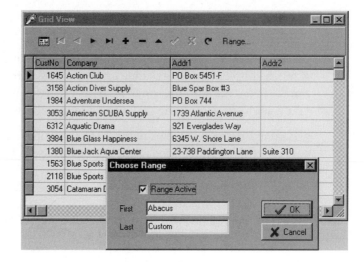

Custom Table Filtering

Besides giving the Table component a range of values to work on, you can set a custom filtering algorithm. Simply set the `Filtering` property of the Table component to `True`, and for each record the `OnFilterRecord` event will be called. In the method connected with this event, you can set a custom filter of your choice. Here is an example:

```
procedure TDataModule2.Table1FilterRecord(
  DataSet: TDataSet; var Accept: Boolean);
begin
  if (Table1Country.Value = 'US') or
      (Table1Country.Value = 'US Virgin Islands') or
      (Table1State.Value = 'Jamaica') then
    Accept := True
```

```
    else
        Accept := False;
end;
```

Again, we have connected this filtering rule to the data module, and it will affect each of the two views. Besides writing a fixed rule, as in the case above, we can allow the user to build his or her own rule, using the range dialog box for this further customization of the data module. This is what I've done in the TwoView3 example (which includes also the code above, commented out).

The new Choose Range dialog box has another check box and two list boxes (see Figure 17.15), filled with the names of the countries and the states when the form is created:

```
procedure TFormRange.FormCreate(Sender: TObject);
begin
  with DataModule2 do
  begin
    Table1.First;
    while not Table1.EOF do
    begin
      // add unique values
      if ListBoxCountries.Items.IndexOf (
          Table1Country.AsString) < 0 then
        ListBoxCountries.Items.Add (Table1Country.AsString);
      if ListBoxStates.Items.IndexOf (Table1State.AsString) < 0 then
        ListBoxStates.Items.Add (Table1State.AsString);
      Table1.Next;
    end;
    // reset the table
    Table1.First;
  end;
end;
```

This code checks to see whether the value of the current record is already present in the list box. If it is not, the value is added to the proper list box. These two lists should be updated each time a new record is added to the database table, or whenever an existing record changes. I've omitted this capability, but it should be quite simple for you to implement it by handling the AfterPost event of the table and writing two lines of code similar to the body of the while loop above.

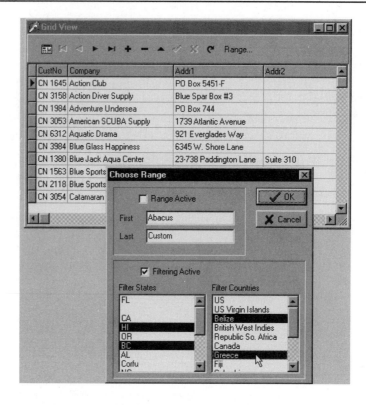

FIGURE 17.15

The new dialog box of
the TwoView3 example,
with advanced filtering
capabilities.

Once the program has filled the list boxes, they are displayed along with the
range options. The custom ChooseRange method of the data module should show
the dialog box again, check the range, set the filters, and refresh the table. This is
necessary because if table filtering was already active but the rules change,
Delphi will not automatically recompute the current active records. Here is the
new version of the code of this method:

```
procedure TDataModule2.ChooseRange;
begin
  with FormRange do
    if ShowModal = mrOK then
    begin
      if CheckBoxRange.Checked then
        Table1.SetRange ([Edit1.Text], [Edit2.Text])
      else
        Table1.CancelRange;
```

```
      Table1.Filtered := CheckBoxFiltering.Checked;
      Table1.Refresh;
    end;
  end;
```

The most important piece of code, however, is the handler of the OnFilterRecord events, which now checks to see if the country or state of the current record is one of the selected items of the two list boxes (which allow multiple selection, but not extended selection). Here is the code:

```
procedure TDataModule2.Table1FilterRecord(
  DataSet: TDataSet; var Accept: Boolean);
begin
  {if the item corresponding to the country in the
  listbox is active, then view the record}
  with FormRange.ListBoxCountries do
    if Selected [Items.IndexOf (Table1Country.AsString)] then
      Accept := True
    else
      Accept := False;
  with FormRange.ListBoxStates do
    if Selected [Items.IndexOf (Table1State.AsString)] then
      Accept := True;
end;
```

Notice that in the second if statement, the value of Accept should be added to the previous one with an or statement. Actually, I can simply set it to True regardless of the previous value (since an or with True always returns True), or let it maintain its current value (since an or with False keeps the existing value).

Custom Filtering and Client/Server Development

If you browse the code of the last example, you'll see that the program interacts with the database data a lot. There are methods scanning the values of a table, looking for the highest value or for the distinct strings. There is also some filtering code written in Object Pascal. As we have seen, most of this code is not directly connected with the user interface but logically belongs to a separate data module. This might look like a correct three-tier approach, but it can also be a bad client/server approach.

In fact, by basing this code heavily on data modules, we have loaded the client application with further computation, leaving the server with little to do (well, we used a Paradox table, so this made sense, but I'm trying to discuss a more general case here). If the table were a SQL Server table containing a large amount of data, our program wouldn't have been very efficient. In such a case we should still use the data module, but we would try to add several queries (executed by the server) replacing our data-related methods (computed by the client).

For example, we might add to the TwoView3 example queries computing the highest customer number, getting all the distinct State and Country names, and write a complex where statement to filter the records or choose a range. I'm not going to write this new version of the program, but you might consider it a more complete three-tier approach, placing the computational load of the intermediate tier on the server as much as possible. Writing a stored procedure on the server is the next step of this approach.

To summarize, Delphi 3 lets you identify the three tiers (the data view, the intermediate rules, and the actual data access) and also provides good help in partitioning such an application between the client (Object Pascal code), the middle layer (Object Pascal code in the form of a data module running on a server) and the database server (SQL code). How you implement this strategy is up to you and your experience, because it is not always easy to determine the best solution from an architectural point of view and still try to make it work as fast as possible.

The Data Dictionary

It is very common to use fields with a similar layout (for example, the same display mask) throughout a single application or in different applications. If you use integer numbers, decimal numbers, percent values, phone and fax numbers (possibly the same number with different extensions) and other standard fields, it is extremely tedious to set each one of them from scratch. For this reason, Delphi includes a Data Dictionary. This is a sort of database that stores the properties of fields. You can define the properties of these standard fields using the Dictionary, or you can simply copy them from existing fields (of course, you can also use the existing entries in the Data Dictionary without further work).

In a client/server environment (with several Delphi programmers), the Data Dictionary can reside on a remote server for additional sharing of information.

NOTE The default Data Dictionary is implemented using a Paradox table, but you can define a new one based on a SQL server table.

The Data Dictionary and the Fields Editor

Most of the operations involving the Data Dictionary take place in the fields editor of a table or query component. The local menu of the Fields Editor, in fact, has five commands related to the use of the Data Dictionary (see Figure 17.16).

FIGURE 17.16

The local menu of the Fields Editor, with the menu commands used to interact with the Data Dictionary.

Here is what they do (I've listed them in a more logical order):

Operation	Meaning
Associate Attributes	This command is used to associate an attribute set with a given field. In practice, you can select one of the attribute sets from the Dictionary to use with the current field. When you associate a field with an attribute set from the Data Dictionary, the attributes will actually be copied to the properties of the field.

Operation	Meaning
Unassociate Attributes	This command is the reverse of the Associate Attributes operation. It breaks the association between the field and the attribute set.
Retrieve Attributes	This command is used to get the current values from the related attribute set. It can be used only while the field is associated with an attribute set. You can think of this as a loading command.
Save Attributes	This command is the reverse of the Retrieve Attributes operation. It copies the values of the properties of the current field to the associated attribute set. If no attribute set is associated, it will prompt you for a new name, as does the Save Attributes As command below.
Save Attributes As	This command is used to associate the field with a new attribute set, for which you have to provide a name in the dialog box that appears.

These commands should be quite intuitive, and I suggest that you work with the Data Dictionary to learn how to use them. You'll get used to the Dictionary quickly. Defining an association between an attribute type and one or more fields of the tables of a database forces Delphi to use the proper attributes every time you use a table with one of those fields in an application. For example, all the "Phone" fields (such as phone number and fax number) of a table can be associated with a specific attribute set, so that every time you use that table in a program Delphi will automatically set the proper input mask of the field object, as well as other attributes. This also works if the field is retrieved as part of a query, but only if you create the field objects at design-time.

What's in an Attribute Set?

In the previous section, I used the term *attribute set* several times. An attribute set is an entry (a *record*) of the Data Dictionary. An attribute set refers to several properties of a TField object, but also includes other general properties. Many of the properties of the attribute set correspond to properties of the various TField subclasses; these should be quite simple to understand. Here is a list of these properties:

Alignment	DisplayWidth	ReadOnly
BlobType	EditFormat	Required
Currency	EditMask	Transliterate
DisplayFormat	MaxValue	Visible
DisplayLabel	MinValue	
DisplayValues	Precision	

Of course, if you set a property as Precision (a value used only for floating-point numbers), and then associate the attribute set with a TStringField, the value will be ignored.

A few other values of the attribute set define the general behavior of a field, and are used to determine how to create a new field object for a given field of a table or query:

Attribute	Usage
TField Class	Indicates the type of field (the TField subclass) to create when a field is added to a data set.
TControl Class	Determines the type of data-aware component Delphi will create when you drag a field from the Fields Editor to a form. If no value is provided, Delphi will use a standard approach, which depends on the type of the field object.
Based On	This is a value you are asked to provide when you save an attribute set with a new name. It indicates the attribute set upon which the current one is based. This means that if you make a change to an attribute of the original set and this attribute is not overridden by the current set, the change will affect the current set, too. The analogy that comes to mind to explain this is that of styles in word processing programs, which can be based on other similar styles. Of course, this resembles a sort of inheritance, too.

Exploring the Data Dictionary

You can easily define a new attribute set by saving the attributes of a current field from the Fields Editor, as I've mentioned before. However, you can also define new attribute sets, or simply view them using the Database Explorer. Just open this tool, select the Dictionary tab above the left pane, and you'll see the Default Data Dictionary (DefaultDD), based on the BDESDD Paradox table. If you've added new Data Dictionaries, you'll see them all. Under the Dictionary entry, you'll find two subtrees, Databases and Attribute Sets, as you can see in Figure 17.17.

FIGURE 17.17

The Data Dictionary, as you can see it in the Database Explorer.

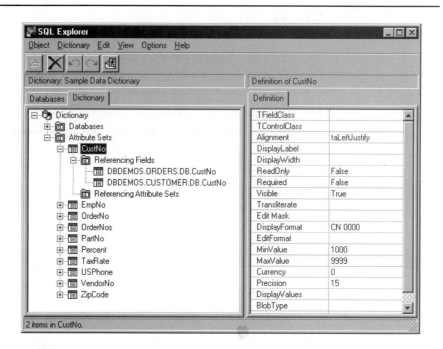

Under Attribute Sets, you'll find a list of these sets, each one with the values of its properties. There are also lists of database tables using each set and of the other attribute sets based on the sets. You can also use the Database Explorer to create new attribute sets or modify them.

The associations between fields of the database tables and the attribute sets can also be seen and modified by exploring the second subtree, Databases. Once you have selected a field of a table, a combo box will allow you to associate it with one of the available attribute sets in the Data Dictionary.

On the whole, when you are starting a new project and you have planned its database tables, I suggest that you start setting up some attribute sets and their associations before starting to work in Delphi. If your plan is not so well defined, though, you should simply use the Fields Editor to build up your Data Dictionary along with your tables, and then use the Explorer to revise the current situation and to document it.

Database Transactions

When you work with a SQL server (but also when working with local database files) you can use *transactions* to make your applications more robust. The idea of a transaction can be described as *a series of operations to be considered as a single, "atomic" whole.* By *atomic* I mean something that cannot be split. An example may help to clarify the concept. Suppose you have to raise the salary of each employee of a company by a fixed rate, as we did in the Total example of the last chapter. Now if during the operation an error occurs, you might want to undo the previous changes. If you consider the operation "raise the salary of each employee" as a single transaction, it should either be completely done, or totally ignored.

Working with database operations as transactions serves a useful purpose: you can start a transaction, do several operations to be considered as a single one, then at the end you can either commit the changes, or roll back the transaction, discarding all the operations done up to now. Typically you might want to roll back a transaction if an error occurred during its operations.

Transaction-handling in Delphi is quite simple. By default each edit/post operation is considered as a single transaction. To alter this behavior you can handle them explicitly. Simply add to a form or data module a Database component, connect each table or query to this form or data module to the database component (we'll see how in a while), and then use the following three methods of the TDatabase class:

StartTransaction	Starts a transaction.
Commit	Confirms the updates to the database done during the transaction.
Rollback	Returns the database to the state prior to starting the transaction.

A Simple Example of Transactions

To show you an example of transaction handling, instead of preparing a complex situation in which transactions would actually be required, I've simply made these three methods into user operations. This is not the standard use of transactions, but it should help you understand how they work.

The form of the Transact example has three buttons in a panel, and a grid covering the client area. This grid is connected with a simple query, which is connected to a database component. Simply place the database component in the form, give a value to its DatabaseName property (which is different from the Name property, which is the name of the component), and then choose this database name as the value of the DatabaseName property of the Query component. Summing things up, these are the properties of the key components of this form, taken from its textual description:

```
object Form1: TForm1
  Caption = 'Transact'
  object DBGrid1: TDBGrid
    Align = alClient
    DataSource = DataSource1
  end
  object Panel1: TPanel
    Align = alTop
    object BtnStart: TButton...
    object BtnCommit: TButton...
    object BtnRollback: TButton...
  end
  object Database1: TDatabase
    AliasName = 'IBLOCAL'
    Connected = True
    DatabaseName = 'MyData'
    Params.Strings = (
      'USER NAME=SYSDBA')
    SessionName = 'Default'
    OnLogin = Database1Login
  end
  object DataSource1: TDataSource
    DataSet = Query1
  end
  object Query1: TQuery
    Active = True
    BeforeEdit = Query1BeforeEdit
```

```
      DatabaseName = 'MyData'
      RequestLive = True
      SQL.Strings = (
         'select * from Employee')
   end
end
```

Now we can look at the code of the example, which is very simple. When the first button is pressed, the program starts a transaction, and enables the other two buttons:

```
procedure TForm1.BtnStartClick(Sender: TObject);
begin
   Database1.StartTransaction;
   BtnStart.Enabled := False;
   BtnCommit.Enabled := True;
   BtnRollback.Enabled := True;
end;
```

The Commit button simply calls the corresponding method of the database object, Database1.Commit, then enables and disables the buttons properly. The last button, Rollback, should also update the contents of the DBGrid. To do this we can re-execute the query, by closing and opening it:

```
procedure TForm1. BtnRollbackClick(Sender: TObject);
begin
    Database1.Rollback;
    Query1.Close;
    Query1.Open;
   BtnStart.Enabled := True;
   BtnCommit.Enabled := False;
   BtnRollback.Enabled := False;
end;
```

If you try running this program, you'll see that you can post some changes to the database, editing several records, and then simply undo the changes by pressing the Rollback button. You should not even press the Start button, because its code is automatically executed each time you start an edit operation:

```
procedure TForm1.Query1BeforeEdit(DataSet: TDataSet);
begin
   // start a transaction, if not already started
   if not Database1.InTransaction then
      BtnStartClick (self);
end;
```

Notice that this code is executed *before* the DataSet is put in edit mode. You can see the effect of a rollback action in Figure 17.18.

FIGURE 17.18

The output of the Transact example before (on the left) and after (on the right) a rollback operation.

Custom Database Login

The Transact example demonstrated another (unrelated) feature, custom database connections. When you start this example, Delphi doesn't prompt you with the usual login dialog box. That's because I decided to handle the OnLogin event of the Database component.

In this event handler you can pass to the database the login parameters, generally customizing the login prompt. In my example I've simply bypassed the login prompt by entering fixed values for the login database parameters.

> **WARNING** Providing hard-coded values for the user name and password bypassed the database security completely. Any user of a computer with this program installed will log in with the same name, and there is no password protection. Working on the local InterBase, this might makes sense. On a real SQL Server platform, of course, this approach is certainly dangerous.

As you can see in the textual description of the form above, a database component has some parameters, with the form:

```
Params.Strings = (
  'USER NAME=SYSDBA')
```

This string is already part of the login parameters you can supply to the database in the OnLogin event handler, by adding new strings to the LoginParams parameter of the corresponding method:

```
procedure TForm1.Database1Login(Database: TDatabase;
  LoginParams: TStrings);
begin
  LoginParams.Clear;
  LoginParams.Add ('USER NAME=SYSDBA');
  LoginParams.Add ('PASSWORD=masterkey');
end;
```

These strings have a special syntax, with two parts separated by an equal sign. There is a little-known feature of the TStrings class, the Value property, which allows you to assign a value to these strings using an array notation. In this case, this notation comes in very handy. We can rewrite the above code as follows:

```
procedure TForm1.Database1Login(Database: TDatabase;
  LoginParams: TStrings);
begin
  LoginParams.Values ['USER NAME'] := 'SYSDBA';
  LoginParams.Values ['PASSWORD'] := 'masterkey';
end;
```

Nice, isn't it? Although this Value property of TStrings is mainly used in conjunction with database parameters and similar values, this is a general technique available to implement some sort of associative string list very easily.

Handling Database Errors

The last feature of database programming we'll explore in this chapter is handling database errors in custom ways. Of course, you can let Delphi show an exception message each time a database error occurs, but you might want to try to correct them, or simply get more details.

While most of the exception classes in Delphi simply deliver an error message, with database exceptions you see a list of errors, showing local BDE error codes, and also the native error codes of the SQL server you are connected with. Besides the Message property, the EDBEngineError class has two more properties, ErrorCount and Errors. This last property is a list of errors:

```
property Errors[Index: Integer]: TDBError;
```

Each item of this list is an object of the class TDBError, which has the following properties:

```
type
  TDBError = class
    ...
  public
    property Category: Byte read GetCategory;
    property ErrorCode: DBIResult read FErrorCode;
    property SubCode: Byte read GetSubCode;
    property Message: string read FMessage;
    property NativeError: Longint read FNativeError;
  end;
```

I've used this information to build a simple database program showing the details of the errors in a memo component. To handle all of the errors, the DBError example installs a handler for the OnException event of the global Application object. This operation takes place in the OnCreate event handler of the form:

```
procedure TForm1.FormCreate(Sender: TObject);
begin
  Application.OnException := MyError;
end;
```

The MyError method simply calls a specific method used to show the details of the database error, in case it is a EDBEngineError:

```
procedure TForm1.MyError (Sender: TObject; E: Exception);
begin
  Beep;
  if E is EDBEngineError then
    ShowError (EDBEngineError (E))
  else
    ShowMessage (E.Message);
end;
```

I've decided to separate the code used to show the error to make it easier for you to copy its code and use it in a different context. Here is the code of the ShowError method, which outputs all of the available information to the Memo1 component I've added to the form:

```
procedure TForm1.ShowError(E: EDBEngineError);
var
  I: Integer;
begin
  Memo1.Lines.Clear;
  Memo1.Lines.Add('Error: ' + (E.Message));
  Memo1.Lines.Add('');
  Memo1.Lines.Add('Number of errors: ' +
    IntToStr(E.ErrorCount));
  Memo1.Lines.Add('');
  // iterate through the Errors records
  for I := 0 to E.ErrorCount - 1 do
  begin
    Memo1.Lines.Add('Message: ' +
      E.Errors[I].Message);
    Memo1.Lines.Add('   Category: ' +
      IntToStr(E.Errors[I].Category));
    Memo1.Lines.Add('   Error Code: ' +
      IntToStr(E.Errors[I].ErrorCode));
    Memo1.Lines.Add('   SubCode: ' +
      IntToStr(E.Errors[I].SubCode));
    Memo1.Lines.Add('   Native Error: ' +
      IntToStr(E.Errors[I].NativeError));
    Memo1.Lines.Add('');
  end;
end;
```

Besides this error-handling code, the example has a table and a query, plus a DBGrid connected with the table. You can use the DBGrid to perform some illegal operations, such as adding a new record with the same key as an existing one. This and other errors can be generated by pressing the four buttons on the left of the memo, as you can see in Figure 17.19.

FIGURE 17.19

The third button of the DBError form generates an exception with 17 database errors!

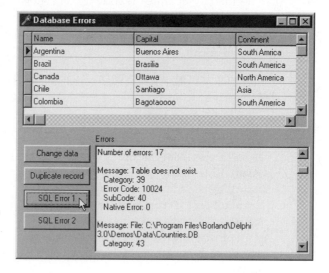

The first button generates an exception which is not generated by the database engine, so it is not displayed in the memo but in the usual message box:

```
procedure TForm1.Button1Click(Sender: TObject);
begin
  Table1.FieldByName ('Name').Value := 'something';
end;
```

This code is not allowed unless the table is already in edit mode. The second button invariably generates a *key violation* error, as you can see in Figure 17.20:

```
procedure TForm1.Button2Click(Sender: TObject);
var
  S: String;
begin
  s := Table1.FieldByName ('Name').Value;
  Table1.Insert;
  Table1.FieldByName ('Name').Value := s;
  Table1.Post;
end;
```

FIGURE 17.20

The second button of the DBError example generates a simple database error, *key violation*.

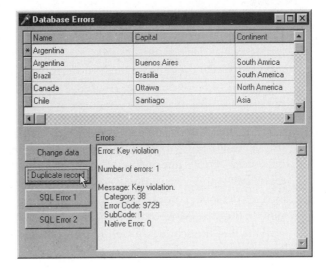

The last two buttons refer to the Query component, and execute illegal SQL queries. In the first case the program tries to work on a nonexistent table (see Figure 17.19 again for the output of the error), in the second case to use a nonexistent record. Here is the code of the two methods:

```
procedure TForm1.Button3Click(Sender: TObject);
begin
  Query1.SQL.Clear;
  Query1.SQL.Add (
    'select * from Countries where Population > 100000');
  Query1.Open;
end;

procedure TForm1.Button4Click(Sender: TObject);
begin
  Query1.SQL.Clear;
  Query1.SQL.Add (
    'select * from Country where Populations > 100000');
  Query1.Open;
end;
```

What's Next?

Client/server programming has been a very hot topic for some time now, and terms such as *downsizing*, *upsizing*, and *rightsizing* are becoming increasingly common (whatever they mean; these terms mean different things to different people). If these were yesterday's buzzwords, today's is *three-tier partitioning*. Again, people use this term to indicate whatever their own system does, as usual.

In this chapter, we have just seen a few things, scratching the surface of the problems and showing some simple practical examples. My goal was simply to make you curious about client/server application development. There is really a lot of work (and a lot of money) involved in this area of programming, which bridges personal computers and bigger machines in a way that has not been possible in the past. Most of the topics I've mentioned require more in-depth study, well beyond the scope of a Delphi programming book.

With this chapter, the database-specific portion of the book ends, although we will examine another database-related tool, report builders, in Chapter 28. In that chapter, we will add report-printing capability to some of the examples developed in this and the previous chapter.

In the next chapter, we will move on to component development and related topics. The focus will move to increasingly complex topics, and the chapter is on the verge of the third and more advanced part of the book. In the first two parts we've discussed the fundamentals, and covered the use of components. Now we start delving into *building* components and working with the OLE and COM technologies. Then, looking further ahead, we'll spend some more time in Part IV on advanced Delphi programming topics.

If you've skipped (partially or completely) Chapters 6 or 7, as I suggested to beginners, now is the time to go back and read them, before you go on with more advanced material.

PART III

Components
and Libraries

Creating Components

- Extending the VCL library

- Writing packages

- Customizing existing components

- Building graphical components

- Defining custom events

- Using array properties

- Placing a dialog box in a component

While most Delphi programmers are probably component users, at times it can be useful to write our own components or to customize existing ones. One of the most interesting aspects of Delphi is that creating components is simple. For this reason, even though this book is intended for Delphi application programmers and not Delphi tool writers, this chapter will cover the topic of creating components, and the next one will introduce Delphi add-ins, such as component and property editors.

In this chapter, I'll give you an overview of writing Delphi components and a number of simple examples. There is not enough space to present very complex components, but the ideas in this chapter will cover all the basics to get you started.

> **NOTE**　　You'll find a lot of more information about writing components in the *Delphi Developer's Handbook*, including data-aware components and many other advanced techniques.

Extending the VCL

When you write a new component, you always extend one of the classes of the VCL. To do this, you use many features of the Object Pascal language that component users seldom need. If you still have doubts about advanced Object Pascal features, you may want to review the overall description of the language presented in Part I of the book. Chapter 7 presented an overview of the VCL, together with some hierarchy graphs and a discussion of the role of properties, methods, and events. If you skipped that chapter or do not feel confident with the basic ideas about the VCL, read it before continuing with this chapter.

Delphi components are classes, and the VCL library is the collection of all the classes defining Delphi components. Each time you add a new package with some components to Delphi, you actually extend the VCL with a new class. This new class will be derived from one of the existing component-related classes, adding new capabilities to those it inherits.

You can derive a new component from an existing component or from an *abstract component class*—one that does not correspond to a usable component.

The VCL hierarchy includes many of these intermediate classes to let you choose a default behavior for your new component and to change its properties. In fact, when you *subclass* a component that has a specific property, you cannot remove that inherited property from the derived component; you can only add new properties. If a component class contains a property you do not want, you should choose a higher-level class in the VCL hierarchy.

From Components to Packages

In Delphi 1 and Delphi 2 the process of adding new classes consisted of adding new units, describing the new classes, and adding the components to the component library file (COMPLIB.DCL in Delphi 1 and CMPLIB32.DCL in Delphi2). These files stored all of the components used at design-time by the Delphi environment. The component's compiled file (the DCU file) was then used at compile time to link the code of the component to that of the application using it.

Delphi 3 uses a completely new approach. Components are added to component packages. Each component package is basically a DLL (a dynamic link library) with a DPL extension (which stands for Delphi Component Library).

Packages have specific compiler options. Two key options, for example, are $DESIGNONLY and $RUNONLY, which determine the role and behavior of a package. The design-only and run-only flags are used only by the Delphi IDE and not enforced in any way by the compiler. When you attempt to install a package, the IDE checks whether it has the design-only or run-only flags, and decides whether to let the user install the package and if it should be added to the list of run-time packages. Since there are two options, each with two possible states, there are four different kinds of component packages—two main variations and two special cases:

- Design-only component packages can be installed in the Delphi environment, and have the role of the component library in past versions of Delphi. The difference is that now you can install several component libraries—or packages—at the same time. Design-only packages contain the design-time parts of a component, such as its property editors and the registration code. They can also contain the components themselves, although this is not the suggested approach. Keep in mind, anyway, that the components of a design-only package can still be statically linked into the executable file, as in the past.

- Run-only component packages are used by Delphi applications at run-time. They cannot be installed in the Delphi environment, but are automatically added to the list of runtime packages when they are required by a package you install. Run-only packages usually contain the code of the component classes, but no design-time support. Run-only packages are important because they can be freely distributed along with applications, but Delphi programmers won't be able to install them in the environment to build new programs.

- Plain component packages (having neither the design-time only nor the run-time only options set) cannot be installed and will not be added to the list of run-time packages automatically. This might make sense only for utility packages used by other packages.

- Packages with both flags set can be installed and are automatically added to the list of run-time packages. Usually these packages contain components requiring little or no design-time support. Keep in mind, however, that users of applications built with these packages can use them for their own development.

TIP
The file names of Delphi's own design-only packages start with the letters DCL (for example DCLSTD30.DPL); file names of run-only packages start with the letters VCL (for example, VCL30.DPL).

In Chapter 2 we discussed the effect of packages on the size of a program's executable file. Now we'll focus on building packages, since this is a required step in creating or installing components in Delphi 3.

When you compile a run-time package, you produce both a dynamic link library (the .DPL file) and a file with symbol information (a .DCP file). The latter file is used by the Delphi compiler to gather symbol information about the units that are part of the package without having access to the unit (.DCU) files. This reduces compilation time and allows you to distribute just the packages without the precompiled unit files. The precompiled units are still required to statically link the components into an application. Distribution of precompiled .DCU files (or source code) may make sense depending on the kind of components you develop. We'll see how to create a package after we've discussed some general guidelines and built our very first component.

NOTE   DLLs are executable files containing collections of functions and classes, which can be used by a main file or other DLLs at run-time. The typical advantage is that if many applications use the same DLL, only one copy needs to be on the disk or loaded in memory, and the size of each executable file will be much smaller. This is what happens with the new Delphi packages, as well. Chapter 20 looks at DLLs in more detail.

Rules for Writing Components

Some general rules govern the writing of components. You can find a detailed description of most of them in the *Delphi Component Writer's Guide*. This manual is certainly required reading for Delphi component writers, but the information in it is somewhat limited. For this reason, it is important to delve into the details of component creation using *Delphi's Component Writer's Help*, a separate help file indexed together with the main Delphi help file. The VCL source code and the VCL reference manual (which are part of the Delphi Developer and Delphi Client/ Server Suite packages) are also important references for component writers.

Here is my own summary of the rules for component writers:

- Study the Object Pascal language with care. Particularly important concepts are inheritance, method overriding, the difference between public and published sections of a class, and the definition of properties and events.

- Study the structure of the VCL class hierarchy and keep a graph of the classes at hand (such as the one included with Delphi).

- Follow the Borland naming conventions. There are several of them for components, as we will see, and following these rules makes it easier for other programmers to interact with your components and further extend them.

- Keep components simple, mimic other components, and avoid dependencies. These three rules basically mean that a user of the components you write should be able to use them as easily as Delphi preinstalled components. Use similar property, method, and event names whenever possible. If users don't need to learn complex rules about the use of your component (that is, if the dependencies between methods or properties are limited), and can simply access properties with meaningful names, they'll be happy.

- Use exceptions. When something goes wrong, the component should raise an exception. When you are allocating resources of any kind, you must protect them with `try-finally` blocks and destructor calls.

- Test each component in a sample form before installing it in the system. Installing a component with serious errors can blow up a package, and even crash Delphi.

- To complete a component, add a bitmap to it, to be used by the Delphi's Components palette. If you intend your component to be used by more than a few people, consider adding a Help file as well.

- Be ready to write *real* code and forget about the visual aspects of Delphi. Writing components generally means writing code without visual support (unless you follow the next suggestion).

- Use a third-party component writing tool to build your components, or to speed up their development. You'll find a very bare tool for writing components in the TOOLS directory of the companion CD. It is much simpler than the professional tools you can buy, but it can still save you a lot of time. Using it will at least give you an idea of what it's like to use a visual tool for component development.

NOTE   Currently, the two main third-party tools available for creating Delphi components are Component Create from Potomac Document Software, and the Component Development Kit (CDK) from Eagle Software. You can find demo versions of both on the companion CD.

Building Your First Components

Before going on with the theory and looking at complete examples of components, I would like to show you a couple of simple, almost trivial, components. The aim of this section, which skips most of the details, is to give you an idea of how easy it is to write new components, and of how to install them in Delphi by creating your first package.

The Fonts Combo Box

Many applications have a toolbar with a combo box you can use to select a font. There was a similar example, ComboBar, in Chapter 12. If you often use a customized combo box like this, why not turn it into a component? It would probably take less than a minute. To begin, close any active projects in the Delphi environment and start the Component Wizard by choosing Component ➤ New Component, or by selecting File ➤ New to open the Object Repository, and then choose Component in the New page. Using either approach, you start the Component Wizard. The new Component Wizard is slightly different from the Component Expert in previous versions of Delphi. As you can see in Figure 18.1, this wizard requires the following information:

- The name of the ancestor type, the component class you want to inherit from. In this case we can use TMd3ComboBox.

- The name of the class of the new component you are building; we can use TFontCombo.

- The page of the Components palette where you want to display the new component, which can be a new or an existing page. We can create a new page, called *Md3*.

- The filename of the Pascal unit where Delphi will place the source code of the new component; we can type FontBox.

- The current search path.

FIGURE 18.1

The definition of the new TMd3FontCombo component with the Component Wizard.

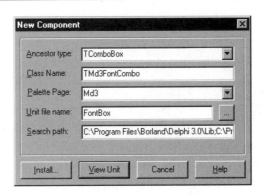

Click on View Unit, and the Component Wizard will generate the following simple Pascal source file with the structure of your component. The other button, Install, can be used to install the component in a package immediately. I prefer looking at the code first, then discuss the installation:

```pascal
unit FontBox;

interface

uses
  Windows, Messages, SysUtils, Classes, Graphics,
  Controls, Forms, Dialogs, StdCtrls;

type
  TMd3FontCombo = class(TComboBox)
  private
    { Private declarations }
  protected
    { Protected declarations }
  public
    { Public declarations }
  published
    { Published declarations }
  end;

procedure Register;

implementation

procedure Register;
begin
  RegisterComponents('Md3', [TMd3FontCombo]);
end;

end.
```

One of the key elements of this listing is the class definition, which begins by indicating the parent class. The only other relevant portion is the Register procedure. In fact, you can see that the Component Wizard does very little work.

Use a naming convention when building components. All the components installed in Delphi should have different class names. For this reason most Delphi component developers have chosen to add a two- or three-letter signature prefix to the names of their components. I've done the same, using *Md3* to identify components built in this book. The advantage of this approach is that you can install my TMd3FontCombo component even if you've already installed a component named TFontCombo.

Now we can start writing code. That's all it takes to build a component without an external tool. Of course, in this example the code is very simple. We need only copy all the system fonts to the Items property of the combo box at startup. To accomplish this, we might try to override the Create method in the class declaration, adding the statement Items := Screen.Fonts. However, if we tried to add this component to the component library, the component would not be usable. The problem is that we cannot access the combo box's Items property, which refers to the strings that will appear in the combo box, before the component is completely constructed. This is because some key properties (such as the Parent property, which refers to the form containing the component) won't be set up correctly until the component construction is finished.

Instead of assigning the new strings in the Create constructor, we must perform this operation in the CreateWnd procedure, which is called to create the window control after the component is constructed. Again, we execute the default behavior, and then we can write our custom code. I could have skipped the Create constructor and written all the code in CreateWnd, but I decided to use both startup methods to demonstrate the difference between them. Here is the declaration of the component class:

```
type
  TMd3FontCombo = class(TComboBox)
  public
    constructor Create (AOwner: TComponent); override;
    procedure CreateWnd; override;
  published
    property Style default csDropDownList;
  end;
```

And here is the source code of its two new methods (the complete source code is available in the FontBox directory on the companion CD):

```
constructor TMd3FontCombo.Create (AOwner: TComponent);
begin
```

```
  inherited Create (AOwner);
  Style := csDropDownList;
end;

procedure TMd3FontCombo.CreateWnd;
begin
  inherited CreateWnd;
  Items := Screen.Fonts;
end;
```

Notice that besides giving a new value to the component's Style property, in the Create method, I've redefined this property by setting a value with the default keyword. We have to do both operations because adding the default keyword to a property declaration has no direct effect on the property's initial value. Why specify a property's default value then? Because properties that have a value equal to the default are not streamed with the form definition (and they don't appear in the textual description of the form). The default keyword tells the streaming code that the component initialization code will set the value of that property.

Creating a Package

 Now we have to install the component in the environment. In Delphi 3, components are always installed in packages. For this example, we can create a new package, or use an existing one, like the default "users package," as we did in Chapter 6. Creating a new package is quite simple, anyway.

In each case choose the Component ➤ Install Component menu command. The resulting dialog box has a page to install the component into an existing package, and a page to create a new package. In this last case, simply type in a filename and a description for the package. Clicking OK opens the Package Editor (see Figure 18.2), which has two pages:

- The Contains page lists the components included in the package (or, to be more precise, the units defining the components to be included in the package);

- The Requires page lists the packages required by this package. You'll generally require the vcl30 package (the main run-time package that contains the fundamental parts of the Delphi VCL), but might also need the vcldb30 package (which includes most of the database-related classes).

FIGURE 18.2

The Delphi 3 Package
Editor.

If you add the component to the new package we've just defined, then simply compile the package and install it (using the two corresponding toolbar buttons of the package editor), you'll immediately see the new component show up in the 'Md3' page of the Components palette. The `Register` procedure of the component unit file told Delphi where to install the new component. By default, the bitmap used will be the same as the parent class, because we haven't provided a custom bitmap (we will do this in future examples). Notice also that if you move the mouse over the new component, Delphi will display as a hint the name of the class without the initial letter *T*.

What's Behind a Package?

What is behind the package we've just built? The package editor basically generates the source code for the package project: a special kind of DLL built in Delphi. The packages project is saved in a file with the DPK (Delphi PacKage) extension. A typical package project looks like this and the following source code:

```
package Md3Pack;

{$R *.RES}
{$ALIGN ON}
{$BOOLEVAL OFF}
{$DEBUGINFO ON}
...
{$DESCRIPTION 'Mastering Delphi 3 Package'}
{$DESIGNONLY}
{$IMPLICITBUILD ON}
```

```
requires
  vcl30;
contains
  FontBox;
end.
```

As you can see, Delphi uses specific new language keywords for packages: the first is the `package` keyword (which is similar to the `library` keyword I'll discuss in Chapter 20). This keyword introduces a new package project. Then comes a list with all the compiler options I've partially omitted from the listing: packages don't use the external option file, but include everything in their source code. Among the compiler options there is a `DESCRIPTION` compiler directive, used to make the package description available to the Delphi environment. In fact, after you've installed a new package, its description will be shown in the Packages page of the Project Options dialog box, a page you can also activate by selecting the Component ➤ Install Packages menu item. This dialog box is shown in Figure 18.3.

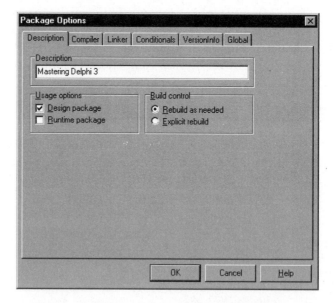

Besides common directives like the "description" one, there are other compiler directives specific to packages. The most common of these options are easily accessible though the Options button of the Package Editor. After this list of options come the requires and contains keywords, which list the items displayed visually in the two pages of the package editor. Again, the first is the list of packages required by the current one and the second is a list of the units installed by this package.

What is the technical effect of building a package? Besides the DPK file with the source code, Delphi generates a DPL file with the dynamic link version of the package, and a DCP file with the symbol information. In practice, this DCP file is the sum of the symbol information of the DCU files of the units contained in the package.

The DPL file and the DCP file are the only two files you need to distribute to make your package available (although you may also distribute the corresponding DCU files of the units contained in the package). These DCU files are still required when you want to statically link the code of the components of the package to an application.

Installing All of the Components of This Chapter

Having built our first package, we can now start using the component we've added to it. Before we do so, however, I should mention that I've extended the Md3Pack package to include all of the components we are going to build in this chapter, including different versions of the same component. I suggest you install this package: The best approach is to copy it into a directory of your path, so that it will be available both to the Delphi environment and to the programs you build with it. The default approach seems to install all the packages into the windows/system directory, which will thus become an even bigger "black hole" taking up a huge part of your hard disk. I suggest you use a different directory whenever possible.

Remember, anyway, that if you compile an application using the packages as run-time DLLs, you'll need to install these new libraries on your clients' computers. If you instead compile the programs statically linking the package, the DLL will be required only by the development environment, and not by the users of your applications.

> **NOTE**　　Besides creating and installing single packages, Delphi can handle collections of packages. The Package Collection Editor (PCE.EXE, in the Delphi BIN directory) allows you to place multiple packages in a single DPC (Delphi Package Collection) file. This file can then be installed in Delphi in the same way you install a stand-alone package.

Using the Fonts Combo Box

Now you can create a new Delphi program to test the fonts combo box. Move to the Components palette, select the new component, and add it to a new form. A traditional-looking combo box will appear. However, if you open the Items Property Editor, you'll see a list of the fonts installed on your computer. To build a simple example, I've added a Memo component to the form with some text inside it (actually, it is the text of the Pascal file defining the new component). The program has little code. When a user selects a new font in the combo box, the new value is used as the Memo component's font:

```
procedure TForm1.Md3FontCombo1Change(Sender: TObject);
begin
  Memo1.Font.Name :=
    Md3FontCombo1.Items [Md3FontCombo1.ItemIndex];
end;
```

At the beginning, the reverse action is performed; the name of the Memo component's font is displayed in the combo box:

```
procedure TForm1.FormCreate(Sender: TObject);
begin
  Md3FontCombo1.ItemIndex :=
    Md3FontCombo1.Items.IndexOf (Memo1.Font.Name);
end;
```

The aim of this simple program (see Figure 18.4 for its output) is only to test the behavior of the new component we have built. The component is still not very useful—we could have added a couple of lines of code to a form to obtain the same effect—but looking at a couple of simple components should help you get an idea of what is involved in component building.

FIGURE 18.4

The output of the DemoFb example.

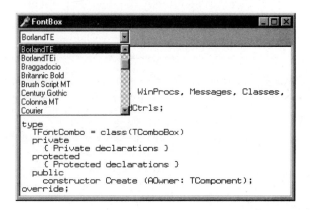

Creating a Tabbed List Box

The Delphi TListBox component lacks a feature that is generally useful in Windows list boxes: the use of Tab characters to display list data in columns. We can build a new, simple component that adds this capability. Since tabbed columns are difficult to maintain, as we will see later in this chapter, Borland's choice is not coincidental. Instead of extending the behavior of list boxes, Borland programmers have chosen a radical solution: the Grid and ListView families of components. Again, our purpose here is simply to demonstrate the process of creating a new component.

A list box can accept Tab characters only if it was created using the lbs_UseTab-Stops window style. So we need some way to change how this control is created. We saw in the earlier example that the window connected to a windowed component is created in a second step, via the CreateWnd method. When this method is executed, we can examine the parameters of the CreateWindow API function and change the values before the actual window creation takes place. We do that by overriding the CreateParams method, whose parameter is a reference of type TCreateParams.

> **NOTE**
>
> Experienced Windows programmers may already know that the TCreate-Params type is a record with fields corresponding to each parameter of the CreateWindow API function. One of the parameters of the wm_Create message is a pointer to this record type.

The CreateParams method is used in Delphi components to change some of the standard values used in component creation. For example, we can write this code:

```
procedure TMd3TabList.CreateParams (var Params: TCreateParams);
begin
  inherited CreateParams (Params);
  Params.Style := Params.Style or lbs_UseTabStops;
end;
```

This code calls the method of the parent class to set the default parameters, and then adds the lbs_UseTabStops flag to the specified window style. Now we can use this list box with Tab characters to display the text in multiple columns. I've opened the Component Wizard and chosen a name for the class of the new component, TMd3TabList; a parent component, TListBox; and a page in the palette, 'Md3'. In the automatically generated Pascal file, I've deleted some useless declarations and written the method above, and its declaration inside the class definition:

```
type
  TMd3TabList = class(TListBox)
  public
    procedure CreateParams (
      var Params: TCreateParams); override;
  end;
```

The code of this example is another demonstration that writing a component can be an easy task. Again, I've written a program to test the new component, the TabTest example (also available in the TabList directory of the companion disk).

Testing the Tab List Component

To test the new Md3TabList component, I've created a new project and added to its main form the component and a normal list box, side by side. The form also has three edit boxes and a button, which are used to add new strings to the list. After adding these components to the form, I entered the new strings for both list boxes, using the same lines of text, including tabs. In Figure 18.5, you can see the text I used for both list boxes with the embedded tabs. In the background of the figure, you can already see how the two list boxes display this text.

FIGURE 18.5

The form of the TabTest example at design-time.

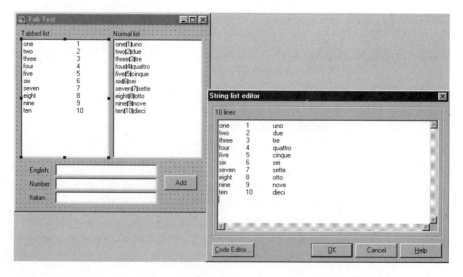

To enter Tab characters while you're in the String List Property Editor, simply press Ctrl+Tab instead of the Tab key alone.

When you run this program to look at the differences between the two list boxes, you can also add new entries. The text of the three edit boxes is used to form a string, with two tabs between the three parts. This string is added to both list boxes, with this code:

```
procedure TForm1.AddButtonClick(Sender: TObject);
var
  NewItem: String;
begin
  if Edit1.Text <> '' then
  begin
    NewItem := Edit1.Text + #9 + Edit2.Text +
      #9 + Edit3.Text;
    Md3TabList1.Items.Add (NewItem);
    ListBox1.Items.Add (NewItem);
  end;
end;
```

You can see an example of the effect of this code in Figure 18.6, where I've added the number 20 to the list boxes of English and Italian numbers. There is no other code in the test program.

FIGURE 18.6

The TabTest example shows the difference between a standard Delphi list box and the tab list component.

Building Brand-New Components

The simple components we have built were just very limited extensions of existing ones. This is what you'll probably do most of the time. At other times, however, you'll want to define brand-new components or components derived from the TCustomXXX generic classes. When you write a brand-new component, you can subclass one of these more abstract classes:

- TWinControl is the parent class of components based on a window. Components that descend from this class can receive the input focus and get Windows messages from the system. You can also use their window handle when calling API functions.

- TGraphicControl is the parent class of visible components that have no Windows handle (which saves some Windows resources). These components cannot receive the input focus or respond to Windows messages directly.

- TComponent is the parent class of all components and can be used as a direct parent class for nonvisual components.

In the rest of the chapter, we will build some components using various parent classes, and look at the differences among them.

> **NOTE**
>
> When you derive a new component from these high-level classes of the VCL hierarchy, it already inherits some properties that are common to all components. Refer to Figure 7.7 to see the properties defined in some of the high-level VCL classes.

A Graphical Component Built Step-by-Step

The graphical component I want to build is an arrow component. You can use such a component to indicate a flow of information, or an action, for example. Instead of showing you the final version of the component, which is quite complex, I've built it in consecutive steps. To avoid updating the package over and over (although this is much faster with Delphi3 packages than it was with the Delphi 2 approach of updating the whole component library), I've tested this component in a program that creates it at run-time. The component I've added to the Md3Pack package is only the final version. As we work through the process of building this component, we'll learn about a number of important concepts:

- The definition of new enumerated properties, based on custom enumerated data types.

- The use of properties of TPersistent-derived classes, such as TPen and TBrush, and the issues related to their creation and destruction, and to handling their OnChange events internally in our component.

- The implementation of the Paint method of the component, which provides its user interface, and should be generic enough to accommodate all the possible values of the various properties, including its Width and Height. The Paint method plays a substantial role in this graphical component.

- The definition of a completely custom event handler, based on a peculiar action the user can do on the component (a double click on the point of the arrow). This will require direct handling of Windows messages and the use of the Windows API for graphic regions.

- The development of a test program along with the component itself, step by step, something very common during the development of a component.

- The inclusion of a bitmap for the component in the Components palette.

> **NOTE**
> Building a test-bed program for components is quite common and very handy. For this reason some third-party developers offer component testing programs, which might come in handy when you're building complex components. The best-known such program is ReAct from Eagle Software, a trial version is included on the companion CD.

Defining an Enumerated Property

After generating the new component with the Component Wizard and choosing TGraphicControl as the parent class, we can start to customize the component. The arrow can point in any of four directions: up, down, left, and right. To express these choices, I've defined an enumerated type:

```
TArrowDirection = (adUp, adDown, adLeft, adRight);
```

This enumerated type defines a private data member of the component and a parameter of the procedure used to change it:

```
TMd3Arrow = class(TGraphicControl)
  private
    FDirection: TArrowDirection;
    procedure SetDirection (Value: TArrowDirection);
    ...
```

Now that we have private data and a method to set it, we can define a corresponding property as follows:

```
published
  property Direction: TArrowDirection
    read FDirection write SetDirection default adRight;
```

The property, which is of the same TArrowDirection data type, is read directly from the FDirection field and is written using the SetDirection procedure. The default value is adRight. We have to use a procedure to update the arrow direction because we have to repaint the component when this property changes:

```
procedure TMd3Arrow.SetDirection (Value: TArrowDirection);
begin
  if FDirection <> Value then
  begin
    FDirection := Value;
    Invalidate;
  end;
end;
```

Notice that the side effect takes place only if the property is really changing its value. Otherwise, the code is skipped and the method ends immediately. This code structure is very common, and we will use it for most of the *Set* procedures of properties.

We must also remember to set the default value of the property in the component's constructor:

```
constructor TMd3Arrow.Create (AOwner: TComponent);
begin
  inherited Create (AOwner);
  FDirection := adRight;
end;
```

In fact, as mentioned before, the default value specified in the property declaration is used only to determine whether to save the property's value to disk. The Create constructor is defined in the public section of the type definition of the new component, and indicated by the override keyword. It is fundamental to remember this keyword; otherwise, when Delphi creates a new component of this class, it won't call its constructor, but the version of the base class. Here is the class declaration:

```
type
  TArrowDirection = (adUp, adDown, adLeft, adRight);
  TMd3Arrow = class(TGraphicControl)
  private
    FDirection: TArrowDirection;
    procedure SetDirection (Value: TArrowDirection);
  protected
    procedure Paint; override;
  public
    constructor Create (AOwner: TComponent); override;
  published
    property Direction: TArrowDirection
      read FDirection write SetDirection default adRight;
  end;
```

Property Naming Conventions

In the definition of the Arrow component, notice the use of several naming conventions for properties, access methods, and fields. Here is a summary:

- A property should have a meaningful and readable name.
- When a private data field is used to hold the value of a property, the field should be named with an *F* (field) at the beginning, followed by the name of the corresponding property.
- When a function is used to change the value of the property, the function should have the word *Set* at the beginning, followed by the name of the corresponding property.
- A corresponding function used to read the property should have the word *Get* at the beginning, again followed by the property name.

These are just guidelines to make programs more readable. The compiler doesn't enforce them. These conventions are described in the *Delphi Component Writers Guide*, and are followed by component writing tools, including the simple one I've built.

Writing the Paint Method

Drawing the arrow is a complex aspect of this example. We'll spend some time working on this Paint method but this should teach you a lot more about the use of the Canvas property and the GDI (Graphics Device Interface) API calls available in Windows. The reason we face so many new output problems here is that it is quite rare to draw directly on the screen in a Delphi program; it is much more common to do the output inside a component. Component writers need to be more experienced in graphical output than other Delphi programmers.

In this example, as in most graphical components, I've overridden the Paint method in the protected section of the type definition (as shown in the listing above), and used the Canvas property (automatically available for each TGraphicControl component). With a series of MoveTo and LineTo calls, you can draw the arrow in the different directions, as shown in Figure 18.7 for the adUp direction.

FIGURE 18.7

The code used to draw the adUp arrow and the resulting effect.

```
1) MoveTo (XCenter, Height-1);
2) LineTo (XCenter, YCenter);
3) LineTo (Width 1, YCenter);
4) LineTo (XCenter, 0);
5) LineTo (0, YCenter);
6) LineTo (XCenter, YCenter);
```

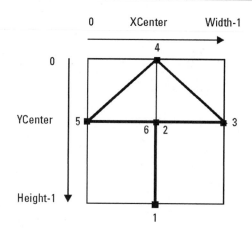

The code computes the center of the component area and uses it to determine the position of the arrow and the division between its two parts (the line and the triangle). Notice that the drawing fills the whole surface of the component, something quite common, since you can then resize the drawing to set the size of the component. Here is the first part of the code of the Paint method:

```
procedure TMd3Arrow.Paint;
var
  XCenter, YCenter: Integer;
begin
  {compute the center}
```

```
YCenter := (Height - 1) div 2;
XCenter := (Width - 1) div 2;

{draw the line and the arrow}
case FDirection of
  adUp:
    with Canvas do
    begin
      MoveTo (XCenter, Height-1);
      LineTo (XCenter, YCenter);
      LineTo (Width-1, YCenter);
      LineTo (XCenter, 0);
      LineTo (0, YCenter);
      LineTo (XCenter, YCenter);
    end;
  adLeft:...
```

You can find the complete listing for the method in the Arrow1 directory on the companion CD, along with the test program.

The Test Program

Instead of installing this component in the palette, we can write a test program that creates an instance of the component at run-time. The test program is called ATest and is in the same directory, Arrow1, that contains the unit defining the component.

The form of this example has other components, which are used to set some of the arrow component's properties. There are two spin edit components used to set the width and height of the arrow, a button to accept these changes (Size), and a second button to turn the arrow (Turn) by changing its Direction property. When the form is built, it creates a new arrow component:

```
procedure TForm1.FormCreate(Sender: TObject);
begin
  A := TMd3Arrow.Create (self);
  A.Parent := self;
  A.Left := 150;
  A.Top := 150;
  A.Width := 20;
  A.Height := 30;
end;
```

In this code, A is simply a private field of the form, of type TMd3Arrow. The program creates the arrow control, and then sets its Parent property to the form itself, to show it inside the form. The arrow component changes when one of the two buttons is pressed. The Size button uses the values of the two SpinEdit components to change the Arrow component's height and size. The other button, Turn, changes the direction of the arrow. It reads the current value of the Direction property we have defined and increases its value by calling the system Succ procedure. When the highest value of the set has been reached, the lowest value is selected (extreme values of the enumeration are computed using the High and Low functions). You can apply this kind of code to any enumerated property to test it. This is the code of the Turn button's OnClick event handler:

```
procedure TForm1.TurnButtonClick(Sender: TObject);
begin
  if A.Direction = High (TArrowDirection) then
    A.Direction := Low (TArrowDirection)
  else
    A.Direction := Succ (A.Direction);
end;
```

As you can see in Figure 18.8 (and test yourself by running the program), the new component works. The problem is that its capabilities are very limited. We have no way to change the size of the arrow point or to act on the colors used and the size of the lines. We will address these problems in the next versions.

FIGURE 18.8

The test bed application of the Arrow1 component.

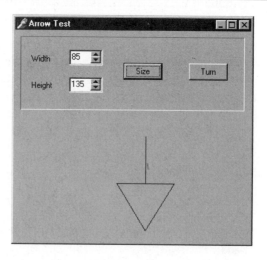

Adding Class-Typed Properties

To determine the aspect of the point of the arrow, I've added some more properties to the component. The first two are two simple properties, ArrowHeight and Filled. Their code is actually quite ordinary, but I've listed it here anyway to underline the idea that component writing is simple, but often a tedious and repetitive work. Here is the new code added to the interface of the TArrow class to define and implement these two properties:

```
type
  TMd3Arrow = class(TGraphicControl)
  private
    FArrowHeight: Integer;
    FFilled: Boolean;
    ...
    procedure SetArrowHeight (Value: Integer);
    procedure SetFilled (Value: Boolean);
  published
    property ArrowHeight: Integer
      read FArrowHeight write SetArrowHeight default 10;
    property Filled: Boolean
      read FFilled write SetFilled default False;
    ...
  end;
```

The ArrowHeight property determines the size of the arrow's point, and the Filled property determines whether it should be colored. The current brush of the canvas determines the color used for the point, so we should add one more property to change the brush. While we are at it, why not add another property for the pen? We have a lot of work to do for the new version of the component.

First of all, we have to implement the two properties above, ArrowHeight and Filled. Both have a corresponding private field in the class, as well as a private access function, as indicated in the declaration of the property. Their code is simple:

```
procedure TMd3Arrow.SetArrowHeight (Value: Integer);
begin
  if FArrowHeight <> Value then
  begin
    FArrowHeight := Value;
    Invalidate;
  end;
end;
```

907

```
procedure TMd3Arrow.SetFilled (Value: Boolean);
begin
  if FFilled <> Value then
  begin
    FFilled := Value;
    Invalidate;
  end;
end;
```

The biggest effect of these new properties, in fact, is on the `Paint` method, which should now correctly display the size of the arrow's point and its color. Here is just one of the `case` branches of the new version of the `Paint` method:

```
adUp:
  with Canvas do
  begin
    MoveTo (XCenter, Height-1);
    LineTo (XCenter, FArrowHeight);
    LineTo (Width-1, FArrowHeight);
    LineTo (XCenter, 0);
    LineTo (0, FArrowHeight);
    LineTo (XCenter, FArrowHeight);
    if FFilled then
      FloodFill (XCenter, FArrowHeight div 2,
        Pen.Color, fsBorder);
  end;
```

You can see a graph with the effect of this code in Figure 18.9 and compare it with the older version in Figure 18.7. To fill a surface with `FloodFill`, you have

---

FIGURE 18.9

A schema of the new version of the Paint code for the up arrow.

1) MoveTo (XCenter, Height-1);
2) LineTo (XCenter, FArrowHeight);
3) LineTo (Width -1, FArrowHeight);
4) LineTo (XCenter, 0);
5) LineTo (0, FArrowHeight);
6) LineTo (XCenter, FArrowHeight);
   if FFilled then
7) FloodFill (XCenter, FArrowHeight
   div 2, Pen.Color, fsBorder);

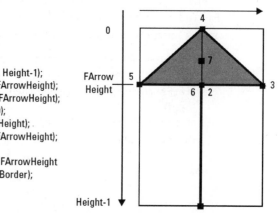

to use the first two parameters to indicate a point inside it. I've chosen a point approximately in the center of the arrowhead, but any other point within the boundaries of the arrow's triangle would do.

The other two new properties are properties of a class type (specifically, of the TPersistent data type, so that they can be automatically streamed by Delphi), so our component will have to create and destroy the corresponding objects. Since users can change the properties of these sub-objects from the Object Inspector, we'll also need to handle one of their events internally in our component. Here is the definition of the two new properties based on objects:

```
type
  TMd3Arrow = class(TGraphicControl)
  private
    FPen: TPen;
    FBrush: TBrush;
    ...
    procedure SetPen (Value: TPen);
    procedure SetBrush (Value: TBrush);
    procedure RepaintRequest (Sender: TObject);
  published
    property Pen: TPen read FPen write SetPen;
    property Brush: TBrush read FBrush write SetBrush;
  end;
```

These properties refer to existing VCL classes, which require some special handling. Both properties are implemented as private fields of the component, and use a set method, with similar code:

```
procedure TMd3Arrow.SetPen (Value: TPen);
begin
  FPen.Assign(Value);
  Invalidate;
end;

procedure TMd3Arrow.SetBrush (Value: TBrush);
begin
  FBrush.Assign(Value);
  Invalidate;
end;
```

Notice the use of the `Assign` method, instead of a plain assignment. Many VCL classes have an `Assign` method that should be used when we need to update the data of these objects, but not to replace them with other objects.

Users will often change one of the properties of the Pen or Brush (using the Object Inspector, for example), instead of replacing all the values at once. How do we keep track of changes to those sub-properties? `TPen`, `TBrush`, and other GDI classes have a specific event for this: `OnChange`. If you assign a method to the `OnChange` event of these components, the method will be called each time one of the properties of the class changes. In the Arrow component, I've added this code to the `Create` method:

```
FPen.OnChange := RepaintRequest;
FBrush.OnChange := RepaintRequest;
```

The `RepaintRequest` handler is declared in the private section of the component as you already saw above. Its effect, as the name suggests, is to repaint the component by calling the `Invalidate` method:

```
procedure TMd3Arrow.RepaintRequest (Sender: TObject);
begin
  Invalidate;
end;
```

Now, to actually use the pen and brush for the drawing, you have to modify the `Paint` method accordingly:

```
procedure TMd3Arrow.Paint;
var
  XCenter, YCenter: Integer;
begin
  YCenter := (Height - 1) div 2;
  XCenter := (Width - 1) div 2;
  Canvas.Pen := FPen;
  Canvas.Brush := FBrush;
  case FDirection of
    adUp: with Canvas do
      ...
```

The last thing to notice is that `FPen` and `FBrush` are two objects, and as with any other objects that are not built-in data types, they must be initialized. For this reason, I've added two more lines to the `Create` constructor. Here is its complete code:

```
constructor TMd3Arrow.Create (AOwner: TComponent);
begin
  {call the parent constructor}
  inherited Create (AOwner);
  {set the default values}
  FDirection := adRight;
  FArrowHeight := 10;
  FFilled := False;
  {create the pen and the brush}
  FPen := TPen.Create;
  FBrush := TBrush.Create;
  {set a handler for the OnChange event}
  FPen.OnChange := RepaintRequest;
  FBrush.OnChange := RepaintRequest;
end;
```

I've also added a destructor to the component and written its code as follows:

```
destructor TMd3Arrow.Destroy;
begin
  FPen.Free;
  FBrush.Free;
  inherited Destroy;
end;
```

This is probably the first time we have needed to use a destructor in an example (destructors were introduced along with constructors in Chapter 5). As I mentioned at the beginning of this chapter, writing components requires the use of many features of Object Pascal that are seldom used in other cases.

Updating the Test Program

To test the new version of the arrow component, still without installing it in Delphi, I've extended the last test example. I'm doing this to show you the common practice of building a component along with its test program, and only installing it when it is finished (and hopefully free of bugs). The new version of the test program has a form with some additional components: some more buttons, a check box, a Color-Dialog component, and a track bar, as you can see in Figure 18.10 at run-time.

FIGURE 18.10

An example of the output
of the Arrow2 component
test program.

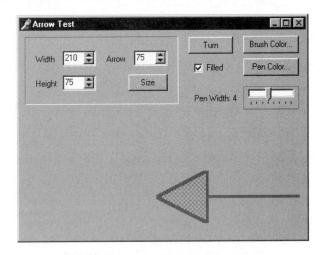

The code of the example is simply an extension of the previous version. The
value of the new Spin Edit control is used when the user clicks on the Size button, while the buttons related to the color of the pen and the brush use a Color-
Dialog component in the standard way. A change in the check box is reflected by
the Filled property, and a change in the track bar in the width of the pen. I'm
going to show you only this last code fragment:

```
procedure TForm1.TrackBar1Change(Sender: TObject);
begin
  PenLabel.Caption := 'Pen Width: ' +
    IntToStr (TrackBar1.Position);
  A.Pen.Width := TrackBar1.Position;
end;
```

The rest of the code of the test program is very simple, and you can find it on the
companion CD.

Defining a New Custom Event

To complete our development of the Arrow component, I want to add a custom
event. Most of the time, new components use the events of their parent classes.
For example, in the third version of the Arrow component, I've made some standard events available simply by redeclaring them in the published section:

```
type
  TMd3Arrow = class(TGraphicControl)
```

```
published
  property OnClick;
  property OnDragDrop;
  property OnDragOver;
  property OnEndDrag;
  property OnMouseDown;
  property OnMouseMove;
  property OnMouseUp;
```

Thanks to this declaration, the above events (originally declared in a parent class) will now be available in the Object Inspector when we install the component. Most of the components will work well enough if you simply redefine existing events, thereby changing their behavior. Anyway, it is interesting to see how you can add a custom event, although this operation is not often necessary.

To define a brand-new event, you first need to add to the class a field of the type of the event. This type is actually a method pointer type. Here is the definition I've added in the private section of the TArrow class:

```
FArrowDblClick: TNotifyEvent;
```

In this case I've used the TNotifyEvent type, which has only the Sender parameter and is used by Delphi for many events, including OnClick and OnDblClick events. Around this field I've defined a very simple published property, with direct access to the data:

```
property OnArrowDblClick: TNotifyEvent
  read FArrowDblClick write FArrowDblClick;
```

Notice again the standard naming convention, with event properties starting with *On.* The FArrowDblClick method pointer is activated (executing the corresponding function) inside the specific ArrowDblClick dynamic method. This happens only if an event handler has been specified:

```
procedure TArrow.ArrowDblClick;
begin
  if Assigned (FArrowDblClick) then
    FArrowDblClick (self);
end;
```

This method is defined in the protected section of the type definition to allow future subclasses both to call and change it. Basically, the ArrowDblClick method is called by the handler of the wm_LButtonDblClk Windows message, but only if the double-click took place inside the arrow's point. To test this condition, we can use some of the Windows API's region functions.

A *region* is an area of the screen enclosed by any shape. For example, we can build a polygonal region using the three vertices of the arrow-point triangle. The only problem is that to fill the surface properly, we must define an array of TPoints in a clockwise direction (see the description of the CreatePolygonalRgn in the Windows API Help for the details of this strange approach).

Once we have defined a region, we can test whether the point where the double-click occurred is inside the region by using the PtInRegion API call. You can see the complete source code of this procedure in the following listing, after the code with the new elements of the type definition of the TMd3Arrow class:

```
type
  TMd3Arrow = class(TGraphicControl)
  private
    FArrowDblClick: TNotifyEvent;
    procedure WMLButtonDlbClk (var Msg: TWMLButtonDblClk);
      message wm_LButtonDblClk;
    ...
  protected
    procedure ArrowDblClick; dynamic;
    ...
  published
    property OnArrowDblClick: TNotifyEvent
      read FArrowDblClick write FArrowDblClick;
    ...
  end;

procedure TMd3Arrow.WMLButtonDlbClk (
  var Msg: TWMLButtonDblClk);
var
  ArrowPoints: array [0..2] of TPoint;
  XCenter, YCenter: Integer;
  HRegion: HRgn;
begin
  {perform default handling}
  inherited;

  {compute the points}
  YCenter := (Height - 1) div 2;
  XCenter := (Width - 1) div 2;
  case FDirection of
    adUp:
    begin
      ArrowPoints [0] := Point (0, FArrowHeight);
```

```
    ArrowPoints [1] := Point (XCenter, 0);
    ArrowPoints [2] := Point (Width-1, FArrowHeight);
  end;
  adDown: ... // similar code
  adLeft:
  begin
    ArrowPoints [0] := Point (FArrowHeight, Height - 1);
    ArrowPoints [1] := Point (0, YCenter);
    ArrowPoints [2] := Point (FArrowHeight, 0);
  end;
  adRight: ... // similar code
end;

{check whether the click took place
in the arrow-point region}
HRegion := CreatePolygonRgn (ArrowPoints, 3, WINDING);
if PtInRegion (HRegion, Msg.XPos, Msg.YPos) then
  ArrowDblClick;
DeleteObject (HRegion);
end;
```

Testing the OnArrowDblClick Event

Now that we have defined the complete version of the component, we can make one last test on the new event before installing it in Delphi. The third version of the test program, saved in the Arrow3 directory, uses the same form as the previous version. Its code, though, contains the new method, ArrowDoubleClick. This procedure is declared in the public portion of the form and is defined as follows:

```
procedure TForm1.ArrowDoubleClick (Sender: TObject);
begin
  ShowMessage ('You have double-clicked ' +
    'on the point of the arrow');
end;
```

It is a handler of the same type as that required by the Arrow component's OnArrowDblClick event, so we use it by setting it at the end of the Create method of the form:

```
procedure TForm1.FormCreate(Sender: TObject);
begin
  A := TMd3Arrow.Create (self);
  A.Parent := self;
  A.Left := 200;
```

```
      A.Top := 200;
      A.Width := 20;
      A.Height := 30;
      A.ArrowHeight := 15;
      A.OnArrowDblClick := ArrowDoubleClick;
    end;
```

The result of this code? If you run the program and double-click inside the triangular point of the arrow, a message is displayed, as shown in Figure 18.11. If, instead, you double-click on the component but outside the arrow point, nothing happens.

FIGURE 18.11

The output message displayed by the test program of the Arrow3 component, when a user clicks on the arrow's point.

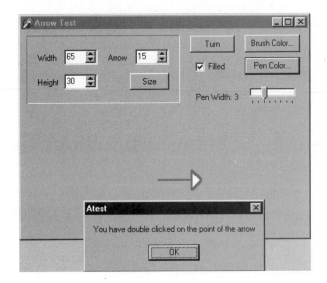

Adding a Bitmap for the Components Palette

Before installing our brand-new component, we have to take one further step: We must define a bitmap for the Components palette. The first two components we defined in this chapter had no specific bitmap, so they used those of their parent class. In this case, since the parent class doesn't have a bitmap, we'll get the default Delphi bitmap. Luckily, defining a new bitmap is easy, once you know the rules. First of all, open the Image editor, start a new project, and select the DCR (Delphi Component Resource) project type.

TIP

DCR files are simply standard RES files with a different extension. If you prefer, you can create them with any resource editor, including the Borland Resource Workshop, which is certainly a more powerful tool than the Delphi Image editor. When you finish creating the resource file, simply rename the RES file to use a DCR extension.

Add a new bitmap to the resource, choosing a size of 24×24 pixels. Now you are ready to draw the bitmap. The other important rule refers to naming. In this case, the rules do not just define a naming convention; they are enforced by Delphi:

- The name of the bitmap resource must match the name of the component, including the initial *T*. In this case, the name of the bitmap resource should be TMD3ARROW. The name of the bitmap resource must also be in all uppercase. Delphi will ignore a bitmap resource named with mixed case (such as *TMd3Arrow*).

- The name of the DCR file must match the name of the compiled unit that defines the component, which is the same as the name of the Pascal source code file. In this case, the file name must be ARROW3.DCR. The file must be saved in the same directory as the unit's DCU file.

When the bitmap for the component is ready, you can install the component in Delphi, by selecting Components ➤ Install Components and choosing a package (or creating a new one); and Delphi should add to the source code of the package a resource inclusion statement for the component bitmap. This doesn't always work, but you can add the {$R arrow3.dcr} statement in the package source code yourself. Even better, you can add the generic statement {$R *.dcr} in the source code of the unit defining the component.

The Final Test of the Arrow Component

If you install this third version of the Arrow component (which is not in the Md3Pack package) you can then try to write a small example to test it. After the installation, you'll be able to use the component like any standard component, setting properties and events with the Object Inspector.

This type of test, after we have written the program, is very important. Often, when you create a component at run-time, some elements may be different from what you would expect. Also, by testing various values for the properties, you can find errors the initial tests did not show. In fact, when testing the component for this example, I found two errors in the code I had written.

The first error is that the component has no default size, so when you place it in a form, its size will be a single pixel. The second error occurs when you select most of the alternative pen styles. In many cases, the filling algorithm doesn't work anymore, as you can see in Figure 18.12. Since these problems are fairly common, I've left the Arrow3 code as it was (that is, with bugs) and made the changes in a new version, Arrow4, which is then installed in the Md3Pack package.

WARNING   Note that you can install only one of the two versions at a time because you cannot have two components—two classes in the components library—with the same name.

FIGURE 18.12

If you try to use a dotted pen in the Arrow3 component, a problem in the filling code emerges at design-time.

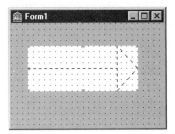

Correcting Bugs in the Arrow Component

The first change in the Arrow component is adding the default values for the Width and Height properties, both in the description of these properties and in the Create method:

```
property Width default 50;
property Height default 20;
```

The above is simply a redeclaration of the properties already defined by the parent class, this time adding a new default value. Actually, providing a default value for the height and width is not common in Delphi components, but I thought it was a good idea anyway. In fact, if the programmer doesn't change these standard values, they won't show up in the textual description of the form.

The other changes are related to the FloodFill function call. If you use Flood-Fill, the region should have a continuous (unbroken) border. Dashed lines don't qualify as continuous borders, so FloodFill *leaks* outside the proper area. As a result, it is time for a complete rewrite of the component's Paint method, using the PolyLine and Polygon methods of the TCanvas class instead of FloodFill. The difference between PolyLine and Polygon is that the first draws a line and the second fills the resulting polygon with the current brush. It doesn't matter what is on the screen; the polygon will be filled properly. So in this case Polygon is a better choice than FloodFill.

We have already seen how to build a polygon with an array of points to test whether the click was on the arrow point. Similar code can be used now. The only problem is that the PolyLine procedure doesn't automatically close the polygon. To draw a triangle, it requires a fourth point in the same position as the first one. Here is a portion of the final version of the Paint method of the Arrow component:

```
var
ArrowPoints: array [0..3] of TPoint;
begin
...
case FDirection of
    adUp:
    begin
    Canvas.MoveTo (XCenter, Height-1);
    Canvas.LineTo (XCenter, FArrowHeight);
    ArrowPoints [0] := Point (0, FArrowHeight);
    ArrowPoints [1] := Point (XCenter, 0);
    ArrowPoints [2] := Point (Width-1, FArrowHeight);
    ArrowPoints [3] := Point (0, FArrowHeight);
  end;
  ...
{draw the arrow point, eventually filling it}
if FFilled then
  Canvas.Polygon (ArrowPoints)
else
  Canvas.PolyLine (ArrowPoints);
end;
```

For the complete listing of the TMd3Arrow class and its methods refer to the ARROW4.PAS unit in the Arrow4 directory. This is the version of the component included in the Md3Pack package.

Arrows and Shapes

Now that everything is working fine, we can test this component in an example project, TArrow (which stands for *Test Arrow*, and is available in the Arrow4 directory on the companion CD). The form of this program has four arrows, four shapes, and a timer. The aim of the example is to see a colored element move around the surface of the form. The colored element, which indicates a hypothetical active element of a process, moves from a square to the following arrow, then to the next square, and so on. To perform the movement at fixed intervals, we'll use a Timer component.

When the form is created, the program stores the four shapes and the four arrows in an array of graphical components, defined as follows:

```
private
  Graph: array [1..8] of TGraphicControl;
```

Here is the code of the FormCreate method:

```
procedure TForm1.FormCreate(Sender: TObject);
var
  I: Integer;
begin
  Active := 1;
  Shape1.Brush.Color := clYellow;
  for I := 1 to 4 do
  begin
    Graph [I * 2 - 1] := (FindComponent (
      'Shape' + IntToStr (I)) as TGraphicControl);
    Graph [I * 2] := (FindComponent (
      'Md3Arrow' + IntToStr (I)) as TGraphicControl);
  end;
end;
```

Well, I've managed to show you something new about the use of components in Delphi even in this example. The FindComponent method simply returns a child component with the given name, if one exists. FindComponent scans the form's Components array to do its job. When this array has been built, you can change the color of the active element quite easily (as you can see in Figure 18.13).

FIGURE 18.13

The output of the TArrow example.

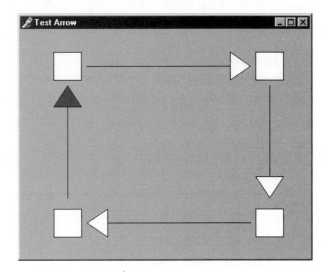

Remember that you also need to restore the color of the element that was active before:

```
procedure TForm1.Timer1Timer(Sender: TObject);
begin
  // disables the active elements
  if Graph [Active] is TMd3Arrow then
    TMd3Arrow (Graph [Active]).Brush.Color := clWhite
  else
    TShape (Graph [Active]).Brush.Color := clWhite;
  // compute the new active element
  Active := Active mod 8 + 1;
  // enables the active element
  if Graph [Active] is TMd3Arrow then
    TMd3Arrow (Graph [Active]).Brush.Color := clRed
  else
    TShape (Graph [Active]).Brush.Color := clYellow;
end;
```

That's all—well, almost. Why not show a message when the user double-clicks exactly on the arrow point of an active arrow? The following method is connected to all four arrow components, using the Object Inspector:

```
procedure TForm1.ArrowDoubleClick(Sender: TObject);
begin
```

```
    if (Sender as TMd3Arrow).Brush.Color = clRed then
      ShowMessage ('Double-click on active arrow');
  end;
```

This example, which might be the output of a simulation program, ends our step-by-step development of the arrow component. Now it is time to move to another component: a digital clock.

The Clock Component

The next component I want to focus on is a digital clock. You'll see the code required to draw an analog clock in an example of Chapter 25, and you might turn that code into a component, if you like. This example has some interesting features. First, it embeds a component (a Timer) in another component; second, it shows the live-data approach.

Since the digital clock will provide some text output, I considered subclassing the TLabel component. However, if you do this, a user can change the label's caption—that is, the text of the clock. To avoid this problem, I simply used the TCustomLabel component as the parent class. A TCustomLabel object has the same capabilities as a TLabel object, but few published properties. In other words, a TCustomLabel subclass can decide which properties should be available and which should remain hidden.

Besides redeclaring some of the properties of the parent class, TDigClock has one new property of its own, Active. This property indicates whether or not the clock is working. As you might have guessed, the clock contains a Timer component. The Timer is not made public through a property, because I don't want programmers to access it directly. Instead, I made the Enabled property of the Timer available, wrapping it inside the Active property of the digital clock. Here is the full type declaration for the component:

```
type
  TMd3DigClock = class (TCustomLabel)
  private
    FTimer: TTimer;
    function GetActive: Boolean;
    procedure SetActive (Value: Boolean);
  protected
    procedure UpdateClock (Sender: TObject);
```

```
public
  constructor Create (AOwner: TComponent); override;
published
  property Align;
  property Alignment;
  property Color;
  property Font;
  property ParentColor;
  property ParentFont;
  property ParentShowHint;
  property PopupMenu;
  property ShowHint;
  property Transparent;
  property Visible;
  property Active: Boolean
    read GetActive write SetActive;
end;
```

Notice that we need methods both to write and to read the value of the Active property, because it is not local data, but rather refers to a member of the embedded component, the Timer:

```
function TMd3DigClock.GetActive: Boolean;
begin
  Result := FTimer.Enabled;
end;


procedure TMd3DigClock.SetActive (Value: Boolean);
begin
  FTimer.Enabled := Value;
end;
```

To make the Timer available, we have to override the constructor of the clock component. The Create method calls the corresponding method of the base class and creates the Timer object, installing a handler for its OnTimer event:

```
constructor TMd3DigClock.Create (AOwner: TComponent);
begin
  inherited Create (AOwner);
  FTimer := TTimer.Create (self);
  FTimer.OnTimer := UpdateClock;
  FTimer.Enabled := True;
end;
```

We don't need a destructor, simply because the FTimer object has the component as owner (as indicated by the parameter of its Create constructor), so it will be destroyed automatically when the clock component is destroyed.

The key piece of the component's code is the UpdateClock procedure, which is just one statement:

```
procedure TDigClock.UpdateClock (Sender: TObject);
begin
  Caption := TimeToStr (Time);
end;
```

This method uses Caption, which is an unpublished property, so that a user of the component cannot modify it in the Object Inspector. The result of this code statement is to display the current time. This happens continuously, because the method is connected to the Timer's OnTimer event.

As usual I've also built a test program for this component. Remember to install the Md3Pack package, which contains the component, before opening this example; it's available in the DigClock subdirectory along with the source code of the component.

Defining an Array Property

Now that we have built some interesting components, the arrow and the two clocks, we can move back to one of the examples introduced at the very beginning of the chapter, the tabbed list box. We can now complete this example using (for the first time) an array property. There is actually nothing strange about the definition of an array property, but this technique is not documented in detail, so I've decided to provide a specific example. When implementing this example, we will face another confusing issue: dialog box units.

To build this new component, I'm not editing the original source code, but creating a brand-new version, with a new name, TMd3TabbedList. By using different names we can install both versions of this component at the same time, place them in the same package, and use them in the same program. This also requires the use of different names for the two units.

The New Tabbed List

The new version of the tabbed list box has a new property, which sets the position of the tabs. This is the definition of the array property:

```
property TabStops [Index: Integer]: Integer
  read GetTabStops write SetTabStops;
```

This property cannot be added to the published portion of the unit because its data type is not a class type or a simple (built-in) type. This means that users of this component can set the property only at run-time, writing some code.

> **WARNING**
>
> If you try to declare this property as `published`, the Delphi 3 compiler will accept it, which seems really odd. Only when you try using the component in Delphi will you get a generic error message.

It would be much better to let programmers set the initial values of the tabs simply by entering the values in the Object Inspector. When you have a list of strings, the standard approach is to use a `TStringList` property. When you have a list of non-string values, instead, the official Delphi solution is to define a `TCollection` property to access to the group of items and a `TCollectionItem` subtype to store each specific item. This approach is far from simple. For this example, I've chosen a simpler nonstandard approach. (By the way, in *Delphi Developer's Handbook* you'll find a complete example using a custom collection property.)

To solve the problem of allowing direct editing of the property at design-time, I've added a new property to the tabbed list box. This is a string with the values of the tabs separated by semicolons. Both this string and the array property access the data stored in a private field, which is an array of integers.

> **NOTE**
>
> It is very important to acknowledge that the data types of the properties do not always match the internal data types used by the class. Separating the interface from the implementation is a key OOP feature, and something properties help you do very easily.

Here is the complete source code of the class of this component:

```
type
  TTabsArray = array [0..9] of Integer;

  TMd3TabbedList = class(TListBox)
  private
    FTabStops: TTabsArray;
    function GetTabStops (Index: Integer): Integer;
    procedure SetTabStops (Index, Value: Integer);
    function GetTabsString: string;
    procedure SetTabsString (Value: string);
  protected
    procedure UpdateTabStops;
  public
    procedure CreateParams (
      var Params: TCreateParams); override;
    procedure CreateWnd; override;
    property TabStops [Index: Integer]: Integer
      read GetTabStops write SetTabStops;
  published
    property TabsString: string
      read GetTabsString write SetTabsString;
  end;
```

The overridden CreateParams method sets the lbs_UseTabStops list box style, as in the previous version of the component. The overridden CreateWnd method initializes the array with fixed values, then updates the actual values of the list box by calling the UpdateTabStops method (a custom method I've added to copy the values from the private array of integers to the actual Windows list box):

```
procedure TMd3TabbedList.CreateParams (var Params: TCreateParams);
begin
  inherited CreateParams (Params);
  Params.Style := Params.Style or lbs_UseTabStops;
end;
procedure TMd3TabbedList.CreateWnd;
var
  I: Integer;
begin
  inherited CreateWnd;
  for I := Low (FTabStops) to High (FTabStops) do
    FTabStops [I] := I * 100;
```

```
    UpdateTabStops;
  end;
```

This method also sets the initial tab values. Now let's look at the two access methods for the property, which have an unusual structure. This time both the Get function and the Set procedure have one more parameter: the index used to access the property. The code of these two methods is quite simple:

```
procedure TMd3TabbedList.SetTabStops (
  Index, Value: Integer);
begin
  if FTabStops [Index] <> Value then
  begin
    FTabStops [Index] := Value;
    UpdateTabStops;
    Invalidate;
  end;
end;

function TMd3TabbedList.GetTabStops (
  Index: Integer): Integer;
begin
  Result := FTabStops [Index];
end;
```

The SetTabStops method simply updates the internal array, calls the Update-TabStops method, and then calls Invalidate to repaint the component. Two more access methods are required to turn the private array of integers into a string, and vice-versa:

```
function TMd3TabbedList.GetTabsString: string;
var
  Text: string;
  I: Integer;
begin
  SetLength (Text, 100);
  Text := '';
  for I := Low (FTabStops) to High (FTabStops) do
    Text := Text + IntToStr (FTabStops ) + ';';
  Result := Text;
end;

procedure TMd3TabList.SetTabsString (Value: string);
```

```
var
  Text: string;
  I, Len : Integer;
begin
  Text := Value;
  for I := Low (FTabStops) to High (FTabStops) do
  begin
    Len := Pos (Text, ';');
    FTabStops [I] := StrToIntDef (Copy (Text, 1, Len), 0);
    Delete (Text, 1, Len);
  end;
  UpdateTabStops;
  Invalidate;
end;
```

The UpdateTabStops method is actually the key element of this component. It sets the tab stops in the list box control that is owned by the component. To accomplish this, a program has to send an lb_SetTabStops message to the list box, passing as parameters the number of tabs you want to set and a pointer to an array of integers with the tab values:

```
SendMessage (Handle, lb_SetTabStops,
  1 + High (ConvertedTabs) - Low (ConvertedTabs),
  LongInt (@ConvertedTabs));
```

Using Dialog Box Units

In the code above, ConvertedTabs is another TTabsArray variable. You cannot pass the FTabStops array directly because the list box uses different units of measurement. In fact, the list box tab stops are expressed in dialog box units, even if you place the list box in a generic window (or any kind of form or container component). However, I don't want to force programmers to use these units; I want to let them work in pixels. For this reason, I've added some conversion code to the UpdateTabStops method.

First of all, dialog box units are a unit of measure based on the dialog's font. They are used to make dialog box measurements independent of the screen resolution or (to be more precise) the default font size. Dialog box units are computed by taking the average character width and height and dividing them by 4 and 8, respectively. Now, how do you make this a conversion to dialog box units? The Windows API function GetDialogBaseUnits returns the base value of the dialog box units (the x in the low word and the y in the high word), so you might think you could write this code:

```
XDialog := XPixels * 4 div LoWord (GetDialogBaseUnits);
```

However, this function is not reliable. It works only for dialog boxes (or list boxes) using the system font. Instead, you can compute the average width of the font in your code. You should use code like the one Windows itself uses, which is based on the GetTextExtent API function. In Delphi, we can use the TextWidth method of the TCanvas class instead. The standard Windows approach is to take the 26 uppercase and 26 lowercase characters, measure the total width, and compute the average by dividing by 52 (twice the number of letters in the US alphabet):

```
HUnits := Canvas.TextWidth (
  'ABCDEFGHIJKLMNOPQRSTUVWXYZabcdefghijklmnopqrstuvwxyz')
  div 52;
```

Of course, you should set the font first, as you can see in the following listing. When you have the base dialog box units, you can easily compute the new value for each of the tabs and set them in the Windows list box control.

So, after this detailed discussion, here is the complete source code of the UpdateTabStops method:

```
procedure TMd3TabbedList.UpdateTabStops;
var
  I: Integer;
  HUnits: Integer;
  ConvertedTabs: TMd3TabsArray;
begin
  {determine the horizontal dialog box units used
  by the list box, which depend on its current font}
  Canvas.Font := Font;
  HUnits := Canvas.TextWidth (
    'ABCDEFGHIJKLMNOPQRSTUVWXYZabcdefghijklmnopqrstuvwxyz')
    div 52;
  {convert the array of tab values}
  for I := Low (ConvertedTabs) to High (ConvertedTabs) do
    ConvertedTabs [I] := (FTabStops [I] * 4) div HUnits;
  {activate the tabs stops in the list box,
  sending a Windows list box message}
  SendMessage (Handle, lb_SetTabStops,
    1 + High (ConvertedTabs) - Low (ConvertedTabs),
    LongInt (@ConvertedTabs));
end;
```

You can now install the component as usual and provide a new bitmap instead of using the one for the list box. Actually, this component (and its bitmap) are part of the Md3Pack package.

> **TIP**
>
> If you want to build the compiled unit of a component, among other approaches, you can open its source file as if it were a project file (using the Delphi Open Project command). When you have done this, you can check the syntax of the component and compile it into the DCU format.

A Header and a Tabbed List Box

Now I want to test the tabbed list box with the most typical example: adding a Header component above it to let the user adjust the position of the tabs at run-time. The positions of the tab stops in the list box are set at the beginning, in the FormCreate method, and in the Header1Sized method each time one of the header separators is moved.

Both procedures are based on a similar array, which computes the tab positions by adding the size of each header to those of the preceding headers. In fact, tabs have an absolute value, while the position of the header component's separators is indicated as the width of each section relative to the previous one. Here is the code common to both methods:

```
for I := 0 to Header1.Sections.Count - 1 do
begin
  Md3TabbedList1.TabStops [I] :=
    Header1.SectionWidth [I] + Last;
  Last := Header1.SectionWidth ;
end;
```

The FormCreate method has another for loop to set the other tab stops to a high value (the actual number used is not important) so that they won't interfere:

```
for I := Header1.Sections.Count to 9 do
    Md3TabbedList1.TabStops [I] := 1000;
```

When you use this code, the list box tabs are automatically resized with the header sections, giving you a nice effect. As you can see in Figure 18.14, this works with any font, not just the system font. The critical code is not in this example, but in the tabbed list box component it uses. That's the power of Delphi components. Notice that we might further extend this example by creating a single component that features a tabbed list box with a header. This would indeed be a useful component, if Microsoft had not added to Windows 95 a specific ListView control with this capability built in.

FIGURE 18.14

The output of the TabTest2 example.

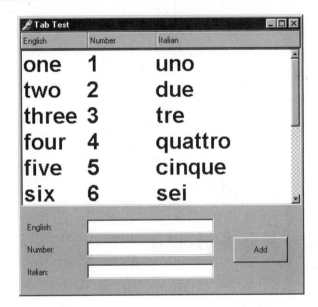

On the down side, notice that the tab characters of the list box are indeed tabs. This means that if you move the second column too close to the first one, some of the tabs will disappear, depending on the length of the words in the first column. You can see an example of this behavior, which is not a bug but is as designed, in Figure 18.15. To solve this problem, you might compute the size of a tab by checking the length of each of the strings in the first column with the current font.

This component is nice but lacks a fundamental feature: although it is possible to provide the initial values of the tabs at design time using the semicolon-separated string, it would be much better (and a little more foolproof) to provide a custom editor for this property. To accomplish this we'll have to write a specific property editor, something that will be described in the next chapter.

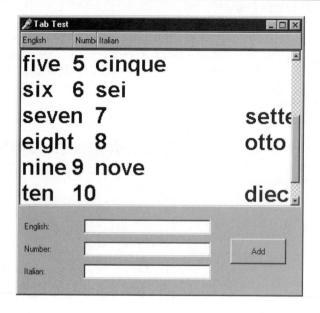

FIGURE 18.15

The behavior of the tabbed list box when tabs are too short.

Building a Nonvisual Component

The last component we'll examine in this chapter is completely different from the ones we have seen up to now. After building window-based controls, and simple graphic components, I'm now going to build a nonvisual component.

The basic idea is that forms are components. When you have built a form that might be particularly useful in a number of projects, you can add it to the Object Repository or make a component out of it. The second approach is more complex than the first one, but it makes using the new form easier, and it allows you to distribute the form without its source code. As an example, I'll build a component based on a custom dialog box, trying to mimic as much as possible the behavior of standard Delphi dialog box components.

A Dialog Box in a Component

The first step in building a dialog box in a component is to write the code of the dialog box itself, using the standard Delphi approach. Just define a new form and work on it as usual. When a component is based on a form, you can almost visually design the component. Of course, once the dialog box has been built, you have to define a component around it in a nonvisual way.

The standard dialog box I want to build is based on a list box, because it is common to let a user choose a value from a list of strings. I've customized this common behavior in a dialog box and then used it to build a component. The simple List-BoxForm form I've built has a list box and the typical OK and Cancel buttons, as shown in its textual description

```
object ListBoxForm: TListBoxForm
  BorderStyle = bsDialog
  Caption = 'ListBoxForm'
  object ListBox1: TListBox
    OnDblClick = ListBox1DblClick
  end
  object BitBtn1: TBitBtn
    Kind = bkOK
  end
  object BitBtn2: TBitBtn
    Kind = bkCancel
  end
end
```

The only method of this dialog box form relates to the double-click event of the list box, which closes the dialog box as though the user clicked on the OK button:

```
procedure TListBoxForm.ListBox1DblClick(Sender: TObject);
begin
  ModalResult := mrOk;
end;
```

Once this form works, we can start changing its source code, adding the definition of a component, removing the declaration of the global variable for the form, and moving the form's type definition to the implementation portion. You can see the result of these operations in the source code of the example.

For components based on a form, you can use two Pascal source code files, one for the form, and the other for the component encapsulating it. In this example, instead, I've decided to place both classes (the form class and the component class) in a single unit. By declaring the form class in the implementation portion of this unit, I also hide it from the users of the component.

The most important of these operations is the definition of the TMd3ListBox Dialog component, a nonvisual component. What determines that this component is nonvisual is that its immediate ancestor class is TComponent. The component has three published properties and a public one. These are the three published properties:

- Lines is a TStrings object, which is accessed via two methods, GetLines and SetLines. This second method uses the Assign procedure to copy the new values to the private field corresponding to this property. This internal object is initialized in the Create constructor and destroyed in the Destroy method.

- Selected is an integer that directly accesses the corresponding private field. It stores the selected element of the list of strings.

- Title is a string used to change the title of the dialog box.

The public property is SelItem, a read-only property that automatically retrieves the selected element of the list of strings. Notice that this property has no storage and no data: it simply accesses other properties, providing a virtual representation of data:

```
type
  TMd3ListBoxDialog = class (TComponent)
  private
    FLines: TStrings;
    FSelected: Integer;
    FTitle: string;
    function GetSelItem: string;
    procedure SetLines (Value: TStrings);
    function GetLines: TStrings;
```

```
public
  constructor Create(AOwner: TComponent); override;
  destructor Destroy; override;
  function Execute: Boolean;
  property SelItem: string read GetSelItem;
published
  property Lines: TStrings read GetLines write SetLines;
  property Selected: Integer read FSelected write FSelected;
  property Title: string read FTitle write FTitle;
end;
```

Most of the code of this example is in the Execute method, a function that returns True or False depending on the modal result of the dialog box. This is consistent with the Execute method of most standard Delphi dialog box components. The Execute function creates the form dynamically, sets some of its values using the component's properties, shows the dialog box, and if the result is correct, updates the current selection:

```
function TMd3ListBoxDialog.Execute: Boolean;
var
  ListBoxForm: TListBoxForm;
begin
  if FLines.Count = 0 then
    raise EStringListError.Create ('No items in the list');
  ListBoxForm := TListBoxForm.Create (self);
  try
    ListBoxForm.ListBox1.Items := FLines;
    ListBoxForm.ListBox1.ItemIndex := FSelected;
    ListBoxForm.Caption := FTitle;
    if ListBoxForm.ShowModal = mrOk then
    begin
      Result := True;
      Selected := ListBoxForm.ListBox1.ItemIndex;
    end
    else
      Result := False;
  finally
    ListBoxForm.Destroy;
  end;
end;
```

Notice that the code is contained within a `try-finally` block, so if a run-time error occurs when the dialog box is displayed, the form will be destroyed anyway. I've also used exceptions to raise an error if the list is empty when a user runs it. This error is by design, and using an exception is a good technique to enforce it. The other methods of the component are quite straightforward:

```
constructor TMd3ListBoxDialog.Create(AOwner: TComponent);
begin
  inherited Create (AOwner);
  FLines := TStringList.Create;
  FTitle := 'Choose a string';
end;

destructor TMd3ListBoxDialog.Destroy;
begin
  FLines.Free;
  inherited Destroy;
end;

function TMd3ListBoxDialog.GetSelItem: string;
begin
  if Selected >= 0 then
    Result := FLines [Selected]
  else
    Result := '';
end;

function TMd3ListBoxDialog.GetLines: TStrings;
begin
  Result := FLines;
end;

procedure TMd3ListBoxDialog.SetLines (Value: TStrings);
begin
  FLines.Assign (Value);
end;
```

Of course, since we are manually writing the code of the component and adding it to the source code of the original form, we have to remember to write the `Register` procedure. This is one of the many changes I've made to the typical structure of a form's code, as you can see from the full listing on the companion CD (in the ListDial subdirectory).

Using the Nonvisual Component

Now that the component is ready, you must provide a bitmap. For nonvisual components, bitmaps are very important because they are used not only for the Components palette, but also when you place the component on a form. Now let's prepare the bitmap, install the component, and write a simple project to test it. The form of this test program has simply a button, an edit box, and our new nonvisual component, as you can see in Figure 18.16.

FIGURE 18.16

The form of the LdTest example, with the new nonvisual component.

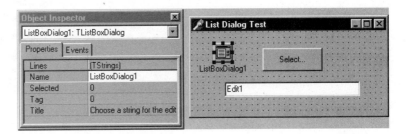

Now you can write a few lines of code, corresponding to the OnClick event of the button:

```
procedure TForm1.Button1Click(Sender: TObject);
begin
  with Md3ListBoxDialog1 do
    if Execute then
      Edit1.Text := SelItem;
end;
```

That's all you need to run the dialog box we have placed in the component, as you can see in Figure 18.17. I think this is an interesting approach to the development of some common dialog boxes.

FIGURE 18.18

The LdTest example can show the dialog box we encapsulated in the ListDial component.

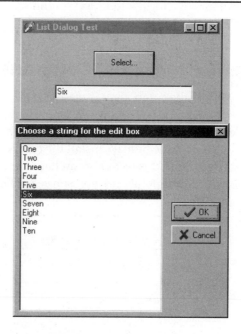

What's Next

This chapter was devoted to the design and creation of Delphi components. We have seen how to define various types of properties, how to add events, and how to define and override component methods. We have seen different examples of components, including simple changes to existing ones, new graphical components, and, in the final section, a dialog box inside a component. While building these components, we have faced some new Windows programming challenges. In general, it is not uncommon to have to use the Windows API directly when writing new Delphi components.

Writing components is a very handy technique for software reuse, but to make your components easier to use you should try to integrate them as much as possible within the Delphi environment. To accomplish this you can write property editors and component editors, a topic discussed in the next chapter. Chapter 19 also provides a general introduction to Delphi's ToolsAPI, which allows programmers to write new Wizards and Version Control Systems.

Components and the ToolsAPI

- Writing property editors

- Writing component editors

- Understanding wizards/experts

- Delphi ToolsAPI interfaces

Writing components is certainly a way to customize the Delphi environment, helping developers to build applications faster without requiring a detailed knowledge of low-level techniques. The Delphi environment is also quite open to third-party extensions. In particular, it is easy to extend the Object Inspector by writing custom property editors, and to extend the form designer by adding component editors. Another option is to create wizards (or experts), which generally involve adding new items to the Delphi menu. Along with these techniques, there are a number of internal interfaces Delphi offers to add-on tool developers. Using these interfaces requires an advanced understanding of how the Delphi environment works, and a fairly good knowledge of the many advanced techniques.

For these reasons, this chapter provides only a general introduction to these topics, giving a few examples but without any claim to completeness. For more advanced information about extending the Delphi environment you can refer to more advanced books, including *Delphi Developer's Handbook*.

Writing a Property Editor

In the last chapter we wrote a tabbed list box component with a special string property that held the values of a series of integers indicating the positions of the tabs. This approach allows users of this component to edit the values at design-time, using the Object Inspector. However, it isn't very convenient to input the sub-strings in a line of the Object Inspector, using semicolons as separators. Instead, we should provide a custom property editor.

Types of Property Editors

Every property editor must be a subclass of the abstract `TPropertyEditor` class, which is defined in the DsgnIntf (*Design Interface*) system unit. However, Delphi already defines some specific property editors for strings (the `TStringProperty` class), integers (the `TIntegerProperty` class), characters (the `TCharProperty` class), enumerations (the `TEnumProperty` class), sets (the `TSetProperty` class), and many others for colors, fonts, pens, string lists, and so on.

In any custom property editor, you have to redefine the `GetAttributes` function so it returns a set of values indicating the capabilities of the editor. You can see some of these attributes in the following table.

Attribute	Description
paValueList	The property editor provides a list of values to display in a combo box of the Object Inspector. The property editor must override the GetValues method to provide the list of values to Delphi.
paSubProperties	The property editor provides some sub-properties, displayed when the user clicks on the plus sign beside the property name. The property editor must override the GetProperties method to define a list of sub-properties.
paDialog	The property editor provides a custom editor in a stand-alone dialog box, deployed when the user clicks on the ellipsis button in the Object Inspector. The property editor must override the Edit method and display the dialog box when the method is called.
paMultiSelect	The property should be listed in the Object Inspector even if the user selects more than one component of the same kind, or components of different kinds sharing that property. This option is quite common.
paAutoUpdate	The property is updated continuously as the user changes a value in the editor (for example, while you type the value of the Caption of a component, you see it change on the screen). If this is not set, the value is updated only at the end of the editing process.
paSortList	The values of the list displayed by the Object Inspector (if paValueList is also set) are alphabetically sorted.
paReadOnly	The Object Inspector doesn't allow you to modify the property in the standard internal editor (that is, the edit area in the right-side of the Object Inspector window). It might still be possible to use a special property editor to change its value, though. Keep also in mind that this doesn't relate to read-only properties, which cannot show up in the Object Inspector. In our example, this is actually what we need in order to show the string with the tabs at design-time, but prevent the user from changing it directly in the Object Inspector.

An Editor for the TabsString Property

In the case of the TabsString property, I want to provide a custom editor in a dialog box. Since the property is of the string type, it is better to inherit the new property editor from the string property editor, as you can see in the definition of my new property editor class:

```
uses
  DsgnIntf;
type
  TMd3IntListProperty = class (TStringProperty)
  public
    function GetAttributes:TPropertyAttributes; override;
    procedure Edit; override;
  end;
```

> **TIP** The default Borland convention is to name a property editor class with a name ending with *Property*, and all Component Editors with a name ending with *Editor*.

The attributes indicate that I want to provide a custom editor in a dialog box, and also forbid a direct editing of the string in the Object Inspector:

```
function TMd3IntListProperty.GetAttributes:
  TPropertyAttributes;
begin
  Result := [paDialog, paReadOnly];
end;
```

I don't want to allow the user to select multiple components, because that would complicate the code of the Edit method. In this code, in fact, I want to access the array of component tabs directly, without having to use the TabsString property (the property the editor will be manipulating). Here is the code of the Edit method:

```
procedure TMd3IntListProperty.Edit;
var
  PEForm: TIntListPEForm;
  Tabs: TMd3TabbedList;
```

```
    I: Integer;
begin
  PEForm := TIntListPEForm.Create (Application);
  try
    Tabs := GetComponent (0) as TMd3TabbedList;
    for I := Low (TTabsArray) to
        High (TTabsArray) do
      PEForm.Memo1.Lines.Add (
        IntToStr (Tabs.TabStops [I]));
    if PEForm.ShowModal = mrOK then
    begin
      for I := Low (TTabsArray) to
          High (TTabsArray) do
        Tabs.TabStops [I] := StrToIntDef (
          PEForm.Memo1.Lines [I], 0);
      // the component data has changed
      Designer.Modified;
    end;
  finally
    PEForm.Free;
  end;
end;
```

This code uses a form I've built in a separate unit (included in this one), which has only a memo component to edit the numbers and three bitmap buttons to accept or reject the changes, or to restore the standard values of the property:

```
object IntListPEForm: TIntListPEForm
  Caption = ' TabString Property Editor'
  object Memo1: TMemo...
  object BitBtn1: TBitBtn
    Kind = bkOK
  end
  object BitBtn2: TBitBtn
    Kind = bkCancel
  end
  object BitBtn3: TBitBtn
    Caption = '&Reset'
    OnClick = BitBtn3Click
  end
end
```

The only code is that of the Reset button, which copies default values into the Lines of the memo:

```
procedure TIntListPEForm.BitBtn3Click(Sender: TObject);
var
  I: Integer;
begin
  for I := 0 to 9 do
    Memo1.Lines [I] := IntToStr (I * 100);
end;
```

Most of the code, in fact, is in the Edit method. If you look back at that listing, you'll see that the property editor accesses the component it is editing, calling the GetComponent method (the 0 parameter indicates the first component, and is useful when an editor is used to update several components at once). Once you begin editing the component, the Edit method can access its TabsStops array property directly, reading its values at the beginning and setting the modified ones at the end.

> **NOTE**
>
> When you modify a property of a component within a property editor, or a component editor, you need to call the Modified method of the Designer object. This object is basically the form designer, and by calling the method we indicate to the Delphi environment that some data is changed. This is fundamental for a correct handling of file saving operations. For example, when closing a modified unit Delphi automatically informs us that the data has changed, asking us if we want to save the changes. Forgetting the Designer.Modified call would mean losing the updates we've made to the components.

This code performs very limited input checking, simply setting values to 0 when the input is invalid. A real tabs property editor should check to make sure that the input is made up only of numbers (and no text) and see whether the relative values are reasonable for the tabs. For example, it should make sure that the values of the tabs are always increasing.

Installing the Property Editor

After you've written this code (you can find it in the PropEdit directory of this chapter on the companion CD), you can install the component and its property editor in Delphi. To accomplish this, you have to add the following statement to the `Register` procedure of the unit:

```
procedure Register;
begin
  RegisterPropertyEditor (TypeInfo (string),
    TMd3TabbedList, 'TabsString', TMd3IntListProperty);
end;
```

This call registers the editor specified in the last parameter for use with properties of type `string` (the first parameter), but only for a specific component and for a property with a specific name. These last two values can be omitted to provide more general editors. This code allows the Object Inspector to inspect the component's properties and use the dialog box called by the `Edit` method to enter new tab stop values, as you can see in Figure 19.1.

FIGURE 19.1

The TabStrings property in the Object Inspector and the corresponding property editor.

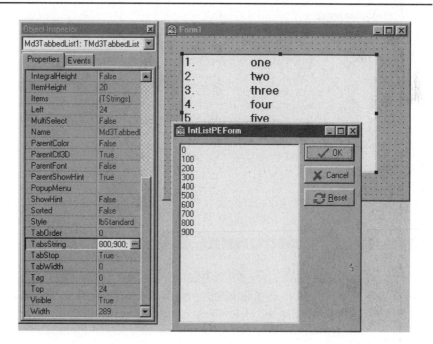

To install this component we should simply add its source code file into an existing or a new package. Instead of adding this unit and the others of this chapter to the Md3Pack package, I've decided to build a second package, containing all the add-ins built in this chapter, named Md3DesPk (which stands for "Md3 design package"). What's new about this package is that I've compiled it using the {$DESIGNONLY} compiler directive. This directive is used to mark packages that interact with the Delphi environment, installing components and editors, but are not required at run-time by applications you've built.

Notice that the unit of the property editor uses the TabList2 unit, which defines the TMd3TabbedList component. For this reason the new package should refer to the existing package. Here is its initial code (I'll add other units to it later in this chapter):

```
package Md3DesPk;

{$R *.RES}
{$ALIGN ON}
. . .
{$DESCRIPTION 'Mastering Delphi 3 DesignTime Package'}
{$DESIGNONLY}

requires
  vcl30,
  Md3Pack;

contains
  PropEdit,
  CompEdit,
  Wizard1,
  IlpeForm;

end.
```

Writing a Component Editor

Using property editors allows the developer to make a component more user-friendly. In fact, the Object Inspector represents one of the key pieces of the user interface of the Delphi environment, and Delphi developers use it quite often. However, there is a second approach you can adopt to customize how a component interacts with Delphi: write a custom component editor.

Just as property editors extend the Object Inspector, component editors extend the form designer. In fact, when you right-click on a form at design-time, you see some default menu items, plus the items added by the component editor of the component. Examples of these menu items are those used to activate the Menu Designer, the Fields Editor, the Visual Query Builder, and other editors of the environment. At times, displaying these special editors becomes the default action of the component when activated with a double-click.

Common uses of component editors include adding an About box with information about the developer of the component, adding the component name, and providing specific wizards to set up its properties.

Subclassing the TComponentEditor Class

A component editor should inherit from the TComponentEditor class. This class has four virtual methods you can override (plus a couple of less important methods I've decided to skip here):

- GetVerbCount returns the number of menu items to add to the local menu of the form designer when the component is selected.

- GetVerb is called once for each new menu item, and it should return the text that should go in the local menu for each.

- ExecuteVerb is called when one of the new menu items is selected. The number of the item is passed as parameter.

- Edit is called when the user double-clicks on the component in the form designer to activate the default action.

Once you get used to this idea that a verb is nothing but a new menu item with a corresponding action to execute, the names of the methods of this interface become quite intuitive. This interface is actually much simpler than those of property editors we've seen before.

A Component Editor for the Tabbed List

Now that I've introduced the key ideas about writing component editors, we can look at an actual example. In my component editor I simply want to be able to show an About box, add a copyright to the menu (an improper but very common use of component editors), and allow users to perform a special action, resetting the tabs. I also want to change the default action to simply show the About box after a beep (which is not particularly useful, but it demonstrates the technique).

To implement this property editor, we have to override the four methods listed above:

```
uses
  DsgnIntf;

type
  TMd3TabListEditor = class (TComponentEditor)
    function GetVerbCount: Integer; override;
    function GetVerb(Index: Integer): string; override;
    procedure ExecuteVerb(Index: Integer); override;
    procedure Edit; override;
  end;
```

The first method simply returns the number of menu items I want to add to the local menu:

```
function TMd3TabListEditor.GetVerbCount: Integer;
begin
  Result := 3;
end;
```

This method is called only once, before displaying the menu. The second method, instead, is called once for each menu item, so in this case it is called three times:

```
function TMd3TabListEditor.GetVerb (
  Index: Integer): string;
begin
  case Index of
    0: Result := 'Md3TabbedList (©Cantù)';
    1: Result := '&About this component...';
    2: Result := '&Reset Tabs';
  end;
end;
```

The effect of this code is to add the menu items to the local menu of the form, as you can see in Figure 19.2. Selecting any of these menu items simply activates the ExecuteVerb method of the component editor:

```
procedure TMd3TabListEditor.ExecuteVerb (
  Index: Integer);
```

```
var
  I: Integer;
begin
  case Index of
    0..1: MessageDlg (
      'This is a simple component editor'#13 +
      'built by Marco Cantù'#13 +
      'for the book "Mastering Delphi 3"',
      mtInformation, [mbOK], 0);
    2: begin
      with Component as TMd3TabbedList do
        for I := Low (TTabsArray) to High (TTabsArray) do
          TabStops [I] := I * 100;
      // data has changed
      Designer.Modified;
    end;
  end;
end;
```

FIGURE 19.2

The custom menu items added by the property editor of the Md3TabbedList component.

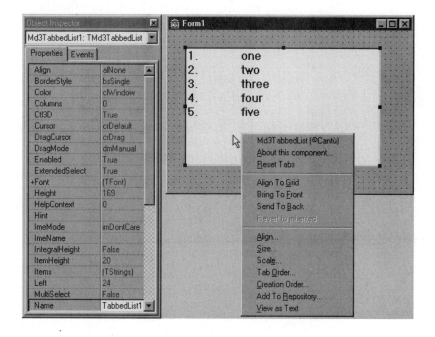

I decided to handle the first two items in a single branch of the **case** statement, although I could have skipped the code for the copyright notice item. The other command changes some of the data, accessing the component we are editing using the Component property of the TComponentEditor class. Knowing the type of the component, we can easily access its property after a dynamic type cast (Component as TMd3TabbedList).

The last method refers to the default action of the component, and is activated by double-clicking on it in the form designer:

```
procedure TMd3TabListEditor.Edit;
begin
  // produce a beep and show the about box
  Beep;
  ExecuteVerb (0);
end;
```

Registering the Component Editor

To make this editor available to the Delphi environment we need to register it. Once more we can add to its unit a **Register** procedure, and call a specific registration procedure for component editors:

```
procedure Register;
begin
  RegisterComponentEditor (
    TMd3TabbedList, TMd3TabListEditor);
end;
```

I've added this unit to the **Md3DesPk** package, which includes all of the work of this chapter. After installing and activating this package you can create a new project, place a tabbed list component in it, and experiment with it.

Writing a Simple Wizard

Wizards (or *experts*, to use the traditional Delphi jargon) are another example of Delphi add-ons. Wizards can add new menu items to the menus of the Delphi environment, or add new items to the Object Repository. The role of a wizard is that of a "hook" the environment offers you to execute a custom procedure: the Execute method of your wizard class. All the rest of the code of an expert, as we'll see, is simply used to install it within Delphi, and to specify its features and its appearance.

From this description you might think that the role of wizards is limited. On the contrary, wizards can be very powerful because Delphi exposes much of its functionality through object oriented interfaces, allowing you to interact with the environment in many complex ways. The details are beyond the scope of this book, but we'll see at least some of the key elements.

Subclassing the TIExpert Class

The ExptIntf unit defines the TIExpert class. This is the class we must inherit from in order to create a new expert or wizard. Unlike the other internal classes we've discussed in this chapter, this class is actually an interface class, as indicated by the initial letters of its name, TI.

> **NOTE** As we'll see in the next two chapters, Delphi can use interfaces to share objects between an executable file and a library. Actually Delphi 3 does the same for plain components, but the internal Delphi interfaces (collectively known as the ToolsAPI) have retained the structure they had in previous versions of Delphi. Note that the term *interface* here has a similar meaning, but no direct connection, to the new interface keyword and other COM-related elements we'll start discussing in Chapter 21.

When you subclass the TIExpert class you can override its virtual methods. Although this is not strictly necessary, it is common to override each of the methods, which are defined as abstract in the TIExpert class. Here is a very short description of each of these methods:

- The function GetStyle returns the type of expert. It can be a standard expert, which appears in the Help menu, a form or project expert which appears in the Object Repository, or an add-in expert, which can install itself in any Delphi menu.

- The function GetName returns the name of the expert.

- The function GetAuthor returns the author of the expert, displayed in the Object Repository when you choose the detailed view.

- The function GetComment returns a description of the expert.

- The function GetPage returns the name of the page of the Object Repository where you want to install the expert.

- The function GetGlyph returns the handle of the icon used by the Object Repository to represent the expert.

- The function GetState returns the status of the expert, which can be enabled (checked)or not.

- The function GetIDString returns a unique string identifier for the expert.

- The function GetMenuText returns the text of the menu item used by a standard expert.

- The procedure Execute contains the actual code of the expert.

Writing a "Stupid" Wizard

With this information available we can now write a simple, totally useless wizard. This wizard will have only one feature, displaying the name of the current Delphi project, if any.

This is the default structure of the class of a wizard:

```
uses
  ExptIntf, Windows;

type
  TMd3Expert = class (TIExpert)
  public
    function GetStyle: TExpertStyle; override;
    function GetName: string; override;
    function GetAuthor: string; override;
    function GetComment: string; override;
    function GetPage: string; override;
    function GetGlyph: HICON; override;
    function GetState: TExpertState; override;
    function GetIDString: string; override;
    function GetMenuText: string; override;
    procedure Execute; override;
  end;
```

The code of most of these methods is terribly simple, and some of them simply return zero or an empty string. Others return something but will never be called, because we are implementing the simplest kind of expert, a standard expert. Skipping these useless methods (you can find their code in the source file, in the Expert1 directory), here is the rest of the code of the wizard:

```
function TMd3Expert.GetStyle: TExpertStyle;
begin
  // show up in the Help menu
  Result := esStandard;
end;
function TMd3Expert.GetName: string;
begin
  // official name
  Result := 'Md3 Expert'
end;
function TMd3Expert.GetState: TExpertState;
begin
  // always enabled, never checked
  Result := [esEnabled];
end;
function TMd3Expert.GetIDString: string;
begin
  // must be unique
  Result := 'MarcoCantu.Md3Expert'
end;
function TMd3Expert.GetMenuText: string;
begin
  // the text of the menu item
  Result := '&Md3 Expert...'
end;
procedure TMd3Expert.Execute;
begin
  // the actual code
  MessageDlg ('Mastering Delphi 3 Wizard'#13#13+
    'Project:'#13 + ToolServices.GetProjectName,
    mtInformation, [mbOK], 0);
end;
```

The effect of this code is quite simple. First, a new menu item is added to the Delphi Help menu, as you can see in Figure 19.3. Second, when you select this menu item, the wizard displays a message box with the name of the current Delphi project, as you can see in Figure 19.4.

FIGURE 19.3

The Wizard1 standard expert adds a menu item under the Help menu of Delphi.

FIGURE 19.4

The simple output of the expert discussed in this section: the only information returned is the name of the current Delphi project.

To access this simple information, the Execute method of the expert uses a method of the internal ToolServices global object. This object, of class TITool-Services, is available only at design time and is an interface to the Delphi environment. The next section gives a short overview of this and other ToolsAPI interfaces.

Other Interfaces of the ToolsAPI

Property editors, component editors, and wizards (or experts) are not the only internal "interfaces" exposed by Delphi to the developers of add-on tools. For example, Delphi exposes an "internal" interface that allows programmers to write their own version control system, which adds its own pull-down menu to the Delphi environment.

There are also many internal interfaces that add-in writers should be aware of. We've already used in very simple ways the `Designer` object of a property in a component editor, and the internal `ToolServices` global object in the code of the wizard. In the following table there is a short summary of the most important internal interfaces of Delphi. Discussing the details of these interfaces and showing examples of their use is far beyond the scope of this book.

Interface	Description
TFormDesigner	Allows property and component editors to inter act with the form designer, and with other components of the current design-time form.
TIToolServices	This interface exposes the status of Delphi, including information on the current project, the editors, the VCL components installed, the menu structure of the Delphi environment, the internal notifications, and many others.
TIModuleInterface	This is the starting point to navigate the current information of a unit, including its editor interface and its form interface (see below) but also to install a *notifier* that will receive events from the system when the user does operations such as loading, saving, or renaming a unit.
TIEditorInterface	Along with TIEditReader, TIEditWriter, and TIEditView, allows programmers to interact with the Delphi editor, reading or modifying the current code. The use of these interfaces is particularly complex.
TIFormInterface	Along with TIComponentInterface allows a programmer to interact with Delphi forms at design-time.
TIStream	The TIStream class and its derived classes are used by other internal routines to access files. They are similar to the standard TStream classes.

Interface	Description
TMenuItemInterface	Allows you to access the items of the Delphi menu, and to modify them or add new ones. You can directly jump to a menu item using the TIMainMenu interface.
TIAddInNotifier	This interface provides global notification, related to operations on projects or the desktop.

Accessing Properties by Name

As you know, the Object Inspector shows a list of the published properties, even for components you write. To do this, it relies on the RTTI information generated for published properties. Using some advanced techniques, an application can retrieve a list of the published properties of an object, and use them.

NOTE This is basically what the Object Debugger tool I've built does. You can find this component in the TOOLS directory of the companion disk. The ideas behind this tool are fully discussed in the *Delphi Developer's Handbook* (by Marco Cantu and Tim Gooch, Sybex, 1997), along with more details about, and examples of, accessing properties by name.

Although this capability is not very well known, in Delphi it is possible to access properties by name simply by using the string with the name of the property, and then retrieving its value. Access to the RTTI information of properties is provided through a group of undocumented subroutines, part of the TypInfo unit.

WARNING The reason these subroutines are not documented is that Borland wants to be free to change them in future versions of Delphi. They have indeed changed from Delphi 1 to Delphi 3, but just a little. If you use them, be aware that you might need to update your code for future versions of Delphi.

Rather than explore the entire TypInfo unit here, we will look at only the minimal code required to access properties by name. Here is an introduction to some of the functions we'll use.

The GetPropInfo function of the TypInfo unit can be used to retrieve a pointer to some internal property information; the type of this pointer is PProfInfo. The GetPropInfo function requires as its parameter a pointer to some internal class information, something you can retrieve using the ClassInfo method of the TObject class. Here is a code fragment, used to access the property information for the Caption property of a button:

```
var
  PropInfo: PPropInfo;
begin
  PropInfo := GetPropInfo (
    Button1.ClassInfo, 'Caption');
```

To access the actual value of the property you can then use the GetStrProp function, which requires as parameters the object and the pointer to the property information structure we've just retrieved:

```
ShowMessage (GetStrProp (Button1, PropInfo));
```

Similar functions, including GetOrdProp and GetFloatProp, retrieve the value of properties of other data types. All of the code above has the same effect as calling ShowMessage, passing as parameter Button1.Caption. The only real difference is that this version of the code is much slower, since normal access to properties is generally resolved by the compiler in a more efficient way. Our step-by-step code, instead, requires a lot of work at run-time. The advantage of the run-time access is that you can make it very flexible, as in the following RunProp example.

This example shows in a list box the value of a property of the string data type for each component of a form. The name of the property we are looking for is provided in an edit box. This makes the program very flexible. Besides the edit box and the list box, the form has a button to generate the output, and some other components added only to test their properties. When you press the button the following code is executed:

```
uses
  TypInfo;
procedure TForm1.Button1Click(Sender: TObject);
var
  I: Integer;
```

```
      PropInfo: PPropInfo;
      Descr: string;
    begin
      ListBox1.Clear;
      for I := 0 to ComponentCount -1 do
      begin
        Descr := Components[I].Name + '.' + Edit1.Text;
        // get property RTTI
        PropInfo := GetPropInfo (
          Components[I].ClassInfo, Edit1.Text);
        if PropInfo = nil then
          // if not found, output a message
          ListBox1.Items.Add (Descr + ' doesn''t exist')
        else if PropInfo.PropType^.Kind <> tkLString then
          // if not a string, output a message
          ListBox1.Items.Add (Descr + ' is not a string')
        else
          // show the value
          ListBox1.Items.Add (Descr + ' = [' +
            GetStrProp (Components[I], PropInfo) + ']');
      end;
    end;
```

Besides demonstrating the GetPropInfo and GetStrProp functions, this method does two more things. It tests whether the result of GetPropInfo is nil, which corresponds to testing whether the property exists. If it exists, it checks the type of the property, using the expression PropInfo.PropType^.Kind. This is used to access some of the internal property information. The code checks this value against tkLString, a constant defining the type of long strings. Here are some other types:

tkInteger	tkEnumeration
tkChar	tkSet
tkClass	tkFloat
tkMethod	

You can see the effect of pressing the Fill List button while using the default 'Caption' value in the edit box in Figure 19.5. You can try other values, such as 'Top', 'Text', 'Name', 'Items', and any other property name.

FIGURE 19.5

The output of the RunProp example, which accesses properties by name at run-time.

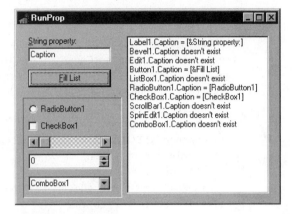

WARNING

Now that I've shown you this example, do not use it instead of other property-access techniques. Use base-class property access first, or use the safe as typecast when required, and reserve RTTI access to properties as a very last resort. This techniques makes your code slower, more complex, and more error-prone, it skips the compile-time type-checking, and it makes the code less portable to future versions of Delphi.

What's Next

The companion CD includes some wizards and some property editors I've built. Some of them, such as my custom component expert, are much simpler and less powerful than commercial third-party tools having the same purpose, but they can be useful.

After discussing components and delving a little into the Delphi environment, the next chapter focuses on Delphi DLLs. We have already met DLLs in many chapters in the past, and it is time for a detailed discussion of their role, and of how to build them. This will serve as a required basis before starting to look into a huge topic, OLE and COM programming. Actually the Delphi interfaces I've just introduced use an approach very similar to COM, as we'll see in Chapter 21. But first, let us cover DLLs.

CHAPTER
TWENTY

20

Dynamic Link Libraries

- DLLs in Windows 95 and NT

- Using a C++ DLL in Delphi

- Using a Delphi form in Word

- Building a DLL of icons

- Calling DLL functions at run-time

Windows executable files come in two flavors: *programs* and *dynamic link libraries* (DLLs). When you write a Delphi application, you typically generate a program file, an EXE. However, Delphi applications often use calls to functions stored in DLLs: each time you call a Windows API function directly, you actually access a DLL. While Delphi 1 and Delphi 2 relied more on static linking than on dynamic linking for their own components and code, Delphi 3 allows programmers to use run-time DLLs also for the component library. When you create a package, you basically create a DLL. Delphi can also generate plain dynamic link libraries. The New page of the Object Repository includes a DLL skeleton generator, which generates very few lines of source code.

It is very simple to generate a DLL in the Delphi environment. However, some problems arise from the nature of DLLs. Writing a DLL in Windows is not always as simple as it seems, and debugging programs with multiple executable files (the main program and one or more DLLs) is often a headache. This chapter covers the basics of DLL programming from the Delphi point of view. As usual, I'll show some examples of what you can place in a Delphi DLL. However, I'll also show a couple of examples using other programming languages and environments, simply because one of the key reasons for writing a DLL in Delphi is to be able to call the DLL from a program written in another development environment and a different programming language.

The Role of DLLs in Windows

Before delving into the development of DLLs in Delphi and in other programming languages, I'll give you a short technical overview of DLLs in Windows, highlighting the key elements. We will start by looking at dynamic linking, then see how Windows uses DLLs, explore the differences between DLLs and executable files, and end with some general rules to follow when writing DLLs.

What Is Dynamic Linking?

First of all, you need to understand the difference between static and dynamic linking of functions or procedures. When a subroutine is not directly available in a source file, the compiler adds the subroutine to an internal table, which includes all external symbols. Of course, the compiler must have seen the declaration of the subroutine and know about its parameters and type, or it will issue an error.

After compilation of a normal—*static*—subroutine, the linker fetches the subroutine's compiled code from a Delphi compiled unit (or static library) and adds it to the executable. The resulting EXE file includes all the code of the program and of the units involved. The Delphi linker is smart enough to include only the minimum amount of code of the units used by the program, and link only the functions and methods that are actually used.

In the case of dynamic linking, which occurs when your code calls a DLL-based function, the linker simply uses the information in the external declaration of the subroutine to set up some tables in the executable file. When Windows loads the executable file in memory, it first loads all the required DLLs, and then the program starts. During this loading process, Windows fills the program's internal tables with the addresses of the functions in memory. If for some reason the DLL is not found, the program won't even start.

Each time the program calls an external function, it uses this internal table to forward the call to the DLL code (which is now located in the program's address space). Notice that this scheme does not involve two different applications. The DLL becomes part of the running program, and all the parameter passing takes place on the stack, as with any other function call.

You can see a sketch of how the program calls statically or dynamically linked functions in Figure 20.1. Notice that I haven't yet discussed compilation of the DLL—because I wanted to focus on the two different linking mechanisms first.

> **NOTE** The term *dynamic linking*, when referring to DLLs, has nothing to do with the late-binding feature of object-oriented programming languages. Virtual and dynamic methods in Object Pascal have nothing to do with DLLs. Unfortunately, the same term names both kinds of procedures and functions, which causes a lot of confusion. When I speak of dynamic linking in this chapter, I am referring not to polymorphism but to DLL functions.

There is another, less common approach to using DLLs, which is even more dynamic than the one we have just discussed. In fact, at run-time, you can load a DLL in memory, search for a function (provided you know its name), and call the function by name. This approach requires more complex code and is generally slower. On the positive side, you don't need to have the DLL available to start the program. We will use this approach in the DynaCall example at the end of the chapter.

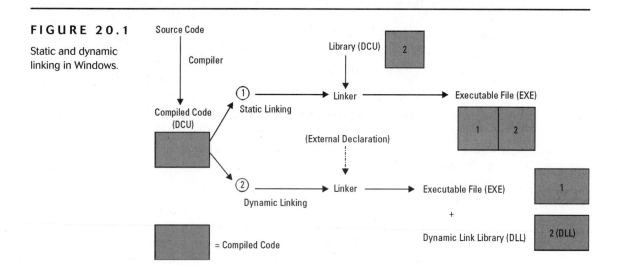

FIGURE 20.1

Static and dynamic linking in Windows.

What Are DLLs For?

Now that you have a general idea of how DLLs work, we can focus on the reasons for using them. Here are some of the reasons to use dynamic link libraries in Windows:

- If different programs use the same DLL, the DLL is loaded in memory only once, thus saving system memory. DLLs are mapped into the private address space of each process (each running application), but their code is loaded in memory only once, using a memory mapped file. In Windows 95, this file is placed at the same address in each process address space.

- You can provide a different version of a DLL, replacing the current one. If the subroutines in the DLL have the same parameters, you can run the program with the new version of the DLL without having to recompile it. If the DLL has new subroutines, it doesn't matter at all. Problems might arise only if a routine in the older version of the DLL is missing in the new one.

Versions of DLL Parameters

The most recent Windows API functions often use as a single parameter the pointer to a data structure, which includes the actual parameters. This approach allows the DLL creator to add new parameters to the data structure, without affecting the existing code. Typically, in these cases, the first parameter of the data structure holds its size, which is used to indicate the *version* of the structure. This way, the DLL can determine which version of the data structure the application refers to, simply by looking at this size/version parameter. This is a useful approach to follow if you think the parameters of a function are likely to change in future versions of the DLL.

For actual examples, you can look at the Windows API functions for the common dialog boxes (such as `GetOpenFileName` or `ChooseColor`) in the Help file, but many other new API func1tions use the same approach.

These generic advantages apply in several cases. If you have some complex algorithm, or some complex forms required by several applications, you can store them in a DLL. This will let you reduce the executable's size and save some memory when you run several programs using those DLLs at the same time.

The second advantage is particularly applicable to complex applications. If you have a very big program that requires frequent updates and bug fixes, dividing it into several executables and DLLs allows you to distribute only the changed portions instead of one single large executable. This makes sense for Windows system libraries in particular. If Borland releases a new version of the Database Engine libraries or writes new SQL Links to access other SQL server databases, you won't need to recompile your application to take advantage of the changes.

Another common technique is to use DLLs to store nothing except resources (Windows resources will be covered in Chapter 27). You can build different versions of a DLL containing strings for different languages and then change the language at run-time, or you can prepare a library of icons and bitmaps and then use them in different applications.

Another key advantage, as I already mentioned, is that DLLs are independent of the programming language. Most Windows programming environments, including most macro languages in end-user applications, allow a programmer to call a subroutine stored in a DLL. This means you can build a DLL in Delphi and call it from C++, Visual Basic, Paradox, dBASE, Excel, WordPerfect, and many other Windows applications.

Understanding System DLLs

The Windows system DLLs take advantage of all the key benefits of DLLs I've just highlighted. For this reason, it is worth examining them. First of all, Windows has many system DLLs. The three central portions of Windows—Kernel, User, and GDI—are implemented using DLLs.

In Windows 95 the three key system libraries are duplicated in 16-bit versions (KRNL386.EXE, USER.EXE, and GDI.EXE) and 32-bit versions (KERNEL32.DLL, USER32.DLL, and GDI32.DLL). These two versions often call each other, in a process called *thunking*. In Windows NT, the system libraries have only 32-bit code. Other system DLLs are operating system extensions, such as the DLLs for common dialog boxes and controls, DDE, OLE, device drivers, fonts, ActiveX controls, and many others.

In the case of Windows itself, using DLLs is extremely important. In fact, DLLs are one of the key technical foundations of the Windows operating systems. Since each application uses the system DLLs for anything from creating a window to producing output, every program is linked to those DLLs. Let's take a minute to look at why you might have different versions of the same library.

First, consider device drivers: when you change your printer, you do not need to rebuild your application, or even buy a new version of the Windows GDI library, which manages the printer output. You only need to provide a specific driver, which is a DLL called by the GDI, to access your printer. Each printer type has its own driver, or DLL, making the system extremely flexible.

From a different point of view, version handling is important for the system itself. If you have an application compiled for Windows 3.1, you should be able to run it on Windows 95. Each version of Windows has different system code (and Windows 95 16-bit support actually corrects some Windows 3.1 quirks), but since each new version contains the older API functions, the old code still works, even though it cannot take advantage of the new API functions. However, old code can indeed take advantage of new features when an existing function's code changes. An obvious example is the user interface: if you build an application for Windows 3.1, you can run it on Windows 95, and it will automatically have different user interface elements. You have not recompiled your program; it used the features of the new system libraries, which were linked dynamically to it.

The system DLLs are also used as system-information archives. For example, the USER DLL maintains a list of all the active Windows in the system, and the GDI DLL holds the list of active pens, brushes, icons, bitmaps and the like. The free memory area of these two system DLLs is usually indicated with the term "free system resources" and plays a very important role in Windows, as we'll see in more detail in Chapter 26.

Using Packages Statically or Dynamically

In Delphi 3, component packages constitute a relevant type of DLL. Packages allow you to bundle a group of components, and then link the components statically (adding their code to the executable file of your application) or dynamically (keeping the component code in a DLL you'll distribute along with your program). We have already seen in the last chapter how to build a package. Now I want to underline advantages and disadvantages of the two forms of linking for a run-time package. There are many elements to keep in mind:

- Using a package as a DLL makes the executable files much smaller.

- Using a statically linked package allows you to distribute only part of its code. Generally the size of the executable file of an application plus the size of the required package DLLs requires is much bigger than the size of the statically linked program.

- If you distribute several Delphi applications based on the same packages, you might end up distributing less code.

- If you run several Delphi applications based on the same packages, you can save some memory space at run-time.

- If you use a package as a DLL, when you have a new, updated version of the package, you'll need to recompile the program or it will display an odd error message at startup and will not run.

- Keep in mind that when you make minor changes to a program, you can use a program to handle patches, so that you distribute only a file with the differences, not a complete copy of the files. This affects both the executable files and the packages themselves.

Differences between DLLs and EXEs

Now that you know the basic elements of dynamic linking and some reasons to use it, we can focus on the difference between a normal executable file (an EXE file) and a dynamic link library (a DLL file). For the most part, the internal structure of an EXE file and a DLL file is the same. It is when a DLL is loaded in memory that things change.

As I mentioned earlier, Windows loads in memory the code of a DLL only once. The same happens with an executable file, even if you run multiple copies. In both cases a module usage count mechanism ensures that the code is discarded when all programs using it terminate.

The key difference between programs and DLLs is that a DLL, even when loaded in memory, is not a running program. It is only a collection of procedures and functions that other programs can call. These procedures and functions use the stack of the calling program (the *calling thread*, to be precise). So another key difference between a program and a library is that a library doesn't create its own stack—it uses the stack of the program calling it. In Win32, because a DLL is loaded into the application's address space, any memory allocations of the DLL or any global data it creates reside in the address space of the main process.

Rules for DLL Writers

What I've described so far can be summarized in some rules for DLL programmers. A DLL function or procedure to be called by external programs must follow these guidelines:

- It has to be listed in the DLL's `exports` clause. This makes the routine visible to the outside world.

- In Delphi 3, exported functions should also be declared as `stdcall`, to use the standard Win32 parameter-passing technique, instead of the optimized `register` parameter-passing technique (which is the default in Delphi).

- In Win32, a DLL can use global data that won't be shared by calling applications. Each time an application loads a DLL, it stores the DLL's global data in its own address space (as we will see in the DllMem example later on).

Win16 and Win32 DLLs

Another important aspect of DLLs is that in Windows, DLLs come in two different flavors. There are Windows 3.1 (Win16) DLLs, and Windows NT or Windows 95 (Win32) DLLs. Libraries written with the 16-bit version of Delphi are of the first kind. Libraries compiled with 32-bit versions of Delphi are of the second kind.

Unfortunately, as I've already mentioned, 16-bit and 32-bit DLLs are *not* compatible. For example, you cannot call a 16-bit DLL from a Delphi 2 program. This is not a Delphi limitation but a general Windows problem. There is actually a solution: you can use Microsoft's thunk compiler to create the proper entry points for the different DLL type. This is what Windows 95 does to call 16-bit system libraries from a 32-bit application, or to call new 32-bit system libraries from old 16-bit applications. However, using the thunk mechanism is quite complex, provides low performance, and requires you to own this specific Microsoft tool. For these reasons, I won't discuss this topic any further.

Using Existing DLLs

Before we start writing DLLs in Delphi, what about using them? We have already done that in a number of examples in the book, when calling Windows API functions. As you might remember, all the API functions are declared in the system Windows unit. In the interface portion of the unit, functions are declared, as shown here:

```
function PlayMetaFile(DC: HDC; MF: HMETAFILE): BOOL; stdcall;
function PaintRgn(DC: HDC; RGN: HRGN): BOOL; stdcall;
function PolyPolygon(DC: HDC; var Points; var nPoints;
  p4: Integer): BOOL; stdcall;
function PtInRegion(RGN: HRGN; p2, p3: Integer): BOOL; stdcall;
```

Then, in the implementation portion, instead of providing their code, the unit refers to the external definition in a DLL:

```
const
  gdi32 = 'gdi32.dll';
function PlayMetaFile; external gdi32 name 'PlayMetaFile';
function PaintRgn; external gdi32 name 'PaintRgn';
function PolyPolygon; external gdi32 name 'PolyPolygon';
function PtInRegion; external gdi32 name 'PtInRegion';
```

The external definition of these functions refers to the name of the DLL they use. The name of the DLL must include the .DLL extension, or the program will work under Windows 95 but not under Windows NT. The other element is the name of the DLL function itself. The name directive is not necessary if the Pascal function (or procedure) name matches the DLL function name.

To call a function that resides in a DLL, you can provide its declaration and external definition, as shown above, or you can merge the two in a single declaration. Once the function is properly defined, you can call it in the code of your Delphi application just like any other function. There is nothing special about the calling syntax; it is just a normal function or procedure call.

As an example of how to call a DLL, I've written a new, very simple DLL in C++, with some useless functions, to show you how to call them from a Delphi application. I won't comment the C++ code in detail (it is basically C code, anyway) but will focus instead on the calls between the Delphi application and the C++ DLL. In Delphi programming it is common to use DLLs written in C or C++.

NOTE With the release of Borland C++ Builder (the Delphi "clone" based on the C++ language), the possibilities of sharing code between C++ and Object Pascal applications have increased exponentially. C++ Builder can directly read Pascal units and use Delphi components. What I'm discussing here is a more generic and traditional approach.

Building the C++ DLL

In the following listing, you can see the source code of the C++ file used to build the CppDll library. You should be able to compile this code with any C++ compiler; I've tested it only with Borland compilers (Borland C++ 5 and C++ Builder). Here is the complete C++ source code of the library:

```
#include <windows.h>

extern "C" __declspec(dllexport)
int WINAPI Double (int n)
{
    return n * 2;
}
```

```
extern "C" __declspec(dllexport)
int WINAPI Triple (int n)
{
    return n * 3;
}

__declspec(dllexport)
int WINAPI Add (int a, int b)
{
    return (a + b);
}
```

This code is very simple: the three functions perform some basic calculations on the parameters and return the result. Notice that all the functions are defined as with the WINAPI modifier, which sets the proper parameter-calling convention, and preceded by the __declspec(dllexport) declaration, which makes the functions available to the outside world.

Two of these C++ functions also use the C naming convention (indicated by the extern "C" statement), but one doesn't. We will see how this affects the way we call these functions in Delphi. The file above is the only source file of the CppDll project. Simply load it in a C++ environment (or load it as a project in C++ Builder), set the proper project options to compile it as a DLL, and the compiler will generate the DLL file. Of course, you can simply use the DLL file provided on the companion CD and concentrate on the real topic of this section, writing a Delphi program that calls a C++ DLL.

Declaring the C++ DLL Functions in Delphi

Now that I've written this DLL in C++, we can write a Delphi program to call it. The example, named CallCpp and stored in the same CPPDLL directory as the C++ DLL on the companion disk, is very simple. Its form has three buttons to call each function of the DLL, two SpinEdit components for the parameters and a read-only edit box to show the result of the sum.

The first thing you must do to write this program is provide a proper definition of the functions. To accomplish this we might first look into the DLL to see the names of the exported functions. If you are running Windows 95 and have installed the viewer for executable files (which comes with the system as an option), you can simply move to the DLL file in the Windows Explorer, click on it with the right mouse button, and choose the Quick View command. The viewer that appears lists some of the low-level technical information available for each executable file. What we are interested in right now is the *Export Table* section, as shown in Figure 20.2.

FIGURE 20.2

Windows 95 Quick View lets you explore a DLL or an EXE file. Here is the Export Table of the file CPPDLL.DLL.

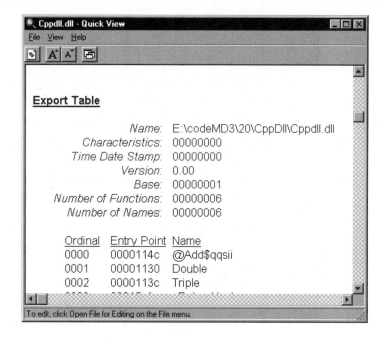

NOTE

Notice that each of the three functions has a name and also an index number (indicated as Ordinal). This index number was generally used for binding DLL functions in Windows 3.1. In Win32, Microsoft suggests that you bind DLL functions by name.

As an alternative to QuickView you can use the TDUMP32 command line program that comes with Delphi, which will give you even more details about the internal structure of the executable file.

The internal names of the three functions correspond to their names in the C++ source code file, except for the Add function. Since we didn't use the extern "C" clause for this function, the C++ compiler used *name mangling*: a technique used to include information about the number and type of parameters in the function name, something the C++ language requires to implement function overloading. The result when using the Borland C++ compiler is a funny function name: @Add$qqsii. This is actually the name we have to use in our Delphi example to call the Add DLL function (which explains why you'll generally avoid C++ name mangling in exported functions, and why you'll generally declare them all as extern "C").

The following is the declaration of the three functions in the Delphi CALLCPP example:

```
function Add (A, B: Integer): Integer;
  stdcall; external 'CPPDLL.DLL' name '@Add$qqsii';
function Double (N: Integer): Integer;
  stdcall; external 'CPPDLL.DLL ' name 'Double';
function Triple (N: Integer): Integer;
  stdcall; external 'CPPDLL.DLL ';
```

As you can see, you can provide an alias for an external function or not. I've done it for the first function (there was no alternative, because the exported DLL function name @Add$qqsii is not a valid Pascal identifier) and for the second, although in the second case it was unnecessary. If the two names match, in fact, you can omit the name directive, as I did for the third function above.

Remember to add the stdcall directive to each definition, so that the caller module (the application) and the module being called (the DLL) use the same parameter-passing convention. If you fail to do so, you will not always get a run-time error, but you will get a random function call, which is the worst outcome, since you might have trouble tracing this bug.

The output of the CallCpp example is very simple. If you click on one of the first two buttons, the value in the corresponding SpinEdit component is doubled or tripled:

```
procedure TForm1.BtnDoubleClick(Sender: TObject);
begin
  SpinEdit1.Value := Double (SpinEdit1.Value);
end;

procedure TForm1.BtnTripleClick(Sender: TObject);
```

```
begin
  SpinEdit2.Value := Triple (SpinEdit2.Value);
end;
```

When you click on the third button, the values of the two SpinEdit components are added, by calling the third function of the DLL, and displayed in the edit box. You can see an example of the output, after each button has been pressed once, in Figure 20.3.

FIGURE 20.3

The output of the CallCpp example when you have pressed each of the buttons.

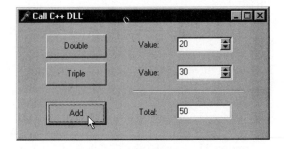

Here is the code of the OnClick event handler for the third button:

```
procedure TForm1.BtnAddClick(Sender: TObject);
begin
  Edit1.Text := IntToStr (Add (
    SpinEdit1.Value, SpinEdit2.Value));
end;
```

Notice that to run this application the DLL should be in the same directory as the project, in one of the directories on the path, or in the Windows or System directories. If you move the executable file to a new directory and try to run it, you'll get a run-time error indicating that the DLL is missing, as you can see in Figure 20.4.

FIGURE 20.4

The error message displayed when you run the CallCpp example and Windows cannot find the required DLL.

Creating a DLL in Delphi

Besides using DLLs written in other environments, you can use Delphi to build DLLs that can be used by Delphi programs, or with any other tool that supports DLLs. Building DLLs in Delphi is so easy that you might overuse this feature. In general, I suggest you try to build components and packages instead of plain DLLs. Packages are based on components, which allow you to write object-oriented code and to reuse it effectively, while placing a collection of subroutines in a DLL is a more traditional approach to programming.

When writing a DLL you generally export subroutines, functions, and procedures, although we'll see in the next chapter that Delphi also allows you to export class methods. Exporting class methods is related to COM, which will be discussed in the next chapter.

In general, when you build complex Delphi applications, you use object-oriented programming techniques to define your application's structure. If you later divide the application's code among DLLs, you lose this advantage.

It is useful to build libraries of small functions if the same functions have to be called from different environments. In particular, you can write DLLs in a compiled language like Object Pascal, and call them from interpreted environments. Of course, whenever possible, it's best to build the whole program in Delphi.

As I've already mentioned, building a DLL is also useful when a portion of the code of a program is subject to frequent changes. In this case you can frequently replace the DLL, keeping the rest of the program unchanged. Similarly, when you need to write a program that provides different features to different groups of users, you can distribute different versions of a DLL to different users.

A First Simple Delphi DLL

Before we study a real example, a form in a DLL, I'll show you a very simple DLL built in Delphi. This is more or less a new version of the DLL we just built in C++. The primary focus of this example will be to see the syntax you use to define a DLL in Delphi. To start, select the File ➤ New command and choose the DLL option in the New page of the Object Repository. This creates a very simple source file that starts with the following definition:

```
library Project1;
```

The `library` statement indicates we want to build a DLL instead of an executable file. Now you can add routines to the library, and list them in a specific `exports` statement:

```
function Triple (N: Integer): Integer; stdcall;
begin
  Result := N * 3;
end;

function Double (N: Integer): Integer; stdcall;
begin
  Result := N * 2;
end;

exports
  Triple, Double;
```

In this basic version of the DLL, I don't need a `uses` statement. I've actually changed the code slightly from the previous version to show a message each time a function is called. There are two ways to show a message. The simplest is to change the code as follows:

```
uses
  Dialogs;

function Triple (N: Integer): Integer; stdcall;
begin
  ShowMessage ('Triple function called');
  Result := N * 3;
end;
```

This code requires Delphi to link a lot of VCL code into the application. If you statically link the VCL, the resulting size will be 197 KB. A better alternative is to show the messages using direct API calls, so the VCL code is not required:

```
uses
  Windows;

function Triple (N: Integer): Integer; stdcall;
begin
  MessageBox (0, 'Triple function called',
    'First DLL', mb_OK);
  Result := N * 3;
end;
```

This change in code brings the size of the application down to only 14 KB. This huge difference underlines the fact that you should not overuse DLLs. In the source code of the example, in the companion CD, you'll find both versions of the library, one of which is commented. Changing the commented section you can easily alter the code and do your own experiments.

Calling the Delphi DLL

How can you use this library? You can call it from within another Delphi project or from other environments. As an example, I've built a new version of the Call-Cpp example, named CallFrst and stored in the FirstDLL directory on the companion CD. This new example has only the upper portion of the form of the previous version, without the Add button or the read-only edit box.

To access the DLL functions I must declare them as external, as we've done with the C++ DLL. This time, however, we can simply copy and paste the definition of the functions from the source code of the Delphi DLL:

```
function Double (N: Integer): Integer;
  stdcall; external 'FIRSTDLL.DLL';
function Triple (N: Integer): Integer;
  stdcall; external 'FIRSTDLL.DLL';
```

These declarations are similar to those used to call the C++ DLL. This time, however, we have no problems with function names. Besides this change and the removal of the third button, the source code of the example remains the same as in the CallCpp example, so I haven't listed it in the book. You can see the effect of the calls to the DLLs of this program (in the VCL based version) in Figure 20.5.

FIGURE 20.5

The output of the CallFrst example, which calls the DLL we've built in Delphi.

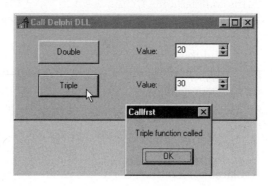

> **WARNING**
>
> If you run the program using the API-based version of the DLL, its behavior won't be correct. In fact, you can press the buttons several times without first closing the message boxes. This happens because the first parameter of the `MessageBox` API call is zero. Its value should instead be the handle of the program's main form. To fix this, you might write an initialization function that saves this value in the DLL data, and then use the value whenever one of the other functions is called. Complex Delphi DLLs often require a similar initialization function. In this case, the important thing is to copy some values from the `Application` global object to the corresponding object of the DLL. In particular, you should copy the `Handle` of the `Application` object of the executable to the same property of the `Application` object of the DLL.

A Delphi Form in a DLL

Besides writing simple DLLs with functions and procedures, you can place a complete form built with Delphi into a DLL. This can be a dialog box or any other kind of form, and it can be used not only by other Delphi programs, but also by other development environments or macro languages.

> **NOTE**
>
> There are two big exceptions to the general statement that DLLs cannot contain Delphi objects. One is the use of packages; the other is the use of the ActiveX and ActiveForm technologies. These technologies allow you to wrap a Delphi object in a special kind of DLL that can act as an OLE in-process server. More on this in Chapters 21 and 23.

To build the FormDLL example, I've started with the form of an existing example, ScrollC of Chapter 8. I've simply added two bitmap buttons to this form and set its `BorderStyle` property to `bsDialog`. The source code of the form, its type definition, and its code have no other changes.

I've only added a new function to the unit which defines the form. In the `interface` portion of the unit I've added the following declaration:

```
function GetColor (Col: LongInt): LongInt; stdcall;
```

The color passed as a parameter is used as the initial color, and the return value is the final color (which is the same as the initial color if the user clicks on the Cancel button). Here is the code of the function, added to the implementation portion of the same unit:

```
function GetColor (Col: LongInt): LongInt;
begin
  // default value
  Result := Col;
  try
    FormScroll := TFormScroll.Create (Application);
    try
      with FormScroll do
      begin
        {initialize the data}
        Shape1.Brush.Color := Col;
        Shape2.Pen.Color := Col;
        ScrollBarRed.Position := GetRValue (Col);
        ScrollBarGreen.Position := GetGValue (Col);
        ScrollBarBlue.Position := GetBValue (Col);
        {show the form}
        if ShowModal = mrOK then
          Result := RGB (ScrollBarRed.Position,
            ScrollBarGreen.Position,
            ScrollBarBlue.Position);
      end; // with
    finally
      FormScroll.Free;
    end;
  except
    on E: Exception do
      MessageDlg ('Error in FormDLL: ' +
        E.MEssage, mtError, [mbOK], 0);
  end;
end;
```

When you want to place a Delphi component (such as a form) in a DLL, you can only provide functions that create, initialize, or run the component or access its properties and data. The simplest approach is to have a single function that sets the data, runs the component, and returns the result, as in the current example. However, for complex cases, you might have to provide complex data structures as parameters, as discussed in the sidebar "Versions of DLL Parameters" earlier in this chapter.

Another important element is the structure of the code of the GetColor function. The code creates the form at the beginning, sets some initial values, and then runs the form, eventually extracting the final data. What makes this code different from the code we generally write inside a program is the presence of exception-handling code:

- The whole function is protected by a try-except block, so that any exception generated by the function will be trapped, displaying a proper message. The reason for handling every possible exception is that the calling application can be written in any language, in particular one that doesn't know how to handle exceptions. Even when the caller is a Delphi program, it is sometimes useful to use the same protective approach.

- The operations on the form are protected by a try-finally block, which ensures that the form object will be properly destroyed, even when an exception is raised.

By checking the return value of the ShowModal method, the program determines the result of the function. I've set the default value before entering the try block to ensure it will always be executed (and also to avoid the compiler warning indicating that the result of the function might be undefined). Notice also that I've passed as a parameter a long integer, which corresponds to the Windows COLORREF data type. Using TColor, a Delphi type, might have caused problems with non-Delphi applications: even though a TColor is very similar to a COLORREF these types don't always correspond. When you write a DLL, I suggest you use only Windows' native data types (unless the DLL is used only by Delphi programs).

Now that we have updated the form and written the code of the unit, we can move to the project source code, which becomes the following:

```
library FormDLL;

uses
  ScrollF in 'SCROLLF.PAS' {FormScroll};

exports
  GetColor;
end.
```

Calling the DLL Form from Delphi

We can now test the form we have placed in the DLL in a Delphi program. On the companion CD, the UseCol example is in the same directory of the previous DLL, FormDLL. The UseCol example is terribly simple. Its form contains only a button. When the user presses the button, the DLL function is called. Here is the definition of this function and the code of the Button1Click method:

```
function GetColor (Col: LongInt): LongInt;
  stdcall; external 'FormDLL.DLL';

procedure TForm1.Button1Click(Sender: TObject);
var
  Col: LongInt;
begin
  Col := ColorToRGB (Color);
  Color := GetColor (Col)
end;
```

Running this program (see Figure 20.6) displays the dialog box, using the current background color of the main form. If you change the color and click on OK, the program uses the new color as the background color for the main form.

FIGURE 20.6

The execution of the UseCol test program when it calls the dialog box we have placed in the FormDLL.

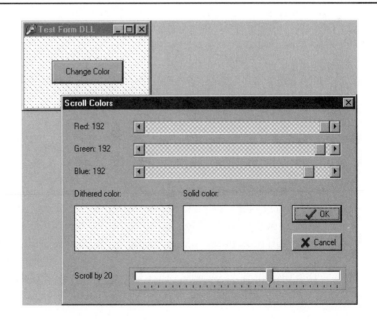

Calling a Delphi DLL from Visual Basic for Applications

We can also display this color dialog box from other programming languages. Calling this DLL from C or C++ is easy. To link this application, you need to generate an import library (using the IMPLIB command line utility) and add the resulting LIB file to the project. Since I've already used a C++ compiler in this chapter, this time I will write a similar example using Microsoft Word for Windows and Visual Basic for Applications instead.

To start, open Microsoft Word, then open its Macro dialog box (with the Tools ➤ Macro menu item or a similar command, depending on your version of Word), type a new macro name, such as 'DelphiColor', and click the Create button. You can now write the following BASIC code, which declares the function of our DLL, calls it, and uses the result to add to the current document (by calling Insert) a description of the color with the amount of Red, Green, and Blue, and to display the total value in the status bar (by calling Print):

```
Declare Function GetColor Lib "FormDLL"(Col As Long) As Long
Sub MAIN
  NewColor = GetColor(0)
  Print "The code of the color is " + Str$(NewColor)
  Insert "Red:" + Str$(NewColor Mod 256) + Chr$(13)
  Insert "Green:" + Str$(Int(NewColor / 256) Mod 256) + Chr$(13)
  Insert "Blue:" + Str$(Int(NewColor / (256 * 256))) + Chr$(13)
End Sub
```

Unfortunately, there is no easy way to use RGB colors in Word, since Word's color schemes are based on fixed color codes. Here is an example of the output of this macro:

```
Red: 141
Green: 109
Blue: 179
```

The nice thing is that I've produced the three lines of text above text by running the macro while I was writing the text of this chapter. You can find the text of this macro in the file WORDCALL.TXT, in the directory of this DLL. If you want to test it, remember to copy the DLL file in one of the directories of the path, or in the windows\system directory first. Of course, you need Microsoft Word to run this program. However, other Microsoft Office applications (and also the macro languages of other office programs) probably require very similar code.

Building a DLL of Icons

Dynamic link libraries in Windows have many other uses. As an example, we'll build a DLL of icons and then load icons dynamically in a program. This will be the first time we access a DLL from an application at run-time, without the usual compile-time link. As a result, the program will run even if the DLL is not available.

To build a DLL from icons or other Windows resources, you need only prepare a resource file and link it to the library. For example, I've prepared a file with three resources, named *Icon_A*, *Icon_B*, and *Icon_C*, representing the corresponding letters. Once the resource file is ready (in this case, it is named ICONS.RES), you can write the simple source code for the DLL:

```
library Iconsdll;
{$R ICONS.RES}
uses
  Windows;
end.
```

The uses statement is required only to avoid complaints from the Delphi environment that the project file structure is invalid. Build this program, and the ICONSDLL.DLL library will be ready to use. Consider this DLL a collection of icons and other resources, such as standard strings for error messages or bitmaps with company logos, to be used by several applications at the same time. In fact, if two applications use this DLL, only one copy of the resources will be in memory. However, if the same resource file is included in several programs, each program will load its own copy in memory.

Loading the Icons from the DLL

Now that we have built the DLL, we have to load it in a program. For this purpose, I've built a simple example, UseIcons (saved in the ICONSDLL directory), which allows users to enter the name of the icon they want to see. The form of this application contains an edit box with a corresponding label, a button, and an image component with a bevel around it. When the form is created, the program tries to open the DLL, calling the LoadLibrary API function:

```
procedure TForm1.FormCreate(Sender: TObject);
begin
  HInst := LoadLibrary ('Iconsdll.dll');
  if HInst = 0 then
    LoadButton.Enabled := False;
    ShowMessage ('Icons DLL not found');
  end;
end;
```

The LoadLibrary function returns the handle to the instance of the library. If this value is 0, it means that an error occurred. (To determine what happened, you'll have to call the GetLastError function.) The library's handle is saved in a private field of the form, HInst, because it is later used in the LoadButtonClick method to load an icon from the DLL (note that the button is enabled only if the library was successfully loaded).

In this event handler, the icon to load is indicated by name, using the text of the Edit component. Once the program has loaded the icon, its handle is used to set the new image (see Figure 20.7):

```
procedure TForm1.LoadButtonClick(Sender: TObject);
var
  HIcon: THandle;
begin
  HIcon := LoadIcon (HInst, PChar(Edit1.Text));
  if HIcon = 0 then
```

```
      ShowMessage ('Icon not found')
   else
      Image1.Picture.Icon.Handle := HIcon;
end;
```

FIGURE 20.7

The output of the
UseIcons program.

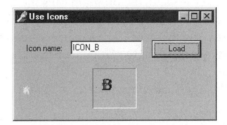

Of course, there's a chance the program won't find the icon. In this case, the
user sees an error message, and the image does not change. The last part of the
program is very important, too. When you load a library manually by using
LoadLibrary, you must remember to free it by using the FreeLibrary call:

```
procedure TForm1.FormDestroy(Sender: TObject);
begin
  FreeLibrary (HInst);
end;
```

If you forget to free the library, it will remain in memory until you exit Windows.

Calling a DLL Function at Run-Time

Now that we know how to access resources in a DLL at run-time, we might want
to use this approach to access a function. I've built a very simple example showing
this and made it quite flexible. Let me show you the example first, and then I'll
describe some general cases when this approach might be useful. The example is
named DynaCall and uses the FirstDLL library we built earlier in this chapter (to
make the program work I've copied the DLL in the directory of the new example).
Instead of declaring the Double and Triple function and using them directly,
this example obtains the same effect with somewhat more complex code. The

advantage, however, is that the program will also be able to access new functions in the DLL without changing its source code and recompiling it.

The form of this example simply contains a button, an edit box, and a SpinEdit component. Clicking the button executes the only method of the program. First, the method calls the LoadLibrary function. Then, if the handle of the library instance is valid, the program calls the GetProcAddress API function. This function searches the DLL, looking for the name of the function passed as a parameter. If GetProcAddress finds a match, it returns a pointer to the requested procedure. Now we can simply cast this function pointer to the proper data type and call it. The output of the program and the effect of this call are visible in Figure 20.8. Here is the (quite complex) code:

```
type
  TIntFunction = function (I: Integer): Integer; stdcall;

procedure TForm1.Button1Click(Sender: TObject);
var
  HInst: THandle;
  FPointer: TFarProc;
  MyFunct: TIntFunction;
begin
  HInst := LoadLibrary ('Firstdll.dll');
  if HInst > 0 then
  try
    FPointer := GetProcAddress (HInst,
      PChar (Edit1.Text));
    if FPointer <> nil then
    begin
      MyFunct := TIntFunction (FPointer);
      SpinEdit1.Value := MyFunct (SpinEdit1.Value);
    end
    else
      ShowMessage ('DLL function not found');
  finally
    FreeLibrary (HInst);
  end
  else
    ShowMessage ('Library not found');
end;
```

FIGURE 20.8

The output of the
DynaCall program.

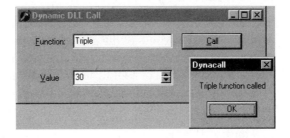

How do you call a procedure in Delphi, once you have a pointer to it? One solution is to convert the pointer to a procedural type and then call the procedure using the procedural-type variable, as I've done in the listing above. Notice that the procedural type you define must be compatible with the definition of the procedure in the DLL. This is the Achilles' heel of this method: there is no check of the parameter types.

What is the advantage of this approach? In theory, you can use it to access any function of any DLL at any time. In practice, it is useful when you have different DLLs with compatible functions or a single DLL with several compatible functions, as in our case. What we can do is to call the Double and Triple methods simply by entering their names in the edit box. Now if someone gives us a DLL with a new function receiving an Integer as parameter and returning an Integer, we can call it simply by entering its name in the edit box. We don't even need to recompile the application.

With this code, the compiler and the linker ignore the existence of the DLL. When the program is loaded, the DLL is not loaded immediately. We might make the program even more flexible and let the user enter the name of the DLL to use. In some cases, this is a great advantage. A program may switch DLLs at run-time, something the direct approach does not allow. Note that this approach to loading DLL functions is common in macro languages and is used by many visual programming environments. Also, the code of the Word macro we saw earlier in this chapter uses this approach to load the DLL and to call the external function. Well, you don't want to recompile Word, do you?

Only a system based on a compiler and a linker, such as Delphi, can use the direct approach, which is generally more reliable, much safer, and also a little bit faster. I think the indirect loading approach of the DynaLink example is useful only in special cases, but it can be extremely powerful.

A DLL in Memory

We can use this technique, based on the `GetProcAddress` API function, to test to which memory address of the current process a function has been mapped. We will use the same example to prove that two Win32 programs can easily access the same global data of a DLL, since they replicate this data in the private address space. This example, called DllMem, is based on two projects: a Delphi DLL and a Delphi application. Here is the full source code of the file `DLLMEM.DPR`:

```
library dllmem;

uses
  SysUtils;
var
  Data: Integer; // global DLL data

procedure SetData (I: Integer); stdcall;
begin
  if I <> Data then
    Data := I
  else
    Beep;
end;
function GetData: Integer; stdcall;
begin
  Result := Data;
end;

exports
  SetData, GetData;
begin
  // initialization
  Data := 1;
end.
```

The program has two simple routines that read or write a global memory location, initialized with a value of 1. When you store the same value again, the library emits a warning sound.

The code of the program using this DLL, UseMem, is very simple. The form of this application has two edit boxes, an UpDown control connected to one of them, three buttons, and a label. The first button saves the value of the first edit box, getting the value from the connected UpDown control:

```
procedure TForm1.Button1Click(Sender: TObject);
begin
  SetData (UpDown1.Position);
end;
```

If you press the second button, the program copies the DLL data to the second edit box:

```
procedure TForm1.Button2Click(Sender: TObject);
begin
  Edit2.Text := IntToStr(GetData);
end;
```

Finally, the third button is used to display in a label the memory address of the SetData function of the DLL:

```
procedure TForm1.Button3Click(Sender: TObject);
var
  HDLLInst: THandle;
begin
  HDLLInst := LoadLibrary ('dllmem');
  Label1.Caption := Format ('Address: %p', [
    GetProcAddress (HDLLInst, 'SetData')]);
  FreeLibrary (HDLLInst);
end;
```

If you run two copies of this program (as shown in Figure 20.9), you can see that each copy has its own value for the global data of the DLL. On the other hand, in Windows 95 each copy of the program will refer to the same memory address for the function, while in Windows NT values might be different. Actually, in Windows 95 this behavior does not prove that the DLL is loaded in memory once and then mapped to the same address in the process space of each application, rather than being loaded multiple times at the same address. In fact, the global memory data is probably at the same address in each process space, but is mapped to different physical memory locations.

FIGURE 20.9

If you run two copies of the UseMem program, you'll see that the global data in the USEMEM .DLL is not shared.

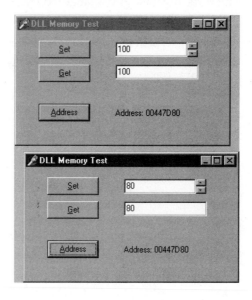

What's Next

In this chapter we have seen how you can call functions that reside in DLLs created in C++ or other languages, and how to create DLLs using Delphi itself. DLLs have been one of the traditional approaches to writing applications using multiple programming languages and environments. Today, COM and OLE provide more advanced techniques. However, this new technology still builds upon the DLLs, so we'll start the next chapter by looking at how we can place classes inside a DLL.

When considering DLLs and other alternatives, keep in mind that although Delphi and Windows share many elements, they also have different "views" of programming. When possible, follow the Delphi object-oriented approach over the Windows procedural-oriented approach, and you'll probably benefit a lot. Actually, the advantages of object orientation are so important that Microsoft has introduced some object-oriented concepts right into the system. In short, OLE and COM are examples of these built-in techniques.

The following chapters are fully devoted to these topics. Chapter 21 introduces COM and OLE, Chapter 22 covers OLE Automation and OLE Documents, and Chapter 23 the development of ActiveX controls. Chapter 24 will then apply some of the ActiveX techniques to Internet programming.

CHAPTER

21

OLE and COM

- What are OLE and COM?

- Objects in DLLs

- COM, GUIDs, and class factories

- Using Delphi 3 interfaces

- Using Windows 95 shell interfaces

According to Microsoft, OLE technology will have a fundamental role in the evolution of the Windows platform. Microsoft has used the term OLE to mean different things, so to understand this claim, we need to look into the details of what OLE is. Afterwards, we'll delve into the object model OLE is based upon, COM. This chapter shows that OLE is simpler than you probably think. OLE seems difficult because there are very few clear descriptions of what OLE is. In this chapter, we'll build our first COM object through a series of steps, starting with a plain Delphi DLL; this will help you understand the key elements of OLE technology. Towards the end of this chapter I'll also show you some examples of using the OLE interfaces included in the Win32 API. Actual applications of OLE will appear in the next and the following chapters.

What Is OLE? And What Is COM?

Part of the confusion related to OLE technology comes from the fact that Microsoft has used this name for different purposes. Everything started with Object Linking and Embedding (OLE, for short) which was an extension of the DDE (Dynamic Data Exchange) model. Using the Clipboard allows you to copy some raw data, and using DDE allows you to connect parts of two documents. Object Linking and Embedding allows you to copy the data from a server application to the client application, along with some information regarding the server, or a reference to some information stored in the Windows Registry. The raw data might be copied along with the link (Object Embedding) or kept in the original file (OLE Linking). We'll discuss this technology in more detail in the next chapter.

> **NOTE** Object Linking and Embedding documents have been renamed as OLE Documents, and now as Active Documents.

Microsoft updated OLE to OLE 2 and started adding new features, such as OLE Automation and OLE Controls. The next step was to build the Windows shell using OLE technology and interfaces, and then to rename the OLE Controls (previously known also as OCX) as ActiveX controls, allowing for lightweight controls suitable for distribution over the Internet.

As this technology was extended and became increasingly important to the Windows platform, Microsoft changed the name to OLE. This is no longer an abbreviation, but simply a name. These changes in naming only partially relate to technological changes and are driven to a large extent by marketing purposes.

What, then, is OLE? Basically, OLE is a technology that defines a standard way a client module and a server module can communicate through a specific interface. Here, "module" indicates an application or a library (a DLL), which can execute on the same or on different computers. There are many possible interfaces, depending on the role of the client and server, and you can even add new interfaces for specific purposes. These interfaces are implemented by server objects. A server object usually implements more than one interface, and all the server objects have a few common capabilities, since they must all implement the IUnknown interface. This is a very short description of the object model used by OLE, the Component Object Model.

By definition, COM is the implementation of OLE. In practice the terms OLE and COM are often used almost interchangeably. COM specifies the technical details of OLE, and any COM-compliant language can be used to write COM/OLE objects. C and C++ were the original languages used to write this code, but Delphi is fully compliant with COM. Actually, by looking at the source code, Object Pascal seems to be easier to use than C++ to write COM objects. This simplicity mainly derives from the introduction of interfaces in Delphi 3. By the way, this same idea of interfaces is used to integrate Java with COM on the Windows platform.

NOTE   For a full description of OLE and COM, the best reference is Kraig Brockschmidt's *Inside OLE*, 2nd edition, published by Microsoft Press. This book is the ultimate guide to OLE—but not a simple one—with examples in C++ and C. The book does not include Delphi code, though.

If OLE is a set of interfaces, it is important to note that these interfaces serve to communicate between two software modules, two executable files, or one executable file and a DLL. Implementing objects in DLLs is generally simpler, because in Windows 95 a program and the DLL it uses reside in the same memory address space. This means that if the program passes a memory address to the DLL, the address remains valid. When you use two executable files, OLE has a lot of work to do behind the scenes to let the two applications communicate. This mechanism is called *marshaling*.

Note that a DLL implementing OLE objects is described as an *in-process* server, while if the sever is a separate executable, it is called an *out-of-process* server. Throughout most of this chapter, we'll look at in-process servers, that is, an OLE server inside a DLL. The next chapters will also cover out-of-process servers. But first we need to learn how a DLL can export an object in Delphi.

Objects in DLLs

As we saw in the last chapter, DLLs are collections of functions. However, it is possible to place a class definition inside a DLL and then use objects of this class in a program that links to the DLL. Actually, a DLL doesn't usually export a class: it exports the virtual methods of the objects of that class.

In other words, the DLL should create the objects of the class. When the DLL has created an object, it can return the object to the calling application. Since every object contains a pointer to its virtual method table (see the section on late binding in Chapter 5), when the DLL returns the object it automatically returns also the memory addresses of the virtual methods of the class of the object. Of course, the executable file should be able to recognize these objects, so it should have a class declaration similar to the one inside the DLL.

Writing the Class in the DLL

In the next example, called DllObj, I'm going to show you how you can define a class inside a DLL and export its virtual methods. The DLL project includes a unit with the definition of the abstract class we want to export and a second unit with the definition of the implementation class. This is the definition of the abstract class in the first unit, called Base:

```
type
  TDllNumber = class
  public
    function GetValue: Integer; virtual; abstract;
    procedure SetValue (New: Integer); virtual; abstract;
    procedure Increase; virtual; abstract;
  end;
```

A class of this kind, with only virtual abstract methods, is often called a *purely abstract* class. This structure is actually very close to an interface, as we'll see in a while.

The TDllNumber class is so simple as to be almost useless, but I want you to concentrate on the techniques used to make it work, more than on the class itself. In this class declaration, you should notice that all the methods must be virtual and abstract. Only virtual methods are added to the VTable (or virtual method table), and only these methods can be exported from the DLL. The implementation class is derived from this abstract class, and is in a separate unit of the DLL:

```
type
  TDllNumberImpl = class (TDllNumber)
  private
    Value: Integer;
  public
    constructor Create;
    function GetValue: Integer; override;
    procedure SetValue (New: Integer); override;
    procedure Increase; override;
  end;
```

The actual code of the class contains nothing special. It is really straightforward:

```
constructor TDllNumberImpl.Create;
begin
  Value := 0;
  inherited Create;
end;
function TDllNumberImpl.GetValue: Integer;
begin
  Result := Value;
end;
procedure TDllNumberImpl.SetValue (New: Integer);
begin
  Value := New;
end;
procedure TDllNumberImpl.Increase;
```

```
begin
  Inc (Value);
end;
```

Besides the class we've just seen, the second unit of the DLL should include a function to create an object of the class:

```
function NewObject: TDllNumber;
begin
  Result := TDllNumberImpl.Create;
end;
```

Again, this function is very simple. It has to be declared as stdcall, and you should also add it to the exports clause of the DLL project file:

```
library DllObj;
uses
  DllClass in 'DllClass.pas';
exports
  NewObject;
end.
```

This is all we need to do to export a Delphi class from a DLL. We could have omitted the base class, and written a single class with all its methods virtual, but the approach I've used (defining an abstract class and an implementation class) is more elegant, and it requires just a little extra effort. This is not already a COM-compliant class, but I'll update it in later examples.

Using a Class from a DLL

Now we can try to use this class in a program, creating a couple of objects. The first thing we must do in the program is to redeclare the class. Since the declaration of the abstract class is in a separate unit, we can simply refer to this unit in the program. However, this time we are not going to write the implementation class, since we'll rely on that of the DLL. In fact the virtual abstract methods of the definition of the base class are used only as a placeholder to build the correct VTable of the DLL's class also in the program using it.

Actually what matters in the client program is to have an interface with virtual methods that have the same parameters and are listed in the same order. In fact I could have even redeclared the abstract class with methods having different names, as in:

```
type
  TDllNumber = class
  public
    function GetValue: Integer; virtual; abstract;
    procedure SetValue (New: Integer); virtual; abstract;
    procedure Inc; virtual; abstract;
  end;
```

The difference here is that I've changed the name of a method, from Increase to Inc. This won't affect the program at all!

WARNING The reason that a change in the method name doesn't affect the behavior of the program is quite complex. We have two class declarations, one in the DLL and one in the program. In these two declarations what matters is the *order* of the virtual methods, and their parameters—not their names. In fact, when a Delphi program calls a virtual function, it calls the function whose address is stored in a given position in the VTable. So if this is the third virtual method of the local copy of the class, it will correspond to the third position in the VTable of the actual class defined by the DLL. This is why it is vital to keep the same order in the two definitions, and why the names have little value. If you change the order of the definitions, writing Inc before SetValue, the executable program will look to the second method of the VTable and find the wrong method!

The test program, using the TDllNumber class declaration in the Base unit, is actually very simple. You can see its form at run-time in Figure 21.1. When the form is created, the program creates two objects of the class TDllNumber (declared as private fields of the class) by calling the DLL function, reads the initial values of the two objects from two SpinEdit controls, and then shows the current values of the objects in two labels:

```
procedure TForm1.FormCreate(Sender: TObject);
begin
  // first create the object
  Num1 := NewObject;
  Num1.SetValue (SpinEdit1.Value);
  Label1.Caption := 'Num1: ' + IntToStr (Num1.GetValue);
```

```
    // create second object
    Num2 := NewObject;
    Num2.SetValue (SpinEdit2.Value);
    Label2.Caption := 'Num2: ' + IntToStr (Num2.GetValue);
  end;
```

The DLL function is redeclared as usual:

```
function NewObject: TDllNumber; stdcall;
    external 'DllObj.dll';
```

FIGURE 21.1

The output of the TestPrj
example used to test the
DllObj library, a DLL
exporting the methods
of a class.

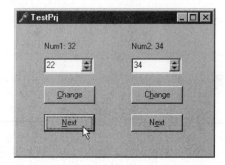

This declaration is actually very important, because makes the DLL get automatically loaded when the program starts. Without this function the executable file and the DLL would have no connection.

Here is the code of the two buttons related to the first object:

```
procedure TForm1.Button1Click(Sender: TObject);
begin
  // change
  Num1.SetValue (SpinEdit1.Value);
  Label1.Caption := 'Num1: ' + IntToStr (Num1.GetValue);
end;

procedure TForm1.Button2Click(Sender: TObject);
begin
  Num1.Increase;
  Label1.Caption := 'Num1: ' + IntToStr (Num1.GetValue);
end;
```

As you can see, once we have asked the DLL to create the object, we use it like any other regular Delphi object. The difference is that the methods we invoke are part of the DLL, not part of our executable file. There is one final event handler in the test program, which is used to destroy the objects:

```
procedure TForm1.FormDestroy(Sender: TObject);
begin
  Num1.Free;
  Num2.Free;
end;
```

In the FormDestroy method, we can call the Free method of each object. The Free method will then call the Destroy destructor of the two objects, as usual. This is important, because Delphi objects have one more virtual method than those listed in the class declaration—the Destroy virtual destructor.

Implementing IUnknown

To turn our simple object into a COM object, we have to implement the IUnknown interface, providing the three standard COM methods: Add, Release, and Query-Interface. Delphi 3 provides built-in support for these features using the new interface keyword, already introduced in Chapter 6. Here is the definition of the IUnknown interface:

```
type
  IUnknown = interface
    ['{00000000-0000-0000-C000-000000000046}']
    function QueryInterface(const IID: TGUID; out Obj): Integer;
stdcall;
    function _AddRef: Integer; stdcall;
    function _Release: Integer; stdcall;
  end;
```

The AddRef and Release methods are used to implement reference counting. The QueryInterface method handles the type information and type compatibility of the objects.

NOTE   In the code above you can see an example of an out parameter, a parameter passed back from the method to the calling program, but without an initial value passed by the calling program to the method.

Implementing IUnknown Methods

Delphi actually implements these methods in a couple of classes. One of them is
TInterfacedObject, a very simple implementation of the interface:

```
type
  TInterfacedObject = class(TObject, IUnknown)
  private
    FRefCount: Integer;
  protected
    function QueryInterface(const IID: TGUID; out Obj): Integer;
stdcall;
    function _AddRef: Integer; stdcall;
    function _Release: Integer; stdcall;
  public
    property RefCount: Integer read FRefCount;
  end;
```

Here is the implementation of the two methods for reference counting, which
are quite simple:

```
function TInterfacedObject._AddRef: Integer;
begin
  Inc(FRefCount);
  Result := FRefCount;
end;

function TInterfacedObject._Release: Integer;
begin
  Dec(FRefCount);
  if FRefCount = 0 then
  begin
    Destroy;
    Result := 0;
    Exit;
  end;
  Result := FRefCount;
end;
```

The most complex method is QueryInterface, which in Delphi is actually
implemented through the GetInterface method of the TObject class:

```
function TInterfacedObject.QueryInterface(
  const IID: TGUID; out Obj): Integer;
```

```
const
  E_NOINTERFACE = $80004002;
begin
  if GetInterface(IID, Obj) then
    Result := 0
  else
    Result := E_NOINTERFACE;
end;
```

The role of the QueryInterface method is twofold:

- QueryInterface is used for type checking. The program can ask an object: Are you of the type I'm interested in? Do you implement the interface, the methods I want to call? If the answer is no, the program can look for another object, maybe asking another server.

- If the answer is yes, QueryInterface usually returns a pointer to the object, using its reference output parameter (out).

To understand the role of the QueryInterface method it is important to keep in mind that a COM object can implement multiple interfaces. When you call QueryInterface you might ask for one of the possible interfaces of the object, using the TGUID parameter.

A COM class, in general, can implement multiple interfaces besides IUnknown, which means we might need to return a specific portion of the VTable. In Delphi 2 this was very difficult to accomplish, while in C++ you can easily obtain it using multiple inheritance. Delphi 3 interfaces solve the problem in a very elegant way. In fact, a single class can have implement multiple interfaces.

Global Unique Identifiers

The QueryInterface method has a special parameter, of the TGUID type. This is an ID which identifies any COM server class and any interface in the system. When you want to know if an object supports a specific interface, you ask the object if it implements the interface which has a given ID (which for the default OLE interfaces is determined by Microsoft).

Another ID is used to indicate a specific class, a specific server. The Windows Registry stores this ID, with indications of the related DLL or executable file. The developers of an OLE server define the class identifier.

Both of these IDs are indicated as GUID, or *Globally Unique IDentifiers*. If each developer uses a number to indicate its own OLE servers, how can we be sure that these values are not duplicated? The short answer is that we cannot. The real answer is that a GUID is such a long number (with 16 bytes, or 128 bits, or a number with 38 digits!) that it is statistically impossible to come up with two random numbers having the same value. Moreover, programmers should use a specific API call, CoCreateGuid (or use an option of their programming environment to call it), to come up with a GUID that reflects the time and date, the network card ID, the calling program, and other information.

Delphi defines a TGUID data type (in the System unit) to hold these numbers:

```
type
  TGUID = record
    D1: Integer;
    D2: Word;
    D3: Word;
    D4: array[0..7] of Byte;
  end;
```

This structure is actually quite odd but is required by Windows. You can assign a value to a GUID using the standard hexadecimal notation, as in this code fragment:

```
const
  Class_ActiveForm1: TGUID =
    '{1AFA6D61-7B89-11D0-98D0-444553540000}';
```

In case you need a GUID, I've written a small program to generate them. The NewGuid example simply calls the CoCreateGuid function and then adds the result to the text of a memo. You can easily copy the definition from the memo into your code.

> **WARNING**
> Besides being careful not to copy the GUID from someone else's program (which can end up in two completely different COM objects using the same GUID), you should never make up your own ID entering a casual sequence of numbers. Windows checks the IDs, and using a casual sequence won't generate a valid ID. An OLE server with an invalid ID is not recognized, but you won't get an error message!

Here is the code of the OnClick event of the only button of the form of the NewGuid example (you can see an example of this code in Figure 21.2):

```
uses
  ComObj, ActiveX;

procedure TForm1.BtnNewClick(Sender: TObject);
var
  ID: TGUID;
  S: string;
begin
  if CoCreateGuid (Id) = s_OK then
  begin
    s := GUIDToString (Id);
    Memo1.Lines.Add (S);
  end;
end;
```

FIGURE 21.2

An example of the GUIDs generated by the NewGuid example. Values depend on my computer and the time I run this program.

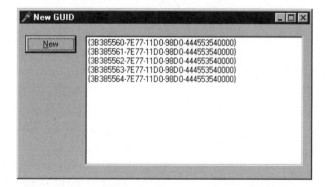

NOTE   The Delphi unit defining OLE functions and data types was called Ole2 in Delphi 2. In Delphi 3 this unit is replaced by the ActiveX and ComObj units, which use the new interface mechanism. You should now use these new units exclusively.

Besides the GUIDToString function, Delphi also includes its opposite, String-ToGUID. You can also use the corresponding Windows API functions, such as StringFromGuid2, but in this case you must use the WideString type instead of the string type. Any time OLE is involved you have to use the WideString type, unless you use Delphi functions which automatically do the required conversion for you. Actually, OLE API functions use the PWChar type (pointer to null-terminated arrays of wide characters), but simply casting a WideString to PWChar does the trick.

By looking at the output in Figure 21.2, or by running the program, you can see that a single application gets a consecutive set of GUIDs. This doesn't depend on time: pressing the button faster or slower always generates numbers in sequence. But if you run another copy of the program, it will have a new sequence of values.

> **TIP**
>
> Keep in mind that GUIDs come in two different forms: Interface ID, which refers to an interface, and Class ID, which refers to a specific object in a server. These two kinds of IDs both use the GUID style, and are often indicated as GUIDs. The difference between these different kinds of IDs is so subtle that the terms are often used interchangeably.

The Role of Class Factories

The first program we have written, with a DLL exporting a class, worked because we were in a closed environment—that is, we wrote the server and the only client which is ever going to use it. To make it a truly standard COM object, we must implement the IUnknown interface, define a GUID, and replace the custom New-Object function with the DllGetClassObject function. In fact, when we register the GUID of the object in the registry, we can use a specific API function to create the object, such as the CreateComObject API:

```
function CreateComObject(const ClassID: TGUID): IUnknown;
```

This API function will look into the registry, find the server registering the object with the given GUID, load it, and, if the server is a DLL, call the DLLGet-ClassObject method of the DLL. This is a function every in-process server must provide and export:

```
function DllGetClassObject(const CLSID, IID: TGUID;
  var Obj): HResult; stdcall;
```

This API function receives as parameters the requested class and interface, and returns an object in its reference parameter. The object returned by this function is a *class factory*.

Now, what is a class factory? As the name suggests, a class factory is an object capable of creating other objects. Each server can have multiple objects. The server exposes the class factory, and the class factory can create one of these various objects. Each object, then, can have a number of interfaces. One of the many advantages of the Delphi 3 simplified approach to COM development is that the system can provide a class factory for us. For this reason, I'm not going to add a class factory to our simple example.

The call to the `CreateComObject` API doesn't stop at the creation of the class factory, however. After retrieving the class factory, `CreateComObject` calls the `CreateInstance` method of the `IClassFactory` interface. This method creates the requested object and returns it. If no error occurs, this object becomes the return value of the `CreateComObject` API.

By setting up all this mechanism (including the class factory and the `DLLGet-ClassObject` call), you gain the advantage of a very simple object creation: `Create-ComObject` is just a simple function call with a complex behavior behind the scenes. What's great in Delphi 3 is that the complex mechanism is handled for you by the run-time system. So it's time, in fact, to start looking in detail at how Delphi 3 makes COM really easy to master.

Using Delphi 3 COM Interfaces

We can now take our example and turn it into the new FirstCom example, which has similar capabilities to the custom DllObj example but uses a standard Delphi 3 COM approach. Here is the definition of the class exported by the library, which is now an interface:

```
type
  INumber = interface
    ['{B4131140-7C2F-11D0-98D0-444553540000}']
    function GetValue: Integer; stdcall;
    procedure SetValue (New: Integer); stdcall;
    procedure Increase; stdcall;
  end;
```

Again, do not copy this IID (Interface ID) in your code, but generate a new one for your examples. After declaring the custom interface, the server declares an actual object implementing the interface:

```
type
  TD11Number = class (TComObject, INumber)
  private
    Value: Integer;
  public
    function GetValue: Integer; virtual; stdcall;
    procedure SetValue (New: Integer); virtual; stdcall;
    procedure Increase; virtual; stdcall;
    procedure Initialize; override;
    destructor Destroy; override;
  end;
```

The TComObject Class

The TD11Number class inherits from the standard TComObject class, provided by the Delphi 3 ComObj unit and implementing a default COM object. This class is similar to the TInterfacedObject class we've seen before, but a little more complex. This is the public portion of the TComObject class declaration:

```
type
  TComObject = class(TObject, IUnknown, ISupportErrorInfo)
    ...
  public
    constructor Create;
    constructor CreateAggregated(const Controller: IUnknown);
    constructor CreateFromFactory(Factory: TComObjectFactory;
      const Controller: IUnknown);
    destructor Destroy; override;
    procedure Initialize; virtual;
    function ObjAddRef: Integer; virtual; stdcall;
    function ObjQueryInterface(const IID: TGUID; out Obj):
      Integer; virtual; stdcall;
    function ObjRelease: Integer; virtual; stdcall;
    function SafeCallException(ExceptObject: TObject;
      ExceptAddr: Pointer): HResult; override;
    property Controller: IUnknown read GetController;
    property Factory: TComObjectFactory read FFactory;
    property RefCount: Integer read FRefCount;
  end;
```

This class implements the IUnknown interface (ObjAddRef, ObjQueryInterface, and ObjRelease methods) and the ISupportErrorInfo interface (through the InterfaceSupportsErrorInfo protected method). It also has a few read-only properties you can use to get information about the class and the status of the object. In our example we simply inherit from this base class, but we do not care too much about the implementation of this base class, which provides us with the basic COM functionality.

Other Delphi COM Classes

Besides the TComObject class we are using in this example and the TInterfacedObject class we've used in Chapter 6 and seen earlier in this chapter, Delphi 3 includes several other predefined COM classes. We'll use them in the following chapters, but here is a list of the most important COM classes of the Delphi VCL (you can see a hierarchy graph of these classes in Chapter 7):

- TInterfacedObject, defined in the System unit, inherits from TObject and implements the IUnknown interface.

- TComObject, defined in the ComObj unit, inherits from TObject and implements both the IUnknown interface and the ISupportErrorInfo interface.

- TTypedComObject, defined in the ComObj unit, inherits from TComObject and implements the IProvideClassInfo interface (beside the IUnknown and ISupportErrorInfo interfaces already implemented by the base class, TComObject).

- TAutoObject, defined in the ComObj unit, inherits from TTypedComObject and implements also the IDispatch interface.

- TActiveXControl, defined in the AxCtrls unit, inherits from TAutoObject and implements a number of interfaces (IPersistStreamInit, IPersistStorage, IOleObject, and IOleControl, to name just a few).

Delphi defines also a class factory for each of these classes. The class factory classes form another hierarchy, with the same structure. Their names are TComObjectFactory, TTypedComObjectFactory, TAutoObjectFactory, and TActiveXControlFactory.

Initializing the COM Object

What we absolutely need to know is that the non-virtual constructor of the TCom-Object class calls the virtual Initialize method. If we want to customize the creation of an object, and initialize it, we should not define a new constructor (which will never be called). What we should do is override its Initialize method, as I've done in the TDllNumber class above. I've also overridden the destructor of the class, because I wanted to test the automatic destruction of the COM objects provided by Delphi. Here is the code for this pseudo-constructor and the destructor:

```
procedure TDllNumber.Initialize;
begin
  inherited;
  Value := 10;
end;

destructor TDllNumber.Destroy;
begin
  inherited;
  MessageBox (0, 'Object Destroyed',
    'TDLLNumber', mb_OK); // API call
end;
```

In the first method, calling the inherited version is good practice, even though the TComObject.Initialize method has no code in this version of Delphi. The destructor, instead, must call the base class version. This is the code required to make our COM object work properly. The code of the other three methods, the custom methods of the INumber interface, is always the same very simple code as in the last two examples, so I won't even list it here.

We must do a few more things to complete the example. First, we should provide a class ID for the server object, possibly using a constant:

```
const
  CLSID_TDllNumber: TGUID =
    '{95D47840-7C4D-11D0-98D0-444553540000}';
```

We also need to provide a class factory. Delphi 3 includes a ready-to-use class factory for TComObject derived classes, called TComObjectFactory. This class implements both the IUnknown and the IClassFactory interfaces, and exports a number of properties, as you can see its public interface:

```
type
  TComObjectFactory = class(TObject,
```

```
    IUnknown, IClassFactory)
  ...
  public
    constructor Create(ComServer: TComServerObject;
      ComClass: TComClass; const ClassID: TGUID;
      const ClassName, Description: string;
      Instancing: TClassInstancing);
    destructor Destroy; override;
    function CreateComObject(
      const Controller: IUnknown): TComObject; virtual;
    procedure RegisterClassObject;
    procedure UpdateRegistry(Register: Boolean); virtual;
    property ClassID: TGUID read FClassID;
    property ClassName: string read FClassName;
    property ComClass: TClass read FComClass;
    property ComServer: TComServerObject read FComServer;
    property Description: string read FDescription;
    property ErrorIID: TGUID read FErrorIID write FErrorIID;
    property ProgID: string read GetProgID;
    property Instancing: TClassInstancing read FInstancing;
  end;
```

All we need to do is to create a global object of this class in the unit defining our COM-compatible class. We can accomplish this in the `initialization` section of the unit:

```
initialization
  TComObjectFactory.Create( ComServer, TDllNumber, CLSID_TDllNumber,
    'Md3.FirstCom', 'Md3 First COM Server', ciMultiInstance);
end.
```

The above code creates an object of the factory class, passing as parameters a `ComServer` object, the class reference to the class we've just defined (`TDllNumber`), the GUID we've just defined for the class, the server name, the server description, and the kind of instancing we want to use.

The global `ComServer` object, defined in the ComServ unit, is a manager of the class factory available in that unit. It uses its own `ForEachFactory` method to look for the class supporting a given COM object request, and keeps track of the number of allocated objects.

There are two more steps required to make our server fully COM-compliant. We must provide the proper interface functions and a registration mechanism.

This is actually quite simple, because the ComServ unit provides these functions for us. So our server should simply export them. Here is the project source code for the FirstCom server example:

```
library FirstCom;

uses
  ComServ,
  DllClass in 'DllClass.pas';

exports
  DllGetClassObject resident,
  DllCanUnloadNow resident,
  DllRegisterServer resident,
  DllUnregisterServer resident;
end.
```

> **NOTE**
> The use of the resident directive for DLL exports is a form of optimization. These functions are always kept in memory, making them fast to call even if they haven't been used for a while (which might cause Windows to move them to a swap file).

To register this server you can simply compile its code, and then use the Run ➤ Register ActiveX Server menu command in Delphi. You do this to register the server on your own machine, with the results you can see in Figure 21.3. When you distribute this server, you should install it on the client computers. This can be accomplished in several ways: you can write a .REG file to install in the Registry, pass the DLL as a command line parameter to Microsoft's REGSVR32.EXE (found in the windows/system directory), or use the similar RegSvr demo program which ships with Delphi.

Now we can turn to the client side of our example. This time the example is called TestCOM and is stored in a separate directory. I've done this to underline that now the program loads the server DLL through the OLE/COM mechanism, thanks to the server information present in the registry, so it's not necessary for the client to know in which directory the server resides.

FIGURE 21.3

The new registered server in Windows 95 RegEdit.

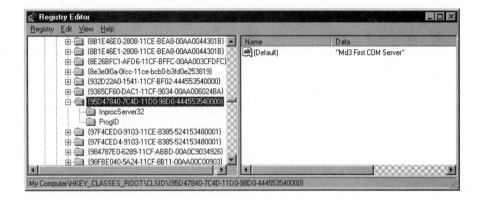

Updating the COM Client Program

In the client program I must redeclare the interface and the COM server GUID (although I could have placed them in a common unit, used by both the server and the client, I decided not to do this extra work in such a simple example):

```
const
  CLSID_TDllNumber: TGUID =
    '{95D47840-7C4D-11D0-98D0-444553540000}';

type
  INumber = interface
    ['{B4131140-7C2F-11D0-98D0-444553540000}']
    function GetValue: Integer; stdcall;
    procedure SetValue (New: Integer); stdcall;
    procedure Increase; stdcall;
  end;
```

Of course the code of the FormCreate method of the example should now be updated. The program starts with all the buttons disabled (at design-time), and enables them only after an object has been created. This way, if an exception is raised while creating one of the objects, the buttons related to the object won't be enabled:

```
procedure TForm1.FormCreate(Sender: TObject);
begin
  // create first object
  Num1 := CreateComObject (CLSID_TDllNumber) as INumber;
```

```
      Num1.SetValue (SpinEdit1.Value);
      Label1.Caption := 'Num1: ' + IntToStr (Num1.GetValue);
      Button1.Enabled := True;
      Button2.Enabled := True;

      // create second object
      Num2 := CreateComObject (CLSID_TDllNumber) as INumber;
      Label2.Caption := 'Num2: ' + IntToStr (Num2.GetValue);
      Button3.Enabled := True;
      Button4.Enabled := True;
    end;
```

Notice in particular the call to CreateComObject and the following as cast. The API call starts the COM object-construction mechanism I've already described in detail. This call also dynamically loads the server DLL. The return value is an IUnknown object. This object must be converted to the proper interface type before assigning it to the Num1 and Num2 fields, which now have the interface type INumber as their data type.

WARNING To downcast an interface to the actual type, *always* use the as cast (as shown in Chapter 6). This provides some protection, because it raises an exception if the interface you are casting to is not supported by the given object. In the case of interfaces, the as cast is the only way to *extract* an interface from an object. If you write a plain cast of the form

```
    INumber(CreateComObject (CLSID_TDllNumber))
```

the program will invariably crash, even if the cast seems to make sense as in the case above. Casting an interface pointer to another interface pointer is an error. Period. Never do it.

In Figure 21.4 you can see the output of this test program, which is very similar to the previous versions. Notice that, this time, Num2 shows the initial value of the object at startup, as set up in its Initialize method. Notice also that I've added one more button, which creates a third temporary COM object:

```
procedure TForm1.Button5Click(Sender: TObject);
var
  Num3: INumber;
begin
  // create a new temporary COM object
```

```
Num3 := CreateComObject (CLSID_TDllNumber) as INumber;
Num3.SetValue (100);
Num3.Increase;
ShowMessage ('Num3: ' + IntToStr (Num3.GetValue));
end;
```

FIGURE 21.4

The output of the TestCom example, which is very similar to previous examples, but uses a fully COM-compliant approach.

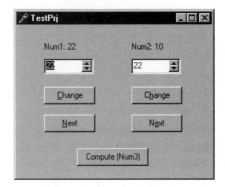

Pressing this button, you simply get the value of the number following 100. The reason I added this method to the example actually doesn't relate to its output. (You already knew that 100 plus one is 101, didn't you?) If you press the button, after the message showing the result, however, you get a second message indicating that the object has been destroyed. Simply letting an interface object go out of scope, the `Release` method of the object is automatically called, the reference count of the object is decreased, and the object is then eventually destroyed if its reference count reaches zero. I have already described this reference-counting mechanism in Chapter 6, so you can refer to that chapter for more details.

The same happens for the other two objects as soon as the program terminates. Even if the program doesn't explicitly destroy the two objects in the `FormDestroy` method, they are indeed destroyed, as the message shown by their `Destroy` destructor clearly demonstrates. This happens because they were declared to be of an interface type.

Using Interface Properties

As a further small step, we can improve the example by adding a property to the `INumber` interface. When you add a property to an interface you indicate the data type, and then the read and write directives. You can have read-only or write-only properties, but the read and write clauses must always refer to a method because interfaces don't hold anything else but methods.

Here is the updated interface, which is part of the PropCom example:

```
type
  INumberProp = interface
    ['{B36C5800-8E59-11D0-98D0-444553540000}']
    function GetValue: Integer; stdcall;
    procedure SetValue (New: Integer); stdcall;
    property Value: Integer
      read GetValue write SetValue;
    procedure Increase; stdcall;
  end;
```

I've given this interface a new name and, what's even more important, a new interface ID. Then I updated the server class declaration simply by writing:

```
type
  TDllNumber = class (TComObject, INumberProp)
    ...
```

Also this class has a new server object ID. The client program, saved in the Test-Prop directory, can now simply use the Value property instead of the SetValue and GetValue methods. Here is a small excerpt from the FormCreate method:

```
Num1 := CreateComObject (CLSID_TDllNumberProp) as INumberProp;
Num1.Value := SpinEdit1.Value;
Label1.Caption := 'Num1: ' + IntToStr (Num1.Value);
```

The difference between using methods and properties for an interface is only syntactical, since interface properties cannot access private data, as class properties can. By using properties we can make the code a little more readable.

NOTE   You can also define array properties, and even choose an array property as default array property for the interface, but these are advanced topics that we won't explore.

Using a Shell Interface

In the last section we built a fully standard COM object, packaged it as an in-process server, and used it from a standard client. However, the COM interface we implemented was a custom interface we'd built. Now we can try to build clients and servers related to the Windows 95 shell interfaces, which are all COM.

> **NOTE**
>
> I'm going to build two simple examples, because in-depth coverage of the Windows 95 shell would require at least a couple of chapters (there are entire books devoted to this subject). Among other books, you'll find a more detailed description of using Windows 95 shell interfaces in the *Delphi Developer's Handbook*.

Creating a Shell Link (or Shortcut)

One of the simplest shell interfaces we can use in a client application is the IShell-Link interface. This interface relates to Windows 95 shortcuts and allows programmers to access the information of an existing shortcut or to create a new one.

In the ShCut example, I'm going to create a new shortcut to the program itself. Of course, once you understand how to do this, you can easily extend the example. The example has an edit box and a button. When the button is pressed, the text of the edit is used as the name of a new shortcut:

```
uses
  ComObj, ActiveX, ShlObj;

procedure TForm1.Button1Click(Sender: TObject);
var
  AnObj: IUnknown;
  ShLink: IShellLink;
  PFile: IPersistFile;
  FileName: string;
  WFileName: WideString;
begin
  // access the two interfaces of the object
  AnObj := CreateComObject (CLSID_ShellLink);
```

```
    ShLink := AnObj as IShellLink;
    PFile := AnObj as IPersistFile;
    // get the name of the application file
    FileName := ParamStr (0);
    // set the link properties
    ShLink.SetPath (PChar (FileName));
    ShLink.SetWorkingDirectory (PChar (ExtractFilePath (FileName)));
    // save the file, using a WideString!
    WFileName := ExtractFilePath (FileName) + Edit1.Text + '.lnk';
    PFile.Save (PWChar (WFileName), False);
  end;
```

The most important code is at the very beginning of this method. The Create-ComObject call creates a system object, as indicated by the GUID passed as parameter. The result of this call (which is an IUnknown interface) is converted both to an IShellLink interface and to an IPersistFile interface. Actually, we could have written the code using this shortcut form:

```
ShLink := CreateComObject (CLSID_ShellLink) as IShellLink;
PFile := ShLink as IPersistFile;
```

If you look at similar examples built in Delphi 2 or in other languages, you'll notice that to access the IPersistFile interface the programs use custom calls to the QueryInterface method. The two as expressions basically call QueryInterface for us.

Once we have two interfaces relating to a single server object, we can call some of their methods, such as SetPath and SetDirectory, and then Save. This last call (which creates the physical .LNK file) requires a "pointer to wide char" parameter. The simplest way to obtain this in Delphi 3 is to declare a long string and then cast it to a PWChar.

WARNING Do not try casting a plain string to PWChar —the compiler will not complain but the program won't work!

The effect of running this program and pressing the button is that in the directory of the project, Windows 95 will add a new link. You can see an example of the program in Figure 21.5.

FIGURE 21.5

The simple user interface of the ShCut example, and some shortcuts created with it in the project folder.

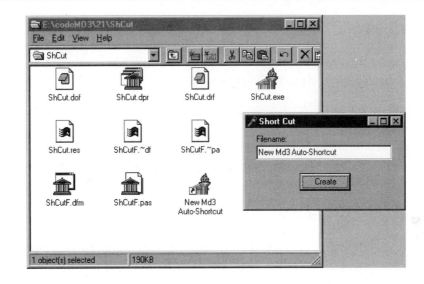

A Copy Hook for Pascal Files

As a second example of integrating a program with the shell, we can now write a simple server. Again, I've decided to implement a very simple example, a *copy hook*, which is a server that implements the ICopyHook interface and registers it into the system. A copy hook server registered into the system is triggered whenever you copy, move, or delete a folder or directory (but not when you do one of these operations on a file). The name of the example is PasCHook.

To start building a new server we can simply select the File ➤ New command of Delphi, and in the ActiveX page choose ActiveX Library. This generates the code for an empty COM server, which corresponds to the project source code we've already used:

```
library Project1;

uses
  ComServ,
  Unit1 in 'Unit1.pas';
exports
  DllGetClassObject,
  DllCanUnloadNow,
  DllRegisterServer,
  DllUnregisterServer;
```

```
{$R *.RES}
end.
```

Now we can simply get rid of the resource inclusion directive and start writing the code of the secondary unit. In the new unit we should create and register a new class, with a custom GUID:

```
uses
  ShellObj;
const
  CLSID_PascalCopyHook: TGUID =
    '{80A06FA0-7DF2-11D0-98D0-444553540000}';
type
  TPasCopyHook = class(TComObject, ICopyHook)
  public
    function CopyCallback (Hwnd: THandle; wFunc, wFlags: UINT;
      pszSrcFile: PAnsiChar; dwSrcAttribs: DWORD; pszDestFile:
      PAnsiChar; dwDestAttribs: DWORD): UINT; stdcall;
  end;
```

The ICopyHook interface we want to implement has just one method and is defined as follows:

```
type
  ICopyHookA = interface(IUnknown)
    function CopyCallback(Wnd: HWND; wFunc, wFlags: UINT;
      pszSrcFile: PAnsiChar; dwSrcAttribs: DWORD; pszDestFile:
      PAnsiChar; dwDestAttribs: DWORD): UINT; stdcall;
  end;
  ICopyHook = ICopyHookA;
```

This interface is an exception to the other shell interfaces, because it directly uses the name of the source and destination folders. Other shell extension servers, instead, receive a block of memory with file information, using a specific interface. If you try implementing them, be warned that they require much more code than this copy hook example.

Here is the code of my implementation of the copy hook CopyCallback method, which should return id_Yes to allow the specific folder operation, id_No to indicate that the specific folder operation should not be completed, and id_Cancel to abort the remaining operations if we are working with multiple folders. In this case, in fact, the method is called once for each folder. Here is the code, based on a case statement that produces a slightly different output depending on the type of operation:

```
function TPasCopyHook.CopyCallback (Hwnd: THandle;
  wFunc, wFlags: UINT; pszSrcFile: PAnsiChar; dwSrcAttribs: DWORD;
```

```
        pszDestFile: PAnsiChar; dwDestAttribs: DWORD): UINT; stdcall;
var
  Msg: string;
  MessType: TMsgDlgType;
begin
  Application.Handle := Hwnd;
  Msg := '';
  MessType := mtConfirmation;
  case wFunc of
   FO_COPY: Msg := Format (
     'Are you sure you want to copy the %s ' +
     'folder to the %s destination?', [pszSrcFile, pszDestFile]);
   FO_DELETE:
   begin
     Format ('Caution... the folder %s is ' +
        'about to be deleted, unless you say no.', [pszSrcFile]);
     MessType := mtWarning;
   end;
   FO_MOVE: Format (
     'Are you sure you want to move the %s ' +
     'folder to the %s destination', [pszSrcFile, pszDestFile]);
   FO_RENAME: Format (
     'Are you sure you want to rename the %s ' +
     'folder as %s', [pszSrcFile, pszDestFile]);
  end;
  if Msg <> '' then
    // ask for confirmation
    Result := MessageDlg (Msg, MessType, mbYesNoCancel, 0)
  else
    Result := id_Yes;
end;

initialization
  TComObjectFactory.Create(ComServer, TPasCopyHook,
    CLSID_PascalCopyHook, 'PasalCopyHook',
    'CopyHook Demo from Mastering Delphi 3', ciMultiInstance);
end.
```

Notice the statement at the beginning, `Application.Handle := Hwnd`, which allows us to use the `MessageDlg` function properly. In fact, the `CopyCallBack` method received as parameter the handle of the window to use as the owner window for our dialog boxes. If you use the `MessageBox` Windows API, you simply pass that handle as first parameter; if you use a VCL function you should use this parameter to set the `Handle` property of the `Application` object.

Once you have written and compiled this program, you are ready for the most complex step, registering the application. This time you need to write a specific .REG file to hook the server DLL into the shell. Basically, you can register a shell extension for a specific file or for any file. A shell extension for folders is indicated in the Registry with the Directory entry. Under this entry you should add a new key for CopyHookHandlers and give it the value of the GUID of our server. Of course, you should also register the CLSID of the server (as accomplished by the first group of statements). Here is the .REG file:

```
REGEDIT4

[HKEY_CLASSES_ROOT\CLSID\ ➦
  {80A06FA0-7DF2-11D0-98D0-444553540000}]
@="PascalCopyHook"
[HKEY_CLASSES_ROOT\CLSID\ ➦
  {80A06FA0-7DF2-11D0-98D0-444553540000}\InprocServer32]
@="e:\\codeMD3\\21\\PasCHook\\PasCHook.dll"
"ThreadingModel"="Apartment"

[HKEY_CLASSES_ROOT\Directory\shellex\CopyHookHandlers]
@="PCopyHook"
[HKEY_CLASSES_ROOT\Directory\shellex\CopyHookHandlers\PCopyHook]
@="{80A06FA0-7DF2-11D0-98D0-444553540000}"
```

Notice that to fit the printed page I had to split a couple of long lines (marked with the ➦ symbol and indented in the listing above), but you cannot do that in the actual .REG file. Registration files require single long lines of text for an entry within square brackets, and single lines for the various commands.

WARNING Besides writing long lines, you should also update the listing above by using the name of the directory where you've placed the DLL. I've left my own directory name in there so you can see the use of *double* back-slashes to indicate the path of the server.

As an alternative to using a .REG file, you can also update the Windows Registry using the specific API. Delphi actually provides a specific class for this, TRegistry. You'll learn how to use this class in Chapter 25.

Once this program is properly compiled and you've merged its registration file into the Windows Registry—simply executing the REG file usually does the trick—you should reboot the system (although sometimes you can skip this step). Now every time you do one of the folder operations indicated above (move, delete, copy, or rename) you'll be asked to confirm the operation. You can see an example of the output in Figure 21.6.

FIGURE 21.6

The output of the PasCHook example, when you are trying to move a folder.

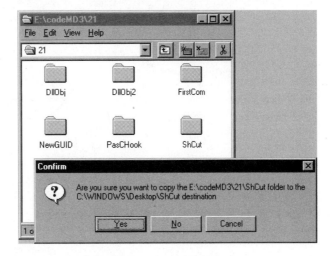

It probably makes more sense to ask for confirmation only for delete operations, and only if the folder contains specific files: now that you understand how to make a shell copy hook in-process server, you can extend it any way you like. When you want to remove the copy hook handler, you can simply remove it from the list of keys under the `Directory\shellex\CopyHookHandlers` of the `HKEY_CLASSES_ROOT` section of the Windows Registry. Installing another copy hook handler, in fact, adds it to the list, and doesn't replace the current one.

What's Next

In this chapter we've focused on the foundations of OLE and COM. We've seen how to place objects in a DLL, how to turn them into COM objects, and how to implement a server that interacts with the Windows 95 shell.

In the coming chapters we'll focus on other kinds of servers supported directly by Delphi 3: automation servers, Active Documents (or OLE Documents), ActiveX, and ActiveForm. We'll cover these features without going into detail, because covering each of these interfaces, and their many related topics, is beyond the scope of this book. For example, we'll learn to write OLE Automation servers and ActiveX controls in Delphi 3, without studying how Delphi makes them work.

OLE Automation and OLE Documents

- OLE Automation: clients and servers

- Making OLE applications interact

- Using type libraries

- A simple OLE Document container

- OLE Documents in-place editing

- Loading and saving OLE Documents to files

The last chapter covered the foundations of OLE and COM. Now we can start looking at the practical applications of this technology. In Delphi you don't need to master the details of COM to write applications, because the environment and its tools hide most of the complexity. This is particularly true for the two topics covered in this chapter.

The first topic is OLE Automation; that is, the development of server programs that expose an OLE interface to other programs, and client programs (OLE Automation *controllers*) that use these interfaces. In Chapter 21 the server was invariably a DLL; now it will be a plain executable file. OLE Automation support has been highly enhanced from Delphi 2. The second topic of this chapter is OLE Documents, or the use of the OleContainer component of Delphi. We'll see some simple examples; this component is not much different than in Delphi 2.

OLE Automation

In Windows, applications don't live in separate worlds. Users often want them to interact. As we'll see in Chapter 30, the use of the Clipboard and DDE allows applications to interact. However, more and more programs offer an OLE Automation interface to let other programs drive them. The advantage is that these interfaces are completely language-neutral, so you can use Delphi, C++, Visual Basic, or a macro language to drive an OLE Automation server regardless of the programming language used to write it.

Our focus, of course, will be on using OLE Automation servers from Delphi applications, and on writing our own servers in Delphi. We will actually write an OLE Automation controller to drive our own OLE Automation server, mainly because I can't anticipate which OLE Automation servers you may have installed on your computer. However, I'll also show you the basic techniques by writing a simple controller for Microsoft Word, which is a widespread application.

OLE Automation is so simple to implement in Delphi that you can use it as a tool to make your programs interact, even though there are other techniques you can use when building both the client and the server programs.

In Delphi 2 OLE Automation support was made available through the TOleAuto class of the OleAuto unit. This unit is still present in Delphi 3, for compatibility reasons, but the new and more powerful OLE Automation support is now provided by the TOleAuto class of the ComObj unit. The examples in this chapter focus on the new approach. The two classes (in the two units) are highly compatible, so porting the examples from Delphi 2 to Delphi 3 was straightforward.

Sending Data to Word

Before showing you how to write an OLE automation server, let me start with a simple Delphi example of an OLE controller. This program extracts some data from a database table and uses it to build a Microsoft Word document, driving Word though its OLE Automation interface.

The basic idea is that you can easily manipulate an OLE server by declaring a variable of the variant data type and assigning the OLE object to it:

```
procedure TNavigator.BtnMasterWordClick(Sender: TObject);
var
  VarW: Variant;
begin
  VarW := CreateOleObject ('Word.Basic');
  VarW.FileNew;
  VarW.AppShow;
  VarW.Insert ('Mastering Delphi');
  VarW.FileSave;
end;
```

Microsoft Word is localized into many languages, and Microsoft also translates some of the OLE automation interfaces in each foreign language, making it difficult to write a generic program. In the following example, I'll use the English version of Word, which means the example might not work if you have a localized version.

The call to CreateOleObjects starts the server, if it is not already running, and returns a reference to the requested object. Now you can call any method or access any properties of the *Word.Basic* OLE server. You can use all the macro commands documented in the WordBasic Help files. The statements above simply create a new file (you can skip this if you want to insert the text in the current file), move the server into the foreground, insert a line of text, and then save the file.

This last operation opens the Save As dialog box of Word itself. Without the AppShow call, the dialog wouldn't have been shown, but the title of the application and its TaskBar icon would have started to flash: the dialog would have been displayed only after the user activated the application. In general you should not show dialog boxes from a server, because if the server is not active they'll remain in the background. You might actually change the code above to call FileSaveAs instead of FileSave. The FileSaveAs call, in fact, directly saves the file, using the parameters you supply. If you pass no parameters, the file is saved with a default name in a default directory.

It is important to notice that at the end of the method the variant variable goes out of scope. As discussed in the last chapter, this removes a reference from the object. If Word was already running, this has little effect. If Word was opened by the CreateOleObject call, then as soon as the variant goes out of scope, the server is closed. This is not a *normal* closing operation; the server is *terminated*. This means, among other things, that the modified files are not automatically saved.

Sending Database Data to Microsoft Word

The code above is actually part of a more complex example, called DbToWord (short for Database to Word). This is a new version of the Navig1 example of Chapter 16, a very simple form showing a record of the COUNTRY.DB table. Besides the Mastering Delphi -> Word button, implemented with the code we've just looked at, this program's form has a button you can use to open a copy of Word, another to send a report of the table to it, and a third to save the file, asking the user for a directory within the controller application.

The variant is declared as a private field of the form. This way it will go out of scope, and the server will be closed, only when the controller terminates. The first button, *Open Word*, creates the server object:

```
procedure TNavigator.BtnOpenClick(Sender: TObject);
begin
  // create the automation object
  try
    VarWord := CreateOleObject ('Word.Basic');
```

```
    VarWord.AppShow;
    VarWord.FileNew;
    BtnPrint.Enabled := True;
    BtnSave.Enabled := True;
    // keep the program in front of Word
    Application.BringToFront;
  except
    ShowMessage('Microsoft Word not found');
  end;
end;
```

If the operation succeeds it enables the two buttons and brings the program back in front of Word, to make it more obvious to users what is going on. Otherwise, a user would have to reactivate the program manually before pressing one of the other two buttons. Here is the code of the second button, *Print to Word*:

```
procedure TNavigator.BtnPrintClick(Sender: TObject);
var
  Bookmark: TBookmark;
begin
  // disable the UI
  Table1.DisableControls;
  try
    // store the current position
    Bookmark := Table1.GetBookmark;
    try
      // insert the title (in bold font)
      VarWord.Bold;
      VarWord.Insert ('American Capitals from ' +
        Table1.TableName + #13);
      // scan the database table
      Table1.First;
      while not Table1.EOF do
      begin
        // send the two fields
        VarWord.Insert ('The capital of ' +
          Table1.FieldByName ('Name').AsString + ' is '+
          Table1.FieldByName ('Capital').AsString + #13);
        Table1.Next;
      end;
    finally
      // go back to the bookmark and destroy it
      Table1.GotoBookmark (Bookmark);
      Table1.FreeBookmark (Bookmark);
```

```
      end;
    finally
      // re-enable the controls
      Table1.EnableControls;
    end;
  end;
```

This method inserts a title caption with the name of the database table, using a bold font, and continues adding a line of text for each record of the database table. Notice the use of the newline (#13) character. You can see the result of this code in Figure 22.1.

FIGURE 22.1

The form of the OLE Automation controller example, DbToWord, with the Word document it produced in the background.

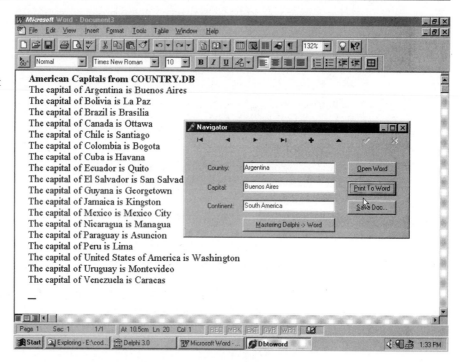

The last button, *Save Doc*, uses a standard Delphi dialog box to request a path and filename for the document, and then saves it:

```
procedure TNavigator.BtnSaveClick(Sender: TObject);
begin
  if SaveDialog1.Execute then
```

```
    VarWord.FileSaveAs (SaveDialog1.FileName);
  end;
```

Using the Delphi dialog box you have more control over the user operation. In fact if the user presses the Cancel button on the Word File Save dialog box displayed by the *Mastering Delphi* button, the server returns an error message to us.

Writing an OLE Automation Server

While it is very simple to write an OLE Automation controller, with Delphi 3 it also very easy to write an OLE Automation server. To create an OLE Automation object, you can use Delphi's Automation Object Wizard.

> **NEW**
>
> OLE Automation servers in Delphi 3 are very different than in Delphi 2. Delphi 3 supports the notion of a type library. You can still write a server by hand, but using the Wizard and the type library editor make everything much simpler.

Start with a new application, open the Object Repository by selecting File ➤ New, move to the ActiveX page, and choose Automation Object. In the resulting dialog box enter the name of the class (without the initial *T*, because this will be added automatically for you), and press the OK button. Delphi will now open the Type Library Editor. But what is a type library?

Introducing Type Libraries

 A type library is basically a collection of type information. This collection generally describes all of the elements (the objects, the interfaces, and other type information) made available by a server. The key difference between a type library and other descriptions of these elements (such as some C or Pascal code), is that a type library is language-independent. The type elements are defined by OLE as a subset of the standard elements of programming languages, and they can be used by any development tool. Why do we need this information?

The OLE Automation controller we wrote before had no type information about the server it was using. This means that, behind the scenes, every function call had to be dispatched to the server using IDispath.Invoke, passing the function name as a string parameter, and hoping the name corresponded to an existing function of the server. The compiler had no way to check whether the methods existed. Doing all the type checks at run-time is risky, because if you make even a minor spelling error in a function name, you get no warning whatsoever of your error until you run the program and reach that line of code.

The OLE IDispatch interface supports this approach. However, it is also possible for a server to export the description of its interfaces and objects, using a type library. This type library can then be converted by a specific tool into definitions written in the language you want to use to write your client or controller program. This makes it possible for a compiler to check whether the code is correct.

Once the compiler has done its checks, it can use two different techniques to send the request to the server. It can use a plain VTable (that is, an entry in an interface type declaration), or it can use a dispinterface. We used an interface type declaration in the last chapter, so it should be familiar. A dispinterface, instead, is something new. It is basically a way to map each entry in an interface to a number. Calls to the server can then be dispatched by number. We can consider it an intermediate technique, in between dispatching by function name and using a direct call in the VTable.

NOTE   The term *dispinterface* is actually a new Delphi 3 keyword. I won't cover it in detail, but I'll show you a dispinterface generated by the Type Library Editor. Along with dispinterface Delphi 3 uses other related keywords: dispid indicates the number to associate with each element; readonly and writeonly are optional specifiers for properties.

The term used to describe this ability to connect to a server in two different ways, using a more dynamic or a more static approach, is *dual interfaces*. This means that an OLE controller can choose to access the methods of a server in two ways: it can use late binding and the mechanism provided by the dispinterface, or can use early binding and the mechanism based on the VTables, the interface types.

It is important to keep in mind that, among other elements, different techniques result in faster or slower execution. Looking up a function by name (and doing the type checking at run-time) is the slowest approach, using a `dispinterface` is much faster, and using the direct VTable call is the fastest approach.

The Type Library Editor

We can now go back to our simple example, and use the Type Library Editor. You can see its window, after I've added some input, in Figure 22.2. The Type Library Editor basically allows you to add methods and properties to the OLE Automation server object we've just created. Once this is done, it can generate both the type library file and the corresponding Object Pascal source code.

FIGURE 22.2

The Type Library Editor.

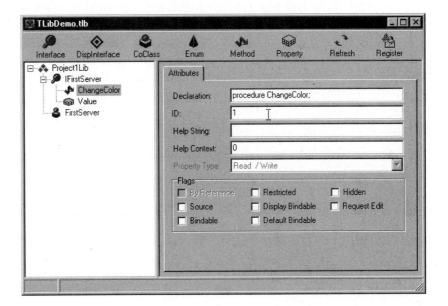

To build a simple example, we can add to the server a property and a method. In the editor we actually add these two elements to the interface, which should be called `IFirstServer`. Simply select it, and then press the Method button of the toolbar. Now you have to give it a name, such as:

```
procedure ChangeColor;
```

Now press the Property button, and give it a name and a data type, as in:

```
property Value: Integer;
```

> **NOTE**
>
> Since this OLE automation interface should be accessible by programs written in any language, we need to limit the data types used for the properties and parameters or return values of methods to those supported by OLE. These include basic data types such as Integer, SmallInt, Byte, Single, Double, WideString, Variant, and WordBool (but not Boolean).

Now we can close the type library editor, saving the changes. This operation adds to the project three items: the type library, a corresponding Pascal definition, and the declaration of the server object.

The type library is connected to the project using a resource inclusion statement, added to the source code of the project file:

```
{$R *.TLB}
```

You can always reopen the Type Library Editor by selecting the proper TLB file in the normal File Open dialog box of Delphi.

The type library is then converted into an interface definition and added to a new Pascal unit. This unit is quite long, so I've listed in the book only its key elements. The first part is, certainly, the new interface declaration:

```
type
  IFirstServer = interface(IDispatch)
    ['{89855B42-8EFE-11D0-98D0-444553540000}']
    procedure ChangeColor; safecall;
    function Get_Value: Integer; safecall;
    procedure Set_Value(Value: Integer); safecall;
    property Value: Integer read Get_Value write Set_Value;
  end;
```

This class simply lists the elements we've visually built with the Type Library Editor. The two extra methods are required by the definition of the property, as we saw in the last chapter.

> **NOTE**
>
> The methods of this interface use the `safecall` calling convention. This basically wraps a `try-except` block around each of the methods, and provides a default return value, as we've seen in the last chapter.

Then comes the dispinterface, which associates a number with each element of the IFirstServer interface:

```
type
  DFirstServer = dispinterface
    ['{89855B42-8EFE-11D0-98D0-444553540000}']
    procedure ChangeColor; dispid 1;
    property Value: Integer dispid 2;
  end;
```

All the declarations of this file (there are some others I've skipped) can be considered an internal, hidden implementation support. You don't need to understand them fully, and you should not edit them directly.

Finally, Delphi generates a file with the declaration of the actual object. This unit is added to the application and is the one we'll work on to finish the program. This unit declares the class of the server object, which must implement the interface we've just defined:

```
type
  TFirstServer = class(TAutoObject, IFirstServer)
  protected
    function Get_Value: Integer; safecall;
    procedure ChangeColor; safecall;
    procedure Set_Value(Value: Integer); safecall;
  end;
```

Delphi even provides us with the skeleton code of the methods, so you only need to fill the lines in between. This is the final code of the methods of the server object of the TLibDemo example:

```
function TFirstServer.Get_Value: Integer;
begin
  Result := Form1.Value;
end;
procedure TFirstServer.ChangeColor;
begin
  Form1.ChangeColor;
end;
procedure TFirstServer.Set_Value(Value: Integer);
begin
  Form1.Value := Value;
end;
```

In this case the three methods simply refer to a property and two methods I've added to the form. In general, I don't think it is correct to add code related to the user interface inside the class of the server object. It is better to refer to a user interface element, such as a form class, and let it perform the actions.

I've added a property to the form because I want to change the Value property and have a side effect (displaying the value in an edit box). The alternative approach, writing inside the server object the code that produces the side effect on the form, seems too confused to me. The server object, in this example, simply exposes some properties and methods of the application. Here is the part of the declaration of the TForm1 class I've edited manually:

```
type
  TForm1 = class(TForm)
    ...
  private
    CurrentValue: Integer;
  protected
    procedure SetValue (NewValue: Integer);
  public
    property Value: Integer read CurrentValue write SetValue;
    procedure ChangeColor;
  end;
```

The implementation of these methods is quite straightforward, and you can easily guess what their code looks like. What's important is the SetValue method, which might produce a side effect:

```
procedure TForm1.SetValue (NewValue: Integer);
begin
  if NewValue <> CurrentValue then
  begin
    CurrentValue := Value;
    UpDown1.Position := CurrentValue;
  end;
end;
```

The form of this example has an edit box with an associated UpDown component, plus a couple of buttons to show the current value and change the color. You can see this form at design-time in Figure 22.3.

FIGURE 22.3

The form of the TLib-Demo example at design-time.

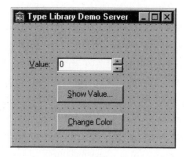

Registering the Automation Server

The unit containing the server object has one more statement, added by Delphi to the `initialization` section:

```
initialization
  TAutoObjectFactory.Create(ComServer, TFirstServer,
    Class_FirstServer, ciMultiInstance);
end.
```

This is not much different from the creation of class factories we saw in the examples of the last chapter. Combined with the call to the `Initialize` method of the `Application` object, which Delphi adds by default to the project source code of any program, the `initialization` code above makes the registration of this server straightforward.

You can add the server information to the Windows Registry by running this application on the target machine (the computer where you want to install the OLE automation server), passing to it the */regserver* parameter on the command line. You can do this by selecting Start ➤ Run, by using the Explorer or File Manager, or by running the program within Delphi after you've entered a command-line parameter (using the Run ➤ Parameters command). Another command line parameter, */unregserver* is used to remove this server from the Registry.

Writing a Client for Our Server

Now that we have built a server, we can prepare a simple client program to test it. We could, of course, use the same approach and code as the initial example of this chapter. However, since we have the type library for this server we can choose a different approach.

Create a new application—I've called it TLibCli—and then open the type library file of the server, after (optionally) copying it to the project's directory. Simply save the type library file, using Delphi's File ➤ Save menu command, and a new version of the interface declarations will be generated for you. Of course, in this case you could have grabbed the Pascal declarations from the server source code, but in my description, I'm trying to follow a more general approach, which applies also to servers you haven't written.

WARNING Do not add the type library to the application, though, because we are writing the OLE Automation controller, not a server. The Delphi project of a controller might include a type library, but it will be the type library of the server it connects to.

You can simply refer to the Pascal file generated by the type library editor in the code of the main form:

```
uses
   Project1Lib;
```

One of the elements of this unit generated by the type library is the *creation* class, a special class with two class functions (or static methods, as described in Chapter 5):

```
type
   CoFirstServer = class
      class function Create: IFirstServer;
      class function CreateRemote(
         const MachineName: string): IFirstServer;
   end;
```

You can use the first of these two functions, `Create`, to create a server object (and possibly start the server application) on the same computer. You can use the second function, `CreateRemote`, to create the server on a different computer, as long as your version of the operating system supports remote OLE Automation (or *DCOM*, *Distributed COM*).

In my example I'm going to use the first function call. When you create the server object you get as return value an `IFirstServer` interface. You can use it directly, or store it in a variant variable. Here is an example of the first approach:

```
var
  MyServer: Variant;
begin
  MyServer := CoFirstServer.Create;
  MyServer.ChangeColor;
```

This code, based on variants, is not very different from that of the first controller we built in this chapter. Here is the alternative code, with exactly the same effect:

```
var
  IMyServer: IFirstServer;
begin
  IMyServer := CoFirstServer.Create;
  IMyServer.ChangeColor;
```

As I mentioned in the section introducing type libraries, one of the differences between these two approaches is speed. It is actually quite complex to assess the exact performance of each technique, since there are many factors involved. I've added to the TLibCli example a simple test, just to give you an idea. Here is the code of the test, a loop that accesses the Value of the server twice, simply dividing these two values to invariably produce 1, so that the final value of K stores the total number of repetitions of the loop. This value is then displayed in a label along with the elapsed time:

```
procedure TForm1.BtnIntfClick(Sender: TObject);
var
  I, K: Integer;
  Init: TDateTime;
begin
  Screen.Cursor := crHourglass;
  try
    Init := Now;
    K := 0;
    for I := 1 to 1000 do
      K := K + IMyServer.Value div IMyServer.Value;
    Label1.Caption := IntToStr (K) + ' - ' +
      FormatDateTime ('nn:ss', Now - Init);
  finally
    Screen.Cursor := crDefault;
  end;
end;
```

You can see the output from calling this method, and the corresponding version based on a variant, in Figure 22.4. Obviously the timing depends on the speed of your computer, and you can also alter the results by increasing or decreasing the maximum value of the loop counter. Before you click either of the two Compute buttons, you should move to the server and set the value to something other than zero.

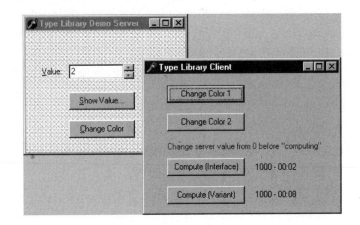

FIGURE 22.4

The TLibCli OLE Automation controller can access the server in two ways, with different performance results. Notice the server window on the background.

What Is an OLE Document?

As I mentioned in the last chapter, the original form of OLE is now called *OLE Document*. This is what takes place inside applications such as Word or Excel when you insert an object from an external server. OLE Documents actually have two different capabilities: *embedding* and *linking*:

- Embedding an object in an OLE Document corresponds to a smart version of the copy and paste operations you make with the Clipboard. The key difference is that when you copy an OLE object from a server application and paste it into a container application, you copy both the data and some information about the server (its GUID). This allows you to activate the server application from within the container to edit the data.

- Linking an object to an OLE Document instead copies only a reference to the data and the information about the server. You generally activate object linking by using the Clipboard and making a Paste Link operation. When editing the data in the container application, you'll actually modify the original data, which is stored in a separate file.

This is the reason why the server will be activated in a stand-alone window, and it will relate to the entire original file, not just the data you've copied. When you have an embedded object from an OLE 2.0 server, instead, the container might support visual (or *in-place*) editing, which means that you can modify the object in context, inside the container's main window. The server and container application windows, their menus, and their toolbars are merged automatically, allowing the user to work within a single window on a number of different object types—and therefore with a number of different OLE servers—without leaving the window of the container application.

Another key difference between embedding and linking is that the data of an embedded object is stored and managed by the container application. The container saves the embedded object in its own files. By contrast, a linked object physically resides in a separate file, which is handled by the server exclusively, even if the link refers only to a small portion of the file.

In both cases, the container application doesn't have to know how to handle the object and its data—not even how to display it—without the help of the server. Accordingly, the server application has a lot of work to do, even when you are not editing the data. Container applications often make a copy of the image of an OLE object and use the bitmap to represent the data, which speeds up some operations with the object itself. The drawback of this approach is that many commercial OLE applications end up with bloated files (because two copies of the same data are saved). If you consider this problem along with the relative slowness of OLE and the amount of work necessary to develop OLE servers, you can understand why the use of this powerful approach is still somewhat limited, compared to what Microsoft envisioned a few years ago.

There are basically two kinds of OLE Document servers:

- Full servers are stand-alone applications, which have file support and are available for any possible use of OLE.

- Mini-servers are servers that reside in DLLs, which cannot be executed by themselves and don't provide their own storage (they use the storage of the host application). Mini-servers support only embedding, not linking.

On the other side, OLE Document containers can support OLE in varying degrees. Without considering the different versions, there are several ways you can place an object in a container:

- You can insert a new object, using a specific menu command to create an embedded object.

- You can paste an object from the Clipboard, creating a new embedded object.

- You can paste-link an object from the Clipboard, creating a new linked object.

- You can create a new object from a file generated by a server. This can result in either an embedded object or a linked object.

- You can drag an object from a server to a container, if the two applications support OLE drag-and-drop.

- You can create an object inside another object, if the server application can also act as a container.

Once the object is placed inside the container, you can then perform operations on it, using the server's available *verbs*, or actions. Usually the *edit verb* is the default action—the action performed when you double-click on the object. For other objects, *play* is defined as the default action. You can typically see the list of actions supported by the current contained object by right-clicking on it. The same information is available in many programs via the Edit ➤ Object menu item, which has a submenu that lists the available verbs for the current object.

Using the OleContainer Component

Delphi provides no *visual* support for building OLE Document servers. You can always write a sever implementing the proper interfaces. OLE Document container support, instead, is easily available through the OleContainer component. To explore the use of this component I'll build a simple example step by step, providing most of the OLE container techniques described in the last section.

NOTE

OLE container support in 32-bit Delphi is quite different from its earlier 16-bit Delphi counterpart. The name of the component is the same, but the unit defining it has changed, the OLE helper functions have disappeared (replaced by new methods of the `TOleContainer` class), and the creation of new OLE objects is completely different.

A Minimal OLE Container

To create a simple OLE container application in Delphi, place an OleContainer component in a form. Then select the component and right-click to activate its local menu, which will have an Insert Object command. When you select this command, Delphi displays the standard OLE Insert Object dialog box. This dialog box allows you to choose from one of the registered server applications, as shown in Figure 22.5. The list of servers that appears in this dialog box depends on the OLE applications and OLE Controls installed on your system and stored in the registration database.

FIGURE 22.5

The standard OLE Insert Object dialog box allows you to insert an OLE object from one of the servers installed on your system.

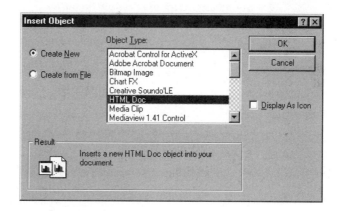

Once the OLE object is inserted in the container, the local menu of the control container component will have several more custom menu items. The new menu items include commands to change the properties of the OLE object, insert another one, copy the existing object, or remove it. The list also includes the verbs of the object (such as Edit, Open, or Play). Once you have inserted an OLE object in the container, the corresponding server will launch to let you edit the new object. As soon as you close the server application, Delphi updates the object in the container and shows it at design-time in the form of the Delphi application you are developing.

I haven't made any other relevant changes to this program, named OleCont1, besides aligning the OLE container to the client area and setting its SizeMode property to smCenter (to show the OLE object in the center of the container component). If you look at the textual description of this form (using the View as Text command of the form's local menu), you'll notice a Data property, which contains the actual data of the OLE object. Although the client program stores the data of the object, it doesn't know how to handle and show that without the help of the proper server. This means that the OLE object is *embedded*. The data of an embedded OLE object is stored inside the form, which is then stored in the executable file of the program. This can increase the size of the program a lot, depending on the type of server you're using and the amount of data. Another problem is that you can run this program only on a computer that has the required server installed. Otherwise, you'll get a run-time error when the OLE container tries to launch the server application to edit the object.

> **NOTE**
> This is true also for this sample program, OleCont1. You can run it only if the Microsoft Paint server is installed on your computer. (This server is included in the default Windows installation, so it should be there.)

When you run the OleCont1 example, you can simply double-click on the OLE container component, and the server window will show up *inside* the window of your application, as shown in Figure 22.6.

FIGURE 22.6

The OleCont1 example at run-time, with visual editing in action.

Object editing becomes active when you double-click on the object because of the value of the AutoActivate property, which is aaDoubleClick by default. Other alternatives are aaGetFocus and aaManual. When the value is aaManual, you can use the Active property to start the server via code; when the value is aaGetFocus, the server is activated as soon as you move the input focus to the object (for example, by clicking on it).

> **NOTE**　You cannot always use the Active property to end editing; if the server has its own window, the user must generally close it.

To improve visual editing by importing the menus from the server application, you can add a menu bar to the form, as we'll do in the next section.

Adding a Menu to the OLE Container Demo

To build a better version of the sample OLE container application, OleCont2, I've created a new form, which includes an OLE container component, a menu, and a panel with a combo box. In this version, the container does not contain an OLE Document object at design-time. A new OLE object will be created when you select File ➤ New, one of the few menu items that are actually enabled.

An important feature of an OLE container application that provides menus and supports in-place editing is *menu merging*. When the OLE object is activated in-place, some of the pull-down menus of the server application's menu bar are added to the menu bar of the container application. At the same time, some of the corresponding pull-down menus of the container application will disappear. OLE menu merging is handled almost automatically by Delphi. You only need to set the proper indexes for the menu items of the container, using the GroupIndex property. Basically, the menu items with an odd index number are replaced by the corresponding elements of the active OLE object.

More specifically, the File (0) and Window (4) pull-down menus belong to the container application. The Edit (1), View (3), and Help (5) pull-down menus (or the groups of pull-down menus with those indexes) are taken by the OLE server. A sixth group, named Object and indicated with the index 2, can be used by the container to display another pull-down menu between the Edit and View groups, even when the OLE object is active. In our example, the GroupIndex properties are 0 for File, 1 for Edit, and 5 for Help. Figure 22.7 shows an example of menu merging, using a Paint OLE object.

FIGURE 22.7

The menu merging of an active OLE object, in the OleCont2 example (only the File menu is that of the container application).

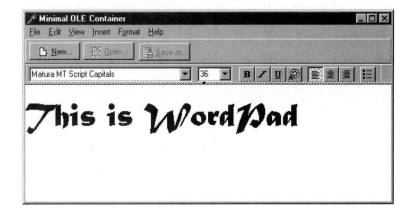

The only menu item we need to code is the New command, which we'll use to insert a new OLE object in the container. To accomplish this you can call the `InsertObjectDialog` method of the `TOleContainer` class, which displays the standard Insert OLE Object dialog box (the same dialog box we saw in Figure 22.5).

The `InsertObjectDialog` method shows the dialog box, takes care of deleting the previous OLE object, and provides the new object initialization. However, it doesn't automatically activate the OLE object. For this reason, it is common to write the following code to activate the object:

```
procedure TForm1.New1Click(Sender: TObject);
begin
  if OleContainer1.InsertObjectDialog then
    OleContainer1.DoVerb (OleContainer1.PrimaryVerb);
end;
```

Once a new object has been created, you can execute its primary verb using the `DoVerb` method. The program also displays a small toolbar, with some bitmap buttons. I placed some `TWinControl` components in the form to let the user select them and thus disable the OleContainer. To keep this toolbar/panel visible while in-place editing is occurring, you should set its `Locked` property to `True`. This forces the panel to remain present in the application and not be replaced by a toolbar of the server, as we will see in the next version of the example.

Visual Editing and Toolbars

As I've just mentioned, the OleCont2 example keeps its toolbar even when you activate an OLE object in-place (which may or may not be possible, depending on the kind of server you are using). In the following version, OleCont3, I've added a second panel, with some more buttons. Since this time I don't set its Locked property, this new toolbar will be replaced with that of the active OLE server. When in-place editing launches a server application that displays a toolbar, that server's toolbar replaces the container's toolbar, as you can see in the lower part of Figure 22.8.

FIGURE 22.8

The second toolbar of the OleCont3 example (top) is replaced by the toolbar of the server (bottom).

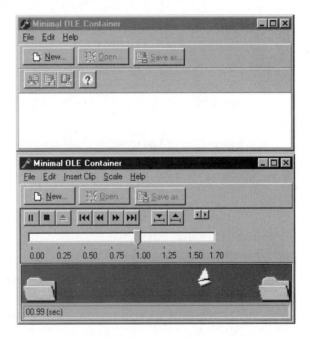

> **TIP**
>
> To make all the automatic resizing operations work smoothly, you should place the OLE container component in a panel component and align both of them to the client area of the form.

The OLE Standard Dialog Boxes

In the previous examples, we created new OLE objects at run-time using the InsertObjectDialog method. However, there are other ways to create OLE objects. One way is to use a similar function, PasteSpecialDialog. Another way to create an OLE object is by dragging, but we won't explore that technique in the book. In the fourth version of our example, named OleCont4, I've added Paste Special support and some other Clipboard support to the OLE container. (I'll cover Clipboard support in Delphi in more general terms in Chapter 30, so here I'll just show you the code, skipping some of the details.)

Another addition to the example is its handling of OLE links. This is another operation available via a standard dialog box, wrapped in a Delphi function. There are several standard dialog boxes in OLE. Some of them are directly available in Delphi using special methods, such as InsertObjectDialog, ObjectPropertiesDialog, and PasteSpecialDialog.

The OleCont4 example uses essentially the same form as the previous version, with a new Object Properties item in the Edit pull-down menu. Here is the code triggered by this menu item:

```
procedure TForm1.Object1Click(Sender: TObject);
begin
  OleContainer1.ObjectPropertiesDialog;
end;
```

You can see an example of the resulting standard OLE dialog box in Figure 22.9. Obviously, this dialog box changes depending on the nature of the active OLE object in the container.

In addition, the program now handles the Clipboard, using cut, copy, paste, and paste special operations. Here is the code for these methods (which are used to handle both menu commands and toolbar buttons):

```
procedure TForm1.Paste1Click(Sender: TObject);
begin
  OleContainer1.Paste;
  UpdateUI;
end;
procedure TForm1.PasteSpecial1Click(Sender: TObject);
begin
  OleContainer1.PasteSpecialDialog;
  UpdateUI;
end;
procedure TForm1.Copy1Click(Sender: TObject);
```

```
begin
  OleContainer1.Copy;
  UpdateUI;
end;
procedure TForm1.Cut1Click(Sender: TObject);
begin
  OleContainer1.Copy;
  OleContainer1.Destroy;
  UpdateUI;
end;
```

FIGURE 22.9

The standard OLE Object
Properties dialog box,
available in the OleCont4
example.

The most important of these four methods is `PasteSpecial1Click`, which
shows another standard OLE dialog box, as you can see in Figure 22.10.

FIGURE 22.10

The standard OLE Paste
Special dialog box.

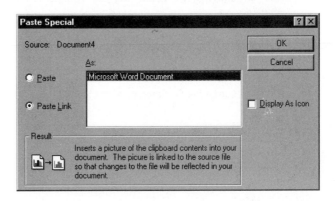

Each of these handlers (and also the `Edit1Click` method that responds to the selection of the Edit pull-down menu) calls an `UpdateUI` procedure I've added to the form:

```
procedure TForm1.UpdateUI;
begin
  Cut1.Enabled := OleContainer1.State <> osEmpty;
  Copy1.Enabled := OleContainer1.State <> osEmpty;
  Object1.Enabled := OleContainer1.State <> osEmpty;
  Paste1.Enabled := OleContainer1.CanPaste;
  PasteSpecial1.Enabled := OleContainer1.CanPaste;
  PasteSpeedButton.Enabled := Paste1.Enabled;
  CutSpeedButton.Enabled := Cut1.Enabled;
  CopySpeedButton.Enabled := Copy1.Enabled;
end;
```

This private method of the form simply enables or disables the menu items and the toolbar buttons depending on the value of the `State` property of the Ole-Container component and the result returned by its `CanPaste` method.

Loading and Saving Objects in Files

The last enhancement we'll make in the series of OLE container examples involves adding support for files. This is actually one of the simplest additions we can make, because the OLE container component already provides file support. The form of the new example, OleCont5, has two standard OpenDialog and SaveDialog components, and its source code adds just a few more lines:

```
procedure TForm1.Open1Click(Sender: TObject);
begin
  if OpenDialog1.Execute then
    OleContainer1.LoadFromFile (OpenDialog1.FileName);
  UpdateUI;
end;
procedure TForm1.SaveAs1Click(Sender: TObject);
  begin
  if SaveDialog1.Execute then
    OleContainer1.SaveToFile (SaveDialog1.FileName);
end;
```

Again, the code calls two methods of the `TOleContainer` class. There is another method, `CreateObjectFromFile`, which has a completely different meaning from the LoadFromFile method. LoadFromFile is simply used to reload files saved with the SaveToFile method. In this example, I've used these methods and I've given these files the extension .DOL (for Demo OLE files). By contrast, CreateObjectFromFile is used to insert new OLE objects into the container, loading their data from a file. That file is generated by the server, and its extension is used to determine the server type.

The program incorporates a lot of OLE features, although it still isn't a complete sample of all the available capabilities. For example, the program doesn't support creating objects from files or OLE object drag-and-drop. Instead of further extending the example in this direction, I want to explore a different case, an example that allows the creation of multiple OleContainer components, relating to different servers.

Multiple OLE Containers

All of the previous examples we've created could display only one OLE object at a time, because we created one permanent OLE container component in each example. Our next example, named MultiOle, shows how to manipulate multiple OLE container components in the same form. (You can compare the approach in this example with the MDI approach in Delphi's own example.)

The MultiOle example can create and display both edit boxes and OLE containers. Components of these two types are created when the user double-clicks on the surface of the form, and they are placed in the position of the click event. The example also has other capabilities. You can move each edit box or OLE container and still click on an OLE container to activate it. You can also select an OLE container and then use its pop-up menu to call its verbs.

The choice between the two components depends on the status of the two speed buttons of the toolbar, which behave like radio buttons (they have the same value of the GroupIndex property). The OnClick event handlers of these two buttons simply set the value of the Boolean OleObj field of the form to True or False.

One of the key elements of the source code is the FormDblClick method, which is used to create new components when the user double-clicks on the surface of the form. You can see the effect of executing this code several times in Figure 22.11.

FIGURE 22.11

With the MultiOle example, you can create several OLE containers and edit boxes.

Actually, there is another related event-handling method, FormMouseDown, used to store the current position of the mouse in the X1 and Y1 fields of the form. I have to do this because the OnDblClick event provides no information regarding the mouse position. The FormDblClick has two distinct parts: the creation of an edit and the creation of an OLE container. Here is the code related to the creation of the OleContainer component:

```
procedure TForm1.FormDblClick(Sender: TObject);
var
  OleCont: TOleContainer;
  Pan: TPanel;
begin
  if OleObj then
  begin
    // create a panel to host the OLE container
    Pan := TPanel.Create (self);
    Pan.Parent := Self;
    Pan.SetBounds (X1, Y1, 100, 100);
    // create an OLE container, with unique name
    OleCont := TOleContainer.Create (self);
    OleCont.Parent := Pan;
    OleCont.Align := alClient;
    Inc (OleCount);
    OleCont.Name := 'OleContainer' + IntToStr (OleCount);
    // insert the actual object
    OleCont.InsertObjectDialog;
```

```
  end
  else ...
```

We have already seen similar code is other examples, so I won't describe it in detail here. Actually, this program has one more feature. It allows a user to drag one of the Edit or OleContainer controls to a different position on the form. To accomplish this, when I create the controls at run-time I set their `OnMouseDown` event to a handler that simply calls the `BeginDrag` method. I've also written a handler for the `OnDragDrop` event of the form, as follows:

```pascal
procedure TForm1.FormDragDrop(
  Sender, Source: TObject; X, Y: Integer);
var
  Control: TControl;
begin
  if Source is TOleContainer then
    // move the panel hosting the control
    Control := (Source as TControl).Parent
  else
    Control := Source as TControl;
  Control.Left := X;
  Control.Top := Y;
end;
```

You can see the complete source code of this example on the companion CD, as usual.

What's Next

In this chapter we have focused on two implementations of the Microsoft OLE technology, OLE Automation and OLE Documents. As we have seen, both are well supported in Delphi 3. They were supported also in Delphi 2, though in different and less powerful ways.

What is brand-new in Delphi 3 is a capability we will explore next: the ability to create ActiveX controls and ActiveForms visually. These two new features are based on the same technology, ActiveX, but are intended for two different uses. ActiveX controls are controls you can use in other development environments besides Delphi; ActiveForms are Delphi forms you can embed in an Internet document. Actually the boundary between the two technologies is not so well-defined, but these are the most typical uses, as we'll see in the next two chapters.

CHAPTER TWENTY-THREE

Using and Creating ActiveX Controls

- ActiveX controls and Delphi components

- Installing and using ActiveX controls

- Turning a component into an ActiveX

- Building an ActiveX from scratch

Microsoft's Visual Basic was the first program-development environment to introduce the idea of supplying software components to the mass market. But the concept of reusable software components is older than Visual Basic, and it's well-rooted in the theories of object-oriented programming. However, OOP languages never delivered the reusability they promised, probably more because of marketing and standardization problems than for any other reasons. Although Visual Basic does not fully exploit object-oriented programming, it applies the concept of a component through the definition of a standard way to build and distribute new controls that developers can integrate into the environment. The first technical standard promoted by Visual Basic was VBX, a 16-bit specification fully available in the 16-bit version of Delphi. Moving to the 32-bit platforms, Microsoft has replaced the VBX standard with the more powerful and more open ActiveX controls.

> **NOTE**   ActiveX controls used to be called OLE Controls (or OCX). The new name reflects more a new marketing strategy from Microsoft than a technical innovation. Technically, ActiveX can be considered a minor extension to the OCX technology. Not surprisingly, ActiveX controls are usually saved in files with the OCX extension.

Introducing ActiveX Controls

From a general perspective, an ActiveX control is not very different from a Windows, Delphi, or Visual Basic control. A control is always a window, with its associated code defining its behavior. The key difference between various families of controls is in the interaction between the control and the rest of the application, the interface of the control. Typical Windows controls use a message-based interface, VBX controls use properties and events, OLE Automation objects use properties and methods, and ActiveX controls use properties, methods, and events. These three elements are also found in Delphi's own components.

Using OLE jargon, an ActiveX control is a "compound document object which is implemented as an in-process server DLL, and supports OLE Automation, visual editing, and inside-out activation." Perfectly clear, right? Let's see what this definition actually means.

An ActiveX control uses the same approach as OLE server objects, which are the objects you can insert into an OLE Document, as we saw in the last chapter. The difference between a generic OLE server and an ActiveX control is that OLE servers can be implemented in three different ways:

- as stand-alone applications (for example, Microsoft Excel).

- as out-of-process servers—that is, executables files that cannot be run by themselves, but can only be invoked by a server (for example, Microsoft Graph and similar applications).

- as in-process servers, such as DLLs loaded into the same memory space as the program using them.

ActiveX controls can only be implemented using the last technique, which is also the fastest. Furthermore, ActiveX controls are OLE Automation servers (also discussed in the last chapter). This means you can access properties of these objects and call their methods. The OLE Automation interface lacks events, which are added in the ActiveX. This makes the ActiveX interface specification similar to that of Delphi components.

You can see an ActiveX control in the application that is using it and interact with it directly in the container application window: this is the meaning of the term *visual editing*, or *in-place activation*. A single click activates the control, rather than the double-click used by OLE Documents, and the control is active whenever it is visible (which is what the term *inside-out activation* means), without having to double-click on it.

As I've mentioned before, an ActiveX control has properties, methods, and events. Properties can be state identifiers, but they can also activate methods. (This is particularly true for ActiveX controls that are *updated* VBX controls, because in a VBX there was no other way to activate a method than by setting a property.) Properties can refer to aggregate values, arrays, sub-objects, and so on. Properties can also be dynamic (or read-only, to use the Delphi term).

In an ActiveX control, properties are divided into different groups: stock properties that most controls need to implement; ambient properties that offer information about the container (similar to the `ParentColor` or `ParentFont` properties in Delphi); extended properties managed by the container, such as the position of the object; and custom properties, which can be anything.

Events and methods are … well, events and methods. *Events* relate to a mouse click, a key press, the activation of a component, and other specific user actions. *Methods* are functions and procedures related to the control. There is no major difference between the ActiveX and Delphi concepts of events and methods.

ActiveX Controls versus Delphi Components

Before I show you how to use and write ActiveX controls in Delphi, let's go over some of the technical differences between the two kinds of controls. ActiveX controls are DLL-based. This means that when you use them, you need to distribute their code (the OCX file) along with the application using them. In Delphi, the code of the components can be statically linked to the executable file, or dynamically linked to it using a run-time package, so you can always choose.

Having a separate file allows you to share code among different applications, as DLLs usually do. If two applications use the same control (or run-time package), you need only one copy of it on the hard disk and a single copy in memory. The drawback, however, is that if the two programs have to use two different versions of the ActiveX control, some compatibility problems might arise. An advantage of having a self-contained executable file is that you will also have fewer installation problems.

Now, what is the drawback of using Delphi components? The real problem is not that there are fewer Delphi components than ActiveX controls, but that if you buy a Delphi component you'll be able to use it only in Delphi and Borland C++Builder. If you buy an ActiveX control you'll be able to use it in multiple development environments from multiple vendors. If you develop mainly in Delphi and find two similar components based on the two technologies, I suggest you buy the Delphi one because it will be more integrated with the environment and easier to use for a Delphi programmer. The native Delphi component will probably be better documented (from the Pascal perspective), and it will take advantage of Delphi and Object Pascal features not available in the general ActiveX interface, which is traditionally based on C and C++.

Using ActiveX Controls in Delphi

Delphi comes with some preinstalled ActiveX controls, and you can buy and install more third-party ActiveX controls easily. (In fact, the ActiveX controls included in Delphi have been developed by third parties, not by Borland.) Since the ActiveX controls are not available in the Standard edition of Delphi, I will describe how ActiveX controls work in general and show you only a couple of very simple examples.

Installing an ActiveX Control

After you've installed an ActiveX control library on your computer, following the vendor's instructions, you need to install it in Delphi to make the controls visible to the development environment. I'm using the term ActiveX control library, because this is the precise description of an OCX file. This file, in fact, can contain multiple ActiveX controls.

The Delphi installation process is very simple. Select Components ➤ Import ActiveX library in the Delphi menu. This opens the Import ActiveX Library dialog box (see Figure 23.1). In this dialog box, you can see the list of ActiveX control libraries registered in Windows. If you choose one, Delphi will read its type library, list its controls, and suggest a file name for its unit. If the information is correct, simply press the Create Unit button to view the Pascal source code file created by Delphi as a *wrapper* for the ActiveX control. Press the Install button to add this new unit to a Delphi package and to the Components Palette.

Whichever button you press, Delphi generates an Object Pascal source code file, which contains the definition of a class for each ActiveX control of the library. For each control there is an `interface` and a `dispinterface` type declaration. For example, installing the WebBrowser component selected in Figure 23.1, Delphi generates a unit with the following declarations (among several others):

```
type
  IWebBrowser = interface(IDispatch)
    ['{EAB22AC1-30C1-11CF-A7EB-0000C05BAE0B}']
    procedure GoBack; safecall;
    procedure GoForward; safecall;
    procedure GoHome; safecall;
    ...
```

```
DWebBrowser = dispinterface
  ['{EAB22AC1-30C1-11CF-A7EB-0000C05BAE0B}']
  procedure GoBack; dispid 100;
  procedure GoForward; dispid 101;
  procedure GoHome; dispid 102;
  ...

TWebBrowser = class(TOleControl)
private
  FIntf: IWebBrowser;
public
  procedure GoBack;
  procedure GoForward;
  procedure GoHome;
  ...
```

FIGURE 23.1

The dialog boxes used to install new ActiveX controls in Delphi.

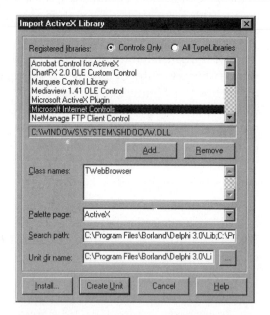

The basic idea is that Delphi declares an interface, and then subclasses the TOleControl class. This new class, TWebBrowser, doesn't implement the new interface. Instead, it includes an interface object as a local private field. The resulting TWebBrowser class has the same properties, methods, and events as the ActiveX control itself (plus a few properties inherited from the TOleControls class and shared by every Delphi component).

Delphi tries to keep the original names of the properties, but this is not always possible. At the beginning of the Pascal files generated during the installation of the components (such as the one above), you'll find a *Conversion log* indicating which names Delphi had to change. For example, in this file we can find the line:

```
{Warning: 'Type' is a reserved word.
IWebBrowser.Type changed to Type_}
```

If you are planning to use ActiveX controls, follow the procedure outlined here to install them. Then you can study (and eventually print) the Object Pascal source code file for the control to see how it is defined. At the beginning of the file you'll also find the lists of constant values for the specific properties.

The TOleControl Class

For each new ActiveX control you install, Delphi defines a new Object Pascal class, derived from the TOleControl class of the VCL. What is this class for? It encapsulates the basic behavior of ActiveX Controls, defining all the code needed by its subclasses to access properties and other information. The class also has some public methods and properties, including the BrowseProperties method and the OleObject property (a read-only property of the variant data type). You can use this property to access the internal OLE object that defines an ActiveX control. This approach gives you direct access to the control object, but it makes the code more difficult to write. So most of the time, using the Delphi interface of the control is better than direct access.

Using ActiveX Controls

Once installed (whether manually or as part of your version of Delphi), an ActiveX control can be added to a form just like any other Delphi component. You can set its properties, handle its events, and work with it almost exactly as you work with other Delphi components.

The first example I'll build, called Spell, uses the VSSpell ActiveX control from Visual Components, available in the Professional Edition of Delphi 3. I've taken an old Notepad-like application (from an older edition of this book), and added this spelling checker to it. Here is how the component looks in the textual description of the form:

```
object VSSpell1: TVSSpell
  ControlData = {000002000101010000000000.....}
end
```

Although these numbers aren't easy to interpret, this `ControlData` property demonstrates that ActiveX controls are really *embedded* objects. Their data is stored in the application containing the control. This numeric value is the result of some simple settings on the ActiveX control. You can set these values with the Object Inspector, or use the custom property editor of the whole ActiveX control, which is available via the Properties command of the component's local menu or by double-clicking on it. In Figure 23.2, you can see both the Object Inspector and the VisualSpeller Control Properties dialog box.

FIGURE 23.2

Two ways to set the properties of an ActiveX control: the Object Inspector or the specific control properties editor.

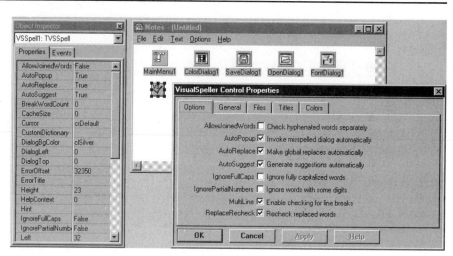

In the Spell example, I've added a menu item to the program's form to activate the spelling component and I've written the following code for its OnClick event handler:

```
procedure TNotesForm.Spelltext1Click(Sender: TObject);
begin
  VSSpell.CheckText := Memo1.Text;
  if VSSpell.ResultCode = 0 then
    // the spelling was properly executed
    Memo1.Text := VSSpell.Text;
end;
```

When you run this program and select Options ➤ Spell text, the ActiveX control will display a dialog box, which allows you to perform standard spell-checking operations. You can see the program running in Figure 23.3.

FIGURE 23.3

The VSSpeller ActiveX
control in action.

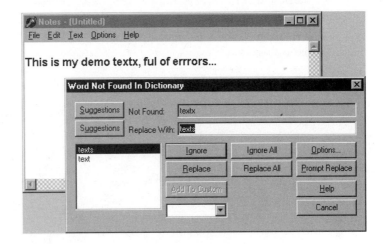

You might be tempted to add the VSSpeller control to an application that works with formatted text, like the RichNot2 example we built in Chapter 10. The problem is that this component is not designed to work with formatted text: although it is very simple to extract the plain text from a RichEdit control, and check its spelling, you'll lose all the formatting.

Building a Chart

Besides the TeeChart component covered in Chapter 11, Delphi includes three different ActiveX controls for charting: ChartFX by Software FX, Graph Custom Control by Bits Per Second, and First Impression by Visual Components. These are powerful components (although the versions you find in Delphi have reduced capabilities), and I've chosen one of them just to show you how easy it is to use a *visual* ActiveX.

In general, the only difficulties you'll find relate to the Help files of the ActiveX controls. You can find these files in the Delphi 3.0/OCX directory, but they are mainly addressed to Visual Basic programmers, so the examples are not always easily applicable to Delphi.

To demonstrate how the First Impression component can be used, I've built another simple program, called XChart. This example is very similar to the Chart example that demonstrated the TeeChart Delphi component in Chapter 11. As shown in Figure 23.4, there is a chart in the top portion of the screen, with a string grid below it, and a push button used to copy the numeric values of the string grid to the chart.

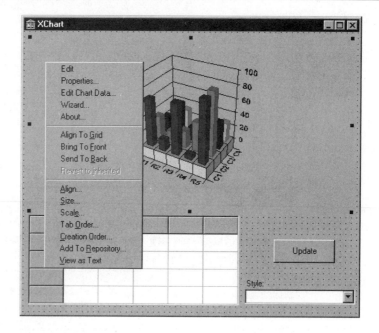

FIGURE 23.4

The form of the XChart example at design-time, with the local menu of this graphical ActiveX control.

The form also has a combo box you can use to choose the type of graph. As in the previous version, the core of this example is the `UpdateButtonClick` method. To copy the data to the chart ActiveX control, you need to set the value of the Row and Column properties to indicate the item you want to modify, and then set the Data property to change the value of the current item:

```
procedure TForm1.UpdateButtonClick(Sender: TObject);
var
  I, J: Integer;
begin
  for I := 1 to 5 do
  begin
    VtChart1.Row := I;
    for J := 1 to 4 do
    begin
      VtChart1.Column := J;
```

```
        VtChart1.Data := StringGrid1.Cells [I, J];
      end;
    end;
  end;
```

Writing ActiveX Controls

 Besides using existing ActiveX controls in Delphi 3, you can easily develop new ones. Although you can write the code of a new ActiveX control yourself, implementing all the required OLE interfaces (and there are many), it's much easier to use the ActiveX Control Wizard. This Delphi tool turns a VCL control you provide into an ActiveX control, with very little work on your part.

To create a new ActiveX you start with an existing VCL component, which must be a TWinControl descendant, and then wrap the ActiveX around it. During this step Delphi adds a type library to the control. Wrapping an ActiveX control around a Delphi component is exactly the opposite of what we did to use an ActiveX inside Delphi.

Another optional step is to prepare a property page for the control, a sort of property editor used to set the initial value of the properties of the control in any development environment. It is a sort of alternative to the Object Inspector in Delphi. Since most development environments allow only limited editing, it is more important to write a property page than it is to write a component or a property editor for a Delphi control (we focused on this topic in Chapter 19). Figure 23.2, earlier in this chapter, shows the property page of the VCSpell ActiveX control.

Building an ActiveX Arrow

As an example of the development of an ActiveX control, I've decided to take the Arrow component we developed in Chapter 17 and turn it into an ActiveX. Actually, we cannot use that component directly, because it was a graphical control, a subclass of TGraphicControl. However, turning a graphical control into a window-based control is usually a straightforward operation. In this case, I've just changed the base class name to TCustomControl (and changed the name of the class of the control as well, to avoid a name clash):

```
type
  TMd3WArrow = class(TCustomControl)
  ...
```

The TWinControl class has very minimal support for graphical output. Its TCustomControl subclass, however, has basically the same capabilities as the TGraphicControl class. The key difference is that a TCustomControl object has a window handle.

After installing this new component in Delphi, we are ready to start developing the new example. To create a new ActiveX library, simply select File ➤ New, move to the ActiveX page, and choose ActiveX library. Delphi creates the bare skeleton of a DLL, as we have already seen in Chapter 21. I've saved this library as XArrow, in a directory with the same name, as usual.

Now it is time to use the ActiveX Control Wizard, available in the ActiveX page of the Object Repository—Delphi's New dialog box. In this Wizard (shown in Figure 23.5) you simply select the VCL class you are interested in, customize the names shown in the edit boxes, and click OK; and Delphi builds the complete source code of an ActiveX control for you.

FIGURE 23.5

Delphi's ActiveX Control Wizard.

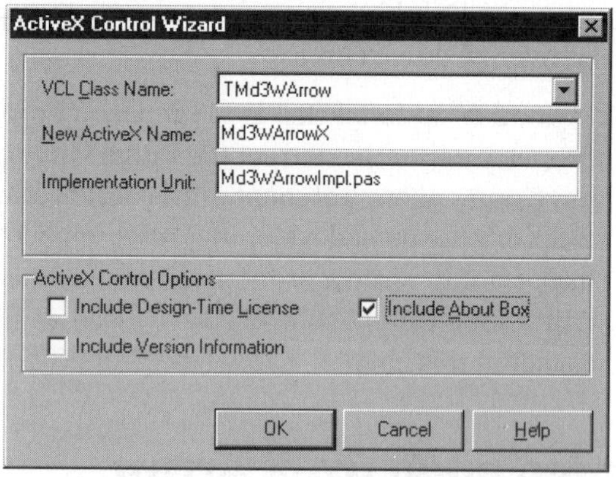

The use of the three check boxes at the bottom of the ActiveX Control Wizard window may not be obvious. If you include design-time license support, the user of the control won't be able to use it in a design environment without the proper *license key* for the control. When you check the Include Design-time License box, the ActiveX Control Wizard creates this license key, and stores it in an .LIC file. The second check box allows you to include version information for the ActiveX, in the OCX file. Version information is discussed in Chapter 27. If the third check box is selected, the ActiveX Control Wizard automatically adds an About box to the control. In this example I've decided to select only the last check box, to have the About box generated automatically. Actually, this requires a little manual intervention on the About box form itself (editing the default captions of the labels).

It is important to look at the code the ActiveX Control Wizard generates. The key element of this Wizard is the generation of a type library. You can see the library generated for our arrow control in Delphi's type library editor in Figure 23.6. From the type library information, the Wizard also generates an import file with the definition of an interface, the dispinterface, and other types and constants.

FIGURE 23.6

The Type Library Editor with the type library of the demo ActiveX control I've created.

In this example the import file is named XArrowLib.pas. The first part of this file includes a couple of GUIDs, one for the library as a whole, one for the control, and other constants for the definition of values corresponding to the enumerated types used by properties of the Delphi control, for example:

```
{ TxArrowDirection }
const
  adUp = 0;
  adDown = 1;
  adLeft = 2;
  adRight = 3;
```

The real meat is the declaration of the IMd3WArrowX interface, and the corresponding DMd3WArrowX dispinterface. Here are two small excerpts from their declarations:

```
type
  IMd3WArrowX = interface(IDispatch)
```

```
  ['{401A3602-9099-11D0-98D0-444553540000}']
  function Get_Direction: TxArrowDirection; safecall;
  procedure Set_Direction(
    Value: TxArrowDirection); safecall;
  ...
  procedure AboutBox; safecall;
  property Direction: TxArrowDirection
    read Get_Direction write Set_Direction;
  ...
DMd3WArrowX = dispinterface
  ['{401A3602-9099-11D0-98D0-444553540000}']
  property Direction: TxArrowDirection dispid 1;
  ...
  procedure AboutBox; dispid -552;
end;
```

There is actually a second dispatch interface for the events of the control:

```
IMd3WArrowXEvents = dispinterface
    ['{401A3603-9099-11D0-98D0-444553540000}']
    procedure OnClick; dispid 1;
    procedure OnArrowDblClick; dispid 2;
end;
```

> **NOTE**
> The final part of the import unit includes the declaration of the
> TMd3WArrowX class. This is a TOleControl-derived class you can use to
> install the control in Delphi, as we've seen in the first part of this chap-
> ter. You don't need this class to build the ActiveX control. You need it to
> install the ActiveX control in Delphi. The class used by the ActiveX
> server has the same class name, but a different implementation.

The rest of the code, and the code you'll customize, is in the main unit, which in
my example is called XArImpl.pas. This unit has the declaration of the ActiveX
server object, TMd3WArrowX, which inherits from TActiveXControl and implements the specific IMd3WArrowX interface. Here is a small part of this declaration:

```
type
  TMd3WArrowX = class(TActiveXControl, IMd3WArrowX)
  private
    FDelphiControl: TMd3WArrow;
    FEvents: IMd3WArrowXEvents;
    ...
```

```
protected
  procedure InitializeControl; override;
  procedure DefinePropertyPages(
    DefinePropertyPage: TDefinePropertyPage); override;
  function Get_ArrowHeight: Integer; safecall;
  procedure Set_ArrowHeight(Value: Integer); safecall;
  procedure AboutBox; safecall;
  ...
```

Before we customize this control in any way, we can see how it works. You should first compile the ActiveX library, and then register it using Delphi's Run ➤ Register ActiveX Server menu command. Now you can install the ActiveX control as we've done in the past; or you can also use a faster approach.

Since you have the import library unit, which already includes the client TOleControl subclass declaration, and the registration code, you can simply add this unit to an existing or new package. After you install this component, it will show up by default in the ActiveX page of the Components Palette. Grab it, place it in a new form, and you'll be able to edit the properties of the component, and use its local menu to show the About box, as you can see in Figure 23.7. Actually, this ActiveX control is not a perfect clone of our original VCL control. The more complex properties, such as properties based on VCL objects as TBrush or TPen, in fact, are not available.

FIGURE 23.7

The ActiveX control we've just created in a Delphi form.

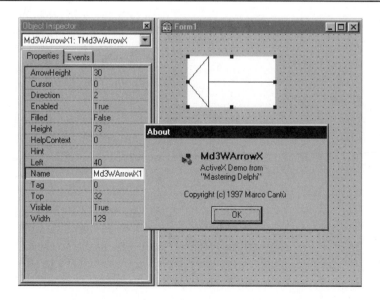

Adding New Properties

Once you've created an ActiveX control, adding new properties, events, or methods to it is—surprisingly—simpler than doing the same operation for a VCL component. Delphi, in fact, provides specific visual support for the former, not for the latter.

You can simply open the Pascal unit with the implementation of the ActiveX control, and choose Edit ➤ Add To Interface. As an alternative you can use the same command from the local menu of the editor. Delphi opens the Add to Interface dialog box (see Figure 23.8). In the combo box of this dialog box you can choose between a new property, method or event. In this example the first selection will affect the IMd3WArrowX interface, and the second the IMd3WArrowXEvents interface.

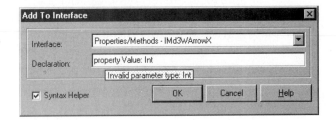

In the edit box you can then type the declaration of this new interface element. If the Syntax Helper check box is activated, you'll get hints describing what you should type next, and highlighting any errors. You can see the syntax helper in action in Figure 23.8. When you define a new ActiveX interface element, keep in mind that you are restricted to OLE data types. In the XArrow example I've added two properties to the ActiveX control. Since the Pen and the Brush properties of the original Delphi components are not accessible, I've made available their color. These are examples of what you can write in the edit box of the Add to Interface dialog (executing it twice):

```
property FillColor: TColor;
property PenColor: Integer;
```

NOTE Since a TColor is nothing but a numeric value, it is legal to use it. TColor is an Integer subrange that defaults to Integer size. In the type library its type is defined as USERDEFINED. This probably means that only Delphi knows how to handle it. I've decided to use it anyway for one property, and use Integer for the other so you can see their effect once the ActiveX control is used in different development environments.

The declarations you enter in the Add to Interface dialog box are automatically added to the control's type library (.TLB) file, to its import library unit, and to its implementation unit:

```
type
  IMd3WArrowX = interface(IDispatch)
    function Get_FillColor: TColor; safecall;
    procedure Set_FillColor(Value: TColor); safecall;
    function Get_PenColor: Integer; safecall;
    procedure Set_PenColor(Value: Integer); safecall;
    ...
    property FillColor: TColor
      read Get_FillColor write Set_FillColor;
    property PenColor: Integer
      read Get_PenColor write Set_PenColor;
    ...
  DMd3WArrowX = dispinterface
    property FillColor: TColor dispid 8;
    property PenColor: Integer dispid 9;
    ...
  TMd3WArrowX = class(TActiveXControl, IMd3WArrowX)
    function Get_FillColor: TColor; safecall;
    procedure Set_FillColor(Value: TColor); safecall;
    function Get_PenColor: Integer; safecall;
    procedure Set_PenColor(Value: Integer); safecall;
    ...
```

This feature is extremely powerful, because editing these three different declarations by hand and keeping them in synch would have been a major effort. All you have to do to finish the ActiveX control is to fill in the Get_x and Set_x methods of the implementation. Here is the code of the example:

```
function TMd3WArrowX.Get_FillColor: TColor;
begin
  Result := FDelphiControl.Brush.Color;
end;

procedure TMd3WArrowX.Set_FillColor(Value: TColor);
begin
  FDelphiControl.Brush.Color := Value;
end;

function TMd3WArrowX.Get_PenColor: Integer;
begin
  Result := ColorToRGB (FDelphiControl.Pen.Color);
end;

procedure TMd3WArrowX.Set_PenColor(Value: Integer);
begin
  FDelphiControl.Pen.Color := Value;
end;
```

If you now reload this control in Delphi, the two new properties will appear. The first, FillColor, is shown in the Object Inspector as any TColor property of a Delphi control, and you can use the corresponding property editor. The second, PenColor, has a plain integer editor, making it quite difficult to enter the value of a new color by hand. A program, by contrast, can easily use the RGB function to create the proper color value.

In other development environments, you'll get the opposite effect, with the Integer property working OK and the TColor property not being recognized. This is particularly true if the host development environment has a window similar to Delphi's Object Inspector.

Adding a Property Page

As it stands, however, other development environments can do very little with our component, because we've prepared no property page—no property editor. A property page is fundamental so that programmers using the control can edit its attributes. However, adding a property page is not as simple as adding a form with a few controls. The property page, in fact, will integrate with the host development environment. The property page for our control will show up inside a property page dialog of the host environment, which will provide the OK, Cancel, and Apply buttons, and the tabs for showing multiple property pages (some of which might be provided by the host development environment).

The nice thing is that support for property pages is built into Delphi 3, so adding one is quite simple. You simply open an ActiveX project, then open the usual New Items dialog box, move to the ActiveX page, and choose Property Page. What you get is not very different from a form. In fact the TPropertyPage1 class (created by default) inherits from the TPropertyPage class of the VCL, which in turn inherits from TCustomForm.

In the property page you can add controls as in a normal Delphi form, and write code to let the controls interact. I've added to the property page a combo box with the possible values of the Direction property, a check box for the Filled property, an edit box with an UpDown control to set the ArrowHeight property, and two shapes with corresponding buttons for the colors. You can see this form at design-time in Figure 23.9.

FIGURE 23.9

The property page of the XArrow ActiveX control at design-time.

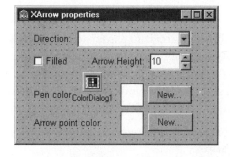

The only code added to the form relates to the two buttons used to change the color of the two shape components, which offer a preview of the colors of the actual ActiveX control. The OnClick event of the button uses a ColorDialog component, as usual:

```
procedure TPropertyPage1.ButtonPenClick(Sender: TObject);
begin
  with ColorDialog1 do
```

```
begin
  Color := ShapePen.Brush.Color;
  if Execute then
  begin
    ShapePen.Brush.Color := Color;
    Modified; // enable Apply button!
  end;
end;
end;
```

What is important to notice in this code is the call to the Modified method of the TPropertyPage class. This call is required to let the property page dialog box know we've modified one of the values, and enable the Apply button. When a user interacts with one of the other controls of this form, this call is made automatically. For the two buttons, however, we need to add this line ourselves.

> **TIP**   Another tip relates to the Caption of the property page form. This will be used in the property dialog box of the host environment as the caption of the tab corresponding to the property page.

The next step is to associate the controls of the property page with the actual properties of the ActiveX control. The property page class automatically has two methods for this: UpdateOleObject and UpdatePropertyPage. As their names suggest, these two methods copy data from the property page to the ActiveX control and vice-versa. Here is the code for my example:

```
procedure TPropertyPage1.UpdatePropertyPage;
begin
  { Update your controls from the OleObject }
  ComboDir.ItemIndex := OleObject.Direction;
  CheckFilled.Checked := OleObject.Filled;
  EditHeight.Text := IntToStr (OleObject.ArrowHeight);
  ShapePen.Brush.Color := OleObject.PenColor;
  ShapePoint.Brush.Color := OleObject.FillColor;
end;

procedure TPropertyPage1.UpdateObject;
```

```
begin
  { Update the OleObject from your controls }
  OleObject.Direction := ComboDir.ItemIndex;
  OleObject.Filled := CheckFilled.Checked;
  OleObject.ArrowHeight := UpDownHeight.Position;
  OleObject.PenColor := ColorToRGB (ShapePen.Brush.Color);
  OleObject.FillColor := ShapePoint.Brush.Color
end;
```

The final step is to connect the property page itself to the ActiveX control. When the control was created, the Delphi ActiveX Control Wizard automatically added a declaration for the DefinePropertyPages method to the implementation unit. In this method we simply call the DefinePropertyPage method (this time the method name is singular) for each property page we want to add to the ActiveX. This method has as its parameter the GUID of the property page, something you can find in the corresponding unit (of course you'll need to add a uses statement referring to that unit). Here is the code of my example:

```
procedure TMd3WArrowX.DefinePropertyPages(
  DefinePropertyPage: TDefinePropertyPage);
begin
  DefinePropertyPage(Class_PropertyPage1);
end;
```

NOTE The connection between the ActiveX control and its property page takes place using a GUID. This is possible because the property page object can be created though a class factory and its GUID is stored in the Windows Registry when you register the ActiveX control library. To see what's going on, look at the initialization section of the property page unit, which calls TActiveXPropertyPageFactory.Create.

Now that we've finished developing the property page, and after recompiling and reregistering the ActiveX library, we can install the ActiveX control inside a host development environment (including Delphi itself) and see how it looks. Figure 23.10 shows an example. (If you've already installed the ActiveX control in Delphi, you should uninstall it prior to rebuilding it. This process might also require closing and reopening Delphi itself.)

FIGURE 23.10

The XArrow ActiveX control and its property page, hosted by the Delphi environment.

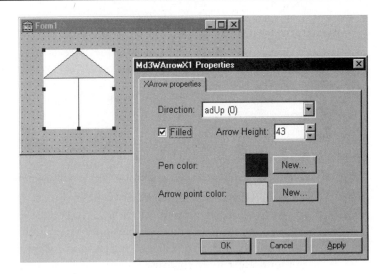

What's Next

In this chapter we have focused our attention on ActiveX controls. We've seen how to use them in Delphi, and how Delphi 3 makes the development of new feature-complete ActiveX controls extremely simple. This is really a very important feature, because it makes Delphi even more suitable for developing the core of an application, letting the programmers who create the user interface and glue together components choose any development environment.

In Delphi 3, along with the support for ActiveX controls, Borland has added support for ActiveForms. These are actually ActiveX controls. The difference is how you develop them, and how you'll generally use them. The development and use of ActiveForms is one of the topics of the next chapter, which is devoted to Internet programming in Delphi. It won't be the only topic, though: we'll see how to view and generate HTML code in Delphi programs, and look at other related topics.

Internet Programming

- ■ Web browsing

- ■ Producing HTML files

- ■ From database tables to HTML tables

- ■ Delphi's ActiveForms

This chapter provides a brief introduction to Internet programming in Delphi. Delphi 3 includes several components aimed at Internet development, particularly in the Client/Server Edition, and this area is actually quite extensive. Complete coverage of Internet programming in Delphi is beyond the scope of this book, but I'll introduce a couple of interesting topics.

We'll start by looking at HTML files, building both a simple browser and a couple of HTML generators. We won't actually cover "live" data—that is, the run-time generation of information from a server (using CGI or ISAPI techniques)—but only the static generation of HTML files. Depending on the version of Delphi you have, in fact, you might use Borland's new Delphi 3 approach or rely on third-party components.

The last part of the chapter will be devoted to the development of some Active-Forms, turning forms from some examples earlier in the book into ActiveForms. This is actually an extension of what we've seen in the last few chapters, since an ActiveForm is nothing but a form wrapped inside an ActiveX and packaged in an ActiveX library.

Browsing HTML Files

The Hyper-Text Markup Language, better known by its acronym HMTL, is a very widespread format for hypertext on the Web, which is an increasingly popular medium. HTML is the format Web browsers typically read. Browsing and generating pages are the main activities that involve HTML. In this section we'll focus on reading existing Web pages and HTML files, while in the next section I'll give you a very short introduction to the HTML format before we develop some HTML-generating programs.

Delphi includes a collection of Internet ActiveX controls licensed from NetManage and called the Internet Control Pack. These components cover several Internet protocols, such as FTP, POP, and UDP. Here I want to build an example of the use of the HTML control, which is basically a fully functioning Web browser. We'll just need to add a toolbar and some other limited capabilities. Using this component to build a clone of one of the popular browsers is not terribly useful. The advantage of using such a control is that you can customize it for specific users, and embed it into your applications. This might be a nice way to let the user of your program read local HTML files and connect to your home page seamlessly.

The form of the WebNav example is quite simple. It has the HTTP control in the middle, a CoolBar control aligned to the top, and a status bar aligned to the bottom. As you can see in Figure 24.1, the CoolBar control has a background bitmap and hosts three components: a toolbar with four buttons implementing common Web browser commands (Previous, Next, Stop, and Refresh), a combo box for entering a URL (Uniform Resource Locator, a string that identifies an Internet resource) and a storing those entered earlier, and an Animate control. This user interface actually clones the Microsoft Internet Explorer, but the user interface of Netscape Navigator is not very different.

FIGURE 24.1

The form of the WebNav example at design-time. Notice the Coolbar and Toolbar controls.

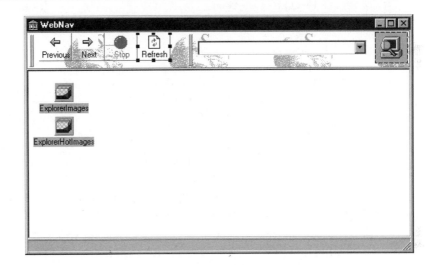

Since I've already covered the use of the CoolBar and ToolBar common Windows controls in Chapter 11, I'll skip the description of their properties and focus on the core of the program, the use of the HTML control. The fundamental element is the call to the RequestDoc method of this ActiveX control. I've wrapped this call inside the GotoPage procedure, since I'm going to call it in several cases:

```
procedure TFormWebNav.GotoPage (ReqURL: string);
begin
  // show the request on status bar and combo box
  ShowCurrent (ReqURL);
  // open the page
  HTML1.RequestDoc(ReqURL);
end;
```

The ShowCurrent method takes care of updating the user interface properly. It adds the requested URL to the Items of the ComboBox, if it is not already there, selects that item in the ComboBox, displays it also in the status bar, and disables either the Previous or Next toolbar button if we are at the beginning or at the end of the list:

```
procedure TFormWebNav.ShowCurrent (ReqURL: string);
var
  Curr: Integer;
begin
  // add the item to the combo, if not present
  Curr := ComboURLs.Items.IndexOf(ReqURL);
  if Curr = -1 then
    Curr := ComboURLs.Items.Add(ReqURL);
  // select the items
  ComboURLs.Text := ReqURL;
  StatusBar1.Panels[0].Text := ReqURL;
  // enable toolbar buttons
  ToolBtnPrevious.Enabled := Curr > 0;
  ToolBtnNext.Enabled := Curr < ComboURLs.Items.Count - 1;
end;
```

After calling the RequestDoc method of the HTML control, the program will handle a couple of events of this control, OnBeginRetrieval and OnEndRetreival. In the two event handlers the program simply starts and stops the animation, and enables and disables the Stop button:

```
procedure TFormWebNav.HTML1BeginRetrieval(Sender: TObject);
begin
  ToolBtnStop.Enabled := True;
  Animate1.Active := True;
end;

procedure TFormWebNav.HTML1EndRetrieval(Sender: TObject);
begin
  ToolBtnStop.Enabled := False;
  Animate1.Active := False;
end;
```

The other event of the ActiveX HTML control the program handles is the OnDoRequestDoc event, activated when a user clicks on a link inside the document. In this case, in fact, we want to track the new URL, adding it to the ComboBox and to the status bar:

```
procedure TFormWebNav.HTML1DoRequestDoc(Sender: TObject;
```

```
   const URL: WideString; const Element: HTMLElement;
   const DocInput: DocInput; var EnableDefault: WordBool);
begin
  // show the current page
  ShowCurrent (URL);
end;
```

This event actually delivers a lot of information, although we use only the wide string with the requested URL. Now we can go back to the beginning and see how the information retrieval actually starts. When the form is created, the WebNav program loads the DEFAULT.HTM file of the current directory, which provides a sort of introduction to the program:

```
procedure TFormWebNav.FormCreate(Sender: TObject);
var
  Drive: string;
begin
  Drive := ExtractFileDrive (ParamStr (0));
  GotoPage ('file:' + Drive + 'default.htm');
end;
```

Strangely enough, to load a file from the current directory you don't need to provide the full path, but you do need to provide the drive (otherwise the program will work only on drive C). You can see the effect of loading this file in Figure 24.2.

FIGURE 24.2

The default HTML file loaded by the WebNav example when it starts.

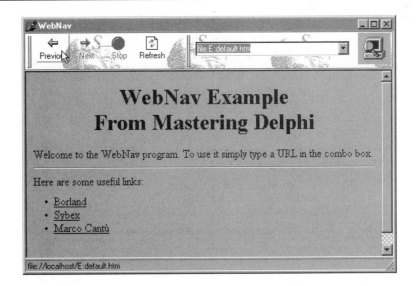

After this initial HTML file has been loaded, you can simply type your requests in the combo box, pressing Enter to send the URL to the HTML control:

```
procedure TFormWebNav.ComboURLsKeyDown(Sender: TObject;
  var Key: Word; Shift: TShiftState);
begin
  if Key = VK_Return then
    GotoPage (ComboURLs.Text);
end;
```

Another call to GotoPage is performed in the OnClick event of the comb box, activated when the user selects one of the existing entries. The remaining elements of the user interface are the toolbar buttons. Here is their simple code:

```
procedure TFormWebNav.ToolBtnPreviousClick(Sender: TObject);
var
  Curr: Integer;
begin
  Curr := ComboURLs.Items.IndexOf(ComboURLs.Text);
  if Curr > 0 then
    GotoPage (ComboURLs.Items [Curr - 1]);
end;

procedure TFormWebNav.ToolBtnNextClick(Sender: TObject);
var
  Curr: Integer;
begin
  Curr := ComboURLs.Items.IndexOf(ComboURLs.Text);
  if Curr < ComboURLs.Items.Count - 1 then
    GotoPage (ComboURLs.Items [Curr + 1]);
end;

procedure TFormWebNav.ToolBtnStopClick(Sender: TObject);
begin
  HTML1.Cancel(Null);
  ToolBtnStop.Enabled := False;
end;

procedure TFormWebNav.ToolBtnRefreshClick(Sender: TObject);
begin
  GotoPage (ComboURLs.Text);
end;
```

In the `ToolBtnStopClick` method above we don't need to stop the animation. In fact, we call `Cancel` and the HTML component will call `OnEndRetrieval` event handler, which stops the animation (see the code above).

We haven't done a lot of work, and we have a working Web Browser. It is indeed very primitive; but again, the purpose of this example was simply to demonstrate Delphi's HTML component, which you can embed in your applications.

Generating HTML Files

If on the client side the main activity is Web browsing—reading HTML files—on the server side you actually generate and make available the HTML pages. At times, it is enough to have a way to produce fixed pages, maybe extracting data from a database table and updating the HTML files frequently. In other cases you'll need to generate pages dynamically based on a request from a user. I'm going to write a couple of examples covering the first case, and then give you an overview of what's involved in the dynamic generation of information.

If you don't know much about the tags included in HTML files, you might read the following sidebar for a fast introduction.

The Format of HTML Files

HTML files are basically ASCII text files. Besides the plain text, an HTML file hosts many tags, which might determine the style of the font, the type of paragraph, and a link to another HTML file or an image, among other things.

Most tags are paired (with the closing tag including a /) to indicate where the style begins and ends. For example, you write `<b>important</b>` to set the word *important* in bold, and you write `<title>Document title</title>` to set the title of a document.

Some tags, however, have no termination, as the `<p>` tag used to separate paragraphs. This is a particularly important tag because the spaces and new-line

Continued on next page

The Format of HTML Files (Continued)

characters in an HTML file are totally ignored. Only by using a <p> tag will you move the following text to a new line.

An HTML document begins with the <html> tag and is divided in two parts marked as <head> and <body>. Each of these three tags requires the corresponding terminator. In the head portion of the HTML file you'll generally write the title (often displayed in the caption of the browser) and a few other generic elements.

In the body you write the contents of the file, generally starting with its visible title. You can have several headings with different levels, marked with the <hX> tag, where X is a number from 1 to 6. These are followed by plain paragraphs (<p>), pre-formatted paragraphs (the tag <pre> is generally used for program listings), various types of lists, and many other elements.

The text will often have links to other pages, or to other parts of the current page, but implementing those links is, again, beyond the scope of this short introduction. HTML is the subject of many books (from Sybex and other publishers), and you can find dozens of HTML tutorials just by browsing the Web.

Building a Plain HTML File

The first example of generating an HTML file will be a variation of the DbToWord example from Chapter 22, which sent some database information to Microsoft Word via OLE Automation. Now we'll use the same structure to produce an HTML file instead, and then pass it to your Web browser. We'll produce very simple output, for the moment; in the next example we'll use HTML tables.

The form of the example, called DbToHTML, has some new components that weren't in the previous version. Besides the database-related components, there are now three buttons, used to perform the various actions, a check box, and a memo control. The memo is used to show a preview of the HTML file we are generating. Actually, the component is also used to hold the HTML code temporarily, before we actually save it to a file.

To avoid repeating code, and to write methods I'll be able to reuse in the other applications, I've added to this example two procedures to generate the initial and the final portion of the HTML file. These are not general-purpose procedures, but have a rather limited scope. Their flexibility lies in the fact that they are not specifically tailored to send the output to the Memo1 component. Instead they receive as parameter a TStrings object, and add the new text to it.

The AddHeader method has a second parameter, a string used both as the title of the HTML file and as the text displayed as the main header of the page. This header is also centered:

```
procedure TNavigator.AddHeader (Str: TStrings; Title: string);
begin
  Str.Add ('<HTML>');
  Str.Add ('<HEAD>');
  Str.Add ('<TITLE>' + Title + '</TITLE>');
  Str.Add ('</HEAD>');
  Str.Add ('<BODY>');
  Str.Add ('<H1><CENTER>' + Title + '</CENTER></H1>');
end;
```

The footer is even simpler, although I've added a custom line, separated from the rest of the text by a line (indicated by the <HR> tag):

```
procedure TNavigator.AddFooter (Str: TStrings);
begin
  Str.Add ('<HR>');
  Str.Add ('Generated by the program DbToHtml');
  Str.Add ('</BODY>');
  Str.Add ('</HTML>');
end;
```

Now we can look at the code of the first button, Print Line. When this button is pressed, the program clears the contents of the memo, calls AddHeader passing as title the value of the first field of the current record, then outputs one line for each of the other fields of the record, and finally adds the footer:

```
procedure TNavigator.BtnLineClick(Sender: TObject);
var
  I: Integer;
begin
  Memo1.Clear;
  AddHeader (Memo1.Lines, Table1.Fields[0].AsString);
  for I := 1 to Table1.FieldCount - 1 do
```

```
        Memo1.Lines.Add (Table1.Fields [I].FieldName + ': ' +
          Table1.Fields [I].AsString + '<p>');
      AddFooter (Memo1.Lines);
      BtnSave.Enabled := True;
    end;
```

As you can see at the end of the method above, once the program adds some data to the memo it enables the Save button. When this button is pressed the DbToHtml application uses a SaveDialog component to save the contents of the memo to a file. The SaveDialog has been customized to look only for files with the HTM extension. At the end, the BtnSaveClick method does something else: it reads the status of the Start Browser check box and, if the box is checked, loads the HTM file in the computer's default browser:

```
procedure TNavigator.BtnSaveClick(Sender: TObject);
begin
  if SaveDialog1.Execute then
  begin
    Memo1.Lines.SaveToFile (SaveDialog1.FileName);
    if CheckStart.Checked then
      ShellExecute (Handle, 'open',
        PChar (SaveDialog1.FileName), '', '', sw_ShowNormal);
  end;
end;
```

Using ShellExecute, in fact, we can simply execute a document, a file. Windows will start the program associated with that extension, using the action passed as the parameter (in this case, *open*). In Figure 24.3 you can see an example of the output of the program, along with its form.

Besides producing the information related to a single country, the program can also produce an HTML file for the complete table, as did the DBToWord example. This is the method executed when the Print All button is pressed:

```
procedure TNavigator.BtnPrintClick(Sender: TObject);
begin
  Memo1.Clear;
  AddHeader (Memo1.Lines, 'Table: ' + Table1.TableName);
  AddAllLines (Memo1.Lines);
  AddFooter (Memo1.Lines);
  BtnSave.Enabled := True;
end;
```

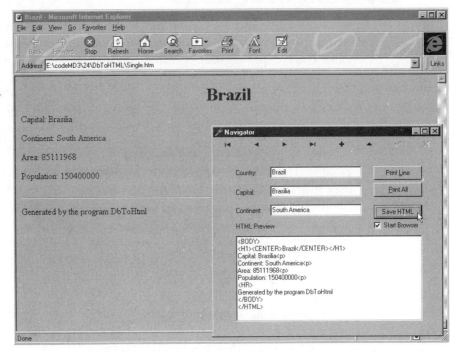

FIGURE 24.3

The DbToHtml example can generate an HTML file and automatically load it in the default browser of the computer, in this case the Internet Explorer.

The program adds a header and a footer and, between them, it calls the AddAll-Lines method. This is essentially a typical while loop which scans the database table after disabling the controls and storing a bookmark. For this reason I won't show you the complete code, but only its central part, the while loop:

```
procedure TNAvigator.AddAllLines (Str: TStrings);
begin
  ...
  while not Table1.EOF do
  begin
    Str.Add (Format ('The capital of %s is %s<p>',
      [Table1.FieldByName ('Name').AsString,
      Table1.FieldByName ('Capital').AsString]));
    Table1.Next;
  end;
  ...
end;
```

Producing HTML Tables

In the last method of the DbToHtml program we produced a simple list of the records of a database table. To improve the output, we might want to use an HTML table. This is a special group of HTML tags, with special formatting capabilities. This approach is a great way to show the output of a database table, so I've applied it to a different program, a new version of the Tables2 example of Chapter 16. The new program is called TableH, and has the same user interface shown in Figure 16.22 (with a new button and a checkbox added to the toolbar panel).

The code related to the generation of the HTML file is similar to that of the last example. However, I've tried to move a step forward. First of all, instead of requiring a memo component, the new version creates a TStringList object in memory. Having decided this, I also wanted to write some generic routines in a separate unit, to make them easier to reuse in other applications. Instead of writing procedures operating on a TStringList object passed as a parameter, I've decided to extend the TStringList class with these new capabilities. (You could further extend this class into a full-blown component.) This is the structure of the new class:

```
type
  THtmlStrings = class (TStringList)
  public
    procedure AddHeader (Title: string);
    procedure AddFooter;
    procedure OutputTable (Data: TDataSet);
  private
    procedure AddTableContents (Data: TDataSet);
  end;
```

The private method is just a *helper* method for the OutputTable method, and for this reason it shouldn't be called from other classes. The AddHeader and AddFooter methods are similar to those in the last example. I've tried to make AddFooter more generic by letting it compute the name of the current program, the producer of the HTML file:

```
procedure THtmlStrings.AddFooter;
begin
  Add ('<HR>');
  Add ('Generated by the program ' +
    ExtractFileName (ParamStr(0)));
  Add ('</BODY>');
  Add ('</HTML>');
end;
```

The call to ParamStr (0) returns the path of the current program, and from the path the program extracts the filename portion. The OutputTable method generates the header of the table, with the names of the fields. Then it calls the helper method AddTableContents, and closes the table definition:

```
procedure THtmlStrings.OutputTable (Data: TDataSet);
var
  I: Integer;
begin
  // start table with borders
  Add('<table border>');
  // new row, with the table headers (tag <th>)
  Add('<tr>');
  for I := 0 to Data.FieldCount - 1 do
    if Data.Fields[I].Visible then
      Add('<th>' + Data.Fields[I].FieldName + '</th>');
  Add('</tr>');
  // new row for each record, with the proper fields
  AddTableContents (Data);
  // done
  Add('</table>');
end;
```

> **NOTE**
>
> The essential tags required for an HTML table are quite simple (although there are many more options I'll skip). The <table> tag indicates the beginning and the end of the table, and its optional border attribute displays borders. The <tr> tag introduces and closes each row, and the tags <th> and <td> indicate a table header cell and a table data cell, respectively. The number of columns depends on the items in each row. Different rows, in fact, can have a different number of items. In this example we have one row for each field of the database table.

The AddTableContents method is based again on a while loop used to scan records of the table. Here is its central portion:

```
procedure THtmlStrings.AddTableContents (Data: TDataSet);
begin
  ...
  while not Data.EOF do
  begin
    Add('<tr>'); // new row, with table data (tag <td>)
```

```
    for I := 0 to Data.FieldCount - 1 do
      if Data.Fields[I].Visible then
        Add('<td>' + Data.Fields[I].DisplayText + '</td>');
    Add('</tr>');
    Data.Next;
  end;
  ...
end;
```

Once we have written this support unit, and saved it as HtmlStr.pas, updating the program becomes quite simple. The only new code is in the OnClick event handler of the new SpeedButton. This method does a few things. It starts by asking the user to name the new HTML file, suggesting the name of the current table but with the HTM extension. Then it creates the THtmlStrings object, and calls its three methods. At the end, it saves the file and destroys the custom string list object (in a protected block, just in case something went wrong). Thanks to the support class, the code is actually very simple for the result you obtain, and it is also easy to understand:

```
procedure TMainForm.SpeedButton2Click(Sender: TObject);
var
  Str: THtmlStrings;
begin
  SaveDialog1.FileName := ChangeFileExt (
    Table1.TableName, '.htm');
  if SaveDialog1.Execute then
  begin
    Str := THtmlStrings.Create;
    try
      Str.AddHeader (Caption);
      Str.OutputTable (Table1);
      Str.AddFooter;
      Str.SaveToFile (SaveDialog1.Filename);
      if CheckBox1.Checked then
        ShellExecute (Handle, 'open',
          PChar (SaveDialog1.FileName),
          '', '', sw_ShowNormal);
    finally
      Str.Free;
    end;
  end;
end;
```

As in the last example, if the check box is selected the method terminates by loading the file in the default Web browser. You can see the effect of this code in Figure 24.4.

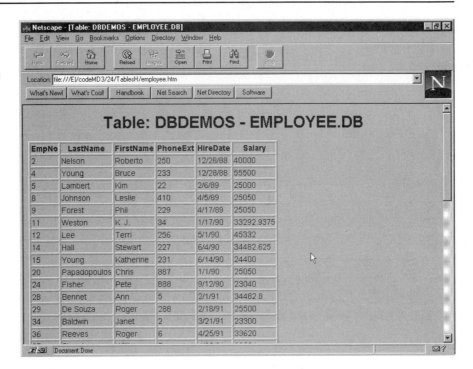

Handling Live Data

The examples we have seen in the last two sections all relate to the construction of HTML files before uploading them to an Internet server. This is very different from letting a server read a request from the user, interactively build an HTML file, and present it to the user.

There are basically two techniques you can employ to accomplish this: use the Common Gateway Interface (CGI), in one of its incarnations, or create a DLL that hooks into the server. In both cases instead of passing to the server a request with the path of the file you are looking for, you pass to it the name of the program (or DLL) and some parameters.

Delphi allows you to create each of these server add-ons, provided the Web server runs on a Windows computer, of course. Actually the Client/Server Edition of Delphi 3 adds specific support for this capability. Using the appropriate Wizard you can generate the structure of an application based on CGI, WinCGI, or a server DLL. If you don't have this edition of Delphi, you can probably rely on third-party components. Again, in this section I'm not going to build examples of the use of these techniques, but only offer you a short overview of each of them:

- CGI, or Common Gateway Interface, is a very widespread Internet technique to process client input, and is supported by most Web servers. Basically the server communicates with the CGI program using environment variables and provides the user input through command line parameters (depending on the command). This technique is built upon the UNIX input/output model and is not terribly efficient. You build a CGI application as a stand-alone console application.

- WinCGI is a variation of CGI, which uses a Windows INI file instead of environment variables to pass the information. Apart from this, the approach is very similar to CGI, although WinCGI applications are Windows executable files.

- ISAPI and NSAPI DLLs are libraries that hook into the Microsoft Internet Server and the Netscape Internet Server, respectively. In both cases the DLL provides specific functions called by the server. Delphi 3 makes the development of these servers much simpler, because it uses a common API (Borland calls this technology WebBridge, because it bridges the two APIs).

With each of these three techniques, to develop a server add-on with Delphi 3 you'll use a WebModule, a specifically configured data module (that is, a subclass of the TDataModule class).

Building ActiveForms

In Chapter 1 we got a glimpse of how simple it is in Delphi 3 to create an ActiveX based on a form, and deploy it on the Internet. Of course, you'll need to view this file with an browser supporting the ActiveX technology. In this section I want to revise the elements of the construction of an ActiveForm, looking more into the technical details, and also create a couple of examples.

The development of ActiveForms invariably starts using the corresponding Wizard. Although it is possible to write the code by hand, it certainly takes a while. The drawback of using the Wizard is that if you've written a complex Delphi application based on a form, you'll need to copy and paste its components and code into a new ActiveForm.

I've created a new example by generating a new ActiveLibrary and then creating a new ActiveForm. The example is called XForm1, and I'll use it to explore the source code automatically generated by Delphi. Then we'll add some capabilities. The first difference from a plain Delphi form is in the declaration of the new form class, which inherits from the TActiveForm class and implements a specific Active-Form interface:

```
type
  TAXForm1 = class(TActiveForm, IAXForm1)
```

As usual the IAXForm interface is declared in the type library, and in a corresponding Pascal file I've named XF1Lib.pas. Here is an excerpt of the IAXForm1 interface:

```
type
  IAXForm1 = interface(IDispatch)
    ['{51661AA1-9468-11D0-98D0-444553540000}']
    // Get and Set methods for TForm properties
    function Get_Caption: WideString; safecall;
    procedure Set_Caption(const Value: WideString); safecall;
    ...
    // TForm methods redeclared
    procedure Close; safecall;
    function CloseQuery: WordBool; safecall;
    ...
    // TForm properties
    property Caption: WideString
      read Get_Caption write Set_Caption;
```

As usual, the Wizard also defines a dispinterface for the form interface, and one for its events:

```
type
  DAXForm1 = dispinterface...
  IAXForm1Events = dispinterface...
```

The code generated for the TAXForm1 class has the implementation of all the set and get methods, which simply change or return the corresponding properties of the form, and the implementation of the events, which again refer to the events of the form. Here, again, is a small excerpt:

```
private
    FEvents: IAXForm1Events;
    procedure ActivateEvent(Sender: TObject);
    procedure ClickEvent(Sender: TObject);
  protected
    procedure EventSinkChanged(
      const EventSink: IUnknown); override;
    procedure Initialize; override;
    function CloseQuery: WordBool; safecall;
    function Get_Caption: WideString; safecall;
    procedure Close; safecall;
    procedure Set_Caption(const Value: WideString); safecall;
```

Notice that the form has a private and a protected section. The interface also has some property definitions, declared as public. Let's look at the implementation of properties first:

```
function TAXForm1.Get_Caption: WideString;
begin
  Result := WideString(Caption);
end;

procedure TAXForm1.Set_Caption(const Value: WideString);
begin
  Caption := TCaption(Value);
end;
```

Now we can look at the events. The TForm events are set to the internal methods when the form is created:

```
procedure TAXForm1.Initialize;
begin
  OnActivate := ActivateEvent;
  OnClick := ClickEvent;
  OnCreate := CreateEvent;
  ...
end;
```

Each event then maps itself to the external ActiveX event, as in the following two methods:

```
procedure TAXForm1.ActivateEvent(Sender: TObject);
begin
  if FEvents <> nil then FEvents.OnActivate;
end;

procedure TAXForm1.ClickEvent(Sender: TObject);
begin
  if FEvents <> nil then FEvents.OnClick;
end;
```

Because of this mapping you should not handle the events of the form directly, but add some code to this default handlers, or simply override the TForm methods that end up calling the events (this is exactly the approach you use when building a Delphi component). Keep in mind, in fact, that the interface properties of the ActiveForm are meant for developers using the ActiveX control, not for final users of the ActiveForm on the Web. This problem refers only to the events of the form itself, not to the events of the components of the form. You can continue to handle the events of the components as usual.

Having studied the internal details, we can use this framework to build a simple example. I want to test the approach I've just described. For this reason I've added a handler for the OnPaint event of the form, double-clicking on the corresponding line of the Object Inspector. Then I've written this code:

```
procedure TAXForm1.FormPaint(Sender: TObject);
begin
  Canvas.Brush.Color := clYellow;
  Canvas.Ellipse(0, 0, Width, Height);
end;
```

The FormPaint method above is totally useless, and will never be executed! If you want to paint something on the form's background, instead, you have to modify the corresponding handler installed by the ActiveForm Wizard:

```
procedure TAXForm1.PaintEvent(Sender: TObject);
begin
  Canvas.Brush.Color := clBlue;
  Canvas.Rectangle (20, 20,
    ClientWidth - 20, ClientHeight - 20);
  if FEvents <> nil then FEvents.OnPaint;
end;
```

As an alternative, you can place a panel or another component on the surface of the form, and handle its events. In this example I've simply added a PaintBox component, with a bevel component behind it to make the area of the PaintBox visible. This makes it quite simple to handle the events for this area of the form, as in the following case:

```
procedure TAXForm1.PaintBox1MouseDown(Sender: TObject;
  Button: TMouseButton; Shift: TShiftState; X, Y: Integer);
begin
  PaintBox1.Canvas.Ellipse (X-10, Y-10, X+10, Y+10);
end;
```

You can see this example in action (inside a browser, of course) in Figure 24.5.

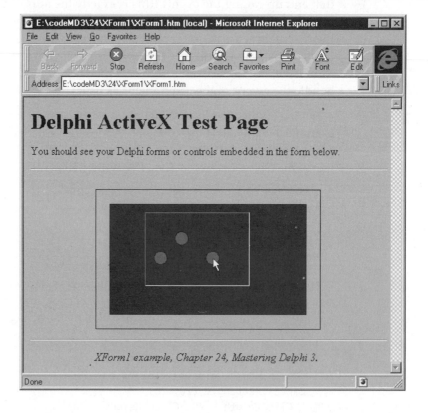

FIGURE 24.5

The XForm1 ActiveForm inside Internet Explorer.

WARNING   Building a Delphi application is usually an interactive process. You start with a simple version, then add new capabilities checking the output from time to time. When you build an active form this can result in a few problems. The Internet Explorer, in fact, has a cache of ActiveX controls, stored by default in the windows/occache directory. Even if you rebuild the OCX file, the Internet Explorer might decide to use the cached version. You can use version information and other related techniques to avoid this problem. It's not very professional, but as a last resort you can simply remove the copy of the file from this cache when everything else fails.

The Role of an ActiveX Form on a Web Page

Before we look at another example, it is important to stop for a second to consider the role of an ActiveX form placed inside a Web page. Basically, placing a form in a Web page corresponds to letting a user download and execute a custom Windows application. There is little else happening. You download an executable file, and start it. (This is one of the reasons the ActiveX technology raises so many concerns about security, but that's not a subject I want to discuss here.)

A simple example can highlight the situation. I've generated a new ActiveForm, added a button and a label to it, and written the following code for the OnClick event of the button:

```
procedure TXUser.Button1Click(Sender: TObject);
var
  UserName: string;
  Size : Integer;
begin
  Size := 128;
  SetLength (UserName, Size);
  GetUserName (PChar(UserName), Size);
  Label1.Caption := UserName;
end;
```

This method simply calls the GetUserName Windows API function, and its effect is certainly not astonishing, as you can see in Figure 24.6. However, this example highlights several important points (which apply both to ActiveForms and ActiveX controls in general):

- In an ActiveX control or form you can call any Windows API function (which also means the user viewing the Web page must have Windows on his or her computer), or some Windows API-compatible libraries.

- An ActiveX can access the system information of the computer, such as the user name, the directory structure, and so on.

- This is why, before downloading an ActiveX, Web browsers check if the ActiveX has a proper authentication, a proper signature. This signature identifies the author of the control, but doesn't prove in any way that the control is safe.

FIGURE 24.6

The simple output of the XFUser example shows that an ActiveX form (or an ActiveX control) can access any information of the computer.

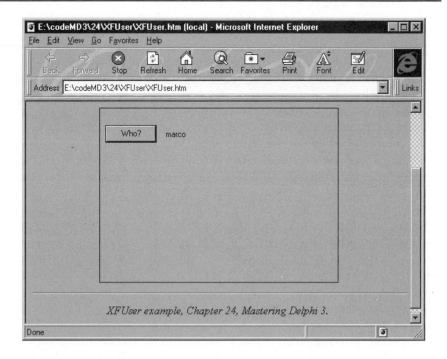

Well, I could continue, but I think my point is clear. ActiveX controls and Active-Forms are a great tool, particularly in an Intranet (an internal company network set up to conform to Internet technical standards). On the Internet, some users might not like having to use ActiveX controls.

Actually the XFUser example demonstrates also another technique. In the Web Deploy options (for users with the Client/Server Edition of Delphi), I've asked for the use of CAB files. These are compressed files which store the OCX file and other auxiliary files like packages, making it easier and faster to deliver the application to the user. A compressed file, in fact, means a faster download.

A Multi-Page ActiveForm

As a final example, I'll take an existing program and turn it into an ActiveForm. We have seen that there are three standard approaches in the development of a complex program, which requires more than one form: MDI, multiple modal or modeless forms, and multi-page forms. This last approach is the one best suited for the development of a complex ActiveForm.

To build the XFMulti example I've basically copied most of the controls and the code of the NoteOnly example of Chapter 14. This was an application based on a notebook. There are several approaches to this copy operation, but the simplest is probably to select all of the components in the original program, build a component template out of them (so that you copy the component properties and their event handlers), and then paste them into a new ActiveForm.

You can see the output of this program by opening the corresponding HTML file in a browser (see Figure 24.7). This is just a simple example, but it highlights an important idea: use the notebook or PageControl components when you want to build a complex ActiveForm.

What's Next

In this short chapter I've introduced you to some Internet-related programming techniques. There are entire books devoted to this complex subject, including some Delphi books. My purpose here was simply to give you an overview of HTML-based development and ActiveForm development in Delphi.

This chapter ends Part III of the book, mainly devoted to component development. We've seen how to build Delphi components, how to extend the Delphi environment to make the new components easier to use, how to build DLLs, how to place classes in DLLs, and how to write COM classes and interfaces in Delphi. Then we focused on several uses of COM, such as OLE Automation, OLE Documents, ActiveX and ActiveForm.

FIGURE 24.7

The output of the XFMulti example: This is a full-blown application running inside a Web browser. It works exactly like the corresponding NoteBook example of Chapter 14.

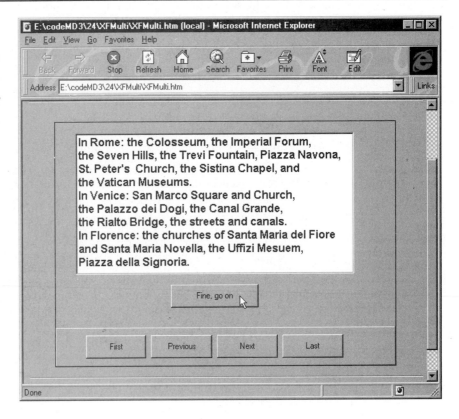

The next part of the book will have a totally different focus. It will help you master some advanced concepts of Delphi development, such as the structure of an application, multithreading, debugging, Windows resources, file access, printing, DDE, and multimedia.

PART IV

Advanced Delphi Programming

C H A P T E R

T W E N T Y - F I V E

25

Discovering the Application Structure

- The role of the Application object

- Programs without components

- Windows command-line parameters

- A graphical clock application

- Background processing and multitasking

- Uses of the Screen object

- Windows INI files and the Registry

We have seen many Delphi applications made up of one or more forms. Everything involves forms and components placed inside forms. However, if you just look at the source code of any project file, another element appears: the `Application` object. This object, which was introduced in Chapter 10, has a role like the director in an orchestra; at the same time, it is also a window. This chapter explores the possible uses of the `Application` object, and of another object we have already used, the `Screen` object. As we explore the roles of these two objects, many related ideas will emerge, including a broad discussion of Windows messages, timers, background computing, and an in-depth introduction to multitasking. I'll also discuss the use of INI files, the Registry, and more.

Using the Application Object

When you create a new, blank application, Delphi generates some code for the project file, which includes the following:

```
begin
  Application.Initialize;
  Application.CreateForm(TForm1, Form1);
  Application.Run;
end.
```

This code uses the global object `Application`, of class `TApplication`, defined by the VCL in the `Forms` unit. This object is indeed a component, although you cannot set its properties using the Object Inspector. But this is not a real problem, since the application has only a few properties. These properties include the name of the executable file, the title of the application (by default, the name of the executable file without the extension), and a few events. You can set some of the properties of the global `Application` object using the Application page of the Project Options dialog box.

Here are some of the properties and events of the `TApplication` component (I've skipped, among others, the properties related to hints, which were discussed in Chapter 12.):

- `Active` is a read-only property indicating whether the application is active.

- `ExeName` is the name of the executable file of the application.

- `Handle` is the handle of the invisible window corresponding to the application object.

- `HelpFile` is the name of the Help file of this application.

- `Icon` is the icon used by the Taskbar, as we'll see in Chapter 27.

- `MainForm` is the main form of the Delphi program.

- `ShowMainForm` indicates whether the main form should be displayed at startup.

- `Title` indicates the title of the application, as displayed in the Taskbar.

And here are all of the events of this class:

- `OnActivate` is called when the user activates the application, by moving the focus to one of its windows. We'll see an example of application and form activation shortly.

- `OnDeactivate` is called when another Windows application is activated.

- `OnException` is called when Delphi's global exception handler is reached. We have used this event in Chapter 17 (in the DBError example).

- `OnIdle` is called when the application has no waiting messages. We'll use this event in an example later in this chapter.

- `OnHelp` is called when the user activates the Help system. The `HelpContext` and the `HelpJump` methods of the `TApplication` class automatically trigger the `OnHelp` event.

- `OnHint` is called when a hint is about to be displayed, as discussed in detail in Chapter 12.

- `OnMessage` is called when a Windows message is posted to the application window, as we'll see in an example shortly.

- `OnMinimize` is called when the application is minimized.

- `OnRestore` is called when the application is restored.

- `OnShowHint` is called to display a hint, as discussed in Chapter 12.

We can start understanding the role of the `Application` object by looking at an example. Create a new application, compile it (saving the files with the default names, UNIT1.PAS and PROJECT1.DPR), and run it. An empty window titled *Form1* appears on the screen, and the corresponding Taskbar icon is named *Project1*, which is the name of the application's main window. Behind the scenes, Delphi creates a window for the Application object and a second window, the main window, which the application window owns. In fact, the application window has zero height and width, and therefore is not visible (although it is not hidden, because that would affect its behavior).

You can perform two additional tests. You can see the name of the main window in the new Windows 95 Tasks application (TASKMAN.EXE in the WINDOWS directory), as shown in the upper-right portion of Figure 25.1. In this window, the program is listed as *Form1*. Now, invoke the Windows 95 Close Program window by pressing Ctrl+Alt+Del. As you can see in the bottom part of Figure 25.1, this window displays a list of the running applications, or processes, and displays the name *Project1* for our new Delphi application.

FIGURE 25.1

Windows 95 has both a Tasks application that lists the main window and a Close Program window that displays a list of the processes, the applications currently running.

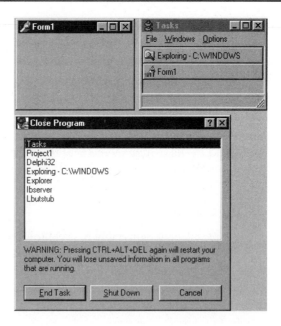

When you're running Delphi itself, Windows 95 displays Delphi's application name in the Taskbar, but it displays the name of the main form in the Tasks window and in the switch window that appears when you press Alt+Tab. Obviously, Delphi behaves in the same way as the applications it generates (because Delphi was built with Delphi itself). When Delphi's main window (the window that contains the menu bar) is visible, you see the name of the project window's caption. However, when you look at the Taskbar, the name of the project is missing. This happens because the Taskbar displays the caption of the application window instead of the caption of the main window. Is this an advantage or a disadvantage? To inexperienced users, seeing two different names can be confusing. However, the application name has the advantage of remaining fixed, while the caption of a program usually changes to reflect the name of the current file or other dynamic information.

You probably should use the initial name of the main form as the name of the application, or make sure that the application and form names are synchronized. To accomplish this, you may need to change the title of the application each time the caption of the main form changes. As soon as you change the caption of the main form, you can write the following code:

```
Application.Title := Caption;
```

You can also write this code at startup (in the OnCreate event of the main form). As an alternative, you can set the initial application name in the Application page of the Project Options dialog box, together with some other properties of the Application object.

Showing the Application Window

There is no better proof that there is indeed a window for the Application object than to display it. Actually, we don't need to show it—we just need to resize it and set a couple of window attributes, such as the presence of a caption and a border. Delphi provides no facilities to accomplish this directly, so we need to perform this work by using Windows API functions to modify the window indicated by Application.Handle. For example, in the ShowApp program I've written the following code:

```
procedure TForm1.Button1Click(Sender: TObject);
var
  OldStyle: Integer;
begin
  // add border and caption to the app window
  OldStyle := GetWindowLong (
    Application.Handle, gwl_Style);
  SetWindowLong (Application.Handle, gwl_Style,
    OldStyle or ws_ThickFrame or ws_Caption);
```

```
// set the size of the app window
SetWindowPos (Application.Handle,
  0, 0, 0, 200, 100, swp_NoMove or swp_NoZOrder);
end;
```

The two GetWindowLong and SetWindowLong API functions are used to access the system information related to the window. In this case, we are using the gwl_Style parameter to read or write the styles of the window, which include its border, title, system menu, border icons, and so on. The code above gets the current styles and adds (using an or statement) a standard border and a caption to the form. You seldom need to use these low-level API functions in Delphi, because there are properties of the TForm class that have the same effect. We need this code here because the application window is not a form.

Executing this code displays the project window, as you can see in Figure 25.2. I suggest that you play with this program a little bit. Although there's no need to implement something like this in your own programs, running this program will reveal the relationship between the application window and the main window of a Delphi program. This is a very important starting point if you want to study the internal structure of Delphi applications.

FIGURE 25.2

The hidden application window revealed by the ShowApp program.

The Application System Menu

Unless you write a very odd example like the one we've just looked at, you will only see the application window in the Taskbar. What you can do with this window is activate its system menu by right-clicking on it. As I mentioned in Chapter 9, when discussing the system menu, an application's menu is not the same as that of the main form. In the SysMenu example in Chapter 9 I added custom items to the system menu of the main form. Now in the SysMenu2 example I want to customize the system menu of the application window in the Taskbar.

First we have to add the new items to the system menu of the application window when the program starts. Here is the updated code of the FormCreate method:

```
procedure TForm1.FormCreate(Sender: TObject);
begin
  // add a separator and a menu item to the system menu
  AppendMenu (GetSystemMenu (Handle, FALSE),
    MF_SEPARATOR, 0, '');
  AppendMenu (GetSystemMenu (Handle, FALSE),
    MF_STRING, idSysAbout, '&About...');
  // add the same items to the application system menu
  AppendMenu (GetSystemMenu (Application.Handle, FALSE),
    MF_SEPARATOR, 0, '');
  AppendMenu (GetSystemMenu (Application.Handle, FALSE),
    MF_STRING, idSysAbout, '&About...');
  // handle application messages
  Application.OnMessage := AppMessage;
end;
```

The first part of the code adds the new separator and item to the system menu of the main form. The other two calls add the same two items to that of the application, simply by referring to Application.Handle. This is enough to display the updated system menu, as you can see by running this program. The next step is to handle the selection of the new menu item. To accomplish this we should provide a handler for the OnMessage event of the Application object, as I've done in the last statement of the FormCreate method above.

To handle form messages we can simply write new message-handling methods, as demonstrated in several earlier examples. We cannot do the same with the application window, simply because inheriting from the TApplication class is quite a complex issue. Most of the time we can simply handle the OnMessage event of this class, which is activated for every message the application retrieves from the message queue, as we'll see in more detail in the next chapter.

To handle the OnMessage event, simply add a new method to the main form, add the proper parameters, install it at run-time (as shown above), and then write its code. In this case we simply need to handle the wm_SysCommand message, and we only need to do that if the wParam parameter indicates that the user has selected the menu item we've just added, idSysAbout:

```
procedure TForm1.AppMessage (var Msg: TMsg;
  var Handled: Boolean);
begin
  if (Msg.Message = wm_SysCommand) and
    (Msg.wParam = idSysAbout) then
  begin
    ShowMessage ('Mastering Delphi: SysMenu2 example');
    Handled := True;
  end;
end;
```

This method is very similar to the one used to handle the corresponding system menu item of the main form:

```
procedure WMSysCommand (var Msg: TWMSysCommand);
    message wm_SysCommand;
...
procedure TForm1.WMSysCommand (var Msg: TWMSysCommand);
begin
  // handle a specific command
  if Msg.CmdType = idSysAbout then
    ShowMessage ('Mastering Delphi: SysMenu2 example');
  inherited;
end;
```

Activating Applications and Forms

To explain clearly how the activation of forms and applications works, I've written a simple self-explanatory example, called Activ. This example has two forms. Each form has a Label component (Label2) used to display the status of the form. The program uses text and color for this, as the handlers of the OnActivate and OnDeActivcate events of the first form demonstrate:

```
procedure TForm1.FormActivate(Sender: TObject);
begin
  Label2.Caption := 'Form2 Active';
  Label2.Color := clRed;
end;
procedure TForm1.FormDeactivate(Sender: TObject);
begin
  Label2.Caption := 'Form2 Not Active';
```

```
    Label2.Color := clBtnFace;
end;
```

The second form has a similar label and similar code. The main form does something else. In the handler of the OnCreate events it installs two further handlers for the two activation methods of the Application object:

```
procedure TForm1.FormCreate(Sender: TObject);
begin
  Application.OnActivate := AppActiv;
  Application.OnDeActivate := AppDeActiv;
end;
```

These two event handlers have very simple code:

```
procedure TForm1.AppActiv(Sender: TObject);
begin
  Label1.Caption := 'Application Active';
  Label1.Color := clRed;
  Beep;
end;
procedure TForm1.AppDeActiv(Sender: TObject);
begin
  Label1.Caption := 'Application Not Active';
  Label1.Color := clBtnFace;
end;
```

If you try running this program, you'll see whether this application is the active one, and if so, which of its forms is the active one. By looking at the output (see Figure 25.3) and listening for the beep, you can understand how each of the activation events is triggered by Delphi. Run this program and play with it for a while to understand how it works.

FIGURE 25.3

The Active example shows whether the application is active and which is the active form of the application.

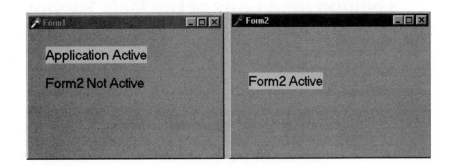

Checking for Multiple Instances of an Application

Probably one of the most common changes programmers make in the source code of a project file is to add a check for the existence of a previous *instance* of the application. Windows 3.1 programmers know that you can test the value of a system parameter, known as HPrevInstance. This is one of the parameters of a standard WinMain function, the entry point of traditional Windows programs written in C. Unfortunately, in 32-bit applications, this parameter is always 0.

In any case, Delphi programmers can use four global variables to retrieve the value of the WinMain parameters passed by Windows to each application:

- HInstance holds an internal Windows value referring to the current instance of an application.

- HPrevInst holds the HInstance value of the previous running instance of a 16-bit application, or zero for the first copy. For a 32-bit application, this value is invariably zero.

- CmdLine contains the command-line parameters passed to the application, such as the name of a file.

- CmdShow in Windows 3.1 contained a display code indicating whether the main window of the application should be minimized or maximized at startup. Under Windows 95 a fixed value is passed each time, and you have to call the GetStartupInfo API function to get the real display code.

These four parameters can be important because they help make your application work seamlessly in the Windows environment.

Looking for a Copy of the Main Window

If you want to run a single instance of an application, the initialization code of the project source file might be written as follows:

```
var
  Hwnd: THandle;
begin
  Hwnd := FindWindow ('TForm1', 'One Copy');
  if Hwnd = 0 then
  begin
```

```
    Application.Initialize;
    Application.CreateForm(TForm1, Form1);
    Application.Run;
  end;
end.
```

The FindWindow API function requires two parameters: the name of the window class (the name used to register the form's window type, or WNDCLASS, in the system) and the caption of the window for which you are looking. You are free to omit one of these two parameters. In a Delphi application, the name of the WNDCLASS window class is the same as the Object Pascal name for the form's class (for example, TForm1). The result of the FindWindow function is a handle to the window, or zero if no matching window was found.

With the above code, the user can start a new instance of the application only if there isn't already a previous instance. If a previous instance exists, nothing happens. Unfortunately, if you run this program from within the Delphi IDE, a window with that caption and class may already exist: the design-time form. Thus, the program won't start even once. However, it will run if you close the form and its corresponding source code file, or if you close the project and run the program from the Windows Explorer.

Activating the Previous Main Form

To improve this program, you can warn the user that this is the second instance, and then activate the main form of the previous instance of the program. This is the behavior of many Windows programs, from several small applications included in the system to some big commercial applications, and it's what I've added to the OneCopy1 example.

To activate the window of the previous instance of the application, you cannot use the SetActiveWindow API function, which was commonly used in Windows 3.1 programs. Instead, you should use the new SetForegroundWindow function, which also works for windows owned by other processes. So you can write an else branch for the if statement above:

```
var
  Hwnd: THandle;
begin
  Hwnd := FindWindow ('TForm1', 'One Copy');
  if Hwnd = 0 then
  begin
```

```
      Application.Initialize;
      Application.CreateForm(TForm1, Form1);
      Application.Run;
    end
    else
    begin
      MessageDlg (
        'You cannot run a second copy of the application!' +
        #13'The form of the older copy will be displayed',
        mtInformation, [mbOK], 0);
      SetForegroundWindow (Hwnd);
    end;
  end.
```

To compile this code, you should add the Dialogs and Windows units to the uses clause of the project source. Again, you might have problems running this program from inside the Delphi IDE.

The OneCopy1 example is a bare program that has a main form with only a single big label. You can see it running in Figure 25.4, where a second instance has been launched. When you click on OK in the message box, the first instance is activated and the second terminates its execution.

FIGURE 25.4

The output of the first and second instances of the OneCopy1 example. When you click on OK, the first instance is activated again.

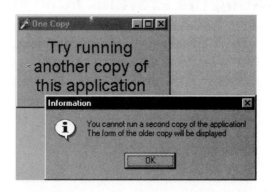

If you want a program that behaves in the same way as many Windows applications, simply remove the message and activate the older instance directly. Notice, however, that the program works only if the main window of the previous instance of the application has not been minimized. When the application is minimized, in fact, the form window is hidden and the activation code has no effect. You could use other functions to show the hidden form, but that creates far more problems than it solves. In fact, you might even end up with the form window and the minimized application window on the screen at the same time (as we saw in the ShowApp program).

Our next example solves this problem in a way that is not elegant, but it works. Although this technique is far from perfect, I've included it simply to demonstrate how to define and respond to user-defined Windows messages.

Handling User-Defined Windows Messages

In the OneCopy2 program, we need to ask the form of another application, the previous instance, to activate itself, even if it is not visible. This can be done by sending a user-defined Windows message to the form—a message that the form can handle in a method we write. We can test whether the form is minimized and then post a new user-defined message to the old window. The following code replaces the code fragment you saw in the last section:

```
begin
  Hwnd := FindWindow ('TForm1', 'One Copy');
  if Hwnd = 0 then
  begin
    Application.Initialize;
    Application.CreateForm(TForm1, Form1);
    Application.Run;
  end
  else
  begin
    if not IsWindowVisible (Hwnd) then
      PostMessage (Hwnd, wm_User, 0, 0);
    SetForegroundWindow (Hwnd);
  end
end.
```

The PostMessage API function sends a message to the message queue of the application owning the destination window, indicated as the first parameter. In the code of the form, you can add a special function to handle this message:

```
public
  procedure WMUser (var msg: TMessage);
    message wm_User;
```

Now we can write the code of this method, which is simple:

```
procedure TForm1.WMUser (var msg: TMessage);
begin
  Application.Restore;
end;
```

Again, if you run this program from the Delphi IDE, it might not work properly, since the FindWindow call may return the handle of the form displayed by the Delphi Form Designer. To test this program, do not merely close this form design window (or hide it), but instead close the corresponding source code file or the entire project and run the resulting program by itself. I'll show you a better version of the program, which does not have this problem, in the next section.

Searching the Windows List

As I just mentioned, the FindWindow API function used in the last example is not always reliable. For example, it cannot discriminate between the form of the previous instance of the application and the form used at design-time in the Delphi environment. To make some improvements, I've written a third version of the example, OneCopy3, which uses a different approach.

When you want to search for a specific main window in the system, you can use the EnumWindows API functions. Enumeration functions are quite peculiar in Windows, because they usually require another function as a parameter, as we saw in Chapter 4. These enumeration functions require a pointer to a function (often described as a *callback* function) as parameter. The idea is that this function is applied to each element of the list (in this case, the list of main windows), until the list ends or the function returns True.

We can replace the initial portion of the program (calling FindWindow) with the new code. Here is the final version of the initialization code of the project:

```
var
  OldHwnd: THandle;
begin
  OldHwnd := 0;
  EnumWindows (@EnumWndProc, Longint (@OldHwnd));
  if OldHwnd = 0 then
  begin
    Application.Initialize;
    Application.CreateForm(TForm1, Form1);
```

```
    Application.Run;
  end
  else
  begin
    if not IsWindowVisible (OldHwnd) then
      PostMessage (OldHwnd, wm_User, 0, 0);
    SetForegroundWindow (OldHwnd);
  end;
end.
```

In this code, OldWnd is a window handle variable, passed by reference, where we will store the result of our search. EnumWndProc is a function I have written that checks the name of each window's class, looking for the string *TForm1*. When an instance is found, the procedure retrieves the module file name (that is, the name of the executable file of the application) of the current program and that of the program owning the matching form. If the module names also match, we can be quite sure that we have found a previous instance of the same program. Here is the full source code of the enumeration function:

```
type
  PHWND = ^HWND;
function EnumWndProc (Hwnd: THandle; FoundWnd: PHWND): Bool; stdcall;
var
  ClassName, ModuleName, WinModuleName: string;
  WinInstance: THandle;
begin
  Result := True;
  SetLength (ClassName, 100);
  GetClassName (Hwnd, PChar (ClassName), Length (ClassName));
  ClassName := PChar (ClassName);
  if ClassName = 'TForm1' then
  begin
    SetLength (ModuleName, 200);
    SetLength (WinModuleName, 200);
    GetModuleFileName ( HInstance,
      PChar (ModuleName), Length (ModuleName));
    ModuleName := PChar(ModuleName); // adjust length
    WinInstance := GetWindowLong (Hwnd, gwl_hInstance);
    GetModuleFileName ( WinInstance,
      PChar (WinModuleName), Length (WinModuleName));
    WinModuleName := PChar(WinModuleName); // adjust length
    if ModuleName = WinModuleName then
```

```
    begin
      FoundWnd^ := Hwnd;
      Result := False;
    end;
  end;
end;
```

Notice that we must define the function as `stdcall`, because it is passed as a pointer to another function, and then called by the system. Windows can properly call only those functions we mark as `stdcall` in the Pascal code, because the system cannot understand the default `register` Delphi calling convention.

Using a Mutex

A completely different approach is to use a *mutex*, or mutual exclusion object. This is a typical Win32 approach, commonly used for synchronizing threads, as we'll see later on in this chapter. Here we are going to use a mutex for synchronizing two different applications, or (to be more precise) two instances of the same application.

Once an application has created a mutex with a given name, it can test whether this object is already owned by another application, calling the `WaitForSingle-Object` Windows API function. If the mutex has no owner, the application calling this function becomes the owner. If the mutex is already owned, the application waits until the time-out (the second parameter of the function) elapses. It then returns an error code.

We can replace the previous project source code file with the following code, which you'll find in the OneCopy4 example:

```
var
  hMutex: THandle;
begin
  HMutex := CreateMutex (nil, False, 'OneCopyMutex');
  if WaitForSingleObject (hMutex, 0) <> wait_TimeOut then
  begin
    Application.Initialize;
    Application.CreateForm(TForm1, Form1);
    Application.Run;
  end;
end.
```

Running this example twice, you can see that a new copy of the application is temporarily created (with its icon appearing in the Taskbar) and then destroyed when the time-out has elapsed.

Programming without Components

Programming with components is not your only choice as a Delphi developer. Components certainly have a central role in this environment, but it is possible to write Delphi applications without any components except forms. (You can also write programs without forms, but that is a very special case.) Which kinds of applications can you write without using components? Windows applications were traditionally written using straight C code, and it is possible to write applications using a similar low-level approach in Delphi, too.

In fact, the question should really be "Which kinds of applications are easier to write without using components?" The answer is that very few applications are easier to write without components and without a visual environment. Both small and large applications benefit from a component approach. Of course, the predefined Delphi components are better suited for some kinds of programs, but by adding the proper custom components to the environment, you can write any type of complex program.

Even if the programs you write have a bare user interface or no user interface at all, like a screen saver or device driver, you can still benefit from Delphi objects like TStreams or TLists. For example, in this chapter we'll build a complex program showing an analog clock; this example will be based on a form but will make very limited use of components, just a timer.

The Smallest Delphi Program?

As you have seen in the previous examples, you can add some code directly to the project file of an application. Projects can be manipulated in Delphi either by using the Project Manager and setting Project Options (the recommended way) or by changing the source code of the project file by hand (the "hacker" way).

It is possible to write any kind of code in the initialization section of the project. Instead of creating a form and running an application, you can produce a beep, display a message box, or run another program. The advantage is that if you do not use forms or the Application object, the size of the executable code shrinks incredibly because the VCL library is not included.

Such programs have a limited use, but in some cases can be handy. You can write simple console applications in Delphi. And you might need to do file operations without showing information to the user. Of course, you can write similar "quick and dirty" programs also with forms, since you probably don't care much for the size of the executable when building a small program for personal use.

Programs like the next example can be defined as the smallest programs you can compile with Delphi, but I don't consider them to be true Delphi programs. They are just small Object Pascal Windows applications that have been written and compiled using the Delphi environment. This is probably the shortest program you can build with Delphi (it's called Beep on the companion CD):

```
program Beep;

uses
  Windows;
begin
  MessageBeep (0);
end.
```

The size of the executable file? Just a few Kbytes, compared to the typical hundreds of Kbytes of a simple Delphi executable file that doesn't use run-time packages. Is it useful? Hardly. It just produces a beep and terminates. To create a small program like this, you should remove every form from a project, using the Project Manager window, and change the default uses statement, as shown in the short Beep program above.

Reading the Command Line

The smallest program that is actually meaningful is a simple example that uses the Windows command-line parameters. Although users seldom specify command-line parameters in a graphical user interface environment, the Windows command-line parameters are important to the system. For example, once you have defined an association between a file extension and an application, you can simply run a program by selecting an associated file. If you double-click on a bitmap file (with the BMP extension), Paintbrush will generally start and load the bitmap file automatically. In practice, when you double-click on a file that has an association, it runs the corresponding Windows program (for example, Paint), and passes the selected file as a command-line parameter. It is up to the program to open the file passed as a parameter, and a well-behaved Windows application should do so.

The following example, called StrParam (for string parameters), demonstrates the use of the command line (or a string command). This statement shows the text of the command line:

```
ShowMessage (CmdLine);
```

If you run it, you'll see that in Windows 95 (and Windows NT) the command line includes the full path of the executable file as first parameter, followed by any other command-line parameters. The program path name is enclosed within double quotation marks. To remove the path name and extract just the parameters, we can scan the string locating the second double quotation mark character.

Accessing the CmdLine string and manipulating it is not the best way to write such code. Delphi, in fact, includes two simple functions to handle the command line parameters: ParamCount and ParamStr. The first of these returns the number of parameters; the second returns the parameter in a given position. Parameters that include spaces can be used if they are delimited by double quotes, as happens with long file names or program paths. Notice that you can use the expression ParamStr(0) to retrieve the full path of the current program. Here is how we can write the code using these functions:

```
begin
  if ParamCount > 0 then
    ShowMessage (ParamStr (1))
  else
    ShowMessage ('No command line');
end.
```

In the source code of the StrParam example, you'll find each of the three versions of the code. You can test this program in several ways. If you run it by itself, without a command-line parameter, the *'No command line'* message is displayed. To provide a command-line parameter during debugging, you can use Delphi's Run ➤ Parameters menu command.

Another technique is to open Windows Explorer, locate the directory that contains the executable file of the program, and drag another file over the executable file. The Windows Explorer will start the program using the name of the dropped file as a command-line parameter. Figure 25.5 shows both the Explorer and the corresponding output.

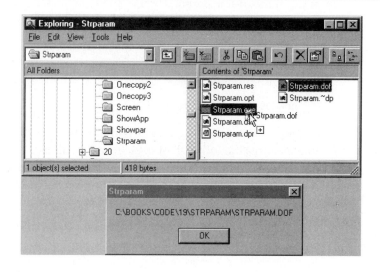

FIGURE 25.5

You can provide a command-line parameter to the StrParam example by dropping a file over the executable file in the Windows Explorer.

Events, Messages, and Multitasking in Windows

To understand how Windows applications work, we need to spend a minute discussing how multitasking is supported in this environment. We also need to understand the role of timers (and the Timer component) and of background (or *idle*) computing. Then we will move on to Windows 95 multithreading and support for this feature in Delphi applications.

In short, we need to delve deeper into the event-driven structure of Windows and in its multitasking support. I won't discuss this topic in detail, since this is a book about *Delphi* programming, but I will provide an overview for readers who have limited experience with Windows (and especially Windows 95) programming.

Event-Driven Programming

The basic idea behind event-driven programming is that specific events determine the control flow of the application. A program spends most of its time waiting for these events and provides code to respond to several of them. For example, when a user clicks one of the mouse buttons, an event occurs. A message describing this event is sent to the window currently under the mouse cursor. The program code that responds to events for that window will receive the event, process it, and respond accordingly. When the program has finished responding to the event, it returns to a waiting or "idle" state.

As this explanation shows, events are serialized; each event is handled only after the previous one is completed. When an application is executing event-handling code (that is, when it is not waiting for an event), other events for that application have to wait in a message queue reserved for that application (unless the application uses multiple threads, each with its own message queue). In the 16-bit versions of Windows, there was a limited multitasking capability, based on the fact that each application took turns responding to its own messages. When an application had responded to a message and returned to a waiting state, it became last in the list of programs waiting to handle additional messages. In Windows 3.1, there was no way to stop an application from executing a complex event handler, and other applications simply had to wait.

Event handling and the message queues are still the core of Windows 95 and Windows NT, but in these 32-bit versions of the environment, after a fixed amount of time has elapsed, the system interrupts the current application and immediately gives control to the next one in the list. Only after each application has had a turn is the first resumed. This is called preemptive multitasking, a feature sorely lacking in Windows 3.1.

Because of the limited multitasking, Windows 3.1 applications used many different techniques to try to divide an algorithm into smaller chunks and execute them one at a time. These techniques include using timers and performing background (or *idle*) computing, and they are still useful. Therefore I'll describe them in the following sections.

By the way, in Win32, just as in Windows 3.1, if an application has responded to its events and is waiting for its turn to process messages, it has no chance to regain control until it receives another message (unless it uses multithreading). This is one reason timers continue to exist (besides 16-bit compatibility). One final note—when you think about events, remember that input events (using the mouse or the keyboard) account for only a small percentage of the total message flow in a Windows application. Most of the messages are the system's internal messages or messages exchanged between different controls and windows. Even a familiar input operation such as clicking a mouse button can result in a huge number of messages, most of which are internal Windows messages.

You can test this yourself by using the WinSight utility included in Delphi. In WinSight, choose to view the Message Trace, and select the messages for all of the windows. Select Start, and then perform some normal operations with the mouse. You'll see hundreds of messages in a few minutes. Of course, WinSight causes Windows to run much slower than usual because of its monitoring. At normal speed, the flow of messages is much faster than you'll see when you run WinSight.

Windows Message Delivery

Before looking at some real examples, we need to consider another key element of message handling. Windows has two different ways to send a message to a window:

- The PostMessage API function, which is used to place a message in the application's message queue. The message will be handled only when the application has a chance to access its message queue (that is, when it receives control from the system), and only after earlier messages have been processed. This is an asynchronous call, since you do not know when the message will actually be received. This API function was used in the OneCopy2 example earlier in this chapter.

- The SendMessage API function, which is used to execute message-handler code immediately. SendMessage bypasses the application's message queue and sends the message directly to a target window or control. This is a synchronous call. This function even has a return value, which is passed back by the message-handling code.

The difference between these two ways of sending messages is similar to that between mailing a letter, which will reach its destination sooner or later, and sending a fax, which goes immediately to the recipient. Although you will rarely need to use these low-level functions in Delphi, you might wonder which one you should use if you do need to write this type of code.

The advantage of using SendMessage is obvious: it provides more control over the system. However, you should generally use PostMessage for a very simple reason: when the messages are posted to the queue, each running application has a better chance to receive control, which makes the entire system behave more smoothly. Delphi includes a specific method, Perform, whose action is very similar to SendMessage.

Building a Clock with a Timer

A good example of the problems that arise in an event-driven environment is creating a clock program. A clock should automatically update its output as time passes. A traditional approach might be to check the current time continuously, reading the value stored in the system clock. Although such a program would probably work well, it would consume a lot of CPU time, depleting the processing power available to other applications.

An alternative is to read the system clock approximately once each second, and then return the control to the system as soon as possible. But how can the application be awakened when each second has elapsed? This is a typical duty for a timer. In Delphi, a Timer component receives an OnTimer event each time a fixed interval has elapsed.

Before continuing with the clock program example, let's take a moment to detail some of the aspects of timer behavior in Windows (we have already used this component, but without examining its behavior). Timers are based on an interrupt, driven by the system clock, and generated at exactly the specified rate.

The problem is that timer messages, like other messages, are posted to a window and are added to the message queue of the application owning the window. This implies that timer messages may not be delivered to the application at the proper rate. If another program takes control of the CPU for a while (for example, during a file-loading operation), timer messages are still generated, but they do not reach the program until it regains control of the system.

In this situation, a second problem arises. Since timer messages can be very frequent (theoretically, each millisecond; in practice, once each 60 milliseconds at most), they don't accumulate in the message queue. If a second timer message reaches the queue and a previous similar message is still there, the first message is overwritten. This means that an application cannot accurately count the number of timer messages received to determine how much time has elapsed. The result is that when you receive a timer message, you know for sure that some time has elapsed, but you do not know how much time.

How can we use a timer to build a clock? Simply place a Timer and a Panel component in a form. Set the timer interval to 1000 milliseconds (that is, one second), select a suitable font for the panel caption, and align the panel with the client area of the form. After you have built this form, write the following code to respond to the OnTimer event of the Timer component:

```
procedure TForm1.Timer1Timer(Sender: TObject);
begin
  Panel1.Caption := TimeToStr (Time);
end;
```

The Time function returns a TDateTime object with the current time, which is converted into a string by the TimeToStr function. You can see the result of this code in Figure 25.6.

As we saw in Chapter 4, the format of the string returned by the TimeToStr function depends on the values of some variables defined in the SysUtils unit. These values depend on the international settings in Windows. For a simple test, start the Clock1 example, open the Windows Control Panel, choose Regional Settings, and select a country different from your own (or move to the Time page and change some values there). Apply the new setting, and notice that the Clock1 example automatically adapts its output to the new time format.

As you have seen in this example, timers can be used to write time-dependent applications. You'll also use a timer each time an application needs to monitor a value. A good example is the Mem program presented in the next chapter. At times, a good alternative to timers is idle computing. We'll investigate this idea a little later in the chapter, after some further refinement of the Clock example.

A Graphical Clock

Now that the basic idea is in place, we can think about expanding the Clock example by adding a number of new features. Digital clocks are not my favorite. How about an analog one, with nice-looking clock hands? I know that Windows comes with a clock program, so there is really no need to make a new one. But everyone has his or her own favorite clock style, and there are dozens of Windows clock applications available. So here comes yet another clock for Windows.

The foundation of the new example is the clock program we have already built. The form we need for the clock with hands is even simpler. It has just a timer, and no panel. Most of the code goes inside the form's OnPaint response method. Since we need to draw three different clock hands, we can add a generic procedure to the TForm1 class. I've called this procedure DrawHand and given it five parameters:

```
procedure DrawHand (XCenter, YCenter, Radius,
  BackRadius: Integer; Angle: Real);
```

The first two parameters represent the x and y coordinates of the center of the clock; then there is the size of the clock hands (that is, the radius of the clock circle), and the radius to extend the hand on the opposite side of the center. The last parameter is the current angle of the hand. The roles of these five parameters are illustrated graphically in Figure 25.7.

FIGURE 25.7

A graphical representation of the output of the DrawHand method of the Clock2 example.

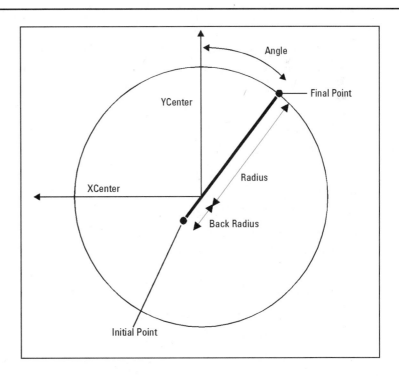

The only way I could work with the analog representation of the clock hands was by using trigonometric functions (cosine and sine), and that's why `Angle` is a real number instead of an Integer. To make things more complex, instead of starting from the center, the hand can extend in the opposite direction, as you can see in the output shown in Figure 25.8. Here is the full source code of the `DrawHand` function:

```
procedure TForm1.DrawHand (XCenter, YCenter,
  Radius, BackRadius: Integer; Angle: Real);
begin
  Angle := (Angle + 3*Pi/2);
  Canvas.MoveTo (XCenter - Round (BackRadius * Cos (Angle)),
    YCenter - Round (BackRadius * Sin (Angle)));
  Canvas.LineTo (XCenter + Round (Radius * Cos (Angle)),
    YCenter + Round (Radius * Sin (Angle)));
end;
```

The change in the value of the `Angle`, at the beginning, serves to move the origin of the angle itself from the horizontal axis to the vertical axis. We can move it forward ¾ turn, and since a complete turn is $2 \times Pi$, we get the expression $3 \times Pi/2$.

In the `FormPaint` procedure, the program calculates the center of the form and the radius of the clock, and then draws the three clock hands after computing their angle. To accomplish this, it uses `Hour`, `Minute`, and `Second`, which are three private fields I've added to the form. Their value is computed in the `OnTimer` response function, using the `DecodeTime` method defined in the Delphi System unit. The `OnTimer` response procedure then calls the `Refresh` method to update the image on the screen:

```
procedure TForm1.Timer1Timer(Sender: TObject);
var
  HSec: Word;  {temporary value, not used}
begin
  {get the system time}
  DecodeTime (Time, Hour, Minute, Second, HSec);
  Refresh;
end;
```

Here is a portion of the `FormPaint` method:

```
{1. Draw the minutes hand: Blue thick pen}
Canvas.Pen.Width := 2;
Canvas.Pen.Color := clBlue;
```

```
Angle := 2 * Pi * Minute / 60;
DrawHand (XCenter, YCenter,
  Radius * 90 div 100, 0, Angle);
{2. Draw the hours hand: Percentage of minutes added to
hour to move the hand smoothly: Same pen as the minutes }
Angle := 2 * Pi * (Hour + Minute / 60) / 12;
DrawHand (XCenter, YCenter, Radius * 70 div 100, 0, Angle);
```

FIGURE 25.8

The output of the Clock2 program. Notice that the second hand extends on the other side of the center.

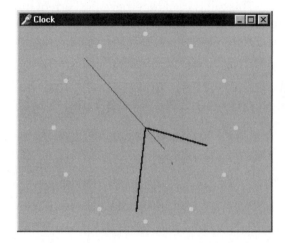

The FormPaint procedure first computes the center of the form and determines the Radius (another private field of the form) of the clock. It then draws each hand. First, it sets the color and size of the clock hand (changing the properties of the Pen selected in the Canvas). Then it computes the angle, converting the numbers from 1 to 60 (for minutes and seconds) into angles in radians (hence the use of Pi).

The code used to draw the hour hand is slightly more complex. To make the hour hand move more smoothly, in fact, the program can add to the hour the elapsed percentage of the next hour (that is, add the current number of minutes divided by 60). The initial portion of the painting method also draws tick marks corresponding to the hour positions to improve the readability of the clock. The program computes the position of these marks in a for loop, again based on the sine and cosine functions (as you can see in the complete source code on the companion CD).

There are two more interesting elements in the program. A call to the Refresh procedure is required each time the form is resized, to repaint the whole form, moving the clock to the center of the screen, and computing a new radius for the clock. The other curious element is a call to the `Timer1Timer` method in the `OnCreate` event:

```
procedure TForm1.FormCreate(Sender: TObject);
begin
  Timer1Timer (self);
end;
```

This call is used to retrieve the current time as soon as the form is created. In fact, soon after the `OnCreate` event, Windows will call the `OnPaint` event. If the current time has still not been computed, the output of the program will be meaningless, until the first timer event.

Painting the Seconds Hand with Raster Operations

The Clock2 program works, but it is far from satisfactory. The clock image is not steady; it flickers a lot. In fact, each second, the whole surface of the form is erased and then repainted again from scratch. This might seem the only possible behavior, since the second hand should move, but it is not. Instead of deleting the whole image, we can delete only the old second hand, and then repaint it.

The problem now is how to delete the line. You might think of painting a new line with the background color, but this would not work, because you might also delete part of the other two clock hands or part of the hour marks.

Understanding Windows Raster Modes

The solution lies in the use of Windows *raster operation* modes, indicated in Delphi by the `Mode` property of the pen objects (we used this approach in Chapter 14 for the splitter line example, Split4). Raster operation modes allow you to indicate the behavior of pens (and, in part, also brushes) during drawing functions. These are some examples of raster operation modes:

- `pmBlack` draws black lines regardless of the pen color you select.
- `pmNot` reverses the color of the current pixels on the screen, again ignoring the pen color.
- `pmCopy` is the default mode to copy the color of the pen to the screen.

The output of a number of these modes depends both on the color of the current pixels of the screen and the color of the pen. You can merge the colors, merge the colors inverting one of them, use a color to mask the other, xor the two colors, and perform many, many more operations with the different modes.

The raster operation mode we need to draw the second hand of the clock example is pmNotXor. Its result is the inverted color of the exclusive or performed between the two colors. The key feature of this drawing mode is that if you draw the same line twice, it disappears. Also, you can draw in color. This is exactly what we were looking for, since we can use it to delete the old line before drawing a new one.

> **NOTE**
>
> Yes, the pmNotXor mode is a little mysterious. But we don't really need to understand how colored pixels are merged and "xored." Our main concern is the *result* of using this mode, not how it works internally.

The New Version of the Graphical Clock

First of all, each time the timer message arrives, we can store the old values of the seconds and minutes in two new private fields of the form: OldMinute and Old-Second. If the value of the minutes has not changed, we use the value of the seconds to delete the old hand and draw the new one:

```
procedure TForm1.Timer1Timer(Sender: TObject);
var
  HSec: Word;  {temporary value, not used}
begin
  {store the old values and get the system time}
  OldMinute := Minute;
  OldSecond := Second;
  DecodeTime (Time, Hour, Minute, Second, HSec);

  {if minutes haven't changed, move the
  seconds hand else redraw the whole clock}
  if Minute = OldMinute then
    DrawSecond
  else
    Refresh;
end;
```

The DrawSecond procedure draws two lines corresponding to the old and the new position of the hand:

```
procedure TForm1.DrawSecond;
var
  Angle, OldAngle: Real;
begin
  {delete the old line, drawing over it again}
  OldAngle := 2 * Pi * OldSecond / 60;
  DrawHand (XCenter, YCenter, Radius,
    Radius * 30 div 100, OldAngle);
  {draw the new line}
  Angle := 2 * Pi * Second / 60;
  DrawHand (XCenter, YCenter, Radius,
    Radius * 30 div 100, Angle);
end;
```

For this code to work properly, you need to set the pmNotXor raster mode. However, you can avoid doing this each time the second hand is drawn by placing it at the end of the painting code. Here is the final portion of this procedure (extracted from the source code of the Clock3 example) with the relevant changes:

```
{3. Draw the seconds hand}
{Red thin pen, with 'not xor' raster mode}
Canvas.Pen.Width := 1;
Canvas.Pen.Color := clRed;
Canvas.Pen.Mode := pmNotXor;
Angle := 2 * Pi * (Second + 45) / 60;
DrawHand (XCenter, YCenter, Radius,
  Radius * 30 div 100, Angle);
```

Avoiding a repetitive call improves the speed of the program. The output of the new version, called Clock3, is actually very similar to that of the previous one, but this time there is no flickering. And there is another difference: when the clock hands are overlapped, the raster mode combines the colors of the two hands. This is something hard to see when reproduced in a black-and-white book, so I suggest you run the two programs and compare their output on the screen.

Idle Computing and Multitasking

An alternative to using timers in a Windows application is to implement some form of background computing. For example, suppose that you need to implement a time-consuming algorithm. If you write the algorithm as a response to an event, your application will be stopped completely during all the time it takes to process that algorithm. To let the user know that something is being processed, you can display the hourglass cursor, but this is not a user-friendly solution.

A better solution is to split the algorithm into smaller pieces, and execute each of them in turn, letting the application respond to pending messages in between processing the pieces. A more radical solution is to use the multithreading capabilities of Windows 95 and NT, starting a separate thread to compute an algorithm, and letting the application process incoming messages *at the same time*.

We will look into some techniques used to implement background computing in a single thread first. These techniques were necessary in Windows 3.1, and can still be useful in Win32 applications. Later on we will explore Delphi's multithreading support and its advantages over background processing, including some synchronization techniques and the capability to set thread priorities.

Background Processing

There are actually several ways to implement background computing, as you'll see in the next example. These are the two most common solutions:

- Call the `Application.ProcessMessages` function each time, so that a waiting message can be processed.

- Execute each step of the program when the `Application` object receives the `OnIdle` event.

These two approaches, which are related to the `Application` object, let the program get more or less system time, depending on the current activity. The difference between calling `ProcessMessages` and using `OnIdle` events is that by calling `ProcessMessages` your code will receive more processing time than it does by using the `OnIdle` approach. Calling `ProcessMessages` is a way to let the system perform other operations while your program is computing; using the OnIdle event is a way to let your application perform background tasks when it doesn't have pending requests from the user.

A third, but less common (and more complex) way to implement background processing is to have the application post a user-defined message to itself at the end of each step in the background process:

```
PostMessage (Handle, wm_User, 0, 0);
```

The application will get this message after a while, so it can execute the next step and then post another message to itself, continuing until the background processing is done.

Computing Prime Numbers (the Dumb Way)

To demonstrate some of these choices, I've written an example named BackProc (for *background processing*). The form of this program has four buttons used to start the processing with four different techniques, four progress bars to report the advances of the algorithm, and four labels to display the results. Above these, there is a SpinEdit control used to set the number of iterations of the algorithm. When you click on one of the four buttons, the program calculates how many prime numbers there are below the value indicated by the SpinEdit control, using a different algorithm for each button. In practice, you can change the value of SpinEdit1 to make the computation last more or less, depending on the speed of your computers.

There are a number of very intelligent algorithms you can use to compute prime numbers efficiently. I've used none of them, because I needed something really slow to demonstrate background computing. For this reason, I've written a simple function to compute prime numbers, which divides a given number by 2, 3, 4, and so on up to the value before the number itself.

The IsPrime function looks at the remainder of each integral division, using the mod operator, and if the result is zero, the number is not prime. When this happens, it stops the loop and returns False:

```
function IsPrime (N: LongInt): Boolean;
var
  Test: LongInt;
```

```
begin
  IsPrime := True;
  for Test := 2 to N - 1 do
  begin
    if (N mod Test) = 0 then
    begin
      IsPrime := False;
      break; {jump out of the for loop}
    end;
  end;
end;
```

With this function, we can compute the prime numbers below a certain value with a simple loop:

```
for Number := 2 to Max do
  if IsPrime (Number) then
    Inc (NPrimes);
```

At the end of the loop, the NPrimes variable contains the result. It's simple, but not efficient. This same algorithm is used four times, with only small changes in the code of the for loop.

The Hourglass Approach

The first button, labeled *Hourglass*, uses the simplest approach. It computes the algorithm, taking whatever time is required, and without explicitly releasing control back to the system. To let the user know something is happening, it shows the hourglass cursor and updates the progress gauge continuously. Figure 25.9 shows the output of the BackProc example when the Hourglass button is chosen.

FIGURE 25.9

The output of the BackProc example when the first button is clicked.

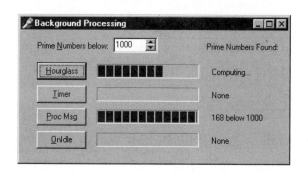

To show the hourglass, this program uses the Cursor property of the Screen object, setting it to crHourglass. You should be careful to reset the normal cursor at the end, and do it in the finally portion of a try-finally block. This approach ensures that the cursor is reset properly, even if an exception is raised in the code.

Two other operations are accomplished before starting the actual algorithm. The label at the right is changed to *Computing*, and the value of the SpinEdit control is copied to the Max variable. This value will be used several times in the following code, so the program reads the value once and stores it. Besides making the code more efficient, this is required by subsequent versions, which allow the user to perform other operations (including changing the spin edit box value) while the algorithm is being performed. Here is the full code of this first version:

```
procedure TForm1.HourButtonClick(Sender: TObject);
var
  Number, NPrimes, Max: LongInt;
begin
  Screen.Cursor := crHourglass;
  try
    NPrimes := 0;
    Max := SpinEdit1.Value;
    HourLabel.Caption := 'Computing...';
    for Number := 2 to Max do
    begin
      if IsPrime (Number) then
        Inc (NPrimes);
      ProgressBar1.Position := Number * 100 div Max;
    end;
    HourLabel.Caption := IntToStr (NPrimes) +
      ' below ' + IntToStr (Max);
  finally
    Screen.Cursor := crDefault;
  end;
end;
```

Each time the loop is executed, the value of the progress bar is updated. This is probably one of the statements that slow down the algorithm, particularly when its effect is to repaint the control. At the end of the routine, the result is copied to the label on the right. I've provided the code of this version mainly to let you know how I changed it in the other versions. The problem with this version is that when you press the Hourglass button, the application will not respond to other messages until the algorithm is done. Contrary to what happened in Windows 3.1, however, you can work on other applications while this application is computing. However, if you hide the form of BackProc behind another window and then you move it to the front again, it won't be repainted properly until the algorithm is done and the application has a chance to process additional messages.

Background Processing with Timers

The Timer button in the BackProc example starts the worst form of background processing. The use of timers makes this code very slow compared to the other solutions. To make good use of a timer, I've "unfolded" the for loop, using one of its cycles for each timer event. The procedure handling the button's OnClick event simply sets the initial value of some private variables (I had to move these variables to the form scope because two different methods need to access them). After this is done, the timer is activated (notice that it is not active at design-time):

```
procedure TForm1.TimerButtonClick(Sender: TObject);
begin
  TimerNPrimes := 0;
  TimerMax := SpinEdit1.Value;
  TimerNumber := 2;
  Timer1.Enabled := True;
  ProgressBar2.Position := 0;
  TimerLabel.Caption := 'Computing...';
end;
```

The real code is in the Timer1Timer method. The for loop is replaced by a plain if statement and a call to the Inc system procedure:

```
procedure TForm1.Timer1Timer(Sender: TObject);
begin
  if TimerNumber < TimerMax then
  begin
    if IsPrime (TimerNumber) then
      Inc (TimerNPrimes);
    Inc (TimerNumber);
  end
  else
  begin
    Timer1.Enabled := False;
    TimerLabel.Caption := IntToStr (TimerNPrimes) +
      ' below ' + IntToStr (TimerMax);
```

```
    Beep;
  end;
  ProgressBar2.Position :=TimerNumber * 100 div TimerMax;
end;
```

You can compare this code with the original version of the algorithm, which is based on a for loop. The rest of the code is easy to understand. No change is made to the cursor, of course, and a simple beep is issued to notify the user at the end.

Notice that while the program is working, the Timer button is not disabled, so the user can restart the algorithm. The user can also click on the Hourglass button, starting the first version of the algorithm, which temporarily stops the timer-based code (as well as any other code of this application).

Processing Messages in the Background

A much simpler and better solution is to let the application (and the whole system in Windows 3.1) process other messages in the background while we are computing the prime numbers. This is much simpler because it only requires adding a single statement to the original version of the algorithm: a call to the ProcessMessages method of the Application object.

This statement is added inside the for loop, so that other events for this application have a chance to be handled on each iteration:

```
for Number := 2 to Max do
begin
  if IsPrime (Number) then
    Inc (NPrimes);
  ProgressBar3.Position := Number * 100 div Max;
  Application.ProcessMessages;
end;
```

This makes the execution smooth. You can do anything on this form, without any real problems—just more slowly. To summarize the code so far, if you click on the Hourglass button, everything within the application stops until processing is complete. If you start the Timer version, the computation will be much slower, but the application will respond to other messages. The higher-priority ProcessMessages version finishes more quickly, and still doesn't halt the application. Also notice that you can restart the ProcessMessages version before it is done (the preceding computation is stopped waiting for the new one to finish).

I suggest that you run the example program and test each method yourself. This will help you to understand the differences between these approaches to

Windows 3.1-style multitasking. Note that you can restart the Timer version while the program is processing, but it will discard the previous results and start over again. The ProcessMessages version, on the other hand, spawns a second computation loop, and restarting it may cause some problems. The biggest problem is that each time you start or *re-enter* this function, a sizable chunk of the stack is used. Starting several computations at the same time may use up all of the program's stack space, something that Windows doesn't like at all (it can bring the system to a complete stop).

As a general-purpose programming technique, code that uses ProcessMessages must protect itself against reentrancy to avoid this kind of stack problem. The best solution is to display a modal status dialog box, so that the main application window (with all its menus) is disabled. In the example program, I've just disabled the corresponding button, to let you start up other versions of the algorithm while this one is running.

Idle-Time Computing

The solution provided by the bottom button in the BackProc example is the only version that really does true background processing, by grabbing idle time from the system. As in the Timer version, the OnIdle method splits the code into two portions. When the OnIdle button is clicked, some initialization code is executed, including setting the OnIdle event handler of the Application object:

```
procedure TForm1.IdleButtonClick(Sender: TObject);
begin
  IdleNPrimes := 0;
  IdleMax := SpinEdit1.Value;
  IdleNumber := 2;
  Application.OnIdle := IdleProc;
  ProgressBar4.Position := 0;
  IdleLabel.Caption := 'Computing...';
end;
```

Again, this code uses some variables declared in the scope of the form (as private fields), and again it uses a test and an increment instead of a for loop. Here is the code of the IdleProc method:

```
procedure TForm1.IdleProc (Sender: TObject;
  var Done: Boolean);
begin
  if IdleNumber < IdleMax then
```

```
  begin
    if IsPrime (IdleNumber) then
      Inc (IdleNPrimes);
    Inc (IdleNumber);
    Done := False;
  end
  else
  begin
    IdleLabel.Caption := IntToStr (IdleNPrimes) +
      ' below ' + IntToStr (IdleMax);
    Done := True;
    Beep;
    Application.OnIdle := nil;
  end;
  ProgressBar4.Position :=IdleNumber * 100 div IdleMax;
end;
```

The second parameter, Done, is used to tell the system whether further idle-time processing is required or the algorithm is finished. When the algorithm terminates, we also disable the event-handler, to avoid receiving additional idle messages when they are not needed.

Notice that in this case, we have very limited control over the execution of our code. We do not know how much time it will take. If nothing else is happening on the computer, this version of the code is as fast as the original one; but if you do other operations, such as executing the version based on the call to the Process-Messages method, the idle processing almost stops.

There is no clear winner among these techniques. For real background computing, OnIdle is the right choice. If you just want the application to respond to other events, even while your program is working hard, use ProcessMessages instead. Using timers is a compromise between the benefits of these two. In contrast, if you want to build a real multithreading application, you must use the threading capability of the Win32 platforms, and the specific Delphi support for this feature.

Multithreading in Delphi

Windows 95 and Windows NT allow us to let two procedures or methods execute at the same time and let our program control them. Before we look at the implementation of multithreading, we should ask ourselves why we might want to have several threads of execution inside a given program. First, consider some of the *disadvantages* of multithreading:

- Multithreading makes a program run slower, unless you have multiple CPUs and the operating system can split the threads among processors.

- Multithreading programs must synchronize access to shared resources and memory, which makes them much more complex to write, as we'll see in many cases.

Fortunately, multithreading also has some advantages. You can run a thread in the background, letting the user continue to operate the program. You can make one thread run faster than others by adjusting its priority, regulate the resource access of different threads, assign local storage to each thread, and spawn multiple threads of the same type.

The TThread Class

Windows provides a series of API calls to control threads (the key one is Create-Thread), but I won't discuss them here because Delphi provides a TThread class that will let us control threads well enough.

The first thing to know about the TThread class is that you never use it directly, because it is an abstract class—a class with a virtual abstract method. To use threads, you always subclass TThread and use the features of this base class. The TThread class has a constructor with a single parameter that lets you choose whether to start the thread immediately or suspend it until later:

```
constructor Create(CreateSuspended: Boolean);
```

There are also some public synchronization methods:

```
procedure Resume;
procedure Suspend;
function Terminate: Integer;
function WaitFor: Integer;
```

The published properties include Priority, Suspended, and two read-only low-level values (Handle and ThreadID). The class also provides a protected interface, which includes two key methods for your thread subclasses:

```
procedure Execute; virtual; abstract;
procedure Synchronize(Method: TThreadMethod);
```

The Execute method, declared as a virtual abstract procedure, must be redefined by each thread class. It contains the main code of the thread, the code you would typically place in a *thread function* when using the Windows API. The Synchronize method is used to avoid concurrent access to VCL components. The VCL code runs inside the main thread of the program, and you need to synchronize access to the VCL to avoid reentrancy problems (errors from reentering a function before a previous call is completed). The only parameter of Synchronize is a method that accepts no parameters, typically a method of the same thread class.

In Delphi 2 applications every operation of a background thread involving the user interface or any other VCL component had to use *synchronized* calls. Delphi 3 includes some native support for multithreading. For example, the TCanvas class has two locking methods, Lock and UnLock, which allow a background thread to paint directly on the Canvas of the main form. Another helpful class is TThread-List, which allow different threads to access the same TList safely and concurrently. Support for threads is available also in graphical objects, including bitmaps.

A First Example

As a first simple example, I've built a program that uses the Synchronize method. The program uses a thread to paint on the surface of a form (the example is called ThOld). The thread class, TPainterThread, overrides the Execute method and defines a custom Paint method. The Paint method is used to access VCL objects, so it is called only from within the Synchronize method. Since the Paint method cannot accept parameters directly and still be a compatible method for the Synchronize method, the class requires some private data. Here is the thread class declaration:

```
type
  TPainterThread = class(TThread)
  private
    X, Y: Integer;
  protected
    procedure Execute; override;
    procedure Paint;
  end;
```

The Paint method marks pixels of the form in red:

```
procedure TPainterThread.Paint;
begin
  Form1.Canvas.Pixels [X, Y] := clRed;
end;
```

This code is very simple, but since it is executed when nothing else in Delphi is running, the synchronized methods should be as fast as possible. The main function of the thread, Execute, randomly updates a pixel by passing the Paint method as the parameter of the Synchronize method:

```
procedure TPainterThread.Execute;
begin
  Randomize;
  repeat
    X := Random (300);
    Y := Random (Form1.ClientHeight);
    Synchronize (Paint);
  until Terminated;
end;
```

Figure 25.10 shows the result of this code. As you can see in the listing above, the thread runs until it is terminated. On the main form, there is a button used to start the thread. By passing False to the Create constructor, the thread starts immediately:

```
procedure TForm1.Button1Click(Sender: TObject);
begin
  Button1.Enabled := False;
  Button2.Enabled := True;
  PT := TPainterThread.Create (False);  // start
end;
```

PT is a private TPainterThread field of the form class. The first button creates the thread and starts it. The second button frees the thread object and toggles the value of the Enabled property of the two buttons.

FIGURE 25.10

The output of the ThOld example: the colored pixels are painted by a background thread.

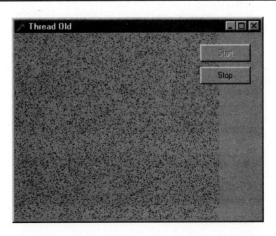

The main form also handles mouse clicks; when a mouse button is pressed on the form, the red pixels of a circular portion of the form around the position of the mouse click are wiped out, repainting the form with its background color:

```
procedure TForm1.FormMouseDown(Sender: TObject;
  Button: TMouseButton; Shift: TShiftState; X, Y: Integer);
begin
  Canvas.Pen.Color := Color; // of the form
  Canvas.Brush.Color := Color;
  Canvas.Ellipse (x - 30, y - 30, x + 30, y + 30);
end;
```

A Locking Example

We can now rewrite the previous example using new Delphi 3 capabilities. In this case, to access the form's canvas we can simply lock it, and avoid the call to Synchronize, simplifying the code. The thread class in the ThLock example has just one method:

```
type
  TPainterThread = class(TThread)
  protected
    procedure Execute; override;
  end;
```

The code of Execute now does everything, including the output, after locking the canvas of the form:

```
procedure TPainterThread.Execute;
var
  X, Y: Integer;
begin
  Randomize;
  repeat
    X := Random (300);
    Y := Random (Form1.ClientHeight);
    with Form1.Canvas do
    begin
      Lock;
      try
        Pixels [X, Y] := clRed;
      finally
        Unlock;
      end;
```

```
    end;
  until Terminated;
end;
```

If you then want to access the Canvas in an event handler other than OnPaint (which handles locking automatically) you should call the Lock method again:

```
procedure TForm1.FormMouseDown (Sender: TObject;
  Button: TMouseButton; Shift: TShiftState; X, Y: Integer);
begin
  Canvas.Lock;
  try
    Canvas.Pen.Color := clYellow;
    Canvas.Brush.Color := clYellow;
    Canvas.Ellipse (x - 30, y - 30, x + 30, y + 30);
  finally
    Canvas.Unlock;
  end;
end;
```

Synchronization Alternatives

The use of the Lock method in Delphi 3 is limited to the few objects which have this capability. The alternative is to continue using the Synchronize protected method of the TThread class, when you expect several threads to need access to a component's properties at the same time. Generally you will use secondary threads for background operations, such as file transfer or number crunching, with little or no need to update the user interface. If you need limited updates of the user interface, there are alternative approaches to the two techniques just mentioned.

First, a thread can update some data structure, which the main thread scans from time to time. You have to take care to avoid read/write. As a second alternative, you can use traditional Windows-based multitasking; the thread can post a message to the main window, asking for an update. Keep in mind that you cannot use SendMessage (which is synchronous, similar to a direct function call) to do this, but should use only PostMessage (which is asynchronous, and uses the message queue). These alternative techniques are not used frequently anyway, compared to the first two I've shown you, so there is no example in the book implementing them.

Thread Priorities

Our third example of threads is an extension of the previous one, but this time uses several threads at the same time, and allows users to change their priorities with some track bars. Here is the new version of the TPainterThread class:

```
type
  TPainterThread = class(TThread)
  private
    Color: Integer;
  protected
    procedure Execute; override;
  public
    constructor Create (Col: TColor);
  end;
```

I've added a constructor to the class to pass an initial color value to the thread. As an alternative, I could have made the Color a public field of the thread class to allow the program to manipulate them directly. Here is the code of the constructor:

```
constructor TPainterThread.Create(Col: TColor);
begin
  Color:= Col;
  inherited Create (True);
end;
```

The constructor initializes the private data, then calls the constructor of the base class, creating the thread in a suspended state. The Execute method of the thread simply scans each screen line, setting each pixel to the given color:

```
procedure TPainterThread.Execute;
var
  X, Y, X1: Integer;
begin
  X := 0;
  Y := 0;
  repeat
    // scan the lines...
    X1 := X + 1;
    X := X1 mod 250;
    Y := Y + X1 div 250;
    Y := Y mod Form1.ClientHeight;
    Form1.Canvas.Lock;
    try
      Form1.Canvas.Pixels [X, Y] := Color;
```

```
    finally
        Form1.Canvas.UnLock;
    end;
  until Terminated;
end;
```

The main form has four check boxes and four track bars (as you can see in Figure 25.11). The form has some local data, too, an array to hold the four thread objects:

```
private
    PT: array [1..4] of TPainterThread;public
```

This array is initialized when the form is created:

```
procedure TForm1.FormCreate(Sender: TObject);
begin
    PT [1] := TPainterThread.Create (clRed);
    PT [2] := TPainterThread.Create (clBlue);
    PT [3] := TPainterThread.Create (clGreen);
    PT [4] := TPainterThread.Create (ClBlack);
end;
```

FIGURE 25.11

The output of the ThPrior example, with four threads updating the user interface concurrently.

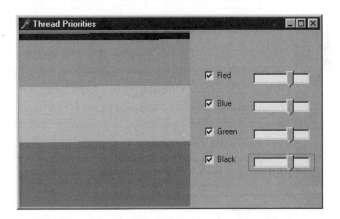

Notice that the program creates the four threads as suspended. They are started when the corresponding check box is checked and suspended again when the check box is cleared:

```
procedure TForm1.CheckBox1Click(Sender: TObject);
begin
    if (Sender as TCheckbox).Checked then
```

```
      PT [(Sender as TCheckbox).Tag].Resume
    else
      PT [(Sender as TCheckbox).Tag].Suspend;
  end;
```

To use the same event handler for all check boxes, I've set the value of the Tag property of each one to the number of the corresponding thread. The same technique is used with the track bars, which are used to set the current priority of the thread:

```
procedure TForm1.TrackBar1Change(Sender: TObject);
begin
  PT [(Sender as TTrackBar).Tag].Priority :=
    TThreadPriority ((Sender as TTrackBar).Position);
end;
```

To set the priority, I simply cast the current Position of the track bar to the corresponding TThreadPriority enumeration value. Then I use the resulting value to set the priority of the corresponding thread, as determined by the Tag property. This program is quite instructive, because you can alter thread priorities and see the effect on screen.

Synchronizing Threads

We have seen that there are two common approaches for synchronizing a thread with rest of the application: the use of the Synchronize method of a thread object, or the use of the Lock method of a VCL class which provides it, such as the TCanvas. In the last example we used the Lock method of the Canvas of the main form also to synchronize four threads which were painting on the screen. This is a very special case. Generally you'll need to use other techniques to synchronize two threads, including low-level techniques available in the Windows API.

In the next section I'll discuss a simple case, waiting for a thread to terminate. In the following sections we will see more complex examples.

Waiting for a Thread

When a thread should wait until another thread is done, it can simply call the WaitFor method of the object corresponding to the thread that should terminate.

Here is a portion of an example, in which a program starts a thread and then waits for its result:

```
Comp := TMyThread.Create (True);
// initialize the thread...
Comp.Resume;
Comp.WaitFor;
// look for final values...
Comp.Free;
```

This code is quite simple to write, but remember you cannot write this code as part of the main thread (for example, in a normal message response function) if the secondary thread has to synchronize with it. If you are waiting in the thread connected to the main form for another thread to finish, and the secondary thread is waiting to access the user interface (hence waiting for the main thread to finish its current job) the program will enter a deadlock!

To avoid this problem, you can use WaitFor to synchronize two threads. A first thread creates a secondary thread, and waits for it to end, without interfering with the main form's thread.

To show you an example of synchronization with multiple threads, I've built a character-counting program, called ThWait. The program computes how many copies of the four characters specified in an edit box are present in the text of a Memo component (you can actually load the text from any file, as long as you do so before starting the computation). The program looks for each of the four characters at the same time, using multiple threads spawned by the main thread. To improve the output, each thread shows its status—that is, how far through the text it has searched—in a progress bar, as you can see in Figure 25.12.

FIGURE 25.12

In the ThWait example, each thread outputs its status in a progress bar.

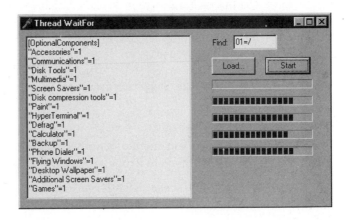

The actual engine of the program is the TFindThread class, which contains the LookFor field to hold the character we are searching for, and a Progress field to store the value of the progress bar and update its status. The result of the computation is placed in the public Found field:

```
type
  TFindThread = class(TThread)
  protected
    Progr: Integer;
    procedure UpdateProgress;
    procedure Execute; override;
  public
    Found: Integer;
    LookFor: Char;
    Progress: TProgressBar;
  end;
```

As usual, the core of the thread is in its Execute method, which scans the lines of the memo, looking for the given character. Notice that we can freely access the properties of the memo without synchronization, since this operation is a non-destructive read—it doesn't affect the status of the Memo component:

```
procedure TFindThread.Execute;
var
  I, J: Integer;
  Line: string;
begin
  Found := 0;
  with Form1.Memo1 do
    for I := 0 to Lines.Count - 1 do
    begin
      Line := Lines [I];
      for J := 1 to Length (Line) do
        if Line [J] = LookFor then
          Inc (Found);
      Progr := I + 1;
      Synchronize (UpdateProgress);
    end;
end;
```

The UpdateProgress method simply updates the status of the progress bar using the value of the field Progr:

```
procedure TFindThread.UpdateProgress;
begin
```

```
    Progress.Position := Progr;
  end;
```

Four copies of this thread are activated by the primary thread, an object of the TMultiFind class. Here is the declaration of this class:

```
type
  TMultiFind = class(TThread)
  protected
    Progr: Integer;
    procedure UpdateProgress;
    procedure Execute; override;
    procedure Show;
  public
    LookFor, Output: String;
    Progresses: array [1..5] of TProgressBar;
  end;
```

This thread class looks for the characters of the LookFor string (there must be four characters for the program to work correctly), using four TFindThread objects:

```
procedure TMultiFind.Execute;
var
  Finders: array [1..4] of TFindThread;
  I: Integer;
begin
  // set up the four threads
  for I := 1 to 4 do
  begin
    Finders[I] := TFindThread.Create (True);
    Finders[I].LookFor := LookFor[I];
    Finders[I].Progress := Progresses [I+1];
    Finders[I].Resume;
  end;
  // wait for the threads to end...
  for I := 1 to 4 do
  begin
    Finders[I].WaitFor;
    Progr := I;
    Synchronize (UpdateProgress);
  end;
  // show the result
  Output := 'Found: ';
  for I := 1 to 4 do
    Output := Output + Format ('%d %s, ',
```

```
      [Finders[I].Found, LookFor[I]]);
  Synchronize (Show);
  // delete threads
  for I := 1 to 4 do
    Finders[I].Free;
end;
```

Notice in particular the `for` loop with the `WaitFor` call. At the end, the `Execute` method shows the result in a synchronized method, `Show`. The program I've written to test these threads is quite simple. As we have seen in Figure 25.12, it has a memo where you can load a file and an edit box containing four characters. The number of characters is checked when the user exits the edit box:

```
procedure TForm1.Edit1Exit(Sender: TObject);
begin
  if Length (Edit1.Text) <> 4 then
  begin
    Edit1.SetFocus;
    ShowMessage ('The edit box requires four characters');
  end;
end;
```

The Start button starts the thread, which in turn immediately spawns the secondary threads:

```
procedure TForm1.Button1Click(Sender: TObject);
var
  I: Integer;
begin
  if Assigned (MainThread) then
    MainThread.Free;
  MainThread := TMultiFind.Create (True);
  MainThread.Progresses [1] := ProgressBar1;
  MainThread.Progresses [2] := ProgressBar2;
  ...
  MainThread.Progresses [1].Max := 4;
  for I := 2 to 5 do
    MainThread.Progresses[I].Max := Memo1.Lines.Count;
  for I := 1 to 5 do
    MainThread.Progresses[I].Position := 0;
  MainThread.LookFor := Edit1.Text;
  MainThread.Resume;
end;
```

Notice that we cannot delete the thread at the end of the method, because we cannot call `WaitFor` on it without creating a deadlock. Take care when writing multithreaded applications, because such a deadlock can freeze the whole system, leaving you with nothing else to do but reach for the reset button.

At the same time, to keep the operating system stable, we must remember to delete the thread, either before creating a second one (as at the beginning of the code above), or when the program terminates. This is also the reason we need to declare the thread object as a private field of the form, and not as a local variable of the method starting it.

Windows Synchronization Techniques

The Windows API functions offer many further synchronization techniques (available in the Win32 platforms):

- *Critical sections* are portions of source code that cannot be executed by two threads at the same time. By using a critical section, you can serialize the execution of specific portions of the source code. Critical sections can be used only within a single process, a single application.

- *Mutexes* are global objects you can use to serialize access to a resource. You first set a mutex, then access the resource, and finally release the mutex. While the mutex is set, if another thread (or process) tries to set the same mutex, it is stopped until the mutex is released by the previous thread (or process). As we have seen in the OneCopy4 example, in fact, a mutex can be shared by different applications.

- *Semaphores* are similar to mutexes but they are counted: you could allow, for example, three and no more than three accesses to a given resource at the same time. A mutex is equivalent to a semaphore with a maximum count of 1.

- *Events* can be used as a mean of synchronizing a thread with system events, such as user file operations. The `WaitFor` method of the Delphi `TThread` class uses an event. Events can also be used to *awake* several threads at the same time.

Building an Example

To demonstrate all of these different techniques I've built the ThSynch example. Suppose we have two threads operating on a string, using its value and updating the string. Suppose also the current value of the string is shared by the two threads. In the example the string initially contains 20 'A' characters, then is updated to contain 20 'B' characters and so on. In the example each thread simply computes the next value of the string than sends it to its own list box.

> **TIP** Of course, threads should tend to avoid using global variables. Delphi helps in this direction by wrapping threads in classes and also by allowing the definition of thread variables, with the `threadvar` **keyword.**

In the ThSynch example there are actually four forms which have two list boxes, with a nonproportional Courier font, and a button to start the related thread. Then there is a main form with four buttons, each showing the corresponding secondary form.

So we end up with four different versions of basically the same form and the same thread class. In each of these forms the Start button simply creates two instances of a thread, associating a list box with each. Here is an example:

```
procedure TForm2.BtnStartClick(Sender: TObject);
begin
  ListBox1.Clear;
  ListBox2.Clear;
  Th1 := TListThread.Create (True);
  Th2 := TListThread.Create (True);
  Th1.LBox := Listbox1;
  Th2.LBox := Listbox2;
  Th1.Resume;
  Th2.Resume;
end;
```

The thread classes are declared in each of the units defining the form, to avoid having too many files. This same unit contain the string variable used by the two thread objects:

```
var
  Form2: TForm2;
  Letters: string = 'AAAAAAAAAAAAAAAAAAAA';
```

Well, this is far from elegant, but in this program I'm looking for some trouble on purpose, so forget the coding style.

The Plain Thread

Here is the thread class and its Execute method in a first simple version:

```
type
  TListThread = class (TThread)
  private
    Str: String;
  protected
    procedure AddToList;
    procedure Execute; override;
  public
    LBox: TListBox;
  end;

procedure TListThread.Execute;
var
  I, J, K: Integer;
begin
  for I := 0 to 50 do
  begin
    for J := 1 to 20 do
      for K := 1 to 2601 do // useless repetition...
        if Letters [J] <> 'Z' then
          Letters [J] := Succ (Letters [J])
        else
          Letters [J] := 'A';
    Str := Letters;
    Synchronize (AddToList);
  end;
end;
```

The AddToList method simply adds the Str string to the list box connected with the thread. I've made each computation artificially long, by increasing each letter 2601 times instead of once: The effect is the same, but there are more changes the two thread will conflict. You can see this effect in Figure 25.13. Even better, you can press the Start button two or three times in a row, starting several threads at once, and increasing the chance of errors.

FIGURE 25.13

The first secondary form
of the ThSynch example
shows some errors in the
values of two list boxes.

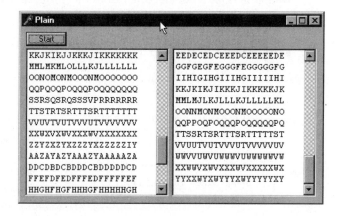

Using Critical Sections

If you want to serialize the operations of the two threads, and have more control
over what the threads do, you can use one of the Windows synchronization
techniques I've discussed before. In this second version I'll use critical sections.
To do this you should add the declaration of another global variable (or a form
class field) for the critical section:

```
var
    Critical1: TRTLCriticalSection;
```

This variable is initialized when the form is created, and destroyed at the end,
with two API calls:

```
procedure TForm3.FormCreate(Sender: TObject);
begin
  InitializeCriticalSection (Critical1);
end;
procedure TForm3.FormDestroy(Sender: TObject);
begin
  DeleteCriticalSection (Critical1);
end;
```

You can use critical sections to serialize specific portions of the code, such as the
code that updates each letter of the string. Here is how I've updated the code of
the Execute method of the thread object:

```
procedure TListThread.Execute;
var
  I, J, K: Integer;
```

```
begin
  for I := 0 to 50 do
  begin
    EnterCriticalSection (Critical1);
    for J := 1 to 20 do
      ... // same code as above
    Str := Letters;
    LeaveCriticalSection (Critical1);
    Synchronize (AddToList);
  end;
end;
```

The effect of this code is that while one thread is computing a new string the other thread will wait before doing the same, so all the output strings will always contain 20 copies of the same character.

Using a Mutex

Now we can write the same code, but using a mutex instead of a critical section. The effect will be the same, but I'd like to show you this technique as well. We simply need to declare the hMutex variable of type THandle, then update the four API calls of the previous example with the following four:

```
// in FormCreate
hMutex := CreateMutex (nil, false, nil);
// in FormDestroy
CloseHandle (hMutex);
// in the for loop
WaitForSingleObject (hMutex, INFINITE);
...
ReleaseMutex (hMutex);
```

Using a TCriticalSection VCL Object

Actually the Client/Server Edition of Delphi 3 offers one further alternative. The SyncObjs unit, in fact, defines VCL classes for some synchronization objects: events and critical sections. So we can build a fourth version of the example, very similar to the second one based on a critical section and Windows API calls. The difference is that now we declare the object as:

```
var
  Critical1: TCriticalSection;
```

and use it as follows:

```
// in FormCreate
Critical1 := TCriticalSection.Create;
// in FormDestroy
Critical1.Free;
// in the for loop
Critical1.Enter;
...
Critical1.Leave;
```

There is very little difference, but the code is a little easier to write. The Sync-Objs units declares the TCriticalSection class along with the THandleObject class, the TEvent class and the TSingleEvent class.

To summarize the ideas described with this long example, a mutex, critical section, or semaphore is required whenever two threads access a shared resource or data. Otherwise, the system may move control from thread to thread before any of them has completed an intermediate operation. In this intermediate state, the data might be invalid, but the other threads will use it anyway. You can access these synchronization objects using simple Windows API calls, or even simpler VCL objects.

Using the Screen Object

We have already explored some of the properties and events of the Application object. However, there are other documented global objects. One of them is the Screen object. This object can be used to access some information about the system display and about the current set of forms in a running application. This object also has a list of the available fonts, which we have already used in some examples (such as the FontGrid example in Chapter 11).

> **NOTE** Other Delphi global objects declared by specific VCL units are Printer and Clipboard, which will be discussed in Chapters 28 and 30, respectively.

Getting Screen Information

Our next example shows some of the operations you can perform with the Screen object. First create a form with some labels and two list boxes. The first list box will be used to provide a list of fonts installed in the system, and the second one to dynamically show the forms of this application.

Both list boxes are filled using array properties of the Screen object. However, maintaining the second list box is more complex because it must be updated each time a new form is created, an existing form is destroyed, or the active form of the program changes. Note that the forms the Screen object references are the forms of the application, and not those of the system. To see how this works, you can create a number of secondary forms by clicking on the button labeled New:

```
procedure TMainForm.NewButtonClick(Sender: TObject);
var
  NewForm: TSecondForm;
begin
  {create a new form, set its caption, and run it}
  NewForm := TSecondForm.Create (self);
  Inc (Counter);
  NewForm.Caption := 'Second ' + IntToStr (Counter);
  NewForm.Show;
end;
```

One of the key portions of the program is the OnCreate event handler of the form, which uses a number of features of the Screen object:

```
procedure TMainForm.FormCreate(Sender: TObject);
begin
  {compute screen size}
  ScreenLabel.Caption := ScreenLabel.Caption + ' ' +
    IntToStr (Screen.Width) + 'x' + IntToStr (Screen.Height);
  {display fonts and forms data}
  FontsLabel.Caption := 'Fonts: ' +
    IntToStr (Screen.Fonts.Count);
  FontsListBox.Items := Screen.Fonts;
  FillFormsList (self);
  {set the secondary forms counter to 0}
  Counter := 0;
  {set an event handler on the screen object}
  Screen.OnActiveFormChange := FillFormsList;
end;
```

Handling the Forms List

As you can see above, the OnCreate event handler fills the list boxes and retrieves the size of the screen. The code used to fill the Forms list box is inside a second procedure, FillFormsList, which is also installed as an event handler for the OnActiveFormChange event of the Screen object:

```
procedure TMainForm.FillFormsList (Sender: TObject);
var
  I: Integer;
begin
  FormsLabel.Caption := 'Forms: ' +
    IntToStr (Screen.FormCount);
  FormsListBox.Clear;
  {write class name and form title to the list box}
  for I := 0 to Screen.FormCount - 1 do
    FormsListBox.Items.Add (Screen.Forms[I].ClassName +
      ' - ' + Screen.Forms[I].Caption);
  ActiveLabel.Caption := 'Active Form : ' +
    Screen.ActiveForm.Caption;
end;
```

> **WARNING**
> It is very important that you remove the handler of the OnActiveForm-Change event before exiting the application; that is, before the main form is destroyed. Otherwise, the code will be executed when no list box exists, and you'll get a system error. To accomplish this, handle the OnClose event of the main form and assign nil to Screen.OnActive-FormChange.

The FillFormsList method fills the list box and sets a value for the two labels above it to show the number of forms and the name of the active one. When you click on the New button, the program creates an instance of the secondary form, gives it a new title, and displays it. The Forms list box is updated automatically because of the handler we have installed for the OnActiveFormChange event. Figure 25.14 shows the output of this program when some secondary windows have been created.

FIGURE 25.14

The output of the Screen example with a number of secondary forms.

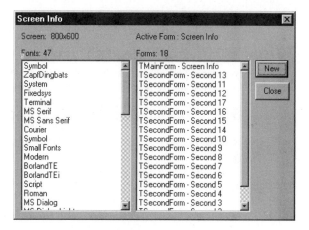

> **NOTE**
>
> Notice that the program always updates the text of the ActiveLabel above the second list box to show the currently active form, which is always the same as the first one in the list box.

The secondary forms each have a Close button you can select to remove them. The code handles the OnClose event, setting the Action parameter to caFree, so that the form is actually destroyed when it is closed. However, this code does not work. Windows moves the focus to a new active form before destroying the old one, so that the list will still contain the name of the form we have closed.

The first idea I had to solve this problem was to call the FillFormsList method directly from the secondary form. This doesn't work, however, because when you make the call, the secondary form still exists. Another idea I had was to use the wm_ParentNotify Windows message, sent to a main form when a secondary form is created or destroyed. Again, this message is sent too early, before the child window is actually destroyed and removed from the Screen.Forms list.

The solution is to introduce a delay, posting a user-defined Windows message. Since the posted message is queued and not handled immediately, if we send it at the last possible moment of life of the secondary form, the main form will receive it when the other form is destroyed.

The trick is to post the message in the OnDestroy event handler of the secondary form. To accomplish this, we need to refer to the MainForm object, by adding a proper uses statement in the implementation portion of this unit. I've posted a wm_User message, which is handled by a specific message method of the main form, as shown here:

```
public
  procedure ChildClosed (var Message: TMessage);
    message wm_User;
```

Here is the code for this method:

```
procedure TMainForm.ChildClosed (var Message: TMessage);
begin
  FillFormsList (self);
end;
```

The problem here is that if you close the main window before closing the secondary forms, the main form exists, but its code cannot be executed anymore. To avoid another system error (a General Protection Fault), you need to post the message only if the main form is not closing. But how do you know that? One way is to add a flag to the TMainForm class and change its value when the main form is closing, so that you can test the flag from the code of the secondary window.

This is a good solution—so good that the VCL already provides something similar. There is a barely documented ComponentState property. It is a Pascal set that includes, among other flags, a csDestroying flag which is set when the form is closing. Therefore, we can write the following code:

```
procedure TSecondForm.FormDestroy(Sender: TObject);
begin
  if not (csDestroying in MainForm.ComponentState) then
    PostMessage (MainForm.Handle, wm_User, 0, 0);
end;
```

With this code, the second list box always lists all of the forms in the application. Note that you need to disable the automatic creation of the secondary form by using the Forms page of the Project Options dialog box.

The last feature I've added to the program is a simple one. When you click on an item in the list box, the corresponding form is activated, using the BringToFront method:

```
procedure TMainForm.FormsListBoxClick(Sender: TObject);
begin
  Screen.Forms [FormsListBox.ItemIndex].BringToFront;
end;
```

Nice—well, almost nice. If you click on the list box of an inactive form, the main form is activated first, and the list box is rearranged, so you might end up selecting a different form than you are expecting. If you experiment with the program, you'll soon realize what I mean. This minor glitch in the program is an example of the risks you face when you dynamically update some information and let the user work on it at the same time.

Saving Status Information

If you want to save information about the status of an application in order to restore it the next time the program is executed, you could use a file and store the data in any format you like. Windows, however, has explicit support for storing this kind of information. In previous versions of Windows, the standard approach was to create an initialization (.INI) file. In Windows 95 (and in Windows NT) you can still use INI files, but Microsoft recommends using the System Registry instead.

In Windows 95, it is important to understand both techniques, because system information is frequently stored in the Registry *and* in the good old WIN.INI and SYSTEM.INI files. I don't want to discuss the advantages and disadvantages of the two approaches here, but only let you know they exist and are easily available within Delphi. To demonstrate both techniques, I've built two versions of a program that saves the position of its main window and restores it the next time it is executed. The first example uses an INI file, and the second uses the Registry.

Using Windows INI Files

Delphi provides a class you can use to manipulate INI files, TIniFile. Once you have created an object of this class and connected it to a file, you can read and write information to it. To create the object, you need to call the constructor, passing a file name to it, as in the following code:

```
var
   IniFile: TIniFile;
begin
   IniFile := TIniFile.Create ('inione.ini');
```

There are two choices for the location of the INI file. If you write the above code, the file will be stored in the Windows directory (unless an inione.ini already existed in the application directory). To be on the safe side, it is better to provide a full path to the `TIniFile.Create` constructor. We can easily extract the path from the first command-line parameter of the program, then use the `ExtractFilePath` method and add the actual file name:

```
var
  IniFile: TIniFile;
  FileName: string;
begin
  FileName := ExtractFilePath (ParamStr (0)) + 'Inione.ini';
  IniFile := TIniFile.Create (FileName);
```

The other solution is to store all the INI files in the Windows directory. This is the default when you provide only a file name, as in the statement above.

WARNING   Although I prefer the application directory approach, in this example I used the Windows directory, to let you run my sample program directly from the CD-ROM, which is a read-only device.

The format of INI files requires some explanation. These files are divided into sections, each indicated by a name enclosed in square brackets. Each section can contain a number of items of three possible kinds: strings, integers, or Booleans. If you are not familiar with the structure of an INI file, you should look at one, using any text editor, such as Windows Notepad.

The `TIniFile` class has three methods used to read each kind of data: `ReadBool`, `ReadInteger`, and `ReadString`. There are also three corresponding methods to write the data: `WriteBool`, `WriteInteger`, and `WriteString`. Other methods allow you to read or erase a whole section. In the Read methods, you can also specify a default value to be used if the corresponding entry doesn't exist in the INI file.

Our example, called IniOne, uses an INI file to store the location, the size, and the status (normal, maximized, or minimized) of the main form. The only real problem in this example is that the value of the state property is not always updated properly by the VCL, so we need to introduce an additional test to confirm whether the form has been minimized.

The main form of the IniOne example is just a plain, blank form, without any components. The program handles two events: `OnCreate`, to create or open the

INI file and read the initial values, and OnClose, to save the status after confirmation by the user. Here is the code of the first method, FormClose, which saves the data to be retrieved the next time the program is run:

```
procedure TForm1.FormClose(Sender: TObject;
  var Action: TCloseAction);
var
  Status: Integer;
begin
  if MessageDlg ('Save the current status of the form?',
    mtConfirmation, [mbYes, mbNo], 0) = IdYes then
  begin
    case WindowState of
      wsNormal: begin
        {save position and size, only if the state is normal}
        IniFile.WriteInteger ('MainForm', 'Top', Top);
        IniFile.WriteInteger ('MainForm', 'Left', Left);
        IniFile.WriteInteger ('MainForm', 'Width', Width);
        IniFile.WriteInteger ('MainForm', 'Height', Height);
        Status := 1;
      end;
      wsMinimized: Status := 2;
        {useless: this value is never set by VCL!}
      wsMaximized: Status := 3;
    end;
    {check if the window is minimized, that is,
    if the form is hidden and not active}
    if not Active then
      Status := 2;
    {write status information}
    IniFile.WriteInteger ('MainForm', 'Status', Status);
  end;
  {in any case destroy the IniFile object}
  IniFile.Destroy;
end;
```

The rest of the code is inside the FormCreate method, which simply reads the saved data and restores the previous situation. The only problem is to restore the minimized form. Setting the wsMinimized style for the WindowState property doesn't work (the form is reduced to an icon, placed over the Taskbar); and calling Application.Minimize doesn't work, either. The solution I've found is to minimize the form soon after it is created, using a Windows API approach: I simulate a user operation (selecting the Minimize command of the system menu) by posting a message. Here is the complete code:

```
procedure TForm1.FormCreate(Sender: TObject);
var
  Status: Integer;
begin
  IniFile := TIniFile.Create ('ini_one.ini');
  {try to read a value and test if it exists}
  Status := IniFile.ReadInteger ('MainForm', 'Status', 0);
  if Status <> 0 then
  begin
    {read position and size using current values as default}
    Top := IniFile.ReadInteger ('MainForm', 'Top', Top);
    Left := IniFile.ReadInteger ('MainForm', 'Left', Left);
    Width := IniFile.ReadInteger ('MainForm', 'Width', Width);
    Height := IniFile.ReadInteger ('MainForm', 'Height', Height);
    {set the minimized or maximized status}
    case Status of
      {1: WindowState := wsNormal;
        // this is already the default}
      2: PostMessage (Form1.Handle,
        wm_SysCommand, sc_Minimize, 0);
      3: WindowState := wsMaximized;
    end;
  end;
end;
```

This code uses a field named IniFile, of type TIniFile, which I've added to the private section to the TForm1 class. I didn't include a figure showing the program's output, because showing you an empty form or an icon is not particularly helpful. Instead, you should simply run the program a number of times to investigate its behavior, resizing and repositioning its window each time. What I will provide is an example of an INI file generated by the program:

```
[MainForm]
Top=359
Left=567
Width=217
Height=201
Status=1
```

Regarding INI files, remember that Delphi uses them quite often, even if they are disguised with different names. For example, the desktop (.DSK) and options(.DOF) files are structured as INI files.

Using the Registry

Now we can write a similar program using the system Registry instead of plain INI files. However, before we do so, I want to spend just a little time discussing the role and the structure of the Registry.

In short, the Registry is a hierarchical database of information about the computer and software configuration, and the user preferences. Windows has a set of API functions to interact with the Registry: you basically need to open a key (or folder) and then work with subkeys (or subfolders) and with values (or items), but you must be aware of the structure and the details of the Registry. The Windows 95 Registry is based on six top-level keys, as you can see in Figure 25.15.

FIGURE 25.15

The Registry Editor program showing the six top-level keys of the Windows 95 Registry.

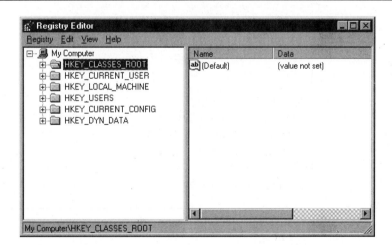

I cannot discuss the role of each part of the Registry in detail here. I recommend that you refer to specific Microsoft documentation (such as the Windows 95 or NT Resource Kit) to get the details of the organization of the Registry and information about where to add your own keys. The importance of the Registry should not be underestimated. The Registry holds crucial information about the system hardware configuration, Control Panel settings, OLE servers, and even statistics about the machine. To study the structure of the Registry and examine the current values of the keys, you can use the RegEdit program under Windows 95, or the RegEdt32 program under Windows NT.

WARNING You can also use RegEdit to edit the values in the Registry, but you'd do better to avoid changing anything unless you are sure about what you are doing. If you damage the Registry, you'll probably have to reinstall Windows from scratch.

In Delphi, there are basically two approaches to the use of the Registry, supported by two VCL classes: TRegistry and TRegIniFile. The first class provides a generic encapsulation of the Registry API, while the latter provides the interface (methods and properties) of the TIniFile class, but saves the data in the Registry instead of using the files. This class is the natural choice for the Registry version of our last program example; by using it we won't have to make too many changes in the source code (a real advantage whenever you have existing code based on INI files). Here are the three changes you have to make to the IniOne program:

1. Use TRegIniFile instead of TIniFile as the class of the IniFile object.

2. Create a new TRegIniFile object, instead of a TIniFile object in the FormCreate method:

    ```
    IniFile := TRegIniFile.Create ('IniOne.ini');
    ```

3. In the uses statement of the interface portion of the unit, replace the IniFiles unit with the Registry unit.

Easy, isn't it? With these simple changes, I've built the Registr example, which has exactly the same capabilities as the previous one, but saves its data to the Registry instead. Actually, when using the TRegIniFile class, Delphi adds a new subkey with the name of the INI file under the HKEY_CURRENT_USER key. We can see the effect of this code by exploring the Registry with the RegEdit application, as shown in Figure 25.16.

Instead of adding your entries directly under the HKEY_CURRENT_USER key you should place them under the *Software* subkey, and perhaps add one more level for your software company, as in *'Software\Soft-House\Demo'*.

FIGURE 25.16

Using the Registr program, you add new entries to the registration database, as you can see with RegEdit.

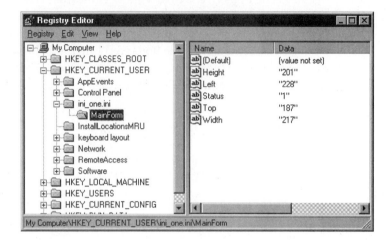

The TRegIniFile class is actually a subclass of the more generic TRegistry class, which has a number of methods very similar to the functions in the Registry API. These functions are not very simple to use, so I suggest that you stay with the simpler TRegIniFile for most cases. To use the TRegistry class, in you usually need to open a key first, and then access its data, including its values and its subkeys.

To show you the basic capabilities of the TRegistry class, I've built a very simple Registry viewer application. This program can show the structure of the Registry and list the values of the keys and items, but it doesn't display the actual data connected with the keys and items. It has just a subset of the capabilities of the RegEdit application, but I think it is an interesting example anyway.

The RegView program is based on a form with two combo boxes and two list boxes. When the application starts, a TRegistry object is created:

```
procedure TForm1.FormCreate(Sender: TObject);
begin
  Reg := TRegistry.Create;
```

```
Reg.OpenKey ('\', False);
UpdateAll;
// select the current root
ComboKey.ItemIndex := 1;
ComboLast.Items.Add('\');
ComboLast.ItemIndex := 0;
end;
```

This code opens the default root key (indicated by the backslash character), and then updates the user interface. At the end, it selects the default root key in first combo box (more on this shortly) and adds the current element to the ComboLast combo box. The UpdateAll method simply copies the current path to the caption of the form and fills the two list boxes with the subkeys and the values of the current key (as you can see in Figure 25.17):

```
procedure TForm1.UpdateAll;
begin
  Caption := Reg.CurrentPath;
  if Reg.HasSubKeys then
    Reg.GetKeyNames(ListSub.Items)
  else
    ListSub.Clear;
  Reg.GetValueNames(ListValues.Items);
end;
```

FIGURE 25.17

The output of the RegView example, showing keys and values of the Registry.

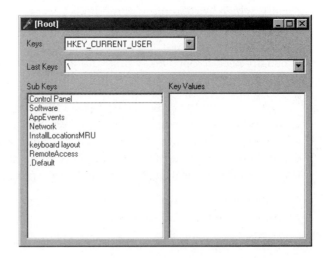

When you select an item from the first list box (ListSub), the program jumps to the selected subkey. To accomplish this, simply write the following code:

```
procedure TForm1.ListSubClick(Sender: TObject);
var
  NewKey: string;
begin
  NewKey := ListSub.Items [ListSub.ItemIndex];
  Reg.OpenKey (NewKey, False);
  UpdateAll;
end;
```

This is enough to navigate the full tree. The two combo boxes add some more capabilities to the program. The first lists the possible root keys for Windows 95. When the selection changes, the corresponding contents are selected as root key of the TRegistry object:

```
procedure TForm1.ComboKeyChange(Sender: TObject);
begin
  case ComboKey.ItemIndex of
    0: Reg.RootKey := HKEY_CLASSES_ROOT;
    1: Reg.RootKey := HKEY_CURRENT_USER;
    2: Reg.RootKey := HKEY_LOCAL_MACHINE;
    3: Reg.RootKey := HKEY_USERS;
    4: Reg.RootKey := HKEY_CURRENT_CONFIG;
    5: Reg.RootKey := HKEY_DYN_DATA;
  end;
  Reg.OpenKey ('\', False);
  UpdateAll;
  ComboLast.Items.Clear;
end;
```

After setting the new root key, the program opens its root item, updates the user interface, and empties the second combo box, which stores the last selected items and can be used to traverse the tree and move up and down, without having to start from the root item each time. This is the code:

```
procedure TForm1.ComboLastChange(Sender: TObject);
begin
  Reg.OpenKey (ComboLast.Text, False);
  UpdateAll;
end;
```

This code is simple, but the code needed to update the list of the items of this combo box is quite complicated. Besides checking whether a path is already present, we have to add a new backslash in front of any path that doesn't have it at the beginning. The problem here is that the method above produces a correct effect, but doesn't set the CurrentPath property of the Reg object properly. To make further selections from that path (once it is added to the list), we need to correct it first. Considering all these issues, here is the final version of the List-SubClick method:

```
procedure TForm1.ListSubClick(Sender: TObject);
var
  NewKey, Path: string;
  nItem: Integer;
begin
  // get the selection
  NewKey := ListSub.Items [ListSub.ItemIndex];
  Reg.OpenKey (NewKey, False);
  // save the current path (eventually adding a \)
  // only if the it is not already listed
  Path := Reg.CurrentPath;
  if Path < '\' then
    Path := '\' + Path;
  nItem := ComboLast.Items.IndexOf (Path);
  if nItem < 0 then
  begin
    ComboLast.Items.Insert (0, Path);
    ComboLast.ItemIndex := 0;
  end
  else
    ComboLast.ItemIndex := nItem;
  UpdateAll;
end;
```

You can see a sample of the items added to the combo box in Figure 25.18.

FIGURE 25.18

The list of recently used
Registry keys of the
RegView example.

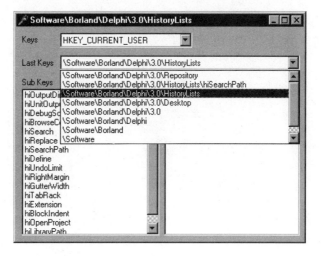

What's Next?

In this chapter, we have seen some of the features of the `Application` global object. We've discussed multitasking, timers, and idle computing. We've also discussed the use of the parameters passed to programs by the system. We also wrote very small programs, without any components or with few of them.

These examples have demonstrated that you can use Delphi to delve into the intricacies of Windows programming, while using very low-level features of the system. To learn more, you can refer to Windows API programming books, and then apply the information to Delphi programming.

The ability to use all the capabilities of Windows is a great feature of Delphi. At times, I must admit, using straight C code for some low-level tasks seems simpler, but that is because the presence of the hidden application window creates some confusion. However, I've still found nothing I could do in C programming that I cannot do in Delphi. The flexibility of Delphi is unusual in a visual programming environment.

We have learned about the `Application` object, but we still have not explored the whole structure of an application. The next two chapters, which cover topics such as memory and resources, will complete the picture.

CHAPTER

TWENTY-SIX

26

Exploring the Behavior
of a Program

- Delphi's integrated debugger

- The Object Browser

- Windows message flow

- Windows memory handling

- Monitoring free memory

Once you compile a program in Delphi and run it, you may think you're finished, but not all of your problems may be solved. Programs can have run-time errors, or they may not work as you planned. When this happens, you will need to discover what has gone wrong and how to correct it. Fortunately, many options and tools are available for exploring the behavior of a Windows application.

Delphi includes an integrated debugger and the Object Browser to let you monitor the result of a compilation process in two different ways. But in order to understand what is happening in a program, you need to know more than just how to use these tools; you should also know how Delphi and Windows use memory. This chapter provides an overview of all these topics, demonstrating the key ideas with simple examples. The first part of the chapter covers Delphi's integrated debugger and the Browser. These sections are not tutorials that describe how to use every feature of these tools; they are technical presentations. The second part of this chapter deals with the key elements of Windows 95 memory handling and internal structure and describes the memory image of a Delphi application.

Using the Debugger

As I've mentioned before, each time you run a program from within the Delphi environment, it is executed inside the internal debugger. (You can change this behavior by disabling the Integrated Debugger option in the Preferences page of the Environment Options dialog box.)

When the program is running in the debugger, clicking on the Pause button on the SpeedBar suspends execution. Once a program is suspended, clicking on the Step Over button executes the program step by step. You can also run a program step by step from the beginning, by pressing the Step Over button while in design mode. Consider, however, that Windows applications are message-driven, so there is really no way to execute an application step by step all the way, as you can do with a DOS application. For this reason, the most common way to debug a Delphi application (or any other Windows application) is to set some *breakpoints* in the portions of the code you want to debug.

Debugging a DLL (and an ActiveForm)

 In Delphi 3 you can also use the integrated debugger to debug a DLL or any other kind of library (as an ActiveX control). Simply open the Delphi project of the library, choose the Run ➤ Parameters menu command, and enter the name of the Host Application (this option is actually available only if the current project is a library). Now when you press the Run button (or the F9 key) Delphi will start the main executable file, which should them load the library. If you set a breakpoint, this will work as expected.

You can use this capability also to debug an ActiveForm. Simply enter the full path name of the Web browser as the Host application, for example *C:\Program Files\Microsoft Internet\Iexplore.exe*, and the full path name of the test HTML file as the Run parameter, for example *c:\codeMD3\24\XForm1\XForm1.htm*. To make this work you should also use the Run ➤ Register ActiveX Server menu command. Once the ActiveX is registered the Web browser will use that version, and not another version available in its OCX cache (as discussed in Chapter 24).

Debug Information

To debug a Delphi program, you must add debug information to your compiled code, which is Delphi's default behavior. You can turn debug information on or off through the Project Options dialog box. As shown in Figure 26.1, the Compiler page includes a Debugging section with three check boxes:

- *Debug Information* adds to each unit a map of executable addresses and corresponding source code line numbers. This increases the size of the DCU file but does not affect the size or speed of the executable program.

- *Local Symbols* adds debug information about all the identifiers defined inside classes, procedures, functions, and methods.

- *Symbol Info* adds cross-reference information about the symbols in a module, to allow the Object Browser to display them.

FIGURE 26.1

Use the Compiler page of the Project Options dialog box to include debug information in a compiled unit.

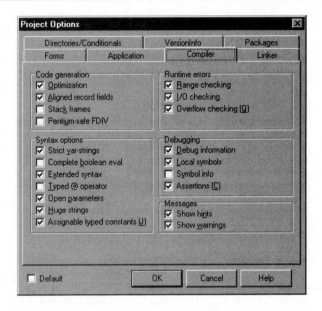

The integrated debugger uses this information while debugging a program. Debug information is not attached to the executable file unless you set the Include TD32 Debug Info option in the Linker page of the Project Options dialog box. Before enabling this option, consider that adding debug information in the executable file has two drawbacks: It increases the size of your program, and it allows someone armed with a debugger to understand how your program was written. You should add debug information to your executable file only if you plan to use an external debugger, such as Borland's Turbo Debugger for Windows (TD32). Do not include it if you plan to use only the integrated debugger; and remember to remove it from the executable file that you ship. This might seem obvious, but there are commercial products on the market that still contain debug information!

Setting Breakpoints

There are a number of ways to set breakpoints in Delphi. In Delphi 3 the simplest method is to click in the gutter of the editor window (the area between the text and the border of the window). As soon as you click on that area, an icon appears near the code, and the line is shown in a different color. Small dots in the gutter indicate the lines where you can place a breakpoint.

You cannot set a breakpoint in just any line of the source code. Basically, a breakpoint is valid only if executable code was generated for the source line. This means that valid breakpoints cannot be placed on comments, declarations, compiler directives lines), or in any other statement that is not executable. Although you can set a breakpoint at an invalid location, Delphi will let you know that it is not correct when you run the program, and mark the invalid breakpoint with a different icon and color.

By the way, since Delphi uses an optimizing compiler, it will not generate any executable code for *unreachable* lines of source code in your program, nor for any other lines that have no effect on the program logic, as in the example below. If you set a breakpoint on a line that didn't produce executable code, the compiler might flag it as an invalid breakpoint. Here is a small portion of the next example:

```
Limit := 3;
Limit := X1;
```

The code generated by the first line has no effect, so it's ignored by the optimizing compiler. Setting a breakpoint on it will be marked as invalid. If you compile the code, the first of these two lines won't have the small dot in the gutter (as you can see in Figure 26.2), which means that no code was generated for that line.

FIGURE 26.2

Some of the lines of this odd example are ignored by the optimizing compiler. You cannot set a breakpoint in the lines that have no point in the gutter.

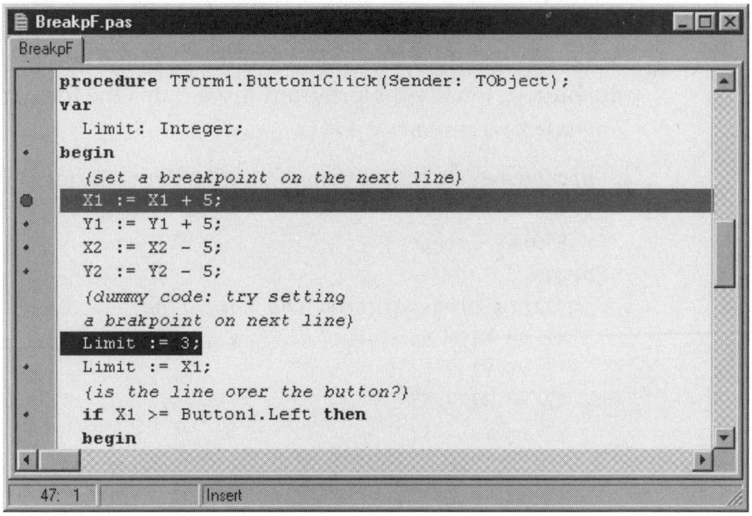

```
procedure TForm1.Button1Click(Sender: TObject);
var
   Limit: Integer;
begin
   {set a breakpoint on the next line}
   X1 := X1 + 5;
   Y1 := Y1 + 5;
   X2 := X2 - 5;
   Y2 := Y2 - 5;
   {dummy code: try setting
   a brakpoint on next line}
   Limit := 3;
   Limit := X1;
   {is the line over the button?}
   if X1 >= Button1.Left then
   begin
```

In fact, if you set an invalid breakpoint and then execute the program step by step, the debugger will skip the line, since it doesn't exist in the optimized version of the compiled code. Except for special cases such as this, once the program execution has reached a line with a breakpoint, the program pauses.

One common use of breakpoints is simply to let you know that a particular event handler has been executed. When you have doubts about a program's execution flow or you are not sure when each handler is being invoked, you can add a breakpoint at the beginning of each method, as suggested in the following BreakP example. This example draws a series of lines around the border of its form. A button in the center of the form allows you to move the lines toward the center, but not over the button. The FormPaint method draws a rectangle using a series of lines:

```
procedure TForm1.FormPaint(Sender: TObject);
begin
  {set a breakpoint on the next line}
  Canvas.MoveTo (X1, Y1);
  Canvas.LineTo (X2, Y1);
  Canvas.LineTo (X2, Y2);
  Canvas.LineTo (X1, Y2);
  Canvas.LineTo (X1, Y1);
end;
```

When the user clicks on the button, the program changes the coordinates of the rectangle, and then checks to see if the rectangle has become too small, overlapping the button. Finally the program invalidates the form, to let Windows send a wm_Paint message:

```
procedure TForm1.Button1Click(Sender: TObject);
var
  Limit: Integer;
begin
  {set a breakpoint on the next line}
  X1 := X1 + 5;
  Y1 := Y1 + 5;
  X2 := X2 - 5;
  Y2 := Y2 - 5;

  {dummy code: try setting a breakpoint on next line}
  Limit := 3;
  Limit := X1;
```

```
{is the line over the button?}
if X1 >= Button1.Left then
begin
  Button1.Enabled := False;
  X1 := Button1.Left;
end;
if Y1 >= Button1.Top then
begin
  Button1.Enabled := False;
  Y1 := Button1.Top;
end;
Invalidate;
end;
```

When the user resizes the form, the program resets the rectangle coordinates:

```
procedure TForm1.FormResize(Sender: TObject);
begin
  {set a breakpoint on the next line}
  Button1.Enabled := True;
  X1 := 10;
  Y1 := 10;
  X2 := ClientWidth - 10;
  Y2 := ClientHeight - 10;
  Invalidate;
end;
```

Once you have set the breakpoints (in the lines following the comments), you can use the Breakpoints command on the View menu to open the Breakpoint List window, as shown in Figure 26.3.

FIGURE 26.3

The Breakpoint List window, with its local menu.

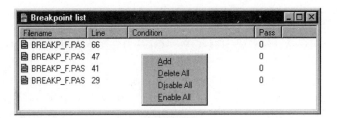

Notice that you can add a condition to a breakpoint, so that the program halts only when the condition is met. You'll see an example with a conditional breakpoint a little later in this chapter.

Once the program has stopped, you can continue executing it by using the Run command. As I've mentioned before, an alternative is to execute the program step by step. The Step Over button on Delphi's SpeedBar allows you to see the execution of statements one after the other. The Trace Into button allows you to trace the methods that are called (that is, to execute the code of the subroutines step by step, and to execute the code of the subroutines called by the subroutines, and so on).

The current line of execution is highlighted with a different color, so that you can see what your program is doing. With the different color (and a small arrow-shaped icon), Delphi indicates the line that is about to be executed.

Note that when you trace subroutines and reach code that exists in a different unit, the new file is automatically loaded in the editor when available. While you're tracing a program, you can see the sequence of subroutine calls currently on the stack with the Call Stack command on Delphi's View menu. By adding a breakpoint in the OnClick event of a button and looking at the stack when the program stops, you get the information shown in Figure 26.4.

FIGURE 26.4

The Call stack window
when a button is clicked.

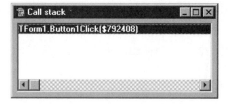

The Call Stack window shows the names of the methods on the stack and their memory addresses. It is particularly useful when you're tracing a series of nested calls.

The CPU Window (or Disassembly View)

Another debug window you can use in Delphi 3 is the CPU view. To enable this window you should add an entry in the Registry. Simply move to the key HKEY_CURRENT_USER and navigate to the subkey:

```
Borland\Software\Delphi\3.0\Debugging.
```

Continued on next page

The CPU Window (or Disassembly View) (Continued)

Move to the right pane, create a new string value, name it "Enable CPU," and give it a value of 1. The next time you run Delphi, the environment will have a new menu command, View ➤ CPU Window. Using this command during debugging you can see a lot of system information: The values of the CPU registers, including special flags, a disassembly of the program, and the Pascal source code included as comments. Here is an example of the output of this window:

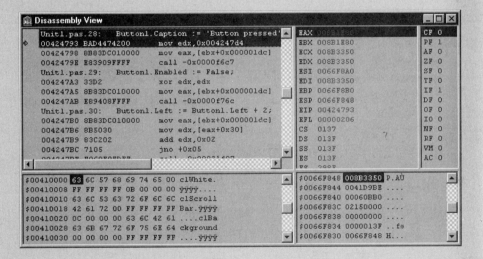

If you have a basic knowledge of assembly language, you can use this information to understand in detail how the program works. You can see, for example, the effect of the Delphi optimizing compiler on the compiled code.

Although it seems bare at first, this Delphi 3 Disassembly View window provides programmers with a lot of power. Using the local pop-up menus, you can even change the value of CPU registers directly! Note, however, that this feature is not *officially* documented by Borland, which means that if it doesn't work as expected you will not get help from their tech support.

Inspecting Values

When a program is stopped in the debugger, you can inspect the value of any identifier (variables, objects, components, properties, and so on) that's accessible from the current execution point (that is, only the identifiers visible in the current scope). In Delphi 2 there were basically two ways to accomplish this: using the Evaluate/Modify dialog box or adding a watch to the Watch List window. We'll look at these two techniques later on.

 Delphi 3 has a brand new feature, *fly-by evaluation hints*. While a program is stopped in the debugger, you can simply move the mouse over a variable, object, property, field, or any other identifier indicating a value, and you'll immediately get a small window showing the current value of the identifier, as you can see in Figure 26.5.

FIGURE 26.5

The best new Delphi 3 debugging feature: Fly-by evaluation hints.

```
BreakpF.pas                                              _ □ ×
BreakpF

  end;

  procedure TForm1.Button1Click(Sender: TObject);
  var
    Limit: Integer;
  begin
    {set a breakpoint on the next line}
    X1 := X1 + 5;
    Y1 := Y1 + 5;
    X2 := X2 - 5;
    Y2 := X2 = 279;
    {dummy code: try setting
    a brakpoint on next line}
    Limit := 3;
    Limit := X1;
    {is the line over the button?}

41: 1                    Insert
```

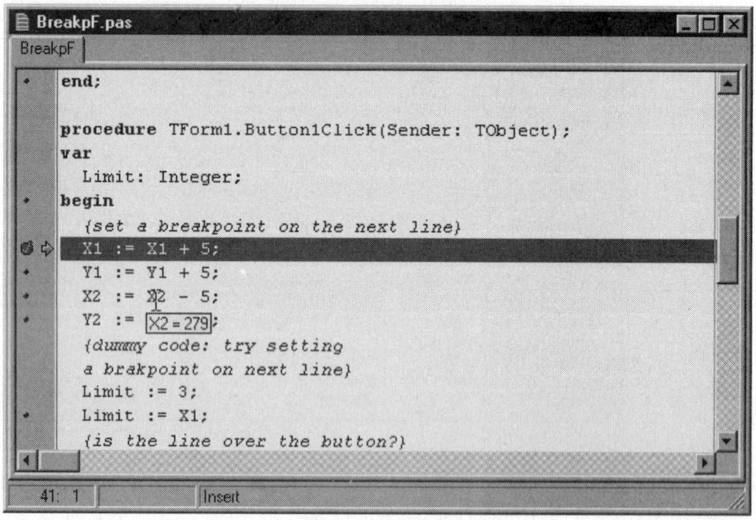

For simple variables, like X1 or Y1, fly-by hints simply show the corresponding value, which is easy to understand. But what is the value of an object, such as Form1 or Button1? If you try inspecting these kinds of values, you'll see that the hint for an object like Form1 includes the list of the private fields I've declared, while for Button1 the information we get refers only to some rarely used properties. The problem is that components have many properties, so Delphi can't list them all.

TIP

TIP You can use the Object Debugger component I've written (included in the TOOLS directory of the companion CD) to get the full list of the values of the published properties of a component at run-time.

In other cases, these fly-by hints are quite odd. For example, when inspecting enumerated values, you might get interesting information such as True=True. Jokes apart, many interesting values can be inspected. If you inspect a color constant, such as clYellow, you get the numeric value of the color.

With the new fly-by hints, the other two available techniques become less useful. The Evaluate/Modify dialog box can still be used to modify the value of a variable or property. The easiest way to open this dialog box is to select the variable in the code editor, and then choose Evaluate/Modify from the editor's SpeedMenu (or press the Ctrl-F7 keys combination). Long selections are not automatically used, so to select a long expression, it's best to copy it from the editor and paste it in the dialog box.

For example, by setting a breakpoint in the OnResize handler of the BreakP example and stepping through the code, you can evaluate and actually change the value of X1, as shown in Figure 26.6. In this dialog box, you can enter complex expressions, as long as there are no function calls involved. You can also enter the name of a constant (such as the color value clYellow) and see the corresponding numeric value.

FIGURE 26.6

The Evaluate/Modify dialog box can be used to inspect the value of a variable and also change it.

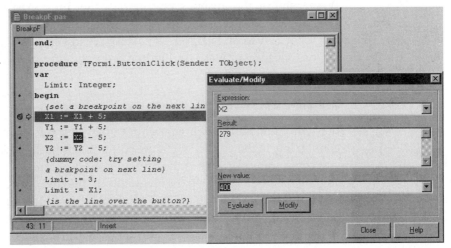

When you want to test the value of a group of variables over and over, using the fly-by hints can become a little tedious. As an alternative, you can set some *watches* (entries in a list of variables you're interested in monitoring) for variables, properties, or components. For example, you might set a watch for each of the values used in the BreakP example's `Button1Click` method, which is called each time the user clicks on the button. I've added a number of watches to see the value of the most relevant variables and properties involved in this method, as you can see in Figure 26.7.

FIGURE 26.7

Using the Watch List window.

You can set watches by using the Add Watch at Cursor command on the editor's SpeedMenu (or just press Ctrl+F5). When you add a watch, you'll need to choose the proper output format, and maybe enter some text for more complex expressions. For simple values, you can just issue the command when the identifier is selected in the editor.

You can see the value of a variable when the program is stopped in the debugger, but not when it is running. Additionally, you can inspect only the variables that are visible in the current scope, because they must exist in order for you to see them! You can also add watches for (or inspect) entire components, but the result is not easy to understand, as you can see in Figure 26.7 above. It is far more common to inspect or watch individual properties of a component.

More on Breakpoints

When a program reaches a breakpoint, Delphi suspends it and shows the current execution line in the editor. When the editor is activated, however, its window might cover some portions of the form of your program. When the code you are going to execute step by step involves output, the form appears from behind the editor but disappears again quickly, without letting you view its new contents. If possible, position the editor window and the form of your program manually so that they do not overlap (or overlap only partially). With that arrangement, you'll be able to execute a program step by step and actually see its output on the screen.

This is particularly important for OnPaint handlers. You can try this with the BreakP example. Open that program again, set a breakpoint in the FormPaint method, and run it. If the editor window and the form overlap, you'll enter an endless series of breakpoints. Each time the form is repainted, the breakpoint stops the program, moving the editor window in front of the form and causing the form to be repainted again, which stops the program on the same breakpoint—over and over again.

The solution is simply to arrange the forms on the screen side by side. In this arrangement, you can see the execution of the FormPaint code step by step and let the program run without any problems. As an alternative, if you only need to know when the OnPaint code is executed, you can disable the breakpoint as it is reached, and later enable it again. In fact, you can add and remove breakpoints easily while the program is stopped in the debugger.

To stop a program only at certain times, you can use *conditional breakpoints*. For example, we might want to stop the Button1Click method's execution (in the BreakP example) only when the lines have moved near the button. You can set a breakpoint as usual; then open the Breakpoint list, double-click on the breakpoint to open the Edit Breakpoint dialog box, and enter this condition:

```
Button1.Top - Y1 < 10
```

The condition is also added to the Breakpoint List window, as you can see in Figure 26.8. Now you can run the program and click on the button a number of times. The breakpoint is ignored until the condition is met (when Button1.Top - Y1 is less than 10). Only after you click several times will the program actually stop in the debugger.

NOTE In Windows, there are some special cases when a message-driven debugger, such as Delphi's integrated debugger, cannot stop at a breakpoint. In these cases, Windows is said to be in *hard mode*. This happens during menu drawing and some kernel operations. When Delphi finds a breakpoint in such a special code area, it will warn you with a message.

FIGURE 26.8

The breakpoint list window, with a conditional breakpoint.

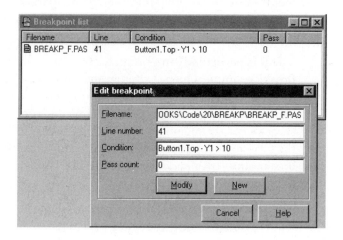

Tracing through the VCL Source Code

If you own the VCL source code, you should know that one of its key uses is in debugging your applications. If you want to know more about the effects of accessing VCL component properties or calling VCL methods than the documentation tells you, you can include the library source code in your program and use the debugger to trace its execution. Of course, you need to be bold enough and have enough free time to delve into the intricacies of the VCL source code. But when nothing else seems to work, this just might be the only solution.

To include the library source code, simply add the name of the directory with the VCL source code (by default, C:\Program Files\Borland\Delphi 3.0\Source\ VCL) in the Search Path combo box of the Directories/Conditional page of the Project Options dialog box. Then rebuild the whole program and start debugging. When you reach statements containing method or property calls, you can trace the program and see the VCL code executed line after line. Naturally, you can do any common debugging operation with the VCL code that you can do with your own code.

As an example, Figure 26.9 shows the Call Stack window after tracing the Invalidate call of the button's OnClick event handler. Notice that you can see a lot of activity before the Button1Click method is called (the topmost element in the Call Stack window is the most recent call, and the highlighted method is almost at the top).

FIGURE 26.9

The Call Stack window when debugging a program that includes the VCL source code.

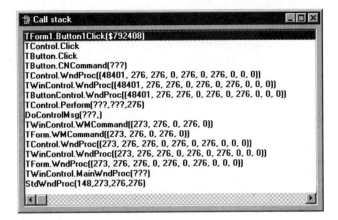

If you compare Figure 26.9 with the contents of the Call Stack window shown earlier in Figure 26.4, you'll see the different level of detail now available. This amount of detail is both an advantage and a disadvantage. It's good because you have all the details you need to get an idea of the status of your program. But it's difficult to pick out the valuable information from all these items, unless you become an expert on the VCL message dispatching mechanism.

Alternative Debugging Techniques

One common use of breakpoints is to find out when a program has reached a certain stage, but there are other ways to get this information. A common technique is to show simple messages (using the ShowMessage procedure) on specific lines, just for debugging purposes. There are many other manual techniques, such as sending the output to a terminal window, changing the text of a label in a special form, writing to a log file, or adding a line in a list box or a memo field.

All of these alternatives serve one of two basic purposes: they let you know that a certain statement of the code has been executed, or they let you watch some values, without actually stopping the program. These approaches avoid the side effects related to stopping and restarting a program (such as the painting problems described earlier), but adding a statement to produce some output is not as easy or fast as setting a breakpoint and removing it.

Debugging with a Terminal Window

Delphi's debugging tools are also much more powerful than most homemade techniques. Being able to step though a program, watching the value of a variable change or tracing through a series of calls—even those made by the VCL source code—is an invaluable programming aid.

However, homemade debugging techniques have their role, too. As an example, consider debugging the BackProc example presented in the last chapter. This program involves a timer, idle-time computing, and other techniques that would be affected by stopping the program in a debugger. To avoid stopping the program, we can display some debug information in a secondary window. This is what I've done in the new version of the program, named Back2.

The Back2 version includes a second form, called DebugForm, which contains a list box covering its entire client area. The unit also includes a procedure you can use to add a line of text to the debugging form's list box:

```
procedure WriteLine (Text: String);
begin
  if not DebugForm.Visible then
    DebugForm.Show;
  with DebugForm.Listbox1 do
    ItemIndex := Items.Add (Text);
end;
```

As you can see, this is not a method, but rather a global procedure, which makes it simpler to use by the code calling it. Now you can simply add a call to WriteLine to each method of the form class, as in the following code:

```
procedure TForm1.IdleButtonClick(Sender: TObject);
begin
  WriteLine ('IdleButtonClick');
  IdleNPrimes := 0;
  {same code as before...}
```

The only place where this code wasn't added is in the IsPrime function, because that function is called too often. Now you can just run the program, and you'll see a lot of output in the debug window. Some of the functions, in fact, are called many times, once for each number to test. In these cases, I've improved the output slightly by adding the current number to the output:

```
procedure TForm1.IdleProc (Sender: TObject;
  var Done: Boolean);
```

```
begin
  WriteLine ('IdleProc' + IntToStr (IdleNumber));
  if IdleNumber < IdleMax then
    ...
end;
```

You can see an example of a debugging session made with the terminal window in Figure 26.10.

FIGURE 26.10

The output of the Back2 example, with its debug window.

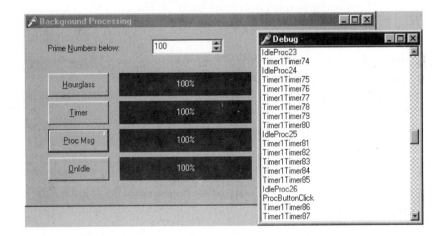

Debug and Release Versions (Using Conditional Compilation)

Adding debugging code to an application is certainly interesting, as the example above demonstrates, but this approach has a serious flaw. In the final version of the program, the one you give to your customers, you need to disable the debugging output, and possibly remove all of the debugging code to reduce the size of the program and improve its speed. At first, you might think that this is too big a problem and that a terminal window is not a professional solution. If you are a C/C++ programmer, however, you may have some ideas on how to remove program code automatically. The solution to this problem lies in a typical C technique known as *conditional compilation*. The idea is simple: You write some lines of code that you want to compile only in certain circumstances and skip on other occasions.

In Delphi, you can use some conditional compiler directives: $IFDEF, $IFNDEF, $IFOPT, $ELSE, and $ENDIF. For example, in our code, we can replace any occurrence of the WriteLine procedure with the following:

```
{$IFDEF DEBUG}
WriteLine ('IdleProc' + IntToStr (IdleNumber));
{$ENDIF}
```

This code is included in the compilation only if there is a DEBUG symbol defined before the line, or if the DEBUG symbol has been defined in the Project Options dialog box, as shown in Figure 26.11.

FIGURE 26.11

Defining a symbol in the Project Options dialog box.

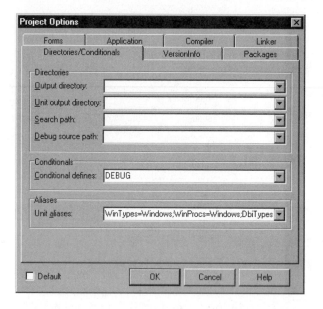

You can even conditionally include the unit defining the debug form, simply by writing the following code into the implementation part of the unit:

```
{$IFDEF DEBUG}
uses
  DebugF;
{$ENDIF}
```

Now you can compile the program, add the DEBUG symbol in the Project Options dialog box, and see the debug output in the terminal window. Then you can remove the symbol definition, choose the Build All command from Delphi's Compile menu, and run it again, this time without the terminal window. The size of the executable file will probably change slightly between the two versions because some source code is removed. Note that each time you change the symbol definitions in the Project Options dialog box, you need to rebuild the whole program. If you simply run it, the older version will be executed because the executable file seems up-to-date compared to the source files.

WARNING   You should use conditional compilation for debugging purposes with extreme care. In fact, if you debug a program with this technique and later change its code (when removing the DEBUG definition), you might introduce new bugs or expose bugs that were hidden by the debug process. For this reason, it is generally better to debug the final version of your application carefully, without making any more changes to the source code.

Using Assertions

Assertions are a new technique you can use in Delphi 3 for custom debugging. An assertion is basically an expression that should invariably be true, because it is part of the logic of the program. For example I might assert that the number of users of my program should always be at least one, since my program cannot run without any user. When an assertion is false, then there is a flaw in the program code. Note: In the *code,* not in the execution.

Delphi 3 includes a new standard procedure, called Assert. The first parameter of this procedure is the Boolean condition you want to test (or *assert*). If the condition is met, the program can continue as usual; if the condition is not met (the assertion fails), the program raises an EAssertionFailed exception.

Here is a simple example, called Assert. Its form includes a progress bar (with the Min property set to 1 and the Max property set to 100) and two buttons, used to increase or decrease the value of a field of the form class (called Number). The two buttons simply increase and decrease the value, and then update the progress bar. The number should never exceed the two limits of the progress bar. This is the condition I test at the end of each method by calling Assert. Here is the code of the Inc button's OnClick event:

```
procedure TForm1.BtnIncClick(Sender: TObject);
begin
  if Number < 100 then
```

```
    Inc (Number);
  ProgressBar1.Position := Number;
  // test the condition
  Assert ((Number > 0) and (Number <= 100));
end;
```

This code is fine. The Dec button's OnClick event, instead, has the wrong test in the if statement, so the assertion can fail:

```
procedure TForm1.BtnDecClick(Sender: TObject);
begin
  if Number > 0 then
    Dec (Number);
  ProgressBar1.Position := Number;
  // test the condition
  Assert ((Number > 0) and (Number <= 100));
end;
```

If you run this program and press the Dec button, an exception is raised, as you can see in Figure 26.12. The output clearly indicates the source code lines where the assertion failed.

FIGURE 26.12

The output of the Assert example when the Dec button is pressed, and the assertion fails.

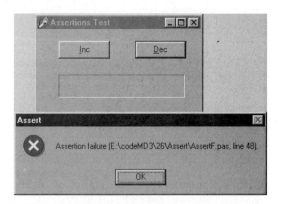

Keep in mind that assertions are a debugging tool. They should be used to verify that the code of the program is correct. Users should never see assertions failing, no matter what happens in the program and which data they input, because if an assertion fails there is probably an error in your code. To test for special error conditions, you should use exceptions, not assertions.

Assertions are so closely linked to debugging and testing that you'll generally want to remove them, by using the $ASSERTIONS or $C compiler directive. Simply add the line

```
{ $C- }
```

somewhere in a source code file, and that unit will be compiled without assertions. This doesn't just disable assertions, it actually removes the corresponding code from the program. To confirm this you can make the following test: compile the Assert example, and look at the legal debugging lines in the editor. The lines with the calls to the Assert procedure will be included. Now disable assertions, recompile the file, and look again at the gutter area. The lines with the calls to Assert won't be valid lines for setting a breakpoint, which means that no code was generated for them.

Viewing a Compiled Program with the Object Browser

Another way you can explore a compiled program is with Delphi's Object Browser. The Browser doesn't show the values of the objects and variables of a program; it shows its data types and classes. Once a program is successfully compiled, you can open the Browser and see the whole hierarchy of classes included in your application, as shown in the example in Figure 26.13. The Browse Objects window displays both VCL classes and those defined by your program.

Delphi's Object Browser is similar to the corresponding tool included in many C++ compilers. Basically, you can use the Browser to see all of the methods, properties, and data fields—both local and inherited—of any class. If you prefer a partial view, you can choose only a subset of the elements of a class by using the Filter buttons at the top of the Browse Objects window. These buttons allow you to filter the definitions according to their kind, their presence in the parent class, and their visibility, as shown in Figure 26.14.

Besides exploring the hierarchy of classes, you can see the elements of each class, and even the details of the definition of each of these elements. You can see when there are references to particular elements in the source code of your application. If you compile the program including the VCL source files, you can see the references to the VCL source, too, and easily reach the definition of each method, property, or class in the source code. In fact when you select a reference, the Browser opens the corresponding source file in the editor, and moves to the proper line.

FIGURE 26.13

An example of the output of the Object Browser.

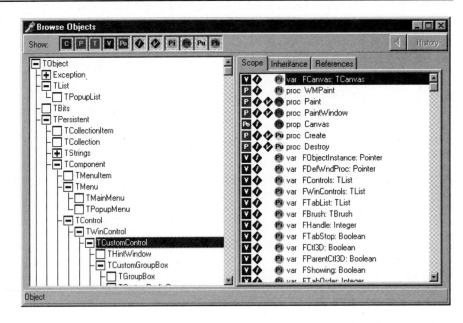

FIGURE 26.14

The Object Browser's speed buttons.

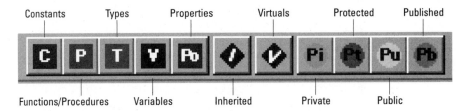

There are other ways to use this tool. The Browser SpeedMenu offers four choices:

- The Objects command shows the class hierarchy, as shown before in Figure 26.13.

- The Units command shows the list of units included in the current project.

- The Globals command shows a list of global symbols.

- The Symbol command lets you enter the name of a symbol and move directly to it.

For example, you can choose the huge Windows unit (it is more than 700 Kb of Pascal code) and see a complete list of the functions of the Windows API and the definition of all Windows constants.

The Browser is a powerful tool that allows you to explore a complex program, or a not-so-complex program written by another programmer (or by you, but a long time ago), because you can easily jump back and forth from it to the editor. Each time you find a symbol in the editor that you don't recognize, you can select it and use the Browse Symbol at Cursor command on the editor's SpeedMenu to jump to the symbol definition in the Browser. There you can see where the symbol is defined or used, and then jump back to that file in the editor. If you include the VCL source code in the compilation, you'll be able to jump to these source code files, too.

The Object Browser lets you explore a program only after you have compiled it. This means that if you change the source code and the program no longer compiles because you have introduced an error while editing, you cannot use the Browser to understand what is happening. To avoid this problem, Delphi lets you save the Browser symbols between sessions. To do this, select the Desktop and Symbols radio button in the Preferences page of the Environment Options dialog box.

Now each time you compile a program, the information required by the Browser is saved to a file with the DSM extension. With this file, you can use the Object Browser for the program, even if it cannot be built anymore due to an error. The Browser can read the DSM file instead of rebuilding the same information in memory. The drawback is that DSM files are very big. Therefore, you might turn on this option only when you really need it; that is, when you are developing a complex program.

Exploring the Message Flow

The two tools we have discussed so far in this chapter, the integrated debugger and the Object Browser, provide common ways to explore the source code of a program. In Windows, however, this is often not enough. When you want to understand the details of the interaction between your program and the environment, other Windows-related tools are handy.

One of them is WinSight, a multipurpose tool included in Delphi. Others are memory-spying programs. Delphi doesn't include this type of program, but they are available from many sources, including shareware, books, and magazine articles.

Using WinSight

We have already seen in previous chapters how WinSight can be used to explore an application. Here, I'll provide a short overview, with some new details and tips. WinSight can be used to build a hierarchical graph of existing windows and to display detailed information about the message flow.

Both operations can be launched by the initial commands on WinSight's View menu: Window Tree and Message Trace. (The third menu item, Class View, was a feature of the 16-bit version of WinSight that is not enabled in the 32-bit version.) You can also choose both views at the same time, placing them in different vertical or horizontal panes, as shown in Figure 26.15.

FIGURE 26.15

The two WinSight panes: the window tree and the message flow.

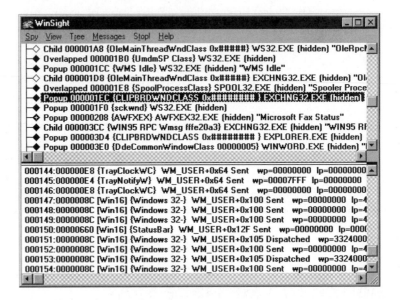

To become a proficient user of WinSight and understand all of the information it delivers, you need to have an in-depth knowledge of the structure of Windows and of Windows applications. Although it might seem beyond the scope of this book, I've decided to give you a brief summary of the information displayed by WinSight, focusing on the information related to Delphi programming.

The Window Tree: Parents and Children

The Window Tree view in WinSight contains a hierarchical tree of windows. The hierarchical view clarifies the relationship between parent and child windows, which is very important both in Windows and in Delphi (see the Parent and Controls properties). An important feature of WinSight is that it also lists hidden windows and other windows that aren't visible (for example, windows reduced to a single pixel). You can also see windows completely covered by other windows, such as a panel covered by a notebook, and obtain some details about a program's user interface structure.

Of course, you can get the details of the user interface structure of any Windows application, even the Delphi development environment or WinSight itself. If you explore an application you have written in Delphi, you'll see the forms and the controls within them. However, notice that some Delphi components don't appear in this list. This is because they are graphical components that don't create their own window. The "one visual element, one window" rule of Windows programming doesn't apply to Delphi or to applications you create with Delphi, which is to our advantage. Non-windowed graphical components tend to be faster and save some system resources.

For each node of the window tree, WinSight first displays the window's type: overlapped, pop-up, or child. Basically, child windows live within a parent window; overlapped and pop-up windows, even if they have a parent/owner window, always use the whole surface of the desktop, and their coordinates refer to the entire screen. The different window types also denote a different default behavior determined by the system.

After the window type comes the value of the window handle, a number in hexadecimal format, such as *28C8*. The handle's value is determined by the system when the window is created. This value is a unique code that the system uses to identify the window. Since this is needed as a parameter for many Window API functions, it is available in Delphi as the Handle property of every TWinControl descendant, a run-time and read-only property.

> **NOTE** Not all Handle properties of Delphi components refer to the handle of a window. There are also icon handles, bitmap handles, menu handles, and so on. Also, not all the other Handle properties are read-only.

Next are the name of the class, the name of the executable file, the position and the size of the window, and its title or caption. You can open a detailed view of the window system data (see Figure 26.16), which includes the handle of the application that created the window (the one stored in the HInstance global variable discussed in Chapter 25), the handle of the menu, the address of the window procedure associated with the window, the client rectangle, and the names of the flags that make up the window style.

FIGURE 26.16

The WinSight window with detailed information about a window and its class; in this case, a Delphi form.

WinSight - Detail 00000894	
Window text:	Breakpoints Test
Process Id:	FFFC4FBB BREAKP.EXE
Application instance:	00400000
Window handle:	00000894
Parent window:	00000080
Window function:	004102E0
Menu handle:	00000000
Window rect in screen:	(9,160)-(306,371)
Window rect in parent:	(9,160)-(306,371)
Client rectangle:	(0,0)-(289,184)
Window style:	16CF0000
#Msgs processed:	135
Overlapped, Visible, ClipSiblings, ClipChildren, SysMenu, ThickFrame, Caption, MinimizeBox, MaximizeBox WindowEdge, Left, LTRReading, RightScrollBar	
Class name:	TForm1
Executable module:	00400000 BREAKP.EXE
Class window function:	004102E0
Icon:	00000000
Cursor:	000014CE
Background brush:	00000000
Window extra bytes:	00000000
Class extra bytes:	00000000
Class style:	00000008
DblClks	

At the end are the details related to the class of the window. This information doesn't relate to Delphi classes, but to Windows classes. To understand what a window class is, you need to understand how the system creates windows and responds to their messages. In short, to create a window of any kind (ranging from the main window of an application to a small control), the Windows environment requires you to specify the class of the window and formally register that class. For this reason, an application written in C often registers a class before creating a window (to ensure that the class will be available). Every window in the system has a class, also known as WNDCLASS, from the type name of the data structure used in the registration code (which is TWndClass in Delphi).

Note that *class* as a Windows term has only a limited relationship with the same term in object-oriented programming languages. Windows' WNDCLASS data structures have a fixed number of fields, one of which is the address of a procedure (called the *window procedure* or WndProc). This single procedure is used to respond to all of the messages sent by the system to the Windows of that class. For this reason, the typical window procedure has a big case statement, with a branch for each message you want to handle. (It is obvious that the object-oriented approach to Windows programming offered by Delphi and some C++ class libraries is far superior to the original approach.)

The class information displayed by WinSight for each window includes the name of the class, the name of the executable file (or dynamic link library) that has registered it, the address of the window procedure for that class, and some style flags for that class.

> **NOTE**
>
> If you are an experienced Windows programmer, you might notice that the window procedure of the class and that of the window do not match. By default, each window uses the window procedure registered for its class unless someone changes this value for that particular window, a technique known as *subclassing* (although it has nothing to do with the definition of a subclass in Object Pascal terms). Subclassing is used extensively in the VCL to let you specify the behavior of a windowed object through event handlers. Windows procedures in Delphi elements are so hidden away in the VCL that you'll seldom notice them. Windows calls the window procedure of the window, and that window procedure takes you directly into the associated object instance. In contrast, traditional Windows programs use a common window procedure for all the instances of a given window class. The Delphi approach has much greater flexibility.

Message Flow and Delphi Events

The main reason I started this analysis of WinSight was to help you understand how to spy the message flow of the Delphi applications. Now we have reached that point. To become an expert Delphi programmer, you must learn to study the message flow following an input action by a user. As you know, Delphi programs (like Windows applications in general) are event-driven. Code is executed in response to an event. Windows messages are the key element behind Delphi events, although there isn't a one-to-one correspondence between the two.

TIP

The programming jargon term *spy* refers to the monitoring of the message flow because the original Microsoft SDK program that allowed this operation was actually named Spy.

In Windows, there are many more messages than there are events in Delphi, but some Delphi events occur at a higher level than Windows messages. For example, in Windows, there is a limited amount of support for mouse dragging, while Delphi components offer a full set of mouse-dragging events. Of course, WinSight knows nothing about Delphi events, so you'll have to figure out the correspondence between many events and messages by yourself (or study the VCL source code, if you have it). WinSight can show you, in a readable format, all of the Windows messages that reach a window, indicating the destination window, its title or class, and its parameters. You can use the Options command from WinSight's Messages menu to filter out some of the messages, and see only the groups you are interested in.

Usually, for Delphi programmers, spying the message flow can be useful when you are faced with some bugs related to the order of window activation and deactivation, or to receiving and losing the input focus (OnEnter and OnExit events), particularly when message boxes or other modal windows are involved. This is quite a common problem area, and you can often see why things went wrong by looking at the message flow. You might also want to see the message flow when you are handling a Windows message directly (instead of using event handlers). Using WinSight, you can get more information about when that message arrives and the parameters it carries.

A Look at Posted Messages

Another way to see the message flow is to trap some Windows messages directly in a Delphi application. If you limit this analysis to posted messages, (delivered with PostMessage) and exclude sent messages (delivered with SendMessage), it becomes almost trivial, since there is a specific event of the TApplication class we can use: the OnMessage event. This event is intended to give the application a chance to filter the messages it receives and to handle certain messages in special ways. For example, you can use it to handle the messages for the window connected with the Application object itself, which has no specific event handlers (as discussed in Chapter 25).

In the MsgFlow example, however, we'll take a look at all of the messages extracted from the message queue of the application (that is, the posted messages). A description of each message is added to a list box covering the form of the example. For this list box, I've chosen Courier font because it is a nonproportional, or *monospaced*, font so that the output will be formatted with the fields aligned correctly in the list box.

The speed buttons in the toolbar can be used to turn message viewing on and off, empty the list box, and skip consecutive, repeated messages. For example, if you move the mouse you get many consecutive wm_MouseMove messages, which can be skipped without losing much information.

To let you make some real tests, the program has a second form (launched by the fourth speed button), filled with various kinds of components (chosen at random). You can use this form to see the message flow of a standard Delphi window. Figure 26.17 shows an example of the output of the MsgFlow program when the second form is visible.

FIGURE 26.17

The MsgFlow program at run-time, with a copy of the second form.

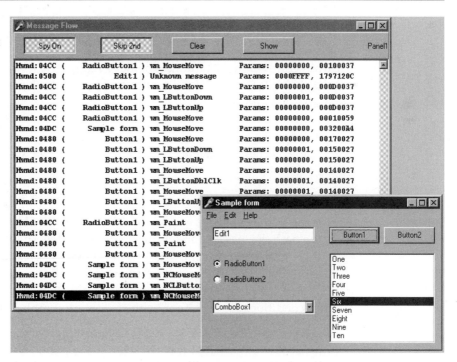

The basic idea of this example is quite simple. Just define a handler for the OnMessage event of the application, and install it in the FormCreate method:

```
type
  TForm1 = class(TForm)
    ...
  private
    Skipping, Spying: Boolean;
    LastMessage: TMsg;
  public
    procedure HandleMessage (var Msg: TMsg;
      var Handled: Boolean);
  end;

procedure TForm1.FormCreate(Sender: TObject);
begin
  Application.OnMessage := HandleMessage;
  Skipping := False;
  Spying := False;
end;
```

Notice the definition and initial values of some Boolean flags corresponding to toolbar buttons. These flags and the value of the last message (I'll describe the TMsg structure below) determine whether a message reaching the application has to be displayed. The core of the HandleMessage method is executed only if three conditions are satisfied:

- The Spying Boolean flag is set to True. A user can easily toggle this Boolean value by clicking on the Spy On button, which behaves like a check box.

- The message is not a message for the list box. This avoids a recursive call, (since adding a new item to the list box generates a series of new messages).

- If the Skipping flag is enabled (by clicking on the Skip 2nd button in the toolbar), the message and its destination window should be different from those of the previous message. Mouse-move messages are often sent in series; with this flag, only the first message of the series is shown.

These conditions are expressed by the following complex if statement:

```
if Spying and (Msg.Hwnd <> Listbox1.Handle) and not
  (Skipping and (LastMessage.Message = Msg.Message) and
  (LastMessage.Hwnd = Msg.Hwnd)) then
  ...
```

In the code of the HandleMessage method, you can add a line to the list box for each message. The goal is to fetch some meaningful information. The parameter of the handler of the OnMessage event, in fact, is of the TMsg type. This is a collection of low-level information about the message, including the handle of the destination window, the code of the message, and some numeric parameters. This is actually the information Windows passes to the application. Instead of using the data directly, I've made it more readable in two ways.

First, the MsgFlow program displays the caption of the window along with its handle. This caption is retrieved using a Windows API function, GetWindowText, which works for any kind of window. This text is formatted in a 15-character space, using Delphi's Format function, and then it is added to the Line string that I'll add to the list box at the end. Before adding the formatted text to the Line string, however, if the string is empty (the window has no caption), the *Unknown* string is used instead. Here is the code of the first part of this method:

```
// output the hex value of the handle
Line := 'Hwnd:' + IntToHex (Msg.Hwnd, 4);
{get the caption from the handle,
using an API function}
GetWindowText (Msg.Hwnd, PChar (Caption),
  Length (Caption));
Caption := PChar (Caption); // recast
if Caption = '' then
  Caption := 'Unknown';
// format the caption in 15 characters
AppendStr (Line, Format (' ( %15s ) ', [Caption]));
```

Notice that I have to cast the string to a PChar and back to a string. (I explicitly cast it to a PChar, and Delphi converts it back to a string before the assignment.) This double-cast forces the compiler to recalculate the string's length by scanning for the null terminator in the original string (as discussed in Chapter 4).

The second key improvement is to output the name of the message, instead of its code. This is not so simple, because message names are not real strings, but are rather names of constants defined in the MESSAGES.PAS system file. Here is an excerpt of this file, with the definition of the first few messages:

```
const
  wm_Null     = $0000;
  wm_Create   = $0001;
  wm_Destroy  = $0002;
  wm_Move     = $0003;
```

This information is important but not usable in our example. However, we can use this text, with some semiautomatic transformations (using search and replace techniques) in an associative list of strings.

The problem is that we cannot simply define an array, because not all of the possible numbers actually correspond to a message. As an alternative, you might recall that the TStringList class has both strings and objects. Storing an object in a TStringList means storing four bytes, so we might use a trick and add the message number instead of a real object. The code above becomes the following:

```
var
  MsgList: TStringList;
...
  MsgList := TStringList.Create;
  MsgList.AddObject ('wm_Null         ', TObject($0000));
  MsgList.AddObject ('wm_Create       ', TObject($0001));
  MsgList.AddObject ('wm_Destroy      ', TObject($0002));
  MsgList.AddObject ('wm_Move         ', TObject($0003));
```

This code (it's actually a couple of pages long) has been obtained by replacing the text *wm* with the text *MsgList.AddObject ('wm*, replacing the equal sign with the typecast code, and adding two parentheses at the end. The typecast used from a number to a TObject is really a low-level trick, the kind of thing I usually hate; in this case, I could find no other simple solution to extract the strings from this list using the message number as the key.

I've placed this code in a separate unit, called MLIST.PAS. The interface portion of this unit also has a function that returns a string corresponding to the message:

```
function GetMessageName (Msg: Integer): string;
var
  N: Integer;
begin
  N := MsgList.IndexOfObject (TObject(Msg));
  if N >= 0 then
    Result := MsgList.Strings [N]
  else if Msg >= wm_User then
    Result := 'wm_User message'
  else
    Result := 'Unknown message'
end;
```

This text is added to the string with the description of the message, followed by the hexadecimal value of the two message parameters. Here is the second part of the `if` statement of the `HandleMessage` method (the first part was shown before):

```
AppendStr (Line, GetMessageName (Msg.Message));
{add the hexadecimal output of the two message parameters}
AppendStr (Line, 'Params: ' + IntToHex (Msg.wParam, 8) +
  ', ' + IntToHex (Msg.lParam, 8));
{add the line, selecting it}
ListBox1.ItemIndex := ListBox1.Items.Add (Line);
{store the message, to compare it with the next one}
LastMessage := Msg;
```

At the end, the string is added to the list. The return value of the Add method is used to select the new item of the list box, to keep it in sight. Then the current message structure is saved, so we can compare it with that of the next messages we receive and eventually decide to skip it if they refer to the same message type.

If you run the program, you'll see only a portion of the messages reaching the windows, since we are scanning only posted messages. Most of these messages will probably relate to mouse actions, and some of them to mouse actions on the form's border (the *nc*, or non-client, messages). Notice that you can see the caption of the panel window. I haven't removed it, to improve the readability of the output of the messages related to this window (since the caption of the window is displayed) and to its speed buttons, which are not Windowed components and do not receive messages by the system. For Windows, clicking on a speed button is like clicking on the panel holding it.

The Memory Image of an Application

In Windows 95 and in Windows NT, each application has a 4 GByte address space in a single huge chunk of memory. Actually, Windows 95 and NT allow a program to use only part of that memory, since other portions are used by system DLLs accessible from the application.

Each application has a similar theoretical amount of memory for code, data, and everything else, but has no way to access the memory of other applications running at the same time. All applications, of course, can access the code (but not the data) of system libraries. In the Win32 systems, the executable files (including the code of DLLs) are loaded in memory using memory-mapped files, so they are visible to all applications. This means that two programs sharing the same executable file (or two instances of the same program) do not need to load it twice in memory.

To get information about the size of the different portions of the memory image of your own application (that is, how your application is loaded in the system memory), you can use the Information command on Delphi's Compiler menu. The Information dialog box (see Figure 26.18) lists the size of the compiled code and of the global data, plus the size of the stack, which depends on project settings. In Windows 95 and NT, there are almost no limits to the memory of an application: you can create very long strings or huge arrays without any trouble (although you need to have enough RAM and free disk space for the swap file).

FIGURE 26.18

The compilation information for the MsgFlow example.

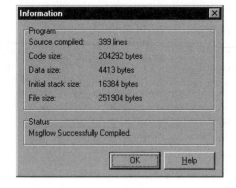

Besides the actual compiled code, the executable file also contains the definition of some resources, such as icons, bitmaps, cursors, tables of strings, and so on. In addition, resources are usually loaded in memory when they are needed, and can be automatically discarded. The use of resources in a Delphi application is the topic of the next chapter.

In addition to the code and resources, which are loaded from the executable file, the memory of an application contains an area for global data, the space for the stack, and a lot of space for dynamically allocated memory. The size of your program's global data area depends on the global variables you've defined in your program and those defined by the VCL. For a small project, you will end up with a few kilobytes in this area. In Delphi, the common way to determine the size of your program's global data is through the Compiler Information dialog box.

The initial size of the stack is indicated by the Linker project options, along with its maximum size (usually a very large number). The stack is traditionally used for procedure, function, and method calls. Local variables, parameters, and return values are stored on the stack temporarily. (The exception to this general rule, is that Delphi default calling convention is the `register` calling, which uses the CPU registers instead of the stack whenever possible.) Even the functions of a DLL, including system libraries, use the stack of the caller application to store their local data.

The rest of the memory, the heap, stores all the dynamically allocated data, including all Delphi objects (instances of a class). Windows 3.1 allowed you to use two different heaps: the small but efficient local heap and the large but slightly less efficient global heap. In Windows 95 and Windows NT, each application has its own local heap, which can be as large as you need. As I mentioned earlier, a common, global heap doesn't exist anymore in Windows 95 and Windows NT.

TIP

You can explore the internal structure of an executable file in several ways. In Windows 95, you can use QuickView from the local menu of the Explorer to have this low-level system information. Delphi includes a command-line tool, TDUMP.EXE, which provides similar details about a program, the functions it exports and imports from DLLs, the resources it contains, and so on. There are also specific programs that extract resources from an executable file, as we will see in the next chapter.

Windows System Memory

Besides requiring memory in its own data segments, a Windows application consumes some system memory, too. For example, the Windows libraries, like any other DLL, have their own memory segments. These were limited to 64 KB each in Windows 3.1, and this limit still applies to some of the system libraries of Windows 95, which are basically still 16-bit DLLs. There are three key libraries in Windows: Kernel, User, and GDI (Graphics Device Interface).

The Kernel DLL creates and maintains a number of small global memory blocks to contain information about processes and modules. The list of modules includes each executable file loaded in the system, including programs, dynamic libraries, system drivers, and many other files in executable format.

The User DLL creates and maintains heaps that store information about windows and menus. In particular, it maintains a heap that has an entry for each window class and each window in the system. This was the cause of many headaches in Windows 3.1 programming, because creating about 700 windows would exhaust this heap, bringing the whole system to a halt. In Windows 95 this limit is higher, around 16,000.

Fortunately, Delphi offers a number of ways to reduce the number of windows used within an application. As we have already seen, not all Delphi components are actual windows. Using windowless components, you can save some memory space in the User heap. Examples of windowless components are the SpeedButton, Image, and Label components, but there are many others. Since all the windowless components are subclasses of TGraphicsControl, you can easily find them by looking at the VCL components hierarchy (see Chapter 7).

The User DLL's heap has one big advantage. When you exit from an application, all the heap entries for the Windows it has created are destroyed automatically, freeing this memory space. Unfortunately, this doesn't happen in GDI heaps.

The GDI DLL stores information about graphic objects, such as pens, brushes, fonts, bitmaps, and so on. Each time you create such an object, you're responsible for deleting it. If you don't delete the graphic object, this system memory won't be released, not even after the application terminates. For this reason, even though GDI objects are usually much smaller than the window structures in the User heap and Windows 95 provides more space, a poorly written program that creates and forgets to destroy a number of these small GDI objects can create problems.

Free System Memory

The GDI and User heaps are known as system *resources*. This is an unfortunate name, because the term *resources* is also used in Windows to denote graphical portions (and other elements) of a program included in its executable file, as discussed in the previous sections. The two uses of the term *resource* have nothing in common at all.

Windows users are familiar with the use of the term referring to heaps, because the standard About box of many Windows applications shows the percentage of *free system resources*. (By the way, we used this same About box in the ShAbout example in Chapter 13.) You can check the system About box occasionally to make sure you're not running out of system resources. However, this is not usually a problem in Windows 95.

I decided to write a simple program that displays global memory status, instead of one that monitors free system resources, because the Win16 functions to access system resources are no longer available in Windows 95. It is still possible to call the 16-bit version of the functions, but this is not very simple.

You can access system memory status information by using the GlobalMemory-Status API function. The form I've built for this example, Mem, has two gauges configured as pie charts (by setting their Kind to gkPie), two labels to describe them, and a timer. It is much better to update the value of the system resources from time to time (hence the need for a timer) instead of asking the user to click on a button or select a menu command to see the new value.

The only actual method of this form is the handler of the OnTimer event of the Timer component. In this procedure, we access some of the values of the structure filled by the call to GlobalMemoryStatus. This function returns (among other information) the total amount of free RAM, the amount of available RAM, the amount of free virtual memory (which includes the swap file), and the available virtual memory. By dividing these values you can get the percentage of free space in these two areas:

```
procedure TMemForm.Timer1Timer(Sender: TObject);
var
  MemInfo : TMemoryStatus;
begin
  MemInfo.dwLength := Sizeof (MemInfo);
  GlobalMemoryStatus (MemInfo);
  RamGauge.Progress := MemInfo.dwAvailPhys div
    (MemInfo.dwTotalPhys div 100);
  VirtualGauge.Progress := MemInfo.dwAvailPageFile div
    (MemInfo.dwTotalPageFile div 100);
  Caption := Format ('Mem: = %d - %d',
    [RamGauge.Progress, VirtualGauge.Progress]);
  Application.Title := Caption;

  {if value is low, turn color to red}
  if (RamGauge.Progress < 5) then
    RamGauge.ForeColor := clRed
  else
    RamGauge.ForeColor := clLime;
  if (VirtualGauge.Progress < 20) then
    VirtualGauge.ForeColor := clRed
  else
    VirtualGauge.ForeColor := clLime;
end;
```

As you can see, the final values are also copied to the caption of the form and to the title of the application. This allows you to see the value while it changes directly on the TaskBar, even if the program has been minimized. Of course, looking at the colored gauges of the form (which is always on top) is much better than simply reading the two numbers. In fact, the color of the gauges changes when their free value is low. You can see an example of the output of this program in Figure 26.19.

FIGURE 26.19

An example of the output of the Mem example.

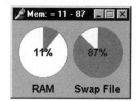

This program is nice, but it would have been much better to see this information in the Icon Tray of the Windows 95 TaskBar, the small area on the left of the TaskBar usually showing the clock, audio, and power management icons. We'll do this in the next chapter, after we've explored how to use icons in Windows.

What's Next?

In this chapter, we have seen that there are a number of approaches you can use to explore a compiled or running application, both by itself and in relation to the Windows system. Windows applications do not live in a world by themselves. They have a strong relationship with the system and, usually less directly, with the other applications that are running. The presence of other running Windows applications can affect the performance of your programs, as well as their stability.

In Windows 95 and NT, applications experience significantly fewer memory problems than in Windows 3.1, although some of the 16-bit Windows problems are still present in Windows 95 (which still replies on 16-bit system libraries). Every application resides in its own large memory space that cannot be accessed by other programs, which eliminates a number of potential problems for programmers.

There is only one concept that we have not discussed yet—the role of resources within an application. I didn't mention this topic in Chapter 25, which covered the Application object, or in this chapter's discussion of the memory structure of an application, because the next chapter will discuss them in detail.

C H A P T E R

27

Using Resources

- **Delphi's Image Editor**

- **Loading Windows resources**

- **Icons for minimized forms**

- **Alternative icons for status changes**

- **Installing a tray icon**

- **Predefined and custom cursors**

- **String tables and language translations**

- **Using version information resources**

As we saw in the previous chapter, the executable files of a Windows application can include special data, known as *resources*. The resources of a Windows program generally include icons, bitmaps, and cursors, which are graphical resources. Other resource types include lists of strings, templates used to build menus and dialog boxes, and other elements. (Again, don't confuse this use of the term *resources* with its other common Windows sense; namely, the amount of available memory for system libraries.)

Most Delphi applications use resources, since at the very least they display an icon. As we have seen in earlier examples, you can add a bitmap to the resource section of an EXE, so that you don't need to ship the bitmap in a separate file. This chapter provides an overview of the use of resources in Windows and in Delphi and includes some interesting examples.

Resources in Windows

In Chapter 26 we discussed the role of resources in Windows from the perspective of memory use. We saw that resources are stored in separate blocks in the executable file of an application, that these blocks are loaded in memory on demand and can be discarded, and that resources can be considered read-only data. However, we still have not described the different types of resources and their individual uses. Table 27.1 provides a comprehensive summary of Windows resources.

TABLE 27.1   Types of Windows Resources

Resource	Description
Icons	Small bitmaps, generally 32 x 32 or 16 x 16 pixels, with a limited set of colors. Used to identify windows and applications graphically.
Cursors	Small bitmaps, generally 32 x 32 pixels, which use only four colors (black, white, transparent, and reverse). Used to indicate the position of the mouse cursor on the screen. Delphi supports a set of predefined cursors, but you can add your own cursors, too.
Menu Templates	Define the structure of a menu. They aren't used in Delphi applications.
Dialog Box Templates	Define the structure of a dialog box. They aren't used in Delphi applications.

TABLE 27.1   Types of Windows Resources (Continued)

Resource	Description
Bitmaps	Define general-purpose bitmaps. Delphi has no direct support for bitmap resources, but you can load a bitmap from the resources instead of from a file.
Fonts	Define new fonts within a single program. Custom font resources are seldom used in Windows. More often, new fonts are installed in the system.
String Tables	Collections of strings, which are placed in resources for flexibility and efficiency, and are used to solve translation problems. Delphi does not directly support string tables, but they can be useful in some situations.
Accelerator Tables	List the shortcut keys of menu commands. They are not used in Delphi applications.
Version Information	A special resource used to indicate the version and author of a program. This is particularly important for DLLs, in which version handling can be a problem. Delphi 3 directly supports version information via Project Options, as we'll see at the end of this chapter.
Custom Resources	Resources in user-defined formats. Although you'll seldom define your own custom resources, Delphi uses a custom resource format for the binary description of forms.

Before looking at special uses of resources in Delphi, let's look at the tools you can use to prepare resources. Delphi includes an Image Editor for bitmap, icon, and cursor manipulation, but in some cases, you might still prefer to use a full resource editor, such as Borland's Resource Workshop (which is not included with Delphi) or one of the shareware resource editors available.

Using Resource Editors

You can activate Delphi's Image Editor by choosing the corresponding command from the Tools menu. Image Editor lets you manipulate four kinds of files. Three of them are file types that contain specific resource types (ICO, CUR, and BMP), and the last is a file format for compiled resource files (RES), which can contain all three kinds of graphical resources. Individual RES files can contain one or more resources of any type (including the graphical resource types). You can add the resources from a RES file to a Delphi application using the $R compiler directive, discussed later in this chapter.

In the Image Editor, you can prepare any kind of icon, cursor, or bitmap. For icons, you can provide a specific bitmap for the standard 32 × 32 image and the Windows 95 16 × 16 image (as shown in Figure 27.1), as well as use a different number of colors. Notice that a single icon resource can contain all these images, not just one. For cursors, you can set the *hot-spot* position, to designate which point in the image is the active one.

FIGURE 27.1

Delphi's Image Editor, with the different kinds of images you can define for an icon resource.

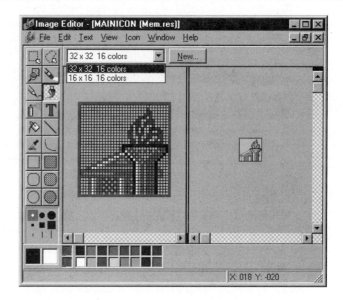

There are basically two ways to use Image Editor:

- Prepare specific files (particularly bitmaps and icons) to be loaded in the Delphi environment at design-time (using properties), or at run-time (using some of the LoadFromFile methods in your code).

- Prepare a number of resource files, and load the resources at run-time in the code, using Windows API calls, as described in the next section. When you work with graphical resource files in Image Editor, a tabbed notebook lets you see a list of elements of each group, as in the example shown in Figure 27.2.

FIGURE 27.2

A list of bitmaps included in a resource file, as displayed by Image Editor (from the Mines example in Chapter 11).

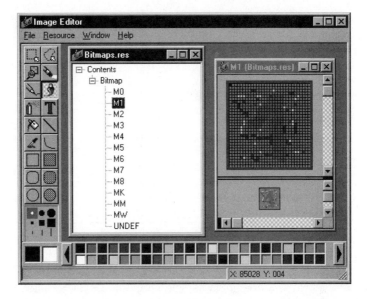

The Image Editor is a useful tool, but its capabilities are somewhat limited. When you need a full-fledged resource editor, you can use Borland's Resource Workshop (or another commercial resource editor). The Resource Workshop lets you open and edit any resource file. You can also use this tool to extract the resources from a compiled program, a DLL, a VBX, or any other executable-format file. (However, this doesn't mean that it is always legal to do so; be sure to determine the copyright status of any image you plan to use.)

If you open a Delphi application with the Resource Workshop, you will discover that it actually contains a series of resources, in addition to the icon present in its RES file. By default, a Delphi application's executable file contains a string table with system messages, captions, and other generic strings (such as the names of the months), binary data in custom resources (describing forms in the custom RCDATA format), some cursors, and one icon. Figure 27.3 shows the list of resources for the Screen example from Chapter 25, which is a relatively simple program. More complex programs may have many more resources, depending on the number of forms, the VCL units you include, the icons and bitmaps you add to the project, and so on.

FIGURE 27.3

The list of resources of a compiled Delphi application in the Resource Workshop (from the Screen example in Chapter 25).

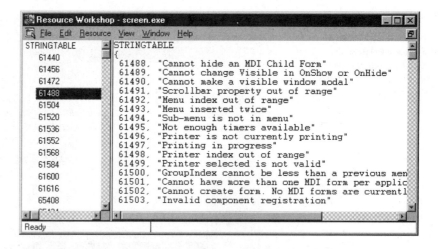

| TIP | Among its sample programs Delphi includes an interesting one named Resource Explorer. This program allows you to open an executable file (EXE or DLL) and see most of its resources, just as Resource Workshop does. Resource Explorer has no integrated resource editors, but with it you can easily copy a resource, which you can then paste into a resource file for your Delphi application, using another resource editor. |

As I've mentioned above, there are basically two ways to define resources and load them in Delphi: by loading them as a form or component property or by defining your own resource file and importing the resources using code.

Loading an Icon or Bitmap as a Property

The simplest approach is to load a resource as a property. Currently, however, the only resources that you can load using properties are icons and bitmaps, and sometimes metafiles. For example, you can place an Image component as the background of a dialog box and load a bitmap into it. Figure 27.4 shows an example of a program, named BackBmp, that uses a bitmap as a background. In this case, the bitmap is an embedded resource of the application, which means that you do not need to ship the original BMP file. (In the example, the original BMP file is in the Delphi Image library, stored by default in the IMAGE subdirectory of Delphi.)

FIGURE 27.4

An example of a program (BackBmp) using a bitmap as a background.

However, in BackBmp and similar examples, the image is not added to the executable file as a stand-alone bitmap resource. It is included in the binary description of the form. The advantage of this approach is that no one can easily use a resource editor to steal your bitmap. However, keep in mind that it is possible to extract a custom Delphi form resource using a tool such as Resource Workshop, save that resource to a RES-format file (but with a DFM extension), and load it back as a DFM file in the Delphi editor. To do this, someone simply needs to know that your application was created using Delphi.

In contrast, form and application icons are placed in the compiled file in a standard resource format, to let applications such as the Explorer or the Windows 95 shell extract them and use them as a hint for the user.

The Manual Approach to Loading Resources

The second technique you can use to access resources in Delphi is the manual approach. For this method, you must first define a separate resource file with the resources you need. The second step is to include the resource file in the project, using the $R compiler directive. In fact, contrary to the typical C/C++ approach, Delphi projects can have a number of resource files.

> **WARNING**
>
> Don't customize the default resource file—the one that has the same name as the project—because sometimes Delphi changes that file, and you might lose your customizations. Simply add other RES files to the current directory, and add a compiler directive to load it.

For example, in the Mines example of Chapter 11 (see Figure 27.2 shown earlier), I added the mine bitmaps to a separate resource file, which I loaded into the program within the implementation section of the form:

```
{$R *.DFM}
{$R BITMAPS.RES}
```

These two lines look suspiciously similar. The first loads a special resource file that has the same name as the Pascal file, but with a DFM extension. This is the form file that corresponds to this unit. In this compiler directive, in fact, the star doesn't mean *any file*, but rather *the file with the same name as this one*. This also shows that Delphi compiled form files are used by the environment as custom resources.

Once you have defined some resources and included them in your application, you can use the following Windows API functions to load resources: Load-Accelerators, LoadBitmap, LoadCursor, LoadIcon, LoadMenu, LoadResource, and LoadString. Each of these functions loads a specific resource type, except for the LoadResource function, which is used for custom resources. The first parameter of these functions is the handle of the application instance, which in Delphi is stored in the HInstance global variable. The second parameter is the name of the resource you want to load. Of course, each application can have a number of icons, bitmaps, and other resources, and you access each of them by name. The LoadString function has some other parameters to specify the buffer in which to copy the string and the size of this buffer.

The other loading functions simply return a handle to the loaded resource as the result. You can assign this handle directly to the corresponding VCL object property, as in the following code:

```
Bmp.Handle := LoadBitmap (HInstance, Name);
```

In this code, Name is a null-terminated string (a PChar) that contains the name of the bitmap, and Bmp is an object of the class TBitmap. This statement is actually extracted from the source code of the Mines example I've mentioned before. Study that example and its description in Chapter 11 to see how you can store several bitmaps as resources of an application and the advantages of using this approach.

Since we have placed bitmaps in the resources of this and other applications in previous examples (including the World2 example in Chapter 11, which loaded a series of bitmaps from the resources into a list), I won't build other bitmap examples now. Instead, we'll focus on the use of icons, cursors, and string tables.

The Icons for Applications and Forms

In Delphi, each application and each form has its own Icon property. When you don't set this property for a form, the program simply uses the value of the Icon property of the Application object. You can see and change this default application icon via the Application page of the Project Options dialog box. This icon is used also by the Windows 95 TaskBar, since the window that appear in the Taskbar for a Delphi application is the Windows of the global Application object.

All these scenarios are demonstrated by a sample program I've written called Icons. The form of this example is divided into two parts: on the left are a label, an image component, and two buttons referring to the icon of the form; on the right there are similar components referring to the icon of the application. In addition, we've added a bevel to separate the two areas and an OpenDialog component that we'll use to browse for icon resource files. Notice that I've defined the Icon property of the form (using the BB.ICO file), as well as that of the application (using the AA.ICO file). I prepared the two icon files using Image Editor. Each time you click on one of the Change buttons, a new icon is loaded from an external file:

```
procedure TForm1.Button1Click(Sender: TObject);
begin
  with OpenDialog1 do
    if Execute then
    begin
      Application.Icon.LoadFromFile (Filename);
      Image1.Picture.LoadFromFile (Filename);
    end;
end;
```

When one of the two Remove buttons is pressed, the corresponding icon is simply removed:

```
procedure TForm1.Button3Click(Sender: TObject);
begin
  Application.Icon := nil;
  Image1.Picture := nil;
end;
```

You can use this program to see how the two icon properties affect the icon of the minimized application. Some examples are shown in Figure 27.5.

1229

FIGURE 27.5

Some of the effects of
the Icons application.

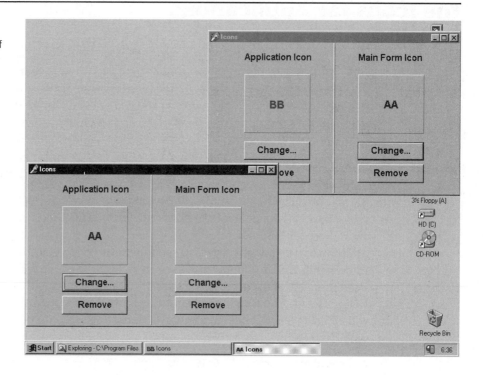

FIGURE 27.5

Some of the effects of
the Icons application.

When you launch the Icons application in the Explorer, Explorer will automatically use the application icon when you minimize the form, and not the icon of the main form. This is because the icon of the form is hidden inside the custom resources describing the form (the DFM file), while the icon of the application is stored in an icon resource that's bound to the executable file in the traditional manner.

Adding Alternative Icons for Different Conditions

In the Icons example, you can change the icon of an application by loading it from an external file. This approach has two disadvantages:

- You need to ship the icon files with your program.

- Loading an external file tends to be slightly slower (although for resources, it won't make much difference).

A technique you may find useful is to add icons to the resources of an application and use them as alternative icons for the program. There are many Windows applications that use different icons to alert the user that the status of the program has changed. For example, mail applications often have an empty mailbox icon and a full mailbox icon. Another common use is in memory monitoring programs, such as the Mem example we built in Chapter 26.

In that program, the title bar of the application changes continuously to show the current level of memory usage, and a gauge turns red when the usage reaches a low level. An improvement would be to switch the Taskbar icon when the gauges on the main form change color. The next example, named Mem2, uses three simple icons representing a green gauge, a yellow gauge, and a red gauge. These three icons are part of a new resource file, named RYG.RES, created with Image Editor. The green color is used to indicate that there is available free RAM, the yellow color is used to indicate the common situation of full RAM but available virtual memory (the swap file) and red indicates an almost-full swap file (a very dangerous state).

Additionally, I've changed the color of the gauges themselves to improve the user interface. I've chosen their foreground color to be green and their background color to be either yellow (for the RAM gauge) or red (for the virtual memory gauge). The reason is that in the Mem example, when you have no available RAM, the RAM gauge is almost completely white, with only the borders in red. In the new version, the gauge becomes completely yellow in this situation. Similarly, when you exhaust virtual memory, the Mem2 virtual memory gauge will become completely red, and you should start to worry!

The default green icon for the Taskbar is loaded at run-time at the beginning of the FormCreate method:

```
procedure TMemForm.FormCreate(Sender: TObject);
begin
  Application.Icon.Handle := LoadIcon (HInstance, 'GREEN');
  {update the output ASAP}
  Timer1Timer (self);
end;
```

Notice that you need to set the default icon before computing the initial value with the call to the timer event handler. Otherwise, the program might prevent the OnTimer event handler from displaying the correct icon, simply replacing it always with the green icon at program startup. In the Timer1Timer method I've removed the code to change the color of the gauges, because of the new approach to colors mentioned before, and added the code to load the proper color icon for the application window, depending on the level of free memory. This code is at the end of the new version of the `Timer1Timer` method:

```
procedure TMemForm.Timer1Timer(Sender: TObject);
var
  MemInfo : TMemoryStatus;
begin
  MemInfo.dwLength := Sizeof (MemInfo);
  GlobalMemoryStatus (MemInfo);
  RamGauge.Progress := MemInfo.dwAvailPhys div
    (MemInfo.dwTotalPhys div 100);
  VirtualGauge.Progress := MemInfo.dwAvailPageFile div
    (MemInfo.dwTotalPageFile div 100);
  Caption := Format ('Mem: = %d - %d',
    [RamGauge.Progress, VirtualGauge.Progress]);

  {copy the form caption to the application title on the taskbar}
  Application.Title := Caption;

  {set icon color}
  if RamGauge.Progress > 5 then
    Application.Icon.Handle := LoadIcon (HInstance, 'GREEN')
  else if VirtualGauge.Progress > 20 then
    Application.Icon.Handle := LoadIcon (HInstance, 'YELLOW')
  else
    Application.Icon.Handle := LoadIcon (HInstance, 'RED');
end;
```

This example is nice, but as I mentioned in Chapter 26 when I built the original version, it would be much better to display the flexible icon in the Icon Tray area of the Taskbar. We'll do that next.

Using the Icon Tray of the Taskbar

Windows 95 has introduced, along with the Taskbar, a new way to display system information, the use of the tray area of the Taskbar. As in the DOS era there were TSR programs and in Windows 3.1 some applications that ran only iconized, in Windows 95 there are programs that run as tray icons. In the lower-right corner of the screen, close to the clock, there is some space (the Taskbar tray) you can use to show your programs or utilities.

There is just one API function involved, Shell_NotifyIcon. This function is very simple. It has two parameters: a pointer to a TNotifyIconData structure, and a flag indicating whether you want to add, remove, or modify the icon. This is the structure:

```
type
  TNotifyIconData = record
    cbSize: DWORD;
    Wnd: HWND;
    uID: UINT;
    uFlags: UINT;
    uCallbackMessage: UINT;
    hIcon: HICON;
    szTip: array [0..63] of AnsiChar;
  end;
```

Here is the description of the fields of TNotifyIconData:

- cbSize is the size of the structure (which is used by the system to determine the version).

- hWnd is the handle of the window to which the TrayIcon should send notifications.

- uID is the identifier of the icon, useful if an application has several tray icons.

- uFlags has three possible flags: nif_Message, nif_Icon, and nif_Tip. They indicate which of the last three fields is valid.

- uCallbackMessage is the number of the user-defined message sent to the window (hWnd) to notify it of a user's action on the icon.

- hIcon is the icon to display in the tray icon area.

- szTip is the text of the tip displayed when the mouse moves over the icon in the Taskbar.

In practice, the fields of this structure (other than the icon and the tip) indicate the window to notify and the message to send it. In fact, when the user interacts with the tray icon, it sends back to the given window a message defined by the program, passing as parameters the action performed by the user on the icon (typically a mouse message) and the ID given to the icon.

Showing the Memory Status with a Tray Icon

Now we'll use this information about tray icons to update the Mem2 example into the Mem3 version, which has a few other new features, as well. The first change I've made to is to show in the two labels the amount of free and total memory, instead of some fixed text, to give more details to the user. Here is the code used to update the first label:

```
Label1.Caption := Format ('RAM:'#13'%s'#13'(%s)',
  [FmtMem (MemInfo.dwAvailPhys),
  FmtMem (MemInfo.dwTotalPhys)]);
```

The FmtMem function is a custom routine I've written to make the information more readable, adding the "KB" or "MB" strings to the proper value:

```
function FmtMem (N: Integer): string;
begin
  if N > 1024*1024 then
    FmtMem := Format ('%.1f MB', [n / (1024*1024)])
  else
    FmtMem := Format ('%.1f KB', [n / 1024]);
end;
```

You can see an example of the updated output in Figure 27.6. But the key change I've made is the creation of the tray icon when the program starts, and the update of this icon when the timer interval elapses.

FIGURE 27.6

The output of the Mem3 example, with more details about the memory status displayed in the two labels, and an icon added to the tray.

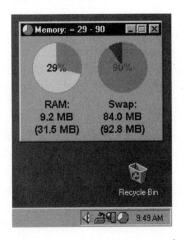

The first thing I've done is to add the ShellApi unit in the uses statement of the interface section of the unit. Next I've added a TNotifyIconData structure to the fields of the form class:

```
private
    nid: TNotifyIconData;
```

When the form is created, the program initializes this data structure, then calls the Shell_NotifyIcon API function to add the icon in the Tray Icon area:

```
procedure TMemForm.FormCreate(Sender: TObject);
begin
  // load the initial icon
  Icon.Handle :=
    LoadIcon (HInstance, 'GREEN');

  // fill the NotifyIcon data structure
  nid.cbSize := sizeof (nid);
  nid.wnd := Handle;
  nid.uID := 1; // icon ID
  nid.uCallBAckMessage := wm_IconMessage;
  nid.hIcon := Icon.Handle;
  nid.szTip := 'Free memory';
  nid.uFlags := nif_Message or
    nif_Icon or nif_Tip;
  Shell_NotifyIcon (NIM_ADD, @nid);

  // update the output ASAP
  Timer1Timer (self);
end;
```

In the OnTimer event handler the program executes the code of the previous version of this example, and then updates the tray icon with the following new code:

```
// update the NotifyIcon structure
nid.hIcon := Icon.Handle;
strcopy (nid.szTip, PChar(Caption));
nid.uFlags := nif_Icon or nif_Tip;
Shell_NotifyIcon (NIM_MODIFY, @nid);
```

This code simply updates the *nid* structure with the icon and the caption (after a cast to PChar), and then updates the icon. In this method the program updates only the few fields that change (this is the reason for declaring the structure as a local field of the form). When the program terminates, in the OnDestroy event handler, the icon is removed with yet another call to Shell_NotifyIcon:

```
procedure TMemForm.FormDestroy(Sender: TObject);
begin
  nid.uFlags := 0;
  Shell_NotifyIcon (NIM_DELETE, @nid);
end;
```

If you forget to remove the icon, it simply disappears the first time you move the mouse over it, but it is certainly better to remove it when the application is closed.

Hiding and Showing the Main Window

The main form of this application should become visible only when the user double-clicks on the icon in the tray. This is not too difficult to accomplish. Simply add a line to the source code of the project:

```
Application.ShowMainForm := False;
```

before you call the CreateForm method. When the user clicks with either mouse button on the icon in the Tray Area, the form receives the wm_IconMessage. I've declared a handler for this message in the form:

```
public
  procedure IconTray (var Msg: TMessage);
    message wm_IconMessage;
```

This method displays a popup menu if the user presses the right mouse button, or simply invokes the default menu item handler (Details1Click):

```
procedure TMemForm.IconTray (var Msg: TMessage);
var
  Pt: TPoint;
begin
  if Msg.lParam = wm_rbuttondown then
  begin
    GetCursorPos (Pt);
    SetForegroundWindow (Handle);
    PopupMenu1.Popup (Pt.x, Pt.y);
  end;
  if Msg.lParam = wm_lbuttondblclk then
    Details1Click (self);
end;
```

The call to SetForegroundWindow serves to display the popup menu properly (that is, in front of everything else). Try commenting out this line of code and you'll see what happens: the popup menu of the tray icon remains on the screen even when you activate another program. By the way, these two choices (right-click for the local menu and left double-click for the default action) are mandatory in the Windows User Interface guidelines.

The Details1Click method is associated with the default item (Details) of a popup menu component I've added to the form. The other menu items are Close and About. The popup menu is not connected to the form, but displayed when a user right-clicks on the icon, as you can see in Figure 27.7:

```
procedure TMemForm.Details1Click(Sender: TObject);
begin
  ShowWindow (Handle, sw_ShowNormal);
  SetForegroundWindow (Handle);
  Show;
end;
```

FIGURE 27.7

The tray icon of the Mem3 example and its local menu.

Again we have to call the SetForegroundWindow function when another application is active and you click the icon. We also need to call the Delphi Show method, so that Delphi realizes what is going on and allows the form to create its windowed controls properly. Removing the call to the Show method doesn't harm this particular example, but if you add a button to the form without that call, the button won't be displayed at all.

The Close menu command closes the program:

```
procedure TMemForm.Close1Click(Sender: TObject);
begin
  Application.Terminate;
end;
```

I call the Terminate method instead of closing the form because when the user closes the form (using the system menu or the Close button in the top-right corner), I want to be able to simply hide the form. For this reason, I've written the termination code above and the following FormClose event handler:

```
procedure TMemForm.FormClose(Sender: TObject;
  var Action: TCloseAction);
begin
  Action := caNone;
  ShowWindow (Handle, sw_Hide);
end;
```

Strangely enough, setting Action to caHide terminates the program, so I call ShowWindow to hide the form. Notice that when you call Application.Terminate the OnClose event of the form is not activated, but the OnDestroy event is.

Hiding the Taskbar Icon

So far we've been able to show a tray icon, update it when the system status changes (using a timer), and let the user select a couple of commands from a popup menu connected to the icon. And we've been able to fix a Windows 95 glitch by calling the SetForegroundWindow function before the popup menu is displayed. However, there is still one big problem. When you run the program, the main form is hidden but the application window is visible, resulting in an application icon in the Taskbar, as well as the icon in the tray area. That is not what this kind of application generally does.

How can we hide the Taskbar icon, representing the application? We might simply hide its window (Application.Handle) but this would mean the Taskbar icon was created and displayed first, and then removed. You would probably notice only a small flicker, but this is far from professional.

An alternative is to disable the creation of the application window, by setting the global variable IsLibrary to True. In fact, looking at the VCL source code in the constructor TApplication.Create you can see the following code:

```
if not IsLibrary then
  CreateHandle;
```

So we can make the Delphi run-time behave as if the program was a DLL and did not require a main window. This is a risky trick, and I've found a strange behavior when you close the program (the OnDestroy event handler is not called). For this reason I've decided to set IsLibrary to True and then set it back to False as soon as possible. But the real problem is to set this global variable to True before the global Application object is created. This happens in the initialization section of the Controls unit. So the question becomes, how can we execute some code before this unit is initialized? Writing something like:

```
IsLibrary := True;
Application.CreateForm(TMemForm, MemForm);
Application.Run;
```

doesn't help at all. In fact, units are initialized before Delphi executes the code of the project file. The solution lies in the fact that units are initialized in the order they are listed in the project file. By default this is:

```
uses
  Forms,
  Resform in 'RESFORM.PAS' {MemForm};
```

However, ResForm includes Forms (which includes Controls), so even in the initialization code of that unit it is already too late. To solve the problem I've added a new unit to the program, with this plain code:

```
unit RunFirst;

interface
implementation
initialization
  IsLibrary := True;
end.
```

Then I've changed the source code of the project file as shown below. Notice that the RunFirst unit is listed first (to initialize it first), and that I set the IsLibrary variable back to False immediately. At the end, this is the complete listing of the project source code:

```
program Mem;

uses
  RunFirst in 'RunFirst.pas',
  Forms, Windows,
  Resform in 'RESFORM.PAS' {MemForm};

{$R *.RES}

begin
  Application.ShowMainForm := False;
  IsLibrary := False;
  Application.CreateForm(TMemForm, MemForm);
  Application.Run;
end.
```

Although I cannot swear everything is OK, I haven't seen any drawback (in such a little program) in disabling the creation of the application window. The effect of this is that as soon as the main form becomes visible, its icon is added to the Taskbar.

Writing tray icon applications is probably the simplest thing you can do to customize the Windows 95 shell (and the Windows NT 4.0 shell, as well). There are many more things you can do; We have seen an example of a shell extension in Chapter 21. Delphi allows you to do just about everything, but at times there are hurdles you have to jump over (or run around) to make things work properly. Needless to say, these challenges can be fun, and they represent a good approach to exploring Delphi architecture in detail.

Using the Cursor in Delphi

Delphi's support for cursors is extensive, so it takes much less work to customize cursors than it does to customize icons. For example, Delphi includes a number of predefined cursors. Some of these are Windows default cursors, but others are added by Delphi. The use of cursors in Delphi is straightforward: simply use the Object Inspector to select the corresponding value for the Cursor property or DragCursor property of a component. If you need to set a global cursor for the whole application for a certain amount of time, you can set the Cursor property of the global Screen component.

However, you can't make this change using the Object Inspector; you have to do it in code. The following code demonstrates a common way to display the wait cursor (the hourglass) for the application while a long task is executing:

```
Screen.Cursor := crHourglass;
try
  {time-consuming code}
finally
  Screen.Cursor := crDefault;
end;
```

This code uses exception handling to ensure that even if something goes wrong in the execution, the default cursor is restored anyway. The Cursor property of the form and other components and the Cursor property of the Screen object are both of type TCursor. If you look up the definition of this data type in Delphi's Help, you are in for a surprise. TCursor is not a class, but rather a numeric type.

Technically speaking, a TCursor is an integer value that references an array of cursor handles, stored in the Cursors property (notice the final *s*) of the Screen object. This array can also be used to load a new cursor from an application's resources.

Designing a Custom Cursor

Our next example, named MyCur, demonstrates how to add a custom cursor to a program, as well as how to use the Cursors property of the Screen object in general. This example uses a new resource file, which contains a new hand cursor, as shown in Figure 27.8. This figure also shows the Hot Spot dialog box for the cursor. When you create a new cursor, always remember to set its *hot spot*. This is a

FIGURE 27.8

When preparing a custom cursor resource, always remember to set its *hot spot*.

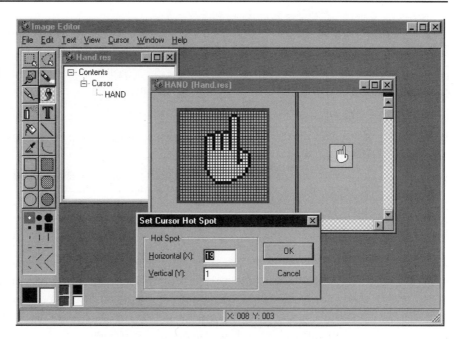

single pixel, within the boundaries of the cursor bitmap, that indicates the exact mouse position. If you are not an artist, remember that you can browse through the collection of cursors available in the Delphi Image Library (located by default in the IMAGES\CURSORS directory).

A resource file named HAND.RES is included in the source code, using the {$R HAND.RES} directive. The example, which is based on a form with two panels and a combo box, displays a list of available cursors, as you can see in Figure 27.9. Here is the textual description of the combo box:

```
object ComboBox1: TComboBox
  Style = csDropDownList
  Items.Strings = (
    'crHand (custom cursor)'
    'crDefault'
    'crNone'
    'crArrow'
    'crCross'
    ...)
  OnChange = ComboBox1Change
end
```

FIGURE 27.9

The form of the MyCur example, with two panels and a combo box, displays a list of available cursors.

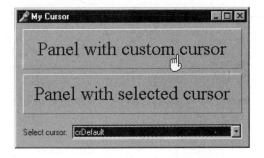

When the program starts, the FormCreate method loads the custom cursor from the application's resources, using the LoadCursor API function. This cursor is then stored in the Cursors array, using a user-defined constant, crHand. The value of this constant is set to 1. By using positive values, you avoid overwriting standard cursors, which use only negative numbers and 0 (we will get to cursor numbering soon). Once the new cursor has been loaded, it can be used like any other cursor. Here is the implementation code:

```
{$R HAND.RES}

const
  crHand = 1;
```

```
procedure TForm1.FormCreate(Sender: TObject);
begin
  {load a custom cursor from the resources}
  Screen.Cursors [crHand] := LoadCursor (
    HInstance, 'HAND');
  {use the new cursor for the first panel}
  Panel1.Cursor := crHand;
  {select the crDefault line}
  ComboBox1.ItemIndex := 1;
end;
```

As you can see above, just two lines of code do the trick. Selecting a cursor for the second panel using the combo box is even simpler—a single line of code:

```
procedure TForm1.ComboBox1Change(Sender: TObject);
begin
  Panel2.Cursor := 1 - ComboBox1.ItemIndex;
end;
```

Strange code, isn't it? As I mentioned before, the Cursors property of the Screen object is an array property that has a cursor handle for each entry. The TCursor type used for the Cursor property is actually an integer. This integer is used by Delphi as the index of the Cursors property to fetch the cursor handle. So when you write this code:

```
Form1.Cursor := crArrow;
```

Delphi translates it as:

```
Form1.Cursor := -3;
```

This is exactly what I have done for the custom cursor; I've defined a constant and used it to specify a cursor within the Screen.Cursors array. With this idea in mind, we can go back to the strange statement above. The trick is that I've added the text identifier of each cursor constant to the Items property of the combo box in the same order as the corresponding constants. Or rather, in the reverse order, since the default Delphi cursors have negative values, ranging from 0 down to –20. Since I've added the custom cursor at the beginning of the list, the first item in the list box (with ItemIndex = 0) corresponds to cursor 1, the second (with ItemIndex = 1) to cursor 0, the third (with ItemIndex = 2) to cursor –1, and so on.

A Flexible Cursor

In the MyCur example discussed in the previous section, you can choose a crNone cursor, which isn't listed in the Object Inspector as a proper value for the Cursor property. This omission is reasonable, because when you select this value, or any index value outside the boundaries of the Screen.Cursors array, the cursor disappears. If you specify this value for the Cursor property of a specific component, the cursor will disappear when you position it over that component and then reappear when you move it over a different component.

This behavior is possible because Windows allows you to define different cursors for some areas of a window. In fact, if a form or a component does not have a specific cursor assigned to it, you can specify the cursor manually in a wm_SetCursor message handler, just as you would in a traditional Windows program.

The next example, FlexCur, shows how this can be done. The form of this application is covered by a blank Image component. This offers us a Canvas connected to a memory bitmap, so that the image we build is saved in memory, and the surface of the window can be automatically repainted. The Image component covers most of the client area, but is not aligned with it, leaving a thin empty border. In a moment, we will see why this border is necessary.

To demonstrate the use of a flexible cursor, this program acts as a circle painter with erasing capability. You can click on the form at run-time to paint a small circle. You can also click on any pixel inside an existing circle to erase that circle. The result of clicking on the form is indicated by the use of two different cursors; that is, the cursor changes state depending on whether the mouse is moving over one of the circles you've painted, indicating that you can delete it.

To accomplish this, the program sets the cursor of the form to crNone and supplies a message handler for the Windows wm_SetCursor message:

```
public
  procedure WmSetCursor (var Msg: TWMSetCursor);
    message wm_SetCursor;
```

Inside this message handler, we perform two tests. First, we need to check whether the mouse is over the client area of the form or over its borders. This can be done using the HitTest parameter of the message and looking for the htClient value, which means that the cursor is over the client area. (For a list of the HitTest codes, see the Windows API Help file, under the wm_NCHitTest message.)

> **NOTE**
> Windows sends the `wm_SetCursor` message to a window each time the mouse changes its position over the window. This is the message that the FlexCur program monitors. By default, Delphi uses the `Cursor` property of forms and components to determine which cursor it should display at the current mouse position, but you can easily change this. A simpler technique is to use the `OnMouseMove` handler to change the cursor. However, in this approach, the cursor will flicker, because the system will display the default cursor (`crNone`) just before you change it.

When the mouse pointer is over non-client areas, the message handler of the parent class is invoked using the `inherited` keyword, to implement the default behavior for Delphi forms. If the cursor is over the client area, we need to check the color of the pixel that's currently beneath the pointer. Since the `wm_SetCursor` message has no coordinate parameters, I've added a call to the `GetCursorPos` API procedure, which returns the cursor position in screen coordinates. The program then translates that point into coordinates of the Image component, and uses these coordinates to check the color of the corresponding pixel, using the `Pixels` array of the Image component's `Canvas` property. Here is the code of this message handling method:

```
procedure TForm1.WmSetCursor (var Msg: TWMSetCursor);
var
  CurPos: TPoint;
begin
  {get the position of the cursor, and
  convert it to client coordinates}
  GetCursorPos (CurPos);
  CurPos := Image1.ScreenToClient (CurPos);
  if Msg.HitTest = htClient then
    if Image1.Canvas.Pixels [CurPos.X,
        CurPos.Y] = clWhite then
      {if the pixel is white}
      SetCursor (Screen.Cursors [crCross])
    else
      {if the pixel is black}
      SetCursor (Screen.Cursors [crUpArrow])
  else
    {if the mouse is outside the client area}
    inherited;
  Msg.Result := 1;
end;
```

As you can see above, depending on the result of the color test, the program calls the SetCursor function of the Windows API, passing as a parameter the handle of the cursor, not its identifier (crCross or crUpArrow). To transform the identifier into a handle, the code uses the Cursors property of the Screen object, accessing the proper item of the array.

Notice that the last line in the code above sets the return value for the message handler (Msg.Result := 1). Return values are seldom used in Windows messages, but if you omit them when they are needed, the system might try to respond to a message you've already handled. With this message, for example, we need to tell Windows that the system should not bother setting a default cursor because we have already set one.

The program uses a cross-hair cursor (crCross) for the white surface and the up-arrow cursor (crUpArrow) for the black pixels. Here, the up-arrow is used as a visual hint for the flood-fill operation that erases the colored area. This erases not just a single circle, but also contiguous ones, as you can see in the two consecutive images shown in Figure 27.10.

If the pixel beneath the location of the mouse click is already black, the FloodFill method is called inside the Image1MouseDown handler in place of the default Ellipse method:

```
procedure TForm1.Image1MouseDown(Sender: TObject;
  Button: TMouseButton; Shift: TShiftState; X, Y: Integer);
begin
  if Image1.Canvas.Pixels [X, Y] = clWhite then
  begin
    {paint a black circle}
    Image1.Canvas.Pen.Color := clBlack;
    Image1.Canvas.Brush.Color := clBlack;
    Image1.Canvas.Ellipse (X-15, Y-15, X+15, Y+15);
  end
  else
  begin
    {erases the contiguous black pixels}
    Image1.Canvas.Brush.Color := clWhite;
    Image1.Canvas.FloodFill (X, Y, clWhite, fsBorder);
  end;
end;
```

By calling FloodFill, we face the risk of also filling the form's border (if it is black) if a circle is too close to it. This is the reason for the thin empty border between the form and the Image component I've mentioned before.

FIGURE 27.10

The FloodFill method used in the FlexCur example erases a group of circles at a time, as you can see by comparing the two images. The bottom image was taken after a single click. Notice the two cursors.

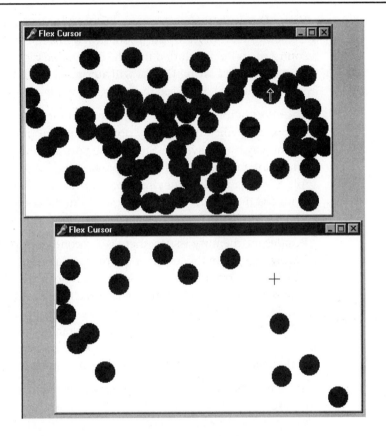

Using String Table Resources

The third kind of resource we will explore in this chapter is the *string table*. String tables have a much bigger role in Delphi 3 than in past versions of this environment. In fact, as we saw in Chapter 4, when you need a string constant in a program, instead of declaring it in a `const` section you can simply declare it in a `resourcestring` section:

```
resourcestring
  Text1 = 'This is some text';
```

When you write this declaration, Delphi automatically adds a new entry to the resource table of the application, stored in a file with the `.STR` extension. This resource file is then included into the executable file. This means that every time you use the `Text1` string Delphi will automatically add the code to load the string from the resources. We'll see this code in a while.

The effect of this change is a different memory layout of the code and data of the program, which is generally positive since resources are handled in a very efficient way by the system. Strings use your application's memory directly, while string tables are loaded in separate, discardable memory blocks that the application loads when they're needed. (Actually the technical reason Delphi 3 introduced this feature is to avoid clashes in the resource identifiers of different packages, but in the end we've got this new feature, and can take advantage of it.)

Besides the memory issues, there is a second reason for using resources in a Windows program: the localization, or translation of a program into another language (such as from English to German). To localize a traditional program, you would have to search through each source file, locate the embedded text, translate the text, and then recompile the entire program. In contrast, when you localize a Windows application that uses string tables, you simply translate the text included in the resources, recompile only the resources (a very simple process), and then bind the new resources to the previously compiled EXE code.

In Delphi, the process of localizing an application is similar. Localizing most of your user interface will involve translating the captions for components by modifying the textual description of form files (opening DFM files using the Delphi code editing window). However, programs usually need to display messages to the user, and you won't want to create a separate form to display each message.

NOTE Borland and other companies sell specific tools to localize Delphi applications. These range from simple inexpensive components that use database tables to complex and very expensive toolkits. Some of these tools allow you to generate different executables files, one for each language, while others also allow you to change the language on the fly, without starting the program again.

A simple approach is to put all of the messages into string tables. This makes your Delphi program as easy to localize as a traditional one that loads the strings using calls to Windows API functions alone. This is exactly what happens in the next example, named StringT. To take advantage of this approach and to let you understand how string tables work behind the scenes, however, the example uses string tables directly, not the new `resourcestring` feature of Delphi 3. The form of the StringT example has two areas marked by two bevels. One area has a button, and the other has a button and a spin edit control (with a label).

The key to the example is in a new resource compiler source file (indicated by the `.RC` extension as usual). This is a text file with some resource statements, documented in the Windows API Help file. Here is the text of the `STABLE.RC` file:

```
STRINGTABLE
BEGIN
  1, "Hello"
  2, "String Table Test"
  11, "First message"
  12, "Second message"
...
  20, "Tenth message"
END
```

To define a string table resource, you need to include the resource statement (`STRINGTABLE`) and a list of identifiers followed by the corresponding strings (the comma separator is optional). Note that the strings must be in C-language format—they must use double quotation marks instead of the Pascal single quotation marks. However, the indicators at the beginning and end of the resource block can be either the Pascal ones (`BEGIN` and `END`, uppercase), as shown in the listing, or the C brackets, { and }.

WARNING You can number the strings as you like, but you must consider that Delphi uses strings itself, as we have seen, so you should be careful to avoid duplicate entries. Delphi generally uses very high values, with string identifiers over 60000; any lower value shouldn't create any problems.

Once you have written this file, you need to compile it into a `.RES` file, the only kind of resource file you can include directly in a Delphi project. This is easier than you might expect, because Delphi includes a full-scale resource compiler,

BRCC32, although it is a command-line tool and not a Windows application. Simply start a DOS session, move to the subdirectory with the project files, and issue the following command:

```
BRCC32 -R STABLE.RC
```

Of course, you should also provide the proper path for BRCC32, which is within the Delphi\3.0\Bin subdirectory. By default, BRC32 tries to bind the resulting .RES file to the corresponding EXE file. The –R parameter tells it to compile the .RC file skipping the binding step. Once the resource file has been generated, we can include it in the code, as usual:

```
{$R STABLE.RES}
```

Now we can actually start writing the code of our program. We'll want to load the first string and display it when the form's Hello button is pressed. The API function is LoadString, which has a buffer for a null-terminated string as its third parameter. The return value of the function indicates the number of characters that have been loaded from the resource, or 0 in case of an error (for example, if the string has not been found). For this reason, we can test the return value:

```
procedure TForm1.HelloButtonClick(Sender: TObject);
var
  Text: array [0..255] of Char;
  N: Integer;
begin
  N := LoadString (HInstance, 1, Text, SizeOf (Text));
  if N > 0 then
    ShowMessage (StrPas (Text));
end;
```

This code works, but it is quite complex. As a much better alternative, we can use Delphi's LoadStr function, which encapsulates the Windows API call and loads a string from the resources directly into a Pascal string. This is the second version of the same method:

```
procedure TForm1.HelloButtonClick(Sender: TObject);
var
  StrMsg: string;
begin
  StrMsg := LoadStr (1);
  if StrMsg <> '' then
    ShowMessage (StrMsg);
end;
```

There is also a second Delphi function used to load strings in Delphi, FmtLoadStr, which uses the string table string as the format template for the given data parameters. It combines the LoadStr and the Format functions. We can call LoadStr again to change the title of the window (and of the minimized window), using the second string:

```
procedure TForm1.FormCreate(Sender: TObject);
var
  StrTitle: string;
begin
  StrTitle := LoadStr (2);
  if StrTitle <> '' then
  begin
    Caption := StrTitle;
    Application.Title := StrTitle;
  end;
end;
```

Besides the Hello button, the program has a second one, Show, with only slightly more complex code. Instead of displaying a fixed string, The ShowButtonClick method uses the current value of the spin edit box to determine which string to use in the range of 10 to 20 (you can see the effect of this method in Figure 27.11):

```
procedure TForm1.ShowButtonClick(Sender: TObject);
var
  StrMsg: string;
begin
  StrMsg := LoadStr (10 + SpinEdit1.Value);
  if StrMsg <> '' then
    ShowMessage (StrMsg);
end;
```

FIGURE 27.11

An example of the StringT program's output when the Show button is pressed.

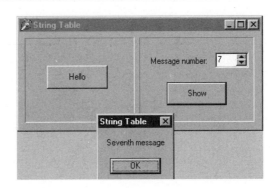

This last method highlights another traditional use of strings. We refer to a group of ten string-based messages, but it is quite simple to add new entries to the string table, increase the value of the SpinEdit component's MaxValue property, and let the program display the new strings without any change to the source code. However, if you change component properties, you'll have to rebuild the project to rebind the custom form resource to the EXE, unless you add the value of the property (MaxValue in this case) in another string and load it dynamically.

Translating the Strings into Another Language

The program we have written works fine, but its real advantage over a program that uses hard-coded strings is that now we can easily localize the application. Simply submit the RC file to a language translator (not necessarily a programmer) and recompile the translated version with the resource compiler. If the translated file has a different name, you can replace the file name in the compiler directive used to include the resources and rebuild the program. That's all you need to do. (You might even skip this minor name change by using the project file's name or by merging the resources with the external resource compiler.)

For this localization, I first translated the strings into another language (my actual first choice, Italian). Here is the result (stored in the file STABIT.RC):

```
STRINGTABLE
BEGIN
  1, "Ciao"
  2, "Prova Tabella Stringhe"
  11, "Primo messaggio"
  12, "Secondo messaggio"
  ...
  20, "Decimo messaggio"
END
```

Then I recompiled the resource file and changed the resource inclusion directive to {$R STABIT.RES}. When we recompile and run this program, it now displays the title of the form and the messages in Italian, as you can see in Figure 27.12.

The program, however, is not completely localized. The Delphi portion (the textual description of the form) should be translated, too, to correct the names of the two buttons as shown in the figure. To accomplish this, you can load the textual description of the form into the Delphi editor and translate all of the strings, such

FIGURE 27.12

The output of the Italian version of the StringT example.

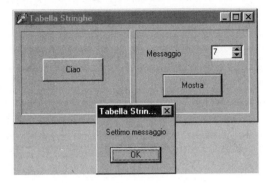

as captions and list items. Do not change the internal identifiers, such as the value of the Name property.

I've performed this operation and saved the new version of the form description in the file STRFIT.DFM. This file is loaded by replacing the statement {$R *.DFM} with the new version: {$R STRFIT.DFM}. Now both the captions and the messages are in Italian, but we use the same source file for the code of the program. To make it simpler to compile either one of the versions from the same source code base, you can use the conditional compilation directives for resource inclusion:

```
{$IFNDEF ITALIAN}
  {$R *.DFM}
  {$R STABLE.RES}
{$ELSE}
  {$R STRFIT.DFM}
  {$R STABLEIT.RES}
{$ENDIF}
```

In a complex program, after this step, you also need to translate the Delphi system strings, such as those you can find in VCL source files (for example, CONST.RC or DBCONSTS.RC). This will complete the program localization.

NOTE Borland sells the Delphi Translation Kit, a simple and economic package that adds a wizard to your Delphi environment, allowing you to choose the language for the system errors, default button captions, default message box captions, and similar items.

There is also another approach to creating multilingual programs. You can prepare different groups of strings, one for each language, using a standard numbering schema. For example, English strings might start from 1, French strings from 10001, German strings from 20001, and so on. Now each time you need to load a string (say, string 235), you can write:

```
MyText := LoadStr (nLanguage * 10000 + 235);
```

In this case, nLanguage is a code corresponding to the current language setting (0 for English, 1 for French, 2 for German, and so on). Then you can add a dialog box to let the user change the language at run-time, setting a new code. The last thing you should consider is that referring to the string by number in the source code is a good way to make it hard to read and easy to break. For this reason, you should define a number of constants corresponding to each string's identifier, and use the constant instead of the numeric code.

Version Information

 The last type of resource I'll focus on in this chapter is version information. Although it was possible to use version information resources also in Delphi 2, Delphi 3 adds specific support for this kind of resource. Simply open the project options, go into the VersionInfo page of the dialog box, and enter the proper values for the resource number, product name, copyright and other information. You can see an example of this dialog box in Figure 27.13.

Version information is required by DLLs and OLE servers (including ActiveX controls) so that installation programs can determine whether you already have the most recent version of a DLL. Without this technique you risk installing an older DLL or control over a newer version. Knowing the details of version information for DLLs is particularly important if you want to make effective use of an installation program (or write your own, comparing the version information of files already present on the hard disk with that of the files you are installing).

Since you can find a good description of the role of version information in Microsoft documentation, I'll skip repeating that. What I want to do instead is to show you a simple use of version information inside an executable program. I'll just add some version information to a program (named VInfo), and then write some code that extracts some of this information to a memo component when the user clicks on the form's Read Version Info button. The problem, as you'll see, is that the API for accessing version information is far from simple.

FIGURE 27.13

The VersionInfo page of the Project Options dialog box.

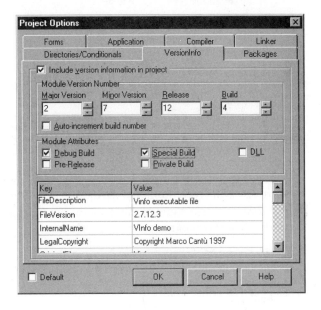

The central API call is GetFileVersionInfo. This function requires as parameters the filename, a pointer to a block of memory to store the data, and the size of this block of memory. To allocate a memory block of the proper size, a program can call the GetFileVersionInfoSize API function first. Here is the first part of the button's OnClick event handler:

```
procedure TForm1.Button1Click(Sender: TObject);
var
  Size, Size2: DWord;
  Pt, Pt2: Pointer;
begin
  Memo1.Lines.Clear;
  Size := GetFileVersionInfoSize (
    PChar (ParamStr (0)), Size2);
  if Size > 0 then
  begin
    GetMem (Pt, Size);
    try
      GetFileVersionInfo (PChar (ParamStr (0)),
        0, Size, Pt);
      ...
    finally
```

```
        FreeMem (Pt);
      end;
    end;
  end;
```

The final part of the code, inside the `finally` block, deletes the memory. In between, the program uses the `Pt` pointer to access version information. We access data by calling the `VerQueryValue` API function, which requires as parameter the pointer to the data, a string with a path indicating the requested information, and a pointer. The function sets this pointer to the requested string or data structure.

The first part of the actual code accesses the fixed portion of the file information, a group of flags and numbers defined by the `TVSFixedFileInfo` structure. Here is the code to access some of this data (in the example on the companion CD you'll find a longer version):

```
// show the fixed information
VerQueryValue (Pt, '\', Pt2, Size2);
with TVSFixedFileInfo (Pt2^) do
begin
  Memo1.Lines.Add (
    'Signature (should be invariably 0xFEEF04BD): '
    + IntToHex (dwSignature, 16));
  Memo1.Lines.Add ('Major version number: ' +
    IntToStr (HiWord (dwFileVersionMS)));
  if (dwFileFlagsMask and dwFileFlags
      and VS_FF_DEBUG) <> 0 then
    Memo1.Lines.Add ('Debug info included');
```

The second part of this code reads some of the strings included in the version information of the program. Each string should be separately accessed, again using the `VerQueryValue` API function. Here are some of these calls:

```
VerQueryValue(Pt,
  '\StringFileInfo\040904E4\FileDescription', Pt2, Size2);
Memo1.Lines.Add ('File Description: ' + PChar (pt2));
VerQueryValue(Pt,
  '\StringFileInfo\040904E4\FileVersion', Pt2, Size2);
Memo1.Lines.Add ('File Version: ' + PChar (pt2));
```

The result of this program is visible in Figure 27.14. The information you can see is not particularly meaningful; the version numbers and other values have just been entered casually. Some applications actually use this approach to show the name and version of the program inside an About box.

FIGURE 27.14

The output of the VInfo example, showing the version information of a program.

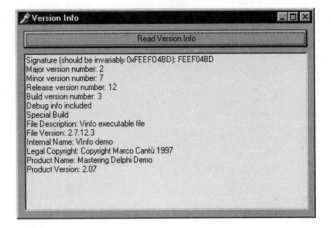

What's Next?

In this chapter, we have examined some details about the role, definition, and use of Windows resources in traditional applications and demonstrated how to use them in Delphi programming. Like many other visual programming environments, Delphi lets you build most of the elements of an application graphically, making use of custom techniques instead of relying on Windows resources and more traditional techniques.

At times, however, resources have a role. We have seen in previous chapters some examples of loading a bitmap from the resources of an application, and in this chapter, how you can load an icon and a cursor. We have also explored a nongraphical resource type that is useful in Delphi as well as other, more traditional environments: string tables. However, building string tables using plain text files is so simple that we can use them quite easily even without specific support from the Delphi environment.

This chapter ends our discussion of the Application object, applications in general, memory, debugging, and resources. With the next chapter, we start exploring other advanced topics that have plenty of specific support in Delphi: printing, files, data exchange, and multimedia. These are the topics of the last four chapters.

CHAPTER

TWENTY-EIGHT

Adding Printing Capabilities to Delphi Applications

- Standard and custom print dialog boxes

- Printing graphics

- Print preview

- Printing text

- Printing database forms

- QuickReport reporting components

- Using ReportSmith

Although we have explored many different Delphi programming topics up to now, including some advanced techniques, there are some important topics we still haven't covered. One of these topics is printing, which is the subject of this chapter. Some printing capabilities are present even in the simplest real-life programs, such as the ones we've built in previous chapters. Many of the examples in this chapter are improved versions of earlier examples, with support for these important capabilities.

This chapter covers two printing-related topics. The first part discusses printing forms, including text and graphics. The second part is about printing reports. Delphi provides plenty of support for both of these printing areas, so adding these features to existing programs is easy to do.

Printing a Whole Form

Printing a form in Delphi at run-time is fairly simple. The TForm class has a Print method, which prints the entire client area of the form and any visual components it contains. Calling this method is all you need to do to print. For example, we might add a Print button to a form and write this code:

```
procedure TForm1.PrintButtonClick (Sender: TObject);
begin
  Print;
end;
```

The effect of this code is to print a bitmap corresponding to the form's client area (the form without its caption and border) using the current printer. To determine the actual size of the printed output, you can adjust the form's PrintScale property before you call the Print method. By default, this property has the value poProportional. This means that the printout will be proportional to the image on the screen, using the PixelPerInch property of the form relative to the screen size and the DPI (dots per inch) setting of the current printer relative to the page size. For example, if the form width is half of the screen, the printout will cover half the width of the printed page.

There are two other possible values for this property: poNone and poPrintToFit. With poNone, no scaling is used. Because of the higher pixels-per-inch capability of printers, the resulting image will generally be quite small. If you use the poPrint-ToFit parameter, the printout will be stretched to fill the whole page, but will maintain its horizontal-to-vertical proportion. With poPrintToFit as the form's

PrintScale property setting, you typically get much bigger images. However, since the bitmap corresponding to the form is stretched for the printed image, the print quality decreases as the image size increases.

A Custom Print Dialog Box

Although Delphi has a specific component encapsulating the standard Windows Print dialog box, to keep this first example simple, I've decided not to use it. Instead, I've built a simple custom dialog box with three radio buttons (actually a radio group with three items), which lets you choose one of the three values of the PrintScale property. I've added this Print dialog box to an application from Chapter 12, ComboBar. The name of the new version is PrnForm. You can see the main form and print dialog box of this example in Figure 28.1. I've added a Print command to the File menu and changed the background color of the label that covers the form's client area to white.

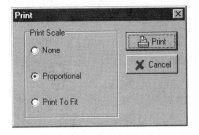

This example has a simple form and lets you change the caption's font in a number of ways and see the effect both on the screen and on paper. The only problem is that the printed output contains not only the label's text, but also the image of the toolbar. If you don't want to print the toolbar, you can hide it by using the Visible command on the Toolbar menu or on the toolbar's SpeedMenu. This way, the program can actually be used to print the text of the caption by itself on a page. Now add a dialog box with an edit or memo field to change the text of the caption, and you can print any text. Why buy an expensive word processor?

The example's code is simple. When the user issues the Print command, our custom dialog box is displayed. If the user clicks on the Print button (which has an mrOk value for its ModalResult property), the current scaling selection is set via the PrintScale property, and the form is printed:

```
procedure TToolbarForm.Print1Click(Sender: TObject);
begin
  if PrintDlg.ShowModal = mrOk then
```

```
begin
  case PrintDlg.RadioGroup1.ItemIndex of
    0: PrintScale := poNone;
    1: PrintScale := poProportional;
    2: PrintScale := poPrintToFit;
  end;
  Print;
  end;
end;
```

The dialog box itself requires no code other than the class definition generated by Delphi. If we wanted to go further, we could add a panel that displays a preview of the printed image. In fact, the TForm class defines a GetFormImage method, which returns a bitmap of the form. This is the same bitmap that is sent to the printer when you call the Print method's code.

What is not simple is simulating the print scaling that shows the form's bitmap inside an area corresponding to the printed page. You'll see an example (PrintBmp) that includes a print preview dialog box later in this chapter. You could use that code to improve the Combo2 example, too.

The Standard Print Dialog Boxes

As an alternative to the custom Print dialog box used in the PrnForm example, you can use the two standard Windows dialog boxes related to printing that are encapsulated in Delphi's PrintDialog and PrinterSetupDialog components.

This is the approach we'll take in the next version of our example, named PrnForm2. This example has the same dialog box as in the previous version, this time used as a Print Options dialog box, plus the standard Print and Printer Setup dialog boxes. To reflect these additions, the example's File menu has been rearranged, as you can see in Figure 28.2.

The two new components for the two dialog boxes have no special properties and are used in a simple way. To set up the printer, you just call the Execute method of the PrinterSetupDialog1 component:

```
procedure TToolbarForm.PrinterSetup1Click(
  Sender: TObject);
begin
  PrinterSetupDialog1.Execute;
end;
```

FIGURE 28.2

The File menu of the Prn-
Form2 example viewed
in Delphi's Menu
Designer.

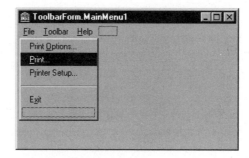

In contrast, when you call the PrintDialog component's Execute method, you need to check the return value to see if the user really wants to print. I've also added code to support the only Print dialog box option that is always present: the selection of the number of copies. The PrnForm2 example does not print all the copies automatically. It prints the first one, checks to see if the user requested more than one copy, and then asks if the user really wants to print the remaining copies:

```
procedure TToolbarForm.Print1Click(Sender: TObject);
var
  I: Integer;
begin
  if PrintDialog1.Execute then
  begin
    Print;
    if (PrintDialog1.Copies > 1) and (MessageDlg (
        'Do you actually want to print ' +
        IntToStr (PrintDialog1.Copies - 1) +
        ' more copies?', mtConfirmation,
        [mbYes, mbNo], 0) = mrYes) then
      for I := 1 to PrintDialog1.Copies - 1 do
        Print;
  end;
end;
```

Notice that the Print dialog box can activate the Printer Setup dialog box, as you can see in Figure 28.3. We could have omitted the Printer Setup command and the corresponding dialog box component without any real problems.

FIGURE 28.3

The standard
Windows 95 Print dialog
box used by the
PrnForm2 example.

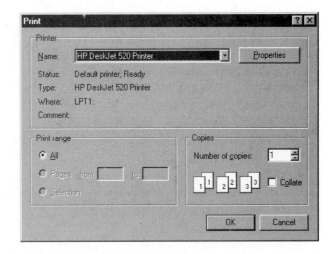

When the user selects the Print Options command, the custom dialog box from
the previous example appears and the `PrintScale` property is set, but nothing is
printed:

```
procedure TToolbarForm.PrintOptions1Click(Sender: TObject);
begin
  if PrintDlg.ShowModal = mrOk then
  begin
    case PrintDlg.RadioGroup1.ItemIndex of
      0: PrintScale := poNone;
      1: PrintScale := poProportional;
      2: PrintScale := poPrintToFit;
    end;
    if PrintDlg.PrintRequest then
      Print1Click (self);
  end;
end;
```

This code doesn't call the `Print` method, but eventually activates the
`Print1Click` method. The dialog box, in fact, has now three buttons, OK, Cancel, and Print. The OK and Cancel buttons work as usual, the Print button has
the `ModalResult` property set to `mrOK`, but its `OnClick` event handler sets the
value of the `PrintRequest` public field of the form to `True`. Therefore, when
this button is pressed the dialog box is closed, but the Print dialog box starts
immediately.

Accessing the Printer Object

For all but the simplest operations (such as printing the whole form), you'll use the global `Printer` variable to manipulate a printer from a Delphi program. Actually, `Printer` is the name of a global function; it returns an object of class `TPrinter`, defined in the Printers unit.

> **NOTE**
>
> In 16-bit Delphi, `Printer` was the name of a global object of the `TPrinter` class. In 32-bit Delphi, there is still a global object of class `TPrinter`, but it is now local to the printer unit. To access this global object, you can use the `Printer` function. This makes the new code highly compatible with the older ones. For example, you can still write `Printer.Canvas.Font` to change the current printing font for text. The reason for this change is that Delphi now also has a `SetPrinter` function, which can be used to change the global object. This allows you to create more than one printer object (with different settings) and assign one of them to the "current printer object" as needed. It is also useful for installing an object of a `TPrinter` descendant class.

You can use the object returned by the `Printer` function to access some global properties related to the printer, such as a list of installed drivers or printer fonts. However, its key property is its canvas. You can use the canvas of a printer the same way that you use the canvas of a form; that is, you can print text, graphics, and everything else. To use this canvas, you need to call the printer's `BeginDoc` method to start the printing job, use the canvas methods to produce the output, and then call the `EndDoc` method to send the output to the printer. As an alternative, you can call the Abort method to discard the print job, or call the `NewPage` method to send the output to the printer and start working on a new page.

A Print Preview of Graphics

Our first example of the use of the global printer object (using the `Printer` function) is a simple application you can use to print bitmaps. Basically, this is an extension of the TabOnly example presented in Chapter 14. That example used a TabControl component to let the user browse though a series of bitmaps. As shown in Figure 28.4, the PrintBmp example has a preview form, with a toolbar with four buttons at the top, and a ScrollBox component that contains an Image component. If the image is bigger than the form, you can use the ScrollBox component to scroll the image without affecting the toolbar.

FIGURE 28.4

The Print preview form of the PrintBmp example at design-time.

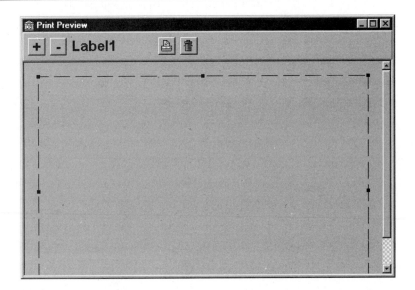

This preview dialog box is opened from the new File ➤ Print command. The preview form lets you compare the size of the resulting bitmap with the printed page (indicated by the size of the image component) and scale the bitmap as necessary, to increase its size.

> **NOTE** Changing the image size affects the screen output in both the preview form and the printed output. The reason for scaling a bitmap prior to printing is that bitmaps printed at their standard pixel-per-inch ratio tend to appear quite small on the printed page.

The code is based on the StretchDraw method of the TCanvas class, which I've used to generate the preview bitmap and the actual output bitmap. The Stretch-Draw method has two parameters: a rectangle, indicating the output region, and a graphic object (the source image). The result is an image stretched to fit the output rectangle. Now let's review some of the code. The main form responds to the Print command by initializing and running the Preview form:

```
procedure TForm1.Print1Click(Sender: TObject);
begin
  {double-check whether an image is selected}
  if Image1.Picture.Graphic <> nil then
  begin
    {set a default scale, and start the preview}
    PreviewForm.Scale := 2;
    PreviewForm.SetPage;
    PreviewForm.DrawPreview;
    PreviewForm.ShowModal;
  end;
end;
```

The test at the beginning could have been omitted, since the Print menu item is disabled until an image file is selected, but it ensures that a file is selected in any case. This code sets a public field of the PreviewForm object (Scale), calls two methods of this form (SetPage and DrawPreview), and finally displays it as a modal form. Figure 28.5 shows an example of the Print Preview form at run-time.

FIGURE 28.5

The PrintBmp example's Print Preview form, with the program's main form in the background.

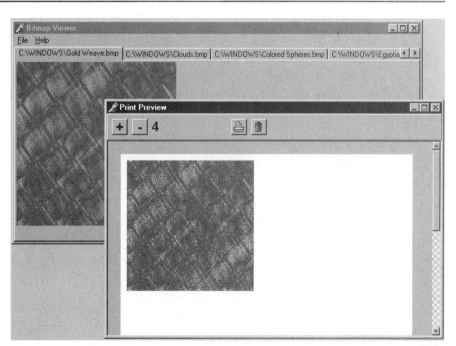

The SetPage method sets the size of the Print Preview form's Image component, using the size of the printed page:

```
procedure TPreviewForm.SetPage;
begin
  Image1.Width := Printer.PageWidth div 5;
  Image1.Height := Printer.PageHeight div 5;
  {output the scale to the toolbar}
  Label1.Caption := IntToStr (Scale);
end;
```

The size of the page is divided by five to make it fit into a reasonable area of the screen. You might use a parameter instead of this fixed value to add a zooming feature on the preview page. However, it seemed confusing to have one button to increase the size of the printed image and another button to increase it only in the preview, so I decided to skip the zooming capability.

The heart of the preview form's code is in the DrawPreview method, which has three sections. At the beginning, it computes the destination rectangle, leaving a 10-pixel margin, scaling the image, and using the fixed zoom factor of five (as you can see in the following listing). The second step erases the old image that is still on the screen by drawing a white rectangle over it. The third step calls the StretchDraw method of the canvas, using the rectangle calculated before and the current image from the image component of the main form (Form1.Image1.Picture.Graphic). To access this information, we need to add a uses clause in the implementation portion of the code referring to the Viewer unit which declares the TForm1 class. Here is the code for this method:

```
procedure TPreviewForm.DrawPreview;
var
  Rect: TRect;
begin
  {compute the rectangle for the bitmap preview}
  Rect.Top := 10;
  Rect.Left := 10;
  Rect.Right := 10 +
    (Form1.Image1.Picture.Graphic.Width * Scale) div 5;
  Rect.Bottom := 10 +
    (Form1.Image1.Picture.Graphic.Height * Scale) div 5;
  {remove the current image}
  Image1.Canvas.Pen.Mode := pmWhite;
  Image1.Canvas.Rectangle (0, 0,
    Image1.Width, Image1.Height);
  {stretch the bitmap into the rectangle}
```

```
Image1.Canvas.StretchDraw (Rect,
    Form1.Image1.Picture.Graphic);
end;
```

All of this code is executed just to initialize the form. The startup code is split into two methods, but only because DrawPreview will be called again later. When initialization is done and the modal form is visible, the user can click on the four toolbar buttons to resize the image, print it, or skip it.

The two resize methods are simple, because they just set the new scale value and call the DrawPreview procedure to update the image:

```
procedure TPreviewForm.ScalePlusButtonClick(
    Sender: TObject);
begin
  Scale := Scale * 2;
  Label1.Caption := IntToStr (Scale);
  DrawPreview;
end;
```

The PrintButtonClick method of the preview form is almost a clone of Draw-Preview. The only differences are that the destination rectangle is not zoomed by the five factor and the bitmap is sent to the printer in a new document (a new page):

```
procedure TPreviewForm.PrintButtonClick(Sender: TObject);
var
  Rect: TRect;
begin
  {compute the rectangle for the printer}
  Rect.Top := 10;
  Rect.Left := 10;
  Rect.Right := 10 +
    (Form1.Image1.Picture.Graphic.Width * Scale);
  Rect.Bottom := 10 +
    (Form1.Image1.Picture.Graphic.Height * Scale);
  {print the bitmap}
  Printer.BeginDoc;
  try
    Printer.Canvas.StretchDraw (Rect,
      Form1.Image1.Picture.Graphic);
    Printer.EndDoc;
  except
    Printer.AbortDoc;
    raise;
  end;
end;
```

Sharing the Output Code

Instead of printing a whole form or copying an existing bitmap to the printer canvas, you can paint on the printer canvas as if it were a form or component canvas. Since you can execute the same methods on a printer canvas as on any other canvas, you can write programs with two output methods—one for the screen and one for the printer—using similar code. Even better, you can write a single output method to use for both kinds of output.

As an example of this approach, I've built a new version of the Shapes4 program from Chapter 10, which stored the description of a list of shapes in memory and later used this description in the OnPaint method. The new version is named Shape6 (a Shape5 example already exists in Chapter 11). As with the other examples in this chapter, the only change in the description of its form is a new Print command in the File menu.

The interesting point is that I've moved the code of the FormPaint example into another method I've defined, called CommonPaint. This new method has two parameters, the canvas and a scale factor, and it outputs the list of shapes to the canvas passed as parameters, using the proper scale factor:

```
procedure TShapesForm.CommonPaint (
  Canvas1: TCanvas; Scale: Integer);
var
  I: Integer;
  CurShape: ShapeData;
begin
  for I := 0 to ShapesList.Count - 1 do
  begin
    CurShape := ShapesList.Items;
    with CurShape do
    begin
      Canvas1.Pen.Color := PenColor;
      Canvas1.Pen.Width := PenSize;
      Canvas1.Brush.Color := BrushColor;
      if Circle then
        Canvas1.Ellipse (
          (X-Size) * Scale, (Y-Size) * Scale,
          (X+Size) * Scale, (Y+Size) * Scale)
      else
        Canvas1.Rectangle (
          (X-Size) * Scale, (Y-Size) * Scale,
```

```
                    (X+Size) * Scale, (Y+Size) * Scale);
      end;
    end;
  end;
```

Once you've written this code, the FormPaint and Print1Click methods are simple to implement. To paint the image on the screen, you can call CommonPaint without a scaling factor:

```
procedure TShapesForm.FormPaint(Sender: TObject);
begin
  CommonPaint (Canvas, 1);
end;
```

To paint the contents of the form to the printer instead of the form, you can reproduce the output on the printer canvas, using a proper scaling factor. Instead of letting the user choose a scale (in a simple Print dialog box with a SpinEdit or a ScrollBar component), I decided to compute it automatically. The idea is to print the shapes on the form as large as possible, by sizing the form's client area so that it takes up the whole page. The code is probably simpler than the description:

```
procedure TShapesForm.Print1Click(Sender: TObject);
var
  Scale, Scale1: Integer;
begin
  Scale := Printer.PageWidth div ClientWidth;
  Scale1 := Printer.PageHeight div ClientHeight;
  if Scale1 < Scale then
    Scale := Scale1;
  Printer.BeginDoc;
  try
    CommonPaint (Printer.Canvas, Scale);
    Printer.EndDoc;
  except
    Printer.Abort;
    raise;
  end;
end;
```

Of course, you need to remember to call the specific commands to start printing (BeginDoc) and commit the output (EndDoc) before and after you call the CommonPaint method. If an exception is raised, we call Abort to terminate the printing process anyway.

Printing Text

In the two previous examples, we used the global printer object's canvas to print graphics. At the beginning of the chapter, we saw another example that could be used to print text, but its code was far from adequate. Printing text is really an important topic, so it deserves some attention.

One approach to printing text from a Delphi program is similar to the one we used in the PrnForm example. If you prepare the text in a form (or, in general, in a bitmap), you can later print the corresponding image to the screen. This is useful in a few cases, such as when you have text in a data-entry form, but it is not generally useful because you can only print a limited amount of text and the print quality is usually quite poor.

Another approach to printing text is to draw the text, using the `TextOut` method of the canvas or other text-related drawing functions. This allows you precise control over the text's position, and you can obtain high-resolution output. The drawback is that there is a lot of work involved, since you must determine the length and position of each line on the page, the height of the font, and many other details. Power never comes free.

The free ride, however, comes from two more approaches. First, if you have to print the text of a RichEdit control, you can simply call its `Print` method. An example of this technique was shown in the RichNot2 example of Chapter 9. The other approach is to use the printer as an output file for text.

In Delphi, you can associate a file with the printer, and then print to the file—send text to the printer—using the standard `Write` and `Writeln` procedures. This is much simpler than the other methods because the system automatically determines the height of the lines, relieving you of much of the work. The print resolution is good, but the control you have over the output is less precise. Long lines are automatically wrapped to the next line, which is helpful but can produce wildly unformatted output.

To build this example, I've updated the Notes example from Chapter 8. This was quite a bare example, so I've added to it file-handling capabilities, font and color dialog boxes, and many other options. In such a simple example, which uses a single font for the whole text and has no special page-handling capabilities (page numbers, header and footers, and so on), using the `Writeln` procedure on a file connected to the printer is a reasonable approach.

Technically, the key to this approach is the use of the AssignPrn procedure, which connects a file with the printer. After starting the print process, you can start using Write and Writeln to print the text by calling the Rewrite procedure. In the PrnNotes example I simply print each of the Memo component's lines, using a for loop from the first to the last line:

```
procedure TNotesForm.Print1Click(Sender: TObject);
var
  PrintFile: TextFile;
  I: Integer;
begin
  if PrintDialog1.Execute then
  begin
    {assign the printer to a file}
    AssignPrn (PrintFile);
    Rewrite (PrintFile);
    try
      {set the font}
      Printer.Canvas.Font := Memo1.Font;
      {copy all the text of the memo to the printer file}
      for I := 0 to Memo1.Lines.Count - 1 do
        Writeln (PrintFile, Memo1.Lines[I]);
    finally
      CloseFile (PrintFile);
    end;
  end;
end;
```

WARNING   Whenever you need to copy the current font of a component or a form to the printer, consider that not all screen fonts are available as printer fonts. A notable example is the MS Sans Serif font often used by default: this font won't print properly. I suggest that you use only True-Type fonts when the printer is involved, because you can be sure these fonts are available on both the screen and the printer.

I could have easily customized this printer function, adding a dialog box to select the range of lines to print, but I decided to use the standard Print dialog box, as you can see in Figure 28.6.

FIGURE 28.6

The standard Print dialog
box used by the
PrnNotes example.

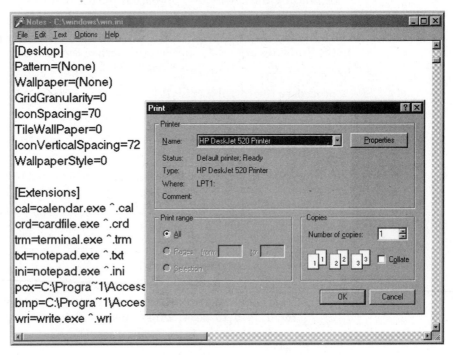

FIGURE 28.6

The standard Print dialog
box used by the
PrnNotes example.

Adding support for page selection is more complex. First, we must compute
the number of lines per page, using the printer's PageHeight property and the
height of the font of the printer canvas. Once this calculation is made, we need to
check whether each line of text will fit in a printed line or be wrapped to the next
line (or even the next two lines), and modify the number of lines in the memo
field on a given page.

When you want to start a new page, however, you cannot call the printer object's
EndPage method. If you do, the printer will eject the page, but the remaining output will begin in the middle of the next page, as if nothing happened. To start a
new page when using an output file connected to the printer, you can simply
close the output file, and then reopen it again. Closing the file terminates the current page. The new page will start from the first line (after a custom header and
the page number).

Printing Database Records and Tables

Using Delphi's printing capabilities, we can easily output our program's database-related forms. Basically, if a form shows a record from a database table, you can use the form's Print method to output the data. Of course, if you intend to print your data, you might as well build the form and arrange the components so that the printed output will look good.

As an alternative to printing a bitmap corresponding to the full client area of the form, you might develop a print function that temporarily removes the form's toolbar and the status bar, prints the whole surface of the form, and then restores the toolbar and status bar. Even better, you can open up a preview form, copy the bitmap of the form, and print only a portion of that bitmap, excluding the toolbar, status bar, and other extraneous elements.

This is not the only approach you can use to print records (or full tables, if they fit on the screen) using database-related forms. You can also apply any of the techniques described in the previous section to print text. In particular, using the file-printing approach, you can print the name of the field and its value on each line of a page, printing one or all of the table's records.

Our first example of database-related output is the PrintNav application, which is an extension of the Navig1 example from Chapter 16, and is similar to the DbToWord example of Chapter 22 and the DbToHtml example of Chapter 24. As in these last two versions, the form of the PrintNav example has some buttons, as shown in Figure 28.7.

FIGURE 28.7

The form of the PrintNav example at design-time.

The three buttons perform different actions involving some type of printer output. The first button simply prints the data of the current record's two visible fields, using the text of the two labels and two edit boxes:

```
procedure TNavigator.PrintButtonClick(Sender: TObject);
var
  PrintFile: TextFile;
begin
  {assign the printer to a file}
  AssignPrn (PrintFile);
  Rewrite (PrintFile);
  try
    {set the font of the printer, and output each element}
    Printer.Canvas.Font := Font;
    Writeln (PrintFile, Label1.Caption, ' ', DBEdit1.Text);
    Writeln (PrintFile, Label2.Caption, ' ', DBEdit2.Text);
    Writeln (PrintFile, Label3.Caption, ' ', DBEdit3.Text);
  finally
    {close the printing process}
    CloseFile (PrintFile);
  end;
end;
```

This code follows the usual assignment of the printer output to the `PrintFile` file. What is new in this method is that the database access and output operations are executed within a `try-finally` block (to avoid skipping the code that closes the print job in case of an error). The code of the second button, Print All, is more complex. It prints the two visible fields for each database record, not just the current one. The program scans the whole table, just as in the DbToWord and DbToHtml examples. As you can see below, at the beginning it sets a bookmark and disables the controls; then it scans all of the records in a `while` loop. For each record, the program outputs a caption followed by the field's text. The program extracts the field with the table's `FieldByName` method and reads its text using the `AsString` property of the `TField` class. Here is the full source code of this method, which uses three nested `try-finally` blocks to take care of every possible exception:

```
procedure TNavigator.PrintAllButtonClick(Sender: TObject);
var
  Bookmark: TBookmark;
  PrintFile: TextFile;
begin
  {assign the printer to a file}
```

```
AssignPrn (PrintFile);
Rewrite (PrintFile);
try
  {set the font of the form}
  Printer.Canvas.Font := Font;
  {store the current position, creating a new bookmark}
  Bookmark := Table1.GetBookmark;
  try
    Table1.DisableControls;
    try
      Table1.First;
      while not Table1.EOF do
      begin
        {output the three fields and a blank line}
        Writeln (PrintFile, 'Country: ',
          Table1.FieldByName ('Name').AsString);
        Writeln (PrintFile, 'Capital: ',
          Table1.FieldByName ('Capital').AsString);
        Writeln (PrintFile, 'Continent: ',
          Table1.FieldByName ('Continent').AsString);
        Writeln (PrintFile);
        Table1.Next;
      end;
    finally
      Table1.EnableControls;
    end;
  finally
    Table1.GotoBookmark (Bookmark);
    Table1.FreeBookmark (Bookmark);
  end;
finally
  System.CloseFile (PrintFile);
end;
end;
```

The Print Form button has the simplest code. To print the output of the form, the PrintFormButtonClick method simply calls the form's Print method. I've added this last button to the program simply to let you test the three different ways to output the data from a database form. You can improve each of these methods by adding headers and comments, printing other fields, and so on. This example is intended to give you an idea of the basic code involved.

By expanding on this idea, you can build complex and sophisticated kinds of output, and also create custom reports and different versions of printed output. As an alternative, you can use specific tools included in Delphi to generate reports: the Delphi QuickReport components or ReportSmith.

The QuickReport Components

The professional editions of Delphi includes QuickReport, a collection of reporting components tightly integrated with Delphi and licensed to Borland by QSD AS (a Norwegian company). Similar Delphi components are available from other third-party companies, but I'll focus on this simply because it will be readily available to most Delphi developers.

> **NOTE** Similar alternatives to the QuickReport reporting component set include ReportPrinter, Piparti, ACE Reporter, and many others, some of which have samples included in the companion CD-ROM.

QuickReport uses a form to build a report visually and in a way very similar to the way you build normal forms. However, you'll use this report form only to develop the report; it is never actually shown on screen at run-time. To print or display the report, you can call the `Print` or `Preview` methods of the Quick-Report component, which you place on each report form. (Placing a QuickReport component on a form turns that form into a report form.)

Using QuickReport, a report is constructed from *bands*, or horizontal regions of information. You can use a band to output data, to provide a header and footer in each printed page, or to include totals and other special information. To build a report, you simply place the QuickReport component in a secondary form (not the application's main form), add one or more bands, and then place on those bands some of the QuickReport data-aware reporting components, which connect to a Delphi data source in the usual way. The data can come from one or more tables or queries, as in the standard data-access components.

A Quick Example

To demonstrate the QuickReport component, I've extended the main form of the last example (PrintNav) by adding a full report to it. I've named the new example QrNav. Besides adding another button to the three printing buttons already available, I've added a new form named ReportForm to the project. The new form has a QuickReport component and three QRBand components, as shown in Figure 28.8.

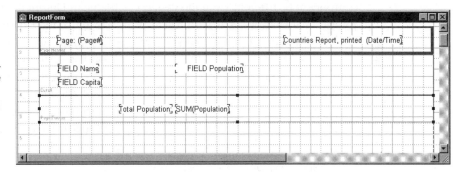

One of the key properties of the QRBand component is BandType, used to indicate the role of the band in the report. In this example, the first band is of type rbPageHeader, the second of type rbDetail, and the third of type rbPageFooter. Other types of bands you can use include rbTitle, included before or after the first page's header; rbSummary, printed only at the end of the report; rbGroupHeader and rbGroupFooter for groups defined with the specific QRGroup component; rbColumnHeader for multicolumn reports; and a few others.

In the example, I've placed two QRSysData components in the first band (the page header). The QRSysData components display the page number, date, and time, and have a description in their Text property. You can print many other types of system information using this component, as indicated by its Data property. I've also set a border for the enclosing band, using its Frame property.

The second band contains the real data from the database. As a detail band, it is replicated on the report for each record that appears in the data source, so you have to specify the dataset for each report component. In this case, I've used the Table1 from the program's main form (after choosing File ➤ Use Unit). This same dataset is also connected with the three QRDBText components placed in the second band.

1279

> **TIP**
>
> In addition to the `DataField` property they share with the standard Delphi data-aware components, the report components also have some formatting capability. If you try setting the value '*###,###,###*' for the `Mask` property, the numbers will be output with thousand separators.

In the last band, I've added a QRExpr component to display the total population of the countries in the report (actually in all the records up to the current page). This component is different from the version available in Delphi 2, and can do more complex calculations. The simplest approach is to use the `Expression` property to indicate the kind of operation (such as sum, min, max, average, count) and the related field (such as *'Population'*). The `Expression` property has a special editor you can use to create the expression, instead of typing it. Remember, however, to set the `Master` property to the report component, `QuickRep1`, because this is the only way to connect the calculated value with the proper dataset. The report is based on a form, so let's look at an excerpt of the form's textual description:

```
object ReportForm: TReportForm
  object QuickRep1: TQuickRep
    DataSet = Navigator.Table1
    ReportTitle = 'Countries Report'
    object QRBand1: TQRBand
      BandType = rbPageHeader
      object QRSysData1: TQRSysData
        Data = qrsPageNumber
        Text = 'Page: '
      end
      object QRSysData2: TQRSysData...
    end
    object QRBand2: TQRBand
      BandType = rbDetail
      object QRDBText1: TQRDBText...
      object QRDBText27: TQRDBText...
      object QRDBText3: TQRDBText
        DataSet = Navigator.Table1
        DataField = 'Population'
        Mask = '###,###,###'
      end
    end
    object QRBand3: TQRBand
      BandType = rbPageFooter
```

```
        object QRExpr1: TQRExpr
          Expression = 'SUM(Population)'
          Mask = '###,###,###'
        end
        object QRLabel1: TQRLabel...
      end
    end
  end
```

Having designed the report, you can test it by simply double-clicking on the report component. This displays the print preview form, which you can use directly to print the report without even compiling the program. You can obtain the same print preview at run-time (see Figure 28.9) by writing the following in the main form's code:

```
procedure TNavigator.ReportButtonClick(Sender: TObject);
begin
  ReportForm.QuickReport1.Preview;
end;
```

FIGURE 28.9

The print preview form of the QrNav example, based on the QuickReport component.

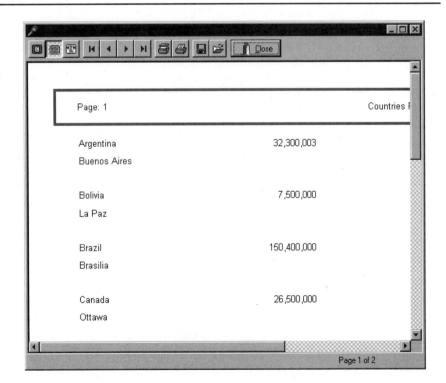

Creating ReportSmith Reports

As an alternative to the use of VCL-based report components, you can use external report engines, such as ReportSmith or Cristal Report. In this section I'll show you an example of the use of ReportSmith. Again, I've chosen this tool because it's a former Borland product, which was included in the Client/Server version of Delphi. Delphi still includes an interface to this engine, in the form of the Report component, which is not installed by default.

This component is not particularly rich by itself. Its properties include the name of the report file you want to print, its directory, and some other information. You can call the Report component's Run method to view a report (using the ReportSmith run-time engine) and to print it. The stand-alone version of ReportSmith, on the other hand, is a very powerful reporting tool that you can use by itself (with no connection to Delphi). ReportSmith has more capabilities than the QuickReport component, but it requires a big set of run-time DLLs (which you must install along with your program), and it requires a fair amount of RAM to achieve a decent speed.

In contrast, the QuickReport reporting components require no run-time DLLs (unless you use the corresponding package as a separate DLL) and are very fast, but they also have more limited reporting capabilities. QuickReport is also more integrated with Delphi; it accesses databases using the Table and Query Delphi components, while ReportSmith uses it own independent approach.

> **NOTE**　The comparison above isn't limited specifically to QuickReport and ReportSmith. The same differences generally hold also for other native Delphi components, and other external reporting engines.

Just to test ReportSmith's behavior, I've written a bare program, named RsPrint, which loads and runs a report (a file with the RPT extension). When you call the Report1 object's Run method, the ReportSmith engine is loaded, and you can see and print the report. This is because the Report component's Preview property is set to True. When the Preview property is set to False, the report is printed as soon as you call the Run method.

As an alternative, once the report is loaded in memory using the Run method, you can use the Print method to send a Dynamic Data Exchange (DDE) message to the ReportSmith engine, asking it to print the report. Do not call Print before running the report, because it will have no effect. The PrintRpt example's form has four components: an "open file" dialog box to let the user select a report, a Report component, a check box to select the preview mode, and a button to start the operation. When you click on the Report button, the program opens the dialog box so that you can select a file, and then runs the engine:

```
procedure TForm1.ReportButtonClick(Sender: TObject);
begin
  Report1.Preview := PreviewCheckBox.Checked;
  if OpenDialog1.Execute then
  begin
    Report1.Reportname := OpenDialog1.FileName;
    Report1.Run;
  end;
end;
```

Since I've set the AutoUnload property, the ReportSmith run-time engine is automatically unloaded from memory when the report terminates. Otherwise, you must add a specific statement in the form's OnClose event, calling the Report component's CloseApplication method.

As I mentioned above, the effect of this code depends on the status of the Preview check box. If the Preview property is set to False, the ReportSmith run-time engine immediately starts printing. Otherwise, the ReportSmith Run_Time window is displayed as shown in Figure 28.10. The ReportSmith window will appear in the same screen position as it was the last time you used it, and you can see the output, which is the preview. From the preview, you can make changes, choose the pages you want to print, and select from many other options.

The connection between Delphi and the ReportSmith run-time engine is somewhat loose. ReportSmith is a stand-alone reporting application, which can be driven by Delphi, but can also be used independently. What you cannot do is see the report preview inside a Delphi window; our next example will add that capability.

FIGURE 28.10

The report preview takes place inside the Report-Smith Run-time window. Notice the form of the RsPrint example above it.

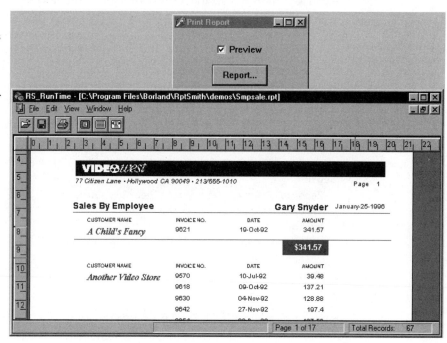

Building a Custom Report

Using the RsPrint program, you can print (or preview) any existing report, but you cannot create new ones. In other words, if you use this approach in your own applications, users will not be able to create their own reports, unless they own a copy of ReportSmith. In that case, of course, they will be able to print any existing report file.

NOTE

Actually, you can use Delphi to create new reports using DDE or the new API to drive the ReportSmith Run-time without having the stand-alone package, but that is not the easiest way to build a report, and I won't cover it in the book.

In general, you will need to build one or more reports when you are developing your program, attach them to the Delphi application, and let the user print them using menu commands.

Building a new report is not really a Delphi programming task. You start ReportSmith (the full version, not the engine) and prepare a report by choosing one of the standard layouts, accessing one or more database tables, and designing a proper layout. For more information about ReportSmith's features, refer to the manuals or online Help files. Here we will take a look at two examples of reports and their connection with a simple Delphi program.

Our first ReportSmith example is a new version of another program presented in Chapter 16, called HandGrid. This new version, RsGrid, has the same grid as the previous version, plus a menu that lets you print a couple of reports in different ways. The structure of the program is simple. There is a DBGrid connected to a table (again COUNTRY.DB). The program has a plain Print command, which uses the standard dialog box just to let the user confirm the action:

```
procedure TForm1.Print1Click(Sender: TObject);
begin
  if PrintDialog1.Execute then
    Print;
end;
```

The other three menu items (two in the File menu and one in the Table menu) are related to two reports. You can either print the first report directly or open it in preview mode, using the File menu's two commands. The second report always has the Preview property set to True, and is activated using the Table menu's only command. All three menu command handlers have the following structure:

```
procedure TForm1.PrintReport1Click(Sender: TObject);
var
  CurrentPath: String;
begin
  // set the report path to the application path
  CurrentPath := ExtractFilePath (ParamStr(0));
  Delete (CurrentPath, 1, 1);
  Report1.ReportDir := CurrentPath;
  Report1.Preview := False;
  Report1.Run;
end;
```

Before printing the report, you have to indicate its directory properly. Since I don't want to use a fixed directory, it is better to extract its name from the full path name of the application, passed as the first command line parameter (see Chapter 25).

What changes in the other two cases is the value of the Preview property and the Report component used. The form and the code of this program are simple. All of the work to build the two reports is actually done with ReportSmith. I'll discuss the first report here and the second one in the next section, because the second report uses some advanced features of ReportSmith.

The first report I've built for the RsGrid example, COUNTRY.RPT, does nothing more than output the contents of the database, using a label format. To rebuild it, start ReportSmith, create a new report, choose the label style, and select the proper database table (notice that the BDE aliases are not available here). Next, drag some of the fields to the report page, and add a standard label with the proper check box. You can see a step of the report's creation in Figure 28.11.

FIGURE 28.11

Creating a report in ReportSmith is as simple as dragging a few labels.

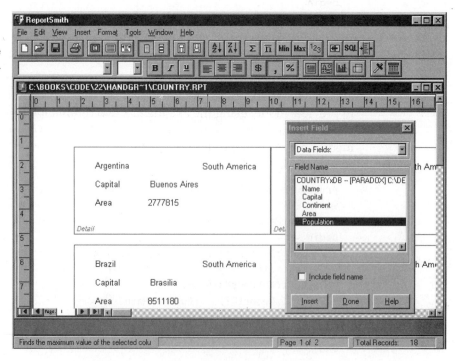

When you are done with the report's layout, save the file and enter its name in the `Report1` component's `ReportName` property in the HandGrid3 example. Now you can run the program and print or preview the report. It really is that simple.

> **WARNING**
>
> In the report file and in the RsGrid program, there are some hard-coded directory names, particularly the name of the directory that contains the database table used by the report. If your installation does not use the default Delphi directories, you might have problems running the program without modification.

Writing a ReportSmith Macro

The RsGrid example's second report, `TABLE.RPT`, is more complex. It uses a columnar report format rather than the label style. Select the table (again `COUNTRY.DB`), and all of its fields are arranged in columns. You can resize the columns to make them fit on the page and set a proper format for the numeric output, such as including thousand separators, as you can see in Figure 28.12.

FIGURE 28.12

The initial development steps of the new report include resizing the columns and choosing proper formats.

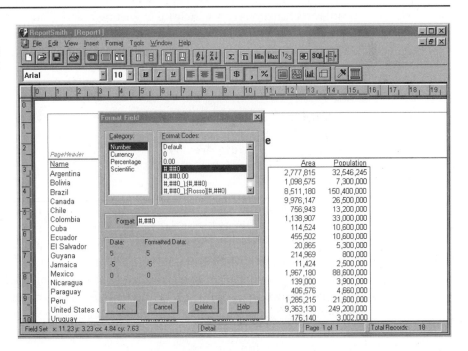

Continue building the report, entering a proper title, sorting it by continent and by name, and grouping the report by continent. Then add a footer to each of the report's groups. In the footer, place a count of the countries for each continent, the total population of each continent, and the total surface of each continent.

Finally, you can move to the tough part: adding a calculated field to show the population density, as we did in examples in Chapters 16 and 17. The problem here is that you cannot use a SQL statement with the definition of the calculated field, because this feature is not supported by ReportSmith for Paradox tables. The only technique available is to define a ReportSmith macro. You can use the Derived fields command on the Tools menu to add a new field name, defined by a ReportBasic macro. I've used the name Density. Then you can give the macro a name, such as GetDensity, and write its code.

When you click on the New or Edit buttons in the Choose a Macro dialog box, the Edit Macro dialog box appears, as shown in Figure 28.13. You can write the text of the macro directly in this macro editor, or you can use the three list boxes at the top to select table fields, commands, functions, and so on. Notice that each of the three list boxes has a combo box above it. You can use each combo box to select a group of elements for the corresponding list box. For example, the last list box can display four different groups of elements: Basic Functions, Basic Statements, Dialog Box Functions, or Branching & Looping. Using these lists of available commands and functions can be helpful in writing macros, but you still need to know at least the basics of the language of the ReportSmith macro editor, ReportSmith Basic. In general, if you want to take advantage of the power of ReportSmith, some background in BASIC will help.

Here is the code of the macro for the new field:

```
Sub GetDensity()
Pop1 = Val (Field$("Population"))
Area1 = Val (Field$("Area"))
DerivedField Str$ ( Pop1 / Area1 )
End Sub
```

This code defines two temporary variables (no declaration is necessary in BASIC), and stores the value of two fields in those variables. The Field$ function returns the text of the field's contents for the current record, and the Val function extracts the numeric value from the string. The last statement computes the population density and transforms it back into a string, using the Str$ function. This value is assigned to the DerivedField identifier, which automatically refers to the field we are computing with the macro. You can see the result of this effort in Figure 28.14, which shows the final report displayed by the RsGrid example in the ReportSmith Run_Time window.

FIGURE 28.13

The ReportSmith macro
editor, where you can
write code in BASIC for a
Delphi application.

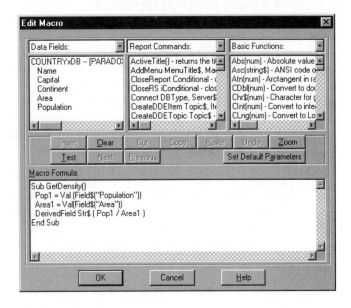

FIGURE 28.14

The preview of the
TABLE.RPT report shown
by the RsGrid example.

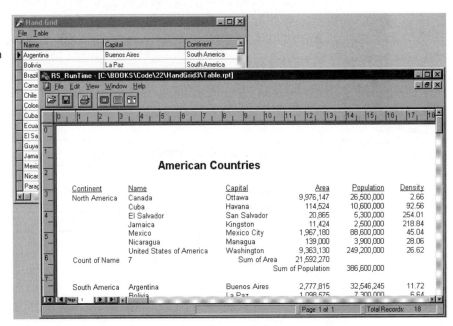

Quicker than ReportSmith

We have seen how much trouble it takes to write this custom report, using calculated fields in ReportSmith. As I mentioned, the problem is the loose integration ReportSmith has with Delphi. Are there better solutions than the one outlined in the RsGrid example? Actually, there are two. The first is to use Delphi to build a new database table containing the actual data you want to output. In this case we need to create a temporary database table with the population density field, and then we can copy the data to it before starting a report that uses the temporary table as data source.

Another solution is simply to forget about ReportSmith and use the Quick-Report components, or another native VCL reporting component. As we saw in the QrNav example, it is very simple to add totals to this type of report. We can also use the QuickReport component to group records and print the totals of each group, obtaining an output very similar to that of the last ReportSmith report, but with less work.

To make this test, I've taken the Calc example from Chapter 16 and turned it into the new QrCalc example. The new report is based on the reporting form shown in Figure 28.15. The report consists of four bands: a title band (rbTitle), a QRGroup component used as a header band, a plain band (rbDetail), and a group footer band (rbGroupFooter) connected with the QRGroup component. The group component is part of the report, and groups the items according to its Expression property, in this case set to Continent to group by that dataset field.

FIGURE 28.15

The QuickReport form of the QRCalc example at design-time.

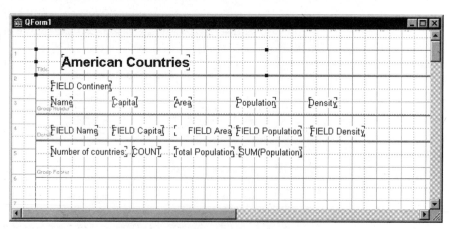

The different bands have various label components (QRLabel), database text components (QRDBText), and calculated components (QRExpr). The detail band has the values of the fields, with the continent name in the header band along with a few labels. The footer band displays the number of records of the group, plus the total population. You can see the details by opening the form of the example (available as usual on the companion CD), and looking at its textual description to see all of the relevant properties.

It is quite simple to build a similar QuickReport form, but connecting it to the COUNTRY.DB table won't work. The records in the table are sorted by name, so you'll end up with many groups made of just a few records, and with repeated groups for each continent. In fact, the QRGroup component simply starts a new group each time the value of the monitored field changes.

To solve this problem, I could have added a secondary index to the Paradox table. Instead, I decided to use a Query component to access the data, and sort the countries by continent inside the SQL query:

```
select * from country
  order by continent, name
```

After this change, I had to define the fields of the query, add the new calculated field (*Density*), and modify the OnCalcFields event handler to refer to Query fields instead of Table fields. You can find the details of this code on the companion CD: It is very similar to the code of the Calc3 example, although this time the program uses a Query component instead of a Table component.

What is the result of this effort? We can now use the QuickReport components to access the calculated field, just like any other field of the Query. Compared with the ReportSmith approach, this is much simpler (and *quicker*). In addition, the result is almost the same, as you can see in Figure 28.16.

Actually, I could have used a different (and probably better) solution. Since I'm using a SQL query to retrieve the data, I could have let the query add the calculated field, as in:

```
select country.*, (Population / Area) as Density
from country
order by continent, name
```

I left the code as it is, because one purpose of this example was to highlight the fact that you customize a ReportSmith report with BASIC code, and a

QuickReport report with Object Pascal. Besides this, SQL is quite limited when you need to compute something even slightly more complex, and you'll often need to add code in another language anyway.

FIGURE 28.16

The report with groups built using the Quick-Report component in the QrCalc example.

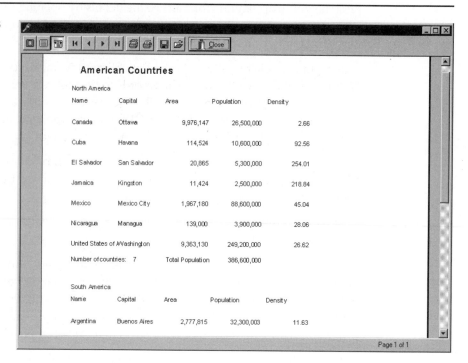

What's Next

In this chapter, we have explored Delphi's printing support. We have seen that it is easy to output the image of a form or to connect a text file with the printer and output data. The Canvas property of the Printer object can also be used to build all types of output, even complex ones. In Delphi, you work with a canvas to produce both advanced screen output and printer output. This means that you can share the code of these two operations, to produce a WYSIWYG ("What You See is What You Get") application, as we saw in the Shape6 example. When you work with database-related forms, you can produce printer output using three completely different approaches: You can drive the printer directly, use Delphi's QuickReport reporting components, or use the ReportSmith application included in Client/Server Delphi to build more complex reports. These three techniques offer increasing capabilities, but the simplest one to implement is probably to use QuickReport components.

Having discussed how to print from a program, we need to focus next on another important aspect of an application, saving data to files. In fact, both in database applications and in other Delphi programs, you'll often need to use files to save information for the next time the program is executed.

CHAPTER

TWENTY-NINE

Adding File Support
to Applications

- ■ Handling text files with Object Pascal

- ■ A text case conversion program

- ■ Delphi's file system components

- ■ Delphi's file stream support

- ■ Component persistency

Saving and loading data to files is vital for most of the programs you write. We have already seen several techniques for saving and loading data in Delphi, and also a number of examples that use the standard file open and save dialog boxes. Although we've covered several aspects of file support, Delphi provides many ways to interact with files.

We can broadly categorize Delphi file support in three areas:

- Object Pascal language file support—identified by the file keyword and by other data types and functions defined in the System unit.

- VCL file support—offered by the TStream and TComponent classes, by the TIniFile class, and by the file loading and storing methods present in several components.

- Database support—provided primarily for file-based formats, such as dBASE and Paradox tables.

In this chapter, we'll explore the first two approaches in detail. Database support was the topic of Chapters 16 and 17.

Files and the Pascal Language

One of the peculiarities of Pascal compared with other programming languages is its built-in support for files. As you might recall from Chapter 4, the language has a file keyword, which is a type specifier, like array or record. You use file to define a new type, and then you can use the new data type to declare new variables:

```
type
   IntFile: file of Integers;
var
   IntFile1: IntFile;
```

It is also possible to use the file keyword without indicating a data type, to specify an untyped file. Alternatively, you can use the TextFile type, defined in the System units to declare files of ASCII characters. Each kind of file has its own predefined routines, as we will see later in this chapter.

Once you have declared a file variable, you can assign it to a real file in the file system using the AssignFile method. The next step is usually to call Reset to open the file for reading at the beginning, Rewrite to open (or create) it for writing, and Append to add new items to the end of the file without removing the older items. Once the input or output operations are done, you should call CloseFile. This operation should typically be done inside a finally block, to avoid leaving the file open in case the file handling code generates an exception.

Delphi includes many other file management routines, as you can see in the list below:

Append	FileClose	Flush
AssignFile	FileCreate	GetDir
BlockRead	FileDateToDateTime	IOResult
BlockWrite	FileExists	MkDir
ChangeFileExt	FileGetAttr	Read
CloseFile	FileGetDate	Readln
DateTimeToFileDate	FileOpen	Rename
DeleteFile	FilePos	RenameFile
DiskFree	FileRead	Reset
DiskSize	FileSearch	Rewrite
Eof	FileSeek	RmDir
Eoln	FileSetAttr	Seek
Erase	FileSetDate	SeekEof
ExpandFileName	FileSize	SeekEoln
ExtractFileExt	FileWrite	SetTextBuf
ExtractFileName	FindClose	Truncate
ExtractFilePath	FindFirst	Write
FileAge	FindNext	Writeln

Not all of these routines are defined in standard Pascal, but many of them have been part of Borland Pascal for a long time. You can find detailed information about these routines in Delphi's Help files. Here, I'll show you three simple examples to demonstrate how these features can be used.

Handling Text Files

One of the most commonly used file formats is that of text files. As I mentioned before, Delphi has some specific support for text files, most notably the TextFile data type defined by the System unit. We used text files in the previous chapter to output text to the printer, by simply assigning the printer to the file variable using the AssignPrn procedure. In a similar way, we can output text to any file, simply assigning an actual file to a file variable.

For this reason, our first example is an extension of the PrintNav application presented in Chapter 28. The new version, named PrnNav2, has the same form with the addition of a PrintDialog component and a SaveDialog component. The Print to File check box of this dialog box determines whether to output the text to a file or to print it. To do this, simply set the value of the poPrintToFile flag of the Options property of the PrintDialog component to True.

In this new version of the example, clicking on the form's Print button opens the Print dialog box (with the Print to File check box, as you can see in Figure 29.1) instead of printing immediately. You can test whether Print to File is checked by looking at the value of the Print dialog box's PrintToFile property. In this case, instead of sending the text file to the printer, the program asks the user to choose a file (using the File Save dialog box) and then writes the text to that file.

The key operation is assigning the text file to the file variable:

```
AssignFile (PrintFile, SaveDialog1.FileName);
```

FIGURE 29.1

The Print dialog box opened by the PrnNav2 example. Notice the Print to File check box activated by setting the corresponding option of the PrintDialog component.

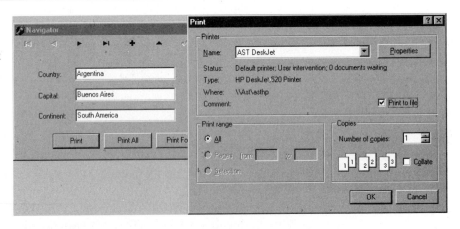

Now you can write to the file, after a call to the Rewrite procedure:

```
Rewrite (PrintFile);
Writeln (PrintFile, Label1.Caption, ' ', DbEdit1.Text);
Writeln (PrintFile, Label2.Caption, ' ', DbEdit2.Text);
CloseFile (PrintFile);
```

As I mentioned before, to make things safer, you can use a try block for the output operations and place the CloseFile call in a finally block, so that it is executed even if there is an input/output error. In addition, since the actual output code is duplicated for printing and file output, I've rearranged the code to write the output operations only once, as you can see in the full source code of the PrintButtonClick method:

```
procedure TNavigator.PrintButtonClick(Sender: TObject);
var
  OutputFile: TextFile;
begin
  {show the Print dialog box}
  if PrintDialog1.Execute then
  begin
    {if the Print to File check box is selected}
    if PrintDialog1.PrintToFile then
    begin
      {choose a file name}
      if SaveDialog1.Execute then
        {output the text to a file}
        AssignFile (OutputFile, SaveDialog1.FileName)
      else
        Exit;
    end
    else
    begin
      {output the text to the printer}
      AssignPrn (OutputFile);
      {set the printer font to the form font}
      Printer.Canvas.Font := Font;
    end;
    Rewrite (OutputFile);
    try
      {save to file or print}
      Writeln (OutputFile, Label1.Caption, ' ', DBEdit1.Text);
      Writeln (OutputFile, Label2.Caption, ' ', DBEdit2.Text);
      Writeln (OutputFile, Label3.Caption, ' ', DBEdit3.Text);
```

```
    finally
      CloseFile (OutputFile);
    end;
  end;
end;
```

The other button, Print All, has more complex output operations, so I've decided to follow a slightly different approach, writing a procedure that outputs the database table to a text file, which can either be connected to the printer or associated with a real file. Here is the core part of the output method, which is based on the usual while loop scanning each record, and enclosed in two further try-finally blocks (missing in the following listing) to disable and re-enable the controls connected with the table and to get and then reset the current position (using a bookmark):

```
procedure TNavigator.TableToFile (var TFile: TextFile);
begin
  ...
  Rewrite (TFile);
  try
    Table1.First;
    while not Table1.EOF do
    begin
      {output the two fields, and a blank line}
      Writeln (TFile, 'Country: ',
        Table1.FieldByName ('Name').AsString);
      Writeln (TFile, 'Capital: ',
        Table1.FieldByName ('Capital').AsString);
      Writeln (TFile, 'Continent: ',
        Table1.FieldByName ('Continent').AsString);
      Writeln (TFile);
      Table1.Next;
    end;
  finally
    CloseFile (TFile);
  end;
  ...
```

In the code of the PrintAllButtonClick method, if you've selected the Print to File check box, the program calls the TableToFile method, passing to it an actual file or one associated with the printer:

```
procedure TNavigator.PrintAllButtonClick(Sender: TObject);
var
```

```
      File1: TextFile;
begin
  if PrintDialog1.Execute then
    if PrintDialog1.PrintToFile then
    begin
      if SaveDialog1.Execute then
      begin
        {assign the output to a real file}
        AssignFile (File1, SaveDialog1.FileName);
        TableToFile (File1);
      end;
    end
    else
    begin
      {assign the printer to a file}
      AssignPrn (File1);
      {set the font of the form, and output the file}
      Printer.Canvas.Font := Font;
      TableToFile (File1);
    end;
end;
```

You can run this example, save a table to a text file, and then open the resulting file (even in the Delphi editor, as you can see in Figure 29.2).

FIGURE 29.2

The text file produced by the PrnNav2 example, if you choose to print all the records to a file.

A Text File Converter

In the first example of handling files, we produced a text file using the contents of a database table. In our next example, we'll process an existing file, creating a new one with a modified version of the contents. The program, named Filter, can convert all the characters in a text file to uppercase, capitalize only the initial word of each sentence, or ignore the characters from the upper portion of the ASCII character set.

The form of the program has two read-only edit boxes for the names of the input and output files, and two buttons to select input and output files using the standard dialog boxes. The form's lower portion contains a RadioGroup component and a bitmap button (named ConvertBitBtn) to apply the current conversion to the selected files. The radio group has three items, as you can see from the following portion of the form's textual description:

```
object RadioGroup1: TRadioGroup
  Caption = 'Conversion'
  Items.Strings = (
    '&Uppercase'
    'Capitalize &sentences'
    'Remove s&ymbols')
```

The user can click on the two buttons to choose the names of the input and output files, displayed in the two edit boxes:

```
procedure TForm1.Button1Click(Sender: TObject);
begin
  if OpenDialog1.Execute then
    Edit1.Text := OpenDialog1.Filename;
end;
```

The second button activates the SaveDialog1 dialog box. The real code of the example is in the three conversion routines that are called by the bitmap button's OnClick event-handler. These calls take place inside a case statement in the middle of the ConvertBitBtn button's OnClick handler:

```
case RadioGroup1.ItemIndex of
  0: ConvUpper;
  1: ConvCapitalize;
  2: ConvSymbols;
end;
```

Once again, you can see the entire source code on the companion CD. Before calling one of the conversion procedures, the `ConvertBitBtnClick` method displays a dialog box (ConvertForm) with a ProgressBar component, to show the user that the conversion is taking place (as you can see in Figure 29.3). This method does most of the work related to handling the files—it opens the input file as a `file of bytes` (a file storing data as plain bytes) the first time, so that it can use the `FileSize` procedure, which is not available for text files. Then this file is closed and reopened as a text file.

FIGURE 29.3

The conversion procedures update the secondary form's progress bar to let the user see the percentage of the file already processed.

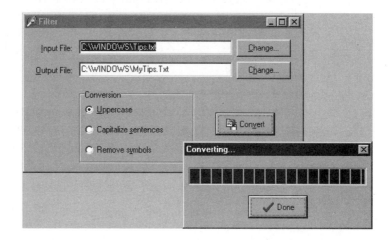

Since the program opens two files, and each of these operations can fail, it uses two nested `try` blocks to ensure a high level of protection, although using the standard dialog boxes to select file names already provides a good confirmation of file selection. Now, let's take a look at one of the conversion routines in detail. The simplest of the three conversion routines is `ConvUpper`, which converts every character in the text file to uppercase. Here is its code:

```
procedure TForm1.ConvUpper;
var
  Ch: Char;
  Position: LongInt;
begin
  Position := 0;
  while not Eof (FileIn) do
  begin
    Read (FileIn, Ch);
```

```
      Ch := UpCase (Ch);
      Write (FileOut, Ch);
      Inc (Position);
      ConvertForm.ProgressBar1.Position :=
        Position * 100 div FileLength;
      Application.ProcessMessages;
    end;
  end;
```

This method reads each character from the source file until the program reaches the end of the file (Eof). Each single character is converted and copied to the output file. As an alternative, it is possible to read and convert one line at a time (that is, a string at a time) using string handling routines. This will make the program significantly faster. The approach I've used here is reasonable only for an introductory example.

The conversion procedure's actual code, however, is complicated by the fact that it has to update the dialog box's progress bar. At each step of the conversion, a long integer variable with the current position in the file is incremented. This variable's value is used to compute the percentage of work completed, as you can see in the code above.

The conversion procedure for removing symbols is very simple:

```
while not Eof (FileIn) do
begin
  Read (FileIn, Ch);
  if Ch < Chr (127) then
    Write (FileOut, Choose);
  ...
```

The procedure used to capitalize the text, in contrast, is really a complex piece of code, which you can find on the companion CD. The conversion is based on a case statement with four branches:

- If the letter is uppercase, and it is the first letter after an ending punctuation mark (as indicated by the Period Boolean variable), it is left as is; otherwise, it is converted to lowercase. This conversion is not done by a standard procedure, simply because there isn't one for single characters. It's done with a low-level function I've written, called LowCase.

- If the letter is lowercase, it is converted to uppercase only if it was at the beginning of a new sentence.

- If the character is an ending punctuation mark (period, question mark, or exclamation mark), `Period` is set to True.

- If the character is anything else, it is simply copied to the destination file, and `Period` is set to False.

Figure 29.4 shows an example of this code's effect; it shows a text file before and after the conversion. This program is far from adequate for professional use, but it is a first step toward building a full-scale case conversion program. Its biggest drawbacks are that it frequently converts proper nouns to lowercase, and capitalizes any letter after a period (even if it's the first letter of a filename extension).

FIGURE 29.4

The result of running the Filter example's Capitalize conversion.

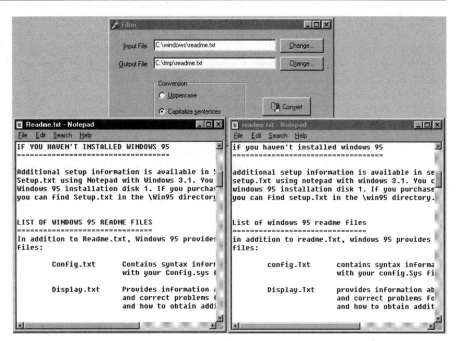

Saving Generic Data

In addition to using text files, you can save other data types to a file, including integers, real numbers, arrays, and records. (You cannot save objects directly. We will discuss Delphi's support for saving objects and components later in this chapter.) Using a custom file type instead of a text file may be an advantage because it might take less space (the textual representation of a number usually takes much more space than its binary value), but this approach won't let the user browse through the files using a text editor (which might be an advantage, too).

Examining the examples in previous chapters, I found one that might benefit from file support—one that is based on a file of integer values rather than on a text file. Our next example, Graph3, builds on the Graph application from Chapter 11. This program used the TeeChart component to display the collected data in a grid. Since the data is basically a series of numbers, it makes sense not to save it as text, although the grid actually stores the values of the items as a table of strings. The form of the example now has a menu with a File pull-down menu and a Help menu with the About command. The key elements are the three file-related commands: Open, Save, and Save As. The rest of the code has just a few changes from the older version.

How do you save a series of integers to a file? First you have to define a file as shown:

```
SaveFile: file of Integer;
```

Then you need to assign the real file to the file variable, open the file, operate on it inside a try block, and close it in a finally block. The program uses two local fields of the form, a string to hold the name of the current file (CurrentFile), and a Boolean value to track whether the data has changed (Modified). First I set the Modified flag to True in the methods that affect the data (pressing the Update button or changing the selected graph type in the combo box). This flag is used by the Save1Click method:

```
procedure TForm1.Save1Click(Sender: TObject);
var
  SaveFile: file of Integer;
  I, J, Value: Integer;
begin
  if Modified then
    if CurrentFile = '' then
      {call save as}
      SaveAs1Click (self)
    else
    begin
      {save to the current file}
      AssignFile (SaveFile, CurrentFile);
      Rewrite (SaveFile);
```

```
  try
    {write the value of each grid element}
    for I := 1 to 5 do
      for J := 1 to 4 do
      begin
        Value := StrToIntDef (Trim (
          StringGrid1.Cells [I, J]), 0);
        Write (SaveFile, Value);
      end;
    Value := Integer (ChBoxMarks.Checked);
    Write (SaveFile, Value);
    Modified := False;
  finally
    CloseFile (SaveFile);
  end;
  end;
end;
```

To save the data to a file, the program saves each value of the string grid (after converting it into a number), and then saves the status of the check box (after converting the Boolean Checked property to an integer value). To accomplish this, the program uses two nested for loops to scan the grid and then appends the code of the combo box selection at the end of the file. Notice the use of the temporary Value variable: the Write and Read procedures require a parameter passed by reference (var), so you cannot pass a property, since it doesn't correspond directly to a memory location.

Of course, the data should be read in the same order it is written, as you can see in the Open1Click method:

```
procedure TForm1.Open1Click(Sender: TObject);
var
  LoadFile: file of Integer;
  I, J, Value: Integer;
begin
  if OpenDialog1.Execute then
  begin
    CurrentFile := OpenDialog1.Filename;
    Caption := 'Graph 3 [' + CurrentFile + ']';
    {load from the current file}
    AssignFile (LoadFile, CurrentFile);
    Reset (LoadFile);
    try
```

```
{read the value of each grid element}
for I := 1 to 5 do
  for J := 1 to 4 do
  begin
    Read (LoadFile, Value);
    StringGrid1.Cells [I, J] := IntToStr(Value);
  end;
  Read (LoadFile, Value);
  ChBoxMarks.Checked := Boolean(Value);
finally
  CloseFile (LoadFile);
end;
ChBoxMarksClick (self);
UpdateButtonClick (self);
Modified := False;
  end;
end;
```

At the end of the above code, the program updates the combo box (to make the current selection effective) and copies the data to the grid (simulating a click on the Update button). The third method of the group is used to handle the File ➤ Save As menu command:

```
procedure TForm1.SaveAs1Click(Sender: TObject);
begin
  if SaveDialog1.Execute then
  begin
    CurrentFile := SaveDialog1.Filename;
    Caption := 'Graph 3 [' + CurrentFile + ']';
    {call save}
    Modified := True;
    Save1Click (self);
  end;
end;
```

As you can see, the Save1Click and SaveAs1Click methods call each other. Save1Click calls the other method to ask for a file name when the file has changed and no file name has been assigned to the CurrentFile variable. This string is also copied to the caption of the form each time it changes (both when you load a file and when you save the current one with a new name). SaveAs1Click, in turn, calls Save1Click to actually save the file once a new file name is provided.

To complete file handling, you must set the properties of the SaveDialog and OpenDialog components. They both have a special filter, *'Chart files (*.chr)'*, and some standard options. (The CHR file extension is my own invention, used only by this program; it is not related to the TeeChart component.) You can see one of the two standard dialog boxes used by the Graph3 program in Figure 29.5.

FIGURE 29.5

Saving a file with a new name in the Graph3 example.

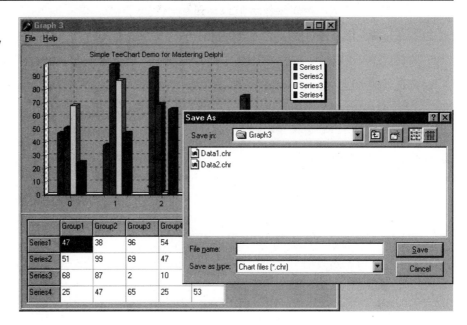

The last portion of the code I want to show you is the check done when the user tries to close the program:

```pascal
procedure TForm1.FormCloseQuery(Sender: TObject;
  var CanClose: Boolean);
var
  Code: Word;
begin
  if Modified then
  begin
    Code := MessageDlg (
      'Data has changed, do you want to save it?',
      mtConfirmation, mbYesNoCancel, 0);
    if Code = idYes then
```

```
          Save1Click (self);
        if Code = idCancel then
          CanClose := False
        else
          CanClose := True;
      end
      else
        CanClose := True;
    end;
```

Depending on the user input, the form closes or stays open, and the user can save the file before exiting.

File Support in Delphi Components

Besides the standard Pascal language file support, Delphi includes a number of other options for manipulating files. Several components have methods to save or load their contents from a file such as a text or a bitmap file, and there are other specific classes to handle files. Many component classes have the SaveToFile and LoadFromFile methods. In this book, we have used these methods for TBitmap, TPicture, and TStrings classes (used in TMemo, TListBox, and many other component classes). They are also available for some data-aware components (TBlobField, TMemoField, and TGraphicField), for other graphic formats (TGraphic, TIcon, and TMetaFile), for OLE (Object Linking and Embedding) containers, and for outlines.

Similar methods are available in the TMediaPlayer class. These methods are named Open and Save, and they have a slightly different syntax and meaning than their LoadFromFile and SaveToFile counterparts. Another file-related class we've already used (in Chapter 25) is TIniFile. This class is a file wrapper specifically intended for Windows initialization files, or for any custom file using the same format. The new topics we will cover here are file system components, streaming components, and the components that implement object persistency.

File System Components

The Delphi file system components are located in the System page of the Components palette: TDirectoryListBox, TDriveComboBox, TFileListBox, and

TFilterComboBox. We have used these components in the TabOnly2 example in Chapter 14. These components are well-known to many Delphi programmers. However, what isn't well known is that the same FileCtrl unit that defines these components also contains three interesting routines:

- DirectoryExists, which is used to check whether a directory exists.
- ForceDirectories, which can create several directories at once.
- SelectDirectory, which shows a predefined Delphi dialog box.

Our next example demonstrates the use of these little-known routines. The example, named Dirs, has a simple form with an edit box and three buttons, as you can see in Figure 29.6. The first two buttons are disabled at design-time, and they are automatically enabled only when there is some text in the edit box:

```
procedure TForm1.Edit1Change(Sender: TObject);
begin
  if Edit1.Text <> '' then
  begin
    TestButton.Enabled := True;
    CreateButton.Enabled := True;
  end
  else
  begin
    TestButton.Enabled := False;
    CreateButton.Enabled := False;
  end;
end;
```

FIGURE 29.6

The output of the Dirs example when the current directory exists.

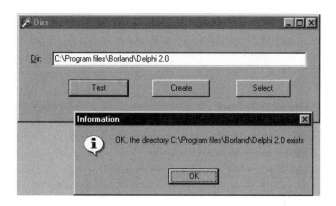

The method associated with the first button tests the existence of the current directory and produces a corresponding message (shown in Figure 29.6):

```
procedure TForm1.TestButtonClick(Sender: TObject);
begin
  if DirectoryExists (Edit1.Text) then
    MessageDlg ('OK, the directory ' +
      Edit1.Text + ' exists', mtInformation, [mbOk], 0)
  else
    MessageDlg ('Sorry, the directory ' + Edit1.Text +
      ' doesn''t exist', mtError, [mbOk], 0);
end;
```

The method associated with the second button asks the user to confirm the operation, and then creates the directory (or at least it tries to; the specified path might be invalid):

```
procedure TForm1.CreateButtonClick(Sender: TObject);
begin
  if MessageDlg ('Are you sure you want to create the ' +
      Edit1.Text + ' directory', mtConfirmation,
      [mbYes, mbNo], 0) = mrYes then
    ForceDirectories (Edit1.Text);
end;
```

The last button's OnClick event handler, which is always enabled, simply displays Delphi's Select Directory dialog box, as you can see in Figure 29.7. The three flags passed to the SelectDirectory function let the dialog box create a new directory, prompting the user for confirmation:

```
procedure TForm1.SelectButtonClick(Sender: TObject);
var
  Text: String;
begin
  Text := Edit1.Text;
  if SelectDirectory (Text, [sdAllowCreate,
      sdPerformCreate, sdPrompt], 0) then
    Edit1.Text := Text;
end;
```

FIGURE 29.7

The Select Directory dialog box is a little-known Delphi system dialog box.

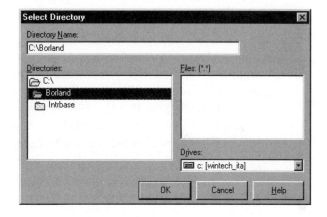

Streaming Data

Another interesting topic is Delphi's support for file streams. The VCL defines the abstract TStream class and three subclasses: TFileStream, THandleStream, and TMemoryStream. The parent class, TStream, has just a few properties, but it also has an interesting list of methods you can use to save or load data.

The various methods are described in Delphi's Help file, but it's not easy to find them. To help you locate the information, you can search the method names in Delphi Help file one by one. The following list of class methods will help you locate the information:

```
function Read (var Buffer; Count: LongInt): LongInt;
function Write (const Buffer; Count: LongInt): LongInt;
function Seek (Offset: LongInt; Origin: Word): LongInt;
procedure ReadBuffer (var Buffer; Count: LongInt);
procedure WriteBuffer (const Buffer; Count: LongInt);
function CopyFrom (Source: TStream; Count: LongInt):
  LongInt;
function ReadComponent (Instance: TComponent): TComponent;
function ReadComponentRes (Instance: TComponent):
  TComponent;
procedure WriteComponent (Instance: TComponent);
procedure WriteComponentRes (const ResName: string;
  Instance: TComponent);
procedure ReadResHeader;
```

Most of these functions relate to components and are used only by component writers, but some of them, such as `ReadBuffer` and `WriteBuffer`, can easily be used by anyone.

Creating a `TStream` instance makes no sense, because this class provides no support to save data. Instead, you can use the two file-based streams to load data from or store it to an actual file. `THandleStream` is used when you already have the Windows handle for a file. Use `TFileStream` when you have just a file name. Both classes have special Create methods used to pass file information. The third stream class is `TMemoryStream`, which manipulates memory locations and not an actual file. However, this class has special methods to copy its contents to or from another stream, which can be a file stream. Creating and using a file stream is as simple as creating a variable of a type that descends from `TStream`:

```
var
  S: TFileStream;
begin
  if OpenDialog1.Execute then
  begin
    S := TFileStream.Create (OpenDialog1.FileName,
      fmOpenRead);
    try
      {use the stream S ...}
    finally
      S.Free;
    end;
  end;
end;
```

As you can see in this code, the `Create` method for file streams has two parameters: the name of the file and a flag indicating the requested operation. In this case, the operation is reading the file (`fmOpenRead`). Streams can actually be used instead of traditional files, although they might be less intuitive to use at first. A big advantage of streams, for example, is that you can work with memory streams and then save them to a file, or you can perform the reverse operation. This might be a way to improve the speed of a file-intensive program. Here is a snippet of code, a file-copying function, to give you an idea of how you can use streams (notice that this code should be protected with two nested `try-finally` blocks):

```
procedure CopyFile (SourceName, TargetName: String);
var
  Stream1, Stream2: TFileStream;
```

```
begin
  Stream1 := TFileStream.Create (SourceName, fmOpenRead);
  Stream2 := TFileStream.Create (TargetName,
    fmOpenWrite or fmCreate);
  Stream2.CopyFrom (Stream1, Stream1.Size);
  T.Free;
  S.Free;
end;
```

Another important use of streams (both file streams and memory streams) is to handle database BLOB fields or other large fields directly. In fact, you can export such data to a stream or read it from one by simply calling the corresponding method.

Streaming Numbers

To show you an example of the use of streams, I've updated the Graph3 example, to use streams instead of plain files. The effect of the two programs is exactly the same. This example, Graph4, uses a very simple approach: create TFileStream objects to save and load the data, and then use the Write and Read methods of the stream class. Both of these methods require as parameters some data (a data buffer) and the size of the data. Since we are working with integers we can simply use the expression sizeof(Integer).

Here is the new version of the code of the Save1Click method, based on a file stream:

```
procedure TForm1.Save1Click(Sender: TObject);
var
  SaveStream: TFileStream;
  I, J, Value: Integer;
begin
  if Modified then
    if CurrentFile = '' then
      {call save as}
      SaveAs1Click (self)
    else
    begin
      {save to the current file}
      SaveStream := TFileStream.Create (
        CurrentFile, fmOpenWrite or fmCreate);
```

```
    try
      {write the value of each grid element}
      for I := 1 to 5 do
        for J := 1 to 4 do
        begin
          Value := StrToIntDef (Trim (
            StringGrid1.Cells [I, J]), 0);
          SaveStream.Write (Value, sizeof (Integer));
        end;
      Value := Integer (ChBoxMarks.Checked);
      SaveStream.Write (Value, sizeof (Integer));
      Modified := False;
    finally
      SaveStream.Free;
    end;
  end;
end;
```

You can compare this method with the corresponding one of the Chart2 example, shown earlier in this chapter. Similarly, Open1Click has been updated to use a stream to read the file:

```
procedure TForm1.Open1Click(Sender: TObject);
var
  LoadStream: TFileStream;
  I, J, Value: Integer;
begin
  if OpenDialog1.Execute then
  begin
    CurrentFile := OpenDialog1.Filename;
    Caption := 'Chart [' + CurrentFile + ']';
    {load from the current file}
    LoadStream := TFileStream.Create (
      CurrentFile, fmOpenRead);
    try
      {read the value of each grid element}
      for I := 1 to 5 do
        for J := 1 to 4 do
        begin
          LoadStream.Read (Value, sizeof (Integer));
          StringGrid1.Cells [I, J] := IntToStr(Value);
        end;
```

```
      LoadStream.Read (Value, sizeof (Integer));
      ChBoxMarks.Checked := Boolean(Value);
    finally
      LoadStream.Free;
    end;
    ChBoxMarksClick (self);
    UpdateButtonClick (self);
    Modified := False;
  end;
end;
```

Streaming Components

A particularly interesting characteristic of streams is their ability to stream components. All the VCL component classes are subclasses of TPersistent (a special class used to save objects to streams) and they have methods for saving and loading all of the properties and public fields. For this reason, all TComponent descendant classes can actually save themselves to a stream, or they can be created automatically when loaded from a stream. A program can use the WriteComponent and ReadComponent methods of a stream to accomplish this, as we'll see in the next example, CRef2.

> **NOTE** For a more detailed discussion of streaming, see *Delphi Developer's Handbook*, which includes an extension of the CRef2 example presented in this section.

As its name suggests, this example is the second version of an older program, ClassRef from Chapter 6. With the original example, a user could create several components of three different types inside a form. With the new version, a user can also save these components to a file or load them from an existing file.

The form of the CRef2 example is quite simple. It has only a panel with three radio buttons. As in the older version, the example uses class references to determine the kind of component to create each time a user clicks in the form's client area. This portion of the code is similar to the original version. What's new is the code of the method related to the menu commands: New, Open, SaveAs, Exit, and About.

The New1Click method deletes all of the existing components, except for the panel used as the toolbar. To accomplish this, it scans the form's Controls array in reverse order (downto). In fact, each time a new component is removed, the Controls property changes. Using the reverse order, the changes are limited to the controls that have an order above the loop counter value (I), so they have no influence on the following operations. Notice that this method resets the component's Counter value, too:

```
procedure TForm1.New1Click(Sender: TObject);
var
  I: Integer;
begin
  {delete all existing components, except the panel}
  for I := ControlCount - 1 downto 0 do
    if Controls.ClassName <> 'TPanel' then
      Controls.Free;
  Counter := 0;
end;
```

The SaveAs1Click method uses a standard loop to save each of the components to a stream, as described earlier. Again, the code skips the TPanel component. The program uses a try-finally block to close the stream even if an error occurs:

```
procedure TForm1.SaveAs1Click(Sender: TObject);
var
  S: TFileStream;
  I: Integer;
begin
  if SaveDialog1.Execute then
  begin
    {open or create the stream file}
    S := TFileStream.Create (SaveDialog1.FileName,
      fmOpenWrite or fmCreate);
    try
      {save each component except the panel}
      for I := 0 to ControlCount - 1 do
        if Controls[I].ClassName <> 'TPanel' then
          S.WriteComponent (Controls[I]);
    finally
      S.Free;
    end;
  end;
end;
```

In Figure 29.8, you can see the Save As dialog box displayed by this program's SaveAs1Click method. The Open1Click method is not much different. This time, the program loops until it reaches the end of the stream. In the loop, it calls the ReadComponent method, passing a nil parameter to indicate that it needs to create a new component. Instead of creating a new component, you can assign the value read from the stream to an existing component (which must be of the same type):

```
procedure TForm1.Open1Click(Sender: TObject);
var
  S: TFileStream;
  New: TComponent;
begin
  if OpenDialog1.Execute then
  begin
    {remove existing controls}
    New1Click (self);
    {open the stream}
    S := TFileStream.Create (OpenDialog1.FileName,
      fmOpenRead);
    try
      while S.Position < S.Size do
      begin
        {read a component and add it to the form}
        New := S.ReadComponent (nil);
        InsertControl (New as TControl);
        Inc (Counter);
      end;
    finally
      S.Free;
    end;
  end;
end;
```

Each time a new component is loaded, it is added to the form list of controls, using the InsertControl method (which requires a parameter of TControl type, of course). Then, the counter is increased to avoid creating duplicate names later on when you add new components to the form.

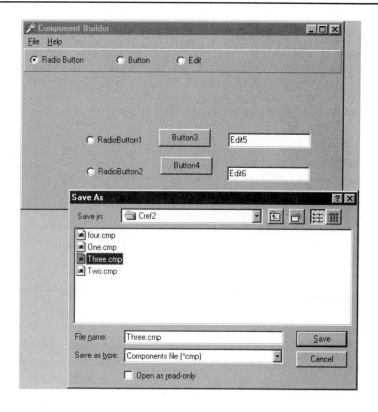

To make the stream reading operations possible, I've added a call to the Register-Classes system procedure to the initialization section of the unit, which creates a list of class names and class references used by the stream reader. This means that the program can read only files with the component types registered in this function. If you want to extend the program with new components, you can add the corresponding classes to this list:

```
initialization
  RegisterClasses ([TRadioButton, TEdit, TButton]);
end.
```

Once you have saved a single component's data, there is little you can do with it. A better alternative might be to save the entire form using the standard Delphi DFM format. In other words, we want to save the whole form with its components in a Windows resource file, the standard format used by Delphi. In fact, DFM files are just RES files that contain custom resources.

The code we use to accomplish this is actually much simpler than what we have seen. You can simply call the WriteComponentResFile procedure, which requires a filename parameter (not a stream) and the name of the form you want to save. This is the sample code from the File ➤ Save Form File command of the CRef2 example (which uses a second SaveDialog component):

```
procedure TForm1.SaveAs2Click(Sender: TObject);
begin
  if SaveDialog2.Execute then
    WriteComponentResFile (SaveDialog2.Filename, self);
end;
```

Once you have saved a form using this method, you can open it in a Delphi editor as a DFM file. Of course you'll find all of the components, including the panel and the menu, but you'll be unable to use this file unless you create the header of a corresponding Pascal source code file.

What's Next

Manipulating files is a key function of most applications, and you'll find plenty of file support available in Delphi. Several components have specific methods to save their contents (usually text or bitmaps) to a file, and there are several specific classes related to files, such as the stream classes and the TIniFile class.

In addition, you can always use traditional Pascal file support, which is a key feature of the language. However, an important concept in Delphi is that each component class is persistent—it can save itself to a stream or a file. This leads to a number of interesting options for writing Delphi add-on tools (something that is beyond the scope of this book).

Typically, files are used to save data for a later use, but they are also a means of data exchange between different applications, provided that they can read and write the same file format. However, there are several other features you can use to exchange data between programs in Windows, including the Clipboard and DDE. These two features are the subject of the next chapters, while another powerful technique, OLE automation, was discussed in Chapter 22.

Exchanging Data

- Working with the Windows Clipboard

- Adding Clipboard support to your programs

- An overview of DDE

- Adding DDE support to your programs

- Simple client/server applications

- An automatic server and graphical DDE client

Windows users frequently run several applications at a time. Each application typically has its own window, and each window seems to be isolated from the other application windows. However, from a technical point of view, this is far from true. As a result, users can benefit from various forms of data exchange between applications available in Windows.

The three main Windows features that implement data exchange are the Clipboard, DDE (Dynamic Data Exchange), and OLE (Object Linking and Embedding). These three features have many differences, for both the user and the programmer. We looked at OLE Documents in Chapter 22; the focus of this chapter is on the use of the Clipboard and DDE. As you'll see, these data-exchange techniques frequently work cooperatively, and it is not always easy to draw a clear line to separate them.

What Is the Clipboard?

Basically, the Windows Clipboard is a storage area for a unit of information. This information can be a portion of text, a bitmap, some data in a proprietary format, an OLE object, and so on. Since there is a specific format for any given data type, each time an application copies data to the Clipboard, it also must specify a Clipboard format. This can be one of the standard formats or a new Clipboard format defined by the application. Actually, the situation is even more complex. The unit of information in the Clipboard can be available in several different formats at the same time, since an application can copy data in custom formats *and* in standard formats. The application accessing this data can use the custom formats if it knows how to handle them. If not, it can take the copy in the standard formats, usually losing some of the information.

As an example, consider the case of passing data from your favorite word processor to the Windows Notepad. The word processor copies the data with font and text format information, but Notepad cannot access that information; it can only retrieve the basic text, which the word processor copied to the Clipboard as a second version of the data in plain text format.

To see the contents of the Clipboard, you can use the Clipboard Viewer application, which shows the data in one of the standard formats and also lists all of the currently available formats, as you can see in Figure 30.1. If you are new to Clipboard programming, the Clipboard Viewer can help you understand how the Clipboard works.

FIGURE 30.1

The Windows 95 Clipboard Viewer, with a list of formats available for the current Clipboard contents. In this case I've captured and saved to the Clipboard a bitmap image of the screen containing the Clipboard Viewer itself, with a Delphi component inside.

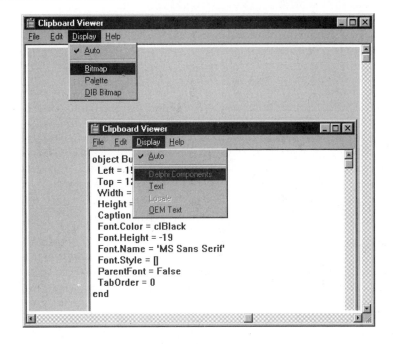

The Clipboard offers *user-driven data exchange*. The user must copy (or cut) data to the Clipboard from the source application, switch to the destination program (if that's different from the source), and paste the data there. The user has control over the entire operation. A drawback to this approach is that if the original data changes, the user needs to repeat the whole process again to keep the copy updated. DDE and OLE were developed to overcome this limitation. In two completely different ways, these techniques can connect data directly to the source application.

Another key element is that the Clipboard supports a single-copy/multiple-paste operation. This means that when you copy new data to the Clipboard, the previous contents are lost, but the paste operation is nondestructive—after you have pasted some data to an application, it is still available in the Clipboard for another paste operation.

As you know, the Clipboard-related commands are located in the Edit menu of an application. These commands are named Cut, Copy, and Paste, and have the shortcut keys Ctrl+X, Ctrl+C, and Ctrl+V, respectively. The same Edit menu often contains other Clipboard-related commands, such as Paste Link and Paste Special, which are actually DDE and OLE commands, as we will see later in the chapter.

The Clipboard in Delphi

In Delphi, Clipboard support comes in two forms:

- Some components have specific Clipboard-related methods. For example, TMemo, TEdit, and TDBImage, among other components, have the CopyTo-Clipboard, CutToClipboard, and PasteFromClipboard methods.

- There is a global Clipboard object of the TClipboard class, which has a number of specific Clipboard features. For full Clipboard support, the use of the Clipboard object, defined in the Clipboard unit, is required.

A program can use the Clipboard object to see if a certain format is available (using the HasFormat method), to list all the available formats, and to place data in the Clipboard (when this function isn't handled directly by other components). The Clipboard object can also be used to open the Clipboard and copy data in different formats. This is the only case in which you need to open and close the Clipboard in Delphi—something that is also required when using the Windows API directly.

Copying and Pasting Text

Our first example using the Clipboard is a new version of the PrnNotes program from Chapter 28, called ClipNote. We don't need to do much to add Clipboard support to this program. Simply enable the Cut, Copy, and Paste commands, set their shortcut keys properly, and write the following three simple methods:

```
procedure TNotesForm.Copy1Click(Sender: TObject);
begin
  Memo1.CopyToClipboard;
end;


procedure TNotesForm.Cut1Click(Sender: TObject);
begin
  Memo1.CutToClipboard;
end;


procedure TNotesForm.Paste1Click(Sender: TObject);
begin
  Memo1.PasteFromClipboard;
end;
```

Now you can run the program and work with the Clipboard. Notice that the first two commands, Cut and Copy, operate on the text selected inside the Memo component. Paste can either replace the current selection (if any) or add the text at the current insertion point. The program works, but these three commands don't always perform their intended tasks. For example, when there is no selection, there is nothing to copy or cut; and when the Clipboard doesn't hold data in text format, there is nothing you can paste. The solution is to enable only the menu items that are appropriate, by testing the current selection and the current contents of the Clipboard.

But where do we write this code? We can't insert the test in the event-handlers of the menu items, because that is too late in the program execution. It can't be when responding to a user action in the Memo component, because we won't know if another application has changed the contents of the Clipboard. The correct location for the test is in the OnClick event of the Edit pull-down menu itself. When we add the Edit1Click method to the form, the program behaves as it should:

```
procedure TNotesForm.Edit1Click(Sender: TObject);
begin
  {if some text is selected in the memo,
  enable the cut and copy commands}
  if Memo1.SelLength > 0 then
  begin
    Copy1.Enabled := True;
    Cut1.Enabled := True;
  end
  else
  begin
    Copy1.Enabled := False;
    Cut1.Enabled := False;
  end;
  {if the Clipboard contains some text,
  enable the Paste command}
  if Clipboard.HasFormat (CF_TEXT) then
    Paste1.Enabled := True
  else
    Paste1.Enabled := False;
end;
```

To compile this program, remember to add a uses statement referring to the Clipbrd unit. You can test the effect of this code by running the program. Figure 30.2 shows an example of the program when no text is selected but the Clipboard has data in text format.

FIGURE 30.2

The ClipNote program, when no text is selected but the Clipboard had text format data.

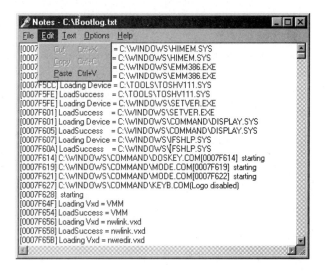

In the listing above you can see a first example of the use of the global **Clipboard** object. The Delphi Help file documents five different formats for the `HasFormat` method: `CF_TEXT`, `CF_PICTURE`, `CF_BITMAP`, `CF_OBJECT`, and `CF_METAFILE`.

These are the formats typically used by Delphi and by VCL components. The Windows API, however, defines many more formats, including the following:

CF_BITMAP	CF_DSPMETAFILEPICT
CF_OWNERDISPLAY	CF_SYLK
CF_DIB	CF_DSPTEXT
CF_PALETTE	CF_TEXT
CF_DIF	CF_METAFILEPICT
CF_PENDATA	CF_TIFF
CF_DSPBITMAP	CF_OEMTEXT
CF_RIFF	CF_WAVE

You can use these Windows formats without any particular problems, although there isn't specific support in Delphi to retrieve these types of data. In this example, we have used two methods of the TMemo class to perform the Clipboard operations, but we could have accomplished the same effect with some of the text-related features of the TClipboard class. For instance, we could have used the **AsText** property (used to copy or paste strings), and the SetTextBuf and GetTextBuf methods (used to handle PChar strings). The TClipboard class has specific support only for text. When you want to work with other elements, you need to use the Assign method or work with handles.

Copying and Pasting Bitmaps

The most common technique for copying or pasting a bitmap in Delphi is to use the Assign method of the TClipboard and TBitmap classes. As a slightly more advanced example of the use of the Clipboard, I've made a new version of the PrintBmp example from Chapter 22, called ClipBmp.

The new example can show bitmaps from a selected file or from the Clipboard, if available, and print them (with the Preview dialog box). The structure of the form is always the same, with a TabControl component covering the whole form and an Image component inside it. The menu, however, is slightly more complex, because it now has the commands from the Edit pull-down menu.

When you select the Edit ➤ Paste command of the ClipBmp example, a new tab named Clipboard is added to the tab set (unless it is already present), as you can see in Figure 30.3. Then the number of the new tab is used to change the active tab:

```
procedure TForm1.Paste1Click(Sender: TObject);
var
  TabNum: Integer;
begin
  {try to locate the page}
  TabNum := TabControl1.Tabs.IndexOf ('Clipboard');
  if TabNum < 0 then
    {create a new page for the Clipboard}
    TabNum := TabControl1.Tabs.Add ('Clipboard');
  {go to the Clipboard page and force repaint}
  TabControl1.TabIndex := TabNum;
  TabControl1Change (self);
end;
```

At the end of the Paste1Click method, the program calls TabControl1Change, the event-handler associated with the selection of a new tab, which can load the bitmap from the current file or paste it from the Clipboard:

```
procedure TForm1.TabControl1Change(Sender: TObject);
var
  TabText: string;
```

```
begin
  Image1.Visible := True;
  TabText := TabControl1.Tabs [TabControl1.TabIndex];
  if TabText <> 'Clipboard' then
    {load the file indicated in the tab}
    Image1.Picture.LoadFromFile (TabText)
  else if Clipboard.HasFormat (cf_Bitmap) then
  begin
    {if the tab is 'Clipboard' and a bitmap
    is available in the Clipboard}
    if Image1.Picture.Graphic = nil then
      Image1.Picture.Graphic := TBitmap.Create;
    Image1.Picture.Graphic.Assign (Clipboard);
  end
  else
  begin
    {else remove the Clipboard tab}
    TabControl1.Tabs.Delete (TabControl1.TabIndex);
    if TabControl1.Tabs.Count = 0 then
      Image1.Visible := False;
  end;
end;
```

FIGURE 30.3

The Clipboard page of the ClipBmp example tab set shows the current contents of the Clipboard if it is a bitmap. Notice that I've again placed an image within the image, as in Figure 30.1.

Notice that if the `Picture` property of the Image component is still not initialized, you must create the bitmap before calling the `Assign` method. If you forget to create the new bitmap and no graphic is associated with the picture, the `Assign` operation will fail (raising an exception). This is because the `Assign` method isn't a constructor; it is a method of an object; and if the object has not been created, you'll get a GPF error when you try to call one of its methods.

> **NOTE**
>
> The `Assign` **method doesn't make a copy of the actual bitmap. Its effect is to let two** `TBitmap` **objects refer to the same bitmap memory image and the same bitmap handle.**

Notice that this program pastes the bitmap from the Clipboard each time you change the tab. The program, in fact, stores only one image at a time, and has no way to store the Clipboard bitmap. However, as soon as the Clipboard content changes, if the bitmap format is no longer available, the Clipboard tab is automatically deleted (as you can see in the listing above). If no more tabs are left, the Image component is hidden.

An image can also be removed using either of two menu commands: Cut and Delete. Cut removes the tab after making a copy of the bitmap to the Clipboard. In practice, the `Cut1Click` method does nothing besides calling the `Copy1Click` and `Delete1Click` methods. Delete simply removes the current tab.

```
procedure TForm1.Delete1Click(Sender: TObject);
begin
  with TabControl1 do
  begin
    if TabIndex >= 0 then
      Tabs.Delete (TabIndex);
    if Tabs.Count = 0 then
      Image1.Visible := False;
  end;
end;
```

The `Copy1Click` method is responsible for copying the current image to the Clipboard:

```
procedure TForm1.Copy1Click(Sender: TObject);
begin
  Clipboard.Assign (Image1.Picture.Graphic);
end;
```

The rest of the code has to do with opening new files and adding them to the tabs as in the previous versions of the program, and enabling and disabling menu items in the File1Click and Edit1Click methods:

```
procedure TForm1.File1Click(Sender: TObject);
begin
  Print1.Enabled := TabControl1.Tabs.Count > 0;
end;

procedure TForm1.Edit1Click(Sender: TObject);
begin
  Paste1.Enabled := Clipboard.HasFormat (cf_Bitmap);
  if TabControl1.Tabs.Count > 0 then
  begin
    Cut1.Enabled := True;
    Copy1.Enabled := True;
    Delete1.Enabled := True;
  end
  else
  begin
    Cut1.Enabled := False;
    Copy1.Enabled := False;
    Delete1.Enabled := False;
  end;
end;
```

Copying Delphi Components to the Clipboard

Along with using text and bitmaps, you can copy any other kind of data to the Clipboard, including custom data. In fact, Delphi does this when it copies components. Actually, when Delphi copies a component to the Clipboard, it copies both the custom definition (binary code) and the textual description, which can be read with any text editor, as we saw in Chapter 2. The specific commands to copy or paste components to the Clipboard are the GetComponent and SetComponent methods of the TClipboard class. At first I thought these methods could be useful for programmers writing Delphi add-on tools, but they are really not very helpful, as we will see later.

We can use these methods to extend the CRef2 example presented in the last chapter (the new example is CRefF3). The form of the example remains the same, with the addition of a new pull-down menu containing the Copy and Paste commands. When a user issues the Copy command, the program displays a list of available controls to choose from, as shown in Figure 30.4.

FIGURE 30.4

The Paste command of the CRef3 example opens a dialog box with a list of available components.

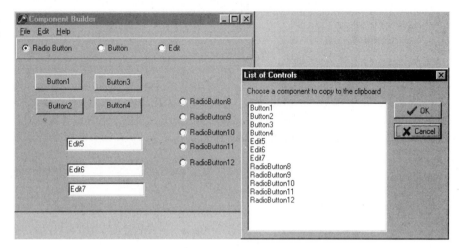

The dialog box includes a default list box, a label, and two standard bitmap buttons inside a new form, named ListForm. All of the code to manipulate this form is in the Copy1Click method of the main form:

```
procedure TForm1.Copy1Click(Sender: TObject);
var
  I, Index: Integer;
begin
  {fill the list of the dialog box}
  ListForm.Listbox1.Clear;
  for I := 0 to ControlCount - 1 do
    if Controls[I].ClassName <> 'TPanel' then
      ListForm.Listbox1.Items.Add (Controls[I].Name);
  if ListForm.ShowModal = mrOk then
  begin
    Index := ListForm.Listbox1.ItemIndex + 1;
    {copy the component and change its name}
    Clipboard.SetComponent (Controls[Index]);
    Controls[Index].Name := Controls[Index].Name + 'C';
    Controls[Index].Width := Controls[Index].Width + 10;
  end;
end;
```

The ItemIndex property of the list box—which identifies the position of the selected element—is used as a counter of the Controls array. The trick here is to add 1 to the ItemIndex to allow for the presence of the panel, which is always the first control of the array.

Notice that once the component is copied, its name is changed (by appending a C) to avoid any problem in case the copy is pasted back to the same form, as shown in Figure 30.5. This happens each time; therefore, if you copy the same component several times, many Cs are added to the name. An alternative would be to set the Name property to an empty string and give a meaningful value to the Caption property, but I preferred to adjust the names in both methods to try to give each component a unique identifier.

The Paste1Click method simply pastes the current component on the Clipboard, changing its position, name, and width (to accommodate the longer name):

```
procedure TForm1.Paste1Click(Sender: TObject);
var
  New: TComponent;
begin
  {retrieve the component, moving it slightly}
  New := Clipboard.GetComponent (self, self);
  if New is TControl then
    with TControl (New) do
    begin
      Left := Left + 50;
      Top := Top + 50;
      Inc (Counter);
      Name := Name + 'P' + IntToStr (Counter);
      Width := Width + 10;
    end;
end;
```

FIGURE 30.5

When you copy a component with the CRef3 example, the name of the original object is changed. Pasted objects are indicated with a P.

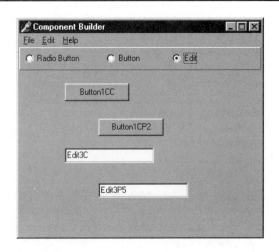

The most complex piece of code is in the `Edit1Click` method, which enables or disables the Copy and Paste commands. To determine whether to enable the Copy menu item, we check to see if the form contains any components other than the panel. To do so, we test whether `ControlCount` is greater than 1. To determine whether to enable the Paste menu item, we need to verify that there is a component in the Clipboard. By using the Clipboard Viewer, you can see the name of the Clipboard format defined by Delphi, and then write the code accordingly. To check whether a component format is on the Clipboard, we can call the `RegisterClipboardFormat` function of the Windows API, passing the name of the format as a parameter. The return value is a system-wide format code. This means that if two applications use the same format name, they end up with the same format code:

```
procedure TForm1.Edit1Click(Sender: TObject);
var
  Format: Cardinal;
begin
  Format := RegisterClipboardFormat ('Delphi Component');
  Paste1.Enabled := Clipboard.HasFormat (Format);
  Copy1.Enabled := ControlCount > 1;
end;
```

The CRef3 program can be improved in a number of ways. For example, if you paste the same component twice, the older object is covered. However, the major problem is that the format used by this `Clipboard` method is not the same format used internally by Delphi's form editor. Besides the fact that it also copies the textual description of the component, the Delphi form editor uses a different format, *Delphi Components*. Unfortunately, this format is not compatible with the *Delphi Component* (without the *s*) format used by the `SetComponent` method of the `TClipboard` class. Therefore, this program is probably not a good example of how to develop add-on tools for Delphi.

Copying Custom Data to the Clipboard

Our next example adds Clipboard support to a program with a generic, custom data type. To accomplish this, we can use the `SetAsHandle` and `GetAsHandle` methods of the `TClipboard` class, which in turn call the `SetClipboardData` and `GetClipboardData` functions of the Windows API. These methods manipulate a handle for a Windows global memory block, allocated via the `GlobalAlloc` function. (For advanced uses of the Clipboard, we need to learn how to handle Windows memory blocks, something that will be useful for DDE, too.)

The goal of this example is to prepare a memory block with the information in a custom format. To accomplish this, we need to call some Windows API functions to allocate some memory (this is the easy part) and then fill the memory block with the data. The most common approach for this is to use a pointer to set or retrieve values from the memory area.

This example is a new version of the Graph3 example from Chapter 29. This version, named ClipGrph, has a new Edit menu, with Copy and Paste commands and the usual three functions connected to Copy, Paste, and the selection of the Edit pull-down menu itself. Apart from these changes, the form of the application is exactly the same as in the previous version. The most interesting part of the program is probably the Copy1Click method.

As mentioned, you can allocate a memory block in Windows using the Global-Alloc function, which requires two parameters: a flag indicating the type of memory, and the size of the block. The return value is a handle to the memory block, which can be passed to the GlobalLock API function to return a pointer to the first location of the memory block:

```
HMem := GlobalAlloc (ghnd, 25 * Sizeof (Integer));
PInt := GlobalLock (HMem);
```

Note that in Delphi you skip these two steps and simply create an object. However, in this case, we actually need to bypass Delphi memory management, because we need a standard memory block for the Clipboard. When we pass this block to the Clipboard, it becomes the owner of the block, and we have no more rights to it. Once we have a valid PInt pointer, we can iterate the memory block and fill it with values. This is generally done using pointers to integers; that is, treating the block of memory as if it is an array of integers. In our case, we end up calling these two statements over and over (inside a loop):

```
PInt^ := Value;
Inc (PInt);
```

The first statement stores a value in the memory location referred to by the pointer, and the second moves the pointer to the next memory slot. When the memory block is ready, we can simply call the SetAsHandle method of the Clipboard object, as shown by the full code of the method:

```
procedure TForm1.Copy1Click(Sender: TObject);
var
  ClipForm, HMem: Cardinal;
  Text: String;
```

```
    PInt: ^Integer;
    I, J, Value: Integer;
begin
    {register a custom Clipboard format}
    ClipForm := RegisterClipboardFormat ('Chart_Data');
    {allocate a memory block and retrieve a pointer to it}
    HMem := GlobalAlloc (ghnd, 25 * Sizeof (Integer));
    PInt := GlobalLock (HMem);
    Text := '';
    {build the data, in both versions}
    for I := 1 to 5 do
      for J := 1 to 4 do
      begin
        {add the number for each cell of the grid}
        Value := StrToIntDef (
          Trim(StringGrid1.Cells [I, J]), 0);
        PInt^ := Value;
        Inc (PInt);
        AppendStr (Text,
          StringGrid1.Cells [I, J] + ';');
      end;
    {add the status of the check box}
    Value := Integer (ChBoxMarks.Checked);
    PInt^ := Value;
    AppendStr (Text, 'Marks:' + IntToStr (Value));
    {open the Clipboard to copy multiple versions of the data}
    Clipboard.Open;
    try
      Clipboard.SetAsHandle (ClipForm, HMem);
      Clipboard.AsText := Text;
    finally
      Clipboard.Close;
    end
end;
```

The code above has another feature. The program copies the current information to the Clipboard in two different formats: a custom format and a textual format (a string). To copy two formats of the data to the Clipboard, you need to hold control of it for the time required for all operations, by using the Open and Close methods of the TClipboard class. Otherwise, the second data format you copy to the Clipboard will delete the previous one. Instead, using these methods, you can copy several versions of the data, as you can see in Figure 30.6 in the Clipboard Viewer window.

Notice also that I've declared a custom Clipboard format, *'Chart_Data'*. I need this custom format also in the `Edit1Click` method, to check whether the proper type of information is available in the Clipboard:

```
procedure TForm1.Edit1Click(Sender: TObject);
var
  ClipForm: Cardinal;
begin
  {if the proper format is available, enable Paste}
  ClipForm := RegisterClipboardFormat ('Chart_Data');
  Paste1.Enabled := Clipboard.HasFormat (ClipForm);
end;
```

FIGURE 30.6

The ClipGrph data can be pasted to a text editor, because the program copies data to the Clipboard using two different formats.

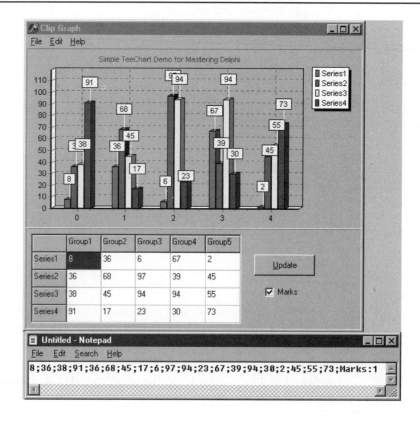

The program could be improved to accept text data input (from the Clipboard), too. However, scanning the string to see if the data is in a valid format and extracting the proper information is somewhat too complex for this example. For this reason, only a *'Chart_Data'* memory block can be pasted back, as you can see in the code of the `Paste1Click` method:

```
procedure TForm1.Paste1Click(Sender: TObject);
var
  HMem, ClipForm: Cardinal;
  PInt: ^Integer;
  I, J, Value: Integer;
begin
  {get the memory block from the Clipboard}
  ClipForm := RegisterClipboardFormat ('Chart_Data');
  HMem := Clipboard.GetAsHandle (ClipForm);
  PInt := GlobalLock (HMem);
  {read each number}
  for I := 1 to 5 do
    for J := 1 to 4 do
    begin
      Value := PInt^;
      StringGrid1.Cells [I, J] := IntToStr(Value);
      Inc (PInt);
    end;
  {read the graph type}
  Value := PInt^;
  ChBoxMarks.Checked := Boolean(Value);
  {update everything}
  ChBoxMarksClick (self);
  UpdateButtonClick (self);
end;
```

The Paste command handler performs basically the reverse operation of the Copy command handler. It iterates through the memory block, again using an integer pointer, and retrieves the data. More specifically, the program retrieves the handle to the memory block from the Clipboard, then uses the `GlobalLock` function to access it. Note that you should not attempt to store the memory handle the Clipboard passes to your program. You need to read it immediately (as I've done in this example), or make a copy in a new memory block. In fact, the next time you copy some information to the Clipboard, it will release the memory block.

Dynamic Data Exchange (DDE): A Technical Overview

As stated at the beginning of this chapter, the Clipboard is basically user-driven. If you want to allow an application to move data to another application automatically, without a specific action by the user, the standard approach is to use Windows Dynamic Data Exchange (DDE). DDE allows two applications to establish a connection and use this connection to pass data. There are various actions DDE can perform, such as sending data on request or continuously updating a changing data item.

The first version of DDE was primarily used as an add-on to MS Excel spreadsheets. It was a message-based protocol, which means that applications sent special Windows messages to each other to exchange information. The protocol was basically a set of message rules you could use to communicate with applications written by other programmers.

Over time, DDE has become an integral part of Windows. A second version, named DDEML (DDE Management Library), was added to Windows 3.1. DDEML has a sort of repository storing information about the current DDE activities. Instead of communicating directly with another application, DDEML works as an intermediary between the two connected programs, solving problems that arise. This makes DDE far more reliable.

DDE Conversations

DDE is used to let two applications conduct a *conversation*. One application acts as the server, and the second as the client. The server is basically the information provider; the client is the application that controls the process. A DDE compatible application can act as a server to multiple clients, as a client for multiple servers, or as a client and a server at the same time. You can see a graphical example of some DDE conversations in Figure 30.7.

Roles of the Server and Client

What roles do the server and client play? What can happen when a DDE conversation is active between two applications? The role of the server is essentially to send data to the client upon request. The role of the client is to start the conversation, request the data from the server, send unsolicited data to the server (*poke*), or ask the server to execute commands (*execute*). (DDE execute commands were popular in the past; nowadays applications use OLE Automation instead.)

FIGURE 30.7

Examples of DDE
conversations.

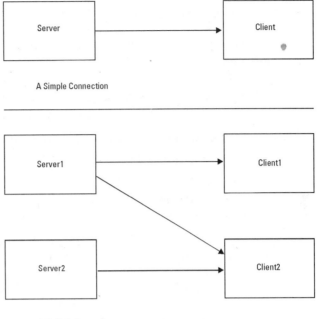

A Simple Connection

A Multiple Connection

The central task is certainly sending data. Once a conversation is active, the client can ask for data from the server (*request*) or start an *advise loop*. Starting an advise loop means that the client can ask the server for notification of any change to a certain piece of data. The server will forward either a notification or a new copy of the data each time it changes. To determine which server you can connect to and the subject of the data exchange, DDE uses three elements:

- *Service* is basically the name of the DDE server application. It can be the name of the executable (without the extension), but it can also be a different name determined by the server itself.

- *Topic* is the global theme of a conversation. It can be a data file, a window of the server, or anything else. A DDE conversation is established between a client and a server about a certain topic.

- *Item* is an identifier of a specific data element. It can be a field of a database, a cell of a spreadsheet, or a stock in an exchange market. Within a single conversation and topic, a client and a server can exchange data about multiple items.

DDE in Delphi

With this general introduction, we can return to Delphi and explore its DDE support. The System page of the Components palette contains four DDE-related components:

- DdeServerConv handles a description of the conversation (including the name of the topic) from the server side, supporting execute operations.

- DdeClientConv handles a conversation from the client side, specifies the current server and topic, and is required to start a conversation.

- DdeServerItem refers to a data item within a conversation for the server. This is the data that is usually sent to the client, or received from it in the case of a poke operation. The name of this component specifies the DDE item.

- DdeClientItem refers to data received from the server (or sent to it with the poke operation). It refers to the DDE item of the server, and relates to a conversation.

A Simple Example of DDE

To build a DDE server and client, you can simply place some of these components in two different forms of two different applications, and write a few lines of code. Of course, the aim of DDE is to let different applications communicate with each other. However, since I don't know which DDE-enabled programs you have on your computer, several of our examples here will include both the server and client applications. I'll also show you examples of the use of different clients and servers.

Our first program for this example is probably the simplest possible server, which will soon be connected to the simplest possible client. Then the application will evolve into a more complex one.

Building a Simple Server

The form of the first server (FirstSer) example has an edit box and a DdeServerItem component. This form doesn't include a DdeServerConv component, since this is required only to provide a custom name and to handle *execute* commands. In the absence of a DdeServerConv component, the service name will be the name of the application, without the .EXE extension, and the topic name will be the title of the form containing the DdeServerItem.

The code of this program is extremely simple. It copies the contents of the edit box to the DdeServerItem's Text property each time the Edit component changes:

```
procedure TForm1.Edit1Change(Sender: TObject);
begin
  DdeServerItem1.Text := Edit1.Text;
end;
```

You can run this server application, but it will be far more interesting after we build the client application.

Building a Simple Client

The first client application, FirstCli, is just slightly more complex than the first server program. The form of this example has both a DdeClientConv and a Dde-ClientItem component, plus an edit box. The DdeClientItem1 component is connected to the conversation component (DdeClientConv1), using the DdeConv property, but there is no design-time connection from DdeClientConv1 to the server. The connection is initialized when the form is created:

```
procedure TForm1.FormCreate(Sender: TObject);
begin
  if DdeClientConv1.SetLink ('firstser', 'First Server') then
  begin
    ShowMessage ('Connected');
    DdeClientItem1.DdeItem := 'DdeServerItem1';
  end
  else
    ShowMessage ('Error');
end;
```

The program calls the SetLink method, passing as parameters the service (the name of the server) and the topic (the title of the form). If the connection is successful, besides showing a message, the application connects the DdeItem property of the client item to the server item. When the connection is set and the link is active, the server application starts sending data to the client each time the data on the server changes. The client application can simply copy the data it receives to its own edit box:

```
procedure TForm1.DdeClientItem1Change(Sender: TObject);
begin
  Edit1.Text := DdeClientItem1.Text;
end;
```

When the connection and the link are established (when both the client and server programs are running), everything the user types in the server edit box is automatically copied to the client edit box. Figure 30.8 shows an example of a server edit box change and the corresponding change in the client edit box. (Of course, you should run both of these programs yourself to fully appreciate their capabilities.)

Notice that the DDE link is between the DdeServerItem component of the server application and the DdeClientItem component of the client application. Each time the Text property of the server item changes, this change is automatically reflected in the Text property of the client item. However, since we have established a link between the text of the two Text properties of the DDE items and the corresponding properties of the two Edit components, in effect, we have connected the two edit boxes via DDE.

FIGURE 30.8

When the connection and the link are established, everything you type in the server edit box is copied to the client edit box.

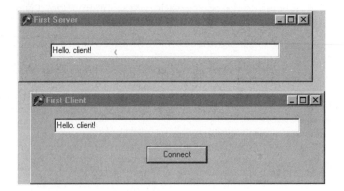

> **NOTE**
>
> What we have built in these DDE applications in Delphi is a DDE advise loop (also known as a *hot link*) using the DDEML library. Writing the same code in C takes a while, because DDEML is not exactly the simplest Windows API. Delphi's support for advise loops makes this program even simpler than a DDE conversation based on a request by the client, which is based on the RequestData method of the DdeClient-Conv component.

Design-Time DDE Connections

In this DDE example, we made the connection at run-time. However, in Delphi it is also possible to make DDE connections at design-time. To test this, run the server application, open the client project, select the DdeClientConv1 component, and open the property editor of the DdeService or DdeTopic property. In the dialog box that follows, enter the required information, as shown in the example in Figure 30.9.

FIGURE 30.9

The property editor of the DdeService and DdeTopic properties of the DdeClientConv component.

Now you can select the client item, select the proper conversation, and enter the name of the DdeItem property, and the connection is established. Make a change in the server, and you'll see the new text in the Object Inspector, as in Figure 30.10.

FIGURE 30.10

If the server is running (see the lower-right corner) when you set the connection and the link, the Text property of the client item is automatically updated with the server text.

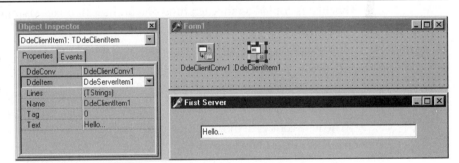

If you set the connection and the link at design-time, you can actually remove the Connect button and its code. Simply running the client program sets up the DDE connection, and the application will work immediately (as long as the server is running). In general, I prefer the run-time connection approach, which doesn't require the user to start the two applications in a fixed order.

Copying and Pasting DDE Links

Our next step will be to add the DDE version of Copy and Paste support to the DDE program, by changing it a bit and enabling its interaction with other third-party applications.

Copying Link Data to the Clipboard

As when we started, the first step in building a new version of the DDE example is to build a server. The form of the new paste server program (PasteSer) has three edit boxes, three DdeServerItem components, and three buttons. This version also uses a DdeServerConv component. The code of this program is still quite simple, although a bit more repetitive. When the form is first created at run-time, the text of the edit boxes is copied to the corresponding server items:

```
procedure TForm1.FormCreate(Sender: TObject);
begin
  DdeServerItem1.Text := Edit1.Text;
  DdeServerItem2.Text := Edit2.Text;
  DdeServerItem3.Text := Edit3.Text;
end;
```

This text is copied again each time one of the edit boxes changes. Here is one of the three methods:

```
procedure TForm1.Edit2Change(Sender: TObject);
begin
  DdeServerItem2.Text := Edit2.Text;
end;
```

The new code is in the OnClick handlers of the three buttons. When the user clicks on a button, the text in the edit box and the link are both copied to the Clipboard:

```
procedure TForm1.CopyButton1Click(Sender: TObject);
begin
  Clipboard.Open;
  try
    Clipboard.AsText := DdeServerItem1.Text;
    DdeServerItem1.CopyToClipboard;
```

```
finally
   Clipboard.Close;
  end
end;
```

The copy operation of the server copies information about the link. This information is not the actual data, the text. If you only copy the link, many third-party applications won't recognize this data, because you don't specify anything about its format. For this reason, both copies are needed.

With this code, you can copy the text of one of the edit boxes from this program and paste it into almost any DDE client. For example, in Microsoft Word for Windows, you can either Paste or Paste Link this data. Simply run the PasteSer program, copy one of the messages, open a Word document, and choose Edit ➤ Paste Special. In the Paste Special dialog box, select the Paste Link radio button and click on OK to establish a connection.

Now the text is inserted into your Word document, but when you move to the server and change the text, it will change in the Word document as well. This should not surprise you, since this is equivalent to our previous example. You should be able to obtain the same effect with many other Windows applications, using menu commands named similarly to Paste Special or Paste Link.

DDE with Timers and Graphics

Most of the DDE examples in Delphi use text as a data-exchange element. This is because Delphi has specific support for text items. It is possible to use Delphi DDE support and call some functions of the DDEML API, to overcome this limit. However, it is generally easier to convert data to and from text and then use DDE support than to try to use undocumented Delphi features and direct API calls.

To test Delphi's DDE capabilities beyond handling text items, I've built an example that involves graphics, although the data exchange passes a string. This example differs from the previous ones in two ways. First, the server data is automatically updated, using a timer. Second, the client shows a graphical version of the data.

The Automatic Server

The server, named DataServ, has a simple form with a read-only Memo component, a timer, a Copy button, and a DdeServerItem component. When the form is created, it starts the random number, calling the Randomize function. Each time the timer interval elapses, the values of the five lines of the memo are changed by adding a random value between –10 and 10 (adding or subtracting a number from 1 to 10). At the end of the handler, the text of the memo is copied to the DdeServerItem:

```
procedure TForm1.Timer1Timer(Sender: TObject);
var
  I, Value: Integer;
begin
  for I := 0 to 4 do
  begin
    Value := StrToIntDef (Memo1.Lines , 50);
    Value := Value + Random (21) - 10;
    Memo1.Lines  := IntToStr (Value);
  end;
  DdeServerItem1.Lines := Memo1.Lines;
end;
```

The other method we'll write is a copy-to-Clipboard operation you should already be familiar with. Besides copying the data, we also copy the DDE link:

```
procedure TForm1.CopyButtonClick(Sender: TObject);
begin
  Clipboard.Open;
  try
    Clipboard.AsText := Memo1.Text;
    DdeServerItem1.CopyToClipboard;
  finally
    Clipboard.Close;
  end;
end;
```

When we copy from this server and paste-link the result in any application, the data will change automatically, without any user assistance.

A Graphical DDE Client

Showing the numbers that change automatically in a third-party application is certainly interesting, but this is just text. The client application that works with this server will show the data graphically. The form of the ViewData client contains just the two typical DDE client conversations and DDE client item components, without any special property set.

Since the form is so bare, you might expect the code to be complex, and it really is. When the form is created, the DDE connection is established:

```
procedure TForm1.FormCreate(Sender: TObject);
begin
  if DdeClientConv1.SetLink ('dataserv',
      'Data DDE Server') then
    DdeClientItem1.DdeItem := 'DdeServerItem1'
  else
    ShowMessage ('Start the server before the client');
end;
```

Instead of simply showing a message, you might try to actually run the server, using the WinExec API. However, this can get complicated if the server doesn't reside in the same directory or in one of the directories of the system path.

Each time the DDE item data changes, the new values are extracted from the string and copied to an array of integers, defined as a private data member of the TForm1 class:

```
Values: array [0..4] of Integer;
```

At first, I thought that the lines of the server item were copied to the lines of the client item, so that this code simply needed to extract and convert each string. But the program ended up with a single string containing all of the numbers. After some trial-and-error, I found the solution. The FormatChars property of the DdeClientConv component should be set to True, to prevent it from skipping the newline characters. When you have set this property, simply write the following code:

```
procedure TForm1.DdeClientItem1Change(Sender: TObject);
var
  I: Integer;
begin
  {extract the numbers}
  for I := 0 to 4 do
    if I < DdeClientItem1.Lines.Count then
  Values  := StrToIntDef (DdeClientItem1.Lines, 50);
  Invalidate;
end;
```

The if statement might seem redundant, but it is not. This method is called at startup, when the values are still not there. Now for the core code. The last line of the OnChange event handler of the DdeClientItem component, above, calls Invalidate to repaint the form.

The FormPaint method is quite complex. If you want to study it, you can find it on the companion CD.

You can see the result of this painting code in Figure 30.11, where two copies of the program are running to show that the image is automatically scaled to the form size. The bars of the ViewData example change automatically over the time, without any user assistance, both on the client program and on the server application.

FIGURE 30.11

Two examples of the output of the ViewData program.

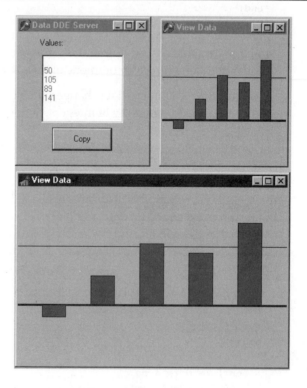

What's Next

In this chapter, we have seen how you can add Clipboard and DDE support to existing or new Delphi programs, and we have seen the similarities and differences between the two features. The use of the Clipboard is very common in Windows applications, and those you write should be no exception. Fortunately, adding Clipboard support is generally quite simple (even when you write Windows programs using the API). In contrast, DDE support can be a significant enhancement to your program. Letting a user copy and paste links, and not only data, between two programs you have written is certainly interesting. Even better, with DDE links, users of your programs can exchange data with other popular Windows applications. Implementing DDE in Delphi is simple, particularly if you compare it with the code behind the scenes. The only drawback is that Delphi's DDE support is not very well documented, and not all of the DDE features are easily accessible. Delphi's support, however, is good enough for most programs.

Now, it is time to move to the final topic of the book, multimedia programming in Delphi. Although it won't be an in-depth discussion of the topic, the next chapter will help you understand how to add some sound and video capabilities to your applications, as a last final touch.

CHAPTER
THIRTY-ONE

31

Multimedia Fun

- Windows default sounds

- From a beep to music

- The Media Player component

- Playing sounds and running videos

- Applications for audio CD drives

Since we've already discussed the printer and the file system (Chapters 28 and 29), I want to focus on other devices that might be attached to your PC, such as a sound card or a CD-ROM drive. (Of course, besides being physically connected to your computer, these devices must be properly installed in Windows for your Delphi applications to access them.)

Windows provides a specific API, known as the *Multimedia API*, to handle external devices such as video, MIDI, and CD drives. Delphi includes a corresponding Help file along with an easy-to-use component, the Media Player, to manipulate most multimedia devices. Before discussing this component, which is the main topic of the chapter, we'll look at some simpler ways to produce sound in Windows, beyond the simple beeps we have used previously.

Windows Default Sounds

In the book's earlier examples, every time we wanted to notify the user of an error or a specific event, we called a Delphi system procedure (Beep) or a Windows API function (MessageBeep). The Beep procedure is defined in the Delphi run-time library as follows:

```
procedure Beep;
begin
  MessageBeep(0);
end;
```

It simply passes the value 0 to the MessageBeep API function. Besides the values 0 and -1, both used to produce a beep with the internal speaker of the computer, the MessageBeep function can also accept other values, and play the corresponding sounds with your sound board. Here are the acceptable constants and the corresponding Windows sounds they produce (these are the sound names available in Control Panel):

mb_IconAsterisk	SystemAsterisk sound
mb_IconExclamation	SystemExclamation sound
mb_IconHand	SystemHand sound
mb_IconQuestion	SystemQuestion sound
mb_Ok	SystemDefault sound

You can change the association between system events and sound files using the Control Panel (see Figure 31.1), which lists the sounds under the names shown in the right column above. These associations are stored in the Windows System Registry.

Notice that these constants are also the possible values of the MessageBox API function, encapsulated in the MessageBox method of the TApplication class. It is common to produce the corresponding sound when the message box is displayed. This feature is not directly available in the Delphi MessageDlg function (which displays a message box with a corresponding icon), but we can extend it easily by building a SoundMessageDlg function, as demonstrated by the following example.

Every Box Has a Beep

To show you the capabilities of the MessageBeep API function, I've prepared a simple example, Beeps. The form of this example has a RadioGroup with some radio buttons from which the user can choose one of the five valid constants of the MessageBeep function. Here is the definition of the RadioGroup, from the textual description of the form:

```
object RadioGroup1: TRadioGroup
  Caption = 'Parameters'
  ItemIndex = 0
  Items.Strings = (
    'mb_IconAsterisk'
    'mb_IconExclamation'
    'mb_IconHand'
    'mb_IconQuestion'
    'mb_Ok')
end
```

The program plays the sound corresponding to the current selection when the user clicks on the Beep Sound button (one of the push buttons of the form). This button's OnClick event-handler first determines which radio button was selected, using a case statement, and then plays the corresponding sound:

```
procedure TForm1.BeepButtonClick(Sender: TObject);
var
  BeepConstant: Cardinal;
begin
  case RadioGroup1.ItemIndex of
    0: BeepConstant := mb_IconAsterisk;
    1: BeepConstant := mb_IconExclamation;
    2: BeepConstant := mb_IconHand;
    3: BeepConstant := mb_IconQuestion;
    4: BeepConstant := mb_Ok;
  else
    BeepConstant := 0;
  end;
  MessageBeep (BeepConstant);
end;
```

The else clause of the case statement is provided mainly to prevent an annoying (but not dangerous) compiler warning. To compare the selected sound with the default beep sound, click on the second button of the column (labeled *Beep –1*), which has the following code:

```
procedure TForm1.BeepOneButtonClick(Sender: TObject);
begin
  MessageBeep (Cardinal (-1));
end;
```

You can also pass the corresponding $FFFFFFFF hexadecimal value to the MessageBeep function. There is actually no difference between the two approaches. To test whether a sound driver is installed in your system (with or without a sound card, since it is possible to have a sound driver for the PC speaker), click on the first button (labeled *Test*), which uses a multimedia function, WaveOutGetNumDevs, to perform the test:

```
procedure TForm1.TestButtonClick(Sender: TObject);
begin
  if WaveOutGetNumDevs > 0 then
    SoundMessageDlg ('Sound is supported',
      mtInformation, [mbOk], 0)
  else
    SoundMessageDlg ('Sound is NOT supported',
      mtError, [mbOk], 0);
end;
```

To compile this function, you need to add the MmSystem unit to the uses clause. If your computer has no sound driver installed, you will hear only standard beeps, regardless of which sound is selected. The last two buttons have a similar aim: they both display a message box and play the corresponding sound (see Figure 31.2).

FIGURE 31.2

The output of the MessageBox call, accompanied by sound (above), and the output of the SoundMessageDlg function, which plays a system sound and shows a Delphi message box (below).

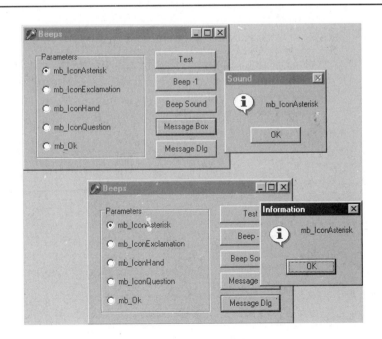

The OnClick event handler of the Message Box button uses the traditional Windows approach. It calls the MessageBeep function and then the MessageBox method of the Application object soon afterward. The effect is that the sound is 1played when the message box is displayed. In fact (depending on the sound driver), playing a sound doesn't usually stop other Windows operations. Here is the code related to this fourth button:

```
procedure TForm1.BoxButtonClick(Sender: TObject);
var
  BeepConstant: Cardinal;
begin
  case RadioGroup1.ItemIndex of
    0: BeepConstant := mb_IconAsterisk;
    1: BeepConstant := mb_IconExclamation;
    2: BeepConstant := mb_IconHand;
    3: BeepConstant := mb_IconQuestion;
  else {including 4:}
    BeepConstant := mb_Ok;
  end;
  MessageBeep (BeepConstant);
  Application.MessageBox (
    PChar (RadioGroup1.Items [RadioGroup1.ItemIndex]),
    'Sound', BeepConstant);
end;
```

If you click on the last button, the program calls the SoundMessageDlg function, which is not an internal Delphi function. It's one I've added to the program, but you can use it in your applications. The only suggestion I have is to choose a shorter name if you want to use it frequently. SoundMessageDlg plays a sound, specified by its AType parameter, and then displays the Delphi standard message box (see again Figure 31.2):

```
function SoundMessageDlg (const Msg: string;
  AType: TMsgDlgType; AButtons: TMsgDlgButtons;
  HelpCtx: Longint): Integer;
var
  BeepConstant: Cardinal;
  begin
  case AType of
    mtWarning: BeepConstant := mb_IconExclamation;
```

```
    mtError: BeepConstant := mb_IconHand;
    mtInformation: BeepConstant := mb_IconAsterisk;
    mtConfirmation: BeepConstant := mb_IconQuestion;
  else
    BeepConstant := mb_Ok;
  end;
  MessageBeep(BeepConstant);
  Result := MessageDlg (Msg, AType,
    AButtons, HelpCtx);
end;

procedure TForm1.MessDlgButtonClick(Sender: TObject);
var
  DlgType: TMsgDlgType;
begin
  case RadioGroup1.ItemIndex of
    0: DlgType := mtInformation;
    1: DlgType := mtWarning;
    2: DlgType := mtError;
    3: DlgType := mtConfirmation;
  else {including 4:}
    DlgType := mtCustom;
  end;
  SoundMessageDlg (
    RadioGroup1.Items [RadioGroup1.ItemIndex],
    DlgType, [mbOK], 0);
end;
```

SoundMessageDlg is a simple function, but your programs can really benefit from its use.

From Beeps to Music

When you use the MessageBeep function, your choice of sounds is limited to the default system sounds. Another Windows API function, PlaySound, can be used to play a system sound, as well as any other waveform file (WAV). Again, I've built a simple example to show you this approach. The example is named ExtBeep (for Extended Beep) and has the simple form shown in Figure 31.3.

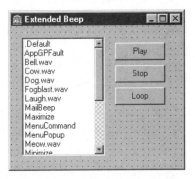

The form's list box shows the names of some system sounds and some WAV files, available in the current directory (that is, the directory containing ExtBeep.exe itself). When the user clicks on the Play button, the PlaySound function (defined in the MmSystem unit) is called:

```
procedure TForm1.PlayButtonClick(Sender: TObject);
begin
  PlaySound (PChar (Listbox1.Items [ListBox1.ItemIndex]),
    0, snd_Async);
end;
```

The first parameter is the name of the sound—either a system sound, a WAV file, or a specific sound resource (see the Win32 API Help file for details). The second parameter specifies where to look for a resource sound, and the third contains a series of flags, in this case indicating that the function should return immediately and let the sound play asynchronously. (An alternative value for this parameter is snd_Sync. If you use this value, the function won't return until the sound has finished playing.) With asynchronous play, you can interrupt a long sound by calling the PlaySound function again, using nil for the first parameter:

```
procedure TForm1.StopButtonClick(Sender: TObject);
begin
  PlaySound (nil, 0, 0);
end;
```

This is the code executed by the ExtBeep example when the user clicks on the Stop button. This button is particularly useful for stopping the repeated execution of the sound started by the Loop button, which calls PlaySound passing as its last parameter (snd_Async or snd_Loop).

The only other method of the example, FormCreate, selects the first item of the list box at startup, by setting its ItemIndex property to 0. This avoids run-time errors if the user clicks on the button before selecting an item from the list box. You can test this example by running it, and by adding the names of the other WAV files or system sounds (as listed in the registration database). I suggest you also test other values for the third parameter of the function (see the API help files for details).

Adding Default Sounds to Delphi Applications

If you run a Delphi application, you may notice that minimizing and restoring its main form don't produce the Windows default sounds connected with these events (you can establish this connection by using the Sounds editor of the Control Panel). Maximizing and restoring a form, however, do work properly.

NOTE Delphi applications don't produce the default sounds because of the presence of the hidden application window and the internal use of complex nonstandard code to handle multiple forms.

Adding the proper sounds to a program is fairly simple, and it requires only a few changes. Youy need to handle the two corresponding events of the Application object, OnMinimize and OnRestore, and use the PlaySound API function with the proper parameters. You can see an example of the required code in the AppSound application. Its main form includes two custom methods:

```
type
  TForm1 = class(TForm)
    Label1: TLabel;
    procedure FormCreate(Sender: TObject);
  public
    procedure AppMini (Sender: TObject);
    procedure AppRestore (Sender: TObject);
  end;
```

The two methods are connected with the corresponding events of the application object inside the FormCreate event handler. Here is the code of the three methods:

```
procedure TForm1.FormCreate(Sender: TObject);
begin
```

```
  Application.OnMinimize := AppMini;
  Application.OnRestore := AppRestore;
end;
procedure TForm1.AppMini (Sender: TObject);
begin
  PlaySound ('Minimize', 0, snd_Async);
end;
procedure TForm1.AppRestore (Sender: TObject);
begin
  PlaySound ('RestoreUp', 0, snd_Async);
end;
```

Paste this code into any of your programs, and it will comply with the default Windows sounds that users expect.

By browsing through the other API functions related to multimedia in the Windows API Help file, you can learn many other techniques for playing sounds and controlling external media devices.

The Media Player Component

Now let's move back to Delphi and use the Media Player component. The Delphi TMediaPlayer class encapsulates most of the capabilities of the Windows Media Control Interface (MCI), a high-level interface for controlling internal and external media devices.

Perhaps the most important property of the TMediaPlayer component is Device-Type. Its value can be dtAutoSelect, indicating that the type of the device depends on the file extension of the current file (the FileName property). As an alternative, you can select a specific device type, such as dtAVIVideo, dtCDAudio, dtWaveAudio, and many others.

Once the device type (and eventually the file) have been selected, you can open the corresponding device (or set AutoOpen to True), and the buttons of the Media Player component will be enabled. The component has a number of buttons, not all of which are appropriate for each media type. There are actually three properties referring to the buttons: VisibleButtons, EnabledButtons, and ColoredButtons. The first determines which of the buttons are present in the control, the second determines which buttons are enabled, and the third determines which buttons have colored marks. By using the first two of these properties, you can permanently or temporarily hide or disable some of the buttons.

The component has several events. The OnClick event is unusual because it contains one parameter indicating which button was pressed and a second parameter you can use to disable the button's default action. The OnNotify event later tells the component whether the action generated by the button was successful. Another event, OnPostClick, is sent either when the action starts or when it ends, depending on the value of the Wait property. This property determines whether the operation on the device should be synchronous.

Playing Sound Files

Our first example using the Media Player is very simple. The form of the MmSound example has some labels describing the current status, a button to select a new file, an OpenDialog component, and a Media Player component with the following settings:

```
object MediaPlayer1: TMediaPlayer
  VisibleButtons = [btPlay, btPause,
    btStop, btNext, btPrev]
  OnClick = MediaPlayer1Click
  OnNotify = MediaPlayer1Notify
end
```

When a user opens a new file, a wave table, or a MIDI file, the program enables the Media Player, and you can play the sound and use the other buttons, too:

```
procedure TForm1.NewButtonClick(Sender: TObject);
begin
  if OpenDialog1.Execute then
  begin
    FileLabel.Caption := OpenDialog1.Filename;
    MediaPlayer1.Filename := OpenDialog1.Filename;
    MediaPlayer1.Open;
    MediaPlayer1.Notify := True;
  end;
end;
```

Since I set the Notify property to True, the Media Player invokes the corresponding event handler, which outputs the information to a label:

```
procedure TForm1.MediaPlayer1Notify(Sender: TObject);
begin
```

```
    case MediaPlayer1.NotifyValue of
      nvSuccessful : NotifLabel.Caption := 'Success';
      nvSuperseded : NotifLabel.Caption := 'Superseded';
      nvAborted    : NotifLabel.Caption := 'Aborted';
      nvFailure    : NotifLabel.Caption := 'Failure';
    end;
    MediaPlayer1.Notify := True;
  end;
```

Notice that you need to set the `Notify` property to `True` every time the `OnNotify` event handler is called in order to receive further notifications. Another label is updated to display the requested command, as you can see in Figure 31.4.

```
procedure TForm1.MediaPlayer1Click(Sender: TObject;
  Button: TMPBtnType; var DoDefault: Boolean);
begin
  case Button of
    btPlay: ActionLabel.Caption := 'Playing';
    btPause: ActionLabel.Caption := 'Paused';
    btStop: ActionLabel.Caption := 'Stopped';
    btNext: ActionLabel.Caption := 'Next';
    btPrev: ActionLabel.Caption := 'Previous';
  end;
end;
```

FIGURE 31.4

A notification message displayed by the MmSound example.

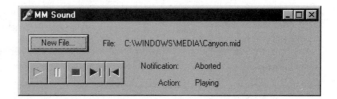

Running Videos

So far, we have worked with sound only. Now it is time to move to another kind of media device: video. You indeed have a video device on your system, but to play video files (such as AVI files), you need a specific driver (directly available in Windows 95). If your computer can display videos, writing a Delphi application to do so is almost trivial: place a Media Player component in a form, select an AVI file in the FileName property, set the AutoOpen property to True, and run the program. As soon as you click on the Play button, the system opens a second window and shows the video in it, as you can see in Figure 31.5, where I've chosen the DELPHI.AVI file distributed by Borland.

Instead of playing the file in its own window, we can add a panel (or any other windowed component) to the form and use the name of this panel as the value of the Media Player's Display property. As an alternative, we can set the Display and the DisplayRect properties to indicate which portions of the output window the video should cover. For example, the MmVideo example has the output shown in Figure 31.6.

FIGURE 31.6

The output of an AVI file into a panel. Compare this figure with the previous one, which shows a video in a default window.

Although it is possible to create a similar program writing no code at all, to do so I would have to know which AVI files reside on your computer, and specify the full path of one of them in the FileName property of the Media Player component. As an alternative, I've written a simple routine to open and start playing a file automatically. You only have to click on the panel (as the caption suggests).

```
procedure TForm1.Panel1Click(Sender: TObject);
begin
  if OpenDialog1.Execute then
  begin
    MediaPlayer1.FileName := OpenDialog1.Filename;
    MediaPlayer1.Open;
    MediaPlayer1.Perform (wm_LButtonDown, 0, $00090009);
    MediaPlayer1.Perform (wm_LButtonUp, 0, $00090009);
  end;
end;
```

After opening the Media Player, I could have called its Play method immediately to start it. But that would not have enabled and disabled the buttons properly. So I decided to simulate a click in position 9 on the *x*-axis and 9 on the *y*-axis of the Media Player window (instead of building the 32-bit value including both coordinates with a function, you can use the hexadecimal value directly, as in the code above). To avoid errors, I disabled all the buttons at design-time, until the simulated click takes place. I also automatically close the player when the application is closed (in the OnClose event handler).

A Video in a Form

The Media Player component has some limits regarding the window it can use to produce the output. You can use many components, but not all of them. A strange thing you can try is to use the Media Player component itself as the video's output window. This works, but there are two problems. First, the Media Player component cannot be aligned, and it cannot be sized at will. If you try to use big buttons, their size will be reduced automatically at run-time. The second problem is that if you click on the Pause button, you'll see the button in front of the video, while the other buttons are still covered. (I suggest you try this approach, anyway, just for fun.)

One thing you cannot do easily is display the video in a form. In fact, although you cannot set the form as the value of the Media Player's Display property at design-time, you can set it at run-time. To try this, simply place a hidden Media Player component (set the Visible property to False) and an OpenDialog component in a form. Set a proper title and hint for the form itself, and enable the ShowHints property. Then write the following code to load, start, and stop the video when the user clicks on the form:

```
procedure TForm1.FormClick(Sender: TObject);
begin
  if MediaPlayer1.FileName = '' then
    if OpenDialog1.Execute then
    begin
      MediaPlayer1.FileName := OpenDialog1.FileName;
      MediaPlayer1.Open;
      Playing := False;
    end
    else
      exit; // stop if no file is selected
  if Playing then
  begin
    MediaPlayer1.Stop;
    Playing := False;
    Caption := 'MM Video (Stopped)';
    Hint := 'Click to play video';
  end
  else
  begin
    MediaPlayer1.Display := self;
    MediaPlayer1.DisplayRect := ClientRect;
    MediaPlayer1.Play;
    Playing := True;
    Caption := 'MMV (Playing)';
    Hint := 'Click to stop video';
  end;
end;
```

In this code, Playing is a private Boolean field of the form. Notice that the program shows the video using the full client area of the form. If the form is resized, you can simply enlarge the output rectangle accordingly:

```
procedure TForm1.FormResize(Sender: TObject);
begin
  MediaPlayer1.DisplayRect := ClientRect;
end;
```

The best way to view a video is to use its original size, but with this program you can actually stretch it, and even change its proportions, as you can see in Figure 31.7.

FIGURE 31.7

A stretched video (with very poor resolution) and the hint indicating the current effect of a click.

Of course, the Media Player can also stop when it reaches the end of a file or when an error occurs. In both cases, we receive a notification event:

```
procedure TForm1.MediaPlayer1Notify(Sender: TObject);
begin
  Playing := False;
  Caption := 'MMV (Stopped)';
  Hint := 'Click to play video';
end;
```

Working with a CD Drive

In addition to audio and video files, the MCI interface is generally used to operate external devices. There are many examples, but the most common MCI device connected to a PC is probably a CD-ROM drive. Most CD-ROM drives can also read audio CDs, sending the output to an external speaker or a sound card. You can use the MCI interface and the Media Player component to write applications that handle such a device. Basically, you need to set the DeviceType property to dtCDAudio, making sure no file is selected in the FileName property, and be ready with a CD player.

In fact, just by placing a Media Player component in a form, setting the above properties, and compiling and running the program, you end up with a fully functional audio CD player. When you start customizing the player, though, not everything is as simple as it seems at first glance. I've built an example using some more capabilities of this component and of Windows multimedia support related to audio CDs. The form of this program has a couple of buttons, some labels to show the current status, a timer, and a SpinEdit component you can use to choose a track from the disk.

The idea is to use the labels to inform the user of the number of tracks on a disk, the current track, the current position within a track, and the length of the track, monitoring the current situation using the timer.

In general, if you can, use the tfTMSF value (Track, Minute, Second, Frame) for the TimeFormat property of the Media Player component to access positional properties (such as Position and Length). Extracting the values is not too complex if you use the proper functions of the MmSystem unit, such as the following:

```
CurrentTrack := Mci_TMSF_Track (MediaPlayer1.Position);
```

Here are the two functions that compute the values for the whole disk and for the current track:

```
procedure TForm1.CheckDisk;
var
  NTracks, NLen: Integer;
begin
  NTracks := MediaPlayer1.Tracks;
  NLen := MediaPlayer1.Length;
  DiskLabel.Caption := Format (
    'Tracks: %.2d, Length:%.2d:%.2d', [NTracks,
    Mci_TMSF_Minute (NLen), Mci_TMSF_Second (NLen)]);
  SpinEdit1.MaxValue := NTracks;
end;

procedure TForm1.CheckPosition;
var
  CurrentTrack, CurrentPos, TrackLen: Integer;
begin
  CurrentPos := MediaPlayer1.Position;
  CurPosLabel.Caption := Format ('Position: %.2d:%.2d',
    [Mci_TMSF_Minute (CurrentPos),
    Mci_TMSF_Second (CurrentPos)]);
  CurrentTrack := Mci_TMSF_Track (CurrentPos);
```

```
TrackLen := MediaPlayer1.TrackLength [CurrentTrack];
TrackNumberLabel.Caption := Format (
  'Current track: %.2d, Length:%.2d:%.2d', [CurrentTrack,
  Mci_MSF_Minute (TrackLen), Mci_MSF_Second (TrackLen)]);
end;
```

The code seems complex only because of the many conversions it makes. Notice in particular that the length of the current track (stored in the TrackLength property) is not measured using the default format, as the online help suggests, but with the MSF (Minute Second Frame) format. The result of displaying this information is visible in Figure 31.8.

FIGURE 31.8

The CDPlayer example at run-time.

The global values for the disk are computed only at startup and when the New CD button is clicked:

```
procedure TForm1.FormCreate(Sender: TObject);
begin
  MediaPlayer1.TimeFormat := tfTMSF;
  MediaPlayer1.Open;
  CheckDisk;
  CheckPosition;
end;

procedure TForm1.NewButtonClick(Sender: TObject);
begin
  CheckDisk;
  CheckPosition;
end;
```

The values for the current track and position are computed this way each time the timer interval elapses, by calling the CheckPosition method. This is far from perfect, because if you want to play an audio CD while using other programs, a timer accessing the Media Player information often slows down the system too much. Of course, this mainly depends on your hardware. Besides telling the user what is going on, the form has the Media Player component to allow the user to start and stop playing, change tracks, and so on. The operations on this component activate and halt the timer:

```
procedure TForm1.MediaPlayer1PostClick(
  Sender: TObject; Button: TMPBtnType);
begin
  if MediaPlayer1.Mode = mpPlaying then
    Timer1.Enabled := True
  else
    Timer1.Enabled := False;
  CheckPosition;
end;
```

You can also use the Go button to jump to the track selected in the SpinEdit component, where the MaxValue property is set by the CheckDisk method. Here is the code I've written:

```
procedure TForm1.GoButtonClick(Sender: TObject);
var
  Playing: Boolean;
begin
  Playing := (MediaPlayer1.Mode = mpPlaying);
  if Playing then
    MediaPlayer1.Stop;
  MediaPlayer1.Position :=
    MediaPlayer1.TrackPosition[SpinEdit1.Value];
  CheckPosition;
  if Playing then
    MediaPlayer1.Play;
end;
```

A good extension to this program would be to connect it to a CD database with the title of each CD you own and the title of each track. (I would have done that if it hadn't been for the time it would have taken to enter the title and track of each of my disks.) Remember, anyway, that a similar program is already available in Windows 95.

Epilogue

In this chapter, we have seen how to add some audio and video capabilities to Delphi applications. We have seen how to add sound effects to respond to user actions. We have also seen examples of how to use the Media Player with sound files, video files, and an external device (an audio CD). With computers and CD-ROM players becoming faster every year, video is becoming an important feature of many applications. Don't underestimate this area of programming simply because you are writing *serious* business programs.

Delphi is a great programming environment. Now that you have mastered Delphi, enjoy it. And if you want further information, the new advanced book I've written with Tim Gooch, *Delphi Developer's Handbook*, is awaiting you. As I mentioned in the Introduction, check my home page, at

```
http://ourworld.compuserve.com/homepages/marcocantu
```

and the Sybex home page, at

```
http://www.sybex.com/update.html
```

for corrections and updates to this book; my home page also has links to other great Delphi sites, where you'll find documentation and third-party components. You'll also find many links on the companion CD.

I really hope you've enjoyed reading the book as much as I've enjoyed writing it, and if you have any suggestion or request, feel free to post it to my e-mail address (in English or Italian):

```
marcocantu@compuserve.com
```

A

A Quick Overview of OOP Concepts

- Abstraction in programming languages

- The OOP concept of class

- Inheritance and class definitions

- Object polymorphism

- Types of OOP languages

The Delphi language, Object Pascal, is an object-oriented programming (OOP) language. Chapter 5 describes the object-oriented features of the language, but it doesn't include much information about OOP concepts in general. This appendix provides an overview of the key elements of OOP.

Abstraction in Programming Languages

The foundation of OOP lies in the idea of *abstraction*. Programming languages were invented and are used to describe a process at a higher level than the CPU machine code. Traditionally, the abstraction offered by programming languages could be divided into two categories, related to the representation of data and control structures.

The fundamental idea of abstraction in the representation of data is the concept of the *data type*. Historically, the first generation of programming languages introduced the concept of type, and the second generation (including the original Pascal language) added the idea of user-defined data types, such as records and arrays. Later on, the idea of the data type evolved into the concept of the *abstract data type*, a type associating the representation of data with the operations used to manipulate it. In an abstract data type, the representation of the data is usually hidden from its users. In these languages, a new data type is perceived as an extension of the type system provided by the language. Classes, as defined by OOP languages, can be considered an extension of the concept of abstract data types.

On the side of control structures, the first programming languages introduced statements for jumps, branches (such as case or if-then-else statements), and loops (such as for or while statements). Then came the idea of subroutines (in the form of procedures and functions). With the advent of subroutines, many programming models were developed, including *functional top-down decomposition*. The abstraction of subroutines is illustrated by the fact that you can call them and know *what* they do, but you don't need to know *how* they do it. Like abstract data types, new subroutines can be considered extensions of the programming language.

Classes

The first key element of OOP is the concept of *class*. A class can be defined as the abstract description of a group of objects, each with a specific state but all capable of performing the same operations.

For instance, a bottle is an object that has a state (it can be empty or full and can have different contents, often indicated by a label) and that allows some operations, such as filling it, pouring it, opening it, closing it, changing its contents, and so on. Of course, some operations depend on the state—pouring from an empty bottle doesn't make much sense. In other words, a class is a type definition that has some fields (the data representing the status of an object of that class) and some methods (the operations), whose behavior depends on the object's status.

NOTE Note that in OOP, the term *class* refers to the data type and the term *object* to an instance of the data type, a variable. Unfortunately, some OOP languages (including older versions of Object Pascal) use different terminology.

Within a program, classes have two main purposes:

- A class defines the abstraction it relates to. You can use classes to describe real-world entities, no matter how complex they are. If the entity is very complex, you can use classes to describe some of its sub-elements (or subsystems). As I mentioned, you can view classes as extensions of the data types of the program. In the same way, you can consider the new Delphi components you write to be extensions of the original VCL shipped with Delphi.

- Classes are the basis of the modularity of a program. In Object Pascal, you can place each new class (defining a form or another element) in its own unit, dividing even a big application into small, manageable pieces. The way Delphi handles the source code of forms naturally leads to this kind of approach.

Being based on classes is not the only requirement for defining a language as object-oriented. Two other key features are inheritance and polymorphism.

Inheritance

Using *inheritance*, you can build a new class by defining it in terms of another existing class, instead of building the class from scratch. A subclass inherits both fields and methods from its parent class.

Extending our example of the bottle class, you can inherit from the generic bottle subclasses such as plastic bottles, glass bottles, or specific ones (beer or wine bottles). Each bottle has its own physical form, is handled in a different way, and might have a different kind of liquid inside. However, all the bottles share some common characteristics, properties, and methods.

Inheritance is a very powerful language construct, but it is not always easy to understand and use. Here are some guidelines and tips:

- In theory, inheritance represents *specialization*. You can consider a subclass as a special case of the parent class. This is often expressed using an *is a* relationship (as in "a plastic bottle *is a* bottle").

- At times, inheritance is used to express *generalization*. If you have a class for managers, one for secretaries, and one for accountants, you can come up with a generic employee class you can use as the parent class for each other class. You can use this parent class to share the common elements, as well as some common code.

- In practice, inheritance is a way to avoid code duplication. Instead of using copy-and-paste techniques to build two similar classes, it is much easier to use one as the parent class of the second. Besides saving some code, you can save some debugging time and handle future changes more easily because there is only one version of the code.

- Another reason to use inheritance is that the compiler *does* understand it. A parent class and a subclass have some form of type compatibility, as described in the next section.

Polymorphism

The third key feature of OOP languages is *polymorphism*, which literally refers to the ability of an object to take many forms. In programming terms, polymorphism allows you to refer to objects of different classes by means of the same program variable. It also allows you to perform operations on that variable in different ways, according to the class of the object currently associated with that variable at the moment. In other words, polymorphism allows you to apply an operation on an object, and let the object respond in a way appropriate for its type.

For example, I can declare a generic variable of the bottle class (say, `MyBottle`) and then assign to it objects of the `TWineBottle` or `TBeerBottle` classes (the *T* in front of the class name is a common Borland coding convention, which stands for *Type*, but probably originally was also for *Turbo*). Now suppose every class has an `Open` method, each with a different implementation. Suppose also that this method uses *dynamic binding* (also called *late binding*), which means the compiler won't decide which function to call, but will delay the final decision until run-time. In Object Pascal, to obtain this behavior you have to declare the method in the parent class as `virtual` or `dynamic` (as discussed in Chapter 5) and redefine it with the `override` keyword in the derived classes.

Once you've done this, when you apply the `Open` method to `MyBottle`, what happens? The `Open` procedure of the current type of the object is called. If `MyBottle` is currently a `TWineBottle` object, the cork is extracted using a proper opener. Opening a beer bottle involves a different action and a different tool.

You can use inheritance and polymorphism together to build programs based on class hierarchies. Writing and extending hierarchy-based code is probably the ultimate OOP approach, and is what writing Delphi components is about.

A Definition of OOP

Now that we know what classes, inheritance, and polymorphism are, we can define an OOP language as one that has at least these three key capabilities. To be more precise, there are three degrees of object-orientedness:

- *Object-based* languages support objects—that is, elements with a set and a state.

- *Class-based* languages have both objects and classes. Every object is an instance of a class, which defines the operations and the representation of the data.

- *Object-oriented* languages also have inheritance and polymorphism, two elements that are often related.

There are other more complex and complete definitions of OOP, but each author tends to gear them toward the language he or she prefers, giving a biased opinion.

OOP Languages

There are many OOP languages, and some of them have been around for a while: Simula was the first language to introduce the concept of class, back in 1967, and Smalltalk was the first language to implement all of the key OOP features, around 1980. Then came hybrid languages (that is, OOP languages built on existing languages), such as C++, Objective-C, CLOS (a LISP derivative), and Object Pascal. Other important, and more theoretically sound, OOP languages include Eiffel and Sather. But new OOP languages appear frequently, with Java being the most recent case.

You can use three key categories to group OOP languages: pure versus hybrid OOP, dynamic versus static type checking, and traditional versus reference object model.

Pure versus Hybrid OOP

- Pure OOP languages are languages that do not allow other programming models. In these languages you cannot write a function by itself if it is not part of a class. You cannot declare a global variable. Examples of pure OOP languages are Smalltalk and Java.

- With hybrid languages, you can do whatever you want, including forgetting to apply OOP principles completely. Examples of hybrid OOP languages are all those compatible with an existing one, such as C++ or Object Pascal.

Static versus Dynamic Type Checking

- Statically typed languages are based on the notion of the data type and perform much compile-time type-checking. Object Pascal, C++, and Java are all examples of OOP languages with strong compile-time type checking. Statically typed languages are generally compiled.

- Dynamically typed languages generally have a weaker notion of type and perform most of the checks at run-time. Dynamically typed languages, such as Smalltalk, are generally interpreted.

The Object Model: Traditional versus Reference

- Many traditional OOP languages, particularly C++, allow you to declare an object in global memory, on the stack, or on the heap. Creating objects on the stack means the system manages object allocation and destruction more easily, but it is not so intuitive to use polymorphism with these objects.

- The more recent group of OOP languages, including Object Pascal and Java, feature an object reference model. All objects are dynamically allocated (generally by writing a corresponding call, such as the explicit use of a constructor), and you should keep track of their destruction. In Java destroying objects is not required, thanks to the built-in "garbage collector." In Delphi the most elegant solution to automatic disposal of unused objects is component ownership. The two main advantages of the object reference model are that it better supports polymorphism and that it simplifies passing objects as parameters.

Object-Oriented Analysis and Design

You can use an OOP language in many ways, particularly when it is an extension of an existing language. However, to exploit the full power of OOP languages, particularly in complex projects, you should probably analyze the requirements and design the program following object-oriented principles.

There are several methodologies of object-oriented analysis (OOA) and many approaches to object-oriented design (OOD), and discussing these topics in detail would require a separate book in itself. Here I just want to underline that object-oriented programming requires the proper conceptual approach, in addition to the proper language and programming environment. You can refer to the extensive literature on these specific subjects for more information.

Do not underestimate the role of OOP in Delphi. If you are not familiar with OOP in general, spend some time learning it. A clear comprehension of OOP concepts will allow you to better understand Delphi's inner structure and to write better programs.

Classes in general and components in particular are great tools for reusability, but without proper design, any complex application can get terribly messy. To gain the benefits of OOP (such as reusability and easy maintenance), you must use OOP techniques properly, something this book has tried to exemplify. Of course, the starting point is learning the language: so if you still haven't done so you can turn to Chapter 5, which discusses Object Pascal in detail.

APPENDIX

B

An Introduction to SQL

- A definition of SQL

- The Select statement and its clauses

- The `distinct` keyword for eliminating duplicates

- Multiple table joins

- Other SQL statements

When you use the Query component in a Delphi database application, to define the query you need to write a SQL statement for the component's SQL property, as we saw in Chapter 16. If you own the Client/Server version of Delphi, you can use the Visual Query Builder tool instead of writing a SQL statement from scratch. In both cases, you need to understand the SQL language. In Chapters 16 and 17, we used some simple SQL statements without describing them in detail.

This appendix serves as an introduction to the basics of SQL programming for programmers who have never used SQL. You can test these SQL statements using the Database Desktop tool. All the SQL statements in this appendix work with the Database Desktop, provided you have selected the proper alias (*DBDEMO*) with the Alias command of the SQL menu.

What Is SQL?

Before looking at SQL statements and how SQL works, we should have a definition of what SQL is. The acronym *SQL* stands for *Structured Query Language*, but is often pronounced according to its former name, *SEQUEL*. SQL is the standard language used to construct and access relational database management systems (RDBMS) of different kinds and on many hardware platforms. Although it is a standard language, there are differences among the SQL dialects implemented in SQL databases.

Here, I'll refer to just a few elements of the language, which, as far as I know, are common to each SQL dialect. Note that although its name refers to queries, SQL is a tool for many other operations besides queries, including updating a database or deleting records.

The Select Statement

The most important SQL statement is probably Select, which is built around three clauses:

- The select clause indicates a list of fields you want in the result of the query; by using the asterisk symbol instead of a list of fields, you can select all the fields in the table.

- The from clause indicates the tables you want to consider in building the query.

- The where clause indicates criteria for selecting records. If the where clause is missing, all the records are selected.

For example, this statement selects all the rows (or records) of the COUNTRY.DB table:

```
select * from Country
```

This statement selects only the specified columns (or fields) from that table:

```
select Name, Capital
from Country
```

And this statement selects those fields from rows (records) that meet the specified condition:

```
select Name, Capital
from Country
where Population > 20000000
```

This last statement returns only the countries that have more than 20 million inhabitants. In the where clause, you can write several different expressions, including an expression to look for a single element. You can also merge two conditions with and to indicate that they must both be met, or use or to select records that meet one of the conditions:

```
select *
from Country
where Continent = "South America"
and Population < 10000000

select Name, Capital
from Country
where Name <= "Brazil"
or Capital >= "Ottawa"
```

The first statement selects the South American countries with fewer than 10 million inhabitants. The second statement selects the countries that have a name alphabetically preceding *Brazil* and those that have a capital whose name follows *Ottawa*.

Avoiding Duplicates

Now suppose you want a list of the continents in the Country table. You can write this statement:

```
select Continent from Country
```

However, this will return each continent several times—once for each country in the continent. To avoid duplicate elements in a query result when you know that multiple records have the same value in a given field, you can add one more SQL keyword, distinct, which forces duplicate removal:

```
select distinct Continent
from Country
```

Making a Join

In many cases, SQL statements need to refer to two or more tables. When you work with two tables, you can join them or use the result of a table to express the condition used in the second one. When you work on two or more source tables, you'll generally join them. In SQL, there is no specific statement or clause to express a join (although this is possible in some RDBMS dialects of SQL, including InterBase).

You can simply work on two tables and join them properly using the where clause to match the value of two fields. For example, we can join the Orders and Customer tables to find the date of each order and the company involved by writing the following code:

```
select Orders.OrderNo, Orders.SaleDate,
   Customer.Company, Customer.Contact
from Orders, Customer
where Orders.CustNo = Customer.CustNo
```

In exactly the same way, you can join three tables using two conditions. In this case, we also want to know the name of the employee who processed the order:

```
select Orders.OrderNo, Orders.SaleDate,
   Customer.Company, Customer.Contact,
   Employee.LastName
from Orders, Customer, Employee
where Orders.CustNo = Customer.CustNo
   and Orders.EmpNo = Employee.EmpNo
```

With the following SQL statement, we retrieve the amount paid by each customer who ordered something by *Johnson:*

```
select Orders.AmountPaid, Customer.Company
from Orders, Customer, Employee
where Orders.CustNo = Customer.CustNo
  and Orders.EmpNo = Employee.EmpNo
  and Employee.LastName = "Johnson"
```

Choosing an Order

Another SQL clause is order by, which determines the order of the values in the resulting query. The following statement returns a table with countries ordered first by continent and then by name:

```
select *
from Country
where Population > 10000000
order by Continent, Name
```

Computing Values

In the select clause, instead of a field of a table, you can have the result of a computation. For example, you can compute the number of employees with this statement:

```
select count (*)
from Employee
```

For a more complex example, you can compute the number of orders taken by an employee, the total amount, and the average:

```
select Sum (Orders.AmountPaid),
  Count (Orders.AmountPaid), Avg (Orders.AmountPaid)
from Orders, Employee
where Orders.EmpNo = Employee.EmpNo
  and Employee.LastName = "Johnson"
```

Defining Groups

Besides making a computation on the result of a query, you can compute a value for each group of elements, as indicated by the group by clause. The result of the following query is a list of employees, each with the total dollar amount of the orders that employee has taken:

```
select Employee.LastName, Sum(Orders.AmountPaid)
from Orders, Employee
where Orders.EmpNo = Employee.EmpNo
group by Employee.LastName
```

Beyond Select

Select is probably the most often-used statement in SQL. However, there are other SQL statements you should be aware of. Here are the most important ones:

- Insert adds data to a table. Generally, it is also possible to insert the result of a sub-table into a table, although the Database Desktop doesn't allow this.

- Update changes the values of a table.

- Delete removes some of the rows of a table.

- Create Table defines a new table.

- Alter Table restructures an existing table, adding or removing columns.

INDEX

NOTE: page numbers in italics refer to figures or tables; page numbers in bold refer to primary discussions of the topic

SYMBOLS & NUMBERS

A

B

(

G

I

L

M

N

Q

R

S

T

U

V

X

Z